MANAGING SOCIAL AND ECONOMIC CHANGE WITH INFORMATION TECHNOLOGY

Edited by

Mehdi Khosrowpour, D.B.A
Pennsylvania State University at Harrisburg

Proceedings of
1994 Information Resources Management Association
International Conference
San Antonio, Texas May 22-25, 1994

IDEA GROUP PUBLISHING

Innovators in information technology publishing

Harrisburg   •   **London**
U.S.A.   U.K.

Senior Editor:	Mehdi Khosrowpour
Managing Editor:	Jan Travers
Printed at :	Kutco Printing

Published in the United State of America by
> Idea Group Publishing
> 4811 Jonestown Road, Suite 230
> Harrisburg, Pennsylvania 17109
> Telephone: (717) 541-9150
> FAX: 717-541-9159

and in the United Kingdom by
> Idea Group Publishing
> 3 Henrietta Street
> Covent Garden
> London WC2E 8LU
> Telephone: 071-240-1003
> Fax: 071-379-0609

Printed in the United States of America

3 2280 00494 2892

British Cataloguing in Publication Data
A Cataloguing in Publication record for this book is available from the British Library.

ISBN: 1-878289-26-8

The views expressed in this publication are those of the authors but not necessarily of the Information Resources Management Association or Idea Group Publishing.

Table of Contents

4

6

Section One

The Human Side
of Information Technology

Investigating Information Technology
Barriers in Saudi Public Organizations

Abdulla H. Abdul-Gader and Khaled H. Alangari
Department of Accounting and MIS
King Fahd University of Petroleum and Minerals
Dhahran, Saudi Arabia

ABSTRACT

The role of Information Technology (IT) to the economic development process in the developing world is contingent on real assimilation of information technology products and applications into organizational processes. There are a number of IT assimilation problems that may hinder effective IT utilization. Using a Delphi method, this paper probes 25 IT experts views on what are the major IT assimilation problems in a developing nation public sector. Out of 30 IT barriers, IT planning and human resources related problems were the most troublesome barriers. Level of centralization has received the least importance score. The findings and their implications are discussed.

1. INTRODUCTION

The world has spent 351 billion US dollars in 1990 on computer hardware, computer software, and computer services (Organization for Economic Cooperation Development, 1992). In the developed countries, information technology absorb half of a firm's capital expenditures in many organizations (Cooper and Zmud, 1990). Following the same trend, several developing countries have been pouring huge investments into IT resources in order to reap the fruits of this "transferable." Some developing nations rely heavily on computerization to support their develop effort (Bhatnagar, 1990). With favorable financial resources, Saudi Arabia micro and minicomputer market, for example, exhibits growth rates similar to the trend American market (U.S. Department of Commerce, 1985).

Despite the inestimable role of information technology to the economic development process in the developing world, it has not received enough attention. There are scanty scholarly reports on IT issues and problems pertaining to organizations in developing countries. The richness of IT literature has primary focused on organizations in the developed hemisphere. Even in the sporadic literature on IT in developing countries, one rarely encounters scholarly reports on IT assimilation problems in countries' organizations. Most studies are descriptive in nature.

Acknowledgment: The authors are grateful for the financial support provided by K of Science and Technology (Grant # AR-25-11). Thanks are also due to the admin students of King Fahd University of Petroleum and Minerals.

The importance of Information Technology (IT) management to developing nations stems from the central role of information resources in modern economic development. The role of IT to the economic development process in the developing world is contingent on real assimilation of information technology products and applications into organizational processes. Developing countries' scarcity of resources prompts for more attention to IT assimilation issues.

This study examines a number of problem areas that have been identified in the literature as barriers to IT assimilation. The objective is to assess the relevance and applicability of these barriers in a culture fundamentally different from those developed countries (e.g., U.S.). Using a Delphi method, this paper investigates experts views on what are the major IT assimilation problems in a developing nation public sector.

The emphasis of this paper is on problems that may embed IT assimilation in Saudi Arabian public sector. Therefore, problems that need to be identified are not specific systems problems. Instead, they are aggregate problems of the portfolio of systems resulting from a number of possible individual and organizational problem areas.

It is of paramount importance to a developing country's managers to identify and study the variables that may promote or hinder attaining the full potential of these considerable investments. This study would also benefit the increasing number of multinational corporations involved in business arrangements in Saudi Arabia. There are almost 300 joint projects between Saudi Arabia and United States (Saudi Arabia C of Commerce, 1988).

IT assimilation research is reviewed in the next section. Based on this background, a taxonomy of IT assimilation problems is adopted. This is followed by a discussion of the methodology used in this study. Next, the data are analyzed and discussed.

2. BACKGROUND

The literature related to IT evaluation, successes, problems, etc. is abundant, multidimensional, and very difficult to characterize. Many studies have been conducted to reveal causes for failure and success of IT assimilation and the extent of either way. A group of researchers has studied users' characteristics that influence acceptance behavior (Davis, et al., 1989; Robey, 1979). A second group has tried to develop an understanding of the impact of external barriers such as the system's technical attributes (Norman and Draper, 1986), system developer values (Kumar and Welke, 1984), design methodologies and user involvement (Lucas, 1975), and the influence of organizational characteristics on users' acceptance and usage behavior (Abdul-Ga 1990).

Since the objective of this paper is to identify the barriers that may limit IT assimilation into the Saudi public sector, an extensive review of IT assimilation was necessary .[1] Special attention is given to assimilation studies in developing countries. Although it would be unfeasible to review all studies, a large number of them have pointed to at least 34 assimilation barriers; a large number indeed. As shown in Table 1, these barriers were listed by more than one reference.

To systematically categorize IT barriers in Table 1, each barrier was assigned one or more of Ives et al. (1980) frame work variables. They have listed nine five environments, three processes, and the portfolio of IT systems. The environmental variables involve the resources for and constraints of systems development, operation and use processes within the organizational and the external environment. These two environments enclose three IT systems environments (development, operations, use). Within environmental constraints, selection and application of organizational resources marks IT system development process. The physical operations of IT systems and tasks accomplishment denote operations and use processes. Table 2 shows the variables in Ives et al. (1980).

IT assimilation can be hindered by problems stemming from one or more of the five environments, one or more of the three processes, or the IT systems themselves. There are problems in the environments, problems in the processes, and problems systems. These problems are inter-related. Thus an environmental problem (constraint) may cause some development, use and/or operational process problems that may res a problem in IT systems.

IT assimilation problems that are identified in the literature are classified into nine categories. Such categorization will help in combining related problems to more concise problem list for this study. The last column of Table 1 delineates classification.

This was important to put the barrier within the context of the reference(s) that has(ve) mentioned it. The objective is to construct a starter list for the Delphi method discussed in the following section.

3. ASSESSMENT OF IT EXPERTS VIEWS

The literature review in the previous section clearly indicates the magnitude of barriers that can impede IT assimilation into organizations. The main objective study is to assess the relative impact of these barriers on public organizations in

Saudi Arabia. It is essential to aggregate, rephrase, and adjust these barriers to mirror three dimensions:

1. that the barriers are operating in a developing nation;
2. that the organizations are from public sector; and
3. that national relevancy must be ensured. The developing country is Saudi Arabia.

Table 3 depicts context specific IT assimilation barriers based on the barriers drawn from the literature.

To assess the importance of these barriers, Delphi method was utilized. The Delphi method is a technique for systematically eliciting experts' opinion and synthesizing group judgment (Evans, 1973). It is basically a series of linked questionnaires initiated with a basic questionnaire. Refinements are reflected in subsequent rounds. The basic questionnaire can be "blank" open-ended questions or (for faster convergence) a comprehensive list of the relevant issues. Each subsequent round contains statittical summary of previous round's results. It may also contain rationale for extreme and detail explanation of each item. The participants are asked to re-evaluate previous opinion based on the new input. The process stops when the group reach acceptable consensus. The Delphi method was first introduced in the early 1960's. It was initially used for forecasting and estimation, but later it was utilized in other fields. Niederman et al. (1991) utilized this method to gage the relative importance of facing IT managers.

For this study, Delphi method was initiated by constructing a simple questionnaire that included a cover letter explaining the objective of the inquiry and the required action from the participants. It also included the starter list of barriers that appear in table 3. Although all the participating experts speak English, the barriers were presented in Arabic and English to minimize possible misunderstanding. This has enhanced the clarity of the statements.

The questionnaire was sent by facsimile to a sample of Saudi IT experts who were selected carefully to represent IT academicians, vendors, and managers. Therefore, an IT expert is defined as a native academician, vendor, or manager who is studying, supplying or managing IT in local organizations. The sample included 25 experts. Seven of these were management information systems and computer science professors from two major Saudi universities. The sample also included 5 IT vendors and 13 IT managers in public sector.

The participants were asked to assign an importance score to each statement in Table 3. The scores ranged from 1 to 10 where higher scores represent higher de limiting IT assimilation. The experts were also requested to add new items they consider as a barrier to IT assimilation in public organizations.

Twenty-three experts responded to the first round of the survey. Input from the first round was analyzed and the mean and standard deviation for the degree of importance of each barrier was computed. To reach a better consensus, a second round of probing was necessary. The list of barriers for the second round has incorporated the finding the first round by:

Table 1: IT Asimilation Barriers Classification

	Barrier	Reference	Category
1	Lack of infrastructure (reliable telecommunication network).	Lu et. al. (1988); Matta and Boutros (1989)	External Environment
2	Restraining external environment	King et. al. (1989)	External Environment
3	Lack of vendor support	Waema and Walsham (1990); Walsham et. al. (1988); Woherem (1992)	External Environment
4	Lack of top management awareness of IT impact on organizational processes.	Madon (1992); Perez (1980); Walsham and Han (1992); King et. al. (1989)	Organizational Environment
5	lack of top management support	Abdul-Gader (1990); Sideridis (1988); King et. al. (1989)	Organizational Environment
6	Small organization size	Abdul-Gader (1990); Ein-Dor and Segev (1988)	Organizational Environment
7	Poor IT Planning	Perez (1980); Alavi et al. (1988); Cheney et al. (1986); King et. al. (1989); Kraemer and King (1986); Porter and Gogan (1988)	Organizational Environment
8	Decentralization in the organization	Montazemi (1988)	Organizational Environment
9	Poor organizational structure to assimilation information technology	Perez (1980)	Organizational Environment
10	Budgetary constraints	King et. al. (1989)	Organizational Environment
11	Astigmatic concentration of emphasis on hardware procurement	Woherem (1992)	Organizational Environment
12	Lack of management commitment to IT implementation	Perez (1980)	Organizational Environment
13	Lack of top management involvement in computerization	Abdul-Gader (1990); Delone (1988); Ein-Dor and Segev (1988)	Organizational Environment
14	Incompetent IT management	Waema and Walsham (1990); Walsham et. al. (1988)	Organizational Environment
15	Lack of management IT literacy and use	Abdul-Gader (1990); Lu et. al. (1988); Bhatnagar (1990); Perez (1980); Waema and Walsham (1990); Walsham et. al. (1988); Delone (1988); Ein-Dor and Segev (1988)	Organizational Environment
16	Lack of IT standards	Lu et. al. (1988); Woherem (1992)	Organizational Environment

Table 1: IT Assimilation Barriers Classification (cont.)

	Barrier	Reference	Category
17	Inter-managerial power struggle (Power conflict and politics within the organization)	Robey et al. (1990); Waema and Walsham (1990); Walsham et. al. (1988); King et. al. (1989); Madon (1992); Walsham and Han (1992); Markus, 1983)	Organizational Environment
18	Meager IT budget	Ein-Dor and Segev (1988)	Organizational Environment
19	Low rank of information system function	Raymond (1985)	Organizational Environment
20	Lack of in-house applications development	Raymond (1985)	Development Environment
21	Scarcity of IT professionals in the organization	Abdul-Gader (1990); Lu et. al. (1988); Avgerou (1990); Madon (1992); Perez (1980); Sideridis (1988); Woherem (1992); King et. al. (1989); Montazemi (1988)	Development Environment Operations Environment
22	Lack of appropriate technical support	Woherem (1992); King et. al. (1989)	Operations Environment
23	Insufficient user training	Abdul-Gader (1990); Lu et. al. (1988); King et. al. (1989); Kraemer and King (1986)	User Environment
24	Lack of users' perceived needs	Bhatnagar (1990)	User Environment
25	Lack of user computer literacy	Abdul-Gader (1990); Montazemi (1988)	User Environment
26	Users' perceived threats from the system.	Robey et al. (1990)	User Environment
27	Ignorance of socio-organizational barriers	Abdul-Gader (1990); Robey et al. (1990); Woherem (1992)	Development Process
28	Lack of management and developer/user commitment to follow guidelines in developing system	Perez (1980)	Development Process
29	Weakness of information requirement analysis	Perez (1980); Woherem (1992); Montazemi (1988)	Development Process
30	Lack of good project management to implement IT projects	Perez (1980); Robey et al. (1990); Woherem (1992)	Development Process
31	Lack of user involvement	Madon (1992); Robey et al. (1990); Sideridis (1988); Walsham and Han (1992); Kraemer and King (1986); Montazemi (1988)	Development Process
32	Lack of formalized design process	Perez (1980)	Development Process
33	Improper hardware maintenance management.	Madon (1992)	Operations Process
34	Poor system design	Madon (1992); Robey et al. (1990); Walsham and Han (1992)	Development Process Systems

Table 2: Ives et. al, (1980) Framework Variables

Variable	Meaning
External environment	The resources and constraints that affect IT systems from sources outside the organization. Social, political, cultural and economic issues.
Organizational environment	The organizational resources and constraints that influence IT systems. Organizational environment includes organizational culture, goals, tasks, structure, and management philosophy and style.
User environment	The immediate environment surrounding users of IT systems. It is marked by user's characteristics, user's peers, and user's tasks.
System development environment	The development resources and constraints that affect IT systems development. Within an organization, it includes development methodology's profile, development tools such as CASE tools, system development team skills and knowledge, and the organization and management of development function.
System operations environment	The resources available for IT system operations and constraints that confine operations in an organization. It includes hardware, software, operations team skills and knowledge, and the organization and management of operations function.
Development process	Selection of resources for development
Operations process	Use of IT resources to operate IT systems
User process	User utilization of IT systems to accomplish user tasks
IT systems	The content, presentation form, and timing of systems

1. Ranking the barriers according to the mean score of importance. If there was the mean, then the one with less variability was ranked higher.

2. Dropping any barrier that has a mean scored of less than five (out of ten) in degree of importance. Three barriers did not meet the 5 limit. Hence, they were dropped.

3. Adding the barriers that have been mentioned by two or more experts in the first round. Five barriers were appended to the initial list.

Each of the participating experts was sent a customized questionnaire containing a list of all remaining barriers from the first round (25 barriers) and the newly barriers (5). The list ranked the 30 barriers based on their mean importance score. Beside each barrier, its first round importance score and the particular experts importance score were reported. Comparing his scores with the groups, each expert was requested to re-evaluate the barriers that have appeared in the first round. If he wishes he can adjust the importance score for each barrier after observing the whole groups evaluation. Newly added barriers were also to be judged and given importance scores.

All participants in the first round except two responded to the second round. Rank order of IT assimilation barriers for the whole sample is shown in Table 4.

4. DISCUSSION

By far, lack of appropriate IT planning was viewed as the most stumbling block toward successful IT assimilation. Planning has been always regarded as the first ranked IT issue for many years (Ball and Harris, 1982; Dickson et al., 1984; Brancheau Wetherbe, 1987). Furthermore, lack of organizational strategic planing was also third in limiting IT assimilation.

Evidence suggests that developing countries striving towards computerization are constrained in their efforts by scarcity of competent work force (Abdul-Gader, 1 et al., 1988; Avgerou, 1990; Madon, 1992; Perez, 1980; Sideridis, 1988; Woherem, 1992). To adjust for the lack of endogenous skilled human resources, Saudi Arabia relies heavily on imported technology and foreign work force. This has created another type of problems. It is becoming too difficult to fulfill the demand for IT know how. The experts have assigned high rating to IT human resources management issues (e.g., professional availability, training, and management knowledge). Ranks 2, 4, 5, 8, and 13 reflect these dimensions.

Table 3: A Modified List of IT Assimilation Barriers

	IT Assimilation Problem	Category
1.	Problems with government budgeting process.	External Environment
2.	Hardware and software high prices.	External Environment
3.	Weakness of the technology to support Arabic use.	External Environment
4.	Inappropriate vendor support after sale.	External Environment
5.	Insufficient financial support to meet the needs.	External Environment
6.	Lack of management confidence in IT feasibility.	Organizational Environment
7.	Work task's characteristics are not suitable to IT.	Organizational Environment
8.	Lack of appropriate IT planning.	Organizational Environment
9.	Lack of standards and specifications (e.g., documentation).	Organizational Environment
10.	Weak relation between top management and IT management.	Organizational Environment
11.	Insufficient IT professionals training and career development.	Organizational Environment
12.	Lack of sufficient computer knowledge within middle and top management.	Organizational Environment
13.	Rigidity of organizational procedures.	Organizational Environment
14.	Non conducive organizational culture.	Organizational Environment
15.	The public sector is too centralized.	Organizational Environment
16.	Low top management involvement in IT projects.	Organizational Environment
17.	The IT department has low organizational power.	Organizational Environment
18.	Low management motivation to use IT.	Organizational Environment
19.	Difficulty of Software maintenance.	Development Environment
20.	Lack of appropriate software development tools.	Development Environment
21.	Costly IT application development.	Development Environment
22.	Scarcity of qualified work force.	Development Environment Operations Environment
23.	Low users' motivation to use IT.	Use Environment
24.	Lack of need for Information Technology (IT) among users.	Use Environment
25.	Insufficient user training.	Use Environment
26.	User perceived threats from IT.	Use Environment
27.	User negative attitude toward IT.	Use Environment
28.	Hardware operation and maintenance problems.	Operations Environment

Top management involvement with computerization is often identified as one of the critical factors (Abdul-Gader, 1990; Delone, 1988; and Ein-Dor and Segev, 1988). "Low top management involvement in IT projects was ranked sixth in the list. Similiarly, low organizational power of IT department also has been viewed as a significant IT assimilation. The "IT department has low organizational power" was the seventh in the list. Whereas, [w]eak relation between top management and IT management was the eleventh. This in congruence with a large number of studies that has argued for importance of organizational power dimension (Robey et al., 1990; Waema and Walsham, 1990; Walsham et. al., 1988; King et. al., 1989; Madon, 1992; Walsham and Han, 1992 Markus, 1983).

The ninth and the tenth barriers are" [i]nsufficient financial support to meet needs" and "[p]roblems with government budgeting process." The Saudi public sector budgetary system is highly centralized and usually there would be no separate budget for organizational units within each public institution. Hence, IT operational, development, and administrative expenses are drawn from a unified pool of fund. This may explain the relative high importance score of budgetary and financial barriers. King et al. Dor and Segev (1988) were among many scholars pointing to lack of financial resources and restraining budgetary constraints.

Moving to the most inferior barriers, centralization lies at the bottom of the Montazemi (1988) asserts that centralization hinders the way to a more supportive organizational climate for successful systems. Contrary to Montazemi's assertion degree of centralization of the decision making in Saudi public sector has been found to be the least significant IT barrier. The participants judgment provides support t to Abdul-Gader's findings (Abdul-Gader, 1990). He has surveyed a number of Saudi private organization and failed to show any significant impact of the level of centralization on system success.

Table 4: Second Round Rank Order of IT Assimilation Barriers

Rank	Barrier	Mean	SD
1	Lack of appropriate IT planning.	8.762	1.261
2	Insufficient IT professionals training and career development	8.333	1.238
3	Lack of organizational strategic plan	8.238	1.261
4	Lack of sufficient computer knowledge within middle and top management.	8.190	1.167
5	Scarcity of qualified work force.	7.857	1.014
6	Low top management involvement in IT projects.	7.714	1.419
7	The IT department has low organizational power.	7.667	1.238
8	Insufficient user training.	7.524	1.470
9*	Insufficient financial support to meet the needs.	7.476	1.167
10*	Problems with government budgeting process.	7.476	1.834
11*	Weak relation between top management and IT management.	7.238	1.546
12*	Rigidity or organizational procedures.	7.238	1.921
13	Insufficient IT management skills and experience	7.190	1.504
14	Poor coordination among different branches and divisions	7.143	1.062
15	Lack of specialized consulting organizations	6.952	2.110
16*	Low users' motivation to use IT.	6.619	1.161
17*	Lack of standards and specifications (e.g., hardware purchase).	6.619	1.658
18	Low management motivation to use IT.	6.571	1.248
19	Weakness of the technology to support Arabic use.	6.429	1.912
20	Inappropriate procedures to define user requirements	6.350	1.565
21	User perceived threats from IT.	6.333	1.560
22	Lack of management confidence in IT feasibility.	6.286	2.004
23*	Non conducive organizational culture.	6.143	1.526
24*	Inappropriate vendor support after sale.	6.143	1.682
25	Costly IT application development.	5.810	1.078
26*	Lack of need for Information Technology (IT) among users.	5.619	1.203
27*	Difficulty of Software maintenance.	5.619	1.322
28	User negative attitude toward IT.	5.476	1.569
29	Hardware operation and maintenance problems.	5.238	1.513
30	The public sector is too centralized.	5.000	2.236

*	Tie in importance means: the barrier with the lower standard deviation is first.

It is surprising to see that" [u]ser negative attitude toward IT" barrier at the bottom of the list. Actually, the participants assigned low importance scores to users related problems such as negative attitude (28th) and lack of need for IT (rank 26). It seems that the participants viewed external and organizational environmental barriers as having more impact than user environment problems.

5. SUMMARY AND CONCLUSION

This paper provides an overall perception of a sample of experts regarding the major barriers to assimilating IT into the public sector in Saudi Arabia. Probllems related to planning and human resources have received the highest rankings. These findings point to the need to pay more attention to these issues.

Planning can lead to better allocation and utilization. Yet as has been shown by Abdul-Gader (1990), planning is not a common practice at Saudi organizations. A practice that needs to be reversed.

Limited Saudi endogenous IT human resources demand more effort for training and IT professional career development. Increasing management and users IT knowledge is a much needed effort.

Future studies may empirically test the barriers of IT assimilation that were identified in this paper. Case oriented and other qualitative research methods can help study the impact of the barriers on different settings.

6. REFERENCES

1. Abdul-Gader, A. (1990) "End-User Computing Success Factors: Further Evidence from a Developing Nation," Information Resources Management Journal, Volume 3, Winter pp. 1-13.

2. Alavi, M., Nelson, R., and Weiss, L (1988), "Managing End-User Computing as a Value-Added Resource," Journal of Information Systems Management, Summer, pp. 26-35.

3. Avgerou, C. (1990), "Computer-Based Information Systems and Modernization of Public Administration in Developing Countries," In Bhatnagar, S. and N. Bjorn-Andersen (Eds.). Information Technology in Developing Countries. North-Holland: Amsterdam.

4. Ball, L., and R. Harris (1982), SMIS Members: A membership Analysis, MIS Quarterly, 6, 1, pp. 19-38.

5. Bhatnagar, S. (1990), "Computers in Developing Countries,". In Bhatnagar, S. and N. Bjorn-Andersen (Eds.). Information Technology in Developing Countries. North-Holland: Amsterdam.

6. Brancheau, J., and J. Wetherbe (1987), Key Issues in Information Systems Management, MIS Quarterly, 11, 1, pp. 23-45.

7. Cheney, P., Mann, R., and Amoroso, D. (1986), "Organizational Factors Affecting the Success of End-User Computing," The Journal of MIS, Volume 3, pp. 65-80.

8. Cooper, R and R. Zmud (1990), "Information Technology Implementation Research: A Technological Diffusion Approach", Management Science, 36, 2, pp.123-139.

9. Davis, F., Bagozzi, R., and P. Warshaw (1989), "User Acceptance of Computer Technology: A Comparison of two Theoretical Models" Management Science, 35, 8, PP. 982-1003.

10. Delone, W. (1988), "Determinants of Success for Computer Usage in Small Business," MIS Quarterly, pp. 51-61.

11. Dickson, G., Leitheiser, R., Wetherbe, J., and M. Nechis (1984), Key Information Systems Issues for the 1980s, MIS Quarterly, 8, 3, pp. 135-159.

12. Ein-Dor, P. and E. Segev (1988), "Information Resource Management for End User Computing: An Exploratory Study," Information Resource Management Journal, Volume 1, pp. 39-46.

13. Evans, L. (1973), Production Technology Advancements: A Forecast to 1988, Industrial Development Division, Institute of Science and Technology, The University of Michigan.

14. Ives, B., S. Hamilton, and G. Davis (1980), A Framework for Research in Computer-Based Management Information Systems, Management Science, 26, 9, pp. 910-93.

15. King, W., V. Grover, and E. Hufnagel (1989), "Using Information and Information Technology for Sustainable Competitive Advantage: Some Empirical Evidence," Information & Management 17, pp. 87- 93.

16. Kraemer, K. and J. King (1986), "Computing of Public Organizations," Public Administrative Review, pp. 488-496.

17. Kumar, K. and Welke, R. (1984), "Implementation Failure and System Developer Values: Assumptions, Truisms and Empirical Evidence", Proceedings of the Fifth International Conference on Information Systems. Tucson, Arizona, pp. 1-13.

18. Lu, M., Q.Youzin, and T. Guimaraes (1988), "A Status Report of the Use of Computer-Based Information Systems in PRC," Information & Management, 15 , pp. 237-242.

19. Lucas, H. (1975). Why Information Systems Fail. New York: Columbia University Press.

20. Madon, S. (1992), "The Impact of Computer-Based Information Systems on Rural Development: A Case Study in India", Paper presented to IFIP Working Group 9.4 Conference, Nairobi, Kenya.

21. Markus, M. (1983), "Power, Politics and MIS Implementation," Communication of the ACM, 26, 6, pp. 430-445.

22. Matta, K. and Boutros, N. (1989) "Barriers to Computer-Based Message Systems in Developing Countries," Computer & Society, 19, 1, pp. 1-6.

23. Montazemi, A. (1988), "Factors Affecting Information Satisfaction in the Context of the Small Business Environment", MIS Quarterly, pp. 239-256.

24. Niederman, F., Brancheau, J., and Wetherbe J. (1991), "Information Systems Management Issues for the 1990s," MIS Quarterly ,15, 4, pp. 474-500.

25. Norman, D. and Draper, S. (1986). User Centered System Design: New Perspectives on Human-Computers Interaction. Hillsdale, New Jersey: Erlbaum Associates.

26. Organization for Economic Cooperation and Development (OECD) (1992). Information Technology Outlook OECD: Paris.

27. Perez, V. (1980), "Factors Challenging Information Technology Applications in Developing Countries," Information and Management, 3, pp. 141-147.

28. Porter, L. and Gogan, J. (1988), "Coming to Terms with End-User Systems Integration," Journal of Information Systems Management, pp. 8-16.

29. Raymond, L. (1985), "Organizational Characteristics and MIS Success in the Context of Small Business," MIS Quarterly, pp. 37-52.

30. Robey, D.(1979), "User Attitudes and Management Information System Use", Academy of Management Journal, 22, pp. 527-538.

31. Robey, D., S. Gupta, and A. Rodriguez-Diaz (1990), "Implementing Information Systems in Developing Countries: Organizational and Cultural Consideration,"In Bhatnagar, S. and N. Bjorn-Andersen (Eds.). Information Technology in Developing Countries. North-Holland: Amsterdam.

32. Saudi Arabia Chamber of Commerce (1988). The Yearly Report of Trade and Corporation, annual publication, Riyadh, Saudi Arabia.

33. Sideridis, A. (1988), "Informatics and Municipalities: The Greek Approach," Information and Management, 14, pp. 183-188.

34. U.S. Department of Commerce (1985). Mini and Micro Computer Systems Market in Saudi Arabia. Washington: International Trade Administration.

35. Waema, T. and G. Walsham (1990), "Information Systems Strategy Formation in a Developing Country Bank", Technological Forecasting and Social Change, 38, pp. 393-407.

36. Walsham G. and C. Han (1992) "Information Systems Strategy Formation and Implementation: The Case of a Central Government Agency", Management Studies Group Research Paper Series, Engineering Dept., Cambridge University, Number 18.

37. Walsham, G., Symons, V. , and T. Waema (1988), "Information Systems as Social Systems: Implications for Developing Countries" Information Technology for Development, 3, 3, pp. 189-204.

38. Woherem, J. (1992), "Strategies for Indigenisation of IT in Africa," Proceedings of the IFIP International Conference on the Social Implications of Computers in Developing Countries, Nairobi, March 23-25.

Endnote

[1]For discussion of the references refer to Abdul-Gader, A. and K. Alangari (for Information Technology Assimilation in the Government Public Sector: An Empirica report. King Abdulaziz City for Science and Technology, Funded project # AR-11- 9

Organizational Maturity in the Context of IS Management and Use

Timo Auer and Mikko Ruohonen

Turku School of Economics and Business Administration, Finland

1. ABSTRACT

The "IS maturity" of the organization is usually evaluated on the basis of hardware/software composition. However, we also need to evaluate the human side of organizational maturity. The skills, knowledge and views of organizational actors affects how IS is managed and put to work. The human side of IS-related organizational maturity is understood here as a state of organizational learning, which consists of the management and user components (i.e. state of learning) and the quality of interaction between those components and a technical component. Our objective is to assess the human side and construct instruments for that purpose. This paper makes use of a number of experiences from longitudinal case studies in which maturity had a central role to play. Two tools are presented here: first the Information Management Knowledge and Motivation Inventory (IMI) for stakeholder evaluation, and second a tool for User Organization Abilities Analysis (UOA) to use IS.

2. ORGANIZATIONAL MATURITY

Several models have been developed to define and predict the growth of IT in organizations [e.g. 10, 15, 23, 24, 30, 44]. Traditionally, these "stages of growth" models have put more emphasis on the technological side than the human side, as they focus on the rapidity of IT diffusion. Fortunately, some models have taken the human side into account as well. For example, the Galliers - Sutherland [23] "seven S" - based on Pascale and Athos [45] - model tries to describe what is needed to progress through to the more mature stages of growth. The "seven S" theme represents strategy, structure, systems, staff, style, skills and superordinate goals. In this model the human side plays a central role, but concentrates more on DP personnel and senior management's abilities and views in IT management than on those of user organizations. One problem with these growth models lies in their validation as only the authors themselves - if anyone - have validated them. Also, since Nolan's "stages of growth" models have been invalidated [8, 34] the academic world has almost dispensed with the "maturity" term because the model's final stage is maturity.

So, what does the term "maturity" imply? In a dictionary "maturity" is defined as a state of being fully developed or adult. In our view, the term *IS related organizational maturity implies the current IS in use and - more importantly - what has been achieved to date in a variable learning process.* Furthermore, we state that absolute maturity is an ideal position that cannot be achieved, since no further development would then

be possible. We do not define or use previously defined maturity stages because they are far too simplified generalizations and counterparts, as such, cannot be found in the real world. Earl's idea [15] that S-curves of learning are repeated for new technology gives us our starting point. The basis of our definition of maturity is how IT is put to work. Maturity is related to three main components and their interaction. *First, the social component* is related to user organizations' abilities to utilize information systems in their daily work (i.e. what skills and knowledge are required to utilize IS?). *Secondly, the technical component* includes both hardware (computers, networks etc.) and a software perspective. *Thirdly, the management component* is the mediating component in our maturity definition. *Human maturity* is an area of the management and social components that includes their mutual interaction as well as their interaction with the technical component.

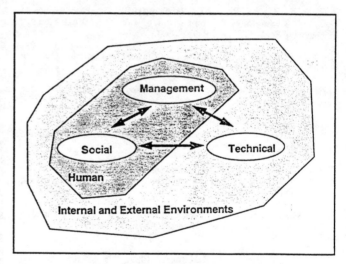

Figure 1:Organizational maturity in the context of IS management and use

2.1 The Social Component of Maturity

The quality of organizational actors is an important factor in the effective use of IT [see e.g. 1, 2, 6, 7], since the adoption of some technologies involves a substantial knowledge burden on would-be adopters [18]. Also, adopters - rather than making a binary decision to adopt or reject - may choose differing levels of IT use (see the overview of Fischman [18]) or slow and halt its assimilation [25, cited in 39]. The social component of maturity is a product of individual and organizational level learning. According to Nelson [43], learning is a relatively permanent change in behavior occurring as a result of experience. Kim [33] defined the term "learning" as *an increasing capacity to take effective action* where knowledge or skill is acquired. Learning consists of two parts: what people learn (know-how) and how they understand and apply that learning (know-why). Argyris and Schön [3] stated that organizational learning takes place via individuals whose actions are based on shared models. In his model, Kim explains the interconnections between individual and organizational learning as follows [33]:

Although the meaning of the term "learning" remains essentially the same as in the individual case, the learning process is fundamentally different at the organizational level. A model of organizational learning has to resolve the dilemma of imparting intelligence and capabilities to a nonhuman entity without anthropomorphizing it. ...The individual learning cycle is the process through which those beliefs change and those changes are then codified in the individual mental models. The cycles of individual learning affect learning at the organizational level through their influence on the organization's shared mental models.

2.2 The Technical Component of Maturity

The technical component (i.e. hardware and software) is a platform for IS development but is not sufficient for organizational maturity. The technical component of maturity is the "traditional" view of organizational computing that describes what kind of technology is in use and to what extent. Take for example the "stages" model for end-user computing developed by Nolan, Norton & Co. [28]. In this model, even networked organizations are described based on the technology in use (Client/Server, Cooperative Processing, Open Architectures). In our organizational maturity definition we see the technical component as an artifact that has to support organizational goals. Organizational learning makes possible the effective use of new as well as older innovations.

2.3 The Management Component of Maturity

The management component of maturity is also a product of individual and organizational learning. It therefore needs multiple views from different stakeholders (i.e. individual level mental models) and their interaction to achieve common goals (i.e. shared mental models at organizational level). The management view, knowledge and skills affect how the IS function is organized and how organizational objectives and needs are aligned between technical and social components. A number of IS researchers have either been worried about the dysfunctional gap between different managers and managerial groups, emphasized the importance of education and training or introduced group-work for improved IS planning [11, 14, 20, 52]. In the IS strategy formulation process, both human and technological sides of organizational maturity should be understood, as IS strategy consists not only of IT strategy, but also of strategies for change management and human resource management [see 21]. Earl [16, 17] states that the unsuccessful features of strategic level IS planning vary, depending on the differing views of stakeholders.

Based on the Leonard-Barton and Deschamps [39] findings, people whose characteristics incline them to adopt an innovation will do so without management support, but people with low adoption characteristics seem to wait until management issues a directive to adopt. Following an organizational decision to adopt an innovation, active people tend to make the decision whether or not to adopt without managerial direction [see also 37]. The successful performance of companies can often be attributed to their management, but it is a fact that activities must be implemented for goals to be promoted. Management has to be aware of technological possibilities, and at what rate organizations can achieve changes in the way they are working. This implies that competitive advantages have to be linked to human resources, which is an evolutionary process where short-cuts cannot be taken.

2.4 The Internal and External Environments of Maturity

Maturity and its components are understood in their context [36]. The internal environment includes, for example, organizational settings such as organizational structures, work processes, tasks and the division of labor. The external environment includes, for example, an organization's customers, suppliers, competitors and state regulations.

3. A CONCEPTUAL FRAMEWORK AND TOOLS PRESENTATION

The human side of organizational maturity can be evaluated via the six general areas of knowledge and skills required by all employees (see Table 1). Nelson [42, 43] used this classification, suggested by Zmud [56], to assess educational and training needs.

In this classification, organizational and functional learning are separated and they have special meanings. Areas of organizational learning are related to organizational goals and objectives, while areas of functional learning are in a specific domain or work unit (e.g. marketing, finance or information systems) [43, 56]. As can be seen from Table 1, data has been collected using multiple methods, in order to collect both qualitative and some more formal (i.e. quantitative) data to support the conclusions drawn. The framework to measure organizational maturity in the use of IT consists of three process phases (see Figure 2): 1) scanning the organization, 2) stakeholder distance analysis and 3) user organization abilities analysis. The evaluation of organizational maturity provides us with the initial phase and is followed by alternative organizational development routes. The alternative development routes (see the Figure 2) are social (e.g. user skills and knowledge intensive), managerial (e.g. Strategic IS Planning) or technical (e.g. Investments in hardware and software projects) specific. The selected development route is dependent on which component has been identified as lacking and in need of development.

3.1 Constructing Measurement Instruments

Scientific rigor requires reliable and valid testing instruments. Qualitative methods have been noted to be especially

	Organizational Scanning	User Organizations' Abilities Analysis		Stakeholder Distance Analysis
	Participation and interviews	Laboratory experiment	Question-naire	Self-assessment
Organizational overview - objectives, purpose, opportunities, constraints, and internal and external functioning	X			
Organizational skills - interpersonal behavior, group dynamics and project management	X			X
Target organizational unit - objectives, purpose, functions, resources, links with other internal and external units, and problems	X		(X)	X
General IS knowledge - hardware and software concepts, IS potential, organizational IS policies and plans, and existing IS applications	X		X	X
Technical skills - methods and techniques required to perform IS-related tasks		X	X	
IS-product - purpose, design, required procedures and documentation		X	X	

Table 1.Topics and data collection methods in the evaluation of maturity

problematic, as no statistical coefficient and reliability measurements can be performed. Researchers using quantitative methods have also worried about the scientific rigor of survey measures, however. Lee [38] presented a methodology for conducting a single case study that satisfies the standards of the natural science model of scientific research (controlled observations, controlled deductions, replicability and generalizability). Contrary to Lee, Zmud [57] and Galliers [22] have stated that it is unlikely one could validate any information systems technique in a one-shot research project, but that validation is possible under a scientific paradigm through the adoption of a long-term, multi-study perspective. According to Benbasat et. al. [9], single-case study projects are most useful at the outset of theory generation and late in theory testing. Furthermore, as the actual process of constructing a measurement instrument is a long and costly learning process, it must be divided into several studies (see the overview of Sethi - King [53]). Another solution is to use multiple methods i.e. pluralism to make better observations and draw better conclusions. Multiple methods in data collection offer the opportunity for triangulation and lend greater support to the researcher's conclusions [9], although there are no clear answers as to how to take full advantage of each approach [19, 22, 27, 35, 55].

It is our opinion that a measurement instrument can be validated through a long process based on multiple methods, but construction has to be achieved in a controlled fashion based on deep knowledge of the research area. Several studies made in sequence allows for critical evaluation of the tool itself, as well as of the findings and experiences gained through using the tool (see Figure 3).

3.2 Organizational Scanning

Organizational scanning (see Figure 2.) has two objectives. First, the researchers learn about the object organization's internal and external operations and organizational principles and goals. The second objective is the assessment of skills and knowledge related to the organizational overview, organiza-

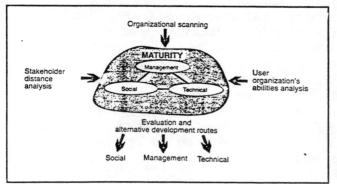

Figure 2: The development processes based on organizational maturity

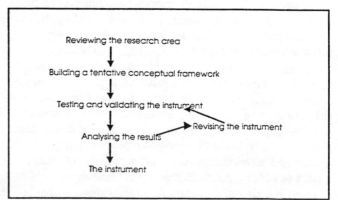

Figure 3: Building, testing and validating a measurement instrument through multiple sequence cases

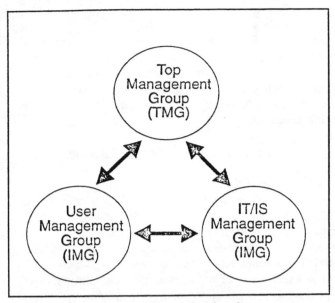

Figure 4:Critical stakeholders in the planning process

tional skills, target organizational skills and general IS knowledge (see Table 1.). Learning the organization under scrutiny is a crucial step, because misunderstanding will affect later phases and results [53]. Furthermore, studies evaluating IS generally assume that the system under study has become stable, instead of examining how the process of developing and implementing the system from its very origin affects outcomes [32, 49]. Our data collection methods involved semistructured interviews and participation. A selected list of questions was used to structure the interviews, and the questions chosen at each interview depended on the interviewee's organizational position.

3.3 Stakeholder Distance Analysis

Three critical stakeholder groups strongly affect the IS planning process and its outcomes (see Figure 4., more in Ruohonen [50]). The actors' knowledge and motivation changes during the development process. This is evaluated by a special instrument called the Information Management Knowledge and Motivation Inventory (IMI). IMI is a self-assessment questionnaire for the support of IS planning processes.

3.3.1 The Structure of the Information Management Knowledge and Motivation Inventory (IMI)

The inventory includes three sections or parts. Each has a special purpose and they can be used together as a multi-assessment tool. The tool deal with the analysis of organizational skills, the target organizational unit and general IS knowledge (see Table 1).

Background; First Part

The first part collects data about the respondents' background. The following were considered in this case study [51]: 1) stakeholder group, 2) background education, 3) IT/IS training received during the last 3 years, 4) previous experience on a PC/different application software and 5) previous participation in IS development.

Learning Issues; Second Part

The next part was designed to present critical learning issues (LIs) concerning IT, information management and IS organization. The IMI consisted of 35 LIs on which managers were asked to comment. LIs were derived from literature concerning information management and the strategic use of IT [40, 41, 47, 48]. The IMI instrument should assess the change of awareness/refocusing on emerging IS issues after management education sessions. The selection of learning issues was aligned with the contents of educational sessions in the case company. It was not intended to be a comprehensive and universal collection of information management issues (see Appendix A for the IMI structure). The inner dimensions of the IMI learning issues were identified through expert analysis. Two dimensions were selected as being important, namely the traditional management vs. technical perspective dimension and the operational value vs. strategic value dimension. The operational value of the LI refers to business objectives, which are mainly related to cost-efficiency and technical feasibility. The strategic value of an LI refers to its potential for use for competition purposes and in support of business strategy. The LIs were selected according to their position within these dimensions, in order to cover the two-dimensions.

The positioning of LIs was executed by five professional department members from the authors' university. They were asked to position each LI in one of the four categories. With the help of a cluster analysis, a 2x2 matrix was created and each LI roughly situated in the matrix. LI categories are naturally overlapping, but some patterns can be found in the analysis of the IMI results [51]. Categories were identified as follows:

1. Applications and Organization, to refer to issues dealing mostly with operationally important management issues.
2. Information Technology, to refer to issues dealing with separate technical issues that have, however, mainly operational value.
3. Management and Strategy, to refer to issues dealing with management issues of strategic value, that have emerged from the evolution of the strategic use of IT and become critical for business.
4. IT Architecture, to refer to issues dealing with large-scale IT infrastructure issues of strategic value, which cannot be handled as separate technical matters.

Open Comments vs. Self-Assessment; Third Part

Open comments/answers naturally produce a rich set of expression but are very often superficial or at least unstructured. Each LI was therefore designed to include a self-assessment element (SA). The SA element requests an assessment by the respondent of his/her knowledge about and motivation towards the issue. The assessment scale used was a 5-step semiordinal scale.

3.3.2 The Modes of Processing; the Use of Cluster Analysis

Cluster analysis was used in this case to measure similarities between stakeholder groups. Cluster analysis is a procedure for detecting natural groupings of objects. Hierarchical clustering was the preferred method in this case study, a hierarchical cluster consisting of that which completely contains other clusters that completely contain other clusters etc. Differentiation of clusters was achieved via similarity measures. Similar objects appear in the same cluster and dissimilar objects in different clusters. Similarity measures also imply the distances between clusters. A percentage distance index and single linkage method (nearest neighbor) were used to produce comparisons of values resulting in contrasts between two profiles [see for more details 29, 54]. The cluster display (i.e. tree) is printed in a manner such that every branch is lined up with the most similar objects closest to each other (unique ordering). The tree produces a one-dimensional ordering of the data [26].

3.4 User Organization Abilities Analysis (UOA)

The purpose of the UOA tool is to assess the user organization's human side of organizational maturity, since we are interested in how organizations are able to utilize IS. The instrument concentrates more on the social component than the management component, although some relevant topics from the latter are included. The term "utilize" has a twofold meaning in this context. First, the users' skills in using software packages and applications, and secondly, the way in which the potential of IT is understood and implemented to support organizational goals. Laboratory experiment, questionnaire and interview methods were used. Both the laboratory tests and questionnaire were used to assess technical skills and IS product-related topics. In addition, the questionnaire assessed general IS knowledge, and to a lesser extent, topics related to the target organizational unit. The interviews were used in follow-up studies to connect quantitative results to work processes (see Table 1).

The UOA tool was used twice in the same company. In our view, in order to construct an instrument, the tool changed greatly in nature due to development based on experience (see Figure 3). The company under scrutiny was a conglomerate operating in foodstuffs, animal feed and chemicals. The first version of the tool concentrated only on end-user computing and microcomputer software packages. On the first occasion, the tool was used to reveal the current level of microcomputer use, and to discover the possibilities that might exist for its improvement. The second time, the tool also included applications and a deeper insight into the company, which made it possible to understand the organization's information systems and link the findings to real-life.

3.4.1 The Structure of the UOA Tool

In order to measure a user organization's IS-related organizational maturity, the use of organizational scanning is required as expressed in Figure 2. The UOA tool itself consists of the following parts: 1) organizational use of applications and software packages, 2) laboratory tests, 3) questionnaire and 4) follow-up.

Organizational Use of Applications and Software Packages

The purpose of the definition of the organizational use of applications and software packages was to select a set of software packages and applications - both micro and mainframe - as indicators. This selection was based on their organizational importance and the number and type of their users. The selection represented the object organization's IS, and different types of software applications and packages (operational, control, planning, communication etc.) were included. The selected software was studied in its environment, to ensure a comprehensive understanding of the situation in which it was being used.

Laboratory Tests

Computing skills, both in micro and mainframe computing, were measured by testing. The microcomputer software packages chosen for testing, were commonly used types of corporate software (e.g. word processor, spreadsheet, graphics) and the operating system. One hundred and five (of the 120 invited) mainframe and sixty (of the 80 invited) microcomputer users participated in the laboratory tests. The population consisted of active users and the selection was based on random sampling. The software application tests measured users' skills in utilizing the most important business applications; see Appendix, tables B and C, more in [4, 5]. In general, a laboratory test measures simulations of work processes rather than real ones. Therefore, a broader view was needed, and the tasks for each software application and package in the laboratory tests were based on the following topics:

- The work chains, people, organizations and other applications related to the tasks supported by an application or a package.
- The users' primary and secondary tasks.
- The tasks supported by an application or package.
- The functions of an application or package.

A laboratory test comprised 7 to 15 exercises, with a different set time allocated to each exercise. For example, in one exercise users were required to construct a report and determine columns, rows and groups; in another they had to print a basic report from an application. Applications and software packages required different sorts of test because of their respective natures. The utilization of software packages requires an ability to determine how to use them in different situations. Applications, on the other hand, fulfill operational tasks that occur time after time, and the users employ completed programs. They don't have to be able to determine and develop their own applications to solve a problem (see examples in Appendix B).

Questionnaire

The purpose of the questionnaire was to gather information about participants, organizational factors and information systems (see Table 2). The questionnaire is constructed based on several research papers [see for example 12, 13, 31, 46] and experiences gained from organizational computing. Through the questionnaire, users estimated their own ability to utilize IT in their work and, in so doing, exposed the gap between actual and imagined skills in computing. Background information was collected to describe the case study and the usage environment, as well as important facts about the users themselves. As attitudes are important to the way individuals and organizations utilize IT, it was also worthwhile collating users' opinions of and satisfaction with information systems, their support, and IS organization. Users' opinions about management's abilities in managing IT, and management's opinions about employees' abilities in utilizing IT were also sought, as we were interested in the interaction between maturity components.

Follow-up

In the follow-up, the preliminary findings gained through laboratory experiment and the questionnaire were reflected to real situations. The researcher interviewed people from the organizational functions that participated in the laboratory tests. Interviews also included white-collar workers from organizations or departments that cooperated with the object function to gain a broader view. The discussion themes were collated from the items included in the laboratory tests and questionnaire. Further information was collected from the practices and goals of the organizational functions.

3.4.2 The Analysis Process

The results obtained with the UOA tool had to be analyzed in line with the data collected in the organizational scanning phase. The data analysis was executed in three phases. First, the diffusion of IT was described based on the frequency and amount of use. Secondly, the maturity of the social component was analyzed in relation to the overall use of IT as brought out by the questionnaire and laboratory tests. Thirdly, quantitative data was bound with the qualitative data collected in the follow-up studies, and final conclusions were drawn. When we used this tool in real situations, the results were judged in relation to the object organization's internal and external environments, and this required both quantitative and qualitative analysis. Laboratory tests of microcomputer software packages may be generalized, but applications laboratory tests are always unique. However, the comparisons between organizations have to be made verbally, taking into account organizations' cultures and environments.

4. DISCUSSION

Our numerous case studies (both with and without measurement instruments) and literature review reveal that it is vital to understand organizational maturity in computing, in order to make focused development plans (see Figure 2). A proper understanding requires more rigorous measurement tools. On the other hand, quality of interaction is very difficult and laborious to measure, and so should be evaluated using qualitative methods i.e. participant observation and interviews. The tools presented in this paper make it possible to obtain both quantitative and qualitative information about the organization, combined with real-life planning processes.

The IMI instrument allows researchers to obtain richer data for the analysis of managers' knowledge about and motivation towards IS. This is evident when compared with other techniques such as a purely structured questionnaire or open-answer formulae. Every manager's self-assessment of knowledge can be analyzed together with his/her background information. A knowledge assessment can be validated and compared with open answers in order to discover a manager's obvious level of knowledge and his/her opinion of it, which improves internal validity. An assessment of motivation may open up the level of resistance to change caused by IT, and can be analyzed with open answer and/or background information. Finally, all three parts of the IMI (open comments/ answers, knowledge and motivation assessments) can be

Questionnaire themes	Examples
Personal resources (i.e. Skills)	Skills to utilize software packages, software applications and operating systems
Experience with IT	Amount and frequency of use, years of experience with IT
Tasks	Work description, tasks supported with IT
Attitudes about IS resources	Effectiveness, efficacy, and satisfaction (IS systems, IS organization, Support, IT)
Organizational factors	Managerial support, Managerial IS competence, Employees competence (Managerial view)
Other background information	Age, education, gender, Experience with the company, SBU, Organizational function

Table 2. Topics in the questionnaire

comprehensively evaluated together to create a coherent view of the perspectives of each manager. Stakeholder views are grouped according to personal managerial views.

The UOA tool made it possible to obtain both qualitative and statistically relevant quantitative information about the organization. Degree and frequency of use cannot be put to work to measure actual skills and organizational maturity. In some instances, putting familiar equipment to only limited use can induce a feeling of monotony, which hinders learning. The human side of IS-related organizational maturity can be identified through the use of multiple methods. The laboratory tests, questionnaire, interviews and participation (scanning and follow-up) made it possible to obtain a both broad and deep view from the organization under scrutiny. The results culled from the UOA tool may be divided into two categories. First, a better understanding of the current situation, and second, the potential for improved effectiveness. The organization might thus attain a realistic overview of its current level of individual and organizational learning, both in general and within different organizational units.

Most IS research areas lack previously defined measures. Both of the tools described were found to be applicable and useful in our research projects. They provided more formal support to the overall qualitative analysis of case companies and their maturity. However, they are still very context-dependent and should be tailored for forthcoming studies. Future effort should be directed towards developing more generally applicable tools e.g. for a specific industry. The learning issues of the IMI tool should be carefully defined with a larger sample and validated following the principles of constructing measurement instruments. This was not possible within a single case study. The UOA tool should be developed to be more general, especially the laboratory tests of microcomputer software packages, and the questionnaire should be generalized. However, measurement research in the IS management and use area is vastly underdeveloped, and these two examples represent a good starting point.

References:

[1]Abrahamson E. (1991) Managerial Fads and Fashions: The Diffusion and Rejection of Innovations, *Academy of Management Review*, Vol. 16, No. 3, pp.586-612

[2]Amoroso D.L. (1991) The Effect of Task Characteristics on Intended and Actual Utilization of Emerging Technologies, *Proceedings of the 24th Hawaii International Conference on Systems Sciences*, January, Vol. IV, pp. 479-486

[3]Argyris C. - Schön D.A. (1978) *Organizational Learning: Theory Action Perspective*. Addison-Wesley

[4]Auer T. (1993), Assessing the State of Learning in Utilizing Information Systems, *Proceedings of the 16th IRIS Conference*, August, Part III, pp. 756-769

[5]Auer T. (1993), An Approach to Measuring an Organization's Ability to Utilize Computer Supported Routines, in: *Knowledge Formation in Management Research*, Åbo Akademi Ser. A:405, ed. Christer Carlsson

[6]Beatty C.A. - Gordon R.M. (1988) Barriers to the Implementation of CAD/CAM Systems, *Sloan Management Review*, Vol. 30, No. 1, pp. 25-34

[7]Beer M. - Eisenstat R.A. - Spector, Bert (1990) *The Critical Path to Corporate Renewal*, Harvard Business School Press, Boston

[8]Benbasat I. - Dexter A.S. - Drury D.H. - Goldstein R.C. (1984) A Critique of the Stage Hypothesis: Theory and Empirical Evidence, *Communications of the ACM*, Vol. 27, No. 5, pp. 476-485

[9]Benbasat I. - Goldstein D.K. - Mead, M. (1987) The Case Research Strategy in Studies of Information Systems, *MIS Quarterly*, Vol. 11, September, pp. 369-386

[10]Brown C.V. - Bostrom R.P. (1989), A Contingency Model for the Management of End-User Computing: Model Development and Exploratory Validation, *Proceedings of the 22nd Hawaii International Conference on Systems Sciences*, January, Vol. IV, pp. 70-77

[11]Cash J. - McFarlan F.W. - McKenney J.L. (1988) *Corporate Information Systems Management- Issues Facing Senior Managers*, Dow Jones Irwin, Illinois.

[12]Davis F.D. - Bagozzi Richard P. - Warshaw Paul R. (1989) User Acceptance of Computer Technology: A Comparision of Two Theoretical Models, *Management Science*, Vol. 35, No. 8, pp. 982-1003

[13]Davis G.B. - Collins Rosann Webb - Eierman Michael - Nance William D. (1991) *Conceptual Model for Research on Knowledge Work*, Revision, Minneapolis

[14]Earl M.J. (1988) IT and Strategy: Reflections and Directions, in *Information Management - The Strategic Dimension*, ed. Earl, M.J., Clarendon Press, Oxford, pp. 275-290

[15]Earl M.J. (1989), *Management Strategies for Information Technology*, Prentice Hall International

[16]Earl M.J. (1990) Approaches to Strategic Information Systems Planning - Experience in Twenty-one United Kingdom Companies, *Proceedings of the Eleventh ICIS*, December 16.-19., Copenhagen, Denmark, pp. 271-277

[17]Earl M.J. (1993) Experiences in Strategic Information Systems Planning, *MIS Quarterly*, March, Vol. 17, No. 1, pp. 1 - 24

[18]Fischman R.G. (1992) Information Technology Diffusion: A Review of Empirical Research. *Proceedings of the Thirteenth ICIS*, December 13-16, Dallas, Texas, USA, pp. 195-206.

[19]Fitzgerald G. (1991) Validating New Information Systems Techniques: A Retrospective Analysis, in *Information Systems Research: Contemporary Approaches & Emergent Traditions*, eds Nissen H.-E. - Klein H.K. - Hirschheim R., North-Holland, Amsterdam, pp. 657-672

[20]Galliers R.D. (1988) Information Technology Strategies Today: The UK Experience. In *Information Management - The Strategic Dimension*, ed. Earl M.J., Clarendon Press, Oxford, pp. 179-201

[21]Galliers R.D. (1991) Strategic Information Systems: Myths, Reality and Guidelines for Successful Implementation. *European Journal of Information Systems*, Vol. 1., No. 1., pp. 55-64.

[22]Galliers R.D. (1991) Choosing Appropriate Information Systems Research Approaches: A Revised Taxonomy, in *Information Systems Research: Contemporary Approaches & Emergent Traditions*, eds. Nissen H.-E. - Klein H.K. - Hirschheim R., North-Holland, Amsterdam, pp. 327-345

[23]Galliers R.D. - Sutherland A.R. (1991) Information Systems Management and Strategy Formulation: the 'stages of growth' model revisited, *Journal of Information Systems*, Vol. 1, No. 2, pp. 89 - 114

[24]Gibson C.F. - Nolan R.L. (1974) Managing the Four Stages of EDP Growth, *Harvard Business Review*, January-February, Vol. 52, No. 1, pp. 76-88

[25]Gruenfeld L.W. - Foltman F.F. (1967) Relationship Among Supervisors' Integration Satisfaction and Acceptance of a Technological Change, *Journal of Applied Psychology*, Vol. 51, pp. 74 - 77

[26]Gruvaeus G. - Wainer H. (1972) Two additions to hierarchical cluster analysis. *The British Journal of Mathematical and Statistical Psychology*, 25, pp.200-206

[27]Gummesson E. (1988), *Qualitative Methods in Management Research*, Studentlitterature Chartwell-Bratt, Lund

[28]Halloran J.P. (1993) Achieving World-Class End-User Computing, *Information Systems Management*, Vol. 10, No. 4, pp. 7-12

[29]Hartigan J.A. (1975) *Clustering algorithms*, John Wiley & Sons Inc., New York

[30]Henderson J.C. - Treacy M.E. (1986) Managing End-User Computing for Competitive Advantage, *Sloan Management Review*, Winter, Vol. 27, No. 2, pp. 3-14

[31]Igbaria M. (1990) End-User Computing Effectiveness: A Structural Equation Model, *Omega International Journal of Management Science*, Vol. 18, No. 6, pp. 637-652

[32]Kaplan B. (1991) Models of Change and Information Systems Research, *in Information Systems Research: Contemporary Approaches & Emergent Traditions*, eds. Nissen H.-E. & Klein H.K. & Hirschheim R., North-Holland, Amsterdam, pp. 593-611

[33]Kim D.H. (1993) The Link Between Individual and Organizational Learning, *Sloan Management Review*, Fall, Vol. 35, No. 1, pp. 37-50

[34]King J.L. & Kraemer K.L. (1984) Evolution and Organizational Information Systems: An Assessment of Nolan's Stage Model, *Communications of the ACM*, Vol. 27, No. 5, pp. 466-475

[35]Klein H.K. - Nissen H-E - Hirscheim R. (1991) A Pluralistic Perspective of the Information Systems Research Arena, *in Information Systems Research: Contemporary Approaches & Emergent Traditions*, eds Nissen H.-E. & Klein H.K. & Hirschheim R., North-Holland, Amsterdam, pp. 1-20

[36]Kling R. (1987) Defining the Boundaries of Computing Across Complex Organizations, in *Critical Issues in Information systems research*, eds. Boland, R.J. - Hirschheim R., John Wiley & Sons, New York, pp. 307-362

[37]Kwon T.H. (1990) A Diffusion of Innovation Approach to MIS Infusion: Conceptualization, Methodology, and Management Strategies, *Proceedings of the Eleventh ICIS*, December 16-19, Dallas, Texas, USA, pp. 139-147.

[38]Lee A.S. (1989) A Scientific Methodology for MIS Case Studies, *MIS Quarterly*, Vol. 13, March, pp. 33-50

[39]Leonard-Barton D. - Deschamps I. (1988) Managerial Influence in the Implementation of New Technology, *Management Science*, Vol. 34, No. 10, pp. 1252-1265

[40]McFarlan F.W. (1984) Information Technology Changes the Ways You Compete, *Harvard Business Review* 62 (3), pp. 98-103.

[41]McFarlan F.W. - McKenney J. (1983) *Corporate Information Systems Management - Issues Facing Senior Managers 1. edition*, Dow Jones Irwin, Homewood IL.

[42]Nelson R.R. (1989) Education and Training: Prescriptions for Organizational Learning, *Proceedings of the 22nd Hawaii International Conference on Systems Sciences*, January, Vol. IV, pp. 86-95

[43]Nelson R.R. (1991) Educational Needs as Perceived by IS and End-User Personnel: A Survey of Knowledge and Skill Requirements, *MIS Quarterly*, Vol. 15, No. 4, pp. 503-525

[44]Nolan R.L. (1979) Managing the Crises in Data Processing, *Harvard Business Review*, March-April, Vol. 57, No. 2, pp. 115-126

[45]Pascale R.T. - Athos A.G. (1981) *The Art of Japanese Management*, Penguin, Harmondsworth

[46]Pentland B.T. (1989) Use and Productivity in Personal Computing: An Empirical Test, *Proceedings of the tenth International Conference on Information Systems*, December, pp. 211-222

[47]Porter M.E. (1980) *Competitive Strategy*, Free Press

[48]Porter M.E. (1985) *Competitive Advantage*, Free Press

[49]Rogers E.M. (1983) *Diffusion of Innovations*, New York, Free Press

[50]Ruohonen M. (1991) Stakeholders of Strategic Information Systems Planning - theoretical concepts and empirical examples, *The Journal of Strategic IS*, Vol. 1, No. 1, pp. 15-28.

[51]Ruohonen M. (1991) *Strategic Information Systems Planning - Analyzing Organizational Stakeholders and Planning Support Activities*. Publications of the Turku School of Economics and Business Administration A-2:1991

[52]Scott-Morton M.S. (1988) Strategy Formulation Methodologies and IT. in *Information Management - The Strategic Dimension*, ed. Earl, M.J (ed.) (1988), pp. 54-70

[53]Sethi V. - King R (1991) Construct Measurement in Information Systems Research: An Illustration in Strategic Systems, *Decision Science*, Vol. 22, No. 3, July/Aug, pp. 455-472

[54]Sokal R.R. - Sneath, P.H.A. (1963) *Principles of Numerical Taxonomy*, W.H. Freeman and Co., San Francisco

[55]Wynekoop J.L. - Conger S.A. (1991) A Review of Computer Aided Software Engineering Research, *in Information Systems Research: Contemporary Approaches & Emergent Traditions*, eds Nissen H.-E. & Klein H.K. & Hirschheim R., North-Holland, Amsterdam, pp. 301-325

[56]Zmud R.W. (1983) *Information Systems in Organizations*, Scott, Foresman and Company, Tucker

[57]Zmud R.W. (1991) Bias in Information System Design: Discussant's Remarks, in *Information Systems Research: Contemporary Approaches & Emergent Traditions*, eds Nissen H.-E. & Klein H.K. & Hirschheim R., North-Holland, Amsterdam, pp. 699-702

Appendix:

Table A: The questions in the IMI tool

No.	Question	No.	Question
1.	The integration of business and IS strategies	19.	The use of viewdata systems in business
2.	The potential of IT in business operations and management	20.	The value chain and the role of IT in its development
3.	Management information systems, Decision Support Systems	21.	The importance of software maintenance and its costs
4.	Centralization of information processing and distributed information processing	22.	An organization's database and its utilization
5.	IS potential in comparison with 10 years ago	23.	The use of telecommunications in business
6.	Interorganizational networks and their use	24.	Office automation, factory automation
7.	Independent use of EUC	25.	Mainframe, mini and microcomputer
8.	Electronic mail	26.	Application and application generator
9.	Expert systems and their use in business	27.	Personal workstation and opportunities for its use
10.	Customer terminals and their importance	28.	The information management function and the difference with IS Dept.
11.	Efficiency of information processing activities	29.	The formulation of information management
12.	Effectiveness of information processing activities	30.	Joint hardware, software and data resources
13.	IT as a part of a product	31.	The functions of an IS-based reporting system
14.	IT in customer relationships management	32.	Local area network, wide area public network
15.	IT in supplier relationships management	33.	Interorganizational information systems (IOS), an example of the IOS organization
16.	IT in creating entry barriers	34.	Chief Information Officer
17.	IT in the structural change of an industry	35.	Infocenter
18.	IT as support for competition		

Table B: Number of participants in the laboratory tests (UOA tool)

Mainframe		Microcomputers	
- Purchasing, agricultural raw materials	8	- Word Processor	51
- Purchasing, other goods	22	- Spreadsheet	32
- Order taking	13	- Graphics	14
- Marketing	24		
- Accounts payable	11		
- Stock accounting	9		
- Internal accounting and commercial bookkeeping	18		
- E-mail	60		

Table C: Examples of exercises (UOA tool)

Spreadsheet	Purchasing, other goods
- Save a file	- Make an order suggestion
- Type numbers into a table	- Make an order
- Format columns and cells	- Browse an order
- Write formulas (+, -, *, /, sum, average)	- Cancel an order
- Copy formulas and table	- Check the order number
- Print a table	- Approve a delivery
- Make and modify a graph	

New Questions for Information Resource Management

John Gessford, Ph.D.
Associate Professor
Information Systems Department
California State University, Long Beach
Long Beach, CA 90840
(310) 985-7881

ABSTRACT

The rethinking of business management that is taking place relies on information systems to make possible new forms of organization and management. Concurrent engineering, continuous process improvement, and reengineering, for example, all rely on information systems to accomplish their goals.

In this environment, what does managing the information resources of an organization entail? The paper argues that it includes more than just providing access to data for the existing organization. It must include redesigning the organization to make the best use of all the data potentially available. The organization should no longer be taken as a given by information resource managers.

Three of the major questions that arise when this new perspective is taken are examined. First, the possibility is considered of improving corporate performance by consolidating processes and making single individuals responsible for these macro-processes. Second, the strategy of making parallel processing possible by providing access to a shared database is examined. Third, disaggregating a distributed process and centralizing a part of it is described as a means of getting the best of both centralization and decentralization.

It is concluded that the IRM paradigm needs to be updated if IRM is to survive as a professional area. A Drucker prediction that only information system specialists and general business executives are needed is cited to evidence that information systems managers are not presently seen as providing the vision of new information system possibilities. The need to change what is taught in business schools about IRM is also noted.

INTRODUCTION

The phrase Information Resource Management (IRM) has been in use for more than two decades. It originated in the 60's with the development of computer files and databases. Originally, it referred only to managing data in a way that made it more widely available to those who could benefit from it in a business. The focus was on enabling managers to get at transaction data for purposes other than merely processing transactions. The development of file management systems, and later database management systems, made this possible.

By the 80's the meaning of information resource management had broadened to include all of the resources involved in collecting, processing and delivering data to information system users. It had become synonymous with information systems management. It retained, however, the connotation of seeking to maximize the benefits obtained from the data files. The glossary in Stair has this definition for IRM: The control and use of a company's data and information so that the greatest possible benefit can be obtained.

It is the thesis of this paper that the rethinking of business management by American executives, caused by the successful penetration of American markets by foreign competitors, is leading to another expansion in the meaning of IRM. This rethinking manifests itself in Concurrent Engineering, Total Quality Management (TQM), Continuous Processing Improvement (CPI), Business Re-engineering and other related management philosophies that redefine responsibilities and roles in the corporation. These new perspectives have profound implications for IRM. The traditional first IRM question, What information is needed to effectively execute a process? becomes secondary. The primary question becomes, how should processes be designed to effectively use information technology. Business processes become variables to be manipulated to maximize the use of data.

Information resource managers given the opportunity to take this new perspective face new questions. New methods of analysis are needed to find answers. This paper surveys these new questions and the answers being found.

Processes

The concept of a process is central to many the new management approaches. Concurrent Engineering attempts to coordinate and overlap design processes with manufacturing process planning. TQM makes process management the basis for all management and control. Continuous Process Improvement makes the measurement of process output and the adjustment of process inputs and activities to improve output quality and reduce costs the key to long term survival and success. Business reengineering identifies the processes that are most vital to achieving the objectives of the organization, defines jobs and responsibilities so that these processes get appropriate attention and invests in the information technology required to perform the new jobs.

So it is appropriate to begin by considering what constitutes a process. In the following paragraphs, the basic characteristics of processes are briefly reviewed. Further discussion and analysis of processes can be found in many books and articles on the new management philosophies.

By definition, a process consists of actions taken to achieve a result. The definition implies that a process has a purpose or intent. Thus, the phrase "random process" is an oxymoron. A process whose output is entirely random is not a process.

There are normative and actual process results. This is where the idea of managing a process comes into play. A process is managed by defining what the results should be and then designing, building and controlling the process to achieve the desired result. To define what the results should be, benchmarking is often used. Benchmarking is the process of studying competing products and customer needs and then defining a "result" that is competitive and appropriate for the market. The feedback loop of a process compares actual process results to the ideal.

The "actions" of a process may themselves be viewed as processes. Thus, a process may consist of subprocesses. This characteristic makes it possible to aggregate and disaggregate processes. This is an important dimension in the design of processes and jobs in reengineering.

A process may have inputs of parts and materials, skilled manpower, and information. These inputs are outputs of other processes. Thus, two processes may be related in the sense that the output of one is input to the other. This relationship occurs whenever the inputting process is not considered to be part of the process that receives it outputs. From this perspective, aggregating processes simply causes the input-output relationships between the aggregated processes to be ignored.

A process exits in an environment consisting of procedures, facilities, equipment, and the effects of other processes, such as training programs, business and human relationships, and feedback information concerning process outputs. When the environment is defined in this way, the difference between a process and its environment becomes a matter of pace, or timing. The processes that define the environment of a process operate much more slowly than the process. For example, the effects of a drill press operator training program occur over a period of years whereas the output effects of operating a drill press can be measured each hour.

The feedback loop of a process is often considered to be part of the process. A process without a feedback loop is not manageable from the perspective of TQM and CPI. When we consider large aggregated processes, however, such as a college bachelor degree program, the feedback loop is likely to involve many types of surveys, tests and analyses and can itself legitimately qualify as a process aggregate.

New Questions

In defining processes that maximize the use of information by an organization, several questions may be relevant. One is the extent to which processes should be aggregated. Another is the extent to which processes should be performed simultaneously instead of serially. A third, is whether a process being executed independently by many different units needs to be disaggregated so that part of it is performed centrally in a way that coordinates of the work of the distributed units. By carefully considering these questions, information resource managers can find ways to achieve major gains for their organizations.

The basic change in circumstance that makes consideration of these questions worthwhile is the progress being made in information technology. The ease with which data and knowledge in all its forms can be communicated and shared makes obsolete the rationale for many of the existing processes of an organization. It is incumbent on information resource management to point out the new possibilities and their advantages.

Each of the questions is considered in more detail in the following subsections. We point out the information limits that led to the old formulation of processes. The use of information systems to eliminate the information limits is described and the benefits of changing the processes of the organization are outlined.

Process Aggregation

Important fundamental processes in business have been disaggregated in many companies because different steps in the process involve different subjects. Each subject is the specialty of a separate department and each department defines a separate process to carry out its part in the fundamental macro-process of the business. The prime example of this is the process of responding to a customer order. In many companies this involves processes in the sales, finance, purchasing, production, warehousing, shipping, accounting, customer service and collections departments. Each department has its customer order process. Together these subprocesses compose the order processing system of the company.

In cases where the cause of the disaggregation of a process (of major importance to the business) is the fact that it involves several different subjects, information systems may be constructed that make the disaggregation unnecessary. In such cases the advantages of process aggregation can be gained by implementing the integrated information system.

A major advantage of process aggregation is the focussed attention to successful execution of the aggregate process that results. If one person is clearly responsible for responding to one customer's order, for example, it is more likely that the order will be delivered and payment collected quickly than if several people are responsible for different parts of customer order processing. From the customer's viewpoint, the business is likely to respond more intelligently and expeditiously to any glitch in the order fulfillment process if one person is responsible for the customer's order than it will if many persons are responsible for different parts of order fulfillment.

In *Reengineering the Corporation*, Hammer and Champy cite IBM Credit Corporation as an example of the benefits of aggregating a series of processes. Prior to aggregation, IBM Credit responded to a request from an IBM field salesperson for a credit quotation with a sequence of five processes. The first process recorded the request for a quotation. The second checked credit worthiness. The third modified the standard loan covenant to suit the customer. The fourth priced the loan and the fifth prepared the quotation letter and mailed it to the salesperson. Each process was executed by a separate department. The average time to respond to the field salesperson was six days. By aggregating these five processes into one and empowering the "deal structurer" who executed this one process with an information system that provides all the data required to handled most requests, IBM Credit reduced the time to respond by 90% and increased productivity a hundred-fold.

Simultaneous Processes

The fact that information on paper can only be in one place at a time often leads to a series of sequential processes. Each process starts when the paper-based information (a document) is received and ends by passing the document to the next processing unit. In cases where some of the processes could be done simultaneously if the document could be in more than one place at a time, there is an opportunity to quicken the total processing time by introducing a new information system.

Progress in word processing and desktop publishing software makes the handling by computer of composite documents, which include text, tables and graphics, quite possible. Also, image processing systems and CAD/CAM software are available to manage graphical information in computer systems. These developments make it possible for multiple processes to simultaneously access and modify an electronically stored document.

When multiple experts can work on a document simultaneously rather than serially two benefits can result. One is a reduction in elapsed time to complete work on the document. The other is improvements in the quality of the work as a result of increased communication between the experts simultaneously working on the project.

An example of using information systems to enable this kind of process improvement is Kodak's product development process. Hammer and Champy report that Kodak cut the time in half that it takes to develop a new camera by establishing an integrated product design database and enabling the engineers working on different parts of the camera to simultaneous access the design database. Kodak was also able to overlap product design and manufacturing process design by giving the manufacturing engineers access to the same database. The quality improvements resulting from increased interaction between product designers and between product and process designer are at least as significant as the reduced development time. They estimate it reduced tooling and manufacturing costs by 25%.

Disaggregate and Centralize

Traditionally, geographical separation has caused information to be available only locally. Branch sales offices, branch banks, factories, and R&D centers all tend to develop processes that accomplish the same result but have differences in detail (remember, the devil is in the details). A major reason for allowing geographically isolated units to develop their own processes is to avoid the delays and inflexibility that centrally controlled processes cause. People at a central location usually do not have all the information available locally that is relevant to a decision about local operations.

Developments in telecommunications tend to reduce the localization of information. Information can be transmitted to headquarters and headquarter information can be accessed remotely in real time, if necessary. ATMs at branch bank and other locations, for example, transmit patron requests to a central location in real time. They also access centrally maintained account information and make it available to the patron at the remote location.

By using telecommunication systems, organizations can have the advantages of both decentralization and centralization. By linking remote locations to headquarters, the subprocesses that are best handled locally because of the human interactions involved can be done locally. Those that are best handle centrally can be executed from the central location.

Hewlett-Packard saved at least $50 million annually by disaggregating its purchasing process and performing a portion of it centrally.

It had traditionally let each operating division handle its own purchasing because they knew their own needs best. But this was causing H-P to miss volume discounts available from vendors. To get the best of both decentralized and centralized purchasing, they developed a standard purchasing system and installed it on computers in each division. The system accesses a central purchasing database to get information on blanket purchase contracts negotiated centrally and to report on shipment releases issued to vendors locally.

Other Questions

If information resource managers would begin asking only the three questions already discussed, they would totally change the image of the profession and pay for their salaries in savings many times over. Most organizations have processes that can be shown to be obsolete by the light of one of these three questions.

These are not the only questions raised by advances in information technology, however. There are many other profitable questions to consider. The following is a brief list, given to show the broad implications of information technology advancements.

EDI: Could the company's relationships with its suppliers and customers be improved through Electronic Data Interchange services?

Expert systems: Are experts executing processes that could be done by generalists?

Activity-based costing: Do product managers have the cost

data they need to set prices and modify processes so that the business is not unintentionally selling product at a loss?

Portable computers and wireless communication: Could field personnel be more effective if they had better access to corporate data and better communication with others?

Continuous process improvement: Do process managers have the authority and data they need to intelligently control and continuously improve their processes?.

Interactive videodiscs: Could more cost-effective marketing processes be developed by using videodiscs?

Simulation: Are operational plans always obsolete because they are not continuously updated?

Conclusions

The information resource management paradigm needs to be updated. It is not sufficient to focus on the control and use of the company's data and information. The focus needs to be on the processes of the business and how they use information. Business process should not be taken for granted by IRM.

Only a decade ago, information engineering was the hot new paradigm in the information systems field. James Martin and others told us to focus on the data rather than the procedures of data processing. The first step was to determine what information users needed. Now we find that view myopic. We must make another paradigm shift.

In a *Wall Street Journal* article, Peter Drucker distinguishes between being computer literate and information literate. He dismisses "information specialists" as tool makers who are computer literate but not information literate. Information resource managers will be lumped in with the other information specialists unless they demonstrate their information literacy. Drucker characterizes an information literate executive as one who asks, "What new tasks can I tackle now that I have all these data? Which old tasks should I abandon? Which tasks should I do differently?" Information resource managers need to be seen asking these questions for the corporation as a whole as well as for the information systems department.

College and university business degree programs should be in the vanguard working to make the paradigm shift. The change in the description of what an information resource manager does needs to be communicated to the current generation of students in the classroom. Also, radically different ways of thinking and working are required to formulate the best processes for a business. Every year of delay is a year of delay in furnishing industry with graduates prepared to work effectively in an increasingly competitive world marketplace.

References

Drucker, Peter. (1992) "Be Data Literate -- Know What to Know." *The Wall Street Journal*, December 1, 1992

Hammer, Michael & James Champy. (1993) *Reengineering the Corporation.* New York City: HarperBusiness.

Kaplin, Robert S. (1988) One cost system isn't enough. *Harvard Business Review*, Jan-Feb. 1988, 61 - 66.

Malcolm Baldrige National Quality Award: 1993 Award Criteria, Gaithersburg, MD 20899: National Institute of Standards and Technology, U.S. Dept. of Commerce

Martin, James. (1989) *Information Engineering, Books I, II, III.* Englewood Cliffs: Prentice-Hall.

Stair, Ralph M. (1992) Principles of Information Systems, A managerial Approach. Boston: Boyd & Fraser.

Tumey, Peter B. B. (1992) *Common Cents: The ABC Performance Breakthrough*, Hillsboro, OR: Cost Technology, Phone: 1-(800) 368-COST.

Technological Change and Economies of Scale of Mainframes

Young Moo Kang
Department of Management Information Systems
School of Business
Dong-A University
Saha-gu, Busan 604-714
Korea
Tel: (82)051-200-7479
Fax: (82)051-200-7481

INTRODUCTION

There have been many economic analyses of computer hardware price and performance throughout computer history. Some of the representative papers are [1, 3, 6, 10, 11, 12, 22, 23, 24, 26, 27, 28, 30, 31]. One reason for the continuing interest is the important implication of these analyses for computing resource management. Although more attention is being given to the economics of software development and operation as unit costs of hardware continue to decline, the expense of hardware nevertheless remains a significant and constant portion of the total data processing budget over the years [16]. Therefore, as organizations make decisions about centralization or decentralization of CPU resources, knowledge about economies of scale can help in choosing alternatives to be seriously considered. Knowing the growth rate of technology is also vital to data processing (DP) managers since this rate directly affects the timing of decisions on computer obsolescence. Consequently, a thorough understanding of the economic implications of computer performance is necessary in order to make rational decisions on computer resource management.

Most previous studies have been based on Grosch's statement [15]. According to this, the increase in the cost of computing power is proportional to the square root of the power increase. This implies that the economy of scale for computing power is two. Some studies [10, 11, 26, 27, 31] support Grosch's statement. Other studies [1, 22, 23, 28] show that the statement is no longer valid. In this paper, I examine the economic implications of computer performance by emphasizing two issues. The first is technological changes in computers. The second is the form of the performance function.

I will look at the technological changes in computers by utilizing cross-section and time-series data. Since computer technology is changing very rapidly, the bias resulting from a shift of only one year may be serious. Figure 1 shows the effect on estimates of the economies of scale of ignoring improvements in computer technology. The curve labeled Computer i is obtained by plotting the performance level of a computer incorporating Technology i (where i=1, 2) for increase in Characteristic A while all other computer characteristics are held constant.

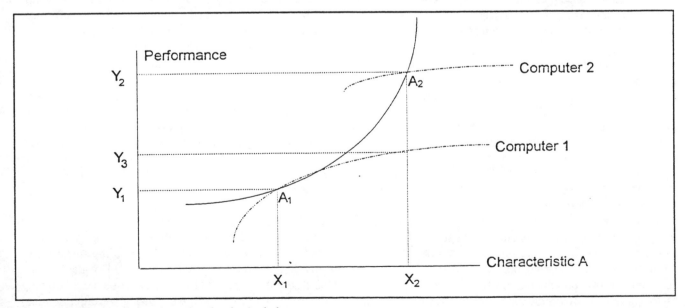

Figure 1: Economies of scale and technological change

By naively observing the two points A_1 and A_2, it may be concluded that doubling Characteristic A (from X_1 to X_2) results in quadrupled performance (from Y_1 to Y_2). However, if the analysis includes the fact that Computer 1 uses old technology and that Computer 2 uses new technology, one can recognize that the above conclusion is incorrect. I can correctly analyze the relation only by examining computers using the same technology. If only Computer 1 is considered, doubling Characteristic A (from X_1 to X_2) will result in a performance increase from Y_1 to Y_3. Therefore, if technological change is not considered properly, the estimate of the economies of scale will be biased by $(Y_2 - Y_3)$. This increase in performance from Y_3 to Y_2 is a result of the technological change.

Technological change measures the increase in computer performance due to shifts in the performance function over time for given computing resources. On the other hand, the economies of scale refers to a relative increase in the performance with respect to a proportional increase in all computing resources for a given technology. Failure to account for these two different effects will result in an incorrect analysis of computer performance. Typically, if the analysis does not include technological change explicitly, then the estimate of economies of scale will be biased upward. This occurs because increases in output due to technological progress are incorrectly considered to be the result of economies of scale.

The second issue I would like to address is the choice of functional form applied to computer performance analysis. For empirical research, the choice of model to be estimated is critical, since the results may depend significantly upon the model selected. However, past studies of computer performance analysis were mostly based on a form of log-linear function, called the Cobb-Douglas function [1, 3, 6, 10, 12, 23, 24, 26, 27, 28, 30, 31]. The popularity of this model is understandable, since it combines some attractive properties with simplicity. (For a detailed discussion of this subject, see [5, 9].) Nevertheless, these conveniences should not have priority over the soundness of the model. One of the major concerns of using the Cobb-Douglas function for computer analysis is the imposition of a restrictive assumption. Applying the Cobb-Douglas function for the analysis implies that each computer characteristic, such as computing speed or memory capacity, contributes a fixed fraction to computer performance over the years, across different systems. This fraction is determined by the coefficient in the Cobb-Douglas function, which is independent of technological changes in computers. Considering the dramatic changes in computer technology, it is desirable to avoid this restriction if possible.

In this paper, I develop a computer performance model using a translog function, which includes the Cobb-Douglas function as a special case. The translog model does not assume fixed performance contribution. In addition to the flexible functional form, our model incorporates vendor specific factors in order to overcome such problems as buyers' loyalty to specific vendors, and different configurations for different vendors. The model developed was applied to the mainframes

available during 1981-1985.

MODEL SPECIFICATION

Assume that each computer's performance (Q) depends mainly upon computer characteristics X_i, where $i=1,...,I$; then the performance function can be written as:

$$F(lnQ, lnX_1,..., lnX_I, T)=0, \quad (1)$$

where T indicates a state of computer technology. I fully differentiate Equation (1) in order to express the total change in performance with respect to the changes in computer characteristics and technology. Following the definitions of technological growth by Caves et al. [2], I define technological change (TECH) as the rate at which performance can grow over time when holding the level of inputs constant. In other words,

$$TECH=(dlnQ/dT), \text{ for } dlnX_i=0 \text{ where } i=1,...,I. \quad (2)$$

Economies of scale (EOS) are defined in terms of the increase in performance resulting from a proportional increase in the level of all inputs for any given technology. In other words,

$$EOS=(dlnQ/dlnX_i), \text{ for } dT=0. \quad (3)$$

By employing specific functions, I may obtain explicit forms for technological change and economies of scale. First, I will use the Cobb-Douglas function and demonstrate its limitations. Second, I will use a flexible translog function. Third, I will examine the relationships of these two functional forms. The Cobb-Douglas function is used to express computer performance as follows:

$$lnQ=_0+_i lnX_i+_1 T+, \quad (4)$$
$$i$$

where Q is a measure of computer performance, X_i is a measure of computer characteristic i, where $i=1,...,I$, T is a measure of the state of computer technology and is an error term. By totally differentiating Equation (4) and applying it to Equations (2) and (3), the technological change and economies of scale which are expressed in terms of the coefficients of the Cobb-Douglas performance function are:

$$TECH=_1 \quad (5)$$
$$EOS=_i \quad (6)$$
$$i$$

From Equations (5) and (6), I can see that the Cobb-Douglas function assumes constant technological change and EOS for all systems over the years. If the model is specified with a single computer characteristic, then the EOS will be the coefficient estimate of that variable. Some of the previous studies use one characteristic such as MIPS [10, 24, 26, 27, 28, 31]. Others have used more than one characteristic [1, 6, 11, 12, 23, 30].

Next, I will use a translog function to express computer performance. The functional form of a translog model is the second order Taylor linear approximation. The advantage of the translog function compared to the Cobb-Douglas function is its flexibility, which will be explained below. Modifying Christensen and Greene [4], the translog performance function is written as:

$$lnQ = _0 + _i lnX_i + (1/2)(_{ij} lnX_i lnX_j) + _0 T + (1/2)_1 T^2 + _i T lnX_i +, (7)$$

where the variables are the same as defined previously. By totally differentiating Equation (7) and applying it to (2) and (3), the rate of technological change and the economies of scale under the translog performance function can be written as:

$$TECH = _0 + _1 T + _i lnX_i (8)$$

$$EOS = _i + _{ij} lnX_j + _i T (9)$$

The above expressions indicate that under the translog specification, technological change is not a constant, but rather a function of computer technology (T) and various computer characteristics (X_i, for $i = 1,...,I$). If technological changes are indeed the same for different models over the years, then the coefficient estimates of $_1$ and $_i$'s (for $i = 1,...,I$) will turn out to be statistically insignificant. Consequently, the translog specification will become identical to the Cobb-Douglas specification.

Similarly, the economies of scale under the translog function includes not only the $_i$'s (for $i = 1,...,I$), as in the case of the Cobb-Douglas specification, but also the computer characteristics (X_i, for $i = 1,...,I$), the state of computer technology (T), and their coefficient estimates. If the true economies of scale for computer performance are the same for different models over the years, then the coefficient estimates of $_{ij}$'s and $_i$'s (for $i, j = 1,...,I$) should be statistically insignificant. I formally test this hypothesis in the Estimation Results Section.

DATA

I need to decide what types of computers are to be included in the model developed. It is reasonable to assume that computer users evaluate different categories of computers by different criteria. Therefore, the same computer characteristics may not be applied to the analysis of different computer categories. Ein-Dor [10] showed that the EOS can be applied only within each category of computers. Kang et al. [24] showed that the EOS are not the same for all categories of computers. In order to eliminate any problem caused by mixing non-homogeneous products, I decided to limit our analysis only to the mainframes.

One difficulty in the economic analysis of computing is to determine a reasonable measure of performance. The problem is that computer performance is inherently heterogeneous. Just as a single characteristic, such as miles per gallon, cannot capture the essence of an automobile, performance result on a single task cannot meaningfully characterize the overall performance of a computer system. Therefore, instead of directly quantifying performance, the price of a computer is used as a measure of its performance. Cale et al. [1, p. 232] concluded that price is the best single measure of computer performance.

The price approach is valid only if the computer market is perfectly competitive. In reality, computer price depends not only upon those computer characteristics which affect performance, but also upon other factors, such as the users' perceptions of the computers. These factors are not related to computer performance, but do affect computer price.

In order to obtain a measure of computer performance, the effects of non-performance-related characteristics on the price should be eliminated, while the effects of performance-related characteristics are preserved. The theoretical model for this approach, called the hedonic model, was developed and applied by Griliches [14] and Rosen [29]. The framework is derived from the idea that consumption of different kinds of goods or services can be analyzed by disaggregating them into more basic units that better measure the characteristics of what is purchased. The hedonic model has been applied to the economic analysis of computers by Chow [3] and Cole et al. [6].

In order to use the hedonic approach, I first classify the performance-related characteristics of computers into three categories. They are: processing speed, main storage capacity, and input/output (I/O) capability. After considering factors such as how appropriately the characteristic represents the computer system, whether the characteristic has been used in other studies, and the availability of the characteristic in the data set, I select one key variable from each category. They are millions of instructions per second (MIPS) for the measure of computing speed, main memory size for primary storage capacity, and number of I/O channels for I/O capability.

The computer purchase prices, MIPS, main memory size and number of I/O channels are obtained from Computerworld [17, 18, 19, 20, 21]. The computer purchase price refers to the list price of the minimally configured system, which includes - in addition to CPU and main memory - the minimal peripherals and features required, such as minimum I/O channels, the console, and the power supply unit. The main memory is the minimum main memory size configured for the computer. The I/O channel is the minimum number of I/O channels. The prices are discounted by the annual inflation rate in order to obtain real computer prices. The inflation rate was obtained from the Survey of Current Business [32].

Next, three non-performance-related factors are identified. The first is the individual vendor's effect. Different manufacturers may have different basic system configurations. Users may value computers made by different manufacturers differently, perhaps based on the firm's reputation or the user's past experience. Cale et al. [1, p. 231] have noted different pricing practices by various manufacturers for computers with the same characteristics. Our model contains dummy variables for each computer manufacturer in order to remove any systematic vendor effects on computer price.

The second factor is the effect of IBM compatibility. Previously, Kang [23], Kang et al. [24] and Mendelson [28] have shown a positive effect of IBM compatibility on computer price. The dummy variable will remove the effect on computer price of IBM-compatibility which is not related to hardware performance.

As a third factor, I include a system's year of introduction. Some of the previous studies have used the introduction year as a measure of computer technology [1, 12, 23, 24, 26, 27, 28].

If the computer market is efficient, similar or lower prices should prevail for older model computers with the same characteristics. However, past studies indicate that a system's introduction year negatively affects its price, and the older models are priced higher. The variable "System introduction year" will control the effect of the introduction year on computer price. The introduction year for each model was obtained from the Datapro 70 [8], from the Computerworld Buyer's Guide [7], or by contacting each vendor.

One way of estimating the technological progress of computers is to analyze the decrease in computer prices over the years, where the computers compared have the same characteristics. I have used time-series and cross-section data for this purpose. With this data set, I can capture the effect of time on computer price since similar computers can be compared over the years. The variable called "Data observation year" is included for this purpose. In the past, Cole et al. [6] and Kang [23] have used this type of data set.

The number of observations available for estimation is 332. The systems were introduced from 1977 to 1985. The prices for these systems were collected from 1981 to 1985. Unfortunately, I was not able to include more current data for my analysis because Computerworld has recently changed Hardware roundup reporting format significantly.

ESTIMATION RESULTS

First, I want to test whether the model specification of the translog functional form is equivalent to the specifications of the Cobb-Douglas form. For this purpose, I analyze two regressions results after including the non-performance related variables in Equations (4) and (7).

With Equation (4) for the Cobb-Douglas function, the sum of squared residuals is 43.641 with 318 degrees of freedom. With Equation (7) for the translog function, the sum of squared residuals is 38.510 with 308 degrees of freedom. The test is a standard F-test comparing the relative change in the sum of squared residuals of the two specifications. (For the detailed discussion of this test, see [3].) The F-test statistic is 4.105 with (10, 308) degrees of freedom. This result indicates that these two models are statistically different at the 1 percent

significance level. Therefore, I reject the hypothesis that the Cobb-Douglas functional form is equivalent to the translog form for representing computer performance. The variables used for estimation are explained in Table I.

Since the test result indicates that the translog specification is more general and cannot be simplified into the Cobb-Douglas specification, I will use the estimation results of the translog function for the remaining discussion. The results estimated with the translog model of Equation (7) after including the non-performance related factors are:

$$PRICE = 6.279 \, (CNST) + 1.075 \, (MIPS) - .171 \, (MEMO) + .101 \, (CHAN)$$
$$ (.204)^{**} (.103)^{**} (.115) (.037)^{**}$$

$$-.048 \, (MIPS)^2 + .021 \, (MEMO)^2 - .007 \, (CHAN)^2$$
$$ (.026)^* (.026) (.011)$$

$$-.019 \, (MIPS)(MEMO) + .074 \, (MIPS)(CHAN) - .038 \, (MEMO)(CHAN)$$
$$(.028) (.040)^* (.028)$$

$$-.160 \, (YEAR) - .033 \, (YEAR)^2 - .098 \, (YEAR)(MIPS)$$
$$(.087)^* (.014)^{**} (.029)^{**}$$

$$+.130 \, (YEAR)(MEMO) + .010 \, (YEAR)(CHAN) - .061 \, (INTR)$$
$$(.036)^{**} (.012) (.018)^{**}$$

$$-.023 \, (IBMC) + .166 \, (MFG1) + .436 \, (MFG2) + .414 \, (MFG3)$$
$$(.144) (.108) (.155)^{**} (.162)^{**}$$

$$+.279 \, (MFG4) + .414 \, (MFG5) + .528 \, (MFG6) + .605 \, (MFG7)$$
$$(.083)^{**} (.098)^{**} (.157)^{**} (.146)^{**}$$

The degrees of freedom is 308. The correlation coefficient (R^2) is .950. The sum of squared residuals is 38.510. The * and ** indicate estimates statistically different from zero at the 5 percent and 1 percent significance levels, respectively, using a one-tailed test. Numbers in parentheses are standard errors.

First, I compute the technological change and EOS from the estimates of the translog model. The results are reported in Table II. Only the estimates which are statistically significant at the 5 percent level were included for computation.

The change in computer technology over the years is computed by applying Equation (8). The estimated average annual rate of technological change is 30.2 percent with a standard error of 0.007. Similarly, the EOS is obtained by applying coefficient estimates to Equations (9). The estimated EOS is 1.160 with a standard error of 0.008.

Symbol	Interpretation
PRICE	ln(Computer price deflated with inflation rate)
CNST	Constant term
MIPS	ln(Millions of instructions per second)
MEMO	ln(Main memory)
CHAN	ln(Number of I/O channels)
YEAR	Data observation year
INTR	System introduction year
IBMC	Dummy variable for IBM compatibility
MFG_i	Dummy variable for manufacturer i, where i=1,...,7

Note: Since the relevant variables are transformed into natural logarithms, the units of measurement are immaterial.

Table I. Variables Used for Estimation

NAMES	COEFF	S.E.
Technological change	0.302**	0.007
Economies of scale	1.160**	0.008
Price rigidity	-0.061**	0.018
IBM compatibility	-0.023	0.144

Notes: COEFF stands for Coefficient estimates. S.E. stands for Standard Errors. ** indicates coefficients significantly different from zero at the 1 percent level using a one-tailed test.

Table II: Estimates of EOS, Technological change, IBM compatibility and Price adjustment.

The estimation results indicate that computer price is not flexible enough to adjust to market forces. For any given time, the computer introduced one year earlier and available currently is about 6 percent more expensive than the comparable computer introduced this year. This phenomenon is quite possibly the result of vendors' pricing strategies which may optimize returns by slowing the rate of decline of prices. No positive effect of IBM compatibility on computer price was observed.

CONCLUSIONS AND MANAGERIAL IMPLICATIONS

The 30 percent annual rate of technological change implies that the MIS managers can buy a comparable computer system at about half the original price at the end of the second year. This rate can be used for making decisions on how to allocate computing resources over time. This result can be particularly useful for planning computer acquisition or replacement by explicitly including the rate of technological change into the decision model.

The estimate of EOS is close to 1, which is about half the values many previous studies [10, 11, 15, 24, 26, 27, 31] have reported. This result supports the findings of Kang [23] and Mendelson [28]. Since there is no significant gain from the economies of scale for mainframes, a cheaper unit processing cost cannot be realized by simply acquiring larger computers. Therefore, the current trend toward decentralized processing power reflects rational behavior on the part of the users. Furthermore, additional factors such as increasing popularity of end-user computing and rapidly growing network technology will continue to make decentralization an attractive approach.

The observed low economies of scale and high rates of technological change indicate that the best strategy for the DP managers is to optimize incremental computing power acquisition with minimum excess computing resource available. For this purpose, organizations should be more concerned about system modularity to allow incremental changes in computing power. The DP managers should also plan for systematic component purchases rather than whole system purchases in order to meet the need for additional computer power. Many traditional organizations may not be able to exercise the incremental computing power approach because of organizational constraints. However, due to significant potential savings, most organizations will benefit in the long run by adapting the modular approach for computing resource allocation.

The analysis shows that computer models older by one year cost about 6 percent higher than newer models with the same characteristics. This result indicates that computer prices do not decrease at the same rate as market forces dictate. Therefore, purchasing newly-introduced models is more cost effective than purchasing older models when other factors are the same.

The estimation results indicate that the IBM compatible systems are less expensive than non-IBM compatible systems after all other factors are controlled, but this result is not statistically significant. I would like to point out that this result does not contradict previous studies. Kang [23], Kang et al. [24] and Mendelson [28] have reported that IBM compatible systems are more expensive than non-IBM compatible systems. However, the above studies either did not consider the manufacturer's effect on computer prices or used different computer categories. Once the manufacturer effects are incorporated into the model, the premium paid for the IBM compatibility disappears. One possible reason for this phenomenon is high competition among IBM compatible mainframe manufacturers.

Lastly, future researchers in this area would benefit by initially examining flexible model specifications before they decide upon a more restricted model. Flexible forms, like the translog function, do not impose restrictions which are unavoidable with less flexible forms such as the Cobb-Douglas function. Consequently, flexible functional forms can represent the technology of computers more appropriately. If the underlying technology seems to behave like the Cobb-Douglas function, then I can always test these two specifications and choose the simplified form based on test results rather than on an assumption.

ACKNOWLEDGEMENT
Financial support from the 1993 Dong-A University Academic Research Fund is gratefully acknowledged.

REFERENCES
1. Cale, E. G., Gremillion, L. L., and McKenny, J. L. Price/Performance Patterns of U.S. Computer Systems, *Communications of the ACM* 22, 4 (Apr. 1979), 225-232.
2. Caves, D. W., Christensen, L. R., and Swanson, J. A. Productivity Growth, Scale Economies, and Capacity Utilization in U.S. Railroads, 1955-74, *American Economic Review* 71, 5 (Dec. 1981), 994-1002.
3. Chow, G. C. Technological Changes and the Demand for Computers, *American Economic Review* 57, (Dec. 1967), 1117-1130.
4. Christensen, L. R. and Greene, W. H. Economies of Scale in U.S. Electric Power Generation, *Journal of Political Economy* 84, 4 (Aug. 1976), 655-676.
5. Cobb, C. W. and Douglas, P. H. A Theory of Production, *American Economic Review* 18, Supplement (1928), 139-165.
6. Cole, R., Chen, Y. C., Barquin-Stolleman, J. A., Dulberger, E., Helvacian, N., and Hodge, J. H. Quality-Adjusted Price Indexes for Computer Processors and Selected Peripheral Equipment, *Survey of Current Business* 66, 1 (Jan. 1986), U.S. Department of Commerce, Bureau of Economic Analysis, 41-50.
7. *Computerworld Buyer's Guide to Large Systems Hardware*, CW Communications Inc., Framingham, Mass., 1984.
8. *Datapro 70. (the EDP Buyer's Bible)*, Datapro Research Corp., Delran, N.J. 1985.
9. Douglas, P. H. Are there laws of production?, *American Economic Review* 38, (1948), 1-41.
10. Ein-Dor, P. Grosch's Law Re-revisited: CPU Power and the Cost of Computation, *Communications of the ACM* 28, 2 (Feb. 1985), 142-151.
11. Ein-Dor, P. and Feldmesser, J. Attributes of the Performance of Central Processing Units: A Relative Performance Prediction Model, *Communications of the ACM* 30, 4 (Apr. 1987), 308-317.
12. Fedorowicz, J. Comments on Price/Performance Patterns of U.S. Computer Systems, *Communications of the ACM* (Sep. 1981), 585-586.
13. Fisher, F. M. Test of Equality between Sets of Coefficients in Two Linear Regressions: An Expository Notes, *Econometrica* 38, 2 (Mar. 1970), 361-366.
14. Griliches, Z. Hedonic Price Indexes for Automobiles: An Econometric Analysis of Quality Change, in *Price Indexes and Quality Change: Studies*

in New Methods of Measurement, Cambridge, Mass: Harvard University Press, 1971.

15. Grosch, H. A. High Speed Arithmetic: The Digital Computer as A Research Tool, *Journal of the Optical Society of America* 43, 4 (Apr. 1953), 306-310.

16. Gurbaxani, V. and Mendelson, H., Software and Hardware in Data Processing Budgets, *IEEE Transactions on Software Engineering* SE-13, 9 (Sept. 1987), 1010-1017.

17. Henkel, T. Hardware roundup, *Computerworld* 15, 26 (Jul. 13, 1981), 11-19.

18. Henkel, T. Hardware roundup, *Computerworld* 16, 31 (Aug. 2, 1982), 23-33.

19. Henkel, T. Hardware roundup, *Computerworld* 17, 32 (Aug. 8, 1983), 29-39.

20. Henkel, T. Hardware roundup, *Computerworld* 18, 34 (Aug. 20, 1984), 23-40.

21. Henkel, T. Hardware roundup, *Computerworld* 19, 33 (Aug. 19, 1985), 23-37.

22. Kang, Y. M., Response to "Economic Analysis of Computer Hardware Performance: Some Theoretical and Methodological Observations" by P. Ein-Dor, R. Giladi and A. Tishler, *Communications of the ACM*, 34, 12 (Dec. 1991) 115-117.

23. Kang, Y. M., Computer Hardware Performance: Production and Cost Function Analyses, *Communications of the ACM*, 32, 5, (May 1989) 586-593.

24. Kang, Y. M., Miller, R. B., and Pick, R. A. Comment on "Grosch's Law Re-revisited: CPU Power and the Cost of Computation", *Communications of the ACM* 29, 8 (Aug. 1986) 779-781.

25. King, J. L. Centralized versus Decentralized Computing: Organizational Considerations and Management Options, *Computing Surveys* 15, 4 (Dec. 1983), 319-349.

26. Knight, K. E. Changes in Computer Performance, *Datamation* 12, 9 (Sep. 1966), 40-54.

27. Knight, K. E. Changes in Computer Performance 1963-1967, *Datamation* 14, 1 (Jan. 1968), 31-35.

28. Mendelson, H. Economies of Scale in Computing: Grosch's Law Revisited, *Communications of the ACM* 30, 12 (Dec. 1987) 1066-1072.

29. Rosen, S. Hedonic Prices and Implicit Markets: Product Differentiation in Pure Competition, *Journal of Political Economy* 82, 1 (Jan.-Feb. 1974), 34-55.

30. Sircar, S. and Dave, D. The Relationship between Benchmark Tests and Microcomputer Price, *Communications of the ACM* 29, 3 (Mar. 1986), 212-217.

31. Solomon, M. B. Jr. Economies of Scale and the IBM System/360, *Communications of the ACM* 9, (June 1966), 435-440.

32. U. S. Dept. of Commerce, Bureau of Economic Analysis, *Survey of Current Business* 66, 3 (Mar. 1986).

Ergonomics in Office Automation: High Touch for High Tech

Omar E. M. Khalil, University of Massachusetts,
N. Dartmouth MA. 02747, (508)999-8443

Executive Abstract

INTRODUCTION

The rapid deployment of microcomputers, video display terminals (VDTs), and other information technology (IT) tools into the office over the last two decades has changed the ecosystem of the office in unanticipated ways. These striking technological advances have overlooked the office workers who are a vitally important factor in the success of the automation of the office. The lack of a corresponding "high touch" component to the application of "high tech" to the office has raised many concerns over potential threats to workers' health and productivity.

Productivity is bound to suffer when the workplace is poorly designed and workers become bleary-eyed and sore after sitting all day in inappropriate chairs, staring at poorly lit screens, and typing with improper keyboards. This paper briefly discusses some of the office automation's threats to health and productivity and explores an ergonomic approach that management can adopt in response to the challenge.

THREATS TO HEALTH AND PRODUCTIVITY

The integration of IT into the office has brought with it a new wave of threats to the health and productivity of white-collar workers. Repetitive stress injuries (RSI), radiation-related illnesses, and vision impairments are three such threats. While white-collar workers may not operate forklifts or spend long hours on an assembly line, the information technology tools they do use and the ways they use them pose varying degrees of risk. Forcing information technology tools into the office has led to a disruption of the work environment and a mismatch between job demands and what the human mind and body can provide. Thus, the absence of high touch--ergonomics considerations--in the new workplace environment makes it potentially hazardous and has a direct negative impact on corporate expenses and productivity.

AN ERGONOMICALLY-BASED APPROACH TO THE PROBLEM

A successful "high tech" application must be accompanied by a "high touch" response to compensate for the impersonal nature of technology. an ergonomically-based approach to create an ergonomically correct computing environment in the office is the proper response to the challenge. Not only would the workers benefit from a more comfortable and pleasant computing environment, but organizations, too, would find cost savings and higher productivity.

This ergonomically-based approach requires the integration of the efforts of many interested groups--i.e., management, legislators, standards organizations, information technology dealers and manufacturers, research institutes, employees, and unions--in order to combat the computer-related threats to health and productivity. Management, however, has to take the lead in: (1) cooperating with the other groups' efforts to foster the development of ergonomics standards and ergonomically-built equipment, and (2) adopting ergonomics programs to design an ergonomically correct workplace. Successful adoption of such programs necessitates, among others, the following requirements:

1. Top management commitment to and information systems' experts involvement in ergonomics programs;
2. Ergonomically designed workplace and correct work habits;
3. Employees' ergonomics awareness; and
4. Utilization of available ergonomics Knowledge (e.g., standards, legislation, equipment catalogues, etc.).

CONCLUSION

Offices are flooded with microcomputers, video display terminals, and other IT tools. Automation has changed the ecosystem of the office and has brought with it new level of stress. This change, unfortunately, has not been matched with a sufficient change in job design and job processes. Consequently, computer-related injuries are on the rise, and productivity is bound to suffer. Management cannot afford to wait for the issue to resolve itself. The potential lost work time, liability suits, and workers' compensation costs associated with the change in office technology call for prompt action. The "high tech" must be accompanied by "high touch"--high human factor considerations to compensate for the impersonal nature of office automation. Workstations, tools, and jobs must be ergonomically designed to fit the individual operator.

Healthy, safe, and comfortable employees are more productive ones. As we move further into a service and information-based economy, it is crucial that we understand the changing environment in which people work and the need for compatible offices. The ultimate winners will be not only the workers, but the employers who will realize how much of an impact these issues will have on productivity and act accordingly in a proactive way.

A Proposed Study of Attitude and its Effect on Electronically Mediated Interpersonal Communication

Kathryn A. Marold
Metropolitan State College of Denver
Takashi Kosaka
The University of Denver
Gwynne Larsen
Metropolitan State College of Denver

INTRODUCTION

In the decade since personal computers, FAX machines, voice mail, and other technical means of computer-mediated communication have become commonplace in our culture, interpersonal communication has undergone subtle changes. The level of human communication that takes the individual into consideration, that serves to link us with our fellow man, relied heavily in the past on immediate interaction and on face-to-face presence. In the field of communication, years of study focused on the nonverbal elements of interpersonal communication. Listening skills were promoted. Summative studies were done on interpersonal communication within dyads. Disclosing, decentering, relationship maintenance, intimacy, communication apprehension, social exchange theories, and metacommunication took up much of our scholastic endeavors. Then suddenly face-to-face interaction and real-time exchanges were not the only interpersonal communication game in town.

Asynchronous (time-delayed) mediated communication introduced new variables into our exchanges with others. The standard paradigm of interpersonal speech communication no longer fits. It now behooves interpersonal communication scholars to take another look at our field and to examine when and how electronically mediated interpersonal communication will be generally accepted. Of all the variables that contribute to user-acceptance of communication technology, one's attitude toward it may be a greater predictor than any other. How a person feels about using computer-mediated communication for interpersonal reasons figures heavily into when and how often he/she will use it.

This theory does not mean that we abandon all we have learned about interpersonal communication since Murray, Barnlund, Bales, Beavins, Jackson, Watzlawick and others began studying this level of human communication. The study of interpersonal communication has advanced immeasurably in the fifty years since it became a recognized area of human communication (Dance, pp. 172-192.) The studies of electronically-mediated communication in general that Innis, McLuhan, Ong, Carey and other scholars have compiled in the last forty years have given us a good foundation for looking at electronically-mediated interpersonal communication. From the broad array of variables that influence the use of Electronically Mediated Interpersonal Communication(EMIC),

let us focus on what we already know about attitudes in general, and apply that to EMIC.

Definition of the Phenomenon

Electronically mediated interpersonal communication can be most aptly described as asynchronous human communication in which messages are transmitted through electronic devices for the purpose of information exchange between individuals. The term interpersonal communication usually is taken to mean communication between individuals at a level where the individual is taken into account. This is the distinction Miller and Steinberg espoused (Dance and Larson, pp. 123-125.) The communication can take place within a dyad or small group. The number is not the distinction, but the emphasis is. That is, when applied to computer communication, if messages are directed to and are heard or read by more than one other individual, as in a small group bulletin board chat session, they are not meant as a "group" message, but are directed to individuals. They are exchanges between distinct personalities. This qualifies them as interpersonal communication.

The term **asynchronous** refers to a delay in transmission. Literally it means transmitting one byte at a time (Marold and Larsen, p.3.) In the sense that Everett Rogers used the term in 1986, it is communication that is not in real time, but one in which the sender and receiver experience a delay, even if slight. All computer mediated communication systems are asynchronous by their nature. Some systems provide hours or days of lag-time, and some provide only a few seconds, but there is some delay with all electronically mediated human communication (Black, p. 62.) Rogers says:

The asynchronicity of computer-based communication means that individuals can work at home on a computer network and thus make their workday more flexible. The new media often have the ability to overcome time as a variable affecting the communication process (p. 5.)

It is clear from these characteristics that electronically mediated interpersonal communication is a subset of what has come to be commonly known as CMC, or computer mediated communication. This term has become very popular over the last few years. There are books, bulletin board services, special interest groups, and professional study groups devoted to this more general phenomenon. Chesebro emphasizes that when using the term computer mediated communication, we are viewing a computer as a link with others where humans dominate the computer system, using it for its transmission function (p.97.) CMC refers to any type of human communication that is electronically mediated, at all levels and within all functions. EMIC concentrates on just the interpersonal aspect of mediated communication: it can include electronic mail, voice mail, chat mode on various systems, facsimile transmission, groupware interaction, on-line bulletin board discussions, or even what Markus and her colleagues have termed "multi-media" CMC--concurrent access to fax, vmail, and email, in addition to traditional nonelectronic communication channels (Markus, p. 207-8.)

Attributes

To summarize the phenomenon that is being studied, EMIC, or electronically- mediated interpersonal communication, is communication between individuals at a level where the individual is taken into account, whether it is in a dyad or in a small group. It is mediated in the sense that the go-between is an electronic layer or interface between sender and receiver. The mediation is a channel for human communication. EMIC is computerized communication that requires a central processor to complete the transfer, and it may use computer input, output or storage devices. It is asynchronous, which refers to a delay in transmission, however brief. And it is half-duplex. In order to exchange messages, the individuals must take turns; they cannot "speak" at the same time. There can be an absence from physical presence, meaning face-to-face proximity is not required. Finally the form of interpersonal communication differs from face to face communication; it is either in text or graphic form, or recorded audio. When these conditions are present, there is electronically mediated interpersonal communication (EMIC.)

Factors Affecting the Use of EMIC

Table 1 divides some of the variable units of electronically mediated interpersonal communication into four main categories. There are those variables that are **skill** related. These are often dependent on social and demographic conditions (Chen, p. 25-27.) How well one interacts with technical innovations, the level of keyboarding skills, the level of computer literacy often reflect one's education level, age, social class, country of residence, economic level, and other demographic features. Whether one is familiar with computers or can type comfortably most obviously will determine whether he or she will use electronically mediated interpersonal communication. One's level of computer literacy, whether it be novice, beginner, competent, proficient, or expert will affect EMIC use (Bodker, p. 83.) Joseph Schmitz and Janet Fulk found a significant positive correlation between electronic mail use and medium expertise (Schmitz, p. 492.) Experience with computing and keyboard skills were good predictors of the amount of time spent using electronic communication. Lack of media related skills inhibited use

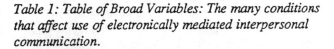

Skill related:	Time Related:	Predisposition Related:	Cognition Related:
technical dexterity	length of time it's been available	ATTITUDE	potential to learn
computer literacy level	general availability	mandated use	communication apprehension
quality of the interface	diffusion (potential receivers also use it)	disability	self efficacy
secondary orality comfort level	frequency of use	general disposition	self concept

Table 1: Table of Broad Variables: The many conditions that affect use of electronically mediated interpersonal communication.

(Schmitz, p. 490.)

It has been shown that the quality of the computer interface, or the way the computer screen appears to the user, has bearing on the use of EMIC (Marold, p. 35-39.) The comfort level with secondary orality, a non-oral medium of any type, impacts use. Ong and others have written extensively on the change that takes place from primary orality to a secondary orality, which concentrates on the text mode, whether it be chirographic or print. The electronic word requires a basic adjustment in cognitive processes (Ong, p. 83.) These variables are referred to as Skill Related.

The second category in Table 1 refers to **time-related** variables. Some cultures and geographic areas have had computers available longer than others. The longer a technology is with us, the more likely we are to use it. The "new" media technologies that Everett Rogers and others wrote of in the 1980s are not so new anymore to many, yet they are still quite foreign to others. Schaefermeyer found that for one to use a computer for communication, it must be available at least 90% of the time (Schefermeyer, P.118.) Now that personal computers are common on the desktop, we can expect EMIC to increase. Markus and Rice in particular have applied the economic and statistical theories of diffusion to communication technology. That is, the degree to which computers and fax machines are diffused within a culture will determine frequency of use. If a society does not have saturation, if very few with whom one interacts use the email, vmail, or fax communication technologies, there is no one to communicate with. Once a group approaches critical mass, where most are using the new technologies, then use will be almost universal (Markus, p. 492-510.) We have seen the use of fax transmission literally mushroom over the last few years. Markus and Rice's theory is a common-sense application of an already proven theory of diffusion, but it says a great deal about the pervasiveness of EMIC. Finally, the more one uses a technology, the more inclined one is to use it again. Repeated use is cyclic; practice makes perfect. Forestor points out that it often takes as long as two years for individuals to adjust to computer technology (Forester, p. 370.) So strong are the time variables with communication technologies that it is suspected that they and attitude are the primary predictors of use.

The fourth category of variables in Table 1 refers to those cognitively related to the use of EMIC. (The discussion of predisposition related variables will be delayed until the **cognitively-related** ones are covered, since attitudes are the focus of the study.) Although there has been a tremendous decrease in the steepness of the learning curve since the introduction of personal computers and more "user-friendly" software (Marold, pp. 37-40), electronic communication still requires complex cognitive processes. EMIC requires a certain capacity to learn, a certain level of potential. This definitely does not mean that the more intellectual capacity one has, the greater the chance the he/she will use EMIC, or even that a individual with a low capacity to learn cannot successfully use EMIC. We all know instances of those with limited intellectual ability who are computer "wizards". Nevertheless, one's capacity to learn is a factor in the use of electronic communication.

The degree of communication apprehension is also a factor in EMIC; however, the severely apprehensive person may be more comfortable with an electronic setting than with a face-to-face or telephone setting. This person has less of what Christie, Short and Williams term "social presence"(p. 65.) The perception of social presence within types of computer mediated communication varies with attitude (Ibid), but nevertheless, the degree of communication apprehension one possesses influences the use of EMIC. The opposite may also be true: someone with very low communication apprehension may deem EMIC as not possessing enough social presence for the occasion.

Variables cognitively related to EMIC include self-efficacy and self-concept--one's view of how successful the communication is, and one's sense of identity. Schmitz and Fall found that individuals' views of the richness of certain media varied. Generally, instead of being media rich, email was perceived as being moderately lean. They say, "Individual variation in media richness is then linked to differences in the communication media patterns of individuals" (Schmitz, p. 491.) Self efficacy and other cognitive variables influence one's use of EMIC. The actual perceptions one has of these cognitive processes spill into the final category--the category that this study focuses on.

The Behavior Related Variables

The **predisposition-related** category in Table 1 includes, along with the chosen variable of attitude, the presence of general disposition, the perception of one's disability with regard to technology, and mandated use. These factors are all perceptual; therefore, they are individual and within oneself. They are not directly measurable because they are inferred from the behaviors they influence (Hovland, p. 1.) One's general outlook toward all objects, the general outlook on life, and the presence of optimism or pessimism reveal general disposition. Whether one is a cheerful, generally happy or upbeat person, or whether one is skeptical, cautious, and more

subdued by nature is one's general attitude. Halloran notes that the overall constellation of a person's general attitude influences formation of specific attitudes (p. 23.) Whether, on the whole, the person is a negative or positive person, whether he/she is innovative or timid by general will influence the attitude toward computers and toward electronically-mediated interpersonal communication. General attitudes toward a class of objects are sometimes termed "values." Rose noted that values, when considered subjectively, are attitudes (Hovland, p. 20.) The nature of the attitude system (i.e. values) will affect behavior in a certain situation (Krech, p. 23.) The nature or overall pattern or constellation of attitudes about other things affect specific attitudes and subsequent behavior toward new things.

Mandated use refers to imposed conditions. Either one's superior dictates that EMIC must be used, or the pressure to conform to what is the standard process of EMIC in one's environment is so great that it is used, even against one's will. Schmitz in 1987 found that electronic mail use by co-workers and by one's immediate supervisor are positive predictors of an individual's frequency of electronic mail use:

Individuals with close work associates who are high users of electronic mail should be more likely to consider electronic mail more useful. Co-workers who model electronic mail use facilitate the acquisition of positive evaluative beliefs (attitudes) by their peers....Coworkers' attitudes toward the usefulness of electronic mail may influence the attitudes of their close associates (Schmitz, p. 494.)

Kelman's studies on processes of social influence showed that when use is mandated without accompanying attempts to change attitude, public conformity and limited compliance result (Trenholm, p. 136-145.) Nevertheless, when the use of EMIC is mandated, there will be an increase in its use, whether permanent, long-lasting, and complete, or not. It is definitely a factor that affects use.

All of the behavior-related variables in the fourth column of Table 1 can in some way be related to attitude; therefore, this study concentrates on **attitude**, the central and crucial variable in the use of electronically mediated interpersonal communication. Indeed, it is the author's proposition that attitude, more than any of the many factors that influence the use of EMIC, is a higher predictor of its use.

The Focus Variable--ATTITUDE

As has already been noted, attitude is a predisposition to behavior. Many studies in the areas of communication, behavioral psychology, sociology, and all social sciences in general have been done. We know a great deal about attitude and how it influences behavior. Attitude has been termed "a mental and neural state of readiness, exerting a direct influence on an individual's response" (Allport, p.8.) Thurstone has called attitude " a system of positive or negative predispositions" (p.531.) Osgood considered attitude an emotional reaction--positive or negative feelings toward an object. Attitudes are predispositions to respond in a particular way toward a specified class of objects. Trenholm calls attitudes a "complex cluster of cognitions" (p. 7.) Leonard Doob described an attitude as an "implicit drive-producing response considered socially significant in the individual's society" (Fishbein, p. 43.) Mueller noted that there are so many definitions of attitude that in everyday language, there is no clear definition at all (p. 2.) It seems that attitude is one of the most slippery, yet intriguing areas of the social sciences; however, because it is so crucial to our actions, its study can never be laid to rest. Although there are innumerable definitions of attitude, most will agree that it is a "mental predisposition toward an object, a readiness to act, think, and feel about it in a given way" (Trenholm., p. 8.) No matter what definition of attitude is employed, or what dimension of it one concentrates on, there is the realization, as Petty and Cacioppo point out, that attitudes *do* affect behavior (Insko, p. xiii.) When the use of electronically mediated interpersonal communication is analyzed, we **must** look to attitude for insight into when and how it will be adopted. The answer will never be complete without it.

We know that attitudes are not innate; they are learned. They develop and are organized from experience (Halloran, p.14.) They are related to behavior, but in complex ways. Katz noted that when an attitude is balanced, when the three elements of it are in equilibrium, it is safe to predict behavior from attitude (p. 140-141.) If an attitude has a balance of all three dimensions (cognitive, affective and behavioral), there is internal consistency among all three components. Halloran holds that even if every element of attitude individually does not strongly predict the behavior that follows it, it does not invalidate the basic law that attitudes influence behavior. (p.20-21).

We know that attitudes are relatively enduring, but they are modifiable and subject to change (Halloran p. 14.) and do predict behavior to one degree or another (Krech, p. 23.) Possibly, then, attitudes toward computer-mediated communication can predict subsequent behavior more accurately than any other factor we have discussed.

The Three Components of Attitude

There is fairly standard agreement among social science scholars on the three dimensions of attitude. They are the **cognitive**, **affective**, and **behavioral** components. What is *not* standard is the degree to which each of these dimensions forms attitude. In the newer research on attitude, James Dillard claims that attitudes "arise casually from one or more of these types of information" (p. 94.) However, from the first definitive study of attitudes that Krech, Crutchfield, and Ballachey summarized in their behavioral psychology text, most scholars have concentrated on the various aspects of these three elements of attitudes. These same components can be applied to attitudes toward electronically-mediated interpersonal communication. If we are to examine users' attitudes toward EMIC, looking at these three elements can aid in putting values on something as abstract and unobservable as attitudes.

The **cognitive** component of attitude has to do with beliefs about an object, including evaluative beliefs that something is good or bad (normative), appropriate or inappropriate. The cognitive portion of attitude does not predict behavior as well as the other elements (Krech, p. 144;) that is, one could know that communication via computers is a good thing, but that knowledge won't greatly influence the tendency to use EMIC. The cognitive aspect of attitude is largely a set of expectations about how one's values are served through the object; for example, one's system of core beliefs and values is employed (Trenholm, p. 6-8.) One's view of how easy or difficult EMIC is, or how efficient or adequate a means of interpersonal communication it is would be cognitive aspects of one's general attitude toward computer mediated communication.

The **affective** or feeling component of attitude has to do with likes and dislikes. This is the emotional element, the aspect that can be voluntary or involuntary, verbal or nonverbal. One can be aware of an emotional reaction, or completely unaware and unable to control the response to an object. One's immediate "gut response" to an attitude object is the affective portion. Research on affective and cognitive elements of attitude generally shows great reliability and validity. The famous Yale studies found internal consistency between cognitive and affective aspects of attitude studies (Hovland, p. 15.)

The **behavioral, or action,** tendency of attitude includes the readiness or predisposition to behave in a certain way. The behavioral element is associated with an attitude, but it does not cover the actual behavior itself, only the tendency. Halloran says it is the **readiness** of an individual to behave in a certain way (p. 21.) Research has shown that the behavioral tendency is strongly correlated with the affective element, and with the cognitive element as well (Hovland, p. 16.)

The imbalance between knowing the efficiency of the technology and personally feeling negative about it makes the behavioral element a poor predictor of use. Some people feel that computer systems are social systems, that interaction that was hitherto impossible is now possible, that self-disclosure is easier with asynchronous communication free from physical presence (Adelman, p.283-284.) Yet those same individuals may not have a strong opinion on how efficient or helpful computer communication is; thus, scores on their attitude scales may indicate an imbalance in the other direction.

METHODOLOGY FOR THE STUDY

Thurstone and Osgood both developed scales to measure attitudes. Thurstone's, which is commonly referred to as the psychophysical, or rational, scale, is an opinion scale that ranks attitude on a continuous scale. It concentrates on the cognitive dimension of attitude (Fishbein, p. 10-11.) Osgood's semantic differential scale with bipolar adjective pairs concentrates on the affective dimension. Osgood's scale is useful where respondents have strong emotional reactions to a topic, but not well-thought out opinions (Henerson, p. 89.) The scale was developed in 1957, and has seven scales for each pair of adjectives. There is proven validity and reliability for this scale that measures the evaluative dimensions of a topic (Fishbein, p. 183.) Measuring attitudes of users toward electronically mediated interpersonal communication would be best done with a semantic differential scale.

In order to construct a measure for EMIC, dividing attitude into two dimensions would be a better way to measure attitudes when using a semantic differential scale. If there are pairs of bipolar adjectives that denote the affective/behavioral aspect of attitude and another set that denote the cognitive/behavioral aspect, a more accurate representation of one's attitude might be obtained. The Two Dimensional ABC Adjective Pairs shown in Table 2 represent the chosen bipolar pairs proposed for the study. They are the general pairs developed primarily by DeVesta, Osgood, and Fitz-Gibbon (Henerson, p. 89-91.)

The data necessary to test these propositions could be obtained by polling respondents' rankings on specific EMIC topics. Possible topics to use are listed beneath Table 2; these are somewhat unique to the field of computer-mediated communication. Using these two-dimensional pairs seems to simplify a complex measurement, allowing for the construction of a survey that is brief, clear, and easy to administer. This survey can be more representative of one's general attitude toward EMIC than one that separates the cognitive, affective, and behavioral dimensions. The respondent indicates on a seven-point scale where his/her attitude lies in a positive or negative direction.

Table 3: Electronic Comminication

A sample of possible survey format is shown in Table 3.

A survey would be constructed using the table of cognitive/behavioral and affective/behavioral pairs in Table 2 to measure a respondent's attitude toward how personal or impersonal electronic communication is, and to relate it to his/her use. A representative sample would be polled to provide some conclusions about the relationship of attitude to the use of EMIC. The relationship between those who feel that computer messages are inadequate, inconvenient, or confusing and their use of EMIC would be shown. The relationship between those who like computers and feel that they are worthwhile, (that bulletin board services with conversation mode are useful, and so forth,) and their frequency of use of EMIC would also be shown. The results of the study would help define the use of computer-mediated communication between individuals and also accurately predict which individuals would be most likely to use EMIC, all other factors (listed in Table 1) being equal.

Frequency of use would be measured by asking each

TWO DIMENSIONAL ABC ADJECTIVE PAIRS

COGNITIVE/BEHAVIORAL	AFFECTIVE/BEHAVIORAL
INCONVENIENT/CONVENIENT	HATE/LOVE
HELPFUL/HARMFUL	DISLIKE/LIKE
USEFUL/USELESS	FRIENDLY/UNFRIENDLY
OLD/NEW	AWKWARD/COMFORTABLE
CONFUSING/CLEAR	PERSONAL/IMPERSONAL
SIMPLE/CLUTTERED	GOOD/BAD
DIRECT/MEANDERING	
EFFICIENT/INEFFICIENT	
BORING/INTERESTING	
EASY/HARD	
ADEQUATE/INADEQUATE	
SLOW/FAST	

Table 2: Two Dimensional ABC Abjective Pairs

respondent to mark the number of times he/she has used email, vmail, chat, conversation mode, fax, or has been the commentor in a groupware package during a fixed period of time. The frequency would then be related to the values collected for the attitude. Thus, the relationship between attitude and frequency of use of EMIC could be demonstrated empirically, and conclusions could be drawn.

SUMMARY

Technology has irreversibly altered our communication patterns. Interpersonal communication that formerly relied on face-to-face presence has led to different forms of interaction, finally providing for electronically-mediated communication. The horizons of interpersonal communication have been irrevocably expanded. It is proposed that the time EMIC has been present and one's attitude toward it should prove to be higher predictors of use than any of the other factors involved. The results of the proposed study should show that there is a greater than chance probability that attitude toward EMIC influences the frequency of its use.

REFERENCES

Allport, G.W. "Attitude," in Handbook of Social Psychology. ed. C. Marchison, Clark University Press, Worchester, 1935, pp. 798-844.

Bodker, Suzanne. Through the Interface. Lawrence Erlbaum Associates. Hillsdale, NJ. 1991.

Black, S.D., J.E. Levin, H. Mehan, and C.N. Quinn. "Real and Non-real Time Interaction: Unraveling Multiple Threads of Discourse." Discourse Processes. 6 (1986): 59-75.

Cacioppo John T. & Petty Richard E. Attitudes and Persuasion Classic and Contemporary Approaches. Wm.C. Brown Company Publishers. Iowa. 1981.

Chen, Milton and William Paisley. Chidren and Microcomputers: Research on the Newest Medium. Sage Publications. Beverly Hills, CA. 1985.

Chesebro, James W. and Donald Bonsall. Computer Mediated Communication. New York. 1989.

Christie, Bruce, John Short, and Ederyn Williams. The Social Psychology of Telecommunications. New York. John Wiley and Sons. 1976.

Dance, F.E.X. and Carl Larson. The Functions of Human Communication: A Theoretical Approach. Holt, Rinehart and Winston. New York. 1976.

Dillard, James. "Persuasion Past and Present: Attitudes Aren't What They Used to Be." Communication Monographs. 60(1) 1993: 90-97.

Fishbein, Martin. Attitude Theory and Measurement. John Wiley & Sons, Inc. New York. 1967.

Forester, Tom. Computers in the Human Context. MIT Press. Cambridge, MA. 1989.

Halloran J.D. Attitude Formation and Change. Leicester Univ. Press, NY: 1967.

Henerson, Marlene, Lynn Morris, Carol Fitzgibbon. How to Measure Attitudes. Sage Publications, CA, 1978.

Hovland, Carl, Communication and Persuasion: Psychological Studies of Opinion Change. Yale University Press, New Haven, CN, 1960.

Insko, Chester A. "Foreword," in Petty and Cacioppio's Attitudes and Persuasion:Classic and Contemporary Approaches. Wm. C. Brown Publishers. Iowa. 1961.

Katz, Daniel. "The Functional Approach to the Study of Attitudes" Public Opinion Quarterly. 24(1960): 163-204.

Krech, Crutchfield and Ballachey. The Individual in Society. McGraw-Hill. Chicago, IL. 1962. 137-179.

Markus, M. Lynne, Tora K. Bikson, Maha E-Shinnawy, and Louise L. Soe. "Fragments of Your Communication: Email, Vmail, and Fax." The Information Society. 8(4) 1992: 207-241.

Markus, M. Lynne. "Toward a 'Critical-Mass' Theory of Interactive Media: Universal Access, Interdependence, and Diffusion." Communication Research. 14(1987): pp. 491-511.

Marold, Kathryn A. and Gwynne Larsen. " The Asynchronous Nature of E-mail and Its Effect on Interpersonal Communication." Proceedings of the Ninth Annual Conference of Office Automation Systems International. June 9, 1993.

Marold, Kathryn A. "Microcomputer User Interfaces and Intrapersonal Communication." Interface: The Computer Education Quarterly. 15(1)1993: pp. 33-40.

Ong, Walter. Orality and Literacy: The Technologizing of the Word. Routledge. New York. 1982.

Osgood, Charles, George Suci, Percy Tannenbaum. The Measurement of Meaning, University of Illinois Press, Urbane, IL, 1957.

Rice, R.E. ed. The New Media: Communication, Research, and Technology. Sage Publications. Beverly Hills, CA. 1984.

Schaefermeyer, J. and F. Sewall. "Communicating by Electronic Mail." American Behavioral Scientist. 32 (2): 1988. 112-1   123.

Schmitz, Joseph and Janet Fulk. "Organizational Colleagues, Media Riches, and Electronic Mail." Communication Research. Vol 36. (4): 1991. 487-521.

Rosenberg, Milton, Carl Hovland, William McGuire, Robert Abelson, and Jack Brehm. Attitude Organization and Change. ed. Hovland and Rosenberg, Yale University Press. 1960.

Thurstone, L.L. "Attitudes Can Be Measured." American Journal of Sociology. 3:529-54.

Trenholm, Sarah. Persuasion and Social Influence. Prentice Hall. Englewood Cliffs, N.J. 1989.

Practice Critical Thinking with a Simple Flowchart Exercise

Elbert L. Menees
Professor of Information Management
School of Business & Economics
University of South Carolina
at Spartanburg
Spartanburg, South Carolina 29303
TEL: (803) 599-2583

Executive Abstract

BACKGROUND INFORMATION

Teaching students to think critically and logically has a high priority in most academic missions. For the quantitative fields like math and computer systems, the method of choice has always been symbolic reasoning. Flowcharts, structure charts, data flow diagrams, decision tables and other graphical presentation methods are the tools of analysis.

Students are normally taught how to use these tools with simple examples. It is rare, indeed, when a simple tool example has multiple solutions that vary so much in degrees of difficulty that nearly everyone can solve the problem but few can optimize the solution.

The MECHANICAL MAN exercise described herein has been used very successfully over a long period of time for computer literacy courses, computer systems design and analysis courses and even MBA courses. The exercise is a simple, non-threatening flowchart example, but it has for years intrigued, cajoled, engrossed, frustrated and confounded students, many of whom get resolutely entrapped by its apparent simplicity. There are a limited number of easily recognizable solutions of varying complexity, but only five or six students out of thousands have found one of the optimum solutions, which, incidentally, were unknown to the exercise developer until discovered by students.

STATEMENT OF THE EXERCISE PROBLEM

MECHANICAL MAN is an early, first generation, mobile computer; a robot with very limited capabilities. The device is more like a programmable calculator than a full service computer. MECHANICAL MAN has only one memory accumulator (called the TOTAL) and a primitive instruction set that permits him only to move slowly from place to place in a straight line. MECHANICAL MAN has been equipped with sensors in his hands and feet, so that he can determine if contact has been make with an obstruction. MECHANICAL MAN can turn away from an obstruction at a right angle and walk in a different direction when instructed to do so.

While walking, the raised arms of MECHANICAL MAN will make contact with an obstruction before his raised feet, and when arm contact is made, the feet will stop moving unless arm contact is followed by an instruction to take another step. This is critical to his protection, because the sensors in his feet have been armed for self-destruction when they contact an obstruction.

These are the instructions in the MECHANICAL MAN instruction set:

**	STAND UP	(into erect position, without moving feet)
**	SIT DOWN	(into sitting position, without moving feet)
**	TAKE ONE STEP	(forward only, fixed length, only when standing)
**	RAISE ARMS	(into fixed position, straight ahead)
**	LOWER ARMS	(into fixed position, straight down at his sides)
**	TURN RIGHT	(in place, 90 degrees, without taking a step)
**	ADD ONE	(to the accumulator TOTAL)
**	SUBTRACT ONE	(from the accumulator TOTAL)
**	IS TOTAL POSITIVE?	(TOTAL > 0)?
**	IS TOTAL NEGATIVE?	(TOTAL < 0)?
**	IS TOTAL ZERO?	(TOTAL = 0)?*
**	IS TOTAL EQUAL TO	

SPECIFIED AMOUNT?   (TOTAL = 47)?
** ARE RAISED ARMS TOUCHING ANYTHING?
** ARE RAISED FEET
TOUCHING ANYTHING? (triggers self-destruct mechanism)

MECHANICAL MAN is seated in a chair, with arms lowered, directly facing a wall an unknown distance away (between 0 and 999999999 steps). Program MECHANICAL MAN (construct the necessary flowchart) to enable him to rise, proceed to the wall and return to a sitting position with arms lowered. Make this happen with maximum efficiency, i.e., the minimum number of flowchart instructions. The chair in which he sits is too low for him to touch with his raised arms. If MECHANICAL MAN touches the chair or the wall with his feet, he will self-destruct.

SOLUTION TESTING AND REINFORCEMENT

The solutions that students submit can be tested in two parts. First, test the solution by assuming that MECHANICAL MAN started 0 steps from the wall, then test the solution by assuming that he started 3 steps from the wall. Any solution that works for 0 steps and 3 steps will work for any other number of steps.

Some solutions will fail the 0 step test at the beginning of the flowchart, because students will start MECHANICAL MAN walking (self-destruction occurs immediately) before first checking to see if his raised arms are touching anything. These are students whose critical thinking skills or problem comprehension skills need to be seriously questioned.

Experience has shown that a number of undergraduate students, perhaps as many as 30%, will either not be able to conceptualize a solution at all or will submit a solution that does not work. The majority of students, perhaps 60-65% will submit the standard 17-step solution, and the remainder will submit one of the efficient 16-step solutions. Only rarely does a student discover or figure out one of the optimum 15-step solutions, even though many students have reported spending up to 100 hours with this exercise. So far, 6 different 16-step solutions and 3 different 15-step solutions have been discovered in addition to the standard 17-step solution.

Even students who fail to derive a solution will benefit from seeing how easily the logic is unmasked and laid bare with modest effort. When students see the optimum solutions, they are usually led to wonder why anyone should have so much difficulty with such a simple problem. This, in itself, is a critical thinking breakthrough.

CONCLUSION

Everything should be made as simple as possible but not too simple. It is easier for most people to practice their critical thinking skills with problems that have few ambiguities. Simple flowchart problems may be ideal for this purpose, provided they are not too simple. The MECHANICAL MAN exercise is a gem, a made to order challenge for critical thinking on every level. Few will get the best of it, but most will think they can and all will benefit by trying. The clear possibility exists that there is a 14-step solution to the MECHANICAL MAN exercise. Please share it with the rest of us when you have the answer.

Isolation Without Privacy

Michael J. Paul, John E. Gochenouer and G. Trevor Foo
Andreas School of Business
Barry University
Miami Shores, Florida
(305) 899-3518
PAUL@buvax.barry.edu

EXECUTIVE ABSTRACT

We are on the threshold of a new era in communications which will have a far greater impact on our lives than the invention of the telegraph in 1837. The technology currently exists to develop a seamless web of communications between computers, databases and consumer electronics that can lead to instant access to any and all information. Certainly, the implementation of such a network has the prospect of profoundly changing the way people live, work, and interact with each other. Taking advantage of this technology implies a future where physical isolation is the norm. People will no longer be required to leave the comforts of their homes in order to work, shop and be entertained. Indeed, the cost of transportation, soaring crime, and necessity of timely access to information, may make the majority of the modern work force prisoners in their own homes. In addition, the reliance on a *public* information superhighway raises significant security concerns. Distrust of business and government and their potential for abuse of computer technology has already fueled fears of privacy loss. Our future may inevitably be characterized by *"isolation without privacy"*.

High-performance computing and high-speed networks have made it possible to link the components of information technology regardless of physical location. This web of communication is referred to as "cyberspace". Cyberspace, however, is far more than the interconnection of physical facilities for transmitting voice, data and images. It personifies telecommunication and implies that the synergy created by massive information exchange will result in an entity that will be greater than the sum of its parts. In fact, cyberspace may be the catalyst for the greatest transformation of society and commerce since the invention of the automobile.

It is estimated that two-thirds of U.S. workers are in information-related jobs, and the rest are in industries that rely heavily on information. Enhanced access to information will clearly provide advantages. For example, workers can avoid wasting the time normally spent traveling to and from the workplace by "telecommuting" (i.e. the partial or total substitution of telecommunications and/or computer technology for the daily commute to work).

New communications technology also has the potential to dramatically impact the way we play and socialize with each other. Imagine that you had a device that combined a tele-phone, a TV, a camcorder, and a personal computer. No matter where you went or what time it was, your child could see you and talk to you, you could watch a replay of your team's last game, you could browse the latest additions to the library, or you could find the best prices in town on groceries... Cyberspace could be a couch potato's dream come true. Even now the average adult sits for an average of 3-4 hours a day in front of a TV. As recreational and social applications of the cyberspace increase, there will be a greater temptation to extend this time or relative isolation.

The development of "virtual reality" and its subsequent incorporation into the cyberspace conjures up fantastic images of a vicarious society. The ability to see, hear, touch, feel and smell programmed "experiences" and interactions with other persons without real physical contact will further reinforce isolation. There will be little need to venture out of the home. Ultimately, even intimate contact could be accomplished via a virtual reality hookup to the cyberspace. Maybe someday we will turn on our "cybercenter" and see an advertisement staring Karl Malden expounding "American Express Virtual Reality - Don't leave home...Ever".

It will be tempting to sit in front of your cybercenter to work, be entertained and to communicate. It will be easier to choose isolation over the efforts necessary to physically interact with other humans. In addition to technological developments, there are a number of other issues that could fuel a trend toward isolation, such as the growing threat of crime, the increasing traffic congestion in our cities, and the cost of transportation.

In the past 50 years, American society has already become the victim of more self imposed isolation than in any period of history. Social gatherings and talking have been replaced by TV and video games as the primary vehicles for entertainment. Physical interaction in the work place has been replaced by telephones and computers. Working in groups has yielded to solitary labor. When we have the technology to produce the virtual reality of all we need and desire, the temptation to stay home will be great.

Increased reliance on cyberspace will create new vulnerabilities. Electronic databases may be broken into and copied. It may be possible to monitor personal and sensitive proprietary data transmissions across the superhighway. Information vital to government, industry and personal welfare may be corrupted or destroyed through accident, sabotage or catastrophic natural disaster. The privacy which the employee hoped to gain by isolating himself/herself will probably be an illusion. For example, supervisors at American Express have retained the ability to monitor employees who have signed up for the Hearth program (working at home) to ensure tight control.

There will certainly be a debate over what information should be public and what should be private. With high performance computing capabilities, information that was once considered public or benign may become an important part of your profile in some marketing research company's database. The potential for abuse is great. Packaging and selling information about a company's customers would be of increased value. This could easily invade what we now consider to be private. For example, employment decisions may be based on an individual's preference in video rentals, on book borrowings from the library or on non-prescription drug purchases.

As we stand at the brink of a new technology that promises to significantly alter our society, what questions should we ask ourselves? Will enhanced communications afford the opportunities of better interaction with our fellow man? Or will it cause us to cower in isolation -- afraid to venture from our homes -- content with our electronic addictions? Will it safeguard privacy or will it cause our lives to become open books to those who would manipulate us?

Pay for Value

Robert Rodgers
Martin School
University of Kentucky
Lexington, Kentucky 40506-0027
(606) 257-4026

Executive Abstract

BACKGROUND INFORMATION

CD-Interactive is a computer-based multimedia presentation platform that is ideally suited for self-paced study. The content of each presentation is converted onto a CD-Interactive file (which looks in appearance like a CD disc) that contains the full range of presentation possibilities - text, creative graphics, animation, still photography, music, voice, and video. Typical CD-Interactive titles (or discs) are played on a CD-Interactive player (rather than a CD player). The user (or presenter) "navigates" through the presentation using a infrared remote control while viewing a TV monitor.

DISCUSSION OF THE ISSUES

As with many new and exciting information technologies, the creation of CD-Interactive titles using conventional production methods has proven to be very expensive. It is not uncommon for a production company to charge hundreds of thousands of dollars to produce a single CD-Interactive title. The number of CD-Interactive title releases has fallen far short of expectations, despite an investment by SONY, Phillips and other large corporations of over $2 billion to develop the hardware needed to run CD-Interactive titles.

This presentation introduces the organizing concept of Pay for Value, a novel approach which is currently being used to produce CD-Interactive titles. Many different individuals and resources collectively pool their resources and talents together to produce a final product in the form of a CD-Interactive title. Conventional boundaries that suffocate most organizations are removed, using Pay for Value principles for organizing the production process.

Pay for Value requires a radical adjustment to conventional thinking about how people can be compensated and investors rewarded for the risks they assume. No individual is paid for their services on a contract basis. There are no "employees" who are employed by a "company". Rather, entrepreneurial partners are paid for the value that they add to the product or service. Payment is received after the value is realized, not before.

FINDINGS

A CD-Interactive title was released in December of 1993 that was produced using the Pay for Value organizing principles. The Communicable Disease Center, a federal agency, was one among a number of other entrepreneurial partners who contributed value toward the production and distribution of a title on bloodborne pathogens, or AIDS. Production of the title was commissioned by the Association for Managerial, Professional and Educational Development (AMPED), a nonprofit organization in Atlanta, Georgia.

The title to be demonstrated has generated total revenues of $9,000 for the three month period from December, 1993 through February, 1994. All revenues that accrue from the sale of CD-Interactive titles will be distributed to CDC, as well as all of the other entrepreneurial partners who collaborated in the production of the titles. The CDC can use the revenues that accrue from the sale of the title to supplement its research programs.

CONCLUSION

Pay for Value is a particularly useful approach for organizing and facilitating the production of many different types of information technology products in Russia, Asia and Eastern Europe, where jobs are scarce and job hunters plentiful. Instead of hoping to secure full time appointment on a "Pay for Service" basis, "Pay for Value" provides the opportunity for any enterprising individual to participate in the production of a product that yields value in the marketplace. Pay for Value affords the opportunity to empower the skills of the unemployed and underemployment, and thereby keep their hopes alive for a better future.

The major difference between "Pay for Value" and "Pay for Service" is realized at the point when the product no longer realizes value. In the case of a production process that has been organized around the conventional principles of Pay for Service, there is a universal recognition of complete failure when the product no longer realizes value in the marketplace. In the case of an entrepreneurial venture organized using the Pay for Value organizing principles, product demise is just as likely. The venture dies when the product no longer sells at a price to keep the entrepreneurial partners interested. Entrepreneurial partners do not lose a "job" however. They simply redirect their energies to the development of new product opportunities that have the potential of realizing value in the marketplace.

Human Factors in Design and Implementation of Information System

Ali R. Salehnia   Sung Y. Shin

Computer Science Department
South Dakota State University
Brookings, SD 57007
Phone: (605) 688-5717
E-Mail: SALEHNIA@MG.SDSTATE

Hassan Pournaghshband

Southern College of Technology
Computer Science Department
Marietta, GA 30060-2896

Executive Abstract

Human-computer interaction involves transducers between humans and machines and because humans are sensitive to response times, viable human interfaces are more technology sensitive than many parts of information systems. Human-computer interaction arose as a field from intertwined roots in computer graphics, operating systems, human factors, ergonomics, industrial engineering, cognitive psychology, and the systems part of computer science.

Human-computer interaction studies human and machine communication and it draws from supporting knowledge on both the machine and the human side. On the machine side, techniques in computer graphics, operating systems, programming languages, and development environments are relevant. On human side, linguistics, social sciences, cognitive psychology, multi-culture translation, and human performance are relevant. The importance of understanding human-machine interaction and perspective within these development methods is essential and it should provide an excellent complement to any design and implementation effort.

Alternative system development processes such as waterfall model, participatory design, life-cycle model, iterative design, prototyping, and fourth generation consider the following steps necessary and essential for development and implementation of any information system. These steps (requirement and specification, analysis, design, implementation, testing, acceptance, operations and maintenance) are all mostly looked at from the technical point of view rather than user-interaction.

However, "The first fundamental element in the design of effective systems is an understanding of the tasks users need to carry out. The second fundamental element is an understanding of the people performing the tasks. The third element, the computer, includes the technology of visual displays, manual input devices, sound and gesture recognition, gaze-tracking, interaction styles and techniques, and user interface development environments and tools." (Sison, 1992).

Analysis of interaction between users and a system can provide a highly informative and effective means of evaluating usability. Usability can be defined in terms of the efficiency and satisfaction with which specified users can achieve specified work goals in given environments. It takes the view therefore that human considerations, such as job satisfaction, task definition, morale and so on, are just as important as technical considerations. The task for the systems designer is to produce a 'good fit' system, taking into account people and their needs and the working environment on the one hand, and the organizational structure, computer systems and the necessary work tasks on the other.

Once human-computer interfaces have been defined, the technical requirements to fulfil these can also be designed. These technical requirements become the output of this stage and the input to the design stage of technical subsystems. As the computer hardware prices decrease and more reusable software become available, the human-computer interface definition becomes a major output of any system development methodology. This task will be more important especially when the designers have to design a system to used in a multi-culture environment.

Hefley, (1992) suggested that Human-computer interaction is affected by the forces shaping the nature of future computing. These forces include: Decreasing hardware costs leading to larger memories and faster systems; Miniaturization of hardware leading to portability; Reduction in power requirements leading to portability; New display technologies leading to the packaging of computational devices in new forms; Assimilation of computation into the environment; Specialized hardware leading to new functions; Increased development of network communication and distributed computing; Increasingly widespread use of computers, especially by people who are subside of the computing profession; Increasing innovation in input techniques; Wider social concerns leading to improved access to computers by currently disadvantaged groups.

It is important to understand about human information-processing characteristics, how human action is structured, the nature of human communication, and human physical and physiological Hefley (1992) also indicated that "Anthropometric and physiological characteristics of people and their relationship to workspace and environmental parameters.

The systems designer should also consider the characteristics of input/output devices such as weight, portability, bandwidth, sensory modality and the technical construction of devices for mediating between humans and machines are essential when designing an information system.

Many information systems do not realize their full potential to enable users to accomplish tasks easily and efficiently. They should be available for use interactively on a terminal connected to a mainframe computer or using a microcomputer. When designing a new information system, the design team should consider the importance of the human-machine interaction, the physical and psychological, and the background and culture characteristics of the users. Today, systems designers and implementors should consider these characteristics seriously they should emphasize more on the users's need than the technological requirement.

Eight Ways to Help Boost a Sagging Change Effort

Ronald E. LeBleu
Managing Partner
Software People Concepts, Inc.
Five Science Park
New Haven, CT 06511
203/786-5075

Roger T. Sobkowiak
Managing Partner
Software People Concepts, Inc.
Five Science Park
New Haven, CT 06511
203/786-5075

Executive Abstract

INTRODUCTION AND BACKGROUND

As a student of change, you know that organizations have an array of models they can subscribe to to help them through a change process. These each generally offer a well-reasoned way to scope out the required change as well as steps to enable an organization to achieve the desired future state. The classic model of change is Lewin's in which he calls for periods of unfreezing, discovery and re-freezing. But with all the models around, why do so many change efforts seem to fall short of expectations? What's missing? We think the answer is complex, but to our way of thinking, the models frequently treat change as a snapshot in time and fail to account for two human phenomena. The first is a negative force. It is when people and organizations start to lose interest as the triggering event fades in time. People and organizations simply move on to something else. The second phenomenon is a positive force, best captured by the words "spirit of renewal". It is the ability of a person or an organization to rekindle his/her/its interest and recharge his/her/its drive. Therefore, a successful change model must be able to function not merely as a snapshot, but as a video, not just at the start-up, but during the full life cycle of a change initiative. We believe that at least eight discrete characteristics can be used as indicators of a successful change effort and as pointers for renewal:

- Will
- Altering the way of work
- Manager role models
- Engineered successes
- Communications
- Rewards and recognition
- Use of development
- Tools

Think of these eight characteristics as a way of checking your own change initiatives and applying any corrective actions that might be required to propel it into the winner's circle instead of the "also-ran" category.

DISCUSSION

The eight characteristics are offered in order of the significance of their impact. To say it another way, if you want to place your change initiative in jeopardy start by falling short on the first five characteristics - and kiss your project goodbye. Although each quality has stand-alone importance, our studies have taught us that all eight qualities together are absolutely critical to the success of a change initiative. Each characteristic that is minimized, trivialized or ignored at any time in the life of the project increases the probability that the project will fall far short of expectations or fail completely. Specific real-life events illustrating each characteristic will be used to highlight this point.

CONCLUSION/DIRECTIONS FOR FURTHER RESEARCH

In identifying the characteristics we also offer a prescription for addressing the problems associated with them. As a quick one-minute check of your own situation, you can take the quiz that accompanies this article. As you rate the presence of each attribute on a scale of "0 to 10" and if you find that a project under your auspices is lacking in more than two of the qualities cited, then take corrective actions now! But the knowledge base about how to go about this work continues to grow. The actions you take will, of course, reflect your own distinctive working environment. Allow the eight characteristics to provide a template for the action, research and change initiatives you are driving. We believe you will soon notice a distinct increase in your success rate!

About the authors: Ronald E. LeBleu and Roger T. Sobkowiak are managing partners of Software People Concepts, Inc., a New Haven, Connecticut, consulting firm specializing in the management of change arising from restructuring, redirecting and reengineering organizations.

A Study of the Career Experiences of Men and Women in the Information Systems Field

Mary Sumner and Kay Werner
Department of Management Information Systems
Southern Illinois University at Edwardsville

The number of women participating in the computing field is still proportionately low, according to a panel of academic professionals addressing the issue of female participation in computing at a conference entitled "Scholarship on Women and Society." (McMullen, 1992). However, as women enter the work force in increasing numbers, more and more are choosing careers in the information systems field. In addition, more and more women are completing academic programs in information systems and computer science.

Even with these recent gains in participation in the MIS field, many writers have pointed to the "glass ceiling," that prevents women from advancing beyond lower or middle-level management positions (Morrison, White, and Van Velsor, 1987). It is important to determine if the "glass ceiling" is a phenomenon influencing women's participation in careers in the information systems field, or if MIS careers provide a different kind of context and opportunity for women.

In an early study of discrimination within organizations and its effects on opportunities for minority members such as women, Kanter argued that groups such as women have low access to power and opportunity (Kanter, 1979). Without access to power, women are often restricted to lower-level assignments and excluded from informal social networks. Excluded from these opportunities, groups such as women may lower their aspiration level and may find themselves unable to influence the course of their own careers.

There is evidence in the research that women have been the object of "treatment discrimination." This translates into fewer rewards, fewer resources, and fewer opportunities. While treatment discrimination may be manifested in terms of tangible outcomes such as fewer promotions, salary increases, training opportunities, and assignments, it may also lower feelings of acceptance into the work group and limit chances to obtain social support from supervisors and peers (Ilgen and Youtz, 1986).

With these views in mind, it is interesting to examine the career experiences of women and men in the information systems field. As a growing profession, the information systems field offers many opportunities. Prior research does show differences between information systems professionals and other professionals in terms of such factors as the need for growth, social need, and need for achievement (Cougar, 1988; Cougar and Zawacki, 1980). There is also some evidence that information systems personnel have difficulty moving into managerial positions and often face limited advancement opportunities because of the technical nature of their field (Tanniru, 1983). Although the career experiences of informa-

tion systems personnel have been investigated, there is almost no research which compares the experiences of men and women in information systems positions.

THE PURPOSE OF THIS STUDY

This study will address two research questions:

1. What is the impact of gender differences on the career experiences and career success of information systems professionals?
2. What skills and capabilities gained from educational preparation and work experiences are viewed as most critical to successful performance in positions in information systems, as viewed by both men and women in the field?

A FRAMEWORK FOR CAREER EXPERIENCES

This study will analyze the career experiences of information systems professionals with respect to a number of variables originally proposed by Greenhaus, et.al. (1990) and later extended by Igbaria and Wormley (1992) in their study of how race differences affect the career experiences and the success of MIS professionals. The framework for describing career experiences includes the following variables: feelings of acceptance, job discretion, met expectations, career support received from one's supervisor, participation in technical training and management development programs, career satisfaction, and organizational commitment.

Feelings of Acceptance by the Organization

Acceptance into the organization's informal networks can increase a sense of power and belonging. Feelings of acceptance in the informal network may encourage an employee to work harder and to be more effective (Woodruff, 1983). Acceptance in informal business activities with peers, subordinates, and superiors is important.

Feelings of acceptance are important to MIS professionals, who are sometimes outside the mainstream of the organization (Barkol and Martin, 1982). Women, too, sometimes encounter difficulty breaking into the organization's informal networks, particularly the "old boy" network. To be successful, women need to feel accepted; they cannot be "too macho" or "too feminine" (Morrison, et.al., 1987). They need to be "easy to be with," able to fit in by making others comfortable, and willing to provide a new kind of interactional leadership by "hosting informal social events" (Rosener, 1990).

Job Discretion

The amount of discretion an employee possesses is a factor influencing how much influence or power he or she can exercise. Job discretion is manifested in authority, decision-making power, budgetary control, and the ability to take independent action. Job discretion motivates high levels of effort, and provides decision-making skills that can enhance performance (Hackman and Oldham, 1976).

Since MIS professionals exhibit a high need for autonomy and dominance, job discretion is especially important (Couger and Zawacki, 1980). In Morrison's view, job autonomy is also a critical success factor for women. Moving into high-risk jobs and taking career risks are key strategies influencing the career success of women (Morrison, et.al., 1987).

Met Expectations

The idea of met expectations measures the extent to which an individual's initial expectations for achieving promotions, career opportunities, and salary increases, are actually met. In other words, are actual advancement opportunities different from what was expected? Met expectations are a source of career satisfaction, especially if the expected outcomes are valued by employees (Greenhaus, et.al., 1983). Unmet expectations may produce feelings of unfairness and inequity, and may cause employees to reduce their efforts (Couger, 1988; Couger and Zawacki, 1980).

Since MIS professionals have a higher need for achievement than most other professionals, their ability to realize their met expectations may be particularly important (Couger, 1990). In the case of women, the evidence that few women reach higher-level positions sends the message that talent and hard work don't pay off and creates morale and productivity issues (Morrison, et.al., 1987).

Career Support from One's Supervisor

Career support or sponsorship received from one's supervisor is clearly a motivating factor. Supervisors can provide sponsorship, acceptance, challenging assignments, visibility and constructive feedback. Sponsorship contributes to effective job performance of both men and women by increasing motivation and chances for upward mobility (Bova and Phillips, 1981; Burke, 1982).

Without question, career support is a determinant in the success of MIS professionals (Couger, 1990; Couger and Zawacki, 1980; Ferratt and Short, 1986; Turner and Baroudi, 1986). Career support, particularly mentoring, is critical for women as well. Successful women in several studies point to having the advantage of higher-level executives as supporters and advocates (Hennig and Jardim, 1977; Morrison, et.al., 1987). Women who have mentors are likely to be better paid and to have better career mobility than women without mentors (Fitt and Newton, 1981; Combs and Tolbert, 1980). Male mentors can effectively support the career development and visibility of women because they are still in higher, more influential positions (Berry, 1983).

Participation in Technical Training and Management Development

Access to training and development provides opportunities for growth that foster career success (Kanter, 1979). Training is particularly important for the development and retention of MIS employees, because rapid technological changes require the updating of technical skills (Bartol and Martin, 1982; Couger, 1980; Kirkley, 1988). MIS professionals also need business-oriented knowledge and managerial skills in order to understand the business context for information systems development and to manage projects successfully (Bartol and Martin, 1982; Kirkley, 1988).

In the case of women, training and development opportunities are equally important. The ability to polish skills and to develop state-of-the-art knowledge is critical to women's ability to succeed (Morrison, et.al., 1987).

Career Satisfaction

Career satisfaction results from challenging assignments, recognition, career support, and progress toward achieving professional goals. Since MIS professionals have a high need for achievement, opportunities for challenging work, consistent training, and salary increments are all associated with career satisfaction. In the case of women, career progress results from the opportunity to take on challenging assignments, the ability to adapt, the drive to succeed, and the ability to work collaboratively with colleagues (Morrison, et.al., 1987).

Organizational Commitment

Job satisfaction is closely related to overall organizational commitment (Baroudi, 1985; Bartol, 1983). Career satisfaction resulting from challenging opportunities, career support, training, and acceptance will enhance organizational commitment.

Organizational commitment is one of the most important factors influencing whether MIS employees leave an organization (Baroudi, 1985; Bartol, 1983). Several studies indicate that MIS professionals exhibit little loyalty to their organizations (Tanniru, 1983; Woodruff, 1980), which may be related to their desire to find highly motivating positions. Studies of the career progression of women professionals illustrate that women who achieve upward mobility demonstrate a good deal of organizational commitment over time (Morrison, et.al., 1987; Hennig and Jardim, 1977). However, complications of women's biological role (e.g. maternity, child-rearing) makes it necessary for them to balance career and family. Women who want to have the flexibility to balance their career and family obligations may be viewed by men as not having adequate commitment to the organization. This poses a dilemma for women which expects them to choose between organizational commitment and family (Schwartz, 1989).

RESEARCH METHODOLOGY

Procedure and Sample

This research is an exploratory study to determine gender differences in career experiences in the information systems field. The population surveyed included all of the graduates of a Master of Science program in Management Information Systems. The respondents to the study graduated between 1981 and 1993. There have been 102 male graduates of the M.S. in MIS program and 46 female graduates.

The procedures for conducting the study included developing a questionnaire and an interview guide. The questionnaire was sent to all M.S. in MIS graduates, and a random sample of ten graduates (five women and five men) were selected for in-depth interviewing. It was felt that the interviewing process would provide some insight into career development issues.

Development of the Questionnaire. The questionnaire was designed to provide information on the respondents' educational background, job history, salary range, age, and career experiences. Questions from a number of validated instruments were used to measure feelings of acceptance, job discretion, met expectations, career support received from one's supervisor, career satisfaction, and organizational commitment.

Interview Guide. As noted, ten of the graduates were randomly selected for in-depth interviews in order to gain further insight into career experiences in the MIS field. The interview guide included open-ended questions in each of these areas: Feelings of Acceptance, Job Discretion, Met Expectations, Career Support, Participation in Technical Training, Career Satisfaction, Organizational Commitment, and Education.

Measures

The measures used in this study were selected from a number of prior studies in which career experience variables were investigated, and all measures have been tested and found to be reliable. Open-ended questions were used to obtain the respondents' views of training opportunities and critical skills and capabilities needed for successful job performance.

Perceived Acceptance by the Organization was assessed with 12 items (e.g. "I am accepted in informal business activities with my boss") taken from the "corporate fit" scale developed by Nixon (1985a). Responses to the 12 items, each with a five-point scale from "strongly agree" to "strongly disagree" were averaged to produce a total Acceptance score.

Job Discretion was measured with nine items (e.g. "I have very little responsibility in my job") taken from a longer "job power" scale developed by Nixon (1985b). Responses to these items were averaged to produce a total Job Discretion score.

Met Expectations was measured by a four-item scale (e.g. "My rate of promotion has been much quicker than I expected it to be"). The areas of rate of promotion, salary increases, career opportunities, and training and development

experiences were taken into account. The Met Expectations scale was developed by Igbaria and Wormley (1992). Responses were averaged to produce a total Met Expectations score.

Career Support was measured by a scale developed by Greenhaus, et.al., 1990. The nine-item scale was used to measure agreement or disagreement on a five-point scale with the degree of career development support they received from their supervisor (e.g. "My supervisor takes the time to learn about my career goals and aspirations.") Responses to all nine items were averaged to produce a total Career Support score.

Career Satisfaction was measured by five items developed by Greenhaus, et.al. (1990). Individuals were asked to indicate their agreement/disagreement with each statement on a five-point scale ranging from "strongly agree" to "strongly disagree" (e.g. "I am satisfied with the progress I have made toward meeting my goals for advancement.") The five items were averaged to create a Career Satisfaction score.

Organizational Commitment was measured using a seven-item scale developed by Alutto, et.al. (1973). Each item required the respondent to indicate the probability of leaving the organization for an alternative job given increases in pay, status, and the friendliness of co-workers. A five-point scale, ranging from "1" I would definitely change to "5" I would definitely not change, was used. Responses were averaged to produce a total Organizational Commitment score.

Participation in Technical Training and Management Development programs was indicated by two items dealing with the nature and duration of training opportunities which the graduates reported. Technical training programs were defined as programs which were designed to teach specific job-related information and skills. Management development programs were defined as programs designed to teach broad managerial skills such as supervision, coaching, decision-making and strategic policy-making.

Critical Skills. Open-ended questions were designed to obtain information about the skills and capabilities gained from educational experiences which the graduates considered to be most critical to their job performance. One question asked which skills and capabilities gained from work experience were most critical for job success.

Data Analyses

The data from respondents' educational background, job history, and career skills were tabulated and presented in tables. The scores for each of the career experience variables (e.g. feelings of acceptance, job discretion, etc.) were calculated, and an overall mean for the men and for the women respondents' for each of these variables was derived. A t-test to determine if the difference between the means for the men and for the women on each of the career experience variables was statistically significant at the .05 level was then determined.

A discussion of interview findings relevant to career experiences, job success, and educational factors contributing to career success was also developed. While this analysis was based upon a limited number of respondents, it was helpful in obtaining insight into gender-related issues in career expectations and experiences.

RESULTS OF THE STUDY

The findings are organized into sections entitled Background Characteristics, Career Experiences, Training Experiences, Critical Skills, and Interview Findings.

Background Characteristics

The background characteristics reported by the 34 respondents described their education, job history, and age distribution. Of these 34 respondents, 25 were male and 9 were female. The overall response rate was 23 percent, with 25 percent of the males and 20 percent of the females responding to the survey. The low response rate of women graduates may be partly explained by the likelihood that some women have interrupted their careers in MIS because of family commitments. See Table 1.

	Men	Women	Total
Total Number of Respondents	25	9	34
Age Distribution			
25 - 34	7		14
35 - 44	12	1	13
45 - 55	6	1	7
Degree Completion Date			
1981 - 1984	3	1	4
1985 - 1988	10	3	13
1989 - 1993	12	5	17

	Men	Women	Total
Job Title			
Supervisor	12	0	12
Systems Analyst	4	4	8
Programmer/Analyst	3	2	5
Systems Engineer	2	0	2
Project Leader	1	1	2
Other	3	2	5

Table 1: Background Characteristics of the Respondents

Career Experiences

The career experience scores for the male and female respondents for each of the career experience variables were averaged, and a t-test to determine if the difference between the means for the men and the women was statistically significant at the .05 level was conducted. The findings showed that the difference in career experience scores for the men and the women in the sample for each of the variables studied was not statistically significant. See Table 2:

One of the first reasons why the experiences of men and women in the information systems profession may be comparable in terms of their perceptions of their career experiences has to do with the nature of the field. Men and women are

	Male	Female	t-value
Feelings of Acceptance	1.73	1.76	-.16
Job Discretion	1.93	2.25	-1.11
Met Expectations	2.93	2.81	.40
Career Support/Sponsorship	2.27	1.91	1.34
Career Satisfaction	2.29	2.13	.46
Organizational Commitment	3.79	3.61	1.36

Table 2: Career Experiences of Men and Women in Information Systems

recruited into the MIS profession largely because of technical knowledge, and their job performance is based upon technical competence—particularly at the lower levels.

Since the items were reverse-scored for each of the career experience variables, mean scores in the "1" and "2" range represent positive assessments. The mean scores for Acceptance (e.g. 1.73 for the men and 1.76 for the women) indicate positive feelings of "Acceptance." This may be based upon the fact that expectations for technical competence are relatively straightforward, and that both men and women are on an "even playing field" with respect to their ability to demonstrate technical expertise as members of a project team.

The mean scores for Job Discretion (e.g. 1.93 for the men and 2.25 for the women) represent a positive viewpoint. The respondents' view of Job Discretion may be based upon the nature of the work itself, since systems work is characterized by chances for problem-solving and analysis.

The mean scores for the variable Met Expectations suggest that career opportunities, promotions, and salary increases are viewed less optimistically. There may be slight frustration with advancement opportunities because corporate downsizing is decreasing opportunities for upward mobility. Some information systems professionals may reach a technical plateau and not find opportunities to advance to management.

In the area of Career Support, both men and women seemed to indicate that sponsorship was a relatively positive element in their career experiences, with the women's view of sponsorship slightly more positive than the men's. This factor may be influenced by the predominance of project teamwork as a strategy for managing systems development projects. On a team, all members have a relatively equal footing and can find opportunities for sponsorship. Women who demonstrate technical expertise become valued contributors.

The issue of organizational commitment was less positive, with both the men and the women expressing willingness to leave their current positions for increases in status and pay. The overall uncertainty in the profession, combined with the search for opportunities which might provide greater upward mobility, may be influencing this lesser commitment. This is consistent with studies that indicate that MIS professionals may willingly leave an organization to find positions which are highly motivating and which offer growth potential (Tanniru, 1983).

In terms of overall Career Satisfaction, the respondents expressed a neutral view. A number of the factors which may be related to this view, including challenging opportunities, career support, expectations, and the changing nature of the profession, will become more apparent in the discussion of the interview findings.

Technical Training and Management Development

In their responses about training opportunities, both the men and women respondents indicated that they participated in technical training and management development programs. Technical training was more frequent, with 22 of the 36 respondents (61 percent) participating, compared to management development, with 11 of the 36 (31 percent) reporting that they participated in these types of programs. Roughly the same percentages of women and men participated in both types of training programs.

Most of the technical training programs were hardware/software specific, including: Novell networking, fourth generation tools, database administration, data dictionary, and other technical topics. In contrast, management development topics included: supervisory skills, making meetings work, leadership education, effective presentation skills, and employee evaluation.

Critical Skills

Each of the respondents described the three skills which they felt were most critical to their success. As you can see from Table 3, effective communications, teamwork, analytical skills, and programming skills were considered critical to job success.

As you can see from these findings, both male and female respondents emphasized the importance of communications and analytical skills. Perhaps the greatest differences occurred in the assessment of the importance of teamwork and organizing. A larger percentage of males than females considered these skills critical to their success.

Critical Skills gained from Education in MIS

In response to the question regarding skills and capabilities gained from educational preparation in MIS which were most critical to successful job performance, the respondents noted systems analysis and programming skills as most important. See Table 4:

As you can see from these findings, a greater percentage of women mentioned the importance of systems analysis and communications skills.

	Males n=25		Females n=9		Total n=34	
	Num	%	Num	%	Num	%
Communications	15	.60	8	.89	23	.68
Analytical	14	.56	3	.33	17	.50
Teamwork	12	.48	1	.11	13	.38
Programming	11	.44	2	.22	13	.38
Organizing	9	.36	1	.11	10	.29

Table 3: Critical Skills

	Males n=25		Females n=9		Total n=34	
	Num	%	Num	%	Num	%
Systems Analysis	12	.48	7	.78	19	.56
Programming	10	.40	5	.56	15	.44
Communications	6	.24	4	.44	10	.29
Database Mgmt	8	.32	1	.11	9	.26
Program Mgmt	8	.32	1	.11	9	.2

Table 4: Critical Skills gained from Education in MIS

	Males n=25		Females n=9		Total n=34	
	Num	%	Num	%	Num	%
Communications	14	.56	6	.67	20	.59
Business Under	11	.44	1	.11	12	.35
Computing	8	.32	2	.22	11	.32
Analytical	6	.24	5	.56	11	.32
Programming	7	.28	2	.22	9	.26
Project Mgmt	6	.24	3	.33	9	.26

Table 5: Critical Skills Gained from Work Experience

Critical Skills gained from Work Experience

The respondents generally felt that the most critical skills gained from their work experience included communications skills, business understanding, knowledge of computing and its applications, programming, and project management. See Table 5.

Slightly greater emphasis was placed upon "business understanding" by the men in this sample, whereas the women mentioned analytical skills as critical more frequently. In general, however, women and men in the sample agreed on the importance of the communications skills gained from their work experience.

Interview Findings: The Career Experiences of Women

Of the five women who were interviewed, four had achieved promotions to senior systems analyst or project leader in major corporations. In all four cases, they reported receiving career support from a sponsor who served as a supervisor and mentor. In addition, these four women reported having a considerable amount of job autonomy and latitude in accomplishing tasks.

Although they felt "accepted," most of the women interviewed pointed to the "old boy network" within their corporations and thought that they might not get "picked for the team" when special projects and assignments occurred. In one case, a woman witnessed outright sexism and harassment. Even though she viewed this as a byproduct of the "company mentality," she was quite unhappy in her job and shunned the "social side" of the work place. The only compensating factor, she felt, was that many of the men who had been there much longer than she respected her competence and consulted with her whenever they had questions on technical issues.

With respect to the issue of "met expectations," four of the five women were confident that they had achieved relevant career goals by mastering technical challenges. One had become an EDI (electronic data interchange) expert, while several others had mastered 4GL's (fourth generation languages). While they derived a considerable amount of career satisfaction from these technical challenges, and had received promotions based upon technical merit, most of these women did not have a clear view of the next step in their career paths.

Although each of the four women reporting successful progress was committed to the organization, none of them aspired to achieve a management position. One was attempting to balance family and career plans and did not want a management role because of the overtime and administration. One held a marketing support position and did not see management as the next step. Another pointed to the fact that managerial opportunities in her company were severely limited, because an entire layer of mid-management was being eliminated. Another felt that her progress managing an EDI project had been good, but viewed future prospects as very limited; she seemed to be at a plateau. She admitted that upward mobility might depend upon making a lateral career move into a business unit, and then making progress on a slightly different career track.

In all five cases, educational background and ongoing technical training were key factors in job success. Four of the five respondents pointed to the importance of programming, networking, and other technical skills as a part of their MIS academic program. In all cases, the women had received on-the-job technical training in areas (e.g. EDI, 4GL's, software) relevant to accomplishing their job responsibilities. Part of the "problem" these women were experiencing with career uncertainty may be related to the MIS profession itself. As already noted, many MIS jobs rely upon technical skills. Once these technical skills are achieved, an individual can reach a career plateau, with the only way out being a lateral step into a business unit. The other complicating factor was corporate downsizing, which was eliminating a layer of middle-level management.

Interview Findings: The Career Experiences of Men

One of the interesting findings from these interviews was the similarity between the career experiences of the men and women. The men who were interviewed had a variety of careers in MIS: as project leaders (two), a consultant, and an internal auditor. One had left the MIS field altogether and was now pursuing a career track in the mortgage operations end of the insurance business.

One of the interesting aspects of the men's career progression was their mobility. One individual had made a transition from a programming position in a large MIS shop to an end-user consulting position. The end-user consulting position provided him with the opportunity to make a lateral move into the business side as a "systems" person; and once there,

he was able to find a sponsor who was willing to teach him the "business" side. In another case, an individual landed a position as a "re-engineering" consultant with a Big-6 accounting firm after a series of positions as a systems specialist—both within MIS groups and within business units.

In contrast to the two men who had made numerous job moves, the other three reported career stability. One had risen to project manager after almost ten years of programming; another was an internal auditor; and another was "plateaued" as a programmer/analyst at a government agency. Interestingly enough, the latter individual felt that his organization was deliberately promoting women and minorities, and "leaving white males behind."

On the issue of "feelings of acceptance," only one of the men felt part of an "old boy network." Three felt that men and women were on a level "playing field" in the MIS profession, because career success at the lower levels depends primarily upon technical knowledge and intelligence, not "informal networking." Women were clearly part of the "team," one project manager noted.

In terms of job discretion, the men who were interviewed reported having considerable job autonomy. This was particularly true of the jobs in end-user computing, project management, and consulting. However, the technical plateau was still a reality for the men, as it was for the women. Three of the five men were not making a transition into management, and in two cases this was intentional. In each case, they had made career progress based upon technical expertise and had reached a plateau.

Training and professional development opportunities were good in almost every case. The men who were interested in a technical career stressed the importance of ongoing technical training over and above the need for management development. Only two of the men interviewed had a clear view of a career track leading into management. One of them was being encouraged to move into management; another had moved into a business track under the auspices of a mentor.

In terms of what was learned at school, the men participating in the interviews pointed to the importance of both technical skills (e.g. programming, database, and networking) and "people skills" (e.g. making presentations, politics, teamwork, and communications). Having MIS training in the context of a business program was viewed as important in the minds of the men who were pursuing careers as systems analysts and consultants within functional areas of the business.

CONCLUSION

The study of the career experiences of men and women in the information systems field provides some interesting insights. Both men and women felt acceptance and reported having opportunities for job discretion, problem-solving, and decision-making in their positions. Sponsorship and career support were viewed as positive influences in their career development.

Both the men and the women were making progress because of their ability to master the technical challenges, but they were "uncertain" about their opportunities for upward mobility, both because of reaching a technical plateau and because of limited management opportunities in the field. Some were primarily interested in a technical career and did not aspire to management. For others, making a transition into providing information systems support within a functional line of business was a strategy which could provide greater career mobility. It was clear that key skills in information systems careers included effective communications, business understanding, and teamwork.

REFERENCES

Alutto, J.A., Hrebiniak, L.G., and Alonso, R.C.. "On Operationalizing the Concept of Commitment," *Social Forces*, V. 51, No. 1, June 1973, pp. 448-454.

Baroudi, J.J. "The Impact of Role Variables on IS Personnel Word Attitudes and Intentions," *MIS Quarterly*, V. 9, No. 4, December 1985, pp. 341-356.

Bartol, K.M. "Turnover Among DP Personnel: A Causal Analysis," *Communications of the ACM*, V. 26, No. 10, October 1983, pp. 807-811.

Bartol, K.M. and Martin, D.C. "Managing Information Systems Personnel: A Review of the Literature and Managerial Implications," *MIS Quarterly*, Special Issue, 1982, pp. 49-70.

Berry, Patricia. "Mentors for Women Managers: Fast-track to Corporate Success," *Supervisory Management*, V. 28, No. 8, August, 1983, pp. 36-40.

Bova, Breda M. and Phillips, Rebecca R.. *The Mentor Relationship: A Study of Mentors and Proteges in Business and Academia*, ERIC 208 233, 1981, 14 pp.

Burke, Ronald. "The Role of Mentors and Sponsors in Management Development," *CTM: The Human Element*, V. 15, No. 2, December, 1982, pp. 10-13.

Combs, Jeanne M. and Tolbert, E.L.. "Vocational Role Models of College Women," *Journal of the National Association for Women Deans, Administrators, and Counselors*, V. 43, No. 1, 1980, pp. 33-38.

Couger, J.D. "Motivators vs. Demotivators in the IS Environment," *Journal of Systems Management*, V. 39, No. 6, June 1988, pp. 36-41.

Couger, J.D. and Zawacki, R.A. *Motivating and Managing Computer Personnel*, Wiley, New York, NY, 1980.

Fernandez, J.P. *Racism and Sexism in Corporate Life: Changing Values in American Business*. Lexington Books, Lexington, MA, 1981.

Ferratt, T.W. and Short, L.E. "Are Information Systems People Different? An Investigation of How They Are and Should Be Managed," *MIS Quarterly*, V. 12, No. 3, September 1988, pp. 427-443.

Fitt, L.W. and Newton, D.A. "When the Mentor is a Man and the Protogee a Woman," *Harvard Business Review*, V. 59, No. 2, March-April 1981, pp. 56-60.

Gill, Patricia and Butler, Janet. "Asleep at the Switch," *Chief Information Officer Journal*, March-April 1993, pp. 34-39.

Greenhaus, J.H., Seidel, C., and Marinis, M. "The Impact of Expectations and Values on Job Attitudes," *Organizational Behavior and Human Performance*, V. 31, No. 3, June 1983, pp. 394-417.

Greenhaus, J.H., Parasuraman, S., and Wormley, W.M. "Race, Organizational Experiences and Career Outcomes," *Academy of Management Journal*, V. 33, No. 1, March 1990, pp. 64-86.

Hackman, J.R. and Oldham, G.R. "Motivation Through the Design of Work: Test of a Theory," *Organizational Behavior and Human Performance*, V. 16, No. 2, April 1976, pp. 250-279.

Harlan, A. and Weiss, C.L.. "Sex Differences in Factors Affecting Managerial Career Advancement," In P.A. Wallace (Ed.), *Women in the Workplace*, Boston: Auburn House, 1982, pp. 59-100.

Helgesen, Sally. *The Female Advantage*, New York: Doubleday, 1990.

Hennig, Margaret and Jardim, Anne. *The Managerial Woman*, New York: Simon and Schuster, 1977.

Ilgen, D.R. and Youtz, M.A. "Factors Affecting the Evaluation and Development of Minorities in Organizations." In K. Rowland and G. Ferris (Eds.) *Research in Personnel and Human Resource Management: A Research Annual*. Greenwich, Conn.: JAI Press, 1986, pp. 307-337.

Igbaria, M. "Job Performance of MIS Professionals: An Examination of the Antecedents and Consequences," *Journal of Engineering and Technology Management*, V. 8, No. 2, August 1991, pp. 141-171.

Igbaria, Magid and Wormley, Wayne. "Organizational Experiences and Career Success of MIS Professionals and Managers: An Examination of Race Differences," *MIS Quarterly*, December 1992, pp. 507-529.

Kanter, Rosabeth Moss. *Men and Women in the Corporation*, New York: BasicBooks, 1977.

Kanter, R.M. "Differential Access to Opportunity and Power, " in *Discrimination in Organizations*. R. Alvarez, (ed.), Jossey-Bass. San Francisco, CA, 1979, pp. 52-68.

Kirkley, J. "MIS Profession is Not What it Used to Be," *Computerworld*, March 21, 1988, pp. 80-81.

Levitin, T., Quinn, R.P., and Staines, G.I. "Sex Discrimination against the American Working Woman," *American Behavioral Scientist*, V. 15, 1971, pp. 238-254.

McMullen, John. "Panel discusses 'Women and Computers' (Scholarship on Women and Society Conference)," *Newsbytes*, June 8, 1992.

Morrison, White and Van Velsor. *Breaking the Glass Ceiling: Can Women Reach the Top of America's Largest Corporations?* Addison Wesley, 1987.

Nixon, R. *Black Managers in Corporate America: Alienation or Integration*, National Urban League, Washington, D.C. 1985a.

Nixon, R. *Perceptions of Job Power Among Black Managers in Corporate America*, National Urban League, Washington, D.C. 1985b.

Olsen, C.A. and Becker, B.E. "Sex Discrimination in the Promotion Process," *Industrial and Labor Relations Review*, V. 36, 1983, pp. 624-641.

Rhode, Deborah. *Justice and Gender*. Cambridge, MA: Harvard University Press, 1989.

Rosener, Judy B., "Ways Women Lead," *Harvard Business Review*, November-December 1990.

Schwartz, Felice N.. "Management Women and the New Facts of Life," *Harvard Business Review*, January-February 1989.

Sumner, Mary, et.al.. "An Assessment of the Attitudes of Graduates and Employers toward Competencies Needed for Entry-Level MIS Positions," *Proceedings of ISECON 1990*, Chicago, 1990, pp. 129-134.

Tanniru, M.R. "An Investigation of the Career Paths of the EDP Professionals," *Proceedings of the 20th Annual Computer Personnel Research Conference*, Charlottesville, VA, November 17-18, 1983, pp. 87-101.

Terberg, J.R. and Ilgen, D.R. "A Theoretical Approach to Sex Discrimination in Traditional Masculine Occupations," *Organizational Behavior and Human Performance*, V. 13, 1975, pp. 352-376.

Turner, J.A. and Baroudi, J.J. "The Management of Information Systems Occupations: A Research Agenda," *Computer Personnel*, V. 10, No. 4, 1984, pp. 61-68.

Woodruff, Charles K. "Data Processing People: Are They Satisfied/Dissatisfied with Their Jobs?" *Information and Management*, V. 3, 1980, pp. 219-225.

Factors Affecting Computer Anxiety and Its Effects on Ease of Use of Business Software

Jennifer Thomas (Ph.D.Student)
Faculty of Commerce and Administration
Concordia University, Montreal, Canada

Executive Abstract

BACKGROUND

Computer Anxiety refers to the extent of fear or aversion to computerization and/or interaction with computers that is manifested in people. (Parasuraman and Igbaria, 1990). Different factors may influence the level of anxiety evoked. This, in turn, may have an affect on performance and/or perception.

DISCUSSION OF ISSUES

Howard and Kernan (1990) identify computer anxiety, alienation and attitudes as being distinctly separate constructs which may affect users' performance with software. They argue that past studies have mixed these constructs which has resulted in conflicting findings. Studies by Igbaria (1990) and Gilroy and Desai (1986) indicate that performance can be improved if computer anxiety is addressed in training and attempts made to overcome it. In Gilroy and Desai's study (1986), it was found that undergraduate and MBA students, who had used a wordprocessor in an English Composition course over a semester, experienced a reduction in anxiety measures from the beginning to the end of the semester, compared to those who had, instead, followed a programming course. Both groups exhibited less anxiety at the end of the semester than those who had had no exposure to computers. Women seemed to exhibit higher anxiety levels than men, while race and age were not found to have significant effects.

A questionnaire survey, conducted by Howard and Smith (1986) to investigate computer anxiety among managers from various firms, found it to be minimal. Age and sex were not correlated with computer anxiety, neither were locus of control, cognitive style, or trait anxiety. Computer anxiety was negatively correlated to favourable attitudes to the computer and its impact on society, and even more so to actual computer experience. High anxiety levels were also found to be related to high Math anxiety levels.

The studies by Shneiderman (1982) also indicate that using less threatening terminology in system messages can reduce anxiety and improve performance. The tone and specificity of these messages was shown, in four experiments, to have an effect on performance. Clear, specific, courteous messages improved performance. Apart from the benefits of the clarity of the messages, there is some indication as well that this contributes to reducing computer anxiety. The use of less obscure technical terminology resulted in the interaction being perceived as less intimidating and threatening.

We conducted an exploratory study of student users in actual use of one of three statistical package treatments to determine the effect of various factors on ease of use of packages of this nature. In this paper, we present the results which were found with respect to computer anxiety. In particular, we were interested in:

Question 1:What are the factors that impact computer anxiety, and does this change over time?

Question 2:Does computer anxiety have an effect on ease of use, as measured by user performance?

FINDINGS OF PAPER

Question 1:

We found that computer anxiety was a function of the type of package experience, extent of microcomputer experience, gender, and perceived competence in quantitative courses. These findings were expected, since several researchers, Igbaria (1990), Howard and Smith (1986) and Gilroy and Desai (1986), to name a few, have also found computer experience levels to be negatively related to computer anxiety. Males had lower anxiety scores on average than Females, which agreed with the findings of Gilroy and Desai's (1986) study of undergraduate and MBA students. Howard (1986), however, did not find gender to be correlated with anxiety in their survey of managers. Equating math anxiety with competency in quantitative courses, it was not surprising that we found those rating themselves as having average and excellent competence in quantitative courses having lower anxiety than those rating themselves as having poor competence. Howard (1986) had found anxiety to be correlated with math anxiety. In the space of a week after experience with an unfamiliar package, the only change in these results was that quantitative competence no longer had a statistically significant impact on anxiety.

Question 2:

We found that computer anxiety had a statistically significant effect on performance and that the higher the computer anxiety score the lower the performance, which is consistent with findings by Shneiderman (1982). Relative to the other factors, however, its impact on performance is small.

CONCLUSION

While computer anxiety was found to be a factor in determining ease of use of a package, in terms of performance, it does not seem to be the definitive factor. Others are more pertinent, in particular, package design characteristics. Level of experience seems to be instrumental in reducing computer anxiety, that is, use overcomes initial fears. Nonetheless, the results indicate that if initial exposure is unfavourable enough, this will have a debilitating effect on performance. It, therefore, should not be ignored, even if its impact seems to be less than other factors. The results also suggest that the problem is more marked for females than for males, indicating the need for greater sensitivity to ways of alleviating the unspoken anxieties of females being initiated to the computer environ-ment, as this anxiety also translated into reduced performance. While our sample was undergraduate students and, therefore, the results cannot be assumed to be transferrable to users in the work place, these students will be future entrants into this environment. They will be bringing these traits with them, which from the results, promises to adversely affect their performance with software and, hence, productivity. This is always a negative in business. It behooves software designers to be cognizant of these findings and, therefore, to seek out and implement those design characteristics which can alleviate this problem and for trainers to likewise seek ways to minimize this potential problem.

Ethical Attitudes of MIS Personnel

Jennifer L. Wagner

Walter E. Heller College of Business Administration

Roosevelt University, 430 S. Michigan Avenue, Chicago IL 60605

(708) 437-9200 x231

ABSTRACT

This paper describes a preliminary study of MIS employees' attitudes toward ethical issues in information systems. The 40 subjects were part-time students studying for a masters in information systems in an evening program at an urban university, while working full-time in the MIS profession.

The subjects read twelve information systems-based scenarios and were asked to classify the nineteen behaviors described in them as Unacceptable, Questionable, or Acceptable. This study used the same instrument as studies by Benham (1994), Paradice (1990) and Morris, Jones, and Rubinsztein (1993), which used undergraduates as subjects. The replication of their earlier work with a different subject group provides the foundation for the present study.

The MIS personnel in the present study demonstrate a great sensitivity to ethical issues in information systems.

INTRODUCTION

An area of great interest to the business community, to the academic community, and, in fact, to the population at large is 'business ethics'. Those of us who teach, study, and practice in management information systems (MIS) are concerned about software piracy, access to confidential data, and use of company computers for an individual's private purposes. The ethical attitudes of MIS personnel are of great concern to business managers and to society as a whole. MIS educators have been asked to improve these attitudes before the workers enter the workplace.

Many educators and researchers have assumed both that a problem exists and that MIS students hold the same ethical attitudes as MIS personnel. This paper describes a preliminary study of MIS employees' attitudes toward ethical issues in information systems, which tests the first of these assumptions. This study used the same instrument as studies by Benham (1994), Paradice (1990) and Morris, Jones, and Rubinsztein (1993), which used undergraduates as subjects. The replication of their earlier work with a different subject group provides the foundation for the present study and will allow comparisons in a later study, which will test the second assumption. All of these studies intend to discover the ethical attitudes of future and present information systems personnel in order that educators and managers may attempt change these attitudes if such action is felt to be necessary.

In order to discuss ethics in MIS, we must first define 'ethics'. Each individual seems to know what he means, but his understanding is not always shared by others. Authors who discuss ethics frequently provide circular definitions, definitions dependent upon understanding even more complex concepts, or, most likely, no definition at all. A recent dictionary provides:

(1) a system of moral principles;
(2) the rules of conduct recognized in respect to a particular class of human actions or a particular group, culture, etc.;
(3) moral principles, as of an individual" (Random House, p. 453).

All three of these dictionary meanings are useful in discussing ethical issues in MIS. The first establishes the parallel between ethics and laws. The second allows us to examine the idea of a code of ethics for MIS professionals. And the third is consistent with such descriptions as "he has ethics" or "he is an ethical person" which frequent the MIS press and literature. This 'dictionary definition' of ethics will be in force throughout the remainder of this paper.

METHODOLOGY

The subjects read twenty information systems-based scenarios and were asked to classify the 31 behaviors described in them as Unacceptable, Questionable, or Acceptable. The Appendix shows the scenarios. The original developers of the instrument included several scenarios that were familiar to students, along with some exclusively from the business world.

The 40 subjects were part-time students studying for a masters in information systems in an evening program at an urban university, while working full-time in the MIS profession. At the time of the survey, the MIS personnel were enrolled in a graduate level systems analysis and design course; ethics was not a major topic of discussion in the course.

RESULTS

The results of this study are presented in Table I. The MIS personnel in the present study demonstrate a great sensitivity to ethical issues in information systems. Earlier researchers, who used undergraduates as substitutes for information systems personnel, have expressed concern over the ethical leniency of their respondents. This is apparently not as great a concern as previously thought, once students enter the workplace. The actual MIS personnel find many actions to be unacceptable or questionable, rather than acceptable. They are not ethically lenient.

Ethical issues abound in MIS. Even more issues are unnecessarily drawn into the ethical arena when legality is not considered. By simultaneously considering both the ethical and the legal aspects of an issue, we can develop an appropriate solution for many situations more rapidly. Those situations which are both ethical and legal (e.g., scenario 11a) need no further examination, nor do those which are both unethical and illegal (e.g., scenario 20c). Those which are ethical, but illegal (perhaps scenario 20a) may result in a change of law. Those which are unethical, but legal (most of the scenarios on the survey instrument) may likewise require a change in the laws. A discussion of "right" and "wrong" answers is, of course, impossible for many of the situations.

Several actions were considered unacceptable by at least 90% of the subjects. These include scenarios 2a (92.5%), 2c (97.5%), and 7 (92.5%). Scenarios 2a, 2b, and 2c involve a computer virus, with 2b describing a somewhat innocuous result. Scenario 7 involves a programmer at a bank altering a system so that he would not be charged a service fee. All of these scenarios describe actions which are clearly illegal.

Scenario 11a was identified as acceptable by 92.5% of the MIS personnel. This scenario involves the negotiation over liability between a programmer and an engineer before a contract is signed. This scenario is certainly within the realm of legality.

Three scenarios stand out because of the diversity of responses. These are 3a, 9, and 17. In each of these roughly one-third of the subjects responded in each category. Scenario 3a describes a student searching for a computer loophole; 9 involves the FBI and convicted criminals; and 17 describes an employee using a company computer for non-work, but non-monetary, purposes. Scenarios 3a and 17 are situations to which thought must be given. Since their legality is not at all clear, ethical judgements are truly involved. The action described in scenario 9 is not only legal, but currently being carried out. The subjects' mixed response probably reflects concerns over an individual's privacy rights.

FURTHER RESEARCH

The results from this study will be compared to the results from the similar studies using undergraduate students as surrogates for MIS personnel.

APPENDIX: ETHICAL SCENARIOS

[Subjects were asked to circle A (acceptable), Q (questionable), or U (unacceptable) at the conclusion of each scenario.]

A student had access to the university computer system because a class she was taking required extensive computer usage. The student enjoyed playing games on the computer and frequently had to request extra computer funds from her professor in order to complete her assignments.

1. Was the student's usage of the computer to play games:

A virus program is a program that performs tasks that a user has not requested, or does not want to perform. Some virus programs erase all files on a disk, some just print silly messages. Virus programs always copy themselves on other disks automatically, so the virus will spread to unsuspecting users. One day, a student programmer decided to write a virus program that caused the microcomputer to ignore every fifth command entered by a user. The student took his program to the university computing laboratory and installed it on one of the microcomputers. Before long, the virus had spread to hundreds of users.

2a. Was the student's action infecting hundreds of users' disks:
2b. If the virus program outputs the message "Have a nice day", would the student's action infecting hundreds of users' disks have been:
2c. If the virus erased files, would the student's action infecting hundreds of users' disks have been:

A student suspected and found a loophole in the university computer's security system that allowed him to access other students' records. He told the system administrator about the loophole, but continued to access others' records until the problem was corrected two weeks later.

3a. Was the student's action in searching for the loophole:
3b. Was the student's action in continuing to access others' records for two weeks:
3c. Was the system administrator's failure to correct the problem sooner:

A university student obtained a part-time job as a data entry clerk. His job was to enter personal student data into the university's database. Some of this data was available in the student's directory, but some of it was not. He was attracted to a student in his Algebra class and wanted to ask her out. Before asking her, though, he decided to access her records in the database to find out about her background.

4. Was the student's action in accessing a fellow student's personal information:

A manager of a company that sells computer processing services bought similar services from a competitor. She used her access to the competitor's computer to try to break the security system, identify other customers, and cause the system to "crash" (cause loss of service to others). She used the service for over a year and always paid her bills promptly.

5. Was the manager's action:

A telephone system employee saw an advertisement in a newspaper about a car for sale. The car sounded like a good buy to the employee. The advertisement listed the seller's telephone number, but not the seller's address. The telephone system employee knew he could determine the seller's ad-

Table 1: Responses to Ethical Scenarios (n=40)

scenario number	"Acceptable"	"Questionable"	"Unacceptable"
1	3	12	25
2a	3	0	37
2b	2	6	32
2c	1	0	39
3a	17	13	10
3b	2	6	32
3c	2	13	25
4	1	10	29
5	3	4	33
6a	4	17	19
6b	3	6	31
7	1	2	37
8a	2	4	34
8b	5	12	23
9	15	16	9
9a	6	12	22
9b	3	14	23
10	3	22	15
11a	37	3	0
11b	4	20	16
12	1	11	28
13	8	13	19
14	3	8	29
15	5	15	20
16	9	12	19
17	13	17	10
18	4	22	14
19	6	17	17
20a	7	17	16
20b	5	13	22
20c	3	3	34

dress by accessing the seller's telephone records. He did this and went to the seller's house to discuss buying his car.

6a. Was the telephone system employees action:

6b. If you know the seller wanted to screen potential buyers over the phone, was the telephone system employees action:

A programmer at a bank realized that he had accidentally overdrawn his checking account. He made a small adjustment in the bank's accounting system so that his account would not have an additional service charge assessed. As soon as he made a deposit that made his balance positive again, he corrected the bank's accounting system.

7. Was the programmer's modification of the accounting system:

An MIS employee at the county courthouse had access to all the county records in the county database. Over the past few weeks, she had become suspicious about her neighbor's buying habits. The neighbor had repainted the house and purchased new lawn furniture and an expensive new car. She decided to access her neighbor's records to determine how these purchases could be afforded.

8a. Was the MIS employee's action:

8b. If the MIS employee suspected that the neighbor might be involved in criminal activity, would this make her actions:

The FBI wants to build a database to maintain information about all persons convicted of a crime. Any person convicted of a crime would be required by law to provide the information requested by the FBI. The data would be maintained for the life of the person.

9. Would this FBI action be:

The FBI want to maintain information on all persons charged with a crime. Any person charged with a crime would be required by law to provide the information requested by the FBI. The data would be maintained for the life of the person.

9a. Would this FBI action be:

The FBI want to maintain data on all persons with a Ph.D. Their reason is that these persons present a significant national resource that may be desperately needed in times of crises. Any person who earned a Ph.D. would be required by law to provide the information requested by the FBI.

9b. Would this FBI action be:

The owner of a small business needed a computer-based accounting system. He identified the various inputs and outputs he felt were required to satisfy his needs. He showed his design to a computer programmer and asked the programmer if she could implement such a system. The programmer knew she could implement the system because she had developed much more sophisticated accounting systems in the past. In fact, she felt this design was rather crude and would soon need major revisions. But, she did not say anything about this because the business owner did not ask her, and she thought maybe she could be the one hired to implement the needed revisions later.

10. Was the programmer's decision not to point out the design flaws:

An engineer needed a program to perform a series of complicated calculations. She found a computer programmer capable of writing the program, but would only hire the programmer if he agreed to share the liability that might result from an error in her calculations. The programmer said he would be willing to assume any liability due to a malfunction of the program, but was unwilling to share any liability due to an error in the engineer's calculations.

11a. Was the programmer's position in this situation:
11b. Was the engineer's position in this situation:

A bank was interviewing a customer with respect to a loan application. The banker was tired and was not paying close attention when the customer told him her highest education level. He did not want to appear inattentive, so he guessed that she probably said that she had earned a Bachelor of Science degree. That was the most common response in his experience, so that is what he recorded on his evaluation.

12. Was the banker's action:

A scientist developed a theory that required construction of a computer model to prove. He hired a computer programmer to build the model, and the theory was shown to be correct. The scientist won several awards for the development of the theory, but he never acknowledged the contribution of the computer programmer.

13. Was the scientist's failure to acknowledge the computer programmer's contribution:

A university student was hired to conduct a survey at a local shopping mall. The amount of money he was paid was based on the number of surveys that were completed. The company conducting the survey wanted to obtain input from shoppers regarding "family-oriented issues". The student's instructions were to obtain responses from persons with children, although he noticed that none of the questions specifically asked about a person's child. He saw a group of friends in the mall, and since he had not been too successful obtaining responses from shoppers, he convinced each of his friends to complete a survey.

14. Was the student's action:

A Computer user called a mail-order computer program store to order a particular accounting system. When he received the order, he found out that the store had accidentally sent him a very expensive word processing program as well as the accounting package that he had ordered. He looked at the invoice, and it indicated only that the accounting package had been sent. The user decided to keep the word processing package.

15. Was the user's decision to keep the word processing package:

A telephone operator received a call requesting the telephone number of Dennis Barak. As he was entering the request into his information system, he could not remember whether the request was for Dennis Barak or Dennis Barat. He decided to have the system return the number for Dennis Bara*; The system would match any number of letters where the asterisk appeared. The system would automatically give the number of the first name that matched. If it was wrong, the caller could just call the operator again.

16. Was the telephone operator's action:

A computer programmer enjoyed building small computer systems to give to his friends. He would frequently go to his office on Saturday when no one was working and use his employer's computer to develop systems. He did not hide the fact that he was going into the building; he had to sign a register at the security desk each time he entered.

17. Was the programmer's use of the company computer:

A computer store was having a sale on a limited number of computer systems. A person who bought one of the systems was so pleased with the purchase that he convinced a friend to buy one too. The friend called the store, described the system in detail to a salesman, and asked whether she could obtain a system identical to her friend's system. The salesman said yes, so the woman agreed to come to the store. When the woman arrived at the store, she found that the salesman had configured a system with a different monitor. When she asked about the difference, the salesman told her it was "functionally equivalent" to her friend's monitor. The only difference was that her friend's monitor had some switches that allowed the monitor's characteristics to be changed, whereas the monitor in her system relied on software signals to switch characteristics. Otherwise the monitors were equivalent and had the same cost.

18. Was the salesman's response during the telephone conversation:

A computer programmer built small systems to sell. This was not his main source of income; he worked for a moderately sized computer vendor. He would frequently go to his office on Saturday when no one was working and use his employer's computer to develop systems. He did not hide the fact that he was going into the building; he had to sign a register at the security desk each time he entered.

19. Was the programmer's use of the company computer:

A student at a university learned to use an expensive spreadsheet program in her accounting class. The student would go to the university microcomputer lab, check out the spreadsheet, complete her assignment and return the software. Signs were posted in the lab indicating that copying software was forbidden. One day, she decided to copy the software anyway so she could work on her assignments at her apartment.

20a. If the student destroyed her copy of the software at the end of the semester, was her action in copying the software:

20b. If the student forgot to destroy her copy of the software at the end of the semester, was her action in copying the software:

20c. If the student never intended to destroy her copy of the software, was her action in copying the software:

REFERENCES

Axline, Larry and Mark Pastin, "The High-Ethics IS Manager", Information Executive, Fall 1989, pp. 21-25.

Benham, H. C.; "Ethical Attitudes in Information Systems: A Study of a Small College's Business Students"; Journal of Computing in Small Colleges; vol. 9, no. 4; March 1994; pp. 149-160.

Christiansen, Donald, "Ethical judgments", IEEE Spectrum, February 1989, p. 25.

Gellerman, Saul W., "Managing Ethics from the Top Down", Information Executive, Fall 1989, pp. 27-33.

Information Executive, "Ethics -- Doing More Than Just the Right Thing: An Interview with William C. Norris", Fall 1989, pp. 34-7.

Little, Joyce Currie, "Self-Regulation of Computer Professionals: Can It Be Done?", Information Executive, Fall 1989, pp. 14-20.

Morris, A., G. Jones, and J. Rubinsztein; "Entry-Level Information Systems Personnel: A Comparative Study of Ethical Attitudes"; Proceedings of the 1993 ACM SIGCPR Conference (M.R. Tanniru, editor); pp. 8-17.

Paradice, D. B.; "Ethical Attitudes of Entry-Level MIS Personnel"; Information and Management; 18, 1990; pp. 143-151.

Random House Dictionary of the English Language (College Edition), Random House, 1969, p. 453.

Sardinas, Joseph L., Mark Blank, and George Spiro, "Data Processing: Towards a Social Responsibility", Journal of Systems Management, May 1986, pp. 14-19.

Spiro, Bruce E., "Ethics in the Information Age", Information Executive, Fall 1989, pp. 38-41.

Will, Paul J., "Promoting Computer Ethics: The Next Generation", Information Executive, Fall 1989, pp. 42-45.

Winninghoff, Ellie, "A Question of Ethics", Entrepreneur, May 1989, pp. 69-74.

The Case for a Discrepancy-Based Model of User (Dis)satisfaction in Information Systems

Jon B. Woodroof and George M. Kasper
Information Systems and Quantitative Sciences
College of Business Administration
Texas Tech University
Lubbock, Texas 79409-2101
(806) 742-3167

Executive Abstract

BACKGROUND

Research has been done on the construct of satisfaction and its relationship to performance for over fifty years. This research has spanned many disciplines and applications, including health care (patient satisfaction / health care success), marriage and family (marital satisfaction / marital success), organizational behavior (job satisfaction / productivity), marketing (consumer satisfaction / product success) and information systems (user satisfaction / system success). Despite this effort, the results have been mixed and inconclusive, and the relationship between satisfaction and performance remains unclear.

While research on user satisfaction (US) in information systems (IS) has been plagued by many problems, perhaps the most central and compelling problem is the lack of adequate conceptual development. This lack of conceptual development for the construct of US in IS may explain why many researchers have obtained results that are inconclusive and sometimes even inconsistent, and thus, why so few organizations are actually measuring US.

This paper addresses these conceptual concerns by proposing the need for a comprehensive model of US in IS. Based on the notion of discrepancy, the proposed model accounts for different user standards, allows for a distinction between US and user dissatisfaction (UD), and provides a framework within which US can be better conceptualized and more carefully measured.

THE NEED FOR A DISCREPANCY-BASED MODEL OF US IN IS

A discrepancy-based model of US is needed for several reasons. First, a discrepancy-based model of US makes sense. Whether one is evaluating a car, a tennis racket, or an information system, satisfaction is innately relative. What is being experienced is compared to some referent standard, and the resulting discrepancy illicits an affective (emotional) response. One way to define this affective response is in terms of satisfaction or dissatisfaction. People use different standards against which to evaluate satisfaction, and thus it is too simplistic to assume some common yardstick. A discrepancy-based model of satisfaction considers the impact of this relative evaluation.

Second, several foundational theories and approaches have been developed in an attempt to understand satisfaction. The notion that is common to many of these theories and approaches to understanding satisfaction is the concept of discrepancy. Among the theories of satisfaction incorporating a discrepancy approach are theories of social comparison, adaptation theory, aspiration theory, and expectancy theory.

Third, a discrepancy-based model of satisfaction has been suggested as important to an investigation of US. Several IS researchers have discussed the importance of a discrepancy-based model of US, but none has developed one.

Finally, a discrepancy-based model of satisfaction has been utilized extensively and found to be useful in the referent disciplines of organizational behavior and consumer behavior.

APPLICATION OF A DISCREPANCY-BASED MODEL OF US

Applying the discrepancy approach to an IS context, a user forms beliefs about certain attributes of a particular system. The formation of these beliefs may be influenced by several sources - the user's experience with other systems, information from peers, or promises by vendors. The user then interacts with the system and experiences first hand the actual performance of the system. The user's perception of the actual performance is influenced by his or her predispositions. The performance perceived by the user is then compared to some standard (or combination of standards) that the user may have developed prior to usage.

If the user perceives that the system performed in accordance with the standard, confirmation occurs. Alternatively, if the user perceives that the system performed differently from his or her standard of comparison, disconfirmation occurs in one of two directions. If the system is perceived to have performed better than the standard used for comparison, there is positive disconfirmation, which may lead to satisfaction. However, if the system is perceived to have performed worse than the standard, there is negative disconfirmation, which may lead to dissatisfaction.

USER DISSATISFACTION

There is evidence from the referent disciplines of organizational behavior and consumer behavior that satisfaction and dissatisfaction may be related but separate constructs. This assertion has intuitive appeal as it specifically relates to US and UD in IS. The items or situations that contribute to satisfaction may not necessarily be the same as those that promote dissatisfaction.

A review of IS literature suggests that in IS, the UD construct may be more salient than the US construct. In fact, the work on dissatisfaction may have particular relevance to research in IS in that users seem much more likely to detect and express frustration with an IS than they are to express delight and elation. Wittingly or unwittingly, information systems are often oversold and users are rarely pleasantly surprised by the efficiency of the system that is actually delivered. In this way, satisfaction is not increased because the system simply performs as the designer claimed it would. Rather, users become dissatisfied when the system fails to meet their understanding of the designer's claims. Therefore, users may have more of a capacity to be dissatisfied by an IS than they do to be satisfied.

In addition, the nature of the effect of a dissatisfier may be different from that of a satisfier. The experience of one dissatisfying occurrence may have the ability to undermine the satisfaction of a user, even though he or she may have experienced a number of satisfying occurrences. Satisfiers may

not have that same power.

CONCLUSION

By incorporating the notion of discrepancy, the proposed model of US yields a framework within which US can be better conceptualized and more carefully measured. The model also highlights the importance of dissatisfaction and suggests that in IS, UD may be a more salient attribute than US. Perhaps IS designers should be more concerned with minimizing dissatisfaction than maximizing satisfaction. A discrepancy-based model of US provides a framework for investigating these and other important US issues.

By utilizing a discrepancy-based model of US, a number of research questions can be addressed. For example, incorporating a discrepancy approach to understanding and measuring satisfaction allows three options for increasing satisfaction or decreasing dissatisfaction: 1) perceived performance could be increased, 2) the standard of comparison could be manipulated, and/or 3) the perception of discrepancy could be influenced. Each of these options needs further research within a discrepancy-based model.

The utilization of a discrepancy-based model of US may also help render the results of future studies of US more consistent, and promote a stream of research on US in IS that is purposeful, cumulative, self-correcting, and replicable.

Section Two

Issues of Global Information Technology Management

Distributing Global Information Systems Resources in Multinational Companies -- A Contingency Model

Dr. Janice M. Burn
Department of Computing
Hong Kong Polytechnic
Hung Hom
Hong Kong
Tel no.: (852) 766 7247
Fax no.: (852) 774 0842
csjburn@comp.hkp.hk

Mr. H. K. Cheung
Department of Computing
Hong Kong Polytechnic
Hung Hom
Hong Kong
Tel no.: (852) 766 7311
Fax no.: (852) 774 0842
cscheung@comp.hkp.hk

ABSTRACT

The recent realignment of national boundaries and the restructuring of national economic policies around the world have highlighted the need for effective management of international Information Systems (IS). This article re-examines the issue of IS resource management with regard to the distribution of resources within the international dimension. Previous debate on this issue has centred around conflicting views on the need for headquarters to assume control and subsidiaries to exercise freedom, supporting two forms of IS structure - centralized and decentralized. However, the authors argue that centralization and decentralization of IS should constitute the two extremes of a continuum and this continuum relates to the extent to which the organization adopts a multinational company (MNC) structure or a global one. This contingency view of IS and organizational alignment is presented and related to theories on organizational fit and information sharing. This article examines the question of IS resources distribution from the following aspects : the drive for internationalization, the differences between an MNC approach and a global approach, a continuum model for MNC structures and the IS services alignment in MNCs. Finally, a number of research areas are identified based on the continuum model and a particular direction proposed for further study.

Keywords: centralization, decentralization, multinational company (MNC), global, international, organizational structure, IS alignment.

1. INTRODUCTION

In the last decade, the role of information systems (IS) has moved quite dramatically from organizational support systems to strategic weapons in the organizational portfolio. With recognition of the value of IS to the organization the question of how best to manage the information resources has also assumed greater importance to practitioners and researchers alike [Wiseman, 1988; Niederman, et al., 1991; Clark, 1992]. This is not the first time the issue has been raised and, as such, it may be too easily dismissed as a continuation of the debate with regard to the extent of centralization / decentralization

appropriate for information services support ongoing since the seventies [Dearden, 1987; Edwards, et al., 1989; Feeny, 1989; Owen, 1990; Morison, 1991]. A number of other factors, however, have combined to refocus the issue as one of critical concern for the nineties.

The very recent realignment and removal of national boundaries around the world has been accompanied by a restructuring of national economic policies which opens many new routes for international co-operation. As a result, organizations are now in need of IS which transcend local operations and facilitate the development of international trades [Roche, 1992]. This intensifies the problems faced in IS management by introducing the issue of international management across a number of cultural rather than political barriers, coupled with the sheer immensity of multinational IS services.

Over the same time period, we have also witnessed a technology initiated change in organizational structures through the utilisation of telecommunication networks. The logical control and communication structures can now be effectively managed without the problems of physical restructuring. This "logical" organization structure has not only greatly enhanced the drive towards globalization, but also created logical and physical problems for IS resource management. Since these now relate not only to IS services, but also to the whole decision making network which represents the organization.

In this article, the authors propose to re-examine the issue of IS resource management with regard to distribution of resources within the international dimension. Previous debate on centralization issues has centred around conflicting views on the need for headquarters to assume control and subsidiaries to exercise freedom. The authors contend that it is too simple to resolve the issue from such traditional arguments and, instead, it is argued that centralization and decentralization should constitute the two extremes of a continuum. This continuum relates not to freedom or control but to the extent to which the organization adopts a multinational company (MNC) structure or a global one. A major tenet of this article is that the differences between these two organizational concepts has not been fully recognized in previous studies on organization of IS services.

The authors examine the question of distribution of IS resources from the following aspects: the drive for internationalization, the differences between an MNC approach and a global approach, a continuum model for MNC structures and the IS services alignment in MNCs. Finally, a number of research areas are identified based on the continuum model and a particular direction proposed for further study.

2. THE DRIVE FOR INTERNATIONALIZATION

In recent years, it has been argued [Deans & Kane, 1992] that the worldwide economic situation has been transformed from one of regional economies into one of global economy. Companies have to compete not only with their regional and domestic competitors but also with their global rivals. A number of factors have contributed to this change.

Many organizations cite "growth" and "world leadership" as their corporate objectives. This not only reflects a desire to be "number one", but also recognises the advantages of economies of scale [Ives & Jarvenpaa, 1991; Neo, 1991]. Economies are not only restricted to operational assets, but also include company expertise and experience. In this way, headquarters can transfer experience, expertise and technology to subsidiaries in order to deal with similar situations but in different markets. Whilst direct transfer may not be possible without some retailoring for the local market, the overall investment is generally considerably lower than that required for a start-up operation. MNCs can both increase their market population and serve their customers more effectively [Neo, 1991]. Operating in a number of geographic regions normally allows the MNCs to operate around the clock and gives them considerable competitive advantage [Keen, 1989; Ives & Jarvenpaa, 1991]. It is therefore hardly surprising that the last 30 years have witnessed the emergence of the world's biggest corporate structures. More recently, however, additional impetus for international expansion has come from external forces.

During the past five years, the world has experienced a shift in global alignments. The unification of the European Community markets in 1992, the success of the democratic movement in Eastern Europe in 1990's, the restructuring of the political and economic systems of Soviet Union and its transformation into the Commonwealth of Independent States, and the opening of a vast China market to other countries have combined to offer worldwide opportunities. The result has been a dramatic emergence of high potential new markets to companies and a concerted thrust towards an international focus. In many cases, this has been accomplished through a series of complex alliances across a number of geographic and cultural boundaries, redefining the whole concept of organizational structure. IS which was designed to support simple organizational models are no longer relevant to the new multidomestic companies.

The thrust towards internationalization, however, is also a product of the application of information technology itself. With the assistance of computer networks and advanced technologies, people can communicate and receive messages from others instantaneously without the constraint of geographic locations and time. This advancement of computing technologies also allows IS to perform very large scale data exchange activities much more effectively and efficiently. Systems such as these have already begun to blur national boundaries within international operations and have opened the way for the development of standardized global IS [Deans & Kane, 1992].

It would seem therefore that these thrusts have been complimentary and should facilitate the growth transition of organizations from national to international operators and the development of even larger MNCs. A major inhibitor, however, may be the misalignment of organizational structure with IS services, since MNCs cannot be regarded as part of a homogenous group but can adopt several very disparate configurations. Before exploring the alignment issues, it is necessary to define the concepts of MNC which the authors use throughout the remainder of this article.

3. MULTINATIONAL COMPANIES (MNCs)

There has been a renewal of interest in IS research with regard to the IS support needs of global organizations [Buss, 1982; Bartlett, 1987; Deans & Kane, 1992]. In much of these literatures the terms 'International Company', 'Multinational Company' and 'Global Company' are used interchangeably. They are employed casually to portray companies with some foreign components in their operations. From a review of the organizational and management literature, however, a clear distinction can be drawn.

An International Company can be defined as a company that engages in business with customers who are in other domestic regions [Deans & Kane, 1992]. Therefore, companies involved in the export or import of materials or services to other domestic regions can be addressed as international companies.

A Multinational Company (MNC) can be defined as a company that has operations in more that one domestic areas, that is, at least one foreign subsidiary exists in the company [Neo, 1991; Deans & Kane, 1992].

A Global Company can be defined as a company that has a philosophical view of the world as a single market (global view on the worldwide market). Thus, the global company will try to sell its standardized products worldwide without considering the regional variations [Farley, 1986; Caldwell and Bere, 1987; Higgins, et al., 1991]. There is no requirement for this kind of company to involve itself in any foreign operations, since their standardized products can be sold by licences or through foreign authorized agencies and dealers.

The relationships of these types of companies are illustrated graphically in FIGURE 1. As we can see the international company includes all companies engaging in business with foreign customers. So, both the MNCs and global companies fall into this category. The overlapping area of MNCs and the global companies indicates that companies can be classified as both MNCs and also global companies when they contain some foreign operations and also have a global world view.

In this article, the authors focus the discussion on the MNCs and their structural alignment along a continuum model. This is developed in the following section.

4.MNC CONTINUUM MODEL

One of the major problems faced by MNCs in doing international business is how to overcome the regional differences in promoting their products in foreign markets. The differences include languages, cultures, currencies, legal systems, political structure and so on [Neo, 1991]. These regional differences can cause a serious conflict between the headquarters in the home country and the subsidiaries in the host countries. Subsidiaries frequently demand more local autonomy for the modification of products or operations in order to fit into the different requirements of local markets. On the other hand, the headquarters require more central control to reduce the variations in the subsidiaries operations for easier co- ordination among subsidiaries and alignment with headquarters' policies. The extent to which decision making authority should be delegated to subsidiaries is generally the main source of conflict within the MNC and is traditionally solved by developing two forms of MNCs : multidomestic and global [Freedman, 1985; Neo, 1991].

The Multidomestic MNCs view the world as a composition of a number of different domestic markets, therefore they will delegate / decentralize all the decision making authority to their subsidiaries. Each subsidiary acts as a single entity without recourse to maintain coordination with other groups within the MNC. The subsidiary can be regarded as a fully autonomous unit. This represents one extreme end of a continuum and is defined as the decentralized MNC within this article.

At the other extreme, Global MNCs view the world as a single market, therefore they attempt to control all the subsidiaries as a single entity and ignore the differences contingent to each subsidiaries' markets. Consequently, the decision making authorities are centralized in the headquarters and this form of MNC is referred to as the centralized form of MNC in the continuum model.

However, the authors contend that both central control / coordination and local autonomy are essential to MNCs and each MNC, to a certain extent, should have these characteristics incorporated into their companies' structures, strategies and policies. Therefore, this article argues that the balance between centralization and decentralization should be considered during the building of the MNC. A simple continuum model shown as FIGURE 2 is constructed to illustrate this argument.

Multidomestic MNCs and global MNCs are placed at the two extremes of this continuum to represent the fully decentralized and centralized structure of MNCs respectively. The degree of centralization and decentralization will vary as the companies locate between the two extreme types of MNC structure.

The authors further propose four types of factors which may determine the positions of the MNCs in the MNC continuum : company adopted strategies [Garnier, 1984; Habib & Victor, 1991; Karimi & Konsynski, 1991; Tavakolian, 1991], nature of company business [Garnier, 1984; Gates & Egelhoff, 1986; Habib & Victor, 1991], company philosophy [Garnier, 1984; Tavakolian, 1991] and host countries' environment [Garnier, 1984; Gates & Egelhoff, 1986].

When establishing foreign subsidiaries, the strategies adopted by the MNC may affect the degree of decentralization of authority to the subsidiaries. Companies which adopt strategies which emphasize the similarities within different regions or standardization in operations or products, will decrease the demand for local autonomy [Farley, 1986]. Hence, MNCs will organize themselves into a more centralized form as a global MNC.

To a certain extent, regional differences will have a greater effect on MNCs in the manufacturing sector than MNCs in the servicing sector. As an example, the formula of toothpaste manufactured for U.S. may not be suitable for Middle Eastern countries, since the Middle Easterners prefer toothpaste that tastes spicy [Grune, 1989]. Therefore, manufacturing MNCs may be forced to adopt a more decentralized structure (multidomestic), while servicing MNCs may find it easier to provide standard services from a centralized base (global).

The company philosophy (shared beliefs, norms or culture) also has an influence on the organization of the MNC. MNCs emphasizing effectiveness will tend to organize themselves into a decentralized forms, but efficiency orientated MNCs will be organized into centralized form. This is because the effectiveness of MNCs is interpreted as the ability to overcome the problems induced by changes in local markets and so favours decentralized structures which allow subsidiaries a large measure of flexibility. On the other hand, efficiency is interpreted as the ability of the MNC to implement corporate strategies in the subsidiaries. In a centralized environment, subsidiaries are directly controlled by the headquarters and it is easier to carry out corporate strategies in the subsidiaries without risk of distortions in the perceptions of the subsidiaries management.

The national stability of the host country is another factor which may determine the MNC structure. The greater the uncertainty the greater the demand of local autonomy required by the subsidiaries in order to reduce the effects of the changing environments of the local markets on the MNC as a whole. Moreover, the demands of the host countries' governments on the MNCs to integrate their foreign subsidiaries' activities more closely into local economies will also impose pressure on the MNC to decentralize. FIGURE 3 summaries the impact of these determinants on MNC structures.

5. ALIGNMENT OF IS SERVICES IN MNCs

Most discussion on the alignment of IS services within an organization focuses on the centralization / decentralization issue but without a consensus opinion on appropriate alignment models [Dearden, 1987; Owen, 1990; Morison, 1991;

Stokes, 1991]. A recent review of IT managers found that whilst 45% are preparing to decentralize the IS functions, 28% were in the process of recentralization [Niederman, et al., 1991]. Organizations now have available technology to implement either centralized or decentralized IS reporting relationships but these must reflect the communication channels throughout the organization.

Centralization of IS is a response to the demand for strong headquarter (central) control on IS and the IT infrastructure. Strong centralized IS control can minimize the problems of hardware and software incompatibility throughout the whole enterprise. A reduction in the duplication of IS assets or efforts can also be achieved when all the IS development is located in the headquarters. Finally, the alignment between the enterprise IS plan and the corporate business plan can be more easily accomplished and related to the organizational plan for information architecture.

However, centralization of IS in MNCs may also introduce a series of problems. Centralized IS decreases the flexibility which subsidiaries may require to respond to the different or changing environments of the local markets. It may also inhibit the development of appropriate technologies, knowledge and skills in the local environments.

It is generally argued [Zmud, 1988; Edwards, et al., 1989; Bacon, 1990; Hodgkinson, 1990; Owen, 1990] that a more desirable option for MNCs lies in controlled decentralization giving subsidiaries more IS autonomy to carry out their business locally yet not to the extent of introducing incompatible systems. Various alternatives have been proposed such as international, global, multinational / regional, collaborative and transnational [Roche, 1992]. Very few guidelines have been developed however to assist the MNC in selecting and implementing appropriate IS resource management structures.

The strength of this article lies in the application of the continuum model for MNC structure to the analogous structure for IS resource management. FIGURE 4 shows that the position of the IS structure in the continuum should correspond with the positioning of the MNC.

This assumes a contingency view of IS and organizational alignment and is supported both by arguments on organizational fit [Leifer, 1988] and information sharing [Lee & Leifer, 1992].

The 'organizational fit' concept argues that the alignment between the IS structure and the organization is extremely important for the organization to perform its business activities successfully. The concept holds that the IS structure depends on the company structure, the mismatch of these two will decrease the effectiveness and efficiency of the company in carrying out its business operations [Ein-Dor & Segev, 1982; Ahituv, et al., 1989; Butler Cox Foundation, 1986; Leifer, 1988; Tavakolian, 1991].

Although, this argument was originally proposed using a conceptual company model organized into a divisional structure and further assumes that all divisions are in the same domestic area as the headquarters, empirical research has more

recently given this theory strong support [Burn, 1989; Earl, 1990; Burn, 1992]. The authors have tried to extend this argument to encompass MNCs such that the IS structures in MNCs also depend on the organizational structure of MNCs and assumes that the geographic locations of the divisions (subsidiaries of the MNCs) only has a minimal effect on the argument.

On the other hand, the 'information sharing' concept argues that the location of the information processing and storage should depend on the degree of sharing of the information throughout the whole corporation. The higher level of data (information) sharing will cause the greater the need to place the processes and the data in the central headquarter; otherwise the processes and the data should be placed in the local subsidiaries [Lee & Leifer, 1992]. The philosophy of this approach of process and data allocation is that users should take full responsibilities for their own data (information). Therefore data (information) should be situated near to the users; however, shared data should be the responsibility of a third party.

In global MNCs, most data (information) is shared throughout the whole corporation, therefore, all the data (information) and the IS functions should be established as a central function. However, in multidomestic MNCs, no data sharing is expected and only the report summaries need be uploaded to the headquarter, so IS functions and data should be decentralized into local subsidiaries.

As the authors have argued that different positions in the MNC continuum represent different degrees of combined centralized and decentralized environments, it implies that different levels of information sharing is expected. So, the IS functions should be organized as a mix of centralized and decentralized functions. However, the levels of this mix depends on the position of the MNCs in the MNC continuum and this is determined by a number of organizational variables. The IS resource management structure is therefore directly contingent on these organizational variables and cannot be determined in isolation.

6. CONCLUSIONS

This article has argued that the alignment between IS resource management structures and MNCs structures is of critical importance in a globalised business environment. In identifying two different models for MNCs as multidomestic and global, the authors also proposed a simple MNC continuum model for determining their structures. This continuum model can also be related directly to IS resource management structures based on the need for organizational alignment and information sharing. The ideas put forward in this article are conceptual and need further research to support the model. As a preliminary study, the authors intend to verify the extent to which organizational factors impact on MNCs in their positioning along the continuum model. This will also be directly related to the IS resource management structure.

In order to pursue this research, the authors have proposed

an IS resources management model [adapted from Tricker, 1992] which will be used as the framework for subsequent studies to identify the relationships between the organizational factors impacting the MNCs structures and the IS resources management structure.

Should these studies support the research model as proposed then detailed studies can take place to identify the role and responsibilities of central and satellite IS functions in different positions along the continuum. It is anticipated that this will also allow us to evaluate the role of IS in MNC growth and the effectiveness of IS management in supporting that growth and development.

REFERENCES

AHITUV, N., NEUMANN, S. and ZVIRAN, M., Factors Affecting the Policy for Distributing Computing Resources, *MIS Quarterly*, December 1989, pp. 389-401.

BACON, C.J., Organizational Principles of Systems Decentralization, *Journal of Information Technology*, 1990, Vol. 5, pp. 84-93.

BARTLETT, C.A. and GHOSHAL, S., Managing Across Borders : New Strategic Requirements, *Sloan Management Review*, Summer 1987, Vol. 28 No. 4, pp. 7-17.

BURN, J.M., The Impact of Information Technology on Organizational Structures, *Information & Management*, 1989, Vol. 16, pp. 1-10.

BURN, J.M., A Contextual Approach to IS Strategies through Organizational Behaviour Analysis, *Proceeding of 2nd International Conference on Organization Behaviour and Information Systems - Curtin Perth, Austrialia*, December 1992.

BUSS, M.D.J., Managing International Information Systems, *Harvard Business Review*, September - October 1982, Vol. 60 No. 5, pp. 153-162.

BUTLER COX FOUNDATION, Organizing the Systems Department, *Research Report 52, Bulter Cox & Partner Limited*, July 1986.

CALDWELL, P. and BERE, J.F., The Making of a Global Manager, *Director & Boards*, Winter 1987, Vol. 11 No. 2, pp. 6-16.

CLARK, T.D., Jr, Corporate Systems Management : An Overview and Research Perspective, *Communications of the ACM*, February 1992, Vol. 35 No. 2, pp. 60-75.

DEANS, P.C. and KANE, M.J., *International Dimensions of Information Systems and Technology*, Boston : PWS-Kent Publishing Company, 1992.

DEARDEN, J., The Withering Away of the IS Organization, *Sloan Management Review*, Summer 1987, Vol. 28 No. 4, pp. 87-91.

EARL, M.J., Approaches to Strategic Information Planning Experience in 21 U.K. Companies, *Proceedings of 11th ICIS Conference*, Demark, December 1990.

EDWARDS, B.R., EARL, M.J. and FEENY, D.F., Any Way Out of the Labyrinth for Managing IS ?, *Research and Discussion Papers RDP89/3, Oxford Institute of Information Management, Oxford University*, 1989.

EIN-DOR, P. and SEGEV, E., Organizational Context and MIS Structure : Some Empirical Evidence, *MIS Quarterly*, September 1982, Vol. 6 No. 3, pp. 55-68.

FARLEY, L.J., Going Global : Choices and Challenges, *Journal of Consumer Marketing*, Winter 1986, Vol. 3 No. 1, pp. 67-70.

FEENY, D.F., EARL, M.J. and EDWARDS, B.R., IS Arrangement to Suit Complex Organizations : An Effective IS Structure, *Research and Discussion Paper RDP 89/4, Oxford Institute of Information Management, Oxford University*, 1989.

FREEDMAN, D.H., Managing Information Systems at Multinational, *Infosystems*, January 1985, Vol. 32 No. 1, pp. 58-62.

GARNIER, G., The Autonomy of Foreign Subsidiaries : Environmental and National Influences, *Journal of General Management*, Autumn 1984, Vol. 10 No. 1, pp. 57-82.

GATES, S.R. and EGELHOFF, W.G., Centralization in Headquarters - Subsidiary Relationships, *Journal of International Business Studies*, Spring 1986, Vol. 17 No. 2, pp. 71-92.

GRUNE, G.V., Global Marketing : Global Opportunities, *Vital Speeches of the Day*, 15 July 1989, Vol. 55 No. 19, pp. 580-582.

HABIB, M.M. and VICTOR, B., Strategy, Structure, and Performance of US Manufacturing and Service MNC : A Comparative Analysis, *Strategic Management Journal*, 1991, Vol. 12, pp. 586-606.

HIGGINS, L.F., MCINTYRE, S.C. and RAINE, C.G., Design of Global Marketing Information Systems, *The Journal of Business and Industrial Marketing*, Summer / Fall 1991, Vol. 6 No. 3-4, pp. 49-58.

HODGKINSON, S.L., Distribution of Responsibility for IT Activities in Large Companies : A Survey, *Research and Discussion Papers RDP 90/5, Oxford Institute of Information Management*, Oxford University, March 1990.

IVES, B. and JARVENPAA, S.L., Applications of Global Information Technology : Key Issues for Management, *MIS Quarterly*, March 1991, pp. 33-49.

KARIMI, J. and KONSYNSKI, B.R., Globalization and Information Management Strategies, *Journal of Management Information Systems*, Spring 1991, Vol. 7 No. 4, pp. 7-26.

KEEN, P.G.W., Information Technology and Organizational Advantage : The Next Agenda for Research, *An ICIT Briefing Paper*, International Center for Information Technologies, 1989.

LEE, S. and LEIFER, R.P., A Framework for Linking the Structure of Information Systems with Organizational Requirements for Information Sharing, *Journal of Management Information Systems*, Spring 1992, Vol. 8 No. 4, pp. 27-44.

LEIFER, R., Matching Computer-Based Information Systems with Organizational Structure, *MIS Quarterly*, March 1988, pp. 63-73.

MORISON, R.F., Beyond Centralized and Decentralized IS : Virtual Centralization, *Information Strategy : The Executive's Journal*, Spring 1991, Vol. 7 No. 3, pp. 5-11.

NEGANDHI, A.R. and PALIA, A.P., The Changing Multinational Corporation-Nation State's Relationship : The Case of IBM in India, *Priism Working Paper, No. 87-002*, 1987.

NEO, B.S., Information Technology and Global Competition : A Framework for Analysis, *Information & Management*, 1991, Vol. 20, pp. 151-160.

NIEDERMAN, F., BRANCHEAU, J.C. and WETHERBE, J.C., Information Systems Management Issues for the 1990s, *MIS Quarterly*, December 1991, pp. 475-500.

OWEN, D.E., A Graphic Equalizer for Sophisticated IRM Control, *Information Strategy : The Executive's Journal*, Summer 1990, Vol. 6 No. 4, pp. 20-24.

ROCHE, E.M., *Managing Information Technology in Multinational Corporation*, Macmillan Publishing Company, 1992, pp. 2-13.

TAVAKOLIAN, H., The Organization of IT Functions in the 1990s : A Managerial Perspective, *Journal of Management Development*, 1991, Vol. 1 No. 2, pp. 31-37.

TRICKER, R.I., The Management of Organizational Knowledge, in GALLIERS, R. (ed), *Information Systems Research : Issues, Methods and Practical Guidelines*, 1992, Blackwell Scientific Publications, pp. 14-27.

STOKES, S.L., Jr., IS Without Managers, *Information Strategy : The Executive's Journal*, Fall 1991, Vol. 8 No. 1, pp. 11-15.

WISEMAN, C., Strategic Information Systems : Trends and Challenges Over the Next Decade, *Information Management Review*, Summer 1988, Vol. 4 No. 1, pp. 9-16.

ZMUD, R.W., Building Relationships Throughout the Corporate Entity, in ELAM, J.J., GINZBERG, M.J., KEEN, P.G.W. and ZMUD, R.W. (eds), *Transforming the IS Organization*, International Centre for Information Technologies Press, 1988, pp. 55-82.

The Ethics of Global Out-Sourcing of Application Development: A Case Study and Analysis

Eli B. Cohen
Eastern New Mexico University
ELI_COHEN@ACM.ORG

ABSTRACT

This paper analyzes the ethical issues in a case study of the TATA Consultancy Services contracts with Indian programmers to produce software for Hewlett Packard. It is drawn from the Internet messages of a working group on Issues in Developing Countries (IFIP WG 9.4). To apply the ethical analysis, this paper develops a framework of ethical issues in technology derived from the thoughts of various writers.

Recently, the public's eye was directed toward one such controversy — the out-sourcing of programming to programmers in less-developed countries. This paper deals with the case that engendered that concern — TATA Consultancy Services' (TCS) contract with Hewlett Packard. This case has, within the last twelve months, been featured in the media at least three times: the cover page of the New York Times (Gargin, 1993), an article in Computerworld (Kruse & Bounincontri, 1993), and an exposé on the television program "60 Minutes".

This paper first describes the allegations against TCS, then establishes a framework for ethical analysis and reviews classical and neoclassical ethical systems. The paper concludes with an ethical analysis of the case.

ALLEGATIONS AGAINST TCS

TATA Consulting Services (TCS) of India provides contract programming, primarily to firms outside India. India has a rising revenue in the export of programming, based in part on the quality of its well-educated English-speaking workforce trained in technical areas. The software available to Indian programmers includes state-of-the-art development tools as well as third-generation programming languages. One example of a U.S.-based firm using Indian programmers is Texas Instruments' (TI) employment of Indians trained in TI's advanced Computer-Assisted Software Engineering tool to develop systems used in the U.S. The export of software is an important and growing source of hard currency for India. Nearly 60% of this revenue is derived from Indian firms sending programmers abroad. The growth of Indian Software Exports in millions of U.S. dollars is exponential.

Indian programmers working abroad are paid their full base Indian salary (which ranges from $350 - $800 per month) plus a subsistence allowance. The allowance for those stationed in the U.S. ranges around $1,500 - $2,000 per month. TCS charges the firm it contracts with around $3,500 per month per programmer, which considerably undercuts American competition. Up to this point, as an overseas firm TCS has avoided paying the same taxes and following the same regulations that drive up the costs to U.S.-based firms.

Hewlett Packard (HP) used the services of TCS to acquire custom software. TCS brought Indian programmers to the U.S. to develop this software for HP. "Californians for Population Stabilization" sued TCS, contending that TCS made fraudulent visa application statements in its assertion that no American workers could do this work. The suit further contends that the contract violates U.S. law regarding worker exploitation because each programmer's contract with TCS calls for a $30,000 fine for any worker who fails to return to work with TCS in India. The courts will decide whether any of these accusations have legal bearing. This paper, as noted above, focuses its attention on the ethical dimensions of the situation. To do so, this paper will assume that the facts as reported are accurate.

Combining the perspectives of various authors, this paper's framework for analysis. The framework analyzes global ethical issues of business in terms of sovereignty/political/community, market/economics/customers, individual's rights/labor, and social equity/owners' rights and responsibilities, each related through technology.

INTERRELATIONSHIP OF ETHICS AMONG ALL FOUR COMPONENTS

All four components of the framework are interrelated through technology. Prior work by this author has dealt with some of these interrelationships and is described briefly in the following paragraphs.

Ethics and Sovereignty. Ethical systems that hold that ethics transcends culture, i.e. what is right or wrong is right or wrong everywhere and throughout time, regardless of culture, are classified by ethicists as following "cultural absolutism". In contrast, cultural relativism holds that ethical behavior is dependent upon the cultural mores. A belief in cultural absolutism has impact on sovereignty/political issues. To the extent that different peoples' cultural beliefs of right differ, they may believe the others' cultural norms to be unethical.

Ethics and Economic Systems. Also, ethical systems are closely related to economic systems. Western banking (with the charging of interest on loans) runs counter to the Sharia, Islamic law. Likewise, the utilitarian ethical system is closely linked to capitalism.

AN ETHICAL ANALYSIS

Ethical analysis is the application of various ethical systems to a dilemma at hand. Each ethical system is limited; by applying a variety of ethical systems, the analyst can arrive at a more complete analysis than by applying any single system.

RELATING THE TCS CASE AND ETHICAL ISSUES

The framework provides us with four issues on which to analyze the ethics in the TCS case: (1) rights of the individual/labor, (2) social equity/rights and responsibilities of the owner, (3) sovereignty/politics/community, and (4) market/economics.

CONCLUSION

In my opinion, none of the ethical systems described in this paper would find fault, on balance, with the issues of the TCS case. Nations, such as India, develop and educate their workforce to compete globally. Global competition can create difficult ethical problems. The TCS case was not one of them.

However, the TCS case has served as a vehicle for international debate and analysis of global information technology issues. The issues in this case were quite specific. I have been given good advice that the larger (and perhaps more important) issues in global ethics are not so easily analyzed. These larger issues include questions about human rights as a limitation on sovereignty and the role of culture-based religion in enforcing limits to human rights. It may be the work of futurists to predict the role that Information Technology will play in this future war of values.

Some Ideas About An Electronic International Trade Network—
The Marketplace

David W. Conrath
Professor of Management Sciences
University of Waterloo
Waterloo, Onario
Canada N2L 3G1

ABSTRACT

This paper is a conceptual/think piece about a computer-based network designed to facilitate the involvement of small and medium sized businesses in international trade. The MarketPlace provides a means for identifying and contacting people with whom one would like to do business. Using the system's software and databases a firm could specify requirements or state its capabilities, negotiate contracts and obtain support services (e.g. arranging shipping, customs clearance and financing) that would enable them to undertake trade that would otherwise seem out of reach. A previous paper [Conrath, 1993] focused on research issues. This one, while mentioning certain problems that must be resolved before such a system could become operational, contains a number of suggestions about the features that the initial MarketPlace ought to possess. These cover everything from product/service specification and language issues, to the technology that ought to be used and the potential sources of revenue that would be available to the operators of the MarketPlace.

INTRODUCTION

The MarketPlace is a computer-based world-wide network of small and medium sized businesses, the purpose of which is to facilitate trade among them. Its components are: personal computers, located in or available to the various businesses; a network connecting these computers; a directory of all the businesses on the network, indicating the type of commercial transactions in which they are interested; a market where one can post informa-tion about products and services one would like to provide or obtain; software on the network that enables interested parties to get in touch with each other, and to negotiate and finalize contracts; and ancilliary support that provides information and services on such things as customs regulations, shipment of goods, financing and the like.

The argument for developing such a system is straightforward. Most small and medium sized businesses do not have the means to get involved in international trade. Both national and local governments generally encourage such trade with a variety of support activities. However, it is difficult for them to help commercial organizations, especially small ones, make the personal contacts that are needed before such trade can take place. Since small businesses seldom have the means to establish such contacts on their own, they expend little if any

effort to participate in international commerce. The barrier to entry is perceived to be too great despite the potential benefits that many of them recognize. The objective of the MarketPlace is to overcome this barrier.

This paper will present ideas about the first steps one might take to launch the MarketPlace. We commence by examing aspects of international commercial transactions that would have to be handled by the MarketPlace, and how these might be provided. Next, we discuss the processes that would take place, such as searching for a counter-part and negotiating a contract, and how the system might conduct these services. This leads to a discussion of the technology involved, including hardware, software, databases and networks. We close with a discussion of the management of the system, covering those issues that have to be resolved if the MarketPlace is to be a successful commercial enterprise in its own right.

SPECIFICATION

There are two aspects of a commercial transaction that require specification. One is the product and/or service that is to be exchanged. The other concerns the conditions of the transaction, such as the price, quality and delivery dates. All such factors have to be well understood by both buyers and sellers. This is easier said than done, even when the people involved have the same mother tongue. When languages and cultures differ, which will often be the case in international trade, the difficulties in achieving mutual understanding are substantially increased.

The first step toward a common understanding is to establish universal formats for all commercial transactions that are to take place in the MarketPlace. This suggest that these formats would have to encompass all of the data that would be required for a given type of commercial transaction. EDI (electronic data/document interchange) standards have already been determined for some commerical transactions (e.g. TradeNet in Singapore and EDIFACT in Europe). Some merely define precisely the content of the electronic transmissions (EDIFACT: Berge, 1991). Others also specify where in the document (location of field on the screen) a particular element (e.g. quantity) belongs, and how the units are to be expressed. Whether or not any of the existing standards could be used for a system which would be open to a wide variety of goods and services is another question. At the least, existing approaches could be used as guides to the establishment of a universal one.

Specifying the quality of goods and services, and establishing the method of payment for them, pose considerable difficulty, especially since payment may be contigent upon approval of the quality. These are the most common sources of litigation in North America, and hence language *per se* is not the issue; the lack of a common understanding is. The MarketPlace should not be expected to eliminate such problems, but it could attempt to standardize the expression of quality specifications and testing. The attempt would not be in the form of legal documentation. Rather it would be engineering based, and defined in terms of specifications and their measurement, which admittedly poses a problem for services.

This raises the general issue of product/service specification. This typically involves both language and graphics. Regarding language, it should be as simple as possible and yet sufficient to express all significant details of a product or service. While there will always be problems of semantics, these are generaly much easier to overcome than problems of syntax (grammer). Hence, there are distinct advantages to using languages that are vocabulary rich and grammatically simple. English satisfies this requirement. It possesses a vocabulary greater than any other language, and it can be used in a highly structured format. One such restriction, for example, is to limit its use to nouns and modifying adjectives, and where verbs are needed they are expressed using the present tense in declarative sentences.

English has another advantage. It is the most common language used in the world of commerce. Witness its widespread use within the Common Market, and this occurred even before the entry of Great Britain. Recognizing that it would still be desirable to present specifications (and many other aspects of the commercial transactions that are to take place) in the mother tongue of the users of the MarketPlace, perhaps structured English could be the basis into which and from which all translations would be made. The feasibility of this approach remains to be tested, yet at this point there do not appear to be alternatives that would be superior. Thus, one could start the MarketPlace using just structured English, adding other languages as the facilities grow to translate them to and from English. More elaborate schemes would have to await the success of the current research on computer-based translation.

Graphics present a simpler issue. While the saying that "a picture is worth a thousand words" may be contentious, drawings, with appropriate markings and measurements, certainly make the specification of many products a great deal easier. In many cases drawings are essential to mutual understanding. Accompanied by standard metric measures and structured English, graphics should not pose many problems. This suggests that a graphics capability ought to be inherent in the system.

Consistent screen and document formats, perhaps augmented with the use of simple icons, are also needed to aid mutual comprehension. Location of data entries is the key.

Fields (blanks where data are to be entered) should be organized according to a logical flow so that their completion does not require much, if any, backtracking. For example, the typical invoice goes (left to right) from product description, to price per unit, to the quantity of units, to total price; special conditions and discounts follow. Standard formats would have to be established, based on what is easiest to follow and the least confusing to the greatest number of potential participants.

TRANSACTION PROCESSES

There are a number of transaction processes which ought to be supported by the MarketPlace. These would include: searching the Directory for appropriate counterparts, searching the Market for possible opportunities, responding to either inquiries or oppor-tunities, selecting counterparts for further consideration, negotiating with a counterpart, drawing up a contract. Each involves somewhat different elements, and all require research before appropriate software could be developed.

Searching the Directory and the Market

An effective means to search the Directory requires work on both database design and retrieval software. To be useful to the user, the retrieval process has to be able to uncover a reasonable number of alternatives, all of them if the number is very small. More impor-tantly, it has to ensure that the vast majority of the alternatives presented are appropriate. If one finds that many of the enterprises retrieved do not possess the capabilities that one seeks, the system will fall into disuse. The cost of weeding out the good from the bad will be perceived to exceed the value of the MarketPlace. On the other hand, as long as there is an adequate number of acceptable alternatives, the failure to include all of those that should be considered is not only of little consequence to the seeker, it may be a positive advantage. If the number of alternatives retrieved is very large, it may be difficult to narrow the list to a useful number. To summarize, the system will need both effective retrieval **and** filtering software (Belkin & Croft, 1992).

To minimize the chance of useless retrievals, the seeker has to be able to specify his or her requirements (seeking products or services) or interests (seeking potential purchasers of products or services) in a manner that rules out the irrelevant. Complete specifications are out of the question as this would make the system too onerous to use. However, some system of meta-specification appears to be needed. In other words, there should be a mechanism whereby one could state requirements or interests that would be able to encompass the capabilities of satisfying those requirements. How this might be done is an open question, but one possibility would be to have capabilities stated as processes, and requirements as products and services that could be produced by these processes. The retrieval software would then recognize those processes that would be satisfactory in all of the implied dimensions, and enterprises possessing those capabilities would be presented to the seeker. Likewise, interests would be stated in terms of products and services, and those seeking to satisfy them would retrieve organizations which would have the appropriate processes.

The Market, a sort of electronic bulletin board, would make use of the same retrieval processes found suitable for the Directory. The difference between the two is that the Market provides the means to let everyone on the system know that one is seeking. The use of the Directory, like the telephone directory, allows one to seek others without their knowledge. Presumably, those posting items in the Market will use the same means for describing products, services, capabilities and interests that are developed for the Directory. Hence retrieval can be conducted on the same basis. However, since the Market is intended to be proactive, there is no need for it to remain passive. It could actively scan the Directory, and let all those in it that satisfy stated capabilities or interests know of the opportunities posted in the Market. If the system had a great many members further screening would undoubtedly be required so that users would not be overburdened with the "opportunities" presented to them. [The December, 1992 issue of the *Communications of the ACM* is devoted almost entirely to the state-of-the-art of information filtering.]

Responding, Selecting, Negotiating and Contracting
All three of these processes concern social as well as economic issues. The goal of the respondent is to establish a trusting and comfortable relationship with the seeker so that the capabilities of the respondent will be given fair consideration. A listing of capabilities by itself is not likely to be sufficient, though it would be in a pure economically rational world. The key is to get the seeker to believe that these capabilities can deliver what is sought. This suggests that, at least at the start, the respondent should provide a proposal that should satisfy the seeker's requirements. Such a proposal, however, can be complete only to the extent that the initial require-ment statement is complete, which for many seekers is unlikely to be the case. Hence, the format and language used by respondents should be flexible so that it can accommodate everything from rough outlines of what one might do to complete proposals. Furthermore, it should allow one to express him/herself (via translation) in a manner that enhances the seeker's ability to "know" the respondent.

Selecting, has to do with narrowing the list of respondents to those with whom one might wish to negotiate a possible contract. Initially, the only information which a seeker has to make such a determination is obtained from the response itself. There should be the opportunity, however, for the seeker to ask the respondents for additional information. Ideally, one would like to make this type of interaction as open as possible. On the other hand, when different languages are involved, either translation facilities have to be provided and/or the interaction has to be highly structured.

Negotiating and finalizing a contract are difficult under the best of circumstances. When these processes have to be conducted remotely, the difficulties are compounded. Still, there may be an advantage to restricting the interactions to commercial issues, for this would lessen the problems associated with personality and cultural differences. The resulting structure, which is needed to minimize ambiguity and thereby foster mutual understanding, has to handle two separate aspects of the processes. One is the ability to negotiate, to make tradeoffs among the variables involved in a commercial transaction. This should be apart from but completely integrated with the other aspect, the contract itself.

The variables subject to negotiation can be delimited quite easily, though they might vary from transaction to transaction. Universal ones would be: price, quantity, product/service specification, quality and how it is to be verified, delivery date(s), and method and timing of billing and payment. The format of negotiating has to indicate how a change in one or more of these variables would affect another. As simple examples, the format has to allow one to describe how quantity discounts would work, or how changes in the delivery date and/or quality would affect the price. Some preliminary research will have to be undertaken to determine the best presentation scheme for various tradeoffs.

The contract itself, as we have noted before, has to be understood fully in terms of all its implications, by all parties to it. This is a goal, and seldom is it achieved, even by elaborate contracts that rely on batteries of lawyers. Nevertheless, there has to be some mechanism to indicate that agreement is reached, and that the terms of the agreement are acceptable to all parties concerned. Signatures are the most common form of indicating agreement, and a means to establish an acceptable authenticating signature could easily be developed for use on the computer. But this is not sufficient. Signing a document does not assure that mutual understanding and agreement exist in fact. The lack of such assurance may be acceptable for contracts made within a language, cultural and political domain, but we need something more substantial when these domains differ between the two parties. How this is to be accomplished remains to be determined. One suggestion for the case when two different languages are involved is to translate the more difficult to comprehend aspects of a contract, for example those concerned with quality control and performance assurance, into a common language, say English. The two translations could then be compared by a third party to determine if they are equivalent. Retranslation to the original language is a common practice to evaluate the accuracy of the initial translation.

This raises the question of quality assurance. This is an important issue since many contracts withhold the payment of invoices until quality testing procedures have been satisfied. The problem is that it is hard for a foreign enterprise to be sure that the proce-dures actually used are legitimate. This goes back to an issue raised much earlier, that of establishing an environment of trust. Trust is enhanced when the measure of determining quality, or performance in the case of a service, is objective and when the means of measurement are both understood and acceptable to both parties. Objectivity in many instances is very difficult to assure. Thus, the understanding and acceptance of the precedures to be used to determine quality/performance by everyone concerned has to be made a primary goal of the contracting process.

TECHNOLOGY

It is not our intention to discuss technology at a level that would be needed for an RFP (request for proposal). Rather, high priority aspects are described, along with suggested solutions, in sufficient detail so that the reader can understand the underlying issues. We start with terminals, and then move on to software, network configuration and databases.

While dumb terminals could be used, with all of the computing power residing in the network, given the relatively low cost of personal computers (pc) and the additional uses to which they could be put, the use of dumb terminals would seem to be a foolish option. It would also put an unnecessary burden on the network. Hence, the MarketPlace would operate on the presumption that all users would have personal computers as their input/output devices. Furthermore, the network should be capable of handling the more popular pc protocols. Particular features, such as memory capacity, processing speed, and screen size and resolution, would depend on the requirements of the individual user. At the high end would be a manufacturer that needs CAD/CAM (computer-aided design/computer-aided manufacturing) facilities. In the future, when multi-media systems become the vogue, other options may have to be reconsidered, especially if video is deemed to be cost-effective. It is also possible that if the MarketPlace becomes sufficiently popular, microcomputers specifically designed for use on the network might be developed.

Most of what needs to be said about software can be inferred from what has already been written, especially that which is needed to support the processes. In fact it should be obvious that the primary challenge to launching the MarketPlace is software development. Some of this will be far from easy as existing software does not possess some of the characteristics we seek. To elaborate this statement, we group the software requirements into three general categories: search and retrieval, interpersonal communication and establishing a viable contract.

Search and retrieval from a large database is probably the highest hurdle that has to be crossed, especially since the state of the art is far from satisfactory (see the July, 1991 issue of *ACM Transactions on Information Systems*, which is devoted to the topic). If one knows exactly what one is looking for, the problems are trivial. At the other extreme, if one is not sure what he/she seeks and the database to be searched is unstructured and large, the problems are enormous and the solutions non-existent. We have to take as a given that the databases (the Directory and the Market) will eventually be large, for that is inherent in the value of the MarketPlace. Clearly, as mentioned before, we need to provide some structure, for without it we would be facing years of research before a suitable retrieval mechansim could be developed. At the same time, the structure cannot be so rigid that it inhibits the users of the system from adequately expressing either their capabilities or their interests. Elaborate classification schemes already exist (e.g. Sweden's job classification code), and these may well provide useful insights. The use of these, however, demands that one know the nomenclature. This is too restrictive for our purposes. Another possibility is to develop a retrieval scheme based on the word profiles used to express capabilities and interests. Early research results suggest that this might be a promising avenue (Turtle & Croft, 1991).

Interpersonal communication software can be based on current e-mail systems, recognizing that expressing oneself in a foreign language will be a problem for many users. Again, this indicates that a certain amount of structure is needed, at least in early versions of the software that will be used for the interaction aspects of responding, negotiating and contracting. Once automatic translation facilities are available the structure can be relaxed, but not eliminated. Certain protocols that govern communication behavior exist in virtually every culture, and these cannot be completely ignored. Some of them, especially those pertaining to the opening and closing of an interaction, ought to be maintained and made as universal as possible.

The software designed to control the contract has to ensure to the extent possible that the contents of the contract are mutually understood. This will require a considerable amount of structure and the use of structured language (English at the start) for such things as product/service specification. The biggest challenge is to develop the ability to allow the negotiants to suggest tradeoffs among the various elements of a contract. This would be most useful to the participants if they had their own software that would indicate to them the implictions of various tradeoffs before they suggested alternatives or had to respond to them.

There are several network design issues. One is configuration. At the start there will be no need for anything other than a completely centralized star network, with all of the databases and software residing at a single computer center. As the system grows, particularly geographically, a distributed system makes more sense. The actual location and distribution of software and databases will reflect not only the actual and predicted traffic patterns, but available bandwidth and the legal environment as well. If the demand for services offered by the MarketPlace grow rapidly, bandwidth may become a significant constraint, especially if parts of the network are not digital. This would limit the extent to which interactions could take place in real time, and thus might inhibit both social and negotiation processes.

Initially there is no point to use anything but the public telephone network. It is very pervasive, and it is hard to image businesses being interested in the MarketPlace that would not have a telephone. With the exception of very few places in the world, this would require modems to convert digital to analogue signals and back again, which greatly restricts the volume of traffic that can be carried. This poses no problem for asynchronous communication, especially of alpha-numerics (text), and these should be the bulk of early traffic. Once graphics and images begin to be used, however, and negotiations are conducted in real-time, the constraints posed by an analogue network are substantial. The question is whether ISDN services would be sufficiently widespread that they could be used or would there be other, more desirable, alternatives. There are other factors that would also enter into the decision to develop a separate network or to use an existing value-added network to handle MarketPlace type services. These include: security, flexibility and cost.

A feasible alternative would be to use a commercialized version of an existing digital network - Internet (Markoff, 1992). At present this meta-network is used primarily to link networks of academics and researchers over the world. However, there is discussion of how it might be extended to businesses and even residences. The initial problem is that it is far from pervasive with respect to the prospective clientele of the MarketPlace. Its advantage is that Internet is digital, and there are plans to make it extremely fast so that it could handle digitized video and all of forms of multimedia interactions.

Databases are the last of the technological issues to be discussed. Those for the Directory and Market have already been covered in adequate detail, with but one exception, how to keep them current. If they are out-of-date, much of their value is lost. Since there is little motivation for businesses to remove outdated entries (unless there is a time-dependent fee for entries; and to encourage use we would suggest otherwise), some system that depends on usage ought to be put into operation. As examples: if an organization neither initiates nor responds to any inquiries for a period of x months, it would have to be reinserted into the Directory before it could use the services of the MarketPlace; and listings in the Market would be for a fixed duration. While this would not ensure invalid entries, it would place limits on the problem.

The other significant database issue is what services, in addition to the Directory and Market, ought to be part of the MarketPlace? Small and medium sized organizations are likely to need advice regarding customs regulations and clearance requirements, and information regarding the transport of goods. Furthermore, they would like to know who is available to help them solve these problems.

Another area of interest is financing and a number of different roles could be played here. One is access to capital to finance a purchase or to produce items for which an order exists. Another that would be of interest to both sides of a contract is assuring the means of payment. For example, banks and other financial institutions might participate in the MarketPlace as escrow agents, assuring that payments will be made subject to the conditions expressed in the contract being satisfied. This would a big boost to the trust element of contract negotiations. Whether financial institutions would be willing to get involved in this way is another question, but if money is to be made, they will. A third role would be that of a venture capitalist, someone willing to invest in transactions for a proportion of the profit.

This is a different type of financing and it might be of interest to firms negotiating contracts that have a level of risk that is unacceptable to more conservative financial institutions.

Making information about its users' legal environments would appear to be a very useful service, especially since small and medium businesses all too rarely make *a priori* determinations of the legal implications of their actions. This could be done in several ways. One would be to have an independent operator offer such a service to the customers of the MarketPlace. A second way would have the MarketPlace provide a legal reference service that one could scan to see if there were laws that might affect a particular commercial transaction. The organization of such a database for naive users would require some research before such a service could be put into operation. An elaboration of either approach would be an expert system that would detect whether or not one should be aware of the legal implications of a pending transaction. This would be the most useful of all the alternatives if it proved to be feasible.

MARKETPLACE MANAGEMENT

Management covers a very broad spectrum of topics, so we will limit our discussion to three: economics, organization and the pragmatics of starting up. The first is essential, for if one cannot make money from developing and operating the MarketPlace it will exist only as a concept. The question then is how might one make money? While there are many possible approaches, two will be discussed.

One is to charge for each and every service. Thus, a firm using the MarketPlace would pay separate fees to use the communication system, to browse through the Directory, to place items in the Market, to access the other databases, etc. This would be a "pay as you go" approach, with participants being billed each month for the services used. This would encourage people to provide value added services to the repertory of the MarketPlace, and they could do so as long as the services added were consistent with the architecture and intent of the system. It might lead to problems of coordination and confusion when services are overlapping or competing, but it would be the epitome of the open market. It could also lead to the problem of data overload to the point that potential participants would avoid the MarketPlace.

An alternative pricing strategy would be to charge only for completed transac-tions, the charge to be a percentage of the value of the transaction, the percentage declining as the value increases. This would be the analgous to the income of wholesalers, jobbers, manufacturers' agents and sales people who work on commission. Most services would be covered by this fee, and businesses pay only when there is a realized benefit. In fact, the fee could be built into the price structure, for with appropriate software the seller would see the price received and the buyer the price to be paid, the difference being the return to the MarketPlace. In other words, what you see is what you agree to. In this case there would need to be a financial intermediary to assure that such a scheme would work. The biggest threat is the possibility that users would bypass the system for the final contract. Mechanisms would have to be added to penalize such behavior, or to provide so many value added services, such as logistics and legal support, that it would not benefit the parties to a contract to finalize it outside of the system.

The specific organizational structure of the MarketPlace would depend in part on the nature of the services provided. Nevertheless, most aspects of structure would be independent of this issue. For example, once the MarketPlace became global it would be very difficult to operate within a highly centralized framework. National and regional differences would require that persons with an understanding of the cultures involved be in a position to respond to local interests. Government regulations would also affect the structure, for in some instances to operate within a country a firm has to establish a subsidiary with majority control belonging to local nationals. Decentralization does raise problems of coordination. However, if the MarketPlace possesses effective interpersonal communication tools, it ought to be able to use these for its own ends.

We close with some comments about getting going. With the exception of the software needed for effective retrieval from the Directory and the Market, everything else mentioned that is needed to get the MarketPlace underway should be able to be developed within a year to eighteen months. Certainly a prototype ought to exist by then if the necessary resources were made available; and the lack of appropriate retrieval software would not be a major issue until there are a substantial number of participants.

Since it is suggested that the dominant language in the early stages be English, it should be launched where this would not be a handicap. Since cultural issues may be an important factor in system usage, the MarketPlace ought to be tried in several different regions. Logical places to start would be in the NAFTA countries, especially the United States and Canada, Europe within the CEC, since English is the governing language of the Commission, and the ASEAN countries, with Singapore as the leader since English is used widely. Experience from these three areas would provide feedback on a number of major issues. These include the effects of using just English for transactions, cultural acceptance and rejection of the system or specific features, and the demand for various services.

Who would be interested in underwriting the MarketPlace? That is the biggest question. Individual elements, especially services, could be developed rather easily and without great cost. The infrastructure, however, would require a major investment. An organization would have to be convinced that it is in its best interests, either for profit or strategic reasons, to undertake such a financial commitment. There is little question, however, that over the long run something like the MarketPlace is going to exist, and that it will eventually become world-wide.

REFERENCES

Belkin, N.J. and Croft, W.B., 1992. "Information Filtering and Information Retrieval: Two Sides of the Same Coin?," *Communications of the ACM, 35* (12), 29-38.

Berge, J., 1991. *The EDIFACT Standards*, Manchester: NCC Blackwell.

Conrath, D.W., 1993. "The MarketPlace: Concepts and Issues," *Journal of Small Business & Entrepreneurship, 10* (4), 69-80.

Markoff, J., 1992. "The Staggering Scope of the Internet: a Thicket of Networks Wound 'round the Globe," *Digital Media: a Seybold Report, 20* April, *1* (11), 19-24.

Turtle, H. and Croft, W.B., 1991. "Evaluation of an Inference Network-Based Retrieval Model," *ACM Transactions on Information Systems,*" *9* (2), 187-222.

Data Transmission in Transnational Corporations

Maeve L. Cummings
Computer Science and Information Systems
Pittsburg State University
Pittsburg, KS 66762
(316) 235-4543
cummings@mail.pittstate.mail.edu

Jan L. Guynes
Information Systems and Management Sciences
University of Texas at Arlington
(817) 273-3502

Stephen E. Lunce
Dept. of Accounting and Information Systems
Texas A&M International University
(210) 722-8001 x 320

ABSTRACT

Transnational corporations face a more complicated environment when transferring data between company units than do corporations operating domestically. Difficulties may be associated with any or all of the cultural, technological, legal, or political circumstances present in the countries in which foreign subsidiaries operate.

This study investigates the question of whether these challenges are sufficiently daunting that transnational corporations have different patterns of data transmission for domestic and foreign subsidiaries. The U.S. oil and gas industry provided the data for this study. The study found that there was no significant difference in the frequency of data transmission between the parent and its U.S.-based and non-U.S. subsidiaries, except in marketing data. The results also showed that the frequency of data transmission from the subsidiaries to the parent was much higher than in the opposite direction, for both U.S. and non-U.S. subsidiaries.

DATA TRANSMISSION IN TRANSNATIONAL CORPORATIONS

The flow of information is vitally important to the functioning of any company, so that any circumstances which constrain that data flow are of major concern. A transnational corporation, with subsidiaries in different countries, faces a much more heterogeneous environment than the company operating only domestically. Problems can arise from any number of differences. For example, not all countries in the world share the U.S. philosophy that information should flow freely and without restrictions. Nations exhibit varying levels of technological sophistication, which affects the availability and reliability of computer and telecommunications equipment and service. Fringe benefits for qualified personnel may be expensive, if personnel are available.

Generally, the conditions which hamper the efficient and effective implementation and management of information systems (IS) outside the U.S. exist in one or both of two forms. The first is local conditions, which comprise the societal culture; the level of technological sophistication; and the economy of the country in which the subsidiary is operating. The second form involves restrictions imposed by governmental or regulatory agencies.

The imposed restrictions take various forms. High import duty, or outright bans, on hardware or software may cause standardization anomalies. Companies are sometimes reluctant to develop software in, or send software to, a country where copyright protection on software is not recognized or severely restricted. Constraints targeting the transmission of data, especially name-linked data, may have a serious impact on the organization's data processing procedures. Data may be subject to taxation, or laws may prohibit the processing of name-linked data outside the home country. Telecommunications difficulties usually take the form of outrageous pricing of services, or regulations on the types of equipment that may be used by the subsidiary, or sub-standard service.

This paper presents the results of an empirical study which investigated whether the overall effect of these differences associated with geographic location is sufficient to cause companies to have different data transmission patterns for U.S. and non-U.S. subsidiaries. Specifically, two research questions are addressed here. Firstly, whether the frequency of data transmission is different when the parent company is sending data to or receiving data from U.S. subsidiaries, as opposed to when the parent is sending data to or receiving data from non-U.S. subsidiaries. Secondly, is the frequency of data transmission the same when data is transmitted from the parent to the subsidiaries as when it is transmitted from the subsidiaries to the parent, and is this the same for both U.S. and non-U.S. subsidiaries?

RELEVANT RESEARCH

Researchers in transnational IS generally seem to agree that an information system is strongly impacted by the external environment when operating outside the relatively homogeneity of the home base (4,7,10,11,13,15,21). Karimi and Konsynski (15) propose that a system that crosses national boundaries faces variation in business environments, availability of resources, and technological and regulatory environments.

Palvia, Palvia and Zigli (17), using a framework of technological sophistication, ranked the issues that were most important to groups of countries. The found that many countries in the world are still concerned about operational types of issues, such as the obsolescence of hardware. Of the 4.5 billion people in the world, only 800 million are covered by global phone networks and about 75% of this coverage is absorbed by nine countries (17). Signalling systems, bandwidth standards, and analog to digital conversion conventions differ from place to place (19). Kedia and Bhagat (16) found that societal culture always affects the transfer of technology from one country to another, and showed that it is the most important factor in the transfer of technology from industrialized countries to developing ones.

Transborder issues have been dealt with at length (1,2,3,5,20,23). In an empirical study of U.S.-based transnational corporations, Kane and Ricks (14) found that transborder restrictions, while they were not considered a major problem, were important factors in decision making. Deans (14) reported similar findings when investigating the most important issues for IS executives in transnational corporations. Both studies suggested that corporations adjust to accommodate differences.

MODEL .

Figure 1 presents the framework which was the basis for this study. The three major components are the parent company, U.S.-based subsidiaries and non-U.S. subsidiaries. The parent company determines the organizational structure of the entire organization, and is the source and destination of the three types of data studied: accounting, marketing, and production data. The data transmission will be determined to a large extent by the organizational structure (9,12) Each subsidiary is engaged in a particular line of business and is also the source or recipient of the three types of data. The non-U.S. subsidiaries are impacted by the local environment of the country in which they are located. The arrows indicate data transmission.

METHODOLOGY

Because of the exploratory nature of this research, it was deemed appropriate to select one industry in the United States, with an eye to keeping the number of variables that might influence the results as small as possible, and to explore that industry in depth. The industry chosen was the oil and gas industry.

U.S.-based transnational oil and gas companies form a relatively homogeneous industry which supplies all sectors of society. Companies in this category are small in number so it was possible to get data from subsidiaries of all ten of the major players.

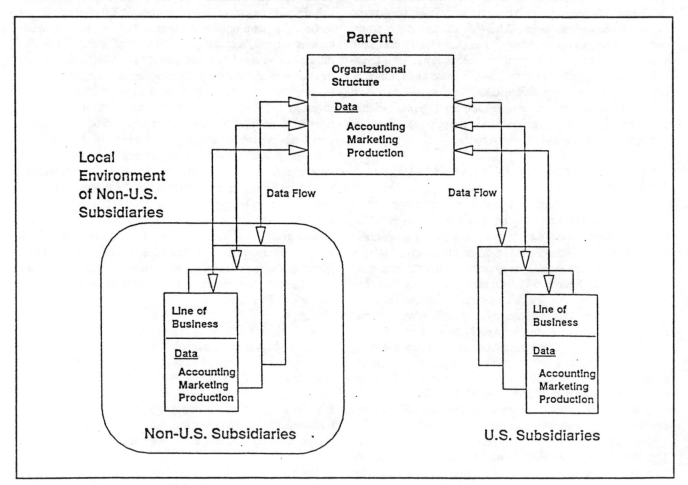

Figure 1: Data Transmission Framework

This is a very mature industry, where the raw materials have been in the earth for millions of years and all companies are searching for and retrieving the product with essentially the same tools. Apparently, the oil and gas companies consider IS to be a significant factor in their success, since they are among the top investors in IT in the United States and in Europe. All ten corporations in this study were listed as having an installed IT base estimated at between $100 million and $950 million (18), with seven of them being among the top sixty investors in IT in the U.S. IT base is defined as the estimated current value of all equipment and IS groups.

Each of these companies in this study had five or more subsidiaries outside the U.S., with at least twenty employees on site. Each company had revenues in 1992 of between $5 billion and $120 billion. Their employees numbered between 8,000 and 145,000.

After a pilot phase to develop the research instrument, the primary study was divided into two phases. The first phase consisted of a survey mailed to the U.S. and non-U.S. subsidiaries of the ten companies. These surveys established the structuring of IS activities within each of the subsidiaries. The second phase of this research was to interview willing respondents of the mailed survey by phone. These phone conversations with the self-selected sample furnished background information on answers provided in the survey and also on factors affecting the subsidiary locally, such as local regulation, and cost and availability of equipment and communications links.

The survey asked about the frequency of transmission of accounting, marketing, and production data. Each question had a fixed set of responses, ranging from "daily and significant" to "none".

PRESENTATION OF FINDINGS

Table 1.—Response Rate of Usable Mailed Surveys

	Surveys Mailed	Surveys Returned	Response Rate
U.S. Subsidiaries	119	21	18%
Non-U.S. Subsidiaries	181	43	24%
Total	300	64	21%

Table 2.—Surveys by Continent

	Surveys Mailed	Surveys Returned	Response Rate
North America (Excluding U.S)	23	8	35%
South America	18	4	22%
Africa	6	0	0%
Asia	14	7	50%
Australia	11	4	36%
Europe	109	20	18%
Total	181	43	24%

Sample

Out of 300 mailed surveys, sixty-seven surveys were returned, a response rate of 22.3%. Of these, sixty-four were usable. The other three were inappropriate for inclusion since the companies were no longer subsidiaries of any oil and gas organization. Twenty-one of the usable surveys were from subsidiaries in the United States, and forty-three were from subsidiaries outside the United States. The response rates are shown in Tables 1 and 2. Responses were received from U.S. and non-U.S. subsidiaries of all ten companies.

RESULTS

The framework presented in Figure 1 suggests that two factors, besides the location of the subsidiary, might reasonably be expected to affect the data transmission patterns between the parent and subsidiaries in an organization. These are the organizational structure of the company and the line of business of the subsidiary.

Because the oil and gas industry was chosen for this study, the question of organizational structure is simplified. More similarity than difference exists in the organizational structures of the companies in this industry. Almost all companies were involved, to some degree, in chemical operations, oil and gas exploration and production, gas and gas liquids, and coal mining and minerals. These operations were generally distinct from each other, and from any other interests the company might have.

The line of business of the respondents is shown in Table 3. This leads to the first hypothesis:

Hypothesis 1.

H0: The types of business in which the U.S. subsidiaries are engaged are the same as the types of business in which the non-U.S. subsidiaries are engaged.

Ha: U.S. and non-U.S. subsidiaries were not engaged in the same types of business.

A chi square analysis, done on the data in Table 3, resulted in a calculated chi square value of 7.36 which is far below the table value of $X^2 = 14.07$ ($p < 0.05$). Thus, there the is no evidence to suggest that the distribution of types of business interests is significantly different for the U.S.-based and non-U.S. subsidiaries in the study.

Table 3.—Line of Business of Responding Subsidiaries

Line of Business	U.S.		Non-U.S.		Ttl	
Raw materials processing	3	14%	8	19%	11	17%
Products for local market	13	62%	23	53%	36	56%
Products for parent market	-	0%	1	2%	1	2%
Both parent and local markets	-	0%	4	9%	4	6%
Both raw materials and local markets	1	5%	-	0%	1	2%
Service	4	19%	4	9%	8	13%
Exploration	-	0%	3	7%	3	5%

Based on these two results, any differences detected in data transmission patterns between U.S. and non-U.S. subsidiaries cannot be shown to be due to the organizational structure of the company or the line of business of the subsidiaries.

Data Transmission

The types of data considered here are accounting data, marketing data, and manufacturing data. Most subsidiaries surveyed reported at least some data transmission between the subsidiaries and parent companies.

Data Transmission from Parent to Subsidiaries

As shown in Table 4, fifty-eight percent (the sum of 5% receiving data daily, 10% weekly, and 43% monthly) of the U.S. subsidiaries receive accounting data from the parent, at least monthly, compared with only 33% (7%+5%+21%) of non-U.S. subsidiaries. The remaining subsidiaries reported accounting data from the parent to be very limited or non-existent. U.S. subsidiaries reported more accounting data from the parent than did the non-U.S. subsidiaries.

Only 19% of U.S. subsidiaries received marketing from the parent company, at least monthly, while 28% (7%+7%+14%) of non-U.S. subsidiaries did. No U.S. subsidiary received marketing data daily or weekly from the parent, but 14% of non-U.S. subsidiaries did. Eighty-one percent (43%+38%) of U.S. subsidiaries and 72% (58%+14%) of non-U.S. subsidiaries received little or no marketing data from the parent company. Non-U.S. subsidiaries reported receiving more marketing than U.S. subsidiaries did.

Production data were transmitted with the least frequency of all three categories. Eighty-five percent (33%+52%) of U.S. subsidiaries, and 75% (14%+61%) of non-U.S. subsidiaries reported little or no production data coming from the parent. As was the case with marketing data, non-U.S. subsidiaries reported receiving production data more often than U.S. subsidiaries.

Data Transmission from Subsidiaries to Parent

Table 5 shows that all U.S. subsidiaries sent data to the parent, with 71% sending the data monthly. Eighty-six (14%+9%+63%) percent of the non-U.S. subsidiaries sent data, periodically, to the parent, with 63% transmitting on a monthly basis. A small number (13%) of non-U.S. subsidiar-

Table 4—Data Transmission FROM PARENT to Subsidiaries

Frequency	Accounting		Marketing		Production	
	U.S.	Non-U.S.	U.S.	Non-U.S.	U.S.	Non-U.S.
Daily	5%	7%	0%	7%	0%	9%
Weekly	10%	5%	0%	7%	5%	7%
Monthly	43%	21%	19%	14%	10%	9%
Insignificant	14%	21%	43%	14%	33%	14%
None	29%	47%	38%	58%	52%	60%

Table 5—Data Transmission FROM SUBSIDIARIES to Parent

Frequency	Accounting		Marketing		Production	
	U.S.	Non-U.S.	U.S.	Non-U.S.	U.S.	Non-U.S.
Daily	10%	14%	5%	9%	0%	19%
Weekly	19%	9%	0%	7%	5%	7%
Monthly	71%	63%	43%	51%	33%	40%
Insignificant	0%	5%	52%	12%	38%	14%
None	0%	9%	0%	21%	24%	21%

ies reported sending very little or no data to the parent. Respondents indicated that "insignificant" means once a year or so.

Forty-eight percent (5%+43%) of U.S. subsidiaries sent marketing data periodically to the parent, compared to 67% (9%+7%+51%) of non-U.S. subsidiaries. It is interesting to note that only one U.S. subsidiary reported sending marketing data more frequently than once a month, but seven non-U.S. subsidiaries did.

Thirty-eight percent (5%+33%) of U.S. and 66% (19%+7%+40%) of non-U.S. subsidiaries sent production data to the parent company periodically. However, production data is still the lowest of the three categories for data transmission from subsidiary to parent. This is probably because most of the subsidiaries in this study produce for the local market.

Not all respondents specifically indicated future trends, but those who did, for the most part, projected that data transmission would remain as is. A few exceptions were found, however. Three U.S. subsidiaries and two non-U.S. subsidiaries indicated that, in the future, they expect data transmission to increase in all the categories in which they transmit data. No subsidiary expressed the belief that data transmission in any category would decrease.

ANALYSIS AND CONCLUSIONS

This section attempts to draw some conclusions from the data presented above. The basic research questions asked about data transmission to and from the parent and its U.S. and non-U.S. subsidiaries. Four more hypotheses are presented to address these issues.

Hypothesis 2 deals with whether there is a significant difference between the frequency of data transmission from U.S. subsidiaries to the parent and from non-U.S. subsidiaries to the parent. The three types of data are considered separately.

Hypothesis 2.
H0: The frequency of data transmission from the U.S. subsidiaries to the parent is the same as the frequency of data transmission from non-U.S. subsidiaries to the parent.
Ha: The frequency of data transmission from the U.S. subsidiaries to the parent is not the same for U.S.

subsidiaries as it is for non-U.S. subsidiaries

The third hypothesis concerns differences in the frequency of data transmission from the parent to the subsidiary.

Hypothesis 3.

H0: The frequency of data transmission from the parent to U.S. subsidiaries is the same as the frequency of data transmission from the parent to non-U.S. subsidiaries.

Ha: The frequency of data transmission from the parent is not the same for U.S. subsidiaries as it is for non-U.S. subsidiaries

Table 6 shows the calculated chi square values for each type of data transmission from both groups of subsidiaries to the parent, and from the parent to both groups of subsidiaries. Data transmission from the parent to the U.S. subsidiaries did not appear to be different than data transmission from the parent to non-U.S. subsidiaries.

The only significant result was for marketing data from subsidiaries to the parent. In other words, the frequency of data transmission from U.S. and non-U.S. subsidiaries is not significantly different for accounting and production data, but it is for marketing data. These results are consistent with the findings of Kane and Ricks (14) and Deans and Ricks (7) that difficulties in the management of a transnational IS are important, but solutions are found to achieve the goals and objectives of the organization. It is not unreasonable that marketing data, especially from the non-U.S., to the parent, would be sent more frequently. Of the three types of data, marketing is probably the most affected by cultural differences, and the area where more input from the subsidiary would be necessary.

Hypothesis 4 considers whether the frequency of data transmission is the same in both directions between the U.S. subsidiaries and the parent.

Hypothesis 4

H0: The frequency of data transmission from the parent to U.S. subsidiaries is the same as from the U.S. subsidiar-

ies to the parent.

Ha: The frequency of data transmission from the parent to the U.S. subsidiaries is not the same as from the U.S. subsidiaries to the parent.

Hypothesis 5 considers whether the data transmission is the same in both directions between non-U.S. subsidiaries and the parent.

Hypothesis 5.

H0: The frequency of data transmission from the parent to non-U.S. subsidiaries is the same as from the U.S. subsidiaries to the parent.

Ha: The frequency of data transmission from the parent to the non-U.S. subsidiaries is not the same as from the U.S. subsidiaries to the parent.

Table 7 shows the calculated chi square values for Hypotheses 4 and 5. In this case, the only non-significant case was that of production data transmission between U.S. subsidiaries and the parent. In all other cases, the transmission of data from subsidiaries to the parent was much more frequent than from the parent to subsidiaries. This was especially true in the case of non-U.S. subsidiaries.

SUMMARY

The main results of this study show that for the sample companies having similar organizational structures, where the distribution of line of business is the same for both the U.S. and non-U.S. subsidiaries that:

1. the frequency of data transmission, for all three types of data, from the parent is the same for both U.S. and non-U.S. subsidiaries.

2. marketing data was transmitted more frequently from non-U.S. subsidiaries to the parent than from U.S. subsidiaries. The data transmission was the same for accounting and production data.

3. the frequency of data transmission from U.S. subsidiaries to the parent was greater than the frequency of data transmission from U.S. subsidiaries to the parent, for accounting and marketing data. Production data transmission was the same in both directions.

Table 6—U.S. vs Non-U.S. Subsidiaries

Functional Area	From Parent To Subsidiary	From Subsidiary To Parent
Accounting	T = 4.51	T = 4.38
Marketing	T = 9.29	T = 15.81 ***
Production	T = 4.83	T = 7.98

Note: *   Significant at 5% level, i.e. p < 0.05
    **   Significant at 1% level, i.e. p < 0.01
    ***   Significant at 0.5% level, i.e. p < 0.005
    ****   Significant at 0.1% level, i.e. p < 0.001

Table 7—Parent vs Subsidiary

Functional Area	U.S. Subsidiaries	Non-U.S. Subsidiary
Accounting	T = 11.50 *	T = 24.90 ****
Marketing	T = 11.12 *	T = 16.91 ***
Production	T = 5.09	T = 17.64 ***

Note: *   Significant at 5% level, i.e. p < 0.05
    **   Significant at 1% level, i.e. p < 0.01
    ***   Significant at 0.5% level, i.e. p < 0.005
    ****   Significant at 0.1% level, i.e. p < 0.001

4. the frequency of data transmission from non-U.S. subsidiaries to the parent was much greater than the transmission from the parent to non-U.S. subsidiaries. This was true for all three types of data.

Since most of the sample data came from well-developed countries, the problems encountered were mostly cost and regulatory difficulties. It would appear that the heterogeneous environments associated with transnational corporations do not necessarily cause major differences in the frequency of data transmission. Companies may simply absorb the cost and make the necessary arrangements to maintain uniformity among all the subsidiaries.

REFERENCES

1. Basche, J. "Information Protectionism". Across the Board, 20 (November 1983): 38-44.

2. Buss, M.D.J. "Legislative Threat to Transborder Data Flow. Harvard Business Review, 62(3), 1984: 111-118.

3. Butler, R.E. "The ITU's Role in World Telecom Development and Information Transfer". Telephony, 203 (August 22, 1983): 49,52.

4. Cash, J.I.; McFarlan, W.F.; and McKenney, J.L. Corporate Information Systems Management. Richard D. Irwin, Inc., Homewood, Illinois, 1988.

5. Chandran, R., Phatak, A. and Sambharya, R. "Transborder Data Flows: Implications for Multinational Corporations". Business Horizons, 30 (1987): 74-82.

6. Deans, P. C. "The Transfer and Management of Information Systems Technology in the International Environment: Identification of Key Issues for MIS Managers in U.S.-Based Multinational Corporations." Ph.D. Dissertation, University of South Carolina, 1989.

7. Deans, P.C. and Ricks, D.A. "MIS Research: A Model for Incorporating The International Dimension." The Journal of High Technology Management Research 2 (Spring 1991): 57-81.

8. Dhir, K.S. "The Challenge of Introducing Advanced Telecommunication Systems in India" in The Global Issues of Information Technology Management Palvia, S., Palvia, P and Zigli, R.M. (eds). Harrisburg, PA: Idea Group Publishing, 1992.

9. Egelhoff, W. "Strategy and Structure in Multinational Corporations: A Revision of the Stopford and Wells Model." Strategic Management Journal 9 (January-February 1988): 1-14.

10. Freedman, D.H. "Managing Information Systems at the Multinational." Infosystems 32 (January 1985): 58-60.

11. Freedman, D.H. "Tying it Together at the Multinational." Infosystems 32 (February 1985): 28-32.

12. Galbraith, J.R. Organization Design. Reading, MA: Addison-Wesley, 1977.

13. Ives, B. and Jarvenpaa, S.L. "Applications of Global Information Technology: Key Issues for Management." MIS Quarterly 15 (March 1991): 33-49.

14. Kane, Michael H. and Ricks, David A. "The Impact of Transborder Data Flow Regulations on Large United States-Based Corporations." Columbia Journal of World Business 24 (Summer 1989): 23-29.

15. Karimi, J. and Konsynksi, B.R. "Globalization and Information Management Strategies." Journal of Management Information Systems 7 (Spring 1991): 7-26.

16. Kedia, B.L. and Bhagat, R.S. "Cultural Constraints on Transfer of Technology Across Nations: Implications for Research in International and Comparative Management." Academy of Management Review. Vol. 13, October 1988, 559-571.

17. Palvia, P.C., Palvia, S. and Zigli, R.M. "Global Information Technology Environment: Key MIS Issues in Advanced and Less-Developed Nations" in The Global Issues of Information Technology Management Palvia, S., Palvia, P and Zigli, R.M. (eds). Harrisburg, PA: Idea Group Publishing, 1992.

18. "Rank and File." Information Week, no. 392 (September 21, 1992): 20-35.

19. Sankar, C.S and Prabhakar, P.K. "Key Technological Components and Issues of Global Information Systems" in The Global Issues of Information Technology Management Palvia, S., Palvia, P and Zigli, R.M. (eds). Harrisburg, PA: Idea Group Publishing, 1992.

20. Sauvant, K.P. (1990). "The Growing Dependence on Transborder Data Flows". Computerworld, 18 (June 25): ID19-ID24.

21. Selig, G.J. "Approaches to Strategic Planning form Information Resource Management (IRM) in Multinational Corporations." MIS Quarterly 6 (June 1982): 33-45.

22. Selig, G.J. "A Framework for Multinational Information Systems Planning." Information and Management, 5, (June 1982): 95-115.

23. Tsanacas, D. "The Transborder Data Flow in the New World Information Order: Privacy or Control". Review of Social Economy, 43 (1985): 357-370.

Facing the Local-Global Challenge: An IT Platform Model for the Networking Firm

Liliane Esnault
Professor of Information Systems and Organization
Groupe ESC-Lyon (Lyon Graduate School of Business)
23 Av. Guy de Collongue - BP 174
69132 ECULLY Cedex - France
Tel (33) 78 33 78 00 - Fax (33) 78 33 61 69

Abstract

Enterprises today face the challenge of operating in an environment which demands conflicting local and global views. Old forms of organization are too rigid, are not sufficiently reactive or flexible, or don't have the critical size for meeting this challenge. A possible response for ensuring success and performance is new forms of networking enterprises. The management of the Information Technology (IT) resource is a strategic one in this type of organization. None of these networking enterprises could deal with their structural, economic and social complexity without being structured around sophisticated IT networks. In addition, the management of the IT resource is much more complex now and requires a new vision. A contingent IT Platform model is proposed for supporting the management of the IT resource in the new forms of networking enterprises. Some European examples are given of how the IT Platform model can be used to describe the IT perspective of networking firms.

Acknowledgment :

I am very indebted to Penelope Ann Tunnell, who played a major part in issuing the English version of this paper.

Introduction

The aim of this paper is to present some conceptual thoughts on a framework for the Information Technology (IT) support of a firm, the IT Platform, in particular for those firms where the IT systems have complex structures because the firms themselves have complex, volatile structures, known as networks.

The first part of the paper briefly suggests an organisational form which firms must develop in order to meet the real challenges of their economic environment, and which I call the "networking firm". I have proposed a typology of the networking firm which seemed to be relevant to me while developing the IT Platform model (ITP) for networking firms.

The second part discusses the importance of a new vision for the management of the IT resource. Although organizational networking is not only a problem of IT support, the role of IT in networking is a very important one, and the IT systems involved in a networking structure are often complex and intricate.

In the third part, I present my ITP model, in an attempt to clarify how a networking organization can deal with the management of its IT resources. This model allows one to keep a global view of the four elements of the ITP : strategy; organization; architecture; and economy ; while doing the groundwork with "building block" strategies in organisational learning project groups. A few European examples of how the ITP model can be used for networking organizations are given.

As I mentioned above, this paper is still at the conceptual level. Further research must be undertaken, especially in the "real world", to validate the utility of such a model, and the refinements required for improving it. This is discussed in the conclusion to this paper.

The Networking Firm, a New Organization

Facing the local + global challenge

For many years now, it has been shown that organizations are open systems, highly dependent on their environment (Mintzberg 1979). This environment now includes some new critical features such as :

- a compelling requirement for quality coupled with an equally compelling need to reduce costs and delays ;
- the globalisation of markets, requiring not only large resources, but also a specific ability for ensuring reactivity and flexibility, which can more easily be provided by local units;
- an exigency to decrease production costs coupled with an equal exigency to meet a short-term specific customized demand ;
- a demand for modern fashionable low-cost products coupled with an equal demand for the natural craftsman's quality and originality of "the olden days" ;
- the use of high-tech transnational technology coupled with the need to employ local manpower ;
- etc.

These requirements, which would have been considered as contradictory fifteen years ago, now all have to be met at the same time by a firm if they want to be competitive or even just

Figure 1: Graphic overview of the paper's structure

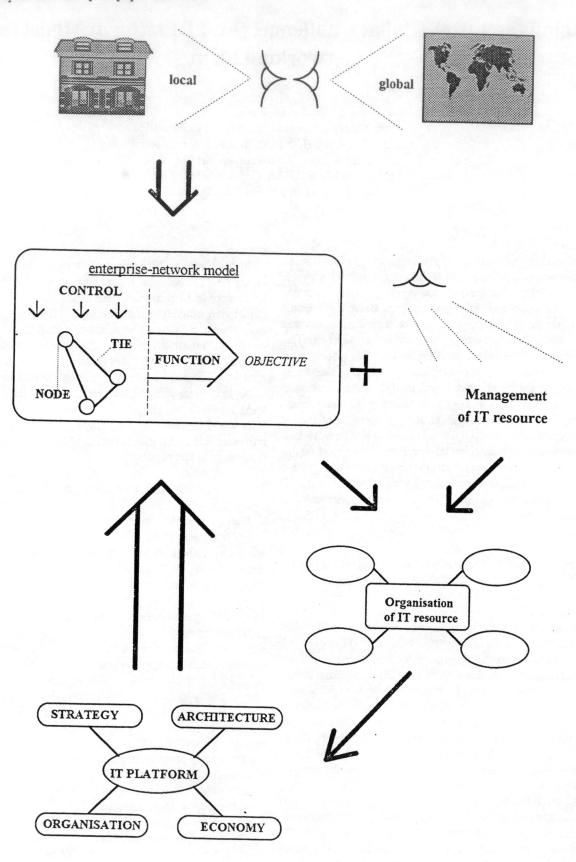

survive. They have to be successful both on the global front - by being able to supply their customers, to work with confidence with their suppliers, and to cope with competitors all around the world - and on the local front - by being efficient within a country, by employing nationals, and by conquering local markets with reliable and knowledgeable relationships. (See, for example, Ohmae, 1990 ; Brown and Watts, 1992 ; Senn, 1993 ; Benjamin and Blunt, 1992).

Networking to succeed

The traditional forms of organization cannot cope with all these new challenges at the same time. Firms have had to, and still have to, design and implement new frameworks for creating flexibility, reactiveness, competitiveness, and performance. A possible response is the network-**ing** organization (or networked - Scott Morton 1991, or network - Nohria and Eccles 1992, or federalist - Davenport and Eccles 1992 or Handy 1992). The choice of "network-**ing**" refers to the fact that it is not a definite stable state, but a continuous learning process, something that is always being built dynamically.

As a network, an organization can be described in terms of :

* *nodes* - the pro-active poles of the network ;

* *links or ties* - the place and support for interactions between nodes ;

* *a control structure* - that which makes the nodes and links work according to their objectives. The control structure manages the structure of the network, the nature and flow of "traffic" and the rules for that traffic, the way the network ensure its functions, the "status" of the network users, and the "procedures" for their "access" to the network ;

* *a set of functions or services* - provided by the network to its users to achieve their common objectives.

Naturally, there is not only one possible response in terms of the structure of the networking firm. Several different processes for networking, for example, can result in different types of structures. For the purpose of this work, the following typology (Esnault 1994) seems to be a relevant one, certainly in regards of its usefulness for discussing the IT point of view :

* *the scattered firm* - for example, the result of "de-s" (decentralization, de-localization, de-concentration, de-legation, etc.) applied to a traditional large company. Consider the many multinationals which have been reorganised in the last ten to fifteen years ;

* *the extended firm* - for example the result of the transversal integration of several partners of a firm into a service-oriented relationship. Consider Value-Added Networks like those supporting EDI (Electronic Data Interchange) ;

* *the associated firm* - for example, the result of an often temporary association between either small firms or units of large firms, public establishments or local communities, or perhaps the realization of a synergy between local resources in order to reach a specific strategic common goal. Consider all "joint organizations" (joint research projects, for example) ;

* *the virtual firm* - for example, the result of a "quasi-

dematerialization" of the networked firm due mainly to intense use of IT. Two of the largest computer manufacturers, IBM and DEC, have announced recently that they were getting rid of thousands of square feet of offices in the center of big cities in Europe (Paris, Stuttgart, etc.). These offices had been mainly used by sales staff, maintenance technicians and engineers, who have become "nomads" with only an "electronic office", which links them into their firm's network from anywhere in the world, including customers' offices, hotels, homes, cars, etc.

The Strategic Role of Information Technology in the Networking Firm

It is evident, as is often shown in the literature (e.g. Nohria 1992), that networking organizations are much more than the simple use of electronic networks to do everyday tasks. In the same way, studying networking organizations is not simply observing that there are networking processes in all kinds of organizations. Being a networking organization implies a permanent structuring of a rather thick web of identified (though sometimes not completely formalized) interactions between "active nodes" to reach a common goal or achieve a common temporary strategy. According to this "definition" one can imagine that the role of IT in the creation, building, functioning, reinforcement and maintainance of the organizational network is not an ancilliary one.

No networking firm without an IT network

The role of the communication systems between the nodes of the networked firm is evidently an important one. Through high tech networks one can deal with :

* the need to overcome geographic distances between nodes;

* the need to eliminate global delays along the value chain;

* the need to reduce transaction costs ;

* the repetition of transactions due the increasing use of Just-in-time ;

* the multiplication of transactions due to the "atomization" of the units involved in these transactions ;

* the need for an "ad-hoc" cohesion between the units in the information process ;

* etc.

There is also an evidence that there is a need for a formal, fast and reliable support mechanism for these communications and information exchanges. Moreover, this kind of technology already exists, as well as the means for implementing it. However, its implementation is often extremely complex, for several reasons :

* the technology for "interconnecting" is miscellaneous, heterogeneous, and ill-assorted. There are not only a variety of systems but there are also a variety of technological ages and countries (regulations, monopolies, legal restrictions, etc) ;

* the technology is evolving at an incredible speed. No sooner has a system become operational than another is announced, naturally a much better one. The main result of this is

a retardation of project development, which gives rise to a wait and see attitude ;

* the actors involved in the process vary according to their professional connection (to the firm or some internal "units", to a manufacturer, to a consultancy firm or a software house, to a telecommunication operator, etc.), according to their skills (DP, telecommunications, hardware, software, databases, practitioners or managers, specialists or "hybrids", etc.), and according to their "size" (individuals, groups of individuals, more or less formal, international groups, SMCs, public or private organizations, etc.). There is also a huge disparity among regions and countries.

The IT network structures and even creates the networking firm

Not only are the IT networks essential to the survival of the networked firm, but often they are also its backbone, as in the case of EDI. Furthermore, some firms create or restructure themselves into network service providers. Numerous instances are to be found in "L'entreprise virtuelle ou les nouveaux modes de travail" (Ettighoffer 1992) and in professional journals.

One can cite, for example, SEITA, the French national tobacco company. Tobacco retailing in France used to be done through small specialized shops or kiosks well placed throughout France in the large city centres as well as in the small villages. SEITA provided these shops or kiosks with a sophisticated network of interconnected cash registers that dealt with automatic invoices and stock inventory. Now SEITA is applying this savoir-faire to developing the shops and kiosks by introducing the sales of other low volume items (tickets, electronic cards, candies, shaving blades, batteries, game tickets, etc...) combined with a very high level of service for customers throughout the whole country. SEITA is metamorphosing from being a tobacco company to being a VAN supplier company.

Networking the management of the IT resource

For networking firms, more so than for traditionally organized firms, IT represents a critical resource which has to be organised and managed optimally. The organization of the IT resource requires knowledge of organization theory, management of the technology, management of the information systems, and knowledge of IT itself for the definition of a set of methods and tools for organizing and managing IT in each firm.

How the management of the IT resource is organised has been evolving since computers first came into commercial existence. Life with the computer was much simpler in the early days, those of the Data Processing (DP) era. A one or even two-dimensional view could be taken in regards of this management function. The accelerated evolution of computer technology has made life with the computer much more complicated today. A four-dimensional view at the very least must be taken (see Fig 2).

Figure 2: The driving forces in the organization of the IT Resource

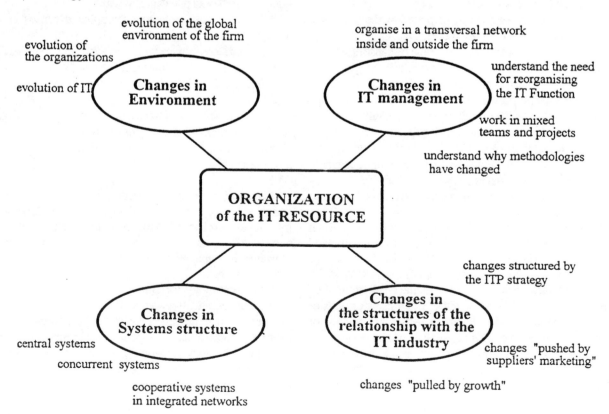

In the DP era, DP was managed by DP specialists just as telephone exchanges were managed by telephone specialists. There was a clear division not only between between the DP specialists and their users but also between the tasks within the DP function. At the same time, the structure of the computer industry (hardware and software suppliers) was clearly defined and relatively stable. There were well known "rules of the game" although its players were highly competitive.

The first "revolution" occurred with the arrival of the micro-computers accompanied by an enhanced role for the users of computer systems and a fundamental restructuring of the industry. There was a three-way battle between the micro-computers, the mini-computers and the mainframe. The choice was which one of the three routes should be taken.

Now this debate is no longer topical, as hardware configurations can consist of mixtures of any of the three sizes of computers. The choice is further complicated by a greater variety of computer in each category in terms of both specialization and stage of evolution. Moreover, a combination of computers can be linked by networks which in turn can be integrated with Local Area Networks (LANs) or Wide Area Networks (WANs) which can have a national or international dimensions. These complex hardware configurations are associated with intricate applications which may have been constructed with a multiplicity of databases, tool kits, standard software products, or specific applications.

The skills required for the construction and maintenance of such a complex hardware, software and telecommunications system cannot exist in the mind of one specialist. Such a system requires not only cooperation, in the form of teamwork, between a number of IT specialists but also the involvement of IT literate users, who must be also part of the same team. These latter could be called "hybrids" as they must have skills which cross the boundaries of the business and IT functions. Furthermore, all these skills may not exist within one company but, as with other IT services and products, may have to be brought in from external sources or companies.

Managing such a complexity requires the construction of a transversal network which covers a firm and its external partners. Designing and maintaining such a strategic network requires a clear vision of the appropriate IT support for a firm, its architectural and organisational implications, and the economic considerations. This can be achieved through the IT Platform model.

The IT Platform Model

The ITP is the framework within which the management of the IT Resource will operate. It is the collection of the minimal specifications that will "bound" the eventual choices of the different actors in the firm who are involved in the design and management of the information systems. It is very essential, given the numerous solutions now available, to ensure a minimum of compatibility and interoperability between all the components of the IT network (nodes, links, control structure,

functions and services) if one wants this network to be operational and provide the minimum services necessary for ensuring a networking firm's competitiveness.

The ITP must be designed with regard to its links with the firm's strategy. It is characterized by its architecture. It is implemented and managed through an ad-hoc structure and organization. It obeys economic rules (see Fig 3).

The four components

Strategy

The links between the strategy of the networked firm and its IT platform are numerous. We saw above that the IT network is often a sine qua non condition of the networking firm. There are numerous instances where the IT platform gave a firm a strategic edge. A given selection of architecture and organization can "make the difference" in a time of increasing competitiveness. In the case of the networking firm, these selections are strategic ones. Moreover, they are usually short-lived and have to be continuously questioned in order to ensure the continuing adaptation of the firm to its environnment.

Organization

This component refers to the organization of the ITP, the organization of the IT department, and also the organization of the use of IT in the whole firm.

The organization of the management of the ITP follows the organization of the whole firm, and, in the case of networking organization, should be articulated around a dual network, the network of the actors and the network of the projects.

The network of the actors includes the Information System or IT Department, those responsible for the information systems in the operational or functional "local" departments, and the partners of the firm (manufacturers, suppliers, services suppliers, software houses, consulting groups, private or public organizations, etc.). The IT department itself tends to be reduced to the smallest number of people, with new skills : the IS manager, one or more network architect(s), administrators (of networks, of databases), some experts (systems, telecoms) and some internal consultants (training, advice for the end users and local management). The local managers are mainly "hybrids", i.e. people with compound skills, information systems plus their own speciality (for instance, ELF Sanofi, a French subsidiary of the oil company ELF which deals with pharmaceuticals, recruits its IS executives from the operational units). The external actors are more often involved in partnership-like relationships, which are based upon confidence and mutual commitment rather than on simple "invitations-to-tender" processes as was customary several years ago.

The network of the projects is the collection of all the projects connected with information technologies that are being developed at a certain time. These projects need to build mixed teams with representatives of each kind of actor. They have been planned, have a definite agenda, a negotiated budget, coherent objectives and a commitment to results. The structuring in the "project mode" allows the implementation of a "constructivist" methodology, in which each step is a framed experiment, with a limited risk and of great benefit to the next steps (expertise acquisition for the team, validation by the end users, benchmarks for the executives).

This kind of organization is an action learning organization. Each project is a way not only of improving the skills of the actors involved within, but also the global ability of the network which enables its evolvement and adaption to new situations.

Architecture

Architecture is that which allows the layout of the different components of the information system, and takes into account :

* the requirements of the network "map-making", i.e. the physical representation, on a map, of the distribution in space and time of the systems involved in the firm, their mutual connections, and their connections with other systems ;

* the importance of norms and standards, for the networks (technologies, protocols, interconnection, administration) as well as for the systems (hardware, software, methodologies). It is the consensus of the market upon these norms and standards which allows the huge heterogeneous international networks to run effectively, which allows EDI and the outsourcing, and which assures the functioning of Just-in-time in the extended firm ;

* the increasing importance of "cabling systems" that build up a relatively normalized infrastructure ;

* the end-user orientation of the workstations, which allows anybody to link into highly sophisticated and integrated networks (voice, data, video) from almost anywhere including mobile situations (cars, planes, etc.) ;

* the distributed and cooperative organization of softwares, databases or applications.

This architecture has to be organised around open systems (i.e. open to the communication with other systems), in a relationship of the client-server kind. In such a relationship, each system does what it knows best to do :

* the micro-computer is the workstation of the end user, user friendly, and able to provide the most customized presentation of the information (including the use of simulation and decision support tools) ;

* the other systems are used as "service providers" (servers) : file servers, data communications servers, document management servers, file storage servers, program servers, etc., which allow the user, whether it be a human or a computer, to choose the most appropriate system ;

* the exchanges are supported by the network logic, which insures not only the "transport" but also the unavoidable "translation" between systems, and assures service continuity, performance, reliability, and security.

The administration of the system is assured via a collection of tools :

* the tools for network administration,

* the tools for database administration,

* the special tools for the specific sub-systems administration,

* etc.

Economy

The economic models are the least advanced part of the ITP organization management. The classical budget models have largely proved to be insufficient, but few new models have appeared to date (Lorino 1977). These models are no longer based only on account indicators, but they try to define economic indicators that can help managers in making strategic choices. They have to deal not only with costs and benefits, but also with risks and advantages, with performance criteria based on specific, short-term, physical tools of measure, and with heuristics.

The advantages of the ITP model

The global vision

The ITP model provides a global vision of the IT system. This implies that, at each level of refinement of each component, one can keep in mind the global representation and context of the four components.

If one is thinking of implementing new software, or buying a new model of computer, one must ask oneself if such a proposal serves the general or specific goals assigned to the relevant department or project, if the necessary skills are available among the users, if it implies a reorganization of project teams, and what kind of economic indicators should be derived to justify the investment.

Put another way, if one learns about the introduction of a new type of IT "tool" (miniaturized PDAs, interconnected multimedia, e-mail, etc.), one should ask oneself, if this tool could be used to exploit a strategic opportunity for enhancing the firm's competitiveness or reactiveness. One must also ask oneself if the appropriate staff and skills are available to form a team to carry out such a development.

However, at the same time, the ITP model shows that there is nothing to be gained in a complex refinement of the architecture, if due thought is not given to the appropriate organization (people, skills, structure, training, management issues, etc.) which is necessary for ensuring a successful implementation.

The "constructive" vision

Maintaining a mental global vision does not imply that everything has to be done at the same time. On the contrary, having defined a broad, first level description of the ITP, that is, the infrastructure requirements (the interfaces) of the architecture, an outline of requisite organization, the main goals to be met, and the rough economic indicators which should be used, one can use a "building block" strategy. Thus one can locally optimise each sub-system within the ITP on a modular basis (a sub-system can be the ITP of a department, a project, or a manufacturing plant, for example).

The "scale invariance" of the model

The "scale invariance" of the ITP model is its potential for simultaneously providing not only a broad representation of the IT systems for a firm but also representations of each of the sub-systems within, to any level of detail. This facility appears to be an important one for networking organizations. Indeed, it must be quite unlikely that one could design and develop a global IT system at one time for such loose and widespread organisations. Thus, the ITP model provides a consistent means of representing the association of the sub-systems within the system as a whole. It also allows one to focus on the interfaces which have to be precisely defined in order to give some relative autonomy to the sub-systems. This is applicable for the physical IT systems as well as for the definition of goals and sub-goals, for team and sub-team building (or projects and sub-projects), and for the definition of global economic indicators as a concatenation of local economic indicators (instead of a generalization of the detailed indicators).

Some Examples of the Use of the ITP Model for Describing Networking Firms

An increasing numb   of examples can be found in the literature of the success of networking firms. Unfortunately, the authors are often not interested in the IT architectural part of the problem. Yet it would certainly be very interesting to see to what extent the performance of these firms is based upon a suitable and reliable "hard network", or what is the effective role of organization versus architecture to achieve the strategic goals in meeting the economic requirements.

In the examples cited below, it would be interesting to do further research on specifying more accurately the ITPs and

their role in the performance of the firms.

Scattered MNCs

The scattered MNCs are probably well known examples of networking firms, because they are often recognized worldwide, and also because many people are interested in what they are doing to try to maintain their "excellence". The two examples below, ABB and Benetton have been documented in the literature.

The IT platform of Asea Brown Boveri (ABB)

[The information for this example has been taken from "The New Organization : Growing the Culture of Organizational Networking" (Hastings 1993)].

Asea Brown Boveri is a transnational corporation formed by the merger of a Swedish company in robotics and a Swiss multinational in the electrical engineering and electronic industries. It is composed of about 1,200 local companies, employing more than 200,000 people in more than 4,500 profit centres in 16 countries.

Strategy :

When carrying out the merger between the Swedish ASEA and the Swiss Brown Boveri, the chairman of ASEA and his colleagues had the will to design a new species of organization based on a radical decentralization, one which would be opera tive at both the global and local levels.

Organization :

The local interests are managed by the countrys CEOs. They ensure that, at the national level, ABB is perceived as a local company, by interfacing with local customers, government and medias, and by organizing an efficient service. The global optimization of activities is achieved through the Business Area Leaders. They plan the production of the different factories for

Fig 3 - The four components of the ITP

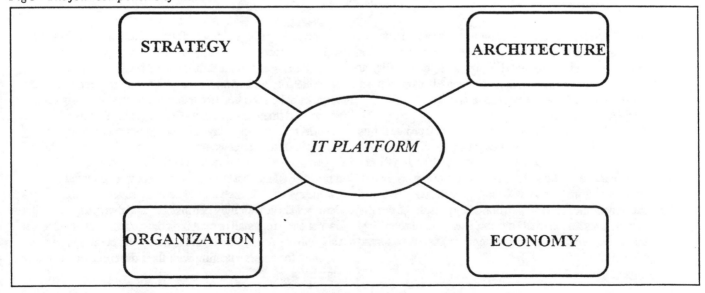

the product line within their area of responsibility. They allocate the resources (financial and human) and define the markets. There is a small number of Business Area Leaders (5 to 10), but their role is critical in ensuring the global coordination. There is only a small team of managers at the headquarters in Zurich, Switzerland. It is responsible for defining the core activities and goals of the "group strategy". They also provide an efficient communication infrastructure and have implemented a rigourous and strong centralized reporting mechanism.

Architecture :

The hard network supports electronic communications such as EDI and the reporting functions, and provides efficient low-tech communications such as fax and telephone. But the networking in ABB is mainly "soft networking", due to the role of the two cross-structures (the Business Area Leaders and Country CEOs), and is maintained through a continuous exchange of people, knowledge and experience, and what they call "overcommunication".

Economy :

It appears that, after four years, the firm has proved to be successful in its markets. The main difficulties occurred in the process itself of building the new organization and in looking for "network skills" among the managers.

The IT Platform of a "vertically de-integrated company" : BENETTON

[The information for this example has been taken from "Strategic Networks : Creating the Borderless Organization" (Carlos Jarillo 1993)].

Benetton is an Italian fashion company, focused on a youth segment which is middle income, and which has a strong fashionable self-image. It has sales of more than $2 billions in more than 6,000 shops in over 40 countries.

Strategy :

Luciano Benetton defines his company's strategy as developing "industrial fashion" with the necessary economies of scales but one which offers good design and good quality at moderate prices while maintaining an extremely close contact with its customer and a fast response to changes.

Organization :

Benetton directly employed only about 1,000 people for its $2 billions sales in 1992. "The design of garments is done outside the company by free-lance stylists.... More than 80 per cent of the manufacturing is done outside the company by 650 subcontractors (more than 10,000 employees). ...Logistics and distribution activities are also performed by outsiders... Finally the company uses an external sales organization of about 100 agents that take care of a retailing system of 6,000 shops spread over the world" (Jarillo 1993).

Architecture :

For example, Benetton uses high technology computer facilities for the design and cutting of the garments, the machines being directly linked to micro-computers with CAD-CAM software. At the other end of the chain, a sophisticated network ensures that any shop in the world can receive a "re-assort" in less than 3 days. This can only be achieved by running the firm - and its Information Systems - as a whole (this being commonly known as the "Benetton system") and having an active prescence throughout the business sytem in planning, direct coordination and unification of goals.

Economy :

Despite the great numbers of subcontractors, the production costs in Benetton factories are 20 per cent below those for other garments of a similar quality in Europe. Shop owners have no legal contracts with the company. They receive the articles directly from the central warehouses, and pay Benetton directly. A small number of agents constitute the interface between Benetton and the shop owners. They choose the new shop locations, select the new shop owners, review the new collections, help the shop owners to start up their business, manage their shops and choose the goods, etc. They don't belong to the company and are simply paid a 4 per cent commission on the value of goods shipped to the shops in their territory. But the whole system is remarkably performative. It seems that the process whereby Benetton select the agents who in turn select the shops is a critical one. Every relationship is based on an entrepreneurial spirit and trust (the same is true for the production subcontractors), so that the network is managed in the most efficient way possible for optimizing the coordination (transaction) costs of the whole system.

Extended and virtual firm

The IT platform of the value-added EDI supplier DDP
DDP is a small French company that has developed the concept of an Electronic Trade Center (ETC).

Strategy :

The concept of Electronic Data Interchange (EDI) is now well developed in in many industry sectors. In general, it consists of the electronic transmission, between a customer and a supplier, of standard messages which form the elements of the commercial transaction (for example, orders, shipping orders, acknowledgments, invoices). EDI appears to provide great benefits by reducing delays in sending transactions, by cutting the costs of transactions, and by improving the reliability of information transmission. The main barriers to the implementation of EDI are that there is no one complete standardization for the systems of exchange. There are several sectorial standards which are not fully compatible, and there may be a high cost of entry for small or medium companies. In the latter case, this will be dependent on how many different systems are required for communicating with their different customers or suppliers.

DDP feels that it can remove all these barriers by providing a complete EDI service through a value-added network. The subscribers of the networks are either suppliers of goods or services of general interest (tools, office stationery, travel agencies, hotels, etc...) or their customers, mainly rather large companies such as energy suppliers, state agencies, railroads, administrations, oil-companies, or other industrial companies.

Organization :

Suppliers' catalogues are digitalized by DDP and transmitted to potential customers who in turn send their orders through the ETC. The goods are shipped directly from supplier to customer. The shipping orders and acknowledgments are also sent through DDP's network. In the near future, if the banks of both parties are also subscribers of the ETC, the payment process will also be completely incorporated.

DDP consists of a number of salespersons devoted to finding ETC subscribers (suppliers and their customers), and a small number of high-tech specialists for maintaining and developing the hardware, software and telecommunication platform that make up the EDI server. In the medium-term, it is possible that DDP will give up the operation of the network to a Facilities Management company, thus becoming a quasi-virtual firm.

Architecture :

The hardware platform consists of a telecommunication front-end which is able to communicate with all the main public networks in Europe (from telephone to ISDN including traditional data networks and videotex), and a data processing network of workstations in a multi-server architecture. The system can be interfaced with any kind of standard computer configuration at the subscriber's office (PC, Workstation, terminal, Minitel, even a telephone).

The software platform consists of five main modules : a monitor, an EDI server (based on the European EDIFACT norm and providing the translators from other EDI standards), a server of transactions, a server of storage (to ensure the continuing reliability and traceability for transactions) and a telecom server. It also includes the provision of the subscriber's application software (client part) and all the necessary databases.

The system is open and very modular and has been developed with today's concepts of architecture, so that any new emerging technology in telecommunications or end-user workstations could be added as an interface to the system. It is also fault-tolerant and highly secured.

Economy :

Each subscribers pays an initial fee. Then the customers pays an annual fee and DDP takes a commission on every transaction from the suppliers. The first stages of the system became operational at the end of 1993. The pre-commercialisation simulations showed a rapid return on investment, for the first technical implementations.

Associated firm

The IT platform for a network of projects within a big project, the RENAULT-TWINGO car
[The information for this example has been taken from "L'auto qui n'existait pas : management des projets et transformation de l'entreprise" (Midler 1993)].

Strategy :

Since 1986, Renault has been wondering whether or not they should offer a second small car (in addition to the CLIO) to their customers. Therefore they initiated a project, named code X06, whose objective was to build a low cost but not a "cheap" car . Nobody knew if this was really feasible. Successive CEOs (this was a time when one CEO, Georges Besse, was murdered by terrorists) alternatively supported the project either very enthusiastically or not very enthusiastically at all. Finally they decided not to decide anything, and instead entered a "go no-go" process. At each project review, they decided whether they should proceed to the next stage or cancel the project altogether, depending on the ability of the teams to meet the projects goals : low costs; high quality; and an attractive design. The final decision was made in spring 1990, and the car, named TWINGO, was first commercially introduced in January 1993.

Organization :

The whole project was developed according to a strategy of integrated engineering (or concurrent engineering), i.e. the simultaneous involvement of all the actors of the different stages from the marketing to the production functions. The project was divided into a web of sub-projects, according to the different 'macro-tasks' determined by the project manager. All the sub-projects, including those involving subcontractors were physically located together in a specific place called the project platform. This project platform was first installed near the design departments, and then moved to the production plant when the project was in the last stages before production. The project platform supported all the technical, IT, and office tools and equipment which would be useful for the project's actors. It provided a comfortable communication area so that the actors could meet, exchange points of views, and solve problems.

The network of projects worked on the basis of a few management principles :

* provide the best means for communications for all the actors in the project, all the sub-projects, and between the project and the "rest of the world" ;

* decentralize the decision mechanisms vertically so that the decisions are taken as close to the field as possible ;

* encourage innovation (not only technical, but also organisational) in order to solve problems in "the best way possible for the project", that is, so that the project can meet its declared goals ;

* maintain the "memory and passion" of the project teams.

Architecture :

Renault did not emphasize the role played by IT in the success of the Twingo project. They only said that all the relevant available tools were given to the teams for optimal performance. One can probably assume that tools such as the sophisticated CAD-CAM facilities, simulators, PDM (Processing Data Managment), project management tools, integrated networks (including the connections with suppliers and sub contractors from throughout the world), robots, etc. were integrated into the project platform. Nevertheless, it would be of great interest to have further details on the actual architecture of this ITP.

The project manager said that he did not encounter technical problems as the technical tools existed and were well known. The main problems were in organizing such a large project, among the first at Renault's, and those were difficult to master.

Economy :

All the economical challenges of the project were met and even surpassed. The project manager concluded that this was a consequence of the fact that there were no formal contracts between the projects and subprojects, and few with the projects which included subcontractors. Everyone was then obliged to "do one's best", which was often better than one could have imagined before the project started.

Conclusions and Further Research

As mentioned earlier, few details about the architectural level can be found in the literature for these examples (except for DDP on which I am working personally).

Thus it would be very useful and interesting to undertake further research (or exploit research in progress) to :

* determine the key features of the ITP of networking organizations and analyse why things are working well (key success factors) or less well (explicit barriers or implicit requirements) ;

* determine the role of IT and IT personnel in the organization of the networking process ;

* determine the degree of competences in IT necessary for a networking organization. Is there a high degree of "hybridiza-tion" (i.e. competence both in a line profession and the IT domain) required for the managers of such networking organizations? It seems that people involved in personal networking have to have more "information skills" than in traditional organizations (see, for example, DEC in Hastings, 1993). What are the actual skills to be developed ?

* determine the management issues which can be derived from observing networking organization and their implication for management education.

References

Benjamin,R.I. and Blunt, J. "Critical IT Issues : The Next Ten Years", Sloan Management Review, Summer 1992, pp7-19.

Brown, J.H. and Watts, J. "Viewpoint. Enterprise Engineering : Building 21st Century Organizations", Journal of Strategic Information Systems, Vol 1 No 5 December 1992, pp243-249.

Carlos Jarillo, J. Strategic Networks : Creating the Borderless Organization, Butterworth-Heinemann, 1993

Davenport, T.H. and Eccles, R.G. "Information Politics", Sloan Management Review, Fall 1992, pp 53-65

Esnault, L : "The Networking Organization", unpublished paper 1994

Ettighoffer, D L'entreprise virtuelle ou les nouveaux modes de travail, Odile Jacob, 1992

Handy, Ch "Balancing Corporate Power : A New Federalist Paper", Harvard Business Review, Nov-Dec 1992, pp59-72

Hastings, C. The New Organization : Growing the Culture of Organizational Networking, McGraw-Hill Book Company Europe, 1993

Lorino, Ph. L'économiste et le manageur, La découverte, 1977

Midler,Ch. L'auto qui n'existait pas : management des projets et transformation de l'entreprise, InterEditions, 1993

Mintzberg, H. The Structuring of Organizations, Prentice-Hall International Editions, 1979

Nohria, N. and Eccles, R.G. Networks and Organizations : Structure, Form and Action, Harvard Business School Press, 1992

Ohmae, K The Borderless World, William Collins & Co, 1990

Senn, J.A. "Drivers of Globalization : the Intertwining of Business and IT" in Global Information Technology Education, edited by M. Khosrowpour and K.D. Loch, Idea Group Publishing, 1993

Scott Morton, M.S. The Corporation of the 1990s, Oxford University Press, 1991

Planning Efficient and Effective Data Security System

Lech J. Janczewski
Department of Management Science and
Information Systems
The University of Auckland
New Zealand

Executive Abstract

INTRODUCTION

From time to time we may witness that quite elaborate data security systems fail to prevent a hacker to penetrate an important data processing system. Careful analysis usually pinpoints flaws in the design or implementation of the system securities. These errors may have sources in the following areas:

* Flaws in the design of the system securities;
* Security investment was not completed due to a lack of financial resources;
* Lack of a proper training.

These three data security flaws are well know in the literature. However, there is another factor, which may be equally important, but which is much less recognised:

*Cumbersomeness of data security mechanisms;

The last point may be generalised by a statement that a security mechanism must not only be adequate to the protected resources but also must allow proper functioning of the facilities. Violation of this principle may lead to the deactivation of some parts of the security mechanism. The suggested methodology takes that into consideration.

PARAMETERS OF EFFECTIVE AND EFFICIENT DATA SECURITY SYSTEM

Broadly speaking, an effective and efficient data security system means a system which takes care of:

* Value of protected information;
* Existing vulnerabilities;
* Security management;
* Security economics;
* Contingency planning and insurance;
* Legal issues.

On the basis of all these factors the methodology of designing a data security systems is presented and discussed.

PHASE I - PREPARATIONS

During this phase a number of tasks are performed which will allow smooth completion of the other parts of the project. These include:

* Management decision to set up a data security planning project;
* Appointment of the project leader and formation of a task force;
*Preparation of the term of references for the task force including the preliminary time table;

*Securing financial support for the task force.

Phase I is clearly focused on the management of the enterprise: their involvement at this stage is essential as without clear top level support no effective data security system can be designed and implemented.

PHASE II - POINT OF ATTACK INVENTORY

This phase of the project is aimed at listing all the points where a particular security violation may take place. Breaching security at a particular part of an information processing system does not imply damage is limited to that part of the system. As a matter of fact the damage may happen in a place on an opposite side of the world, as it may result from the activity of a telecommunication systems.

PHASE III - THREATS INVENTORY

Inventory of threats (T) is perhaps one of the most confusing activity in the field of data security. Almost each author presents different list of such T. It seems that the following general list of threats is the best:

*Environmental problems;
*System error;
*Operator error;
*Fraud/Vandalism;
*Espionage;
* Theft.

PHASE IV - CONTROLS & SAFEGUARDS INVENTORY

This list of Control and Security Safeguards (CS), includes all data processing equipment, software, procedures, office and other equipment which may increase the security of data processing.

PHASE V - GENERATION OF DATA SECURITY MATRIX

After identification of the POAs, Is and CSs, the next step of the methodology is to place them in a matrix, where columns are labelled by Is, rows by POAs, while CSs are located in appropriate cells depending on which resources they are protecting and against which threats. From this matrix one may find out that, for instance, computer hardware at the premises is protected against unauthorised access by card operated locks and security guards.

PHASE VI - GENERATION OF RISK ASSESSMENT MATRIX

Development of the Risk Assessment Matrix is probably the most difficult and imprecise part of the described methodology. The main problem is that assessments of many risk factors will only rarely be supported by verifiable data. It is due to this fact that the procedure is applied prior to the system implementation or prior to a particular security break happening. The format of the Risk Assessment Matrix is identical with those of the Data Security Matrix.

PHASE VII - GENERATION OF COST MATRIX

Possible damages specified in the Risk Assessment Matrix may be nullified by security measures described in the Data Security Matrix. However there is a strong relationship between possible damages and measures introduced to counter them. To define that relationship the Cost Matrix is generated. The headings of this matrix are identical with those of the Data Security Matrix.

PHASE VIII - SERVICES DEGRADATION MATRIX

A practical relationship between the effectiveness of a security measure and the degradation of the quality of operation exists: The quality of a security measure is inversely proportional to the degradation of the quality of service. On the basis of this relationship a Services Degradation Matrix is generated. The headings of this matrix are identical with those of the Data Security Matrix.

There are three type of entries in this matrix.

*There are crosses in those cells which correspond to the crossed cells of the basic Data Security Matrix.

*"0"s are assigned to cells in which, in the opinion of the Delphi team, the introduced security measures do not degrade the system performance.

*All the other entries are calculated on the following basis: the time required to perform a given activity is compared to the time needed to do the same operation with the security in place. For instance, if a door lock doubles a time require to pass the door, then the degradation factor in the appropriate cell is equal to 0.5.

In case of multiple CSs located in a single cell and not interfering with each other the resulting service degradation factor is a product of the individual factors.

PHASE IX - FINAL ANALYSIS

After completion of the Base Data Security Matrix, the Risk Assessment Matrix, the Cost Matrix, and Services Degradation Matrix, the final analysis of a suggested data security system may be performed.

CONCLUSION

The described methodology is a modified and expanded version of a methodology developed by a team headed by John Beatson from the DATABANK, New Zealand. The original methodology was implemented in a number of Data Security audits (Oracle, Hong-Kong, ASB Bank and others). The modification results from suggestions made after the performing of these audits.

IT Diffusion & Socio Economic Change in Egypt

By
Sherif H. Kamel
The Cabinet of Egypt, Information & Decision Support Center
&
London School of Economics & Political Science

ABSTRACT

Although new information handling technologies have recently been widely disseminated as tools for socio-economic development, they cannot be used in the same ways as in the industrialised countries for which they were designed. Three things at leat distinguish the experience of developing countries. The first is the context of their bureaucratic, administrative, managerial and political systems and the differing expectations of users. The second is attitude towards information technology and the resources which must be used to implement ambitious systems. The third is the content of information analysis and use in developing countries, where both application areas and interpretive assumptions are likely to be radically different from the experiences of managers and administrators in industrialized countries.

This paper describes and analyses the experience of the Egyptian government in spreading the awareness of information technology and its use in managing development planning for socio-economic change. The experience has been one of building multiple information handling and decision support systems in very messy, turbulent and changing environments. The successes over the past eight years by the Cabinet in implementing and sustaining state of the art decision support systems in Egypt's governorates [local administrations] as well as for central governmental decision making holds many lessons for the implementation of sophisticated systems under conditions of extreme difficulty.

The analysis of these experiences offers insight into a variety of problems for designers, implementors and users of information and decision support systems for managing socio-economic change. This paper concludes with analytical methods and guidelines for the future implementation of similar projects in developing countries which may with to benefit from the successes of Egypt's Cabinet Information and Decision Support Center.

Introduction

Egypt's history dates back to around 5000 years BC. It is the largest country in the middle east with 60 million inhabitants sharing Arabic as the common language. The population of Egypt is growing at a rate of about 2.8 percent annually. The majority of the population is concentrated in 6 percent of the land which has a total of 1 million km2. Most of the population reside on the two banks of the river Nile which extends from the south of the country in the borders with Sudan to the north on the Mediterranean representing a length of over 1000 km. The urbanization is about 45 percent with only three large cities of over 2 million population which are Giza, Alexandria in addition to Cairo which has a total population of about 12 million.

Egypt is considered one of the developing countries. Its gross domestic product has been 35 billion US dollars in 1992. The gross domestic product has been growing for the last decade at a rate of 2-3 percent. The GDP is divided mainly among industry and agriculture where the first account for about 40 percent and the later accounts for 15 percent. Egypt has a rather low per capita income on the international scale due to the ever increasing population rate which accounts for around US$ 610. The major sources of finance of the Egyptian economy reside in four main aspects. They include: the remittances of the Egyptians working abroad mainly in the Arab countries, the tourism sector, earnings from the Suez Canal and Oil. However, Egypt faces a number of economic problems that could be characterized by a wide trade deficit that is currently estimated to be around US$ 4 billion. Moreover, Egypt has a large international debt totalling around US$ 33 billion.

The decision making process at the strategic level addresses a variety of socio-economic development issues. It is characterized by ill-structured and messy issues, interdependent, complex, multi-sectoral, and operates within a turbulent and dynamic environment. Moreover, it involves conflict resolution, crisis management and fast response. Therefore, the level of information needs for the design and development of information systems and/or decision support systems at that strategic level represents a challenge since the nature of information needs is mostly qualitative, lacks documentation, and gathered from an unlimited number of sources. This usually leads to an information overload to different decision makers. Hence, the information collected needs to be well integrated across multiple sources and should be well defined in terms of format and quality requirements that should be determined and related to the decision making process.

Decision support systems, since their inception in the 1970s, were differently defined and conceptualized by vendors, researchers as well as academicians. However, there were general guidelines and interpretations defining them as computer-based systems that help decision makers confront ill-structured problems through direct interaction with data and analysis models. The literature show that the focus of research and applications of decision support systems is to a large extent on studying the individual and organizational decision processes. Decision support systems represent a set of opportunities directed towards improving the effectiveness and productivity of managers and professionals, boosting the competitive edge, and rationalizing the decision making process within an organizational context. They aim at realizing the desire for accurate, timely and relevant information to help support various organizations to deal with an increasingly turbulent economic environment and stronger competition pressures. The focus during the last two decades at both the research and application levels was on the effect of decision support systems on the management's role of various profit-oriented organizations. These systems were mostly related to issues such as organizational planning, organizational competitive advantage and administering client's portfolios. In that respect, most of the literature on decision support systems developed during the last two decades were focusing on their uses in organizational contexts. However, much less emphasis was given to their use in socio-economic development planning issues and introducing change into to the society.

In that respect, this paper provides new grounds and research opportunities for one of the advanced techniques of information technology: decision support systems research and application through the demonstration of their use by a non-profit organization: the government of Egypt in rationalizing the decision making process, better allocating the scarce resources, and for introducing socio-economic change for development planning purposes. The focus of the paper is one of the national projects developed and implemented by the government of Egypt, Information and Decision Support Center (IDSC) and aiming at introducing and diffusing the use of state of the art information technology tools and techniques at the governorates level to realize socio-economic change and development.

The Cabinet Information & Decision Support Center (IDSC)

Egypt, faced with the classical problems of developing countries such as heavy foreign debt, balance of payment deficit, high illiteracy rate, poor technological infrastructure, lack of financial resources and unemployment has been striving to implement a nation-wide strategy to support the realization of its targeted socio-economic development program. In that respect, the government of Egypt adopted in the mid 1980s a far reaching supply-push strategy for the introduction, implementation and institutionalization of large information and decision support systems projects aiming to improve top level decision making at the Cabinet level with respect to socio-economic development planning. The strategy had to be tailor-made to the decision making needs at the Cabinet level which addresses a variety of socio-economic development issues. These issues include public sector reform, administrative reform, balance of payment deficit, debt management, and privatization. The concept of information needs and decision making at the Cabinet level was defined in terms of the following aspect; data rich and information poor, DSS/OR/MS specialists and experts were isolated from the decision makers, and the use and application of computer

systems were viewed as end means rather than information technology tools that can support in decision making. Moreover, the focus was more on technical issues rather than decision outcomes. Therefore, the urgency and criticality of the decision making level necessitated the importance of providing information and decision support services to support the decision making process through the use of the most appropriate state of the art information technology tools and techniques.

In this respect, the government of Egypt has realized the importance of establishing a comprehensive information base which can provide support for the Cabinet and top policy and decision making requirements. To achieve such a strategic objective, the Cabinet of Egypt, late in 1985 has initiated a program that was designed for the optimum goal of improving the strategic decision making process at the Cabinet level. It consisted of a number of projects namely the information and decision support systems projects. The number of projects have reached 428 projects in september 1993 covering an expansive variety of major economic, social, managerial and technological domains that are of vital importance to Egypt. Among the projects were; the debt management project, the national resources project, the education reform project, the legislation project, the international trade project and the governorates information and decision support centers project.

The objectives of the program included; the establishment of a center for information and decision support systems for the Cabinet in addition to supporting the establishment of decision support systems in different ministries, sectors and governorates and to assist in making more efficient and effective use of the available informatics resources. Therefore, the idea of the Cabinet Information & Decision Support Center (IDSC) was initiated to provide the Cabinet with both information and decision support. Thus, in 1985, the Cabinet of Egypt established the Information & Decision Support Center (IDSC). Its mission is to provide information and decision support services to the Cabinet for socio-economic development planning. The objectives of IDSC include: firstly, to develop information and decision support systems for the Cabinet and top policy makers in Egypt. Secondly, to support the establishment of decision support systems/centers in different ministries and make more efficient and effective use of the available information resources. Thirdly, to initiate, encourage and support informatics projects that could accelerate managerial and technological development of Egyptian ministries, sectors and governorates. Finally, to participate in international cooperation activities in the areas of information and decision support.

The framework of IDSC is divided into three levels. The first level represents the Cabinet base where information and decision support systems projects are developed to support the strategic policy and decision making processes in development planning. The second level represents the national nodes where IDSC links the Cabinet with existing information sources within the ministries, national organizations and agencies and academic institutions and research centers. The third level represents the international nodes where IDSC extends its activities by accessing major databases worldwide through state-of-the-art information technology and telecommunications facilities.

The role of IDSC differs according to its four operational levels; the Cabinet, sectoral, national and international. Firstly; on the cabinet level, IDSC provides information and decision support, crisis management support, modelling and analysis and multi-sectoral information and databases. Secondly; on the sectoral level, IDSC provides assistance in the development of decision support centers, advisory and consultancy, sectoral database development and project financing and support. Thirdly; on the national level, IDSC provides assistance in policy formulation and drafting, legislative reform support and in the infrastructure development. Finally; on the international level, IDSC provides the facilities for technology transfer to Egypt, the establishment of a DSS model for developing countries and it also supports establishing cooperation link and opening communication channels with international information agencies.

The areas of scope of IDSC projects covered is grouped along four dimensions which encompass the activities of IDSC; decision support systems for strategic issues, building sectoral decision support centers, information infrastructure development and management and technological development. It is within the scope of this paper to cover one of the largest projects implemented by the Cabinet IDSC within the information infrastructure development programme which is the governorates information and decision support centers project (GIDSC).

The GIDSCs Project

The interest of the strategic, executive and political power in information technology and its impacts on socio-economic development in Egypt, especially at the Cabinet level has started over a decade ago. The idea of enhancing the decision making process at the governorates level might have been there well before that date but it had only been materialized with the initiation and development of the governorates information and decision support centers project which took place during 1987 through a project implemented by the Cabinet IDSC and supported by the ministry for local administration.

The idea of improving the decision making process at the governorates level through the provision of relevant and timely data had started in 1981 when a presidential decree was officially announced which necessitated the establishment in each of Egypt's 26 governorates of a Governorate Information & Documentation Center (GIDC). The role of the GIDCs was mainly the collection of data from different sources in the governorate which includes the local administration offices i.e the representatives of the central ministries. This period lasted from 1981 until mid 1987 and was characterized by the lack of systematic steps and procedures and where each local administration office staff strongly rejected the dissemination of data as their source of power. Thus, the role of the GIDCs

was minimal in terms of development planning. In that respect, the role of the GIDCs was insignificant and of minimal value to the governorates development programs as well as to the decision making process at the governorates level. Moreover, in various occasions the data flow from different local administration offices lacked smoothness, relevancy, timeliness and accuracy. Moreover, the GIDCs did not provide any support in upgrading and enhancing the follow-up and evaluation mechanisms within the governorates nor they introduced change to the administrative systems as it was planned as being one of the main activities of the GIDCs. On the contrary, some of the GIDCs became the resort to some of the governorates' employees that were known for being unproductive and worthless in other central and local government agencies. Hence, they were transferred to these newly emerging GIDCs since their role was visioned as of having secondary significance even at the governorates level. In that respect, one could see that not only the GIDCs did not produce the desired objectives but moreover, they were not given the chance to realize their targeted goals and fulfil their mandated obligations since the staff of the GIDCs were not trained or had the knowledge and/or experience of handling various types of data to be provided to the decision makers at the right time and in the right way to use them in their decision making processes. The failing role of the GIDCs and the need for managerial, administrative and technological development at the local level, in addition to the need to make better use of the available resources mainly information aiming at the rationalization of the decision making process necessitated the move towards a better solution and a concrete action.

Therefore, in April 1987, the ministry of local administration in cooperation with the Cabinet IDSC have initiated the idea of an informatics project namely the Governorates Information & Decision Support Centers (GIDSCs). The mission of the project was to develop information and decision support systems focusing on socio-economic high priority issues at the governorates level. The aim of which was to introduce socio-economic change using state of the art information technology. One major characteristic of the project was that it was the first time in Egypt that an information technology project would be implemented outside Cairo: the capital. The changing focus from Cairo to the rest of the country through the introduction of information technology tools and techniques within the 26 governorates and the use of computer technology in local governorates where some of them are rural and others are urban have presented a large and significant set of challenges to the Cabinet IDSC in the implementation of the project. These challenges were formulated due to managerial, administrative, technological and cultural aspects.

The planned intention of the project and the initial plan was to start with the Governorates Information & Documentation Centers (GIDCs). This was done to avoid any duplication in the efforts that were already exerted, although minimal, during the implementation of the GIDCs. The aim was to support the GIDSCs in performing their leading role in providing information and effective decision support services besides providing support in the follow-up and evaluation of the impacts of such information/decision support services at the governorates level. The project is financed jointly between the ministry of local administration through the Cabinet IDSC and the 26 governorates. The planned time-schedule of the project was four years from 1988 until 1992 to be able to cover all of Egypt's 26 governorates through a phased implementation plan that started with a pilot project in June 1988 with one governorate, Suez. After the full implementation of the first phase and the establishment of the Suez GIDSC, the second phase was launched with the establishment of 6 GIDSCs. Next, the third phase started with a massive and parallel establishment of 20 GIDSCs to cover all remaining governorates and the city of Luxor GIDSC.

Objectives

The objectives of the GIDSCs project aim for socio-economic development that falls within the scope of the governorates level in Egypt. These objectives include:

· To contribute in enhancing and improving the effectiveness of administrative development at the regional level through the development of information and decision support systems to support the decision making process at the top policy and managerial levels in the governorates.
· To upgrade the level of services and increase both the level and value of production at the regional level through the provision of information and decision support systems capable to rationalise decisions at the governorates level together with the related local administrative departments.
· To contribute in diminishing the pressure off the constituency and decrease the waste from the different production and service operations at the regional level through the provision of effective systems to follow-up, control, evaluate and determine decision making indicators.
· To provide socio-economic information related to both products and services in the different governorates for the purpose of building a national information system based in the Cabinet IDSC and linked through a governorates-wide information network linking all GIDSCs. From the above mentioned objectives, we could conclude that the overall objective of the GIDSCs project is to try, backed by and through the efforts of the GIDSCs staff in various governorates, to support the establishment and the development of the governorates information and decision support systems in the different governorates aiming at introducing socio-economic change.

Framework

The framework of the GIDSCs project is divided into three major parts according to both its geographical and sectoral dimensions. The geographical framework of the project covers all of Egypt's 26 governorates and the city of Luxor. The coverage of the governorates include all the cities, areas, villages and districts with a focus on the economic, social and political priority issues to the governor at the local level and to the Cabinet at the national level. The sectoral framework of the project represents the major sectors in the economy that are determined by the Cabinet IDSC and included in the GIDSCs project document. These sectors represent the major sectors in the comprehensive sectoral information system that is designed and developed by the Cabinet IDSC and located in each GIDSC. The framework of operations includes all laws and decrees that guarantee the effective, efficient and timely flow of information into the GIDSCs from different data sources within the governorate's boundaries as well as from outside agencies and organizations both regionally and centrally.

Moreover, the data items in the different sectors are selected and built according to a priority list which defines the level of data types which at the same time defines the depth and the level of comprehensiveness of such data. In that respect, a time plan and an agenda for the steps and procedures is usually determined by the governor for data collection and data updating. The time and contents of each sector in each governorate might be slightly different than in other governorates depending on the needs of the governor and the type of data being updated. One should note that the changes in the sectoral information system from one governorate to the other is minimal which was intended to provide macro level indicators at the national level based on the aggregation of the data produced from the 27 GIDSCs. In that respect and following the framework of responsibilities, the relationship between the Cabinet IDSC and the GIDSCs passed through two major phases. The first phase included setting the plan for development, its implementation and ended with the inauguration of the GIDSCs. This phase was highly characterised by in-depth cooperation and support by the Cabinet IDSC as an implementing and executing agency through a time plan and fixed agreements between the Cabinet IDSC and each GIDSC. The second phase included the post-implementation phase of the GIDSCs which was characterised by extensive cooperation and support by the Cabinet IDSC to the GIDSCs through periodical assessment and evaluation of performance and monthly field visits according to a planned schedule to get the feedback from the GIDSCs staff as well as the GIDSCs users.

Duties & Responsibilities

The framework of cooperation and the support provided by the Cabinet IDSC to the different GIDSCs could be illustrated as follows:

· The provision of technical and practical expertise presented to the governorates to transform and develop the GIDCs to become GIDSCs.
· The provision of information technology tools and techniques that guarantee the provision of an effective information and decision support services to decision makers at the governorates level.
· The provision of documented systems for gathering and controlling the channels of data from various sources to ensure their proper flow into the GIDSC.
· The design and production of application programs which represent the governorates' information system installed

in the GIDSCs.

· The planning, financing and implementation of training and human resource development programs for the GIDSCs staff as well as information officers in the governorate's offices and departments.

· The provision of the technical infrastructure from hardware and software needed to establish the GIDSC.

· The transfer and dissemination of expertise gained from the application of various informatics projects in an attempt to draw generalizations and learn from the experiences occurring in similar projects.

Development phases

The development of the GIDSCs project given the limited financial and technical resources necessitated a phased development and implementation approach. Thus, the development of the project passed through a set of phases in the design and development of its different applications and through the development of prototypes. The sectoral database was easy to develop due to the similarity of the basic needs across the different governorates. One of the major characteristics of the sectoral database is that it is developed in a transferable/ portable manner so that what applies on one governorate would apply to the others. The sectoral database programs and applications were developed through a phased development plan using the technical and managerial expertise of the Information Resource Management department in the Cabinet IDSC.

The design and development of the systems applications took a period of nine months including the testing and the analysis of the users needs through continuous interaction with the users and the development and alteration of the programs and applications based on their needs. The first phase included seven applications: housing and construction, health, agriculture and irrigation, infrastructure, youth and sports, labor and tourism. The second phase included two applications: industry and education and it lasted for three months. The third phase included four applications: administration and organization, internal supply, population and social insurance. The data sources in the governorates included the departments of the governorate's general administration, the specialized technical and experts departments and offices affiliated with the governorate's general administration in addition to the local administration offices that exist on different levels in the governorates such as the areas, cities and the villages.

Although in each GIDSC the sectoral database includes the data related to the governorate only, the comprehensive database available in the Cabinet IDSC covers the aggregated model of all 27 GIDSCs. The aim of which is to support the Cabinet on national socio-economic issues and priorities at the national level. This represents in a sense the ultimate objective of the project which is to develop national socio-economic indicators. For example, the data developed regarding the local administration for education in each governorate represents the level of data available in the GIDSC which, gathered together with other governorates, would produce indicators for the ministry of education at the national level which represents the level of data available in the Cabinet IDSC. Thus, the comprehensive sectoral database was designed to fit both the national domain and the local domain baring in mind the importance of keeping standardization and systemization of the different components and the logical structure of the sectoral database along the 27 GIDSCs to serve two purposes. Firstly, to be able to develop local indicators as a first step to develop nation-wide indicators related to the various important issues to the society to be able to serve higher policy making levels such as the ministers and the Cabinet in the national planning programs. Secondly, to work as a first step in the formulation of a nation-wide information-base network linking all the GIDSC databases together having as a main-hub the Cabinet IDSC.

The flow of data through the development of the GIDSC takes three modules. The first data flow takes place from different data sources and local administration offices and ends at the statistics unit in the GIDSC. The second data flow takes place within the GIDSC itself between its internal units (the statistics, decision support, computer resource, publications and documentation & library units) and the Cabinet IDSC. The third data flow takes place after the analysis, processing and formulation of decision support cases between the GIDSCs and the different users. In the first data flow, the data collection process begins at the local administration offices then it is transferred into the information units newly installed in the governorate's general administration. These information units have direct access to the GIDSCs and act as feeding units to the GIDSC's statistics unit. Moreover, these information units have direct access and links with the ministry's information systems and they also feed them with data. The data is then transferred from each ministry's information system into the different departments of that ministry and to the ministry for local administration. The ministry for local administration is fed with the data for the purpose of updating its governorates-wide indicators regarding each sector. As for the ministries, each ministry is updated for the purpose of updating its files and records regarding the related issue. Finally, each ministry feeds the Cabinet IDSC with the newest updates regarding its related issues.

The second data flow takes place within the GIDSCs where data after being collected from the different data sources through the statistics unit is cross-checked and verified with various sources such as the local administration offices and the ministry in concern at the central level. The next step within the GIDSC is that data are transferred to the computer resources unit where the data is entered into the GIDSC sectoral database and the updating of the governorates system is done. Upon requests coming into the GIDSC data is transferred to the decision support unit for the analysis, issue formulation and problems identification in addition to the development of alternatives and solutions regarding the issues in hand. Finally, the last step in the data flow within the GIDSC is that upon the completion of a certain information and/or a decision support case, a copy of the final report is kept in the library and documentation unit for future reference. Moreover, another copy of the report goes in the form of a case to be published in the monthly newsletter to be distributed among other GIDSCs which is produced by the publications unit.

The third data flow occurs post to the GIDSC phase which takes the information after its processing and feeds it into the ministry for local administration comprehensive database which is working as the main-hub for the governorates-wide information-base network covering the 27 GIDSCs. Next, the ministry for local administration feeds the Cabinet IDSC with information for its use in supporting the Cabinet and top policy makers in their decision making processes.

The GIDSC Project Implementation phases

The GIDSC project followed a phased implementation approach which was developed including four major phases: initiation, base building, institutionalization and sustained growth phases.

The initiation phase

In the initiation phase, the project team spent nine months in 1987 and early 1988 studying the decision making environment in the 26 governorates in details, evaluating and assessing the available resources and opportunities for the establishment of the GIDSCs. The Suez governorate located in the Canal region was selected for the establishment of the first GIDSC which would be the pilot project. There were defined successful criteria for the selection of the Suez governorate which was selected due to the following reasons:

· The governor had expressed strong interest and belief in the use of information technology and decision support in introducing socio-economic change and development planning in the governorates level.

· Suez comprises a mix of rural and urban populations which would provide the project team with a variety of experiences from various fields.

· Suez is close to Cairo which made it easier to get access to the GIDSC for maintenance and follow-up in both the implementation and institutionalization phases. Moreover, it provided more opportunities for the staff to get them trained in the Cabinet IDSC and to live the experience in its different departments.

· Suez is considered one of the strategic governorates both economically and politically; hence, the model of the Suez governorate serves the need in defining the role of the GIDSC.

Strategies

The strategies implemented during the initiation phase are characterized as being mainly dependent on a supply-push strategy. The use of information technology and computers was almost non-existent in local administration in Egypt. The bulk of information technology is concentrated in Egypt in the governorates of Cairo, Giza and Alexandria. It was very

difficult for the constituency in the local governorates to identify the needs and requirements from information technology while their comprehension of the whole technology environment was merely minimal. The awareness of the benefits and outcomes of the use of information and computer technology on the socio-economic development programs in the governorates level was also minimal or even non-existent. Following this illiterate and opposing constituency by nature due to the resistance to change and fear of losing jobs to automated machines, the Cabinet IDSC had to implement a supply-push strategy through the establishment of the GIDSC and actively show its uses with its information and decision support systems in high priority issues related to the governorates development programs and to show the GIDSC's actual impact on the decision making process and the better allocation and use of the scarce resources. During the initiation phase the sectoral database along with its different applications and programs could be characterized as of having a portability character. This portability aspect was due to the transfer of the system from one GIDSC to the others to develop standardization. This is because the information system in Suez comprised the sectors of population, industry and education and while the GIDSC collected data from local sources covering the education sector, the project team collected data from the local sources covering the population and the industry sector which represented the division of data collection in this phase.

The organizational structure and the internal steps and procedures of the GIDSC in that phase were prototyped and still evolving. Therefore, the specifications of the GIDSC units and the clear defined steps, procedures and services especially those of the decision support and publication units were evolving and under amendments and changes according to the needs of the various users. Moreover, the GIDSC's information system was prototyped including the GIDSC's database applications, framework, structure, and outputs. The prototype developed and used in the governorate of Suez in the initiation phase became the model for future implementation in the next phases in the establishment of the other GIDSCs. It is very important to note that the prototype of the GIDSC information system, the amendments and the changes in the organizational structure, steps and procedures and the success of demonstrating the experience of the Suez GIDSC had a positive impact in the future development and implementation of other GIDSCs.

Therefore, the project team was under severe pressure by the Cabinet IDSC management levels to quickly demonstrate the benefits of the use of information technology in the Suez GIDSC in attempt to do the following:

· To prove to the governor of Suez that his initial trust and belief in information technology was worth the time and effort invested which was very important because the conviction of the governor was essential for guaranteeing his continuous support.

· To set the example for other governorates to proceed with implementing the GIDSC project in other governorates.

· To meet the pressure of the Cabinet IDSC's top management considering that the GIDSCs project is one of the largest and most important information and decision support systems projects implemented by the Cabinet IDSC.

To overcome these issues, the project team developed model reports that had the fastest and strongest impacts on the governor and that encouraged him to continuously support the GIDSC. These reports usually covered very important and sensitive sectors to the constituency such as education and health. Moreover, the project team tried to bridge the technological gap and to impress the governor by the least and simplest hardware such as stand-alone personal computers, standard and user friendly software applications such as database and spreadsheet packages that are easy to be taught and used. The inauguration of the GIDSC in the governorate of Suez represented the marketing and the promotion of the organization as well as the organizational visibility at the local, regional and national levels. In that respect, and as a strategy set by the project team which was inspired from other projects developed and implemented by the Cabinet IDSC, the project team adopted a strategy were the inauguration of the GIDSC was organized to become a local event where all major organizations, agencies and authorities attend it. The inauguration of the GIDSC was presented as a highly supportive tool to its beneficiaries which included, the governor, the secretary general of the governorate, the councils and the business sector in the governorate. Moreover, the inauguration of the Suez GIDSC was attended by the prime minister and a number of ministers such as the minister for local administration and other key positions. This has given the inauguration both the social and political weight in addition to the proper mass-media and promotion needed to promote its objectives and diffuse its awareness. The organization of the inauguration of the GIDSC led to an excellent marketing and public relations opportunity. Moreover, it led to the feeling among the constituency that there could be an organization in the governorate that is close and supportive to them as individuals. The event also led to drawing the public attention to the GIDSCs' activities and rendered their existence legitimate which led to the formulation of a constituency at the local level that represented the users of the GIDSC.

Impacts

The impacts of the Suez GIDSC were felt even before its inauguration which took place in June 1988. It represented a significant take-off phase of the GIDSCs project since it was the first breed of a whole year of initiation, planning, design, development, prototyping and implementation. The experience was to be witnessed through the decision making process which differed dramatically in comparison with the previous approach used in the collection of data and its representation upon request to the governor by the GIDC. The change induced by the GIDSC relative to the GIDC affected the basic and grounded ingredients such as the mechanisms and structure for data collection, analysis and information dissemina-

tion within the GIDSC and the GIDSC's continuous interaction with its different users. Through the GIDSC, the statistics unit began to systematically collect data from various local administration offices through following the structured steps and procedures defined by the GIDSCs project document. The role of the statistics unit, through gathering the data from various sources had its direct and positive effect which was felt at the governor level in the sense that nowadays the governor deals with one entity which is the GIDSC for information access instead of dealing with up to 30 local administration offices prior to the implementation of the GIDSCs project. Moreover, the library and documentation unit through the collection of reports and studies related to the governorate's issues and socio-economic development needs served as an institutional memory and at the same time minimized the duplication of time, effort and cost when conducting new studies. There were a number of challenges faced by the project team during the initiation phase which included:

· The definition and representation of outputs in the form that would trigger the interest of the governor in order to encourage him to use the GIDSC services.
· The definition of the areas of focus of the GIDSC which should be inspired by two major aspects: the issues of interest to the governor and the issues of interest to the constituency which were developed in a way to tackle major sectors such as education, health and infrastructure.
· The definition and design of information systems was one of the concerns of the project team in the sense of knowing how to develop easy and user friendly systems that would trigger the interest of the users as well as to deliver the objectives of such information systems.
· The ability to obtain data from different sources within the governorate of Suez was originally dealt with through personal interactions. However, nowadays there is a set of steps and procedures that are developed to systemize the access to data that would be used in the services provided by the GIDSC.
· The access to the governor and the governorate's offices was easy in the case of the governorate of Suez. However, for the future implementation of other GIDSCs, there was a clear need to develop a proper interaction with the governors to be able to approach them and convince them with the idea of the GIDSC.
· The selection of the GIDSC director and how to understand the mission of the GIDSC and transmit it to his staff and being able to meet the requests of the governor.
· The definition of the proper organizational structure of the GIDSC was dealt with through the implementation of the organizational structure developed by the project team.
· The definition of the GIDSC human and technical infrastructure and how to select the proper human resources qualified to meet the needs and the objectives of the GIDSC.

The Base building

The second phase represented the model building phase which began immediately after the success that occurred with the inauguration of the Suez GIDSC. The phase began during early 1989 with the construction and establishment of 6 GIDSCs. These GIDSCs were in the governorates of Sharkeya, Port-Said, South Sinai, North Sinai, Ismailia and Red Sea. They were all selected because they shared the social, political and economical problems and issues. The implementation of the base building phase changed from the one that occurred during the initiation phase which was attributed to the following:

· The governorates are now aware of the GIDSCs project and are anxious and keen to follow the experiences that has proved to be successful and promising through the implementation of the Suez GIDSC.

· Within the project team, the staff became more aware of the methods and techniques to use while dealing with the staff at the governorates level which has led to the changing vision across time.

· The structure of the project team was changed by adding the concept of the account executives whose main job is to conduct periodical visits to the GIDSCs, meet the requirements of the staff.

· The inclusion of additional and more advanced courses.

· The concept a refreshment program was introduced that represents a continuation of the training program and aims at continuously update the GIDSC staff with the latest advances in information technology.

· The initiation of a prize presented to the best achievements in the courses in the form of a monetary reward.

· The design of the sectoral database, windows and menus of options in addition to the depth of data included were changed to introduce more simplicity to the uses of the system.

Strategies

The strategies implemented were mostly the same as in the initiation phase in addition to a number of new strategies that were introduced in the base building phase. The new strategies were developed and drawn from the experiences and lessons learnt from the initiation phase. The emerging strategies of the base building phase included the increasing interest and investment both in time and effort in training and human resource development and the priority given to these programs in shaping the skills and knowledge of the GIDSC staff besides improving the quality of the performance of the GIDSC staff. The strategies implemented affected the quantity and quality of the training and human resource development programs in terms of training hours in addition to the depth and level of the programs given which passed the level of simple applications related to the computer usage to advanced courses in statistical analysis, systems analysis and design and courses in information systems management. The systems implemented and prototyped in the governorate of Suez were amended after the experiences witnessed in the

application of different information and decision support cases and the observations made explicit by the project team and the needs that were developed and requested from the GIDSCs staff. This process of learning from the experience of the Suez GIDSC and the transfer of these lessons to the implementation of the project in the following GIDSCs led to the development of version #2 of the GIDSC's software application. The new version not only included changes in the design of the databases themselves but also it witnessed the expansion both vertically and horizontally in the size and scope of these databases which was possible since the project management team from the inception of the project and since the initial design and development phases of the governorates systems have put into account both levels of development since there was a general feeling among the project team that if the project proves to be successful additional sectors will be added.

The expansion in the databases were tailor-made to the application environment i.e. to the governorates. Example of which is the case of the governor of Sharkeya, later on minister for local administration and the Cabinet member responsible for the GIDSC project. He is originally a surgeon; hence, he had requested from the GIDSC of the governorate and through his personal relationship with the GIDSC project manager as well as his close friendship with the Cabinet IDSC Chairman of the board to focus and expand the details in the database that concern and are related to the health sector. In that respect, the level of details in the health sector database were expanded much more than in other GIDSC's systems. Later on and through learning from other GIDSC's experience exchange program developed and encouraged by the Cabinet IDSC, other previously established GIDSCs were required to add the new additions on the health application.

The expansion strategy has touched not only the magnitude and level of the GIDSCs system but also the scope of users of the GIDSCs. The strategy used for promoting the existing operation, uses and benefits of the GIDSC which represented the organizational visibility was increased during the base building phase and the result of the strategy was more awareness of the GIDSC as a concept which was seen and felt in all governorates. This was achieved through the formulation of local and regional seminars covering various issues related to the GIDSC's scope, role, activities and plans for the future. The level of the presentation was also expanded at the governorates level to include other public and private entities interested in the activities of the GIDSCs. With the expansion of the number of GIDSCs inaugurated, the project team had to develop a strategy to monitor and control the activities, performance and outcomes of the GIDSCs. In that respect, the concept of account executives inspired from the marketing and advertising fields was used through the development of periodical and upon request visits on a monthly basis to the GIDSCs to assess their performance and to maintain the systems, answer the requests and inquiries of the GIDSCs staff.

Impacts

By the end of 1989, the new 6 GIDSCs in addition to the Suez GIDSC established in the initial phase were intact. This represented 26% of the total scope of the GIDSC project. Yet, it could be seen that the phase to which the GIDSCs project have reached through the systematic collection of data could be easily defined as being accurate, timely and efficient. However, this did not yet show the shift to the ultimate and strategic goal of providing information that is analyzed, prepared and presented in a manner that could be positively used in the decision making process of the governor. This could be due to factors such as:

· The inability of the GIDSCs staff to provide such a service probably due to the lack or inadequacy of the training and human resource development required. Or that the experience and culture of information and decision support was new at the governorates level.

· The lack of comprehensiveness of most of the key decision makers in the governorates i.e. the governors, to the uses of information technology in the decision making process and how to depend on the output of a machine as an input to their decisions.

The second phase, the base building phase, witnessed the fall of the success previously achieved by the first phase i.e. the pilot GIDSC in the governorate of Suez. The continuous inflow and information support provided by the Suez GIDSC was provided but at the same time the deep analysis of information and the problems faced by the governorates were not properly met due to the capabilities available in the GIDSC. The change in the success story of the Suez GIDSC was due to the change of the governor of Suez into a governor who was not interested in the idea of the project which had its negative and drastic impacts on the concept, image and the performance of the GIDSC. The GIDSC due to not being on the priority list of the governor led to a change in the user definition of the GIDSC. Thus, the focus was switched to other priorities rather than using the GIDSC in development and in rationalizing the decision making process.

Institutionalization/Diffusion

The third phase leads us to the confusion of choosing a title for whether it is diffusion, expansion and/or institutionalization. The actual definition of the phase includes the three components. During the third phase the remaining governors were jealous and eager to establish their own GIDSCs after the remarkable, although initial and growing, success of the already established GIDSCs. The chairman of the board of the Cabinet IDSC with the consultation of the project team developed a plan to expand the project on a parallel strategy to inaugurate the remaining 20 GIDSCs including the city of Luxor. The strategy was backed and advocated by the minister for local administration, previously the governor of Sharkeya. The plan was set to establish 20 GIDSCs within 1 year.

Strategies

The strategies that were implemented during the institutionalization/diffusion phase included in addition to the already carried out strategies from both the first and the second phases. Some of them were amended according to the prevailing circumstances and needs and some were newly developed to meet the expanding establishment of the 20 GIDSCs remaining. Among these strategies were the better selection and staffing of the GIDSCs where a newly developed decree necessitated a minimum level of both managerial and technical skills that was set for the recruitment of the GIDSC staff. Another strategy that was implemented was the extensive training and human resource development programs that were developed and enforced both by the project team at the Cabinet IDSC and also by the governors themselves. Moreover, the training programs included for the first time courses for the pre-selection of the staff in addition to the continuous programs that were presented to the GIDSCs staff as part of their job and represented on the job training. The reason behind this was to try, through the human resources available which represent the most precious resource available, to reach the level of efficiency and effectiveness of use of the GIDSCs capabilities and produce the quality outcomes, planned, targeted and required. The capacity building programs; thus, were much more advocated and encouraged. Therefore, the plan was intensified by the project team in coordination with the Cabinet IDSC training and human resource development experts. The program was added to the Dbase 3+, spreadsheet, word processors, in addition to the advanced programs and applications in software development. This included rapid application development and advanced 4th generation languages generation in addition to newly developed courses in management functions and selected topics in sociology, economics and environments. Moreover, there were courses in systems analysis and design and skills development. But at the same time, the decision support domain was not yet emphasized. There was no theoretical background that was provided which had to do mainly with cultural problems which faced the Cabinet IDSC in many of its informatics projects throughout the country.

Another strategy implemented by the project team is the cross-fertilization that was taking place through the organization of brainstorming sessions between the GIDSCs staff. The documentation of the cases applied and the sharing of the decision support cases implemented were among the main characteristics of this phase. The presentation of remarkable as well as failure cases is organized so as to diffuse the experience of the GIDSCs and both the success and failure reasons through the formulation of seminars and workshops on an annual basis to be attended by the GIDSCs staff and the experts from the Cabinet IDSC together with information systems analysts and experts from various Egyptian universities. The sharing of some applications developed across more than one governorate with the support of the Cabinet IDSC also led to the innovation, development and exchange of ideas across different GIDSCs. Finally, one of the very successful strategies that was developed in this phase and that had enormous impacts on the GIDSCs staff and performance was the development of incentives from the Cabinet IDSC to the GIDSCs staff other than the incentives presented from the governorate itself. The fact that the salaries of the government staff is low and therefore the GIDSCs staff used to be paid low rates led them to look for other jobs after their working hours in the GIDSCs which extends from 09:00 a.m. until 02:30. This has proven during the first and second phase that it leads to the lack of concentration of the GIDSCs staff in their quality of work developed and produced. This represented a barrier to the governors because even at the government regulations level, the law ensured a low ceiling on the bonuses paid by the governor to his employees. Thus, the project team at the Cabinet IDSC developed an incentives scheme to increase the GIDSCs staff salaries and to enhance their motivation.

The incentives were presented on a set of conditions that could be categorized either according to the best performance by the GIDSC and/or by the production of the best newsletter per month. In that respect, the best newsletter every month was presented an award in addition to the publications unit staff were presented with monetary motivations. On the other hand, the GIDSC based on their performance and presentation of reports covering decision support cases were presented with monetary incentives based upon their monthly performance. Finally, the best performance and grades in the training and human resource development programs were presented with extra monetary incentives.

Impacts

The impacts of the third phase which witnessed the inauguration of the remaining 20 GIDSCs was greatly felt throughout the country. By the end of this phase, a whole stage of the GIDSC project was completed. This phase also witnessed the inclusion of three additional sectoral databases. Moreover, the support presented by each governor was easier to obtain due to the fact of the establishment of the GIDSCs in all governorates which created a kind of competition among the governors. Therefore, each governor wanted that his own GIDSC would perform better than the others. The impacts of this phase were more concentrated on the development of the human resources through the training and human resource development programs. This phase showed the need of the project team at the Cabinet IDSC to develop the skills and capabilities of the GIDSCs in various related aspects. In that respect, a more thorough institutionalization plan needed to be developed in order to develop the GIDSC in a way to serve the community at the local level as it was planned and designed but unfortunately the implementation did not deliver the expected outcomes.

Sustained growth

The focus in the fourth phase was the sustainability of the growth, development and institutionalization of the GIDSCs. This included more focusing on the training and development of the human resources, better formulation of links and connections with the various data sources, agencies and local administrations office at the local level. Moreover, it included boosting the morale of the GIDSC staff, try to build career path development for each and every position in the GIDSC and finally ensuring the diffusion of the GIDSC's services across the different users in the governorate.

Strategies

The strategies of the fourth phase included a number of newly developed concepts that are described as follows. The formal establishment of the concept of the account executives where five account executives were assigned from the Cabinet IDSC to work in the project in order to establish monthly visits to the different governorates to inspect the databases for data verification, regular updating, assure the quality of the reports and ensure the efficiency and the effectiveness of both information and decision support services. Moreover, the account executives are responsible for visiting the GIDSCs whenever required by the GIDSC staff. The stress on the monetary motivation was more emphasized during the fourth phase especially regarding the production of the newsletter, the quality of the contents of the databases and the issues analyzed and formulated in the GIDSCs which has led the Cabinet IDSC to give awards in cash every month for the best performing five GIDSCs. To market the services of the GIDSC and to diffuse its technology among the constituency in the governorates and to increase the number of users of the GIDSCs especially among the business sector, the production of the monthly newsletter and the control and the assessment of the contents of the newsletter was clearly emphasized as one of the basic marketing tools to be used in the institutionalization of the GIDSCs within the governorate and to spread the knowledge of its services.

Managing institutionalization and the strategy implemented regarding this issue was inspired from the experiences learnt from the implementation of other information technology projects in Egypt developed and implemented by the Cabinet IDSC. The institutionalization process is managed beyond the development and implementation of the GIDSCs in the sense that it includes information technology transfer, adaptation, diffusion, adoption, value assessment and evaluation in addition to the continuous monitoring, tracking and implementation of state of the art technologies. In other words, it includes:

- The cultural interface represented the adaptation aspect of the society and the implementation of decision support systems to meet the context needs. Adaptation dealt with various modifications to fit both contextual and cultural characteristics of the environment. Thus, the cultural interface was designed and implemented in Arabic which entailed training of users, managing the users learning process and teaching users modelling capabilities.
- The organizational interface represented the diffusion of information technology knowledge within the society and the overcoming of the resistance to change. Diffusion dealt with spreading the use of decision support systems at

various organizational levels which could be measured by the frequency of use of effective decision support systems.

· The user interface represented the adoption of users and the use of the decision support tools and techniques in the decision making process. Adoption dealt with the personalized use of decision support tools by managers and decision makers and by the support staff which led to customized systems according to users needs.

· The evaluation and assessment of the impacts of decision support systems dealt with evaluation and assessment of utilization, identification of operational problems and measurement of value added benefits to strategic decision making. It involved the assessment of the impact of decision support systems, technical evaluation, analysis of risks and costs incurred, documentation and maintenance.

· The monitoring and tracking dealt with the parameters of critical issues, assumptions, priorities, data and information in addition to the changes in information technology and their impacts on decision support.

· Value assessment dealt with how decision support systems have greatly improved strategic decision making in Egypt and both the values and benefits that could be demonstrated in terms of tangible and intangible efforts.

Impacts

The impacts of the fourth phase were felt during the first quarter of 1992. This was developed due to the fact that in this period each governorate was ready to present a description of the socio-economic development status and what needs to be done in the future to improve the current plans in addition to the proposition of projects and development activities that needs to be done and that are not currently under consideration. The challenges of the fourth phase included the following:

· The management of the institutionalization of the 27 GIDSCs.

· The monitoring of their outputs and the justification of their existence and their expenses to the Cabinet through the positive and concrete outputs presented by the GIDSC in the socio-economic development activities.

The clear impact of the phase was the organization of the first national conference for the GIDSCs namely "local administration in the information age" which was attended also by the prime minister, the concerned ministers, the governors and experts from various related fields. The organization and the attendance of this massive policy and decision makers representing the first and second executive bodies of the country represented a positive and nation-wide approval of the role of the GIDSCs at the governorates level in boosting the socio-economic development programs and in rationalizing the decision making process.

In summary, the experience of such new form of information-based organization in Egypt i.e. the GIDSCs and the implementation of sectoral information and decision support systems led to the rationalization of the decision making process at the governorates level and supported in the socio-economic change and development programs. The new opportunities developed from the use of decision support systems in such an environment have increasingly contributed to the conviction of the top level policy making level in Egypt on the advantages of the use of various information technology tools and techniques in socio-economic change and development purposes.

References

Davis, G.B., "Strategies for information requirements determination"., *IBM Systems Journal* 21 (1) 1982.

El-Sherif, H., "Managing institutionalization of strategic decision support for the Egyptian Cabinet", *Interfaces*, 20,1, January-February 1990.

El-Sherif, H., "Managing large information & decision support systems projects", *IFORS*, 1988.

El-Sherif, H. and El-Sawy, O., "Issue-based decision support systems for the Cabinet of Egypt", *MIS Quarterly*, 12, December 1988.

Handy, C., "On Cultures and Structures", Understanding organizations, London 1992.

Hirschheim, R and Klein, H.K., "Four paradigms of information systems development.", *Communications of the ACM* 32, October 1989.

Katz, R.L., "Explaining information sector growth in developing countries", *Telecommunications Policy*, September 1986.

Keen, Peter G. and Scott Morton, Michael S. 1978, Decision Support Systems: An organizational perspective, Addison-Wesley Publishing Company, Inc., Philippines.

Liebenau, J and Backhouse, J., "The primacy of social organization", Understanding Information, London, 1990.

Harindranath, G and Liebenau, J., (eds) "Information technology policies and applications in the commonwealth developing countries", London 1993.

Markus M.L. and Robey, D., "Information technology and organizational change: causal structure theory and research", *Management Science* 34 (2) 1988.

Mintzberg, H., and Waters, J., "Deliberate and emergent IS strategies" *Strategic Management Journal*, (6:3), 1985.

Olson, M.H., "New information technology and organizational culture", *MIS Quarterly*, 6 (1982).

Robey, D., "Implementation and the organizational impacts of information systems", *Interfaces*, Vol 17, No. 3, May-June 1987.

Sprague, Ralph H. Jr and Watson, Hugh J., Decision Support Systems: Putting theory into practice, Prentice-Hall, New Jersey, 1986.

Whisler, T. L, The impacts of computers on organizations, Praeger Publishers, New York, 1970.

Biography of author

Sherif H. Kamel

Sherif H. Kamel is the head of the Regional Information Technology Institute (RITI) at the Regional Information Technology & Software Engineering Center (RITSEC). Also, he is currently part-time employed at the Cabinet Information & Decision Support Center (IDSC) in its international cooperation department. He is a Ph.D research student at the London School of Economics and Political Science, University of London since 1991. He holds a Master Degree in Business Administration and a Bachelor of Arts in Business Administration from the American University in Cairo. His professional areas of interest includes; management information systems, decision support systems, crisis management and information technology transfer into developing countries.

A Process Management System to Support International Work Flow

Brenda L. Killingsworth
Decision Sciences Department, School of Business
East Carolina University
Greenville, NC 27858
(919) 757-6235

P. Candace Deans
World Business Department
Thunderbird American Graduate School of International Management
Glendale, Arizona
(602) 978-7608

Ronald Mueller
Hampton Industries
2000 Greenville Highway
P.O. Box 614
Kinston, NC 28502-0614
(919) 527-8011

ABSTRACT

This paper describes an extension of the Network Expert System Management System (ESMS) model proposed by Killingsworth, Madabhushi, and Deans (1993) that includes a knowledge representation scheme to ease assessment of ISO 9000 certification as well as an interface to decision support facilities to support international work flow and organizational decision making. This model, the Process Management System, includes three key design elements: (1) a knowledge representation permitting linkage of knowledge with objects in the organization, (2) a corporate calendar overlaying timing and synchronization requirements on the processes within the organization, and (3) integration of knowledge to the decision support facilities available. A description of a case study on features incorporated in a process management system of an international-based Apparel Company is presented as well.

INTRODUCTION

Many international-based organizations are confronted with the need to document processes related to their quality systems and, if selling in the European Community, often the requirements of ISO 9000. However, even organizations with only local sales markets are recognizing the critical importance of evaluating their processes and attempting to improve the effectiveness and efficiencies of those processes. Documenting procedures for ease of evaluation and reference is essential for ensuring that effort required to track quality does not become so overwhelming as to cause the demise of the organization itself.

Global competitiveness places a new emphasis on integrating information systems and documentation to ensure consistent application of processes within an organization. Many of the organizations providing services and products in the European Economic Community are facing the need to be certified as meeting the International Standards Organization (ISO) 9000 series standards, a requirement imposed by supplies by many of the organizations throughout the world. ISO 9000 requires a quality system model demonstrate a supplier's capacity to design, produce, install and service the product (Dupont, 1992). Organizations must go through recertification every six months and must ensure that their documentation is kept up-to-date. If procedures change during the six-month interval of recertification, the organizations must be able to map the performance data to the procedure used.

Some organizations have turned to continuous process improvement and total quality management to identify ways to better manage their processes. Improving processes by reducing the number of tasks that don't add value as well as reducing the number of document transfers within an organization can help. However, well-integrated information technology can provide the competitive edge needed to compete in a global marketplace and to ensure that the time to complete a process is minimized.

This paper describes key features of a system, referred to as the Process Management System, which permits integration of ISO 9000 documentation within a corporate information system. A case study at a major manufacturer in the apparel industry in the southeastern part of the United States is used to describe this process-based approach to information andknowledge systems design. The Process Management System incorporates a frame-based design permitting a modular design and expansion of the network and extends the expert system management system (Killingsworth, et al. 1993) to the process management problem. Section II provides an overview of the International Organization for Standardization's (ISO) ISO 9000 series standards and on decision making within organizations and information system design issues. Section III identifies implications of ISO 9000 on the design of information systems. Section IV presents features incorporated in the design of a network Process Management System. Section V offers final remarks of the paper and directions for continued research in supporting the networking of information systems technologies in international settings.

THE INTERNATIONAL ORGANIZATION OF STANDARDS (ISO)

The International Organization for Standardization (ISO) is headquartered in Geneva, Switzerland. ISO was founded in 1946 to develop and promote standards. Since its inception, over 8100 international standards and technical reports have been issued. Currently, 91 nations are members of ISO. ISO 9000, published in 1987, is a series of international standards and guidelines designed (1) to provide a standard against which a customer could evaluate a supplier's quality system as well as (2) to provide guidance to suppliers for improving the effectiveness of their quality system. The guidelines and standards of this series are generic, not product specific. They are applicable to all processes within an organization that are germane to the quality of a product or service. These standards specify the minimum quality requirements but do not specify how to accomplish or specifically implement those standards.

Currently, 55 nations have adopted the ISO 9000 series, including the EuropeanCommunity. The European economic area treaty, ratified in January 1993, has 12 European community (EC) member states -- Belgium, Denmark, France, Germany, Greece, Ireland, Italy, Luxembourg, Netherlands, Portugal, Spain, and the United Kingdom. In addition, it has 7 European free trade association (EFTA) countries -- Austria, Finland, Iceland, Liechtenstein, Norway, Sweden, and Switzerland. The European Community was set up to promote common quality standards, the removal of trade barriers, reciprocal recognition, and reduced costs of audits.

The ISO 9000 series is composed of five standards, prepared by Technical Committee ISO/TC 176 on Quality Assurance in the interest of merging or harmonizing the immense number of national and international standards. The first, ISO 9000 provides *guidelines* used in by organizations in selecting and using the other four standards in the series. The second, ISO 9001, is a *standard* used when compliance to specified requirements is to be guaranteed by the supplier during product/service design and development, production, installation, testing and service operations. ISO 9002, is a *standard* used when compliance to specific requirements is to be guaranteed by the supplier during production, installation and testing. ISO 9003, is a *standard* for use when compliance to specified requirements is to be guaranteed by the supplier at final inspection and test. Finally, ISO 9004 provides *guidelines* for quality management and quality system elements.

IMPLICATIONS OF ISO 9000 AND THE QUALITY MOVEMENT ON INFORMATION SYSTEMS DESIGN

There are twenty quality system elements as specified by ISO 9004. While all of these elements are closely tied to an organization's information system, six of these elements have major implications. These key elements that significantly impact the design of aninformation system include: (1) the existence, of a quality system that is well-documented and actually adhered to in practice, (2) employees have skills and training appropriate for their work, (3) document control, (4) traceability, (5) process control, and (6) inspection capabilities and measurement.

Most companies that have been ISO 9000 certified have developed manual documentation of their quality systems. One of the difficulties in maintaining ISO 9000 certification is the maintenance of the voluminous documentation when changes in processes occur. In addition, an organization must prove that the documentation is actually adhered to in practice. That means that employees must be well trained in the process and that no deviation from the process exists that is not documented in the quality system manual. When the documentation of processes is provided in the form of huge manuals, employees may be unwilling to refer to the documentation when attempting to complete their tasks within standard process times. Thus, this documentation needs to be on-line and used to enforce process adherence. The last four measures, are natural elements of an information system. The difficulty in adhering to the ISO 9000 standards is that companies must manage change control so that assessors from the registrars can trace the impact and quality of processes that existed prior to a change. For instance, an assessor may want to trace a process or object through a process in existence six months ago, prior to several changes to a process. In essence, a company must maintain prior environments, in addition to the normal current processing and testing environments. Finally, additional data regarding time stamps and unquality events is required to document and permit evaluation on the quality of a system.

A common problem in international information systems management is the coordination of distributed systems. Often these distributed system share a common database. However, with ISO 9000's emphasis on process control, the need for integrating processes across geographic regions as well as in the same organizational facility is quite evident. One reason for the lack of integration may be tied to organizations' emphases on designing information systems as application-based systems rather than process-based systems. Application-based systems group programs according to a functional area. With this approach to information system design, an individual may have to utilize several applications just to perform a sequence of tasks, often moving between applications several times before completing a job. Also, with application-based systems, there are few controls on the sequence or timing in which an individual performs a set of tasks. Further, no interface exists between applications which provides guidance on the priority of working on a given document or task. Typically, an individual will (1) attempt to run an application and learn that the database is not in the proper state for completion of the application, (2) view the state of the database to determine if it is appropriate for a given task, or (3) rely on another individual or team within the organization to send an E-mail message or voice message to indicate they have completed their portion of the process. The time delay between processing tasks can quickly add up when accumulated over the full path of the process.

DESIGN OF A PROCESS MANAGEMENT SYSTEM

There have been several conceptual frameworks proposed to network multiple expert systems ranging from supporting fixed links between specific functional areas (Rauch-Hindin, 1986) to permitting more flexible access to multiple expert systems (Davis and Smith, 1983; Malone, Fikes, and Howard, 1983; Erman, et al., 1980; Fox, 1981; Jacob and Pirkul, 1990; Killingsworth, et. al. (1992, 1993)). The process management system model presented in this paper integrates concepts found in previous communication models (Jacob and Pirkul, 1990; Ho, Hong, and Kuo, 1986; Woo and Lochovsky, 1986) and in the group decision making approach found in the Hearsay-II systems (Erman, et al., 1980; Fox, 1981) which use a blackboard for knowledge sources to communicate within the network.

Three design issues arise from the ISO 9000 series that need to be addressed in the conceptual framework of a process management system to support synchronization of processes in an international organization; process modeling and representation, corporate calendaring, and base time stamps.

Process Modeling and Representation

Knowledge and tasks are typically modeled by knowledge engineers in terms of individual decision makers. ISO 9000 requires that knowledge be viewed in terms of processes. The ability to trace the origin of an object or document through the process requires the linking of knowledge and tasks among experts involved in the processing of that object or document. The model proposed here expands on the concept of on-line help by using the knowledge to enforce process adherence.

The model implemented in this case study represents each expert's knowledge as frames of knowledge that consists of tasks performed by the expert. Knowledge stored about each task include: the purpose of the task (classified as value-added, supplier failure, staging, rework, and inspection) and the estimated time for completion. Any task can be performed by more than one expert. In turn, each task contains a set of

steps needed to accomplish that task. The steps can be linked to an object (such as a document, a computer application, or a graphic object.) Finally, processes within organizations are composed of a sequence of tasks. Process knowledge includes task sequence, the overall begin and end time of a process cycle and the begin and end times for each task in the process.

Process Synchronization and Scheduling: A Corporate Calendar

A key issue in the design of a process management system to support organizational decision making is the synchronization and prioritizing of the multitude of processes within the organization. As indicated, notification of a completed task within a process requiring organizational effort is typically done through E-mail, voice mail or viewing the state of the database to see if work has been accomplished. It is often up to the priorities of the individual to determine which object or task to complete first. The time delay from the use of this approach can be significant given its dependency on manual efforts.

By modeling information systems in terms of processes rather than applications, automatic notification of work can be achieved, thus eliminating the time delay from conventional approaches. This research proposes the use of a corporate calendar and process frame-based knowledge system to coordinate processes within an organization. A frame-based representation of knowledge is chosen in this design because frames permit a modular specification of knowledge. Ideally, frames are designed to represent objects, actions (i.e., manual tasks or computer applications), or events (i.e., receipt of an object, the occurrence of a specific state of an object...). An added advantage of using a frame would be that procedures can be linked to the frame itself.

A corporate calendar stores knowledge about the synchronization between and prioritization of processes (and objects) within the organization. With process knowledge and automation of the corporate calendar, at any point in time, the expected completion date and available slack time of a process for any given object can be calculated (using the current date, the process end base time and the expected durations of each task remaining).

Base Time Stamps

A third design issue facing knowledge engineers supporting international-based organizations is the synchronization of time between expert nodes (and decision makers) scattered throughout the world given the different time zones of its branch offices and plants. The approach followed in this design uses a base time stamp. All transactions are recorded using the base time at corporate headquarters while local time is displayed at each of the other nodes through the use of a time zone conversion algorithm.

FINAL REMARKS

Modeling process knowledge is gaining increased attention for organizations striving for ISO 9000 certification and/or maintaining certification. This paper has described features incorporated in an international-based apparel manufacturing organization in its attempts to reduce ensure a quality system is adhered to consistently. Research issues that are currently being addressed to improve the Process Management System include the design of analytical features for analysis of process changes and the application of object-oriented principles to process documentation.

REFERENCES

Davis, R. and Smith, R.G. (1983) "Negotiation and metaphor for distributed problem solving," *Artificial Intelligence*, Vol. 20, pp. 68-109.

Date, C.J. (1990) *An Introduction to Database Systems*, 5th Edition, Reading: Massachusetts, Addison-Wesley.

DuPont, (1992) "ISO 9000 is here." Quality Management and Technology Center, E.I. du Pont de Nemours and Company, Newark, DE.

Erman, L.D., Hayes-Roth, R., Lesser, V.R., and Reddy, D.R. (1980) "The Hearsay-II speech-understanding system: integrating knowledge to resolve uncertainty." *Computing Surveys*, 12(2), 213-253.

Fox, M.S. (1981) "An organizational view of distributed systems," *IEEE Transactions on Systems, Man, and Cybernetics*, Vol. SMC-11, No. 1, pp. 70-80.

Ho, C.S., Hong, J.C., and Kuo, T.S. (1986) "A society model for office information systems," *AMC Transactions on Office Information Systems*, Vol. 6, No. 2 pp. 106-131.

Howard, H. Craig, and Rehak, Daniel R. (1989) "KADBASE - interfacing expert systems with databases" *IEEE Expert*, Fall, pp. 65-76.

Jacob, Varghese S. and Pirkul, Hasan (1990) "A framework for networked knowledge-based systems" *IEEE Transactions on Systems, Man, and Cybernetics*, Vol. 20, No. 1., January/February, pp. 119-127.

Killingsworth, B.L., Madabhushi, S., and Trumbly, J. (1992). "Design of a hierarchical knowledge-based system management system (KSMS) for multiple domains." In the *Proceedings of the National Decision Sciences Institute Conference.* San Francisco, CA., November 1992.

Killingsworth, B.L., Madabhushi, S., and Deans, P.C. (1993). "Managing knowledge and quality procedures through the design of a network expert system management system (ESMS) for multiple domains." In the *Proceedings of the Information Resource Management Association Conference.* Salt Lake City, Utah, May 1993.

Malone, T.W., Fikes, R.E., and Howard, M.T. (1983) "Enterprise: a market-like task scheduler for distributed computing environments," working paper, Cognitive and Instructional Sciences Group, Xerox Palo Alto Research Center.

Rauch-Hindin, N.B. (1986) *Artificial Intelligence in Business, Science, and Industry, Vol. I,II.* Englewood Cliffs, NJ: Prentice Hall.

Woo, C.C. and Lochovsky, F.H. (1986) "Supporting distributed office problem solving in organizations," *ACM Transactions on Office Information Systems*, Vol. 6, No. 3, pp. 185-206.

Global Information Technology: Impact on Organizational Technology: Impact on Organizational Performance

Anil Kumar
Prashant Palvia
Memphis State University

ABSTRACT:

This paper presents a conceptual model to find the impact on organizational performance of firms using different Information Technology (IT) structures, in a global environment. An attempt is made to answer the following research question: Does the impact on organizational performance vary with different IT structures? A prototype study was conducted using graduate students as subjects. The results suggest that there are several other factors besides organizational structure which drives the IT structure in a subsidiary of a firm operating in a global environment. It was also found out that the business performance of organizations is affected by information technology. The paper provides rich qualitative information, which can be used for future research.

1. INTRODUCTION:

With businesses going global, a key to success for companies in 1990s may be the establishment of an Information Technology (IT) infrastructure that effectively supports an enterprise's global presence. IT when used as a tool in different business environments around the world can enable global enterprises to use information and systems internally and externally to gain competitive advantages. The advantages gained give the company an edge over indigenous host country firms that have extensive local market knowledge. Further with the spread of an organization over geographical regions there is an increased need for global coordination and control between headquarters and subsidiaries. This has also placed greater demands on information requirements and communication. Investment in IT provide firms with a basis for increased coordination and control.

Organizations which operate in the global arena have different strategies to optimize performance and operations. Based on these strategies, the organizations have different organizational structures. For IT to be used effectively as a tool there is a compelling need to harness IT properly with respect to an existing global business strategy. "Misalignment of information technology with global business strategy can severely hamper a firm's efforts to seek global pre-eminence" (Ives and Jarvenpaa, 1991). Does one conclude from this that there is a perfect match between global business strategy and IT strategy or are there other factors which could influence the IT strategy in global firms? Once the fit between global business strategy and IT strategy is achieved, how does it impact the performance of an organization? Do organizations which achieve a fit between organizational structure and IT structure perform better than organizations with a misfit?

This study was initiated to look at these questions specifically,

Q#1 Does organizational structure at HQs drive the IT structure worldwide (in subsidiaries)?

Q#2 What are some of the other factors that might influence the IT structure in a subsidiary?

Q#3 Does the impact on organizational performance vary with different IT structures?

The paper is organized as follows. The next section reviews the relevant literature to date. The third section presents a research model and the research questions being addressed in this prototype study. The fourth section describes the research methodology. In the fifth section results are presented and discussed. Finally the paper concludes with implications for further work in this area.

2. LITERATURE REVIEW:

In this paper, two different streams of research are being reviewed. One looks at the various frameworks, that have been proposed by several scholars, which align organizational structures with the IT structure in subsidiaries. The other stream of research looks at the advantages that are derived from the use of IT in a global environment.

2.1 Frameworks

Alavi & Young (1992) provide an integrated framework for aligning a firm's business and information technology strategies when the headquarters and subsidiary units are separated by national borders. The multinational, global, and transnational forms of international business strategies are defined and are shown to differ in organizational structure, strategic objective, transaction scope and locus of management. These three international strategies are then integrated with the dimensions of information technology including the technology architecture, data architecture, telecommunications architecture and information technology management. Simon & Grover (1993) explore the use of information technology in conjunction with a popular framework, the Integration-Responsiveness (IR) framework of international business. The IR framework developed by Prahalad and Doz (1987) is then operationalized adopting the strategic dimensions developed by Miller (1987). The four dimensions are complex innovation, marketing differentiation, breadth and conservative cost control. The authors state that there is considerable supporting research for these strategic dimensions in the strategy, management and international business literature (Doz, 1985; Porter, 1980; Bartlett & Ghoshal, 1989; Roth & Morrison, 1990). Using the IR framework and the strategic dimensions, the authors propose their own framework and demonstrate how the fit between a firm's strategic decisions and IT applications can be used to attain competitive advantages in the international environment . Specific examples of companies in each group are mentioned by the authors.

Ives and Jarvenpaa (1993) use information processing theory as the basis for examining alternative organizational designs for information technology in a globally competing firm. The authors of this study contend that the overall organization's structure, including the decision-making structure, controls the flow of information within the firm. They use the general patterns of decision-making structures of the Bartlett and Ghoshal (1989) models, to find the fit between global business models and global information technology configuration. The results of the study conducted by the authors showed that in nearly half of the organizations, the way information technology activities are organized is inconsistent with the way the organization is reportedly structured. Breukel and Simons (1993) present a theory-based model in which they show that a company's performance depends on the fit between the competitive strategy, the organizational structure and the IT. They conducted a series of explorative interviews (five business managers) to confirm the validity of this fit for successful IT-usage and the necessary role of the managerial decision-making for the realization of such a fit.

2.2 Impact of IT on organizations:

A perusal of the literature reflects that there are many options available to a multinational firm to enhance competitive advantages through the application of IT in its overall strategy (Bartlett and Ghoshal 1989, Galbraith 1977, Johnson and Vitale 1988, Farrell and Song 1988, Ives and Learmonth 1984, Neo 1991). Parsons (1983) presented the impact of Information technology on three levels i.e. industry, firm and strategy. The use of IT as a mechanism to coordinate the firm's value chain activities is suggested by Porter and Miller(1985). Their view on the strategic impact of IT on organizations is that IT can improve the business functions of the firm, can add more information (technology) to the products the company offers, and that it can change the industry in which it competes. Huff (1991) says "IT in global firms can dramatically compress time and distance, facilitate the coordination and movement of worldwide goods and services, allow for the sharing of human expertise and other resources, and provide the infrastructure necessary for operating new services that generate real competitive advantages". For example, the Society for Worldwide Interbank Financial Telecommunications (SWIFT) system electronically moves money freely and rapidly across national boundaries and towards those investments that offer the greatest return. The system allows credit transfers between some 1500 banks in approximately 70 countries. In a given day, as much as $700 billion is transmitted through the system (Ohmae, 1990). Hamilton (1986) argues that information technology in the financial services industry has created a totally new system of world finance:

"The growth of international communications, the development of the data-processing capability of the big computer and the personal desk-top facility, and the arrival of the day of the wired society have revolutionized the way in which finance is transacted". IT is also transforming the international transport and logistics businesses (Browne, 1991).

Mason, Ives, and Jarvenpaa (1993) talk about firms using computer and communications technology to extract the information components from tangible products, or substitute knowledge for material, and then instantly transport the electronically represented information or knowledge worldwide. Value can be added or an information based product can be used at the most economically advantageous location. The time delays, high costs, and lack of customer responsiveness associated with transportation, reproduction, and inventory can be reduced or even eliminated. This instantaneous "world reach" produces major changes in order management, manufacturing, and marketing cycles.

In this prototype study the business performance measures, being used were taken from the GLOSCIT model (Palvia,1992). It is pertinent to mention here that only qualitative measures were used and the study does not involve any statistical analysis.

3. RESEARCH MODEL:

The business models of Bartlett and Ghoshal (1989) were modified to a certain extent and based on that a research model is being proposed in this paper (figure 1). The model is used to derive the research questions mentioned earlier on in the paper. The emphasis in this study is to find out if the impact on organizational performance varies with different IT structures? The model uses the organizational structures of Bartlett and Ghoshal (1989) which have been re-classified into three groups, based on the decision-making patterns i.e. Multinational, Global and Transnational. Since the main difference between an International firm and a Transnational firm is the flow of innovation (e.g. unidirectional and bidirectional respectively) they have been grouped into one category for simplification. Corresponding to each organizational structure is an IT structure i.e. decentralized, centralized, and distributed processing IT approaches. The business performance measures are taken from the GLOSCIT model (Palvia, 1992).

4. RESEARCH METHODOLOGY:

The study was conducted by using the interview methodology and a structured interview was used to get responses. However, at times based on the responses, additional questions were asked of respondents. The intent was to get as much information as possible. The total number of responses used was seven. All subjects used were graduate students. Of the seven respondents there were six PhD students and one M.B.A. student. All the students had previously worked for international companies in different parts of the world. Out of the seven companies represented in the study there were two multinational companies, three global companies, and two

Figure 1: A Conceptual Model

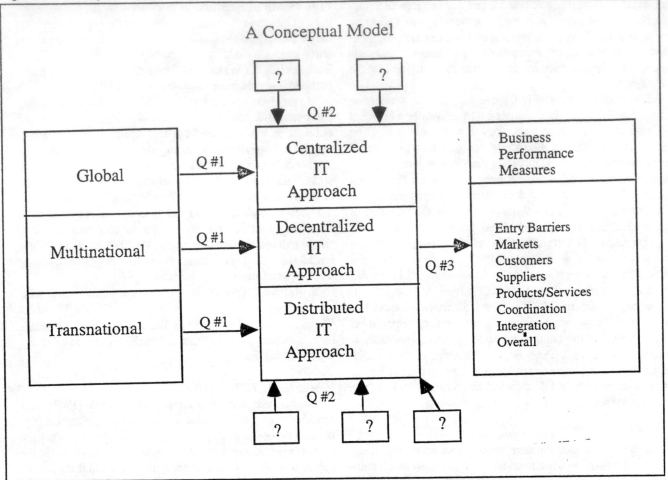

transnational companies. Four of these companies were from the service sector whereas three companies were from the manufacturing sector.

5. RESULTS:

There were three questions which were addressed in this study. The results are reported in the same sequence as shown in the model.

5.1 Organizational structure-IT structure fit:

Does organizational structure at headquarters drive the IT structure worldwide (in subsidiaries)? In general the organizational structure-IT structure fit was seen to be present in five of the seven companies in the sample. The other two companies in the sample did not have a fit between their organizational structures and IT structures. The misfit cases reported were:

i) A global company with a decentralized IT approach. For a global company to have a decentralized IT approach seems very surprising. However from the discussion, the point that came out was the fact that "Integration is not deemed necessary at this time. A small number of financial applications are shared, but these are few. Integration will take place slowly".

ii) A transnational company with a decentralized IT ap-

proach. The transnational company reporting a decentralized IT approach has evolved from a multinational to a transnational and it still needs to integrate its IT structure.

5.2 Factors influencing IT structure:

The factors that emerged as influencing the IT structure in subsidiaries in addition to the organization structure at headquarters are shown in figure 2. A brief discussion of these factors follows (in order of importance):

Human Resource Availability: Organizations must have a supply of trained, qualified, and skilled professionals. Without an abundant supply of skilled human resources, the organization will have a hard time achieving its goals. For countries to have skilled professionals the role of universities, schools, and training institutes is very important. Subsidiaries which are located in those parts of the world where there is a lack of skilled manpower will find it difficult to implement a desired IT solution.

Socio-Cultural Factors: reflect the demographic characteristics and the value systems within a society. Values and norms are very important components of cultures and cannot be ignored. Organizations that have subsidiaries in places of high inequality (power distance) among people, the people in power do not like the idea of others having access to informa-

Figure 2: Factors Influencing IT structure

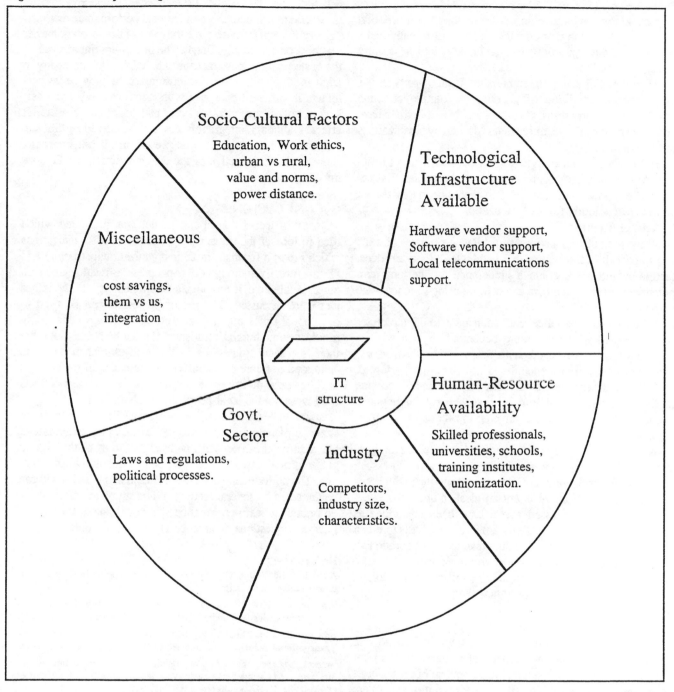

tion. This may be considered intimidating as information is a major asset of the people in higher positions. There is a resistance on the part of the powerful members in such a society for using information technology. Cultures which have a high power distance may resist the use of information technology as it is perceived to reduce the power distance (Kedia & Bhagat, 1988).

Technological Infrastructure Available: The technological infrastructure that impacts the IT structure in a subsidiary falls into two main categories:

i) local telecommunications support: lack of good communications support would lead to an unreliable communication network in turn hindering efforts to coordinate and integrate activities in an organization.

ii) hardware and software vendor support: lack of such support in subsidiaries would lead to incompatible systems and hardware, in turn effecting implementation of useful systems.

Government: The government includes the regulatory, legal and political systems that surround the organization. If the government in a particular country forbids use of particular technology it will have an impact on the IT structure of a subsidiary located in that country. India, until recently had a policy that did not permit foreign technology into the country easily.

Though not directly related but significant, nonetheless, is the economic condition of a country. Volatile economic changes in a country restrict business and growth and can have an impact on the IT investment that is desired by organizations in subsidiaries.

Industries: Major competitors in the industry can influence an organization's decision to adopt a particular IT structure to keep up with the competition even though it might not be the ideal solution for an organization.

Miscellaneous:

i)Pressures of cost savings to achieve economies of scale can impact the IT structure that is adopted. Short-term cost factors should not become a hinderance for the long-term potential benefits that a firm can achieve using IT to integrate activities.

ii)Subsidiary resistance can contribute to IT structures being adopted which are more decentralized than what is required. Care must be taken to see that the "them vs us" syndrome does not influence the IT structure that is adopted.

iii)In countries where a subsidiary is very small, adopting an IT structure consistent with other subsidiaries might not be economically viable and can have an impact on the IT structure.

iv)Organizations have different levels of need for integrating the IT structures in subsidiaries worldwide. For such organizations, following an IT structure consistent with headquarters- driven structure is not an ideal solution.

These factors discussed above have been mentioned as having an effect when adopting a particular IT structure in a subsidiary. An organization should take into consideration all of these factors and adapt to the environmental characteristics when making a decision about the IT strategy in a subsidiary, rather than just go by the headquarter-driven structure.

5.3 Impact on performance:

The results for the third question are given in the following Table. This table lists the number of respondents who believed that IT had an impact on one or several of the business performance measures. The fit cases (five out of seven) are those where the organizational structure matches the IT structure. In case of a misfit the organizational structure is different from the reported IT structure (two out of seven firms). Each

cell indicates the number of respondents who reported an impact on the particular organizational performance measure.

As is evident from the table the role of IT as an entry barrier was not considered significant. The maximum impact was on the customers business measure i.e. helping the company to learn more about worldwide customers, helping serve customers in different countries with different needs etc. Markets, suppliers, products/services, and coordination were all affected, although integration was not considered significant. The overall impact of IT was present in all but one case, showing that irrespective of the different structures, IT does impact performance.

6. CONCLUSION:

In this paper a conceptual model was presented which tried to look at the impact on performance of organizations which report a fit/misfit in their organizational structure and IT structure. Even though the paper presents results which are purely qualitative, it provides a useful insight into the issues that were discussed. The prototype results can be used to develop a full study in the future. Although this study provides some interesting results, it must be pointed out that there are some limitations in this study which need to be addressed in future research. The sample size of the study is not large enough to make generalizations, and the respondents used were not the ideal people for such an study.

It would be desirable to interview the MIS managers or the strategic planning group managers to get richer information. Quantitative measures must be used in a study of this type to get empirical validation, in addition to qualitative information. The performance of an organization in the real world can be impacted by several factors. In this study, the effect of IT on organizational performance was not isolated. Finally the interview questions need to be rigorously validated.

References:

Alavi M. and Young G., "Information technologies in International Enterprise:An Organizing

Framework",**The Global Issues of Information Technology Management**, edited by Palvia, Palvia & Zigli, Idea Group Publishing, 1992.

Bartlett C. and Ghoshal S., **Managing Across Borders: The Transnational Solution**. Boston:Harvard Business School Press,1989.

Breukel, Ad., and Simons, J.L., "Competitive Strategy and Organizational Structure: Key Factors for Competitive Advantage with IT", **Proceedings of the 1993 IRMA Conference**, pp. 311-319.

Browne M.J., "Prospective Freight Mega-Carriers: The Role of Information Technology in Their Global Ambitions", **Proceedings of the Hawaii International Conference on Systems Sciences**, IEEE Computer Society (1991), pp.192-201.

Doz I., **"Strategic Management in Multinational Corporations"**, Oxford:Pergamon Press. 1985.

Farrell C., and Song J.,"Strategic Uses of Information Technology", SAM **Advanced Management Journal**, Winter 1988,pp.10-16.

Galbraith J., **Organizational Design**. Addison-Wesley Publishing Co.,1977.

Hamilton A., **"The Financial Revolution"**, The Free Press, New York (1986),pp.33.

Business Performance Measures	Fit cases (5)	Misfit cases (2)
Entry barriers	1	-
Markets	3	1
Customers	4	2
Suppliers	3	-
Products/services	3	1
Coordination	3	1
Integration	1	1
Overall	5	1

Huff, S. L., "Managing Global Information Technology", **Business Quarterly**, Vol:56, Autumn 1991, pp.71-75.

Ives B. and Learmonth G., "The Information System as a Competitive Weapon", **Communications of the ACM**, 27(12), 1984, pp.1193-1201.

Ives B. and Jarvenpaa S.L., "Organizing for Global Competition: The fit of Information Technology", **Decision Sciences**, Vol:24, May/June 93, pp. 547-580.

Ives B. and Jarvenpaa S.L., "Applications of Global Information Technology:Key Issues for

Management", **MIS Quarterly**, Vol. 15, No.1, March 1991.

Johnson H. and Vitale M., "Creating Competitive Advantage with Interorganizational Information Systems", **MIS Quarterly**, 12(2), 1988, pp.153-165.

Kedia B.L.,and Bhagat R.S., "Cultural Constraints on transfer of technology across nations:

Implications for Research in International and Competitive Management", **Academy of Management Review**, Vol 13, No. 4, pp.559-571, 1988.

Mason R.O., Ives B., and Jarvenpaa S.L., "Global Business Drivers: Aligning Information

Technology to Global Business Strategy", **IBM Systems Journal**, Vol. 32, No. 1, 1993. pp. 143-161.

Miller D.,"The Structural and Environmental Correlates of Business Strategy",

Strategic

Management Journal, 8: 1987 pp.55-76.

Neo B., "Information Technology and Global Competition", **Information and Management**, 20(2), 1991, pp.151-160.

Ohmae K., **"The Borderless World"**, Harper Press, New York (1990), pp.162.

Palvia, P.,"GLOSCIT: A Comprehensive Model for Global Strategic and Competitive Impact of Information Technology", **Working Paper**, Dec., 1992.

Parsons G.L., "Information Technology: A New Competitive Weapon", **Sloan Management Review**, Fall 1983, Vol. 25, no 1, pp. 3-14.

Porter M., **"Competitive Strategy"**, New York: The Free Press. 1980.

Porter M. and Miller V., "How Information gives you Competitive Advantage",**Harvard Business Review**, 62(4), 1985, pp. 149-160.

Prahalad C.K., and Doz I., **"The Multinational Mission: Balancing Local Demands and Global Vision"** New York: The Free Press. 1987.

Roth K., and Morrison A., "An Empirical analysis of the Integration-Responsiveness Framework in Global Industries", **Journal of International Business Studies**, 21(4):pp.541-564, 1990.

Simon S.J. and Grover V., "Strategic use of Information Technology in International Business: A Framework for Information Technology Application", **Journal of Global Information Management**, Vol:1, Spring 1993, pp.29-42.

Infrastructure Enhancement and Multinational Corporate Structures

Laura Lally
BCIS/QM Department
134 Hofstra
Hofstra University
Hempstead, New York 11550
516 463 5351

ABSTRACT

In the emerging global environment, enhancements in the information infrastructure will allow new organization structures to evolve. Two very different structures proposed in the literature, the Global Web and the Ethnocentric MNC are compared on the dimensions of: 1) type of information infrastructure required, and, 2) potential positive and negative impacts. An infrastructure based tool, electronic data interchange (**EDI**) is compared along the same dimensions to determine which structure it best supports and its positive and negative impacts. Research questions are proposed to address managers' key concerns in developing the best infrastructure for a multinational firm.

NEW ORGANIZATIONAL FORMS EMERGE

In the emerging global environment, multinational corporations (MNCs) will be able to do business with less regard for geographical and national boundaries. An enhanced information infrastructure, permitting real time exchange of data, voice and images is becoming available that will enable new business processes, less constrained by time and space. New organizational structures are likely to evolve to support these new processes.

This study will present two contrasting theoretical views of what the structure of the multinational firm of the future will look like, Reich's "Global Web" (Reich, 1992) and Roche's "Ethnocentric MNC" (Roche, 1992). Although the technology can be designed to support either structure, the structures are radically different. A comparison will be made between the key elements of the Global Web and Ethnocentric MNC structures, and their potential positive and negative impacts on the organization's efficiency, its workforce, and on the host countries in which the organization does business.

The evolution of new organizational structures will also be influenced by the infrastructure-based tools that are made available to management. To provide further insight into evolving structures, one currently available tool, electronic data interchange (**EDI**) will be examined in terms of whether it supports the idea of a "Global Web" or an "Ethnocentric MNC," and its relationship to workforce and host country issues.

Finally, the analysis will yield a number of research questions aimed at providing insight to management as to: 1) which organizational structures are most likely to emerge, 2) what the constraints on designing these structures will be, and 3) how to design the best structure for a given organization.

REICH'S "GLOBAL WEB"

Secretary of Labor, Robert Reich, in his recent book, "The Work Of Nations," (Reich, 1992) argues that global business will evolve away from centralized, hierarchical structures, and operate instead as "Global Webs". These webs will be composed of individuals and groups forming ad-hoc alliances to take advantage of ever changing market conditions (see Figure 1). Decision making in Global Webs will be distributed to whichever individual is most qualified or may be shared among groups of experts, regardless of their geographical location. Organizational processes in Global Webs are continually re-designed to reflect the best way of getting the job done. Reich considers most large, centralized organization structures as historical artifacts of a manufacturing based economy. The webs will allow the more flexible business arrangements and greater responsiveness to local markets required by the service based, "value-added" economy of the future.

The key individuals in these webs will be what Reich calls "symbolic analysts," -- knowledge workers of three types: 1) problem identifiers who seek new opportunities, 2) problem solvers who design solutions to take advantage of the opportunities and 3) strategic brokers who co-ordinate the resources necessary to implement the solutions. The resources -- raw material, labor and investment capital -- will be acquired on the world market at the best price.

Information technology supports the work of all three types of symbolic analysts by providing information and analytical models to support their decision making and the infrastructure to communicate with other analysts. Real-time information exchange will give rise to worldwide networks of expertise where the knowledge of an analyst can be applied where it is most needed. Reich cites some successful examples of these webs: Arthur Andersen consulting, WPP Group advertising, and Baker & McKenzie legal services. (Reich, p. 133).

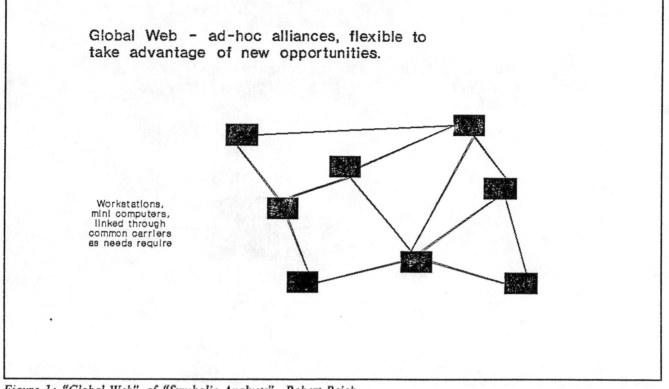

Global Web - ad-hoc alliances, flexible to take advantage of new opportunities.

Workstations, mini computers, linked through common carriers as needs require

Figure 1· "Global Web" of "Symbolic Analysts" Robert Reich

Reich believes that the unique abilities of the symbolic analysts will transcend cultural differences and make expertise the base of power in the evolving MNC. He sites Sony's recent takeover of Columbia as an example. Although company ownership had become Japanese, the symbolic analysts, executives with marketing know-how and the recording artists were still American and they still represented the firm's power base, as evidenced by their exorbitant salaries. The recent abdications of Jon Peters and George Michael provides some evidence against Reich's predictions (Emmot, 1993).

Reich states that through information technology groups of symbolic analysts will form their own "virtual communities." These groups of physically separate but logically united knowledge workers share common problems and perspectives. Although symbolic analysts represent the elite of the laborforce, they are in one way similar to assembly line workers. "Symbolic analysts rarely come into direct contact with the ultimate beneficiaries of their work." (Reich, p. 178).

This distancing from the physical and emotional aspects of life can result in alienation. Symbolic analysts are likely to develop a greater sense of community with one another than with individuals in their immediate physical environments and "secede" from the problems of their community and nation. They are also more likely to view the customers, labor force and other human variables in their problem solving as abstractions. The social gap between the well paid analysts and the people who represent labor "resources" they manipulate is likely to grow.

ROCHE'S "ETHNOCENTRIC MNC"

Roche, as part of his book, "Managing Information Technology in Multinational Corporations," presents an empirical study that indicates an entirely different multinational corporate structure emerging. His study indicates that multinational corporations tend to have centralized information technology infrastructures. The multinational firms he examined were more likely to keep their processing power (which can be viewed as a surrogate for problem solving) and storage devices (which can be viewed as a surrogate for corporate memory) in their home country (Roche, p. 165). Furthermore, Roche argues, MNCs are likely to grow even more centralized as legislative restrictions regarding transboarder data flows and host country processing requirements ease. Therefore, in an age of downsizing from mainframes to LANs in domestic firms, MNCs are likely to be "upsizing" -- transferring regional applications up to a centralized home country mainframe.

A centralized infrastructure is vastly different than Reich's Global Web, it consists of relatively permanent connections between home country mainframes and smaller, less powerful, host country computers (see Figure 2). Hierarchical decision making and power relationships are supported by these structures.

Centralized structures may lead to what Roche calls "Eth-

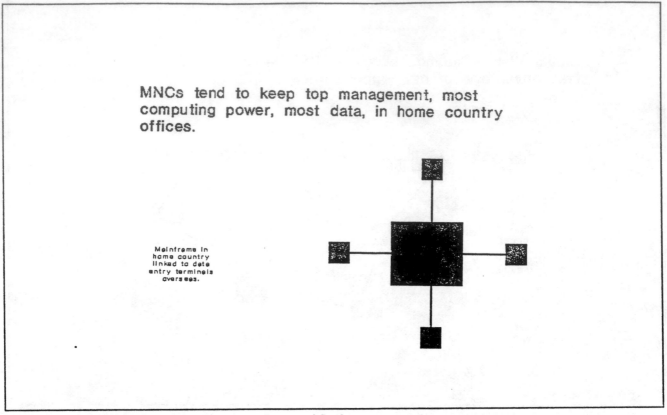

Figure 2: Ethnocentric MNCs Edward Roche - Empirical Study

nocentric MNCs," organizations that adopt imperialist business practices in dealing with host countries. There is a long history of conflict between host countries and MNCs due to charges of imperialism. Host countries argue that MNCs exploit them by depleting their natural resources, and keeping their labor force in low level jobs. Roche found that in Ethnocentric MNCs only 1.6% of top corporate management is foreign (mostly those in marketing).

A centralized infrastructure can help support imperialistic business practices. Managers and professionals can stay at home and still micro-manage a global operation. The labor force is removed from their direct experience by great distances, cultural and language barriers. The tendency to treat labor as abstract variables in a problem grows even more severe.

EDI AND ORGANIZATIONAL STRUCTURE

A infrastructure-based tool, EDI, is currently beginning to have an impact on organizational structures. Do the changes enabled by EDI move the organization more toward the Global Web or Ethnocentric model? EDI is a frequent tool used by "re-engineers" in streamlining business processes (Hammer, 1993). When used within an organization EDI can support the streamlining of process and lead to decreased labor and paper costs. EDI used between companies, such as customers and suppliers (and their banks), makes connections between the firms more permanent as they adopt common forms and ordering procedures (Figure 3). Used in this

manner, EDI can lead to great improvements in short-term efficiency resulting from faster order cycles.

EDI is still more widely used in the U.S. than in Europe and its further growth will depend on untangling a number of problems with standards (Trauth, 1993). However, the technology exists to create EDI links across national boundaries to support within firm and between firm processes of MNCs.

One potential problem of EDI is that it can lead to long term inefficiencies due to the limitations its use can impose on the free market system where competition encourages the best product at the lowest price. Companies linked to their suppliers through EDI are less likely to "shop" elsewhere. Requiring EDI raises the cost of market entry to small, niche suppliers who may be the source of innovations.

COMPARING STRUCTURES AND EDI

Table 1 compares the Global Web and Ethnocentric MNC structures on the basis of infrastructure, processes, decision making, and impact on the workforce and home country. The use of EDI is compared to the structures along the same dimensions to determine which model EDI best supports.

Reich's Global Web requires a flexible infrastructure to support flexible processes within organizations and flexible relationships between them. The Ethnocentric MNC requires a more fixed infrastructure and processes. The use of EDI within an organization tends to favor the fixed model since it requires that processes be fixed so that they can be automated. Between organizations, EDI is likely to lead to more fixed,

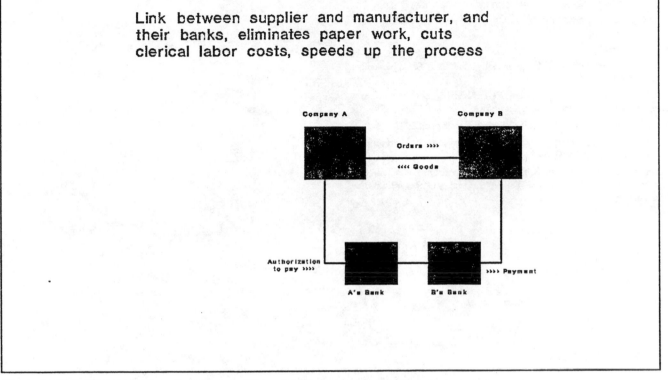

Link between supplier and manufacturer, and their banks, eliminates paper work, cuts clerical labor costs, speeds up the process

Figure 3: EDI - Electronic Data Interchange Allows for "Re-engineering"

rather than ad-hoc relationships, increasing the possibility of oligopolies.

The Global Web requires distributed decision making in contrast to the hierarchical structure favored by the MNC. EDI does not appear to play a major role in an organization's decision processes, unless it is used to bypass layers of management.

The Global Web may have some indirect negative impacts on the workforce as symbolic analysts form stronger alliances with one another and lose touch with their fellow man. The negative impact of the ethnocentric MNC, however, is much more direct. Workers are explicitly seen as factors of production to be acquired at the lowest price and micro-managed solely in terms of bottom-line efficiency. EDI permits the elimination of clerical jobs, another bad sign for labor.

The Global Web supports the development of companies in remote areas since the expertise and capital required becomes more easily transportable. Local symbolic analysts can combine their regional expertise with home country analysts. These collaborations can lead to a transfer of managerial expertise to less developed countries. The Global Web of analysts as a worldwide community also has its brighter side in terms of societal impacts. Taking part in a worldwide community of knowledge is likely to make symbolic analysts more enlightened people. Symbolic analysts are also likely to

be influential members of their home country societies, with the result that more enlightened political policies may emerge. Although this vision is many steps from realization, it at least sounds promising on paper.

The Ethnocentric MNC, in contrast, is likely to exacerbate the problems currently experienced between MNCs and home countries. Local legislators will be less likely to yield to the requests of MNCs for easier data transfer if more imperialistic business practices are the result. Therefore, the relationship between conceptual structures and emerging tools may be two way. Not only will the structures depend on available tools, but the tools made available by the home countries may depend on the structure and associated business practices local politician feel are likely to emerge.

EMERGING RESEARCH QUESTIONS

This preliminary analysis of evolving MNC organizational structures yields a number of promising research questions:

What other factors influence the structure of the MNC?
   Are manufacturing firms more likely to be ethnocentric than service firms?
   Will structure depend on the relative degree of technological sophistication between home and host countries?

How do we best support the work of symbolic analysts?
Tradeoffs between individual and co-operative work.
How do we minimize the potential for alienation?

What new factors must we consider when designing
computer systems for MNCs?

REFERENCES

Emmot, Bill., "How Japan Got Mugged in Hollywood," *N.Y. Times*, November 26, 1993, p. A35.

Hammer, Michael., and James Champy, *Re-engineering the Corporation: A Manifesto for Business Revolution*, (Harper Collins: New York), 1993.

Reich, Robert., *The Work of Nations*, (Knopf: New York), 1992.

Roche, Edward M., *Managing Information Technology in Multinational Corporations*, (Macmillan: New York), 1992.

Trauth, Eileen, M., and Ronald S. Thomas, "Electronic Data Interchange: A New Frontier for Global Standards Policy," *Journal of Global Information Management*, Fall, 1993., Vol. 1, No. 4, pp 6-18.

	Global Web	Ethnocentric MNC	EDI
Impact of Structure on:			
Information Infrastructure Required	Flexible	Fixed	Fixed
Processes	Flexible	Fixed	Fixed
Decision Making	Distributed	Hierarchical	No direct impact
Workforce	Indirectly Negative	Directly Negative	Probably Negative
Host Country	Mostly positive	Mostly negative	No direct impact

Table 1

Creating a Global Information Technology Infrastructure: Issues, Approaches and Solutions

Amarnath Prakash
Department of MIS and DS
Fogelman College of Business and Economics
Memphis State University
Memphis, TN 38152
Telephone # : 901-678-2462

Suvojit Choton Basu
Department of MIS and DS
Fogelman College of Business and Economics
Memphis State University
Memphis, TN 38152
Telephone # : 901-678-2462

Executive Abstract

INTRODUCTION

Few organizations these days can avoid the effects of the globalization of markets, sources of materials, technology, and intellectual capital. An organization unable to adapt to the emerging worldwide economy will probably severely constrain its prospects for success in the twenty-first century. Information systems managers are likely to find themselves in the vanguard of their firm's efforts to cope with the added complexity of the global organization. This shift to a global organization raises a number of new and challenging issues for information systems management.

BACKGROUND

Carefully crafted investments in global IT offer firms an opportunity to increase control and enhance coordination while opening access to new global markets and businesses. Globalization produces dramatic changes in key markets, major competitors, and products. Information technology is a critical component in managing this profound change. IT on a global scale compresses time and space and permits the duplication and sharing of scarce corporate expertise. Such capabilities provide firms with an opportunity to leverage advantage in both market size and geographical scope while they simultaneously provide the means to respond rapidly to the unique requirements of national markets. It is in this context that the alignment of IT with the business strategy takes on monumental importance. A misalignment of IT with a firm's global business strategy can severely hamper a firm's efforts to seek global pre-eminence. Before building an IT infrastructure in a global environment there are a host of organizational, technological, cultural, and strategic issues that need to be addressed. A global IT application is different from a traditional local-bound application not only in its scope and span of control, but also in terms of strategic and operational impact on the organization. A global IT application contributes to achieving a firm's global business strategy by using IT platforms to store, transmit, and manipulate data across cultural environments.

DISCUSSION OF ISSUES

The role of IT in supporting and enabling the globalization of business has been understated and certainly under-ex-

plored. Application of information technology transcends national boundaries. A firm should structure its information systems function to operate in a 'mixed mode'. Different suites of applications will support different business strategies and will therefore require varying degrees of commonality across borders. Inflexible minds presiding over installed bases of unconnected applications software and incomparable data will retard the organization's ability to successfully integrate IS with the organization's mainstream. IT can propagate new business strategies, but a more common goal is to effectively harness IT to an existing global business strategy. Such alignment requires a shared understanding of the firm's overall global strategy.

Critical IT business drivers that constitute a critical component of a responsive global IT structure have to be identified and considered. Some of the global business drivers are joint resources, rationalized and flexible operations, risk reduction, global products, quality suppliers and customers. These global drivers can address both the firm's internal value chain and its external partners and constituents. Managing the firm's own internal value chain more efficiently and effectively on a global scale cannot be overemphasized. Addressing issues of interorganizational interdependence and its impact on the design of a global IT infrastructure is of paramount importance. Technology is not socially neutral ; it usually introduces some changes to the norms that exist in an organization. For example, it may lead to extensive changes in the organization structure; it may alter departmental procedures and affect jobs and people. Social and cultural issues are important focal-points that have to be focused upon while building the global IT structure.

Organizational interdependencies are driving firms toward major internal transformation. IT is a key enabler of these transformations. Creating a global IT structure that propels the business towards excellence and innovation is the challenge. Various approaches to building a responsive global IT structure exist and the best approach depends on the type of industry, business environment, and nation-specific factors.

CONCLUSION

Identification of impact areas in business is an important

consideration in an international environment. The validity of the global IT structure should be established by using global constructs. Those constructs can then be further disaggregated to pinpoint individual factors impinging directly on the selection of impact areas for IT implementation on a global scale and context until we reach a level of understanding rather than prediction.

DIRECTIONS FOR FURTHER RESEARCH

The dynamic global business environment entails a flexible IT infrastructure to support changing operations. A variety of both environmental and organizational factors impinge on the evolution and maintenance of an IT structure. Possibilities of future research exists in the areas of culture impact on organizational IT structure, and technology impact on organizational infrastructure.

Informative Economy:

A Shift from Information Economy

Andrew S. Targowski
Professor of Computer Information Systems
Department of Business Information Systems
WESTERN MICHIGAN UNIVERSITY
Kalamazoo, MI 49008
(616) 375-5406
fax (616) 375-8762
targowski@hcob.wmich.edu

Executive Abstract

The post-industrial economy (service or information economy) is defined in literature by the criterion of the number of information workers employed in the economy. The information substance of work determine information economy. In the year 2000 the number of information workers will decline and service economy will shift into service-industrial economy. Despite of the fact that the number of computers and networks in use will increase. It means that material cannot be replaced by information like steel by plastic. Quantitative and qualitative measures of information economy are discussed. The attributes of informative economy (way of doing business) are presented under the form of the Porter-Targowski model.

Goals and roles of computers and networks in informative economy are presented. Four informative economy environments: automated, electronic, on-line, and virtual are presented under the form of system architectures. Rethinking business in informative economy are analyzed in two major and ten optional steps. In conclusion, in global economy, the post-industrial economy or service economy is not a model to copy by the nations. Otherwise, production of goods should be allocated outside of the Earth. A model of service-industrial economy (informative model) is the model to be used by the majority of successful nations.

Tackling Information Management Issues Through an Information Infrastructure

Roelof J. van den Berg   Theo J. W. Renkema
Section Information and Technology
Graduate School of Industrial Engineering and Management Science
Eindhoven University of Technology
P.O. Box 513
5600 MB Eindhoven
The Netherlands
Tel: +31 40472592/472290

BACKGROUND INFORMATION

In the past few years the level of turbulence in most markets has significantly increased due to a number of factors. Many regard increased globalization as the root cause of change in the 1990s. The societal responsibility of organizations has increased, e.g. environmental issues take a prominent position in decisions where it was possible to exclude them until recently. Due to the rise of individualism an attuned human resources policy has become of increased importance as well. For the same reason companies see themselves confronted with a customer who is much more unpredictable than he was a decade ago. The rapid evolution in information technology (IT) application is also one of the major drivers of the shifts in competitive power. We now have entered "The Wired Society"; the current state of IT allows for interconnecting of organizations.

IT is not only a cause of turbulence but can also be used proactively. Distributed systems have become a powerful leverage in breaking down the traditional hierarchy by offering information accessibility for all organizational members, working in small flexible units.

However, to effectively manage this kind of IT application, the traditional paradigm of top down planning in a centralized computer environment, as solidified in methods like BSP and ISP, is no longer adequate. As a result of the developments discussed, a new type of information management approach is needed.

ISSUES

We propose an alternative paradigm centred around an *information infrastructure*. The basic purpose of this approach is *to provide a set of common IT provisions that enable the subsequent development of information systems serving the needs of individual organizational units*. The information infrastructure comprises a collection of common and standardized provisions of all the four components. As such, it enables its users to develop their own information systems within the limits imposed by the information infrastructure. The following issues receive special attention:

· Which elements constitute the information infrastructure?
· How can the decision making process regarding investments in the information infrastructure be conceptual-

ized?
· How can this decision making process be supported?

FINDINGS

Components of an information infrastructure

The concept of an information infrastructure is not entirely new, but up till now it is has been given quite different meanings. Traditionally the term infrastructure has a rather technological connotation, often referring to the centralised hardware environment. New views have included telecommunications based provisions as an analogy to the public infrastructure. Others see the infrastructure as all the facilities, standards and policies to enable dispersed or end user computing.

Our view of the information infrastructure is a more comprehensive one. An information infrastructure consists of several components:

· a hardware infrastructure;
· a data infrastructure;
· an application infrastructure;
· an organizational infrastructure.

A conceptual model of the decision making process

Based upon the descriptive decision-making literature and case study research we propose a conceptual model of the decision making process regarding investments in the information infrastructure. In this model, investment decisions are taken on different levels. Outcomes of decisions at a certain level set constraints on the alternatives for IT application at lower decision levels. This results in a layered information infrastructure. Furthermore, it is assumed that decisions with respect to the different components of the information infrastructure are partly taken independently. Consequently, the actual shape en content of an information infrastructure permanently changes as a result of the different ongoing decision-making processes. In such an environment a tool which would allow for unambiguous modelling and simulation of the various investment alternatives and their consequences can significantly contribute to enhancing the productivity of the communication between the various colewort and consequently the decision making process as a whole.

Decision support with ExSpect

ExSpect (Executable Specification tool) was developed at Eindhoven University of Technology to support formal specification of systems. It uses coloured Petrinets for specification of processes and their inputs and outputs. To specify the active components in these processes it uses a typed functional language, similar to Z. The ExSpect specifications are executable. Primarily to overcome the disadvantage of low accessibility of formal specifications for non-experts: a prototype of the system can be run to enable the clients/users to validate the system specification. Although ExSpect was developed primarily for information system specification, it has been used for modelling and simulating other types of systems as well. The Dutch Railway Organization for instance uses ExSpect to support the decisions on adjustment of their infrastructure.

As an example of ExSpect's modelling capabilities and its use as a communication tool in decision processes regarding information-infrastructures we conducted a case-study of the Dutch GBA-system (= Municipal Base Register of Population).

The project was initiated by the Dutch central government in 1984 to achieve a higher level of uniformity in the systems for registration of population that were used in the more than 650 municipalities in the Netherlands. The resulting infrastructural system consists of a network, a minimum set of data every municipality has to keep of every member of its population and procedures for sending messages between municipalities and other institutions interested in the data (e.g. the tax agency). Within these standards it allows a municipality to fit its Register of Population to its own needs.

CONCLUSIONS AND DIRECTIONS OF FURTHER RESEARCH

In the current turbulent environment in which organizations operate, the traditional approach of information management based on top down planning in a centralized computing environment proves to be increasingly inadequate. An alternative paradigm centred around an information infrastructure is presented and relevant issues are discussed.

Further research should be directed towards finding the essential criteria to evaluate infrastructural IT-investments and incorporating them into a communication support system. In the continuation of our research we will contribute to this through participatory case study research.

Role of Culture in the Development and Transfer of Information Technology

Venky Venkatachalam
and
Barry Shore
The Whittmore School of Business and Economics
Department of Decision Sciences
University of New Hampshire
Durham, NH 03824

ABSTRACT

The systems development life cycle methodology fails to consider the role of national culture in the development of IS applications. Neither does it consider the role of culture in the transfer of applications from one culture to another. This paper draws upon three major frameworks from the IS literature to develop a cross cultural view of the systems development life cycle. First, the differences among cultures are explored using the Hofstede framework. Second, the role of international competition is considered using Porter's framework, and third, the role of the work process or task is considered using the Gorry and Scott-Morton framework. Finally, these frameworks are combined to develop a conceptual model of the development and transfer of information technology.

INTRODUCTION

An increasing number of information system (IS) applications are implemented across national and cultural boundaries. The literature on systems analysis and design, however, has been developed primarily in the United States and may be culturally biased when this framework is used to develop applications in other cultures or when applications are developed in one culture and transferred to another.

Broader Framework

A broader framework is needed to acknowledge how the dimensions of culture can affect the development process from requirements planning through implementation. But developing such a framework is fraught with problems. How can culture be measured? What role does international competition play in the forces that drive an organization to adopt IT? Does culture impact all applications? And finally, how does culture affect these applications? Problems notwithstanding, it seems appropriate at this stage in the development of a theory of global information technology to formulate a general framework which identifies the major issues affecting development and information technology transfer. The risks of working in this ambiguous arena hopefully outweigh the risks of proceeding without an integrative framework.

Once developed, a framework promises several benefits. First, it can identify the dominant issues in the development and transfer of applications across national cultures. Second, it can provide insight into the way in which these issues are related. Third, it can help clarify which problems need attention. And finally, it can establish a basis for comparability of research.

Comparability is an issue of concern . Many studies have already been reported in the literature[Ein-Dor, Segev, Orgad, 1993]. As Palvia has stated, "Such descriptive and comparative studies are of great value to both practitioners and researchers." [Palvia, 1993, p. 3]. These studies however usually take a "country-specific" frame of reference. As a result, comparability among different studies, a next step in the research trail, is difficult because no agreement on a frame of reference exists. Palvia states "..I would like to exhort the international MIS researchers to go several steps beyond such descriptive studies in order to develop further insights into the nature of country issues as well as differences among countries." [Palvia, 1993 p, 3]. This paper is attempt to address this challenge.

Three Factors

It is becoming clear that culture does indeed influence the development and transfer of IT across national boundaries.

"Computers, the products of western civilization, are adjusted to the culture of their developers. African cultures are quite different and as a result, their implementation may lead to psychological stress. Developers of information technology should be aware of this fact and adjust their systems accordingly." [Janczewski, 1992]

But there are other factors which affect this process. Alavi and Joachimsthaler [1992] suggest that those 'contextual variables' which influence implementation success include the external factors such as competitive considerations, organizational factors such as management support, task type or task complexity, and user factors such as cognitive style and personality.

From this we will identify three factors which appear to dominate the development and transfer process. The first is national culture, the second is the competitive environment, and the third is the nature of the task or problem itself.

While organizational factors (organizational culture) may have an effect on the development and transfer of information technology, we have decided to omit them from the framework in the interest of keeping the focus on differences between cultures rather than on differences within cultures. Nonetheless, organization culture may explain why one organization in a culture has a different experience with the development and transfer of IT than another organization in the same culture.

This paper is organized into three sections. The first section defines the three factors, the second discusses the interaction among these factors, and the third draws conclusions and suggests directions for future research.

FACTORS AFFECTING IT TRANSFER

National Culture

Cross-cultural differences have been explored in many studies, but the model developed by Hoftstede dominates the literature and therefore seems to be a reasonable starting point. Hofstede [1980] defines culture as the

"Collective programming of the human mind that distinguishes the members of one human group from those of another. Culture in this sense, is a system of collectively held values."

Do these 'collectively held values' influence the management process?

"There is something in all countries called 'management', but its meaning differs to a larger or smaller extent from one country to the other, and it takes considerable historical and cultural insight into local conditions to understand its processes, philosophies, and problems. If already the word may mean so many different things, how can we expect one country's theories of management to apply abroad." [Hofstede, 1993].

While Hofstede and others address management in general our interest is on the cultural affect on the management of IT development and transfer process. Babington states:

"Many development projects have failed as consultants and aid officials have attempted to transport sophisticated American and business methods to developing countries." [Babington, 1987]

Consider also the experience encountered in the United States in the transfer of IT intensive Japanese management strategies such as Total Quality Control, Just-in-Time, Kaizen (continuous improvement), and cost management systems to American and Japanese-owned firms. The conclusion in an article by Young suggests that

"US firms and Japanese-owned firms in the United States will be much more successful in adopting and implementing Japanese manufacturing practices, respectively, if they pay more attention to the differences in practices and modify them accordingly [Young, 1992].

Research therefore suggests that culture does have an impact on the transfer of in Information technology.

Studying national culture, Hofstede [1980] identified four dimensions by which national cultures differed. From his analysis of 116,000 questionnaires he found they differed

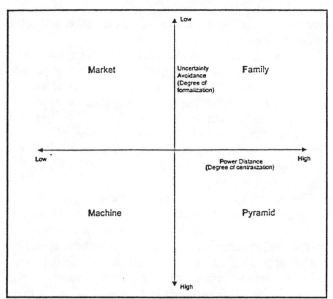

Figure 1: Organizational Cultural Profile (OCP)

by:
- Power distance,
- Uncertainty avoidance,
- Individualism-Collectivism, and
- Masculinity-Femininity

Power Distance indicates "the extent to which a society accepts the fact that power in institutions is distributed unequally."

Uncertainty Avoidance is the extent to which a society feels threatened by uncertain situations and avoids these situations through career stability, establishing formal rules, and not tolerating deviant ideas.

Individualism-Collectivism suggests a loosely knit social fabric in which people take care of themselves contrasted with a social fabric in which groups take care of the individual in exchange for their loyalty.

Masculinity-Femininity reflects whether the dominant values are associated with the collection of money and things (masculine) as contrasted with values associated with the caring for others and the quality of life (feminine).

The research data compared beliefs and values of employees from a multinational corporation with facilities in 40 "wealthy" and "more prosperous third would countries." It concluded that these dimensions are valid measures of cultural differences among these countries.

Of these four dimensions power distance and uncertainty avoidance are considered dominant in studying organizations within a particular culture [Hofstede, 1981]. We will consider the same two in developing a framework for studying the interaction between culture and systems development stages.

Hofstede [1980], describes four classifications of culture measured by combinations of power distance and uncertainty avoidance, which we refer to as the organizational cultural profile (OCP) (see Figure 1). The degree of power distance is reflected by the degree of centralization in organizations within a given culture, while the degree of uncertainty avoidance is reflected by the degree of formalization and rules within those organizations.

The four quadrants in the OCP represent regions into which organizations within a specific culture can be placed. The first quadrant, called the family by Hofstede, is characterized by cultures displaying a high degree of centralization combined with a lower level of formalization ("the need for formal rules and specialization, the assignment of tasks to experts,"[Hofstede, 1980, p365]. Organizations in less developed countries would be expected to fall in this quadrant, for example, organizations in India and Iran.

The second quadrant, called the market, represents cultures which are neither centralized nor formalized. Organizations in Great Britain may be expected to fall in this category.

The third quadrant, called the machine, is characterized by a high degree of formalization and decentralized power. Organizations in Germany would fall in this category as the power is vested in the role not in the person filling the role.

The fourth quadrant, called the pyramid, is both centralized and formal. Examples would include organizations in France.

This framework is particularly useful in helping us to understand the differences in the use of IT applications across national cultures. Verstraete studying organizations in Eastern Europe concluded:

> One overwhelmingly predominant feature of Eastern European organization universally mentioned is its extreme emphasis on centrality, with decision making emanating from the top and seldom allocated to lower echelons. Within such an environment, the personal computer will serve a far different role than it has in the west, where its introduction enhances individual autonomy[Verstraete, 1992, p.69.].

This suggests that in cultures with high centrality (high power distance) the transfer of certain applications may be problematical. While culture may play a significant role in the transfer of IT, it can also be argued that the influence of technology and task is so pervasive that national cultural values are forced to change as an application is introduced into the organization. For example, the implementation of an accounting system may force the change in methods and procedures which would otherwise be rejected by the prevailing culture. Indeed, the argument has been made that technology will ultimately force culture to change.

> "...we do not contend that the studies in cross-cultural management are obsolete, but we do feel the logic of technology is taking over man's differing beliefs and value orientations." [Negandi, 1983]

But Hofstede contends, "Culture..is often difficult to change; if it changes at all, it does so slowly" (Organizational Dynamics 1980 p.348).

How, then, does culture affect systems development and transfer? The answer we contend cannot be answered by considering culture alone. It can be answered only in the context of the competitive nature of the industry and the nature of the task. Nonetheless, it may be possible to hypoth-

esize that some cultures, perhaps classified as 'family' and 'pyramid' may resist the consequences of IT. Justification for this may be in the fact that they exhibit a large power distance and accessible technology may interfere with the balance of power. In others, perhaps classified as 'market' or 'machine' the transfer of IT may be somewhat easier to accomplish.

Competitive Environment

There are many models that have been developed to explore the competitive environment of the firm. Perhaps the most widely used topology is that of Porter [Porter, 1980, 1986] [Sundaram and Black, 1992]. Porters framework suggests that the forces driving industry competition include the rivalry among firms, the bargaining power of suppliers, the bargaining power of customers, the threat of new entrants, and the threat of substitute products.

Rivalry among firms is the jockeying for position using such tactics as price competition, advertising battles, product introductions and increase customer service or warranties. All firms are threatened by the *substitute products* sold by computers. The more attractive the price-performance of the substitute product the greater is the sense of competition. *Buyers* affect the competitive nature of the industry by forcing prices lower, bargaining for higher quality or more services, and playing competitors against one another. Suppliers affect competition within the industry by threatening to raise prices or deducing the quality of purchased goods and services. *New entrants* to the market can bring new resources and capacity as well as redistribute market share.

Collectively, these forces affect the competitive nature of the market place. The level of competition among industries can vary considerably. Porter suggests that competition is intense in industries like tires, paper and steel, and relatively mild in industries like oil-field equipment and services. Competition may be minimal in fields such a government services and education.

How does the competitive environment affect IT development and transfer? We suggest that organizations will face increasing pressure to speed cultural accommodation in the interest of meeting increasing levels of national and international competition.

Information Hierarchy

IT applications can be classified in many ways. Gorry and Scott-Morton [1971] classify applications according to the level in the management hierarchy they support. Accordingly, applications can be described as supporting transaction processing, operations planning and control, management planning and control, and strategic planning. For example, Airline reservation systems represent transaction processing, Production planning systems such as MRP would represent operational planning and control systems, spreadsheet budgeting would represent a management planning and control system, and a system with access to industry and economic data would represent a strategic planning system. In addition, applications can also be characterized by the degree of structure in the problem domain. Two extremes are structured and unstructured problems.

Transaction processing applications are very structured and represent a class of problems where the procedures of the task dominate the problem domain. However, as the applications migrate from operations planning and control to strategic planning and as applications move from structured to unstructured, intangibles play an increasing role in the development and use of the application. As the application moves from transaction processing toward strategic planning and as the application moves from structured to unstructured, the degrees of freedom available to the systems analyst increases. For example, a systems analyst in one organizational environment may design a manufacturing planning and control system very differently from a systems designer in another organization.

How does the task or nature of the application affect IT development and transfer? We suggest that as the application moves up the information hierarchy the ambiguity of the problem domain increases, culture has a greater range to impact the development and implementation process.

INTERACTION AMONG FACTORS

Figure 2 suggests how these three factors interact to influence the system development and transfer problem. First, the competitive environment of the industry and the position of the application in the information hierarchy interact with the culture to influence or modify the national culture. Table 1 suggests the direction of these influences. In a highly competitive environment together with a task which is low in the information hierarchy (very structured), the influence on culture will be low as the task and competitive forces dominate culture. When the competitive environment is high but the application is in the higher ranges of the information hierarchy (strategic planning) the influence on culture will be

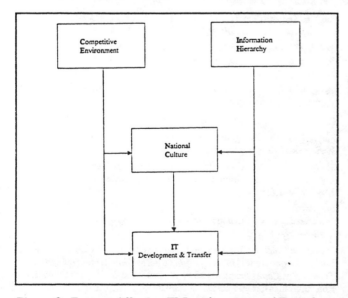

Figure 2: Factors Affecting IT Development and Transfer and their Interaction

Competitive Environment	Information Hierarchy	Cultural Influence
High	Low	Low
High	High	Moderate
Low	Low	High
Low	High	Very High

Table 1: Influences of Competitive Environment and Information Hierarchy on Culture

moderate as the ambiguous nature of the problem provides the degrees of freedom necessary for cultural difference to increase its role in the development and transfer process.

When the competitive forces are low and the application is in the low range of the information hierarchy, for example a billing system in a government owned public utility, the influence of culture will be high as the lack of competitive urgency and uncertainty avoidance serve to inhibit significant changes in the national culture. When the competitive forces are low and the application is in the higher ranges of the information hierarchy the influence of culture can be very high as the ambiguous nature of the problem together with lack of urgency and uncertainty avoidance tolerate a strong cultural influence.

We have suggested the way in which competition and hierarchy can influence culture. At the bottom of Figure 2 culture together with competition and hierarchy are shown as influencing IT development and transfer.

IT Development and Transfer

The *development* of an IT application includes the stages of project definition, systems study, design, and programming. [Hosseini, Shore, Venkatachalam, 1993] Since programming is a structured task it seems reasonable to conclude that this activity is relatively unaffected by culture. In addition, the influence of technology such as relational data base management systems and CASE tools has significantly standardized certain design stages and has contributed toward an increase in the standardization of the design process. This leaves the stages — definition and study — as the two stages most likely influenced by national culture. The degree of this influence, however, will be determined by the interaction of culture with competition and the location of the application in the information hierarchy.

The *transfer* of IT applications includes the phases of implementation and use. It might be suggested that countries characterized by a high degree of power distance and uncertainty avoidance, classified as belonging to the pyramid quadrant, would resist the development of new applications or the transfer of applications. These application would threaten established work methods. Verstraete [1992] studying information systems in the Soviet Union and Eastern Europe found the transfer of accounting systems (transaction applications) 'overwhelming'. Indeed Hofstede [1993] classifies Russia as very high (the highest in his study) in power distance and uncertainty avoidance (the second highest in his study). Cultural issues in Verstraete's study involved underground economies, official and unofficial systems, avoidance of documentation, and even manipulation of data to support beliefs. Transferring applications to these cultures would be expected to be met with resistance.

Our framework provides some insight into Verstraete's example. First, the competitive environment and the nature of the problem are expected to have an impact on the national culture. That is, the culture may have to change if the system is to work. But as Hofstede points out culture may change slowly. At the same time culture as it exists now, competition, and the task, all affect the current state of the information system. So we may conclude that while the competitive environment may dictate one type of accounting system, cultural forces acting at the present time may dictate another. The question is how to bridge the gap and encourage the changes in culture necessary to respond to nature of the problem in a specific competitive environment.[Shore, Venkatachalam, forthcoming].

CONCLUSION

While a considerable body of work has developed around the management of information technology in multinational corporations and multicultural environments, a review of the literature suggests that very little work, if any, has been done linking national culture with theories of information systems design.

The purpose of this paper has been to suggest how links can be drawn between the literature on culture, competitive advantage and tasks and their influence on IT development and transfer. The degree of cultural influence on the process of IT transfer is affected by the nature of competitive environment in which an organization operates and the level at which the application fits the information hierarchy.

This paper suggest the interaction of the three factors namely culture, competitive environment, and Information hierarchy, and their influence on It development and transfer. However, the links proposed in the framework need to be corroborated with industry studies. Organizations experienced in cross cultural transfer of IT need to be involved and their experience studied in order to validate the framework suggested in this paper.

A second direction for future research include the identification of variables for each of the three factors and empirical study of the relationship among them. Culture can be measured by Hofstede's framework, namely, a combination of power distance, uncertainty avoidance, individualism-collectivism, and masculinity-femininity. Competitive environment can be represented as a combination of number of competitors, number of suppliers, size of the customer base, and the extent of threat from substitute products and services. The application's position in the information hierarchy can be classified as either highly structured or poorly structured.

The degree of success of the IT transfer process is related to the extent to which the end-users are satisfied with the use of the application. Past studies in the area of end-user computing satisfaction including the measures suggested by Doll and Torkzadeh [1988] can be used in conjunction with the cultural, competitive, and hierarchical variables identified earlier in order to develop a model of the IT development and transfer process. Such a study would certainly lead us to a better understanding of the IT transfer process and be of use to practitioners as well.

REFERENCES

Ackermann, W.," Cultural Values and Social Choice of Technology", Int.Soc.Sci.J,Vol. XXXIII, No.3, 1981.

Alavi, M. , E.R. Joachimsthaler," Revisiting DSS implementation Research: A Meta Analysis of the literature and suggestions for researchers", MIS Quarterly, March 1992, pp. 95-116.

Babington, E. A., "Installing a Computerized Planning System in Ghana", Long Range Planning, Vol. 20, No. 4, 1987, pp. 110-117.

Doll, W. J. and G. Torkzadeh, The Measurement of End-User Computing Satisfaction, MIS Quarterly, June 1988, pp. 259-273.

Ein-Dor, P., Segev, E., and Orgad, M. "The Effect of National Culture on IS: Implications for International Information Systems, Journal of Global Information Management, Vol 1, No 1, Winter 1993, pp. 33-44.

Gorry, G. A. and M. S. Scott-Morton, A Framework for Management Information Systems, Sloan Management Review, Fall 1971, pp. 55-70.

Hosseini, Jinoos, B. Shore and V. Venkatachalam, Revisiting Systems Analysis and Design: A Cross-Cultural Approach, Proceedings of the 1993 Information Resources Management Association, Salt Lake City, 1993, pp 25-31.

Hofstede, Geert, Motivation, Leadership, and Organization: Do American Theories Apply Abroad?, Organizational Dynamics, Summer 1980.

Hofstede, Geert, Culture and Organizations, International Studies of Management and Organizations, Vol X, No 4, 1981, pp. 15-41.

Hofstede, Geert, Cultural Constraints in Management Theories, Academy of Management Executive, Vol. 7, No. 1, 1993, pp. 81-94.

Janczewski Lech J., Relationships Between Information Technology and Competitive Advantage: In New Zealand Businesses, Proceedings of 1992 Information Resources Management Association, Charleston, 1992. pp. 357-364.

Laudon, Kenneth C. and Jane P. Laudon, Management Information Systems: Organization and Technology, Macmillan, NY, 1994

Negandhi, Anant R., Management in the Third World, in Managing in Different Cultures, Edited by Pat Joynt and Malcolm Warner, Norwich, London, 1985, pp. 69-97.

Palvia, Prashant, Preface, Journal of Global Information Management, Vol.1, No.2, Spring 1993, pp. 3-5.

Porter M. E. Competitive Strategy, New York, Free Press, 1980.

Porter, M. E. The Changing Patterns of International Competition, California Management Review, Vol. 28, No 2, pp.5-13.

Shore, B. and V. Venkatachalam, Prototyping: A Metaphor for Cross-Cultural Transfer and Implementation of IS Applications, Information and Management, (forthcoming).

Sundaram, Anant K., J. Stewart Black, The Environment and Internal Organization of Multinational Enterprises, Academy of Management Review, Vol 17 No.4, 1992, pp.729-757

Verstraete, Anthony, Information Systems in the Soviet Union and Eastern Europe: Opportunities Under Perestroika, in The Global Issues of Information Technology Management, edited by Shailenra Palvia, Prashant Palvia, and Ron Zigli, Idea Group Publishers, Harrisburg, Pa, 1992, pp.55-72.

Young, S. Mark, A Framework for Successful Adoption and Performance of Japanese Manufacturing Practices in the United States, Academy of Management Review, Vol. 17, No 4. pp. 677-700.

Executive Information System and Decision Support System: A Framework for Integration

David C. Yen
Department of Decision Sciences
Miami University, Oxford, Ohio 45056
(516) 529-4827

Alex N. Chen
Management Sciences and Information Systems
Penn State Altoona Campus
Altoona, PA 16601, (814) 949-5248

H.L. Tang
Dept. of BIS
Western Michigan University
Kalamazoo, MI 49008   (616) 387-5479

Executive Abstract

This paper examines the integration of Decision Support Systems (DSS) and Executive Information systems (EIS). The integration of these two systems is still at a stage of experimental research. Middle managers have widely used DSS on doing data and model analysis. Top management has found EIS particularly helpful from the structured and well-informed information provided. The importance of this topic is supported by the potential benefit to effective management decision making and support. The understanding of this framework would benefit future studies in this area.

Development of computer technology, data communication, and various decision support applications will have considerable impact on this integration framework.

BACKGROUND INFORMATION

Decision support system offers strong support to middle managers and professional systems. It enhances decision making by providing capabilities of modeling and data analysis. Executive information system is intended to help senior executives access wide-ranged information and assist them in implementing decisions. Being aware of the environmental changes of the competitive position of the organization, executives make decisions in a well informed and effective manner. A significant development in management decision support is the integration of different kinds of decision support systems such as DSS, EIS, Office Automation (OA), and Expert System (ES). Integration of complementary systems can provide high quality and effective decision support. The purpose of this paper is to examine the roles of DSS and EIS in management decision support, and to present the feasibility and potential framework to integrate EIS and DSS.

DISCUSSION OF THE ISSUES

EIS and DSS have their distinctive capabilities and components. It is their distinctive features that would make the integration significant. EIS and DSS have the same nature with regard to their generic goal — management decision support. EIS provides senior executives various sources of information in a descriptive way. Communication is a distinct feature of EIS.

DSS addresses the functional analysis needs from managers. DSS is driven by models and users have high involvement in the process. Information is relatively not very diversified and mostly comes from functional departments. EIS and DSS have the similar components: Database management; Model base system; Dialog management; and Users are managers. Data communication and office support are two components of less significance in DSS.

FINDINGS OF THE PAPER

The paper, based on the common components of EIS and DSS, proposes a framework from two perspectives:

(1) Enhance — incorporate the components into the system and generate improved result;

(2) Coupling — integrate the component into the system by communication mechanism.

The proposed integrated system has components of Database System, Model Base System, Dialogue Management, Data Communication, OA, and Users.

Expert System (ES) has also been applied to domains in

which adoption of the intelligent "thinking" is necessary. A complete management support system cannot be achieved without ES that is considered a technology to enhance the intelligent aspect of the system.

CONCLUSION

The integration of EIS and DSS provides a potential framework for a comprehensive management decision support system. The implementation of this framework is not easy because:

(1) The research and application of EIS are still at an experimental stage.

(2) System complexity. It is a complicated task to combine all components into an organization framework.

(3) Technology constraints. The application of AI technology has not been widely accepted.

Some new developments will have potential influence on the integration framework:

(1) GDSS. GDSS can be integrated into the framework to support group decision making.

(2) AI. AI brings the "intelligence" to the framework.

(3) Integrated Service Digital Network (ISDN). ISDN transmits text, graph, and digits over a communication network simultaneously.

(4) Distributed Database. A distributed database system provides a scheme for a decentralized organization information process.

This paper provides a potential framework for a comprehensive management decision support system. Future studies about this topic are imperative.

Section Three

Strategic Information Technology Management

Project Management for Business Process Redesign

Robert W. Bryan
Dr. Michael L. Gibson

415 West Magnolia Avenue
Department of Management
College of Business
Auburn University
Auburn, AL 36849-5241
(205) 844-6538/6525

ABSTRACT

Business process redesign (BPR) is vital to enhance the ability to compete. Radical redesign needs to be guided by sound project management (PM) principles. These principles and procedures were developed for the management of innovative, unfamiliar projects. Recommended steps in BPR are considered. Steps for managing BPR as a project are recommended, and the relationship between PM and BPR explored.

The urgency of the competitive environment mitigates against formal use of PM methods, although its principles are essential. The experience of Xerox in a recent redesign project highlights the use of work teams. The project provided incentive for Xerox personnel to bid competitively for the work against inside and outside providers.

Insights are offered for new techniques and methods for BPR project teams. These emphasize telecommunications and standardized interfaces to improve communication and coordination.

Information Technology Innovations and Healthcare Industry

Edward T. Chen
Management Department
Southeastern Louisiana University
Box 350, SLU Station
Hammond, LA 70402

Hsin-Ginn Hwang
Computer Office Information Systems
Northeast Louisiana University
Monroe, LA 70209

ABSTRACT

The purpose of the following research paper is to provide a summary of prior research on information technology innovations and the Healthcare industry. The paper covers topics including the background information on the two industries, exploration of computerized patient records, recent electronic billing systems, medical information networks, the evolution of information technology innovations in medical field, and practices in this field. With the onset of healthcare reform proposed by President Clinton, there are several problems that have arisen and even more will surface as reform is carried out. The integration of the current management information systems and hospital systems is a necessity to achieve the health reform goals. This paper also suggests some system development methodology available to the design of an integrated medical delivery system.

INTRODUCTION

The annual Industrial Outlook released at the end of 1993 by the Commerce Department predicted the healthcare spending would top $1 trillion in 1994. If effective cost constraints are not carried out and current healthcare policy is not changed, the report suggests that the spending will grow at an average rate of thirteen and half percent annually for the next five years. These estimates add a strong momentum to the healthcare reform movement. The challenge of healthcare industry is to reduce the rate of growth. President Clinton's healthcare reform plan aims to reduce the rate of increase in healthcare spending to that of inflation with an adjustment for population growth. His reform plan also intends to limit the private insurance premiums and to cut federal healthcare programs. The public financial concerns will force healthcare executives to look closely on the relation between how healthcare institutions are paid for services and how they are managed. The significance of national expenditures on healthcare has raised legislative concern on the general issue of cost control and quality treatment. Techniques and practices motivate promising cost reduction and treatment improvement will be popular.

The essence of healthcare reform is providing quality healthcare while lowering costs simultaneously. Politicians and business leaders are looking for ways to stop rising healthcare costs. They seem to believe that information systems could be the cure. However, the only true presence of information systems in the healthcare industry is in the form of billing and other back office operations. A survey of 400 information systems hospital managers showed that eighty-three percent of them believe that hospitals are far behind in the use of computers (Betts, 1993).

Traditionally, automation has come in the area of bookkeeping. However, experts see that future information systems investments will help doctors and nurses improve productivity and enable them to upgrade the quality of healthcare provided to their patients. In addition, the cost of most information systems projects is very high and the average hospital is finding it very difficult to raise the necessary funds.

Healthcare industries have certain distinctive characteristics. Kimberly (1982) indicates that (1) the raw material of healthcare institutions is human; (2) healthcare work is guided by a trial-and-error paradigm not an empirically validated theory, therefore, it is art rather than science; (3) measurement of the performance of healthcare providers raises a problem on the standard of quality of care; (4) the key production worker is usually not employees of the institution such as physicians use hospital resources but are generally paid by patients; and (5) the ideology of patient care often conflicts with the ideology of efficient managerial practice. Increasing efficiency may be inherently pernicious to patient life. With the basic understanding of the healthcare industry, we argue that the new information technology innovations should not be considered solely as managerial competitive weapons. Instead, the whole healthcare community should look these new information technology innovations as opportunities of joint venture to achieve mutual benefits.

The purpose of this paper is to provide a summary of some advanced information technology innovations that can be applied to the healthcare field to achieve these goals. Computerized patient records, electronic payments and claims, and fiber optics and information network are the major investigations of this paper. These innovations may incur some high costs at the early adoption stage. They would be paid off soon after their implementation. Some caveats are also mentioned in the paper.

COMPUTERIZED PATIENT RECORDS

Patient records must be stored up to twenty-five years, depending on state laws. Davidson (1992) points out that ninety-nine percent of patients records are currently kept on paper. The paper records make them cumbersome to access, vulnerable to error and misplacement, and often illegible. As a result, costly duplication is common and decision making becomes slow. Without a timely access to the patient's health record, the physician is frustrated, the patient is suffering, staff time is being wasted and costs are mounting.

Recording patient's data in an electronic form will provide the physicians with the ability to consult with healthcare professionals anywhere in the country. Through data communication, current patient information can be available simultaneously to both parties. E-mail, teleconferencing, and videoconferencing assist healthcare professionals improve their communication and produce less paper circulation. Employees also can spend less time in meeting and more time in their work. Computerized patient records are building blocks for several benefits. Physicians and healthcare practitioners can reach a new level of productivity by working together more creatively and collaboratively. Medical record department can improve patient data collection, retrieval, display, and storage.

These new records will draw scattered patient information into an integrated system, which is the key to the healthcare reform package. Potential benefits include increased billing turnaround time and reduced support staff. The United States Government demands that all hospitals participating in Medicare must convert to computerized patient records by January 1, 1996 (Cornelius, 1993). Many hospitals expect their information technology budgets to grow largely due to the new standards that will be required.

Computer-based Patient Record Institute (CPRI) was formed in 1992 to promote and facilitate development, implementation and distribution of the computerized patient records. Codes and structure, confidentiality, privacy and legislation, professional/public education and financing are the important considerations of their projects.

Skeptics believe that money and people's resistance to change are holding up the use of the computerized patient record. However, to implement this plan the entire organization must be re-engineered (Steward, 1993). That means changing the fundamental business process to promote coordinated care instead of allowing reimbursement to influence the type and site of treatment (Morrissey, 1993a). There are many obstacles that stand in the way of a true computerized patient record. There are lack of funds, technology, government standards, and clinician interest, no hospital commitment, too many state regulations and hospital policies.

Critics are worried about the issues involving security and patient confidentiality. However, there is a medical audit trail within the system that tracks who has accessed that particular record. Computerized patient record could provide more in the way of access security. The data management must be accurate, complete, accessible, timely, and coordinated (Tan, McCormick, and Sheps, 1993). Personnel may be required to use passwords, keys or cards to access the system. The predominant barrier is the attitude of healthcare executives toward the cost of computerization. They should not look at the creation and conversion of patient records as overhead. Instead, the computerization of patient records is the key to many other efficient and effective practices such as timely available patient information and automatic billing. The computerized patient records can be a long-term savings and patient care benefits.

Healthcare costs could be modified by using computer-based patient records to reduce the number of redundant tests performed because previous test results were unavailable. The National Academy of Science's Institute of Medicine is demanding that a database be created to consolidate records for one particular patient. These computer-based records also would foster research on the effectiveness of patient care. Quality and utilization review can be easily assessed through captured patient data (Tan, et al., 1993). Healthcare providers, payers, and patients become the ultimate beneficiaries.

A few questions and issues must be resolved in order to measure computerized patient record productivity. Cornelius (1993) recommends that information systems managers ask the following questions before adopting the new approach:

· Can the hospital centralize and standardize the record system from admissions to closure?
· Check with other area hospitals to see if they have found an effective way of revamping the record system.
· Meet with physicians, nurses, technical departments, and record staffs to examine where duplication and useless information documentation occurs.
· Determine which records and reports are proprietary and check how non-proprietary information could be shared electronically to reduce paper flow.
· Did management create a paperless administrative office as an example toward computerization?
· Meet with information systems experts to determine the best methods for communication and data transfer.

Positive responses to these questions and statements indicate movement toward a true computer-based patient record system.

The computerized patient record should have multi-faceted role in the healthcare industries. Shortliffe and Perreault (1990) point out that these records could serve several critical functions:

· Patient care--the main purpose of the medical record is to facilitate patient care by summarizing the patient's history and documenting care services.
· Legal and financial requirements--the medical record is a legal document, and that must be preserved as a record of medical activities and the justifications for those activities.
· Research support--the rapid analysis of large sets of patient

records will provide a new source of new knowledge.

ELECTRONIC PAYMENTS AND CLAIMS

Healthcare Financial Management Association announced that hospitals have to switch over from the old UB-82 format to the new UB-92 for billing Medicare by April 1, 1994. In the meantime, the Workgroup on Electronic Data Interchange, a healthcare industry task force established by the Bush administration, recommended in the middle of 1992 that the healthcare institutions convert to ANSI-837 standards for all healthcare transactions including Medicare billing by the end of 1994. This one standard would replace the seemingly one hundred different ways of electronically sending and receiving claims that already exist. The ANSI-837 was created by a committee of the American National Standards Institute and gives providers a uniform format for processing all healthcare transactions and especially bills.

UB-92 is a paper billing form on a screen that can be converted to an electronic form that is a flat file. It takes a fixed-length format for each transaction. The ANSI-837 can do a lot more than the UB-92. It is not a uniform bill. It is a set of rules to tie together all the data items of a bill. ANSI standards utilize variable lengths for both fields and records. The blank fields will not be transmitted. Therefore, the ANSI-837 format will take less time to transmit and less space to store than the UB-92 flat file. The ANSI-837 contains all of the information of UB-92 and can handle a variety of bills. Switching from UB-92 to ANSI-837 should not be a big pain from the management standpoint. The reprogramming, retraining of staff, reexamining billing procedures should be planned well. According to a 1993 study of the Healthcare Financial Management Association, total savings from automation and standardization of billing procedure can add up to 2.6 to 5.2 billions (Gardner, 1993).

Both organizations call for federal legislation mandating healthcare providers to convert to the new standards. The automatic billing system will revolutionize data entry in many medical transaction processing systems. The standardization of electronic data interchange should not be considered only as processing bills more efficiently. The reliability and accuracy of the transmitted data will provide audit and control of healthcare system (Hansen, 1989). It would also promote strategic relationships between healthcare trading partners (Roche, 1991). Currently the United States and Canada use the ANSI X.12 protocol and Europe uses a standard called EDIFACT. The converge of these two standards and the support of a consistent international data communication protocol should be concerned. Multinational companies need internal systems that support EDI across all of their sites.

FIBER OPTICS AND INFORMATION NETWORK

Fiber optics technology offers two-way transmission of voice, data, image, and video across a single line. Medical information can be exchanged between healthcare professionals anywhere within seconds. Diagnostic images then can be accessed by physicians on-line. A patient's condition can be displayed in a high resolution project screen in front of a surgical team. Medical students can experience the surgical procedure through video transmission.

Fiber optics will be a backbone support system behind the new computerized healthcare system. It helps provide timely and accurate quality treatment while keeping costs low. However, the systems that exist now are private networks. Only members are allowed access. What is needed is a public fiber optic network that would provide benefits to all. Because of its transmission capacity, fiber optics can provide a wider variety of services than are now available. However, the U.S. lacks a uniform telecommunications policy, which presently is a major roadblock to a nationwide fiber optic network (Holliday, 1991).

The enormous communication capacity of fiber optics can be used to construct an information network. The network with fiber optics is able to provide timely and quality treatment and in measuring performance. Airline and banking industries have formed information network to share information and assist travelers. Healthcare industry needs a public information network to fulfill their ultimate goal-- providing quality service at lower cost.

Healthcare reform will provide unemployed and uninsured people access to the federal healthcare programs. This will demand a new information delivery system among healthcare providers, insurers, patients, and government agencies. Most traditional communication networks are proprietary or owned by healthcare providers or payers. These traditional networks are designed to serve a comparatively small scope group. They will show many limitations on facing the national healthcare challenge. So far, several states and healthcare institutions have formed many community health information networks, or called CHINs.

Healthcare industries face a life or death situation over the availability and integrity of data. Many factors, including patient well-being, economic and funding pressures, are forcing healthcare organizations to develop integrated information systems if they are to survive.

The challenge of the design and development of a healthcare integrated system will be the integration of diverse applications into a common computing environment. Max Hopper (1990) coined "information utility" to describe this desired level of integration. He states that the development cost will be so expensive and no organization can afford. This integrated healthcare delivery system requires a joint effort organized through trade groups. Funding of this project from government is a necessity.

Before hospitals create an integrated delivery system, they must have a way to identify, share and store clinical information so it will be accessible to any healthcare provider throughout the system. At Baystate, Sharp Healthcare in San Diego, they have done just this. They reorganized their institutions and component provider departments. They broke down barriers to interaction and formed an open system. They settled on one set of operating procedures that took the place of a "hodgepodge" of clinical reporting regulations and record keeping (Morrissey, 1993b).

In order to work, an integrated system must have departments and facilities that operate cohesively. The first steps toward an integrated system should be:

1. Create a way to identify a patient throughout the system.
2. Reach a consensus on which information should be included in a patient's record.
3. Create a way to computerize the hospital departments and outlying offices that provide the system with information.

Some helpful devices in accomplishing this goal are a "master patient identifier" and a "data repository". A "master patient identifier" stores data under different identifiers to the same location. A "data repository" integrates information from diverse departmental systems into a common language, which avoids the need to link the systems in every way. Each system can then access the database and retrieve information from other component parts in the system. However, these are not the only plausible answers. A data dictionary can retrieve information from separate systems and display it on-screen for the user requesting it. Patient information is entered only once and can be called up from the database for patient histories or to update patient files.

The establishment of integrated national healthcare communication networks could link the entire healthcare systems electronically. However, this cooperative network can only work if individual hospitals put their own systems on-line and use an open system architecture.

The recent development in computer-aided software engineering (CASE) presents solutions that can be shared by almost all the organizations in a given industry. The amount of information utilized in the practice of medicine is immense, and systems to merge and manage these data are critical in the healthcare community. The CASE approach to generate a multimedia information repository with reusable applications that can be readily modified for a particular need. An object-oriented user interface or graphical user interface will make the integrated system even more user friendly.

GTE Government Systems Corporation, a unit of GTE corporation was awarded a six-year contract worth $19 million to design and develop a new information network to save Medicare $200 million a year. The Medicare Transaction System is to begin operating in late 1996 and be fully implemented by 1998. Data regarding eligibility, other insurance coverage and prior claims will be available to healthcare providers instantaneously.

Medicare recipients would present a Medicare card for their healthcare services. This card will allow hospitals and doctors to submit the claim to Medicare electronically and be paid automatically. Medicare recipients will receive a copy of the bill and care information. This system also allows the patient's Medigap insurer to be billed simultaneously. Medigap policies cover medical costs not covered by Medicare. The federal information network system may also help Medicare officials detect fraud and abuse in the Medicare program.

SUGGESTIONS AND IMPLICATIONS

Hopper (1990) asserts that technology alone cannot provide an enduring business advantage. Warner (1987) even describes information technology as a business competitive burden. Information technology innovations that are competitive advantages today may easily become tomorrow's liability. Healthcare industry has its unique characteristics in terms of utilizing information technology innovations. Stages of the evolution of information technology in relation to expenditures should be well planned (Gibson and Nolan, 1979). The value chain can be used as an analytical framework to examine value-adding activities in the information innovation application (Porter and Millar, 1985). The life cycle for each information technology innovation depends on the fit of the organization and the industry. The more an organization understands its own value chain as well as the value chain of the customer, the greater the ability to create value for the customer. Information technology innovations should help both parties understand each other better and enhance the primary and support activities of the healthcare providers.

From the above research, it is easy to surmise that there are revolutionary things happening in the healthcare industry. This revolution is the result of many factors. They are the election of a democratic president, the onset of reform of the very nature of how healthcare is provided, and the demand of all Americans for quality healthcare provided at an affordable price. At the heart of the reform is information systems technology.

Information technology holds the key to unlocking the flood gates of reform and cost effectiveness. It will only be those hospitals and healthcare providers that employ information technology and properly manage their information systems departments that will survive in the future. Those who fail to realize information systems importance to the healthcare industry will fall by the waste side. It is suggested that all healthcare providers invest in their information systems departments and move toward a completely computerized system. Those who do so will find that their profits will rise and their costs will decline.

CONCLUSIONS

Information technology and the healthcare industry will be forever married in harmony. In an effort to stop rising costs, the entire organization must be re-engineered through a disciplined approach. In the center of this new organization is the information systems department. In order to have an integrated delivery system, all departments must work cohesively. New government standards have forced healthcare providers to change how they do their accounting and how they record patient information. Already right now the average hospital spends fifty percent of its information systems budget on hardware and software combined. In the future, this percentage is expected to rise. Soon every hospital will have truly computerized patient records. In the future, innovations like fiber optics will make it possible for healthcare providers to use an enormous database filled with diagnoses, treatments and other various patient information. Further research should be conducted to show hospitals how to integrate these innovations into their existing systems. This would complete the revolution by allowing hospitals to come full circle with their information technology. All these innovations are creating a system where quality healthcare can be provided at an affordable rate.

REFERENCES

Betts, Mitch, "Rx for health costs: A dose of IS," *Computerworld*, July 1, 1993, pp. 47-48.

Cornelius, Mark, "Why endure frustration? Medical records need cooperative overhaul," *Modern Healthcare*, March 1, 1993. p. 33.

Davidson, Richard J., "CPR--The Key to Reform," *Health Systems Review*, Vol. 25, No. 6, 1992, pp. 18-22.

Gardner, Elizabeth, "Electronic Billing Entering New Era," *Modern Healthcare*, May 17, 1993, pp. 39-48.

Gibson, C. F. and Richard N. Nolan, "Managing the Four Stages of EDP Growth," *Harvard Business Review*, January-February 1974, pp. 76-88.

Hansen, James V. and Ned C. Hill, "Control and Audit of Electronic Data Interchange," *MIS Quarterly*, Vol. 13, No. 4, December 1989.

Holliday, Clifford, "Fiber optics: Health care needs a public network," *Hospitals*, November 20, 1991, p. 64.

Hopper, Max, "Rattling SABRE--New Ways to Compete on Information," *Harvard Business Review*, May-June, 1990, pp. 118-125.

Kimberly, John R., "Managerial Innovation and Health Policy: Theoretical Perspectives and Research Implications," *Journal of Health Politics, Policy and Law*, Vol. 6, No. 4, 1982, pp. 637-652.

Morrissey, John. "Steps toward Standardization Raise Questions about Priorities," *Modern Healthcare*, December 6, 1993, p. 56.

Morrissey, John. "Integrating the incompatible," Modern Healthcare, October 11, 1993, pp. 39-42.

Porter, M. J. and V. E. Millar, "How Information Gives You Competitive Advantage," *Harvard Business Review*, July-August, 1985, 149-160.

Roche, Edward M., *Telecommunications and Business Strategy*, Dryden Press, Chicago, IL., 1991.

Shortliffe, Edward and Leslie Perreault, *Medical Informatics: Computer Applications in Health Care*, Addison-Wesley, Reading, MA., 1990.

Steward, Thomas A., "Reengineering--The Hot New Managing Tool," *Fortune*, August 23, 1993, pp. 41-48.

Tan, Joseph K. H., Edward McCormick, and Samuel B Sheps, "Utilization Care Plans and Effective Patient Data Management," *Hospital & Health Services Administration*, Vol. 38, No. 1, Spring 1993, pp. 81-99.

Warner, Timothy, "Information Technology as a Competitive Burden," *Sloan Management Review*, Fall 1987, pp. 55-61.

Case Studies on the Exploitation of Electronic Messaging Systems in International Enterprises

Kai Jakobs and Klaus Lenssen
Technical University of Aachen
Informatik IV, Computer Science Department
Ahornstr. 55, D-52056 Aachen, FRG
Tel.: +49-241-80-21405l37;
Fax: +49-241-80-21429
e-mail: jakobslklaus@informatik.rwth-aachen.de

Executive Abstract

1. BACKGROUND

As a service for their member organizations, the European Electronic Messaging Association (EEMA) commissioned the authors of this paper to prepare a report on "Successful Applications of Electronic Messaging in International Organizations". The organizations cover a broad range of business areas, including finances, chemistry, aviation, hauliers, and others. They employ some 500,000 people and represent about 120,000 internal users, with additional 120,000 external terminals. This paper provides a summary of the report.

2. WHY MESSAGING?

Let us consider the major reasons for introducing electronic messaging. These include: •cost reductions •time savings •simultaneous delivery of information •post-processing of documents possible •simplification •enhanced reachability •information sharing •satisfying requests from customers or business partners

3. INTRODUCING E-MAIL

It has come very clear that large, international enterprises typically do not make overall strategic decisions concerning IT technology in general and messaging services in particular. Typically, IT-related decisions are made at department level, if not at an even lower one. Obviously, this does soon lead to very heterogeneous IT environments. Thus, it is little wonder that global, enterprise-wide strategies were normally not employed from the very beginning. Rather, it turns out that such strategies are defined at some later stage. That is, the number of users has to reach a "critical mass" before it is realized that a central management action is urgently required. The following introduction "strategy" holds for two thirds of the organizations considered: For one reason or another, some groups happen to get a messaging tool. The new service soon becomes popular with its users. The number of users increases steadily. Still, this does typically not happen at organizational level, but at departmental or site-level. However, at the same time very similar developments take place at many sites, obviously resulting in an extremely heterogeneous environment. This typical approach may be referred to as "bottom-up". Subsequently, at some stage, some central entity takes over and tries to harmonize the different services. "Top-down" is obviously another straightforward approach. However, it has turned out that only very few of the organizations considered had adopted this approach. In fact, it were the smaller ones who did.

4. BENEFITS IDENTIFIED

The three major benefits unanimously identified were: •enhanced cooperation and information sharing •cost savings •time savings Use of standardized forms and documents, for example, contribute considerably to a much more efficient communication. Post-processing of documents and far better print quality are other important features enabled by use of electronic messaging. This holds particularly when compared to the "normal" way of document transmission via fax. In general, the improvement of internal processes, based on the consistent use of electronic mail throughout an organization, is one of the major benefits identified. In addition to savings due to better cooperation and information sharing, cost savings include for instance the ongoing replacement of phone and telex by electronic mail. Moreover, use of message-based EDI contributes considerably to both, time and cost savings. Calculations done by one of the organizations reveal a significant and, in fact, astonishing superiority of e-mail to fax transmissions. Additional, straightforward time savings result, for instance, from e-mails capability to overcome time-zone problems to a great extent (compared to the phone), and far shorter transmission times (compared to a letter).

5. FUTURE DEVELOPMENTS

Please note that this refers to envisaged developments within the different organizations rather than future technical progress. At present, the organizations are in a transition phase. Most are considering X.400 based messaging as the system of choice. However, X.400 will mainly be employed as a mailbackbone, used to interconnect the single LAN-based systems of the different sites. In relation to X.400, a number of open issues have been identified, most of them common to all organizations (with different priorities, though), These include: •integration of mobile users •uniform directory service •integration of authentication functionality •integration of mail into the user's office environment Especially integration an (X.500 based) directory service is a most important issue. Whilst directory services are being used by every organization, these exhibit a similar heterogeneity as did the messaging services before.

6. LESSONS LEARNED

All organizations considered have now gathered substantial experiences in electronic messaging. A number of applications appear to be crucial to the success of messaging: •interpersonal messaging •application to application messaging EDI being the most prominent application in this area. •access to telematic services Most important, access to the fax service has to be provided. In addition, however, telex continues to be in use in some business areas. Due to the difficult and complex task of introducing and maintaining an electronic mail service, it is little wonder that problems and open issues have been encountered, some of which rise from the common lack of a central IT department. These include: •multiple communication protocols used •proprietary or vendor specific solutions •security problems •naming issues •directory services In addition, difficulties also arise if standards are to be used: •which standard? Besides the internationally standardized X.400 recommendation series, there is at least one more de-facto standard to be considered, the Internet mail. The major argument for the latter being the considerably larger number of users. The most prominent argument against the Internet is "hacker's delight", that is, security issues and reliability. •X.400 issues Most

service providers only offer X.400 (84). This old version offers very limited services, for instance in terms of directory utilization and support of distribution lists. Moreover, this leads to problems concerning undefined body-parts, ie. body parts, that are not supported by all ADMDs. Some ADMDs refuse to relay messages originating from another ADMD and destined to a third one. This continues to be a major obstacle for global X.400 connectivity.

7. SOME CONCLUDING REMARKS

From the reports assembled it may well be deducted that electronic messaging has successfully made its way into the offices of major international organizations. The current situation can be described as follows: the first stage of providing messaging services has been completed. This phase was usually characterized by the (bottom-up) introduction of e-mail systems, their spread throughout the organization and, finally, the establishment of a central entity in charge of managing electronic messaging on an enterprise-wide basis. LAN-based systems are installed at most sites. The second phase, which typically has been started more recently, will focus on homogenization. This will in most cases be done by employing X.400 as a backbone service, interconnecting the single in-house systems. Subsequently, it is planned to increase utilization and friendliness of messaging. The first will for instance include integration of mobile users, the latter primarily refers to introduction of a uniform directory service. To summarize: especially organizations operating on an international or even global basis have definitely identified messaging as being fundamental in the business world.

Standardizing Degree Terminologies in Information Technology Certification

Elive Likine
College of Business Administration
University of Detroit Mercy
Detroit, Michigan 48219

Kiumi Akingbehin
Department of Computer and Information Science
University of Michigan-Dearborn
Dearborn, Michigan 48128

Executive Abstract

INTRODUCTION

This paper examines the wide variation in names of information technology certification. The problems associated with this non-standardization are highlighted. The results of a recent study of the situation in Michigan are discussed. Indications are that the situation in Michigan is representative of the nation as a whole, and is probably international. Some approaches are suggested towards standardization.

THE SURVEY

A preliminary survey followed by a more comprehensive survey of Michigan institutions was conducted in 1993. Specifics of the survey are as follows:

1. Period of Survey: May-July 1993
2. Institutions Included: 2-year and 4-year Colleges/Universities
3. Number of Institutions that Responded: 50 (approximately)
4. Media Used: Telephone, Fax, Mail
5. Specific Information Requested:
    (a) list of all IT-related degrees/programs/disciplines
    (b) unit in which each is housed
    (c) exact degree/title awarded
    (d) list of required core courses for each

RESULT OF SURVEY

The most popular undergraduate degrees (awarded by two or more institutions), in order of popularity are:

BS in Computer Science
BA in Computer Science
AS in Computer Science
AA in Computer Science
AB in Data Processing
BS in Computer and Information Science
BAA/AS in Computer and Information Systems
BS/AD in Computer Information Systems
BS/AD in Computer Information Science
BS/BA in Computer Aided Design

Other degree majors (less popular, offered by only one institution) are:

Applied Science
Microcomputer Business Technology
Office Systems Administration
Management Information Systems
Computer Integrated Manufacturing
Computer Technology
Computer Aided Design
Math and Computer Science
Information Systems
Information Science
Office Information Technology
Computer Analyzing
Computer Operations
Computer Programming
Word Processing
Computational Mathematics
Data Processing Programming
Data Processing Microcomputer Applications
Computer Aided Design Technology
Computer Science/Management
Computer Engineering
Information Processing Specialist
Computer Aided Drafting

Computer for Business
Computer Aided Design
Electronic Data Processing
Business Computer Programming
Management Information Systems
Information Systems Management
Management/Computer Information Systems
Computer Information Systems Teacher
Computer Aided Design Technology
Computer Applications Technology
Local Area Network Administration
Computer Engineering Technology
Computer Information Systems Management
Business Data Processing
Computer Numerical Control Technology
Business Computer Programming
Mathematics/Computer Science
Computers
Computers Maintenance Technology
Business Computers
Computer Systems
Business Systems
Computer Aided Design and Industrial Technology
Computer Science Education

THE PROBLEMS AND POSSIBLE SOLUTIONS

The variation and virtually uncontrolled use of terminologies in information technology curricula causes problems for students, employers, institutions, faculty, and businesses. Some of these problems are:

1. Students are frequently overwhelmed by the multitude of degrees and options available and may subsequently enroll in the wrong programs.

2. Employers usually have a more difficult time recruiting the right candidate for the job. Employment decisions cannot be based on degree alone.

3. Institutions frequently have to deal with unnecessary internal competition and overlaps. This invariably results in inefficient use of resources.

4. Faculty frequently teach topics which are duplicated in other courses.

5. Businesses sometimes have a difficult time deciding which degrees or programs are the best for the initial or continuing education of their personnel. It is also difficult to decide which training is the best for solving the various problems encountered in day-to-day operation.

It may safely be said that far fewer IT degrees and programs are needed. This is particularly true when one considers the fact that the difference between two degrees is frequently less than five courses out of a total of around forty courses. Activities that can lead to better standardization of information technology curricula and contents include:

1. More conferences and meetings, such as the present conference, where IT education issues are discussed.

2. Formation of additional accreditation bodies for IT curricula.

3. More liaison between the different groups involved in IT education.

4. The formation of a single body or task force to oversee IT education.

CONCLUSION

This paper has discussed the wide range of terminologies used in information technology education and the resulting problems. The results of a survey of Michigan institutions are included. Suggestions are also included on activities that can promote the standardization of the terminologies. It is obvious that information technology transcends and spans an increasingly broad area involving several other disciplines and will continue to do so. This makes the job of standardization increasingly more difficult and challenging. The authors of this paper hope they have been able to sensitize the readership to this emerging problem. The tasks that need to be done remain enormous and require the cooperation and contribution of everybody.

IRM Within a Federal Agency:

A Primer

Shirley Linde
Division Assistant
The MITRE Corporation
1120 NASA Road 1
Houston, Texas 77058

Executive Abstract

WHAT IS IRM?

Information resource management has effected the operation of federal agencies since the passage of the Brooks Act in 1964 and especially since the passage of the Paperwork Reduction Act in 1980 and 1986. There still confusion, however, on what IRM really is and what implementing it means. Part of implementing IRM requires an understanding of these basic IRM concepts.

WHY IRM?

The federal government has a huge investment in information resources; the National Aeronautics Space Administration (NASA) alone has invested many billions of dollars. For a federal agency like NASA there are multiple reasons why IRM should be practiced, both economic and regulatory. This paper will discuss the current implementation of IRM within NASA and one of its installations, Johnson Space Center, in Houston, Texas.

IMPLEMENTATION OF IRM AT JOHNSON SPACE CENTER

Johnson Space Center is responsible for training astronauts and supporting real time mission operations for manned space flight. Consequently, it has several large computing facilities and thousands of support contractors. Most of this automated information processing equipment, software, and personnel are subject to federal IRM regulations and NASA policies and procedures.

The IRM federal regulatory process begins with Congress' passage of public laws and the creation by oversight federal agencies of appropriate federal regulations which implement them. The two major oversight agencies are the Office of Management and Budget (OMB) and the General Services Administration (GSA). Each of these agencies has its own areas of IRM responsibility, but because of poor communication, there are inconsistencies among federal regulatory requirements.

NASA as a federal agency must comply with federal regulations and respond to information requests by federal oversight agencies. Consequently, NASA IRM personnel have interpreted federal regulations and established a NASA IRM program. As required by regulation, a Designated Senior Office has been appointed, and a second level of IRM management, the Institutional Program Offices, has been delegated responsibility for managing IRM within the set of NASA installations assigned to them. The Center Directors at each installation have, in turn, been delegated responsibility for appointing a Senior Installation IRM Official (the third level of IRM management) who is responsible for implementing and executing an IRM program at his/her installation.

The Senior Installation IRM Official at Johnson Space Center has implemented an IRM program which establishes good management practices and meets federal regulations and NASA policies and procedures for IRM. This program is structured around an IRM life cycle model. Several major initiatives have been undertaken as part of the JSC IRM Program to increase the effectiveness of IRM at Johnson Space Center: IRM Program documentation and compliance, IRM budget planning, savings opportunities, standards, automated information systems security, and acquisition.

IRM Program Documentation and Compliance. IRM personnel have established the Johnson Space Center IRM Program by defining and documenting key areas of the Program. IRM responsibilities were identified in existing federal regulations, NASA IRM policies, and Johnson Space Center policy documents. Areas of inconsistencies were resolved, and the final list of responsibilities was documented and each responsibility assigned to an organization or civil servant. In addition a documentation tree was established and missing/incomplete sections were completed.

Part of the federal IRM program includes IRM audits and reviews by the General Services Administration. NASA's approach to meeting the requirement for IRM reviews has been to implement IRM self-assessments at the installation level. JSC established its own self-assessment approach which included developing a survey based on existing GSA recommendations, establishing peer review, and using existing data whenever possible.

IRM Budget Planning. The growing awareness of the size and impact of the investment in information resources and regulatory requirements for budget reporting resulted in the integration of IRM budget planning with the existing budget process. A tool was developed to integrate the data and to enable data analysis and speed publication of the Johnson Space Center Information Systems Plan. The data contained in the Plan are used to respond to external (NASA and federal) requests for data and to ensure compliance with regulations. The data are also used to determine information technology issues, quantify planned information technology investments, identify consolidation opportunities, and establish budget priorities.

Savings Opportunities. A team was established to identify ways to reduce IRM costs, more effectively utilize information technology, and improve the quality and efficiency of information resources. Ideas were screened for potential return on investment. Those selected were then evaluated using continuous improvement teams. Several major consolidations were implemented based on the teams' recommendations, saving millions of dollars in cost avoidance.

Standards. Johnson Space Center must comply with Federal Information Processing Standards which are mandatory for all information technology procurements. In addition the Center has established an integration standards program to increase its return on investment and improve interoperability. The program includes all Johnson Space Center-funded commercial-off-the-shelf software and hardware products.

Automated Information Systems Security. The Automated Information Systems Security Program focuses on the security of sensitive applications and data processing installations, personnel, training, and incident response and reporting. According to NASA policy, a Center Computer Security Manager has been appointed to execute the program at Johnson Space Center. He has established an Automated Information Systems Security Committee with representation from all major organizations. This group reviews and provides input to the Security Manager for all automated information systems security matters at the Center.

Acquisition. Regulations for acquisition of information resources by a federal agency have recently (1990) been augmented by the Federal Information Resources Management Regulations. In addition the threshold for the requirement to request a Delegation of Procurement Authority from the General Services Administration has been lowered substantially ($2.5 million for NASA). These two factors have increased the workload and lengthened to the time required to procure information resources at Johnson Space Center. Several initiatives were undertaken to alleviate these problems: the procurement process was reengineered saving months of processing time, and an expert system tool was developed to speed the generation of required forms. The tool has been so successful that it has been distributed to other federal agencies.

IRM CHALLENGES AT JOHNSON SPACE CENTER

IRM managers at Johnson Space Center have many of the same issues and challenges facing managers in industry:

- Currently, Centerwide IRM staff are viewed as "bureaucrats" and the Centerwide IRM program as overhead with no real added value.
- There is no clear understanding of the Centerwide IRM staff's role, and they are often viewed as competitors with IRM staffs which have evolved within individual organizations.
- In these days of "business process reengineering", IRM staffs must understand the business processes supported by information resources and bring business-like disciple to the analysis of information resources investments.
- IRM staff must keep up technically with the rapid growth and change in information technology to retain the respect of their customers and to be able to plan for the technological changes, e.g., the transition from mainframe applications to client-server architectures.
- Traditionally records managers have not been considered part of IRM resulting in inconsistent/conflicting information management policies and procedures.

IRM focus in the future will be on meeting these and other unforeseen challenges and maintaining the existing IRM program.

Paradox and Learning in the Strategy Making Process:
A Holistic Model for IT Enabled Transformation in the 1990s

Jane McKenzie
Research Fellow
Henley Management College
Greenlands, Henley on Thames
RG9 3AU
United Kingdom
712 Deerwood Drive
Stockbridge GA 30281
USA
Phone 1 404 474 0407

Executive Abstract

INTRODUCTION - LIMITATIONS TO TRANSFORMATION

The 1990's is expected to be a decade of continuous revolutionary change in business. Organisations are being encouraged to radically rethink their methods of operation and to use the potential of information and technology to transform their relationships with others inside and outside their value chain. Looking back over the evidence of the past thirty years, it is an unfortunate fact that conventional approaches to strategic planning rarely produce the sort of truly radical thinking necessary to stimulate revolution. Generally the result is incremental change rather than quantum shift. This is the inevitable result of viewing the world through the selective screen of traditional management perspectives and conventional concepts of strategy. Assumptions of rationality, order and predictability can be dangerously misleading. Prescriptions for success extrapolated from past experience quickly become blinkers upon open mindedness. In today's world, we can no longer expect 'perfect' information', however exhaustive our analysis; we can no longer make rational predictions with any degree of certainty. In other words, the business conditions characterized in many of the paradigms of the '60's '70's and '80's differ substantially from the chaotic condition prevailing in the 1990's. Discontinuity is already a new dimension to be managed. Programs of sustained transformational change can only exacerbate the problem. Coping with the consequent complexity, unpredictability and ambiguity requires updated management techniques and a strategic orientation that better approximates environmental conditions.

PARADOX AND LEARNING_ - NEW AIDS TO STRATEGIC MANAGEMENT

Radical change amidst complexity and unpredictability predicates two specific conditions - conflict and a capacity to learn. Conflict is necessary to challenge the assumptions and mental ties that bind us to the old order. Capacity to learn from that conflict enables us to effectively explore the complexity and unpredictability and adapt to change. By combining both conflict and learning into a paradigm for revolutionary strategy making, we can create a management process that is better adapted to the prevailing chaotic conditions. Paradox is the essence of mental conflict. The dictionary defines it as a self contradictory proposition or an opinion that conflicts with common belief. As such it would seem an ideal tool to help management revolutionaries challenge the old order. Further, there is a fundamental synergy between paradox and learning. The creative tensions inherent in dilemmas force people to confront the barriers to learning; once reconciled, the paradoxical solution interferes with other parameters to create further dilemmas. Thus more conflict must be confronted and further learning achieved. Religious truths are often presented in paradoxical format, for this very reason. They challenge the listener to extend their thinking outside of narrow channels and see greater possibilities. Christianity, for example, asks believers to die so that they can live. History shows that many of the great advances in science and art are the result of creative people accepting such apparently contradictory propositions as being simultaneously viable, and developing a new frames of reference that encompasses both alternatives. Extending our thinking and developing new frames of reference is a good description of business objectives in the 1990's. By following the precept that synergy is more effective than selection, both/and is more powerful than either/or, we should be able to accelerate the rate of learning and change to create stable process for lasting revolution.

FIFTEEN STRATEGIC PARADOXES - THE KEY DIMENSIONS OF SUCCESSFUL IT ENABLED TRANSFORMATION.

As part of a three year research alliance between Henley Management College in the UK, and Coopers and Lybrand's London office, the author has produced an integrative framework centred on paradox and designed to promote learning, change and durable business growth. The model synthesises the dilemmas inherent in ten distinct aspects of business strategy and twenty recognised inadequacies in the Strategic Information Systems Planning (SISP) process into a virtuous circle of strategic learning. The ten different approaches to strategy form five contradictory propositions. These become five interdependent dimensions that can be used to measure the organisational learning capacity. The twenty major failings of the SISP process produce 10, interrelated, IT specific frictions which, unresolved, can seriously impede revolutions of the learning circle. Rate of change (R) is one major difference between evolution and revolution, so the model seeks to increase the rate of change by removing the natural impediments. A derivative diagnostic tool allows users to pinpoint the major obstacles to learning and evaluate which areas of organisational weakness require priority attention during the transformation process. Each of the generic paradoxes can be interpreted in the context of an organisations contingent circumstances so as to provide a customised metric to monitor the success of a change program. Once an organisation's unique combination of problems has been diagnosed, the model also provides a logical guide to the selection of suitable technological and behavioural tools that will help realise the desired changes. A preliminary statistical analysis of responses to the diagnostic questionnaire shows that companies who best reconcile the fifteen identified dilemmas, and use the appropriate behavioural tools, get more benefits from their investments in strategic information systems and are more satisfied with the outcome. The results also show clearly that the organisations who have most successfully reconciled the key dilemmas, are those that consistently challenge cultural 'givens'. Case studies indicate that successful organisations address all the dimensions interdependently and simultaneously; the more holistic their approach, the better they perform.

CONCLUSION - A HOLISTIC PROCESS SATISFIES THE COMPLEX DEMANDS OF THE 1990'S

A more holistic process for developing strategies for transformation is more appropriate in complex environments. Several important benefits can be derived from a holistic paradigm centred on paradox and learning. They stimulate the necessary challenge to organisational inertia. They provide a meaningful measure of the intangible obstacles that hinder radical change programs. They tackle the problems of business and IT strategy simultaneously in one process, which is expected to improve strategic alignment. The process addresses the conflicts inherent in the management literature and builds on past learning. In summary, a more integrated paradigm is better suited to the development of revolutionary strategies in the chaotic environmental conditions of the 1990's.

FUTURE RESEARCH DIRECTIONS

Empirical testing of the model in different industries will provide valuable data to refine what is currently a generic model. Long term comparative studies of organisations who adopt a more holistic approach are necessary to validate the expected performance improvements over more conventional management approaches. Since the dilemmas were collected primarily from western sources, inter cultural comparisons of the key dilemmas is also needed

Influences on Specialty Retailers' Adoption of Quick Response

Jonathan W. Palmer
The Claremont Graduate School
165 E. Tenth Street
Claremont, CA 91711-6186
(909) 621-8193 (Phone)
(909) 621-8009 (Fax)
palmerj@cgsvax.claremont.edu

Executive Abstract

Quick Response (QR) has been proposed as a critical use of technology for competitive advantage in the retail industry. QR involves a suite of technologies including electronic data interchange (EDI), point of sale (POS) systems, and several types of interorganizational systems. The paper explores the specialty retailing industry's use of QR. Based on an initial study of eight specialty retailers, QR's advantage and adoption are found to be influenced by the number of suppliers, product mix, and the specialty retailers' concentration on elements of the retail pipeline.

BACKGROUND

Quick Response (QR) strategy is the retailing industry's equivalent of just-in-time The QR circle uses technology to include retailer, manufacturer, transporter, mill, and bank. In understanding each other's market goals, QR can allow each of these companies to work as one organization in serving the ultimate consumer.

Potential results of adopting QR include higher inventory turns, fewer markdowns, better in-stock position and higher profitability. As QR moves to a more sophisticated level and the level of trust between the retailer and suppliers grows, QR has the opportunity to outsource much of the decision making re: assortments, fixtures, sales associate training.

In a recent survey, Kurt Salmon & Associates (1993), identified four levels or stages of QR. The first level involves automated point-of-sale (POS), bar coding universal product codes (UPC), automatic price look-up and electronic data interchange (EDI) for order entry and inventory management. A second level involves automatic replenishment by suppliers, forecasting and electronic invoicing. EDI at this stage includes order status, invoicing and advance shipment notices. Enhancements in stage three include using the information gleaned through the elements of the earlier stages for pre- and post-season planning, shipment container marking and arrangement. In the fourth stage, suppliers actually take over inventory management functions, this stage also includes seasonless retailing, and space management.

DISCUSSION

Quick Response technologies provide the potential for a number of competitive advantages. By emphasizing transaction efficiency, QR focuses on managing all elements of the retail pipeline. These implementations attempt to bring greater levels of efficiency and shorten the response times from product manufacture to stocking of retail shelves to eventual sales and service. In some cases this transaction efficiency is blurring the lines between suppliers and retailers; using information technology to avoid intermediaries and reduce transaction costs across the pipeline.

Quick Response systems often cover the full upstream channel and involve orders to manufacturers, suppliers, and vendors and the subsequent delivery of materials. EDI applications allow quick order processing and order tracking. A number of systems vendors have put together packages of hardware and software aimed at expediting the interface between suppliers and retailers. These systems often involve the use of bar coding and related devices for automated data capture. Typically these devices are handheld and move easily with retailing staff responsible for ordering and inventory. Some specialty retailers concentrate heavily on the final distribution of stock keeping units (SKUs). The focus is on the distribution center to retail outlet portion of the pipeline. These implementations include dynamic stock picking, on-line order replenishment and delivery mechanisms, and electronic inventory management.

Specific transaction efficiency implementations include electronic invoicing and ordering; dynamic or automatic replenishment; private labeling; electronic inventory; and support for cross-docking. Typical technology includes EDI, point-of-sale, and satellite linkages. In most cases, these IT implementations require EDI-compatibility between the specialty retailer and the various manufacturers, vendors and distribution centers. Vertically integrated firms would have the same basic configuration, although with an internal EDI system.

FINDINGS

An initial study of eight specialty retailers explored the use of information technology, focusing on the use of Quick response, EDI, and interorganizational information systems. The initial survey responses, phone and personal interviews raised the question as to the use of Quick Response by

Key Influences on Quick Response Adoption

Dimension	QR adopters	QR non-adopters
Product Mix	Commodity	Fashion
Number of suppliers	Smaller	Larger
Use of IT to Support Retail Pipeline		
Supplier	Heavy	Moderate
Internal	Heavy	Moderate
Customer	Moderate	Light

specialty retailers and identified several dimensions which might explain the choice to pursue Quick Response.

The critical dimensions which distinguished adopters and non adopters were: product mix, number of suppliers, and their use of IT in support of the retail pipeline. Those companies with more stable, commodity-like products found QR more useful, while those with more fashion oriented products were less likely to adopt QR. It was also clear that the larger the number of suppliers, the more difficult the economic justification for QR. The concentration of specific elements of the retailing pipeline also drove QR choices.

CONCLUSIONS

QR concentrates very heavily on the supplier and internal aspects of the retail pipeline. There must be a greater concentration on the customer side to achieve more significant advantage. QR has not achieved wide spread adoption, often because of the lack of compelling business cases for retailers. In some cases, large numbers of smaller suppliers makes the economics of QR unworkable. In other situations, the type of product, the rapidity of inventory turn and the flexibility in reordering capabilities diminish the attractiveness of QR.

Those adopting QR have not typically moved to the most advanced stages of QR envisioned by QR advocates. The non-technological issues involved in sharing information with suppliers regarding inventory and sales has often stood in the way of allowing suppliers to truly manage inventories and participate fully in the concept of seasonless retailing.

Given its focus on a particular product, customer segment or geographic market, specialty retailing is particularly susceptible to changes in corporate strategy. As retailing moves from using IT as merely a delivery mechanism to greater dependence on IT and as the retail pipeline changes through technology, specialty retailing is struggling with designing appropriate corporate and IT strategies. Many specialty retailers are looking to IT to level the playing field with both the larger national chains and the local mom and pops. In appropriate situations regarding the number of suppliers, product mix and pipeline focus, Quick Response can provide an effective IT solution.

Information Systems Outsourcing Pros and Cons: Towards a Balanced Understanding

Prashant Palvia
Don Lim
Memphis State University

Executive Abstract

The option of outsourcing the information systems (IS) function is being exercised increasingly in corporate America. The question of "return on IS investment" has constantly alluded MIS researchers and practitioners, which at least partially explains the current emphasis on outsourcing. Existing published reports of IS outsourcing outcomes generally point to its many benefits. One should, however, recognize a reporting bias in the published accounts. Most reports have been based on the accounts of senior executives or outsourcing "survivors"; all of these people have a vested interest in making their decisions look good. This paper discusses the various advantages and pitfalls of IS outsourcing. It provides a more balanced view, as it is based on a real case study as narrated by two people who were on opposing sides of the fence: one was an outsourcing "survivor", and the other was an outsourcing "casualty" and was terminated after the outsourcing action.

Various issues in outsourcing have been discussed in this paper from these two perspectives. These issues include: what to outsource; motivation, benefits and pitfalls of outsourcing; and the outsourcing process. On most issues, the two views are diametrically opposite. For example, according to the survivor, only the operations and hardware should be outsourced and application development work should be retained in house. According to the casualty, all systems, people and operations should be turned over to the vendor in order to obtain economies of scale.

According to the survivor, the decision to outsource is clearly motivated by strategic reasons. One of the strategic goals for the institution was to maintain a position of independence so that it could return to an independent processing mode upon sudden termination of the contract. Another goal was to allow it to compete with big national rivals. Another was the ability to respond to customers in a very rapid fashion. And, of course, cost containment and reduction was an important factor. However, according to the casualty, the primary reason for exploring outsourcing options was the obvious cost containment. There was a lot of money being spent on the IS function. The institution was going through some hard financial times because of tremendous loan losses. As such there was an incredible pressure to show a substantial cost reduction. Related to the cost reduction motivation was the bank's fixation on return on equity (ROE). Another very important reason according to the terminated employee was to influence control over MIS operations. The IS structure had become unwieldy, with no clear sense of direction. While the survivor felt that the outsourcing action was an overall success, according to the terminated employee, it provided very short-term gains and was not a great strategic move.

According to the survivor, the process used for outsourcing was very objective and rational. Many of the steps described in the literature were explicitly used. For example, a task force was formed with appropriate representation, computerized financial models were built, extensive what-if analysis was performed, and the final vendor was selected carefully and objectively. However, this is not what the terminated employee said. According to him, the process was largely politically driven. In his own words, it "was a very strange little piece of organizational dynamics". A tentative decision was made very early on, and lines formed very quickly. Once the two opposing internal players were known, then the lines were just solid. The dynamic organizational change did not help the process at all. It actually made effective decision making worse. The final decision was not a pure economic decision. According to him, this was a political exercise as much as it was a business exercise.

In summary, while most published reports of outsourcing paint a rosy picture of the benefits of outsourcing, this paper has provided a number of pitfalls and problems during the outsourcing process. One should recognize a reporting bias in current reports. These reports have generally been based on the accounts of either senior executives, outsourcing vendors, or survivors in the MIS organization. These people have a stake in defending the decisions that they made or benefitted from, as such the validity of their claims can be questioned. This paper, based on the accounts of two people who were on opposite sides of the fence, has provided a more balanced view of outsourcing pros and cons.

Is The Use of Information Technology in the Specialized Semiconductor Industry Driven by The Product Life Cycle ?

Edward M. Roche
Assistant Professor
Computing and Decision Sciences Department
W. Paul Stillman School of Business
Seton Hall University
South Orange, New Jersey 07079
&
Adjunct Associate Professor
Leonard Stern Graduate School of Business
New York University

ABSTRACT

This paper reports a study of the strategic use of information technology in the specialized semiconductor industry — production of highly customized analog/digital devices. The results of the analysis show that the role of information technology in these organizations is best guided by knowledge of how the company has positioned itself on the product innovation life cycle. These findings agree with the observations of Link, Tassey and Zmud[1] who performed an empirical assessment of the Utterback and Abernathy Model[2] in so far as the role of information technology might be said to change at different points along the life cycle. The role of information technology changes as a function of what strategy the firm adopts to address the rapidly changing demands of the semiconductor industry. In brief, companies at the leading edge of the product innovation cycle do not need heavy emphasis on information technology. Companies which concentrate more heavily on production and manufacturing have a corresponding heavier reliance on information technology.

THE SPECIALIZED SEMICONDUCTOR INDUSTRY

As a rough approximation, we can generalize that there are two basic types of semiconductor manufacturing companies: the merchant producer and the custom house. The merchant semiconductor manufacturers are easily recognizable: Nippon Electric Corporation, Hitachi, Toshiba, Texas Instruments, Intel, and Motorola are some of the famous names. These companies have distinguished themselves by mass production in very high quantities — millions and tens-of-millions — of memory chips. These companies concentrate on large production volumes in order to lower the cost per unit of the chip, for it is cost per unit as well as market entry timing which determine success in the marketplace. As a result of this need for high volume production, the chip being produced is designed as a least common denominator — suitable for use in the widest possible range of products; both consumer and military.

The specialized semiconductor industry is entirely different. Instead of lot sizes of millions, production volumes are many times measured only in the thousands, or tens of thousands. Instead of chips which have relatively simple designs, but which nevertheless are highly compact; the custom houses tend to produce highly complex chips.[3] Instead of attempting to design general chips which have the widest possible range of uses, the custom houses design chips which are individually tailored, many times for a single application. In addition, the general design process is different. For the custom houses, a great premium is placed on working with the customer and co-designing the chip according to specifications. Highly profitable systems integration work generally accompanies the creation of a specialized semiconductor.

Within the family of specialized semiconductor manufacturers, this paper reports on a study of a specific group: producers of analog-digital devices. The companies studied were Burr-Brown, Crystal Semiconductor, ComLinear, Maxim, Analog Devices, Precision Monolithics, Linear Technology — seven companies in all.

This family of companies is involved in production of analog-digital converters (A/D), a widely-used chip which takes analog information and converts it to digital or vice-versa. For example, for CD players, an A/D converter takes the laser scanned information from the disk and converts it to analog information for amplification. Another device might take temperature information, for example, and convert it into digital form for interpretation by a computer. A/D converters are one of the most widely-used, but least known, type of semiconductor in the world. The creation of many A/D converters involves their merging with highly specialized circuits, even the creation of hybrid semiconductor devices. The specifications for this type of semiconductor are generally derived from very close cooperation and coordination with the customer. For most companies, no single customer or product accounts for more than 2%-3% of sales.

Background on Cases Examined

The companies studied are highly variable in their size,

strategy, history and use of information technology. Some are rapidly growing start-ups, others have been in the semiconductor business since its beginning in the days of Philby and Noyce.

Analog Devices

Analog Devices is the largest of the companies studied. It was founded in 1965 by Ray Stata and Matt Lorser, graduates of MIT. It now employees 5,200 people worldwide with 2,700 in Massachusetts, where it is based. In addition to making specialized semiconductors, AD makes a wide range of products. It is one of the world's leaders in product innovation, and operates with a well-defined set of strategic 5-year plans. AD has concentrated heavily on customer relations and has developed four programs to carry out its mission: Customer Ordering System; Manufacturing Excellence Through Quality Improvement Process Programs; Customer partnership Program; and other programs to address the need of recruiting and training high quality engineering talent. AD focuses both on high performance/high price chips but also on high volume/low price chips.

Investments in information technology are aided through a Central I.S. Steering Committee. AD views all of the information systems as ideally working together an integrated fashion and creating competitive advantage by helping with on-time delivery, reducing defects in manufacturing (statistical process control); and by reducing the averge order cycle time for products wanted by the customer.

Burr Brown

Burr Brown produces a narrower product range than Analog Devices, but has several unique processes for manufacturing which keep it out front in the manufacture of specialized semiconductors, including its ability to adjust circuitry at the microelectronic level using lasers. BB was founded by Paige Burr and Tom Brown in 1956 in Tucson, Arizona. By 1959 it was manufacturing transistorized component parts known as operation amplifiers which aided in ranger missle experiments on the moon. Approximately 70% of BB's sales are international, and it has manufacturing and technical facilities in Livingston, Scotland and Atsugi, Japan in addition to headquarters in Tucson, Arizona. Its sales have risen from $12m to $180m from 1975 to 1989. It makes a very broad range of products from precision integrated circuits; modular electronic power supplies; data entry and display terminals; microcomputer input/output systems; instrumentation systems; and LAN limited distance modems.

ComLinear

Comlinear specizlizes in the design and manufacture of high-performance analog signal processing components. More than 60% of its sales is to the military, and it has a sophisticated statistical quality control program in place to keep its "1772 certification" for high-level defense contracts. In 1989, its sales reaches $16m. It is a small and generally secretive (discrete)

firm with a strong corporate culture. Most of its products are produced in small batches of 1000 to 10,000 units, confirming its positioning in the specialized semiconductor field.

Crystal Semiconductor

Crystal is a fast growing, aggressive start-up company based in Austin Texas. Crystal is small, and aims to provide highly customized, high performance circuits for companies which can not be served by the larger seimconductor manufacturers. Crystal attempts to engineer its products to last much longer than those of other companies. It has only 125 employees, but is working hard on developing an information system which will remain totally integrated regardless of how large the firm grows in the future.

Linear Technology

LT's 400% growth rate over the past 5 years is based on their ability to customize products and provide a high level of on-time delivery of product. LT both designs and manufactures its products, and appears similar in some respects to Burr Brown. It spends a minimum amount of resources on information technology out of its $64m sales. Its mission is to be the world's leader in the design, manufacturing and marketing of linear integrated circuits.

Maxim Integrated

Maxim has concentrated on being a broad line supplier in the rapidly growing mixed signal cmos market. 1989 sales were approximately $55m. In addition to providing design and manufacturing for customized semiconductors, Maxim also acts as a second sourcer for various components which are in short supply. Interviews indicate that Maxim has a reputation of being able to deliver on time for orders which have been placed.

Precision Monolithics

PMI is a smaller specialized company which manufacturers advanced, standard, and custom monolithic linear integrated circuits; including switches/multiplexers; line-interface units; matched transistors; voltage folowers/buffers, references, and comparators; analog-to-ditital and ditital-to-analog converters; and sample and hold, instrumentation and operational amplifiers. Sales in 1989 were approximately $90m, with 50% going into the military. PMI concentrates on producing well-established products, and uses information technology to maximize the efficiency of its manufacturing processes.

Given the type of industry being studied, we sought to examine the strategic role of information technology, and how it relates to the organization of the semiconductor company.

Methodology

The study involved approximately 75 persons,[4] in addition to the many persons who helped in the interviews. See Figure 2.

The project involved four phases of analysis: (1) Phase I —

Information Scanning and Structuring of Problem; (2) Phase II — Business and Technological Analysis of Each Company; (3) Phase III — Sub-Team, Team, and Group Summaries; (4) Phase IV — Strategic Analysis.

During the first and last phases of the project, the group work as a whole. However, during the middle parts of the project, the group was divided up into teams: roughly 10 persons per company team, and roughly 5 persons on the business and 5 persons on the technological sub-teams.

During Phase I, the group as a whole went through an accelerated learning curve regarding competition in the semiconductor industry. Two tours of semiconductor manufacturing facilities were arranged. Also, a wide-ranging selection of industry studies were handed out and discussed. After this general information was collected, the group worked together to create a general structuring of the problem.

The problem was structured into both technological and business oriented areas of analysis, including:
• The Overall Strategic Mission of the Company
• The General Corporate Strategy
• The Competitive Structure of the Industry
• The Nature of Sales and Customer Service, which we had determined was a leading indicator of competitive success
• The Organization of Operations
• Engineering
• The Information Systems Budget and How It Is Controlled
• The Future Prospects and Strategy of the Corporation.

In Phase II, the group was divided up into 7 teams — one team for each of the companies being studied. Each team was further divided up into two sub-teams; one to study the general business strategy and positioning, the other to study the use of information technology. Each person was given a specific piece of the problem. There was a great deal of sharing of information between the different persons within groups, but limited sharing of information between groups.

After the team assignments were made, each team went through a process of determining the sequence of analysis to use, determining the major questions which needed answering; assign team members to each of the relevant portions of the problem; coordinating the research effort (since the number of contacts made with each of the companies being studied had to be carefully controlled so as to not dry up sources of information); and swapping of information.

The teams then began to analyze and collect their data, the major data sources being:
• Personal and Telephone interviews with the companies
• Scanning and study of publication information and data on the company (credit reports; annual reports; articles; product brochures; etc.)
• Review of summary materials which summarize other research which has been conducted on the semiconductor industry
• Review of printed materials gathered from the companies being studied
• Interviews with customers of the companies being studied, to determine how good and responsive the company was in meeting market demands
• In some cases, interviews with sales representatives of the companies being studied.

In Phase III, the teams began to summarize the findings to increasingly higher levels of abstraction and generalization. First, each sub-team made conclusions regarding the findings on its company. In the next step, the business and technological sub-teams got together and created a general team summary. In the next phase, all of the teams were put together into the Group Decision Support Systems facility at The University of Arizona for two brainstorming sessions, called Superbowl I and Superbowl II, which formed Phase IV.

In Phase IV, all of the groups were back together working as one large team. Superbowl I involved an electronic brainstorming session which attempted to answer six major questions about the specialized semiconductor industry:

Business Domain[5]
1 Where is the Industry Going?
2 How are competitors attacking each other?
3 What are sources of competitive advantage
    Technological Domain
4 What is the role of information technology in the industry?
5 Given this role, how well are companies meeting the challenge?
6 Given this challenge, what should companies do to get competitive advantage?

In Superbowl II, the group was asked to identify the key variables and sub-variables for utilization of information technology in the specialized semiconductor industry, weight these variables, then score each company as to how well it was accomplishing its mission.[6]

Findings[7]

The results of the study show that the companies differed amongst themselves as to how they were positioning themselves on the product innovation curve. In general, there were four types of companies in this regard:
• Type I — Leading Edge Design House
• Type II — Systems Integrator and "Job Shop" Manufacturer
• Type III — Cream Skimmer & Second Sourcer
• Type IV — Integrated Supermarket

The Type I company specializes in the design of the chips, but avoids manufacturing, which is usually "sent out" to a silicon foundry for production. In this way, the Leading Edge Design House can concentrate on design and systems integration, which has a higher value added, and at the same time pick-and-choose the foundry with the quickest turnaround time, so as to beat out the competition. The Type II company does the design and systems integration activities of the Type I firm, but also manufacturers. Due to limited lot sizes of most products, between 1,000 and 10-100,000 items, the production tended to be highly decentralized. It is ironic that in spite of the "high tech" nature of the Type II Systems Integrator and "Job Shop" Manufacturer, the manufacturing set-up resembles a medieval

Figure 2: Phases I and II of the Analysis

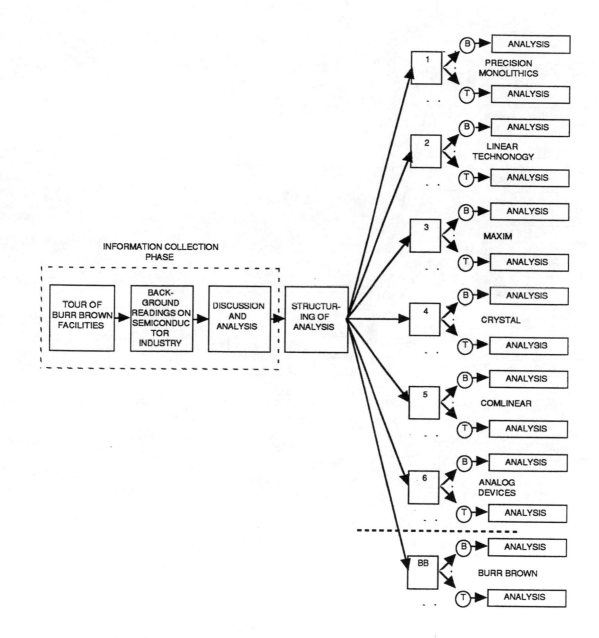

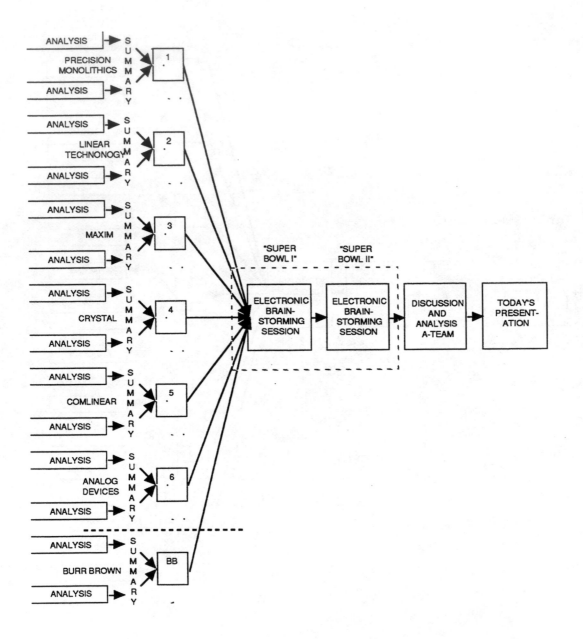

guild: limited size lots, labor and skill intensive, not too much similarity from one job to the next. The Type II firm covers the product cycle from the very bottom up through the middle of the first slope. As soon as a product matures, it "hops" onto the next innovative product cycle.

The Type III firm avoids getting very involved in the innovation, systems integration, or job-shop manufacturing process. Instead, it waits until a product has been proven commercially successful by someone else, then jumps into the production cycle at the peak of the curve. Sometimes as a "second source" (a company which fills in manufacturing demand for other companies which temporarily can not fill demand) or as a full scale manufacturer. In the latter case, the Type III Creme Skimmer concentrates on highly efficient manufacturing so as to gain competitive advantage from low-cost manufacturing.

The Type IV Integrated Supermarket does it all. It operates successfully over the entire range of the product cycle curve: it it active in systems integration, design, and highly efficient manufacturing at either medium sized or large production runs. In addition, it can be a low cost producer for large orders. Only one firm wc studied was a Type IV: Analog Devices in Massachusetts.

Type I, I, III, and IV firms encapsulate the basic family of strategies which are identifiable from the cases examined here.

In addition to finding that the different firms manufacturing specialized A/D semiconductors had very different strategies for attacking the product innovation cycle, the study found that they were *radically different* in their approach to and utilization of information technology. Even though these companies were producing essentially the same products, their information systems varied from which might be termed *primitive* to *highly sophisticated and integrated*.

Some of the firms had virtually no information technology system all: one or two persons serving in the "MIS Department" with no relationship between job scheduling, customer service, and inventory control. Other firms had a great deal of information technology spread over the world in different manufacturing sites (typically the Far East, North America and Western Europe), but with no or very poor integration. These firms had a decentralized style of manufacturing and also of information technology. Many decisions regarding information technology are being made on a divisional or departmental basis, rather than from the point of view of the corporation as a whole.

Other firms, some of widely different scale and business range, had highly sophisticated systems which link together all

Figure 1: Types of Companies and the Semiconductor Product Cycle

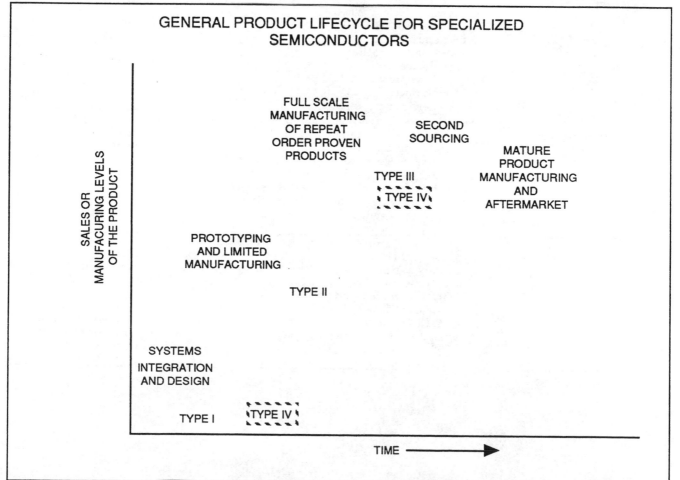

Table 1: Type and Characteristics of Specialized Semiconductor Manufacturers

GROWTH TYPE	CHARACTERISTICS	TYPE OF PRODUCTS	ROLE OF INFORMATION TECHNOLOGY
Type I Leading Edge Design House	Small: 5-50 Employees. No manufacturing; use of external custom "Silicon foundries" for manufacturing. Limited Production Runs: 1,000 or less to 1x,000 units. Concentrates only on the leading edge of the Production Innovation Curve. Avoids involvement at any other part of the Product cycle.	Design of Advanced circuits. Close consultation and "co-design" with customers. Value-added through systems integration.	Heavy use of CAD. Limited or almost zero use of other information technology systems.
Type II Systems Integrator and "Job Shop" Manufacturer	Medium: 50-x,000 employees. "Job shop" manufacturing based on orders received from customers. Generally small production runs of 1,000 to 1x,000 for most customized chips. Concentrates on the initial and middle parts of the product Innovation cycle; When a product is "proven" frequently jumps off curve onto another innovative product curve, after manufacturing competition sets in.	All services of Type I, plus manufacturing. Also provides systems integration using products from other companies. Complete circuit boards in addition to single semiconductors.	Heavy use of CAD. In addition, much automation of individual departmental functions. Difficulties in providing overall integration of the firm between functions.
Type III Cream Skimmer & Second Sourcer	Small: 5-250 Employees Concentrates on manufacturing only of products which have been established in the marketplace by someone else; thus staying at the Top of the Product Innovation Curve.	Manufacturing services, including second sourcing. Does not provide design or systems integration services, except on a highly limited basis.	Concentration on systems which are used for manufacturing control, including Statistical Process Control; and Inventory Control; Customer Service Automation.
Type IV Integrated Supermarket	large: xx,000 Employees Provides entire range of manufacturing from small orders to large. Highly Automated and World Class Manufacturing. Covers the entire range of the Product Innovation Cycle.	All Services from "Cradle to Grave" for Semiconductor Products.	Highly automated in all respects: Customer Service, Manufacturing Automation, Statistical Process Control. Has integration between different functions (not characteristic of Type III Firm)

aspects of the customer service, scheduling and manufacturing process. In addition, the highly critical element of statistical process control was also integrated into the systems.[8]

These observations lead to questions about the relationship between the commercial strategy of the firm and its use of information technology:

• Is there a correlation which can be drawn between the firm's approach to the product innovation cycle and the use of information technology?

• How can firms which have the same approach to the product innovation cycle use completely different approaches to the use of information technology? Can this be explained?

Summarizing the observations on the seven cases yields the following, under an ideal conditions model, which does not take account of the contradiction which was found in some firm strategies, mentioned above.

These observations suggest a general "evolution" or "development path" for use of information technology in this type of semiconductor manufacturing firm. It would suggest the following logic: For firms which concentrate on the very leading edge of the production innovation curve, massive amounts of information technology are not needed because manufacturing is subcontracted away and inventory control is not complex because of limited inventory numbers in orders, and the relative short life span of the product.

As this type of firm grows greater capabilities, for example by taking on manufacturing (perhaps it develops a proprietary manufacturing process, as the companies in this group studied here in fact have); then the role of information technology increases sharply and the task is made much more complex. First of all, control of the general manufacturing process and the required statistical process control and accounting add great complexity. Second, the company has limited batch "job shop" type orders and is therefore typically manufacturing several different products simultaneously; thus raising the complexity of scheduling, resource allocation, and delivery lead time calculations. The automation required for customer service and price quotation also raises the cost of automation. The problem with this situation is that as the orders increase, and as the firm grows to take on more and various types of assignments, the information technology overhead may become a great burden, since it tends to be highly decentralized.

For the cream skimmer firm, the task of information technology is streamlined in the sense that it can concentrate almost solely on efficiency in manufacturing. The complexity of scheduling is decreased, since the production runs are more stable. In addition, the number of products being handled is smaller, thus yielding further simplification. This type of firm, however, has limited growth possibilities because it is ultimately dependent upon "overflow" from other companies and their proprietary designs, which are never produced by the cream skimmer. The cream skimmer is always a follower.

The integrated supermarket firm does everything of the job shopper except in larger numbers and with a much higher level of integration. The integrated supermarket appears to be the final stage of growth and evolution for the job shopper. It can compete not only on innovation, and limited lot size manufacturing, but does not have to "jump off" the product innovation curve to seek for higher value added innovations because it is also able to manufacture efficiently. The integrated supermarket has the innovation of the design house, and the ability to produce limited run batches of the job shopper; but it also has the manufacturing efficiencies of the cream skimmer. The information systems are able to control all aspects of the firm and are a truly critical strategic asset for the firm. Assuming that a firm might grow through the stages of the product innovation curve, then our research suggests that it is easier to grow from being a design house to being a job shopper than it is to grow from being a job shopper to being an integrated firm. In the first case, the growth is essentially agglutinative in nature: different production lines are added one at a time, typically with their own information systems. The job *shopper become* in nature: different production lines are added one at a time, typically with their own information systems. The job shopper becomes the sum of a large number of limited scale operations. In the second case, however, the task becomes taking a highly decentralized information technology environment and making into an integrated system. Our research shows that this is an extremely formidable task, and two of the companies studied appeared to be "stuck" in a technological trap: having built up efficient job shop operations, they are unable to suddenly turn around to a completely different philosophy and integrate the systems.

The contradiction in our observations turns out not to be a contradiction at all. We found one company which is a Type I, but which was building an information systems capability similar to a Type IV, although everything was in a prototype stage. Interviews revealed that the firm was consciously building into their systems from a very early stage the ability to eventually operate as efficiently as a Type IV firm. On the other hand, we found other Type I firms which seemed to be following the path of the job shopper: they were heading towards an uncontrolled, and uncoordinated decentralized computing environment.

In summary, the mapping of the firm positioning against the product innovation life cycle within the context of explaining their information technology strategies has yielded these conclusions: that is a clear relationship and that firms which appear to understand this relationship at the early stages of their development have a greater chance of growing into large integrated firms than those that fail to recognize this and adopt a different course.

Implications for Literature[9]

Wasson (1978), Wells (1972) and Hirsch (1972) have all pointed out different aspects of the product life cycle. Wasson divides the cycle up into 8 phases. Wells and Hirsch used a different dividing system. The main point of these explanations is that over time the role of different activities on the part of the firm changes in relation to the maturity of the product. Mesher

Table 2: Information Systems Characteristics of Seven Specialized Semiconductor Manufacturers

Company	Location	Sales	Strategy Type	Is/As % Of Revenues	Is $/ Employee	Is $ / Chip	Type Of It System
Analog Devices	Massachus etts	$1,000m	Type IV	4%	$3,487	$0.60	VAX
Burr Brown	Tucson, Arizona	$185m	Type II	1.6%	$1,900	$0.11	VAX and HP
ComLinear	Ft. Collins, Colorado	$16m	Type II	1.3%	na	na	Prime 2450 CPU with PCs
Crystal Semicondu ctor	Austin, Texas	$3.5m	Type I	1.1%	$1,760	$5,641	VAX with Sun4 work-stations.
Linear Technology	Santa Clara Valley, California	$70m	Type II	<1%	$1,000	na	Minimal IS, PC-based
Maxim Integrated	Sunnyvale, California	$50m	Type II with some Second Sourcing	1.19%	$1,761	$1,449	VAX 6000 with PCs and ter-minals.
Precision Monolithic s	Santa Clara,Calif ornia	$90m	Type III	5%	$,5,861	$4,069	VAX with HP 3000 system

(1990) notes some of these factors: "demand for the products ... number of manufacturers, type of labor used to manufacture a product, capital intensity..."

The Hirsch analysis divides up the characteristics of the product life cycle into three phases: early, growth and maturity. For each of those phases of the cycle, Hirsch discusses the characteristics of technology being used, the capital intensity required for manufacturing, the general industry structure, including the relationship to the ease of entry into the market, the critical human inputs, particularly the role of management skills, and the general demand structure, showing how the product is marketed.

Mapping the findings here against the work of Hirsch would yield another column of the analysis: the role of information technology. (Although in this case, we are considering a specialized part of a unique industry, whereas Hirsch was considering industry in general.) Even given these obvious limitations to the analogy, we could place the Type I, Type II, and Type IV information technology characteristics against the framework provided by Hirsch. An exception would have to be made for Type III firm, although it would fit in with Hirsch's discussion of barriers to entry into an industry in the sense that a firm would be required to have access to very up-to-date manufacturing automation and statistical process control technology to jump into the product life cycle along with other Type III firms.

In addition, the type of product cycle most characteristic of the specialized semiconductors produced by the firms studied here would fit into Wasson's "high learning product life cycle".

Mesher quotes Davis (1989) and McIvor (1989) in their discussion of the unique conditions present in the product life cycle for semiconductors. Their discussion agrees also the Okimoto (1989) and others. Generally, semiconductors have accelerated the pace of technological innovation, with decreasing lengths of product life cycles. It is a shorter and shorter time between each introduction of a new generation of semiconductors. Davis and McIvor are speaking generally of the merchant semiconductor industry, such as DRAMS. Their analysis does not hold as true for the specialized semiconductor industry, which is driven by customization and systems integration rather than by mass production in a highly cost-competitive market. None of the writers consulted have discussed the role of information technology in the firm in relation to the product life cycle.

In the MIS area, Parker and Benson's (1988, 1989) concept of *information economics* has direct relation to the study here. Their argument is that the selection of the best investments for information technology are found by a careful analysis of factors which lie in what they call the *business domain* and the *technology domain*. Their analysis of investment strategies served as a basis of this study. It is for this reason that each team was divided up into a business sub-team and a technology sub-team. Their analysis as well as the analysis during this project lend further evidence to the idea that the business objectives and strategies should play a very great part in determining the investment priorities for information technology.

Although it is logical that the firm's positioning of itself against the product innovation cycle is a business and strategic imperative which should have a great impact on the investment priorities for information technology — a sequence which would agree with the concepts of *information economics* —

Table 3: Parallels Between Utterback and Abernathy Model and Specialized Semiconductor Manufacturing

Utterback and Abernathy	Specialized Semiconductor Manufacturing Strategies
Fluid	Type I
Transition	Type II
Specific	Type III

Parker and Benson have not referred to the product innovation life cycle, only to the general external environmental conditions which shape a firm's strategy.

In addition, the extensive reviews of the strategy literature by Laudon (1989) Lucas (1988) and Laudon and Turner (1988) have shown that the external conditions being faced by the firm can go far in shaping the role of information technology. However it appears that no one has discussed the role of information technology in the semiconductor industry and how it can match the firm's approach to the product innovation cycle.

It appears that study of the relationship between the role of information technology and how the firm approaches the product innovation cycle is both a valid and potentially new line of inquiry which may help in understanding the specific conditions of some high technology firms, such as specialized semiconductor manufacturers. The work of Utterback and Abernathy has suggested the relationship between the firms innovation process and the use of technology by the firm and its competitors. If we take information technology as a type of "technology" used by the firm, then we can see parallels between the Utterback and Abernathy Model, as described by Link, Tassey and Zmud. Their description of the model discusses the relationship between the stage of process development and the product characteristics, process characteristics and how a decision is made about whether to induce or purchase improved technology.

Link, Tassey and Zmud conclude that "Further empirical and theoretical research examining the validity and implications of such a formulation is highly encouraged. .... firm characteristics as well as industry characteristics were observed to be significant." Within this context, this research suggests a bridge with the Utterback and Abernathy model, as explained by Link, Tassey and Zmud.

There is, however, a small variation in the model. The Type IV firm which is the Integrated Supermarket does not fit precisely because it is involved in being on many different product innovations curves simultaneously. In addition, it makes many types of "plays" in providing a type of universal service to potential customers.

Another factor is that the movement from Type I to Type II

or from Type II to Type IV is suggested and confirmed by the Utterback and Abernathy model.

This analysis suggests the following conclusions:
• Information technology strategy can be guided by product strategy in the semiconductor industry, and in particular by how the firm attacks the product innovation cycle.
• The role of information technology appears to be less important in the more innovative firms which seek to get the greatest part of their value added through innovation and customization.
• Firms in the specialized semiconductor industry can be caught in an information technology "trap" of decentralization and lack of integration if they fail to plan ahead for taking a position covering the entire production innovation curve.

Sources of Error in Data and Suggestions for Further Research

There are several points of weakness and possible error in this data and the concluding observations which might suggest ares for further research:
• We do not know if the same results would be found in other industries which depend heavily upon innovation and other similar product innovation cycles. For example, consumer electronics.
• Some firms' position against the product innovation curve is actually composed of many different products (several thousand) each at different positions of innovation, growth and maturity. Therefore, the type-casting of the companies is a generalization, and may have a significant number of internal contradictions.
• Are the seven companies here enough to develop these conclusions? It may be enough for this portion of the specialized semiconductor industry, simply because all of the major companies have been covered; but it may not be enough for the entire industry.
• In the future, therefore, it would perhaps be profitable to study more sectors using the same approach to compare results.
• The data suggests a need for more empirical precision in follow-on research: product cycles are highly generalized and the ascribed role of information technology may be too general.

References

Abernathy, W.J. Production process structure and technological change. Decision Sciences, 1976, 7, 607-619. also The productivity dilemma. Baltimore, Md.: Johns Hopkins University Press, 1978.

Davis, Dwight B. "Beating the Clock", *Electronic Business,* May 29, 1989, pp. 21-28.

Hirsch, Seev. "The United States Electronic Industry in International Trade," in *The Product Life Cycle and International Trade.* HBS. 1972, pp 37-52.

Jewkes, John, David Sawers, and Richard Stillerman. *The Sources of Invention.* London: MacMilan & Co., 1958.

Laudon, Kenneth C. *A General model for Understanding the Relationship Between Information Technology and Organizations.* Center for Research on Information Systems. New York University. working Paper Series No. 199. January 1989.

Link, Albert; Gregory Tassey, and Robert W. Zmud. *The Induce Versus Purchase Decision: An Empirical Analysis of Industrial R&D.* Decision Sciences, 1983, Vol. 14.

Lucas, Henry C., Jr. *Integrating Information Technology and Strategic Planning.* Center for Research on Information Systems. New York University. working Paper Series No. 174. March 1988.

McIvor, Robert. *Managing for Profit in the Semiconductor Industry.* Englewood Cliffs, N.J: Prentice Hall, 1989.

Mesher, Gene. *The Product Life Cycle.* mimeo. MIS Department, MOSAIC Group, The University of Arizona. n.p .Spring 1990. This term paper summarizes much of the literature on the product life cycle.

Okimoto, *Competition in the Semiconductor Industry.* Stanford University Press, 1989.

Parker and Benson. *Information Economics.* 1988 and 1989..

Roche, Edward M. *An Information Economics Analysis of Competition in the Semiconductor Industry.* forthcoming, based on the same experiment.

Turner, Jon A. and Kenneth C. Laudon. *Information Technology and Management Strategy.* Center for Research on Information Systems. New York University. Working Paper 178, February 1988.

Utterback, J.M. Successful industrial innovations: A multivariate analysis. *Decision Sciences,* 1975, 6, 65-77

Wasson, Charles R. *Dynamic Competitive Strategy and Product Life Cycles>* Austin, Tx: Lone Star Publishers, 1978.

Wells, Louis T. "International Trade: The Product Life Cycle Approach" The Product Life Cycle and International Trade. Harvard Business School, Division of Research, 1972, pp. 3-33.

NOTES

[1] Link, Albert; Gregory Tassey, and Robert W. Zmud. *The Induce Versus Purchase Decision: An Empirical Analysis of Industrial R&D.* Decision Sciences, 1983, Vol. 14.

[2] Utterback, J.M. Successful industrial innovations: A multivariate analysis. *Decision Sciences,* 1975, 6, 65-77; Abernathy, W.J. Production process structure and technological change. *Decision Sciences,* 1976, 7, 607-619. also *The productivity dilemma.* Baltimore, Md.: Johns Hopkins University Press, 1978.

[3] Measurement of chip "complexity" is difficult. For this project, we used "number of models for a single chip." This measure gives an estimation of complexity, since it requires more complex chips to perform many different functions. The best measure would be number of logic elements on a chip, and number of different types of logic elements; however, it was impossible to collect this type of information for the thousands of types of chips.

[4] I would like to thank the following persons for help in this research: Mr. Dan Mittleman, Mr. Mark Fuller, and Doug Vogel who led the group decision support sessions. Ms. Karen Lorentzen at Burr Brown was instrumental in getting the research project approved and supported at Burr Brown. I would also like to thank Mr. Mark Finklestein at Burr Brown who helped in compiling the many bibliographic references on the different companies being studied. Thanks also goes to all of my students who performed the many analyses of this project under my supervision.

[5] The term "domain" is taken from Parker and Benson's book "Information Economics".

[6] For results of this, please see Edward M. Roche "An Information Economics Analysis of Competition in the Semiconductor Industry".

[7] This paper reports only those findings related to the product cycle and the corresponding use of information technology. Other data is still under analysis.

[8] Highly advanced SPC methods are critical in getting the various levels of military certifications needed for contracts involving the most sophisticated integration projects being built for the military.

[9] I would like to give credit to Mr. Gene Mesher, my graduate student, for his research and summarization of much of the literature on the product life cycle.

Integrating Strategic Management and Information Resources Management in U.S. Hospitals -- A Prescription for Managing Strategically under Healthcare Reform

Lauren C. Thompson, Ph.D.
Practice Director, Healthcare Business and Information Engineering
Birch & Davis Associates, Inc.
8905 Fairview Road
Silver Spring, MD 20910
(301) 650-0381/(703) 823-0795

Executive Abstract

INTRODUCTION

Hospitals face many challenges in providing cost-effective healthcare services in a dynamic and competitive environment. The nature of the healthcare industry is changing, and along with it, the basis of competition. Information resources (information and information technology) are valuable, but as yet under-utilized, organizational assets in the quest for competitive advantage and enhanced performance in hospitals. When appropriately aligned with the strategies and environmental context of hospitals, and managed as strategic assets, information resources have the potential to provide competitive advantage, enhance hospital performance, and facilitate cooperative efforts toward community-based patient care.

Exploratory in nature, this study examined the relationships between strategic orientation, information resources management (IRM) orientation, and performance in acute care hospitals in the United States. The objectives of the study were two-fold: (1) to investigate a hypothesized pattern of relationships between strategic orientation and IRM orientation in hospitals, and (2) to examine the performance implications of differing alignments of strategic orientation and IRM orientation in those hospitals. Further, the study sought to validate in the hospital industry the Miles and Snow typology of strategic orientation, refine the use of the information systems strategic grid as a research construct of IRM orientation in hospitals, and correlate these typologies thereby establishing an empirical linkage between business- and functional-level strategies and management orientations.

BACKGROUND

The Miles and Snow typology of strategic orientation, which provides a categorization of organizations by type of business strategy pursued, was used to measure the strategic orientation of study hospitals. The typology describes four organizational types--Prospector, Analyzer, Defender and Reactor--and their underlying business strategy and strategic management orientation, differentiated along three dimensions: the orientation of the organization to the marketplace; how the organization coordinates, plans and implements its strategies; and the technological and engineering processes supporting production, research and development. The information systems strategic grid, adapted for use as a research construct in this study for measuring IRM orientation, provides a framework for identifying the IRM type of an organization (Strategic, Turnaround, Factory, or Support) based upon the strategic relevance of the current and future information systems applications portfolios and associated planning characteristics. Since a commonly accepted measure of hospital performance is not readily available, a composite measure of hospital performance was developed for use in the study to assess three aspects of performance -- efficiency, profitability, and access to care. Quality, increasingly used as a measure of performance, was excluded from the composite measure because of a lack of consensus regarding the definition and use of quality measures in hospitals at this time.

Data was gathered from CEOs in a nation-wide random sample of acute care hospitals over 200 licensed beds stratified on the basis of hospital ownership/control, and membership in a healthcare system. CEOs were surveyed on their strategic planning and management processes, IRM practices, and performance relative to peer hospitals. Investigator-developed decision rules were used to classify hospitals into categories of strategic orientation and IRM orientation, and determine overall performance based upon weighted component measures of each variable. Chi-square analysis was used in examining relationships between strategic orientation and IRM orientation. Analysis of variance was used to examine the influence of strategic and IRM orientation on performance. Both the independent and interaction effects of strategic and IRM orientation on hospital performance were examined.

DISCUSSION

The study postulated a strategic role for information resources in hospitals, maximized when IRM strategies and management context are optimally aligned with, and fully integrated into, the hospital's business strategies and general management context. Synchronization of business planning and IRM planning processes, alignment of IRM strategies with business objectives and strategies, involvement of the senior information resources manager in the hospital's strategic management planning and management process, and involvement of the chief executive in strategic planning for information resources were hypothesized to enhance alignment. It was hypothesized that certain strategic types would be associated with certain IRM types. These hypothesized combinations of types were Prospector-Turnaround, Analyzer-Strategic, Defender-Factory, and Reactor-Support.

It has been suggested that the performance of organizations whose strategic and IRM orientations are aligned can be enhanced. In the context of this study, hospitals that leverage information technologies and application support to realize their strategic objectives have greater potential for performance improvements than those that do not. Thus, it was further hypothesized that Analyzer-Strategic hospitals would perform better than Prospector-Turnaround hospitals, which would perform better than Defender-Factory hospitals, which would perform better than Reactor-Support hospitals.

Certain factors may influence the ability of an organization to optimize the utility of the information resources at its disposal and thus realize its strategic potential. Among these factors are the nature and extent of the specific business and IRM strategies pursued, the extent and functional nature of information systems support within hospitals, and the availability of slack resources to invest in information resources. In order to accommodate the possibility that different combinations of organizational types and performance effects would occur as a result of these or other factors, alternative hypotheses, more general in nature, were specified. These hypotheses were: (1) that a statistically significant pattern of relationships between strategic and IRM orientations would be found (although not necessarily those combinations previously discussed), and (2) that hospitals with a Strategic or Turnaround IRM orientation, in combination with any strategic orientation, would perform better than hospitals with a Factory or Support IRM orientation, in combination with any strategic orientation.

FINDINGS

The results of the study suggest that a pattern of relationships exists between strategic orientation and IRM orientation in acute care hospitals. A statistically significant general association between strategic orientation and IRM orientation was found, as well as significant associations between five combinations of types: Prospector-Strategic, Prospector-Turnaround, Analyzer-Strategic, Analyzer-Turnaround, and Defender-Factory types. Other combinations of strategic orientation and IRM orientation were found that were not significantly related: Prospector-Factory, Analyzer-Factory, and Defender-Turnaround types. These results suggest that hospitals with more comprehensive and institutionalized strategic management practices, and which more aggressively pursue new markets and develop new services, were also more advanced in their view of the strategic utility of information resources, incorporated information resources strategies in their strategic business plans, and emphasized alignment of their IRM function with the organizational context.

The study findings also indicated that, independently of one another, both strategic orientation and IRM orientation influence hospital performance. When the performance of hospitals with differing combinations of strategic and IRM orientation was examined, the results were mixed but generally did not support a statistically significant performance effect of any combinations of types with two exceptions -- Prospector-Strategic hospitals differed significantly in performance than all other hospital types except Prospector-Turnaround, and Analyzer-Strategic hospitals and Prospector-Turnaround hospitals differed significantly in performance from Prospector-Factory and Analyzer-Factory hospitals. These results suggest that hospitals with a more market-focused strategic orientation, more future-oriented and market-based IRM strategies, and in which the senior executive views information resources as strategic assets may perform better in a dynamic environment.

CONCLUSION

The healthcare industry is undergoing dramatic upheaval as a result of reformation of the fundamental policies and structure of healthcare delivery and financing systems. The transformation is being facilitated by innovative application of information technologies in support of health care delivery and management. Hospitals are most threatened by the changes, and must learn how to adapt to the new environment, and to optimally utilize information resources in shaping their delivery systems and management strategies to their advantage.

The results of this study offer hospitals some prescriptions for maximizing their competitive advantage and ultimately enhancing their performance. This study benefits health care, strategic management and IRM practitioners, policy makers and researchers by offering tools for diagnosing strategic orientation and IRM orientation, suggesting strategies that may influence hospital performance, and offering possible prescriptions for policies and management incentives designed to achieve widely accessible, cost-effective, high quality health care.

For researchers, this study validates the use of the Miles and Snow typology and the information systems strategic grid as research constructs in measuring strategic and IRM orientation, respectively, and a method for assessing overall hospital performance using a multiple measures approach. Additional research is needed to validate the findings of this study in hospitals, in other healthcare sectors and in other industries. Longitudinal research would aid in examining the effect of changes in business and IRM strategy on performance, and the relationships between orientations, over time. Further, this study did not examine causal relationships between strategic orientation, IRM orientation and performance, examination of which would be beneficial in future research.

Issues in Strategic Information Systems Planning

Vincent C. Yen

Department of Management Science and Information Systems

Wright State University

Dayton, Ohio 45435

INTRODUCTION

One of the critical issues for information exectives today continues to be the strategic information systems planning (SISP) (Brancheau and Wetherbe, 1987, Moynihan, 1990). Well planned and effectively executed SISP can help organizations achieve their objectives. However, ill-executed SISPs could lead to wasted resources and time, and decreased staff moral. A number of surveys have been conducted in the past to ascertain the critical attributes of success of SISP in practice. Lederer and Sethi (1988), and the recent article by Earl (1993), both studied the SISP success factors or features. They all pointed out that receiving top management acceptance or support is one of the success factors. It is easy to understand why lack of top management support could contribute to failure. However, with respect to this deficiency in SISP, there has been no study to determine why the top management behaved as such. And, of course, a cure cannot be prescribed under the circumstances.

Surveys conducted so far have revealed many critical factors for consideration by both practitioners and researchers alike. However, these surveys do not necessarily include all the critical factors for a successful methodology and implementation. For example, Breukel and Simons (1993) hypothesized that "in information-intensive industires with a good fit between competitive strategy, IT and organizational structure, will have a higher performance than organizations without such a fit". Although their hypothesis was partially confirmed through the use of a small sample, it does suggest that the degree of "fit" may prove to be an important factor.

This article first reviews the definitions of SISP and problems with SISP methodologies and implementations. Then with respect to the issue on "the lack of top management support", a series of hypotheses are suggested as the new dimensions of future research. Similarly, a set of new hypotheses for the problems of SISP is posed for research.

DEFINITION OF SISP

A good and concise discussion on the meaning of SISP is given by Lederer and Sethi (1988). Earl (1993) summarized various ways used in the literature and recommend that a SISP should emphasize the following areas:

". Aligning investment in IS with business goals.

. Exploiting IT for competitive advantage.

. Directing efficient and effective management of IS resources.

. Developing technology policies and architecture."

In this article, SISP is defined as the process of developing a portfolio of computer-based applications to assist an organization to realize the above features.

SISP METHODOLOGIES

A variety of SISP methodologies are available and commonly used. Vitale, et al. (1986) classified them into two categories: *alignment* and *impact*. In the *alignment* category, the methodology "aligns" MIS objectives with organizational goals. The representative ones are: Business Systems Planning (IBM, (1975)), Strategic Systems Planning (Holland Systems, (1986)), and Information Engineering (Marting, (1982)). In the "impact" category, the methodology may help create and justify new uses of IT, thus impacting SISP. The prominent ones are Competitive Strategies, Value Chain Analysis (Porter (1985)), and the Customer Resource Life Cycle (Ives and Learmonth, (1984)).

PROBLEMS WITH METHODOLOGIES

However, the methodologies available today have several drawbacks for implementation. First is the *cost*. Rockart (1979) noted that SISP may be very costly due to its comprehensive nature of data analysis. Second is *skills*. It requires skilled management expertise and IS technical competent staff (Zachman, 1982, and Vacca, 1983). Boynton and Zmud (1984) pointed out that users of the methodologies must be well trained. Third is the *limitations of the methodologies* itself. King (1988) noted that SISP fails to effectively establish strategies in such areas as the organizational, technological, legal, and external environments. Sullivan (1985) noted that existing SISP methodologies do not adequately address architectural issues. And the fourth is the *lengthy process of information requirements determination* (Cowman, Davis, and Wetherbe 1983). Yadav (1983) pointed out that SISP often fails to assess the organization and its environment, structure, constraints and policies.

The success of SISP is hampered by not only the flawed and impractical methodologies but also by managerial factors. Lederer and Sethi (1988) noted *the lack of top management commitment* as one of the problems for SISP. So does Earl (1993). Another important factor that could determine the outcome of SISP is *the user-IS relationship*. Earl (1993) reported that the user-IS relationship is one of the unsuccessful features of SISP.

The problems stated above are primarily unveiled through surveys of large organizations. Lederer and Sethi (1991) used an exploratory factor analysis to ascertain the underlying dimensions of SISP problems. Implicitly they assumed that some formal SISP methodologies were used by the targeted organizations. They came up with five factors: The *organization, implementation, database, hardware and cost*. In contrast to Lederer and Sethi, (1988 and 1991), Earl (1991) made no such assumptions on his survey that was based on interviews with IS directors, general managers and a senior line or user manager. Since he was interested in the variety and richness of planning behavior the respondents experienced, he obtained a taxonomy of five SISP approaches in practice. These are *business-led, method-led, administrative, technological, and organizational approaches*.

Up to this point, the problems of SISP have mostly been identified through theses surveys. These problems may be conveniently called the first order issues of SISP. It is conjectured that these problems will not disappear unless the causes of these problems are well understood. The causes of these problems are hereafter referred to as the second order issues of SISP. The purpose of the paper is to present the second order issues. These issues are posed in the form of hypotheses as they need to be tested in the future.

HYPOTHESES ON THE LACK OF MANAGEMENT SUPPORT

Since the lack of management support in SISP is always ranked high in the above mentioned surveys, it may be the single most important issue for research. The aim is to find the causes or factors that influence the top management decision-making in SISP. These causes or factors are proposed in the form of the following hypotheses.

Hypothesis 1. The strategic necessity hypothesis:
Top management will not support SISP unless it is considered strategically necessary to the business.

Hypothesis 2. The minimum hypothesis:
Top management will not support SISP unless the minimum requirement to effectively run the business is deficient. Example systems are accounting system, budgeting systems, transaction systems, and personal system, etc..

Hypothesis 3. The innovation hypothesis:
Top management will not support SISP if it is considered uninnovative.

Innovations are new ideas in IT applications; it is not simply an application of new technology.

Hypothesis 4. The incremental hypothesis:
Top management will not support SISP if it goes too far from the current capabilities.

Hypothesis 5. The synopsis hypothesis:
Top management will not support SISP if it is not a comprehensive plan.

Hypothesis 6. The profit hypothesis:
Top management will not support SISP if it can not result in an acceptable amount of profit or return on investment.

Hypothesis 7. The efficiency and effectiveness hypothesis:
Top management will not support SISP if it can not demonstrate significant improvements in efficiency and/or effectiveness.

Hypothesis 8. The state-of-the-art hypothesis:
Top management will not support SISP if it is not considered state-of-the-art.

Hypothesis 9. The wait and see hypothesis:
Top management will not support SISP if it has not been adopted by the majority in the business.

Hypothesis 10. The short term hypothesis:
Top management will not support SISP if the it is considered as "long term" in nature.

Earl (1991) also revealed an important fact that many firms may employ a variety of techniques and procedures in SISP. This suggests that SISP is dynamic in nature. Top management can change SISP whenever they see it fits.

THE IT ENVIRONMENT

In the seventies and eighties, IBM's business systems planning methodology was the dominant force in large business corporations. Information technology during that time was relatively stable. Today, we all experience a rapid change in information technology, paradigm, and market structure. Personal computers have now entered into their fifth era. The power of these PC's exceeds those mainframes of the early seventies. Client/server computing is swiftly making inroads into what was traditionally mainframe territory. Computer aided systems engineering (CASE) tools leapfrogged from simple functions to integrated teamwork packages. As a result, the information technology industry is quite different from ten years ago. Such rapid changes in the computing environment may contribute to unwillingness to adopt any formal SISP approaches. The rapid progress whcih causes instability in the technology selection may act as another factor in getting management commitment.

It is conceivable that one can add other potentially influential factors for consideration, further demonstrating the richness of this research field.

CALL FOR STUDY OF THE SECOND ORDER FACTORS.

To improve the chance of success of SISP, it is time to research into the second order issues. The hypotheses given in this paper are directed to the issue of the lack of commitment by top management. Similar hypotheses may be studied on other issues such as organization, implementation, database, etc. Reevaluation of the key factors on each of the second order issues will positively identify the problems and help formulate new strategies for more successful SISP.

REFERENCES

Bergeron, F., Buteau, C. and Raymond, L. (1991), Identification of Strategic Information Systems Opportunities: Applying and Comparing Two Methodologies, MIS Quarterly, March, pp. 89-101.

Bowman, B, Davis, G., & Wetherbe, J. (1983) Three state model of MIS planning. Information and Management, 6(1), pp. 11-25.

Boynton, A. C., & Zumd, R. W. (1984) An assessment of critical success factors. Sloan Management Review, 1984, pp. 17-27.

Breukel, A. and Simons, J. L. (19933) Competitive strategy and organizational structure: Key factors for competitive advantage with IT, 1993 Information Resource Management Association Conference Proceedings. pp. 311-319.

Earl, M. J., (1993), Experiences in Strategic Information Systems Planning, MIS Quarterly, Vol. 17, No. 1, March, pp. 1-20.

Fredrickson, J. W. (1983), Strategic Process Research: Questions and Recommendations, Academy of Management Review, Vol. 8, No. 4, pp. 565-575.

Hagmann, C. and McCahon, C. S., (1993), Strategic Information Systems and Competitiveness, Information and Management, 25, pp. 183-192.

King, W. R. (1978), Strategic planning for management information systems. MIS Quarterly, 2(1), pp. 27-37

King, W. R. (1988), How effective is your information systems planning?, Long Range Planning, 21(5), pp. 103-112.

Lederer, A. L. and Sethi, V., (1988), The Implementation of Strategic Information Systems Planning Methodologies, MIS Quarterly, September, pp. 445-461.

Lederer, A.L. and Sethi, V., (1991), Critical Dimensions of Strategic Information Systems Planning, Decision Sciences, Vol. 22, pp. 104-119.

Rockart, J. F. (1979), Chief executives define their own data needs. Harvard Business Review, 57(2), pp. 215-229.

Sullivan, C. H. (1985), Systems Planning in the information age, Sloan Management Review, 26(2), 3-13.

Vacca, J. R. (1983) BSP: How is it working? Computerworld, March .

Yadav, S. B. (1983), Determining an organization's information requirements: A state of the art survey. Data Base, 14(3), pp. 3-20.

Section Four

Information Technology Management in Developing Countries

Does Information Systems Education Prepare Professionals for the Real World?

Janice M Burn, Eugenia M W Ng Tye, Louis C K Ma, Ray S K Poon
Department of Computing, Hong Kong Polytechnic,
Hung Hom, Kowloon, Hong Kong

Executive Abstract

Globalization increasingly highlights the need to understand cultural differences worldwide. This is particularly relevent to Information Systems (IS) personnel who, by the very nature of their job, have to participate in the development of systems which transcend cultural barriers. The global nature of IS, however, also means that organizations have to formulate corporate IS personnel policies which must take into account the different expectations and motivational patterns of IS staff worldwide.

This paper reports on a cross-cultural study which addresses some of these issues. The study examines the expectations of graduating IS professionals with the perceived reality of the IS profession through the eyes of past graduates. Hong Kong (HK) based IS professionals are compared at both stages of the study against their US counterparts. Not only is there a severe mismatch between the expectations and their realization but significant differences exist between the two cultures. This has been a number of implications for IS personnel policies and for IS education worldwide.

The Results Analysis of Current Graduate Expectations

The respondents were asked to rate 20 questions on Job Characteristics using a 5 point Likert-scale with 1 as "strongly disagree" and 5 as "strongly agree" (see Figure 1). The questions were adapted from a similar study by Smiths et al. (1993). The job characteristic questions were used to assess the respondent's self-description of work-related traits.

In general, the HK respondents gave a lower and narrower range of scores than their US counter-parts for the questions related to job characteristics. The results ranged from 3.15 to 4.12 for HK respondents but ranged from 3.25 to 4.67 for US respondents. However, the HK respondents gave lower scores

Figure 1 : Comparison of Job Characteristics between Hong Kong and US Graduate

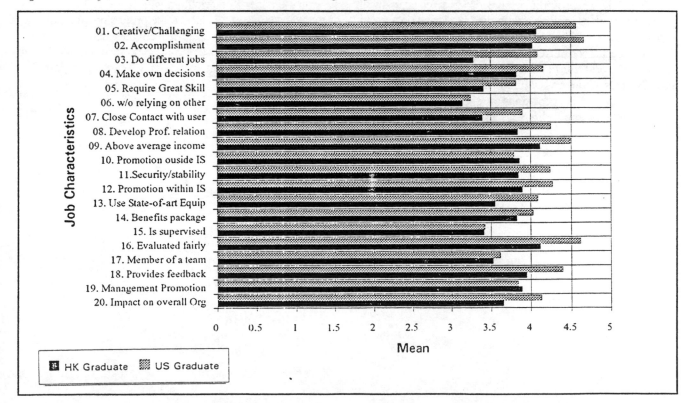

Source: "IS curriculum development through career progression analysis", Research Working Paper, Department of Computing, Hong Kong Polytechnic.

for all eighteen out of the twenty questions asked. The two job characteristics rated higher by HK respondents are "promotion outside IS" and "management promotion". Three other characteristics of HK respondents, which were rated only slightly below the US counterparts, are "without relying on others", "is supervised" and "member of a team". All the other 15 Job Characteristics were rated significantly lower by HK respondents.

Comparison with Job Characteristics of Past Graduates

In a previous study by the authors IS graduate professionals (drawn from the IS student graduate population over the last five years) were asked to rate the job characterisitics of an IS professional using the same set of questions as the current study. Jobs do not live up to the expectations of IS graduates. The scores for job characteristics of pre-graduates are significantly higher than graduated professionals. The mean scores are 3.74 from pre-graduates and 3.17 from graduates. This is in line with the US results although the US differences between the pre and post graduate populations are less (0.35). However, once again the scores from US respondents, from both pre-graduates and graduates, are higher than those in HK.

Conclusion.

This paper has examined the results from two separate stages of a longitudinal research study examining the job expectations and career development of IS graduate professionals in HK. These findings have also been compared with the results from a similar study in the US. The initial conclusions suggest that there is a considerable mismatch between the job expectations of fresh graduates and their actualization in the real world. Further the disparity is greater for HK IS professionals compared with their US counterparts even though their overall expectations are significantly lower. This has a number of implications for IS career development and management. There is strong evidence to suggest that a changing IS paradigm will impact on the role of IS professionals in the 1990s. The IS professional will be integrated into different business units within the organization and play a stronger role in user support and business analysis. The findings in this study, however, suggest that these views have not been implemented in practice either by the academic community or IS management. The majority of students at the time of graduation seek jobs with technical orientations and place a low emphasis on user interaction and team working skills. While these views change after employment the HK IS professional then finds the job environment highly limiting with little opportunity to do different jobs, gain promotion or move outside the IS field. Strong similarities existed within the US and HK data sets implying that these were global issues and not solely local issues. Significant differences seem, however, to relate to the job environments where HK IS professionals find their prospects more limited. This coupled with their lower overall expectations implies that few HK organizations are gaining maximum productivity from their IS staff or utilizing them as effectively as they could. Unfortunately this is likely to inhibit the effective development of global IS since few HK IS professionals would appear to have the opportunity to develop the breadth of business expertise which would be required to make significant contributions to corporate re-engineering. In conclusion, the challenge for the future is two-fold. The academic community must attempt to develop a broader IS curriculum which reflects the IS needs of the 90s and also to influence the professional IS community. IS managers must in turn recognize that they have a major part to play in fostering the new IS professional and creating an environment in which IS career development plays an intrinsic part.

Critical Factors Influencing Utilization of Information Technology—Case Studies from Pakistan's Textile Industry

Syed Zahoor Hassan
Graduate School of Business Administration
Lahore University of Management Sciences
Lahore, Pakistan

ABSTRACT

Factors that influence utilization of information technology (IT) by a specific organization have been studied by a large number of researchers. This paper focuses on understanding how Pakistan's textile industry has utilized IT and the factors that have significantly influenced the extent and effectiveness of these efforts. In depth case studies of four organizations with more than five years of computerization efforts have identified a number of key factors that influence effective utilization of IT. The analysis of these case studies has shown that business characteristics, and management structure influence the IT utilization process, and the degree of IT utilization in turn influences the management structure of organizations. The most important variables were found to be rate and nature of growth that the company is going through, the degree of dependence on vendors and suppliers, the management style of top management, the degree of professionalism of senior managers, the state of company's planning, training, evaluation and reward systems, and the methodology employed for identification and development of IT applications.

1. INTRODUCTION

There has been growing interest in studying the utilization of information technology (IT) in developing countries (Palvia, 1992). Special country specific studies have been carried out to understand what factors influence success of computer based information systems (CBIS). Odedra (1993) presents a good overview of various studies done to identify the critical factors affecting success of CBIS. It also presents the success factors emerging from five case studies of African organizations. A number of other recent studies have also focused on the approaches being used in developing countries for implementing information technologies (Doukidis, 1992) (Hassan, 1991). The infrastructure constraints in implementing information technologies in Pakistan have been discussed in Hassan (1993). In this paper we focus on understanding the utilization of CBIS in Pakistan's textile industry.

Pakistan's industry has seen a rapid growth in the use of computers. The imports of various types of computers in Pakistan increased from 29,468 units worth Rs 238 million (one US $ = Rs 30, approximately) in 1981-82 to 65,387 units worth

Rs 857 million in 1989-90 (Memon, 1991). Apart from other factors, this rapid growth has been due to greater affordability of the computer hardware, lifting of import duty from computers in 1986 (Kazmi, 1990), and greater awareness about the utility of information technology for businesses. The textile industry is the most important private sub-sector in Pakistan. It employs about 35 per cent of the industrial labor force, produces nearly 30 per cent of manufacturing industrial output, and accounts for about 75 per cent of manufactured exports. Nearly 40 percent of the textile mills in the organized sector are integrated mills, that is, mills that convert ginned cotton to yarn and also make cotton (Saigol, 1993). Hence, the focus of this study is on the integrated or composite textile companies.

In the next section, the research methodology followed for this study is described. Section 3 describes the finding from the studied companies and also includes analysis of each company's situation. The overall analysis of data from the four companies is presented in section 4. Main conclusions from this study are presented in section 5.

2. RESEARCH METHODOLOGY

Study of twenty companies in a number of different industrial sectors of Pakistan, has indicated that apart from environment and organization related factors, specific industry characteristics also strongly influence IT utilization (Hassan, 1994). Hence it becomes important to focus on a specific industry sector and study how it has utilized IT. Textiles, the most important industry in Pakistan, was identified for in depth study. Also, over the last five to ten years a large number of firms in this industry have tried to utilize IT. Moreover, this industry is regarded as one that has not utilized IT as much it should have, given its resources and favourable business conditions that have resulted in high growth in this sector. In many ways Pakistan's textile industry is also the most typical Pakistani indigenous industry - there are no multinationals or joint venture firms in this sector. But on the other hand, Pakistani textile industry is heavily export oriented, and this makes it even more unusual that IT is not more widely used.

A case study methodology was adopted to gather data. Structured interviews were conducted to collect information in three broad areas: business characteristics, management structure, and the IT utilization processes from four firms. A number of earlier studies have shown interdependence between information technology and organizational structures (Burn, 1989), and influence of work procedures on success of information systems implementation (Joshi, 1990). Nosek (1989) presents the idea of interplay between organizational structure, task design, people, reward system and information processes to understand how IT can be effectively utilized by organizations.

Exhibit 1 provides details of the main areas that were explored in the study through these interviews. More than forty managers were interviewed. These included members of the top management team, senior and first level managers from the user functional areas, and the managers in the information systems area. This approach was used to refine the key issues and variables that need to be focused upon (Benbasat, 1987; Yin, 1989). Later data could be collected from a larger number of companies to further refine the results. The four selected firms have more than five years of IT utilization experience and are all well established, large, vertically integrated firms (composite units that start processing with ginned cotton and produce finished fabric, or in some cases even made-ups like bed sheets). All of these firms belong to different business groups, and are representative of management practices and styles that prevail in Pakistan's textile industry. Two of these firms are located in the main textile industrial city of Pakistan, Faisalabad, while one is located in the Karachi, the largest industrial centre of the country. The fourth firm is located away from the major industrial centres in the north of the country.

We would be referring to the studied firms as Company 1, Company 2, Company 3 and Company 4.

Company 1: This was the largest integrated textile mill in the country in 1993. This company's main strength was quality and it obtained a premium of 10-15% on the prices of its products due to its relatively better quality as compared to the average Pakistani textile firm. In 1993 it employed nearly 6000 people and had a total of 12 stand alone personal computers (PCs) and two 386 based computers with ten terminals running Unix operating system. With annual revenues of Rs 3,688 million and after tax profit of Rs 223 million in 1992, the total investment in computer hardware at the company was nearly Rs 500,000 and the salary budget of the computer section was about Rs 720,000 per annum.

The computerization at this mills started nearly six years ago with the arrival of a new Executive Director of Finance who had prior experience with computers. At the same time the company's auditors also encouraged computerization. The company bought a computer and a financial package (General Ledger, Debtors Balance, Trial Balance and other related modules) from their auditing firm. The company had problems in getting the system updated with new features due to high turnover of staff at the software vendor company and the management started looking for other options. Another software company was given the task to develop a custom payroll package. Even with the lapse of nearly a year and a payment of

Rs. 100,000 to the vendor no working system was delivered. Again the main problem was the high turnover of staff at the vendor company. At this time there was also a change in the senior management in the Finance department (that was involved in the computerization efforts). The new head of the Finance department had come from a large manufacturing company that had successfully developed computer based information systems through an in house team. A number of new software vendors were evaluated. On each new contact with a vendor company new faces would be representing it. This was due to high turnover of employees. Due to this situation the management decided that a computerization would have to be done with an in house team. An EDP manager was hired to develop applications. This person who had a Master's in Computer Science and several years of applications development experience, adopted and modified the applications that were earlier obtained from the auditing firm. He also developed new applications for Payroll and Stores Inventory. In mid-1993 more applications in the accounts area were planned to obtain timely information on the quantity and value of exports. This would help in timely recovery of export rebates, and provide information needed to verify expenses, allowing computation of profits.

The main motivations of the top management in computerization was to get information quickly, assist in the annual audit process, and avoid computational errors. During the last two years the firm had increased its cloth production by more than 50% and now it was focusing on overcoming operational problems and saving labor costs.

Over the last few years the company had recruited a number of MBAs to work in various departments, specially in export marketing, purchasing, and some production departments. These MBAs initiated development and use of computer based systems. A computer based system was developed for the purchase department but the old employees resisted its implementation. When the MBA posted in this department was transferred the situation reverted to the old manual system. Now another attempt was being made to implement that computer based system. A computer based system had been implemented in the folding department to generate accurate information on the wastage in the printing department. As the incentive of the section incharge was linked to control of wastage, he was eager to use the system as it helped him address the problems in time.

There was no formal push or encouragement from the top management to computerize but significant latitude was given to managers who showed initiative for computerization. At the same time, focus on short-term and immediate results was emphasized. "How will it help increase production?" was the question that the chief executive always asked. He would say, "get as large a computer as you want as long as it delivers higher production that justifies its cost. " The top management's philosophy was to delegate almost all of the operational decision making to managers. Even new hires with no prior work experience were given this authority. In the words of one such

Exhibit 1: Areas explored during the field study

A. Business Characteristics:

What are the main areas of focus for the company to retain competitiveness?

Has the company followed a growth approach aggressively?

What is impact of government regulatory policies on the company?

To what extent does the company have a totally self contained and integrated production process?

What is the role of vendors and suppliers in company's operations?

Which technologies are important for company's competitiveness?

To what extent has the company relied on new technologies?

and how have the business characteristics changed over the time that company has utilized information technology?

B. Management Structure:

What is the management structure of the company?

What are the educational and professional background of the managers?

What planning (both short term and long term) processes are used?

What are the evaluation and incentive systems for workers and managers?

What are the distinct values and style of the top management?

and how has the entire management set up evolved since the start of the computerization process?

C. IT Utilization Processes:

How and by whom was computerization initiated at the company?

What were the motivations and initial areas for using IT?

How much money was spent on IT implementations?

Is there a strategic IS plan? If so, who has formulated it?

How were the IT priorities determined and by whom?

What specific hardware and software technologies were employed?

What process was followed for IT implementation?

To what extent were outside consultants used?

What was the role of the end users in IT utilization process?

What have been the major benefits and issues in IT utilization?

and how have the above evolved since the inception of computerization?

young manager, 'it is basically a swim or drown approach.' The company had concluded that use of outside consultants did not give results as they did not understand the business details and suffered from high employee turnover in a high growth environment. The company's main approach has been to hire people with little background in computers (like the new MBAs) and encourage them to learn by doing.

The company did not prepare any formal strategic or annual plan all the planning was done by the principal owner, and chief executive, on an ad-hoc basis and had a very short term focus (see Exhibit 2 for a profile of top management in each of the four companies). Some departments had very recently started making own plans. The exports department had recently prepared an annual budget for the first time. Funds were allocated on need basis - if the immediate boss could be convinced money could be obtained to buy computer equipment.

There was no human resource policy at this company. Most departments had no formal evaluation system. One of the MBAs who was heading the export department had initiated an evaluation system in his department. The company did not consider formal training of its managers a key investment. It was very rare that a manager was sent on an executive education program.

Analysis of main issues:

The case highlights a number of interesting aspects of IT utilization and corresponding issues. Some of these are: * The computerization efforts at this company have been very closely tied to individual rather than company policy or strategy. It was the induction of new individuals with prior exposure to computer based systems that triggered initial computerization efforts or subsequent changes in its specific implementation approaches. * There is lack of systems development expertise in the functional departments that are involved in developing computer based systems. This situation raises the issue of the quality of the design and coding of these systems. * Due to the totally decentralized systems development and data processing, there is duplication of data entry. * The high emphasis on immediate results could lead to poor overall analysis and inefficient systems in the long run. Most managers would try to quickly put together a system that would give them the information that they currently require without any thought of what other information could also be generated that can help in improving the over all efficiency and effectiveness of the organization. In such an environment the question of investing time and efforts into a large long term effort, to develop a system that can provide strategic advantage, would never arise. * The firm basically followed a prototype like approach to systems development for nearly all of its non accounting systems. * On the positive side, one could argue that with its results oriented approach, that employed eager and highly motivated young managers, the company was learning at a very low cost. But with the absence of proper human resource systems (evaluation and incentive programmes), it was highly questionable whether the company would be able to capitalize on this learning by

retaining these managers for a longer period.

Company 2:   This company was the second largest textile unit in Pakistan in 1993. Since early 1980s the company had been implementing Quality Circles (QC) and by 1993 nearly 40 such circles were working quite actively. The company had invested heavily in training and top management had identified development of computer based information systems a key priority area. After undergoing a major expansion phase the company was in the consolidation phase with focus on process improvements and efficiency enhancement. It had been recently selected by a large Japanese company as an equity partner in setting up of a new large textile unit in Pakistan. Acquisition of technology was a key element of this company's long term strategy.   The computerization efforts at this company started in early 1980s when with the investment of Rs 500,000 a top management bought a Novell Network system and asked the finance controller to learn the technology and use it. He was not eager to use the system and left the company in the process. This system was never utilized but top management felt it had sent the message that information technology is coming to the company. In 1985 the company decided to give PCs to all managers who asked for it and nearly Rs 500,000 were spent in acquiring 12 PCs for this purpose. In 1987 a management consulting firm was hired to study a management systems, and develop and implement information systems. This effort that cost several hundred thousand rupees was not successful as the junior and middle level management staff did not cooperate with the consultants. Later a US trained IS professional was hired as an MIS manager. He developed some ideas to develop applications but was not able to build proper rapport with user groups. A three-day in house training course was organized for all the managers to introduce them to a MIS concepts and to teach them to use spreadsheet and database packages. At this time top management gave managers in various production departments six months to learn to use a PCs or leave the company. The Director Operations also learnt to use PC and started using it extensively.

By 1989 most of the management staff had become computer aware through use of PCs and when the company appointed another consulting firm to help in deciding the systems that had to be developed, the consultants received cooperation from the staff. The consultants, who were also IBM resellers, recommended that the company should buy an AS/400 machine and link all the existing PCs to it. With the financial controller as the chairman of the computerization committee, a software development work started on the newly acquired AS/400. The total charges for development of the financial systems were nearly Rs one million. During the next 18 months the consultants worked on developing the systems without much tangible progress. The main reason for the slow progress was the lack of experience of the consultant staff with the AS/400 environment. Moreover, the consultants also lacked understanding of company's systems. In July 1991, a new financial controller was hired who had prior experience with computerization projects. He decided to use Xenix for applications

Exhibit 2: Top Management Profiles and Priorities

	Education	Personality/Style	Association with Information Technology	Priorities
Company 1	BA	Very aggressive, results oriented, delegates operational decisions	No direct interaction with computers.	- growth
Company 2	MBA	Long term focus, almost emphasis on quality. Hands on style, not micro-management	Extensively using PC for spread sheet models Views IT as necessary	- Development of capabilities and systems - Quality consciousness - Worker involvement
Company 3	B.S Eng..	Micro-management focus. Non-assertive style.	Does not use a computer directly. Never asks for new reports.	- survival key concern
Company 4	B.Sc (IE & OR)	Details oriented, focus on control for efficient operations. Keen for new technologies	Involved in design of all new IS application. Very active user of PC- Carries a notebook computer. Uses spread sheet models for making management decisions.	- Focus on technology competitive weapon - Building of human and professional management.

All the four companies top management belongs to the owner family. In case of Company 1, the chief executive is not involved in day to day management. In all the remaining three cases the top management retains involvement in operational management decisions.

development and invested Rs 300,000 in a new 486 machine with four terminals. An MIS manager/analyst was hired along with two junior programmers. Work continued on the AS/400 applications but the analyst and one junior programmer in a span of nearly one year computerized all the financial systems in the Xenix environment. The salaries, wages, personnel records, fixed assets, and weaving efficiency systems were developed on the AS/400. Only previously existing manual procedures were computerized and the modifications suggested by consultants were not implemented. Inventory and a number of sales related applications were also under implementation. In early 1993 plans were underway to convert Xenix systems to the AS/400 to facilitate the integration of applications that was required for generation of management reports. There were also plans to link the DOS based PCs to AS/400. A number of CBIS had been developed by the staff in the production departments on their own. These included systems for monitoring the production of yarn and cloth. Some of these departments had several PCs. In one department a four-node Novell network was also being employed. The staff in these departments had learned to develop applications primarily on their own initiative and had almost no formal training. Those departments that had shown effective usage of their existing PCs had no difficulty in getting funds for additional equipment. As a result of the recently implemented CBIS, more timely and specific accounting information (profitability by each area, for example) was now available. A 20% reduction in inventory levels had also been achieved (from Rs 100 to Rs 80 million), timely salary disbursement, 2% reduction in wastage, availability of salary information during the union negotiation, availability of information on financing resources, and availability of data on quality improvements were some of the other benefits. The company developed a plan for next 12 months but had no long term strategic plan. Integration of the production and costing systems through conversion to AS/400 was planned for 1993. The major constraint in the speed of computerization was the availability of people for the development work.

Analysis of Main Issues:

* Due to lack of a properly planned and well thought out approach to computerization the company had wasted valuable time and money. Top management though eager to employ IT, was not willing to spend the time to learn and manage the process of IT utilization. Their reliance on outside consultants, who had very little understanding of the business and possessed limited IT skills, though intended to fasten the pace of IT implementation, actually caused delays.

* Individuals that joined the organization with prior knowledge of IT implementation issues that enabled the company to derive results from IT. It was only when the company had acquired in house expertise in development and management of IT that it obtained any meaningful results from its computerization efforts and IT investments.

* Top management felt that by encouraging the production departments to develop their own applications the pace of computerization had increased but the corporate IS department's control had weakened, making integration of systems more difficult. Significant amount of repeated data entry was now needed to consolidate information for several managerial reports.

* The quality of the applications developed by the self-trained functional department staff would be a key issue, especially when efforts will be made to integrate the applications.

* Currently managers are the people who have an interest in computerization. Clerical workers are still reluctant to be involved as their work load has increased in some cases due to the additional data entry work, as the manual records are still being kept.

* The systems have been developed in three environments: Xenix (a flavour of Unix), AS/400 environment, and DOS. Although for future the focus is on moving the Xenix applications to AS/400, the ease of development in the prototype-like environment of PCs and urgency to quickly computerize maximum number of areas can lead to continued applications development in all environments making the ultimate integration of systems harder.

Company 3: This company is located in the northern part of the country, more than a hundred miles from the main textile manufacturing city, Faisalabad, where companies 1 and 2 are located. It had sales of Rs 1,078 million, after tax profit of Rs 37 million and work force of nearly 3,100 in 1992. It is one of the oldest integrated textile mills in Pakistan. For a very long period the company did not invest in new equipment and technology. Nearly 10 years ago it faced serious labor problems that resulted in a major restructuring. Since 1985 the company has invested in new technology by upgrading its spinning and finishing process equipment. In 1993 the company was planning to go into textile made-ups. The company had invested nearly Rs 2 million in hardware and was spending nearly Rs 350,000 annually on salaries of the computer staff and equipment maintenance. A server and 24 networked workstations in various departments formed the hardware set-up. The EDP manager was the only systems developer.

The use of computers at this company started when the Sales manager realized computers could help him. He had to frequently send lengthy cables to his customers. He had a small data base developed to keep track of his customer communications. On seeing this system the Managing Director decided to computerize the company operations. A formal request for proposal was advertised and a consulting firm was selected to study the company's systems and develop information systems. The primary objectives were to reduce the more than 20 days delay in the reporting of monthly accounts, improve accuracy of reporting and document systems and procedures. The consultants documented all existing systems, suggested improvements and made a system manual. A local area network based hardware was acquired on a consultant's recommendation. Development work on the suggested computer based information systems (CBIS) was initiated by the consultants. Implementation of a financial package and a Stores Inventory system was started in 1990. At this stage an EDP manager was also hired. Due to the consultants being based in Lahore, nearly 200 miles away, required frequent changes became very difficult to manage. The company did not have the source code and was totally dependent on consultants for making any change in the systems. After nearly six months of effort it was decided to rewrite the applications in house. During this process it was discovered that the functional area managers had not provided correct and relevant information to the consultants. There was lack of co-operation from the heads of departments who suspected that the CBIS would threaten their jobs. Some managers never believed computerization would actually happen and never took the consultants seriously. In some cases the managers did not even bother to read the consultants report before approving it. At this stage the support provided by the Managing Director to the EDP manager sent a clear signal that computerization was there to stay. The EDP manager also developed cordial relations with the department heads and their clerical staff through one-on-one meetings. It was through these efforts that he was able to rewrite the original applications and also add new ones in a relatively short period. Less resistance was encountered from the old-guard in production departments as they knew they were indispensable to the organization and would not be affected by the computerization. On the other hand the managers on the shop floor were not keen while the managers in the main corporate office were very supportive of computerization efforts. In this whole process the Finance manager left when the Managing Director supported the EDP manager in his efforts to implement systems. But after this the MD clearly told the EDP manager that he was on his own and should not expect intervention from him in future.

In 1993 Finance, Purchase and Stores departments were fully computerized and implementation of the CBIS in Sales department was in progress. A production monitoring system was also being implemented through an outside consultant.

During the computerization process, efforts were made by the EDP manager to learn from the experiences of other textile companies. He visited Company 1 and Company 2, but felt could not learn much from them as they were developing stand alone systems while his company's systems were all integrated. There was no program to train the managers in use of PC-based applications. When the systems were developed for an area the EDP manager sat with the related manager and explained its operations.

The company had no formal systems. There was no budgeting systems or process for performance evaluation. The MD was very closely involved with operations and spent nearly four hours every day on the factory floor during two detailed tours. The organizational structure of the company had not changed for the last fifteen years. The main challenge faced by the company was to survive at a time when demand for its products had reduced due to recession in Europe and US, its primary markets. The MD felt that due to excess labor, because of too many layers of company management, older less efficient machines, and old management structures costs were too high. He looked at IT as a means to overcome some of these problems. Without a clear vision for the specific role of IT and no long term IS plan, he was not clear how to proceed. He realized that without professional management no progress would be possible but the main challenge was how to put together such a group and to develop and implement systems that would be needed to retain and utilize it effectively

Analysis of main issues:
* The Managing Director felt the entire computerization process was too dependent on one person, the EDP manager. *
The delays in reporting of information was still there though much less.

* The value of some of the information generated from the computer applications was seriously compromised due to very lax and somewhat inadequate procedures for ensuring proper and timely data entry. In one instance a person did not enter 'issue notes' in the stores system for several months only when he left the company were these discovered unentered in his office drawer.

* The reluctance in streamlining and changing the management processes to enable proper realization of benefits was another major issue. An inventory system developed to obtain accurate and timely information on use of consumables like dyes was still not providing the desired benefits. All incoming materials were not recorded as received until they were approved by the ordering department. In the case of dyes, the finishing department waited until they had consumed all the supply and found it of proper quality before they would certify its acceptance. This was due to bad experience in the past when some genuine and some counterfeit products had been supplied in the same lot. Hence the accounting department did not get accurate information on consumption of dyes for two to three weeks after the end of the month. This problem could have been solved by making use of decision support systems that relied on past vendor performance and item consumption data. But instead the company decided to set up a more extensive testing facility and a separate warehouse to shorten the acceptance testing time. The option of rethinking the company-vendor relationship was not pursued.

* Lack of formal management processes has also caused low effectiveness of IT applications. The company had no formal planning, or even meetings among the departmental heads. Hence there was no forum where issues related to overall management of the company could be discussed and new ideas debated. Philosophy was to focus on immediate problems. Whoever had something to discuss with the MD would walk into his office.

* The organization structure of the company reflected the predominant production focus. All the department heads reported to the Resident Director who was a production person with little understanding or appreciation of other areas. The MD, being an engineer by training, was also production oriented.

Company 4

With sales of Rs 626 million and profits of Rs 25 million and a reputation for innovation and effective technology utilization, this company is one of the leading textile mills in Pakistan. Though much younger in age compared to companies 1,2, and 3, this company has the longest history of utilizing IT. It had served as an inspiration and reference for other companies in the use of information technology.

Computerization at this company started when a son of the owner returned after completing his education in US in industrial engineering and operations research. As he got involved in streamlining operations he realized the need for CBIS to provide the relevant information. The first computer application, weaving production control system, was developed to monitor and enhance the efficiency of the weaving section.

An IBM system 34 was purchased and staff recruited to develop applications in house more than ten years ago. The computer section consisted of a person with an M.Sc in Computer Sciences and experience of systems development at a bank, an individual with bachelor's in accounting and some exposure to computer, and one experienced textile engineer. Later MAPICS package was also bought from IBM but it was found not suitable to the production processes at the company. The experience gained in implementing this package helped the company's computer staff to develop other applications in house. An extensive training program was conducted for the managers to introduce them to various PC packages in 1985. Since that time PCs are being used extensively in a number of areas, especially for costing purposes. The incentives of user department mangers and workers were tied to the effective use of the IS applications. For example, in the weaving section a system helped supervisors monitor the efficiency on two-hourly basis and their incentive bonus was tied to the level of efficiency. Once they realized that the system can help them increase efficiency there was no resistance to its use. But in the beginning the chief executive had to discuss with them the efficiency figures of their section with the help of the computer system output report to emphasize how it could be of help. The top executive who had initiated the computerization process has stayed very closely involved with the design and implementation of all applications. All applications have been initiated by him. The IS department has been called the office of computer services (OCS) to emphasize the user orientation in all the applications development work. The company hired fresh trainees with 12 or 14 years of education and used them as computer operators. These people were utilized to maintain systems initially and those who were good were moved to software development projects. Except for the first group the company had not hired any trained software developer from outside. The hardware was later upgraded to an AS/400 in 1988. During the process of conversion to new hardware it became clear that there was lot of duplication in the applications as in some cases several programs existed to generate the same report. This had happened primarily due to lack of any formal planning and documentation in the OCS area. Whenever the top management wanted a report, whoever was available in the OCS department at the time wrote a program to generate it. A total of over 4000 programs were located at this time. Instead of converting them to the AS/400 native environment most of the applications were run in the 3X emulation mode, resulting in highly inefficient hardware utilization. At this time a joint project was started with IBM to develop the weaving production control application in the AS/400 environment. IBM supplied the systems development expertise and the company the process related knowledge. More recently, Oracle based applications are also being developed in the PC environment with the help of outside consultants. As the company had to acquire the services of consultants to train its computer staff in relational data base concepts and Oracle, it decided to also have a system developed with their help and active involvement. The company had also developed certain systems that it viewed as strategic. One such system scheduled jobs in the finishing department. Through this system the latest status of specific orders could be traced. This was important because the company also performed finishing operations for a number of other companies A new system was being developed to automate the design and printing process for various fabric patterns. With this system the company would be able to offer significantly shorter turnaround time to its customers on new fabric designs enabling it to compete in the high value fashion segment where designs changed very frequently and shorter delivery time was a critical success factor.

Analysis of Main Issues

* Due to lack of proper planning and documentation in the IS department, there was significant duplication in programs. Most of the development work had been done by only one person. In the absence of documentation the company was vulnerable to this person leaving it.

* Hardware utilization was not very efficient. As the applications were moved from the S/34 to AS/400 without proper redesign, they were basically emulating S/34 environment on the AS/400.

* Due to the home-grown nature of the IS staff, the IS applications design skills in the company were not very good. Moreover, the applications lacked integration resulting in duplication of effort in data entry. For, example the costing system, that was PC based required input data from the production systems that resided on the mini computer. This data had to rekeyed into the PCs.

* Lack of IS planning had resulted in inefficient utilization of the available IT resources. The top management had never formally reviewed the business processes in the company to identify opportunities for IT utilization. Hence, it was also not aware of what it could accomplish if it had a stronger IS design and development team.

* The over-centralization of IS related decision making, including the identification and design of applications, had stifled the assimilation of IT by the organization. All ideas for new applications were coming from the top, and the applica-

Table 1: Major issues faced by the four companies and the related characteristics

	Co. 1	Co. 2	Co. 3	Co. 4
Business Characteristics	- High growth - Focus on short term profits - No significant pressure to cut costs due to favourable regulatory - Suppliers mostly small and with low bargaining power - Located in the main Textile industrial city. - Investment in latest equipment and use of foreign technicians.	- Steady growth - Focus on development of systems to obtain long term competitiveness - Very limited use of vendors for Manufacturing. - Very high focus on quality - An extensive quality circles programme that involves top management as well as workers.	- No growth - High cost structure due to old equipment - Trying to reduce costs and excess labour to become more competitive - Not located in the Textile industry region-no access to vendors for outside manufacturing	- Steady growth - Forward looking and progressive, technology oriented approach. - Focus on sustaining long term steady profitability - Located in the largest industrial centre--easy availability of work force. - Focus on value-added exports. - Willingness to take calculated risks with new technology.
Management Structure	- Decentralised operational decision making - Hiring of young MBA's in different departments - No formal evaluation or incentive systems for management - Willing to recruit from outside for senior positions.	- Some systems in place for evaluation - Very limited use of young MBAs - Mostly long term employees - More direct involvement of top management in operational decisions	- No planning systems - No evaluation or incentive systems - Informal process for co-ordination - Mostly long term employees and very few young MBAs	- Focus on developing systems. - Formal systems for evaluation and incentives - Highly professional and well trained management team - Formal delegation of responsibility

Table 1 (continued)

	Co. 1	Co. 2	Co. 3	Co. 4
IT Utilization Process	- No specific interest or encouragement from top management. Initiated by a new Finance department head on advice of auditors. - Driven by junior managers, mostly MBA, and the Finance General Manager - EDP manager reports to GM Finance - Most IT applications in Finance area. - Prototype like development approach used.	- Personal interest taken by Top mgt. in computerization - Initially focused on use of consultants for SW development, now developing in house - A formal committee monitors MIS - Planning process exists - MIS department reports to G.M Finance - Corporate MIS focused on developing Finance applications. Production develops applications independently. - Prototype based development approach.	- A Formal system study done. - Focus on an integrated system - No MIS steering Committee - EDP manager reports to the Resident Director - Focus on Finance and Inventory systems - Initially the traditional SDLC approach followed. Later more proto-type based development.	- Started with in-house development. - Focus on IT as a service-- department called office of computer services (OCS) - Top management involved in even detailed design of applications - Top executive considers IT as a means of attaining competitive advantage - Focus on production management area IS application. - Prototype based development.

Table 2: Factors Influencing IT Utilization

	Factors	Companies
A.	Lack of IS Planning and ad-hoc software development	1,2,3,4
B.	Shortage of skilled IS people, especially scarcity of system design expertise.	1,2,3,4
C.	Lack of top Managements IT vision	1,2,3
D.	Lack of Strategic planning	1,2,3
E.	Lack of Top management's willingness to be actively involved in IS activities	1,2,3
F.	Informal and ad-hoc management structure	1,3
G.	Poor choice of consultants low business and/or IT skills of chosen consultants.	2,3
H.	Lack of evolution in management decision systems to enhance IT utilization effectiveness.	1,3
I.	Lack of proper evaluation and reward system	1,3
J.	Over reliance on outside consultants for too long	2
L.	Low level of professionalism in user functional area	3
M.	Total Centralisation of IT decision making with top management	4
N.	User resistance	3

tions developers had to get the design (including input and output formats) approved from the top executive. In a way the top executive who had been instrumental in introducing and utilizing IT at the company, had through his over possessiveness of this function, stifled its growth - he was hugging it too tightly resulting in a 'bear hug'.

4. COMBINED ANALYSIS OF THE DATA FROM THE FOUR CASE STUDIES:

A number of issues relating to effective utilization of Information Technology (IT) have been highlighted by the specific experiences of the four companies studied above. Broadly, the issues lie in three main areas: Business characteristics, Management Structure and the IT utilization processes. Table 1 gives a summary of these issues for the four companies.

The major factors that have influenced the IT utilization process in each of the four companies are listed in Table 2. Exhibit 2 provides a summary profile of the top management of the four companies. Combined study of Table 1 and Exhibit 2 reveals the strong influence of the top management on the extent, effectiveness and areas of IT implementation. The most interesting aspect is the heavy involvement of top management in the design and development of IT applications. It seems to indicate that at times, if the involvement becomes excessive then it might become detrimental. Some of these factors dominate the IT utilization process making the other factors

irrelevant. Hence, it cannot be said that only the observed factors are relevant. It is very likely that if one or more of these dominating factors is removed then the importance of other factors will he highlighted. For example, in the case of Company 4 the over-involvement of the top executive in the detailed design of applications had become a major bottleneck and shortage of system design skills in the company or issues related to its recruitment policy were not seen to be that critical.

Apart from the environment and organization specific factors, a number of industry specific characteristics have also shaped the process of IT utilization at these companies:

1. The lack of focus on professionalization of management. Over the years Pakistan's textile industry has utilized the old-guard people who have learned through experience over a period of many years and have in quite a few case had no college education. One reason for this situation is the extremely difficult work environment on the typical textile factory floor. Over the years a strong 'party-system' has also developed where the spinning masters and supervisors have established strong loyalty bonds with the workers. This has resulted due to hiring of totally unskilled workers as apprentices and their coaching and protection by supervisors over years. It is not uncommon to find all the workforce in a unit belonging to the same native village or extended family. The spinning masters, hence, have a lot of influence on the work force and it is not uncommon that when such a person leaves

Exhibit 3: The Proposed Model for Factors Influencing IT Utilization

BUSINESS CHARACTERISTICS

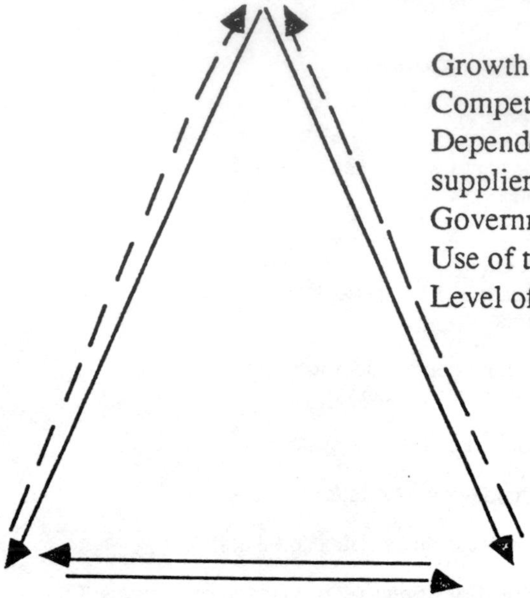

Growth *
Competitiveness
Dependence on vendors &
suppliers
Government regulations
Use of technology
Level of vertical integration

MANAGEMENT STRUCTURE

People (Backgrounds)
  - CEO
  - Functional Managers *
  - MIS staff

Organizational structure*
Systems

  - Planning*
  - Training*
  - Evaluation*
  - Reward

Values

IT UTILIZATION

Motivations
Development Process*
HW & SW technologies employed
Role of CEO*
Role of user dept mgrs*
Role of MIS managers*
Area (s) of IT application
IT Budget Allocations

ENVIRONMENTAL/INFRASTRUCTURE FACTORS

Availability of IS professionals
Availability of Professional Managers
Access to reliable SW and HW Support
Degree of enforcement of laws and regulations*

Note: Variables mark with an * were observed to be more important.

a company to join a new one, he also takes a large number of other senior supervisors and workers with him. The young trained professionals find it difficult to adjust in such an environment.

2. There is also a significant pay and incentive difference between the unit managers and supervisors. This has generally resulted in the senior managers' efforts to retain the existing management practices and the supervisors and junior managers' eagerness for implementation of new systems. This clear difference in perspectives has caused internal conflict and hindered utilization of IT for implementation of new systems.

3. Due to its very large share in the total Pakistani industry and very effective lobbying trade association, Textile industry has always managed to obtain significant and liberal support from the government in the form of loans, high import duties for protection from imported textile products, export rebate subsidies, and favourable export duty structure. It is rumored to have the clout to cause devaluation of the national currency. Presence of all these support facilities has led to a lower focus on enhancing efficiency and building systems to become more competitive. Also being primarily export oriented and focussed on selling only commodity products, like yarn and grey cloth, in the past, the industry has lacked the internal competitive culture that usually spurs efforts to modernize and use technology for enhancing competitiveness.

5. CONCLUSION

The study of the four textile companies efforts to implement information technology has indicated the hypothesis that the effective utilization of IT in an organization is determined by the interplay of factors in three areas: Business characteristics, Management structure, and the IT utilization processes. There are a number of infrastructure and environmental factors that also influence the dynamics of this interplay. Exhibit 3 depicts this interaction. The direction of arrows shows the influence of the three areas on each other. It is interesting to note that business characteristics seem to influence both management structure and IT utilization process but these two only influence each other. Another important hypothesis that has emerged from this study is the effectiveness of these prototyping approach to systems development. It has been seen that systems development and utilization was only effective when an in house IS group was present. Even those companies that started computerization efforts by relying on an outside software consultant had to eventually establish in house capabilities. This need for prototyping and the consequent requirement for in house development group is most probably due to the unstructured, informal and ad-hoc processes that exist in these companies. One reason for this state of affairs is the unstable economic and regulatory environment. Hence, in most cases these processes are also quite dynamic. In this regard the experiences of developing countries in adaptive development of software could be of benefit to the organiza-

tions in developed countries that are now beginning to face unstable economic conditions and need to follow a more adaptive software development approach.

A more extensive study will be conducted to verify the hypotheses that have emerged from this initial study. It will include a broader range of textile companies, especially the relatively new and more modern units that focus on only one aspect of the textile production process like spinning (manufacture of yarn) or weaving (manufacture of cloth from yarn). These newer units, not encumbered by most of the historical organizational legacies that have prevented the older units from fully utilizing the potential of IT, should be in better position to attain greater benefits from IT.

REFERENCES

Benbasat, I., Goldstein D.K. and Mead, M. "The Case Research Strategy in Studies of Information Systems," MIS Quarterly (11:3), September 1987, pp. 369-388.

Burn, J. M. "The Impact of Information Technology on Organizational Structures," Information & Management, 16, 1989, North-Holland, pp. 1-10.

Daukidis, G.I., Smithson, S. and Lybereas, T. "Approaches to Computerization in Small Businesses in Greece," Proceedings of the Thirteenth International Conference on Information Systems, Dallas, Texas, December 13-16, 1992, pp. 139-148.

Hassan, S. Z. "Use of Computer Technology in Production Management -Evolution Stages and Guidelines for success," Proceedings of the Third International Production Management Conference on Management and New Production Systems, Goteborg, Sweden, May 27-28, 1991, pp. 330-345.

Hassan, S. Z. "Infrastructure Constraints in Implementing Information Technologies in Pakistan," Proceedings of 1993 Information Resources Management Association International Conference, Salt Lake City, Utah, May 22-26, 1993, pp.

Hassan, S. Z. "Factors influencing the success of CBIS: Cases from Pakistan," To be presented at Third Annual World Business Congress, June 16-18, 1994, Penang, Malaysia

Joshi, K. "Reorganization of the Work System for Successful Information Systems Implementation," Information & Management, 19, 1990, pp. 271-284.

Kazmi, W. "Computers and High-Tech Products," Pakistan and Gulf Economist, Vol. IX No. 3, January 20-26, 1990, pp. 25-26.

Memon, N.A. "Technology and Information, "Pakistan and Gulf Economist, Vol X, No. 45, November 9-15, 1991, pp. 9-11.

Nosek, J. T. "Organization Design Strategies To Enhance Information Resource Management," Information & Management, 16, 1989, pp. 81-91.

Odedra, M. "Critical Factors Affecting Success of CBIS: Cases from Africa," Journal of Global Information Management, Vol. 1, No. 3, Summer 1993, pp. 16-31.

Palvia, P., Palvia, S. and Zigli, R. "Global Information Technology Environment: Key MIS Issues in Advanced and Less-Developed Nations" in S. Palliate, P. Palliate and R.M. Sigil (Esd) Global Issues of Information Technology Management, Idea Group Publishing, 1992, pp. 2-34.

Saigol, T. S. "A peep into Pakistan's Textile Industry," Business Recorder, April 19, 1994.

Yin, R.K. "Research Design Issues in Using the Case Study Method to Study Management Information Systems," Harvard Business School Research Colloquium, The Information Systems Research Challenge: Qualitative Research Methods, Vol. 1, Chapter 1, pp. 1-6.

Information Technology and

National Development in Third World :

A challenge of creating technological convergence for Asian and African countries

Goel Kahen and B. McA. Sayers
IC-Parc, William Penney Laboratory
Imperial College of Science, Technology and Medicine,
London SW7 2AZ   England
Tel: +44-71-225 8930 e-mail: {gk,bms}@doc.ic.ac.uk

Executive Abstract

Introduction

During the last three decades technology transfer to Third World has been an important issue for many research institutes and universities. Research over the past ten years has provided substantial evidence to show that national economic development leads to the generation of a sizable information workforce. This phenomenon signals the emergence of an information sector in national economies; this sector contains an increasingly widespread and sophisticated domain of Computer-based Information Technology.

At present, acquiring and using appropriate information technology is a fundamental requirement for the progress of developing countries. These countries need to use and coordinate information technology to promote their industrial and socio-economic development as speedily as possible. The weakness of social, education, economic, health and other social services, as support functions, in developing countries has increased the need for the transfer of information technology (IT) to Third World nations. The trend towards increasing information sector activity is greater than for other sectors (i.e. Agriculture, Industry, Services) across the developing world (Katz 1986). However, only 10-12% of the population in developing countries has any contact with a product/service which is an output of a computerised process (Bhatnagar 1990). Many Third World countries experience similar problems with the utilisation of information technology; accordingly, after highlighting some of the problems of usage of the computer-based systems, the paper categorises a set of common factors.

Barriers to Successful Transfer of IT

The literature on information technology and computer-based systems in developing countries traces many problems which inhibit such countries from achieving substantial benefits from the potential of IT. We can summarise some important problems and factors responsible for low usage or misuse of IT systems in developing countries. For example, lack of plans for documented systems; low computer literacy amongst people especially staff and managers; shortage of capital; lack of indigenous experts; inadequate data and information; poor infrastructure (i.e. inadequacy of the communication infrastructure keeps many types of IT applications beyond the realm of feasibility; the electric supply is erratic and the quality of power is poor); IT systems maladjustment or unsuitability because of ergonomic problems in design.

Due to the replacement of labour by technology in Western countries, the development of systems and technology reflects needs and levels of satisfaction in developed countries, rather than the specialised needs of underdeveloped countries (i.e. the existing training programmes in developed countries are inappropriate to the needs of developing countries). Compared with industrialised countries, technology in developing countries is generally labour intensive and workforce cost is lower. In fact, some conflict often arises from using IT products from developed countries. So, the particular socio-economic, ergonomic, environmental, and cultural conditions of a recipient country "require consideration to ensure that any transfer of technology is appropriate to the needs of that country" (Eres 1981).

Country Convergency versus Country Divergency

While there is no universal culture within developing countries, local IT practitioners need to devise appropriate ways of coping with the features of local and regional culture. The existence of shared ideological and religious similarities within a group of countries in a zone or region (Iran, Pakistan, Bangladesh, or Iraq, Jordan, Syria) could be convenient in establishing a convergency strategy of IT transfer for the zone. Inter-country political and economic cooperation is another context for convergency. The maturity of one country, in some aspects of computerisation relative to one or more other countries, may provide the opportunity for utilisation and production of a coordinated strategy for their information sectors. The optimisation of processes for allocation of limited resources is a crucial factor in development planning, and could gain from this knowledge-based inter-country collaboration.

Creating a convergence strategy

Examination of the situation in various countries suggests that a converging strategy for promoting IT within Asian or African countries can be identified. The availability of some types of indigenous capabilities for infrastructure development in some countries within the zone, can provide a convenient context of fundamental progress in IT from country to country. Regional cooperation in communication and power utilities may have tangible contributions to national IT development. Where this has been done effectively it has contributed to national economic development. This convergency between countries provides a relevant opportunity for the mutual transfer of IT experience which supports a trade-off in both scientific and computer-based technology transfer. Approaching such a contributions to national socio-economic development requires a systematic research effort and detailed academic analysis.

Applying a Strategic Planning Model to Developing Countries

Laura Lally
Hofstra University
BCIS/QM Department
134 Hofstra
Hempstead, NY 11550
516 463 5351
and
Anne T. Murray
Hofstra University
BCIS/QM Department

Executive Abstract

THE POSITION OF DEVELOPING COUNTRIES IN THE GLOBAL ECONOMY

Information technology is transforming the earth into a place where information can be transferred in real time, regardless of the nature of the information and the distance it must travel. This transformation will impact developing countries in two important ways.

Social Impacts. Developing countries already receive 100 times more information from developed countries than they send in return. This bombardment is likely to increase further as more of communication channels become available. Concerns grow about the erosion of traditional cultural values brought about by continual media based exposure to the lifestyles of developed countries.

Economic Impacts. Although the evolving information infrastructure can support a wide range of organizational structures, early evidence suggests a tendency toward greater centralization among multinational firms. Multinational firms (MNCs) are using an enhanced information exchange infrastructure to centralize managerial decision making and increase managerial spans of control. The likely impact of greater centralization is that imperialistic business practices will increase and that there will be an even greater tendency for MNCs to view developing countries and their citizens as abstract entities, valuable only in terms of their ability to enhance corporate profits by serving as sources of cheap labor, raw materials, or consumers of products. Centralized global structures are not likely to support the transfer of technology, managerial know-how, or investment capital to developing countries.

Developing countries, therefore, must take a **proactive strategy** in defining their role in the emerging global economy or risk the negative impacts of being the passive recipients of the media broadcasts of developed countries and the strategic plans of MNCs. This paper proposes a model drawn from the strategic management literature and applies it to the planning process of developing countries with the goal of helping them define an active role for themselves in the emerging global economy.

APPLYING STRATEGIC MANAGEMENT TO DEVELOPING COUNTRIES

At the end of the 20th Century many developing countries are at the level of economic development of advanced nations prior to 19th century industrialization. In order to close the gap and bring these nations up to the technological level of advanced economies, industrialization completed in ten generations must be compressed into one generation. To meet this awesome challenge, governments and the people they lead must make the best use of their country's resources to achieve national goals.

Strategic management techniques, long utilized in the business environment, can provide government leaders with a dynamic framework for development of objectives, assessment of strengths and weaknesses and implementation of strategies to achieve successful transfer of technology. Less developed countries with marginal economies need to optimize scarce resources and must develop long range planning so that decisions for technological development can be based on quantitative analysis and other strategic tools.

THE MODEL AND ITS APPLICATIONS

The following steps are recommended in applying a strategic planning model to developing countries:

1. *Identify a National Mission* -- an ideological declaration of the national philosophy. The mission defines the image and character the country wishes to present to itself and to other nations. With a mission statement in effect, a standard exists against which proposals can be evaluated and strategic choices made. The focus of the mission statement must be on population needs and abilities, providing guidelines for strategic decisions rather than a list of unachievable ideals. The statement must be clear, leaving the door open to action. But most of all, the mission statement provides a mechanism for self-control.

2. *State Government Objectives* --Objectives help define and legitimize the goals of government to the population served and to the global community, attracting capital and qualified individuals who identify with the objectives to work

for their achievement. Objectives are also more tangible targets than mission statements and provide standards for assessing performance.

3. *Examine the External Environment for Threats and Opportunities* -- Environmental analysis and diagnosis gives strategists time to anticipate opportunities and to plan to take optimal responses to them. This process also helps strategists develop an early warning system to prevent threats or develop strategies which can turn a threat into an opportunity.

4. *Examine the Internal Environment for Strengths and Weaknesses* -- This analysis enables the strategist to exploit opportunities, meet threats and modify the weaknesses which could compromise a strategy or place the country at a competitive disadvantage.

5. *Identify Strategic Alternatives and Choices* -- The government may wish to pursue an purely internal strategy, highly unlikely in the case of a less developed nation. An external approach would seek involvement of advanced nations or MNCs and may be more appropriate for a developing country. A combination strategy in the form of a joint venture is another viable choice for the emerging country.

6. *Evaluation and Modification of Plan* -- The strategic management process does not end with the adoption of a strategic plan. The government must establish a methodology for periodically evaluating the success or failure of the new plan and respond accordingly.

Towards an Information Technology Management Framework for Developing Countries - Investigating the *Keiretsu* Model

Hans Lehmann
Department of Management Science and Information Systems
University of Auckland
Private Bag 92019
Auckland, NEW ZEALAND
Tel 64 9 373 7599 x 8659
Fax 64 9 373 7430
Email h.lehmann@auckland.ac.nz

Abstract:

Information Technology Management methods evolved and designed in western, first world countries are not appropriate for third world countries. Furthermore, they are now becoming inadequate because the current thinking on management theory - upon which Information Technology Management is defined - is changing significantly. The salient points of this shift in the paradigm of strategic management are outlined and an indication is given of how this will impact the management of information technology, with specific regard to the requirements of developing countries. An outline of an adapted model is attempted, using a simple four-component framework. The area of information technology planning will need to change. Systems acquisition will need to develop new, proprietary methods, tailored to development levels. The character of the day-to-day management, however, is most significantly affected, mainly by an increased use of external agents in what will probably be new and innovative forms of alliance. The concept of an information technology *keiretsu* is investigated as a useful model for how such alliances could be structured and how they could act as a catalyst for accelerated learning and thus lead to more effective transfer of skills and technology for Information Technology Management.

The importance of the right management model

Although there is common agreement that information technology is a powerful agent of development for lesser industrialised nations, there is also widespread evidence that it has been of mixed success in developing countries. Furthermore, for management to be effective, the structures and processes it applies must be appropriate to the nature and characteristics of what it is managing. Information Technology itself has been changing at a rapid pace during the last ten years. Even more significant is the change in its role within the business process. It is argued that the model for the management of information technology in use now is inadequate for the demands placed on it in general, but particularly with reference to developing countries. There are three reasons for this

- The management model was developed by western, industrialised countries, based on assumptions which are now not valid for developing countries;
- But even within the first world, the model is based on assumptions about the nature of information technology which are now incomplete;
- The fundamental paradigms of strategic business thinking upon which information technology management rests, seem to changing.

This exploratory paper first gives an overview of some issues of cultural differences affecting information technology in developing countries. The change in the nature of information technology is discussed next. Thirdly, the perceived paradigm shift in the theory of strategic management will be described in brief. In the main part of the paper, an attempt is made to set out where and how the model for information technology needs to be adapted for developing countries. The structure of an information technology *keiretsu* is investigated and proposed as a useful construct for developing countries. Lastly, areas for further research are sketched out.

Cultural issues in information management

That differences in the cultural environment are an important issue in the management of information technology in developing countries has been well established, specifically in the field of international information systems.

Robey & Rodriguez-Diaz (1989) found that cultural differences such as the different ways in which information systems are interpreted and are given meaning proved a significant impediment to the management of an accounting system in one of two Latin American countries. The difficulties could be overcome by inclusion of the stakeholders in the project team at a second implementation project, changing and adapting the

Table 1. Comparison of the Traditional Information Management model with the Requirements of Developing Countries

Data Processing Management Model	Developing Countries *Real Requirements* Mainly <u>smaller</u> enterprises
Processes and structures are geared towards the <u>large</u> corporation/enterprise	
Predominance of <u>custom development</u> of application systems in-house	Lower degree of sophistication means *off-the shelf systems* will suffice for most applications at present
Availability of large numbers of <u>skilled staff</u>	Shortage of <u>skilled staff</u>, both systems staff and users
Systems which are mainly of the <u>'Support'</u>[1] type	Most systems of high priority for developing countries can have <u>'Strategic'</u> elements[2]

management framework. Heitzman (1990), in a study on the acceptance and the influence of information technology in the third world, particularity in South East Asia, also sees the regionalisation/localisation of development and implementation efforts as a way to ameliorate the otherwise steep difficulties experienced in managing information technology across cultural and developmental divides.

These findings were confirmed in a wide ranging analysis of issues in information technology in less developed countries (Sarawat & Gorgone, 1991). They also found a political element to the management issue, where lack of involvement sometimes was interpreted as using information technology as another means of the assertion of first world dominance. Skills deficiency, lack of indigenous technology content and concern over employment issues (e.g. clerical displacement) were cited as other issues.

Whereas these and other studies found in the literature concentrate mainly on the effect of different levels of development on the day-to-day management and also on the management of systems implementation, there is also a second element of straight difference in culture, ie in the way in which value systems, business philosophies (especially ethics) and general living habits diverge, often substantially, between different implementations of an international system. Goodman & Green, (1992) demonstrate this with their analysis of the information technology environment in the Middle East.

From this background, it can therefore be concluded that a useful model for Information Technology Management for the developing nation should be adapted to its individual level of development and should take their cultural identity into account.

The changing nature of information technology

The frameworks for the management of information technology stem from the early 1970s (Cash et al. 1988). As they are based on the body of experience built up during the 1960s, they are rooted in the era of data processing, which is different from that of information technology. Data Processing was then characterised by a dominance of centralised mainframes, with restricted facilities for on-line terminals and a subsequent orientation for batch-type, repetitive calculation oriented

workload. These expensive computers were situated mainly in large companies, administered by substantial departments of skilled technical specialists. Users of computers were in the main fully dependent on the technicians and demand for computer services often outstripped supply. The majority of systems were custom-built in-house.

These characteristics of Data Processing determined the framework for its management. And although updated to recognise some changes, the traditional Information Technology Management model is still based on the above assumptions, which makes this model particularly inappropriate for developing countries. Table 1 shows this:

Nolan, Norton & Company (1985), however, predicted that by the mid-1990s at most about a third of the information technology expenditure would be attributable to data processing of the Data Processing type.

Changes in the strategic management of information technology

Although Wysocki & Young (1990) claim that Information Technology Management is not so much a framework but a body of 'tribal knowledge', it is clearly modelled on the broader tradition of general business (Cash et al. 1988).

Changes in the way in which general business views strategic management are therefore of influence for information management. Current strategic management thinking is shaped by the planning-doing-cycle. First, the enterprise determines what it wants to do (the 'end', to use terminology introduced by Hayes, 1985), then it specifies a strategy to get there (the 'ways') and lastly it develops a detailed strategic plan to marshall the necessary resources (the 'means') to carry it out. Oversimplifying somewhat in the interest of clarity, this 'ends-ways-means' paradigm implies three axiomatic assumptions:

• The environment can be <u>forecast and predicted</u> sufficiently well so that a strategic fit can be distilled from it;

• The firm itself is <u>inherently stable</u> and will not change fundamentally over the planning horizon;

• Top management steers the enterprise in 'command-and-control' mode like the general in an army.

This paradigm, basically reactive in nature, has served business seemingly well until the last decade. Then it became obvious that the pace of change, not only in technology but also in politico-economical developments lead to unpredictable sea changes in the environment which, together with a rapidly increasing number of market operators and the closeness of markets in the 'global village' had made those basic assumptions untenable. The now well established notion of concentrating on the 'core competence' of an enterprise (Prahalad & Hamel 1990) together with several other concurrent developments in general management thinking (Kanter 1989) is increasingly, and profoundly, influencing the basic paradigm of strategic management and re-formulates the basic three axioms differently:

• Strategic intent on shaping the environment replaces reactively fitting in with the world (Hamel & Prahalad 1991);
• Core competencies (and 'core capabilities', a complement introduced by Stalk, et al, 1992) provide a better focus and means to cope with the vagaries of an increasingly unpredictable universe;
• Learning organisation (Senge, 1990) to cope with fast change (Drucker 1988) add stretch and leverage (Hamel & Prahalad, 1993) to the strategic intent.

The implications of these notions for developing countries are set out in Table 2 below.

This changed strategic management thinking is at present in the process of being consolidated into a cohesive framework and is also being translated into information technology management frameworks. The implications for Information Technology Management in developing countries together with a possible outline of an adapted Information Technology Management model is developed in the following section.

Towards an information technology management model for developing countries

It is firstly necessary to introduce a simple nomenclature for the main components and functions of the information technol-

ogy management process so that the adaptations suggested can be clearly demonstrated. This describes the functions of information technology management in four base activities, ie planning, buying and making (technology and services) and finally running the information technology management function.

In the following paragraphs the implications of the new strategic management thinking for each of these information technology management functions will be discussed. This is an overview version of a more detailed treatment provided elsewhere (Lehmann, 1992 and 1993).

THE 'PLAN' FUNCTION

Strategic planning for information technology traditionally is a subset of, and via a process of 'alignment', dovetails into, corporate strategic planning.

The new strategic management substitutes this reactive strategic planning with statements of strategic intent, based on core competencies and capabilities of the enterprise. Analogously, information technology planning needs to base its strategy and vision on an analysis of how information technology can leverage these core competencies in the first instance, and subsequently determine how to develop their own core competencies to support, complement, enhance, or, as is increasingly the case, create or transform the enterprise's core competencies. Two iterative steps (shown in Figure 1) make up this planning process:

• identifying where core competencies are in relation to the value generated by the activities using them; Schoemaker (1992) suggests a practical framework on how to do this; and, secondly

• re-engineering the operations with the use of information technology and identifying the information technology intensity of each core competence; as a framework suitable for the analysis and definition of leverage points for information technology Porter's value chain model (Porter and Millar 1985) seems a suitable candidate; Hammer (1990) supplies a discussion of business process redesign and Davenport and Short (1990) elaborate more on the specific aspects of

Table 2. Relevance of the New Management Thinking for Developing Countries

New Management Paradigm	Implications for Developing Countries
'Strategic Intent'	Improve upon reactive commodity selling by strategically marketing value added products
'Core competencies and capabilities'	Discover, define/refine and develop as required by the new shift to 'products'
'Learning organisations' for 'stretch and leverage'	Using the same mechanisms for accelerated learning and technology and skills transfer

Figure 1: Coupling the core competencies of information management and the enterprise

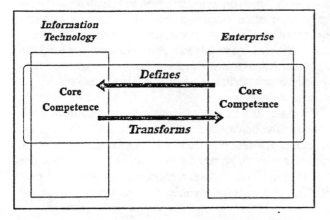

Figure 2: Analysis of the availability of "Commodity" versus "Tailored" software for general business applications of informaiton technology

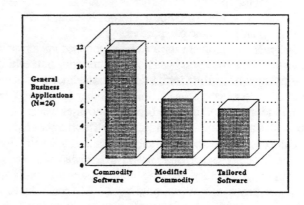

enhancing it with information technology.

A study of ASEAN countries (Check-Teck et al, 1992) found that much of the strategic planning was of the traditional kind. For developing countries, the core competence based planning, however, would need some adaptation:

- In many developing countries the core competencies needed in its industries and for each of the contenders within an industry need to be determined and established in a process which probably more resembles 'discovery' than the refinement type of definition referred to in the literature applicable to an industrialised environment;
- Similarly, in analyzing the leverage gained through information technology the ease of access to available technology will be a integral part of the core capabilities determination and not so much a process of derivation.

THE 'BUY' FUNCTION

The traditional management model is based on the presumption of custom development by technical specialists as the norm and packaged software the exception.

This needs adapting to the present reality which is characterised by a flood of pre-written software, especially for the mini and micro computer platforms. An analysis of the availability of packaged software versus the need to custom-write systems for general business functions (Lehmann, 1992) shows that pre-written 'packages' cover a significant proportion (11 out of 26 application areas) of the basic business support required from information technology. There is a high percentage of applications where adjustments from a standard package will suffice. The number of areas where full tailoring is required is relatively small - only about one in 5. Figure 2 shows these statistics.

The concentration of efforts on the 'core competencies' coupled with the need to be flexible puts heightened emphasis on selecting and making packaged software work.

Developing countries often have - at least initially - a relatively simple business administration structure. It is thus very likely that pre-written business software packages will provide sufficient functional fit with requirements.

An overview of the main issues a with a management model for dealing with pre-written software is provided in more detail by Lehmann (1993). There are, however, specific issues for developing countries in the context of acquiring applications systems:

- Systems need to run on proven hardware, adequately supported in the developing country
- Use should be made of tele-support facilities (over international communications links) for software packages to limit the need for skilled support personnel in the developing country itself.

THE 'MAKE' FUNCTION

The traditional Systems Development Life Cycle[3] is fairly cumbersome. There is also some doubt whether the traditional model can cope with anything other than incremental change (Chandler 1991). The high risk and the long lead times for in-house developed software also seem to become less tenable in an environment where business undergoes rapid change, such as a developing country.

The main factor in deciding about 'making' systems in a developing country is often the shortage of skilled development staff. Even where there is skilled technical staff around, original development is often not frequent enough to make it feasible to employ large technical staff in-house. In-house staff also are more involved in maintaining (repairing and enhancing) existing software. Large systems projects would thus take too long to complete with in-house staff. Third party development is therefore an essential component of the new management model for the development activity. However, there are also strategic reasons why outsourcing of systems development may or may not be advantageous: where information technology application is at the heart of the enterprise's core competence/capability in-house expertise is a strategic requirement. Richmond et al (1992) provide a rigorous investigation of this issue from an economic perspective.

Original development for a fully customised system will, however, only be necessary whenever the enterprise is breaking new technological ground or if information technology is at the heart of the core competence. In most other cases it will be enough to create additional processing modules which interface with standard, pre-written software. This may be crude in a technical sense, but the inelegance is balanced by lesser effort and the fact that cheaper, more powerful hardware can tolerate such inefficiencies. Using new concepts such as 'megaprogramming' (Wiederhold, et al, 1992) could also provide a more simple way of application development. For practical reasons, eg to maintain product guarantees, such add-ons should be developed externally by the supplier of the original piece of software.

External suppliers, however, cannot be expected to provide the user training required to make the system work in the specific environment of the individual user. Providing user training and often eduction too, is thus an imperative aspect of application building, particularly in developing countries. Research on small firm computing (Cragg et al, 1993) confirms that limited education is a major source of de-motivation and a strong inhibitor to the growth of information technology application.

Providing the infrastructure for i.e. the technical and software standard platform systems, too, is essentially an in-house management function and an important component in the strategic planning process sketched out above.

Given these considerations as a premise, a practical management model for systems development in developing countries will most likely have the following key elements

• Defining the strategic <u>outsourcing balance</u> between in-house and external development;
• <u>Project skills</u> to manage the external activities.
• The main area of systems development should not be the application systems itself, but first and foremost to set up a <u>technical infrastructure:</u>

THE 'RUN' FUNCTION

'Production' and 'Operation' used to be the traditional core of the day-to-day management of information technology. However, as information technology is more and more disseminated to the users and as they are now running their own systems, production management tends to be refocused on the provision of technology services with the objective to ensure a 'transparent' infrastructure for the end-users. The rapid development of information technology has, however, lead to an ever increasing level of sophistication and variety of technologies

which need to be supported. This has meant that the corresponding demands on technical skills, in variety as well as in depth, have often outgrown the information technology department's in-house resources, for economical reasons and because they are not readily available. Nowhere has this been more conspicuous than in developing countries, where attracting and holding technical talent is of particular concern for business.

The skills to mix internal with external resources while increasing the quality of services provided to users and the systemic use of third party suppliers, in a multiplicity of roles, are thus at the very heart of the new model for the day-to-day management of information technology, and are of specific criticality in developing countries.

Critical Success Factors for developing countries

The critical success factors for the management of information technology, with specific reference for developing countries are summarised in Table 3 below.

Towards an appropriate co-operation structure for developing countries

There are a number of ways in which co-operation with an external supplier can be structured and managed. In the western, industrialised countries of America and Europe the traditional way is the contract-based, arms-length relationship between customer and supplier. The contract is supposed to stipulate comprehensively the sum-total of both parties' obligations under a single, individual deal. This model has been found wanting, however, as the deals became more complex and the dependence between the deal partners grew - the formulation of contracts to cover imponderable uncertainties is not always possible and the use of contracts to force parties to perform was found rather limited.

Table 3. Summary of critical issues for information technology management in developing countries

Function	Critical Factors for Developing Countries
PLAN	• "Discovering' core competencies and capabilities required for 'stretching' towards value added products • Integrating information technology into these 'core' activities
BUY	• Assuring proven hardware and technology is available • Innovative support methods (eg international tele-support)
MAKE	"Technical infrastructure establishment and enhancement • Outsourcing balance between in-house and external supply • Project skills to manage external efforts
RUN .	• Managing a variety of alliances Maintaining a learning environment

In the context of developing countries the 'contract' model is even less satisfactorily as

- often the legal infrastructure is not in place to process complex agreement constructs
- even if contract enforcement were possible legally, practically it may not be possible because the skills or other wherewithal may be non-existent

Furthermore, the general lack of technology literacy needs mutual assistance between customer and supplier. The basically antagonistic contract model is diagonally juxtaposed to this notion.

In industrialised nations, subsequently, interested parties started joint-venture projects and, particularly in manufacturing, closer relations such as 'preferred supplier' status were introduced. All had their fair share of problems, as had the next development, the notion of a strategic alliance (Lei & Slocum 1991).

A very successful form of alliance, however, has its origins in the East: the Japanese *keiretsu* (and to a certain extent its Korean counterpart, the *chaebol*).

Descendants[4] of the earlier family groupings (the *zaibatsu*), they were formed after the second world war (in response to US occupation rules) around either around a bank or as supply groups around a large manufacturing company. The Japanese government encouraged them because they tended to accelerate development of all members in the group as well as at the same time ensure competition among them. Both types of grouping are very tight alliances, with interlocking directorates and 'executive clubs' to ensure communication among the key staff of the various members. Cross-shareholdings between members - and mutual non-selling agreements - are a fairly common bond. In this way, mutual shareholdings account for about 30% of the company stock of any member of the *keiretsu*. Because a large percentage of shares are thus never traded, managers need not worry about take-overs. This structure puts therefore less emphasis on short-term profitability, encourages re-investment and is thus focused firmly on quality-based, long-term growth.

The origins of both types of consortia are in the development phases of countries, when co-operation, typically to master new developments, was found more beneficial than competition.

Most developing countries are in a state of urgent development needs where information technology is concerned. Mastering the technology as a nation is therefore as important as the notion of information technology as a competitive weapon for individual industries. This would make the formation of information technology *keiretsus* a sensible thing to consider.

Centered around a 'hub' from an information technology intensive industry (such as a bank), the functions of such an information technology *keiretsu* would include taking on such roles as

- Local supplier/distributor of software; this should include a

'brokerage' for sourcing and selecting international software;
- Local technical support for software and focal point for the maintenance of the tele-support technology with the original supplier of international software;
- Hardware/technology supplier and technical support for infrastructural systems and equipment (e.g. operating systems, wide area and local communication networks, etc.);
- Development and implementation of software, ie the normal functions of a software house; specific emphasis would, however, be placed on
- Education and training of application systems users and/or user/supporters, as well as the provision of ongoing management education for both technical and business management.

Figure 3 depicts such an information technology *keiretsu*.

The close relation between a number of suppliers (hardware, software, services) and their customers across different, non-competing industries would work well towards ensuring that an optimal balance between outsourcing of non-critical activities and strengthening essential, 'core competence' skills in-house can be struck for each member. Cross ownership within the *keiretsu* would provide a strong incentive for this form of consortium to concentrate on mutually beneficial objectives.

Such an information technology *keiretsu*, even where most of its members are small enterprises, would be of sufficient size to attract good technical people and hold them. Their multi-industry character would enable interdisciplinary and cross-business learning for the information technology professionals. On the other hand, the *keiretsu's* comprehensive coverage of a wide spectrum of mature and emerging technologies should foster accelerated absorption of the technology by business managers, who would be able to get intensive exposure to all aspects of information technology.

Table 4 (overleaf) summarises the potential advantages of an Information Technology *Keiretsu* for developing countries.

Figure 3: The composition of an Information technology Keiretsu

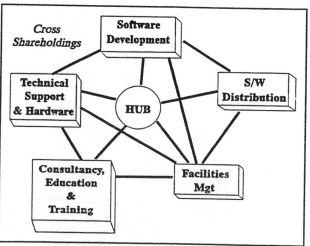

Suggestions for further research

The areas of a new information technology management model of most significance to developing Countries are the planning and the day-to-day management of information technology. Research should therefore concentrate on

- Developing a methodology for the 'discovery' process of core competence definition more commonly needed in developing countries
- Investigating whether the value-chain approach is the most appropriate for analyzing and defining the leverage of information technology on the business' core competencies;
- Exploring the economical, political and social corollaries of the notion of an information technology *keiretsu* in developing countries;
- The emphasis onto the area of managing the acquisition and support of packaged software in often remote areas of developing countries necessitates research into innovative but simple methods of managing and operating this process.

Whilst most of these research areas can be adequately dealt with in individual, focused projects using traditional research methods, the establishment of a pilot project will be necessary to investigate the internal dynamics of such a grouping. More radical research methodology, such as action research, would probably be more appropriate for such larger scale projects.

Conclusion

The traditional model of information technology management is inappropriate for developing countries. In addition, current thinking on management theory is changing and this will impact information technology management as a matter of course.

In part this impact will lead to critical re-examination of current management practices and to align them with the new business thinking. The most influence will be felt in the area of information technology planning. The character of the day-to-day management is also affected, mainly by an increased use of external agents in what will probably be new and innovative forms of alliance.

The needs of developing countries are better served with the new management model, but a mechanism for accelerated learning and increased penetration of the technology into developing countries' businesses is desirable.

The idea of an *information technology keiretsu* seems to have merit in that it could be of advantage in most of the areas of information technology management which have been shown to be critical to developing countries.

A secondary, but probably more lasting consequence of such a *keiretsu* structure should be a change in role for information technology in developing countries.

Discovering, defining and building core competence through information technology could well mean that it will be absorbed

Table 4. Potential advantages of an Information Technology Keiretsu *for Developing Countries*

Function	Critical Issues for Developing Countries (Table 3)	Advantages of an Information Technology KEIRETSU
PLAN	• 'Discovering' core competencies Integrating information technology into core activities	• Experience eschange within interlocking executive and staff groups
BUY	• Assuring proven hardware	• Hardware and Technical support are group members with shared interests
	• Innovative support methods	• ·Technical group members can invest into longer term plans with backing from the user-members
MAKE	• ·Technical Infrastructure	• Facilities Mgt. member has interest to make user-members independent (their profitability is his income too)
	• Outsourcing balance	• Shared interest allows more outsourcing for user-members
	• Project skills	• More opportunity to gain these skills through higher exposure to external projects
RUN	• Managing alliances	• Interlocking management communication at all levels
	• Learning Environment	• Management/Staff rotation among the members increases exposure to technology and business issues

far more comprehensively into the operation and the running of business in developing countries than its present state of 'integration' indicates. If core competencies are the engines of the enterprise in a developing nation, than it looks as if information technology is set to be the very fuel that fires them.

Endnotes

[1] In the sense of McFarlan's 'categories of strategic relevance' (McFarlan 1983)

[2] eg as in enabling international trade via the use of an EDI systems such as reported by Lee and Donaldson Dewitz (1992)

[3] ie, of establishing user requirements, translating them into software, testing to see whether the software indeed fulfils the requirements and finally the installation of the system into the users' business environment.

[4] Anchordoguy (1990) provides a good, brief history of Japan's *keiretsu.*

REFERENCES

Anchordoguy M (1990). A Brief History of Japan's Keiretsu. *Harvard Business Review*, July-August 1990, 58-59

Barsoux, J.-L. (1992). Following the Leaders. *International Management*, 47, 7, 40-41.

Cash J I, McFarlan W F, McKenney J L and Vitale M R (1988) *Corporate Information Systems Management: Text and Cases*. Irwin, Homewood, Illinois.

Chandler R (1991) Why Systems Analysis Methodologies Fail to Respond to Strategic Change. In *Business Strategy and Information Technology* (Sutherland E and Morieux Y, Eds.) Routledge, London.

Check-Teck F, Grinyer P H and McKiernan P (1992) Strategic Planning in the ASEAN Region. *Long Range Planning*, Oct 1992, 80-90.

Cragg P B and King M (1993) Small-firm Computing: Motivators and Inhibitors. *MIS Quarterly*. Mar 1993, 47-60

Davenport T H and Short J E (1990) The New Industrial Engineering: Information Technology and Business Process Redesign. *Sloan Management Review*, Summer 1990, 11-20

Drucker P (1988) The Coming of the New Organisation. *Harvard Business Review* Jan-Feb, 45-53.

Earl M J (1989) *Management Strategies for Information Technology*. Prentice Hall, London.

Frenzel C W (1992) *Management of Information Technology*, Boyd & Fraser, Boston.

Goodman, S. E. & Green, J. D., (1992). Computing in the Middle East. *Communications of the ACM*, 35, 8, 21-25.

Hamel G and Prahalad C K (1991) Corporate Imagination and Expeditionary Marketing. *Harvard Business Review* July/August, 81-92.

Hamel G and Prahalad C K (1993) Strategy as Stretch and Leverage. *Harvard Business Review* March-April 1993, 64-74

Hammer M (1990) Reengineering Work: Don't Automate, Obliterate. *Harvard Business Review*, July-August 1990, 104-114

Hayes R H (1985) Strategic Planning - Forward in Reverse? *Harvard Business Review* Nov-Dec, 111-134

Heitzman, J. (1990). Information Systems and Development in the Third World. *Information Processing & Management (UK)*, 26, 4, 489-502.

Hopper M D (1990) Rattling SABRE - New Ways to Compete on Information. *Harvard Business Review* May-June, 118-125.

Kanter R M (1989) The New Managerial Work. *Harvard Business Review* Nov/Dec, 171-177.

Kearney A T (management consultants)(1984) The barriers and opportunities of information technology - a management perspective; *Report to the Department of Trade and Industry in the UK*, London.

Lee, R. M., Donaldson Dewitz, S. Facilitating International Contracting: AI Extensions to EDI. *International Information Systems*, Vol 1, Nr 1, January 1992, 94-123

Lehmann H P (1992) *Towards a paradigm shift in Information Management?* Working Paper No 9 of the University of Auckland, April 1992.

Lehmann H P (1993) Core Competence and Learning Aliances - the New Face of Information Management? *Journal of Information Technology*, 8, 217-225

Lei D and Slocum J W (1991) Global Strategic Alliances: Payoffs and Pitfalls. *Organisational Dynamics*, 1st quarter, 44-62.

McFarlan F W and McKenney J L (1983) *Corporate Information Systems Management - The Issues Facing Senior Executives*. Richard D. Irwin Inc, Homewood, Illinois.

Nolan, Norton & Co (1985) The economics of computing in the advanced stages. *Stage by Stage*, European Issue.

Nolan R (1982) *Managing the Data Resource*, West Publishing Company, Minnesota.

Porter M E and Millar V E (1985) How information gives you competitive advantage. *Harvard Business Review*, July-August, 149-160.

Prahalad C K and Hamel G (1990) The Core Competence of the Corporation. *Harvard Business Review*, May/June, 79-93.

Richmond W B, Seidmann A and Whinston A (1992). Incomplete Contracting Issues in Information Systems Development Outsourcing. *Decision Support Systems*, Sep 1992, 459-477.

Robey, D. & Rodriquez-Diaz, A. (1989). The Organizational and Cultural Context of Systems Implementation: Case Experience from Latin America. *Information & Management (Netherlands)*, 17, 4, 229-239.

Rowbrey-Evans P (1991) An alternative Model for the corporate IS function. *The Computer Bulletin*, Series IV, Vol 3, Part 8, Nov/Dec.

Saraswat, S. P. & Gorgone, J. T. (1991). Multinational Issues in Information Technology: A Perspective from Less Developed Countries. *Information & Management*, 21, 2, 111-121.

Schoemaker P J H (1992) How to Link Strategic Vision to Core Capabilities. *Sloan Management Review*, Fall 1992, 67-81

Senge P M (1990) The Leader's New Work: Building Learning Organisations. *Sloan Management Review* Fall, 7-23.

Stalk, G., Evans, P. and Shulman, L. E. Competing on Capabilities: The New Rules of Corporate Strategy. *Harvard Business Review*, March-April 1992, 57-69

Wiederhold G, Wegner P and Ceri S (1992). Toward Megaprogramming. *Communications of the ACM*, Nov 1992. 89-99

Wysocki R K and Young J (1990) *Information Systems - Management Principles in Action*. John Wiley & Sons, New York.

An Evaluation of Information Systems Development Practices in Singapore

Shailendra C. Palvia
and
M. Gordon Hunter
Information Management Research Centre (IMARC)
School of Accountancy and Business (SAB)
Nanyang Technological University (NTU)
Singapore 2263

INTRODUCTION

Organizations are faced with identified as well as hidden application development backlogs. In-progress IS development projects are generally behind schedule and/or over budget. When completed, the information systems do not necessarily solve all the original problems and are very difficult and costly to use and maintain. Improvements in software development methodologies, techniques, and tools lag far behind advances in hardware. Software development and maintenance costs are the major share of total Information Technology (IT) budget.

This research focuses on two key resources for development of information systems — people and methods. People include IS professionals and IS users. Methods are comprised of methodologies, techniques, and tools. We argue that these resources are the key contributors to the productivity of the IS development process and also the quality of the IS produced. We tie together these concepts in our model for IS development. This paper provides a status report on the current state of IS professionals, methodologies, techniques, and tools which are the key resources in productive development of quality information systems. A comparison with utilization of methodologies, techniques, and tools in the U.S.A. is also provided.

LITERATURE REVIEW

This section provides a broad survey of current literature focusing on a) software development and maintenance problems, and the consequent need for improvement in productivity and quality, b) changing IS professionals roles and skills mix, and c) ever evolving methods to develop information systems more efficiently and effectively.

Software Development and Maintenance Problems

According to Kendall (1992) it is generally known there is an excess demand for IS development. Applications development backlogs averaging up to 30 work-months have been reported by some data processing managers. It has also been suggested (Senn,1985; Yourdon,1989; and Kendall,1992) that in addition to this identified backlog, there also exists a hidden backlog, which represents those users' plans which are not even submitted because of delays resulting from the identified backlog. When this hidden backlog is taken into consideration, delays of up to four to seven years have been projected in the development of information systems (Yourdon,1989). Within individual projects there also exists concerns regarding completion on time and within budget. According to Laudon and Price Laudon (1991) some development projects can be as much as 30 percent over budget, eventually requiring 50 percent more time than originally estimated.

Beyond the above delays and cost-overruns during systems development, major problems unfold after the system has been developed and implemented. According to Hussain and Hussain (1988), statistics suggest that 50 percent of data processing budgets are allocated to maintenance. Kendall (1992) suggests the maintenance phase consumes up to 70 percent of all programmer effort. Furthermore, 40 percent of that maintenance effort is the result of errors, not enhancements (Rush,1985). Kendall (1992) also suggests that these errors have resulted from problems created in phases prior to programming. Yourdon (1989) supports this contention suggesting that 50 percent of errors and 75 percent of the cost of the removal of these errors can be attributed to errors which occur in the analysis phases. This problem is further confounded by the fact that the later in the Systems Development Life Cycle (SDLC) that an error is discovered, the more it costs to fix (Boehm, 1981).

It is our belief that the principles of Total Quality Management (TQM) have a significant relevance to IS development. Oates (1992) suggests that to ensure accuracy of systems specification, IS professionals should apply the principles of TQM. The principles of TQM in relation to information systems, as suggested by Oates, are as follows:

1. Understand and document the detailed requirements to produce analysis stage specifications.
2. Document the criteria to judge the quality of the work steps through life-cycle quality metrics.
3. Train employees to perform these detailed work steps and recognize defects in the work steps.

It should be noted that quality is defined with respect to conformance to specification in all tasks. That is, the more an IS conforms to that which has been specified, the higher the quality. A measurable standard of performance may be developed through a focus on the identification of defects. Oates (1992) suggests the most critical aspect of any quality improvement program is the ability to recognize a defect. A defect may be defined as, a deviation from specification.

Changing Roles and Skills Mix of IS professionals

A series of articles have described research relating to motivation and satisfaction of systems analysts and to a limited extent, the other IS professionals included in this article. (Couger,et,al,1979; Goldstein and Rockart,1984; Ein-Dor and Segev,1986; Couger,1988; Couger and Adelsberger,1988; Garden,1988a and 1988b; and Couger,et al.,1989). These authors are trying to determine how to increase motivation and satisfaction for IS professionals. This increase, some authors suggest, may lead to an increase in productivity. Another approach (see Hunter, 1992, 1993 and 1994) is to identify the characteristics of an "excellent" IS professional. Having done that, the productivity in IS development may be improved by selecting and training individuals who more closely reflect the local or corporate interpretation of "excellent".

Articles by Lyons(1985), Smith(1988), and Buie(1988) discuss the personalities of systems analysts. All three articles used the Myers-Briggs Type Indicator (MBTI) questionnaire. The research results indicated the distribution of systems analysts relative to personality types are different from the general population. Systems analysts, according to Smith, "... need to have strong interpersonal skills linked with conceptual thinking ability and an inquiring mind." (Smith,1988:14). However, Smith's research results indicated systems analysts "... have a strong technical orientation and a very conservative outlook." (Smith,1988:14). These results were supported in the other articles (Lyons,1985 and Buie, 1988).

Other research has attempted to determine the major components of the job of systems analysis. (Arvey and Hoyle,1973 and 1974; Cheney and Lyons,1980; Vitalari,1985; Cheney,1988; and Cheney,et,al,1989). In general, the following conclusions were reached. "The trend for systems analysts/designers is toward increased knowledge of people and problem-solving skills, and away from developing application software." (Cheney, et al, 1989:335). Cheney (1988), in a follow-up to a 1980 study (Cheney and Lyons, 1980) indicates that human relations skills seem more important as a result of increased user involvement.

Another series of research projects is aimed at obtaining a better understanding of systems analysts and what they do. (Benbasat,et,al,1980; Vitalari and Dickson,1983; Crocker,1984; Litecky,1985; Barrett and Davis,1986; Maxwell,1986; Guinan,1988; and McCubbrey and Scudder,1988). Some of these projects indicate the importance of a specific skill. Other projects identify trends in the importance of a skill over time. Still other projects identify "highly rated" systems analysts, and then proceed to investigate a specific skill. Some of these projects highlight skills categories but do not indicate a level of importance. Unfortunately, based on the results of this series of projects, it is not possible to identify the relative importance of a skill in relation to an entire set of skills, in sufficient detail to support further action. Thus, little data are available with which to be able to differentiate systems analysts.

Hunter (1992, 1993 and 1994) has attempted to determine what differentiates "excellent" systems analysts. He has conducted research which takes a qualitative approach to determining an interpretation of what constitutes the qualities of an "excellent" systems analyst. This research project included 53 participants from 2 companies in Canada representing 5 groups of individuals, or audiences, who interact with systems analysts. The data were gathered using Kelly's RepGrid technique and represent audience perceptions of what constitutes an "excellent" systems analyst. Overall, the more important aspects which emerged from the research include communicate, attitude, knowledge, investigate, and experience as the key characteristics of an "excellent" systems analyst. The detailed definitions of these aspects varied among different stakeholders. For instance, User audiences emphasized content related aspects, such as knowledge. Systems Analysts and their supervisors differentiated on process related aspects, such as investigate. Each stakeholder has its own interpretation of the relative importance of what constitutes an "excellent" systems analyst. Based upon these research findings, the companies involved in the research project have revised their approach to hiring and training systems analysts.

Information Systems Development Methods

Since the early eighties, several research publications have dealt with effectiveness of different modes of presentation and use on problem solving and decision-making. Previous research on effectiveness of different modes of presentation in different problem solving contexts has not provided any definitive answers about the overall superiority of any mode. DeSanctis [1984], in a comprehensive review of the literature, found that 12 studies showed tables are better than graphs, 7 studies showed graphs outperform tables, and 10 studies showed no meaningful differences between these two presentation modes.

Most research has substantiated the role of task characteristics in determining the role of presentation methods. Umanath et al (1990) emphasize the importance of task in the choice and preference for a presentation method. Tan and Benbasat et al (1990) have reemphasized the importance of task characteristics by developing a taxonomy of tasks for understanding, measuring, and evaluating the relative merits of different forms of graphical representation. Most recently, a study on the role of mode of use in the different stages of solving Decision Analysis problems has been published (Palvia and Gordon, 1992).

Research has not been limited to graphical and tabular modes. There have also been studies about the effectiveness of different modes during different phases of IS development [Juhn and Naumann, 1985; Wells and Naumann, 1985].

Naumann and Palvia [1982] evaluated different system development tools in the program design phase, and found that pictorial modes — Hierarchy Input Processing Output (HIPO) charts, and Warnier/Orr (W/O) diagrams — were preferred over the other two modes — Chapin Charts and Decision Tables. Palvia and Palvia [1990], while evaluating the effectiveness of modes of data, procedures, and logic representation in the different phases of systems development life cycle, found data flow diagrams to be superior for information flow representation; structured English to be superior for information processing representation; system flow charts, structured English, and data flow diagram (in that sequence) to be superior for ease of use and ease of learning; system flow charts to be superior for communication to the programmer analysts; and narrative descriptions to be superior for communication to the users. Vessey and Weber [1986], in analyzing decisions made by programmers, found that structured English outperforms decision tables when the task is to taxonomize (identify the conditions that evoke particular actions), but decision tables outperform structured English in sequencing (converting the taxa to a linear sequence of program code).

Some empirical studies on the use of methodologies, techniques, and tools in organizations have direct relevance to our research. Mahmood (1987) documents his results as a result of responses from 61 organizations in the U.S. The research was aimed at investigating the impact of systems development methods — SDLC and prototyping — on a system's success measured by 24 criteria for two broad categories of stakeholders — designers and users. The broad finding was that development method should be based on the characteristics of the project, task, users, and designers. Necco et al (1987) focused on how organizations use different tools, techniques, and methodologies to perform systems analysis and design. Usable responses to an extensive 20-page questionnaire were received from 97 organizations. The major findings of this research were: organizations use a combination of methodologies (SDLC, prototyping, End User Computing etc.) and within each approach they use a mixture of techniques and tools.

THE MODEL

The problems of the software crisis, low productivity, and low IS quality cited in earlier sections are further exacerbated by the continually changing environment, both in technology and corporate structure and scope. Rapid advances in technology have caused changes in the means by which IS are developed and maintained. This environment seems to be continually changing as a result of the introduction of such concepts as end-user computing, supported by information technology (IT); and information engineering which promotes the use of fourth generation languages; object oriented analysis, design, and programming; and prototyping.

As is clear from the above discussion, people and methods are the inputs to the systems development process. People are represented by five different IS professionals — Project Manager, Systems Analyst, Communications Specialist, Database Specialist, Programmer; and IS users — end-users, user mangers. These people typically constitute a project team to develop IS. The methods are comprised of methodologies, techniques, and tools. Exhibit-1 provides definitions of these IS professionals and methods. The right choice of people and methods will affect the productivity of IS development and will also impact the quality of the IS delivered. Exhibit-2 depicts this model.

Exhibit-1: Definitions of Different IS Professionals and Methods

Systems Analyst
Works with end-users to define information systems requirements Designs information systems to performed defined requirements.

Programmer
Designs, codes, and tests computer programs based on information systems specifications. May also enhance and make changes to existing programs based on IS specifications.

Database Specialist
Defines and controls the database for an IS applications or the overall organization including physical database design. He/she may also be responsible for the operation, maintenance, and performance monitoring of the DBMS software.

Communications specialist
Develops and manages telecommunications links. Responsible for interconnecting computers and peripheral equipment to form network or networks which support the movement of data from one node to another.

Project Manager
Estimates the expected costs, benefits and time schedules for a project, followed by the application of appropriate control measures throughout the life of the information system project in order to ensure adherence to estimates.

Methodology
A systematic procedure to develop an IS from conception till implementation. A methodology may utilize one or more techniques to accomplish different phases of systems development. Some examples of methodology include the use of specialized manual procedures and tasks described in vendor provided methodologies like Spectrum, SDM, Pride, and now some specialized prototyping and object-oriented methodologies.

Technique
A specialized narrative, graphic, pictorial, or tabular approach to accomplish a particular procedure or task in systems development efficiently and effectively. Examples are Data Flow Diagram, Decision Tree, Decision Table, Pseudocode etc.

Tool
A tool, generally computerized, helps in efficient use of a technique. Examples include Data Dictionary processor, Code Generator, CASE tool etc.

Exhibit-2: Quality and Productivity in Information Systems Development: Role of People and Methods

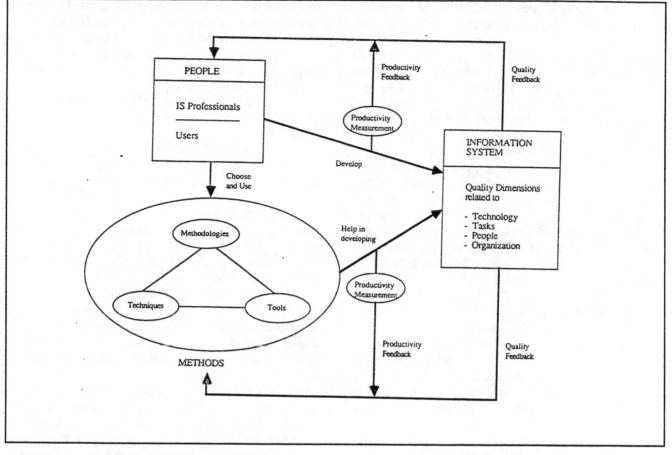

The computer industry is approximately 45 years old. We have witnessed several mini-revolutions or stages of development within this short period. These changes have been driven by hardware and software generations and have resulted in a continually changing skills-mix of people who develop, maintain, and use the information systems. The entire IT industry is constantly in a state of change. This model for productive development of quality information systems, we contend, is relatively stable and independent of the continual changes in information technology.

The focus has shifted from the first generation when detailed technical knowledge of the internals of computer hardware was required, to the current generation when it is possible to specify what is to be done (i.e., knowledge about the business) rather than how it is to be done by the IS. Now we are in the age of end-user computing or distributed computing when software development occurs in a central IS group and/or in decentralized business groups and/or on the desk-top PCs of individuals. In short, the job roles, job descriptions, the required and desirable skills-mix of IS professionals have been changing faster than the supply side can cope with. The proposed model suggests that a right mix of people skills on the systems development team can contribute significantly towards improving productivity of people and in enhancing the quality of information systems developed. Hunter (1992, 1993 and 1994) suggests that to improve

productivity systems analysts should be more carefully selected and should be trained according to their relative skill deficiencies. The basis for systems analyst selection and training will vary from one organization to another. The same conclusion, we contend, should also apply to other IS professionals.

Methods include the use of the systems development process (methodology), techniques (data flow diagrams, structure charts etc.), and tools (data dictionary processor, code generator, and CASE tools etc.). These systems development aids (methods) have been also evolving during the last four decades. IS management and staff choose and later use the methods to develop information systems. Our contention is that not all methods suit all people.

People and methods in combination develop information systems. The use of the right mix of people and the right combination of methods will improve the productivity of IS development process and the quality of IS produced. The model suggests the need for defining and measuring productivity of people and methods in developing information systems.

What is quality and how do we measure quality? International Standards Organization for Standardization, defines quality as: "the totality of features and characteristics of a product or service that bears on its ability to satisfy stated or implied needs" [ISO, 1987]. Putting it into the context of IS,

Schulmeyer and McManus [1987, p.10] suggest that quality is "the composite of all attributes which describe the degree of excellence of the computer system ... so as to assure that the system meets its stated requirements." Tobin (1990) suggests that in order to implement Total Quality Management (TQM) concepts, IS professionals must develop a new definition of quality, expand methodologies, develop new systems, and expand into the business environment. Further, Zadrozny and Tumanic (1992), when discussing the principles of TQM as applied to an IS environment, suggest a focus on customers, zero defects, and people and processes rather than technology. While measuring the quality of IS delivered, practitioners and researchers generally tend to focus on technical quality and ignore the social aspects of the system. We must adopt a sociotechnical perspective in measuring or evaluating the quality of an information system. The sociotechnical perspective will include not only the technology aspects of the IS but also the impact on tasks, people, and organization (Conrath and Sharma, 1992).

RESEARCH ISSUES

Based on the proposed model and prior literature survey, this research aims at investigating the following for Singapore:

1. The skills mix of advertised IS professionals positions
2. The skills mix of IS professionals employed
3. Methodologies utilized for IS development
4. Techniques utilized for IS development
5. Tools used for IS development

RESEARCH METHODOLOGY

The research methodology employed is a rigorous one using questionnaire survey approach. The questionnaire itself was developed based on past research by the authors. The initial draft of the questionnaire was pre-tested by our colleague researchers at the School of Accounting and Business. The improved questionnaire was field-tested by seven systems development managers of Information Management Research Centre (IMARC) corporate sponsors. This questionnaire is organized in three sections.

Section "A" contains questions regarding the use of various methodologies, techniques and tools for IS development by the organization. The definitions of Methodology, Technique, and Tool were also provided separately as Glossary of Terms for the convenience of the respondents.

Section "B" collects data on the hiring, promotion, evaluation, and training criteria used for IS professionals by an organization. The respondents were requested to list in priority order the criteria used for hiring, promotion, evaluation, and training. For their convenience, a list of criteria (Crocker, 1984) was also provided. Furthermore, the respondents were requested to send a copy of each of his/her organization's Performance Appraisal forms used for the five IS professional groups: Project Manager, Systems Analyst, Communications Specialist, Database Specialist, and Programmer. (see Appendix-1 for definitions of these IS professionals).

Section "C" collects data about the organization's experiences in developing IS applications in the last two years. Of special interest to us was the IS development group's satisfaction with the IS professionals who developed the applications and the methodologies, techniques, and tools that were employed to help the group in productive development of quality information systems.

Finally, section "D" collects data about the company, the information systems department of the company, and also about the respondent.

To explore the skills-mix requirements for IS professionals in the Singapore market, an analysis of the position advertisements of two Saturdays — January 9 and January 16, 1993 and May 1 and May 8, 1993 was performed. This analysis will be performed eventually for a longer period of time and will include the ASEAN and the North American region.

DATA ANALYSIS

In what follows, the data from position advertisements of major newspapers is analyzed with respect to the first research issue, and 65 valid questionnaire responses (over 25% response rate) received from organizations — are analyzed with respect to each of the remaining seven research issues described earlier. The responses were received from different sizes of companies having several different types of business and were centralized or decentralized to different levels. The IS departments had number of employees ranging from below 15 to more than 100 and the IS budgets of responding organizations also varied significantly. The respondents themselves were generally in the age group 35-50 and held positions varying from systems analyst to systems development manager to IS manager to CIO.

Research Issue One: The skills mix of advertised IS professionals positions

This issue is supported by the analysis of a survey of position advertisements in the January 9 and 16, 1993 and May 1 and May 8, 1993 issues of the Singapore Straits Times. The objective was to document what companies are looking for when position advertisements are placed in local newspapers.

Table-1 presents the data gathered in the survey. In general, it should be noted that detailed item counts may not equal the number of advertisements because of multiple items identified per advertisement. The most prevalent criteria for Education was for a technical Degree. From the data gathered a degree in Computer Science was the most requested. Very few non-technical degrees were encountered. This is perhaps to be expected for the more technically oriented information systems professionals such as Communication Specialist and Programmer. However, it is somewhat surprising for the more people oriented information systems professionals of Project Managers and Systems Analysts. Both of these positions require a mixture of a technical and people skills.

Table-1: *PILOT SURVEY*

STRAITS TIMES - JANUARY 9 AND 16, 1993 STRAITS TIMES - MAY 1 AND 8, 1993					
Item	Communication Specialist	Database Specialist	Project Manager	Programmer	Systems Analyst
Number of ads	5	1	4	44	23
EDUCATION					
Degree					
Technical	4	1	2	20	16
Non-technical	0	0	2	2	2
Diploma	0	0	0	15	4
'A' Level	1	0	0	1	0
EXPERIENCE					
Average	2.40 yr	2.00 yr	4.50 yr	1.98 yr	3.17 yr
Range	1-5 yr	0-2 yr	2-6 yr	1-4 yr	1-5 yr
Hardware					
Micro	2	0	0	5	3
Mini	0	0	1	22	12
Mainframe	0	0	0	1	1
Networks	5	0	1	7	2
Software					
Operat. Sys.	1	0	1	35	11
Word Proc.	1	0	0	1	2
Spreadsheet	1	0	0	3	2
Database	0	0	0	14	5
3 G/L	1	0	1	36	16
4 G/L	0	1	2	20	10
Data Comm.	2	0	0	4	6
SKILL					
Communicate	3	1	2	14	11
Attitude	1	3	0	16	7
Experience	0	0	1	6	13
Knowledge	5	0	1	5	10
Interpersonal	0	1	1	5	5
Thorough	0	0	0	4	3
Plan	1	0	1	0	0
Investigate	0	1	2	1	0
Involve User	0	0	0	1	1

The average years of experience requested varied across all information systems professionals categories, where data were available. Programmers required the least average years experience at 1.98 years, followed by Database Specialists at 2.00 years and Communication Specialists at 2.40 years. The average years experience for Systems Analysts was 3.17 years and then 4.50 years for Project Managers. This sequence of increasing average years of experience also seems to follow the traditional approach to a career path. That is, usually Programmers are promoted to Systems Analysts who are, in turn, promoted to Project Managers.

The emphasis regarding Hardware Experience was on mini-computers. This may simply be a reflection of the general size of the companies placing position advertisements during the pilot survey period.

Software Experience was mainly requested for Programmers and Systems Analysts positions. Justifiably there was emphasis for Programmers to have experience with specific Operating Systems as well as programming languages - both 3G/L and 4G/L. With regards to Systems Analysts, it is noted there was a relatively equal emphasis on 3G/L and 4G/L. For both of these information systems professional categories, the 3G/L and 4G/L comparison reflects the status of companies incorporating this technology into their information systems development process. That is, while their still remains a large portfolio of 3G/L applications, 4G/L's seem to be making inroads into some companies.

The skills identified in the survey, in general, relate to non-technical items requested by the companies which placed the positions advertisements. The majority of these types of skills were requested for Programmers and Systems Analysts. Within these two information systems professionals categories "Ability to communicate effectively" was mentioned most often. Examples of detailed requests within this category are as follows:

"able to communicate effectively with all levels of users",

"write technical specifications", and

"make technical presentations".

For programmers the second most frequently mentioned skill was attitude. Some detailed examples are as follows:

"prepared to travel",

"self starter", and

"prepared to work long hours".

For systems analysts the second most frequently mentioned skill was experience. Some detailed examples are as follows:

"MIS experience in a manufacturing/Sales and Marketing environment",

"Phone systems",

"Manufacturing and distributed systems", and

"Warehousing and procurement applications".

Further, for systems analysts the third most frequently mentioned skill was knowledge. Some detailed examples are as follows:

"project estimating",

"cost/benefit",

"knowledge of open systems technology", and

"knowledge of Client-Server technology".

The results of this Skills section of the survey indicate what companies are looking for when they place position advertisements. That is, the skills included in the position advertisements represent an initial attempt, on the part of the company, to identify items which will differentiate potential candidates, and will assist in the selection process.

Research Issue Two: The skills mix of IS professionals employed

Table 2 through 5 present the data gathered as part of a questionnaire survey of Singapore companies in the spring of 1993. A list of skills was provided in the questionnaire based

TABLE 2: *Selection Information Systems Professionals' Skills Questionnaire Survey - Singapore*

TABLE 3: *Promotion Information Systems Professionals' Skills Questionnaire Survey - Singapore*

TABLE 4: *Evaluation Information Systems Professionals' Skills Questionnaire Survey - Singapore*

TABLE 5: *Training nformation Systems Professionals' Skills Questionnaire Survey - Singapore*

PRELIMINARY ANALYSIS	PRELIMINARY ANALYSIS	PRELIMINARY ANALYSIS	PRELIMINARY ANALYSIS
PROJECT MANAGER(36)	PROJECT MANAGER (31)	PROJECT MANAGER (28)	PROJECT MANAGER
1. Project Planning (23)	1. Project Control (19)	1. Project Control (20)	1. Project Planning (13)
2. Project Control (17)	2. Project Planning (16)	2. Project Planning (15)	2. Project Control (13)
3. Decision Making (11)	3. Decision Making (16)	3. Decision Making (13)	3. Dealing with People (7)
4. Dealing with People (11)	4. Dealing with People (12)	4. Dealing with People (13)	4. MIS (7)
5. Verbal Communication (8)	5. Progress Monitoring (10)	5. Progress Monitoring (12)	5. Human Behavior (6)
			6. Negotiations (6)
SYSTEMS ANALYST (33)	SYSTEMS ANALYST (35)	SYSTEMS ANALYST (32)	
1. Interviewing (8)	1. Project Control (12)	1. Dealing with People (11)	SYSTEMS ANALYST (33)
2. Verbal Comm. (8)	2. Dealing with People (12)	2. System Testing (9)	1. Tech.Doc.Preparation(8)
3. Program Suite Design (7)	3. Project Planning (8)	3. Project Control (8)	2. Project Planning (7)
4. Dealing with People (6)	4. Progress Monitoring (7)	4. Progress Monitoring (7)	3. Project Control (7)
5. Information Structures (5)	5. System Testing (7)	5. Tech.Doc.Preparation (7)	4. Data Structures (5)
6. Software Package Evaluation (5)			5. Measure.Sys.Perform.(5)
7. Application Packages (5)	COMMUNICATIONS SPECIALIST (23)	COMMUNICATIONS SPECIALIST (22)	6. Cost/Benefit Analysis(5)
8. Project Planning (5)	1. Computer Network (9)	1. Computer Network (14)	7. verbal Comm. (5)
9. Tech. Doc. Preparation (5)	2. Telecomm. (9)	2. Telecomm. (13)	8. Other Computer Applications within org. (5)
	3. Microcomp.Tech. (7)	3. Microcomp.Tech. (6)	
COMMUNICATIONS SPECIALIST (26)	4. Presentation Prepar. (5)	4. Dealing with People (5)	
1. Computer Network (16)	5. Dealing with People (5)	5. Project Planning (5)	COMMUNICATIONS SPECIALIST (21)
2. Telecomm. (16)	6. Cost/Benefit Analysis (5)	6. Project Control (5)	1. Computer Network (15)
3. Microcomp.Tech. (10)			2. Telecomm. (14)
4. Install.Configuration (7)	DATABASE SPECIALIST (21)	DATABASE SPECIALIST (20)	3. Microcomp.Tech. (6)
5. Compatible Hardware (5)	1. Database (9)	1. Database (11)	4. Tech.Doc.Preparation(5)
	2. File Design (5)	2. File Org. (7)	5. Project Planning (5)
DATABASE SPECIALIST (23)	3. Data Structures (5)	3. Data Structures (6)	6. Project Control (5)
1. Database (15)	4. System Security (5)	4. File Design (6)	
2. File Design (8)	5. Dealing with People (5)	5. Data Control (6)	DATABASE SPECIALIST(22)
3. Data Structures (7)		6. System Security (4)	1. Database (15)
4. File Org. (5)	PROGRAMMER (37)		2. File Design (6)
5. Interviewing (5)	1. Program Design (13)	PROGRAMMER (33)	3. Measure.Sys.Perform.(6)
	2. Programming (12)	1. Programming (16)	4. Data Structures (4)
PROGRAMMER (39)	3. Structured Prog. (9)	2. Program Design (12)	5. Data Control (4)
1. Programming (21)	4. System Testing (7)	3. Other High Level Lang. (8)	6. System Security (4)
2. Prog.High Lev.Lang.(18)	5. Appl.Packages (7)	4. Structured Prog. (7)	7. Dealing with People (4)
3. COBOL (13)		5. Test Data Design (7)	
4. Structured Prog. (11)		6. System Testing (6)	PROGRAMMER (33)
5. Appl.Packages (11)			1. Programming (10)
			2. Soc.Impact of Syst. (9)
			3. Database (7)
			4. Program Design (6)
			5. System Testing (6)
			6. Appl. Packages (6)
			7. Tech.Doc. Preparation(6)

upon previous research by Crocker. While 64 responses were received, 45 have been used to conduct the preliminary analysis, because they had consistently used Crocker's list. The other 19 responses either did not respond to the skills section of the questionnaire or the response was too general to be included in the preliminary analysis. Further, it is noted that not all information system professional categories were represented within all 45 usable responses. Thus, as Tables 2 through 5 indicate the response counts for each of the four criteria within all five information systems professional group is less than 45. The number in brackets following each criteria and each skill represents their respective count of occurrence. The sequence of skills listed within each criteria represents a priority ranking based upon occurrence for the 45 used responses. In general, the data from this preliminary analysis seems to reflect the generic interpretation of the four criteria. That is, the skills identified for each criteria seem to represent the inherent objectives of that criteria. For instance, the skills identified for SELECTION represent those skills necessary for entry level requirements. This is the case for all five information systems professionals. Also, the skills identified for TRAINING represent those further requirements to either perform the job or to more appropriately match specific individual assets with requirements of the organization. Further, the skills identified for EVALUATION represent a combination of SELECTION and TRAINING criteria. This seems appropriate from a generic human resources perspec-

Table-6A: Status of Systems Development Methodologies in Singapore

	Have now in Place	Under Are now Implemen- -ting	Not Active Evalu- -ation	yet consi- -dered	Has been Rejected	Do not know the term
a. Sequential Systems Development	48%	5%	1.5%	14%	1.5%	30%
b. Prototype Systems Development	43%	21%	14%	21%	1%	0%
c. Formal Post-Implementation Review (PIR)	40%	16%	15%	24%	2%	3%
d. Return On Investment (ROI) Analysis	36%	8%	5%	44%	2%	5%
e. Net Present Value (NPV) or Internal Rate of Return (IRR) Analysis	21%	6%	5%	58%	5%	5%
f. Application Prioritization Method	60%	8%	6%	10%	8%	8%
g. Chargeout System	28%	0%	13%	32%	8%	19%
h. Change Control System	63%	11%	6%	10%	0%	10%
i. Feasibility Studies	78%	13%	1.5%	6%	0%	1.5%
j. Formal System Development Methodology	35%	19%	1.5%	21%	0%	1.5%

Graph 6: Systems Development Methodology Status in Singapore

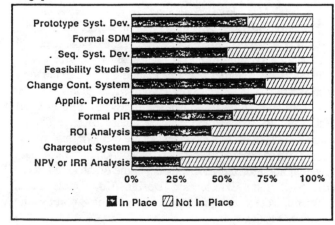

tive. Evaluation is based upon the initial base (identified in SELECTION) and what has been added (identified in TRAINING). Another factor could be experience, but it was not measured in this survey, because we did not gather data about individuals but rather data based upon information system professional groups. Finally, the skills identified for PROMOTION represent those requirements to perform at the next level either within the information systems professional group or as a series of progressions from one group to another. For instance, the data suggest that promotion for Communication Specialists and Database Specialists is within the respective group. While within group promotion occurs for the other three groups, it is also possible to progress from Programmer to Systems Analyst to Project Manager. This progression represents the traditional career path identified within information technology in general. The data gathered in the preliminary analysis suggests the traditional approach is being taken by those who responded to this section of the questionnaire.

Research Issue Three: Methodologies utilized for IS development

Table-6A gives detailed percent frequencies of the responses regarding broad methodologies employed and specific approaches utilized for information systems development. Graph-6 provides the summary after aggregating some responses. These results are significant in demonstrating the use of state-of-the-art approaches in Singapore.

Sixty four percent of the respondents said that they were either using or implementing the prototype approach for systems development as opposed to 53% using or implementing the traditional (sequential) systems development approach. Conducting formal post implementation review was also the practice of fifty six percent of the respondents. As many as sixty eight percent of the respondents said they were using or planning to use application prioritization methods, indicating there must be more requests than can be acted upon. The most gratifying result is that ninety one percent of the respondents said that they were using feasibility studies during the systems development approaches. About half the respondents said they were using formal systems development methodologies — most of these were in-house developed, only a few were using vendor supplied methodologies like SDM-70, Method-1 etc. Almost three-fourth of the respondents said they were using control system to manage changes during or after systems development. During feasibility studies, forty four percent utilized return-on-investment analysis, while twenty seven percent used net present value approach.

Table-6B provides a comparison of the methodologies used in Singapore with those used in U.S. during 1986 (Necco et al, MISQ, 12/1986). Even though there is a time gap of 7 years, the results are worth comparing. For one thing, it points to the fact that the use of traditional SDLC approach must be on the decline in U.S.A. also because of the inherent inflexibility of the approach. At the same time, the use of prototyping

TABLE-6B: Systems Development

Methodologies Used – U.S.(1986) and Singapore(1993)		
Method	U.S.(1986)	Singapore(1993)
Traditional SDLC	69%	53%
Prototyping SDLC	46%	64%
Feasibility Studies	–	91%
Formal PIRs	–	65%
Application Priority	–	68%
Shailendra Palvia, 1994		

approach must be on the rise. We do not think the differences are due to country, but they are rather due to the 7 years gap.

Research Issue Four: Techniques utilized for IS development

Table-7A depicts the status of the use of techniques in Singapore. About three-fourth of the respondent companies are using or planning to use data flow diagrams, system flow charts, program flow charts, and data dictionary. About half of the respondents are using entity relationship diagrams, pseudocode, decision tables, decision trees, and structure charts. Use of other techniques is insignificant. Graph-7 depicts the same results in more summarized form.

Table-7B provides a comparison of the techniques used in Singapore with those used in U.S. during 1986 (Necco et al,

Table-7A: Status of Systems Development Techniques in Singapore

	Have now in Place	Under Are now Implemen- -ting	Active Evalu- -ation	Not yet consi- -dered	Has been Rejected	Do not know the term
a. Data Flow Diagrams	57%	16%	9%	16%	2%	0%
b. System Flow Charts	78%	8%	5%	8%	0%	1%
c. Entity Relationship Diagrams	54%	13%	6%	24%	1.5%	1.5%
d. Decision Trees	42%	8%	4%	34%	9%	3%
e. Decision Tables	46%	6%	3%	34%	8%	3%
f. HIPO Charts	25%	1%	5%	40%	16%	13%
g. Warnier/Orr Charts	0%	3%	3%	48%	13%	33%
h. Structure Charts	41%	6%	6%	36%	3%	8%
i. Chapin Charts	0%	1.5%	1.5%	44%	5%	48%
j. Jackson Charts	9%	2%	5%	45%	11%	28%
k. Program Flow Charts	72%	6%	0%	14%	6%	2%
l. Pseudocode	55%	1.5%	0%	33%	1.5%	9%
m. Data Dictionary	63%	11%	11%	12%	0%	3%
n. Object Oriented Anal. (OOA)	10%	3%	20%	59%	0%	8%
o. Object oriented Design (OOD)	11%	3%	15%	55%	8%	8%

Graph-7: Systems Development Techniques: Status in Singapore

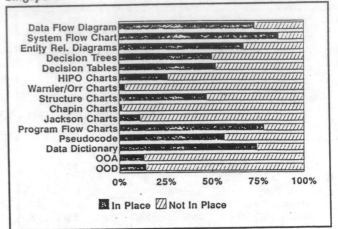

MISQ, 12/1986). Even though there is a time gap of 7 years, the results are worth analyzing. The use of most of the structured analysis and design techniques — data flow diagrams, data dictionary, structured english, structured charts, HIPO charts — was more widespread (and must still be) in U.S.A. than in Singapore. This confirms the fact that there is a time lag in transfer of technology (techniques in this case) from advanced nations to the not advanced nations including newly industrialized nations.

TABLE-7B: Systems Development

Techniques Used -- U.S. (1986) and Singapore (1993)		
Method	U.S. (1986)	Singapore (1993)
Data Flow Diagrams	80%	73%
Data Dictionary	97%	74%
Structured English	58%	57%
Decision Tables	42%	50%
Decision Trees	32%	50%
Warnier/Orr Diagrams	32%	3%
Structure Charts	75%	47%
HIPO Charts	30%	26%
System Flow Charts	–	86%
ER Diagrams	–	67%
OOA OOD	–	14%
Shailendra Palvia, 1994		

Research Issue Five: Tools used for IS development

Table-8A provides a summary of the tools utilized for systems development in Singapore. By far the most used tool is structured programming — eighty seven percent of the respondents were either using or planning to use in the very near future. The other tools employed or planned to be employed shortly are top-down testing (68%), screen/report design facility (63%), and data dictionary package (51%). About one-third of the respondents were using or implementing the use of program generator, application generator, data flow diagram aid, and CASE tools. Some of the CASE tools utilized include Excelerator, Design-Aid, Oracle Case, Silverrun, Microsoft Workbench, IEF. Graph-8 portrays the summary results.

Table-8A: Status of Systems Development Tools in Singapore

	Have now in Place	Under Are now Implemen- -ting	Active Evalu- -ation	Not yet consi- -dered	Has been Rejected	Do not know the term
a. Structured Programming	78%	9%	5%	3%	0%	5%
b. Object Oriented Programming (OOP)	14%	3%	24%	54%	2%	6%
c. Program Generator	29%	5%	20%	39%	2%	5%
d. Application Generator	23%	6%	15%	48%	3%	5%
e. Data Dictionary Package	42%	9%	12%	31%	0%	6%
f. Screen/ Report Design Facility	55%	8%	10%	20%	0%	7%
g. Top Down Testing	57%	11%	3%	21%	0%	8%
h. Data Flow Diagram Aid	32%	1%	14%	48%	0%	5%
i. Structure Chart Aid	21%	3%	10%	58%	1%	7%
j. Computer Assisted Software Engineering (CASE) tools	27%	7%	22%	36%	3%	5%

Graph-8: Systems Development Tools: Status in Singapore

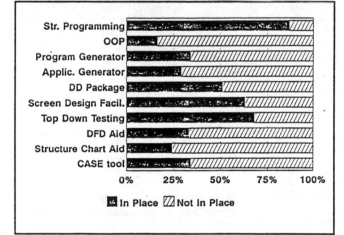

Table-8B provides a comparison of the tools used in Singapore with those used in U.S. during 1986 (Necco et al, MISQ, 12/1986). Even though there is a time gap of 7 years, the results are worth analyzing. The use of the automated tools— program generator, application generator, data dictionary processor, screen design facility, data flow diagram aid, and structure chart aid — was more widespread (and must still be) in U.S.A. than in Singapore. This confirms a well

TABLE-8B: Systems Development

Tools Used -- U.S. (1986) and Singapore (1993) Method	U.S. (1986)	Singapore (1993)
Program Generator	43%	34%
Application Generator	32%	29%
Data Dictionary Pkg	86%	51%
Screen Design Facilty	91%	63%
Data Flow Diagram Aid	52%	33%
Structure Chart Aid	38%	24%
OOP	–	17%
CASE Tools	–	34%
Shailendra Palvia, 1994		

documented fact that there can be a significant time lag in transfer of technology (tools in this case) from advanced nations to newly industrialized or developing or underdeveloped nations.

CONCLUSIONS AND SUGGESTIONS FOR FUTURE RESEARCH

1. Previous research studies have been fragmented in the sense that either they looked at only methods or only at people (and here too usually systems analyst only). These studies were usually descriptive. We have investigated both the resources (methods and people) together as providing synergy to the systems development process. Organizations must focus on the interaction effect of methods and people. This focus should be further enhanced by consideration of specific organizational and IS project characteristics.

2. We are planning a more rigorous cross-cultural research on practices of people and methods in the ASEAN region and North America. It may point to certain differences in practices which are perhaps caused by political, economic, social, and cultural differences. So, promoting one standard choice of people mix and methods mix in any national or cultural setting may not be a practical idea. In this research, we have provided some comparison between methods practices in U.S.A. and Singapore and have found significant differences (some of these may be attributed to the time difference of data). Even though we do not have any conclusive evidence, we do confirm that there can be significant time lag in transfer of technology (in this case methodologies, techniques, and tools for information systems development) from advanced nations to the not advanced nations.

REFERENCES
Arvey, Richard D. and Joseph C. Hoyle, "Evaluating Computing Personnel", Datamation, July, 1973, pp.147-150.

Arvey, Richard D. and Joseph C. Hoyle. "A Guttman Approach to the Development of Behaviorally Based Rating Scales for Systems Analysts and Programmer/Analysts", Journal of Applied Psychology, Vol.59, No.1, 1974, pp.61-68.

Barrett, Robert A. and Bruce C. Davis. "Successful Systems Analysts Hone Their Communication Skills", Data Management, April, 1986, pp.18.

Benbasat, Izak, Albert S. Dexter and Robert W. Mantha. "Impact of Organizational Maturity on Information System Skill Needs", MIS Quarterly, March, 1980, pp.21-34.

Boehm, Barry. Software Engineering Economics. Englewood Cliffs, New Jersey, Prentice- Hall, 1981.

Buie, Elizabeth A. "Personality and System Development What's the Connection", System Development, Vol.8, No.1, January, 1988, pp.1.

Cheney, Paul H. "Information Systems Skills Requirements: 1980 and 1988", Management of Information Systems Personnel Proceedings of the 1988 ACM SIGCPR Conference, Awad, E. (Chr.). ACM, New York, 1988, pp.1-7.

Cheney, Paul H., David P. Hale and George M. Kasper. "Information Systems Professionals: Skills for the 1990s" in Sprague, Ralph H. Jr. (Ed.), Proceedings of the 22nd Annual Hawaii International Conference on Systems Sciences, Washington, D.C., IEEE Computer Society Press, 1989, pp.331-336.

Cheney, Paul H. and Norman R. Lyons. "Information Systems Skill Requirements: A Survey", MIS Quarterly, Vol.4, No.1, March, 1980, pp.35-43.

Conrath D.W. and Sharma R.S., "Expert System Evaluation: a Model and a Method," working paper, Information Management Research Centre, Nanyang Technological University, 1992.

Couger, J. Daniel. "Motivators vs. Demotivators in The IS Environment", Journal of Systems Management, Association of Systems Management, June, 1988, pp.36-41.

Couger, J. Daniel and Heimo Adelsberger. "Comparing Motivation of Programmers and Analysts in Different Socio/Political Environments: Austria Compared to the United States", Computer Personnel, ACM Press, Vol.11, No.4, September, 1988, pp.13-17.

Couger, J. Daniel, Israel Borovitz and Moshe Zviran. "Comparison of Motivating Environments for Programmer/Analysts and Programmers in the U.S., Israel and Singapore", in Sprague, Ralph H. Jr. (Ed.), Proceedings of the 22nd Annual Hawaii International Conference on Systems Sciences, Washington, D.C., IEEE Computer Society Press, 1989, pp.316-323.

Couger, J. Daniel, Robert A. Zawacki and Edward B. Oppermann. "Motivation Levels of MIS Managers Versus Those of Their Employees", MIS Quarterly, Vol.3, 1979.

Crocker, Patricia Susan. Systems Analysts - Training and Experience. Manchester, England, NCC Publications, 1984.

DeSanctis Gerardine, "Computer Graphics as Decision Aids: Directions for Research", Decision Sciences, 15/4, Fall, 1984.

Ein-Dor, P. and E. Segev. "Attitudes, Association and Success of MIS: Some Empirical Results from Research in the Context of a Business Game", The Computer Journal, Vol. 29, No.3, 1986, pp.212-221.

Garden, Anna-Maria. "Behavioural and Organisational Factors Involved in the Turnover of High Tech Professionals", Computer Personnel, ACM Press, Vol.11, No.4, September, 1988a, pp.6-9.

Garden, Anna-Maria. "Maintaining the Spirit of Excitement in Growing Companies", Computer Personnel, ACM Press, Vol.11, No.4, September, 1988b, pp.10-12.

Goldstein, David K. and John F. Rockart. "An Examination of Work-Related Correlates of Job Satisfaction in Programmer Analysts", MIS Quarterly, June, 1984.

Guinan, Patricia J. Patterns of Excellence for IS Professionals - An Analysis of Communication Behavior. Washington, ICIT Press, 1988.

Hunter, M Gordon. The Essence of "Excellent" Systems Analysts: Perceptions of Five Key Audiences. Doctoral Dissertation, Department of Management Sciences, Strathclyde Business School, University of Strathclyde, Glasgow, 1992.

Hunter, M Gordon, "A Strategy for Identifying "Excellent" Systems Analysts", The Journal of Strategic Information Systems, Vol.2, No.1, March 1993, pp.15-26.

Hunter, M Gordon, ""Excellent" Systems Analysts: Key Audience Perceptions", Computer Personnel, (forthcoming), 1994.

Hussain, Donna and K.M. Hussain. Managing Computer Resources. 2nd Ed. Homewood, Illinois, Richard D. Irwin, Inc., 1988.

ISO 9004:1987, "Quality Management and Quality System Elements - Guidelines," CAN/CSA-Q420-87, Canadian Standards Association, Toronto, June 1987.

Juhn Sung H. and Nauman Justus d., "The Effectiveness of Data Representation Characteristics on User Validation", Proceedings of the Sixth International Conference on Information Systems, Indianapolis, Indiana, December 16-18, 1985.

Kendal, Penny A. Introduction to Systems Analysis and Design: A Structured Approach. 2nd Ed. Dubuque, IA, Wm.C. Brown Publishers, 1992.

Kraemer Kenneth L., Gurbaxani Vijay, King John Leslie, "Economic Development, Government Policy, and the Diffusion of Computing in Asia-Pacific Countries", Public Administration Review, 52/2, March/April 1992.

Laudon, Kenneth C. and Jane Price Laudon. Management Information Systems, A Contemporary Perspective. New York, MacMillan publishing Co., 1991.

Litechy, Charles R. "Better Interviewing Skills", Journal of Systems Management, June, 1985, pp.36-39.

Lyons, Michael L. "The DP Psyche", Datamation, August 15, 1985, pp.103-110.

Mahmood Mo A. "System Development Methods - A Comparative Investigation", MIS Quarterly, 11/3, Sept. 1987.

Martin, Merle P. Analysis and Design of Business Information Systems. New York, MacMillan Publishing Co., 1991.

Maxwell, Paul David. A Critical Analysis of the Personal Characteristics of Successful Information Systems Analysts. Ph.D. Dissertation, Boston University, 1986.

McCubbrey, Donald J. and Richard A. Scudder. "The Systems Analysts of the 1990's", Management of Information Systems Personnel, Proceedings of the 1988 ACM SIGCPR Conference, Awad, E. (Chr.), New York, ACM, 1988, pp.8-16.

Nauman, Justus D. and Shailendra Palvia. "A Model for Selection of System Development Tools", MIS Quarterly, March, 1982.

Necco Charles R., Gordon Carl L., and Tsai Nancy W., "Systems Analysis and Design: Current Practices", MIS Quarterly, 11/4, Dec. 1987.

Palvia Shailendra and M Gordon Hunter, "Systems Analysis and Design Practices in the ASEAN Region", Proceedings of the 1193 DSI Conference, November 1993.

Palvia Prashant and Palvia Shailendra, "Applicability and Ergonomic Characteristics of System Development Techniques", Interface - The Computer Education Quarterly, March, 1990.

Palvia, Shailendra C. and Steven R. Gordon, "Tables, Trees, and Formulas in Decision Analysis", Communications of the ACM, Vol.35, No.10, October, 1992.

Rush, Gary. "A Fast Way to Define System Requirements". Computerworld, Vol.XIX, 40, October 7, 1985.

Senn, James A. Analysis and Design of Information Systems. New York, McGraw-Hill Ltd., 1985.

Smith, D.C. "The Personality of the Systems Analysts: An Investigation", Computer Personnel, ACM Press, Vol.12, No.2, December 1988, pp.12-14.

Schulmeyer G.G. and McManus J.I. (editors), Handbook of Software Quality Assurance, Van Nostrand Reinhold, New York, 1987.

Thachenkary Cherian S., "Information Technology (IT) Expenditures and U.S. Productivity: On the Fundamentals of Information Economy", EDI Europe, 1/2, 1991.

Umanath, Narayan S., Richard W. Scamell and Sidhartha R. Das, "An Examination of Two Screen/Report Design Variables in an Information Recall Context", Decision Sciences, Vol.21, 1990, pp.216-240.

Vessey, Iris and Ron Weber, "Structured Tools and Conditional Logic: An Empirical Investigation", Communications of the ACM, January, 1986.

Vitalari, Nicholas P. and Gary W. Dickson. "Problem Solving for Effective Systems Analysis: An Experimental Exploration". Communications of the ACM, Vol.26, No.11, November, 1983, pp.252-260.

Vitalari, Nicholas P. "Knowledge as a Basis for Expertise in Systems Analysis: An Empirical Study", MIS Quarterly, September, 1985, pp.221-241.

Wells, Connie E. and Justus d. Naumann, "An Empirical Comparison of User Understanding: System Flow Charts and Data Flow Diagrams", Proceedings of the Annual Meeting of the American Institute for Decision Sciences, Las Vegas, November 11-13, 1985.

Yourdon, Edward. Modern Structured Analysis. New York, Yourdon Press, 1989.

The Impact of Culture on the Information Needs of Manager of Manufacturing Firms in Developing Countries

Timothy Shea, Boston University
David Lewis, University of Massachusetts/Lowell

BACKGROUND

To be competitive in the 1990's, manufacturing companies from Germany to Japan to the United States are reengineering their organizations. New levels of cooperation, such as shared supplier-customer information systems and cross-functional teams within companies, are yielding significant benefits.

Managers have been particularly affected. Many managers have been reengineered out of jobs, and for those which remain their jobs have changed. Two common changes include a broader span of control and broader decision making powers. Both changes require significant changes in information needs. As a result, to successfully function in the lean and mean era of the 1990's managers must be able to access different information sources than in the past and, in growing proportions, use the desktop computing and networking available to them for the information.

However, while prescriptions for success are evolving for companies in highly industrialized countries, there is less understanding about their applicability to developing nations.

This research, using survey data, will explore information needs of manufacturing managers in a developing country. The following sections will specify the research questions, review the relevant literature, and detail hypotheses and methodology.

RESEARCH QUESTIONS

Three research questions are relevant. First, *what information is necessary for managers of a manufacturing company in a developing country?* For example, within an organization, how much cross-functional information sharing is needed? Integration of internal information systems is feasible today, but the challenge is managing limited resources by identifying essential information needs. Additionally, in a changing environment, external information, such as industry benchmark information and developments in production technology, is more essential than ever.

The second question, given an organization gathers the needed information, is *how well are organizations getting needed information to managers.* The ease with which managers can access the information they need and the quality of the information they access affects their ability to do their jobs. The use of computer supported information is a related question.

The third question, and the source of the major hypothesis for the current research is that another variable, cultural context, is important in the determination of information needs. Specifically, *does the cultural context significantly*

determine manager's information needs. The next section reviews the literature in these areas, followed by a description of the research instrument, and data analyses that are to be undertaken.

LITERATURE

Information Needs of the 1990's Manager

Managerial information can be viewed as three categories -- vertical, lateral and external (Kantor, 1983). Vertical information comes from within the traditional, functional hierarchy, either up or down. Lateral information originates within the company, but outside the department or vertical line of command. External information refers to information gathered outside the company.

Greater use of external and lateral information are indicative of the downsized, decentralized, cross-functional team oriented, world-class manufacturing company of the 1990's (Frohman and Johnson, 1993). Conversely, reliance on vertical information is common within a traditional hierarchical company interfacing with a relatively stable environment. In such a company, integration among departments as well as environmental scanning is handled at the executive level. Therefore, different organizational forms dictate different information processing capabilities for its managers, which in turn, significantly affects information flows (Galbraith, 1977).

The Usefulness of Information

The usefulness of information sources is largely determined by the amount an information source is used. For individuals, it has long been established that use is largely determined by the quality and accessibility of the source (O'Reilly, 1982; Pfeffer & Salarcik, 1978; Allen, 1977). These studies show that, with managers and non-managers alike, higher quality information is used more frequently, as is more accessible information.

Unfortunately, while computer and network technologies open up expansive new pools of information, successful distribution of that information is nontrivial. In the United States, where the trend for decentralization dictates wider information distribution, over 62 percent of middle managers in a nationwide survey "disagreed or strongly disagreed with the statement that 'The quality of information I receive ... is good." (Harcourt et al., 1991, p. 354).

Cultural Variables

There is a vast literature describing cultural differences and its impact on management. One early area concerned differences in decision making style. Differences were found on how much individuals depended on others (the Japanese, for example rely heavily on others), bottom up versus top down, and whether decisions are made by individuals or groups (see Burger and Bass, 1979, for the comparisons of twelve diverse countries).

Other research has helped identify the nature of the cultural differences. These studies include work related values (Hofstede, 1980, found cultures could be compared on four dimensions: power distance, uncertainty avoidance, individualism, and masculinity), cultural universals (Hofstede, 1980, found view towards time, harmony with nature, etc., to be different in different countries), leadership style (Haire, Ghiselli, and Porter, 1966, looked at eight items depicting classic or democratic managerial style), needs and beliefs (Newman, 1970, for example, found American managers have a need for precise, accurate data, and value of planning), differences in risk preferences (Burger and Bass, 1979, found risk taking much higher in the US and Japan as compared to Germany), differences in leader's backgrounds (British managers are promoted on the basis of job performance whereas French managers are chosen from the graduates of elite schools according to Granick, 1972), to name a few.

Unfortunately, while cultural variables have been identified and refined, most managerial research that has been conducted in the United States has been by American researchers on American managers (Phatek, 1992). Up to the last decade, for example, American management ideas were promoted and exported to other countries through returning graduates. These ideas were sometimes not readily accepted due to cultural differences.

We shall base our study of managerial information on empirical data drawn from businesses within a developing country and seen through the filter of a culturally influenced leadership style. The following section describes the research model and hypothesis.

RESEARCH MODEL AND HYPOTHESIS

Our premise is that the mix of information that managers use--lateral, vertical, and external--at least partly depends upon the cultural setting of the managers. We are focusing on the cultural variable of leadership style. Leadership is appropriate because how a manager interacts with his employees and what role the leader is expected to play in the organization could significantly impact the type of information used.

We anticipate, given the Latino culture of Costa Rica, a more autocratic leadership style will be common (Haire, et al, 1966; Hofstead, 1980). Such a leadership style would be more suited to a traditional hierarchical organizational structure which places an emphasis on vertical information flow and little on the use of lateral or external information. Pictorially, this can be represented as follows:

This contrasts with the trend for companies in industrialized countries to emphasize lateral information in order to support a participative, cross-functionally oriented leadership style.

In order to examine this relationship we plan to test the following hypothesis:

H1: Managerial leadership style (autocratic versus democratic) effects a manager's use of information (vertical, lateral, and external)

In addition, we will examine two other research questions through descriptive analysis: (1) the mix of vertical, lateral, and external information by manufacturing managers and how it matches against perceived information needs, and (2) any hindrances to information use due to poor information access or quality. The next section details the survey methodology and analysis approach to be used.

METHODOLOGY AND ANALYSIS

Data collection will be via questionnaire. The questionnaire will be drawn from a previously validated leadership instrument (Haire, Ghiselli, and Porter, 1966) and an infor-

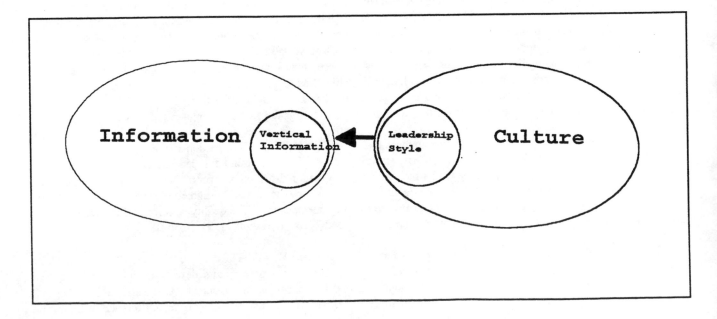

mation questionnaire which the authors have pretested extensively on American companies through the fall of 1993. The sample was drawn from a variety of sources including American firms doing business in Costa Rica, manufacturers taken from the Costa Rican yellowpages, and a listing of Costa Rican manufacturers. A convenience sample of 500 companies will be drawn in Costa Rica. A Spanish language questionnaire will be sent to the Manager of Production/ Operations, with a return mailer containing a Costa Rican address. Based on similar mailings (Lewis, 1984, 1985), we anticipate a response rate of 10-15 percent. As of this writing, the surveys have been distributed, and we anticipate that we will have the preliminary results to present at the conference. The small sample size, while statistically limited and inadequate for generalization, will provide useful descriptive information about management style, information use, and workstation usage by manufacturing managers in a developing country. Additionally, an indication of the relationship between leadership and information needs will be useful in refining the research in other countries. A copy of the research instrument (both English and Spanish versions) is found in the Appendix.

The first section (questions 1-8) provides useful demographics. This information will be helpful in testing whether other independent variables had an impact on the outcomes. For example, it is expected that there will be a wide variation in the size of the companies and the educational background of the respondents which may have as great an impact as culture on their information needs. This data will also be helpful to compare data in future replications of this study performed in a variety of industrialized and developing sites. The second set of questions (9-21) is related to information needs. We will be able to determine what kinds of information are used, its source, and perceived usefulness. The last section (questions 22-29) measures leadership style on four dimensions, one extreme indicating an autocratic leadership style and the other extreme a democratic style.

Assuming sufficient data is generated, three sets of data analyses are possible. The information needs (section 2) and the leadership style (section 3) areas can be viewed separately, through the demographic variables, as well as analyzed together, which is the main focus of this research.

CONCLUSIONS AND FUTURE RESEARCH

Very frequently we extend the results of research performed in the United States, and assume it has applicability in other countries. The premise of this paper is that there may be a dichotomy in managing companies within highly industrialized countries and developing countries, measurable through cultural variables. In this study, cultural effects, measured through leadership style, will be viewed through the perceived information needs of manufacturing managers.

In the future, based on the results of this study, we plan to refine our data collection. By collecting empirical data from manufacturing managers in Costa Rica on leadership style and information needs, we will be able to compare current managerial practices in a developing company to prescriptions for world class manufacturing developed in highly industrialized nations. Differences would be important to all practitioners offering either management advice or computer hardware and software to developing countries, reemphasizing the need to understand the culture before offering solutions. Culture, here viewed through leadership style, may impact the information use and needs of manufacturing managers. These differences, if ignored could lead to some very costly mistakes in business decision making. In an era where seemingly every computer software ad and every academic article about management speak to the value of integrated efforts, introducing integrated software systems and the like, may be inappropriate and counterproductive to the culture within developing countries.

In the future, we plan to review the instrument, review the effectiveness of leadership as our cultural variable, then continue collecting data from different countries, beginning with Mexico in the summer 1994.

BIBLIOGRAPHY

Allen, T. J., *Managing the Flow of Technology*, Cambridge, MA: MIT Press, 1977.

Burger, P. and Bass, B., *Assessment of Managers: An International Comparison*. New York, N. Y. Free Press, 1979.

Frohman, Alan L. and Leonard W. Johnson. *The Middle Management Challenge: Moving from Crisis to Empowerment*. McGraw-Hill, Inc., 1993.

Galbraith, J. *Organization Design*. Reading, Mass.: Addison-Wesley. 1977

Granick, D., *Managerial Comparison's of Four Developed Countries: France, Great Britain, United States, and Russia*. Cambridge, Ma., MIT Press, 1972.

Haire, M., Ghiselli, E. E., and Porter, L. W. "Cultural Patterns in the Role of the Manager," *Industrial Relations*, vol. 2, no. 2., (February 1963), p. 95-117.

Harcourt, Jules, Virginia Richerson and Mark Wattier. "A National Study of Middle Managers' Assessment of Organizational Communication Quality,"; *Journal of Business Communication*, Vol. 28, Iss 4 Fall 1991, pp. 348-365.

Hofstede, G., *Culture's Consequences: International Differences in Work-Related Values*. Beverly Hills, Ca. Sage Publications, 1980.

Kanter, R. M., *The Changemasters*. New York: Simon and Schuster, 1983.

Lewis, D., "Managerial Attitudes: A Cross Cultural Comparison," *Proceedings of the Segundo Simposio de Internacional Ingeneria*, 1984, pp. 213-228.

Lewis, D., "Leadership Style: The Case of Puerto Rico," in *Production and Inventory Management*, February 1985, p. 19-21.

O'Reilly, C. A., "Variations in Decision Makers' Use of Information Resources: The Impact of Quality and Accessibility of Information," *Academy of Management Journal*, vol. 25, 1982, pp. 756-771.

Pfeffer, J. and G. Salancik, *The External Control of Organizations: A Resource Dependence Perspective*, New York: Harper and Row, 1978.

Phatek, A., *International Dimensions of Management*, Boston, Ma. PWS-Kent, 1992.

APPENDIX

Spanish version of questionnaire

Cuestionario

1-8. Las primeras ocho preguntas se refieren a informacion general.

1. Cuantos anos ha estado trabajando en esta industria? ___ anos
2. Cual es el titulo/nombre de su puesto? _____
3. Cuantos empleados hay en la compania? ____ Cuantos le reportan directamente? ___
4. Cuanto dinero puede gastar sin necesidad de obtener autorizacion de su superior?
    _____colones
5. Cuantos anos paso Ud. en la escuela/universidad? ___ anos
6. Mi habilidad general en el manejo de computadoras puede ser descrita como:
    ___ incipiente ___ limitada ___ promedio ___ excelente ___ profesional
7. Los ultima trea anos, estime la tasa de cambio del medio ambiente de su compania para cada una de los siguientes casos:

		No mucho			Mucho	
a.	patrones de compra y requeriminto de las clientes	1	2	3	4	5
b.	comportamiento de los distribuidores	1	2	3	4	5
c.	patrones de precios en la industria	1	2	3	4	5
d.	desarrollo tecnico pertinte con el negocio de las divisiones de la empresa	1	2	3	4	5
e.	estrategia de los competidores	1	2	3	4	5
f.	cambios en los procesos de produccion	1	2	3	4	5

8. Piense en todas las formas de adquirir informacion sobre el trabajo. En general, como las calificaria?

a.	Rapidas	1	2	3	4	5	Lentas
b.	Baratas	1	2	3	4	5	Caras
c.	Confiables	1	2	3	4	5	Dudosas
d.	Completas	1	2	3	4	5	Incompletas
e.	Faciles de usar	1	2	3	4	5	Dificiles de usar
f.	Simples	1	2	3	4	5	Complejas

9-21. El siguiente grupo de preguntas se refieren a la informacion que Ud. necesita. Por favor, conteste las siguientes preguntas rodeando de un circulo el numero de la respuesta que Ud. considera mas cercana a su situacion.

Grado:	Ninguno	Bajo	Mediano	Alto	Muy Alto
9. Hasta que grado dispone de la informacion necesaria para tomar decisiones?	1	2	3	4	5
10. Hasta que punto necesita informacion proveniente de otras partes de la compania?	1	2	3	4	5
11. Hasta que grado obtiene informacion necesaria de otras partes de la compania?	1	2	3	4	5

12. Hasta que punto busca Ud. informacion relacionada con su trabajo utilizando las siguiente fuentes?

a.	consultaria o expecialistas externos	1	2	3	4	5
b.	revista, periodicos o diarios	1	2	3	4	5
c.	reportes de computadoras o bases de datos	1	2	3	4	5
d.	otros gerentes de su area funcional	1	2	3	4	5
e.	otros gerentes fuera su area funcional	1	2	3	4	5
f.	personal especializado de su area funcional	1	2	3	4	5
g.	personal especializado fuera de su area	1	2	3	4	5
h.	subordinados	1	2	3	4	5
i.	contactos personal fuera de su compania	1	2	3	4	5
j.	personal de oficina	1	2	3	4	5
k.	archivos o registros personales	1	2	3	4	5
l.	proveedores o clientes	1	2	3	4	5

13. Hasta que punto se encuentran las registros computerizados?

a. en su area de control	1	2	3	4	5
b. dentro del area de control de su superior	1	2	3	4	5
c. dentro del area de control de alguien mas en su compania	1	2	3	4	5
d. dentro del area de control de agentes externos (fuera de su compania)	1	2	3	4	5

14. Hasta que punto consume su tiempo el obtener la informacion relacionada con su trabajo que necesita?   1   2   3   4   5

15. En una semana tipica, hasta que punto busca Ud. informacion relacionada con su trabajo?   1   2   3   4   5

16. En una semana tipica, hasta que punto utiliza su computadora personal?   1   2   3   4   5

				estoy
desapruebo completamente	no estoy de acuerdo	neutral	estoy de acuerdo	totalmente de acuerdo

17. Las diferentes unidades dentro de mi compania trabajan juntas para alcanzar una meta comun   1   2   3   4   5

18. Las decisiones son delegadas hasta el nivel mas bajo posible   1   2   3   4   5

Muy Adecuado	Adecuado	Neutral	Inadecuado	Muy Inadecuado

19. Que tan adecuados son los sistemas de administracion de informacion computerizados de su compania para proveerle con la informacion que Ud. necesita?   1   2   3   4   5

20. Que tan adequados son los archivos manuales y los sistemas de registro en proveerle la informacion que Ud. necesita?   1   2   3   4   5

21. Piense en todas las formas de adquirir informacion desde su computadora personal en el trabajo. En general, como las calificaria?

a. Rapidas	1	2	3	4	5	Lentas
b. Baratas	1	2	3	4	5	Caras
c. Confiables	1	2	3	4	5	Dudosas
d. Completas	1	2	3	4	5	Incompletas
e. Faciles de usar	1	2	3	4	5	Dificiles de usar
f. Simples	1	2	3	4	5	Complejas

22-29. Esta seccion se refiere a su actitud frenite a los trabajodores

estoy:	muy de acuerdo	de acuerdo	indeciso	en desacuerdo	total en desacuerdo

22. El individuo medio prefiere ser dirigido, elude responsabilidades y tiene, relativamente, poca ambicion   1   2   3   4   5

23. La habilidad de dirigir puede ser adquirida por la mayor parte de las personas, independientemente de sus rasgos y habilidades innatas.   1   2   3   4   5

24. El uso de recompensas (paga, promocion, etc.) y castigos (dejar de promover, etc.) no es el mejor medio para que los subordinados trabajen.   1   2   3   4   5

25. Si en el trabajo los subordinados no pueden ejercer su influencia sobre mi, pierdo entonces cierta influencia sobre ellos.   1   2   3   4   5

26. Un buen lider deberia dar instrucciones completas y
    detalladas a sus subordinados,en vez de darles simplemente
    instrucciones generales y depender de su iniciativa para
    realizar los detalles   1   2   3   4   5
27. El establecimiento de metas de equipo ofrece ventajas
    que no pueden obtenidas por el establecimiento de metas
    individuales.   1   2   3   4   5
28. Un superior deberia da a sus subordinados solamente
    la informacion necesaria para que ellos puedan hacer su
    trabajo inmediato.   1   2   3   4   5
29. La autoridad de un superior sobre sus subordinados, en
    una organizacion, es primordialmente economica.   1   2   3   4   5

Nuevamente le agradezco por participar en este estudio. Por favor, use el sobre incluido para retornarnos el cuestionario.

English Version of Questionnaire

Questionnaire

1-8. The first eight questions are general background information

1. How many years have you been employed in this industry? ___ years
2. What is your job title? _____
3. How many employees in your company? ___ How many report to you? ___
4. How much money can you spend without obtaining higher authority? ____ colones
5. How many years did you go to school? ____ years
6. My overall personal computer skill level is best described as:
    ___ Novice ___ Limited ___ Average ___ Excellent ___ Professional
7. Over the past three years, rate the amount of change you have seen in your company's environment for each of the following items.
    a. Buying patterns and requirements of customers   1   2   3   4   5
    b. Distributors' attitudes   1   2   3   4   5
    c. Industry pricing patterns   1   2   3   4   5
    d. Technical developments relevant to divisions business 1 2   3   4   5
    e. Competitors strategies   1   2   3   4   5
    f. Changes in production processes   1   2   3   4   5
8. Think of the ways you get job related information at work. In general, how would you characterize the ways that you acquire job related information?
    a. Fast   1   2   3   4   5   Slow
    b. Inexpensive   1   2   3   4   5   Expensive
    c. Reliable   1   2   3   4   5   Unreliable
    d. Comprehensive 1   2   3   4   5   Incomplete
    e. Easy to Use   1   2   3   4   5   Difficult to use
    f. Simple   1   2   3   4   5   Complex

9-21. The next set of questions refer to issues dealing with your information needs. Please answer the following questions by circling the number of the response which comes you feel comes closest to your situation:

	No Extent	Little Extent	Some Extent	Large Extent	Great Extent
9. To what extent do you have as much information as you need to make decisions?	1	2	3	4	5
10 To what extent do you need information from other parts of your company?	1	2	3	4	5
11. To what extent do you get the information you need from other parts of your company?	1	2	3	4	5

12. To what extent do you search for job-related
    information using these sources?

a. outside consultants or specialists	1	2	3	4	5
b. magazines, journals, or newspapers	1	2	3	4	5
c. computer reports or databases	1	2	3	4	5
d. other managers within your functional area	1	2	3	4	5
e. other managers outside your functional_area	1	2	3	4	5
f. staff specialists in your functional area	1	2	3	4	5
g. staff specialists outside your functional area	1	2	3	4	5
h. your subordinates	1	2	3	4	5
i your personal contacts not in the company	1	2	3	4	5
j. your clerical staff	1	2	3	4	5
k. personal files or records	1	2	3	4	5
l. suppliers or customers	1	2	3	4	5

13. To what extent are the computer records you search

a. within your area of control	1	2	3	4	5
b. within your superiors control	1	2	3	4	5
c. within the control of someone in another area of your company	1	2	3	4	5
d. from outside your company	1	2	3	4	5

14. In a typical week, to what extent do you
    actively search for job-related information? 1   2   3   4   5

15. In a typical week, to what extent do you
    use desktop computing? 1   2   3   4   5

16. to what extent is it difficult to get access to
    desktop computing? 1   2   3   4   5

	Strongly Disagree	Disagree	Neutral	Agree	Strongly Agree
17. Different units within my company work together to reach a common goal	1	2	3	4	5
18. Decisions are delegated to the lowest possible level	1	2	3	4	5

	Very Adequate		Neutral		Very Inadequate
19 How adequate are your firm's computer-based "management information systems" in supplying you with the information you need	1	2	3	4	5
20. How adequate are your manual files and record-keeping systems in supplying you with the information you need?	1	2	3	4	5

21. Think of the ways you get job related information from desk top computer at work. In general, how would you characterize the ways that you acquire job related information?

a. Fast	1	2	3	4	5	Slow
b. Inexpensive	1	2	3	4	5	Expensive
c. Reliable	1	2	3	4	5	Unreliable
d. Comprehensive	1	2	3	4	5	Incomplete
e. Easy to Use	1	2	3	4	5	Difficult to use
f. Simple	1	2	3	4	5	Complex

22-29. This section relates towards your attitudes towards your workers

	Strongly Agree	Agree	Neutral	Disagree	Strongly Disagree
22. The average human being prefers to be directed, wishes to avoid responsibility, and has relatively little ambition.	1	2	3	4	5
23. Leadership skills can be acquired by most people regardless of their particular inborn traits and abilities.	1	2	3	4	5
24. A good leader should give detailed and complete instructions to his subordinates, rather than giving them merely general directions and depending upon their initiative to work out the details.	1	2	3	4	5
25. A supervisor should give his subordinates only that information which is necessary for them to do their immediate tasks.	1	2	3	4	5
26. In a work situation, if the subordinates cannot influence me then I lose some of my influence on them.	1	2	3	4	5
27. Group goal setting offers advantages that cannot be obtained by individual goal setting.	1	2	3	4	5
28. The use of rewards (pay, promotion, etc.) and punishment (failure to promote, etc.) is not the best way to get subordinates to do their work	1	2	3	4	5
29. The superior's authority over his subordinates in an organization is primarily economic.	1	2	3	4	5

Thank you again for participating in this survey. Please use the enclosed mailer to return this questionnaire.

Is Computer Integrated Manufacturing an Appropriate Technology for the Developing Nations?

Massoud Tabatabai
School of Science, Engineering, and Technology
Penn State University at Harrisburg
Middletown, Pa. 17057

Cyrus Azani
Department of Management
University of District of Columbia
Washington, D.C.

CIM is a computer-based system that automate and integrate the entire design and manufacturing processes in manufacturing organizations. The CIM main purpose is to automate the flow of information from the initiation of design to core manufacturing activities and to integrate the information from marketing, accounting, purchasing, maintenance, engineering, and production. Application of CIM may ultimately lead to the formation of an automatic or humanless factory called the factory of the future.

CIM technology is more suitable for high volume and highly standardized production. However, it is being rapidly utilized in smaller economically-viable batch sizes that will enable the organization to become more competitive in responding to a wider range of demand and product changes.

Modern Integrated Manufacturing technologies are in the process of creating an industrial and social paradigm shift and as nations becomes more and more dependent on these new technologies, the side effects of their application become more and more evident. Such effects can manifest as human depersonalization, alienation, and finally displacement of man the creator of such technologies. At the same time, the tremendous changes brought about by modern computer-based manufacturing technologies will create new challenges and opportunities for the developed as well as developing nations. According to U.S. National Research Council, application of CIM has resulted in the following organizational achievements:

* Productivity enhancement by 40 to 70 percent.
* Quality improvement by a factor of 3 to 4.
* Equipment utilization increase by a factor of 2 to 3.
* Engineering design cost reduction of up to 30 percent.
* Inventory and lead time cutbacks by 30 to 60 percent.
* Improvement of the overall organizational effectiveness.

The CIM technology adoption is not problem free, however. Among the challenges we can identify the following:

* The CIM technology is a very complex technology,
* The cost of assessment, development, and implementation of the technology is staggering,
* The social impacts of CIM utilization in the developed as well as the developing nations are unknown and difficult to assess,
* Massive reorganization efforts and major changes in management philosophy and training is needed.
* Traditional economic analysis of the technology is irrelevant due to the existence of a lot of intangible costs and benefits.

Whether CIM technology is an appropriate technology for the developing nations is to a large extent determined by the effectiveness of the decision makers, and the way the unexpected events are managed during the assessment, installment, and operation of the new technology. The managers responsible for the CIM technology assessment and transfer need to be aware of the causes of the failure as well as the critical factors required for success in implementation of a new technology. Additionally, the barriers to the introduction and implementation of CIM technology experienced by other nations need to be identified and studied in a comprehensive way. Furthermore, adoption of a proactive strategy in identifying the barriers and developing plans to extract them is very essential for effective management of the CIM technology. Finally, the developing nations need to continuously monitor the advancements in the state of the art of CIM technology and periodically evaluate and analyze their national technology strategy and reassess their position with regard to the changes in the global scientific and economic environments.

Impact of Office Automation and IT on Health and Stress: A Singapore Study

Palvia, Shailendra   Tung, Lai Lai

Information Management Research Centre
School of Accountancy and Business
Nanyang Technological University
Nanyang Avenue
Singapore 2263

ABSTRACT

This study[1] reports the results of a survey on the impact of IT on health and stress of 87 Singapore office workers. Results indicate that more than 70% of the office workers reported eye strain and general stress in using IT. There is a positive correlation between age and health problems such as eye strain, stress and backache. There is also a positive correlation between the number of hours spent in front of a computer monitor and eye strain and stress. The top three sources of stress include long hours spent in front of the computer, having to prepare a lot of documents, and not being fully competent with IT. The top three factors crucial to doing a job well in an IT environment include having computer knowledge, having facilities for maintenance of data, and having proper lighting for screen display.

INTRODUCTION

Over the last forty years, information technology has significantly changed the way an office worker performs his/her tasks. The office workers of the past used typewriters for correspondence and file cabinets for information storage, while the modern office workers use office automation (Hirschheim 1985). In Singapore, although the use of office automation is widespread, no systematic study has been conducted to explore how well the modern office workers have coped with office automation. This paper summarizes our research on the impact of this technology on the office worker's job satisfaction, motivation, health, and stress.

Understanding the role of human factors -- the scientific study of people at work -- involves systematically applying knowledge of people's sensory, physical, intellectual, and motivational attributes to the design of the environment of the office (Galitz, 1984). Ergonomics -- the science of fitting the workplace to the worker -- involves the design of furniture and equipment to meet the needs of workers, which is important in improving productivity (Sox 1990). These two types of research are especially significant for a country like Singapore, where labour is one of the most scarce resources. Management must be aware of the importance of an "ergonomically right" office.

When human and ergonomic factors are not taken into consideration in designing an office and its information technology equipments, it becomes difficult for the office worker to be productive and to work without health hazards or stress. Many physical, psychological, and social problems have followed the introduction of video display terminals (VDTs) in offices. Some of the common ailments arising from working in an IT environment include visual problems, postural problems, and various psychosocial problems due to work stress. The next section, the literature review section, describes in detail some of the common health problems that office workers experience in their workplace.

LITERATURE REVIEW

Visual Problems

Numerous field studies in recent years have uncovered a variety of complaints about eye troubles associated with using Video Display Terminals (VDTs). The most commonly reported visual discomforts are eye strain, burning eyes, irritated eyes, and blurred or double vision (Sox 1990). Research by Dainoff (1982) also found that eye strain and back pain have a direct correlation with the number of hours spent working with a computer.

One study (Neal 1989) found that people in their twenties and thirties who work at least six hours a day in front of VDTs have trouble focusing much sooner than if age caused such problems. Another large scale study (Coe et al 1980) reported that eye fatigue was reported by 50% of the VDT operators' group compared with only 33% among the group of non-VDT control operators. Interestingly, this study also reported that fatigue was less (42%) among those VDT operators who were able to take frequent informal breaks (finding something to do which allowed them to look away from the screen) than those who cannot (62%).

To combat these problems, Dainoff and Dainoff (1987) and Springer (1982), among other researchers, suggested several ergonomic factors that are crucial to high performance in an IT environment. Among these factors, the more prominent ones are lighting positioning and workstation design. Palvia and Palvia (1990), while evaluating the effectiveness of modes of data, procedures, and logic representations in the different phases of systems development life cycle, provided information on the ergonomic effectiveness of systems development techniques for different phases.

Postural Problems

Like visual discomfort, many studies have uncovered reports of postural problems associated with using VDTs (Galitz 1984). Many people who work with computers complain of back pain. Other postural problems include shoulder pain, wrist pain, neck pain and body fatigue. Most of these complaints can be remedied with properly designed furniture that is movable and adjustable vertically and horizontally.

Psychosocial Problems

A third area of concern is related to a person's psychological reactions to IT. Limited research evidence now available indicates that some users of VDTs are more prone to stress than their colleagues who do not use VDTs. (Galitz 1984, Brad 1984). Other physical conditions, such as headaches, nausea, and dizziness, may be related to stress and attitudinal problems.

Disoriented sense of time was found to be a major problem for users who have used computers for a prolonged period of time (Josefina 1985).

Emmanuel (1983) suggested that many things affect the amount of stress workers experience. Among a host of reasons, he highlighted users' past experiences with computers and the ages of the users as prominent attributes related to stress. Older employees in particular suffer from psychological stress stemming from fear of computers — fear about not being able to use the machines and fear of failing when competing with younger, better trained workers, or fear of being replaced by them. He also mentioned that stress is often the result of diminished contact with other office workers.

Cohen (1981) found that lack of autonomy and pressures for performance are distinguishing features of highly stressful IT jobs. Problems, such as tension, low morale, poor attitude, isolation, fear, and worry, are also symptoms of psychological stress. Fear of job loss, physical harm, and isolation from co-workers may cause operators of automated equipment to develop any of the aforementioned stress symptoms. Some common causes of work stress resulting from working in an IT environment are (Cohen 1981, Hirschheim 1985, Sox 1990):

i)Lack of control

The lack of autonomy is one distinguishing feature of highly stressful jobs. The IT environments often do not permit workers to exercise control over the manner, order and pace of their work. Tasks must be performed in the prescribed way, prescribed order and at a pace dictated by the computer's response time.

ii)Heavy workloads

Computerisation frequently brings with it calls for high production standards. A person is often asked to perform at maximum rates for long periods of time, sometimes resulting in work fatigue and even job burnout.

iii)Pressures for performance

Pressures for high performance is another distinguishing feature of stressful jobs. Constant pressures to achieve high performance, to achieve a machine-like efficiency, may be both outwardly imposed by management or inwardly imposed by the worker.

iv)Monitored performance

Computerised activities can easily be monitored, be it by keystrokes, pages created, or transactions processed; and this creates undue pressure on the worker.

v)Disrupted social relationships

Computerisation can seriously impair or destroy social relationships that exist in the office. People need to encounter and interact with others. Social reinforcement of the peer group is important to many people.

vi)Concern for career and job future

As computers perform more of the tasks accomplished by clerical personnel, employment opportunities will diminish. Being replaced by a machine is a valid fear expressed by many.

vii)Not fully competent with IT yet

In an automated office, computers take centre-stage. Being competent in working with the machine is an asset to the office worker. On the other hand, not being fully competent with IT yet implies that there will be frequent disruptions to work flow due to problems posed computers, and thus a major cause of stress.

xiii)Long hours spent in front of the computer

As a result of computerisation, the bulk of work carried out by an office worker will be accomplished using computers, resulting in prolonged hours spent in front of the machine.

ix)Fear of not being able to catch up with technology

At the relentless pace with which IT is developing, an office worker cannot afford to remain complacent in his/her computer knowledge as far as working in an automated office is concerned. Knowledge gained during the last 3 - 5 years may be obsolete by now. Trying to catch up with technology has indeed been stressful for many.

RESEARCH ISSUES

Based on the above literature review as well as field interviews with some office staff, the following research issues about the impact of information technology and office automation on the health, and the resultant stress of office workers (clerical and administrative staff) were investigated.

(1)Several health problems of stress, eye strain, headache, backpain and disorientated sense of time may result from working with information technology equipment.

(2)The existence of the above health problems are dependent on the age groups of the office workers.

(3)The occurrence of the above health problems are dependent on the number of hours spent by an office worker using computers and other IT equipment.

(4)The incidence of stress is dependent on the educational background, gender or job position of the office worker.

(5)The main sources of stress for the office workers are related to the length of use of IT devices and the level of competence with IT.

(6) The crucial factor affecting IT users' performance and reduction of stress is having adequate knowledge and skills in using computers.

RESEARCH METHODOLOGY

A total of 250 questionnaires were distributed to companies in Singapore for written responses -- 96 were returned of which nine were incomplete. To maintain respondent anonymity, no identification was asked for and therefore the respondents could not be contacted for clarification. The incomplete questionnaires had to be discarded. The resulting sample size was 87, which amounts to 34.8% usable response rate.

For the greater part of the data analysis, simple tabulations were used (such as table 1 on the profile of the respondents). In some instances, cross tabulations were used to determine relationships between different variables (such as figure 1 on the relationship between a person's age and health problems).

To rank the importance of some variables, (such as table 7 on factors crucial to doing job well in an IT environment), a total scoring method was use. To convert a series of variables from a five-point likert-type format into a ranked order, the following formula is used to compute the total score (TS) of importance of a factor.

$$TS = S1*f(S1) + S2*f(S2) + S3*f(S3) + S4*f(S4) + S5*f(S5)$$

where S1 is the first importance score (5 in our case), and f(S1) is the frequency of occurrence of importance score S1 and so on.

For instance, on a likert type scale of 1 to 5 (1 being the least important, and 5 being the most), a factor is rated "the most important" (score = 5) by 10 respondents, "highly important" (score = 4) by 3 respondents, and "least important" (score = 1) by 6 respondents. For this factor, the cumulative importance rating score will be computed as (5 X 10) + (4 X 3) + (3 X 0) + (2 X 0) + (1 X 6) = 68. Since 19 respondents rated this factor, the maximum possible importance score is 5 X 19 = 95.

The factor with the **highest total score** is the one perceived to be the **most important** by the respondents, the one with the second highest total score is the second most important factor, and so on.

ANALYSIS OF DATA

Table 1 below summarizes the profile of our respondents. In this study, 40.23% of the respondents are involved in clerical and administrative duties, 9.2% sit in managerial positions while the remaining 50.57% are professionals. In addition, the sample was sufficiently balanced in terms of gender. All respondents in the sample were at least 20 years of age, with the majority (more than 90%) falling in the age group of 21 to 40 years old. Among the respondents, graduates dominated (accounting for 43.68%). All respondents have at least an 'O' level qualification[2], as shown.

Other characteristics of respondents pertain to their use of IT-related devices. IT-related devices are peripherals and

Table 1: Profile of respondents.

Profile	Factors	Percentage
1. Positions in Organizations	Clerical and Administrative	40.23%
	Managerial	9.20%
	Professionals (eg. accountants, auditors)	50.57%
2. Age	Less than 20 years	-
	21 - 30 years	41.38%
	31 - 40 years	49.42%
	Greater than 40 years	9.20%
3. Gender	Male	50.57%
	Female	49.43%
4. Education	Graduates	43.68%
	Diploma	19.54%
	'A' and 'O' levels	36.78%

equipment which are electronically configured and serves as a medium for transfer or storage of data. Such devices commonly found in the modern office environment include fax machines, computers, printers, modems, word processors etc. In this survey, all the respondents had computer experience. However, almost half of them picked up the experience only upon joining the current organisation. All respondents utilise IT-related devices in one way or another to do their work, with the majority (82.76%) spending, on average, more than 15 hours each week on such devices in the office. Of these, 9.72% actually continued with more than 5 hours of IT activity back at home. Furthermore, 50.57% of respondents bring home work to do; of these, the number of hours spent on IT devices each week, on average, at home doing office work generally does not exceed 5 hours (84.09% of total respondents who bring home work to do). Thus, the number of hours spent on IT equipment at home is insignificant relative to the amount of time spent on IT devices in the office.

The following is an analysis of the health and stress related problems faced by our respondents.

(1) Several health problems of stress, eye strain, headache, backpain and disorientated sense of time may result from working with information technology equipment.

Common complaints from the users of IT ranged from disorientated sense of time to eye strain and back problems. Among the health problems, the two most commonly cited ones were eye strain and stress, accounting for 77.01% and 72.41% of total respondents respectively. Table 2 below shows the various problems related to use of IT and their impact on users of computers. Other problems cited by respondents include sleepiness and being easily agitated when there is a lot of work to do.

Table 2: Symptoms commonly experienced by respondents

Problems Experienced	Percentage
Eye strain	77.01%
Stress	72.41%
Backache/neck pain/etc	45.98%
Headache	28.74%
Disoriented sense of time	24.14%

Figure 1: Symptoms commonly experienced by respondents in relation to their age

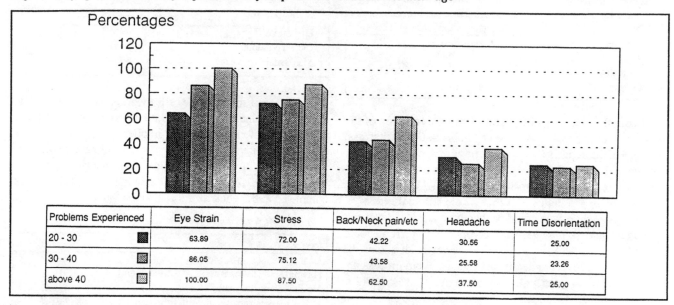

Problems Experienced		Eye Strain	Stress	Back/Neck pain/etc	Headache	Time Disorientation
20 - 30		63.89	72.00	42.22	30.56	25.00
30 - 40		86.05	75.12	43.58	25.58	23.26
above 40		100.00	87.50	62.50	37.50	25.00

(2) The existence of the above health problems are dependent on the age groups of the office workers.

The following cross-classification tabgraph[3] (figure 1) is an attempt to determine if there is a discernible correlation between the common ailments due to IT usage and age.

From figure 1, there appears to be a positive correlation between age and eye strain, age and stress, and age and backache. Such symptoms are much more common among older respondents than the younger ones. However, with respect to headache and disoriented sense of time, the correlation is harder to discern.

(3) The occurrence of the above health problems are dependent on the number of hours spent by an office worker using computers and other IT equipment.

The following cross-classification tabgraph (figure 2) tabulates the correlations between the common ailments due to IT usage and the total length of time respondents spent on IT per week.

From figure 2, it can be seen that except for headache, there is a strong relationship between experiencing health and stress problems with the number of hours spent in front of the computer ie. the longer the number of hours, the more likely such symptoms will occur.

(4) The incidence of stress is dependent on the educational background, gender or job position of the office worker.

There is a commonly held belief that the more highly educated one is, the less stress he/she will experience as far as using computers is concerned.

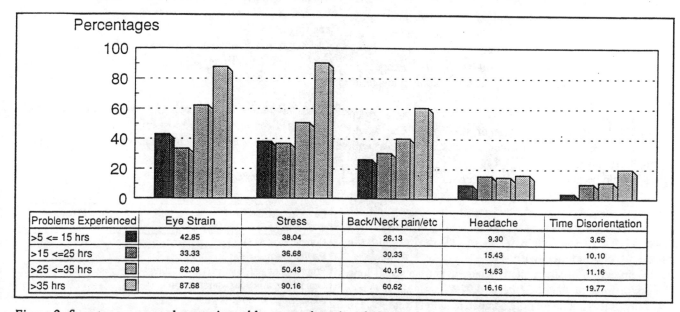

Problems Experienced		Eye Strain	Stress	Back/Neck pain/etc	Headache	Time Disorientation
>5 <= 15 hrs		42.85	38.04	26.13	9.30	3.65
>15 <=25 hrs		33.33	36.68	30.33	15.43	10.10
>25 <=35 hrs		62.08	50.43	40.16	14.63	11.16
>35 hrs		87.68	90.16	60.62	16.16	19.77

Figure 2: Symptoms commonly experienced by respondents in relation to duration of use

Table 3: Correlation of stress with education background

Qualifications	Percentage experiencing stress
'A' Level	84.61%
Diploma	76.47%
Graduates	73.68%
'O' Level	57.89%

From the above findings, the level of education of the respondents appear to have a positive correlation with stress, instead of the negative one that we have proposed earlier on. In fact, only 57.89% of the 'O' level holders reported experiencing stress, compared to 84.81% of the 'A' level holders[4], 73.68% of the graduates, and 76.47% of Diploma holders[5].

One possible reason could be that graduates, 'A' level and diploma holders may be using computers to perform more complex, analytical tasks while 'O' level holders may be using them for low complexity tasks such as word-processing. As a result, the higher task complexity may have raised the incidence of stress reported for the groups of respondents with higher education. Unfortunately, data about the exact type of computer usage was not collected for this study, and hence is unavailable for further analysis.

In addition, there was a common belief that female staff members are usually more prone to stress when using computers than their male counterparts.

Table 4: Correlation of stress with gender

Gender	Percentage experiencing stress
Male	77.27%
Female	67.44%

From table 4, it appears that the percentages of male and female workers who reported experiencing stress are 77.27% and 67.44% respectively. Hence, the data collected in this study do not reflect common belief.

Do people holding high positions experience more stress in using computers than others? From table 5 below, this is found to be inconclusive as professionals (79.55%) and those in clerical and administrative positions (65.71%) appear to experience more stress than respondents holding managerial positions (62.50%).

It is counter-intuitive that the professionals as a group recorded the highest percentage of stress since one would expect that they would be the people that can cope best with computers.

It should be noted that the managerial category of people were rather under-represented in our respondents' profile -- only 9.2%.

(5) The main sources of stress for the office workers are related to the length of use of IT devices and the level of competence with IT.

Main causes of stress cited include having to spend long hours in front of the computer (53.97%), as well as heavy workloads and not being fully competent with IT yet (30.16% each). Table 6 provides the details on various causes of stress.

Table 5: Correlation of stress with position held

Position Held	Percentage experiencing stress
Professional	79.55%
Clerical & Admin	65.71%
Managerial	62.50%

Other causes of stress for the office workers include having to ensure and maintain a high standard of work at the workplace as it is a common belief that IT implies quality. In addition, the office workers find it highly stressful to have to serve so many bosses with so many deadlines, each demanding that his work be done first and each believing that work can be completed at the click of a few buttons.

Table 6: Sources of stress

Reasons	Percentage
Long hours spent in front of the computer	53.97%
Having to prepare loads and loads of documents	30.16%
Not fully competent with IT yet	30.16%
Fear of not being able to catch up with technology	26.98%
Supervisors becoming more demanding	23.81%
Less interaction with colleagues	19.05%
Supervisor having more control over your work	3.17%

(6) The crucial factor affecting IT users' performance and reduction of stress is having adequate knowledge and skills in using computers.

At the rate at which IT development is going, knowledge which one gained 5 years ago would be obsolete by now. In view of such fast pace of development in the IT arena, how does an office worker cope?

The main avenue for coping with IT developments appears to be attending organizational in-house courses (56.32%). Two other ways to cope include keeping up with state-of-the-art IT development by reading relevant periodicals and newspapers (48.28%) as well as through discussions with colleagues (49.43%).

Factors which have an impact on an individual's performance, apart from financial incentives, include environmental (ergonomics) and social factors, as well as attitude and competence.

As can be seen in table 7, being knowledgeable in computer usage has been cited as the most important factor crucial to doing a job well in an IT environment. The other crucial

Table 7: Factors crucial to doing job well in an IT environment

Factors	Total Percentage Points (max=400)
Computer knowledge	378
Facilities for maintenance of data	312
Proper lighting suitable for screen display	300
Opportunity to interact with colleagues	297
Minimal distraction (ie. low noise level)	260
Ability to adjust one's work surface	250

factors found in this study include facilities for maintaining and backing up of data (eg. magnetic tape storage, back-up disks etc.), proper lighting and the opportunity to interact with colleagues. These findings are echoed by the respondents in their solicited open-ended comments.

One respondent commented that organisations should hold seminars on advancements in IT in order to keep staff members informed of the latest developments. Two respondents noted that since they are now so used to the speed and ease with which work can be carried out with the help of IT, they cannot imagine how life would be in a non-IT environment. Interest in IT itself prompted many respondents to stay on in an IT environment. "Without IT, work will be monotonous, tedious, unproductive and less challenging", quoted one male respondent with an 'A' Level qualification. And one respondent noted that "knowing [that] there is more efficient system around and not using it is frustrating." This reflected the respondent's thirst for knowledge on new technologies and the challenges they bring.

Other comments on the open-ended question are concerned with the office's physical equipments. One respondent hoped that more suitable and comfortable chairs will be provided so as to reduce physical fatigue for those who need to work long hours on the workstation. Another respondent mentioned that organisations should constantly upgrade their hardware and software in order to keep pace with technological advancements.

LIMITATIONS AND FUTURE RESEARCH

One of the limitations of this study is its scope. Because of limited resources, only two main areas of the impact of IT are addressed here: the health and stress issues of office workers. Other issues such as the design of the office environment (ergonomics), and the changes in the social and organizational structures are not addressed. Two interesting and potentially rewarding areas to look at, as an extension of this study, are to examine the issues of ergonomics and human factors for the design of a better office environment and to study the ensuing organizational and social changes arising from the introduction of IT.

In addition, one other factor that may affect the health and stress levels of office workers is the nature of the tasks performed by them. The educational background and job position do not necessarily reveal the complexity of the tasks performed by the respondents using IT. Hence, a future study in this area should look at the nature of the task performed by the respondents as a possible correlating factor with stress.

CONCLUSIONS

The use of office automation has been embraced by nearly all the respondents in this study -- more than 90% of the respondents would rather work in an IT environment. IT is advancing at such a fast pace that many respondents felt that it is incumbent on their part to continually keep in touch with technological changes, and the only way that they can gain such ongoing exposure is through working in an IT environment. However, there is a responsibility on the part of the provider of IT to avoid health hazards in the office environment so as to alleviate any potentially adverse effects on the physical and psychological health of the employees.

This study has found that eye strain, stress and back pain are common symptoms of IT users, especially those who work long hours in front of a VDT. In addition, one major source of stress is having to spend long hours in front of the computer. In order to reduce these health problems, users of IT should not work long hours in front of the VDT continuously. Instead, they should take short breaks while doing so. In addition, the correlations between these symptoms and age show that users of IT needs to be educated about the proper use of IT, and they should be given safer and better equipments to handle in the office environment.

In addition, management needs to empower the office worker with knowledge about the computers that are working on in order to reduce their stress level as well as to motivate them to do their job well. This means that continuing IT education for the office workers is a must for these organizations.

This research has pointed out some of the problems associated with the use of IT in the office environment. Management should approach the automated office environment with a proper plan for optimally integrating people, equipment and procedures in the organisation in order to avoid the physical and psychological problems associated with the introduction of IT. While the results of this study may be preliminary, we hope that it will pave the way for other research on the relationship between the office worker's work environment and their health.

REFERENCES

Brad, Craig. *Techno Stress: The Human Cost of the Computer Revolution.* Addison-Wesley, 1984.

Coe, J.B., Cuttle, K., McClellan, W.C., Warden, N.J., and Turner, P.J. *Visual Display_Units report W/1/80.* Wellington, New Zealand Department of Health, 1980.

Cohen, S. "Sound Effects on Behaviour", *Psychology Today.* October 1981.

Dainoff, M.J. and Dainoff, M.H. *A Manager's guide to Ergonomics in the Electronic Office.* John Wiley and Sons, Ltd., 1987.

Dainoff, M.J.; Fraser, L.; and Taylor, B.J. "Visual, Musculoskeletal, and Performance Differences Between Good and Poor VDT Workstation: Preliminary Findings," *Proceedings of the Human Factors Society 26th Annual Meeting,* Santa Monica, Calif., 1982.

Emmanuel, H.M., and Saunders, S. "Plugging into the Open Office." *Today's Office,* June 1983, pp.29-31.

Galitz, W.O. *Humanizing Office Automation: The Impact of Ergonomics on Productivity.* Wellesly, Mass.: QED Information Science Inc, 1984.

Galitz, W.O., and Laska, T.J. "The Computer Operator and His Environment." *Human Factors,* 12, No. 6, 1970, pp. 563-573.

Hirschheim, R.A. *Office Automation - A social and organisational perspective of office work.* John Wiley & Sons Ltd, 1985.

Josefina F.D. *Visual Display Units: Job Content and Stress in Office Work.* International Labour Organisation, 1985.

Neal, E. Boudette. "The New Asbestos?" Industry Week, CCXXXVII, April 3, 1989, pp. 67.

Palvia, S. and Gordon, S. "Trees, Tables, and Formulas in Decision Analysis," Communications of the ACM, October 1992.

Palvia, P. and Palvia, S. "Key Ergonomic Characteristics of Systems Development Techniques," Interfaces, The Computer Education Quarterly, May 1990.

Sox, Charlene W. Introduction to Office Automation, Prentice Hall Inc, (1990).

Springer, T.J. "Emphasize Ergonomics of Office Automation." National Underwriter, September 24, 1982, pp. 376.

ENDNOTES

[1]Acknowledgement: The data for this study is collected by Chee Siew Hong, Lee Hung Ling, and Mike Kew Seng Kiong.

[2]'O' level qualification corresponds to the 10th grade of high school education in the U.S. A.

[3]The term tabgraph was first introduced by Palvia et al (1992). A tabgraph is a combination of a table and a graph to provide maximum utility for diverse users and decision-makers.?

[4]Equivalent to High School diploma in U.S.A.

[5]Equivalent to 2 years of education in a Vocational College after high school.

Survey Sample

A SURVEY ON
THE IMPACT OF INFORMATION TECHNOLOGY

1. Position in organisation:
   - [ ] Clerical & administrative
   - [ ] Managerial
   - [ ] Professional

2. Gender:
   - [ ] Male
   - [ ] Female

3. Age:
   - [ ] Less than 20 years old
   - [ ] Between 21 to 30 years old
   - [ ] Between 31 to 40 years old
   - [ ] More than 40 years old

4. Highest academic achievement:
   - [ ] 'O' Level
   - [ ] 'A' Level
   - [ ] Diploma holder
   - [ ] Graduate

   Others (please specify):_____

5. How many computer programs did you know how to use BEFORE joining your present organisation? (please specify):_____

6. How many do you NOW know? (please specify):_____

7. How many hours each week, on average do you spend on IT- related devices (eg. computers, fax machines) in the office?
   - [ ] Not at all
   - [ ] Less than 5 hours
   - [ ] Between 5 to 15 hours
   - [ ] Between 15 to 25 hours
   - [ ] Between 25 to 35 hours
   - [ ] More than 35 hours

8. Do you take home work to do?
   - [ ] Yes
   - [ ] No

9. How many hours each week, on average do you spend on IT- related devices (eg. computers, fax machines) at home doing office work?
   - [ ] Not at all
   - [ ] Less than an hour
   - [ ] Between 1 to 5 hours
   - [ ] Between 5 to 10 hours
   - [ ] Between 10 to 15 hours
   - [ ] Between 15 to 20 hours
   - [ ] More than 20 hours

10. If you do a lot of work on the computer, do you experience the following?
    - [ ] Disorientated sense of time
    - [ ] Headache
    - [ ] Backache /neck pain /shoulder pain
    - [ ] Eye strain
    - [ ] Stress

    Others (please specify):_____

11. If you experience stress, is it due to any of the following?
    - [ ] Supervisor having more control over your work
    - [ ] Superiors becoming more demanding
    - [ ] Having to prepare loads and loads of documents
    - [ ] Not fully competent yet with IT equipment
    - [ ] Less interaction with colleagues
    - [ ] Long hours spent in front of the computer
    - [ ] Fear of not being able to catch up with technology

    Others (please specify):_____

12. How do you cope with the pace at which IT is developing in your organisation?
    - [ ] Go for special courses on your own initiative eg. Lotus 1-2-3
    - [ ] Read up on IT in periodicals and newspapers
    - [ ] Discuss with colleagues
    - [ ] Attend courses arranged by organisation
    - [ ] Do not bother at all

    Others (please specify):_____

13. How has computerisation affected your productivity?
    - [ ] Reduced significantly
    - [ ] Reduced slightly
    - [ ] No change
    - [ ] Increased slightly
    - [ ] Increased significantly

14. How much weightage would you give to the following factors as crucial to doing your job well in an IT environment? (on a scale of 1 to 5, 1:Least 5:Most)

Minimal distraction (ie. low noise level)
Proper lighting suitable for screen display
Ability to adjust one's work surface
Opportunity to interact with colleagues
Facilities for backing up and maintenance of data
Computer knowledge

15. If given a choice, would you rather work in a non-IT environment?

Yes
No

Why ?_____
_____
_____
_____
_____

16. Please supply any further comments concerning the impact of information technology on your working life.

_____
_____
_____
_____
_____
_____
_____
_____
_____
_____

Optional

_____

If you are prepared to discuss your comments with the researchers, please write your name and contact number below.

_____
_____
_____
_____
_____

WE ARE GRATEFUL FOR YOUR COOPERATION. THANK YOU.

Security and Information Systems
in Latin America: A Pilot Study

Daniel Villarroel, M.I.M.
Area Manager, International Division
Inverness Corporation
17-10 Willow St.
Fair Lawn, NJ 07410
(201) 794-3400

Esther Guthery, Ph.D.
World Business Department
American Graduate School of International Management
15249 N. 59th Avenue
Glendale, AZ 85306-6010
(602) 978-7150

ABSTRACT

This research looks at computer security issues in Latin America. Three different types of companies were surveyed: U.S. Multinational Corporations that have subsidiaries in Latin America, subsidiaries of those same corporations, and domestic companies in Latin America. This pilot study included the following respondents: three U.S. headquarters, three Latin American subsidiaries, and two Latin American domestics. The survey instrument was administered in English, Spanish, or Portuguese. All respondents were MIS directors of their companies. These initial findings show that security of information technology lags slightly behind U.S. standards. Issues addressed by the survey also included who the decision makers are in defining security standards, the importance of political unrest in the decision making process, and importation of security software and hardware.

INTRODUCTION

In this global village where communication links are facilitating commercial transactions, business negotiations, etc., the world finds itself grasping for ways to secure these communications to protect free and fair trade.

Security has evolved from a physical meaning -- safe storage of material and equipment -- to a more technical level involving encryption via algorithms. Today, access to systems by intelligent users utilizing desk-tops, modems, and network systems adds a new dimension to security measures of information systems. Perils facing systems come from both internal and external environmental factors.

The United States and European Community are at the forefront of establishing harmonization of these security standards. In the 1980's, the U.S. and its TCSEC Trusted System Criteria (Orange Book) represented the only formalized system of security controls for confidentiality of information systems installations and programs. Recently, the EC put forth its own proposal for security evaluation, the Information Technology Security Evaluation Criteria (ITSEC), in an attempt to replace individual European national standards by introducing an element of standardization.

Yet, in industrialized countries, the words "computer security" are still often used without a complete understanding of their meaning. And it is these countries -- the ones that are setting the standards -- that have a huge impact on the information systems of developing countries and the "newly industrialized tigers".

In researching information security issues, material about countries other than the U.S. and those in the EC, was virtually non-existent. Given the increased trade with developing countries, it is of vital importance to learn about and discuss the security of their information systems in order to protect and promote free and fair trade. Latin America was chosen for this study because of its recent increased economic importance to U.S. companies and also because it is representative of an area influenced by both U.S. and European policies.

Recent trends in information security will be discussed and the results of questionnaires sent to IS managers in the U.S. and Latin America will be reviewed. Criteria selected for the questionnaires will also be explained.

WHAT IS INFORMATION SECURITY?

The generally accepted definition of information security is the preservation of confidentiality, integrity, and availability of information (Lobel 1986). Information losses are generally said to be from modification, destruction, disclosure and use. In his paper to the IFIP in 1992, Donn P. Parker of SRI International recommends adding authenticity (genuineness, conforming to fact, or correct) and utility (fitness for a purpose) to the definition of information security and replace the loss types with the *inverses* of the definition attributes, e.g., loss of integrity, etc. Since this revision is broader and more fully captures the essence of information security, it is put forth, here, as the definition of information security. (Please note that recent harmonization attempts utilize the "generally accepted" definition of information security.)

We should also keep in mind that while the focus of security is primarily on the protection of data in electronic information systems, a conscious effort should be made to ensure that other forms of information, such as the spoken word and the written word -- including hard copy produced as output from electronic devices -- are not overlooked, as these items can be more vulnerable than electronic data.

Information security is being driven today by technicians

focused on software and hardware development, enhancement and evolution. For example, U.S. President Clinton recently proposed the "Clipper" system as a further development in the encryption of data as opposed to the current Date Encryption Standard (DES) system. DES is a private key system requiring the sender and recipient of an encrypted document to directly and secretly exchange a shared cryptographic key. Equipment using the Clipper, on the other hand, will be issued two keys. One key would go to the end-user, the other would be cut in half and each half held by a (as-of-yet unspecified) government agency in what is called a *key escrow system* database. The purpose of splitting the key is to protect the privacy of Clipper users. By having different agencies store one half of the key, access by a single government worker is remote since the only way to join the split key is under a court warrant.

Security packages offered with most large systems these days provide excellent, sophisticated and (for most people) entirely adequate access control, audit and separation facilities (Smith 1991). Currently, information security tends to be defined more by technology than by training programs for a company's human resources, i.e., it is defined as a "machine problem" as opposed to a "people problem". Because of this tendency toward technical solutions, there remains a widespread ignorance of computer security among non-technical people who generally need to be more familiar on the subject, but are usually overwhelmed by difficult-to-read literature on security.

Therefore, aside from technical approaches to information system security, employees need to be taught security procedures (e.g., care and protection of passwords and/or identity tokens, respect for privacy of marked material, virus alertness, physical care of equipment and media, etc.) to complement technical measures and these procedures also need to be continuously reinforced and updated.

If security issues continue to plague industrialized nations, then we must know how security of information systems is handled in lesser developed countries (LDCs) and developing countries. The *need-to-know* about information security procedures is required to safeguard against the compromising of information systems when conducting business overseas.

WORLDWIDE SECURITY EVALUATION CRITERIA

Security standards are undergoing change given the increased sophistication of computer systems and the need to safeguard these technologies against familiar and/or new threats. However, nationalistic tendencies in the past treated computer security as property of the domestic domain. For example, the "Orange Book" developed at the outset of President Ronald Reagan's anti-Soviet military buildup in the early 1980's, viewed data confidentiality as the sole security concern (Madsen 1992). The Orange Book was designed principally for the evaluation of operating systems used in military systems. Therefore, its application to the evaluation of products such as databases is poor.

The division between the East and West Blocs in the late 1980's brought about increased cooperation between the United Kingdom, Germany, the Netherlands, and France to draft a more standardized and harmonized security evaluation criteria. The result is known as the European Information Technology Security Criteria (ITSEC). The criteria treats integrity, availability, and confidentiality as key components of security evaluation. Furthermore, the ITSEC criteria expand the scope of security beyond operating system security to include networks, electronic data interchange (EDI) and other IT systems. The approach adopted for the production of the ITSEC has been to maintain maximum compatibility with existing work (U.S. Orange Book, German GISA Criteria, etc.) while ensuring flexibility and utility.

Before formal evaluation commences, a Security Target is defined, specifying the security functions of the system or product. The system or product to be evaluated is known as the Target of Evaluation (TOE). Seven evaluation levels (E0 to E6) are defined representing levels of confidence.

The objective of the ITSEC is to create an internationally known procedure for the certification of evaluated products which will provide benefits for both buyers and vendors of secure systems and products. Harmonized criteria will likely lead to improved customer documentation, more secure product distribution methods and better product design. With more emphasis on integrity and availability, the new criteria will be applicable to a wider range of products than was possible under the Orange Book.

With the European incentive serving as a catalyst, the U.S. government plans to replace its guidelines for evaluating the security capabilities of information technology products next year with new criteria that would widen the focus on network and data access products. The new directive, called the Common Criteria, is being developed together with Canada, Europe and Japan and will be submitted to the International Standards Organization (ISO) as the proposed standard. Since all government users must purchase evaluated products to protect security data, the Common Criteria would open an international market in "trusted systems" (Messmer 1993).

ISSUES AFFECTING SECURITY

In the quest to learn what our Latin counterparts are doing to secure their information systems, pertinent issues regarding security affecting Latin America needed to be identified. Since no information exists on this topic, questionnaires were sent to information system managers in Latin America and the United States to learn about various international and external security factors. The questions asked were extrapolated from various worldwide sources of information security. The topics addressed in the instrument included:

· Internal security issues
· External security issues
· Perceptions of comparable processing capabilities and power
· Risk analysis
· Existence of Database Administrator
· Execution of operations-management audits

· Existence of computer security awareness programs
· Access Control Tools and Technology
· Security Policies
· Government Policies Toward Information Protection
· Disaster Recovery Plans

THE RESULTS

Some questions posed to U.S. IS managers were different from those posed to IS managers of U.S. subsidiaries in Latin America. Similarly, some questions asked of IS managers of companies native to their own country (i.e., not a U.S. subsidiary) were slightly different than those asked of their counterparts at U.S. subsidiaries. All questionnaires sent to Latin America were translated into Spanish and Portuguese to allow IS managers to feel comfortable expressing themselves and to allow for maximum comprehension of the requested information.

Most of the U.S. companies had subsidiaries in the larger Latin American countries with potential and/or growing economies: Argentina, Brazil, Chile, Colombia, Venezuela, Mexico, and Panama. These companies represented a broad range of industries: banking, manufacturing, and services. Similarly, the Latin American companies that responded to the questionnaire represented the broad spectrum of industries. All respondents were the MIS directors of their companies.

Respondents to the questionnaires resulted from taking a limited sample of companies procured through the Alumni network of the American Graduate School of International Management. Potential respondents were contacted by telephone and faxed the questionnaire. The categories and numbers of respondents were as follows:

U.S. Headquarters	3
Latin American Subsidiaries	3
Latin American Domestics	2
Total	8

Rankings

Respondents utilized the following scale to rank the importance of system control measures as well as internal and external control measures:

extremely important	important	somewhat important	not important at all
4	3	2	1

The ranked issues and their results were as follows:

	Average	Rank
a. Systems Control measures		
operations systems security	3.63	2
physical security	3.63	2
good password management	3.75	1
encryption	2.50	3

	Average	Rank
b. Internal security issues		
Entry of "bad" data by employees	3.13	3
Destruction of data by employees	3.13	3
Unauthorized access to data/system by employees	3.50	2
Poor control over manual handling of input/output	3.63	1
Inadequate control of media (disks,tapes)	3.63	1

	Average	Rank
c. External security issues		
Access to system by outsiders (hackers, competitors)	3.63	1
Entry into system of viruses, worms	3.63	1
Weak, ineffective, inadequate physical control	3.50	2
Natural Disaster: fire, flood, loss of power, communications	3.38	3
Political unrest that might affect IS operations	2.75	4

An open-ended question was asked of the respondents to gain an idea as to what they felt was the most important internal or external security issue. Therefore, responses were not limited to the above. Two respondents ranked Access control as the most important issue. The other individual responses were:

· Integrity of information
· Efficient Back-up systems
· Communications
· Language Barrier
· Security software not evolving fast enough to meet changing technology (not just a Latin Problem)
· Inadequate control of disks and back-up tapes

Perceptions:

1. · One-third of the U.S. companies perceived that their Latin American subsidiaries had a similar level of processing capability and power as in the U.S.
   · Two-thirds of the Latin American subsidiaries felt they had the same level of processing power as the U.S. head office.
2. · Of those companies with a parent/subsidiary relationship, six out of seven felt confident that the Latin American information systems had the same integrity as in the U.S.
   · One-half of the Latin Domestics felt their systems possess high integrity
3. · Two-thirds of the U.S. companies said the local communication networks in Latin America were as secure as those in the U.S.
   · Two-thirds of the Latin American subsidiaries said they felt their communication networks were secure.
   · Latin American Domestics were asked if they felt their communication networks were properly secured. A Bolivian respondent answered "no", whereas a Colombian respondent said communication networks worked well,

however, they were run by a state monopoly and subject to strikes.

4. · Two-thirds of the U.S. companies were not aware of Risk Analysis done in Latin America. The one company aware of Risk Analysis in Latin America said it was done according to Headquarter's specifications.

· All of the Latin American subsidiary respondents perform Risk Analysis. Two-thirds follow corporate directives, the other follows its own guidelines.

· Both of the Latin American Domestics perform Risk Analysis. One indigenous company responded saying its risk analysis was influenced by German, Swiss and Japanese procedures. The other said they perform risk analysis without any influence from outside entities.

5. All respondents except one Latin American subsidiary said there are Computer Awareness Programs in Latin America.

· Two-thirds of the U.S. companies said these programs are available for Latin IT employees only. The other programs are directed to all employees.

· One Latin American subsidiary said its programs were directed to all employees. The other explained that different programs were directed to different employees.

· Both Latin American Domestics said Computer Awareness Programs were only directed to IT personnel.

6. Security Policy:

· Two-thirds of the U.S. companies said their Latin American subsidiaries followed corporate directives. One said the Latins designed their own.

· Each Latin American subsidiary responded differently. One each said:

  - they designed the policy by themselves
  - they worked with headquarters to design a policy
  - they followed corporate directives

· As for the Latin American Domestics, one said it determined its own policy without help from other (international) entities, whereas the other said it relied on other entities for assistance

7. Selecting Access Control Tools and Technology:

· Two-thirds of the U.S. companies said the Latin American subsidiaries follow corporate recommendations and directives. The other said it was a combination of working with headquarters to determine policy, but usually with more guidance from corporate recommendations.

· Two-thirds of the Latin American Subsidiaries said they follow corporate recommendations. The other said corporate recommendations are taken into consideration, but the design of the plan is up to the subsidiary.

· One indigenous company said it received assistance from international entities. The other said it worked alone.

8. Five-sevenths said the local government does not interfere with the transborder flow of information. Six-eighths said the government does not interfere with the import of technology necessary for security of information systems.

9. All respondents said that Disaster Recovery Plans are in place in Latin America.

· Two-thirds of the U.S. companies said plans were de-

signed by headquarters.

· One-third of the Latin American subsidiaries said they followed headquarter's directives.

· One Latin American Domestic said it designed its own plan without outside (international) assistance. The other said it relied on international entities for guidance.

10. Six-eighths said audits of operations-management are executed.

11. Seven-eighths of the respondents said they use a Database Administrator.

ANALYSIS

Although only a small sample was utilized, the results still proved to be intriguing and are believed to be representative of Latin America. Security of IT, in general, lags slightly behind U.S. standards. Also, companies in Latin America that have been developing economically at a faster pace than their neighbors felt more confident about their information security. Most large MNCs with Latin subsidiaries generally had strong IT security procedures in place, however, there were a few surprising responses.

For example, encryption of data has been an important topic lately given the Clinton Clipper system announcement. It is the bias of the authors that it should have more importance in transborder data flow because information can be compromised during transmission. Yet, it was not ranked as having high importance in this survey. Nevertheless, respondents with a parent/subsidiary relationship felt their systems possessed high security and integrity with equal processing capability and power to headquarters.

Political unrest was another surprising answer. Ranked lowest as an external issue, one respondent said their communication network was subject to strikes because it was a state monopoly. However, it should be noted that this response came from a Latin American Domestic which may not have the same financial resources as a U.S. subsidiary to secure its information systems.

One question not addressed by this study was that of language barriers. It is overwhelmingly recommended that this question be asked in future studies. Two U.S. respondents mentioned "communications" and language barriers as the most important security concerns. This has implications not only on subsidiaries following and understanding corporate directives in implementing established (i.e., written) security procedures, but also on effectively communicating data so as to reduce errors due to language barriers. Lack of foreign language comprehension may encourage the use of external (to the company) language translation services which may affect accuracy of information and defeat the purpose of having security policies in the first place.

There were a few questions where companies were asked if they worked on a certain issue alone or in tandem with their subsidiary or headquarters. In regard to the overall implementation of security policies only one out of all Latin subsidiaries said they worked with headquarters to establish jointly defined policies. Either subsidiaries followed corporate recommendations or headquarters allowed subsidiaries to establish their own policies. A similar response was given to the question of selecting Access Control Tools and Technology.

Disaster recovery plans were defined by everyone. However, of those with a parent/subsidiary relationship, no one said these plans were implemented as part of a joint effort.

From the examples of overall security policies, access control tools, and disaster recovery plans, it can be determined that companies are not communicating effectively to implement security standards that are beneficial to all parties. Most companies require their subsidiaries to strictly follow headquarter's protocol without taking local conditions into account. Others go to the other extreme and direct subsidiaries to implement security policies, but let the subsidiary pursue its own plan. A better understanding of each other's operation is required and jointly devised programs will, no doubt, instill confidence in data transmissions and integrity.

It is noteworthy to point out that some countries still have problems with the transmission of data beyond their borders and importation of security software and hardware due to government regulations. There was one response which specifically pointed out that the exportation of information was still a problem in Brazil, a country which still has strict import/export rules to protect its industries. As was reiterated through the NAFTA debate, those countries which seek protectionist policies negatively affect their economies and the latest news from Brazil still shows it in economic difficulties.

Latin American Domestics realize the importance of information security. It was surprising to note that one worked with countries other than the U.S. to implement security policies. While Latin American Domestics maintain themselves informed of security trends, it appears they lag slightly behind Latin American subsidiaries.

RECOMMENDATIONS FOR FUTURE STUDIES

This being a preliminary research effort, questionnaires were designed in an open-ended manner to solicit as much information as possible to allow for feedback from the pilot study to influence and help design future studies. The following are recommendations for the future:

1. Quantify questionnaires to allow for greater statistical analysis. Questions should be "closed" as opposed to "open-ended". A "comments" section should be added to the end of the survey to allow respondents to add any further thoughts.
2. Add a question as to the type of computer systems utilized: microcomputers, mainframes, networks. Also a question on the types of networks available should be included.
3. Split up the study. One survey should examine headquarters and subsidiary security procedures. The other should examine policies of companies indigenous to Latin America.
4. In whatever questions possible, request information about how the procedure is implemented (headquarters, locally, joint effort, etc.).
5. All companies refused to divulge their Risk Analysis procedures. Instead of an open-ended question asking what is done, probing questions should be asked (e.g., Are security systems checked internally by IT personnel or externally by other entities?).
6. A listing of Latin American countries should be given on the survey for U.S. companies to allow them to check-off countries for expediency in completing the questionnaire and for more accuracy in determining in which countries these companies are actively involved.
7. When asking the question of political unrest, the question should be rephrased to ask about the respondent's perceptions of political implications vis-à-vis its impact on information systems.
8. Utilize new data gathered from open-ended questions to ask new ones, e.g.: To what degree do language barriers affect your operations? (high impact, medium impact, low impact, no impact)

REFERENCES

Cash, James I.; F. Warren McFarlan; James L. McKenney; Lynda M. Applegate. *Corporate Information Systems Management: Text and Cases*, 3rd ed, 1992.

Davies, Donald W. "Information Security -- Theory and Practice." *Information Security*, D.T. Lindsay and W.L. Price, eds., 1991.

Eloff, Jan H.P. "Selection Process for Security Packages." *Computer Security: A Global Challenge*, J.J. Finch and E.G. Dougall, eds., 1985.

Janczewski, L.J., "Data Security Model for Branch Offices of Big Organizations." *IT Security: The Need for International Cooperation*, G.G. Gable and W.J. Caelli, eds., 1992

Lobel, Jerome. *Foiling the Systems Breakers*, 1986.

Loch, Karen D.; Houston H. Carr, and Merrill E. Warkentin. "Threats to Information Systems: Today's Reality, Yesterday's Understanding." *MIS Quarterly*, June 1992, pp. 173-186.

Madsen, Wayne. "International Information Technology (IT) Security Cooperation into the 21st Century." *IT Security: The Need for International Cooperation*, G.G. Gable and W.J. Caelli, eds., 1992.

Messmer, Ellen. "U.S. Government Seeks New Global Security Guidelines." *Network World*, September 6, 1993.

McLean, Kevin. "Information Security Awareness -- Selling the Cause." *IT Security: The Need for International Cooperation*, G.G. Gable and W.J. Caelli, eds., 1992.

Nash, Michael; David Brewer; Bernard Chorley; Richard Lampard; and Fiona Williams. "Criteria, Evaluation and the International Environment: Where Have We Been, Where Are We Going?" *Information Security* D.T. Lindsay and W.L. Price, eds., 1991.

Parker, Donn B. "Restating the Foundation of Information Security." *IT Security: The Need for International Cooperation*, G.G. Gable and W.J. Caelli, eds., 1992.

Salamone, Salvatore. "Clinton's Clipper: Can It Keep a Secret?" *Data Communications*, August 1993, p. 53.

Smith, M.R., Squadron Leader MBE BSc RAF. "Creating and Maintaining the Corporate." 1991.

Straw, Julian. "Commercial Evaluation and the Information Technology Security Evaluation Criteria." 1991.

Taggart, M. *Information Systems, An Introduction to Computers in Organizations*, 1986.

Van Tongeren, H. "Information Security in the Framework of the International Data Flow." *Computer Security*, J.B. Grimson and H.J. Kugler, eds., 1985.

Section Five

European Issues of Information Management

BeMI: A Method for Information Policy Formulation

Jacques S.K.Th. Boersma
Department of Information and Organization
Faculty of Management and Organization
University of Groningen
P.O. Box 800
9700 AV Groningen
The Netherlands
Phone: +31-50-633857
Fax: +31-50-633850
E-mail: S.K.Th.Boersma@bdk.rug.nl

Robert A. Stegwee
Information Systems Center
Martini Hospital
P.O. Box 30034
9700 RM Groningen
The Netherlands
Phone: +31-50-245095
Fax: +31-50-246047
E-mail: R.A.Stegwee@bdk.rug.nl

ABSTRACT

Most current methods for information systems planning are portrayed as methods for strategic planning with respect to information systems support within an organization. The tactical and operational planning levels are occupied by such activities as Business Area Analysis and Business Systems Design. In this paper we argue that most current methods for information systems planning are unsuitable for the requirements of a truly strategic planning process, involving top-managers from all functional areas. As an alternative, we propose to differentiate between information policy and information planning. From the mid-eighties onward, we have developed a comprehensive model and method for information policy formulation, termed BeMI (pronounce "bay-me"). After discussing the rationale for developing a method for information policy formulation, the BeMI method will be presented, as well as some example information policy statements taken from the application of BeMI in a hospital environment.

1. INTRODUCTION

Much has been said and written about strategic information systems planning, information strategy planning, and other forms of strategic planning with respect to the provision of information systems support for an organization. However, most of the methods developed for this purpose adhere to the traditional division made by the Information Engineering school of methods, which positions all information planning activities at the strategic level. The tactical and operational levels are occupied by such activities as Business Area Analysis and Business Systems Design. In this paper we argue that most current methods for strategic planning for information systems support are unsuitable for the requirements of a truly strategic planning process, involving top-managers from all functional areas. Hence, the ever recurring outcry by information managers for top-management support and for linkage between business strategy and information management.

As an alternative, we propose to differentiate between information policy and information planning. An analysis of planning literature will demonstrate the need for this differ-

entiation and will argue that most current methods should be positioned at a tactical information planning level, rather than at the strategic information policy level. As a consequence, information planning should ideally be preceded by information policy formulation. However, methods for information policy formulation are not very well-known. From the mid-eighties onward, we have developed a comprehensive model and method for information policy formulation, termed BeMI (pronounce "bay-me") (Boersma & Hopstaken, 1984; Boersma, 1988; Boersma, 1993). This method is rooted in a number of fundamental premises about organizations and organizational behavior, which differ substantially from the views underlying common methods for information planning. In our experience with the BeMI method, it works quite well, both as a means to interact with top-management on information issues and as a carrier for strategic guidance for the information planning process.

This paper is structured along the following lines. The following paragraph is devoted to a justification of our fundamental critique of current methods for information planning not being strategic. In providing this justification, the basic premises of our research are outlined as well. The end of paragraph 2 presents a definition of (information) policy and planning, focusing on their differences and the way they influence each other. In paragraph 3, the BeMI model for information policy formulation is presented. In order to illustrate the model, examples of information policy statements are presented in paragraph 4. These examples are taken from a hospital environment, in which we applied both BeMI model and method. Finally, paragraph 5 provides some conclusions and indications of on-going research in this field.

2. BACKGROUND

A short excursion into the general field of planning, combined with an overview of information planning definitions, will render an understanding of the need for a distinct set of models and methods to be used in strategic planning with respect to the provision of information systems support. It will therefore clarify the distinction made by us between information policy formulation and information planning.

2.1 Perceptions of planning

This section is devoted to a brief discussion of ideas on the subject of planning. By no means does it claim to be comprehensive; actually, a few specific ideas have been adopted in order to show the necessity of differentiating between distinct levels of planning with respect to information technology application and information systems support within an organization. In his note on planning, Mintzberg coins four definitions of planning, in order to provide a basis for research in planning as part of managerial work (Mintzberg, 1981). These four definitions comprise:
- planning as future thinking,
- planning as integrated decision making,
- planning as formalized procedure and articulated result, and
- planning as programming.

Although Mintzberg himself finds neither of these definitions fully adequate to describe planning as part of managerial work, a similarity can be found with the different levels of planning. It seems the four definitions follow the lines of strategic, tactical and operational planning quite well. Planning at the different levels can be described as follows:
- future thinking with the objective to coordinate decision making belongs to the strategic planning level;
- the process to make and coordinate decisions, using formal procedures and producing articulate results belongs to the tactical planning level;
- the operational planning level consists of programming business activity in such a way as to achieve the goals specified at the tactical level.

These views on planning indicate a resemblance with the distinction between unstructured, semistructured and well structured problems, presented by Boersma (1989, p.19). Moreover, as this distinction has been related to Simon's model of decision making, one can do the same here. Planning as future thinking relies heavily on the intelligence activity of a decision maker and can hence be positioned at a strategic level. A process to make and coordinate decisions using formal procedures and articulate results seems to indicate a focus on the design phase of a decision making process. Finally, programmed decisions focus on the choice phase and must deal with well structured problems. These resemblances are far from perfect, but they provide a general indication of the types of decision making problems to be dealt with at different levels of planning.

In the context of this research these notions of planning have to be applied with respect to information technology application and information systems support for an organization.

2.2 Perceptions of information planning

The number of names used for information planning methods, a couple of which were mentioned in the introduction, indicates the multitude of views and definitions of information planning. Lederer and Sethi define the purpose of information planning, in a fairly restricted sense, as "to identify the most appropriate targets for automation and to schedule their installation" (Lederer & Sethi, 1988, p. 445). This focus on computer based information systems is not uncommon, although Olle explicitly alters his scope of information systems when addressing information systems planning: "The concept of an information system at the information systems planning stage is both broader and less well formed than it will be later in the design process. At this point, no decision has been taken as to whether the information system (or which parts of it) will be given automated support. The general concept is that of a business information system." (Olle et al., 1988, p. 208). This is also the perception used throughout this paper. Information planning has to do with the design of information systems support for an organization. Information systems support contains both the computer based information systems and the manual data processing systems in an organization (Stegwee, 1992).

Comparative studies of methods for information planning try to categorize within the field of information planning. For example, Theeuwes differentiates between
- information strategy planning,
- information architecture planning, and
- information project planning,

based upon the level of planning (compare strategic, tactical, and operational levels) (Theeuwes, 1988, p. 26). Information planning itself is then defined as an overall concept covering the activities to integrate these three elements. Within the three elements, a distinction is made as to planning horizon and planning aspect. Not very often is the distinction made between planning levels, when referring to information planning. Van Waes (1991) refers to "the Dutch school" in defining information management, which includes separate subtasks such as information policy formulation and information planning.

In general, most information planning methods will claim to be positioned at the strategic level. As such, top management involvement is usually stressed by such methods. However, research reports that over 50% of the companies indicated difficulties in securing top management commitment as an extreme or major problem with respect to information planning (Lederer and Sethi, 1988, p. 454). This is hardly surprising, as the level of detail of the models, and the model representations, are very far from the level of concern of top management. Therefore, the distinction between strategic and tactical planning levels is important. Different methods have to be used in information policy formulation (being our terminology for strategic planning of information systems support) and information planning (when defined as tactical planning), as will follow from the discussion of planning in the next section.

2.3 Integration of perceptions

Now it is time to compare Mintzberg's perceptions of planning, as described above, with the perceptions of information planning. Future thinking with the objective to coordinate decision making, being part of strategic planning, can not be governed by formal procedures and pre-defined results, as given by traditional methods for information planning, such as Business Systems Planning or methods from the Information Engineering school of thought. This forms the basis of our argument for a distinction between information policy formulation and information planning. Mintzberg points out that more strict definitions of planning, as given by his last two notions of planning, lead to the conclusion that "planners and planning find their roles more on either side of the strategy making process than at its centre" (Mintzberg, 1981, p. 323). Less formal procedures are necessary to aid in the process of information policy formulation.

Information planning, as advocated by current theory and practice, compares well to the planning definition at the tactical level. Methods for information planning constitute a detailed set of guidelines on the steps to take (see e.g. IBM, 1984; Arthur Young, 1988; Aarts & Janssen, 1989). Moreover, they describe in detail the deliverables of the various phases in an information planning process. As such they meet the requirements of formal procedures and articulated results. Also, information planning constitutes a way of making and coordinating decisions. The deliverables of an information planning project require certain decisions to be made with respect to information technology application and information systems support within an organization. Meanwhile, the scope of a typical information planning project, combined with the various models to be specified for the future, stimulate the coordination of decisions within several distinct fields.

The above description leaves only the operational level of planning to be discussed. Theeuwes (1988) positions traditional systems development methods at this level, which is also indicated by Greveling (1990) who discerns development of information systems support as the operational level planning activity. However, from the definition given above, operational planning has to do more than just realize the information systems as described in the information plan. In the next section we will distinguish between the content of a plan and the implementation of a plan. This implementation itself has to be planned, which is the essence of operational planning when executing a tactical plan. As the core of an information plan is formed by an architecture of information systems, portraying the desired situation, the implementation plan contains the migration path necessary to reach this desired situation.

In the general framework for information planning methods, as depicted in figure 1, the migration from current to desired situation is covered by the specification of a transition path and policy statements, resulting in an information plan. This shows that most information planning methods attempt to cover the range from strategic planning all the way down to operational planning. However, the procedures and techniques used at the different levels vary enormously, as do the

decision makers to be involved. When looking at the content of information planning methods, most emphasis is given to the tactical level, and few guidelines are given for neither the strategic planning level, nor for the specification of a transition path, being the principal ingredient of the operational planning level. The BeMI method attempts to provide guidelines for the strategic planning level with respect to the application of information technology and the development of information systems support. Methods that will cater to the needs of more operationally oriented information planning will not be discussed in this paper.

2.4 Information policy formulation and information planning

Above, we have used the term information policy formulation in conjunction with the term information planning. Information policy formulation has been used to indicate strategic planning with respect to the development of information systems support, whereas information planning has been positioned at the tactical level. However, this does not provide insight into the differences in content of both processes. For a more detailed definition it therefore seems useful to consult literature concerning the terms policy and planning in their general context. Studies devoted to these topics conclude, however, that a "jungle of approaches" exists when discussing policy and planning concepts and that in general the search for an analysis of the differences and the comparison between the terms planning and policy will be in vain. Some of the reasons for this chaos in the terminology are that the definition depends to a high degree on the discipline, on the type of organization, and on the (historical) point in time when the term is used. In order to dodge this broad analysis, definitions have been looked for that distinguish policy from planning, but do consider them to be closely related. The general framework used here is depicted in figure 2.

Policy formulation concerns the essential conditions that have to be taken into account during the planning process and the implementation of the plan. A policy indicates fundamental choices of the management and can be considered as a vision which other decision making processes should respect. Recall, in this context, the notion of future thinking with the objective to coordinate decision making, which has been positioned at the strategic level of decision making. Policy can best be described as:

a framework of statements which provides guidance for the planning process and the implementation of a plan.

The term framework indicates the foundation on which the building rests. Policy is the foundation in the form of statements by the management (e.g. the board of directors) that should be seen as directive by all members of the organization. Depending on the (functional) area of discourse, the term policy is augmented by an adjective: human resource policy, financial policy, information policy, etcetera. Following this definition, the term information policy means:

Figure 1: General framework for information planning methods, as presented by Stegwee and Van Waes (1990).

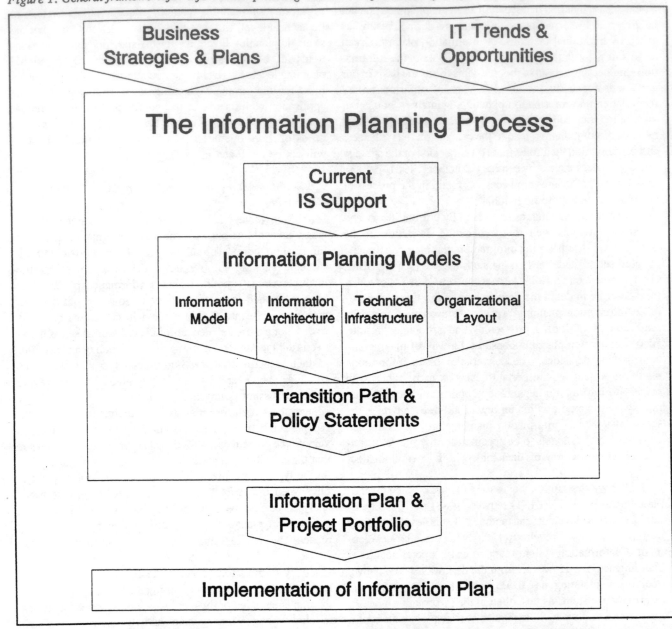

a framework of statements that provides guidance for the information planning process and the implementation of the information plan.

Planning can be seen as a subset of the collection of decision making processes (Bosman, 1984). Specifically, we have earlier used the notion of "the process to make and coordinate decisions, using formal procedures and producing articulated results". According to this conception, planning is a decision making process aiming at the specification of the contents of a plan. Depending on the area of application, the term planning is provided with an adjective, such as personnel planning, financial planning, material requirements planning, information planning, etcetera.

In addition to the contents of a plan we recognize the implementation of a plan. Implementation is a new decision making process that refers to the activities to be executed, the points in time and the resources to be used, as well as the organizational structure employed to realize the plan. In the literature terms such as activity planning, scheduling and network planning are used for such implementation problems. Misunderstandings when using the word planning can therefore be expected. In this paper the term planning is used for the process needed to obtain the contents of a plan. Although determination of these contents and the implementation of the plan should be seen as two separate decision making processes, there is a connection. It would seem very unrealistic to determine the contents of a plan without considering the possibilities to implement and realize the plan. The planning process would result in a "blue sky approach", if

Figure 2: Framework for policy formulation and planning

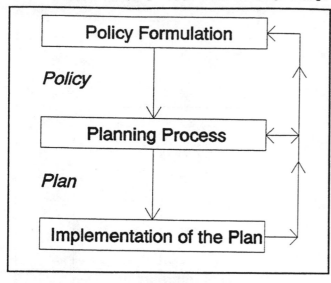

the possibilities for realization would not be taken into consideration.

In agreement with the description of the term planning, information planning is defined as:

the (articulation of a) decision making process aiming at the specification of an information plan, which is to be used as the basis for the development of information systems support as specified by the plan.

The core of an information plan is formed by an architecture of the future information systems support covering the following aspects of the problem formulation: the information aspect, the systems aspect, the technical aspect and the organizational aspect (Stegwee & Van Waes, 1990). In the implementation plan the transition path, among others, is portrayed in order to reach the desired situation. Additionally, statements are made about the necessary input of people and means during the course of the transition.

3. THE BEMI MODEL

It was mentioned earlier that the information policy contains statements made by the top management which refer to the desired information systems support for the organization. These statements should take into account the problems which arise with the development of information systems support, as well as the opportunities that they offer to the organization, the so-called innovation aspect. Possible opportunities that can be thought of are the improved ability to react to external changes through so-called strategic information systems, but also improved coordination. Based in part on these arguments, important relations exist between the information policy on the one hand and the strategic, the organizational, and the resource policies on the other. (Boersma & Hopstaken, 1984; Boersma, 1988, and 1989). These relations are expressed in figure 3. This figure also shows the relation with the information plan and the implementation plan.

The arrows in figure 3 indicate relations in the form of processes: the rectangles indicate the results of these processes. The rectangle 'information policy' is the result of a complex (decision making) process at a high level in the organization where strategic, organizational, and resource problems are discussed, in close coordination with problems in the field of information systems support.

Strategic policy refers to the determination of the (future) goals of an organization as a whole, in terms of the nature and the level of the intended service to the (business) community social, as well as the choice of corresponding approaches toward their implementation. From this description, strategy emerges as a choice of goals and the main approaches of implementation together.

Each organization is characterized by a specific task environment, i.e. by a number of relations with the environment which are specific for the organization. Although it is generally difficult to determine these relations, and especially their influence, a more or less continuous survey and analysis of the environment is important. Such analyses are necessary in relation to the determination or the revision of the goals and for determining the best possible ways of realizing of these goals. Based on an environmental analysis and on knowledge concerning the opportunities of the organization itself, the strategic policy of the organization can be developed. In such a policy, using an integral approach, societal, financial, social, commercial, and technological aspects are discussed, as well as the strategies directed at these aspects.

Organizational policy, among others, aims at the division of functional areas, the coordination and integration of these areas and the extent of (de)centralization of an organization. The policy is realized through organizational structures and procedures. The *resource policy* refers the policy for the use of human resources, financial resources, and technical means.

The rectangle 'information plan' in figure 3 is the result of a decision making process where the information policy is used as a framework. While determining the information policy is a strategic problem for the organization, information planning is seen as a decision making process at the tactical level of the organization. The implementation of the information plan, which can be said to include the development of subsystems, is performed at the operational level.

Figure 3 differs from the usual conceptions, which state that the information policy should be derived directly from the general or strategic policy of an organization. A linear relationship assumes that general policy is present in every organization and that it can be used as a starting point for information policy formulation. In some cases information policy is not considered to be necessary until the developments on the hardware-level require it. A well known example is the purchase of PC's, which is often hard to control. In the case of explosive growth in the number of PC's the financial resource policy will demand an automation policy, which in turn can lead to information policy. In turn, the demand for information policy can lead to impulses for

Figure 3: The place of information policy and information plan in relation to each other and amidst other policy fields.

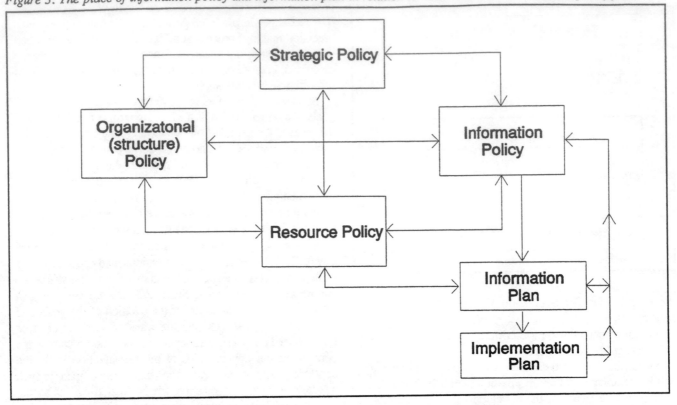

strategic and/or organizational policy formulation. This bottom-up development is one possibility of an urge to formulate information policy and strategic policy.

In contrast to the linear model, figure 3 also indicates that information policy is dependent upon other connections. The figure can be compared with a so-called mobile, a construction of thin iron rods that are set in motion by air currents. When one part starts to move, all other parts will move as well. Correspondingly, this means that a change in one of the policy fields indicated in figure 3 will have consequences for the other fields. It is beyond the scope of this paper to describe all relationships in detail. Please refer to Boersma (1993) for an extensive treatment of these relationships. However, one should bear in mind that the following relationships are essential for a balanced information policy:

- the relationship between strategic policy and information policy,
- the relationship between organizational policy and information policy, and
- the relationship between resource policy and information policy, which can be broken down into relationships with human resource policy, financial resource policy, and technical means policy.

Above, we have used the BeMI model to indicate the subject areas which can be addressed in the information policy of an organization. For each area, a list of issues can be given. However, such a list will never be complete, due to the diversity of organizations. Issues that are crucial to one organization may be irrelevant in a different setting. For example, security and backup systems are of vital importance to airlines

and travel agencies, as their reservation systems are at the core of their operations. These systems are of strategic importance and their availability must be guaranteed. Such issues must be addressed in an information policy. Depending upon the organization certain issues will be added or stressed, while other issues identified on the basis of the BeMI model may have no relevance in a particular situation.

4. AN EXAMPLE FROM A HOSPITAL ENVIRONMENT

Health-care institutions in the Netherlands have faced a major revolution with respect to the way they are being financed. Two elements take up a central position concerning the budget system, namely cost limitation and room for local policy. The element of cost limitation results in the government coming to agreements with individual institutions about cost development, using the budget system. As a result, the government has better control over the cost of health-care at a macro-level. Room for local policy means that institutions can, to a certain extent, determine the distribution of financial resources over the various tasks and the related cost types, with the exception of interest, depreciation and maintenance. Due to the possibility of substitution, an institution can, more than before, distribute the financial means according to their own priorities.

Aside from the introduction of budget financing, the health-care field has been struck, over the last years, with severe budget cuts. With an equal or lower budget, the institutions have to carry out the same, or sometimes even more tasks than before. Hospitals should also consider the changes in finance methods as a result of shifting from specialist intramural health-care to extramural and preventive care. In mental health-care a gradual shift is taking place from a long-term stay of patients to a shorter stay and day-care.

4.1 Relationship between strategic policy and information policy

The external developments mentioned above give rise to several problems for the internal functioning of the institutions. We name three of them:

1.the internal control problem

The role of management changes as a result of the increased emphasis on the responsibility of the institutions for spending a determined budget. Internal budgeting is in some hospitals the result of the external budgeting;

2.the planning problem

The decision problem of the size and contents of the task package (substitution and reallocation) is diverted to the institutions to a higher degree than before.

3.the distribution problem

The complexity of the decision problem of the internal distribution of the budget is increased as a result of the diversity of interests.

An example of the changing role of the management is that in the "old" finance system the decisions were more or less made by the doctors. Their decisions to carry out an operation or to provide certain treatment were automatically translated into costs, as the output of the doctors was the basis for financing the institution. The economic decision was limited to the registration of the consequences in terms of cost of the use of production factors in the medical field. Simply put: the "economist" was a bookkeeper. In the new way of financing, on the other hand, two decision circuits (see figure 4) become mutually dependent. The fixed budget, the input standardization, indicates the borders within which the medical decisions have to take place.

Due to the fact that hospitals today have more degrees of freedom concerning the spending of resources, organizational measures have become necessary. More attention for strategic, financial, social and informational problems are examples of this. Within health-care organizations change processes should be set in motion to accomplish this. A broad basis is essential in order to be able to support the changes.

Information systems are, more than before, necessary to support planning, control, and execution. Financial systems which are limited to bookkeeping are insufficient for input standardization. Examples of information systems to support the three problems mentioned on the above are:

- an internal budgeting system as part of the financial information system and corresponding to the external budgeting;
- a planning system with the goal to calculate substitution effects, including the effects of alternative treatment structures and estimation of the consequences of introducing new tasks;

- an employee allocation system with the goal to calculate various strategies with respect to the distribution of human resources across functions.

We place health-care organizations in the "turn-around" cell in McFarlan and McKenney's strategic grid, implying that current IT applications are not of strategic value, whereas future systems are (McFarlan & McKenney, 1983). Whether the hospital management shares this thought is doubtful, nor does it come forward in the (information systems) literature for health-care, which is lagging behind on the strategic perspective. This literature hardly pays any attention to information systems which improve the effectiveness of the decision making process. In practice, most of the IS budget is devoted to providing registrative systems, which cater to the needs administrative personnel and external institutions. For example, an information system for personnel planning has recently been realized at a group of dutch hospitals, but this system only takes care of the registrative tasks. It is deemed a success by its users, because it relieves many people of a whole lot of paperwork. However, it is doubtful whether hospital management should be very happy with this system, as it does not tackle the issue of effective deployment of personnel, one of the key cost drivers in the hospital.

This very short indication of the strategic issues facing health-care organizations in the Netherlands provide the basis for the following examples of information policy statements that could be developed in an information policy formulation process.

Information Policy Statement 1

The government imposed system of external budgeting, striving for cost control, efficiency improvement as well as deregulation and freedom of funds distribution, requires information systems to support hospital management in realizing these goals. The PAMIS system is an example of such an information system (see Boersma, 1989).

Clarification of statement 1

For the realization of cost control it is necessary that hospital management, responsible for the strategic policy of a hospital, determines the planned activities and the relating costs (the planning elements) for a certain period. During this period management should have timely information on key indicators available in order to be able to react to deviations between reality and the expected (the control element). The information system to be used for this purpose is commonly referred to as an internal budgeting system. Some reasons for the implementation of an internal budgeting system are:

-due to the disappearance of the old form of government financing, there no longer is an external system for cost control; and because of the budget cuts imposed, a substitute system is desperately needed;

-the need to have a system for the distribution of financial means;

-to highlight strategic choices and priorities;

Figure 4: Relations between medical and economical decisions in a situation of output standardization and input standardization respectively (see also: Van der Meer and Van Montfort, 1985).

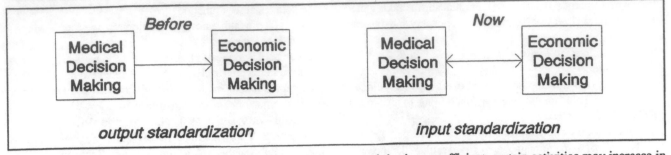

-to have a means of planning the activities throughout the hospital and to be able to account for their realization.

For the fulfillment of the second goal mentioned for external budgeting, i.e. efficiency improvement, other information systems are required than the usual registrative systems which do not contain data about the work processes themselves, except for financial data. The following policy statement is devoted to this issue.

Information Policy Statement 2

In order to gain an insight into the budgeted versus the actual spending of means, in relation to the appropriateness of historically developed situations, information systems are necessary which gather data about the cost drivers of current work processes. Only research into the relation between means and processes will enable management to redirect inappropriate spending. Only then will changes be possible to maintain or improve the quality of care, given the decreasing external budget.

Clarification of statement 2

Current financial systems in hospitals are based on the demands placed on the publication of yearly statements by the Dutch Hospital Board. The data required for producing these yearly statements are processed periodically according to a prescribed system of accounting rules. The resulting figures are comparative indicators with respect to the prevailing budget and with previous years. However, they do not offer any information for obtaining an insight into the *necessary* cost of work processes.

As was portrayed in the introduction to this section, health-care has two important strategic elements in the field of financial management: cost control and local discretion with respect to distribution of funds. External budgets are assigned to hospitals with a certain amount of room for local prioritization. Budget financing thus requires management to obtain information with respect to:

a.insight into the distribution of means and expenditures across the various possible purposes, as a result of which alternatives may surface;

b.insight into the actual amount of spending for the various purposes;

A remark is in order here: information about total cost per

activity is not sufficient: certain activities may increase in volume due to an increased number of patients with a clinical diagnosis corresponding to these activities. Hence the number of patients with a certain diagnosis directly influence the amount of spending on their companion activities.

c.meeting the legal requirements relating to the provision of information to external health-care authorities.

4.2 Relationship between organizational policy and information policy

Hospitals can be categorized as so-called professional bureaucracies in terms of Mintzberg's typology of organizations. This, among others, implies the following characteristics:

- the operating core is the most important component in the organization;
- the most important coordination mechanism is standardization of skills and the related design parameters training and indoctrination;
- a result of the importance of the necessary professionalism is decentralization of decision making:

"horizontal decentralization: power to the experts (...) by virtue of their knowledge" and:

"the more professional an organization, the more decentralized its structure in both dimensions" (Mintzberg, 1979).

Beside the main structure of the professional bureaucracy, a second structure often develops. This second structure consists of the support staff of the professional bureaucracy. This part of the organization provides support services, such as finance and administration, human resources, and the technical services.

This description of hospitals in terms of Mintzberg's configurations, gives rise to a number of information policy statements with respect to the relationship between organizational policy and information policy. One such statement is elaborated here.

Information Policy Statement 3

It is necessary that the hospital's top-management indicates the way in which in the development of information systems support is to take place.

Clarification of Statement 3

Organizations with a high degree of decentralization tend to run the risk that various organizational units will follow their own course in the development of information systems support. For organizational, economical, and technical reasons, standards should be set that apply to all these developments. The topics of standardization are hardware, software, methods, and organization.

The path to be followed in the development of information systems support will generally comprise the following steps:

- developing an information systems plan that outlines the major information systems areas;
- choosing a systems development method for every single information systems area;
- devising methods and techniques to control the systems development activities;
- setting the criteria to be used in the evaluation of alternative hardware and/or software solutions.

Only top-management of a hospital can sanction such an imposed path for developing information systems support and it's accompanying standards for the whole organization. However, it is important that the benefits of such an approach are explained to the members of the organization.

4.3 Relationship between resource policy and information policy

Information Policy Statement 4

Management should determine the annual financial budget available for new developments, in accordance with their wishes with respect to the pace of information systems introduction in the organization.

Clarification of Statement 4

The financial means in hospitals will not be of such proportions, that means can be allocated for information systems development without redistribution of funds. This complication demands that management considers and weighs a large number of factors, both short term as well as long term oriented. One needs to take into account, for example, the importance of other purposes, the level of automation in comparable hospitals, the need for new information systems, the change processes within the organization, and the capacity of the information systems department. Additionally one needs to consider the long-run financial implications of the introduction or adjustment of computer based information systems. Beside the initial investments, the hospital requires the financial capacity to cover operational costs, and additional investments for replacement and expansion.

Information Policy Statement 5

Training is one of the most important means for an organization to foster appropriate responses to a changing environment. In addition to the fact that it boosts the competence of the organization, training programs also reduce the need for external consultants. It is therefore necessary to devise a training program which describes the appropriate educational services for all groups within the organization.

Clarification of Statement 5

The introduction of information issues and the related automation issues brings along some drastic changes for the personnel of an organization. At all levels personnel is faced with questions such as:

-what information do I need to do my job?

-how can an established information need be filled?

-what effects will automation have on my job?

A renewed orientation on the tasks to be completed and the decisions to be taken is necessary. In many cases, the initial education of personnel will not have been devoted to computer science or its applications. Since user participation is an essential condition for successful information systems development, educational programs are a requirement. One can distinguish several categories of users within an organization:. Each of these groups will have different educational requirements which will have to be recognized in the training program.

Information Policy Statement 6

The technical infrastructure in hospitals should be such that decentralized deployment of information technology - geared to the information needs of the end-users - becomes a possibility.

Clarification of Statement 6

In a professional organization such as a hospital, decentralized computer usage offers extra opportunities, such as:

- increase user involvement which in turn leads to a higher expected degree of acceptance of information systems;
- quick local consultation of information systems in order to come to better decisions;
- smaller vulnerability;
- larger flexibility;
- more innovative developments.

Decentralized deployment of information technology fits the hospital organization as a professional bureaucracy, as it strengthens of the individual responsibilities of all management levels. IT-enabled improvements in efficiency and effectiveness can best be realized when they are the responsibility of the management involved. In order for decentralized computer usage to succeed both technically and organizationally, appropriate educational services must be included in the personnel training programs.

6. Conclusion

The description of information policy statements provided above should clarify our distinction between information policy formulation and information planning. Information policy is a much more coarse indication of the roads to follow, the factors to take into account, and the goals to strive for in the development of information systems support for an organization. The approach taken here is clearly different from current methods for information systems planning. The more articulate and systematic approaches toward information systems planning have definitely shown their value in coordinating the IS development activities, but when it comes to defining the strategic goals for information systems support, they are not effective.

The BeMI method presented here has proved itself in a number of practical situations, and it has become a valued consulting instrument. In combination with an elaborate training and awareness program for the top-managers involved, it turns out that the approach proposed by us leads to a better understanding of the relevance of information systems support for strategic issues within the organization. Top-management will take control of the vital aspects of information systems development within their organization and will direct IS development efforts, rather than letting IS staff translate the organizational strategy into technical terms. This also means that a more results-oriented approach is likely to prevail, instead of the infrastructural approach taken by most information plans.

One of the issues open for research is the way in which information policy statements provide guidance to the information planning process. It is one thing to make a clear distinction between strategic and tactical planning with respect to information technology application and information systems support, but the ensuing problem is to get the two processes in line with each other. Current research is tackling this issue by taking both a contingency approach toward information planning and a conceptual modelling approach toward both information policy and planning.

References

Aarts, A.F.H., and P.M.C. Janssen (eds.), *Handboek Informatieplanning (Manual Information Planning; in Dutch)*; Department of Defense, 's Gravenhage (NL), 1989.

Arthur Young, *Computer Systems Methodology : Information Engineering, Planning*; Unpublished Proprietary Material, Arthur Young International, March 1988.

Boersma, Jacques S.K.Th., 'Bedrijfskundige methode voor informatiebeleidsvorming (BeMI) (Managerial method for formulating information policy; in Dutch)'; *Informatie*, vol. 30, no. 2, 1988, pp. 91-99.

Boersma, Jacques S.K.Th., *Beslissingsondersteunende Systemen : een praktijkgerichte ontwikkelingsmethode (Decision Support Systems : a practice based development method; in Dutch)*; Academic Service, Schoonhoven (NL), 1989.

Boersma, Jacques S.K.Th., *Bedrijfskundige Methode voor Informatiebeleid (Managerial Method for Information Policy; in Dutch)*; Lansa, Leidschendam (NL), 1993.

Boersma, Jacques S.K.Th., and Boudewijn Hopstaken, 'Informatiesystemen: Integratie door Beleid (Information Systems: Integration through Policy; in Dutch)'; *Informatie*, vol. 26, no. 3, 1984, pp. 218-224.

Bosman, Aart, 'Planning en administreren (Planning and administration; in Dutch)'; *Ontwikkelingen rond informatiesystemen (Developments in Information Systems)*, Samsom, Alphen aan den Rijn (NL), 1984.

Greveling, Norbert J.W., *Informatieplanstudie: Model voor Strategie (Information Plan Study: Model for Strategy; in Dutch)*; Dissertation, Faculty of Management and Organization, Technical University of Eindhoven (NL), 1990.

IBM, *Business Systems Planning : Information Systems Planning Guide*; Fourth Edition, GE20-0527-4, International Business Machines Corporation, Atlanta, July 1984.

Lederer, Albert L., and Vijay Sethi, 'The Implementation of Strategic Information Systems Planning Methodologies'; *MIS Quarterly*, September 1988, pp. 445-461

McFarlan, F. Warren, and James L. McKenney, *Corporate Information Systems Management : The Issues facing Senior Executives*; R.D. Irwin, Inc., Homewood, Illinois, 1983.

Meer, D. van der, and A.P.W.P. van Montfort, 'Het nut van budgettering ten aanzien van ziekenhuizen (The use of budgeting with respect to hospitals; in Dutch)'; In: *Toevoegen van waarde. Ontwikkelingen in theorie en praktijk (Adding value : developments in theory and practice)*, H.G. Barkema and P.W. Moerland (eds.), Kluwer, Deventer (NL), 1985, pp. 169-177.

Mintzberg, Henry, *The Structuring of Organizations : A Synthesis of the Research*; Prentice Hall, Englewood Cliffs, 1979.

Mintzberg, Henry, 'Research Notes and Communications : What Is Planning Anyway?'; *Strategic Management Journal*, vol. 2, 1981, pp. 319-324.

Olle, T. William, Jacques Hagelstein, Ian G. Macdonald, Colette Rolland, Henk G. Sol, Frans J.M. van Assche, and Alexander A. Verrijn-Stuart, *Information Systems Methodologies : A Framework for Understanding*; Addison Wesley Publishing Company, Workingham (UK), 1988.

Stegwee, Robert A., *Division for Conquest : Decision Support for Information Architecture Specification*, Dissertation, University of Groningen, Wolters Noordhoff, Groningen (NL), 1992.

Stegwee, Robert A. and Ria M.C. van Waes, 'The Development of Information Systems Planning towards a Mature Management Tool'; *Information Resources Management Journal*, vol. 3, no. 3, Summer, 1990, pp. 8-21.

Theeuwes, Jacques A.M., *Informatieplanning (Information Planning; in Dutch)*; Kluwer, Deventer (NL), 1988.

Waes, Ria M.C. van, *Architectures for Information Management : A Pragmatic Approach on Architectural Concepts and their Application in Dynamic Environments*; Dissertation, Free University of Amsterdam, Thesis Publishers, Amsterdam (NL), 1991.

Enterprise and Information Modelling
for the Expression of Organisational Policies

John Dobson
Dept. of Computing Science
University of Newcastle
Newcastle upon TYPE NE1 7RU, U.K.

Mike Martin
Ryton Associates
15 Ryton Hall Drive
Ryton, Tyne and Wear NE40 3QB, U.K.

Executive Abstract

Introduction

One of the major difficulties in the management of information is the expression of policy with respect to the intended use of information. Information policy may stem from goals such as satisfying organisational objectives or changing organisational power structures. It is often difficult to re-express these policies in the engineering terms that a system designer can use and be sure that the policy implications of design decisions are identified early and handled appropriately by the policy makers.

The solution to this kind of problem lies in taking multiple views, or projections, of a computer system, as embodied in the standards for Open Distributed Processing. The purpose of the information modelling architecture is not only to derive the data models that are required, but also to determine all the contextual requirements on the data. By determining such requirements the data needs can be shown to be complete and fit for the purpose in terms of the organisational responsibilities of the data owners and users.

The projections provide a conceptual modelling language and framework from within which it is possible to represent and analyse various organisational issues. These languages function much the same as any other language; their purpose is to act as a medium through which information can be exchanged and consensus built. Each language stresses a particular set of issues and attempts to elucidate and represent their requirements. Consequently each language has a set of unique constructs and also a set of constructs which it shares with the other projection language. Each projection represents a particular perspective of the system with its own interests, objectives and goals. Thus in order to specify completely a system a problem solver must use all of the projections. Each of the projections also allows for multiple views of the problem. In that way it is possible for a system designer to not only understand how each object and module, in the system interacts with each other, but also how the system interacts with its environment.

There are five projections, listed below and described briefly in the following paragraphs.

- The Enterprise Projection
- The Information Projection
- The Computational Projection
- The Engineering Projection
- The Technology Projection

The Enterprise Projection

The principal role of the enterprise projection is to interpret the role of a computer system within an organisation. The enterprise projection describes the overall objectives of a system in terms of agents, actions, resources and policies.

The Information Projection

The primary function of the information projection is the identification and location of information, and the description of the information processing activities. The information projection allows a system designer to express the structure, interpretation and timeliness as well as to examine the relationships that can exist between information objects within the organisation.

The Computational Projection

The purpose of the computational projection is to provide a framework for the description of the structure, specification and execution of application programs.

The Engineering Projection

The primary function of the engineering projection is to provide a framework for the specification of the mechanisms and trade-offs required to support the application programs. Thus the purpose of the projection is to describe the organisation, and the system within it, in such a way that the system designers can reason about its performance.

The Technology Projection

The primary function of the technology projection is to express the system in term of its physical components, hardware, software etc. Thus in the technology projection issues concerned with construction and maintenance can be expressed and discussed.

Using the Projections

We have developed a small but quite complete model based on current practice in quality systems to illustrate the use of the projections. The example shows the enterprise and information projections in detail, and indicates some aspects of the computational projection.

The enterprise model for this particular case has two sub-models. The first of these identifies directing, managing and executing agents, and explores the relationships between them so as to provide the generic vertical structure of the enterprise. Client and supplying agencies provide the external environment for this model. The second sub-model represents quality assurance, quality control, and certification agency and the relationships between them.

There are many approaches to implementing a quality system, which can vary from the concept of completely independent inspection and certification to the concept that quality is the concern of everybody in the enterprise and they must be empowered to discharge this responsibility and to show that they have done so. We show how the underlying model of enterprise management and quality management can be configured to different quality implementation philosophies and how this modifies the mapping of a common information model onto different system implementations. In the case of a quality system, this results in different job and role descriptions on the one hand and different data and transaction models of the corporate information system on the other.

One of the principles of the modelling approach which is presented is that the obligation relationships which are created and discharged by the agents are embodied in the generation and interpretation of information items which are associated with "instruments". Examples of such instruments are the quality manual, quality plans, management accounts and, most typically, contracts to supply. We show that the criterion of completeness of the information projection is that it provides an adequate and appropriate set of instruments to carry all of the obligation relationships presented in the enterprise projection. The criterion for completeness of the enterprise projection is that it represents the division and distribution of responsibility for the enterprise, so that for example all the different failure and success modes can be distinguished and attributed to some role holder.

Conclusions

The importance of this approach is the maintenance of a clear means of tracing design decisions concerning both the organisation and the information system and the representation of information policy. A further benefit is the ability of the approach to support the exploration of policy options while maintaining the distinction of the common invariant elements which represent the constraints and boundaries of the enterprise. All this is part of a broader concept of architecture which the authors believe must be adopted if we are to tackle the increased flexibility and dependability requirements of the information systems we are building today and which will be needed to meet the economic and social needs of the next decade.

Outsourcing in the United Kingdom and Vendor/Client Relationship Issues

Guy Fitzgerald
Department of Computer Science
Birkbeck College, University of London

Leslie Willcocks
Oxford Institute of Information Management
Templeton College, University of Oxford

Executive Abstract

ABSTRACT

This paper reports on a recent detailed research study concerning the outsourcing of information technology activities in the United Kingdom. The study involved a postal survey and a set of 25 detailed case studies based on large and medium sized organisations.

The survey identified that contracts and vendor relationships were key elements in successful outsourcing. Many of the problems encountered by organisations related to the details of the contract; including the definition of service levels, managing the contract, lack of vendor flexibility, staffing, and lack of vendor responsiveness. This resulted in half of the organisations experiencing disputes with their vendor(s). The survey also found that the relationship that clients are adopting with vendors are becoming increasingly contractually based and indicates that one of the responses of organisations to the above problems is to try and more rigorously define and specify the contract. Another way of overcoming the problems was to enter only short term contracts, and the survey showed this to be the case with 95% of contracts being of less than 5 years duration and 49% being of two years or less.

However an important group of organisations adopted a different approach and advocated the establishment of partnership relationships with the vendor which implied a non-reliance on the contract as the basis of the relationship and adopted what was termed a give and take philosophy. This approach is criticised as naiveté on the part of the client, relying on an overgenerous profit for the vendor to make it work, and it is suggested that it is unlikely to survive when problems and disputes are encountered. The only real partnerships were those based on the more normal business definition of partnership, where there was a more up front, well defined, element of mutual economic benefit. This might involve contractual arrangements with incentives for vendors to perform well through to the full sharing of risks and bottom line rewards. Such partnerships were relatively rare.

Thus there seemed to be a number of somewhat conflicting trends and a degree of misunderstanding concerning partnership. The paper argues that notions of partnership cannot be divorced from that of the type of contract, and that the type of contract depends on the type of outsourcing under consideration.

In order to facilitate and explore these issues a framework was developed that plots the degree of contractual definition, on a continuum between loose and tight, against the type of outsourcing. The type of outsourcing is defined as the degree to which the requirements of the client can be fully defined and specified, which includes the initial definition, requirements over the duration of the contract, and the requirements on termination of the contract. The type of outsourcing is also expressed as a continuum between requirements that are basically fully known and understood, and those that are substantially unknown and unknowable. Typical of those that are known are the transaction processing/mainframe type of outsourcing The other end of the continuum is the type of outsourcing that is difficult to specify because of the range of uncertainties both current and future. Typical of this type might be the move to client-server architectures, or open systems, the design and development of new business systems, business process redesign activities, etc., i.e. a degree of business or technical uncertainty, or both. Such circumstances, it is argued, are best dealt with via a contractual arrangement that shares the risks and rewards arising from the uncertainty. There exist various intermediate positions of lesser or greater uncertainty that might involve the variety of incentive type contractual arrangements that the survey identified.

The purpose of the framework is to suggest that certain combinations are more likely to lead to successful and sustainable outsourcing, whilst other positions are more likely to be situations of risk or inefficiency. For example, it is argued that situations of relative certainty should be accompanied by a very tightly defined contract for best results. The tight specification means that the contract is relatively easily and accurately priceable and vendors can be easily compared. Such situations are best organised via a fixed fee type of contract, and the result is likely to be a keen and realistic contract price. To be in a loose contract situation in this position exposes the client organisation to unnecessary risk, i.e. the vendor can charge extras for anything not fully specified in the contract. For the vendor not to be tempted to do this they would have to feel that they were making enough money from the contract not to wish to jeopardise the situation. This is likely to mean that the client is not getting the best deal that is potentially obtainable.

In situations of uncertainty the contractual arrangement should be a looser contract based upon the sharing of risks and rewards. A tight contract is very difficult to achieve in such circumstances, and indeed is likely to be counter-productive. A tight contract will be making various assumptions about the future which are unlikely to be true as we are talking here about possibly fundamental and unpredictable situations, perhaps involving quantum change, rather than incremental developments. The essence of the situation is the need for flexibility and a tight contract is likely to constrain the vendor from reacting in the way that the client may wish. Nevertheless the client cannot just leave the situation open and hope that the vendor will perform in the right way simply on trust or on the basis of a give and take partnership, it would be too risky.

Therefore the risk must be minimised by the use of the sharing of risk/reward type of contractual arrangements but with a looser contractual definition, in terms of service levels and penalty clauses, etc. to ensure flexibility. The incentive for the vendor to do what is best for the client is for them to share the rewards resulting from the combined vendor/client performance (or to minimise the losses).

The paper concludes by suggesting that more serious thought needs to be addressed by organisations entering into outsourcing deals concerning partnership, and although there is an identified trend to move to more tightly defined contracts this may not be appropriate in all circumstances and there are situations where it may be counterproductive. Equally a move towards a partnership relationship may not be appropriate and even dangerous where this is simply an excuse for not fully defining and specifying the contract. In each situation the type of contract is crucial and for situations of uncertainty the shared risk/reward contract may be the only appropriate arrangement.

Information Wards - A New Conceptual Tool for Modelling the Political Implications of Information Systems Development

D.N. Hart

University College, UNSW
Australian Defence Force Academy
d-hart@adfa.oz.au

Executive Abstract

Development of an information system is not only a technological issue but also an organizational one. This is well recognized within the information systems community but often a "rational" picture of organizational behaviour and functioning is assumed. However, such a "rational" picture is rarely realistic and organizations, especially those of any size, are generally political in nature. As the possession and control of information forms an important basis for organizational power, efforts to develop information systems often carry power-modifying and therefore political connotations.

This paper develops a graphical model for representing the political milieu surrounding information systems development and, on the basis of the model, suggests reasons why problems occur and strategies that might be adopted to avoid them. The model is based on two new concepts - "information wards" and "political information wards".

INFORMATION WARDS

In pursuing their organizational roles, different groups within an organization (called "players" in the paper) work with particular data holdings and associated business processes. These are likely to be regarded as being owned by the player concerned. The "information ward" (IW) of an organizational player is defined as this set of owned data and associated business processes. Information wards of different organizational players are not necessarily distinct. They may overlap. This will be the case if, for example, two or more players redundantly operate with identical data and/or processes, or if two or more players both *perceive* that they should each exclusively own and operate with some particular data holding or business process.

It is argued that information wards are not simple. They have an internal structure since a player will generally consider some subset of their total information ward to be central to their organizational identity, role and power. This subset they will defend against any threat of takeover. It is referred to as their "political information ward" (PIW) since such defense may, if it proves to be necessary, include normally illegitimate organizational methods like political action.

If information wards overlap then disagreements over ownership of organizational data and processes may ensue. The severity of such disagreement and the prospects for negotiated or imposed resolution depend on how the wards of the contending players are related (do their IWs or PIWs overlap?).

INFORMATION SYSTEMS AND INFORMATION WARDS

An information system (IS) deals with some subset of organizational data and business processes. That is, an IS will in general overlap the IW and perhaps the PIW of one or more organizational players. How this overlap occurs will determine the level of interest each player has in the IS and the actions taken in regard to it. Overlap of a player's IW implies an influencing or stakeholder role for the player; overlap of a player's PIW implies that they will want an owning or controlling role with respect to the IS. If an IS overlaps the PIWs of two or more players of comparable organizational power then conflict and political strife over the IS may be predicted (even though the PIWs themselves are distinct). If the PIWs of the players overlap too, then the situation for the IS is as grim as it could possibly be.

A case study of a large failed IS project is described in the paper to illustrate the applicability of the IW and PIW concepts. The fate of the project is interpreted in terms of overlap between the scope of the IS and the PIWs of the five organizational players involved. As the ward model would predict, the project became the subject of intense political wrangling and was eventually terminated.

MANAGEMENT IMPLICATIONS

If it is regarded as likely, or it becomes evident, that an IS will generate political controversy then some management recommendations based on the information ward model can be made. These recommendations involve modifying the scope of the IS in such a way as to eliminate overlap with more than one player's PIW. This may be done by splitting the project into sub-projects, each owned by the player whose PIW it overlaps; or by being less ambitious and reducing the overall project scope to avoid the cause of the conflict. If this cannot be done because PIWs themselves overlap then this is a business, not an IS, problem and must be resolved in that light.

CONCLUSION

Information is not only necessary for the functioning of the modern organization but is also a source of organizational power for those who possess or control it. The planners and developers of information systems need to take cognizance of this dual aspect of the raw material with which their systems deal. That is, systems must be planned to be not only organizationally effective but also *politically acceptable* to the organizational players that they will affect. Neglect of either of these aspects of an IS development effort will almost certainly increase the risk of failure. The information ward model described in this paper provides a conceptual basis for modelling the political implications of IS developments as well as suggesting ways in which any risks that might arise could be minimized.

Using Information Systems to Reshape Management Practice in New Market Economies

William K. Holstein
Distinguished Service Professor, School of Business
State University of New York at Albany
Founding Director, Center for Private
Enterprise Development
Budapest, Hungary

Jakov Crnkovic
Associate Professor, Computer Information
Systems Department
College of Saint Rose, Albany, New York

ABSTRACT

The countries of East and Central Europe and the former Soviet Union are rapidly moving from command economies to market economies, but the path is fraught with difficulty. For 45 or more years the goal has been serving the government plan with the production requirements determined by command from above. Now identifying market needs and serving customers is becoming important.

In our experience in several "emerging" economies, improved information systems have proven to be a powerful tool that can help individual companies adapt management practice to new competitive realities. As these countries move out from under previous restrictions at a relatively slow pace, many Western management ideas and systems cannot yet be applied. But improvements in relatively straightforward areas of information systems such as inventory management can be applied. Improvements in such areas can rectify years of problems in logistics and distribution and, we believe, can play an important role in restructuring economies and improving competitive effectiveness.

This paper presents case studies from two companies who have used change in their information subsystems for inventory management in quite different ways. In the first case, a steel producer has obvious inventory problems. The organization of inventory functions causes even more problems. Movement towards a solution is achieved by the development of a marketing information system, which promotes reorganization and changes in management.

In the second case, planning for a new power plant begins with grand plans for an integrated enterprise information system similar to those found in the U.S. and Western Europe. Numerous problems lead the company towards a more feasible solution involving smaller steps, in which two subsystems are central: an inventory management system and a project management system.

INTRODUCTION

The countries of East and Central Europe and the former Soviet Union are rapidly moving from *production* economies to *market* economies. Having spent more than 40 years working under the guidelines of a command economy, the transition is fraught with difficulty and uncertainty. One might think that the economies whose primary goal has been serving the needs of *production* - producing to meet a *quantity* plan and a mix determined by command from above - would

be quite efficient at managing the physical stocks and flows in production and distribution. Now that *marketing* is becoming important - finding what the customer needs and wants, and then serving that need better than under the previous system - perhaps production-oriented management systems and tools should get less attention.

Our purpose is to point out almost exactly the opposite:

- That production- and distribution-oriented management tools and systems are *not* all that well established. This is particularly true of inventory management systems.
- That production and distribution activities, *not* more marketing-related tools such as market research, advertising, and promotion, are the most important keys to short-term success and to make a pathway towards company prosperity in the transition to a market economy.

We wish to share our experience and our views in a general, motivational manner. We hope to share our enthusiasm that information systems, and relatively straightforward subsystems such as inventory and distribution systems can play a very important role in emerging economies.

THE ECONOMIC AND MANAGEMENT SITUATION

During the late 1980s, the economic and political maps of East and Central Europe changed dramatically. The breakup of the Soviet Union added further changes. The members of the Warsaw Pact were inextricably tied economically, politically and militarily with the Soviet Union. Trade within the Warsaw Pact countries was very much a hub and spoke system, with Moscow the hub. Markets for the satellites focused on the Soviet Union and other Pact members. There was little choice of what to produce and no drive for innovation or product improvement. "Meet the production goal and don't ask too many questions" seemed to be the safest strategy for companies in the old system.

New business conditions have developed very quickly. Earlier, trade was almost completely based on barter arrangements. Now, hard currency is the key to trade, and it has become a very scarce commodity. Most enterprises have been left adrift without their former top-down instructions, without their major markets, and stuck with processes, products and designs that in most cases are generations behind Western standards. And, most companies have been left with weak management and organizational structures, often populated with holdovers from the old regime, and with inadequate resources to make dramatic short- or longer-term improvements.

Yet, many tangible moves towards restructuring are underway: privatization, foreign investments, new market institutions, new market conditions, and new financing alternatives are only a few examples. Restructuring, rebuilding, and re-engineering are popular buzz-words now. New technology and new management practices are coming, and the legislative decisions, fiscal instruments, and business regulations to support the new environment are not far behind.

What is not going well in all of these countries is the development of management and information systems infrastructure to operate businesses efficiently and quickly. Clear evidence of this is easy to find in the area of logistics, distribution, and inventory management. Domestic goods still cost too much. This is not because of labor, material, or other costs directly related to manufacturing, but because of the way the whole system of manufacturing and distribution is *managed* - a system that has for far too many years ignored supply and demand. In most organizations, inventories are horribly managed - with too much of the wrong things, and too little of what the market wants. Distribution intermediaries at all levels in the system are small, inefficient and costly. Goods sit, spoil, deteriorate and get damaged and mishandled far too frequently. The waste in the system in most of these countries under the communist system was truly staggering, and much of it remains to be rooted out and eliminated. Shortages of spare parts and raw materials, and the hard currency to buy them, coupled with high inflation and interest rates, have increased the demand for improved materials management.

These observations do not contain new knowledge. More than a decade ago, a government official in Hungary (a country in which inventories were probably better-managed than in most other countries in the region) made the following comments:

> (The reason) *consumption can be smoothly regulated but investment activity cannot* (is that) *consumption relations are regulated by a monetary policy, but investment activity has been controlled in physical terms over a rather long period.* (^{1})

IDEAS FOR CHANGE

The solution to these macro-level problems requires focusing on the same kinds of issues and factors that companies in the U.S., Western Europe and Japan face every day - defining specific markets and market needs, clarifying and simplifying, streamlining and speeding up processes, removing organizational boundaries, being more customer-driven and more quality- and service-oriented. But how are these things to be done? Which management concepts and techniques can be applied? Which cannot, at least in the short term?

We believe that fundamental changes in corporate efficiency (doing the right thing) and effectiveness (doing it right) cannot be done *yet* in the emerging economies by using contemporary U.S. and European management ideas. Let us expand on this thought for a moment.

In the U.S., there is no shortage of ideas on how corporations should restructure and improve. Management gurus put forth a steady stream of concepts such as learning organizations, re-engineering, organizational architecture, time based competition, and leveraging core competencies. (^{2}) In Europe, there is much talk of changes required to meet the needs of the Common Market. (^{3}) Application of many of these ideas requires fundamental and radical organizational change in U.S. and European companies.

In companies operating in the emerging economies, applying these ideas would require even more massive changes - precisely at a time when *any* change is difficult and many externally imposed changes must be dealt with.

Many of the ideas for change in the U.S. and Europe involve the development and deployment of new information systems and technology. The re-engineering ideas of Michael Hammer, for example, follow a dramatic theme as noted in the following quote:

> *If you don't rebuild the business, you're dead, finished, over.* (^{4})

Hammer is talking about U.S. companies, not those in the emerging economies. He notes that many U.S. companies (with vastly more resources and management sophistication than would be found most companies in East and Central Europe) have managed investments in information systems and technology poorly:

> *Heavy investments in information technology have delivered disappointing results - largely because companies tend to use technology to mechanize old ways of doing business. They leave the existing processes intact and use computers simply to speed them up.* (^{5})

Mechanizing old ways of doing business certainly isn't what is needed in the emerging economies. Radical changes and dramatic, new concepts aren't likely to succeed either.

A 1990 paper, reporting on a survey of inventory practices in Hungary, notes:

> *Why can't the majority of our companies apply these successful ideas?* (such as MRP and JIT) *...Companies in shortage economies are in a special "paternalistic" relationship with the state ... a very large proportion of* (their) *income is first centralized and then redistributed. ... The rules of this redistribution are to a great extent "tailor made."*
>
> *The main reason behind the low methodological level of management is therefore that managers are more involved in external "political" activity than in internal development of company operations, which latter can produce results only at the margin, while good relations to central government can result in incomparably higher rewards.* (^{6})

What is needed, in our view, are implementable, incremental approaches that are well-based in theory, well understood, able to deliver significant short-term results, and that speak to real needs. Improved inventory management is precisely such an idea - an idea that can build on existing structures, yield good (and badly needed) results, and pave the way for more sweeping changes and improvements when organizations and the economic system are more amenable to accepting them.

Working on inventory management, logistics, distribution and related topics fits in well with skills and interests that already exist. There is considerable literature in East and Central Europe and in the former Soviet Union dealing with inventory theory and problems, at both the level of the economy and the firm. The problems are nonetheless real - the existence of literature has not meant good solutions and practical application in industry. Indeed, in countries where management, as we know it, is a relatively new concept, it is perhaps too much to expect good theory to be well applied.

RESTRUCTURING ECONOMIES

It takes a leap of faith to go from improvements obtained through better management in individual companies to restructuring and improving the entire economy. Rather than ask for such a leap, we cite Porter's definition of a competitive nation, and his comment on how it is achieved, and let the matter rest:

A nation's competitiveness depends on the capacity of its industry to innovate and upgrade.

Much innovation is mundane and incremental, depending more on a cumulation of small insights and advances than on a single, major technological breakthrough. It often involves ideas that are not even "new" - ideas that have been around, but never vigorously pursued. (7)

In summary, we believe that improvements in the competitiveness of individual companies in the countries that are the focus of this paper will come only through the implementation of *ideas that can work in the present environment.* Replicated often enough in several industries, such ideas can indeed lead to increased international competitiveness for a country.

We turn now to two examples drawn from actual practice. We will argue more categorical points from more specific detail. We will concentrate on the important role that improving information subsystems, such as for inventory management and control, can play in the process of restructuring a company and, if replicated often enough, an entire economy.

The following example is from a government-owned steel mill in Central Europe.

THE STEEL MILL CASE

This mill has been a partner of a major West European automobile manufacturer for years. The mill's sheet, roll and forged products are shipped directly to auto parts and assembly plants throughout Europe.

In addition to the business with the automobile manufacturer, the mill produces fittings and simple castings, general purpose tools and machines, as well as more sophisticated specialty machines and flexible manufacturing systems. Most of the non-automobile-related business was conducted with the Soviet Union and a few domestic customers on a job-shop, custom-order basis.

The Soviet business was based on an agreed list of products to be exchanged, so the mill's "payments" were handled by government accounting for Soviet exports to other customers. This practice of "offsetting exports" was typical in the region. When the Soviet Union was unable to make up trade deficits with wanted export goods or hard currency, the system collapsed, leaving many companies without their largest markets.

When most of the Soviet market was lost, it was quickly obvious that the mill would have to become much more market-oriented. Yet responsibility for marketing and sales activities were split between two organizational units. Marketing activities - promotion, advertising and marketing research - were the responsibility of a small Marketing Department. Sales, purchasing of all materials and parts, maintenance contracts, and all services were handled by the large and powerful Commercial Department.

New market conditions made improved information systems crucial for the mill, yet existing systems were piecemeal, isolated, unconnected transaction processing systems. Systems for managing inventories were a significant problem. Frequently new parts or materials were ordered when adequate supplies existed, but were not tracked, included, or reported by the system. Worse, existing parts that could be used in new products were re-designed, or "re-invented," adding further to inventory problems. This added more difficulty to the existing problems between the sales and production organizations since quotes took a long time to develop, information on existing parts costs was not accurate, and even old prices were not readily available.

Bill of material handling and processing was at the most rudimentary level. The quality of products was quite high and products were competitive. Company used statistical quality control concepts with inspection stations for incoming parts and raw materials and for outgoing products. MRP concepts were relatively unknown - most logic was batch-oriented with excessive buffer stocks to paper over coordination problems. The important connection between inventory management and financial reporting and control was completely lacking. An inflation rate of 200 percent per year caused prices to change daily. Coupled with an order cycle of 12 months or more, palpable havoc and aberrant management coping behavior was clearly in evidence.

In response to these problems, members of the Board of Directors (analogous to the senior management group in U.S. practice) initiated an ambitious program to build a Marketing Information System. A project team, composed of external consultants, the head of Information Services, the chief Marketing officer, and several staff members from Information Services, was formed. Later, members from the Commercial Department and several production groups joined the effort.

The project team conducted a complete systems analysis using IBM's Business Systems Planning methodology - an approach that would be sophisticated even by Western standards. A training program for information services staff and key people in the marketing, commercial and production areas was implemented. The importance of improvements in information systems was highlighted throughout the training, and this phase was considered quite successful. The information system design team was competent and well motivated. The consultants introduced basic TQM concepts which stimulated further improvements and led to a clearer focus on the users of the future information system. (See ([8]) for an example of the methodology used.)

Soon after the start of the project it became clear that significant problems existed between the Marketing and Commercial Departments, and between the selling and purchasing units in the Commercial Department itself. Since the project had strong support at the Board level, changes were made quickly. The two departments dealing with marketing and sales tasks were combined. A new marketing manager with broad responsibilities was appointed. He was instructed to simplify the combined department's procedures, and to improve communication and coordination among the various units within the department.

As the project to develop the Marketing Information System progressed, inventory management, and the "ownership" of inventory became hot political issues that impeded progress. Under the old, production-driven, command system such issues were irrelevant because decisions were "received" rather than "made." Now, "turf" issues and conflicts over "decision making power" in inventory management between Production and the newly integrated Marketing Department threatened disaster.

In our experience, this kind of conflict is almost inevitable in the former communist countries. Some verification is found in ([9]) from which the following quote is taken:

The integration of the sales-production-inventory-purchasing processes in the vast majority of cases goes on under the leadership of a production manager, who is usually at a high level in the hierarchy. The integration is actually dominated by production, the interest of which is a smooth operation, which can be ensured by high input stocks.

Production wanted to take complete responsibility for the inventories of raw materials and spare parts, but to have no responsibility for the management of finished goods. Production's goal was to produce as much tonnage as possible - for example a few large, heavy fittings, rather than a larger number of smaller fittings that might be in higher market demand - reflecting an old emphasis on fulfilling the set plan (in tonnage) as a measure of success, rather than being able to make flexible change and to reach for increased profits.

The consultants proposed putting responsibility for all inventories in the Marketing Department, but Production's objections forced the issue to the Board of Directors level. They did not go further with the reorganization and left responsibility for inventory split. The peaked organizational pyramid remains with heavy, often impenetrable, lines between departments and functions.

Contemporary management concepts, such as Just-In-Time inventory management, were considered by the team, but quickly rejected for practical realities. Meanwhile, the production staff exerted continuous pressure to increase the warehouse stocks of raw materials to overcome the uncertainties of vendor quality and delivery and unreliable transportation.

That an idea such as JIT was considered at all is somewhat unusual. In 1990, the inventory survey referenced earlier noted: *"We do not know about any company which would have tried JIT."* The survey of 78 Hungarian companies indicated that 56.4% had never heard of JIT, and 39.7% had never heard of MRP. ([10])

The new system maintained two financial values for all inventory items - in (relatively constant) local currency, which was useless because of daily price changes due to inflation, and the equivalent in German marks, the base foreign currency used because of extensive German-mark-based sales and purchases. A constant problem was to determine the foreign exchange rate to use - the official rate or the market rate which, at times, was as much as double the official rate. With a production cycle of up to a year for many products, the usually simple task of estimating the costs of materials used in production was a nightmare. Pricing was even more complex. With so many other problems, the project team building the Marketing Information System never really addressed the costing problem. It was left to manual procedures. The system offered only on-line tracking of physical quantities of raw materials and finished goods.

In the end, the new marketing information system was neither that nor a solid collection of reliable sub-systems. Some new elements were added to the old information system, but most departments and units continued on with old systems or adopted only small pieces of the new system.

CAN INFORMATION SYSTEMS CHANGE MANAGEMENT?

Is there a maxim here? We think "yes."

In the changing business environment that is characteristic of the emerging market economies today, too many things are changing inside and outside the business to tackle too much change at once. We see in this example pressing needs for organizational restructuring and new integration and coordination, and yet, except for accounting and some financial reporting, there are no basic systems, no modules *that really work* on which to build.

Rather than tackling large, integrated systems development projects, and then trying to impose the results on a reluctant organization, we suggest that smaller, more focused attempts might be more productive.

In this case, for example, a highly structured and limited effort to improve inventory recording, tracking and costing within the production organization might have paid big dividends. It might also have been possible to install without attracting substantial organizational resistance. Building on the success of a good inventory reporting system, control logic to operate in the highly uncertain environment could have been added. *Then* integration with marketing and sales might have been appropriate.

Can information systems change management? Yes, *if* they have limited, achievable objectives, *if* they can attract sufficient support from lower levels in the organization, and *if* they are properly implemented with clear checks at each stage of development to demonstrate effectiveness. Until these lessons are carefully learned, it is most likely that management will change information systems, with little or no impact on the fundamental problems that plague companies in newly emerging economies.

The following example, drawn from a large power plant construction project, focuses on the modular, "from the bottom" approach to systems development.

POWER PLANT "B"

Power plant "B" is a very large electrical generation plant located on a river in Eastern Europe. At the time of the events described here, the plant was under construction. Power plant "B" was owned by a large government enterprise that included other power generation facilities and several coal mining operations. A strip mine next to the plant provides the coal to fuel the plant's boilers.

The turbines and other equipment used in the plant came from a wide variety of domestic suppliers and foreign equipment suppliers in Canada, Germany, Austria, Russia and other East European countries.

The Board of Directors of the company (senior management) included people from engineering and management. The two groups expressed quite different views and goals. The engineering group had in mind just one objective: Build! The management group, representing three functional areas, personnel, finance, and accounting, was responsible for employee relations, financing, cost control, and budgeting (particularly coping with inflation which, at times during the project, was over 100 percent per year). There was little cohesion between the two groups of managers at the top of the organization, except on one issue - everyone agreed that the company needed an "integrated information system." It was not quite clear who understood what about this concept, but it was popular buzz word at the time. The system was to assist in the management of the construction process, and then would "take over" the regular operation of the plant.

As in the steel mill case, an external consultant was hired - but in this case the entire contract was given to the outside firm, rather than forming a team consisting of consultants, internal management, and technical staff.

Early in the systems analysis phase, serious problems became evident. Real cooperation between the consultants and senior plant managers was almost impossible to secure. Lower-level managers were helpful, but frequently were not allowed by their superiors to "waste" time working with consultants . Project deadlines quickly fell behind, and serious delays were anticipated in the construction schedules.

Once it became obvious that delays in the development of

an information system could slow down the entire construction project, more high-level management attention was focused on the task. Several important problems and fundamental disagreements among the members of the Board were resolved. A key decision was to reduce the scope of, and expectations for, the new information system and to focus attention on two important sub-systems: project management and inventory management.

During the construction phase, the plant had a relatively small number of full-time employees. Most construction activities were staffed by the several contractors working on the project. Yet, during the construction period, project and inventory management were absolutely critical.

The engineering group designed the warehouse system. Some equipment was stored outside, close to the final location where the equipment would be installed. For some expensive parts and equipment, security or protection from the weather was not adequate and the material had to be moved indoors. Tracking the exact physical location of all the bits and pieces that would be needed to bring the plant on-line placed heavy demands on the inventory system. Keeping components of the final system together, both physically and in the inventory system, was a challenge.

Material arrived on rail cars and trucks, in containers, boxes, and often loose. Documentation was frequently missing, poorly recorded, incomplete, or illegible. One Canadian supplier put only the total value for a whole container of over 1,000 different parts in the accompanying documentation, with no details whatsoever to check the contents.

Database design became another problem area. The engineering group wanted to track only unit measures and quantities of all materials. The project team wanted to connect this database to the project management module to keep up with deadlines and to use the system for managing the site. The management group wanted money equivalents for each inventory item. They needed to calculate values for the completed construction elements, and the amount of damage and theft. They also needed a basis for financial reporting and future estimates.

It was extremely difficult to calculate the value, or the cost, or even the cost basis, for many items; not simply because of high inflation and dynamic foreign exchange rates, but because much of the material had no estimated value upon receipt, some material was taken out and returned in damaged or unusable condition, and other material lost considerable real value in storage prior to installation (but gained in current value because of inflation).

After a year of incredibly difficult complications, the company was restructured and a new, smaller Board of Directors, more focused on problem-solving at this particular plant, was installed.

The new Board quickly realized that the unfinished project management and inventory management systems were critical to allow the completion of Plant "B." They further decided to scrap the previous Board's decision to connect the new systems to existing transaction-processing systems on a terminal network with a minicomputer host from one of the company's older power plants. Instead, they specified a LAN-based microcomputer system, and re-hired the consulting firm to pick up the systems development process once again.

The consultants returned with a smaller team and quickly started on a prototyping methodology to deliver the elements of a working system for project management and inventory management.

Using much of the work that had been completed earlier, a prototype was delivered within a few months for on-site testing. The prototype included some decision support system elements and adopted MRP-like ideas to coordinate the timing needs of the construction schedule in the project management module with inventory data in the inventory management and warehouse systems modules.

The earlier problem of physical and financial values in the inventory records was solved by recording unit volumes only, and ignoring cost and value classifications. This decision allowed the project to proceed, leaving the financial connection to a later phase.

The system database was constructed with inventory management and control needs primarily in mind, but keyed to nodes in the project management system. The database also included coded titles from the signed contracts with the various construction companies and financing institutions working on the project in order to coordinate billing and payment activities.

Plant "B" construction is nearing completion, and enhanced versions of the prototype project and inventory management systems are still running. The inventory values question has not yet been resolved.

In this example we observe some of the difficulties faced by companies trying to learn management while building integral information system. Here, difficulties of coping with the environment are compounded by problems with the organization structure, the lack of a clear chain of command, and confusion about goals and the methods for achieving them.

In this internal environment, we believe that the approach adopted here is excellent - to pare expectations and objectives to the bare minimum, to focus on practical systems elements that are essential, leaving knottier problems and other systems elements until later, perhaps much later.

CAN INFORMATION SYSTEMS RESHAPE MANAGEMENT PRACTICE IN NEW MARKET ECONOMIES?

We return to the assertion in the title of this paper. We have seen two examples of how relatively simple information subsystems focused basically on inventory management can help companies in economies that are shifting away from command and toward market forces. We believe that these examples are generalizable and show what can be done with simple, direct approaches that meet real management needs. If enough of these systems are adopted, and enough companies

begin to pay attention to the benefits of information technology applied to relatively (by Western standards) simple systems, we believe that this can have a significant effect on the whole economy, and make it possible to develop a stronger economy more quickly.

Many of the companies in East and Central Europe, even some of the largest, have been running for years with unsophisticated, very often poorly managed information systems. As noted earlier, the theory is there, and there are numerous examples of good practice from the U.S., Western Europe and Japan. Yet it is almost more than we can expect for such companies to suddenly develop and adopt new systems and new technologies for managing the business in the present environment. Perhaps a more realistic expectation would be to do what we see here: Coordinate inventory planning and control with project management activities to ensure that the right materials will be available on time - and leave the rest, including most of the difficult cost analysis and financial reporting tasks. Existing information systems were organized to support management practices that are now often entirely irrelevant. To maintain and support old information systems based on old management needs and out-of-date organizational concepts is very costly and doesn't make competitive sense. Better to move forward with small systems modules that later can be build into larger, more comprehensive systems.

Everything *can't* be done at once, and *shouldn't*. But some things are relatively easy to accomplish and can bring big, and fast, dividends. Developing information subsystems with clear goals and proven quality, like bringing inventories and material flows under control, reducing cycle times, eliminating waste and delays are important, and achievable. Many of the tools and techniques in these areas are precisely the kinds of things that can work in East and Central Europe and in the former Soviet Union.

REFERENCES

(1) Bela Csikos-Nagy, President, Hungarian Board for Materials and Prices, "Some Issues of the Economics of Inventories from the Hungarian Standpoint," Engineering Costs and Production Economics, Elsevier Science Publishers B.V., Amsterdam, Volume 5 Number 4, December 1981, p. 239.

(2) "Management's New Gurus," Business Week, August 31, 1992.

(3) "1992: Moves Europeans are Making," Eric G. Fribert, Harvard Business Review, May-June 1989.

(4) "Reengineering the CEO," Information Week, November 5, 1990.

(5) Michael Hammer, "Reengineering Work: Don't Automate, Obliterate", Harvard Business Review, July-August 1990.

(6) Attila Chikan, University of Economics, Budapest, "Characterization of Production-Inventory Systems in the Hungarian Industry," Engineering Costs and Production Economics, Elsevier Science Publishers B.V., Amsterdam, Volume 18 Number 3, January 1990, p 2.

(7) "The Competitive Advantage of Nations," Michael E. Porter, Harvard Business Review, March-April 1991.

(8) Richard E. Zultner, "TQM for Technical Teams," Communications of the ACM, October 1993, vol. 36, No. 10, pp. 79-91.

(10) Attila Chikan, "Characterization of Production-Inventory Systems in the Hungarian Industry," op. cit., p 2.

(11) ibid. p 2.

Organizational Information Technology Related Innovation:

A Framework For Mapping and Development

of Research Issues

Tor J. Larsen, Ph.D.
Associate Professor
The Norwegian School of Management
P.O. Box 580, 1301 Sandvika, NORWAY
Telephone: (+47) 67 57 08 46
Telefax: (+47) 67 57 08 54
Bitnet: FLG89007 at NOBIVM.EARN

ABSTRACT

The number of issues that may be studied in management information systems (MIS) is vast and the connections among issues are almost infinite. Detailed studies without a clear identification of boundaries that determine where studies belong in the larger picture makes theory building exceedingly difficult. A holistic approach is needed to guide research in MIS. Innovation theory is offered as one possible basis for the development of a framework for mapping present and future research issues.

The innovation process contains two principal dimensions. First, innovation unfolds over time in three distinct phases; the idea phase, the creation phase, and the usage phase. Second, innovation is a product of the interaction among elements: the innovation itself is the articulated information and decision support needs of an organizational setting. The solution to satisfy such needs may be the development of information and decision support systems, requiring the deployment of information technology (IT). IT experts often play a critical part in the development of these information systems. The development and use of information systems can only be understood in context, that is, as they interact with organizational and individual factors.

The framework also forms the basis for a more accurate identification of areas where positive and negative effects from information and decision support systems deployment may occur. In the idea phase actors have perceptions of what the effects of information and decision support innovation might be, in the creation phase the effects are formally identified, and they emerge (intentionally or unintentionally) in the usage phase.

INTRODUCTION

The development and use of information technology (IT)-related innovation in business organizations is a complex phenomenon. A frequent tactic employed to handle the complexity of the field has been to concentrate on specific domains, for example, strategic use of IT, the role of change champions, the diffusion of IT, systems development, end-user computing, or maintenance.

The contribution to knowledge within each of these domains has been of value to both researchers and practitioners. However, from the viewpoint of the organization, the total benefit of IT deployment is the combined utility of all its various uses. The number of issues that may be studied within the field of management information systems (MIS) is vast and the interaction among elements virtually infinite. By focusing on one domain researchers risk leaving out elements that are essential to organizational success. That is, too much focus on detailed studies increases the dangers of reductionism (Lakatos, 1970).

A holistic approach to IT development and use are needed to counteract the dangers of reductionism. This article offers innovation theory as one platform that may assist us in understanding the combined effects of IT development and use, and the identification of research issues.

In the following section a framework for IT-related innovation is developed. Based on the proposed framework, selected research findings regarding MIS, innovation, and IT are discussed. This material is the background for defining future research issues, leading into concluding remarks.

A FRAMEWORK FOR IT-RELATED INNOVATION

In organizational settings, the most commonly used definition of innovation is this:

"An innovation is a new idea, which may be a recombination of old ideas, a scheme that challenges the present order, a formula, or a unique approach which is perceived as new by the individuals involved." (Rogers, 1983; Zaltman, Duncan, and Holbeck, 1984; Van de Ven, 1986, p.591.)

The prerequisite added here is that the innovation utilizes IT to some degree. It should also be noted that the focus of this article is on organizations where the core business is other than the development of IT as the commercial product.

Understanding IT-related innovation involves two dimensions. First, the utilization of IT must be understood in conjunction with the business need for its deployment (Keen, 1991). Second, time is a critical component in the development of an innovation (Van de Ven, 1986). The two dimensions are the basis for the IT-related innovation framework.

The Relationship Between Business Need and IT

The question of what or who are the primary source of IT related innovation in organizational settings is unclear. Are IT innovation in organizational settings are driven by technological advances or by business needs (Zmud, 1984)?

IT as the Source of IT Innovation

Obviously, vendors and software houses have a market potential in mind in their IT product development efforts. Because of the drastic vendor and software houses IT product advancements over time, it must be correct to observe that the possible areas of IT use today is radically larger than what was the case in, for example, the early 1970ies. The development of efficient mass data storage devices, multi media processing, PCs, powerful micro computers, enhanced telecommunication services, and flexible software applications have made people think of a vast range of new areas for IT utilization. In this regard the innovation process is technology driven.

Granted they have resources to do so, ordinary business organizations choose to combine IT products and develop their own applications in unique ways. Otherwise, little competitive benefit can be derived from IT investments. The unique combination of IT elements and the development of organizational specific applications are the organizational IT innovation. In principle, the organizational IT innovation must occur through human agents within the organization. As observed in the field of systems thinking, only people through a "human activity system" can create artifacts (Checkland, 1981; Checkland and Scholes, 1990). This is the focus of the present framework.

IT may directly influence actors' IT innovation behaviors. However, the indication is that this is not necessarily the case. Larsen (1993) found that there was no correlation between hands-on use of computers or delegation of computer tasks among middle managers and IT innovation. The more middle managers were engaged in business innovation, the more they were active in networks discussing IT related issues, and the less varied jobs they held, the more middle managers were responsible for implemented IT change. Seemingly, knowledge about IT through use may not play a decisive role in the IT innovation process.

Actors as the Source of IT Innovation

The first principal question here is the relative role of IT experts versus people employed in the core production process of the organization in IT innovation. It is well documented that users regard as much as 80 per cent of information system implementations as failures (Mowshowitz, 1976; Vowler, 1991). In most cases IT experts are blamed for this sad state-of-affairs. It is claimed that information systems are riddled by technical rather than business considerations.

Keen (1991) argued that the most critical factor in ensuring an appropriate utilization of IT is managers' maturity level in regard to their knowledge about IT business potentials. His view is that in order to avoid the negative impacts of IT experts' influence, line managers must take responsibility for the coupling between business needs and IT solutions and support. Consequently, in defining who among the actors within an organization drive the IT innovation processes it is of paramount importance to differentiate between actors of the organization engaged in "production" and IT experts. Additionally, a framework for the elements influencing IT innovation should clearly demonstrate that the organizational members outside the IT expert domain carry the main responsibility for defining IT business functionality. (In the remainder of the article the term "core" is used to denote organizational activities, structures, and actors outside the IT expert domain.)

The influence on IT innovation from the core organizational setting is not only a question of individual action. People are organized into larger structures for a purpose. The minimum differentiation of structure needed to understand IT innovation is to consider the levels of the organization, groups, and individuals. Each may have its own objectives, motives, knowledge, and needs.

It is often said that some organizations are more innovative than others, a theme that has been studied in its own right (Henderson, 1979; Peters and Waterman, 1982; Kanter, 1983; Lawrence and Dyer, 1983). Consequently, the organizational impact on IT innovation may vary drastically from one organization to another.

The group level should be divided into two types; formal and informal. Formal groups may play a vital role in explaining innovation. These groups exist at all levels of the organization, making decisions on many issues in their regular meetings. Among the formal groups of the organization, there is ample evidence that the power elite is a specifically critical body (Thompson, 1967; Hage and Dewar, 1973; Larsen, 1993). The power elite, because they have decision mandate and resources available, initiate more change than managers lower in the organizational hierarchy. To a large extent, the power elite use innovation to promote their own views and interests (Kling, 1980). Also, they may suffer from self-induced protective behavior (Janis, 1971). It can take considerable pressure to induce them to initiate necessary radical changes (Pettigrew, 1985).

Informal groups exist in every organization. They emerge

because of individual action. For example, when individuals take action to introduce change, they may work as much through informal contacts as through established managerial command chains of the organizational hierarchy (Schein, 1980; Kanter, 1983, Albrecht and Ropp, 1984). The informal groups of the organization may be quite stable over time.

Individual employees, and perhaps specifically middle managers in the core organization, also take action to initiate change (Kanter, 1983; Beath, 1991; Larsen, 1993). Often, individuals employ newly introduced IT before the organization has developed active knowledge and strategies for its use (Brancheau and Wetherbe, 1990).

The essence of this discussion is that factors within the core business area - related to the organization, the formal group, the informal group, and the individual levels and the interactions among them - determine the requirements for IT innovation. Although it may not absolutely be so, this is the best way to think about it; a view that Keen (1991) advocates.

In my experience, actors within the core business do not primarily think of IT. Their concern is that the organization, the formal groups, the informal groups, and the individuals need information to carry out their tasks, remain informed about important business events, and make decisions. Consequently, the most important output from the organizational, group, and individual levels is the need for information to stay informed and the need for information to make decisions.

On a conceptual level, the aim of IT deployment is to facilitate the communication of messages in a manner that optimizes the likelihood for correct interpretation on the part of the recipient. That is, the information is communicated to a user. To make a distinction from human face-to-face interchange, the term "formal communication" is used as a general label for information and decision support. The objective of the core business is, therefore, the articulation of *formal communication needs*. The term covers the whole range of information where IT plays a role, be it data, text, voice, graphics, or live pictures. IT facilitate many, but not all, formal communication needs.

As previously mentioned, IT experts play a vital role in the selection or development of hardware and software components. The IT experts are a buffer between formal communication needs and IT solutions. Again, this does not imply that IT experts may not influence core business needs, the development of formal communication needs, core actors, or any other element. Their contributions are critical in the development and use of appropriate IT solutions. The main reason for the placement of IT experts as a buffer between articulated formal communication needs and IT hardware and software is to maintain the focus of business considerations first and technology related issues as a vehicle to support business second.

The Impact of Time on Innovation

It is quite common to advocate that an innovation develops over time in phases. Using the area of strategy process development as the basis Van de Ven (1992) strongly argues

that researchers should consider their framework for study very carefully. A development process may contain many elements not included in a simple phase model. The process also reiterates phases more often than thought and each reiteration may contain different elements and actors.

Many IT innovations are fairly large and complex undertakings that require the establishment of a formal project organization to develop a solution. However, a project organization is not established in thin air. This formalization can only occur because actors in the organization at an earlier point in time have seen a need for the effort. Additionally, a project organization is not an end, it is a vehicle for creating an IT solution. The demise of a project organization occurs when the product it has made has been transferred to the users in the core organization.

Based on these simple observations it is suggested that most IT innovations develop through three distinct phases. First, actors within the organization give birth to an idea and process it until a decision is made that a project is needed to take care of it. This is the idea phase. Second, the obvious task of the project organization is to test the soundness of the initial idea and carry through the necessary activities needed to create the new IT solution. This is the creation phase. Third, once the new IT solution is developed the IT solution is transferred into the core organization. This is the usage phase.

The idea phase, the creation phase, and the usage phase are the absolute minimum of phases needed to understand most IT innovation processes. The three phases, although of a very general nature, cover the complete process from birth to death. The division of the total process into only three components make the model robust. Also, the chosen names describe the core process within each of the three phases. For example, the traditional label for the creation phase is systems development. However, systems development has a very strong IT flavor. It may make us think about technical issues more than what is appropriate. Because of IT failures, many actors within the core organization react negatively to the term systems development.

The three phases put forward here are fewer than those Cooper and Zmud (1990) suggested. Their stages are initiation, adoption, adaption, acceptance, routinization, and infusion. Cooper and Zmud state explicitly that their model is based on "a technological diffusion perspective." (p. 124). This is a good illustration of the fundamental difference between the basis of the present framework and theories based on the diffusion of technological innovations. The principal element in the present framework is the human component, that is, the human actors within an organization. The anchor of the innovation process is the development of peoples' ideas over time and how these ideas through articulated formal communication support needs attach IT to them as part of the solution. In conclusion, this framework proposes that innovation models should choose people as their primary starting point not IT.

The Idea Phase

Ideas may have many sources; strategic processes, individuals within the line organization, or IT experts. Idea generation is the source of organizational renewal. Thus, organizations must encourage individual creativity as well as provide a structure that may guide and encourage the development of novel business approaches.

Regardless of the source, researchers have been concerned with how an idea may obtain support for its development (Kanter, 1983; Van de Ven, 1986; Beath and Ives, 1989; Beath, 1991). People must buy into the idea, that is, the informal groups of the organization and the power elite must be convinced of its benefits and the allocation of resources for its development. In most cases, the original idea will become better articulated as it goes through the buy-in process.

Thus, the idea phase consists of two sub-phases; idea percolation and idea molding. The term "percolation" reflects the need to let as many ideas as possible be articulated. "Molding" indicates processing the idea through informal groups and the power elite to secure the development and survival of ideas with high potential benefit and the cancellation of efforts with small hope of a desirable contribution.

The Creation Phase

Sometime during the molding phase an idea will have gained enough support for a decision to be made about its implementation. This is the creation phase. The term "creation" is used here to underline that the main objective, in many cases, is to make an information system with novel features. The MIS literature presents a variety of approaches for this phase - for example; systems development, the waterfall model, the socio-technical approach, heuristic development, or prototyping - each containing different and similar phases. In principle, the creation phase consists of two sub-phases; first, a formal testing of the soundness of the underlying idea, and, second, if a solution is found to be both systemically desirable and culturally feasible (Checkland and Scholes, 1990), the creation and implementation of the new formal communication system.

The term for the formal testing of an idea is "change process definition." The first task of the phase is to put a project team into place. A project leader must be chosen and team members signed on. A project plan and control mechanism must be defined before the formal testing of the idea can be carried through.

The traditional phrase for this formal testing is feasibility study. The feasibility study is the first phase of systems development. The two reasons for substituting the term feasibility study with "change process definition" are importance and scope.

Surveys of user opinions indicate that as much as 80% of all systems development efforts are judged as either direct or partial failures (Mowshowitz, 1976; Vowler, 1991). This fact alone justifies lifting out the formal testing of an idea from the mainstream of systems development and formalize it as a necessary preconditional activity. The term "change process definition" more clearly signals that the framework for the actual creation of an information system must be determined up-front.

The scope of the change process definition is wider than for traditional feasibility studies. It contains three elements. First, this is the activity that must build on the outcome of the idea molding phase. An idea, its promoters, and opponents already exists. Second, the idea, alternative technical solutions, and effects of these solutions on the elements of the innovation process (organization, power elite, formal communication support, existing information technology, IT experts, informal networks, and individuals) must be documented on a principal level. Third, the requirements for the detailed development of the system in the next sub-phase must be determined. This would include selection of quality standards, methods, information technology support (CASE), budgeting, scheduling, and mile-stones.

The second element of the creation phase would be change creation. It would span the activities of information requirements development, the detailed evaluation, procurement, and installment of IT, program development and testing, and implementation. The scope of this article is not to weight the pro and cons of quality and appropriateness of various systems development methods.

The Usage Phase

The basis for defining a minimum number of sub-elements in the usage phase is the concept of product life-cycle from the field of marketing (Kotler, 1991). At a minimum, a product goes through initiation, maturation, and decline.

With information systems the sub-phase parallelling initiation is "change anchoring". A new information system is a complex and novel experience for users and IT-experts. Some users may be pessimistic, others overly optimistic. They need time to adapt to the new tool. In this phase IT experts work on fixing errors and making smaller changes. Their task is to stabilize the new information system. The time required for this phase may vary. It cannot be shorter than the time people cognitively and emotionally need to adapt to a new situation. If the information system contains elements used seasonally, a year may be an appropriate time-frame.

Following completion of change anchoring the information system enters its longest period. From an innovation standpoint, the critical aspect of this phase is the continuous changes made to the information system. The term maintenance has been used for this process, however, maintenance implies fixing something that is wrong. A more appropriate view, this author suggests, would be to consider the difference between the concepts of product versus process innovation (Abernathy and Utterback, 1982). The result of the creation phase is the product innovation. Process changes can be made, but these changes would be incremental compared to the relatively radical changes made in the creation phase (Zaltman et al., 1984). In the usage phase refinements are made to the original design. The technical design of the information system largely

Figure 1: A Framework for IT Related Innovation

Elements of the innovation process / Evolvement over time	IDEA PHASE		CREATION PHASE		USAGE PHASE			EFFECTS OF IT DEPLOYMENT
	Idea perco-lation	Idea molding	Change process definition	Change creation	Change anchoring	Change refine-ment	Change termi-nation	
Human activity system view — **Core organization** — Organizational level								Business effects / Organizational effects
Group level — Formal groups								Formal group effects
Informal groups								Informal group effects
Individual level								Individual effects
Formal communication needs: information and decision support								Formal communication needs effects
IT expert level								IT expert level effects
IT -hardware -software								IT hardware and software effects

determines the degree of change that can be made to it in the usage phase.

Because of the inherent design limitations in any information system, and perhaps also because of developments in IT itself, the gap between business needs and deliverables from an information system will increase over the years of use. Therefore, every information system will enter a period where the question of its demise and substitution with a new system surfaces. This is the "change termination phase".

The Framework for IT-Related Innovation

The framework combines the two dimensions of IT-related innovation elements and the development of an innovation over time. Effected areas are also introduced, highlighting the need to keep in mind that innovation processes have a purpose.

The area of organizational effects has been elaborated upon to reflect the difference between business effects and other organizational effects. Business effects, whether external or internal, are the area of most concern to managers. However, organizational effects also occur. IT-related innovation may be combined with organizational development to result in changes in the organizational structure, competence and knowledge changes, or simply a higher degree of organizational efficiency (that is, tasks may be executed with less manpower, less capital cost, etc). These areas contain the basis for identification of economic effects. The framework is presented in Figure 1.

The proposed framework has similarities and differences compared with the classical model for MIS research that Ives, Hamilton, and Davis (1980) proposed. The similarity is that the proposed framework here and the Ives et. al. model contain the elements of the organization, the IT system, and the development of IT solutions. However the present model view IT through the lenses of the core business actors. Additionally, in the present framework the principal development of IT solu-

tions has been specified and areas where IT effects may occur has been included. The proposed framework includes any actor that may have a role in IT innovation. It is not restricted to direct or indirect users of IT. Because of the actor focus, environmental elements, organizational cultural impact, attitudes or beliefs are not explicitly included. These would be a further development of the constructs and variables that may explain how and why actors articulate their information needs the way they do.

MAPPING OF SOME PREVIOUS RESEARCH EFFORTS

The framework is used as a vehicle to identify and classify some of the published material within MIS. Obviously, one article cannot consider the vast material developed in the field. The choices made here are purely personal and intended as illustrations of the purpose of the framework. The phases of the innovation process is used as a template for the presentation of previous research efforts.

The Idea Percolation Phase

New ideas may be a result of organizational as well as individual action. Recently, much attention has focused on how strategic planning may lead to the identification of areas for IT investment that are most critical to the organization (Clemons and Harris, 1991; Morton, 1991; Clemons and Row, 1992).

Since the power elite (e.g. top managers) is more active in initiating business change (Hage and Dewar, 1973; Ettlie, 1983), one might think that this also applies to innovation in information systems. However, this is not necessarily so (Larsen, 1993). Additionally, some evidence suggests that in cases where top management initiate IT innovation, organizations experience more problems than if IS management starts the process (Lederer and Sethi, 1988).

Individuals within the line organization are also important sources of ideas for organizational renewal (Beath, 1988). Middle managers may play a particularly critical role (Kanter, 1983; Larsen, 1993). Younger and better educated employees are more likely to be among the first to try newly developed information technology (Brancheau and Wetherbe, 1990). All these categories of people display a high degree of innovativeness.

IT experts may also forward ideas, although reports about their idea generation activities cannot be found. Perhaps IT experts are more responsible for innovations based on IT development than people in the line organization. This would be an example of the difference between technology push versus technology pull (Zmud, 1984).

The freedom to generate ideas - idea percolation - may vary substantially among organizations. Some researchers argue that nearness to demanding customers is the most effective way to secure innovative behavior (Kohli and Jaworski, 1990; Narver and Slater, 1990). Others point to organizational climate favorable to change (Feldman, 1986; Frost, Moore, Louis, Lundberg, and Martin, 1991; Linstead and Grafton-Small, 1992). In a positive climate people feel free to forward thoughts about new arrangements, know that their incentives are welcomed and acted upon, and that they will not be punished for their efforts (Kanter, 1983; Van de Ven, 1986). According to Kanter, mechanisms the organization may use to foster innovation are job rotation through various departments and rewards as much in the form of recognition as monetary premium or promotion.

The Idea Molding Phase

Kanter (1983) claims that innovative middle managers are particularly concerned with building coalitions to support their ideas. Innovative organizations strengthen coalition building trough the availability of resources - monetary and human. Organizations, she argues, must free resources for innovation. These resources should be spread throughout the organization to ensure that innovators have to negotiate with people outside their own department to secure funding and support. In the process managers use the informal network while engaging the support of their superiors.

The probability of acceptance may depend on the idea's fundamental characteristics. Rogers (1983) defined these characteristics as relative advantage, compatibility, complexity, trialability, and observability. These dimensions have been tested and further developed specifically for the adoption of IT (Moore and Benbasat, 1991). Their analysis indicated that relative advantage, compatibility, ease of use, result demonstrability, image, visibility, trialability, and voluntariness are the most salient characteristics.

In the idea molding phase these dimensions do not relate to installed IT solutions but to thoughts about how a solution might work. These items may also relate to more than one of the elements of the innovation. For example, relative advan-

tage, compatibility, and result demonstrability might be related to formal communication needs (information and decision support). Ease of use, image, visibility, and trialability might be related to IT itself. Voluntariness describes a personal reaction on the part of persons other than the one promoting the idea and might therefore be regarded as a description of the reactions of people in the informal network.

At the organizational level very little is said in the literature about how the idea molding process should be carried out. Writings on the strategic development of IT guidelines for defining participants and their role in the process can be found, although such issues are not explicitly stated as a major focus (Clemons and Sidney, 1991; Scott Morton, 1991; Clemons & Row, 1992). The material usually concentrates on the dimensions of the strategic development in regard to customers, vendors, competitors, the threat of new entrants, and the probability of substitute products, as in Porter's writings (Porter, 1985; Porter and Millar, 1985). In conclusion, writings on IT strategy seem to be dominated by structural- rather than process-oriented views.

The Change Process Definition Phase

One of Kanter's (1983) findings is that innovative middle managers have a specific role in the project phase. Innovators do not take on the role of project managers and they do not take part in carrying out the detailed work of the project. Rather, innovators act as brokers between the project-team and the rest of the organization. Their contributions are their ability to anticipate problems that might surface and take an active role in solving emerging problems and political issues related to the interaction between the project and the organization. Their contribution is to maintain project momentum and keep the effort going. Kanter has coined the term for these activities as "boundary walking." Research findings within MIS indicate that projects have a higher probability of success when a line manager rather than an IT expert takes on the role of project manager (Johnston and Carrico, 1988).

Basic textbooks on MIS contain material with practical advice on the scope, phases, project organization, and evaluation points in feasibility studies (for example: Alter, 1992; Reynolds, 1992; Hicks, 1993). Very little, however, is said about what should be done in this phase to ensure that the personal commitment and outcome from the idea molding phase is taken care of in an appropriate manner. Additionally, the literature rarely says anything about the prerequisites for selection of appropriate methods and techniques for creating a system, although the need for selection in accordance with the particularities of each systems development effort has been clearly articulated (Davis and Olson, 1985; Dickson and Wetherbe, 1985).

Advocates of the concept of total quality management argue that the methods and techniques to be employed in development must be determined up front (Gillies, 1992). Otherwise, individuals are forced to make their own choices resulting in low system quality. Regarding the technical aspects of systems development, researchers advocate that the use of CASE tools must be planned and a structure for their use determined (Swanson, McComb, Smith, and McCubbrey, 1991). If not, incompatible solutions would be the result. Good management and selection of appropriate solutions will lead to higher quality and improved efficiency in the system. Equally important, standardization and selection of appropriate tools are prerequisites for effective and efficient improvements of the system in "the change refinement phase".

The Change Creation Phase

Numerous issues have been identified in this phase: the development of detailed information requirements, user participation, technical design, programming, testing, user training, conversion, implementation, and project management (De Marco, 1978; Mumford, 1983; Olle, Hagelstein, Macdonald, Rolland, Sol, Van Assche, and Verrijn-Stuart, 1988; Swanson, 1988; Westerman and Donoghue, 1989; Snow and Couger, 1991). This illustrates the complexity of the area.

Many of these research issues are examined in Cotteman and Senn (1992). Systems development may be said to be one of the most researched areas within MIS. Despite, or maybe because of this, as many issues seem unresolved or unidentified (for example; securing positive and limiting negative IT effects, the role of user participation, the line management versus IT management role, and appropriate implementation strategies)

The Change Anchoring Phase

People's reactions vary and may depend upon whether that person, on an individual basis, initiated a change effort or whether the innovation is the result of organizational activity. On an individual basis, the probability of adoption would most likely depend on the characteristics of the particular hardware or software under evaluation. In the case of the adoption of spreadsheets, Brancheau and Wetherbe (1990) investigated the differences in person profiles and networking behaviors between early and later adopters. Moore and Benbasat (1991) investigated the critical issues that determined success or failure to adopt personal workstations.

Researchers have often based their investigation on an easily defined example of IT where "..the individual adoption decision is voluntary." (Moore and Benbasat, p. 194). The researchers have not looked into details regarding the kinds of tasks a spreadsheet or a personal workstation may be used for and what benefits or problems people may have with each of these. They have used the name of the innovation (the spreadsheet or the personal workstation) in aggregated questions to tap respondents' reactions.

Organizational systems might contain a much more complex combination of hardware and software in their design. People do not always have a choice whether to use the information system or not. Preparing the ground for successful use of organizational innovations starts in the idea phase and should

be systematically implemented in the creation phase (Swanson, 1988).

The Change Refinement Phase

Although this is the longest, and probably the most important period in a system's lifecycle, relatively little research has been reported. It is symptomatic that in a comprehensive textbook on information systems Wysocki and Young (1990) do not use the word "maintenance", or its equivalent, in the table of contents or in the index. In Cash, McFarlan, and McKenney (1988) maintenance is infrequently found under subheadings in the table of contents and given less than one page of space in the text. Journal articles often have a technical flavor, focusing on professional problems or purely technology considerations (Edwards, 1984; Kim and Westin, 1988). The exception to the rule is the work of Swanson and Beath (1989). Their book gives a comprehensive view of the many issues of maintenance and how it could be better managed.

Regarding end-user computing systems, maintenance is viewed as problematic (Davis, 1989). Seemingly, people in the line organization do not have the discipline needed to analyze their own information requirements, or to test and document their programs properly.

The focus literature on the idea refinement phase has mainly been on how the IS operation should be organized and run (Dearden, 1987; La Belle and Nyce, 1987; Wysocki and Young, 1990). The most important line management concern seems to be calculating the right sum of money that should be paid for IS services (Hufnagel and Birnberg, 1989).

Managerial challenges have been more thoroughly investigated in the area of end-user computing (Nelson, 1989). Frameworks for the evolution of the management of end-user computing over time have also been presented (Henderson and Treacy, 1986). Recent publications have initiated a discussion of the overall responsibilities of line managers (Keen, 1991; Boynton, Jacobs, and Zmud, 1992).

The Change Termination Phase

To the knowledge of this author there is no published work that specifically addresses this issue. Rather, this dimension of a system's life is subsumed under other fields in a structural and technical manner.

When strategic planning or an isolated project effort define an opportunity or a problem, it is automatically assumed that a new system will render an old one obsolete. During implementation the emphasis is on how an old system's data is converted into a new structure and how functional transition from the old to new may be achieved in steps or in one big operation.

The Effects of IT Innovation

Identifying benefits from IT investment is a difficult task. Researchers have investigated efficiency (doing the thing right) and effectiveness issues (doing the right thing). It does not seem from recent publications that researchers have succeeded in delineating principal effect areas, the interrelationships among areas, ways to measure effects, or what types of effects have economical ramifications that can be calculated (Banker, Kauffman, and Mahmood, 1993). This may parallel the situation in the area of organizational impact of the introduction of IS (Attewell and Rule, 1984; Markus and Robey, 1988).

Although attempts have been made to forward coherent frameworks for economical results (Parker, Benson, and Trainor, 1988), more effort seems to have been directed toward the development of the concept of user satisfaction as a substitute for IT effects. Ives, Olson, and Baroudi (1983) developed a scale for organizational systems and Doll and Torkzadeh (1988) developed a somewhat different instrument for end-user computing.

Other researchers have expressed doubt as to whether these instruments tap the right constructs or are stable across research areas (Iivari, 1987; Etezadi-Amoli and Farhoomand, 1991). The difficulty of developing stable research models is illustrated by the excellent work of Goodhue (1986) who claimed that user satisfaction must build on the concept of job satisfaction in behavioral science. Yet, surveys of research in the domain of job satisfaction have consistently reported that the construct is complex and that the relationship with performance may be questionable (Locke, 1976; Lawler, 1983; Fisher, 1983).

FUTURE RESEARCH ISSUES

The critical issue that may determine future success in MIS research is "doing the right thing". It is the opinion of this author that the state-of-the-art today is characterized by "doing the things right", that is, detailed studies. The quantity of publications in MIS is increasing, it seems exponentially, because of the introduction of new journals, textbooks, and books on specific themes with contributions from many authors. Consequently, the traditional and the new publication outlets contain a high number of loosely connected articles. The field has passed the threshold where one person can hope to remain cognizant of published material, even within her or his areas of specialty. As long as MIS research efforts stay on a detailed level, the number of issues and their interconnections will remain infinite.

The innovation model in Figure 1 offers a generic framework for a holistic understanding of research findings within MIS. It also indicates three obvious choices for the definition of broader based research undertakings. First, research projects may include a higher number of the elements of IT innovation, that is, the vertical axis in the model. Second, research efforts may include a wider time-span, that is, a higher number of phases of the innovation process. Third, research might include the concept of IT change effects more often.

The Interaction Among Elements

Research efforts may choose between two strategies. The research design might include the interaction among elements in their core model. The second alternative would be to focus on one of the elements and treat factors of the other relevant elements as controls. Either strategy is valid for any of the phases of the innovation process and within each phase the interaction among elements might be genuinely different. The development of frameworks for these interactions and controls are separate undertakings in their own right.

An example of the need for this type of research is the area of idea development in the idea percolation phase. As discussed earlier, ideas may come from planned organizational action, IT experts, or from individuals in the line organization. Questions we might ask in this respect include: What is the relative importance of idea generation from these sources and what mechanisms organizations should employ to increase the likelihood of idea generation (that is, what are the inhibiting and facilitating factors of idea generation)?

In the idea molding phase, questions regarding tactics for ensuring a sound collaboration on idea development and organizational anchoring would seem critical. In the area of strategy development indications are that organizations where both top management and lower organizational members take an active part perform better (Hart, 1992). Organizations where top management dominate or where lower organizational members have taken over strategy development because of top management abdication perform worse. The processes used for idea molding and the rate of success regarding IT innovation under the three types of strategy development (top management and organizational member collaboration, top management control, and top management abdication) would be an area for investigation.

The Development of IT Innovation Over Time

Research undertakings may be based on a single element or a combination of elements and their development across phases. A good example of an investigation of the impact of a single element over time is the work of Swanson, McComb, Smith, and McCubbrey (1992). They investigated how the careful design of CASE tools and reuse of program modules would result in more efficient execution of programming tasks in systems development and maintenance.

In research on multiple elements, Walls, Widmeyer, and El Sawy (1992) have proposed a generic theory for system design. Their work include, the elements of management, methods for systems development, change velocity, and their relationships with theory building. Although the authors introduced terms (for example, templates & triggers) that are not part of the standard vocabulary of the MIS community and that are quite hard to understand because they of their abstract nature, this is a good example of the type of information the MIS field is in critical need of.

While the article of Walls et. al. includes a definition of principal elements and their interrelationships, it does not raise the issue of how these elements and interrelationships may evolve over time. This may be a crucial issue. What are the mechanisms that would ensure an acceptable and feasible transition from one phase to another? The development of IT innovation contain multiple transitions:

- How to move from the idea percolation phase to idea molding?
- How should an idea move from the molding phase to change creation anchoring?
- What should one do to ensure a smooth and appropriate transition from the anchoring phase to change creation?
- What works and what does not work to ensure effective and efficient transition into the change anchoring phase?
- How does the system move to the change refinement phase?
- What should be done to ensure that organizations can get rid of outdated information systems?

Perhaps the most fundamental question is whether IT innovations develop in distinct phases. Inherent characteristics of the technology itself may determine a natural sequence of events. The innovation process may execute tasks out of sequence, the execution of tasks may be more circular than commonly held, or the process may contain tasks we do not know much about or may put less emphasis on others (Van de Ven, 1992). IT innovation may be different from other types of change efforts.

IT Change Effects

Organizations expect a positive contribution from IT innovation. DeLone and McLean (1992) have presented a thorough survey of the multiple constructs researchers have used to measure information system success. They suggested that organizational impact is the ultimate dependent construct.

However, the term "organizational impact" is imprecise. An elaboration on the effect areas in Figure 1 may assist us in a clearer understanding of the dependent effect construct and the interrelationships among effect areas.

Obviously, positive business effects must be the ultimate objective of IT innovation. Business effects may be an increase in efficiency or effectiveness. Efficiency effects may be related to the business value chain (Porter, 1985). Just in time systems may be impossible without IT; the deployment of information systems leading to reduced need for inventory. IT may speed up the production process. IT may be a critical vehicle for efficient distribution of goods. The automatization of customer order and handling by means of EDI may result in increased market share. IT business effectiveness may be related to increased ability to perform product and market analyses.

Positive business effects may materialize if formal communication needs are satisfied. Formal communication needs satisfaction may be achieved through appropriate information and decision support.

Organizational effects (reduction in manpower needed to execute tasks, degree of reorganization, and knowledge requirements), formal group effects (redistribution of influence, the need for formal organizational structures, changes in attitude among the power elite), informal group effects (changes in social patterns, changes in informal networking), and individual effects (job content changes, degree of job autonomy) may interact among themselves and influence the probability of achieving formal communication needs satisfaction.

IT effects may be the factor behind the scene that has an influence on all these other areas. Examples of IT effects are requirements for IT expert knowledge, the degree of functionality of hardware, software, operation systems, telecommuni-

Figure 2: A Model for Principal Effect Areas and Their Interrelationships.

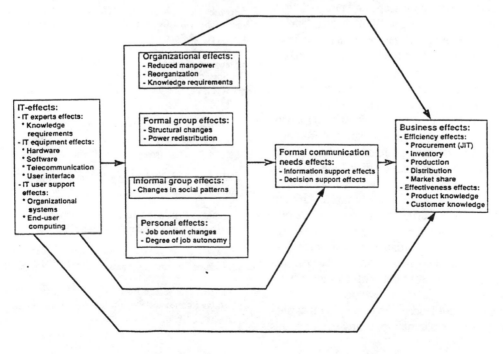

cation, the quality of the user interface, and the quality and availability of user support. Of course, the relationships among business, formal communication, organizational, formal groups, informal groups, individual, IT expert, IT support, and IT hardware and software may be reciprocal. However, the best way to think about them may be to state that the ultimate results are the business effects and that these emerge because of formal communication support. The possibility of achieving this support depends on the effects on the organizational, formal group, informal group, and individual level. The effects here are facilitators or inhibitors to that end. Finally, the multiple IT effects are the elements that influence all other effects. An example of a model for these principal effect areas and their interrelationships is shown in Figure 2.

Obviously, much more work needs to be done to develop good and practical models for the definition of effects. In addition to definitional efforts, the practical measurement of effects, the transition of effects into monetary terms, models that may assist managers in understanding the interrelationships among effects, definition of effects that increase the probability of success, and what effects that may jeopardize IT innovation all need more attention.

Effect recognition itself is not often recognized as an area of study. It would seem obvious that the probability of success would increase if systematic thought was given to innovation effects in the idea phase, thoroughly investigated and documented in the change creation phase, and consciously engineered in the change anchoring phase. The handling of effects must surely also be a critical issue in the change refinement phase. Perhaps the key to successful line management of IT innovation is the planning and control of effects.

CONCLUDING REMARKS

The main objective of this article has been to argue that research in MIS needs to define its scope and place within a coherent framework. This does not at all imply that detailed studies in MIS should be avoided. However, more concern must be given to our research designs and choice of methods to avoid the dangers of reductionism.

Popper's axiom that good theory building resides in efforts to refute a theory rather than prove over and over again that it holds may be the reason why empirical research so easily becomes a jungle of improbable and disconnected findings. The vast majority of MIS publications report correlations, beta values in regression analyses, or loadings from LISREL in the 0.15 to 0.40 range. These are good to excellent results, however, even a finding at the 0.40 level only explains 16% of the variance. Add to this all the difficulties we have with theory, construct, research model, variable and hypothesis development. The operationalization of variables is yet another challenge leading into problematic research design choices. No wonder researchers can easily prove that the theory underlying the findings does not hold.

This criticism should not lead to the conclusion that phenomenological studies is the alternative. Many studies of this nature are of lesser quality than traditional empirical efforts, simply because researchers of the "soft approach" seem to forget basic rules for clarity and flow of argument from problem statement to conclusions. Regardless of research approach, consistency, quality, validity, and reliability must be present.

However, more freedom in what is acceptable for publication may be needed to bring the MIS field forward. We need more think-pieces and discussions on generic frameworks to assist individual researchers in carving out an acceptable domain for scrutiny.

REFERENCES

Abernathy, William J. and Utterback, James M. (1982). "Patterns of Industrial Innovation," in Tushman, Michael L. and Moore, William L. (Eds), Readings in the Management of Innovation. Boston, MA: Pitman.

Albrecht, Terrance L. and Ropp, Vickie A. (1984). "Communicating about Innovation in Networks of Three U.S. Organizations," Journal of Communication, Summer, pp. 78-91.

Alter, Steven (1992). Information Systems: A Management Perspective, Reading, MA: Addison-Wesley Publishing Company.

Attewell, Paul and Rule, James (1984). "Computing and Organizations: What We Know and What We Don't Know," Communications of the ACM, 27(12), December, pp. 1184-1192.

Banker, Rajiv D., Kauffman, Robert J., and Mahmood, Mo Adam (Eds) (1993). Strategic Information Technology Management: Perspectives on Organizational Growth and Competitive Advantage. Harrisburg, PA: Idea Group Publishing.

Beath, Cynthia Mathis (1991). "Supporting the Information Technology Champion," MIS Quarterly, 15(3), September, pp. 355-372.

Beath, Cynthia Mathis and Ives, Blake (1989). "The Information Technology Champion: Aiding and Abetting, Care and Feeding," in Gray, P., King, W. R., McLean, E., and Watson, H. (Eds), The Management of Information Systems. Chicago, IL: The Dryden Press.

Boynton, Andrew C., Jacobs, Gerry C., and Zmud, Robert W. (1992). "Whose Responsibility is IT Management?," Sloan Management Review, Summer, pp. 32-38.

Brancheau, James C. and Wetherbe, James C. (1990). "The Adoption of Spreadsheet Software: Testing Innovation Diffusion Theory in the Context of End-User Computing," Information Systems Research, 1(2), pp. 115-143.

Cash, James I. Jr., McFarlan, F. Warren, and McKenney, James L. (1988). Corporate Information Systems Management: The Issues Facing Senior Executives. Homewood, IL: Irwin.

Checkland, Peter (1981). Systems Thinking, Systems Practice. Chichester, England: John Wiley & Sons.

Checkland, Peter and Scholes, Jim (1990). Soft Systems Methodology in Action. Chichester, England: John Wiley & Sons.

Clemons, Eric K. and Harris, Sidney E. (Eds) (1991). "The Strategic Use of Information Systems (special issue)," MIS Quarterly, 15(3), September.

Clemons, Eric K. and Row, Michael C. (Eds) (1992). "Strategic and Competitive Information Systems (special issue)," Journal of Management Information Systems, 9(2), Fall.

Cooper, Randolph B. and Zmud, Robert W. (1990). "Information Technology Implementation Research: A Technological Diffusion Approach," Management Science, Vol. 36(2), February, pp. 123-139.

Cotteman, William W. and Senn, James A. (1992). Challenges and Strategies for Research in Systems Development, ?; John Wiley & Sons.

Davis, Gordon B. (1989). "Caution: User-Developed Systems Can Be Dangerous to Your Organization," in Nelson, R. Ryan (Ed), End-User Computing: Concepts, Issues and Applications. New York, NY: John Wiley & Sons.

Davis, Gordon B. and Olson, Margrethe H. (1985). Management Information Systems: Conceptual Foundations, Structure, and Development, New York, NY: McGraw-Hill Book Company.

De Marco, Tom (1978). Structured Analysis and System Specification. New York, NY: Yourdon Inc.

Dearden, John (1987). "The Withering Away of the IS Organization," Sloan Management Review, Summer, pp. 87-91.

DeLone, William H. and McLean, Ephraim R. (1992). "Information Systems Success: The Quest for the Dependent Variable," Information Systems Research, 3(1), March, pp. 60-95.

Dickson, Gary and Wetherbe, James C. (1985). The Management of Information Systems, New York, NY: McGraw-Hill Book Company.

Doll, William J. and Torkzadeh, Gholamreza (1988). "The Measurement of End-User Computing Satisfaction," MIS Quarterly, 12(2), June, pp. 259-274.

Edwards, Chris (1984). "Information Systems Maintenance: An Integrated Perspective," MIS Quarterly, 8(4), December, pp. 237-256.

Etezadi-Amoli, Jamshid and Farhoomand, Ali F. (1991). "On End-User Computing Satisfaction," MIS Quarterly, 15(1), March, pp. 1-4.

Ettlie, John E. (1983). "A Note on the Relationship Between Managerial Change Values, Innovative Intentions, and Innovative Outcomes in Food Sector Firms," R & D Management, 13(4), pp. 231-244.

Feldman, Steven P. (1986). "Management in Context: An Essay on the Relevance of Culture to the Understanding of Organizational Change," Journal of Management Studies, 23(6), November, pp. 587-607.

Fisher, Cynthia D. (1983). "On the Dubious Wisdom of Expecting Job Satisfaction to Correlate with Performance," in Steers, Richard M. and Porter, Lyman W. (Eds), Motivation & Work Behavior. New York, NY: McGraw-Hill Book Company.

Frost, Peter J., Moore, Larry F., Louis, Meryl Reis, Lundberg, Craig C., and Martin, Joanne (Eds) (1991). Reframing Organizational Culture. Newbury Park, CA: Sage Publications.

Gillies, Alan C. (1992). Software Quality: Theory and Management. London, England: Chapman & Hall.

Hage, Jerald and Dewar, Robert (1973). "Elite Values Versus Organizational Structure in Predicting Innovation," Administrative Science Quarterly, September, pp. 279-290.

Hart, Stuart L. (1992). "An Integrative Framework for Strategy-Making Processes," Academy of Management Review, 17(2), pp. 327-351.

Henderson, Bruce (1979). Henderson on Corporate Strategy. Cambridge, MA: Abt Books.

Henderson, John C. and Treacy, Michael E. (1986). "Managing End-User Computing for Competitive Advantage," Sloan Management Review, Winter, pp. 3-14.

Hicks, James O., Jr. (1993). Management Information Systems: A User Perspective, Minneapolis/St. Paul, MN: West Publishing Company.

Hufnagel, Ellen and Birnberg, Jacob, G. (1989). "Perceived Chargeback System Fairness in Decentralized Organizations: An Examination of the Issues," MIS Quarterly, 13(4), December, pp. 415-429.

Iivari, Juhani (1987). "User Information Satisfaction (UIS) Reconsidered: An Information System as the Antecedent of UIS," Proceedings of the Eighth International Conference on Information Systems. Pittsburgh, PA, December 6-9, pp. 57-73.

Ives, Blake, Hamilton, Scott, and Davis, Gordon B. (1980), "A Framework for Research in Computer-Based Management Information Systems," Management Science, Vol. 26(9), September, pp. 910-934.

Ives, Blake, Olson, Margrethe H., and Baroudi, Jack J. (1983). "The Measurement of User Information Satisfaction," Communications of the ACM, 26(10), October, pp. 785-793.

Janis, Irving L. (1971). "Groupthink," Psychology Today, November, pp. 378-384.

Johnston, H. Russel and Carrico, Shelly R. (1988). "Developing Capabilities to Use Information Strategically," MIS Quarterly, 12(1), March, pp. 37-47.

Kanter, Rosabeth Moss (1983). The Change Masters: Innovation & Entrepreneurship in the American Corporation. New York, NY: Touchstone.

Keen, Peter G. W. (1991). Shaping the Future. Cambridge, MA: Harvard Business School Press.

Kim, Chai and Westin, Stu (1988). "Software Maintainability: Perceptions of EDP Professionals," MIS Quarterly, 12(2), June, pp. 167-185.

Kling, Rob (1980). "Social Analyses of Computing: Theoretical Perspectives of Recent Empirical Research," ACM Computing Surveys, 12(1), March, pp. 61-110.

Kohli, Ajay K. and Jaworski, Bernard J. (1990). "Market Orientation: The Construct, Research Propositions, and Managerial Implications," Journal of Marketing, 54(April), pp. 1-18.

Kotler, Philip (1991). Marketing Management: Analysis, Planning, Implementation, and Control. Englewood Cliffs, NJ: Prentice-Hall International, Inc.

La Belle, Antoinette and Nyce, H. Edward (1987). "Wither the IT Organization," Sloan Management Review, Summer, pp. 75-85.

Lakatos, Imre (1970). "Falsification and the Methodology of Scientific Research Programs," in Lakatos, Imre and Musgrave, Allen (Eds), Criticism and the Growth of Knowledge. Cambridge, England: Cambridge University Press, pp. 91-196.

Larsen, Tor J. (1993). "Middle Managers' Contribution to Implemented Information Technology Innovation," Journal of Management Information Systems, 10(2), Fall, pp. 155-176.

Lawler, Edward E. III (1983). "Satisfaction and Behavior," in Steers, Richard M. and Porter, Lyman W. (Eds), Motivation & Work Behavior. New York, NY: McGraw-Hill Book Company.

Lawrence, Paul R. and Dyer, Davis (1983). Renewing American Industry: Organizing for Efficiency and Innovation. New York, NY: The Free Press.

Lederer, Albert L. and Sethi, Vijay (1988). "The Implementation of Strategic Information Systems Planning Methodologies," MIS Quarterly, 12(3), September, pp. 445-461.

Linstead, Stephen and Grafton-Small, Robert (1992). "On Reading Organizational Culture," Organization Studies, 13(3), pp. 331-355.

Locke, Edwin A. (1976). "The Nature and Causes of Job Satisfaction," in Dunnette, M. D. (Ed), Handbook of Industrial and Organizational Psychology. Chicago, IL: Rand McNally.

Markus, M. Lynne and Robey, Daniel (1988). "Information Technology and Organizational Change: Causal Structure in Theory and Research," Management Science, 34(5), May, pp. 583-598.

Moore, Gary C. and Benbasat, Izak (1991). "Development of an Instrument to Measure Perceptions of Adopting an Information Technology Innovation," Information Systems Research, 2(3), September, pp. 192-222.

Morton, Michael S. Scott (Ed) (1991). The Corporation of the 1990s: Information Technology and Organizational Transformation. New York, NY: Oxford University Press.

Mowshowitz, A. (1976). The Conquest of Will: Information Processing. Reading, MA: Addison-Wesley.

Mumford, Enid (1983). Designing Human Systems For New Technology.
Manchester, England: Manchester Business School, Printed by Wright's (Sandbach) Ltd.

Narver, John C. and Slater, Stanley F. (1990). "The Effect of a Market Orientation on Business Profitability," Journal of Marketing, 54(October), pp. 20-35.

Nelson, R. Ryan (Ed) (1989). End-User Computing: Concepts, Issues, and Applications. New York, NY: John Wiley & Sons.

Olle, T. William, Hagelstein, Jacques, Macdonald, Ian G., Rolland, Colette, Sol, Henk G., Van Assche, Frans J. M., and Verrijn-Sturart, Alexander A. (1988). Information Systems Methodologies: A Framework for Understanding. Wokingham, England: Addison-Wesley Publishing Company.

Parker, Marilyn M., Benson, Robert J., and Trainor, H. Edward (1988). Information Economics: Linking Business Performance to Information Technology. Englewood Cliffs, NJ: Prentice-Hall, Inc.

Pettigrew, Andrew (1985). The Awakening Giant: Continuity and Change in ICI. Oxford, England: Basil Blackwell.

Peters, Thomas J. and Waterman, Robert H., Jr. (1982). In Search of Excellence: Lessons from America's Best-Run Companies. New York, NY: Warner Books.

Porter, Michael E. (1985). Competitive Advantage: Creating and Sustaining Superior Performance, New York, NY: The Free Press.

Porter, Michael E. and Millar, Victor E. (1985). "How Information Gives You Competitive Advantage," Harvard Business Review, July/August, pp. 149-160.

Reynolds, George W. (1992). Information Systems for Managers, St. Paul, MN: West Publishing Company.

Rogers, Everett M. (1983). Diffusion of Innovations. New York, NY: The Free Press.

Schein, Edgar H. (1980). Organizational Psychology. Englewood Cliffs, NJ: Prentice-Hall, Inc.

Snow, Terry A. and Couger, J. Daniel (1991). "Creativity Improvement Intervention in a Systems Development Work Unit," Proceedings of the Twenty-Fourth Annual Hawaii International Conference on Systems Sciences, IV, pp. 412-418.

Swanson, E. Burt (1988). Information Systems Implementation: Bridging the Gap Between Design and Utilization. Homewood, IL: Richard Irwin, Inc.

Swanson, E. Burt and Beath, Cynthia Mathis (1989). Maintaining Informatio Systems in Organizations. Chichester, England: John Wiley & Sons.

Swanson, Kent, McComb, Dave, Smith, Jill, and McCubbrey, Don (1991). "The Application Software Factory: Applying Total Quality Techniques to Systems Development," MIS Quarterly, 15(4), December, pp. 567-579.

Thompson, James D. (1967). Organizations in Action. New York, NY: Mc Graw-Hill.

Van de Ven, Andrew H. (1992). "Suggestions for Studying Strategy Process: A Research Note," Strategic Management Journal, Special Issue on "Strategy Process Research," 13(Summer), pp. 169-188.

Van de Ven, Andrew H. (1986). "Central Problems in the Management of Innovati n," Management Science, 32(5), pp. 590-607.

Vowler, J. (1991). "A Risky Investment that Business Has To Make," Computer Weekly, Vol. 6 (November).

Walls, Joseph G., Widmeyer, George R., and El Sawy, Omar (1992). "Building an Information System Design Theory for Vigilant EIS," Information Systems Research, 3(1), March, pp. 36-59.

Westerman, John and Donoghue, Pauline (1989). Managing the Human Resource. New York, NY: Prentice Hall.

Wysocki, Robert K. and Young, James (1990). Information Systems: Management Principles in Action. New York, NY: John Wiley & Sons.

Zaltman, Gerald, Duncan, Robert, and Holbeck, Jonny (1984). Innovations & Organizations. Malabar, FA: Robert E. Krieger Publishing Company.

Zmud, Robert W. (1984). "An Examination of 'Push-Pull' Theory Applied to Process Innovation in Knowledge Work," Management Science, 30(6), pp. 727-738.

Evaluating Requirements for Future Information Technology Systems: A Socio Technical Approach

Mrs C W Olphert, Mrs S D P Harker and Professor K D Eason
HUSAT Research Institute, Loughborough University of Technology,
The Elms, Elms Grove, Loughborough, Leics. LE11 1RG, UK
Tel: +44 509 611088

Mr J E Dobson
Department of Computing Science, University of Newcastle upon Tyne
Newcastle upon Tyne, NE1 7RU, UK
Tel: + 44 91 222 8228

Executive Abstract

INTRODUCTION

To exploit information technology in a business context, business leaders need to be able to understand the potential of the technology and apply it to their enterprise. This paper describes the ORDIT methodology, developed in the European ESPRIT programme, which enables business 'stakeholders' to generate and evaluate socio-technical options based on new forms of technology. The paper describes how the use of the methodology handles the emergence of new requirements and conflicts between requirements. It describes three examples of using the methodology to demonstrate its use with different types of socio-technical alternatives.

BACKGROUND

If organisations are to exploit the potential of information technology they have to use it to transform their business processes to win new markets, meet new customer requirements and develop the roles of their staff. Conventional methods for developing information technology systems do not support this process. The analysis methods tend to assume requirements for new systems can be collected or elicited from the study of existing systems. It is also assumed that this is a logical process that can be undertaken by systems analysts. Our view is that major new developments in information technology require an entirely different process. The main 'stakeholders' in the organisation have to be able to review the options for new technology to enable the redesign of their socio-technical systems in order to tackle future challenges. Most of the senior people who are responsible for management are in no position to undertake such exercises. They do not understand new technological developments sufficiently to see their relevance to the future of their organisations and, if information systems specialists try to help them, the usual methods and forms of representation used for systems development hinder rather than help the communication.

The development of major systems depends on a recognition that the process of requirements specification needs to be an active one in which stakeholders are helped to generate requirements which are relevant to the future of the organisation. Consideration of the future gives rise to requirements which are emergent - that is, they are a result of the process of engaging with the options which are available. These issues have been addressed by the ORDIT (Organisational Requirements Definition for Information Technology systems) methodology. This was developed in a recently-completed ESPRIT project, to provide a process and a set of methods by which organisational stakeholders and systems staff can work in partnership to generate and evaluate socio-technical systems options that are made possible by the combination of new forms of information technology and new organisational structures.

DESCRIPTION OF THE ORDIT METHODOLOGY

A central concept of the ORDIT methodology is the notion of the requirements perspective - for example efficiency, staff satisfaction, return on investment, client service, orientation etc. - as a driver of design decisions. These perspectives cannot always be expressed in terms of activities performed or resources used; rather they behave as sources of policy and provide evaluation criteria for selecting between options. Identification of perspectives is thus a vital part of an ORDIT project.

The process of perspective identification serves to uncover possible futures, in the sense that it may reveal alternative ways of grouping responsibilities, and the loci and structures of policy making. Shifts of perspective or concentration on one perspective can often be shown to result in implications which are felt to be undesirable from the perspectives of other stakeholders. Thus the exploration of possible futures and the terms in which such futures are expressed and evaluated relates to the perspectives involved. The information technology system itself may be seen as an agent of change, and the benefits and penalties of the change as seen from each perspective must be evaluated. Many of the concepts and techniques of ORDIT are primarily designed to achieve these evaluations, which serve as a means of driving out an agreed set of organisational requirements.

The methodology provides a process and a set of tools to support the identification of options for evaluation. The application of the methodology is intended to start in the conceptual stage of systems development and may extend alongside the development process. It starts by identifying key stakeholders, the people in or associated with the organisation who could have an interest in a new systems development. The methodology contains methods to help stakeholders generate and evaluate their requirements and to identify shared requirements and those that are in conflict. It also includes processes based upon management of change theories which support user participation, in order that stakeholders can play their role in specifying and prioritising requirements, proposing options, evaluating the impact of options, identifying and resolving conflicts, etc.

There is a facility for modelling enterprises which enables a socio-technical representation to be created integrating the business process, the organisation structures and the information processes. The modelling process is based on the analysis of responsibility and obligation. It recognises that organisations achieve major goals by assigning responsibilities for activities to work roles. This both specifies the rights and obligations of the holder of a particular work role and the relationships that exist between work roles. The responsibilities held by role holders are supported by the information systems, and the representations provided by the modelling therefore provide the bridge between the organisational structure and the information technology. Models can be produced at different levels of abstraction and detail. A model of the existing system can be used as a basis for developing other models to represent alternative socio-technical opportunities based on new requirements. Technical specialists can suggest options that make use of the enabling properties of new technology. The ease with which alternatives can be generated facilitates the evaluation of the costs and benefits of different ways forward.

The aim of the process is to support a debate based on the review of options which may range from minor changes in technology to a major re-orientation of the organisation. Stakeholders are able to explore a wide range of implications, can work through conflicts, introduce new requirements and develop their preferred options in considerable detail. The process of option generation is likely to occur for different purposes at different stages in the use of ORDIT. In the early stages of a project, options may be generated as a way of clarifying the problem, defining system boundaries or identifying levers for change. Alternative options may be generated as part of the requirement definition process (e.g. alternative work organisation or job design options, interface options, technical options) as a way of refining, focussing, checking and confirming requirements. The output is a specification of a future socio-technical system which has the commitment of the major stakeholders, is well understood by them, includes a specification for organisational change and a specification for the required information system.

CASE STUDIES IN THE GENERATION OF SOCIO-TECHNICAL OPPORTUNITIES

The paper presents three case studies to illustrate the use of the ORDIT methodology in different organisational settings:- a utility company, a bank and in the criminal prosecution service.

CONCLUSIONS

By exploring the way in which the tools and process of the ORDIT methodology enabled options to be generated and evaluated, the paper aims to show (i) how stakeholders can play an effective role in the examination of the radical roles might play in their organisation, (ii) how stakeholders become able to contemplate major organisational changes, and (iii) how a specification for future information systems emerges from the process.

The Adoption of Information Systems Methodologies - An Analytical Framework and a Case Study

Chris Sauer & Colleen Lau

Fujitsu Centre for Managing Information Technology in Organisations
Australian Graduate School of Management
University of New South Wales
PO Box 1, Kensington, NSW 2033, Australia

Executive Abstract

BACKGROUND

Information systems development (ISD) methodologies are claimed to bring various benefits including better systems, and better and more standardised development processes. Researchers have concentrated on developing new methodologies and comparing their features rather than evaluating whether in practice they do generate the claimed benefits. Issues such as ease of adoption and use are not discussed. The focus of this paper is on adoption where this means selection, introduction, and integration of an ISD methodology.

The literature is pessimistic of our ability to learn about the practical value of methodologies. However, there is some existing work on the contingencies associated with methodol-

ogy use (Naumann et al 1980, Davis 1982, Episkopou & Wood-Harper 1986). This paper develops and extends their work into a framework which can be used for understanding methodology adoption. It then applies the framework to analyse a case and draws some recommendations and conclusions.

THE FRAMEWORK

The framework identifies six components which are important in influencing adoption (Table 1, col 1). Each component may vary on a number of dimensions (Table 1, col 2).

The framework makes successful methodology adoption dependent on two things. One, there must be a match between the values of the methodology's various dimensions and those

Table 1: Contingency framework for the adoption of IS methodologies

Component	Dimensions
problem solver, problem owner	personality, cognitive style, skills, experience, interests, values, disposition toward methodologies
methodology	cognitive information processing requirements, level of detail, values, epistemological orientation, resource costs, time span
problem solving process	cognitive requirements of established tasks, values, epistemological orientation, malleability of existing processes
problem style	size, complexity, uncertainty, novelty, business system type
intra-organisational context	structures, processes, policies, culture, resources
extra-organisational context	source of contingencies, methodology experience, labour market, consultancy, CASE tools, user groups

of (1) the problem solver, (2) the problem solving process within which the methodology is to be used, and (3) the parameters, or style, of the problem. Two, there must not be contextual factors such as political conflict or resource shortage which regardless of the match hinder adoption.

CASE STUDY FINDINGS

The case studied the efforts made by an Australian state government agency to adopt the methodology, SSADM. Adoption proved to be part of a longer history both of attempts to introduce a methodology and of broader organisational change. By the end of 1992 the adoption process appeared to have halted.

Acquiring and introducing SSADM proved insufficient for continuing integration and use. Although the methodology had the potential to professionalise the development process for the IS department, other factors militated against this. The disposition of developers (problem solvers) towards the methodology was mostly no better than cool. In addition, there were overriding contextual factors. The changing political context imposed severe new demands on users who in turn needed better service from the IS department. In trying to reduce user dissatisfaction ISD management increased user management's influence in projects by agreeing to have user project managers. This undermined the IS department's own ability to influence adoption by marginalising the methodology's champion from decisions as to how much of SSADM should be used in any project. For user project managers, while the methodology offered some benefits, the dominant concern was that it would increase development times and therefore they had little reason

to promote adoption. In permitting SSADM adoption to falter, they were complicit in its tacit rejection by the IS development staff.

CONCLUSIONS

The case study only road tests parts of the proposed framework. Nonetheless, it does help us understand the methodology adoption process. In particular, by highlighting critical components of adoption it gives us a basis for identifying matches and mismatches between those components and the methodology, and hence for recognising likely sources of difficulty.

The case reinforces the conclusion that adoption should be treated as a project in its own right. Adoption does not take place in an historical or political vacuum. An influential methodology champion appears very desirable to give impetus to the adoption project.

Finally, the case also suggests that a failed methodology adoption project may have serious negative effects on future attempts to introduce some other methodology.

REFERENCES

Davis, G.B. (1982) Strategies for information requirements determination, *IBM Systems Journal*, 21, 1, 4-30.

Episkopou, D.M. & Wood-Harper, A.T. (1986) Towards a framework to choose appropriate information system approaches, *Computer Journal*, 29, 3.

Naumann, J.D., Davis, G.B. & McKeen, J.D. (1980) Determining information requirements: a contingency method for selection of a requirements assurance strategy, *Journal of Systems and Software*, 1, 273-281.

Contingency Based Situational Systems Development in Large Organizations

C. van Slooten
School of Management Studies
University of Twente
P.O. Box 217, 7500 AE Enschede
The Netherlands
E-mail: cvs@sms.utwente.nl

S.Brinkkemper
Dept. of Computer Science
University of Twente
P.O. Box 217, 7500 AE Enschede
The Netherlands
E-mail: sjbr@cs.utwente.nl

P. Hoving
School of Management Studies
University of Twente
P.O. Box 217, 7500 AE Enschede
The Netherlands

ABSTRACT

Financial organizations in Europe are continually reorganized due to acquisitions and mergers. The corresponding integration of IT departments requires a new philosophy in systems development: situational methods based on project contingencies. Contingency approaches are discussed from the perspectives of organizational theory and information systems development. We present the construction process of situational methods emphasizing the determination of the project characterization. The theory of contingencies of system development is elaborated. Finally, a migration path for the adoption of situational system development is presented.

Keywords: System development, dynamic organizations, situational methods, contingency approaches

1. INTRODUCTION

In the last two decades many information system development methodologies, including methods, techniques and supporting tools, have been developed (Olle 1986). These methodologies handle different assumptions, encompass often different phases and emphasize different aspects of the system development process. Methodologies arose in an ad-hoc way, e.g. a designer facing a problem in practice and looking for a solution of that particular problem, developed his own methods which may also be applicable in other situations. Furthermore, it has been recognized that organizations have to change their system development methods due to changing situations. Welke and Kumar (1992) state this as follows:

"...we need a formal (as opposed to ad-hoc) and efficient (as opposed to resource and time efficient) methodology for developing ISDMs which are situation appropriate (as opposed to universal) and complete (as opposed to partial) , and at the same time rely upon the accumulated experience and wisdom of the past (as opposed to built from scratch)".

Because methodologies are not universal, not complete and sometimes not appropriate it is often better to adapt the methodology to match the business context. Every time a system development project is running, knowledge and experience must be collected with respect to less or more successful approaches to the development of information systems. "Approach" has here the same meaning as "methodology" or "situational method". In fact, there is a need to change

methodologies and to adapt them to the requirements of the specific situation. Different project situations, e.g. as a consequence of different interest groups, different business cultures, different types of application or different skill levels of participants, may cause a different approach: the application of different methods and different development tasks.

The problems described so far have been experienced very strongly by the financial organization (ING Bank in Amsterdam) where our field study has been accomplished. The ING Bank is a merger of two former banks with their own system development methodologies. Organizations like the ING Bank are characterized by a high level of automation. More than one billion Dutch guilders was spent on automation in 1992. Therefore, it is very important to control the expenses for automation. The business units of the ING Bank are supported by central service departments; one of them is the Department for Information Technology (DIT), the focal department of the field study. The planning, design, construction, maintenance and use of computer-based information systems and technical supplies constitute the domain of this department. The clients of DIT are the business units and the other service departments. Compensation for accomplished services is realized by an internal accounting system. Also in the ING Bank we observe an evolution from one best approach for all projects towards a more situation-specific, contingency-based approach. Different methodologies are already in use with different development strategies, but a situation-specific, contingency-based approach has not been defined. The ING Bank is looking for a solution for the problems with system development. Therefore, the problem statement of the field study is:

How can we proceed in the direction of a fully implemented approach to the development of information systems, which is situation-specific, improving the success of automation?

The goal of the field study is twofold:

- The construction of a framework for implementing a situation-specific approach in large organizations like the ING Bank.
- Outcomes of this field study will support the Method Engineering research project at the University of Twente (Van Slooten and Brinkkemper 1993).

Situational Method Engineering is defined by Van Slooten and Brinkkemper as follows:

"The process of configuring a project scenario for information system development using existing methods, or fragments thereof, to satisfy the factors that define the project context". A scenario, in this context, is an approach to the system development process or a situational method, determined by situation-specific contingency factors. The method engineering approach will be explained in section 3 in the context of situation-specific method construction. Thoughts about contingency approaches in organization theory and information system development, important for our field study, can be found in section 2. Contingency factor determination related to risk analysis and influences of contingency factors will be elaborated in section 4. The migration from the current situation to the desired situation has our attention in section 5. Finally, we will conclude and mention some prospects about further research on this topic at the University of Twente.

2. CONTINGENCY APPROACHES

Contingency theory is a theoretical and rational approach of organizations that are considered by contingency theory as units of analysis (Pfeffer 1982). Nowadays, contingency theory has also been applied on the level of subsystems of organizations, e.g. the application of contingency frameworks like the framework of Naumann et al. (1980) as one of the first. Because an information system development project may be considered as a subsystem of an organization it will be possible to apply a model of contingency approaches in organization theory.

2.1 Contingency Approaches in Organization Theory

Until 1960, one best way of organizing was still dominant. After 1960, since the time of Burns and Stalker (1961) the idea has been put forward that one best way of organizing does not exist. Galbraith (1973) said it as follows:

"there is no one best way to organize and any way of organizing is not equally effective"

Unhappy about existing theories, internal and external circumstances determining the functioning of the organization were elaborated. The idea was that, depending on the situation, certain organizational structures are more efficient and more effective. Burns and Stalker (1961) distinguished two extremities of organizational forms: the mechanistic and the organic form. Organic organizations were supposed to deal with innovative situations. Mintzberg (1979) distinguished five and later more configurations of organizations in different situations. A strong hierarchical organizational structure is not appropriate for an organization in a dynamic environment. In such a case a simple structure will be more effective. A major point of critique against the more traditional contingency approaches is the unidirectional relationship between organizational structure and situation. New contingency approaches emphasize the bi-directional relationship beween both (Weick 1979, Grandori 1987). Lawrence and Lorsch (1967) used contingency theory to make their conclusion evident that in order for an organization structure to be

Figure 1: Model of Contingency Approaches

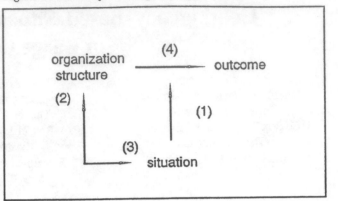

effective (outcome), it must deal with the diversity or uncertainty of the environment (situation), which is illustrated in figure 1 by arrow 1.

The next step was the study of the relationship between the situation (environment and/or technology) and the organizational structure (arrow 2 in figure 1). This relationship is in accordance with the discovery of Woodward (1965) that the most appropriate organizational form for a certain technology is in that particular situation also the most usual organizational form. We have already mentioned the bi-directionality of the relationship between situation and organizational structure (arrows 2 and 3), which completes our simple model of contingency approaches in organization theory.

2.2 Contingency Approaches in Information System Development

Because an information system development project can be assumed to be an organization on the meso-level, we are able to substitute in figure 1 the term "organization structure" with "project approach". The project approach comprises all structural aspects of the project, e.g. development strategy, methods, and roles of participants. In the context of information system development an approach may be defined as the way an information system will be developed: the way of organizing, the way of working, the way of control, the way of thinking, the way of modelling and the way of supporting (Wijers 1991). Depending on the situation there are many ways for developing information systems. Because "situation" is in practice a very complicated concept defined by a large number of factors, there exist, similar to organization theory, many frameworks for contingencies in information system development (e.g. Mc Farlan 1982, Naumann et al. 1980, Burns and Dennis 1985, Saarinen 1990). The mentioned contingency approaches are at most partial solutions for situation-specific information system development. In practical situations there may exist many contingencies and constraints not mentioned by the former approaches and there is no guidance for the selection of specific methods and tools, only a rough direction is offered, which is useful but not enough for a complete project characterization as will be elaborated in the remaining sections of this paper. The calculation of the level of uncertainty does not guarantee a proper choice out of possible alternative measures. If, for instance, uncertainty is caused by the vagueness of information needs, than one may decide to apply functional prototyping; on the other hand, if the cause of uncertainty is a need for high performance of the system, than functional prototyping does not make sense and simulation might be more appropriate. The action to be taken is highly dependent on the reason behind the uncertainty. Furthermore, the before mentioned contingency approaches emphasize the selection of a development strategy or a kind of management of the project, but the selection of appropriate methods, techniques and tools is outside the scope of these approaches.

During the seventies, the aim was to use one so-called "best" methodology or approach for system development in every situation. Such a methodology prescribes precisely what must be done and often also which methods and tools must be applied, independent from the project situation. However, in practice it is often the case that a methodology is not equally suitable in different situations, which is also indicated by arrow (1) in figure 1. In the meantime, many methodologies have been developed and no one is satisfactory in each situation. Many different approaches arise in practice and in publications (e.g. Olle et al. 1991). There exist process-, data-, behaviour- and object-oriented methods and one may choose, depending on the situation, for instance a linear, incremental or experimental strategy for the system development process. The selection of a certain approach, depending on the situation, is depicted by arrow (2) in figure 1. The other way around, the chosen approach may influence the situation. If, for instance, a reverse engineering strategy is selected for a project, then the availability of an appropriate computer aided reverse engineering tool may be a reasonable condition for the application of such a strategy. If such a tool is not available one may decide to acquire it, which means an adaptation of the situation depicted by arrow (3) of figure 1. Consequently, it seems to be important for the selection of an approach that a match arises between the dominant factors of the situation and the important conditions for applying the approach.

3. SITUATION-SPECIFIC, CONTINGENCY-BASED APPROACHES

3.1 The Situational Method Engineering Approach

Van Slooten and Brinkkemper (1993) proposed to support method engineering by a configuration procedure to construct an approach to system development from project characterizations. The starting point is a given dynamic and evolving project environment, being part of a larger organizational setting. The project environment includes the existing information infrastructure, the users, the organizational culture of both the supplier organization and the customer organization. Project or contingency factors, such as application characteristics, external factors, technical factors, and the available development expertise, are determined in some way by form-

ing a project characterization.

The selection or construction of an approach to system development (situational methodology) is mediated by so-called intermediate variables derived from the project characterization. Intermediate variables include aspects of methods (e.g. data- or process-oriented), levels of analysis and design (e.g. object system analysis and design, computer-based information system analysis and design), the development strategy for the project (e.g. linear, iterative) and the constraints for the project (e.g. the budget, time). Based on these intermediate variables, the available method fragments and route maps in a method base (a kind of knowledge base) including the formalized experience of previous projects, the method engineer may be able to construct an appropriate methodology for the project. Method fragments are parts of methods, techniques or tools. Route maps are plans associated with development strategies including the activities to perform and the products to deliver.

In practice, the constructed methodology may not be complete because some decisions may be postponed, e.g. the decision about the kind of computer-based information system that will be developed is often made after the first stages of the development process, which decision may influence the methodology. Moreover, unforeseen contingency factors may arise during the development process necessitating improvements or clarifications of the project characterization and therefore a refinement or adaptation of the methodology. The complete project performance may yield more development expertise, that can be stored in the method base and will be exploited by future projects. Based on this method engineering approach a model for system development has been built for the ING Bank.

3.2 A Model for System Development

The process of providing information to support the business processes is changed by information system development projects. Figure 2 illustrates our model for system development constructed for the ING Bank. Two situations, depicted by "old" and "new" situation, are distinguished by the

Figure 2: Model for System Development

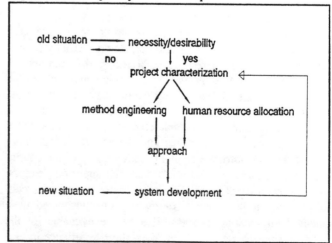

model: the old situation, before the system development process is initiated, and the new situation, after the system development process has been completed. The model does not represent all details and all decision-making during the system development process. The project characterization for instance may happen partly during the system development process depicted by a feed-back loop.

The Old Situation

There may arise some kind of problem in the old situation. The solution of the problem may cause some point of improvement of the business process. A problem in the broad sense is anything with a negative influence on the realization of the business goals or the absence of positive influences, e.g. when electronic banking is not available a client may decide to go to the competitor. Another possibility is that the business goals change, which necessitates an adaptation of the business activities. The project management method of the ING Bank distinguishes the next incentives for starting a new development process: a problem, a point of improvement, a migration plan, a policy for the future and the desire for a new product. Furthermore, it is necessary to describe the problem situation. This description can be used to decide upon the start of the project.

Necessity/Desirability

Before starting the system development process, which means the migration from the current to the desired situation, the rewards have to counterbalance the expenses. The quantification of the rewards is very difficult in many cases, just as a reliable estimate of the expenses for development and exploitation. The input to the process determining the necessity/desirability is the problem description and the output is a decision upon the feasibility of a system development process. When the decision is positive, the system development process will start, otherwise the problem is handled in another way or disappears spontaneously; in any case it makes sense to save the problem situation in a systematic manner, which may be useful in future situations.

Project Characterization

After it has been decided to solve the problem through a system development process the characterization of the project will start. During project caracterization the contingency factors of the specific problem situation are analyzed, for the contingency factors determine a fitting methodology for the project. The stakeholders, e.g. users, commissioners, developers and economists, must characterize the project, for instance during brainstorming sessions. The characterizations of other projects may contribute to this process. Some of the contingency factors are: present methods, techniques, tools and the human resource situation. From the available methods, techniques and tools a methodology can be constructed by a method engineering process. The people available for the project, their capacities, their skills, their experience in system development and the problem domain, and their mutual relationships is contained in the human resource situation. Subsequently, the project characterization within the ING Bank will be elaborated. A list of contingency factors is consulted before the actual start of each project. However, an exhaustive list of contingency factors can hardly be acquired. A classification of contingency factors is based on the next piece of text:

The *client* has a *problem* with a negative influence on the goals of the *organization*. This problem can be solved by the implementation of a computer-based *information system* through *people* in a *project*.

The various categories of contingency factors are printed in italics. The ING Bank has added to each category a non-exhaustive list of contingency factors. Such a long list of contingency factors may be hard to handle in practice. Therefore, the most important and dominant factors should be selected from the list, which may yield a different list of most important contingency factors for each business unit. The importance of a factor is related to the influence of the factor, which is elaborated in section 4. Based on the aspects, mentioned in section 4, the level of importance of the factor can be justified, e.g. a factor with a long influence over time, a large scope of the influence and a direct influence on the effectiveness of the project means a high level of importance. For instance, if the factor "knowledge of the information analyst about the problem domain" is low, then there will be a long influence on projects where the information analyst is involved, yielding bad products for such projects. The last discussion deals with the influence of contingency factors (arrow 1 in figure 1) on the system development process (arrow 4 in figure 1), which is different from the discussion about the influence of contingency factors on the configuration of a methodology for the system development process (arrow 2 in figure 1). A structured analysis of the situation by project characterization may prevent bad influences due to unrecognized contingency factors. In practice, the ING Bank has implemented various approaches to system development, e.g.:

- a standard project management method dealing with software package selection.
- a standard project management method dealing with a standard system development methodology.
- a standard project management method dealing with a standard system development methodology for small-scale new systems.

Actually, there exist more variants and some of the variants are used informally. Furthermore, a project characterization, including a contingency analysis, is not accomplished in the current practice. The method engineering process, depicted by figure 2, can also support the selection from already existing approaches to the system development process. Incidentally, project characterization, method engineering and human resource allocation may also take place during the system development project and not only at the very beginning. In any case, the already existing standard approaches to system development must be accompanied by a set of pre-conditions, which must be fulfilled before the approach can be applied. The addition of such a set of rules to an approach, not established today, will simplify the selection of the approach during project characterization. The Project Start-Up, in the case of the ING Bank, is an initial structured meeting of the project team with other involved stakeholders. This meeting is also appropriate to start the project characterization and to estimate the value of the intermediate variables. Based on the project characterization the human resource allocation and the method engineering can be accomplished yielding the approach or methodology for the system development process.

Method Engineering and Human Resource Allocation

Project characterization provides the input for method engineering and human resource allocation. Method engineering will be supported by a knowledge-based system containing a method base with the stored method fragments, and route maps. The output of method engineering and human resource allocation is a situation-specific approach to the system development process. The intermediate variables, already defined by Van Slooten and Brinkkemper, will simplify the transition from the contingency factors to the configuration of the approach. Intermediate variables are: aspects, levels, constraints and development strategies. The relationship between contingency factors and intermediate variables will be explained by an example. Suppose there is a clearly described problem in a rather simple business situation and the policy of the organization is re-use of a common data model. In such a situation it is appropriate to apply a data-oriented system development approach (the data or information aspect), to re-use the common data model (an organizational constraint) and to develop the system in a linear way with the possibility of skipping some activities during the first stages of the project due to the relative simplicity of the problem domain. Subsequently, the intermediate variables as defined by Van Slooten and Brinkkemper will be cleared up a little.

- The aspects

The well known classification of regulatory, maintenance and primary processes of an organization may be used as a decomposition mechanism for the problem domain or object system, which way of modelling is an example of representing the process-oriented aspect. The construction of activity diagrams according to the ISAC-methodology (Lundeberg 1982) is an example of a technique supporting the process-oriented aspect. Entity-relationship diagrams constitute an example of the information- or data-oriented aspect, whereas Petri nets are an illustration of the behaviour-oriented aspect. Van Slooten and Brinkkemper distinguish also organization- and problem-oriented aspects to represent for instance organization charts and problem solving methods.

- The Levels

Two levels for the analysis and design stage of system development are distinguished: object system analysis and design, and computer-based information system analysis and design. A further refinement is possible through a decomposition process of the object system and the supporting computer-based information systems. The idea is that a more detailed study of the object system requires methods and techniques which are not appropriate at a high level of analysis.

- The Development Strategy

Burns and Dennis (1985) distinguish three strategies: the traditional life cycle, a mixed methodology and prototyping, but more specific development strategies may be appropriate, e.g. more specific ways of prototyping and incremental strategies.

- The Constraints

Sometimes there exist organizational policies and rules limiting the possible approaches directly, e.g. tools available, a standard method, the budget. There may exist so-called hard and soft constraints. Hard constraints cannot be removed, but soft constraints may disappear after possible measures have been taken.

So far we have discussed the intermediate variables defined by Van Slooten and Brinkkemper, but in the situation of the ING Bank a few additional intermediate variables appeared appropriate: the roles of the participants, and the relationship between the project and its environment.

- The Roles of The Participants

What is meant is the kind of user participation, the tuning procedures between analysts and clients, and the roles of other stakeholders, e.g. decision makers, financial experts and organizational specialists. If the project is not about a change of the functionality of the information system, it will be better to assign the user a passive role during the project, but a change of functionality necessitates a more active role for users, particularly during the first stages of the project. Various roles are possible for users, e.g. the user as an information resource, the user participating in a soundboard group, the user in the project organization, and the user as analyst, depending on the contingency factors.

- The Relationship between The Project and its Environment

There may exist other projects related to the project at hand necessitating some coordination. The project may be a sub-project of another project or strongly related to a reorganization project. Many problems of automation are caused by insufficient attention to organizational change and too much emphasis on the information technology aspect. Interdependencies between projects may have a strong impact on the system development approach. The activities of a project will influence decisions upon concurrent and subsequential projects.

Until now the ING Bank has not implemented a contingency-based approach, but in time, after some experience with such an approach, a decision supporting model may emerge. Such a decision supporting model will contain rules for the selection or construction of an approach. A selected approach is always one of the adopted standard approaches already experienced as useful in certain situations. A set of pre-conditions, to facilitate the selection process, must be defined for a standard approach. A more extensive method engineering process is necessary when we have to construct a new approach, but rules about the construction of a new methodology from existing method fragments and heuristic knowledge constitute also the decision supporting model. The explained intermediate variables will be helpful to build a decision supporting model from practice. The possible approaches are characterized by the various activities to be accomplished supported by method fragments, the various products to be delivered from the activities, the allocation of human resources to carry out the activities and the planning and tuning of deliverables with people involved in the project. Over a period of time a limited number of approaches, from which a selection can be made, will emerge in practice. That selection is based on a comparison between the actual situation and the pre-conditions of the approaches. The pre-conditions are derived from the contingency factors of successful projects.

System Development

The system development process will take place by applying the constructed or selected approach. However, in a real situation it happens frequently that the approach as a product of project characterization and method engineering is not complete and not even the best due to unexpected events and contingency factors, which explains the need for the feedback loop from system development to project characterization. Dividing a project into sub-projects may mean the necessity of a specific approach for each sub-project causing project characterizations for the sub-projects during system development. The outcome of system development is a new situation.

The New Situation

After system development some business activities are carried out differently, the intention being to support the business goals better than before. Of course, in the new situation, new problems may arise, causing a new process of change. An evaluation of the system development process, including the applied approach, may cause improvements.

4. CONTINGENCY FACTOR DETERMINATION

We have already mentioned the evolution within the ING Bank from one "best" approach for all projects to a contingency-based approach. The actual situation is the existence of a few alternative approaches, e.g. system development for small projects, an approach for software package selection, system development and prototyping. However, the classification into small and large projects is not clear at all; classifications may be different for different business units. Furthermore, such a classification takes into account only one aspect of the situation: the size of the project. Moreover, there are more important factors, e.g. the experience of the participants and the type of information system, influencing the approach to system development.

4.1 Contingency Factors

In previous sections we have already used various terms pointing to contingency factors, e.g. situational influences, criteria for choice, project characteristics. A short definition of contingency factors is as follows:

Contingency factors are circumstances of the project influencing in some way the selection or construction of an approach (situational methodology) to system development.

This definition is illustrated by an example. Suppose that eliciting requirements specifications for a particular information system is difficult. This contingency factor indicates that a prototyping approach makes more sense than a strictly linear strategy, which emphasizes the influence of the situation on the actual approach depicted by arrow 2 of figure 1, whereas arrow 1 of figure 1 represents the influence of the situation on the application of the approach during system development. However, the analysis of arrow 2 makes use of knowledge about arrow 1. The analysis of arrow 1 can be considered as an evaluation of the project after it has finished.

4.2 Risk Factors

To be prepared for the risks of a project it may be appropriate to accomplish a diagnosis of the project by using a questionnaire, e.g. the Security By Analysis questionnaire (SBA, 1984) distinguishing five categories of risk factors: the size of the project, the level of automation, the technology, the project organization and the project environment. The conclusion is obvious that risk factors are just contingency factors. In the questionnaire, many detailed questions related to the five categories must be answered. Risk factors may establish success or failure behaviour. The ING Bank has already gained some experience with risk analysis, e.g. for one particular project a lot of factors were recognized: good team spirit, involvement of all participants, early and clear decision making, good communication with environment, stable environment, clear boundaries of tasks, uniform expectations about final goals, timely deliverables from concurrent projects. Through controlling recognized risks, measures may emerge that constitute the approach. Consequently, risk analysis and control is an important part of contingency-based situational system development.

4.3 The Influence of Contingency Factors

It is possible to distinguish different aspects of the influence of contingency factors. The estimation of the influence has to deal with a number of aspects: duration, direction, scope, deepness, origin, and mutual relationships.

Duration. Duration is the length in time of the influence during the project. Suppose, a project requires some coordination with other projects. At a certain point in time it may be the case that the other projects are finished. After that particular point in time coordination with the other projects is also finished.

Direction. The question here is whether we have to deal with a failure- or success-behaviour of the factor in connection with an influence on the effectiveness or the efficiency of the project. The contingency factor "informal decision making" may have in a certain context the meaning: informally the managers leave the decision making to the automation people. This situation will cause failure behaviour with respect to the effectiveness of the project, because technical arguments are decisive and organizational aspects are neglected.

Scope. The scope of the influence of a factor may be limited to the project itself meaning a minimal scope, e.g. requirements and desires with respect to the system under development, and no influence on other projects. The contingency factor "quality policy" is an example of a factor influencing all projects of the organization. Sometimes there is even an influence on projects outside one's own organization, e.g. the contingency factor "technological evolution".

Deepness. The question is how deeply the influence of a factor penetrates the project organization. The deepness of a factor can be explained by comparing a project with an organization. In an organization we can distinguish three management levels: the operational level, the tactical level and the strategic level. The factor "project experience" for instance influences all levels.

Origin. The meaning of this aspect will be explained by an example. The factor "involvement of management is low" may be caused by the fact that during previous projects most of the communication with management took place in technical language. Current projects may prevent the failure behaviour of this factor by improving communication between technical people and management.

Mutual Relationships. The question is whether there are strong interdependencies between factors, e.g. during our field-study in the ING Bank we observed that the project organization was less satisfactory when the involvement with the project of the user was less.

4.4 Problems with the Determination of Factors

Problems arising when thinking about contingency factors include: the unit of the factor, the visibility of the factor, the measurability of the factor and the stability of the factor.

The Unit of the Factor. The uniqueness of a problem, for instance, can be represented by a percentage between zero and hundred, the number of involved participants will be expressed by a natural number, the estimated throughput-time by time units and the expertise on the problem domain by: excellent, good, sufficient, bad. The difference of units makes it difficult to assign weights to contingency factors, comparing in this way the influence of factors.

The Visibility of the Factor. The influence of a certain factor may be hardly visible, e.g. the influence of the resistance to change of people in the organization. Resistance to change may not be recognized sufficiently by the project team causing unwillingness of some users to accept the outcome of the project.

The Measurability of the Factor. The problems with respect to the measurability are explained by distinguishing three sub-topics:

- The value of the factor may be difficult to measure. It is for instance difficult to measure the involvement of the users.
- The relationship between factor and success. For instance, the assignment of experienced people may be considered by an organization as a critical success factor, whereas another organization may consider a balanced distribution of experience as successful.
- The measurability of the effect of a factor, acting as a selection criterion for a certain approach, may be a problem. For instance, based on the instability of requirements specifications a prototyping strategy is chosen for the project. However, the effect of prototyping may be difficult to measure, because the comparison with aplying a linear strategy to the same project is not possible. When you want to measure this effect you have to carry out exactly the same project applying a linear strategy and all other variables unchanged.

The Stability of the Factor. The value of a factor may vary over time. For instance, the number of available people with a certain level of experience may change, because other projects with high priority may be started during the project, which influences the assignment of people to the project. Also the relative priority of the project may change.

4.5 Prevention of Risks and Uncertainties

Prevention of risks and uncertainties may be realized by characterizing the project situation. We wish to mention a few possibilities:

- Removing or smoothing the failure behaviour of factors beforehand. For instance, the size of a project influences the project considerable, which may necessitate dividing the project into a number of smaller projects, increasing possible success.
- Increasing or creating the success behaviour beforehand. For instance, improving the attitude of management with respect to the project by transferring relevant information and stimulating the involvement of management.
- Anticipating risks and uncertainties by matching the approach and the situation. During the project start-up an approach is chosen which fits the project situation as well as possible.
- Monitoring the approach of the project based on changes or unforeseen contingencies during the project.

5. MIGRATION OF AUTOMATION

Based on the former sections of this paper we wish to demonstrate how an organization like the ING Bank can migrate from the current situation of system development to a new and better situation. As was discussed already, the system development process itself is a change process for the organization. Consequently, the migration from the current situation to the desired situation for the system development process is a change of a change process. This change process implies a new way of thinking about system development projects and causes changes on different levels of the organization: the Bank level, the Business Unit level and the Project level. Due to the extensiveness of the change process it seems appropriate to start the migration with a pilot project carried out for a certain business unit including a number of carefully selected projects. The pilot project, depicted by stage zero of the migration, consists of the following activities:

- Selection of business unit. Important criteria for the selection are: a positive view towards situational approaches, a willingness to change and the transferability of the outcomes to the other business units.
- Selection of projects. The selection of projects to apply the new way of thinking. The duration of the project, the risk that the project must be stopped due to the new way of thinking and the model function of the project are important criteria for the selection.
- Evaluation of the outcomes of the projects. The question is whether the new approach fits the specific project better than the standard approach used in the old situation.
- Formulation of conclusions about the pilot project. The contribution of the new way of thinking with respect to a better outcome of the project and a more efficient system development process. Try to explain and to analyze potential negative conclusions.

When the conclusions about the pilot project are positive the next stage, stage one, of the migration project can be started.

Stage one, Bank level
- Augmentation of the project with method engineering as explained in the former sections.
- Augmentation of the project management method with a way of working for the exchange of knowledge and experience about approaches of system development. The way of working may include the use of standard forms for the evaluation of projects emphasizing the contingency factors with a relevance to the approach, the contingency factors appearing during the project and the effect of measures based on contingency analysis to increase the success of the project.
- Monitoring of the various knowledge bases on the business unit level and stimulating the learning process between different business units.

Stage one, Business Unit Level
- Determination of important contingency factors for the business unit, because contingency factors may differ for each business unit. Experienced project managers may fill up an appropriate questionnaire comprising a comprehensive list of contingency factors.
- Determination of relationships between contingency factors, method fragments and route maps by using the intermediate variables.
- Evaluation data from the various projects within the business unit will be collected and stored in the knowledge base.

Stage one, Project Level
- Determination of important contingency factors for the

project using the list on the business unit level. However, more specific factors may be added. When specific factors are added to the list, one may decide to extend the business unit list or not. One may continue the contingency analysis process by applying the ideas of the former sections of this paper, in particular a risk analysis may be appropriate.
- The output of the project characterization is used by the method engineer to decide upon an appropriate approach.
- Based on the selected or constructed approach the project team will start the system development process. Adaptation of the approach during the project may happen due to the changing situation or postponed decisions on contingency factors, which may lead to new situational approaches. An evaluation of the project afterwards may require an update of the knowledge base.

Stage two, Bank Level
- Stimulation and coordination of the learning process between business units. Decision making about standard approaches appropriate for all business units.

Stage two, Business Unit Level
- When certain approaches, including pre-conditions, appear to be successful one may decide to nominate them as standard approaches of the business unit. The standard approaches may be selected by projects during the second stage of the migration.
- Evaluations of projects during the second stage may influence the standard approaches.

Stage two, Project Level
- A project characterization will occur during the project start-up, similar to stage one.
- The project situation will be compared to the pre-conditions of the standard approaches to select one of them.
- Based on the selected standard approach the project will start. It is still possible that during the project it is necessary to change the project characterization due to unforeseen circumstances. The evaluation at the end of the project may still yield new knowledge about the situational application of approaches.

6. CONCLUSIONS AND FURTHER INVESTIGATIONS

We think we have answered the question as to how to proceed in the direction of a fully implemented approach to situation-specific development of information systems in the context of the situational method engineering approach proposed by Van Slooten and Brinkkemper. Within the ING Bank organization one agrees about the necessity to approach different projects in different ways. Attention is needed for different approaches as a consequence of different roles of participants, different aspects of system modelling, different levels of analysis and design, and the relationship between the project organization and its environment. Different categories of contingency factors may influence a project: client, problem, organization, information system, project and people, but the classification is not complete and will evolve in the future. The influence of a factor can be expressed by concepts like: duration, direction, scope, deepness, and origin of the factor. The factors may also influence each other. The migration from the current situation to the desired situation has the attention of the ING Bank, but tools to support the project characterization and the method engineering process have been designed (Harmsen et al. 1994) and will become operational in the near future.

Acknowledgements

We are very grateful to the staff of the ING Bank. They spent a lot of time in facilitating the research and criticizing our conclusions and reports. Also the critique of Prof. R.K. Stamper and Drs. F. Wijnhoven was very helpful.

References

Burns, R.N. and A.R. Dennis (1985), Selecting the Appropriate Application. *Database*,Fall Burns, T. and G.M. Stalker (1961), *The Management of Innovation*. Tavistock Publications

Galbraith, J.R. (1973), *Designing Complex Organizations*. Reading (MA): Addison-Wesley.

Grandori, A. (1987), *Perspective on Organization Theory*. Ballinger, Massachusetts.

Harmsen, F., S. Brinkkemper, H. Oei, Situational Method Engineering for Information System Project Approaches. *Technical Report*, University of Twente, Jan. 1994.

Lawrence, P.R. and J.W. Lorsch (1967), Differentiation and Integration in Complex Organizations. *Administrative Science Quarterly*, vol. 12, 1.

Lundeberg, M. (1982), The ISAC Approach to Specification of Information Systems and its Application to the Organization of an IFIP Working Conference. *Information Systems Design Methodologies: A Comparative Review*, North-Holland.

Mintzberg, H. (1979), *The Structuring of Organizations*. Englewood Cliffs: Prentice Hall.

McFarlan, F.W. (1981), Portfolio Approach to Information Systems. *Harvard Business Review*, 59, 5, 142-150.

Naumann, J.D. et al. (1980), Determining Information Requirements: A Contingency Method for Selection of a Requirements Assurance Strategy. *The Journal of Systems and Software*, 1, 273-281.

Olle, T.W. et al. (1986), *Information Systems Design Methodologies: Improving the Practice*. North-Holland.

Olle, T.W. et al. (1991), *Information Systems Methodologies: A Framework for Understanding*. Addison-Wesley.

Pfeffer, J. (1982), *Organizations and Organization Theory*. Massachusetts, Pitman.

Saarinen, T. (1990), System Development Methodology and Project Success: An Assessment of Situational Approaches. *Information and Management*, 19, 183-193.

SBA (1984), *Sarbachets Analys*. Learning Productions Ltd, Surrey.

Slooten, C. van and S. Brinkkemper (1993), A Method Engineering Approach to Information Systems Development. *Information System Development Process*, North-Holland.

Weick, K.E. (1979), *The Social Psychology of Organizing*. Philipinnes: Addison-Wesley.

Welke, R.J. and K. Kumar (1992), Methodology Engineering: A Proposal for Situation-Specific Methodology Construction. *Challenges and Strategies for Research in Systems Development*, Wiley and Sons Ltd.

Wijers, G.M. (1991), *Modelling Support in Information Systems Development*. Thesis Publishers, Amsterdam.

Woodward, J. (1965), *Industrial Organization*. Oxford University Press.

Section Six

Information Technology in Asia-Pacific Countries

Designing a Network System for Managing the Six-Year National Development Plan in Taiwan

David C. Chou
Department of Computer Information Systems
West Texas A&M University
Canyon, Texas 79016

Bob Sloger
Department of Computer Information Systems
Amarillo College
Amarillo, Texas 79178

ABSTRACT

Using a network of computerized forecasting systems for managing Taiwan's Six-year National Development Plan can facilitate the coordination of project planning, implementation, and evaluation. This system depicts the functionalities of distributed AI, decision support, project management, and economic forecasting.

INTRODUCTION

The Republic of China (R.O.C.) on Taiwan (better known as "Taiwan") implements its Six-year National Development Plan in the period of 1991-1996. This plan performs an integrated planning to accelerate the nation's modernization process through a series of important public construction projects aimed at resolving current development bottlenecks and improving the national quality of life. The total capital required for major public development projects in this gigantic plan is estimated around 330 billions of U.S. dollars (*The ROC Six-year National Development Plan in Brief*, 1991).

The six-year national development plan is divided into four principal aspects: (1) macroeconomic development; (2) resources for continued industrial growth; (3) regional development; and (4) national quality of life. This plan consists of 775 projects in total. Most projects need technological supports such as project analysis and design, project management, project evaluation, human resources management, and economic forecasting. In order to efficiently and effectively manage this plan, the adoption of a network system which functioning as an AI-assisted, decision-supported, computerized forecasting system is needed.

This paper proposes an architecture of a network-based, computerized forecasting system for managing Taiwan's Six-year National Development Plan. This system features the functionalities of distributed AI-expert system, decision support system, project management, and forecasting system.

A literature review on the computerized systems is presented next. The structure of Taiwan's Six-year National Development Plan is illustrated after that. The architecture of this computerized forecasting system is constructed and evaluated next. A conclusion is given in the last section.

A REVIEW OF COMPUTERIZED FORECASTING SYSTEMS

Forecasting techniques have gone through revolutionary changes over the past years. The use of computers in forecasting expanded the processing capability and the data accessibility. Forecasters could establish a comprehensive forecasting model without fears of processing speed. The use of statistical packages (such as SPSS, BMDP, SAS, etc.) in forecasting industry promotes the quality of the forecasted outcomes. Moreover, the integration of artificial intelligence techniques adds in a potential development for the automated business forecasting system.

Georgoff and Murdick constructed a 20 by 16's matrix chart for a manager's guide to forecasting (Georgoff and Murdick, 1986). This guide includes sixteen (16) evaluation criteria for business forecasting. Nute, Mann and Brewer borrowed this matrix to build a defeasible reasoning model (reasoning subject to defeat by further information is called defeasible reasoning) for selecting a business forecasting method (Nute, Mann and Brewer, 1988). Kumar and Hsu also integrated this matrix guide to build an expert system for forecasting method selection (Kumar and Hsu, 1988).

The development of business forecasting techniques is under the following two trends: AI-embedded forecasting methodology and expert system-based forecasting method. First of all, the AI-embedded business forecasting technique generates a better prediction by the following reasons:

(1) it can automatically compute the economic indicators and oscillators;
(2) it can use a collection of decision-making strategies for

helping users;

(3) it can allow the user to explore a knowledge base and also allow an increase in knowledge;

(4) it can use a domain-specific language to specify new algorithms and heuristics.

Kandt and Yuenger proposed an AI-embedded financial investment assistant software for business forecasting (Kandt and Yuenger, 1988). This system attempted to improve the process by partially automating the acquisition, analysis, and selection of financial market investment. However, the final goal of this approach is to fully automate the process.

The second approach, expert system-based forecasting method, represents another major path of forecasting technique advancement. This technique emphasizes the selection of a forecasting method based on the merits (rules) of different forecasting methods and user's input to expert system. Kumar and Hsu developed an expert system for the Selector, which is one of the frameworks for an automated forecasting system (Kumar and Hsu, 1988).

The basic process of building an intelligent forecasting model should include the following steps: elicit information from data, select suitable forecasting techniques, and develop a forecasting model. The follow-ups should consist of: forecasting performance evaluation, results validation, model modification, and final conclusion on business forecasting.

Kumar and Hsu's expert system-based Selector has the following distinct advantages over the previous selection techniques:

(1) it reduces incompleteness by filling in where the previous tabular solutions left gaps,

(2) it suggests a combination of appropriate complementary methods to improve the accuracy of the forecast,

(3) it allows for the application of heuristics, and can also show the user the path of reasoning taken to reach the conclusion,

(4) it makes the selection in real time after simultaneously considering the various pertinent factors that affect the decision, and

(5) it is easy to use and free of the biases which often developed by the managers.

Nute, Mann and Brewer used FORE, a prototype expert system to control selection of a business forecasting method (Nute, Mann and Brewer, 1988). This system also proposed the feasibility of using d-Prolog (defeasible Prolog) in a business environment. This prototype expert system adopted Georgoff and Murdick's entire 16 by 20 matrix as its database. This paper also discussed the three approaches to problem solution: absolute reasoning system, probabilistic reasoning system, and defeasible reasoning system. The authors concluded that a defeasible reasoning system represented the appropriate solution for this problem domain.

Chou developed expert system-based business fore-

casting systems for forecasting automation (Chou, 1989; 1991a; 1991b; and 1992). He also developed an AI-based decision support system for economic development planning process (Chou, 1990). The integration of AI-expert system and decision support system for economic development planning thus becomes another challenge in this research area.

STRUCTURE OF SIX-YEAR NATIONAL DEVELOPMENT PLAN

Taiwan's Six-year National Development Plan consists of the following four aspects: macroeconomic development, resources for continued industrial growth, regional development, and national quality of life. The information of this discussion are based on *The ROC Six-Year National Development Plan in Brief*, published by Government Information Office, ROC, in 1991. The structure of this plan is important to the construction of knowledge base and data base of a computerized forecasting system. The domain of objects in national development plan are the foundation of building its knowledge base and data base. Figure 1 summarizes the categories and the numbers of individual projects in Taiwan's six-year national development plan. The goal and structure of each aspect in national development plan are described as following:

1. Macroeconomic development:

The goal of macroeconomic development in Six-year National Development Plan is to keep sustained economic growth in this nation. The various projects in this aspect will stimulate domestic demand, enhance overall productivity, and promote efficient resource allocation to assure nation's stable growth. This aspect includes the following three sectors:

(1) Agriculture: agricultural development will focus on types of production that are technology-intensive and high value-added, entail low environment cost, and have considerable market potential.

(2) Industry: strengthening R&D, promoting production automation, upgrading product quality, and preventing and controlling industrial pollution are the major industrial development targets.

(3) Services: providing modern, high-quality services to meet industrial and consumer's needs. A special emphasis is on manpower planning and training in service industries.

2. Resources for continued industrial growth:

This aspect of the plan focuses on the efficient allocation of sufficient productive resources such as land, water, energy, and transportation facilities during the planning period. The major construction projects consist of the following eight categories:

(1) urban and regional studies on industrial zoning and development;

(2) converting the unproductive farmland to intensive industrial, commercial, residential, and recreational uses;

(3) water resource conservation plans;

(4) human resources management projects to raise labor productivity;

(5) energy management such as diversifying energy sources, keeping rational energy pricing structure, and developing energy technology;

(6) transportation management to raise its efficiency, and develop Taiwan into the transportation hub of the Western Pacific;

(7) telecommunication development and management; and

(8) scientific and technological research and development.

3. Regional development:

This aspect of the plan is to achieve more balanced regional development and to avoid the pitfalls associated with rapid industrialization and urbanization. The plan gives top priority to accelerating the development of backward areas by improving housing, schools, and medical, cultural, and transportation facilities.

4. National quality of life:

The ultimate goal of economic development is to improve the national well-being and quality of life. To realize this goal, 18 living perimeters will be established in proximity to major industrial centers. The planning and development of living perimeters will focus on the following two approaches:

(1) establishing living perimeters to meet the six major social needs of residents: working, housing, recreation, schooling, medical services, and shopping; and

(2) strengthening environmental protection by adopting the following processes: garbage disposal, industrial waste disposal, sewer systems, water pollution control, and air pollution control.

Figure 1 shows the categories and their numbers of projects in Taiwan's Six-year National Development Plan:

Figure 1: Categories and numbers of projects of the ROC Six-year National Development Plan.

Category	Number of Projects
1. Agriculture, forestry and fisheries.	79
2. Irrigation, water conservation and flood control	61
3. Transportation and communications	100
4. Urban development and housing	44
5. Tourism and recreation	30
6. Cultural and education	93
7. Science and technology	67
8. Energy development	77
9. Manufacturing industrial sector	73
10. Service industrial sector	10
11. Environmental protection	67
12. Public health	9
13. Social welfare and security	39
14. Other	26
Total	775

CHARACTERISTICS OF THE NETWORK SYSTEM

The structure of this network system is designed by meeting the following properties of The National Development Plan:

1. The National Development Plan incorporates various social-economic sectors in Taiwan: agriculture, education, transportation, industry, business, cultural, environmental protection, public health, etc. In order to smoothly coordinate the project through various governmental agencies in the nation, a distributed, decision-supported, forecasting-based system is needed. This system should be housed in the central computer center and network-linked with each governmental agencies and administrative departments in the nation. Also, this system should be able to communicate with domestic private sector and foreign countries. Figure 1 illustrates such network environment. Finally, the system is capable of conducting group decision support and assisting group decision-making within its network environment.

2. The National Development Plan includes a large number of projects (775 projects). This computerized system should have the capability of conducting project management. Most projects in this plan are requested to collaborate with governmental agencies. This system is then capable of performing group project management in order to fulfill this functionality.

3. The final goal of this national development plan is to promote the economic growth in the nation. In order to perform the role of monitoring economic development, this system should have the capability of conducting economic forecasting.

4. An AI/expert system-assisted functionality is needed for this forecasting system since this National Development Plan is huge and complex in nature. The knowledge base and data base in central computer's repository stores a tremendous amount of rules and data for modeling, information retrieving, knowledge acquisition, reasoning, and computing. The integration of distributed-AI capability into this system will enhance the effectiveness and efficiency of performing group decision-making and project management.

5. In order to effectively monitor the national development projects, the following systematic operational stages are worth observing for designing project management sub-system:

(a) Project Planning Stage: a preliminary investigation and feasibility studies are conducted for each project during this stage.

(b) Project Scheduling Stage: a careful project scheduling arrangement is necessary in order to meet the correct due days for each project.

(c) Project Design Stage: a comprehensive design process is needed before actual construction stage. An evaluation and testing plan should be arranged during this stage.

(d) Project Construction Stage: a careful project construction is the heart of the National Development Project. Various paralleled construction activities need to be monitored through the project management subsystem. The forecasting system has the capability of conducting the analysis and prediction of economic indicators and their impacts on on-going projects. This early warning system can assist government to identify the inferior projects and then stop them at early step.

(e) Project Evaluation and Testing Stage: the completed evaluation and testing processes need to be done before implementing the constructed projects. The guideline setted in project design stage need to be observed during this stage.

(f) Project Implementation Stage: A completed project will be implemented after final testing. The performance of each project will be recorded and evaluated for later studies of project development and project maintenance.

(g) Project Development and Maintenance Stage: the possible development and maintenance plans will be proceeded in the future. The National Development Plan steering committee will recommend the further development plans for strengthening the national economy.

5. In order to enhance the fruits of the National Development Plan, this network system should deliver the following properties of software quality assurance:

(a) Correctness;
(b) Efficiency;
(c) Integrity;
(d) Maintainability;
(e) Manageability;
(f) Reliability;
(g) Reusability;
(h) Safety; and
(i) Verifiability.

CONCLUSION

Taiwan is striving for cultivating its economic development. The Six-year National Development Plan is a great venture to achieve the goal of enhancing its national economy. In order to successfully monitor this enormous project, a network system is designed to control the various activities on forecasting, decision-making, and project management.

This network system should facilitate the following components: interface programs, inference engine, software (including application programs, DBMS, expert systems shells, and communication programs), data base, knowledge base, and model base.

A network system which is facilitated with the above functionalities can enhance the effectiveness and efficiency of Taiwan's Six-year National Development Plan. This system also applies advanced technologies for fulfilling the expected software quality assurance criteria.

REFERENCES

Chou, D. C., "Knowledge-based expert system for business fluctuation analysis," ORSA/TIMS Joint Conference in New York City, October, 1989.

Chou, D. C., "An intelligent decision support system for economic development planning," ORSA/TIMS Joint Conference in Philadelphia, October, 1990.

Chou, D. C., "Creating a better expert system by modeling economists' forecasting behavior," Advances in Information Systems Research, eds., G. E. Lasker, T. Koizumi, and J. Pohl, International Institute for Advanced Studies in Systems Research and Cybernetics, pp. 435-440, 1991a.

Chou, D. C., "A comparison of computerized forecasting systems," Advances in Information Systems Research, eds., G. E. Lasker, T. Koizumi, and J. Pohl, International Institute for Advanced Studies in Systems Research and Cybernetics, pp. 423-428, 1991b.

Chou, D. C., "Modeling Knowledge base for economic forecasting expert systems, Mathematical Modelling and Scientific Computing, pp. 344-349, 1993.

Georgoff, D. M. and Murdick, R. G., "Manager's Guide to forecasting," Harvard Business Review, (January-February), pp. 110-120, 1986.

Hayes-Roth, F.; Waterman, D. A.; and Lenat, D. B., Building Expert Systems, Addison-Wesley Publishing Co, 1983.

Kandt, K. and Yuenger, P., "A Financial Investment Assistant," Proceeding of the 21st Annual Hawaii International Conference on System Sciences, pp. 510-517, 1988.

Kumar, S. and Hsu, C., "An expert system framework for forecasting method selection," Proceeding of the 21st Annual Hawaii International Conference on System Sciences, pp. 86-95, 1988.

Nute, D.; Mann, R.; and Brewer, B., "Using Defeasible logic to control selection of a business forecasting method," Proceeding of the 21st Annual Hawaii International Conference on System Sciences, pp. 437-444, 1988.

The ROC Six-Year National Development Plan in Brief, Government Information Office, Taiwan, ROC, 1991.

Information Technology and Top Management Support: The Singapore Scenario

Dr Gabriel Goren   Dr Tung Lai Lai
Information Management Research Centre
School of Accountancy and Business
Nanyang Technological University
Nanyang Avenue
Singapore 2263.

ABSTRACT

Top management support is often cited as a critical success factor for the development and implementation of IT-related activities. Yet, the nature and extent of top management support in Singapore is not well understood. This research reports on two studies conducted to determine the type of top management support in existence in Singapore and the extent to which the support is given. The first study surveyed 57 top management and IT specialists for their perception on the importance of top management involvement in a successful MIS development. In addition, their current participation in and outlook towards IT projects are also surveyed. Implications of the results are discussed. The second survey is a part of a nation-wide survey on IT use which looks at the personal involvement and participation of CEOs in IT-related activities. The relationship between the CEOs' involvement and participation and the firms' overall performance is explored. It is hoped that by reporting the state of top management support in a variety of organizations, we can gain an insight to the extent and nature of these activities in Singapore.

INTRODUCTION

Top management support has been hailed as the necessary ingredient for successful Management Information Systems (MIS) development and implementation since the 1960s (O'Toole and O'Toole 1966, Rockwell 1968, Freeman 1969, Adams 1972). The lack of top management support and involvement has been cited as the strongest inhibitors of a company's effort to create strategic applications (King 1986). In the last decade or so, organizations have began to realize that information technology (IT) can also give organizations a strategic edge (Cash et al. 1988, Cash and Konsynski 1985, Porter and Millar 1985). In fact, examples of such strategic IT applications are frequently cited (Keen 1981). Organizations have been quick in recognizing the strategic opportunities from IT, and began to view IT as a component of corporate strategy. The nature and types of top management support for IT applications became a critical issue for these organizations. Suddenly, information systems are no longer just a productivity tool -- they are "too important to leave development in the hands of technicians" (Rockart 1988). A recent survey of IT penetration in Singapore, shows that CEOs consider IT to be very important to their firm overall performance (NCB, 1992).

In spite of the importance of top management support, only a handful of studies have examined the nature and extent of the support required from top management for the successful implementation of IT and for the exploitation of IT for strategic advantage (Jarvenpaa and Ives 1991). In fact, little is known about the existing state of top management support for IS projects in Singapore -- a necessary first step towards understanding the critical nature and extent of top management support and its relationship to the success of the IS projects. There are two types of top management support identified in the literature -- top management involvement and top management participation (Barki and Hartwick 1989). In addition, the Chief Executive Officers' (CEO) personal factors, as well as his organization's technology, industry and organizational factors have been cited as critical in influencing the CEO's involvement and participation in implementing IT (Schein 1994). There is a need to examine the nature of top management support in Singapore from the perspective of their involvement and participation in IS projects. In addition, the underlying factors influencing their involvement and participation is discussed.

This study describes the results of two surveys on the nature of top management support for IT-related activities. The first survey analyzed the results of 57 top management and IT specialists' views on the importance of top management involvement in a successful MIS development (involvement) as well as for their current participation in and outlook towards IT projects (participation). Implications of the results are discussed. The second survey is a part of a nation-wide survey on IT use, which looks at the personal involvement and participation of CEOs in IT-related activities. The relationship between the CEOs' involvement and participation and the firms' overall performance is explored. It is hoped that by reporting the state of top management support in a variety of organizations, we can gain an insight to the extent and nature of these activities in Singapore.

LITERATURE REVIEW

Most of the literature on top management support focused on the importance of such support in pushing IT to become a viable competitive weapon for the increasingly competitive business environment. For example, King's (1986) survey of 51 IT executives found that the lack of top management support was seen as the strongest inhibitors of a company's efforts to create strategic applications. Reich and Benbasat (1988), in a study of eleven strategic IT applications in nine Canadian companies, found that 50% of the respondents reported that CEO's support is "very important" in developing strategic applications, and eighty percent of the systems has been given a high profile by senior management during the development process.

There is also some evidence that the role of IT in organizations has elevated in importance over time (Jarvenpaa and Ives 1990). Brancheau and Wetherbe (1987), for instance, found that respondents viewed the use of information for competitive advantage as a critical issue of information systems management in 1986, although the issue had not arisen in a similar study done three years earlier (Dickson et al. 1984).

More importantly, a few recent studies has began to looked at the different types of top management support in MIS development. Schein (1994), for instance, sees the CEO as a change agent who plays several roles in managing the change process each time a new information technology (IT) or computer system is introduced. Factors that affect this change process includes **personal factors, technological realities, organizational realities, and industry realities.**

Personal factors of the CEO, such as their basic assumptions about IT, vision for IT, background and experience with IT is a "driving force" for the change. A CEO may have the vision to automate -- a way of replacing expensive unreliable human labour with sophisticated robots, systems, and other IT devices. He/she may have the vision to informate (Zuboff 1988) -- making previously concealed parts of a system's processes more visible to people higher up and lower down in the organization. Lastly, he/she may have the vision to transform -- completely transforming their organization and industry through innovations in technology and changes in the organizational structures. These visions and perceptions of IT can directly affect the CEO's involvement in the change process for IT investments.

On top of personal factors, perceptions about technological realities, for example that technology is not yet good enough or cheap enough to deliver on its potential, may affect the development and implementation of IT. In addition, CEO are often unsure about the level of investment for IT, and how to use IT to maximize its potential benefits. Behaviours of the competitors will shape their attitudes and behaviour, since the industrial realities often affect the level of investments of the organization in its attempt to stay even with the industry. Finally, organizational size and age may make a difference to the CEO perception of change. Larger, older, multidivisional companies tended to have CEOs who delegated the major decisions and implementation programs to special task forces and divisional management. In smaller and younger organizations, CEO is said to be directly involved with IT matters at all times since they cannot afford to delegate such decisions or to hire IT staffs. In addition, decentralized organizations often made it essential for the CEO to coordinate the units together, through the use of IT innovations such as electronic mail and common information and control systems. Hence, the CEO's

role becomes much more of a monitor and controller of IT. Finally, the financial conditions of an organization may affect the type and level of IT investments in the organization, since it affects the capability of the organization to invest in IT.

Jarvenpaa and Ives's (1991) study looked at the nature of executive support to determine what type of support exists and may be appropriate for the organization. They took Barki and Hartwick's (1989) work on involvement to break down executive involvement into two different constructs -- **involvement**, which is defined as a subjective psychological state -- and **participation**, which refers to the behaviours and activities performed. Participation is concerned with CEO behaviours related to information systems planning, development, and implementation, which necessitates expanding time and energy in IT-related matters. Involvement, on the other hand, refers to a CEO's perceptions and attitudes concerning IT, i.e., the degree to which the CEO views IT as contributing to the firm's success.

Jarvenpaa and Ives's (1991) operationalized executive participation as CEO's personal participation in the firm's use of IT, his/her role in corporate IT steering committee, knowledge of competitor's use of IT, information contacts with IT management, knowledge of IT opportunities in the firm, and number of levels between IT head and CEO . Executive involvement was defined as CEO's prevailing thinking about IT spending, perception of IT's importance to the firm, vision for IT, and endorsement of applications not meeting traditional criteria. Through their survey of CEOs and information systems executives, they found that executive involvement is more strongly associated with the firm's progressive use of IT than executive participation in IT activities. Factors that influence executive involvement includes the CEO's participation, prevailing organizational conditions, and executive's functional background. CEO's perceptions about the importance of IT in their firms are generally positive, although they participated in IT activities rather infrequently.

SURVEY ON MIS DEVELOPMENT

The first survey[1] consists of two hundred questionnaires sent out by post -- 40 each to small companies, medium companies, public listed companies and statutory boards. These companies are chosen on a random basis from the telephone directory and Stock Exchange of Singapore (SES) listing from the Straits Times. A total of 65 people responded to the survey and these respondents comprised of Chief Executive Officers, Chief Information Officers, Specialists in the IT fields and System Analysts. Table 1 below shows the profile of the respondents.

Top management involvement in the development of a successful MIS was rated extremely or very important by all participants (see figure 1). This corresponds to earlier research in the US on the increasing importance of this factor. Other indications of **involvement** can be seen in table 2. From table 2, it can be seen that 65% of top management (both management and IT specialists) views IT as a strategic invest-

Table 1: Profile of Respondents

Profile	Percent
Male	77%
Female	23%
Age:	
<30 years	12%
30-40 years	25%
41-50 years	40%
>50 years	23%
Management	49%
IT Specialist	51%
Type of Company:	
Small (<30)	8%
Medium (30-100)	12%
Big (>100)	19%
Public Listed Companies	30%
Statutory Boards	31%
No. of years in organization:	
<10 years	10%
10-20 years	46%
21-30 years	30%
>50 years	14%

ment, while only 35% views funds on IT as an expense. In addition, top management in all the organizations surveyed made a long term commitment to provide stable funding for systems development activities, attesting to the involvement of top management to this process. Finally, top management involvement in the IT budgeting process is viewed as important, very important or extremely important by all respondents. None of the respondents disputed the importance of

Figure 1: Importance of Top Management Involvement

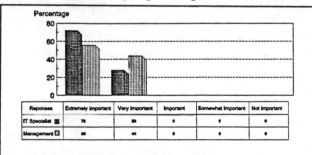
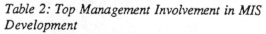

Table 2: Top Management Involvement in MIS Development

Top Management View	Percent
Strategic Investment	65%
Expense	35%
Provision for stable funding	
Make long-term commitment	100%
No long-term commitment	0%
Importance of involvement in budgeting	
Extremely important	23%
Very important	67%
Important	10%
Somewhat important	0%
Not important	0%

top management involvement in budgeting.

In terms of participation, top management is avid in gaining knowledge about IT opportunities and also of competitor's IT innovations. Figure 2 shows the top management keeping themselves somewhat to very informed about these opportunities and innovations. Thirty-eight percent of the respondents indicated that top management are very well informed about IT opportunities and possibilities[2] while the remaining 62% indicated that top management are well informed. None are extremely informed, somewhat informed or weakly informed. Similarly, 25% of the top management in the respondents' organization are very informed of competitors' IT innovations while 63% are well informed and 12% are somewhat informed. None are extremely and weakly informed.

Figure 2: Knowledge of IT Opportunities and Possibilities, and Competitor's IT Innovation

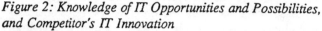
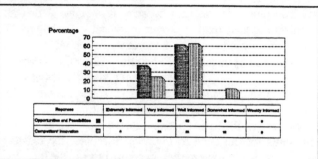

Finally, top management can also participate in the setting of goals and objectives on IT as well as in steering committees. Table 3 shows the extent of top management participation in these activities. Seventy-two percent of the respondents in this study indicated that the top management involved themselves in setting goals, appraising objectives, criteria and priorities before investing in the MIS development. Sixty-three percent of the organizations surveyed have an Executive Steering Committee of top management and functional managers that are involved in setting priorities and/or allocation of resources for system development.

Table 3: Top Management Participation in Setting Goals, Objectives, and Existence of Steering Committee

Response	Percent
Participation in setting goals and objectives	
Yes	72%
No	28%
Existence of steering committee	
Yes	63%
No	37%

IMPLICATIONS OF THE FIRST SURVEY

Top management and IT specialists appear to concur in their opinions of the importance of top management's involvement in the success of MIS development. Figure 1 shows that while more IT specialists rated the top management involvement as extremely important than top management themselves, both parties acknowledged the importance of top management involvement in MIS development as at least very important.

The personal factors of the top management, such as their assumptions, visions and background in IT will affect their involvement in using IT in the organization. This survey has shown that top management in Singapore has the motivation to make such a change. Sixty-five percent of the respondents (see table 2) concluded that top management sees IT as a strategic investment that will benefit the organization as a whole. Those who view IT as an expense need not necessarily be less willing to be involved in MIS developments. However, by treating IT as an expense to be allocated across units, top management may want end-users from various organizational units to be accountable for the amount of IT resources they consume. It can also be seen from table 2 that all organizations have made a provision for stable funding for IT and all of them stressed the importance of top management involvement in budgeting. In addition, 72% of the respondents indicated that top management also participated in setting goals and objectives (see table 3). Top management, by providing stable funding for system development activities, recognizes that the rapid changes in technologies and innovations calls for the need to improve or replace the existing system constantly so as to remain competitive in the industry. By making long term funding commitment, it reinforces the fact that most of the top management sees MIS as a strategic investment that provides long term benefits as opposed to an expense which is beneficial to the organization only in the short run.

Top management's participation in setting goals, appraising objectives, criteria and priorities can also ensure that the MIS development plan will be in line with the overall business plan of the organization. While the planning effort sets a broad framework for the IT activities, the budgeting process ensures fine tuning in relation to staffing, hardware and resource levels. In addition, the budgeting process ensures that organizational consensus is reached on the specific goals and possible short-term achievement for IT activities[3]. These visions and assumptions that top management held indicated that they are highly motivated and involved in supporting MIS developments.

The rapid evolution and spread of information technology has placed a special burden on top management to assess IT opportunities and possibilities in order to gain a competitive edge over its competitors. Such knowledge on technological realities is necessary for organizations to avoid failures, survive and achieve success in this ever changing and competitive environment. Results of this survey shows that 38% of the respondents indicated that top management are very well informed about IT opportunities and possibilities[4] while the remaining 62% indicated that top management are well informed. None are extremely informed, somewhat informed or weakly informed (see figure 2). Knowledge of IT opportunities and possibilities are vital to the top management as it

enables them to make decision regarding the amount of resources to be allocated to the development of new technologies in order to have a competitive edge over the major competitors. When top management are generally well informed of the IT opportunities and possibilities (as shown in this survey), they will be well poised to guide and assist in the exploitation of MIS within the organization.

In addition, top management are also well informed of the IT innovations developed by major competitors[5] (see figure 2) -- that is, the industrial realities. Twenty-five percent of the top management in the respondents' organization are very informed of competitors' IT innovations while 63% are well informed and 12% are somewhat informed. None are extremely and weakly informed. Over the years, top management has come to the realization that they can use IT to cause a significant shift in market share or competitive positioning. Hence, top management are eager to learn about IT innovations developed by major competitors. The successful managers should be able to recognize the potential opportunities to use IT and to apply the technology in a manner consistent with the firm's fundamental business strategy.

Finally, in terms of organizational realities, 63% of the organizations surveyed have an Executive Steering Committee of top management and functional managers that are involved in setting priorities and/or allocation of resources for system development (see table 3). These organizations consists only of the big organizations, public listed companies and statutory boards. Small and medium organizations lack the required funds and manpower to set up an Executive Steering Committee[6]. The existence of an Executive Steering Committee to evaluate and guide IT projects is often an indicator of formal top management participation in IT projects.

SURVEY OF IT USAGE

The second survey is a Singapore nation-wide survey on IT usage held in 1992 by the National Computer Board (NCB). One of the authors was on the team of researchers that conducted the study. The questionnaire for this study included questions related to the participation, as well as involvement, of CEOs in IT. All questions used a likert-type scale of 1 (very low) to 7 (very high). A random sample of 5,326 firms was selected, including firms from manufactur-

Table 4: CEO Questionnaire Response Rate

ResponseRate	Number Sent	Number Received	Response Rate
Manufacturing(Mfg)	1201	381	31.7%
Trade	946	254	26.8%
Transportation(Tpt)	536	124	23.1%
Financial Services(FinSv)	607	158	26.0%
Tourist & Leisure Services(TLS)	297	88	29.6%
Construction & Real Estate(Const)	674	228	33.8%
Government & StatBoards(Govt)	65	51	83.1%
Others	1000	236	23.6%
Total	5326	1520	28.5%

ing, trade, transportation, financial services, tourism and leisure services, construction and real estate, and the public sector. One thousand, five hundred and twenty questionnaires were filled by CEOs from the various sectors in Singapore. Table 4 shows the distribution of respondents by sectors.

Three aspects of CEO involvement in IT and the assessment of its impacts were studied: participation in IT related activities, alignment of IT plans with business plans, and CEOs' perceptions of the impact of IT on their firms' performance.

The following IT related activities were included in the questionnaire:

    a.Planning for IT acquisition and applications beyond a one year time horizon.

    b.Approving major IT projects.

    c.Evaluating technologies not currently used in the organization.

    d.Setting IT policies.

    e.Recruiting key IT personnel.

    f.Selecting vendor.

The mean ratings of CEO participation in these IT activities are presented in table 5. Three questions on the questionnaire focused on the integration of business and IT planning. They were: (1) To what degree does IT manager participate in business planning? Are IT plans incorporated in business plans? and (3) Are business plans used as a basis for IT plans? In terms of the CEOs' perceptions on the business role of IT, three questions were asked: (1) To what degree is IT essential for the firm's present or future success? (2) To what degree is the firm's current operations dependent on IT as a competitive necessity? and (3) How vital is the role IT in the past?

We analyzed the effects of the above three aspects on firm performance. Performance measures included: market share, return on investment, profitability, market/product development, product/service quality, customer relationship, ability to compete globally/regionally, productivity, and quality of decisions. The assumption is that the stronger the link between the different aspects of CEOs involvement and participation in IT related activities and their firms' performance, the more important these activities are.

A regression analysis of the association between CEOs' participation in IT related activities and firm performance gives an R-square of 0.132 (adjusted R-square 0.129). Two of the variables, approving major IT projects and evaluating technologies not currently in use, were found significant at the

Table 5: CEO Participation in IT Activities

IT Activities	Mean Rating (1-7)
IT Planning	49
IT Project Approval	49
Evaluating New Technologies	46
Setting IT Policies	46
Selecting IT Vendor	46
Recruiting Key IT Personnel	42

Table 6: Regression of IT related activities and firm performance

Variables	Beta	T
Planning for IT acquisitions and applications beyond a one year horizon	.059	1.062
Approving major IT Projects	.284	6.207**
Evaluating technologies not currently in use	.116	2.530**
Setting IT policies	.061	1.075
Recruiting key IT personnel.	.022	0.455
Selecting vendor	.044	0.962
R-square	0.132	
Adjusted R-square	0.129	
** Significant at the level of 0.01		

0.001 level. Table 6 shows the results of the analysis. It should be noted that IT is only a small part of a long list of factors contributing to firm performance. As such, we should not expect high levels of R-square (which suggests the proportion of the variation in firm performance accounted for by the regression variables). In addition, when considering the large number of cases, the significance of the results is strengthened.

A different analysis shows a positive association between the degree to which business plans are used as a basis for IT plans and firm performance. The results for the three variables are given in table 7. CEOs are responsible for the firm's business plan. If they are not involved in IT planning, it is very difficult for the IT planners to understand the business plan and make sure that the IT plan is aligned with the business plan. Without CEO's involvement the chances of IT planners to properly incorporate business plan into IT plan are rather slim. Therefore this is another indirect indication for the importance of CEOs' involvement in IT related activities.

Table 7: Regression of the integration of Business and IT Planning and firm performance

Variables	Beta	T
IT manager participates in business planning	.358	9.625**
IT plans incorporated in business plans	.477	1.355
Business plans used as basis for IT plans	.367	1.696
R-Square	.1284	
Adjusted R-Square	.1270	
** Significant at the level of 0.01		

The position of the senior IT manager (Chief Information Officer, MIS manager, or any comparable title) in the firm's hierarchy is also an indication to the importance CEOs attribute to IT. The most common number of reporting levels between the IT manager and the CEO for most firms was one, meaning that the IT managers report directly to the CEOs. For smaller firms, this finding may be related to size; but in larger firms it is an indication of the importance that top management attributes to IT. Table 8 gives the distribution. When we looked at a subset of firms with 100 employees or more, still in more than half of the cases the senior IT manager reported directly to the CEO.

Table 8: Reporting Level of Most Senior IT Manager

Reporting Level	Percent
1 level below CEO	65.3%
2 levels below CEO	26.1%
3 levels below CEO	6.3%
4 levels or more below CEO	2.3%

Most CEOs perceived IT to have a positive impact on their firms' performance. The mean rating of the perceived impact of IT on most factors contributing to firms' performance was around 5 on a scale of 1 to 7. This finding is significant. Most of previous studies on IT's contribution to productivity or other firm performance factors did not find conclusive support for a positive relationship. In recent years, the literature on justifications for the current level of investment in IT indicated that the relationship between investment and payoff is doubtful at best. These studies have had an impact on the CEOs' perceptions on IT (Wilson, 1992). However, the relationship between the CEOs' participation in IT-related activities and their perception of IT payoff is clear in this study. The more they participate the better the chances of payoff are, as shown above. In addition, the better the payoff that they see, the higher their perceptions of IT payoff.

In support of the findings above, other questions addressing the overall role of IT as seen by CEOs. Table 9 shows the distribution of responses. While the role IT played in the past is on the high side - 4.7 of 7 (mean ratings), the role for recent and future success is very high - 6 of 7.

Table 9: Business Role of IT

Role	Mean Rating (1-7)
IT is essential for present/future success	6.0
IT is competitive necessity for operations	5.4
IT played a vital role in the past	4.7

IMPLICATIONS OF THE SECOND SURVEY

The importance of top management involvement and participation in IT is supported by this study. Fifteen hundred CEOs from all major industries and firms of various sizes and types have indicated that IT is of utmost importance to the future of their firms. This study has surveyed the largest number of top executives on that issue in the reported literature to date. The perception of high importance of IT for the present and future success of their firms can not be held without accompanied participation in actual activities. Indeed, as the findings indicate, most CEOs have high degree of participation in IT activities.

This findings suggests that Singaporean CEOs believe that IT is important to their firms, and that they personally need to be involved and participative in IT (see table 5). They have these perceptions in spite of the fact that many previous studies had failed to demonstrate clear payoff for IT investments. The continuous push for IT investments by the government may explain the reason for these perceptions. However, such strong supportive views can not be explained

by this effect alone. Most of the firms surveyed were private, the results are confidential, and there is no reason for so many CEOs to indicate such a strong support for IT unless they really believe in it.

In summary, CEOs in Singapore see IT as an important factor contributing to their firms overall performance. As such, they understand the need to devote more of their time to IT. The more time CEOs devote to IT the better the chances for IT to work well for their firms. These findings reenforce the conclusions of the previous study, and demonstrated the importance of personal involvement of top managers in IT-related activities for their firms.

CONCLUSIONS

While there is a general agreement in the literature concerning the importance of top management involvement and participation in IT-related activities, little is known about the actual behaviour of top managers. The above two studies in Singapore revealed that most top managers strongly believe in IT and actively participate in IT-related activities. Top managers reported that they view IT as very important to their firm's success, that IT is generally viewed as a strategic investment rather than an expense, and that IT contributes to their firms' performance. These perceptions of top managers are supported by actual participation in IT-related activities. Top managers reported participation in the long term planning of IT, in approving major IT projects, in setting IT policies, and in IT budgeting. As a result, they are committed to provide stable long term funding for IT.

Until recently, there were no published studies showing that there is a proven payoff for IT. Yet, the results of this study have shown that top management perceive their involvement and participation to be essential to the continued success of their organizations. The findings of this study may be an indication that previous studies on IT payoffs may not apply to the Singapore scenario.

ENDNOTES

[1] The data for this survey was collected by Ang Suan Choo, Choo Yee Leng, and Lee Yew Wah.

[2] By IT opportunities and possibilities, we mean technological know-how and advancement which the organization can take advantage of to increase the operating efficiency and effectiveness of the organization so as to remain competitive in the industry.

[3] The budget also establishes a framework around which an early warning system for negative deviation can be built -- without a budget, it is difficult to spot deviations in a deteriorating cost situation in time to take appropriate corrective actions.

[4] By IT opportunities and possibilities, we mean technological know-how and advancement which the organization can take advantage of to increase the operating efficiency and effectiveness of the organization so as to remain competitive

in the industry.

⁵ IT innovations developed by major competitors are newly developed tools, equipment, technological know-how ,etc that enables them to effectively cut their cost of production . This allows the competitors to offer customers with more differentiated product at a lower price , thereby giving them a competitive edge over the others.

⁶ Small organizations often purchase software application programs off the shelve rather than develop them in-house, hence reducing the need for a steering committee.

REFERENCES

Adams, W. "New Role for Top Management in Computer Applications," Financial Executives, Apr. 1972, pp. 54-56.

Applegate L.M., and Osborn C.S., "Phillips 66 Company: Executive Information System," Harvard Business School Case no. 9-189-006.

Barki, H. and Hartwick, J. "Rethinking the Concept of User Involvement," MIS Quarterly (13:1), March 1989, pp. 53-64.

Brancheau, J.C. and J.C. Wetherbe, "Key Issues in Information Systems Management," MIS Quarterly (11:1), Mar. 1987, pp. 23-45.

Cash J.I., and B.R Konsynski, "IS Redraws Competitive Boundaries," Harvard Business Review, Mar-Apr. 1985, pp. 134-142.

Cash J.I., McFarlan W.F., and McKenney J.L., "Corportate Information Systems Management: The Issues Facing Senior Executievs," Irwin, Homewood, Illinois, 1988.

Cash J.I., McFarlan W.F., McKenney J.L., Applegate L.M., "Corportate Information Systems Management," third addition, Irwin, 1992.

Dickson, G.W., R.L. Leitheiser, M. Nechis, and J.C. Wetherbe, "Key Information Systems Issues for the 1980's," MIS Quarterly (8:3), Sep. 1984, pp. 17-35.

Doll, W.J., "Avenues for Top Management Involvement in Successful MIS Development," MIS Quarterly (9:1), Mar. 1985, pp. 17-35.

Feeny D.F., Edwards B.R., and Simpson K.M., "Understanding the CEO/ CIO Relationship," MIS Qarterly (16:4), Dec. 1992, pp. 435-467.

Freeman, G.A. Jr., "The Role Top Management Must Play in MIS Planning and Implementation," Proceedings of the Founders' Conference of the Society for Management Information Systems, Society for Management Information Systems, 1969.

Hall G., Rosental J., and Wade J., "How to Make Reengineering Really Work," Harvard Business Review, Nov-Dec., 1993, pp. 119-131.

Jarvenpaa S.L. and Ives B., "Information Technology and Corporate Strategy: A view from the top," Information Systems Research, (1:4), Dec. 1990.

Jarvenpaa, S.L. and Ives, B. "Executive Involvement and Participation in the Management of Information Technology," MIS Quarterly (15:2), Jun. 1991, pp. 205-228.

Keen, P., "Telecommunications and Business Policy: The Coming Impacts of Communications on Management," CISR Working Paper 81, Center for Information Systems Research, MIT, Cambridge, MA, Sep. 1981.

Keen, P., "Shaping the Future", Harvard Business School Press, 1991.

King, W., "Seeking Competitive Advantage Using Information-Intensive Strategies," Proceedings of New York University Symposium on Strategic Uses of Information Technology, May 1986, pg 11-27.

Lederer A.L., Mendelow A.L., "Information Resource Planning: Overcoming Difficulties in Indentifying Top Management's Objectives", MIS Quarterly, Sep. 1987, pp. 389-399.

NCB, Singapore IT Usage Survey, 1992.

O'Toole, R.J.W. and O'Toole, E.F. "Top Executive Involvement in the EDP Function," PMM & CO-Management Controls, Jun. 1966, pp. 125-127.

Porter, M.E. and V.E. Millar, "How Information Gives you Competitive Advantage," Harvard Business Review, Jul.-Aug. 1985, pg 149-160.

Reich, B.H. and I. Benbasat, " An Empirical Investigation of Factors Influencing the Success of Cusstomer-Oriented Strategic Systems," Working Paper 88-MIS-010, Faculty of Commerce and Business Administration, The University of British Columbia, Vancouver, Canada, May 1988.

Rockart J.F., De Long D.W., "Executive Support Systems", Business One Irwin, 1988.

Rockwell, W.P. "MIS: A View from the Top," Dun's Review (92:4), Oct. 1968, pp. 20-22.

Schein E.H., "The Role of the CEO in the Management of Changes: The Case of Information Technology," in: Allen T.J., Morton S.S., (Editors) "Information Technology and the Corportation of the 1990s," 1994.

Sprague R.H., McNurlin B.C., "Information Systems Management in Practice", third addtion, Prantice-Hall, 1993.

Wilson D.D., "Asssesing the Impact of Information Technology on Organizational Performance." In Strategic Information Technology Management: Perspectives on Organizational Growth and Competitive Advantage (Eds. R. Bunker, R Kauffman, and M. Mahmood), Idea Group Pub., Harrisburg PA, 1993.

Zuboff, S. "In the Age of the Smart Machine". New York: Basic Books, 1988.

Quality Assurance in Information Systems Development: A Case Study in Hong Kong IT Environment

Murali Mohan Narasipuram
Department of Information Systems
City Polytechnic of Hongkong, Hongkong
ismohan@cphkvx.cphk.hk

Executive Abstract

INTRODUCTION

Hongkong is the hub of economic activity in the Asia-Pacific region. It is making great strides in application of IT at a macro-level in globalisation of the economy and at a micro-level in making the Hongkong business firms more profitable and competitive. In the process, the IT industry in Hongkong has faced several quality-related issues to be resolved in the information systems development (ISD) process. Certification of quality of an information system by a third party according to an established set of standards has been accepted as a reasonable measure in ensuring quality in ISD. Though ISO9000 is being used in the Hongkong IT environment as a set of guidelines for quality assurance in ISD, there are some users and developers who question the suitability of ISO900 for ISD. Not many software houses in Hongkong have acquired this certificate; and from the user point of view, quality related work is always seen as a large indirect overhead. A study is being conducted to investigate various aspects of ISO9000 for ISD, including the relationship of ISO9000 to TQM, guidelines for implementation of ISO9000 in relation to ISD using a standard methodology such as Structured Systems Analysis and Design Method (SSADM), and the impact of quality assurance certification process on the organizational procedures and its personnel. A questionnaire is prepared based on the Hongkong Quality Assurance Agency's checklist. This questionnaire is about 20 pages and included several descriptive questions too. Quality assurance managers of three multi-national software houses were interviewed. The questionnaire was sent to the interviewees in advance of the interview. In addition to the quality assurance checklist, some general questions are also asked on the quality assurance process and its organization within the enterprise. In this paper, some interim results of the study are presented. Responses of one of the three interviews are analyzed as a case study of quality assurance process and certification in ISD and its impact on business enterprises in Hongkong IT environment. The ISO9000 series of standards was published in 1987 as the definitive quality management system standards for international use. The standards have now been adopted by more than forty countries as their own national standards for quality systems. There are now many thousands of companies throughout the world which have been assessed and certified by second and third parties against ISO9000 standards. Certification and registration of companies which are able to demonstrate capability of meeting all the requirements of ISO9000 is carried out in each country by certification bodies. These certification bodies assess the competence of companies to meet the international requirements for quality management system by means of an initial detailed systems audit and continuous surveillance thereafter. BS5750 is a British initiative, accepted in 1987 as a dual international standard to ISO9000. Development of ISO9000 concepts in Hong Kong, and the role of the HKPC (Hongkong Productivity Council) and HKQAA on the ISO9000 development in Hong Kong is discussed in several earlier works.

IT ENVIRONMENT UNDER STUDY

The organization under study is referred as Company1 for the reasons of anonymity. Company1 is a leading computer software, systems and consultancy company with activities worldwide. The company operates from 12 countries, and projects have been completed in over 50 countries. Company1's broad client base covers a wide range of market sectors including banking, finance, telecommunications, computing, electronics, space and defence. It has Quality Assurance units in each of its offices throughout the world. It had successfully accredited the ISO 9001 certificate with the full scope of "Design, production, installation, supply and maintenance of software system to specific client requirements and standard software products". It had also obtained the certificate of the TickIT Professional Attributes/Performance Standards for Software Quality Management System (QMS) - a side software standards to ISO9001 for Information Technology industry. To conform with the ISO9001 standards, Company1 has prepared the following types of documents - Quality Assurance Manual, Quality System Procedures Manual, Quality Plan, Work Instructions, and Forms, Records, etc. For every project the project manager draws up a quality plan based on the requirements of their quality system. Each plan is specific to the project in hand and is tailored to the technology most appropriate to the project. Drawing up the plan is a well documented process and client participation is solicited. Clients are encouraged to read and comment on the quality plan and are invited to incorporate their own quality standards where appropriate. The quality plan clearly defines all of the quality measures to be employed. This covers not only the standards and methods but also the organizational aspects of : (a) Quality Control - an embedded function within the line structure of a project team (b) Quality Engineering - the function of organizing and coordinating the effective use of the quality control methods within the project (c) Quality Assurance - the independent monitoring and audit activities conducted by the Quality Assurance office throughout all phases of the project. All procedures relating to IS development, in compliance with ISO9001 standards, are documented in the Quality System Procedures Manual. Company1's detailed commitment to quality is aimed at identifying any problems early and resolving these in a timely manner, thereby reducing problems during the test and acceptance phases and demonstrating complete compliance with all agreed requirements. Different recommended guidelines will be used for the development of different projects/systems depending on the agreement with clients and the nature of user requirements. Steps and deliverables recommended in SSADM are used in developing systems where applicable. During quality audit by the HKQAA, the most common problems faced are that the company's quality system may not be fully understood by the quality auditor. Result of quality audit will depend on the degree of understanding by the auditor of the quality related issues and relevant standards applicable to IT industry.

QUALITY CERTIFICATION PROCESS - ORGANIZATIONAL IMPACTS

Company1 has been adopting quality system for many years, and so the ISO9000 process has no special impact on the staff. And also, the ISO9001 certification process did not involve much additional cost to the company. The only additional costs are certification cost, annual certification renewal fee and expenses in surveillance visits by HKQAA. After the certification audit, Company1 clears all non-conformities. To prepare for the future continuous audit, Company1 has to review and improve the quality system from time to time, so as to improve quality, and to comply with ISO9000 standards. Clients derive many benefits from this approach; in particular they can expect (a) a clear view, at the very outset of a project, of the quality measures being employed during the development process to achieve a quality product; (b) that the design will be systematically reviewed and tested at each stage; (c) more effective quality controls and quality engineering support by means of the regular monitoring and auditing undertaken by the independent quality assurance office; (d) delivery of systems on time and within budget which are fully supported with the necessary documentation for the operation and maintenance of the system; and (e) continuous refinement of their quality practices by the active feedback of past project experience. The most important benefit from Company1's quality system is fostering of the quality culture in every one of its staff members. Quality pervades everything they do, and motivates staff to set goals and priorities which are based on client's needs. These goals and priorities are monitored and assessed by the organizational quality standards. In the opinion of the Quality Manager of Company1, it is well-worth for a company to register for the ISO9000 certification. This is because a well-defined quality system is helpful for management control. The ISO9000 process can provide a good chance for quality control, and for reviewing the existing procedures no matter whether the certificate can be successfully accredited or not. On the other hand, with the accreditation of ISO9000 certificate, clients rate the company as more trust-worthy and quality-conscious.

Beyond Industry Policy to Information Society: A Framework for Government Involvement in IT Policy

Felix B Tan

Department of Management Science and Information Systems

The University of Auckland, NEW ZEALAND

email: f.tan@auckland.ac.nz

The scope and direction of information technology (IT) policy in shaping social and economic change vary among nations. In some countries, focus has been on the competitiveness of their IT industry through a broad range of industry policies. In others, the emphasis has moved beyond industry specific policy to one where IT has been identified as the key to the achievement of the 'information society'. This paper discusses the essential elements of IT policy in Singapore - a nation successful in fostering socio-economic changes through state-directed IT efforts aimed at achieving the vision of an "intelligent island". It argues that there are two dimensions to government involvement in IT in Singapore - state push and state pull actions. A framework relating combinations of the above actions is developed. The paper concludes that different options are available to policy makers depending on the priority and impact of IT goals.

I. INTRODUCTION

It has been suggested that there is a link between a nation's overall social and economic developments and its approach to the use and diffusion of information technology (IT) (Porter, 1990; King and Konsynski, 1991; Street, 1992; Malecki, 1991; OECD, 1992; Evenson and Ranis, 1990). This growing awareness of the contribution that IT has made and can make to economic and social wellbeing has brought the subject of national IT policy to the forefront of public discussions in both national and international forums. One area of discussion is the role of government in shaping and directing industry and in particular IT policy and developments. A dichotomy of views exists relating to government involvement in IT policy. On one extreme, the approach is market directed, where the operation of the free market will lead to optimum resource allocation and result in the most desired economic outcomes. On the other extreme, the market is considered a tool for achieving socially and economically desirable objectives and that government has a role in directing the market toward such objectives (Kraemer et al., 1992). While these opposing views have created considerable controversy, some voices are beginning to suggest that it is time to move beyond the ideological debate and attempt to understand how government can influence markets to achieve socially beneficial results (Kraemer and Dedrick, 1993). This paper looks at the essential elements of IT policy in Singapore - a "hands on" government directed programme which extends beyond assistance to its IT industry to the informatisation of society as a whole. The aims are to assess the themes that characterise IT policy in Singapore and to develop a framework to understand how government involvement in IT can be categorised.

Section II discusses the concept of industry policy, particularly IT policy -its role in economic policy and the rationale for government involvement. Section III describes Singapore's vision of an intelligent island and reviews the essential elements of its IT policy - who are the architects? How have they participated directly or indirectly in the nation's IT developments? A framework assessing the themes that characterise IT policy in Singapore is then presented in Section IV. This framework is an attempt to understand how government involvement in IT can be categorised. Section V concludes with comments on the general applicability and implications of this framework.

II. THE CONCEPT OF INDUSTRY AND IT POLICY

Industry policy, "is the sum of a nation's effort to shape business activity and influence economic growth. It's proper concern is the long term structural integrity of a nation's industrial base" (Leone and Bradley, 1981). Much of the current enthusiasm for the notion of industry policy hinges on the premise that a better portfolio management by government is necessary for economic growth (Leone and Bradley, 1981; Scott, 1982; Kantrow, 1983; Bower, 1983; Baradacco and Yoffie, 1983; Levitt, 1984).

IT policy can be regarded as an industry policy specifically concerned with ensuring that firms, consumers,and government have access to appropriate and up-to-date technology at the lowest possible cost; with fostering invention and innovation; with encouraging the diffusion of innovation, new Its; and with ensuring that industry takes advantage of the economic and social advantages offered by developments in IT. IT policy can therefore be viewed as a particular subset of the instruments in a nation's broader economic and social strategy (Barber and White, 1987).

The scope and direction of IT policy in shaping socio-economic change vary among nations (Kraemer and Dedrick, 1993). For instance, IT policy in the United States and United Kingdom can be classified as market-directed, where the approach is marked not by an absence of IT policies, but rather by the absence of a centralised, coordinated strategy. Another approach is more prevalent in Europe, Japan, and the East Asian nations, where the governments influence developments and directions of IT in their industries and society.

A number of rationale have been proposed for government involvement in promoting IT. These can generally be classified into 2 broad areas - economic and social. Monk (1993) argues that micro-level decisions and actions of IT users, investors, and other economic agents take place within a political and economic environment that is strongly influenced by macro-level policy making. Macro-level IT issues relate to the transition of advanced economies from an industrial mode of operation to one based on information (OECD, 1986; Antonelli, 1992). Part of the rationale for macro IT policy formulation is derived from actual or potential implications of the micro-level IT activities of economic agents. Monk contends that IT is not merely a vehicle for generating profits for their corporate owners. IT's significance lies in its role in the operation of economy as a whole. Viewed in this light, the development of a national IT policy will improve the efficiency, effectiveness, and functionality in the economy within which corporate economic agents operate.

The possible social impact of IT (eg. teleshopping, cashless transactions, telecommuting, intelligent buildings, and improved quality of life - electronic information on leisure activities, traffic, business and government services) and the conflicts of interest (eg. issues relating to privacy, ownership of data, copyright, and censorship) that could arise or be intensified warrant the formulation of a policy which addresses both today's issues and develop future goals through the selective use of new IT (Harpham, 1980; National Computer Board, 1992).

III. SINGAPORE: A VISION OF AN INTELLIGENT ISLAND

The *World Competitiveness Report* has, in the recent years, placed Singapore among the top nations in the world to have effectively exploited IT. The island nation is the site of an astonishing economic and technological achievement. Singapore not only embodies what is already perhaps the most technologically advanced nation in the world but is also poised to become the world's first fully networked society - one in which all homes, schools, business, and government agencies will be interconnected in an electronic grid (Sisodia, 1992; National Computer Board, 1992).

Many authors argue that the success so far achieved by Singapore in the application of IT for social and economic change can be attributed to the state-directed IT strategy (Gubaxani et al., 1990; Sisodia, 1992; King and Konsynski, 1991; Long, 1990) and the sociocultural infrastructure (Swyngedouw, 1990; Wong, 1990). Gurbaxani et al. (1990) describe the Singapore government as a regulator and coordinator of IT development and an active participant in developing both the supply side and demand side as well as the necessary IT infrastructure.

Elements of Singapore's IT policy

What, therefore, make up the fabric of the state-directed IT policy in Singapore? Singapore's industry policy since its independence in 1965 has been based on developing the country as an export base for multinational corporations (MNC) (Lim and Associates, 1988; Goh et al., 1993). This approach to "luring" the production of IT products to the island is the focus of Singapore's IT policy.

a. The Architects

The IT policy model adopted by Singapore has been very much state-directed, where policy is usually designed and implemented by a government agency or statutory board. Once IT was targeted as vital to achieving the goal of becoming an information society, the government established a high level ministerial Committee on National Computerisation (CNC) to develop a national IT plan for Singapore. The key agency for the government's IT plan is the National Computer Board (NCB) formed in September 1981 and overseen by the CNC (Economic Development Board (EDB), 1981; Ministry of Trade and Industry (MTI), 1986). A very strong coordination exists between the NCB, EDB, and industry trade association Singapore Federation of the Computer Industry (SFCI).

b. Direct Participation

The Singapore government actively participates in IT developments both at the micro and macro levels through the establishment of the NCB and through the EDB. The objective is to stimulate industries, businesses, and society toward the stated vision.

The NCB was established as a statutory board to act as a focal point, catalyst, and liaison for both public and private sector IT activities (Gurbaxani et al., 1990). The NCB serves as an advisor to the government on computerisation and its mission is to encourage the use and production of IT products and services. As part of Phase I of the national IT plan and to encourage the use of IT, the NCB set up the Civil Service Computerisation Programme (CSCP) to computerise the government ministries. The CSCP was designed to demonstrate the government's strong commitment to computerisation and to lead the national computerisation effort - Phase II (Gurbaxani et al., 1990). To encourage the production of IT related products and services, the NCB promotes initiatives such as market development through the delivery and administration of grants and incentives for new software development and the dissemination of IT knowledge and skill. The NCB also encourages joint development of products, through R&D funding, where it can be established that product outcomes can be exported from Singapore (Hosken, 1992).

The EDB is the marketing arm of the nation. It serves to effectively promote Singapore as a centre for business success and stable nation to invest in. To achieve this end, the EDB facilitates and administers investment incentives through tax relief schemes, loans, and venture capital incentives. The focus is very much on innovation and productivity as well as the encouragement of further enterprise development through the EDB's Industry Development and Small Enterprise Bureaus.

c. Indirect Policies

The very strategy which built the economic miracle of Singapore - emphasis on petroleum, shipbuilding and repair, and construction - has run its course, with these now being considered as "sunset industries". In its place, the government is now encouraging capital intensive and intellect oriented sectors like medical services and IT related industries (artificial intelligence, robotics, and informatics). These have been termed as "sunrise industries". Various forms of policies and incentive schemes have been developed in order to attract local and foreign investment, especially from MNCs, in these "sunrise industries" and to support the seven specific strategic goals identified in the National IT Plan (MTI, 1986). These policies and schemes can be categorised into investment incentives, financial assistance, and export incentives. Details of Singapore's indirect IT policies are summarised in Table 1.

It is also felt that the impact IT has on society warrants the formulation of specific policies which will encourage the adoption and diffusion of IT through the enhancement of IT skills, the nurturing of an IT culture, and the development of an infrastructure which can support IT supply and demand (MTI, 1986; Gurbaxani et al., 1990). A pre-requisite to high productivity and improved business efficiency is to have a better educated and trained workforce. The current *IT Manpower* plan focuses on 2 aspects: (a) the enhancement of existing educational facilities to improve the quality and scope of IT instruction and to strengthen the appeal of IT as an area of study; and (b) the encouragement and support of private sector IT training (eg. through assistance from the Skills Development Fund). Preparing the broader community for an information society meant the nurturing of an *IT Culture*. To increase the society's general appreciation and awareness in IT, IT has been promoted in educational institutions and through co-sponsoring national IT events, like software competition, trade fairs, and conferences. The government has also initiated the Education and Literacy in IT programme to improve IT literacy among the working population. An information-based society requires a reliable and cost effective telecommunications and *IT Infrastructure* in order to ensure its creative and widespread use. The state owned Telecom has been actively building modern telecommunications to support various networks such as TradeNet, MedNet, and LawNet and promoting the widespread use of new and innovative applications. One such application is Teleview, an interactive videotex system that links to computers and televisions in private residences. Teleview offers teleshopping, educational programmes, on-line banking, and much more. Another is to extend Singapore's telecommunications service internationally (eg. extending the ISDN service overseas and assisting Indonesia in setting up networks).

IV. AN IT POLICY MATRIX

The previous section describes the essential elements of IT

Table 1: Indirect IT Policy Instruments

Instruments	Policy Summary
Investment Incentives	Zero tax on company profits for 5 to 10 years.
Pioneer Status	Alternative to pioneer status, where tax-exempt profits are limited to
Investment Allowance	specified percentage (up to 50%) of actual fixed investment.
	A reduced tax rate of 10% on post-pioneer profits.
Post Pioneer Incentive	Concessionary tax rates for royalties paid to non-residents abroad.
Approved Royalties	Five-year tax exemption for 50% of qualifying income.
Warehousing/Servicing Incentive	Expenditure on new technology equipment can be written off against
Depreciation Allowance	taxable profits over 3 years.
	Tax relief for new capital expenditure of more than S$10 million on plant
Expansion Incentive	or equipment to increase production of approved IT products.
	50% write off of the equity against tax if the new technology project
Venture Capital	incurs losses
Financial Incentives	Equity participation (with a buy-back option) and term loans.
Capital Assistance Scheme	Dollar-for-dollar grant subject to a maximum of $10,000 per project.
Product Development Assistance	Low interest loan aimed at upgrading technology of small companies.
Small Industries Finance	Finances the upgrading of skills, subsidising up to 70% of training costs.
Skills Development Fund	Subsidies of up to 90% for manpower and equipment in new knowledge
INTECH	intensive projects.
Export Incentives	Maintains the S$ parity through a managed float.
Exchange Rate Policy	4% tax on export profits for a period of five to fifteen years.
Export Incentive Scheme	A banker's guarantee scheme to cover credit needs of local IT exporters.
Export Credit Facility	Five years concessionary company tax at 20% on export profits.
International Trade	A tax exemption of 50% of export profits for five years.
International Consultancy	

policy in Singapore. How can these policies as a whole be categorised? Are there any themes that characterise IT policy in Singapore?

A number of authors (OECD, 1989; Arnold and Guy, 1986; Gurbaxani et al, 1990) have agreed that IT policy can be conceptualised along two key dimensions: the level of institutional involvement (through influence or regulation) and the nature of that involvement (supply or demand). These dimensions are illustrated in a 2 X 2 matrix (Figure 1).

The level of institutional or government involvement, shown on the vertical axis of the matrix, refers to the character of the government's role in the development of IT. The influence role is the proactive role and the role of greatest involvement in which the government uses its nonlegal influence to spearhead the development of IT. The regulatory role of the government is the legal role in which the government uses legislation to affect IT development.

On the horizontal axis of the matrix, the nature of government involvement refers to the ways in which the government encourages and supports IT development. These are categorised into supply and demand. Interventions involving the supply side are those aimed at spurring innovation or encouraging the local production of products or processes containing those innovations. On the demand side, the interventions are designed to create a need for innovative products and processes, or to enhance the efficiency and effectiveness with which they are used.

The matrix presents six types of IT policy interventions: knowledge building, knowledge deployment, subsidy, mobilisation, standards, and innovation directives. These are categorised into the matrix according to the intended effect of the policy. Gurbaxani et al. (1990) have applied this framework in analysing Singapore and describe the government's role as regulator and coordinator of IT development.

This paper presents an alternative approach in assessing the theme which characterises Singapore's IT policy. Gurbaxani et al. (1990) suggest that the government directly influences and indirectly regulates IT developments. This concept can be interpreted into two broad categories that seek to initiate development - state push actions and state pull actions. State push actions involve the direct participation of the government in IT developments. This takes the form of the creation of the NCB to direct policy and to participate in equity capital of private enterprise with the aim of stimulating growth in IT use and production. State pull actions involve the designing of market mechanisms to induce the required IT developments. These include investment incentives, financial assistance, and export related schemes. As evidenced in this paper and cited works, there is a subtle interplay between government involvement in the form of direct participation and in the form of regulation. These interrelationships suggest that it may be useful to view these two forms of state actions as interdependent rather than separate instruments through which IT goals are pursued.

Taken collectively, these two forms of state actions may be used as dimensions in a conceptual scheme that may be applied to categorise government involvement in IT. The joint actions can be represented on a two-by-two matrix, as illus-

Figure 1: Dimensions of Institutional Intervention (adapted from Gurbaxani et al., 1990)

	Nature of Involvement	
	Supply (production)	Demand (use)
Influence	Knowledge Building Knowledge Deployment Subsidy Innovation Directive	Mobilisation Knowledge Deployment Subsidy
Level		
of	I	II
Involvement	III	IV
Regulation	Knowledge Deployment Innovation Directive Subsidy Standards ·	Subsidy Standards Innovation Directive

Figure 2: IT Policy Matrix

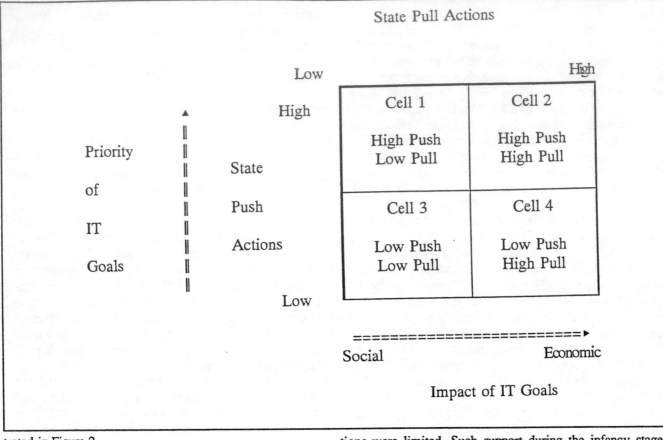

trated in Figure 2.

The underlying theme behind these push/pull actions is that the higher the priority of the IT policy goal and the greater the impact of the goal on economic growth (than social benefits) then the political pressure is for increased intensity of state actions.

High push/low pull actions (cell 1)

A high priority goal from inception is the development of the telecommunications infrastructure. This is being achieved, primarily through active government participation (high push) in telecommunication projects aimed at achieving a fully networked society (the intelligent island) and secondarily through incentives (low pull), which encourage different industries to work with the government in establishing a reliable and cost effective infrastructure. Although goals which fall in this category tend to be extremely risky, the benefits to society tend to outweigh the cost and hence attract greater promotion through direct state influence than indirect policies.

High push/high pull actions (cell 2)

Another high priority goal from the early stages, is the establishment of demand for IT products and services in order to develop economic growth in the IT sector. The state, through NCB, created the market for IT at a time early in its life cycle, when prices are very high and the range of applica-

tions were limited. Such support during the infancy stage helps to nurture development in IT use to the point where the private sector demand is sufficient to sustain growth. As government support is critical in developing the IT industry, both state push and pull actions are most intense.

Low push/low pull actions (cell 3)

There is a set of IT goals which revolve around the nurturing of an IT culture and the continual upgrading of skills through public and private sector IT education and training. It seems that the state initiatives relating to these societal goals are to gently stimulate the normal process of IT awareness and adoption, where it is otherwise retarded. It is encouraging to note that the moderate policies have been prompting developments in these instances and that intense push and pull actions may not have been favourable.

Low push/high pull actions (cell 4)

State actions in cell 4, which consists of strong pull relative to push seem to encourage the supply of IT products and services. Existing competition in the IT industry already induce a high rate of product and service innovations. To attract continual foreign investments in an intensely competitive environment, appropriate market mechanisms and incentives have been designed, thereby ensuring the maintenance of an export base for MNCs.

V. CONCLUSION

The matrix presented in Figure 2 constitutes a framework which focuses attention on the joint impact on a nation's IT developments of the two major categories of government involvement. The matrix is by no means precise as it will require more accurate measurements for assessing the priority and impact of IT policy goals and will need to be tested for its general applicability. This paper does not suggest that a predominantly state push orientation is better than state pull, or vice versa. It concludes that there are different options for policy makers depending on the priority and impact of IT goals. Nevertheless, the patterns reveal by the framework provide useful guidelines for shaping government involvement in stimulating IT developments beyond economic growth in its industries toward a fully networked information society.

REFERENCES

Antonelli, C (ed.) *The Economics of Information Networks,* North Holland, Amsterdam, 1992.

Arnold, E and Guy, K *Parallel Convergence: National Strategies in Information Technology,* Frances Pinter, London, 1986.

Badaracco, J D and Yoffie, D B 'Industry Policy: It Can't Happen Here' *Harvard Business Review,* Nov - Dec 1983, pp.97-105.

Barber, J and White, G 'Current Policy Practice and Problems from a UK Perspective' in *Economic Policy and Technological Performance,* Dasgupta, P and Stoneman, P (eds.) Cambridge University Press, 1987.

Bower, J L 'Managing for Efficiency, Managing for Equity' *Harvard Business Review,* Jul - Aug 1983, pp.83-90.

Economic Development Board (EDB) *Computer Software and Service Firms in Singapore,* July 1981.

Evenson, R E and Ranis, G (eds.) *Science and Technology: Lessons for Development Policy,* Westview Press, Boulder, Colorado, 1990.

Goh, M, Chong, L C and Yeoh, C 'Strategic Management in Economic Development: The Singapore Experience' *International Journal of Management,* June 1993, pp.165-173.

Gurbaxani, V, Kraemer, K L, King, J L, Jarman, S, Dedrick, J, Raman, K S and Yap C S 'Government as the Driving Force Toward the Information Society: National Computer Policy in Singapore', *Information Age,* 1990, pp.155-185.

Harpham, M 'Toward a Communications and Information Policy for New Zealand', *Commission for the Future,* Report No CFFR4/80, November 1980.

Hosken, N 'A Review of the Information Technology Industry of the Asian-Oceanian Region' *Report on the Asian - Oceanian Information Technology Industry,* January 1992.

Kantrow, A M (ed.) 'The Political Realities of Industrial Policy' *Harvard Business Review,* Sept - Oct 1983, pp.76-86.

King, J L and Konsynski, B 'Singapore Tradenet: A Tale of One City' *Harvard Business School Case No 9-191-008,* Boston, Harvard Business School, 1991.

Kraemer, K L, Gurbaxani, V and King J L 'Economic Development, Government Policy, and the Diffusion of Computing in Asia-Pacific Countries' *Public Administration Review,* March/April 1992, pp.146-156.

Kraemer, K L and Dedrick, J 'National Technology Policy and the Development of Information Industries' *Centre for Research on Information Technology and Organisations,* University of California, Irvine, 1993.

Leone, R A and Bradley, S P 'Towards an Effective Industrial Policy' *Harvard Business Review,* Nov - Dec 1981, pp.91-97.

Levitt, A 'Industrial Policy: Slogan or Solution' *Harvard Business Review,* Mar - Apr 1984, pp.6-8.

Lim, C Y and Associates *Policy Options for the Singapore Economy,* McGraw-Hill, Singapore, 1988.

Long, S R 'Singapore: The drive into the 1990's', *Information Age,* September 1990.

Malecki, E J *Technology and Economic Development,* Longman Group UK, 1991.

Ministry of Trade & Industry (MTI) 'The Singapore Economy: New Directions', Report of the Economic Committee, February 1986.

Monk, P 'The Economic Significance of Infrastructural IT Systems' *Journal of Information Technology,* Vol 8, No 1, 1993, pp. 14-21.

National Computer Board (NCB) *A Vision of an Intelligent Island,* NCB, Singapore, March 1992.

Neo, B S, King, J L and Applegate, L 'Singapore Tradenet (B): The Tale Continues' *Harvard Business School Case No 9-193-136,* Boston, Harvard Business School, 1993.

OECD, 'Trends in the Information Economy', Information, Computer and Communication Policy Series, No 11, OECD Paris, 1986.

OECD, *Information Technology and New Growth Opportunities,* Information, Computer and Communication Policy Series, No 19, OECD Paris, 1989.

OECD, *Technology and the Economy - The Key Relationships,* OECD, Paris 1992.

Porter, M E The Competitive Advantage of Nations, The MacMillan Press Ltd, 1990.

Scott, B R 'Can Industry Survive the Welfare State' *Harvard Business Review,* Sep - Oct 1982, pp.70-84.

Sisodia, R 'Singapore Invests in the Nation Corporation', *Harvard Business Review,* May-June 1992, pp. 40-50.

Street, J *Politics and Technology,* Gulford Press, New York, 1992.

Sywngedouw, J 'The Role of Christianity' in Peter, B L and Hsiao, H M (eds.) *In Search of an East Asian Development Model,* Transaction Publications, New Jersey, 1990.

Wong, S 'The Applicability of Asian Family Values to Other Sociocultural Settings' in Peter, B L and Hsiao, H M (eds.) *In Search of an East Asian Development Model,* Transaction Publications, New Jersey, 1990.

Utilization of Information Technology in Hong Kong Organizations

Eugenia M W Ng Tye
Department of Computing
Hong Kong Polytechnic
Hunghom, Kowloon, Hong Kong

Patrick Y K Chau
Department of Business Information Systems
The Hong Kong University of Science and Technology
Clear Water Bay, Kowloon, Hong Kong

Executive Abstract

INTRODUCTION

Hong Kong is one of the fastest growing area in the world and is one of the "four little dragons" in Asia. It is the eleventh largest trading economy in the world and is the world's second busiest container port. The gross domestic product (GDP) has grown by an average of 12% per year since 1979. Hong Kong is not only known as a manufacturer and exporter of goods, it also becomes the major service and sourcing centre for the Asian countries. The tertiary sector is now the largest contributor to GDP.

DISCUSSION OF THE ISSUES

As Hong Kong moves towards a service-oriented economy, the reliance on strategic use of IT in Hong Kong organizations should become more intense. There have been a few studies on IT in Hong Kong, but it was either a few years back or on a small area of interest. Thus, the authors attempt to study the role of IT in Hong Kong business organizations in general by conducting a survey. This study will investigate the following aspects of IT in Hong Kong:

1. level and extent of utilization
2. perceived benefits and problems encountered

METHODOLOGY

This study is based on data gathered through a mail survey. The participants of the survey were chosen from the Hong Kong section of the 1992 Asian Computer Directory. A total of 438 IT managers were included in the mailing list. 116 usable returns are received with a response rate of 26.5%. The respondent are from medium and large companies of major industry groups.

The questionnaire has two major parts. Managers were asked to answer most questions using a 5-point Likert scale with 5 being "strongly agree" and 1 being "strongly disagree". The first part of the questionnaire consisted of ten questions which were related to the utilization of IT in the respondents' organization. The second part of the questionnaire concerned the respondent's background and the demographics of the organization.

RESULTS AND DISCUSSIONS

Level of Commitment

Hong Kong organizations have a high level of commitment of in IT. Most of the respondents have around ten years of IT experience and had computers installed in their workplace before the mid-1980s. More than 80% of the responding organizations have installed mini and micro computers but only about one third of them have installed mainframe computers.

Most of our responding organizations have a fairly small IT department. More than half of them have ten or less personnel in their IT department. Their spending on IT is also small. The responding companies have spent less than 5%, of their annual turnover on IT. The situation has changed gradually and organizations are beginning to spend more.

Extent of IT Penetration

Majority of the responding organizations have more than half of the employees using computers at work. They use IT most extensively in "traditional" applications areas such as accounting, finance, and personnel/human resources. IT is used in a lesser extent in other functional areas such as marketing, sales, production, and general management. The responding companies also use IT extensively to perform various managerial activities. IT is used for budgeting, planning, controlling and monitoring activities but rarely used for finding problems alternatives.

Software Packages

In our sample, word processing is the most popular type of software package followed by spreadsheet packages, data management packages and communication packages. The responding companies use graphical/presentation packages, statistical packages, modelling packages and CASE tools less often.

Benefits and Problems of Using IT

Most respondents acknowledge the benefits of using IT in their organizations. The average scores on the ten benefits listed in the questionnaire are high. They are ranged from 3.91 to 4.72, with 1 being strongly disagree with the stated benefit and 5 being strongly agree with the stated benefit. The highly recognized IT benefits are: to provide better record-keeping; to provide more timely, more accurate and expanded information; and to improve operational procedures. The least regarded benefits of IT are to produce information that existed before computerization at less cost and to facilitate business/organizational growth through computer controls.

The respondents perceive that benefits outweigh the problems when adopting IT. The average scores for all the problems listed in the questionnaire are much lower than the scores for benefits, range from 2.67 to 3.16. The top problem is the lack of financial support. Other problems include the lack of end-user support, lack of experience in using IT, and lack of top management support.

CONCLUSIONS AND IMPLICATIONS

We believe the combination of the growing globalization of businesses, greater complexity of organizations, and more service-oriented economy has driven Hong Kong organizations to rely more on the use of IT to remain competitive in the world market. Most large Hong Kong organizations have adopted IT to support their key business activities.

Although most responding companies appear to be satisfied with the IT utilizations in their companies, the Hong Kong Government could take a more active role to sustain the economic growth. The government could coordinate and promote the use of IT in organizations, apart from promotion through its own consumption. The government may also offer incentives such as tax breaks and subsidies for IT investments. Lastly, IT professional bodies may suggest standards and offer consultancy to assist organizations to adopt IT successfully.

Graduate Computer Education in India and the United States: First Steps in an International Collaboration

Dr. Stuart A. Varden, Dr. Frank LoSacco, Dr. David Sachs
Pace University
Information Systems Department
861 Bedford Road
Pleasantville, NY 10570
Internet Address: VARDENF@DAC.PACEVM.EDU

GREAT COMPUTER POTENTIAL IN INDIA

In recent years, foreign computer companies have been flocking to India's major urban areas. The low cost of labor in India is the main inducement for foreign companies, mainly from United States and Europe, to set up operations in India to develop software products and applications for export to overseas markets. This, coupled with India's own growing information needs, has led to a high demand for skilled software developers and application builders. Tens of thousands of jobs are available, which has stimulated great interest in the field, and thus, in computer education.

LIMITATIONS OF INDIA'S SYSTEM OF HIGHER EDUCATION

Education in India is based largely on the British system. Degree granting institutions are limited in number, which means that available seats are scarce and those which do exist are in very high demand. The numbers of qualified computer science and information systems graduates are far too small to meet the needs of India's rapidly growing computer industry. Moreover, the focus of most university programs is on theory and research, and is not oriented toward applications appropriate to business needs.

THE RISE OF PROPRIETARY COMPUTER SCHOOLS

The lack of appropriate job-related training and professional computer education have stimulated the growth of many successful profit-making proprietary computer schools and training centers throughout India. Such schools serve to bridge the gap between what the traditional educational system is producing and the needs of industry. Many sequences of courses offered by these proprietary schools are designed to prepare students to take the Indian Government's Department of Electronics Accreditation (DOEACC) scheme. Students who pass these examinations are virtually assured professional employment as programmers or application developers.

DESCRIPTION OF APTECH

Apple Industries, through its information technology subsidiary,APTECH, operates over 125 computer training centers throughout India. The large number and increasing growth of these centers is in response to a high demand for computer education in India, running from elementary workshops in microcomputer software applications packages, to semester-length graduate-level courses of study in computer science and information systems. APTECH is authorized to award certificates to students who have taken a sequence of courses and passed examinations covering a particular body of knowledge. APTECH, however, cannot award college academic credit or degrees.

DESCRIPTION OF PACE UNIVERSITY

Pace University is a private comprehensive university with about 16,000 students on campuses in the greater New York City area. The University has six schools including business, art and sciences, education, nursing, law, and computer science and information systems. The School of Computer Science and Information Systems (SCSIS) offers programs in computer science, information systems, telecommunications, and office information systems at both th undergraduate and graduate levels.

THE PACE UNIVERSITY/APTECH PROGRAM

Apple Industries and Pace University have entered into an arrangement regarding the computer science and information systems courses which are taught by APTECH faculty in India. The curricula which they follow approximates that of similar courses which are taught at Universities in the United States. In addition, some SCSIS faculty have travelled to India to orient APTECH instructors regarding the texts and course curricula which are typically used in such courses.

PACE CERTIFICATE EXAMINATIONS — A FIRST STEP

Pace University professors have developed two sets of examinations which focus on subject matter in the areas of computer science and information systems, respectively. Tests are administered in India and returned to Pace University for scoring by the Pace faculty members who designed them. Students who pass the examinations are awarded a continuing professional education certificate from Pace University. Although Pace University does not award credits for courses taken in India, it does award credit by examination to students who have successfully completed their examinations in India, for up to 12 credits, who choose to continue their studies at Pace University in the United States leading to a Master of Science in Computer Science or Information Systems degree. Interest in the Pace University/APTECH program in India has been very high judging from the hundreds of students that attend each information session.

ADVANTAGES OF THE PROGRAM TO PACE UNIVERSITY

Working with colleagues and students in India has provided a general educational and cultural broadening of Pace faculty who have participated. So far six Pace faculty members have gone to India in connection with the program, some more than once. These opportunities for foreign travel and cultural exchange has been very rewarding for all concerned. Faculty have had the opportunity to explore, learn about, and put into practice, an promising form of distance learning. The program also provides an excellent opportunity for faculty to learn about, work in, and become involved with, the emerging industries of global software engineering and applications development, and emerging issues, such as ISO 9000.

CONCLUSION

The APTECH/Pace University program has taken some time to put into place, and much of hard work and learning on the part of institutions on two continents. However, it is fair to say that the first steps are well underway, and appear to be quite successful. Both partners in this international collaboration have learned how to work with one another, and look forward to similar opportunities in the future.

Section Seven

Emerging Technologies Management

Strategic Information Technology Management in State Government Agencies: Strategic Planning for Emerging Technologies

Stephen T. Bajjaly, Ph.D.
College of Library and Information Science
University of South Carolina

Executive Abstract

"Reinventing government," a key objective for public officials and managers in the 1990s, means not only cutting costs and increasing efficiencies but expanding the scope and quality of government services. An integral component of reinvention involves "reengineering" existing work processes to take full advantage of modern information technologies (IT). In both the public and the private sectors, reengineering seeks to uncover breakdowns, bottlenecks, and redundancies in established work processes and to apply IT to change fundamentally the ways of doing business.

Because they change the way business is conducted, reengineering projects are considered strategic IT applications. Inherently proactive, strategic IT applications are designed to achieve positive, consequential outcomes and to enable the strategic value of information to emerge. Since governments at all levels collect, generate, process, and disseminate ever-increasing amounts of information, any effort to change the nature of government should involve the strategic application of emerging IT.

This paper examines the extent to which public agencies today are interested in emerging IT for strategic reasons. By addressing how public agencies are implementing document imaging systems, one of the most prominent of the emerging information technologies of the 1990s, this study examines normative IS concepts developed for the private sector which appear to be applicable to public agencies and which have undergone limited empirical testing, especially within a public sector context.

HYPOTHESES

The research hypotheses were designed to test whether normative concepts of IT planning and management developed in the private sector apply within state government. Although these normative concepts have not been studied empirically within the private sector, they are treated as "conventional wisdom," taken as universal truths. In order to examine these concepts, the following constructs were developed:

- Strategic IS Orientation: The degree to which a state agency is interested in IT to achieve strategic outcomes.
- Formal IS Strategic Planning: Completion of formal, management planning activities to ensure that the use of IT aligns with the organization's strategic goals and that available IT resources are deployed properly.

- Supportive IT Environment: The extent to which a state agency operates in an environment that supports the strategic use of IT in government.
- Document Imaging Adoption: State agencies that have reached the decision to invest the resources necessary to undertake the implementation of a document imaging system.

The following research hypotheses are proposed for testing:

H1: *State agencies which engage in formal IS strategic planning have a higher strategic IS orientation than state agencies which do not engage in formal IS strategic planning.*

H2: *The more comprehensive a state agency's formal IS strategic planning process, the more the agency will operate in an environment supportive of IT.*

H3: *State agencies which have adopted document imaging have a higher strategic IS orientation than state agencies which have not adopted document imaging.*

The basic premise behind testing these hypotheses is that state agencies, while operating in a potentially different environment from their private sector counterparts, nevertheless have the same needs and desired outcomes for their IT investments and so these normative relationships should apply to state government agencies.

METHODOLOGY

Data for this study were collected through a pre-tested mail survey sent to a purposive sample of 438 state agency IT managers nationwide. IT managers for each of the following agencies in each of the fifty states were contacted: motor vehicles, workers' compensation, secretary of state, elections, employee retirement, insurance, state university, court administration, social services, and law enforcement. (The number of contacts was less than the expected 500 since some of the IT managers oversee multiple functions.) These agencies were selected because they were reported as having the greatest interest and adoption likelihood in a recent report on document imaging in state government.

A total of 237 responses to the mail survey was received, for a response rate of 54 percent. At least one IT manager from each of the fifty states responded to the survey. The results are based upon data analyses of the useable set of 234 responses.

CONCLUSIONS

IS strategic planning is touted in the literature as the mechanism to maximize the strategic application of IT within the organization and to ensure an environment which supports the strategic application of IT. . This study considered both the act of IS strategic planning and the extent of IS strategic planning. That is, this study considered not only whether it is necessary for state agencies to engage in formal IS strategic planning but whether merely engaging in formal IS strategic planning is sufficient or if the kind of IS strategic planning makes a difference.

The results of this study generally confirm that these ideas concerning IS strategic planning hold within state government:

- State agencies which engage in IS strategic planning are more oriented to the strategic uses of IT.
- State agencies which engage in IS strategic planning operate in an environment generally more supportive of the use of IT in government.
- The degree of strategic IS orientation within the agency is directly related to the comprehensiveness of its IS strategic planning process. The more comprehensive the strategic IS planning process, the more the agency will have a strategic IS orientation.
- The level of support for IT in which the agency operates is directly related to the comprehensiveness of its IS strategic planning process. The more comprehensive the IS strategic planning process, the more supportive the IT environment.

Groupware: Latest Buzzword or Tool for the New Enterprise?

B. Bonnie Baranowski, Ph.D.
Cambridge College
15 Mifflin Place
Cambridge, MA 02138
(617) 492-5108 x236

Jacquelin R. Dunn, Ph.D.
School of Business
University of South Dakota
Vermillion, SD 57069
(605) 677-5559

Michael W. Varano, Ph.D.
Management Department
College of Commerce & Finance
Villanova University
Villanova, PA 19085
(215) 645-7799

Executive Abstract

Simultaneously, fundamental changes are taking place in corporate structures, business environments and the nature of information technology applications. The new corporation must develop new ways of doing business. Organizations should be restructured around outcomes rather than tasks and treat geographically dispersed resources as if they are centralized; parallel activities should be linked (Huff 1992). The organization structures should be flatter, with fewer middle managers and greater use of formal or ad hoc workgroups (Rappaport 1992).

Information technology will/should play an important role in the re-invention of the corporation, however, it should not be viewed as a solution but as an enabler. Groupware, along with electronic data interchange, image processing, high-bandwidth networks and database management systems, is a powerful tool to help re-engineer a business. The term groupware (or workgroup systems) means different things to different people but it generally refers to software that improves the effectiveness and performance of the group through a streamlining of the process and a reduction of the turn-around time for creating work products. Groupware provides at least some of the following capabilities: information base sharing, message filtering and management, computer conferencing, group scheduling and calendaring, workflow management and project/task management (Kobielus 1993). The most notable of these products are Lotus Notes, WordPerfect Office, Microsoft At Work, Windows for WorkGroups and Digital Equipment Corporation's TeamLinks.

The installation of groupware products is growing fast. As of July 1, 1993 there were over 500,000 Notes users at 2,000 companies up from 350,000 at 1,400 companies six month earlier. Many of the installations are at large financial institutions, consulting firms and the Big Six accounting firms (Wilke 1993). Studies of the implementation of groupware are beginning to appear with mixed results. Banks and insurance companies have reported productivity gains and improved communication processes and flows between the people in different departments at the home offices and between the home offices and field locations (Plotkin 1993; Rabkin 1993). At Price Waterhouse, the primary benefit is easy communications and quick and effective access to shared organizational knowledge (Kiely 1993).

Groupware is more than connectivity, it is a tool to help people work jointly on projects. Co-operative working requires agreed working procedures, clear boundaries, and sharing. The most difficult aspect of the new software is a necessary shift in work methods from individual to team. Many workers are uncomfortable with automatic routing and action deadlines which can create a feeling that "big brother" is watching. If organizations encourage competition among employees and reward individuals, the workers do not feel it is in their best interest to share information. There have been problems of too much data and most companies have had to appoint "expert" editors to review the database. Previous studies of office automation (McLeod and Jones 1987; Jones, Saunders and McLeod 1989; Dunn, Baranowski and Varano 1992) have shown that even when advanced technology is available, managers prefer and use personal verbal contact as the most common form of communication. The potential payoffs from groupware are great but organizations must understand their culture and provide the necessary training for the software and the processes it is designed to support.

METHODOLOGY

To obtain information about the use of groupware and its implementation, a survey was conducted on the Internet. A pilot study of the questionnaire was broadcast in the upper midwestern region of the United States in late winter. The revised form was broadcast internationally in mid/late March. The questionnaire was designed to obtain information about the type of groupware products and features used; composition of the groups; how the groupware is used within the groups; how the software was implemented (training); and the perceived impact (both positive and negative) on the end-user and the organization.

FINDINGS

The results presented in this abstract are from the pilot study. The full analysis and discussion will be presented at the conference. Responses were received from two distinct groups, individuals who currently are using groupware and those who currently do not have access to it but see its value.

The users of groupware included executives, middle managers, professionals (educators, nurses) and secretarial staff. Most worked for government agencies. The organizations ranged in size from under 10 employees to over 500.

WordPerfect Office was used by over 50% of the respondents, Lotus Notes by 35% and Microsoft at Work and Windows for WorkGroups by the rest. Most (over 70%) had been using the products for 6 to 12 months and 25% for less than 6 months; the remaining had used the products for over 1 year. The most commonly used features included information base sharing, application sharing and group scheduling and calendaring. Lesser used features included computer conferencing, project/task management and document tracking. All users were connected to others within the same site and almost everyone was also connected to others across their state.

Everyone felt that they had not received adequate training on the use and features of the software. Concerns about security and privacy are a major issue for all users of groupware. Everyone felt that groupware helps them work collaboratively with others on joint projects. The greatest benefits reported are a reduction in travel time and reduced time for the completion of projects. Groupware has also reduced problems in coordinating schedules. The flip side of these benefits is that the organizations are now expecting tighter deadlines and a reduced time frame for projects.

The individuals who did not yet have groupware were employed in libraries, research councils and transportation groups. They are currently trying to obtain the functionality of groupware by using e-mail, the "sneaker net" and placing information on a common drive. They see the potential of groupware products to meet their needs.

We expect that the wider survey will confirm many of the preliminary findings of the pilot study.

Implementation of a New Paradigm of Organizational Computing: A Case Study

Anol Bhattacherjee and Sam Ramanujan

Decision and Information Sciences
University of Houston
Houston, TX 77204-6282

Post-industrial organizations today are faced with increased competition, increased complexity, and increased need for change. Rapidly changing business and organizational needs, in turn, calls for an increased responsiveness of Information Technology (IT) to changes in the business environment. The dilemma faced by most IT organizations is how to effectively manage the escalating costs of computing with the demand for increased information processing capabilities. Many believe that the evolving client-server architecture is the panacea to this problem. This case study takes a close look at the implementation of client-server systems at a major oil company and illustrates how it is transforming the nature of organizational computing. It identifies the strategic and operational issues associated with this new paradigm and develops a descriptive framework for relating organizational characteristics and information systems structure in the current context of changing business needs. Finally, it highlights some of the critical implications of the new paradigm and its impact on organizational roles and processes.

1. INTRODUCTION

The early 1980's saw the introduction of personal computers and office automation tools to the user's desktop. But mainframe-based systems still commanded the high end database-intensive applications due to their speed, larger memory capacity, and ability to handle large databases (Nully 1993). Since then, rapid advancements in microprocessor technology and the advent of local and wide area networks have brought forth a desktop revolution, and are currently challenging the traditional paradigm of mainframe computing in organizations. Gartner Group, a research and consulting firm in Stamford, Connecticut, estimates that more than one-half of current mainframe users are considering downsizing their information systems (IS) projects. A recent survey by Datamation indicates that 60 percent of large organizations were planning to target PCs and workstations for their longer term application development in 1992, up from 51 percent a year earlier (Francis 1992).

Over the last fifteen years or so, there has been numerous studies on the relationship between IT structure and organizational effectiveness (Olson and Chervany 1980, Ein-dor and Segev 1982, Attewell and Rule 1984, Tavakolian 1989, Lee and Leifer 1991, and so on). However, the findings of these empirical studies are not comprehensive or consistent. The results obtained needs to be re-investigated in the light of current organizational restructuring and changing business needs and re-interpreted in the current context of change in order to gain a better understanding of how IT can help organizations manage the change process. Many organizations believe that client-server architecture is the key to the a highly responsive but cost-effective data processing environment as mandated by the changing nature of business needs (Zeigler 1991). This case study analyzes the implementation of the client-server architecture at X-OIL[1], which is believed to be ushering in a new paradigm of organizational computing. The study focuses on "why" the company adopted the new paradigm and the issues that were addressed in the process. Building upon the findings of the current study, we propose a framework to describe how IS structures in organizations are driven by business needs and point out some of the implications of this framework.

The intended audience of this paper is both IS researchers and the practitioners. The relationship between IS structure and organizational structure and processes has been one of the central areas of interest of researchers in both management of IT and organizational theory. Given the plethora of empirical studies and models in this area, most of which are plagued by limited generalizability, the current study is expected to bring into light some of the current issues that concern IT management in the context of organizational restructuring and changing business needs and stimulate further studies on similar lines. For practitioners interested in implementing client-server architecture, the study points out that this process is not as simple as it apparently seems to be. Client-server is not just another computing architecture, it involves a complete transformation in the way organizations view IS, which means implementing a different type of data model, a different philosophy of application development, and a different role for IS staff using this paradigm. Also of relevance to practitioners will be the close relationship between client-server architecture and re-engineering, business systems planning, downsizing, and other organizational issues that have generated significant interest at present times.

A case study was chosen over other research approaches because the current body of literature in this area is not mature enough to develop research hypotheses that can then be tested statistically. Data collection in this study was accomplished primarily by structured interviews of both IS staff and end-users, and also by using company planning documents, annual reports, and IS situation assessment report submitted by an independent consultant. Company documents and related articles from business and trade journals were used to formulate a set of open-ended questions on which the interviews were based. Each interview lasted 40 to 90 minutes. Follow-up interviews were conducted in certain cases to clarify some of the issues mentioned in the previous interview. The final case report was proof-read by related IT professionals at X-OIL for validity and correctness of content.

This study is organized in six sections. The second section provides a background on the use of IT at X-OIL and its need for a change. The third and fourth sections discusses some of the strategic and operational issues related to the new paradigm, and illustrates how the individual pieces of the client-server puzzle fits into the big picture. Based on existing literature and the findings of this study, a framework for describing IS structure based on environmental variables, business needs, and organizational characteristics is proposed in the fifth section. The sixth and final section discusses some of the critical implications of this new paradigm like empowerment of end-users, and a changed operational and strategic role of the IS staff in organizations.

2. BACKGROUND

Established in 1989 as a joint venture partnership between a U.S. based oil company and a Saudi Arabian oil company, X-OIL specializes in manufacturing, distributing, and selling petroleum-related products. Within the first four years of its operation, X-OIL is already among the top ten retail gasoline marketers in the highly competitive and fragmented U.S. petroleum industry. The company's activities can be divided into two main categories: refining and marketing. It own three large oil refineries at Texas, Louisiana, and Delaware, and its marketing activities are coordinated by four regional marketing offices located in Texas, Florida, Georgia, and New Jersey. As of 1992, the three refineries employ 2600 employees and are capable of processing 600,000 barrels of crude oil every-day. The marketing group has about 9,000 employees, distributing petroleum products through 48 company-owned distribution terminals and 1,550 retail outlets in 26 states.

2.1 Corporate Goals and Policies

X-OIL is a young, dynamic company aspiring to become the leader in the oil refining and marketing industry in the United States. The company believes that in order to succeed in the highly competitive retail gasoline business, its marketers must provide competitively priced products and services that routinely meets customer expectations. The mission statement, as stated in the company profile, is:

"At X-OIL, we strive to be the preeminent refiner/marketer by being proactive and innovative employees who provide quality products and services as measured by our customers' satisfaction, and our company's reputation and profitability."

The company believes that the means to achieving its vision is by developing a culture of innovation, risk-taking, and team effort practiced by a set of highly motivated, well-trained employees imbued with entrepreneurship and a sense of commitment.

Quality is the central tenet in X-OIL's business philosophy. The quality process at X-OIL is viewed as a long-term journey intended to involve all employees in the collective pursuit of excellence in the services the company offers and in the product it sells. The company invests considerable time and money in training its employees on the principles and practice of quality.

Because of its decentralized structure, X-OIL is quick to seize opportunities in the marketplace and maximize its revenues. A dedicated set of wholesale and retail marketers has been X-OIL's vital link to its distribution network. Continuous innovation has been another critical factor for the company's success. Its convenience stores, with advanced merchandising and inventory systems and distinctive signage are turning out to be another industry trendsetter. X-OIL cash machines, which operate much like automated teller machines, can be used for dispensing scrip which is redeemable inside the store for purchases or cash.

2.2 Goals of the Information Systems Department

The Information Services (IS) Department at X-OIL is responsible for providing many of the high value-added services to various business units within the company. Its goal is to provide the company with competitive advantage through the appropriate use of information technology (IT). The mission statement of the IS department is stated as:

"The department strives to be recognized throughout X-OIL as the preeminent information technology organization by providing X-OIL with business driven, value added solutions which will yield significant competitive advantage for the company."

The primary role of the IS department in the company is four fold. First, it provides X-OIL with technical expertise in the definition, evaluation, integration, development, and maintenance of information systems. Second, it engineers and supports a cost-effective processing environment in terms of hardware, software, and telecommunications architecture that enables the company to execute business processes effectively and efficiently. Third, it enhances the skills, use and knowledge of data and systems throughout the company through training and otherwise. And finally, in addition to these operational roles, it also strives to provide X-OIL with competitive advantage by deployment of appropriate information technology.

2.3 Evolution of the IS Department

In 1989, the IS department at X-OIL was a small department of six IT professionals whose functions were not well-defined. The organization, during this time, was in a very fluid stage with no well-defined business units, other than the refining and marketing entities with some amount of work that required the use of computers. The IS staff at that time was primarily responsible for end-user support, that is, run help desk functions for users on an ad-hoc basis. The Director of IS describes the situation as:

"The way I looked at the organization, then and somewhat now, is very similar to wartime when you've got ship captains put on a rough sea, and told to go out on the dark waters, fight, and survive."

Over time, the organization gradually developed a business function based structure comprising of three primary business units: manufacturing (refining), marketing, and finance, all of which were supported by the IS, Human Resources, and Public and Human Affairs departments. The systems used at X-OIL gradually increased in complexity, both in terms of data management and application development.

Because of its small staff size in 1989, IS had to subcontract and outsource many of its IT-related activities. Operational data processing at X-OIL was almost entirely supported by the IS department of its U.S. based parent company. But the outsourcing of X-OIL's financial reporting system was proving to be prohibitively expensive in the 1990's. The escalating costs of mainframe computing and the attractive evolution of client-server technology stimulated X-OIL to rethink its IS strategy and develop an internal, business-driven IS department that can not only manage its IS resources in an efficient manner but can also provide sustainable competitive advantage through effective use of information technology (IT). About 30 formal client-server applications are currently in operation at X-OIL, using a consolidated enterprise-wide data model residing on an UNIX database server at its main production center in Houston. Regional marketing and refining centers can access and process these data and applications via a WAN backbone running TCP/IP.

Currently, the IS department at X-OIL is mapped directly on the business units. It permeates through the user departments, facilitating their daily business operations. In addition to the IS staff at the Houston headquarters, smaller groups of IS personnel are physically located at the regional marketing offices and refineries to support their local, operational IT needs. Marketing, manufacturing, finance, and supply and distribution constitute the major end-user groups. The decentralized structure of the IS organization sometimes causes value conflicts between business units and the central IS department. For example, the IT staff working with a particular marketing department is accountable to the marketing department employing them, even if their local IT plans may not comply with the guidelines prescribed by the central IS department. But the decentralized arrangement does provide for a very responsive and efficient support to X-OIL's decentralized operations.

Despite minor differences in priorities with the central IS department, users of IT at X-OIL are quite satisfied with the overall performance of the IS department. As the Assistant Comptroller of Financial Systems says,

"On a scale of one to five, with five being excellent, I'd rate our IS department as a strong four. They are very capable, very responsive, and sensitive to our needs. They've learnt our business well enough to integrate their thinking with ours. They've reduced computing expense by over 20 percent per year and helped us improve our quality, productivity, and effectiveness at the same time. I also see them as being participative in helping X-OIL redesign or re-engineer its business processes, which I think is very critical for its survival in the immensely competitive oil industry today."

2.4 The Course for a Change

Information Technology expenses at X-OIL accounts for only about 0.8 percent of the total revenue compared to an average of 1.3 percent in the petroleum industry (X-OIL statistics). A big portion of this expense goes into outside services. In 1991, contracting fees comprised 46 percent of the total systems expense and outside computing (processing and network) costs accounted for another 21 percent. Despite its IS spending being much lower than the industry average, because of the competitive state of the oil industry and squeezing profit margins, there has been increasing pressure on the IS department to cut back on IS spending. The current strategy of downsizing mission-critical business applications from mainframes to PC-LAN based environment stems out of the need to reduce IS expenditure. As additional cost-reduction measures, the IS department is trying to cut back on maintenance costs by eliminating change requests to applications that don't have a sufficient business justification and by establishing software releases that are phased over a longer period of time.

The escalating costs of mainframe computing was the primary factor that forced X-OIL to rethink its IT strategy and search for an alternative computing paradigm. In addition, there was a lot of dissatisfaction regarding IT planning, development, and implementation in its mainframe days (see Table 1). Mis-communication between IS and user departments often led to IT strategies being mis-aligned with the client department's business strategies. Since IS essentially plays a supporting role to its client departments, its effectiveness depends on how well it is able to meet the computing needs of the end-users. Keeping in view the changing needs of the business environment and the dynamic nature of technology, it was therefore required that the organization change the way it views the IS function, and hence the development of a new computing paradigm. Some of the IT needs that the new paradigm at X-OIL must support are summarized in Table 2. This paradigmatic shift in viewing organizational computing is closely associated with the change in computing platform from mainframe to client-server environments.

At X-OIL, the IS department currently has an aggressive strategy of renovating and redeveloping most of its applications as they are being migrated from the IBM mainframe environment to the new LAN-based client-server environment. It favors the use of new technologies like workflow automation, image processing, video-conferencing, and Electronic Data Interchange (EDI) as a means of generating competitive advantage. But the principal drivers of IT strategies at X-OIL are process re-engineering and use of an enterprise data model. The data-driven approach is based on planning and implementing a conceptual information structure for the

Table 1: Information management problems with the traditional paradigm

IT planning issues:

1. Inadaquate planning in business units to implement and support IT.
   - Regions are not allocated sufficient IT staff or resources to support new technology.
   - As technology changes, the existing infrastructure of operations changes and so do IS requirements.
   - IS and other business units do not have a working knowledge of each others operations.
2. Standards, procedures, and guidelines not interactively developed.
   - Consistent standards, screens, function keys, and on-line help are not utilized.
   - Effects of new applications on X-OIL's current processes not defined or communicated.
   - Multiple customer numbers for the same customer, and so forth.
3. Responsibility for data and reports not clearly defined.
   - Confusion exists as to who is accountable for the integrity of the data.
   - Procedures should be developed to delete inactive data.
   - Users don't know who to call when they have problems with the data.
4. Timely information not provided.
   - Elapsed time between data requests and data availability is too long.
   - Regions should be provided with current withdrawal statistics on demand.

IS development issues:

1. Projects often under-estimated in time and money.
   - More user participation required in requirements determination.
   - Projects are often headquarters oriented and seldom designed by field-users.
2. Inadequate change control procedures.
   - Applications are not revised to meet changing user needs.
   - All system changes should be coordinated through the controller group.
3. Inflexible applications which require high maintenance.
   - 75 percent of marketing applications are over 10 years old.
   - Most maintenance "patches" the code and makes it less manageable.
   - Older applications should be re-written, not enhanced.

IS Implementation issues:

1. Inadequate end-user training and documentation.
   - Employees do not know what applications are available.
   - Employees do not know what data files are available.
   - Training is not perceived as high priority.
2. Inadequate communication between IS support and users.
   - Information is either not asked for, or when asked for, the response is ignored.
   - Change requests not viewed with users inteactively.
   - Changes implemented to system without least mention to users.
3. Implementation procedures not fully defined.
   - Some applications being put into production are not fully tested or fully functional.
   - New applications should be run in parallel with existing applications for some time.
   - Some applications are put on the mainframe when they should actually be distributed.
4. Rapid changes in the leading-edge technology putting strain on implementation, training, and staffing.

entire organization that would define the data standards to be implemented on different computers on an enterprise-wide network for supporting dynamic user needs. Data standards are defined independent of an individual, department, or of a specific hardware or application system configuration, so that the data is insulated against changes in user requirements or in the technology.

3. THE NEW PARADIGM: STRATEGIC ISSUES

As mentioned earlier, the new paradigm of client-server computing represents a drastic change in the way X-OIL views the IS function. Though the client-server environment has facilitated the new paradigm, the architecture is just a part of a much bigger picture involving a larger set of organizational issues. Some of these strategic issues, considered to be the key pieces of the client-server puzzle, are discussed in this section.

3.1 Integrating IT planning into Business Systems Planning

The IS department at X-OIL is responsible for providing support to a diverse set of functional units. The major problem faced by IT planners is how to manage effectively this wide gamut of applications, and still keep up with the continuous change in the business environment. The solution lies in integrating the IT strategies into X-OIL's business planning process, so that they are coherent with its long-term business strategies. A tight coupling between the company's business processes and IT activities will allow the IS department to deliver technology guidance in a timely manner to compliment the tactical and strategic needs of X-OIL, manage the changes in business direction, and provide a base for justifying future IT investments. To enable the success of its IT planning process, the IS department urges its professionals to be more knowledgeable about the business and its needs and the business units are also taking more active role in IT planning and in setting priorities for systems investments.

Formalized IT planning efforts were initiated in 1990 with the Business Systems Planning for Strategic Alignment (BSP/SA). The goal was to align IT strategies with corporate business processes. Since data strategy forms the core of X-OIL's overall IT strategy, BSP/SA was followed by a second phase called Business System Planning for Architecture (BSP/A) to generate an enterprise-wide data model which

Table 2: IT needs of the future

1. Lower costs of data processing.
2. Improved access to data by end-users.
3. Distributed data processing and support.
4. Data consistency, integrity, and security.
5. Reduced maintainence costs.
6. IT investments in line with business goals.
7. Ability of data/applications to withstand changes in technology and business needs.
8. End-user training to keep pace with technological changes.
9. Flexible applications: easy to modify, accurately reflect user needs.

would form the basis for all future projects or functional data models. The result of BSP/A was a business process architecture, which is a blueprint for the development of integrated databases and applications to support the information needs of the entire organization. It identifies the major processes, data flows, and data stores that need to be addressed by applications, and therefore represents a high level definition of processing requirements. The major processes and information flows between them are described by means of process node trees, data flow diagrams, and process definitions.

Though the BSP process was an excellent high level roadmap for establishing general directions, it did not adequately identify specific projects to be sponsored and funded by various business units within X-OIL. However, it pointed out that the IT planning process should be categorized into three distinct areas: data, application, and architecture, and that explicit strategies must be established for each of the component areas so as to give them a high level direction regarding future IT investments. Some of these areas are highlighted in Table 3 and are also discussed in subsequent sections.

3.2 Business Process Re-engineering

Re-engineering[2] was initiated at X-OIL at a very early stage, even before the word was coined as a popular term. The majority of X-OIL's mission critical systems, including Financial Reporting, Sales Operations, and Inventory Management Systems are old and built around business processes that are no longer the preferred mode of operation. These systems are very important to the business, however they are expensive to operate and maintain, inflexible, and do not provide much of the information needed by the business units. As time passes, maintenance of these systems will become even more costly and the technology utilized by them will become obsolete.

The main purpose of the business process re-engineering efforts at X-OIL was to remodel these processes to better reflect business needs and make better use of the available technology. New or migrated systems built around the re-engineered processes are envisaged to have the potential for creating enhanced value for X-OIL as well as for reducing its IT expenses. To reduce expenses in the process, some of these

Table 3: Strategic concerns

Data	Enterprise data models
	Management of distributed data
	Data warehouse
	Data security: backups, etc.
Application	Legacy systems
	Application development tools
	Prioritizing proper business types
Architecture	Processing power of server
	Network management
	Hardware and software management
	Operational shortcomings: batch scheduling, security, etc.
	Graphical User Interface

projects are targeted jointly with outside organizations of the same group. But each of investment included in the plan has to undergo a detailed analysis of its economic and technical feasibility prior to its approval

X-OIL views re-engineering as a continuous process and realizes that effective re-engineering of key business processes improve operational effectiveness at the expense of scarce resource time. Hence any effort of this nature are carefully prioritized in concert with other ongoing activities in the company. New information technologies can greatly reduce the cost of operating and maintaining re-engineered systems, but X-OIL employees must improve their knowledge of IT in the new environment in order to use the resources productively. The current relation of business process re-engineering to IT strategy is summarized by the Assistant Comptroller of Financial Systems,

"In the past, the traditional IT organization has driven many of the business decisions, either because the IT system was inadequate or that it could not be directed reasonably over a period of time to accomplish business needs. There was a misconceived urge of automating things without really improving on the underlying business process. I believe that business goals and objectives should always be the driver, and IT the enabler. I believe that our IT organization (at X-OIL) is sharing this view and is coordinating their IT planning process with the corporate business planning process, and I fully agree with that."

3.3 Principles-Based Architecture

X-OIL's strategies for each of the three components of the IT planning process (Table 3) stem from a "principles-based" IT architecture. The connotation "principles-based" refers to the fact that a set of organization principles is used to evaluate and manage strategies and set overall directions for the company's data, applications, and architecture. The IT strategy rests on the premise that X-OIL personnel need to acquire skills necessary to effectively utilize and exploit IT as a strategic tool. The role of IS department should be to organize, deploy, and support IT activities in various business units and to effectively manage the competition for corporate resources and priorities among client departments, while that of individual business units should be to actively participate in the development of applications and use them in an effective manner when implemented. The principles related to each of the three components of the IT planning process are discussed next.

Data. X-OIL believes that data is a corporate asset and should be managed as such. Keeping in view its enterprise IT architecture, X-OIL emphasizes the need for developing and maintaining enterprise-wide data models, that are developed independent of applications and storage technology. Distributed database structures are viewed as the means for allowing users easy access to corporate data in a timely manner, but the inherent problems of data integrity, security, and enterprise-wide compatibility still need to be addressed.

Applications. At the application level, principles-based architecture has several implications. First, systems must be developed using formal project management and software engineering tools and techniques to improve quality, decrease development time and allow for faster system modification. Second, applications must be made portable across different hardware and software platforms. Third, in determining IS solutions, all possible options, namely purchased application packages, in-house development, and outsourced services, must be reviewed according to time required, life-cycle costs, functionality, and profitability prior to choosing a specific course of action. Fourth, IS is a corporate asset and must be managed as such. And finally, ITS must encourage end-user computing and provide its users with the information tools and necessary training to improve their productivity.

Architecture. The architectural level of IT planning at X-OIL is of crucial importance because it provides the key linkage between data and application models. The IS department at X-OIL believes that a model-based architecture is required to facilitate cooperative IS development and sharing, and client-server architecture is viewed as the strategic platform to enable distributed data processing while maintaining a high level of connectivity and compatibility. All hardware, software, and communication components of the information architecture must adhere to formal standards adopted by X-OIL. Technological innovations in IT are a strategic source of competitive advantage and hence the IT architecture at X-OIL must be capable of integrating new technologies like imaging, video-conferencing, and work flow automation as and when they are found feasible.

3.4 Enterprise-wide Data Model

One of the major initial activities for IT professionals at X-OIL was to develop an enterprise-wide data model that would accurately describe the current information processing environment as well as provide a base for justifying future IT investments. The purpose of a enterprise-wide data model is to define X-OIL's global data requirements, that is, identify the major entities that it needs information about and the relationships between these entities in form of entity matrix, data models, and business rules. This model is, therefore, a logical representation of the corporate data needs independent of hardware/software implementations and/or performance considerations. This model also supplies the data definitions required to support enterprise-wide user access to corporate data thereby forming the basis for a migration plan for replacing existing legacy systems. The data model is the heart of the company's data strategy and represents a blueprint for implementing databases because all databases in the architected environment are developed from the same corporate data model using data-driven, top-down Information Engineering methodology by James Martin (1989). Computer aided software engineering (CASE) tools are used to automate the collection and storage of meta-data.

The first step towards developing the enterprise-wide data model was to consolidate some of the existing data models that were limited in scope and functionality. A number of local project data models were created at X-OIL over the last several years, with a significant amount of overlap across different models that was often a cause of data inconsistency. In 1992, a three week effort was devoted to consolidate some of the more critical data models into one single, integrated data model, and document the remaining data integration issues for later resolution. At the same time, efforts were made to ensure that ownership of data was not lost between the business units responsible for the initial models for their areas of the merged model, and provided a foundation for a consolidated X-OIL data architecture that could be shared between projects.

The deliverables produced from this project were a single model stored in ORACLE*CASE, a set of subject area diagrams representing the data model, and a set of documented changes made to the project models during consolidation. It was not possible to resolve all the integration issues within the three week effort. Some issues were found to require a substantial amount of analysis and were sufficiently documented so that they can be addressed at a later time. However, the consolidated data model generated by this exercise was found to have enough credibility, scope, and accessibility for project teams to share and manage.

3.5 Downsizing

The primary reason for downsizing[3] in X-OIL was to reduce computing costs. PC-based systems have a much lower cost of processing than mainframes and also require less operations staff. With rapid advancements in computer hardware and LAN technologies, a high-end server today is not only capable of handling large database intensive business applications, but can do so more responsively and at lower costs than many mainframe-based systems. X-OIL believes that correctly designed and properly configured PC-based systems can thus provide a better platform for the new generation of information systems.

Downsizing business applications is still at an early phase. A recent study by Computerworld (Dostert 1993) reveals that only 23 percent of corporate businesses have downsized from mainframe systems, and X-OIL belongs to this group of early adopters. At X-OIL, though all new applications are PC-LAN based, a significant set of legacy applications still run on "glass house" mainframes at high operational costs. X-OIL plans to migrate these mainframe applications to a PC-based client-server environment by 1997, assuming sufficient resources allocated to the task.

Despite the attractiveness and success stories of downsizing, there are some potential problems associated with it. The key limitations of the downsized architectural model are more managerial than technological in nature. Data security and management, which can be of utmost importance for mission-critical applications, is a drawback of PC-based systems owing to the decentralized nature of the stored data. Two other key features that also needs to be addressed in a PC-based environment are concurrency control (which allows concurrent data sharing across multiple users), and data recovery abilities in case of disasters. X-OIL has selected the Data General AViiON processor as its database server, running UNIX operating system and ORACLE7 database management software. This combination provides system failure recovery capabilities, and on-line monitoring and reporting of data usage. The new ORACLE7 environment also provides potential for true distributed data access and robust transaction processing. Successful downsizing also requires adequate planning and management involvement, specifically how well the systems architects understand the business charter of the organization and are able to select appropriate hardware and software products. To this end, the IS department in X-OIL solicits inputs and cooperation from end-users.

3.6 Open Systems Strategy

Open systems refer to standards-based, vendor-neutral IT products that allow application development and portability over a wide range of computer hardware and telecommunication systems and interoperability with other applications on local and remote systems. These systems are also important from the strategic point of view because they can easily adapt themselves to changing business needs like change of data formats, technology upgrades, and/or hardware migration. At X-OIL, open systems are perceived to be desirable in the long-run because they insulate corporate data, applications, and architecture from changes in technology and in business needs. In the context of client-server computing, open systems refers to the capability of applications to access data from different database servers all over the organization and process them without loss in data integrity or consistency.

The IS department at X-OIL chose UNIX as the operating system on the server end because it best meets their open systems strategy and provides an efficient migration path to subsequent processors from other open vendors. Though the general opinion is that UNIX is not user-friendly and is difficult to support, X-OIL believes that commodity UNIX boxes are the best current strategy because they support open systems and provide the required scalability. The IS Director at X-OIL believes that Windows NT might eventually be a potential replacement for UNIX, but also points out that it will take NT at least another 2-3 years to mature sufficiently to handle high-end database-intensive operations, and until then UNIX will be the operating system of choice for most database servers.

3.8 Migration of legacy systems

Legacy systems are the old "bread-and-butter" applications that have been used historically to support specific business functions (Radding 1993). Though these systems are of great importance to the organization, they are expensive to maintain, inhibit seamless data sharing, and restrict the organization's ability to respond to changing data needs. Over time, as business needs changed, a complex set of bridges was built to maintain data consistency across functional areas, but this arrangement locked many companies in a quagmire of

data and application maintenance. Most of the early operational systems used at X-OIL are over twenty years old. Originally developed by X-OIL's parent company, these applications were typically mainframe-based and were made available to X-OIL via contractual agreements. In addition to usage licenses, these agreements provided computer facility to run the applications and also the staff and resources to maintain the applications. X-OIL has three major concerns with the use of these legacy systems. First, the applications were written using a technology that is now outdated and inefficient. Second, these applications allow restricted portability of data and applications and are difficult to adapt to fast-changing business needs. And third, they use expensive mainframe MIPS and DASD storage.

IS has developed a strategy to migrate these applications using open-systems client-server technology. The migration strategy centers around re-engineering the existing systems in the overall context of X-OIL's business. This requires an understanding of the business activities to support, the data they use, and the way they interact. A business model is generated, and existing systems are mapped on to this model to develop a migration plan which lays out the activities to be performed along with their priority and sequence. The business model can also be used to identify whether the activities under consideration require incremental improvements over a long time-frame or a radical overhaul, and whether an internal system development effort, purchased packages, or outsourcing is the best way to approach the task given organizational resource constraints. Business needs therefore drive the technology platform and other resources to be used. A big challenge of this migration plan is to make the new systems flexible enough so that new technologies such as imaging, work flow automation, and object-oriented techniques, can be incorporated into the IT infrastructure in the future with relative ease.

The IS department is aware of the fact that migrating seven million lines of legacy code written in COBOL and PL/1 to the new client-server environment is an uphill task. IS is still struggling with some of the legacy applications inherited from its parent company, and is continually confronted with such problems as multiple definitions of items across the organization, and one entity having multiple definitions. But the IS director is optimistic,

> "I kind of see it as slicing up a pie. What we are doing is moving slices of the pie from a mainframe environment to a client-server environment. And if we do it right, at some point of time, there will be no pie left on the mainframe, and a new pie will be formed on the LAN-based platform. But, however we do it, linking of pieces between IMS applications on the mainframe side and Oracle applications on the other side is a very difficult technical task."

4. THE NEW PARADIGM: OPERATIONAL ISSUES

The key operational IS issues at X-OIL, derived directly

from strategic plans, can be divided into three broad categories: data, applications, and architecture. The strategic data plan is generated from business processes and is based on the data principles established in its principles-based architecture. The data plan rests on the premise that critical data management functions and operation skills should be centralized to improve data consistency and integrity, but the infrastructure should facilitate end-user data access and support distributed data processing at the same time.

On the applications side, based on extensive review of X-OIL's existing applications by users departments with respect to their business importance, functional condition, and technical operation, a general plan for each system was developed, whether to replace, renovate, maintain, or eliminate them. The IT application plan outlines an aggressive approach towards replacement and renovation of most of the major business systems used. It also includes the creation of new systems to improve the company's business operations and sustain its competitive advantage. Existing systems that are important to the business but are in poor functional and/or technical condition received priority in scheduling and funding.

The enterprise architecture at X-OIL is the bridge between the data plan and the application plan. Designed to support new IT investments as well as the migration of existing legacy systems, the architecture plan is based on open systems client-server technology operating on Local and Wide Area Networks (LAN/WAN), and will allow X-OIL to implement business-driven IT solutions quickly and effectively, capitalize on the cost effectiveness of new technologies, and better satisfy user needs. To enable X-OIL realize its mission, the IS department follows a set of implicit strategic guidelines: (a) all enterprise hosts should be compatible and share information consistently (open systems), (b) all data centers, refineries, marketing headquarters, and retail outlets should be connected by high-speed, reliable, multi-purpose communications lines (interconnectivity), (c) the enterprise infrastructure must make the best use of available technology, and (d) end-users should be enabled with enhanced access to corporate data by means of GUI interface.

4.1 Data Management

A critical success factor related to X-OIL's overall data strategy is its ability to manage such a complex architecture in a cost-efficient way. Multiple uses of the same data at different locations often result in duplicated, partitioned, separate-schema, and incompatible data, and can therefore complicate data integrity, consistency, and processing. Other problems related to decentralization of data include data security, data recovery, data ownership, and DBMS upgrades. The IS department proposes "rightsizing" the number of databases and database servers and maintaining centralized control over performance monitoring of different applications, backup and recovery abilities, concurrent use of data, and updates to the databases from its central data center using a cooperative server technology supported by ORACLE7. A

set of data-related standards, procedures, and policies, like repository management and model management procedures, is being used to support later enhancements and updates to the data architecture. Though data is viewed as a corporate asset not owned by any specific business unit, certain business units are allocated responsibility of maintaining the integrity and consistency of specific databases as "data stewards." In addition, X-OIL has established an Information Resource Management (IRM) function using a robust set of automated software engineering tools to provide a high level overview of data-related activity in the company.

Effective data management in a distributed environment is one of the central issues in the client-server environment. A frequent user of IT at X-OIL, has some interesting thoughts on this issue:

"The central role of data in enterprise-wide computing should never be under-estimated. We have to manage our data as a corporate asset and companies that do not control and manage their data will fall apart in the long run. But decentralizing the computing environment does not imply that you have to give up control over your data. I don't see much of a problem in having multiple copies of data coming off central repositories, if the users know that their processed data is not going to be stored back in the corporate data repository. I'd like to see more people accessing data from the centralized repository, making snapshots of it, moving it to their local machines, using it and then throwing it away."

4.2 Client-server Technology

Most corporate applications at present are mainframe-based. Users interact with applications running on mainframes through terminals or PC-based emulators (Sinha 1992). Though mainframe-centric systems accord tight administrative control and comprehensive system management, the applications and data are not generally not portable across hardware platforms. Also they allow little flexibility to the user by restricting their view of data to predefined screens and reports, and causes excessive loading on expensive CPU cycles since all computations as well as user interface control are rendered by the mainframe.

X-OIL views client-server systems as a logically distributed data processing architecture. The driving force behind this architecture is the perceived need for open systems and portability of applications and data so that they can easily be integrated with the overall IT architecture. Client-server systems reduce processing costs by transferring some of the processing workload to the client end and avoiding excessive loading on expensive CPU cycles. At X-OIL, this architecture is viewed as the key technology to cost-effectively manage a distributed data processing environment. Borne out of the need to cut back on escalating costs of mainframe computing, downsizing to a PC-LAN based client-server platform is now revolutionizing the role of IT processes at X-OIL from one of operational support to that of strategic support, and is ushering in a new paradigm of organizational computing.

4.3 New Technologies

As noted earlier, use of new technologies for generating sustainable competitive advantage is an accepted theme of X-OIL's strategy and the IS department is continuously on the watch for new hardware and software related to the business. Hardware upgrades are included in the IT plan to accommodate for increased capacity as business needs expand in the future. Recently one of their disk storage devices was found to be performing at 85 percent efficiency compared to X-OIL's stringent performance requirements of 99 percent. Industry estimates from users running heavy transaction workloads in mission-critical environments indicate that for every hour required disk-based data is not available, companies may lose as much as $100,000, in addition to opportunity costs and productivity losses associated with data inaccessibility (Computerworld, March 8, 1993). To prevent "bottom-line" losses of this nature, the IS department at X-OIL is now using the state-of-the-art fault-tolerant RAID[4] (Redundant Arrays of Independent Disks) storage media to ensure continuous and highly reliable data access. IS believes that the RAID technology will play a dominant role in the new client-server environment in keeping huge databases on UNIX processors up and running.

The IS department at X-OIL is currently conducting a series of prototyping experiments to identify applications that might benefit from the use of new technologies. One such prototype, being implemented in Microsoft Access, is a change request form that can be used by users to send in requests for a change in applications or data stored in the corporate database. Future IS plans at X-OIL include incorporating new technologies like image processing, video-conferencing, multi-media, and object-oriented design into the existing IT infrastructure when they become viable, and using them as a possible means of generating competitive advantage.

5. A FRAMEWORK FOR DESCRIBING THE IS ARCHITECTURE

A descriptive model of the evolution of IS structure in X-OIL is presented in Figure 1. The model explains the dynamics of the adoption of client-server architecture and relates it with organizational characteristics, business needs, and environmental variables. The findings are in conformance with earlier rescarch on IS architecture (for example, Attewell and Rule 1984, King 1983, Olson and Chervany 1980, Tavakolian

Figure 1: A Framework for describing IS Structure

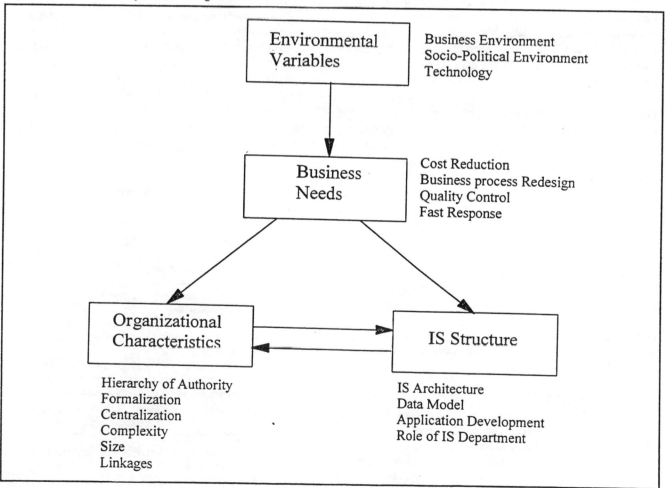

1989, Ein-dor and Segev 1982, and so forth).

According to our proposed model, characteristics of an IS is determined primarily by business needs, which in turn, are affected by the changes in environment variables such as business environment, available technology, and so forth. These business needs impact IS structure both directly and indirectly via organizational characteristics like formalization, centralization, complexity, size, and so on (Robey 1977). In fact, based on previous studies in this area, we propose a reciprocal relationship between organizational characteristics and IS structure, that is, IS structure influences organizational characteristics (Foster and Flynn 1984) and vice versa (Olson and Chervany 1980, Ein-dor and Segev 1982). Components of the IS structure includes the IS architecture, data model, and application development, which are the three key components of X-OIL's principles-based architecture. The fourth component of IS structure, namely role of the IS department, which is the key to the new paradigm, has been supported by Galletta and Heckman (1990).

This model is motivated by our findings in this case study. One of the critical components of the IS structure is the IS architecture that is affected directly by business needs. This is substantiated by the fact that at X-OIL, cost reduction of data processing, business process redesign, higher quality service, and fast system response are the principal drivers of the client-server architecture. The same variables also drive enterprise-wide data model, a high-speed telecommunication network, and extensive use of fourth generation languages by users to develop their own ad-hoc applications. The business needs, in turn are the direct result of the increase in competitiveness of the oil industry, shrinking profit margins, state of the available technology, and so forth, all of which calls for a low cost but a highly efficient and responsive data processing environment that the client-server architecture is expected to provide. Business needs have prompted redesign of the organizational structure at X-OIL, by mandating decentralized but responsive operations, developing a tradition of innovation, and necessitating reduction in size, all of which appear to be interesting correlated with a similar impact on IS structure, for example, distributed data processing and decentralization of IS personnel to remote units, technological leadership in IT, and downsizing of IS staff and applications. The changing role of the central IS department from an operational to a strategic role, relegation of the responsibility of data management and application development to end-users, and enabling them with the tools and the training for the same, and so forth, are all borne out of the stringent nature of the business needs.

6. CONCLUSIONS

Client-server computing has ushered a completely new outlook regarding how organizations perceive the nature and role of IT. Though initially conceived of as merely being a tool to reduce computing expenditures in organizations, it is the theme of this paper that this new paradigm of organizational computing is altering the relationship between end-users and IS staff, and is transforming the operational and strategic role of IS professionals in organizations of the future. Some of the critical implications of this new paradigm are discussed in this section.

6.1 Economic Benefits of the Client-server Paradigm

Some of the IT elements in the traditional mainframe paradigm are compared to those in the new client-server paradigm in Table 4. Distinctive features of the new paradigm are open systems, distributed data processing, central data repository and an enterprise-wide data model. Cost reduction is the single largest benefit of the new architecture at X-OIL. Another major benefit is the improvement in speed and flexibility of data access and processing. Migration of some of the legacy systems to open platforms has helped reduce the costs of data and application maintenance to a great extent. But managing enterprise data with minimal loss in data integrity and maximum security still remains a major problem to be resolved in the near future.

Since the implementation of the new client-server architecture in June 1991, overall computing costs at X-OIL have declined in phases. Also, the ease of data access has increased manifold. At the same time, this architecture is still yet to mature to levels required by the end-users. The Assistant Comptroller of Financial Systems at X-OIL says:

"The most tangible benefit of the client-server environment is definitely reduction in costs. The savings for us has been and will probably continue to be considerable. The first couple of years, we've seen reduction in costs of the order of 20-25 percent, which is a significant amount if you look at X-OIL's overall IT bill. But I think that the most important benefit in getting off the mainframe was that now we have a much greater control over our computing architecture and our day-to-day operations - the new architecture has given us greater flexibility in terms of building and moving systems, and we don't have to worry about where the data is and how it can be accessed. On the other hand, there is a certain amount of concern that we haven't yet compensated for the loss in security and control that we

Table 4: IT elements in the new paradigm

	Traditional Paradigm	*New Paradigm*
Data	Mainframe resident Application dependent Redundancy across departments Access difficult	Reside on database servers Independent of applications Centralized data repository Enterprise-wide data model
Applications	Legacy systems High cost of maintenence	Open systems Supports distributed data processing
Architecture	Mainframe environment High overhead of CPU cycles	Client/server environment Low computing costs

had in our earlier mainframe environment. I also feel that our data communications capability needs to be improved, WANs are still not mature and sometimes cause unforeseen problems. Overall, I think that the non-mainframe world we have out here will still take a while to mature to what the mainframe world has been, but I'm confident that it is a step in the right direction."

6.2 Empowerment of End-users

In the context of today's business environment, information technology is assuming a greater role as a strategic resource in organizations which, if used effectively, can be used to generate sustainable competitive advantage. One interesting aspect of the new client-server paradigm is that it is transferring organizational power over the strategic IT resource from the IS department to the end-users, that is, the end-users will now depend less on the central IS department for their routine data processing needs. In addition, the user departments will be responsible for the data they use, and inappropriate use of the data resources may lead to loss in data consistency, data integrity, and data security. One of the crucial functions of the IS department at X-OIL therefore will be to educate users on how to use the IT resources on their desktop in the most effective and efficient way. Interestingly, the IT director at X-OIL believes that most system development in the future will also be done in the business units themselves, probably by non-professional people, using GUI tools and Fourth Generation Languages.

Empowerment of end-users can be both good and bad to the organization. Effective use of the new IT architecture can help them achieve their business goals and for generating competitive advantage. But if the users are unable to use the enormous computing power on their desktop in the appropriate way, it can lead to problems in data integrity and consistency. The IT director of X-OIL summarizes the situation as:

"IT in organizations throughout American industries are under stress, because the senior managers and ship captains (business unit managers) don't really understand the complexity of the function. The PC, in my opinion, has been both the best and the worst thing to happen in this industry in the last ten years. The bad side of the PC is that it makes everybody believe that they are computer professionals because they know Lotus, Paradox, and so on. And this has caused a data nightmare for the IT department - floppy disks, hard disks, file servers full of data most of which are irrelevant to corporate needs. The IT departments are no longer looked upon as the golden boys that they used to be twenty years ago. A great deal of work remains before the situation can be brought under technical control."

The extent to which end-users should be empowered is a much debated topic. It is also possible that a overload of responsibility for IT resources may be resented by end-users. The line that divides responsibilities between users and IT personnel must be demarcated with great caution and pru-

dence. According to the Assistant Comptroller of Accounting Systems:

"X-OIL has gone through some of the classical mistakes of decentralizing IT to the extent that we gave our users more responsibility over the technical aspects of computing than we should really have. The central IT department should be responsible for setting standards and for helping users determine the best solution for their computing problems, not necessarily to preempt them from doing things that lack overall IT focus. The end-users, today, has a much greater control on a day-to-day basis on their operational computing needs, but in the long term, when you get down to the appropriateness of IT regardless of platform and method of delivery, I still believe that the IT department is in the best position to assess, develop, implement and migrate that technology to make sure that the company stays competitive in the overall use of IT. At the same time, I also believe that the end-users should be more sophisticated so as to make appropriate use of the IT resources made available to them for accomplishing business goals."

6.3 Operational Role of IS Departments

As stressed throughout the earlier discussion, the new paradigm is transforming the nature of IT functions in organizations and therefore calls for a changed role for IS personnel in the future. Most of the data processing MIPS and resources in the new paradigm is currently located outside of the IS department, and this trend is expected to continue in the future. The task of the IS department will be to make sure that the IT resources used by the end-users are up and running and to manage help desk functions. It must also maintain end-user training facilities to enable the efficient use of IT resources by end-users.

A well-engineered, consistent, and well-managed enterprise-wide data model is central to the success of organizations in the new paradigm. In addition to being responsible for creating and maintaining corporate data models, and for performing regular backups and periodic checks to the corporate database, the central IS department must solicit cooperation from the end-users to ensure that corporate data is not being misused in the organization. They must establish a common standard for hardware/software acquisition by business units throughout the organization to maintain compatibility and to cut back on the costs of maintenance of corporate resources. They should be responsible for such issues as licensing agreements that users are typically not able to look into. Some of these strategic and operational functions of IT personnel in the new paradigm are outlined in Table 5.

6.4 Strategic Role of IS Departments

In response to the predicted change in organizations' perception of the IT function, the IT organizations all over the U.S. are currently undergoing a major restructuring phase. Their role in organizations is changing from operational support to one of strategic support. The impact of organizational and business changes on IT departments is unparalleled in any other department. The Director of IS at X-OIL says:

"In my opinion, the IT profession, right now, is the most difficult profession to survive in. Manufacturing, marketing, finance, engineering - all of them are pretty deterministic. Nobody is trying to reinvent their functions under their feet like we are in the IT world."

In addition to their operational role, the IT departments of the future will have a distinct strategic role in the selection of appropriate IT investments, aligning IT strategies with business goals, dealing with personnel issues like training of end-users and career development programs for IT professionals, and so on. With the advancement of new technologies like image processing and video-conferencing, it will be responsible for examining their feasibility and incorporating them into the enterprise IT infrastructure, if considered viable. Organizations may find it cheaper to outsource the routine and repetitive IT operational tasks but the strategic responsibilities will be best served by an internal IT department cognizant of the organization's business needs and the environment it operates in. The increasingly important strategic role of IT in organizations will provide for the leverage of organizational power within the IT departments.

The IS departments of the future must also be dynamic in their own internal skills and continually upgrade it to keep up with the changes in technology and in business needs. Constant change in the leading edge technology implies that organizations utilizing IT as a strategic driver need to continuously adapt themselves to the changing environment to keep themselves ahead of the competition. This will incur a lot of strain on the hiring, training, and staffing of IS personnel so that they are able to continuously provide value-added services to the client departments. It is believed that the client-server paradigm will enable them to this goal to a significant extent. But whether the IS departments are able to live up to their expectations is a question only time can answer.

In summary, it is hoped that this research will stimulate more studies of the relationships between IS structures and organizational structures in the presence of environmental and business constraints. The current case study was exploratory in nature, aimed at uncovering some of the hidden issues

associated with client-server computing. Generalizations drawn from a single case study are of course tentative, and replication of the study under a different organizational context is warranted to validate the results. However, practitioners need to be aware of the broader context of the new paradigm while implementing client-server systems, and must address some of the issues highlighted in this study for effective management of the new technology. Academicians can use the findings of this study as a basis for generating hypotheses for future research.

REFERENCES

Attewell G.W. and Rule, J. "Computing and Organizations: What We Know and What We Don't Know," *Communications of the ACM*, Vol 27, No. 12, December 1984, pp. 1184-1192.

Cafasso, R. "Reengineering," *Computerworld*, Special Report, March 15, 1993, pp. 102-105.

Dostert, M. "Users bring Downsizing Demands to Exposition," *Computerworld*, February 22, 1993, pp. 16.

Ein-dor, P. and Segev, E. "Organizational Context and MIS Structure: Some Empirical Evidence," *MIS Quarterly*, Vol. 6, No. 3, September 1982, pp. 55-68.

Francis, R. "Downsizing: The Application Migration," *Datamation*, November 15, 1992, pp. 36-48.

Foster, L.W. and Flynn, D.M. "Management Information Technology: Its Effects on Organizational Form and Function," *MIS Quarterly*, Vol. 8, No. 4, December 1984, pp. 229-236.

Galletta, D.F. and Heckman R.L. "A Role Theory Perspective on End-user Development," *Information Systems Research*, Vol. 1, No. 2, June 1990, pp. 168-187.

King, J.L. "Centralized versus Decentralized Computing: Organizatioal Considerations and Management Options," *Computing Surveys*, Vol. 15, No. 4, December 1983, pp. 319-350.

Lee, S. and Leifer, R.P. "A Framework for Linking the Structure of Information Systems with Organizational Requirements of Information Sharing," *Journal of Management Information Systems*, Vol. 8, No. 4, December 1990.

Markus, M.L. and Robey, D. "Information Technology and Organizational Change: Causal Structure in Theory and Research," *Management Science*, Vol. 34, No. 5, May 1988, pp. 583-598.

Nully, P. "When to Murder Your Mainframe," *Fortune*, November 1, 1993, pp. 109-120.

Olson, M.H. and Chervany, N.L. "The relationship between Organizational Characteristics and the Structure of the Information Services Function," *MIS Quarterly*, Vol. 4, No. 2, June 1980, pp. 57-67.

Radding, A. "Five Types of Tools get Data from Legacy Systems," *Software*, Vol. 13, No. 2, January Special 1993, pp. 31-41.

Robey, D. "Computers and Management Structure: Some Empirical Findings Re-examined," *Human Relations*, Vol. 30, No. 11, November 1977, pp. 963-976.

Richardson, G.L., Jackson, B.L., and Dickson, G.W. "A Principles-Based Enterprise Architecture: Lessons from Texaco and Star Enterprise," *MIS Quarterly*, Vol. 14, No. 4, December 1990.

Sinha, A. "Client-Server Computing", *Communications of the ACM*, Vol. 35, No. 7, 1992, pp. 77-98.

Tavakolian, H. "Linking the Information Technology Structure with Organizational Competitive Strategy: A Survey," *MIS Quarterly*, Vol. 13, No. 3, September 1989, pp. 309-317.

Zeigler, K. *Distributed Computing and Mainframe: Leveraging Your Investments*, John Wiley and Sons Inc., 1991.

Table 5: Role of IT personnel

TRADITIONAL PARADIGM	NEW PARADIGM
Mainframe support	Distributed systems support
Asset management: proprietary hardware, software	Asset management: distributed hardware, software, LAN
System development/maintenance	System development/maintenance
	Create/maintain enterprise data models
	Data management: security, backups, etc.
	End-user training
	Integrate IT into business processes
	Technology research and assessment
	Upgrade their own skills

END-NOTES

[1]X-OIL is a fictitious name for a large oil production company based in Houston, Texas.

[2]Re-engineering refers to the fundamental re-examination of how companies do what they do and finding out ways of doing it more efficiently, more profitably, and at reduced costs. Generally speaking, re-engineering is initiated in businesses for various reasons: to simplify a business process, to improve an existing proess to make better use of available technology, or to redesign of the entire process for achieving business goals that have changed over time. In a *Computerworld* special report (Cafasso 1993), IS executives from 100 premier companies have reported that re-engineering did result in greater productivity, lower expenses, and higher profitability in their organizations. However, even re-engineering's greatest bppsters say that though the idea is hot, the chances of failure is substantially high (about 70 percent), because the concept is hard to implement, and if done improperly, it can rip up working business processes and irrevocably damage the status quo.

[3]Downsizing, in general, refers to the process of moving applications from mainframe-based systems to smaller systems. The trend of migrating from mainframes began a few years back in an attempt to control the escalating costs of mainframe computing to deliver more computing power to the end-users. Many experts believe that downsizing has a lot of relevance in the context of organizational computing, because it attempts to closely mirror the way an organization's data is stored, processed, and distributed to the actual business needs of the organization.

[4]RAID is a fault-tolerant disk design that relies on redundancy in a set of physical disk drives that is viewed by the operating system as a single logical disk drive. Data is stored across corresponding physical drives of an array. The redundant disk capacity is used to store parity information, which guarantees data recoverability in case of a disk failure. First conceived of at the University of California in an effort to bridge the widening gap between processor performance, RAID is viewed as the future of intelligent storage subsystems and is currently available at six levels, each level reflecting a design architecture (Cafasso 1993).

Managing Local Area Networks and Measuring Their Performance

Dr. N. J. Hard and Mr. K. T. Adams
General Business and Systems Management
East Texas State University
Commerce, Texas 75429
[903] 886-5687

Executive Abstract

Local area networks (LAN) become more important in this era of globalization and business re engineering. Performance management continues to be an important part of the success of any system. Many tools assist with the task of measuring LAN performance as well as alleviating LAN problems. Several LAN consultants were interviewed to determine key issues related to managing LANs and strategies necessary to measure the effectiveness of LANs. This research integrates current literature with the findings of LAN consultants interviewed. Tools for measuring LAN performance are identified and discussed. Additionally, issues related to future problem areas were identified and are addressed. Future problems may impact modification or expansion of existing LANs.

BACKGROUND INFORMATION

As organizations shift from large mainframe systems to LANs, networks become more complex. The management of those systems becomes more critical. The value of performance management increases in an attempt to produce and maintain successful systems. Therefore, the key to having a competitive edge today may be managing LANs.

Tools are available that assist the task of measuring performance. Tools may both identify and alleviate LAN problems. However, LAN personnel need special skills to ensure that they use the tools properly. Along with operators that are in charge of keeping the system running, organizations need to hire and train support personnel for users of the systems. Support personnel may be part of either a help desk or an information center and may provide help for systems users.

Additionally, management must have clear goals and plans when developing LANs. A good understanding of the goals and objectives will alleviate problems that could arise with the LAN. Managing networks has become a growing issue along with the growth in technology.

Managing a LAN starts long before a system is in place. More problems will arise as LANs grow and become more complex. Management must plan ahead to reduce problems and alleviate much of the chaos that occurs with problems. Management can play a significant part of controlling and resolving problems with LANs. As Nadig and Hard [1] point out, performance measurement is not an issue that should be brought up when a problem occurs. Rather, it should be done during the planning stages of the LAN.

DISCUSSION OF ISSUES

LAN managers (system administrators or network administrators) should describe the goals and objectives for the network before its implementation. They must have plans and requirements for the network in order to keep the users up and running. They should consider the number of users on the system and their use of it. They must have knowledge of users' jobs, duties, skills, education levels, and training and must identify the tasks and information needs of the users. They need to know how all employees will be using the network and its software. As users' tasks become more complex, task analysis will become more critical to the performance of the network.

LAN managers must be aware of the structure of the network and its involvement in the entire organization. A LAN manager must plan and implement a recovery plan that will give the fastest restoration of service.

FINDINGS

Many components make up a LAN and effect the performance of the network system. Information networks are frequently composed of a mixture of hardware and software from different manufactures. When hardware and software from different manufacturers are mixed on a network, the LAN manager's job becomes more complex and he or she may need integrated management systems to help them analyze the system. Integrated management systems help LAN managers identify problems across the multivendor environment. As a result, LAN productivity increases and repair time decreases. LAN managers' jobs would be tough without advances in technology and multivendor network management systems capabilities.

For a network to run properly, all of the different devices must run synchronized. Network problems can range from slow response to a bad adapter card. All problems on a network are considered performance problems. The most common LAN problem is a slow response from the server. Slow response may result from high demands on network printers, collisions (packets of data that collide when sent across a network), or increased number of users on the system. Another common problem occurs when a file server for a particular segment goes down. Another problem occurs when a workstation constantly sends data out because of a faulty adapter card. Problem identification and correction remain critical aspects of the LAN manager's tasks.

Many tools measure LAN performance and analyze the activity of the network. Automated tools gather information on problems and historical data related to the problem. A good statistical tool, such as SAS, will help to generate reports on network performance. Diagnostic tools help managers detect and correct problems. Less sophisticated tools are testers, device alarms, and surge protectors

Tools that test the hardware and wiring communications are called time-domain reflectometers (TDRs). If a problem does not exist on the physical layer of the network, an analyzer or monitor may detect the problem. A network technician must be skilled in translating the data captured by the monitor or analyzer. A monitor oversees the activities of a network. Analyzers are tools that help network administrators narrow down problems that are on LANs.

CONCLUSION

Network management becomes more important with the continuous growth of LANs. A network can run properly only with the proper strategies and tools. Performance management should be a pro-active process. Strategies for performance management should be planned during the creation and design of the network. When a network does not fulfill the users' goals, then the network becomes worthless. The performance of a network has a great impact on the entire performance of the organization. LANs are the computer systems of the present and future. Performance management is critical to the ongoing success of a LAN system.

[1] Nadig, D. V. and N. J. Hard, A proposed model for managing local area networks and measuring their effectiveness, *Proceedings of the Twenty-Sixth Hawaii International Conference on System Sciences,* 1993, 538 - 547.

Electronic Mail and Legal Liability:
A Company Policy Perspective

Alvin E. Hammond
Candidate: College of Law
University of Lousville
Lousville, KY 40292
and
Robert M. Barker
Department of Computer Information Systems
College of Business and Public Administration
University of Louiville
Louisville, KY 40292
ph. (502) 852-4779 fax (502) 852-7557

I. INTRODUCTION

Civil law chases current technology. As new technologies have been introduced into our society, both legislative and common law doctrines have been changed to reflect society's interest in protection from abuses, as well as remedies for injuries sustained, as a result of the use of the technology. At the time of its drafting, the framers of the Constitution certainly did not envision many of the modern information technologies we now take for granted. As the Fourth Amendment was written, electronic networks and vast computer database systems for information storage and retrieval were not even a remote consideration. This is where we stand today, however; we are a society where there is increasing dependence on electronic technology to store and transmit information. With an increasing use of new and more effective forms of information technology, inevitably there will be an increased number of legal concerns related to the use of that technology. The information technology to be specifically considered here is that of Electronic Mail (E-mail). What must organizations be aware of when they facilitate the utilization of E-mail? This article is not meant to be a treatise on current law as it relates to E-mail. The intent is to introduce the reader to the possible legal exposures an organization faces when the decision is made to use E-mail within a business environment. Even in relatively small businesses, computers and E-Mail are becoming standard business tools. Managers must be informed of the possible liability one might encounter through the adoption and use of such technology. In a large corporate environment, legal exposure increases and the ability to control abuses can decrease, unless steps are taken to avert possible problems. Organizations may expose themselves to legal liability inadvertently. Employees may expose an employer to litigation, even where there is no intent, knowledge or complicity on the part of the employer. Good management at least entails an awareness of issues arising from, and some basic rules to follow, when E-mail is introduced to business functions. Managers in the age of E-mail also need to be aware of the limits of the use of E-mail in the management of employees. This article explores circumstances that have arisen in the past, and suggests simple preventative measures that can minimize organizational risk exposure.

II. ELECTRONIC MAIL AND THE ISSUE OF PRIVACY

Most of the risk involved in the utilization of E-mail revolves around privacy. The Supreme Court has ruled that the Constitution guarantees an individuals right to privacy in certain circumstances. As new technologies for transmission of information have emerged, the Court has been called upon to interpret the Fourth Amendment many times, in newer and novel ways. Consequently, as private citizens, the Court has ruled we have the right to not have our mail or phone calls intercepted by persons for whom they were not intended. The primary issue in privacy with regard to the transfer of personal information which has constantly been challenged in the courts is conflict which arises between someone who believes s/he has the right to use a particular medium to transfer personal information and some other party who believes s/he has an equivalent "right" to intercept such messages. This second "right" is also supported by the Constitution, within certain circumstances. The rights of the individual, or the employee, conflict with that of the organization. How does one reconcile the two apparent rights?

While originally an issue involving telephone, the introduction of the computer into this situation has exacerbated this question. A computer can store vast amounts of information and retrieve specific items almost instantaneously. Ever since George Orwell conceived of "Big Brother", the persistent fear was one where some faceless government would use computers to invade a citizen's privacy at will. Unfortunately, there have been many instances where Orwell's prediction has become a reality; but Big Brother is much more likely to be one's employer, not the government. Organizations have used increasingly sophisticated methods to surveille employees to ensure efficiency and control, and the monitoring of E-mail has emerged as one of the most popular of those methods.

Just as telephone and video surveillance have been used by companies to monitor employees actions, examining employee E-Mail is fast becoming the preferred choice of organizations for determining what the people within the organization are actually saying to one another. And just as organizations claimed it was their right to use phone taps and video surveillance within the workplace, employers are also claiming it their right to examine an employee's E-mail. Cases where employees challenge these organizations are starting to find their way into the court systems. With the declining cost of the technology, E-mail is becoming increasingly commonplace in the business environment. Companies of all sizes now purchase E-mail systems to increase the efficiency of transmission of correspondences within the organization, as well as to parties on the outside. What remains to be seen is whether the companies adopting E-mail have explicitly considered the issue of employee privacy versus the organization's need to know, and have expressed clear policies concerning the use of the E-mail systems. The following section examines the conflict between workers' and employers' views on this privacy issue.

III. PRIVACY: CONFLICTING EMPLOYER AND EMPLOYEE PERSPECTIVES

Privacy is a social conscience and public policy question, and, as such, generates a great deal of emotion when abuses are perceived to occur. There are those that would argue that under no circumstances should a person or organization be allowed to intercept or peruse an individual's private property. But whose property is inside the computer? The company, of course, owns the computer. The company expends the resources to provide the employee a tool with which to carry out his or her assigned duties. Isn't the company, therefore, entitled to review anything which transpires is within the asset they purchased? On the other hand, the employee expects that "personal" messages transmitted via E-mail are afforded the same right to privacy granted to telephone conversations and personal mail. It is this specific issue which today's courts are being called upon to answer.

Employers argue many sound and logical reasons for using E-mail as a surveillance tool. These reasons offer a more legitimate and reasonable justification for monitoring electronic mail than to simply say, "We own it, therefore we can do with it what we want." These issues include ensuring the security of company secrets and assets; to reduce company liability resulting from employee malfeasance; the need to control organizational network communication costs; and the use of E-mail as a tool to monitor worker performance on the job.

The first issue for monitoring that companies raise is security. In 1990 the U.S. Department of Commerce estimated that businesses lose approximately $40 billion each year to employee theft and that up to 75% of all employee theft may go undetected (9). Secondly, the incidence of industrial espionage is increasing due to the competitive environment

the world's businesses find themselves in. Employees can find it very profitable to divulge organizational secrets to the competition. Consequently, a company might suggest that surveillance of employees via review of electronic mail is a easy and convenient means to ascertain if an employee is acting in the best interest of the company. While it would not seem to be a smart action to transmit sensitive information through the company's own computer, this has indeed happened. For example, two computer programmers who worked for a California software company and were terminated for allegedly disclosing trade secrets to a rival computer company. It was while monitoring electronic mail messages on Internet that the company discovered the divulged information (9).

A second concern is that the use of the company E-mail system for personal use will result in organizational liability exposure. Given the sophistication and expense which can involved with an electronic mail system, many employees do not have the resources to obtain a system of their own. However, they may recognize that using the company system may have great benefit to them. This benefit may range from an seemingly innocent electronic mail transmission sent to a friend far away, to more unscrupulous use which may subject the company to legal liability even when the company had no knowledge nor participation in the activity. For example, one enterprising bank employee was found to be running a sports betting operation on the company electronic mail network (1). Another case involved a worker who used his company computer to send derogatory statements across a national network and identified the sender as the company (1). Both of these activities expose the company to possible financial liability exposure. In the case of the betting ring, the organization may have to defend itself in court for complicity in the illegal activity. In the second case, consider that Company A was the subject of one of the derogatory remarks from the employee of Company B. Furthermore, assume that the derogatory remark made its way into the public domain and the bad publicity caused some detriment to the company (i.e. significant loss of business). It may be argued that the Company B is partially responsible for those damages, given that it was their system and was perpetrated by their employee. Company B, therefore, had a duty to control and regulate the information which originated within the company and went out over the network. IN the past, companies have been found liable for employee actions on many occasions. For example, the brokerage firm of Merrill Lynch, Pierce, Fenner, and Smith Inc. which was ordered to pay $2 million dollars in punitive damages due to the fraudulent trading of one of its brokers, even though the firm was not knowingly involved, had discovered the activity itself, and quickly fired the broker. (*Davis v. Merrill Lynch, Pierce, Fenner, and Smith Inc.*, 906 F 2d 1206 (8th Cir 1990)). The company, therefore, has a duty to protect itself and its' stockholders from such financial exposure.

With regard to the more innocent use of sending private communication, this use becomes a cost issue for the organization. While the marginal cost for a small operation may be minimal, imagine the expense if, for example, every one of E. I. DuPont's 90,000 E-mail users decided to send several personal messages per week. Thus, in order to ensure that the system is being used for only business purposes in an effort to contain costs, a company may want to monitor an employee's outgoing E-mail the same way many companies monitor long distance telephone charges.

Perhaps the most often cited reason for examining E-mail is that it provides an objective way to evaluate employee performance and improve customer service. A common way for a company to assess an employee's abilities on the job is to listen in on an employee's phone calls to determine whether the worker meets objective performance standards. Review of E-mail logically accomplishes the same objective. Furthermore, advocates of electronic monitoring suggest that the practice increases productivity, provides better accountability, and fosters job improvement (5). The theory employed here is that behavior improves because employees never know when they might be watched (5).

Of course, workers may have a diametrically opposed opinion on this matter. The issues from the employee's perspective include the invasive nature of what the company is doing; the question of what the company will do with the information they find during these examinations; and the perception that the company is trampling on the perceived right of privacy, based on Constitutional grounds.

Most employees expect a reasonable amount of privacy in the workplace. Unfortunately, for reasons cited above, employees fail to understand that once they enter the workplace, total personal privacy is a cost that most organizations are not willing to bear. This may not the employee's expectation, however. Because some states have ruled it to be illegal to eavesdrop on private conversations or phone calls even if made on a company owned phone (2), the expectation is that the same privilege will extend to E-mail. Unfortunately, there are few clear rules governing E-mail as it has penetrated the workplace.

Employees also expect that the messages sent via E-mail which are not part of the scope and purpose of their jobs, when deleted, are no longer accessible by the company. This may not be the case either. Sophisticated retrieval programs can recreate messages even if they have been deleted from the current file (6). Consequently, a company can engage in surveillance of electronic mail even when the employee doesn't want the message saved in the system and has purposely purged it. Old personal messages, then, may surface and haunt that employee.

The real issue concerning the employee is what the company does with the information obtained during the monitoring. Given performance standards, if the monitoring reveals that the employee is deficient in his/her duties, termination based on this criteria would seem justified. On the other hand, what if the company dismisses the employee based on nothing more than personal messages critical of management obtained during the monitoring process? The employee may sue based on the fact that the intercepted correspondence, like telephone conversations, is private property and the company had no right to it. The company may be liable, because it cannot dismiss the employee if it shouldn't have had the information in the first place. If the company has already dismissed the employee, the employee can seek compensatory and punitive damages. This argument becomes even more complex when related to criminal activity since the burden of proof is higher in criminal cases and the rules of what is admissible or not is very often a key element of both prosecution and defense. The conflict between employer interests and those of the employee rest within conflicting values perceived by each. The employer seeks to protect the business, and the employees perceive a right to privacy with regard to their communications. The following section will explore specific cases where the monitoring of E-mail has resulted in litigation, and how the courts ruled in those cases.

IV. RECENT CASE EXAMPLES AND THEIR RESULTS

The previous discussion has been somewhat theoretical and general. In an effort to provide guidance to business professionals in the creation of E-mail policies, this section will explore specific cases and what the courts have ruled in those cases. The questions which need to be answered are: What have companies been doing with the information they collected during this surveillance process, and what did the courts rule based on that monitoring? Consider the following cases currently in the judicial system:

Case 1: In 1989 Nissan Motor Corporation U. S. A. hired Bonita Bourke and Rhonda Hall to run the electronic mail network for its Infiniti dealers. The pair trained dealers to use the system and as such they became friendly with some of the dealers. A female supervisor overheard that some of the messages may be "too" friendly for business purposes and began monitoring the women's electronic mail. It was determined that the pair, as well as receiving business communications were also receiving "love letters, soft-core pornography, and horoscopes", in addition to saying some rather disparaging things about the supervisor. The supervisor admonished the two and threatened to discharge them. When the women filed a grievance for invasion of privacy, they were fired. They sued the auto maker. The case was dismissed because the courts found that California privacy laws did not extend to workplace surveillance. The case is currently under appeal (10).

Case 2: Alana Shoars was hired to be Epson Computers electronic mail administrator. She advised 700 employees during training sessions that their passwords were classified and no one other than the intended recipient could read their electronic mail. However, a supervisor set up a gateway between the companies computers and the electronic mail network the company subscribed to so he could read all the electronic mail from outside the company. When Shoars complained she was fired for gross insubordination. This case was also dismissed for the same reason as Case 1 and is also on appeal (10).

Case 3: Borland International has accused ex-employee Eugene Wang of passing trade secrets to a competitor named Symantec. The company's complaint is based on electronic mail messages found on Wang's computer hours after he announced he was leaving Borland for a new job - with Symantec! Wang's argument is that the communications are private and therefore inadmissible (1). This case has not yet been tried.

These are all examples of how monitoring of E-mail can implicate a company in a legal complaint. Even though the companies mentioned above may have been within their rights to do as they have done, they were subjected to the costs of litigation attributed to their monitoring of E-mail transmissions. Unfortunately, there are few clear laws governing E-mail. The question of how E-mail should be managed has emerged as one of the most murky and difficult legal issues of the electronic age. Furthermore, dependent on whose E-mail system is being used, responses differ on what should be allowed. For example, most Americans are not familiar with the use of seized E-mail in the Iran-Contra scandal. A central issue in the case was the White House policy of requiring employees to destroy all E-mail files after a hard copy was produced. Judge Charles Richy rejected the argument that all files had been in fact saved on hard copy and ruled the White House policy was contrary to public interests (2). Consequently, the private E-mail of Oliver North, which North argued was privileged, was one of the principal sources of information used against him (3). Those E-mail messages had been purged by North from his account after the scandal came to light. North believed the messages were destroyed, but they were recovered from tape back-ups by investigators. In the business environment, such issues about accountability to the society are absent. In this situation the question arises of whether or not private messages transmitted over privately owned computers should be considered the property of the originator or the system provider.

There has been no case to date involving electronic mail in the private sector which has reached the Supreme Court, so there are no definitive rulings to provide any guidance. Furthermore, there is no Federal Legislation which covers the monitoring of electronic mail by employers. The Electronic Communications Act of 1986 prohibits "outside" interception of electronic mail without proper authorization but does not cover interception by persons inside the organization. In other words, the organization which supports the cost of the system has the right to use that system in whatever way it sees fit, but passive infiltration of the system from outsiders is expressly against the law.

Senator Paul Simon of Illinois has tried to enact legislation which set guidelines for workplace monitoring of E-mail beginning in 1987. This bill never made it out of committee. Then in 1990 he introduced the Privacy for Consumers & Workers Act. This bill and it companion bill H. R. 2168 would have required employers who engage in electronic monitoring of employees to give advance written notice to

each employee of:
(1) the form of monitoring to be used.
(2) the personal data to be collected.
(3) the frequency of the monitoring.
(4) the use of the data collected.
(5) interpretation of data collected.
(6) existing standards for work performance expectations.
(7) methods for determining production standards and work.

This particular legislation encompassed not only E-mail but all forms of surveillance. Once again, the bill did not pass and he reintroduced it in 1992. It, too, did not pass.

Some states however have taken the initiative and passed laws which do cover certain types of monitoring activities. None however specifically mention E-mail as an area to be protected. In the cases mentioned earlier, the courts in California ruled that their workplace privacy statutes did not extend to E-mail. Bear in mind that as with all common law issues, this can change with the decision of just one case decided against the employer. Typically, as the incidence of the alleged abuse increases, the courts take a stricter look at what the needs of society are and very often rule in the opposite when circumstances suggest time has come to afford greater protection to the public.

In summary, there is little in the way of statutory or case law which would allow an employer to determine what is allowed or what to do to protect itself from exposure if they decide to monitor employees electronic mail. This does not mean organizations can do nothing to lessen the risk exposure. The following section outlines simple policies which should be implemented to limit the possibility that such issues will arisen in the future.

V. WHAT AN ORGANIZATION SHOULD DO TO AVOID LIABILITY

Here is a quote from the legal classic by Rose and Wallace as reported in Syslaw (7):

In the absence of definitive court rulings, most lawyers believe that under current laws, workers do not have privacy rights on company electronic mail systems unless their employers give them those rights. This can happen in two ways. First, if an employer knowingly allows private employee electronic mail to grow and flourish on the company system without opposing it, then an implied agreement can be established, under which employees have a right to expect their private transmissions to remain private. The employer may be able to negate the employees' privacy rights afterward by declaring that electronic mail is not private, but this would likely affect only future electronic mail, and not electronic mail transmitted before the announcement.

Second, employers can affirmatively create employee electronic mail privacy rights by an express agreement with their employees, which will normally take the form of inclusion of such rights in their policy manuals. This is the more generous approach, espe-

cially where employers choose to give their workers express, well-defined electronic mail privacy rights.

The thrust of this statement is that if you inform employees of what the company policy is, the likelihood of avoiding privacy issue lawsuits will increase. (Providing the company consistently follows the policy, of course.) Some companies have recognized the benefit and have established company policies which cover employee use of E-mail, and what the company policy is regarding the monitoring thereof. The fact is, though, less than ten percent of U.S. companies have such a policy, according to Walter Ulrich, managing director of the consulting firm of Arthur D. Little (3).

There are two extremes to consider when drafting a company electronic mail policy. At one extreme, a company can state that all electronic mail is the property of the company and can be accessed by the company at any time, for any purpose. This approach can create an atmosphere of suspicion and mistrust, and may inhibit the use of electronic mail. Thus, any cost savings and productivity increases will be lost. Tom Peters states this about electronic mail monitoring: "It's important to stress that the whole idea of electronic mail monitoring is bull---- strategically. If management is going to act like cops, then they are going to destroy the potential of the system (3)." He did also state that monitoring may be acceptable in the case of proving employee theft or illegal activity. Some companies have adopted this option and developed policies which state that "everything on the computer will be read." Both Kodak and E. I. du Pont de Nemours & Co. have such policies. Interestingly, this type of policy is also advocated by Noel Shipman, attorney for the plaintiffs in the Epson and Nissan cases mentioned earlier. Shipman does not believe that companies should be monitoring employees electronic mail, but admits that companies must maintain that right in order to legally protect themselves (8). Despite the fear that such a policy might restrict the use of electronic mail, Kodak's director of records management said that there has been dramatic growth in electronic mail usage (8). This indicates that employees can come to accept such policies, if they are made explicit and enforced consistently.

At the other extreme, the E-mail policy can be completely privacy oriented and state that all E-mail is private and no employee other than the intended recipient and the sender may view it without the permission of the sender. This approach also poses problems. Total privacy restricts the ability of the company to discover information and thus impedes the company's ability to do business. What if two individuals passed important information about a business matter through the electronic mail system but neither was available to authorize another who needs the information immediately? Consequently, the best policies must fall somewhere in the middle of the extremes.

The consensus may be that a productive electronic mail policy is one that is enforceable, that fits the company culture, and that allows for the incidental and occasional use of E-mail for personal communications (3). Furthermore, a company should reserve the right to monitor E-mail but prohibit employees from reading other employees E-mail except in those situations that require access for legitimate business reasons (3).

Educating the employee as to the ramifications of the policy is just as important as having a policy. A policy allowing monitoring of E-mail would not protect a company if the employees is not aware of it. But how can an organization communicate the policy to employees, and more importantly, how do you prove that the employees have been informed of the policy? United Parcel Service displays a message that spells out the company policy when a user signs on to the network (8). Kodak, on the other hand, requires their employees to sign a statement which says they have read the company policy (8).

Complicating this whole process is the fact that some states are beginning to enact legislation regarding employee monitoring of E-mail. These local statutes may be contrary to company policy. Companies which operate internationally have to consider there may be foreign laws, especially in Europe, which are contrary to company doctrine. These are problems which companies must face as they arise.

VI. DEVELOPING ELECTRONIC MAIL POLICY GUIDELINES

So where does a company turn for assistance in developing an electronic mail policy? Two major areas must be addressed in the formulation of an E-mail policy. The first concerns the issues of E-mail privacy and organizational rights to know. The second deals with the contents of the E-mail messages themselves, concerning what is and is not appropriate content for transmission and storage on the network.

To help in the privacy issue, in a White Paper prepared for the Electronic Mail Institute by John Podesta and David Johnson, several policy options are articulated. They were proposed as general conditions that a company should consider when drafting an E-mail policy. These include:

A. What are the permissible uses of the E-mail system? Can it be used for personal messages and if so must employees take special steps to protect such messages against inadvertent inspection by others?

B. Will the company monitor the messages transmitted on the system as a matter of course or for a particular purpose? Will the company refrain from further inspection if it determines the nature of the message to be private? Will the nature of the routine monitoring be disclosed? Will there be limits on the use of information obtained via monitoring?

C. What grounds will be required to be shown to access E-mail without the consent of the sender?

D. Will the company allow employees to request that their E-mail not be disclosed to others even though company policy may be contrary? What grounds would be required to make such a request?

E. Will the company impose restrictions on the uses to which the results of monitoring can be used? Will these restrictions be disclosed to the employees? Will the policy include provisions regarding termination or discipline based solely on results of monitoring?

F. Will any special restrictions apply to disclosure of E-mail to law enforcement officials?

G. What procedural requirement will be required prior to disclosure? Will a committee decide? An Individual?

Organizations need to consider these privacy questions as applied to their management philosophies and organizational culture, and then choose accordingly. In addition to being made aware of the company policy regarding privacy in the use of E-mail, employees should also be instructed on how E-mail messages should be structured and what types of languages and subjects should NOT appear in the system, in order to lessen liability exposure if the E-mail is subpoenaed in a civil case. Establishing a formal etiquette may prevent problems from occurring initially, and can be used to control for damage, if the medium is subsequently abused by an organizational employee.

John Jessen, Managing Director of Electronic Evidence Discovery Company suggests the following guidelines that E-mail users should be instructed to follow while creating messages. First, employees must be made aware that any message they write could be held against them, as well as the company, as it can be made available to anyone who has access to the company computer. This includes people outside the company as well. For example, a California company dismissed an minority individual who sued the company for wrongful termination due to discrimination. The company in the case lost, primarily because Jesson retrieved a memo sent from one individual to another which stated, "You know how these people are, there not team players." The jury interpreted "these people" as a indication of bigotry. Given that the trial takes place long after the incident and in the sterile environment of the courtroom, it is not always easy to suggest that it didn't mean anything. In the same vein, uppercase letters used for emphasis can make points seem more important than they were intended to be, and should be used with care (6).

Secondly, employees should be told not to joke, be sarcastic, and absolutely never use derogatory or off-color language to discuss company issues. These results can be disastrous for the company. In another case Jesson worked on an employer produced as evidence a "picture perfect" letter of termination that had been given to an employee who sued the company for wrongful termination. Jesson countered with an earlier E-Mail communique he had reclaimed from files presumed to be deleted. The four letter word strewed diatribe from the company's president to its personnel director essentially read, "Dump the bitch (6)." Needless to say, profane letters about fired employees do not make winning a case any easier.

In order to prevent discovery of deleted messages, a company should consider having the entire hard drive storing the E-mail physically erased periodically. While this is an expensive procedure, it can be beneficial in the long run especially if your system is very large and control is difficult. (NOTE: Don't do it AFTER you are sued. This would constitute obstruction of discovery and suppression of evidence, both of which would be disastrous in this case.)

In summary, good policies should encourage fast and free sharing of E-

mail, but still preserve the company's rights to proprietary information and control. It should include references to proper etiquette as well as hardware procedures to afford as much protection as reasonably possible.

VII. BIBLIOGRAPHY

1. *Daily Labor Report*, Bureau of National Affairs, Inc. (Nov. 17, 1992)

2. Elmer-Dewitt, Phillip. "Who's Reading Your Computer Screen?" *Time*. (Jan. 18, 1993). p. 46.

3. Fryer, Bronwyn and Furger, Roberta. "Who's Reading Your Screen?". *PC World*. (Aug., 1993), p. 166.

5. Marx, Gary. "Let's Eavesdrop on Managers". *Computerworld*. (April 20, 1992). p. 29.

6. "The Perils of E-mail". *INC*. (Aug., 1993). p. 38.

7. Rose, Lance and Wallace, Jon. *Syslaw, The Sysops Legal Manual*. (Winona, MN.: 1992). pp. 101-102.

8. Salamone, Salvatore. "Attorney Discusses How To Avoid E-mail Privacy Woes". *Network World*. (March 25, 1991), p. 21.

9. Ulrich, Walter. "Rights of Privacy in E-mail". *Los Angeles Times*. (Sept. 7, 1990). p. D-3.

10. Weigner, Kathleen. "The Trouble With E-mail". *Working Women*. (April, 1992). p. 46.

The Use of 4GLs in Application Development: A Managerial Perspective

Andy C.H. Lam

Hong Kong Polytechnic

ABSTRACT

The purpose of this study was to explore user expectations, limitations and methods of improving productivity of 4GLs (Fourth Generation Languges) in the perspective of managers of different organizations in Hong Kong. Based on interviews with eleven managers and an application consultant with experience with ten different organizations including four 4GL vendors, a hardware vendor, two software houses, a government department and two commercial organizations, the findings from this study provide a better understanding on the reasons why investment in 4GLs does not always give the promised development productivity. Users' and developers' expectations were identified from definition and selection criteria of 4GLs. The major limitations and issues in the use of 4GLs relates to the learning curve, project types, programming experience, resource requirements and performance requirements were discussed. The study also identified methods of improving development productivity in practice and in development.

Acknowledgements

I would like to thank the individuals with whom I spoke for their time, support and their insights into the use of 4GLs.

1. INTRODUCTION

Year after year, many organizations increase their information systems expenditures to cope with information needs. However, their application backlogs still stretch over several years. The maintenance of existing applications continues to consume a large percentage of IS resources. The emergence of 4GLs (Fourth Generation Languages) for over a decade ago was in response to the need of development tools for improving systems delivery. Findings from several papers were encouraging as all reported that 4GLs were more productive than 3GLs (Third Generation Languages) in the development of business applications. 4GLs such as FOCUS, LINC were used in several studies to compare with the productivity of 3GLs. Harel and McLean (1985) compared the programming productivity of FOCUS and COBOL. Their study supported earlier findings that programming tasks are written faster in FOCUS by an average of 3 to 1. Rudolph and Simpson (1984) also reported a significant overall productivity advantage for LINC over COBOL in terms of function point for development productivity. Other comparisons in serveral studies (see for examples, Holtz (1979), Behrens (1983), Duffy (1984), Cobb (1985) and Lehner (1990)) also supported that 4GLs have relative advantages over 3GLs.

However, surveys on development tools reveals some interesting results in the use of 4GLs. The 4GL is not a favourite of all IS (Information Systems) professionals. Doke (1989) conducted a survey on the importance and popularity of application development tools. In his findings, the 4GL was among the ten least popular tools, ranked 23 out of 28 and was not even among the ten most important tools, ranked 19 out of 28. Another survey by Lehman and Wetherbe (1989) on 4GL users and applications reported that only about 5% of the respondents used 4GLs instead of 3GLs. About 80% of the respondents used 4GLs to supplement 3GLs or to supplement application packages. In the survey by Khosrowpour and Lansa (1989), results show that only 14% of programmers preferred to use 4GLs over 3GLs, 40% of the programmers disliked 4GLs and 46% was neutral.

It is obvious that productivity is not simply a question of tools. Investing in 4GLs without achieving the expected rapid returns is one of the major concerns to the management. There must be some neglected issues which have a significant influence on the use of 4GLs in application development. Management must cope with these issues in order to realize the promise of 4GLs. A number of organizations in Hong Kong have accumulated experience in using 4GL's in their application development. This study is designed to identify the expectations, limitations and methods of improving development productivity from a managerial perspective.

2. METHODOLOGY

Since the objectives of the study are to find out expectations, limitations and methods of improving productivity in use of 4GLs, an applied approach was used to collect data for analysis. Though structured interviews may not be considered rigorous, they are appropriate for this study which is a pilot study to clarify on the answers to open ended questions and requires flexibility in restructuring the questions for respondents of different background and experience in application development. This method can also provide the best source of qualitative information on opinions, policies, and subjective descriptions of activities and problems related to IS development.

Eleven managers and an application consultant belonging to ten different organizations with experience in either development, technical support, IS project management, software selection and/or training of 4GLs were interviewed for about 60 to 120 minutes each. The interview time varied because some questions arose as a result of insights gained during the interview. The experience of the respondents ranged from five to sixteen years in the IS profession. All respondents have experience in both 4GL and 3GL projects. The respondents represent both large and small organizations in many different industries. Different organization types were chosen so that the data collected represented a more universal view on use of 4GLs. The characteristics of the respondents is shown in Table 1.

Table 1: Characteristics of respondents

Title	Type of Organization
Regional Director of Technical Services	Hardware Vendor
Manager of Technical Services	Software Vendor A
Customer Support Manager	Sofware Vendor B
Application Consultant	Software Vendor C
Regional Manager	Software Vendor D
Managing Director	Software House A
Systems Manager	Software House B & 4GL distributor
Systems Manager	A government department
Division Manager & Manager of EDP	Engineering Corporation
MIS Manager	Trading and Manaufacturing

During each interview, the same questions were asked. However, many more questions were raised as a result of insights gained during discussion of answers. The key questions are shown in Table 2.

Table 2: Key Questions for The Interview

What is your definition of 4GLs?
What are your major selection criteria of 4GLs?
What are the limitations of 4GLs?
What are the methods of improving development productivity?

All respondents were asked to answer questions in their own views without reference to a particular 4GL. The data collected was quite product-independent.

3. FINDINGS OF THE STUDY

3.1 What is the definition of 4GL?

All respondents was surprised by this question. Most of them considered that it was a difficult question to answer. They preferred to define a 4GL in terms of essential attributes. This is understandable as 4GLs are still evolving and are without a standard definition. Table 3 summarizes the attributes of 4GLs as described by all respondents. The results show that all responents considered a 4GL must be easy to learn, able to improve programming productivity and able to generate reports, screens, menus and forms easily with a set of tools. All respondents but one disagrees that 4GL should have non-procedural feature. This particular respondent preferred to program using procedural language constructs which he suggested provide more flexibility. He had bad experience

Table 3: Features of A Conceptual 4GL

User Defined 4GL Attributes	No. of Responses	Percentage
A set of development tools for report, screen, menu and form generation	12	100%
Improve programming productivity	12	100%
Easy to learn	12	100%
A non-procedural language	11	92%
Include SQL (Strutured Query Language) or a template-driven query language	9	75%
Support client/server computing	8	67%
Work with GUI (Graphical User Interface)	8	67%
Enable end-user computing	7	58%
Can integrate/interface with 3GLs	6	50%
Maintainability	6	50%
User friendly	6	50%
Allow reuse of code	5	42%
Interoprability	4	33%
Application portability	4	33%
A simple and powerful procedural language	4	33%
Object-Oriented functionalities	4	33%
Link with a Data Dictionary	3	25%
Simplify the traditional system development life cycle	3	25%
Can transparently access multiple databases and file systems locally and remotely	2	17%
Automatic generation of program documentation and cross-references	1	8%

with a powerful non-procedural 4GL which he used in the development of a Material Requirements Planning System. According to the respondents, the remaining attributes are dependent on project requirements, software development environment and personal experience. During the discussions, we also discovered that the findings provided the expectations of IS developers in the use of 4GLs as the defined attributes were either used in previous IS projects or was needed but not available from the 4GL used.

3.2 What are the major selection criteria of 4GLs?

Many respondents have experience in the selection of 4GLs for their organizations. Most of them have used previously one or more 4GLs for application development. In some conversations, there were indications that the respondents' selection criteria might evolve from 4GL vendor presentations. New requirements may be developed through a process of learning about alternative techniques and innovative features of the evolving 4GL products. The end-users' requirements also play an important part in the process. The features which can increase application development productivity may not be the most important critera. It is more important to ensure that a 4GL can run efficiently in the current system environment. Response time is always a major requirement from the users. Very often, the expenditures for hardware and software purchases are from budgets of user departments. The technological infrastructure of the organization is another significant factor affecting the choice of 4GLs. Therefore, considerations in the organizational IS/IT plan, software development environment, project requirements and end-user requirements are vital inputs to the selection of 4GLs.

The features which can increase application development productivity are not the most important criteria for all respondents. Respondents also emphasize system performance, vendor support, learning curve, hardware requirements, application maintenance and ability to handle ad hoc reporting requirements. The findings are shown in Table 4.

The results indicate that some selection criteria are also the defining features of a 4GL. Also, the percentage of respondents differed in these items. For example, the importance of interoperability had increased from 33% in the definition question to 67%. Discussion with respondents revealed that end-user requirements were taken into consideration to cause such change.

Extension of this research to include end-users in the future would probably provide a major impact on understanding the factors affecting the use of 4GLs from the end-users' perspectives. Some evidence of including end-users' expectations in the selection criteria of 4GLs are reflected in the current findings.

3.3 What are the limitations of 4GLs?

Several respondents had experienced performance problem with 4GLs. Although developing applications with a 4GL might save developers' time, they required usually more processing time and disk resources. One respondent emphasized that the developers' productivity improvement was a one time gain but the application would be executed daily or weekly causing an accumulated loss of system productivity. Another respondent argued that applications of the 90's required frequent changes to cope with the changing business environment. If applications written in a 4GL can be maintained with ease and in less time, the gains of competitive advantages from the rapid changes could easily offset the loss in system productivity.

Other limitations of 4GLs were lack of capabilities to handle complicated logic, integration problem with existing 3GL applications, steep learning curve in achieving 4GL proficiency and no standards in 4GLs. The limitations of 4GLs were listed in table 5.

Several respondents were disappointed by the experi-

Table 4: Selection of 4GLs

Major Selection Criteria	No. of Responses	Percentage
Short learning curve	12	100%
User friendly interface	12	100%
Ability to handle complex problem	12	100%
Ability to handle ad hoc reporting requirements	11	92%
Vendor technical support	11	92%
Improve application productivity	10	83%
Support Client/Server Computing	10	83%
Compatible with existing software development environment	9	75%
Ability to generate efficient and maintainable code	9	75%
Interoperability	8	67%

Table 5: Limitations of 4GLs

Disadvantages	No. of Responses	Percentage
Unsatisfactory response time	12	100%
High system resources requirements	12	100%
Unable to handle complicated logic	10	82%
Integration problem with existing 3GL applications	6	50%
Steep learning curve to achieving proficiency	6	50%
Evolving without standards	6	50%
Unable to access multiple data bases and file system	2	17%

enced programmers in use of 4GLs. They claimed that the experienced programmers always used the low level procedural constructs of a powerful 4GL and did not benefit from the available non-procedural capabilities. Two respondents commented that trainee programmers could learn to write 4GL programs much better than experienced programmers. They believed that experienced programmers could learn 4GL programming more effectively only after possible brainwashing. The findings also indicated that two respondents had bad experience with the interoperability of the evolving 4GLs. They had difficulties in integrating their applications developed using a 4GL with some external applications. Interoperability has become one of the industry "buzz words", amongst database and 4GL vendors. The growing trend is to separate a 4GL from its DBMS according to Robins (1990). The software environment has become to some extent a components environment. However, findings indicate that many of the available components might not work well together. Another respondents encountered difficulties in the use of non-procedural capabilities to write a batch processing application. It was very time-consuming to write complicated logic with non-procedural constructs. Programmers lost control of their programs written in pure non-procedural code. Therefore, it was concluded that a 4GL might not be suitable for all project types.

3.4 What are the methods of improving development productivity?

It was interesting to know the methods of improving development productivity in use of 4GLs. Respondents were asked to suggest ways to improve productivity further.

In the findings, one respondent suggests the use of object-oriented technology. Object-oriented (OO) techniques are used in the analysis and design of applications. The objects encapsulate the general requirements of a industry. The deliverables of OO systems analysis and design is a class library. An 4GL with OO functionality can be used to develop the applications with further productivity improvement. The application can be sold as a class library to different organizations of the same industry. This can reduce efforts in the analysis and design of the systems development cycle and the object-oriented class library can be reused and maintained easily.

Another respondent recommends the use of packages written in the same 4GL used by the organization to shorten the system development life cycle. The 4GL package must meet at least 70-80% of your requirements. Otherwise the efforts needed to change the package may be too big. As most the changes needed are probably the front-end features, end-user report writer specific to the applications is usually available in such packages. Users can obtain their front-end requirements quite easily with the tailor-made report generator. The back-end functions of the application are quite standard and they could be changed by programmers if required. This approach also reduce the efforts in database design and preliminary investigation. The users have the opportunity to see the functions of the package and define their requirements more easily and accurately to the systems analyst. Thus, the workload of the system analyst can be reduced significantly.

Several respondents use the more conventional method. The development of the application using a new 4GL is performed with the use of an external consultant. The external consultant is contracted to work on the IS project for a number of months depending on the size and complexity of the project. It must be ensured that the consultant must have experience in both the application and the 4GL used. The project team members could shorten the learning curve and improve their productivity through either peer tutoring and discussions. If budget is not available for the contracting of a consultant. Structured walkthroughs of the design and programming works can be arranged with the 4GL vendor. Usually two days before the walkthrough session, design documentation or the 4GL codes are sent to 4GL vendor. The vendor arranges some experienced analyst or programmer to inspect the user works and these personnel would participate the walkthrough session on-site. Feedback from the support personnel of the vendor will improve the proficiency of the project team member in design and programming using the new 4GL and it costs much less than having an in-house consultant. This approach also shortens the learning curve and development cycle. The application developed can evolved into a package for sale to subsidiaries or organizations of the same industry to gain more returns from the investment.

The use of PC (Personal Computers) and 4GLs by non-data processing staff is one of the current development in corporate computing. There are strategies and issues that IS managers need to address. EUC must be planned and it might not be suitable for all organizations. Henderson & Treacy (1986) provided a good framework for addressing the four fundamental issues, namely, technological infrastructure, support infrastructure, data infrastructure and evaluation/justifcation and planning. Three respondents described productivity gains from (EUC) end-user computing. Conceptually, productivity gain is obtained from reducing workload of analysts and programmers. However, there are indications in the conversations to suggest that the use of 4GL for the implementation of EUC is to reduce backlog pressures from users to the IS manager rather than as a mean to improve productivity. In some conversations, there are evidence to suggest that use of 4GL in EUC is still in the initiation stage in Hong Kong.

4. CONCLUSION

Many organizations in Hong Kong have started using 4GLs in application development several years ago. The IS professionals are able to identify factors affecting the success of 4GL applications through their accumulated experience. Their difficulties are related to human factors and organizational IS/IT planning. On the human side, the senior experienced analyst/programmers resist change to a new powerful language because they may lose their 3GL experience and seniority. Some 4GLs did not live up to their promises of productivity improvement. There is evidence to suggest that pure non-procedural language is not suitable for all project types. It is difficult to write complicated logic with a non-procedural language. This lends support to findings of Read & Harmon (1981). A 4GL program can be written over ten times faster than COBOL as defined by Martin (1985). However, most 4GLs required more processing time and disk storage for its execution. System productivity is easily degraded by the powerful language leading to user dissatisfaction and complaint. The use of 4GLs required additional budgets for the upgrade of hardware, contracting of 4GL experts and training. The senior management may not be aware of the cost of improving development productivity. Downsizing is the current buzz word in large organizations. This makes it more difficult to apply for additional budgets for staff development and hardware upgrade. The 4GL vendors are also aware of the problems of their clients. 4GLs have been evolved to be more powerful and more efficient in every new version. Most 4GLs can run under client/server environment. 4GL can now be sold independent of DBMS and provide interoperability and portability capabilities. The only concern is the the use of 4GLs in EUC. There is still a misconception that 4GL can be learnt in days if not hours and is suitable for implementing it in an EUC environment without a strategy. The diffusion of 4GL technologies and the decentralization of computing requires the formulation of an organization strategy for its control and support. However, it seems that management of many organizations are not aware of the cultural and social technical changes created in its work force by 4GLs. As a result, the application of 4GLs in EUC is very limited. Most end-users use a 4GL for data retrieval and simple data manipulation only. As a result of their ad hoc queries to the production system, it creates another performance problem for the IS managers.

References

[1]Behrens, C.A. (1983) "Measuring the Productivity of Computer Systems Development Activities with Function Points," *IEEE Transactions on Software Engineering*, VOL. SE-9, No. 6, pp. 648-652.

[2]Cobb, R.H. (1985) "In Praise of 4GLS," *Datamation*, July, pp. 90-96.

[3]Doke, E.R. (1989) "Application Development Productivity Tools: A Survey of Importance and Popularity," *Journal of Information Systems*

Management (Winter), pp. 37-43.

[4]Duffy, N.M. (1984) "Fourth Generation Languages: Some Planning and Implementation Issues," *Proceedings of the Joint International Symposium on Information Systems*, Sydney, April 9-11, pp. 166-96.

[5]Grant F.J. (1985) "The downside of 4GLS," *Datamation*, July, pp. 99-104.

[6]Harel, E. and McLean, E.R. (1985) "The Effects of Using a Nonprocedural Computer Language on Programming Productivity," *MIS Quarterly*, Vol. 9, No. 2, June, pp. 109-120.

[7]Henderson, J. & Treacy, M. (1986) "Managing End-User Computing for Competitive Advantage", *SLOAN Management Review*, Winter 1986, pp. 3-14.

[8]Holtz, D.H. (1979) "A Nonprocedural Language for On-line Applications", *Datamation*, April, pp. 167-176.

[9]Jeffery D. R. (1986) "A Comparison of Programming Productivity: The Influence of Program Type and Language", *Proceedings of ACC 86*, pp. 383-400.

[10]Khosrowpour, M. and Lanasa, J. (1989) "MIS Professionals' Attitudes Toward and Perceptions of 4GLs", *Journal of Information Systems Management* (Fall), pp. 51-57.

[11]Kull, D. (1989) "Building a 4GL Foundation", *Computer Decisions*, June, vol. 21, no. 3, pp. 44-47.

[12]Lehman, J. and Wetherbe, J. (1989) "A Survey of 4 GL Users and Applications," *Journal of Information Systems Management* (Summer), pp. 44-52.

[13]Lehner, F. (1990) "Cost Comparison for the Development and Maintenance of Application Systems in 3rd and 4th Generation Languages," *Information and Management* 9 (1990) pp. 131-141.

[14]Martin, J. (1985) *Fourth-Generation Languages Volume I - Principles*, Prentice-Hall, Inc., Englewood Cliffs, New Jersey.

[15]Read, N.S. and Harmon D.L. (1981) "Assuring MIS Success", *Datamation*, February, pp. 109-120.

[16]Robins, G. "4GLs, bundled or a la carte", *Computerworld*, March 5, 1990 vol. 24, no. 10, p. 73.

[17]Rudolph, E. & Simpson, G. (1984) "Evaluating of a Fourth Generation Language", *Proceedings of the Joint International Symposium on Information Systems*, Sydney, April 9-11, pp. 148-165.

[18]Sumner, M. & Benson, R. (1988) "The Impact of Fourth Generation Languages on System Development", *Information & Management*, 14:2, pp. 81-92.

Groupware at Work: Users' Experience with Lotus Notes

Hao Lou
Management Information Systems
College of Business Administration
Ohio University

ABSTRACT

Many companies have chosen groupware to support their work groups. How is groupware, such as Lotus Notes, used in organizational settings and what are users' reactions to the use of groupware? This paper reports partial findings from an electronic survey on individuals' acceptance of groupware in three Fortune 500 companies. The results suggest that (1) groupware use is contextual and (2) users' reactions to groupware implementation may depend positively on how groupware is implemented and used in a particular organizational context. Specifically, organizational differences, such as implementation policy and on going education and training may determine individuals' use of groupware. Further, the intensity and scope of groupware use may affect individuals' satisfaction with and perceived benefits of using groupware.

1. INTRODUCTION

A substantial body of management literature supports the general finding that managers and professionals, who make up about 70% of the office workforce, spend well over half of their work day in communication-related activities (Mintzberg, 1973; Rice and Bair, 1984; Panko, 1989). In fact, management communication is the largest single cost factor for U.S. business today (Strassman, 1985; Panko, 1992). Since the managerial and professional labor force represents the greatest portion of costs for labor and these people spend the bulk of their time communicating, improvements in the communication process should be of great interest to organizations.

The importance of communication has been intensified by the recent emphasis on work groups, in which the group is viewed as a basic unit of the formal organization structure (Drucker, 1988; Johansen, 1988). One of the cornerstones of effective group work is communication. Effective communication is a precursor to meaningful collaboration and coordination. The rapid development and widespread availability of personal computers and telecommunication networks (especially local area networks), together with the focus on work group computing, has stimulated a significant increase in the development of groupware.

The term, groupware, was initially used in 1978 by Peter and Trudy Johnson-Lenz, although Douglas Engelbart is credited with conceiving the idea as far back as 1962 while a fellow at the Stanford Research Institute (Johansen, 1988). The groupware concept begun to take the form of a product in 1989 when Lotus Development Corporation introduced Lotus Notes. Lotus Notes (Notes) is a client-server platform for developing and deploying groupware applications. Notes combines electronic mail and computer conference with database features that allow users to access, track, share, organize and view document-oriented information in a variety of ways.

While groupware products are proliferating at work and fueling speculations about their potential to enhance organizational effectiveness, it has been suggested that the implementation of such technologies is more difficult and yields more unintended consequences than is typically acknowledged (Bullen and Bennett, 1990; Grudin, 1988; Kling, 1991; Orlikowski, 1992). If indeed groupware can offer what it has promised, then studying the use of groupware in the workplace should be valuable for understanding how such technology is implemented and used and how its use is affecting productivity in today's organizations.

The questions of whether groupware technologies are being used in organizations and how they are being used in organizations that have implemented this type of technology is important for at least two reasons (Markus et al., 1992). First, how such technologies are used is believed to condition their effects. Second, because people use groupware with other people, one person's choices about how to use groupware may have consequences for other group members.

This paper describes some of the findings from an exploratory field study on the use of Lotus Notes and its organizational impact. The purpose of this paper is to provide partial findings regarding to users' reactions to Lotus Notes. The following sections provide a brief description of the research method, partial research findings, and discussion. For more complete and detailed analysis of the results, including theoretical rationale and hypotheses testing, see Lou (1993).

2. RESEARCH METHOD

2.1 Samples

This study was conducted in three Fortune 500 organizations. For purposes of confidentiality, the three organizations are designated as Company A, Company B, and Company C. Company A operates in the life insurance industry while companies B and C belong to the oil and gas industry.

Users access Notes mainly by means of personal computers located on their desks that are connected to a local area network (LAN). Users in the three companies were primarily white-collar managerial and technical or professional employees. Once installed, use of Lotus Notes was free to employees in all three companies, a policy that may have influenced usage. Nonetheless, since this factor was constant across the three companies, an examination of other independent factors that contribute to variation in the individual level of use remains a valid undertaking.

2.2 Data Collection

An electronic survey via Notes served as a focus for data gathering. The questionnaire was adapted from previous studies on computer-mediated communication systems (CMCS) in general and electronic mail and computer conference in particular (Kerr and Hiltz, 1982; Steinfield, 1986; Markus et al., 1992) and redesigned as a Notes database[1] form. The decision to use Notes to study Notes was based on the view that this tool would provide advantages over a conventional paper and pencil survey, such as instant distribution of the questionnaire to Notes users, automatic collection of responses, and easier monitoring and follow-up. As a research tool, electronic surveys have been found to be as effective for data collection as traditional paper and pencil surveys. A study comparing both types of surveys reveals no significant differences in the rate of participation, number of questions completed, and time spent completing the questionnaires (Sproull, 1986). On the positive side, respondents to an electronic survey are more likely to use the entire range of response categories instead of just the middle categories when compared to traditional surveys (Kiesler et al., 1984; Kiesler and Sproull, 1986). On the negative side, prior studies also confirm that the relevant population for an electronic survey is restricted to those who have access to computers and feel comfortable using them. In the present study, since the relevant population in each company was confined to Notes account holders, this weakness was not viewed as a problem as far as the research objective is concerned.

To solicit participation in the survey, a letter was sent via Notes mail to all Notes account holders' Notes mail boxes on a number of Notes servers at two research sites (Company A and Company C). In Company B, the letter was sent to the potential respondents' electronic mail boxes via Microsoft Mail because company policy did not allow use of the Lotus Notes mail feature - a policy that may also have affected individuals' use of Notes in this company. Within the letter, a brief explanation of the study and instructions for accessing and completing the questionnaire were provided. In addition, a DocLink[2] was created inside the mail document (for Company A and Company C only) to allow respondents to access the survey database directly. In order to complete the survey, a potential respondent was required to add the survey database to his or her desktop workspace[3] and compose a form by using a mouse. Once the form had been completed and saved, all answers were stored in the survey database and available for viewing by the researcher in a variety of ways. The respondents were encouraged to complete the survey in one sitting although it could be saved or aborted in the middle and re-accessed later if desired. The survey responses (views) were not accessible by the respondents to assure confidentiality although one was able to view his or her own responses.

Table 1 - Response Rates[a] by Organizations

	# of E-mail Sent	# of Responses	Response Rate
Company A	270	60	23%
Company B	199	48	24%
Company C	700	87	12%
Total	1169	195	17%

[a]The response rate may actually be higher due to the fact that some Notes account holders may not have opened their mail or even logged into Notes during the time period of the survey.

The survey database was available to Notes users in Company A for only a few days[4] and in companies B and C for about 4 weeks. During the data collection period, reminders to complete the survey were sent to all Notes mailboxes in Company C and to all Microsoft Mail boxes in Company B. Table 1 summarizes the response rates from the three organizations. The actual response rate may be higher due to the fact that some Notes account holders may not have opened their mail or even logged into Notes during the time period of the survey.

3. RESEARCH RESULTS

The partial results of the research project reported here are organized around three dimensions of individual acceptance of computer-mediated communication systems (CMCS) suggested by Hiltz and Johnson (1989). These dimensions encompass organizational members' (1) amount of use of a particular groupware product (which can be viewed as a CMCS for groups), Lotus Notes, (2) subjective satisfaction with Notes as a group communication medium, and (3) perceived outcomes of using Notes.

3.1 Measures of the Amount of Notes Use

Notes utilization measures may focus on (a) "intensity of use" by looking at hours of use within a given time period, or (b) "cumulative use" or experience at a particular point of time. In addition, both measures can be obtained from self-reported and computer-monitored usage data. This study uses the first measure, intensity of use (or amount of use), operationalized as the weekly average number of hours using Notes, collected by both self-reported and computer-monitored usage data. Self-reported use was obtained by asking the respondents to indicate the average number of hours per work week they spent using Notes. On the other hand, the computer-monitored usage data were captured by Notes Logs. Notes Logs contain a group of log files structured as standards Notes applications. Among these logs, one can easily obtain users activity logs, such as number of hours (connection time) each user used Notes, number of reads, and number of writes each user made in using Notes, either on a daily or on a weekly

Table 2 - Summary of the Use (Hours Per Week) of Lotus Notes

	Company A	Company B	Company C
Self-Reported Use			
Number of Responses	61	46	84
Mean	9.8	3.9	4.7
Standard Deviation	9.8	4.3	5.4
Maximum	38.8	20.0	30.0
Minimum	1.0	0.1	0.3
Computer-Monitored Use			
Number of Responses	62	38	88
Mean	5.6	3.8	1.2
Standard Deviation	9.3	5.3	1.4
Maximum	38.7	24.1	9.4
Minimum	0.4	0.1	0.0

[1]Computer-monitored use is measured in terms of number of hours (connection time) per week averaged from 4-5 weeks' Notes Logs.

basis.

Table 2 contains a summary of self-reported use. Self-report response data indicates that the average weekly use per person is 9.8 hours in Company A, 3.9 hours in Company B, and 4.7 hours in Company C. Notes Logs indicate that the average computer-monitored weekly use per person is 5.6 hours in Company A, 3.8 hours in Company B, and 1.2 hours in Company C.

In addition to intensity of use, the respondents were asked to indicate the degree to which they used Notes for various purposes. Previous studies of computer-mediated communication systems (Steinfield, 1986) have demonstrated that

these purposes of using a computer-mediated communication system can be factor analyzed into two dimensions, one defined primarily by task-related applications and the other defined by socioemotional and entertainment applications. Table 3 depicts the questions, the mean response and standard deviation for each question across the three companies. The results indicate that the respondents in Company A use Notes often for task-related applications such as *send a message in place of a phone call* (Mean=4.1, scales range from 1 = Never to 5 = Very often), *distribute/provide information* (Mean=4.1), and *learn about events/things I am interested in* (Mean=3.7).

On the other hand, the respondents in Company A report that they rarely use Notes for socioemotional or entertainment applications such as *participate in entertaining events/ conversations* (Mean=1.7), *keep in touch/maintain relationship* (Mean=1.8), and *organize/coordinate a social activity* (Mean=1.7). The respondents from companies B and C indicate similar purposes of their use of Notes with somewhat lower means when compared to those from Company A. One exception in both Company B and Company C is that they rarely use Notes to *send a message in place of a phone call* (Mean=1.3 in Company B and Mean=2.5 in Company C), a particular task-related application.

3.2 Measures of Subjective Satisfaction with Using Notes

As indicated by Hiltz and Johnson (1989), user subjective satisfaction in the context of computer-mediated communication systems (including groupware) refers not to the product of using a system, but rather to the process of interacting with the system as a communication medium. Nine questions in the questionnaire probed the users' reaction to using Notes as

Table 3 - Items Measuring Purpose of Use

Question[a]	Company A		Company B		Company C	
	M	S.D.	M	S.D.	M	S.D.
- Coordinate projects on which I am working	3.2	1.4	1.9	1.2	2.3	1.2
- Brainstorm/generate ideas	2.9	1.2	2.2	1.2	1.8	0.9
- Monitor progress of projects on which I am working	3.0	1.3	2.2	1.2	2.4	1.3
- Send a message in place of a phone call	4.1	1.1	1.3	0.9	2.5	1.2
- Distribute/provide information	4.1	1.0	3.3	1.2	3.5	1.3
- Keep a record of agreements/interactions	3.0	1.3	2.2	1.4	2.4	1.4
- Seek task information from people I know	3.1	1.1	2.1	1.2	2.5	1.3
- Give/receive feedback on reports/ideas	3.2	1.2	2.7	1.4	2.5	1.2
- Schedule meetings/appointments	2.8	1.2	1.3	0.9	1.6	1.1
- Learn about events/things I am interested in	3.7	1.0	3.0	1.3	3.6	1.2
- Fill up free time	2.1	1.2	1.5	0.8	2.0	1.2
- Take a break from my work	2.0	1.1	1.5	0.6	2.0	1.1
- Participate in entertaining events/conversations	1.7	0.9	1.4	0.7	1.4	0.7
- Keep in touch/maintain relationship	1.8	1.0	1.5	1.1	1.4	0.7
- Organize/coordinate a social activity	1.7	1.1	1.0	0.0	1.0	0.3

[a]*Please indicate the degree to which you use Lotus Notes for the following purposes:* Scales range from 1 = Never to 5 = Very often.

Table 4 - Items Measuring groupware User Subjective Satisfaction

Question[a]	Company A		Company B		Company C	
	M	S.D.	M	S.D.	M	S.D.
Over all, the system is... (1=Extremely bad, 5=Extremely good)	4.1	0.6	3.6	0.7	3.8	0.7
I find using Notes to be (1=Boring, 5=Stimulating)	4.1	0.7	3.4	0.8	3.6	0.9
I find the language of Notes (1=Confusing, 5=Understandable)	3.9	0.9	3.6	1.0	3.3	1.1
I find the language of Notes (1=User unfriendly, 5=User friendly)	3.9	0.7	3.6	1.0	3.3	1.1
Please indicate your reactions to using Notes:						
1=Hard to learn, 5=Easy to learn	4.0	0.8	3.6	1.0	3.6	1.0
1=Impersonal, 5=Friendly	3.9	0.7	3.4	0.9	3.5	0.9
1=Frustrating, 5=Not frustrating	3.8	0.9	3.6	1.0	3.4	1.0
1=Time wasting, 5=Time saving	3.9	0.7	3.5	0.8	3.4	0.9
1=Not productive, 5=Productive	4.2	0.7	3.7	0.8	3.6	0.9

[a]*These questions concern your overall reaction to Lotus Notes as a means of communication and work. They consist of a number of rating scales on which you are to select one number which corresponds to where you would place your own impression of Lotus Notes on that dimension.*

a means of communication and work. These questions focus on the respondents' reactions to the system interface and impressions of Notes. Each of these questions had previously been used in studies of computer conferencing (Hiltz and Johnson, 1989; Vallee et al., 1978).

The results associated with these nine questions appear in Table 4. All the questions are based on a five-point scale with 5 as the most positive and 1 as the most negative responses. Note that all items yield a mean response on the positive side (Mean>3) across all three companies, ranging from 3.8 to 4.2 in Company A, 3.4 to 3.7 in Company B, and 3.3 to 3.8 in Company C. Again, the respondents from Company A seem to be slightly (not necessarily statistically) more satisfied with using Notes than their counterparts from Company B and Company C are.

3.3 Measures of Perceived Outcomes

Ideally one would like to obtain "objective" measures of the productivity-related outcomes or benefits of using Lotus Notes. However, objective measures that would apply to a wide variety of information workers across different departments and organizations are difficult if not impossible to obtain (Hiltz and Johnson, 1989). Therefore, this study relies on self-reports of perceived benefits and changes in communication behavior that have been demonstrated to be related to productivity.

Table 5 lists six items that were used to measure the perceived benefits of using Notes. As shown in Table 5, in Company A, the mean response to each question related to the

perceived benefits of using Notes falls on the positive side of the measurement scale, ranging from 3.2 to 4.1 (scales ranged from 1 = Strongly disagree to 5 = Strongly agree). In companies B and C, the mean responses for the same questions are somehow lower, ranged from 2.7 to 3.7 in Company A, 2.8 to 3.5 in Company C. Once again, the respondents from Company A are somewhat more positive about the perceived outcomes of using Notes.

In addition, seven questions were used to assess the effectiveness of Notes in communication. Table 6 contains a summary of the results where the respondents were asked if the use of Lotus Notes has changed their communications or work patterns.

In Company A, 82% and 88% of the respondents indicated the use of Notes reduced their use of telephone and inter-office mail respectively. Eighty-five percent of the respondents also agreed that the use of Notes made communication with others more efficient. In addition, about half (52%) of them felt that the use of Notes reduced the number of meetings they must attend and 32% considered their use of Notes reduced length of meetings. Moreover, only 18% of the respondents indicated that the use of Notes facilitated meeting new people and 17% of them indicated that their use of Notes reduced use of libraries. Again, noticeable differences from the responses in companies B and C can be observed. For example, only 49% and 45% of the respondents, in Company B and Company C respectively, agreed that the use of Notes made their communication with others more efficient. This is in sharp contrast

Table 5 - Items Measuring Perceived Outcomes

Question[a]	Company A		Company B		Company C	
	M	S.D.	M	S.D.	M	S.D.
- Notes has made it easier for me to reach people with whom I need to communicate	4.0	0.8	2.7	1.2	3.0	1.0
- Notes has provided me with ideas, references, or other information useful in my work	4.1	0.9	3.7	1.1	3.0	1.0
- Notes has increased my stock of ideas	3.7	1.0	3.3	1.1	3.2	1.0
- Notes has increased the efficiency of my work	3.5	0.8	3.0	1.1	2.9	1.0
- Notes has increased the quality of my work	3.2	0.9	3.0	1.1	2.8	1.0
- Overall, Notes is useful for my work	4.1	1.0	3.6	1.0	3.5	1.1

[a]*Please indicate your level of agreement with each statement by selecting the appropriate number.* Scales ranged from 1 = Strongly disagree to 5 = Strongly agree.

Table 6 - Changes in Communications or Work Patterns

Question[a]	Company A % Agree	Company B % Agree	Company C % Agree
- Use of Notes reduces use of telephone	82%	32%	34%
- Use of Notes reduces use of inter-office mail	88%	36%	43%
- Use of Notes facilitates meeting new people	18%	2%	12%
- Use of Notes makes communication with others more efficient	85%	49%	45%
- Use of Notes reduces use of libraries	17%	13%	24%
- Use of Notes reduces number of meetings	52%	36%	18%
- Usc of Notes reduces length of meetings	32%	28%	20%

[1]*Has the use of Lotus Notes changed your communication or work patterns?* 1=Yes/0=No.

to the 85% in Company A. Further, 32% of the respondents in Company B and 34% of the respondents in Company C agreed that the use of Notes reduced their use of telephones and 36% of the respondents in Company B and 43% of the respondents in Company C agreed that the use of Notes reduced their use of inter-office mail.

4. DISCUSSION

Based on the results presented in the previous section, there are observable differences in terms of individuals' use of Notes (both self-reported and computer-monitored usage), their satisfaction with and perceived benefits of using Notes across the three research sites. Because of the complexity of intervening factors (not reported here), the observations made

here have no simple explanations. In addition, neither hypotheses and nor statistical inferences are made in this paper. The purpose of this section is to discuss possible explanations for the observed variations.

4.1 Use of Notes

As indicated in the previous section, Company A had the highest average self-reported and computer-monitored use (9.8 hours and 5.6 hours per week) when compared to Company B (3.9 and 3.8 hours) and Company C (4.7 and 1.2 hours). There are few possible reasons why the average use of Notes in Company A is higher than the average use in the other two companies.

In Company A, Notes was introduced and implemented approximately six months before the survey was administered. In addition to top management support, Company A maintained a special task force providing user education and support, such as an on-line help (HelpDesk in Notes) and regularly scheduled short training classes (at different levels of training). The implementation of Notes was publicized company wide. These characteristics of the Notes implementation in Company A may have, in part, made the average individual Notes usage higher in this organization.

Company B, on the other hand, implemented Notes for a limited number of users on a trial basis only. Although users were encouraged to try out Notes, there was no special requirement for such use. In addition, training was not provided to these users. For example, one respondent in Company B noted,

"If back-and-forth information sharing is not a big part of the message (I'm just informing some one of something), I prefer E-Mail because I know the person will receive the message quickly and realize that the person has specifically been sent a message. Lotus Notes may have some features to overcome these problems, but I haven't received any training so I don't know about it. I just see it as one more technology-of-the-week that we are spending money on and perhaps don't need."

Moreover, the electronic mail feature in Notes was not used at all in Company B because of the company's policy in mandating the use of Microsoft Mail. The fact that the respondents in Company B do not use the mail feature of Notes certainly reduces their use of Notes.

Company C implemented Notes along with a group decision support system product and an audio conferencing system at least one year prior to the administration of the survey. Like Company B, use of Notes was not required in Company C. Since most people in this organization had access to multiple electronic mail systems (PROFS, CEO, VAX NOTES, etc.) and some people perceived Lotus Notes as "just another electronic mail system," Notes was not used to its greatest potential. This is evidenced by several respondents' written comments:

"I have noticed most users new to Notes perceive it as 'just another e-mail package.' This severely limits their acceptance of the product. They continue to use PROFS or Office Vision and not get into Notes."

"Somewhat --PROFS (or OV/VM) accepted as standard; systems exist already in PROFS (i.e., calendar, conference room reservation)."

"In our department we have two e-mails, PROFS and CEO, that are checked regularly. I think that Notes is mostly viewed as just another e-mail system."

Further, several respondents also offered written comments that suggest the lack of training and education may limit their understanding of the capabilities of the technology and their use of the technology. For example, one Notes sever administrator noted,

"If increase Notes use is an objective, the strengths and usefulness of Notes has not been properly marketed within our company (.....at least not at my location)."

Another respondent also commented,

"(Notes is) vary well written, lots of thoughts was put into designing the package. It is so versatile, though, that I don't think we nearly use it to its potential yet. With time and proper training, this tool will become essential to our group, department, and possibly the company as a whole."

As a result of "the company's emphatic position on PROFS," together with the lack of training and education, the use of Notes in Company C was limited to "just another e-mail."

4.2 Users' Reactions to Using Notes

The results of the present study also indicated that the respondents had different reactions to using Notes across the three research sites. In Company A, for example, 88% of the respondents consider the use of Notes reduces their use of inter-office mail, 82% of them agree that the use of Notes reduces their use of telephones, and 85% of them think that the use of Notes make their communication with others more efficient. In contrast to these favorable responses in Company A, much lower percentage of the respondents in Company B and Company C agree that the use of Notes reduce their use of telephone (32% and 34%) and inter-office mail (36% and 43%) and increase their communication efficiency (49% and 45%). The more favorable responses from Company A are also reflected in some comments. For example, the respondents from Company A in general had higher praise for Notes:

"Lotus Notes is an exceptional tool for information transmittal/sharing."

"Good communication tool. As soon as everyone is on Notes, a large improvement can be made in project coordination/control, idea generation, communication, etc."

"Lotus Notes is an asset in accomplishing work and communicating information."

"The various discussion databases (in Notes) provide very good information on what is going on, how things are done, what went wrong, how to correct it. When unable to attend user meetings, these databases provided information (probably more - since others outside of these meetings are able to contribute) that is pertinent to testing."

In contrast, the respondents in Company C had less favorable reactions to the use of Notes. For example,

"Notes is good for understanding what is going on but does not increase productivity beyond any other e-mail system."

"The use of Notes has not greatly enhanced the way I do my job, only given me another way of doing my job. Once I have mastered the use of Notes, I can see the application becoming a viable tool. At this point, I am not a strong enough user to support the application as a GREAT tool."

These results seem to confirm with the contention (Bullen and Bennett, 1990) that as groupware products, such as Notes, are more widely known and used, their inherent value may become more obvious to the users.

5. CONCLUSION

Rice (1992) has argued that new media (Notes certainly can be viewed as a group communication medium) use is contextual. In general, the results of this exploratory study support this contention. Specifically, the results suggest that individuals' use of groupware depends, in part, on contextual factors, such as implementation tactics and users education and training. Further, the intensity and scope of groupware use in a organizational context may affect users' satisfaction with using a groupware product as a group communication tool and perceived outcomes of using it. As a matter of fact, a wide array of factors (not reported in this study) may co-exist in affecting individuals' use and evaluations of groupware. Future studies of groupware should address, (1) at the individual level, factors that have been proposed to explain individuals' adoption, use, and evaluation of groupware and (2) at the organizational level, strategies to implement groupware (Markus, 1987) and organizational structure and culture elements that may interact with other factors to influence how groupware is implemented and used (Orlikowski, 1992). The present exploratory study represents a first step in investigating issues related to implementation and evaluation of groupware.

6. ENDNOTES

[1] A Notes database is an object storage facility through which users can access, track, store, and organize information on their network.

[2] A Doclink is a miniature window embedded in the text of a document, such as a mail document as in this particular case. It indicates a linked reference to another document (the survey document, for instance). Double-clicking with the mouse pointer on a DocLink opens the linked document.

[3] User "workspace" is a graphical user interface that will have a familiar "look and feel" for users of Windows, Macintosh® System 7, OS/2, or UNIX system.

[4] Top management decided to withdraw participation in the study.

7. ACKNOWLEDGEMENTS

The author acknowledges the support for this research made available by the three participating organizations and the Information Systems Research Center (ISRC) at the University of Houston. Special thanks to the persons who provided me access to their Lotus Notes servers and users in the three research sites.

8. REFERENCES

Bullen, C.V. and J.L. Bennett (1990). "Groupware in Practice: An Interpretation of Work Experience." **CISR WP No. 205**, Center for Information Systems Research, Sloan School of Management, Massachusetts Institute of Technology.

Drucker, P.F. (1988). "The Coming of The New Organizations." **Harvard Business Review.** January-February: 45-53.

Grudin, J. (1988). "Why CSCW applications fail: Problems in the Design and Evaluation of Organizational Interfaces." **Proceedings of the ACM Conference on Computer-Supported Cooperative work**, pp. 85-92.

Hiltz, S.R. and K. Johnson. (1989). "Measuring Acceptance of Computer-Mediated Communication Systems." **Journal of the American Society for Information Sciences**, 40(6): 386-397.

Johansen, R. (1988). **Groupware: Computer Support for Business Teams.** New York: The Free Press.

Kerr, E.B. and S.R. Hiltz (1982). **Computer-Mediated Communication Systems: Status and Evaluation.** New York: Academic Press.

Kiesler, S. and L. Sproull (1986). "Response Effects in the Electronic Survey." **Public Opinion Quarterly**, 50, pp. 402-413.

Kiesler, S., J. Siegel, and T. McGuire (1984). "Social Psychological Aspects of Computer-Mediated Communication," **American Psychologist**, 39, pp. 1123-1134.

Kling, R. (1991). "Cooperation, Coordination, and Control in Computer-Supported Work." **Communication of the ACM**, 34(2): 83-88.

Lou, H. (1993). "Computer-Mediated Communication Systems at Work: A Pluralistic View on Their Use, Satisfaction, and Outcomes." Unpublished Ph.D. Dissertation. University of Houston.

Markus, M.L. (1987). "Chargeback as a Tactic for Implementing Office Communication Systems," **Interface.** 17(3): 54-63.

Markus, M.L., T.K. Bikson, M. El-Shinnawy, and L.L. Soe. (1992). "Fragments of Your Communication: E-Mail, V-mail, and FAX." Unpublished working paper. UCLA.

Mintzberg, H. (1973). **The Nature of Managerial Work.** New York: Harper and Raw.

Panko, R. (1989). "Measuring the Office Work Force." **PRIISM Working Paper 89-013**, Pacific Research Institute for Information Systems and Management, University of Hawaii.

Panko, R. (1992). "Managerial Communication Patterns." **Journal of Organizational Computing**, 2(1): 95-122.

Orlikowski, W.J. (1992). "Learning from Notes: Organizational Issues in Groupware Implementation." **Proceedings of the ACM Conference on Computer-Supported Cooperative work**, pp. 362-369.

Rice, R.E. and J.H. Bair (1984). "New Organizational Media and Productivity." In R.E. Rice and Associates, **The New Media: Communication, Research and Technologies**, Beverly Hills, California: Sage, pp. 198-215.

Rice, R.E. (1992). "Task Analyzability, Use of New Media, and Effectiveness: A multi-Site Exploration of Media Richness." **Organization Science**, 3(4): 475-500.

Sproull, L. (1986). "Using Electronic Mail for Data Collection in Organizational Research." **Academy of Management Journal**, 29, pp. 159-169.

Steinfield, (1986). "Computer-Mediated Communication in an Organizational Setting: Explaining Task-Related and Socioemotional Uses." In M. McLaughlin (Ed.), **Communication Yearbook 9.** Beverly Hills, California: Sage.

Strassman, P. (1985). **The Information Payoff: The Transformation of Work in the Electronic Age.** New York: Macmillan.

Vallee, J., R. Johansen, H. Lipinski, K. Spangler, and T. Wilson. (1978). **Group Communication through Computers, Volume 4: Social, Managerial, and Economic Issues.** Institute for the Future, Report R-40.

A Decision Support System (DSS) Framework for Network Organizations Relationship Management

James Otto
IIT Research Institute
4140 Linden Avenue, Ste. 201
Dayton, OH 45432

Anita Lee-Post
Decision Science & Information Systems Dept
College of Business and Economics
Room 425, B&E Building
University of Kentucky
Lexington, KY 40506

ABSTRACT

The business environment has changed dramatically over the last two decades. Two key reasons for this change are the integration of the global marketplace and the rapid pace of technological innovation. An integrated global economy means that there are many more competitors to contend with. The fast pace of technology has accelerated the product innovation cycle and technology has provided many new tools to support operational flexibility. These changes have profound implications for how companies must organize and operate. This paper examines network organizational structures, discusses how information technology can support them, and introduces a framework for designing a decision support system (DSS) to support decisions concerning interfirm relationship management.

1.0 INTRODUCTION

The business environment has changed dramatically over the last two decades. Two key reasons for this change are the integration of the global marketplace and the rapid pace of technological innovation. An integrated global economy means that there are many more competitors to contend with. The fast pace of technology has accelerated the product innovation cycle and technology has provided many new tools to support operational flexibility. These changes have profound implications for how companies must organize and operate. This paper examines network organizational structures, discusses how information technology can support them, and introduces a framework for designing a decision support system (DSS) to support decisions concerning interfirm relationship management.

Treatment of these issues is organized into seven sections. Section two outlines the new business environment created by the effects of technology and integration of the global market. Section three discusses in general terms, how the operational imperative has changed from big and efficient to lean, fast, and flexible. Sections four and five examine organizational structures and how information technology can support them. In section six, a framework for designing a DSS for network organization relationship management is provided. Section seven presents a summary and conclusions.

2.0 THE NEW BUSINESS ENVIRONMENT

The marketplace has gone global. Competitors are everywhere and competition among rivals is intensified. The U.S. and its companies no longer dominate the world economy unchallenged (Refs 22, 23). This situation has come about for a variety of reasons, but the harsh reality is that it has changed the way the corporations must compete. Big and efficient is becoming less important than lean, fast, and flexible, especially in areas that provide the best hope for economic rewards (Refs 1,3,6,23).

Since the 1940's, many economic competitors have been recovering from the devastation that WWII inflicted on their economies. The recovery of these economies, combined with the integration of the world market, rapid advances in technology, and an increase in deregulation have made the world market a much more competitive place.

Technology has accelerated the integration of the world market. Advances in transportation technologies have made it possible to ship products around the world quicker and at lower cost. Communication and information technologies have allowed corporations to efficiently manage and coordinate far flung operations around the globe. Because of these advances, companies can implement different parts of the value chain (such as design, production, marketing, and distribution) in the most productive and efficient locations, even if they are far apart. This means that a product can be designed in one locale, produced in another, and sold in yet another. For example, the Mazda Miata was designed in California, prototyped in England, and assembled in Michigan and Mexico (ref 22).

Technology breeds technology. As new technology becomes available, it helps create the knowledge and tools to engender new technologies. This creates an ever-increasing pace of technology and product innovation which, in turn, reduces product cycle times and increases the velocity of change (ref 24,25).

Deregulation of many industries has significantly increased change and competition in those industries. Witness the rapid changes in the airline and telecommunications industries when they were deregulated in the 1980s. For example, AT&T estimated that it would take until 2010 to convert all of their long distance switching from analog to digital. However, because of competition from companies like Sprint, they were motivated to complete the task by 1990. (Reference 18).

All these changes make it hard for a company (or nation) to erect and sustain competitive advantage and/or market barriers. One effect of instant global communications is that ideas and techniques can be quickly transferred between nations. As competitors can quickly learn and copy ideas and techniques, this source of competitive advantage becomes less effective. Because of the dynamism and competitiveness of the global market, the global transportation infrastructure, and the ease with which information and operations can be transferred around the world, the advantages of location have been reduced. Companies must compete globally.

All of these environmental attributes suggest that a company or nation, if it is to sustain competitive advantage, must concentrate on those areas that do not easily diffuse beyond its boundaries. These areas include infrastructure, relationships, and knowledge (ref 22).

In summary, the world has become much more competitive place. There are more competitors, market barriers are tougher to erect and sustain, the pace of technology and product innovation has accelerated, and product life cycles have shortened. How technology can support decisions that are crucial to competing in this environment is a critical issue. Here we contribute to answering this question by exploring the leveraging of information technology to support the implementation and management of organizational structures and relationships that best fit environmental requirements.

3.0 THE OPERATIONAL IMPERATIVE: LEAN, FAST AND RESPONSIVE

In the era of mass production, efficiency and economies of scale were the predominant competitive strategy. The key was to develop highly efficient (but more rigid) means of production that could produce an individual product at the lowest possible cost. Mass production of single products was preferred in order to amortize the value of the production equipment over many individual pieces. Workers were deskilled or trained in only a very narrow area of production. Vertically integrated bureaucratic governance structures were implemented to control and supervise the most efficient 'scientific method' of production. Change only interrupted efficiency and resulted in cost increases. The result was

Figure 1. Organizational Responses

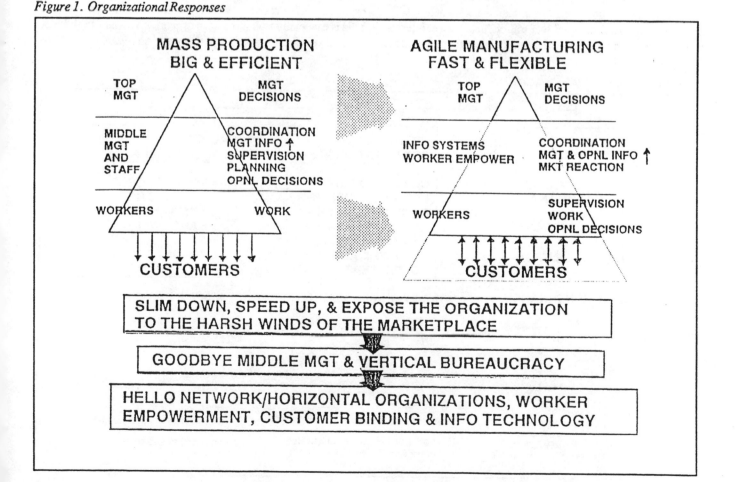

economies of scale and efficiency, but at the cost of responsiveness. (Refs 7, 16)

Today however, with the relentless pace of technology and corresponding compression of product life cycle times, long product runs are less desirable because products can become obsolete quickly. Consequently, companies must organize their structures, relationships, and technologies to meet the realities of the fast changing competitive landscape. In many cases, they must move from a strategy of mass production to one of agile manufacturing; from large and efficient to lean, fast, and flexible. Figure 1 summarizes this shift. A key component in implementing a more dynamic organization is to institute a more flexible firm structure such as a network organization. Information technology can support the realization of this objective.

4.0 ORGANIZATIONAL STRUCTURE

Figure 2 diagrams the organizational governance spectrum, from vertical integration to market control. The network organization attempts to combine the best properties of both. Figure 3 summarizes the general characteristics of the market, vertically structured, and network organizational types. Each of these types of organizational structures is described in the subsections 4.1 through 4.3.

4.1 The Vertically Integrated Bureaucracy

The vertically integrated organization is characterized by tight transactions, functional integration, and market internalization (Reference 2). It is a hierarchical beaurocracy that can be compared to the military command and control model. Decisions are made at the top based upon planning and scheduling and their implementation is supervised by the organization's policies and control structure.

This type of organizational structure is best suited for a stable planning and scheduling environment with a low level of uncertainty. This is because it is not structured to adapt quickly to change. An example of a stable environment might be a regulated marketplace. This type of environment, which also suits a strategy of mass production, does not demand flexibility. In this situation the inertial power and economies of scale that can be generated by a vertically structured organization can provide significant advantages.

Another reason for having a hierarchical beaurocracy is because market transactions can be too complex or involve too much overhead (Ref 15, 9). This is especially true for work that cannot be completely described a priori or where it is hard to measure specific value (such as the activities of a research scientist). Instead of spelling out detailed contracts to cover all possible contingencies (which may be impossible), an arrangement based on some level of trust is established. Since the arrangement is between entities within the same organization, there is an implicit presumption that each will act in good faith and in the best interest of the organization for those areas not explicitly covered by the contract mechanism.

Sometimes, assimilation of an asset (integrating it into the organization) is chosen over acquiring it in the marketplace. This is especially true if the item or work involves a high level of asset specificity or skill. In this case, an organization may

Figure 2. Organizational Spectrum

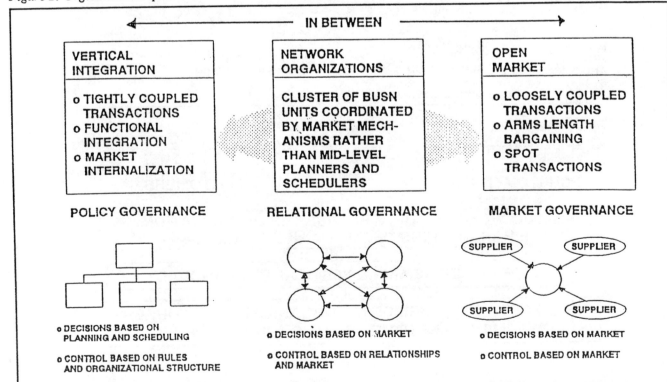

Figure 3. Characteristics of Organizational Types

HIERARCHICAL BUREAUCRACY	NETWORK ORGANIZATIONS	OPEN MARKET
BETTER SUITED FOR ENVIRONMENT THAT WITH:	TRIES TO COMBINE THE BEST OF BOTH	BEST SUITED FOR ENVIRONMENT THAT IS:

· BUREAUCRATIC CONTROL
· STATIC MARKETS
· HIGH MARKET BARRIERS
· LOW UNCERTAINTY
· COST COMPETITION
· INACCURATE METERING
· MASS PRODUCTION
· COMPLEX RELATIONSHIPS
· ASSET SPECIFICITY
· ECONOMIES OF SCALE
· LOW RISK
	---STABILITY/LONG TERM VIEW
	    DYNAMISM---
	---COOPERATION & TRUST
	    MARKET DISCIPLINE---
	---TRANSACTION EFFICIENCY
	    MARKET EFFECTIVENESS---
	---CONTRACT FLEXIBILITY
	---ECONOMIES OF SCALE
	    ECONOMIES OF TIME---
	    SPECIALIZATION---
	---DEPENDENCE
	    INDEPENDENCE---
	---SCOPE
		· MARKET CONTROL
		· DYNAMIC ENVIRONMENT
		· LOW MARKET BARRIERS
		· TIME COMPETITION
		· ACCURATE METERING
		· SPOT PRODUCTION
		· SIMPLE RELATIONSHIPS
		· COMMODITY PRODUCTS
		· ECONOMIES OF TIME
		· HIGH RISK

REQUIRE EFFICIENCY	---THICKER INFORMATION FREER INFORMATION--	REQUIRE EFFECTIVENESS

choose to co-opt the asset rather than bid for it in the open marketplace. Whereas unspecialized items pose reduced risk because there are plenty of alternate suppliers in the market, a highly specialized asset may generate nonmarketability problems for either the buyer or seller. The article might not be available to the buyer (because there are not enough of them on the market) or the item might not be marketable by the seller because it is too specific to a particular buyer.

4.2 The Market Organization

In contrast to the vertically integrated organization, the market mechanism is characterized by loosely coupled transactions, arms length bargaining, and spot market transactions (ref 2). Buyers and sellers come together and bargain for the best price. The advantage of the market control mechanism is that the market introduces discipline (a fair market price) on the transactions. The market control mechanism is more dynamic and adaptable to change because the buyers can switch to different suppliers when the environment requires it. This is especially true when dealing with commodity-type products that are widely available .

These types of transactions are efficient for items for which the value can be easily determined. For products with an unclear value, transaction costs can be incurred in trying to determine a fair price. Other transaction costs may involve search costs (finding the goods in the marketplace), contract administration costs, and performance monitoring costs (ensuring contract compliance) (ref 15).

Unfortunately, market failure can occur for complex, uncertain transactions. This is because in such situations a contract cannot adequately specify all possible contingencies. Given the nature of the mechanism, opportunistic behavior may result. Market failure may also result when there are not enough suppliers in the market (such as for specialized assets) to generate adequate competition (ref 9).

4.3 Network Organizations

The network organization works to combine the advantages of vertically integrated structure with the advantages of market control. It is defined as a cluster of business units involved in long-term relationships and coordinated by market mechanisms rather than by layers of middle-management planners and schedulers (References 1 and 2). Essentially it involves independent entities coming together as a team to work on a project(s). These independent business units can exist within the same company (i.e. an internal network) or be separate companies (i.e. an external network). While we use the term 'network organization', there are many related terms such as joint ventures, strategic alliances, value-added partnerships, equity partnerships, hybrid organizations, collaborative research consortia, licensing agreements, repriprocity deals, satellite organizations, and virtual corporations (References 5, 7, and 16).

Because a number of smaller specialized organizations are coming together to temporarily create a larger organization, the network can combine the flexibility advantages of smaller, specialized companies with the advantages of size. While the combined size of the network organization can be large, each of the network members can concentrate on its own specific area of competence. For example, one member may design the product, another may produce it, and a different one may market and distribute it.

The governance mechanism of the network organization is partly market driven. This instills the dynamism and discipline of the market. If one team member is not performing up to par, the other members are motivated to try and help improve that team member's performance or to find a new member. However, since the team relationships are also based on a certain level of trust, information sharing, and cooperation (general characteristics of integrated companies), this tends to increase transaction efficiency and ameliorate the potential transaction costs and market failures associated with market control mechanisms (ref 9).

Because the network is essentially an voluntary adhocracy, each team member shares a common destiny. This is the glue that keeps the team working together and motivates cooperation among the independent entities. If the team intends to work together for any length of time, then each member is motivated not only by its own interest but also in the interest of the organization. This 'clan' or 'repriprocity' governance mechanism (Reference 9) tends to reduce opportunistic behavior. It is closer to a relationship of interdependence than to one of dependence or independence.

It has also been asserted that the information flow among network members is thicker than information exchanged in the marketplace (because members share more intimate data) and that it is freer than information exchanged within an integrated organization (because it is less hostage to internal organization politics) (ref 7).

Of course, network structures can also have disadvantages. If not properly managed, they may incorporate the worst features of the vertically integrated and market structures instead of the best. If a sufficient level of cooperation is not present, then opportunistic behavior may occur. On the other hand, if the network members become too interdependent and integrated, then network entry (or exit) barriers may increase and a decline in market discipline may result.

Other issues related to network structure, management, and operation involve the relative levels of power and influence among the different members, the value of member contributions to the network versus the value they derive, the level of boundary permeability between the units, and the network architecture. All of these issues must be carefully managed and balanced to ensure that the network fosters appropriate member relationships and behavior (refs 14, 2, 7).

5.0   INFORMATION TECHNOLOGY AND NETWORK ORGANIZATIONS

Information and computer technology is a critical enabling technology of network organizations. Because we are talking about independent business units that may be geographically separated, successful coordination of operations requires significant information transfer and cooperation across unit boundaries. Information technology can support these information transfer needs and hence support the integration of individual companies into a network.

Information technology can also be used to reduce transaction costs for such activities as contract administration, performance monitoring, and value computation (Refs 1, 5, 4, 10, 8).

One motivation for establishing network organizations is to develop the flexibility to implement agile manufacturing. This type of manufacturing, as opposed to mass production, requires the ability to closely monitor customer needs and to quickly react accordingly. This monitoring requires sophisticated information technology to collect and process market information. Manufacturing agility is also dependent on information technologies to automate the factory such as Computer Aided Design (CAD), Computer Aided Manufacturing (CAM), Computer Aided Engineering (CAE), and Computer Integrated Manufacturing (CIM).

All of these knowledge collection and processing tools must be closely linked so that the network can react quickly to changes. Information technology allows for the sharing of process, inventory, and market demand data to facilitate streamlined manufacturing operations. A good example is electronic data interchange (EDI).

One area that has not seen information technology support is in network organization relationship management. Since the relationships between firms in the network are important to the health of the overall network organization, it is the position of the authors that this is an area that deserves attention. In line with this contention, a framework for a Decision Support System to support relationship management is provided in the next section.

6.0 DECISION SUPPORT SYSTEM FRAMEWORK FOR NETWORK ORGANIZATION RELATIONS MANAGEMENT

Relationships are critical to network organizations. In order to cooperate without the protection of market type contractual mechanisms (and their inherent transactional inefficiencies), there must be a strong level of trust among the participants. Each member must feel that every other member is contributing to the network in fair proportion to the benefits that are received. Opportunistic behavior or poor performance by one of the members adversely affects the entire network and every other member. Given the critical nature of network relationships, this is an area that should receive careful management attention. In particular, we contend that a DSS could aid in this management task.

The specific purpose of the proposed DSS is to support a decision by the core firm about what to do about a member that has displayed either inappropriate behavior (such as opportunism) or poor performance. Another implicit objective of the DSS is to encourage behaviors that are healthy for the network. That is, behaviors that increase trust and cooperation, a sense of community, interdependence, a long term view, market discipline, a norm of repriprocity, and a feeling of shared ideals and fate.

Given that inappropriate behavior or poor performance has occurred, it is assumed that there are three fundamental alternatives available to the decision maker: to nurture the member; to discipline the member; or to nurture/switch to a competitor. Another course of action could involve some combination of these three alternatives.

A DSS framework to support relationship management is presented in Figure 4. The DSS consists of databases to track member firm activities, a model to compare member firm performance against other potential member firms, and an expert system to provide advice and consultation on how to best manage member firms. Each of the DSS components is discussed below.

Member Performance Database: This database would contain data relevant to the past, current, and estimated future

Figure 4.DSS Framework for Management of Network Relations Management

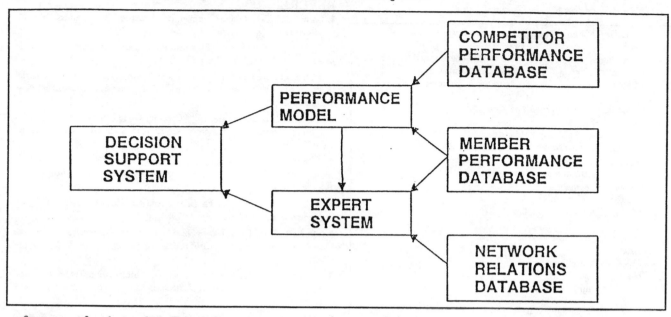

performance of each member. Past and current performance are historical in nature. Projected future performance could be important if a member had invested to upgrade future performance. The member performance database includes objective measures of individual performance such as cost, quality, and responsiveness as well as information related to the team performance of the member. Team performance data would include information about inputs to the network that went beyond membership requirements (such as supporting other members) or inputs that benefitted the network at the expense of the member (such as investing in network specific capabilities). These types of selfless behaviors generate goodwill in the network and should be strongly considered in the overall performance evaluation. As the norm of repriprocity is an important value to networks, these types of behaviors should be rewarded. In fact, it may be the case that even though the individual performance of a member may be poor, the overall value of the member to the network may be high.

Competitor Performance Database: This database would include similar types of data on potential replacements for the members. This information would be needed in order to estimate how well network members are performing relative to similar organizations. However, this data may not be completely available for companies outside the network. This is especially true for information concerning the potential team performance of the company. In this case, an argument might be made for having multiple members with the same or overlapping capabilities in the network. This would provide better access to comparison data as well as provide market competition within the network. It might, however, also reduce the level of cooperation and trust within the network. These tradeoffs would need to be carefully weighed.

Network Relationships Database: This database contains information concerning the types and characteristics of rela-

tionships between the members. This would include information on both formalized (contractual) and informalized (social) relationships among the members in the network. Network cultural and structural information would also be included. Cultural information describes the cultural norms present in the network. For example, does the network place a higher degree of importance on team cooperation or individual member performance? This type of information is important because the success of any actions taken with respect to a network member may be impacted by the network's culture. Structural information portrays the architecture of the organization. An example might be the relative dynamism of the network architecture (internal, stable, dynamic) and how each member fits into the structure.

Performance Model: The purpose of this model is to compare the both the individual and team performance of the network member with other similar companies to arrive at an overall performance measure.

Expert System: The purpose of the expert system is to provide consultation and recommendations concerning the best approach to take to correct the member problem. It would examine the costs and benefits associated with each alternative. The expert system would consider the effects of various actions on the individual member, on the other members in the network, and on the network as a whole. The types of issues that would be considered by the expert system are listed in Table 1.

Decision Support System (DSS): The DSS integrates the databases, performance model, and expert system to provide recommendations to the user for consideration. It also provides an interface to directly access the databases, models, and rule sets in the system.

7.0 SUMMARY

The business environment has changed dramatically over

Table 1. Issues for Expert System Consideration

Alternative: Nurture Member to Improve Performance.
- Costs
  - Training
  - Capital
  - Labor
- Benefits
  - Network Cohesion and Teamwork
  - Avoid Switching Costs
  - Network Reputation

Alternative: Switch to or Nurture Competitor.
- Costs
  - Sunk Costs (Hardware, Relationships)
  - Startup Costs for New Member (Training, Relationships)
  - Contractual Costs
  - Network Cohesion and Teamwork
  - Network Reputation
- Benefits
  - Enforces Network Discipline

Alternative: Discipline Member
- Costs
  - Member Resentment
- Benefits
  - Avoid Nurturing or Switching Costs
  - Enforces Network Discipline

Mitigating Issues to Be Considered:
- Extent of Member Problem
- Past and Potential Future Performance
- Degree of Member Specificity
- Availability of Competent Competitors
- Level of Network Integration
- Network Architecture (Integrated, Stable, Dynamic)
- Has Problem Been Adequately Communicated to Member?
- Has Member Had Opportunity to Fix Problem?
- Reason for Problem
- Network Cultural Impacts
- Attitude and Commitment of Member to Fix Problem
- Attitude of Other Members
- Overall Value of Member to Network

the last two decades. The marketplace has become global and a lot more competitive. Technology is advancing at an ever-increasing pace and product cycle times have decreased dramatically. In order to survive in this environment, companies must adapt their structures and processes to provide tailored products quickly to the marketplace. This paper advocates leveraging information technology to support cooperative project teams (network organizations).

Relationship management is important to networks. This paper has presented a framework for a DSS design to support this activity. Such a system would support judgements about what actions to take to correct inappropriate or poor performance by a network member.

REFERENCES

1. Snow, C., Miles, R., and Coleman, H. "Managing 21st Century Network Organizations," *Organizational Dynamics*, pp. 5-20.

2. Thorelli, H. "Networks: Between Markets and Hierarchies," *Strategic Management Journal*, Vol 7, pp. 37-51.

3. Miles, R. "Adapting Technology and Competition: A New Industrial relations System for the 21st Century," *California Management Review*, Winter 1989, pp. 9-28.

4. Johnston, H. and Vitale, M. "Creating Competitive Advantage with Interorganizational Information Systems," *MIS Quarterly*, June 1988, pp. 153-165.

5. Johnston, R. and Lawrence, P. "Beyond Vertical Integration - the Rise of the Value-Adding Partnership," *Harvard Business Review*, July-August 1988, pp. 94-101.

6. Miles, R. and Snow, C. "Fit, Failure And The Hall of Fame," *California Management Review* (26:3), Spring 1984, pp. 10-28.

7. Powell, W. "Hybrid Organizational Arrangements: New Form or Transitional Development," *California Management Review*, Fall 1987, pp. 67-87.

8. Applegate, L., Cash, J., and Mills, D. "Information Technology and Tomorrow's Manager," *Harvard Business Review*, November-December 1988, pp. 128-136.

9. Ouchi, W. "Markets, Bureaucracies, and Clans," *Administrative Science Quarterly*, March 1980, pp. 129-141.

10. Bakos, J. "Information Links and Electronic Marketplaces: The Role of Interorganizational Information Systems in Vertical Markets," *JMIS* (8:2), Fall 1991, pp 31-52.

11. Hammer, M. "Reengineering Work: Don't Automate, Obliterate," *Harvard Business Review*, July-August 1990, pp. 104-112.

12. Knapp, T. "Hierarchies and Control: A New Interpretation and Reevaluation of Oliver Williamson's 'Markets and Hierarchies' Story," *The Sociological Quarterly* (30:3), pp. 425-440.

13. Drucker, P. "The Coming of the New Organization," *Harvard Business Review*, January-February 1988, pp. 45-53.

14. Borys, B. and Jemison, D. "Hybrid Arrangements as Strategic Alliances: Theoretical Issues in Organizational Combinations," *Academy of Management Review* (14:2), pp. 234-249.

15. Williamson, O. "The Economics of Organization: The Transaction Cost Approach," *American Journal of Sociology* (87:3), pp. 548-577.

16. Davidow W. and Malone, M. *The Virtual Corporation*. New York: HarperCollins, 1992.

17. Peters, T. *Liberation Management*. New York: Alfred A. Knopf, 1992.

18. Coy, P. "How Do You Build an Information Highway," *Business Week*, 16 Sept 1991, p. 112.

19. Wiggenhorn, W. "Motorola, U: When Training Becomes an Education," *Harvard Business Review*, July-August 1990, pp. 77-78.

20. Willett, H. "What Drives Quality at Intel?" *Electronic Business*, 7 October 1991, pp. 29-36.

21. Dumaine, B. "The Bureaucracy Busters," *Fortune*, 17 June 1991, P. 46.

22. Reich, R. "Who is Them?," *Harvard Business Review*, March-April 1991, pp. 77-88.

23. Reich, R. "Who is Us?," *Harvard Business Review*, January-February, pp. 53-64.

A Framework for Researching the Role of Information Technology Enabled Teamwork in Managing Organizational Change

Juha Pärnistö
Turku School of Economics and Business Administration
Institute of Information Systems
Turku, Finland

ABSTRACT

Business organizations are trying to develop their structures towards increased flexibility in order to be able to cope with changes in business environments. Effective work groups, teams, provide possibilities to flexibility and distribution of knowledge in organizations. Information and communications technology has an important enabling role in teamwork. Work in teams is mainly based on communication and cooperation. Managing work flows based on cooperative organization implies the transformation of traditional functional organizations, which prevail among large companies. Information technology should be rethought to support this shift.

A research framework for the evaluation of teamwork in managing organizational changes is constructed for evaluating the effectiveness of teamwork in change processes. The strategic planning perspective in managing teamwork will also be examined. The value-adding activity chains called business processes and major changes in these processes should be defined in business strategy. Team members' values and mental models, the organizational environment, and the technology are also supposed to have a significant effect on team's performance.

1. INTRODUCTION

The changes in business environment have been and will be fast. Companies move quickly in and out of products, markets and sometimes even entire businesses [25]. In such an environment the essence of strategy is not the structure of a company's products and markets but the dynamics of its behavior. Companies should identify their unique capabilities which separate them from their competitors. Dynamic strategies and corporate renewal have become critical for success [23]. Organizational structures should provide flexibility and innovativeness. The knowledge organizations are becoming flattened networks in which the expertise and knowledge are distributed [28]. This is a great challenge to management. The coordination of distributed organizations requires effective management processes and communication tools.

Business process reengineering (BPR) has become an important and widening research area in this decade. The main contents of business process reengineering is identifying main business processes of an organization and redesigning them in order to achieve improved effectiveness and efficiency.

Leavitt and Whisler suggested in the 1950s that in the future information technology would lead to a general restructuring of the organization, ultimately eliminating middle management [15]. Their forecast has not come true, but we are dealing with the same problems today. Lawrence and Lorsch found that successful companies differentiated themselves into suborganizations to allow accumulation of expertise and simpler management processes driven by shared goals and objectives [14]. Galbraith expanded this subject and wrote about managing interaction through people-oriented mechanisms [6]. He also introduced the concept of computer-based information systems as a vertical integrator within the firm. Today this approach appears incomplete [20]. Information technology serves increasingly as a tool for both horizontal and vertical integration.

The articles mentioned above describe the evolution of process thinking in organizations. Of course process concept is not mentioned in all these articles but the same basic thinking lies in the background. Research of work processes and organizational structures has been an important aspect for a long time. But the new opportunities provided by information technology offer also new perspectives to academic research [22].

2. BUSINESS PROCESS REDESIGN AS AN APPROACH TO ORGANIZATIONAL CHANGE

Many organizations have already reengineered their business processes. The industrial manufacturing processes are optimized and effective. The productivity and effectiveness are on a high level. But the effectiveness of management processes is not at the same level. Information management could be more effective and work flows could be more simple and more productive. So far, the use of information technology (IT) has not been very intensive in designing work flows. There has not been tools for group support, the existing tools have been expensive and the technological infrastructure has not been ready for developed productivity tools. The development of microcomputer networks has enabled the distributed information processing. There are also many new technological tools to support and enable the redesign of information processes. Investments in information technology have not always been as successful as expected in office environments, because in many cases companies tend to use technology to mechanize old ways of doing business [10]. Many job designs, control mechanisms and organizational structures came of age in a different competitive environment and before the advent of the computer. Electronic mail, group decision support applications, work flow management products and negotiation tools have the potential to improve the effectiveness of management processes in distributed environments.

The complexity of business environment forces people to work together more effectively. Individuals can not cope with the complexity as well as teams, because their competence is more restricted [12]. In order to innovate, solve problems and work effectively high-levels of group collaboration and interaction are required. Effective work groups are called teams. Katzenbach and Smith define team as follows [11]:

"A team is a small number of people with complementary skills who are committed to a common purpose, set of performance goals, and approach for which they hold themselves mutually accountable."

A team is not just a group of people working together. Teams usually have shared leadership roles and a common purpose. Team work encourages open-ended discussion and active problem-solving meetings. Effective teams develop commitment and a good basis for learning. It should be noted that a team is not necessarily a group of people working in the same place or on the same level in the organization. Team members may be distributed widely in the organization.

The theoretical and empirical research in the area of managing changes, structural problems of organizations and the effectiveness of teamwork is very important and lively at the moment. The significance of the research increasing knowledge about these topics is very useful to business managers as well as academic researchers [1]. The competitive advantage is more and more based on managing core processes effectively. These processes are dynamic and small structural changes happen all the time. Every now and then major changes (a completed redesign) is required to keep the processes competitive and effective.

According to Grover et al. there are three research streams that deal with the business reengineering phenomenon [8]. The research on the relationship between IT and the organization focuses on IT's impacts on human actions and institutional properties of organizations. The integration between corporate planning and IT planning (strategic planning for IT) is another important research area. Organizational innovation is the third research stream. This study has elements from all these streams. Strategic planning is required to guide the changes. The impacts of IT must be understood in wide organizational context in order to implement the changes and organizational innovation is required to maintain the flexibility and effectiveness of action.

3. MODELING THE TEAMWORK IN BPR EFFORTS

3.1 Organizational changes: a systems approach

Business process redesign is often described as a revolutionary change [9]. In systems theory change means transforming a system from one state to another. This transformation is often described with the freezing - change - unfreezing model. For some reason the system, which is in a state of equilibrium (in a stable state) moves into a state of non-equilibrium [24]. This change is irreversible; the system will not return to the original state. As a result of the change the system moves to a new state of equilibrium. Stacey suggests that the change is actually continuing. Some changes are though more far-reaching and significant than others. In the traditional management literature, the state of equilibrium is desirable. This is not necessarily true. There is evidence that innovativeness and creativity occur in the state of non-equilibrium. Stable organizations try to maintain the status quo and are therefore inflexible.

According to Lundeberg, problems and issues can be perceived on different levels of abstraction [18]. Different values and perceptions cause different behavior. Conflicts and misinterpretations are usual in organizational change situations. Time has an important role in changes. The impacts of change are often unpredictable. Managers must cope with uncertainty and incomplete information. Stacey has identified three types of changes [24]. *Closed changes* are highly predictable. They have influences only in a near future or they happen in closed systems. *Contained changes* are much similar to closed changes, but their impacts are known only probabilistically (there are some factors causing uncertainty). *Open-ended changes* are the most "difficult" type. The impacts of open-ended changes can not be predicted. This does not mean that nothing can be said about the impacts, but the system has so many possible states that the exact evaluation is impossible. Open-ended changes are becoming more and more usual in business world.

Change was defined as a transformation in organizational system. According to systems theory (soft systems theory) this system consists of parts that in some way are related to each other. Here the word "system" means the same as human activity system in soft systems methodology [2,3]. It should not be confused with information system. Systems as such do not exist in reality. Only different perceptions about them exist. The system has also other properties (emergent properties) than the sum of the properties of the parts. These are the basic concepts of human activity systems. The change in human activity system can be understood as a transformation process. The input (information, resources, task) is transformed into output (for example plan, recommendations, a refined document). This flow of value-adding activities can be managed and controlled through modern information technology applications. Systems have also objectives or goals. In organizations the objectives are defined in business mission and business strategy. Grover et al. have represented a framework for BPR planning and its connections to strategic planning [8].

This framework describes BPR as an integrated part of corporate planning. It is based on IS strategy and business strategy. Many researchers have identified the implementation phase to be a very difficult for organizations [5,7]. The

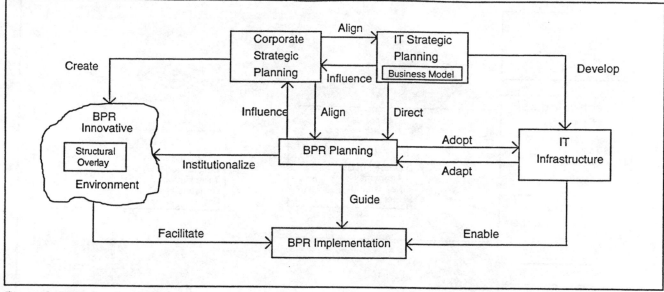

Figure 1. BPR planning framework

significance of BPR could be in structuring the implementation phase. IS strategy, for example, is usually only a blueprint for IS planning. It is not supposed to be a very precise plan, but a directing and long-run plan. The business strategy has a strong influence on these plans. Key business activities and core processes must be identified in business strategy. BPR planning is based on strategic planning and translates the high level plans into specific implementation guidelines. The objective of BPR implementation is to actually change business processes within the parameters defined by BPR planning and the existing IT infrastructure.

Grover et al. define the BPR innovative environment part of their model as an environment that is conducive to organizational change on a continuous basis. It is created as a result of strategic planning in the form of top management support or result of specific BPR planning in which organizational groups are created to identify BPR opportunities [8].

3.2 Some previous models of teamwork

The nature and effectiveness of teamwork has been an important research object in social psychology and organization theory. Kurt Lewin was one of the pioneers of group process research [16,17]. Taylor and Bowers stated that the organization is a structure of groups linked together through which work flows [27]. According to McGrath systems theory provides a framework for accommodating the variables of substantive theories of group behavior [19]. This approach is adopted in this study also.

Dennis et al. have developed a model for researching the effectiveness of IT to support meetings. Figure 2 displays their model [4]. They identified several key elements that affect the meeting situation. However, this framework is restricted to a rather narrow situation. The meaning of the process is to make a decision. The model is restricted to fit for this purpose only. For example Schäl and Zeller define teamwork in a larger context [21]. They have defined three dimension of coopera-

tion in teamwork. Individuals need to *coordinate* their actions with those of others to perform the work processes. Coordination aims to synchronize persons, actions and the consistency of individual actions with respect to the whole process. *Collaboration* refers to individuals working together to achieve a certain goal. Individuals must share knowledge and skills and they must have a common understanding of the goal. *Codecision* means working together in order to make a decision. Each of these forms of cooperation requires support from information and communications technology.

Larson and LaFasto have researched the effectiveness of teamwork [13]. They identified eight dimensions that affect the effectiveness. These are:
- clear, elevating goal
- results-driven structure
- competent team members
- collaborative climate
- unified commitment
- standards of excellence
- external support and recognition
- principled leadership

Based on these factors and the framework in figure 2, Kutsko and Smith developed a new framework in order to examine the effectiveness of teamwork in distributed environments [12]. This framework is represented in figure 3. The eight dimensions of effective teams are included in this model. The members of the teams are not supposed to work within physical proximity of one another, but with decentralized, flattened organizations.

The framework has six components: task, technological support, group, structure, process and outcome. A group performs a task and uses technological support for coordination and communication. Instead of using the term context, Kutsko and Smith use the word structure, because actually all the components belong to the context. Both these terms remain rather unclear, because they are not explicitly defined.

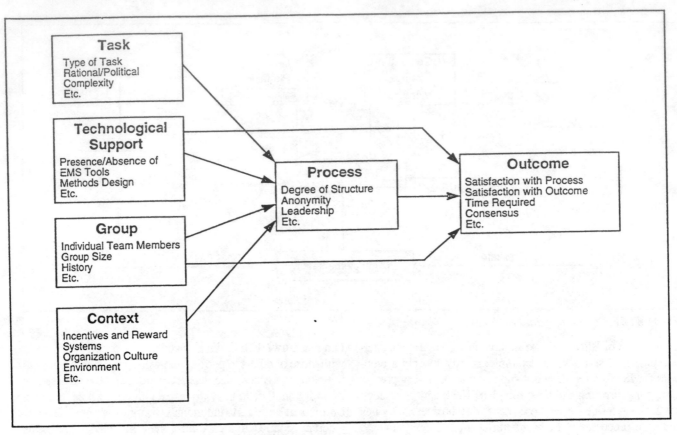

Figure 2. The factors affecting the meeting situation.

Kutsko and Smith refer to Larson and LaFasto research saying that structure includes four of their dimensions. However, this does not clarify the real meaning of structure. Obviously the structure does not have the traditional meaning of organizational or group structure (for example hierarchy, matrix or network). The components mentioned in the model could describe any of these organizational forms. The process refers to work flow of the group. It is the series of activities, which the group performs in order to achieve the goal. The outcome then is the result of the work.

3.3 Teams in organizational change processes: the research framework

The models by Kutsko and Smith as well as Dennis et al. form the basis for this study. These models must, however, be modified in order to fit them into the theoretical background of this study. The modified research framework is represented in figure 4.

First of all, the team is the central research object in this study. Other components of the model are mainly defined by using the team concept. That is why other components are depicted inside the team component. Business and IT strategies define the purpose for the team. The business process may be defined by the team or by the strategy (in the team assignment). Business process defines the target of change. The business process should be defined broadly. It may be complicated and unstructured or very simple and structured (normal customer order).

The technology component includes information systems supporting teamwork (for example e-mail, electronic meetings, work flow management, document management). The communications technology may also work as a platform for developed applications and integrated information management. The integration of telephone and fax systems to organizations' information architecture is becoming more important and it has also a significant influence on teamwork.

Values and mental model of the team has a significant impact on teamwork. The team's perceptions about its own work, decision making and position in the organization create the circumstances in which the team will succeed or fail.

Teams are not closed systems. The environment should provide support to teamwork in the form of open organization culture and cooperation with other teams. Providing the external support is mainly the management's task.

The team's task is to make a change happen. The outcomes of the change may vary depending on the nature of business process and change itself. Tapscott and Caston have identified several levels of impacts that may result from the change process [26]. The team approach and redesign of processes is only the first step towards integrated systems that have the power to transform organization. The highest level is interenterprise computing, which means using IT not only for internal systems but also in external relationships. Information systems are extending the reach of organizations

outward to link enterprises with their suppliers, distribution channels and consumers. Such systems can for example

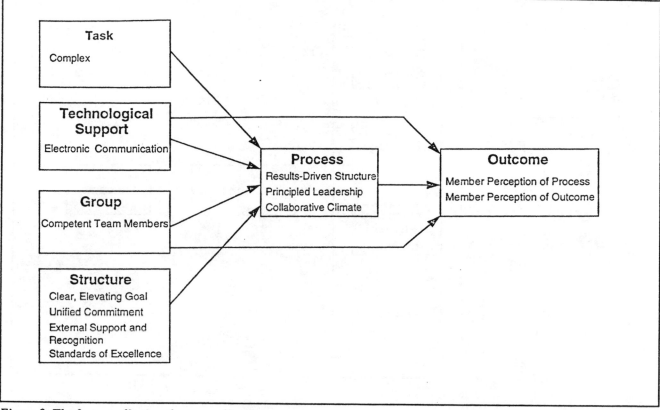

Figure 3. The factors affecting the team effectiveness

strengthen customer loyalty, lock out competitors, speed up distribution of goods and customer service.

Measuring the outcomes of the change process must include both quantitative measures like the cost benefits and qualitative measures like the team members' different perceptions about the change process and process outcomes.

4. THE CASE STUDY

The empirical research will be based on a case study. ICL Data will be the case company. ICL Data is a part of the international ICL corporation, which is a major European software and hardware manufacturer and vendor. Information systems for office environments are the main products of ICL Data. The company has a long experience on group technology and has developed a groupware product called TeamOffice. The main purpose of the TeamOffice system is to increase the productivity of work processes in offices and to improve and facilitate the communication in teams. TeamOffice includes several tools for communication and information management:

- -TeamMail, electronic mail and information carrier
- -TeamForum, electronic conferencing and bulletin boards
- -TeamFlow, task organizer and case routing for work flow management
- -TeamLibrary, document management and sharing
- -TeamCalendar, resource management and scheduling

TeamOffice requires a microcomputer network and a network management system like Novell Netware or Windows NT. Gateway links to several mainframe environments are also available. Application development based on TeamOffice services is also possible. The applications can be designed by using for example Lotus Notes or SQL query generators.

In the first phase TeamOffice will be applied in ICL's own reporting processes. The customer service process will be redesigned by using TeamOffice applications, improving phone and fax services and introducing process thinking in local sales units. The customer service is a very important process to ICL, because the customers are mainly large organizations and they buy complicated service packages. These packages include user training, consultation, expert services, hardware, and software products. A lot of work by several people is required in order to be able to offer these packages to customers. The implementation of office systems requires often different solutions because of different technical solutions in customer organizations.

Several functional units of ICL Data (for example sales, technical support, and systems planning) are usually involved in the customer service process. The coordination of the process requires effective information management and communication between these units. ICL has a lot of experience in developing teamwork. The use of information technology in ICL's internal systems is very intensive and they are very anxious to develop the TeamOffice product further.

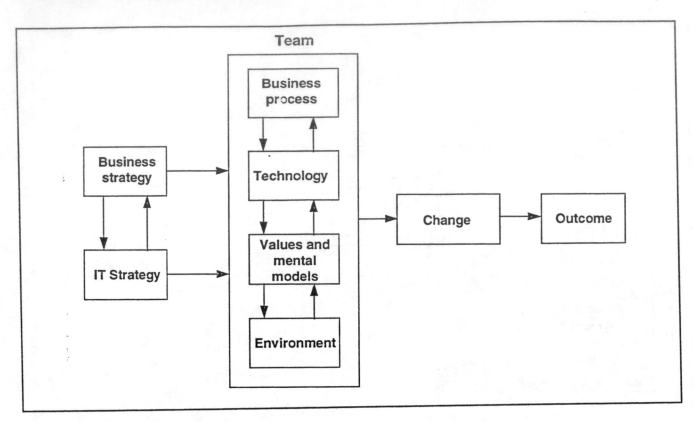

Figure 4. The research framework

REFERENCES

[1] Benjamin, Robert I. - Levinson, Eliot (1993) A Framework for Managing IT-Enabled Change. *Sloan Management Review*, Vol. 34, No. 4, 23-33.

[2] Checkland, Peter - Scholes, Jim (1990) *Soft Systems Methodology in Action*. Wiley.

[3] Checkland, Peter (1981) *Systems Thinking, Systems Practice*. Wiley.

[4] Dennis, A. R. - George, J. F. - Jessup, L. M. - Nunamaker, J. F. Jr. - Vogel, D. (1988) Information Technology to Support Electronic Meetings. *MIS Quarterly*, Vol. 12, No. 4, 591-624.

[5] Earl, Michael J. (1993) Experiences in Strategic Information Systems Planning. *MIS Quarterly*, Vol. 17, No. 1, 1-24.

[6] Galbraith, J. (1977) *Organization Design*. Addison-Wesley.

[7] Galliers, Robert D. (1987) Information Systems Planning in the United Kingdom and Australia - a comparison of current practice. *Oxford Surveys in Information Technology*, Vol. 4, 223-255.

[8] Grover, V. - Teng, J. T. C. - Fiedler, K. D. (1993) Information Technology Enabled Business Process Redesign: An Integrated Planning Framework. *Omega*, Vol. 21, No. 4, 433-447.

[9] Hammer, Michael - Champy, James (1993) *Re-engineering the Corporation. A Manifesto for Business Revolution*. Harper Business, New York.

[10] Hammer, Michael (1990) Reengineering Work: Don't Automate, Obliterate. *Harvard Business Review*, Vol. 68, No. 4, July-August 1990, 104-112.

[11] Katzenbach, Jon R. - Smith, Douglas K. (1993) *The Wisdom of Teams: Creating the High-Performance Organization*. Harvard Business School Press.

[12] Kutsko, Jackie - Smith, Jill Y. (1991) Effectiveness measures for distributed teams using electronic meeting technology: the Larson/LaFasto instrument. *Proceedings of the Twenty-Fourth Annual Hawaii International Conference on System Sciences*, Vol. 4, 458-470.

[13] Larson, Carl E. - LaFasto, Frank M. J. (1989) *Teamwork. What must go right/What can go wrong*. Sage Publications.

[14] Lawrence, P. R. - Lorsch, J. W. (1967) *Organization and Environment: Managing Differentiation and Integration*. Irwin.

[15] Leavitt, H. J. - Whisler, T. L. (1958) Management in the 1980s. *Harvard Business Review*, November-December 1958, 41-48.

[16] Lewin, K. (1951) Problems of research in social psychology. In: D. Cartwright (ed.) *Field theory in social science:* Selected papers by Kurt Lewin. Harper & Row, New York.

[17] Lewin, K. (1943) Forces behind food habits and methods of change. *Bulletin of the National Research Council*, 108, 35-65.

[18] Lundeberg, Mats (1993) *Handling Change Processes*. Studentlitteratur, Lund.

[19] McGrath, J. E. (1984) *Groups: Interaction and performance*. Prentice-Hall.

[20] Rockart, John F. - Short, James E. (1989) IT in the 1990s: Managing Organizational Interdependence. *Sloan Management Review*, Vol. 30, No. 2, 7-18.

[21] Schäl, Thomas - Zeller, Buni (1991) Design Principles for Cooperative Office Support Systems in Distributed Process Management. In: A. A. Verrijn-Stuart - H. G. Sol - P. Hammerley (eds.) *Support Functionality in the Office Environment*. Proceedings of the IFIP TC8/WG8.3/WG8.4 Working Conference on Support Functionality in the Office Environment, 85-101. Canterbury Kent, September 1991. North-Holland.

[22] Smith, H. A. - McKeen, J. D. (1993) Re-engineering the Corporation: Where Does IS Fit In? *Proceedings of the Twenty-Sixth Annual Hawaii Conference on System Sciences*, Vol. 3, 120-126.

[23] Stacey, Ralph D. (1992) *Managing Chaos. Dynamic Business Strategies in an Unpredictable World*. Kogan Page.

[24] Stacey, Ralph D. (1991) *The Chaos Frontier. Creative strategic control for business*. Butterworth-Heinemann.

[25] Stalk, George - Evans, Philip - Shulman, Lawrence E. (1992) Competing on Capabilities: The New Rules of Corporate Strategy. *Harvard Business Review*, Vol. 70, No. 2, 57-69.

[26] Tapscott, Don - Caston, Art (1993) *Paradigm Shift. The New Promise of Information Technology*. McGraw-Hill, New York.

[27] Taylor, J. C. - Bowers, D. G. (1972) *Survey of Organizations: A Machine-scored standardized questionnaire instrument*. Ann Arbor, University of Michigan.

[28] Zuboff, S. (1988) *In the Age of the Smart Machine. The Future of Work and Power*. Basic Books, New York.

System Development Methodologies: Responding to a Changing Environment

Nancy L. Russo
Northern Illinois University

Judy L. Wynekoop
University of Texas, San Antonio

Executive Abstract

INTRODUCTION

Changes in organizational structures, competitive environments, technologies and economies are altering both the types of computer-based information systems that are developed and the process by which these systems are developed. Change itself is not new to the systems development arena. However, the pace and the impact of changes are accelerating, making it both more difficult and more crucial for development methods to respond to these changes.

Technological advances and trends such as client-server architectures, graphical user interfaces, and distributed systems have changed the nature of the systems that are developed. Technologies such as fourth generation languages, application generators, and local area networks have changed the way systems can be developed, facilitating rapid, iterative, user-centered development. Economic pressures have forced organizations to look for less expensive computing alternatives, which has resulted in a change in focus from mainframe environments to networks of microcomputers. Based on this type of platform, the types of systems developed are less likely to require large-scale, long-term development projects, and more likely to be smaller, short-term, incremental types of projects. Increased competitiveness and globalization have had an impact on the structure of today's organizations. The more formal, rigid, hierarchical structures of the past are being supplanted with more fluid, hybrid structures. To assist organizations in meeting the needs of these changing structures, information systems, and the methods for developing them, must also be adaptive and flexible.

Based on these changes in the system development environment, we would expect to see fundamental changes taking place in the development technologies -- methodologies, tools, and techniques -- used to support the development process. However, there is little evidence to indicate that this is happening.

In this paper the research issues and methods which have been used in studying system development methodologies are examined and classified according to research purpose and type. This analysis highlights areas which need to be examined and identifies research methods which may be of particular use in understanding the changes taking place in system development and in the technologies supporting it.

SYSTEM DEVELOPMENT METHODOLOGY RESEARCH

Thirty research papers from various sources were examined. This group of papers represents an initial assessment of the state of the field, and is not assumed to be an exhaustive sample. Each paper was classified based on the research method used and the purpose (explicit or implied) of the research. The research method categories used were case study, field research (field studies and field experiments), action research, laboratory experiment, survey, and normative. Three categories of research purpose were used in this analysis. The first group, *understand/describe*, includes studies which define or describe the features of particular methodologies or methodologies in general. Also included in this category are frameworks for the understanding or comparison of methodologies. The second category, *create/ improve*, includes research that describes the construction of a new methodology or discusses requirements for improving existing methodologies. The third category, *evaluate*, is made up of studies which assess or evaluate the usefulness or impact of one or more methodologies. Frameworks which evaluate methodologies for the purpose of selection are also included in this category.

Seventeen of the thirty papers examined were normative in nature; that is, they described a particular methodology or group of methodologies based on the authors' insights, experience, or opinion. Five of the papers used surveys to collect data, and four used laboratory experiments. Two of the papers were case studies and two were action research.

Exactly half of the papers were placed in the *understand/ describe* category. The vast majority of these (eleven out of fifteen) were normative writings. Only one case study and three surveys were found in this category. Because this category deals with description, we would expect to see normative studies here; however, the lack of research in other categories indicates that our knowledge of development methodologies comes primarily from individuals' opinions and experiences, not from true studies of methodologies in use.

Four studies were classified in the *create/improve* category. All of these papers were essentially normative in nature. Eleven papers *evaluated* methodologies directly or presented frameworks for methodology evaluation. Only three studies actually attempted to evaluate methodology use in real settings (a case study and two action research studies). Surprisingly, no field studies were found in this group. Methodologies, or parts of methodologies, were compared in laboratory experiments in four of the papers, and surveys were used to evaluate methodologies in two of the papers.

CONCLUSION

What can we learn from this type of categorization of research? We see an over-reliance on normative studies, and a paucity of field research. Only four studies out of thirty were conducted in real world settings. This means that our knowledge of how information systems are developed and our understanding of the role and impact of methodologies is derived from the opinions and experience of a few individuals, rather than from a large base of empirical data. If we continue along the same path, how can we expect to meet the challenges of changing technologies, organizations, and economies? If we are to develop methodologies which meet the needs of current system development environments, we must utilize research methods which can more effectively provide information and understanding regarding the process of system development today. To understand the historical and contextual influences on the use/non-use of methodologies, longitudinal field research, including case studies and action research, is necessary. Broad-based surveys are needed to identify the changes taking place in development environments, and field work is necessary to understand how these changes affect the development process. Systematic evaluations of methodologies in use under realistic conditions are needed to understand the effectiveness of existing methodologies and to determine the requirements for future methodologies.

An Expert Multi-Agent Negotiation Support Tool for Electronic Meeting Systems

Ashraf I. Shirani, Ph.D.
Hofstra University
Hempstead, N.Y.
and
Milam W. Aiken, Ph.D.
University of Mississippi
University, MS

ABSTRACT

Research, development, and use of electronic meeting systems (EMSs), group decision support systems (GDSSs), and computer supported cooperative work (CSCW) has steadily been increasing in recent years. A number of studies have documented benefits of these systems to structure and support task and meeting process, as well as foster communication, idea generation, collaboration, problem solving, and decision making. Negotiation and resolution of conflicts in groups, though originally envisaged as a potential application of EMSs, has noticeably lagged behind.

This paper describes the framework and design philosophy of an automated negotiation support tool to work in conjunction with a group decision support system, *GroupForum*, developed at the University of Mississippi. The multi-agent negotiation support (MANS) tool is in effect an intelligent mediation facilitator which may be used by human meeting facilitators to plan and conduct multi-party negotiations.

BACKGROUND

Group decision support systems (GDSSs) and electronic meeting systems (EMS) provide automated support of group work. One of the most comprehensive definitions of a GDSS by Dennis et al. [10] may have set the standard for support and tools that one may expect from a GDSS. The tools thus envisaged included those to support group communication, planning, idea generation, problem solving, issue discussion, negotiation, conflict resolution, systems analysis and design, and collaborative group activities such as document preparation and sharing. The tool described in this paper is meant to provide negotiation support, working in conjunction with *GroupForum*, a GDSS developed at the University of Mississippi.

In order to develop intelligent agents for negotiation support, one must carefully study the role and use of heuristics by human negotiation facilitators. A large body of research offers insights into how agreements are affected by intervention of a third party, the anticipation of such intervention, and the kind of intervention (e.g., [17, 18, 20, 21, 23]). A third party may, for example, act as a mediator and provide a mechanism for negotiators to make concessions without loss of face; this kind of role is often effective even if the third party has a very passive role [17]. Third party may also intervene as an arbitrator by imposing a solution. Other third party intervention techniques that may facilitate an agreement include: increased inter-party communication; negotiating all issues at once rather than one at a time; and methods of identifying underlying issues [20]. Osgood's GRIT model [19] suggests that one way out of deadlocked negotiations may be that one party initiate a small concession and others will most often reciprocate. Given such insights into possible negotiation facilitator's role, an intelligent tool may be built to emulate such a role. The multi-agent negotiation support (MANS) tool described in this paper is an attempt in that direction. MANS is designed to act as a third-party and may also be used by electronic meeting facilitators as their assistant in negotiation deliberations.

SYSTEM OVERVIEW

MANS design incorporates three main components which provide negotiation support for planning, communication, and mediation.

Planning: Preparation, prior to actual negotiation using a GDSS, is crucial in carrying out a successful negotiation session. Ordinarily, meeting facilitators must obtain necessary information on all the negotiation-related issues, negotiators' background and their possible positions and strategies, various alternatives available for the issue on hand, and approximate cost and benefits to various negotiators for different alternatives. MANS provides help in the form of templates to record and store such information. The system uses the templates during a negotiation session.

Communication: MANS supports communication at three levels, enabling a team or a subset of negotiators to deliberate privately or join a public discussion. *Level One - Public Forum:* Public Forum is a discussion and brainstorming mode open to all the participants in a meeting. *Level Two - Team Forum:* In this connectivity mode, members of one negotiating team can engage in discussion without anyone else having access to their deliberations. *Level Three - Negotiators' Forum:* This communication mode connects two or more team leaders/negotiators. Negotiators may instantly switch among all three modes with the push of a key, whereas other participants may switch between Public and Team Forum modes only.

Mediation: The mediation support provided by MANS uses repetitive reformulation of alternatives and gradual consensus building strategies to facilitate an agreement. It dynamically monitors the meeting process and displays appropriate messages, targeted to selected negotiators, or to all participants, as necessary.

CONCLUSION

Very little research in GDSSs has progressed beyond the "surface level". That is, as yet the GDSS technology does not provide effective integration of database, model base, and application programs with GDSSs so users could access data and models to support decision making [7, 12]. The research presented in this paper is an attempt to develop such a "deeper level" GDSS capability. Further research and development will involve empirical tests of the MANS tool. Also, since *GroupForum* already incorporates multilingual communication support, a multilingual negotiation support tool should be another logical step toward its continued evolution as a comprehensive decision support facility.

For references/copy of the full paper, contact Ashraf Shirani, Department of BCIS/QM, Hofstra University, Hempstead, NY 11550.

Hypermedia for Learning -

Improving the Current Methodology

Alok Srivastava, Randy Meinert
Department of Decision Sciences
Georgia State University
(404) 651-4000

Executive Abstract

Computer technology is being used increasingly for as an educational tool in scholastic settings from the elementary level to the college level, and beyond college to specialty areas. For learning, computers have so far taken on one of two roles: they are either used as proxies to provide experiences for the learner in virtual environments, allowing he/she to experiment with concepts that have been taught by an instructor, or they take on the role of instructor to provide the delivery of information.

It is in this second role that hypertext and hypermedia have found some favor. The appeal of hypertext is two-fold. First, it has potential to provide to the user access to potentially large amounts of information. Second, it permits the user to gain access to the information in the order that is based on the user's needs, which sets it apart from traditional computer-based instruction. The combination of these two enhancements to computer-based information delivery has made hypertext the focus much research for computer-based learning environments.

Hypertext is the non-sequential delivery of text. A text need not be scanned linearly, but rather, through links placed within the body of text, may be scanned in one of many arrangements. The links may, or may not be, activated by the user depending on his/her requirements. Each user of the text may therefore follow a different path through the text. Functionally, links available to the user are represented on the computer screen by words or phrases that are differentiated from the rest of the text by color, typeface, or some other flag. The user launches to a new location in the text by, for example, clicking on the flagged word or phrase with a pointing device like a mouse. Hypermedia is an extension of hypertext: the non-sequential access to media other than text, such as still pictures, video, and voice--all now deliverable via the computer.

The nature of hypertext is two-fold. The first and most apparent aspect of hypertext is its look-and-feel to the user. In a hypertext environment, the user has the ability to go directly to a location of interest by activating some form of trigger. Furthermore, the triggering devices are presented in many forms, and can be embedded into text, graphics, charts, lists, etc. for ease of access and to provide contextual information so that the user does not become disoriented. The other aspect of hypertext, which is not necessarily apparent to the user, is its potential for making large quantities of information accessible dynamically. Documents of any size may have any number of embedded links accessible in any arrangement. Combined, these two aspects of hypertext make it powerful for the delivery of information.

The characteristics of hypertext have lead it to be used both in industry and academia. A hypertext information management system developed at the University of Kent at Canterbury is now in use at ICL--a computer and printer hardware manufacturer. The system was conceived to address the problems of a diagnostician while researching answers to phone-in customer problems. Numerous other industrial applications of hypertext are mentioned in the literature many of which address similar problems of accessing large quantities of textual data in an on-line setting. In addition to the employment of hypertext to information intensive environments, there is a thrust of research into the use of hypertext for computer learning environments.

The advantage of hypertext's application to computer-assisted instruction is less from the perspective of hypertext's facility with large amounts of unstructured textual information, but rather its perceived advantage to allow the learner flexibility in the learning process. Several computer "courses" using one of hypertext environment have already been created, tested and reviewed in the literature.

- The Dublin City University created a hypertextual introductory course on databases which consists of the equivalent of 40 lectures for use with third-year undergraduate students.
- Five iterations of tutorial on a state-of-the-art video recorder was created using HyperCard at the University of Idaho for the purpose of evaluating the utility of providing structure and maps to the user.
- Cornell University's Interactive Multimedia Group developed a system to treat the subject matter of the influence of insects on human culture.
- An increasingly well known hypertext project is that of the Perseus Project on classical Greek civilization--a collaborative undertaking based at Harvard University.

An attraction to the use of hypertext in learning environments is the versatility it potentially provides. Earlier iterations of Computer Assisted Instruction have most often been structured, linearly-displayed "courses." The flexibility of hypertext applications extends them also to those users with some degree of domain knowledge who seek specific content or details.

From the studies performed, hypertext learning environments beckon to three levels of users.

- On the most basic level, the user is one who has little or no domain knowledge in the subject matter and seeks simply to learn about it.
- The second level of user is one who has some intermediate level of domain knowledge and who accesses the program with one or several specific intentions.
- At the third level, the hypertext program ceases to be a restricted to a "course" framework, but rather becomes a research tool for those with significant knowledge in a domain related to the subject matter represented in the program.

Each of the hypertext applications mentioned was authored to afford the user several options to access information. They are basically one of four types of navigation currently used:

- The navigational map gives some representation of context, or relationship, of the major concepts of the subject matter, and permits the user to go directly to the starting point of a concept's presentation.
- The list, such as a glossary or an index, uses a strictly textual presentation of keywords, each of which may be found one or more times within the body of concepts.
- The string search offers more flexibility than the list for textual linkages, but it implies by its nature no guarantee of a "hit."
- The visually-based, or image-based navigational aid.

The use of computers to provide effective and efficient hypermedia learning environments faces some challenges. Perhaps the foremost hurdle is the cost of creating a hypertext/hypermedia application--both in terms of time and money. Not unrelated to the issue of cost is another important drawback of the current approach of hypertext application development: the subject matter is inextricably linked to the interface by the design tool. The structures thereby created are not immediately reusable. Finally, perhaps because hypertext for learning is still in an experimental stage, there is no consistent convention for designing the user interface of a hypertext application. Currently, each hypertext author decides what to offer in terms of navigational aids, search mechanisms, structure and context.

In order for hypermedia learning applications to gain widespread use, developers and hypermedia development software must overcome jointly the difficulties alluded to above while offering hypertext/hypermedia applications of worth to all levels of users. These concurrent goals can be achieved by applying some established paradigms to the technology of hypermedia. One regards the distribution of knowledge--teaching--and the other the storage of information--databases.

Separating the meta-knowledge from the subject matter in hypermedia learning applications offers the obvious advantage of the reusability of the vehicle of presentation. Key to this separation is the change of the location of the meta-knowledge of the subject matter. Any meta-knowledge aspect of current designs is "hardwired" as nodes, links, and structures that bind the user interface to the material presented. With the new approach, the required meta-knowledge is designed into the storage of the subject matter.

The basic design for the new approach becomes more distinct and powerful. The major difference exists in the fact that the user interface is not only conceptually separate from the subject matter but it is also physically independent from it. It becomes a separate overlay program which has the capability to recognize and retrieve links among concepts, and present them appropriately to the user in the same manner as would its current counterpart. This physical separation of the user interface mechanism from the subject matter storage mechanism addresses the three challenges spoken of earlier. The user interface would be immediately reusable with other concept databases. In addition, because a singular user interface would be used to present many sets of subject matter, there would be consistency of presentation to the user among all the hypermedia courses displayed by it. Finally, a cost savings would occur over the development of multiple courses because only the subject matter dealing with each new course need be accumulated and arranged into a new concept database. In addition, ease of both maintenance and incorporation of enhancements are additional benefits from developing the user interface as an independent object. The concept database may be updated or made more comprehensive at any time. Any change will be automatically be presented as such by the interface.

The framework of the new approach also enables course material to be geographically divorced from those who use it. A concept database may be placed at a distant server to be used locally by those with a copy of the user interface. Eliminating the need to "package" the subject matter of a course with the means to interact with it allows for option of network installation of the database of information. All network users thereby may have access to the most recent version of the concept database at the same time.

The approach for the design of hypermedia applications suggested in this paper addresses many of the problems associated with the current methodology for the development of hypertext learning applications. The total separation of the user interface from the subject matter offers additional advantages in that each separate entity can be incrementally improved as needed. Furthermore, this design methodology profits from the advantages of both the existing multimedia software technology as well as the latest database technology.

The Effect of Organization Innovativeness and IT implementation Practice on Information Technology Quality Performance Outcomes

Gilles-E St-Amant
University of Québec in Montréal
C.P. 6142, Station Centre-Ville
Québec, Canada
H3C 3P8
Fax: (514) 987-3343

Samia Assaad
University of Québec in Montréal, Québec, Canada

Abstract

This article presents the results of a field study examining the impact of organization innovativeness, rhythm of change, organization size, dependency on EDP and implementation practice of the information technology quality performance outcomes. The data generated by a field study allows us to examine the question of IT payoff. In addition, it highlights organization innovation and implementation issues such as dependency on EDP, relation with EDP staff, user involvement and user know-how, and their relative implications for system planners and managers.

INTRODUCTION

It is documented in the literature that during the 80's fifty percent of all business capital purchases were in Information Technology (IT). With these spending levels, the issues of "benefits", "gain or payoff", and the factors do have an influence on IT Quality Performance Outcomes, have become critical in the 90's.

In addition to addressing these issues we also have consider the following subsequent questions: What is the impact of Information Technology (IT) on business performance? To what extent does IT improve the quality of client service, work relations, business profit and other work related organization factors?

To address these questions, one has to develop a conceptual model that accounts for both quantitative and qualitative outcomes of IT strategies. The model should also take into account organizational change and implementation practice. Such a model is presented in figure (1). The effect of the organizational change aspect related to the internal environment is defined in terms of the degree of innovativeness, rhythm of changes (see Fig [1]). The IT implementation practice is explained in terms of the dependency on EDP, communication with EDP, users involvement and user know-how.

In addition the model presented in table 1 also reflects the latest conceptual changes in the discipline. That is the moving away from using IT as a strategic weapon and moving towards using IT to re-engineer the business internal process, becoming more market-driven and customer-oriented (Ncivclt 1993). For example, Benjamin et al. (1984) and Parsons (1983) studied the competitive advantages and position of the organization. They suggested that information technology can be exploited to gain competitive advantage or improve internal operation. Porter (1980) explained in his model of competitive strategy that exploitation of IT should be aligned with competitive strategy.

IT QUALITY PERFORMANCE OUTCOMES

In our paper, we will consider the competitive position of the organization as one of our IT quality performance outcome variables (dependent variable): "Quality of client service", "Task organization", "Work relation", "Enterprise image", "Employee's productivity", "Quality of work", "Organization competitive position", "Business profit", "Material condition and work environment" and "Work schedule".

Organizations are becoming more aware of the strategic benefits to be gained from adapting business processes to allow for innovative information technological tools to be integrated in their organizations, particularly those that can confer to the organization substantial gain in productivity, quality and efficiency.

ORGANIZATIONAL CHANGE

More research attention has been paid to innovation antecedents than to the black box between input and output (Vande Ven & Poole 1989). An alternative view is that the outcome stems from analyzable traits of participants in the industry and the IT applications (Clemons & Row 1991).

Definitions of innovation vary considerably in the organizational literature. This is often due to the theoretical purpose of the investigator (Bolton 93). West & Farr (1990) provide the following self explanatory definition:

"Innovation is the sequence of activities by which a new element is introduced into a social unit, with the intention of benefiting the unit, some part of it, or the wider society."

In this study, the Organization Innovativeness independent variable is defined in terms of the Innovation Technology variables. The Innovation Technology variables measured were: "Tendency to continually integrate new IT innovation", "Ease of adaptation", "Encouragement of employees' to propose technological innovation", "Management support employees' in their effort to adapt", "Encouragement of employees' to discuss adoption of new technologies", "Use technological innovation to better meet business objectives", "Administrative unit considered as innovative", and "Activities and progress are based on planning".

ORGANIZATION VARIABLES

The discussion related to organization size suggests that large organizations make more use of formal information and control systems (Banbury and Nahapiet 1979. See also DeBarander et al., 1972; Stabell 1976; Christen 1982).

Researchers generally assume that the propensity to innovate is a stable characteristic of firms dependent upon organizational size, structure and leadership (Burns and Stalker 1961; Wilson 1966; Lawerence and Lorsch 1967; Mohr 1969; Hage and Dewar 1973; Baldridge and Burnham 1975; Kimberly and Evanisko 1981; Daft 1982; Damanpour and Evan 1984; Tushman and Romanelli 1985).

THE IMPLEMENTATION PRACTICE

Recent research focuses upon a variety of individual, organizational, and technological forces which are important to IT implementation effectiveness (Cooper & Zmud 1990). Special emphasis has been placed on organizational variables (occupational stress) as important determinants of how new technology is implemented (Amick and Ostberg 1987). The organizational variables included in empirical studies are climate-related and structural related. Climate-related factors centered around themes of supportiveness of climate (Mjrchzak and cotton 1988; Nelson and White 1988), management objectives (Buchanan and Bessant 1985; Chao and Kozlowski 1986), planning adequacy (Ginzberg 1981; Gutek and Bikson 1985) and a general organizational culture concept (Morieux and Sutherland 1988) as potential influences on IT success.

An underlying theme is the discussions of the implementation process for successful system implantation (Hirschheim, 1985; Ives and Olson, 1984; Lucas 1981; Markus 1984). Implementation practices include interaction with EDP staff, general understanding of the system, user involvement, work group and supervisory support for learning and experimentation. (Aydin 1991; Ives and Olson 1984; Johnson and Rice 1987). Successful implementation will influence the success of IT quality performance output.

User resistance (due to lack of user know-how) issue has been studied by Bjorn Anderson and Hedberg (1977), Dutton and Kraemer (1978), Markus (1983), and Newman & Rosenberg (1985). It is anticipated that user resistance for example would lead to continued Information System failure.

HYPOTHESES:

Given the above explanations the following hypotheses were tested in our study:

H1: The organization IT innovativeness (index) is highly correlated with the improved IT quality performance outcomes.

H2: The organization IT innovativeness (innovative climate) is more likely to improve the work related IT outcomes (index) and work relation. (quantitative & qualitative)

H3: The organization innovativeness defined by its innovative climate is more likely to improve its business profit.

H4: The organization innovativeness (innovative climate) is more likely to improve the quality of client service IT outcome. (non quantitative)

H5: The organization innovativeness (innovative climate) is more likely to improve the enterprise image. (non quantitative)

H6: The organization innovativeness (innovative climate) is more likely to improve organization competitive position. (non quantitative)

H7: It is more likely that the organizational change in terms of the rhythm of change is positively correlated with IT quality performance outcomes index.

H8: The larger the organization or the larger the relative size of EDP it is more likely to produce more improvement in the IT quality performance outcome index.

H9: The dependency on EDP and communication with computer staff are positively correlated with IT quality performance outcome index.

H10: User's involvement (participation) in the implementation process will more likely lead to improve IT quality of performance outcome index.

H11: User's resistance is more likely to be negatively associated with improved and successful IT quality performance outcome index.

Figure 1: The Model Research

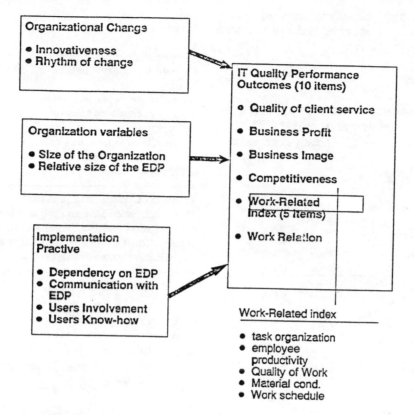

DATA COLLECTION

This study is based on data generated by interviewing 83 organizations in Montreal. A random selection technique was applied to choose 120 organizations or professional employees who best represent the organization administrative unit. The respondent was asked to reflect the opinion of his administrative (finance, personnel, communication) unit rather than his own personal opinion. The interviewers used a structured questionnaire to collect the research data. Each interview lasted about 1 1/2 to 2 hours.

VARIABLES AND THEIR MEASUREMENT

The dependent variable

To study the perceived benefits of IT, six outcomes were studied:

1. Quality of Client Service IT Outcome

The respondents were asked to rate the quality of client service outcome as result of IT. The scale ranged from 1- greatly improved to 7- greatly deteriorated.

2. Business Profit IT Outcome

The respondents were asked whether their business profit improved or deteriorated. The scale ranged from 1- greatly improved to 7- greatly deteriorated.

3. Enterprise image & 4. Organization competitive position

The respondents were asked whether the enterprise image and organization competitive position were improved or deteriorated. The scale ranged from 1- greatly improved to 7- greatly deteriorated.

5. Work related IT outcome index

Seven statements describing the expected work related outcome. All seven questions have seven possible answers stated on the scale form when the interviews were administered as: "greatly improved", "improved", "more/less improved", "neither/nor", "more/less deteriorated", "deteriorated", "totally deteriorated".

The statements were: "task organization", "employee's productivity", "quality of work", "material condition and "work schedule"

These outcomes are compatible with the key roles identified for IT and reported by a large body of research in the literature (Neivelt 1993).

6. Work Relation

The respondents were asked whether their work relation within the organization improved or deteriorated. The scale ranged from 1- greatly improved to 7- greatly deteriorated.

Table 1- Descriptive statistics.

Variables	Mean	Standard Dev.
Work-related IT outcome index		
Q38B - Task organization	2.902	1.243
Q38E - Employees' productivity	2.687	1.168
Q38F - Quality of work	2.398	1.070
Q38I - Material cond. & work env.	2.916	1.027
Q38J - Work schedule	3.829	0.783
Q38A - Quality of client service	2.518	1.243
Q38C - Work relation	3.913	0.830
Q38D - Enterprise image	2.890	0.930
Q38G - Org. competitive pos.	3.098	1.061
Q38H - Business profit	3.183	0.944

Mean scale used in the analysis was the original scale: 1= most positive, 7=most negative response. Scale reversed afterwards for further analysis.
Work-related IT outcome =
(Q38B+Q38E+Q38F+Q38I+Q38J)/5
Work related index internal reliability (alpha) for 5 items was 0.7562.
IT Quality performance Outcome index =
(Q38A+Q38B+Q38C+Q38D+Q38E+Q38F+Q38G+Q38H+Q38I+Q38J)/10. The internal reliability (alpha) test for 10 items scale was accepted at = 0.832.

THE INDEPENDENT VARIABLES

1. Organization innovativeness (Innovative climate)

The index covered 8 statements that were rated by respondents according to their judgment of how the statements apply to their unit on the 7 point scale ranging from "totally agree" to "totally disagree".

Table 2- Descriptive statistics.

Variables	Mean	Standard Dev.
1. Continue integrate new IT	3.024	1.861
2. Adapt Easily	3.073	1.624
3. Encourage employee propose	3.361	1.858
4. Support employee to adapt	2.783	1.616
5. Employee can discuss adopt IT	3.578	1.747
6. Innov. used to meet bus. objectives	2.72	1.451
7. Considered Innovative by others	3.361	1.825
8. Plan new Tech. changes	3.317	1.662

Reliability Coefficient (alpha) for 8 Items was 0.883.
Mean scale used in the analysis was the original scale: 1= most positive, 7=most negative response.
Scale reversed afterwards for further analysis.
Organization innovativeness index = Var1 to Var8.

2. Rhythm of Change

The respondents indicated whether the rhythm of change (speed of implementation) in their opinion was adequate or whether they prefer it to be accelerated, maintained or stopped . The scale ranged from 1- accelerated to 4- stopped in a descending order.

3. Organization Size and 4. Relative size of the EDP

Size of the Organization was measured by the total number of employees in the organization. The size of EDP unit was measured by the number of EDP employees. The relative size of the EDP was calculated by dividing "no of employees in the EDP" by "total number of employees in the organization" times "100".

5. Dependency on EDP

The respondents indicated their agreement as to whether they actually implement Information technology without having EDP participation. The answer categories started were: 1- totally agree 4- neither/nor to 7- totally disagree.

6. Communication with EDP and User involvement

These variables represented two factors of Ives, Olson and Baroudi out of five factors (1983). (See Ives et al. for reliability and validity of these scales). The factor related to communication with EDP staff included "the relationship with EDP responsible", "Attitude of EDP responsible", "Communication with EDP responsible". The factor related to user involvement/participation included "Understanding of the system", and "Feeling of participation in implementation practice".

7.   User know-how

To measure user know-how, the instrument developed and tested by Collerette et Delisle (1984) was used to inquire about user know-how conditions. Two questions were asked, the first one was related to the "fear from new anticipated demand the second one was related to "the mastering of IS system usage". (See Collerete et Delisle for the reliability and validity of these scales). The answer categories started with: 1- totally agree 4- neither/nor to 7- totally disagree.

Table 3 - Descriptive statistics.

Variables	Mean	Stand. Dev.
Fear from new anticipated demand	3.867	1.962
Do not master IS usage	3.639	1.798

Internal Reliability (alpha) for 7 items was 0.7597; Scale: 1= most positive, 7=most negative response. Scale reversed afterwards for further analysis.

FINDINGS

The percentage of small size organizations (< 50 employees) was (5%), (18%) of the organizations were medium size (50-200 employees) and (77%) were large size companies (> 200 employees). The average relative size of the EDP department was evaluated as 15.9% of the total number of employees in the organization. The percentage of innovative companies was 83% and 17% of all organizations were considered as exnovative type.

The data were analyzed using the correlation matrix and crosstabulation statistics.

The findings support hypothesis H1; which states that the organization innovativeness index is highly correlated with the improved IT quality performance outcome (r=0.4896, p < 0.001).

The organization innovativeness (innovative climate) shows a strong positive correlation with work related index of IT outcomes (R=0.4879, p < 0.001). On the other hand, organization innovativeness is also significantly correlated with improved work relation (r= 0.2694, p < 0.02). Based on these findings H2 is supported. (see correlation matrix).

The findings also support hypotheses H3, H4, H5 and H6. The results show that the organization innovativeness described by its innovative climate, is positively associated with improved business profit (r= 0.3666, p < 0.001). There is also positive correlation of (r= 0.3248, p < 0.003) between the

organization innovativeness and the improvement in the enterprise image (correlation value of (r=0.4324, p < 0.001) with improved organization competitive position).

Hypothesis H7 is supported as the correlation shows a positive value of (r= 0.2294, p < 0.05) between the rhythm of change and IT quality performance index.

As for the organizational size and relative EDP size, they were not correlated with IT quality performance outcomes index.

However, when we crosstabulated the innovativeness index with IT quality performance outcome controlling for size of the organization, the Gamma test shows a high value of (Gamma =0.8802) with p < 0.0003 for the large size organizations (>200 employees) . As for the small and medium size no Gamma results were computed due to insufficient data.

The crosstabulation between Organization innovativeness and IT quality performance outcomes controlling for relative EDP size showed a strong Gamma test of 0.75 significant at p < 0.004 for the a relative size of less than 5%. As for higher relative EDP sizes the findings were insignificant.

Hypothesis H9 is partially supported. The communication with computer staff is the only factor that is positively correlated with successful IT quality performance outcome (r=0.3669, p < 0.001).

Both hypotheses 10 and 11 are not supported. The user involvement in the implementation stage as well as user know-how toward the IT are not significantly correlated with IT quality performance outcome (index).

Further statistical analysis was carried out. The correlation between the innovativeness variables and the four IT quality performance outcome variables produced the results in Table 5.

DISCUSSION

Organization innovativeness does influence the IT quality performance outcome index. Innovative climate include the following variables: continuous integration of new IT, ease of individual adaptation, supporting employees to adapt, create an environment where employees can discuss adopting IT and encouraging them to propose innovation in IT. All technological changes should be planned, using innovation to meet business objectives. Finally the organization unit should be perceived by others as an innovative one.

The above innovative climate did create IT quality performance outcomes. Organization innovativeness produced quality of client services, increased business profit, improved work relation and many aspects of work related outcomes. Work related outcomes considered in this study were; improvement and work schedule. It is also important to mention that the innovative climate did improve the organization competitive position and the enterprise image.

Consequently in order to obtain quality performance outcome, it is extremely important for planners and manager to develop an innovative climate as defined in this study.

Table 4: Correlation Matrix

Variable	1	2	3	4	5	6	7	8	9	10	11	12	13	14	15
1. Org. Innov. index	1.00														
2. Rhythme of changes	.27	1.00													
3. Size of the Org.	.10	-.03	1.00												
4. Relative Size of EDP	.06	-.09	-.06	1.00											
5. Dependency on EDP	-.10	.08	-.24*	-.10	1.00										
6. Comm. with EDP staff	.27*	.04	.03	.06	.13	1.00									
7. User involvement	.26	-.06	-.09	.08	.14	.50*	1.00								
8. User resistance	-.23	-.22	-.09	.14	-.05	-.05	-.22*	1.00							
9. Quality of Client Srv.	.49*	.28*	-.05	-.11	.09	.22	.04	-.10	1.00						
10. Work Relation	.27*	.01	.05	-.14	.15	.24*	.26*	-.05	.06	1.00					
11. Enterprise image	.32*	.18	-.04	-.01	.13	.23*	.07	-.00	.38*	.28*	1.00				
12. Org. Comp. position	.43*	-.03	-.02	.00	.04	-.07	.04	-.08	.33*	.23	.53*	1.00			
13. Business Profit	.37*	.03	.08	.08	-.00	.28*	.12	0.04	.17	.28*	.49	.62	1.00		
14. Work-relate index	.49*	.19	-.02	-.10	-.02	.30*	.22*	-.13	.44	.18	.47*	.43*	.41*	1.00	
15. IT Qual Perf Index	.55*	.23	-.05	-.07	.09	.37*	.20	-.01	.58*	.40*	.64	.63	0.58	.79*	1.00

* correlation is statistically significant with ($p < 0.0001$ to $p < 0.05$)

Table 5

Variables	Quality of Client Service	Work relation	Enterp. Image	Org. Com-pet. pos.	Business Profit	Work related index
Continue integrate new IT	.4268 p=.000	.1360 p=.229	.2174 p=.050	.3914 p=.000	.2110 p=.057	.3729 p=.001
Adapt Easily	.3220 p=.003	.1766 p=.117	.1853 p=.096	.2824 p=.010	.1683 p=.131	.3309 p=.003
Encourage employee propose	.3878 p=.000	.2769 p=.013	.2720 p=.013	.2867 p=.009	.3183 p=.004	.4310 p=.000
Support employee to adapt	.5302 p=.000	.1390 p=.219	.2628 p=.017	.2386 p=.031	.2738 p=.013	.5262 p=.000
Employee can discuss adoption of IT	.2422 p=.027	.1196 p=.291	.2742 p=.013	.3134 p=.004	.3663 p=.001	.2034 p=.069
Innov. used to meet business objectives	.3321 p=.002	.2044 p=.069	.3155 p=.004	.4189 p=.000	.3352 p=.002	.3991 p=.000
Considered Innovative by others	.5184 p=.000	.2003 p=.075	.3179 p=.004	.5177 p=.000	.2960 p=.007	.4500 p=.000
Plan new Tech. changes	.2597 p=.018	.3983 p=.000	.2545 p=.021	.2482 p=.025	.2536 p=.022	.3385 p=.002

When rank ordering the innovative climate variables, the following characteristics came first: management support for employees to adapt, followed by the administrative unit must be innovative, continue to integrate IT, ease of employees adaptation and finally innovation must be used to meet pre-planned business objectives.

The rhythm of change was less an important factor in affecting the IT quality performance outcome. The correlation with the IT quality performance index was (r=0.229) and it was only correlated with quality of client service.

As for the size of the organization, it did contribute to IT quality performance outcome. This was specially true with large size of organization (Gamma was 0.880 at p < 0.0004). As for the medium and small size organizations, we were not able to compute the correlation coefficients because of the small size of the response in these two categories.

The size of the EDP was significantly correlated with IT quality performance outcomes. This was only true in the case of relative size of EDP less than 5% of the total organization size. When the size of the EDP exceeded 5%, there was no significant impact.

Regarding the implementation practice, the dependency on EDP was not significantly correlated with the IT quality performance outcomes. However, better communication with EDP improved the IT quality performance outcome (r =0.281). Communication with EDP improved quality of client service,

enterprise image, work relations, organization competitive position, business profit and work related IT outcomes. There was no significant impact on both business profit or the quality of client services.

User know-how was not significantly correlated with IT quality performance outcome. However users involvement was significant at p = 0.07. Users involvement correlation with IT performance quality outcome were weaker than other independent variables (r = 0.21 with p = 0.07). User involvement was only significantly correlated with work related index at (r=0.2209, p =.05) and work relation outcome at (r=.2651, p = 0.02).

CONCLUSION
Quantitative results of this study indicate that both organization innovative climate, rhythm of changes, and communication with computer staff were correlated with improvement of quality of client service outcomes. If management was to create an innovative environment, apply a reasonable rhythm of change, and maintain a good relationship with EDP staff, the IT quality performance outcomes would be better.

In addition, organization Innovativeness (innovative climate), communication with EDP have a positive impact on the work relation.

Again, Organization innovativeness and good relation with

EDP were shown to have a positive impact on the work-related IT outcomes index.

In a more general sense the research contributes to our understanding of the innovation characteristics of an organization and the implementation issues and their implications on successful IT outcomes.

BIBLIOGRAPHY

Amick, B.C. III and Ostberg, O., "Office Automation, Occupational Stress, and Health: A Literature Analysis with specific Attention to Expert Systems", Office: Technology and People, Vol. 3(3), 1987, pp. 191-209.

Aydin, Carolyn E. and Rice, Ronald E. (1991). "Social worlds, individual differences, and implementation: predicting attitudes toward a medical information system", Information & Management, vol. 20, pp. 119-136.

Benjamin, R.L., Rockart, J.F., Scott Morton, M.S., and Wyman, J., "Information Technology: A Strategic Opportunity", Sloan Management Review, 1984, Spring.

Bolton, Michelle Kremen (1993). "Organizational Innovation and Substandard Performance: When Is Necessity The Mother Of Innovation?", Organization Science, Vol. 4(1), Feb., 1993, pp. 57-74.

Baldridge, J.V. and Burnham, R.A. (1975). "Organizational innovation: Individual, Organizational and Environmental impacts", Administrative Science Quarterly, Vol. 20, pp. 165-176.

Banbury, J. and Nahapiet, J.E. (1979). "Towards a Framework for the Study of the Antecedents and Consequences of Information Systems in Organizations", Accounting, Organizations and Society, Vol. 4(3), pp. 163-177.

Bjerknes, G. and Hedberg, B. (1977). "Designing Information Systems in an Organizational Perspective", in Perspective Models of Organizations, TIMS Studies in the Management Sciences, Vol. 5, P. Nystrom and W. Starbuck (Eds.).

Buchanan, D.A. and Bessant, J. "Failure, Uncertainty and Control: The Role of Operators in a Computer-Integrated Production System", Journal of Management Studies, 1985, Vol. 22, pp. 292-308.

Burns, Tom and Stalker, G.M. (1961). "The Management of Innovation", London: Tavistock Publications.

Chao, G.T. and Kozlowski, S.W.J., "Employee Perceptions on the Implementation of Robotic Manufacturing Technology", Journal of Applied Psychology, 1986, Vol. 71(1), pp. 70-76.

Christensen, G.E. (1982). "Information Technology and Organizational Characteristics: A Review of Macro Organizational Issues", Working Paper No. A-82.002, Institute for Information System Research, Norwegian School of Economics and Business Administration, Bergen, Norway.

Clemons, Eric K. and Row, Michael C. (1991). "Sustaining IT Advantage: The role of Structure Differences", MIS Quarterly, Sept 91, pp. 275-291.

Collerete, P. and Delisle, G. (1984). "Le Changement Planifié", Editions Agence D'Arc, 2e édition.

Cooper, Randolph B. and Zmud, Robert W. (1990). " Information Technology Implementation Research: A Technological Diffusion Approach", management Science, Vol. 36(2), pp. 123-137.

Daft, Richard L. (1978). "A Dual Core Model of Organizational Innovation", Academy of Management Journal, Vol. 21, pp. 193-210.

Damanpour, Fariborz and Evan, William M. (1984). "Organizational Innovation and Performance: The Problem of Organizational Lag", Administrative Science Quarterly, Vol. 29, pp. 392-409.

Debrabander, B., Deschoolmeester, D., Leyder, R. and Vanlommel, E. (1972). "The effects of Task Volume and Complexity upon Computers: Memeory, Evocation and Management Information, Omega, Vol. 9(1), pp. 25-32.

Dutton, W. and Kraemer, K. (1978). "Management Utilization of Computers in American Local Governments", Communications of the ACM, Vol. 21(3).

Ginzberg, M.J., "Key Recurrent Issues in the MIS Implementation Process", MIS Quarterly, 1981, Vol. 5(3), pp. 47-49.

Gutek, B.A. and Bikson, T.K., "Differential Experiences of Men and Women in Computerized Offices", Sex Roles, 1985, Vol. 13:3-4, pp. 123-136.

Hage, Jerald and Dewar, Robert (1973). "Elite Values Versus Organizational Structures in Predicting Innovation", Administrative Science Quarterly, Vol. 18, pp. 279-290.

Hirschheim, R.A. (1985). "Office Automation: A social and organizational prespective", NY: John Wiley and Sons.

Kimberly, J.R. (1981). "Managerial Innovation", in Handbook of Organizational Design, P. Nystrom and W.H. Starbuck (Eds.), Oxford University Press, London, Vol. 1, pp. 84-104.

Ives, B. and Olson, M.H. (1984). "User involvement and MIS success: A review of research", Management Science, Vol. 30, pp. 586-603.

Ives, B., Olson, M.H. and Baroudi, J.J. (1983). "The measurement of user information satisfaction", Communications of the ACM, Vol. 26, pp. 785-793.

Johnson, B.M. and Rice, R.E. (1987). "Management organizational innovation: The evolution from word processing to office information systems", NY: Columbia University Press.

Lawerence, Paul R. and Lorsch, Jay W. (1967). "Organization and Environment: Managing Differentiation and Integration", Homewood, IL: W.W. Norton.

Lucas, H. Jr. (1981). "Implementation: The key to successful information systems", NY: Columbia University Press.

Majchrzak, A. and Cotton, J., "A Longitudinal Study of Adjustment to Technological Change: From Mass to Computer-Automated Production", Journal of Occupational Psychology, 1988, Vol. 61, pp. 43-66.

Markus, M.L. (1984). "Systems in organizations: Bugs and features. Boston: Pitman.

Markus, M.L. (1983). "Power, Politics and MIS Implementation", Communications of the ACM, Vol. 26(6).

Mohr, Lawerence, B. (1969). "Determinants of Innovation in Organizations", American Political Science Review, Vol. 63, pp. 111-126.

Morieux. Y.V.H., and Sutherland, E., "The Interaction Between the Use of Information Technology and Organizational Culture", Behavior and Information Technology, 1988, Vol 7(2), pp. 205-213.

Neivelt, Augustus M.C. (1993). "Managing with Information Technology - a Decade of Wasted Money?", Information Strategy: The Executive's Journal, Summer 1993, pp. 5-17.

Nelson, Debra l., "Individual Adjustment to Information-Driven Technologies: A critical Review", MIS Quarterly, March 1990, pp. 79-98.

Newman, M. and Rosenberg, D. (1985). "Systems Analysts and the Politics of Organizational Control", Omega, Vol. 13(5).

Parsons, G.L., "Information Technology: A New Competitive Weapon", Sloan Management Review, Fall, 1983.

Porter, M., "Competitive Strategy: Techniques for Analyzing Industries and Competitors", Free Press, N.Y., 1980.

Stabell, C. B. (1976). "The Organization as an Information Processor: A Note on the information Processing Capacity", Graduate School of Business, standford University, August.

Tushman, Michael l. and Romanelli, Elaine (1985). "Technological Discontinuities and Organizational Environments", Administrative Science Quarterly, Vol. 31, pp. 439-465.

Van de Ven, Andrew & Poole, Marshall (1989). "Research in the Management of Organizations: the Minnesota Studies", Harper Business.

West, 'M.A. & Farr, J.L. (1990). "Innovation at work", In M.A. West & J.L. Farr (Eds.), Innovation and Creativity at Work: Psychological and Organizational strategies. Chichester: Wiley.

Wilson, James Q. (1966). "Innovation in Organization: Notes Toward a Theory", in James D. Thompson (Ed.), Approaches to Organization Design, Pittsburgh: University of Pittsburgh Press, pp. 193-218.

Multimedia Support for an Introductory MIS Course

Nancy Stern
Hofstra University
BCIS/QM Department
134 Hofstra
Hempstead NY 11550
(516) 463 5028
and
Laura Lally
Hofstra University
BCIS/QM Department
134 Hofstra
Hempstead NY 11550
(516) 463 5351

Executive Abstract

THE CHALLENGES OF TEACHING AN INTRODUCTORY MIS COURSE

Teaching an introductory college level MIS course in management information systems is a challenging experience. An initial challenge facing professors is that students may have negative attitudes about computing and MIS. One study showed that many high school students are intimidated by computers, find them dry and abstract, and think that only "nerds" and math experts will do well in MIS courses (Mahwinney and Miller, 1992). One study (Barrier, 1993) has indicated that students attitudes toward computers may actually become more negative after taking an introductory MIS course.

A second challenge for the professor is the wide range of subject matter that must be covered in an introductory course. Productivity tools must be presented in a way that not only teaches students which keys to press, but which highlights their importance in a business context. Technical fundamentals of hardware, software, and telecommunications that are often difficult to visualize, must be conveyed. Finally, concepts presented individually must be integrated in order to convey the impact of information technology on business and on everyday life.

To address these challenges, a multimedia software system, PassPort, was created. The system is a supplement to an introductory MIS textbook, *Computing in the Information Age*, by Robert A. Stern and Nancy Stern and is integrated with the text material. This paper will present the fundamental ideas behind PassPort as a basis for a presentation of the system at this year's IRMA conference.

PASSPORT FEATURES AND HOW THEY ADDRESS THE CHALLENGES

PassPort combines color, graphics, animation, and sound to make classroom presentations more dynamic. PassPort's features include TechTools, TechBytes, and TechTours, each designed to address specific challenges of teaching MIS.

TechTools provides tutorials on productivity tools and their importance in a business context. TechBytes illustrate and often demonstrate interactively how particular applications, such as satellites or laser guns, work. TechTours integrates these concepts to demonstrate their impact in a business context or on daily life. One TechTour demonstrates how the satellites, laser guns and computers presented in the TechBytes help the air express industry speed delivery and improve the tracking of packages.

TechBytes and TechTours are organized around four themes:

1) "The World is Getting Smaller" -- the air express industry example,

2) "The World is Getting Smarter" -- The TechTour explores the Tron House, a "smart house" with electronic components such as computer-aided cooking, electronic storage, environmental controls, and automatic gardening. The related TechBytes are on smart maps, smart cameras, and robotics.

3) "The World is Getting More Creative" -- The TechTour focuses on multimedia and emphasizes how graphics, sound video, animation, and CD-ROMs are changing the way information is presented. The TechBytes are on CAD systems, virtual reality, expert systems, and computer viruses.

4) "The World is Getting More Connected" -- The TechTour is on electronic education and focuses on how electronic networks, computers, video and other technologies are enabling instructors to collaborate with one another to create dynamic course material. The TechBytes are on cellular phones, ISDN, and computing for the disabled.

Table 1 summarizes how PassPort addresses the challenges of teaching an introductory MIS course, and the anticipated results of using the system. An additional, "meta-level" benefit may also result from using innovative information technology to teach information technology -- students may become more comfortable interacting with computers.

Although originally designed as an in-class teaching tool, PassPort can also be made available in student labs to help students review and study outside of class. Controlled experiments measuring differences in final exam scores or attitudes toward computing between classes that use PassPort and those that do not, would provide an indication of the overall success of the package and suggest areas for further refinement.

Table 1

Challenge for Introductory MIS Professor	How Passport Addresses Problem	Anticipated Results
Students fear computers, find them dry, inaccessible.	Combines color, sound, graphics, and animation for more dynamic presentations.	Classroom lectures more dynamic.
Productivity tools, need to go "Beyond Buttonpushing"	TechTools	Better understanding of tools contexts.
Wide range of abstract concepts.	TechBytes	Better grasp of fundamental concepts.
Need for concept integration to illustrate impact on business, daily life.	TechTours	Better integration of concepts and understanding of their impact.

Section Eight

Telecommunications and Networking Technology

Telecommunications and Business Competitiveness: Perceptions in Canadian and United States Businesses

Wendy Cukier
Professor, Administration and Information Management,
Ryerson Polytechnic University
350 Victoria St. Toronto, ONTARIO CANADA M5B 2K3
416-979-5000x.6740 71417.763@compuserve.com
Lis Angus,
Executive Vice President
Angus TeleManagement Group, 3-1400 Bayly St. Ajax ON CANADA L14 3R2
905-686-5050

Executive Abstract

Introduction

For almost a decade, claims have been made about the links between information technology and competitive advantage (Cash and Konsynski, 1985; Clemons and McFarlane, 1986; Porter,1991; Keen, 1988; Tapscott,1993). While debate still focuses on assessing the effects of the technology and the "paradox of stalled productivity" (Vitale, 1986; Clemons and Row, 1991; Pinsonneault and Kramer, 1993;) there is little doubt that information technology, particularly telecommunications, is playing an increasing role in virtually every industry. This paper explores the perceived links between business competitiveness and telecommunications in a series of vertical markets. It also provides illustrative examples of how telecommunications is being used at all stages in the value chain and, in many cases, is becoming part of the product. Finally, it examines similarities and differences in the Canadian and United States contexts.

Methodology

Semi-structured telephone interviews were conducted with a stratified purposive sample of 60 telecommunications and information systems managers from companies in Canada and the United States. Included were small (100 employees), medium (100 - 500 employees) and large (1000 employees) companies, as well as a cross section of segments (financial, insurance, manufacturing, service, etc.) and regional representation. American companies in the "large" category were much larger (3000 - 190,000 employees) than the Canadian companies in the "large" category (1,350 - 60,000 employees), and this may have affected the results. The initial research, with 65 respondents, was sponsored by Canada's Department of Communications and Industry, Science and Technology Canada in 1992. This was supplemented by a literature review and additional interviews with key informants. While the sample was not sufficiently large to be conclusive, and the number of respondents in any category was too small to make comparisons, some interesting themes emerged which suggest areas for

further research.

Findings

There were some differences in the key competitive issues reported by respondents, but customer service was mentioned by virtually everyone regardless of size or sector. Telecommunications is being used to support links to customers, including automatic teller machines, point of sale terminals, electronic credit authorization, in-bound and out-bound telemarketing, customer service and support, order tracking, remote maintenance and customer support. Some respondents, such as banks, and couriers indicated that telecommunications was actually part of their product. For others, such as pizza companies, taxis and the airlines, "order taking" depended on telecommunications. In effect, "a call is a sale". Telecommunications is also used to support links with suppliers. For example, in some companies, Electronic Data Interchange (EDI) is used to exchange documents with trading partners, while others are heavily dependent on more traditional services, such as fax and telephone. Many respondents emphasized the importance of cost control. Within companies, telecommunications is used to support internal operations, for sales tracking, inventory control and price adjustment; for concurrent manufacturing and production; for teleconferencing; electronic mail; distributed teams and work at home. Telecommunications appears to be important at every step in the value chain.

There were some differences in the services reported in Canada and the United States. In Canada more respondents emphasized traditional voice services (800 service, tie line, resellers etc.), whereas in the United States there was more emphasis on higher-speed data networks, such as T-1, fractional T-1, switched 56 services, virtual private networks and frame relay. Next to voice communications, facsimile was the technology which respondents in both countries most frequently considered to be "very important" to their company (88% in Canada and 92% in the United States). Facsimile was followed by electronic mail (53% and 67% respectively); voice messaging (50% and 67%); online data applications (44% and 46%); paging (44% and 25%); LAN to LAN communications (35% and 58%); and audioconferencing (32% and 63%). American respondents ascribed more importance to EDI and videoconferencing than Canadians. Canadians ascribed more importance to cellular than Americans (32% vs.8%). In both countries there were substantial differences between companies with highly sophisticated and integrated networks supporting voice, data and even video communications, and companies with relatively simple voice networks and limited data applications. While some were pushing the technological envelope, many were preoccupied with implementing simple applications, such as voice processing or electronic mail. It should be emphasized that none of these observations can be taken as reflective of differences in the population at largeAbecause of the size and construction of the sample. Nevertheless, they are interesting and warrant further study.

There were also differences in perceptions of service providers. American companies showed slightly higher levels of satisfaction with price, service and products than Canadian companies For example, of Canadian respondents, 52% considered services to be "very expensive" and only 12% othought they were "reasonable". In contrast, only 4% of American respondents considered them to be "very expensive", while 63% considered them to be "reasonable".

There were also some differences in the problems perceived by Canadian and American respondents. For example, most Canadians believed that long distance costs and delays in service offerings were adversely affecting their competitiveness relative to American competitors and argued for a "level playing field". Subsidiaries of American firms seemed particularly aware of the North/South and international differences. In contrast, American companies more often mentioned problems with international services. Administrative and management issues such as billing and network management were regarded as critical in both countries.

Conclusions

Telecommunications and information systems managers, in virtually every industry, and companies of all sizes, in both Canada and the United States, believe that telecommunications is critical to business success. Further research could explore the diffusion and use of telecommunications technologies, and differences across sectors and between countries. One strong impression which could be further explored is the gap between the emphasis on advanced technologies (Asynchronous Transfer Mode, multimedia) in the press and the mundane preoccupations of many managers (facsimile, electronic mail and voice processing).

There seem to be some differences between the United States and Canada which could be further investigated. Certainly there is other evidence to support the claim that Canadian businesses pay more for long distance and high speed services than their American counterparts. Given that long distance competition and substantial price reductions were introduced in Canada in late 1992, it would be interesting to revisit perceptions of price.

While respondents in both countries reported that telecommunications is tied to key competitive factors, this might simply reflect the orthodoxy espoused in the business press. What is less clear is the extent to which telecommunications is actually linked to business success. Further research is needed to better understand not only the extent and ways in which telecommunications is used, but the links to business performance in particular industry sectors.

The Electronic Highway: If they build it, who will come?

Wendy Cukier

Professor, Administration and Information Management,
Ryerson Polytechnic University
350 Victoria St. Toronto, ONTARIO CANADA M5B 2K3
416-979-5000x.6740 71417.763@compuserve.com

Executive Abstract

Introduction

The "Electronic Highway" is a metaphor which has captured the imaginations of the information technology industry, the politicians, the media and many others. However, there are divergent views about the reality which underpins the metaphor, its implications and future directions. Considerable attention is being focused on technological issues and the struggle between competing approaches, but there are a host of social, economic and political issues which also need to be explored. This paper will provide one view of the conflicting interpretations of the "Electronic Highway" metaphor and their implications. In particular, it will focus on the tension between supplier and user perspectives. While market uncertainty is generally regarded as a question best left to the suppliers and their customers, the "Electronic Highway" is unique because of its far-reaching implications for social policy and services and because of the substantial involvement (directly and indirectly) of government resources. This paper offers an analysis of some of the interests and issues at stake, as well as their political, social and cultural implications from a Canadian perspective. A conceptual model of the "Electronic Highway" is proposed which encompasses the key elements and stakeholders associated with the technology, the content and its use.

Methodology:

This paper uses qualitative methods to explore different perspectives of the "Electronic Highway" and to identify some of the questions which surround it. It combines a number of techniques including literature review, unstructured interviews with over 100 potential users from a variety of sectors (education, libraries, government, healthcare, and business), an analysis of media discourse, and observation in key sites. It draws on research which was funded by the Ontario Ministry of Economic Development and Trade, and the Canadian Network for the Advancment of Research in Industry and Education (CANARIE), as well as secondary literature, primary documents and observation at key sites.

Interpretation

The "Electronic Highway" is a metaphor which means many things to many people. While some take exception to the term, I believe that it helps illuminate, at a conceptual level, the significance of telecommunications as the infrastructure which enables delivery of an increasingly wide range of services. In contrast to earlier discussions of the importance of fibre networks, bandwidth, digital versus analogue transmission, and so forth, the "Electronic Highway" is more evocative. It is helping to shift focus from the technology to its applications. However, because it is a metaphor, it is often used to represent (or misrepresent) many things by many people.

Many suppliers appear to see the metaphor as a way to market their current and future network services. Within the telecommunications sector, there are competing models, each with advantages and disdvantages. The telephone companies, for example, tend to envisage the "Electronic Highway" as an expanded version of the telephone network - switched everyone to everyone connectivity on a pay as you go basis. Their principal challenges centre on providing high speed at afforable price ,and overcoming the bottleneck of the "last mile". The cable television companies, on the other hand, are concentrating on adding interactivity to the existing television broadcast networks and this too presents some challenges. Finally, many are proposing The Internet, an international network of networks which supports computer based communications, as the embyonic electronic highway. Each model has advantages and disadvantages, and much of the media attention has been focused on the struggle for "control" - the battle between competing models, industries and companies.

Currently, attention is shifting from who will build the highway to the services and content which will actually run on it. The industry alliances among telecommunications companies, content producers and hardware and software vendors reflects this. The issues surrounding the development of content for electronic delivery - intellectual property, community standards and pricing strategies, for example - are thorny. In Canada there are additional concerns about preserving cultural sovereignty given the dominance of United States entertainment and cultural industries. Finally, not only is the availability of content essential, but the tools needed to adapt it to electronic form, and the means of accessing, organizing, selecting and storing it are critical.

More attention is also being placed on user issues and benefits, but the extent to which suppliers actually understand potential applications and potential demand remains a very large question. The example of multimedia is illustrative: there is a wealth of market research that suggests that about 50% of the multimedia market is in training. It does not, however, follow from this that 50% of the training market is multimedia. There may be a gap between what suppliers want to sell and what users will want to buy. History has shown that we are notoriously bad at predicting when and how a technology will be diffused and adapted. Personal computers, electronic mail, videoconferencing, facsimile, and cellular all evolved in ways that few researchers anticipated. We have seen the transformation of industries and consumer behaviour with the introduction of some technologies. The videogame maket, for example, now exceeds the movie market. It is extremely difficult to project demand for services which do not exist.

There are significant differences within vertical markets - education, health, business, consumer etc., and within any sector. For example, not only is the education sector divided between levels (eg. elementary, secondary, colleges, universities, private training), but within sectors and even institutions. Despite the fact that education in Canada is almost entirely publicly funded, there are historical barriers and differences which produce very diverse perceptions and realities. The perceived needs and available resources of an engineering faculty at a large metropolitan university are quite different than those at a small school on a First Nations reservation in the north. The "Electronic Highway" is often touted as the means of extending education, healthcare and government services to underserved areas. However, locations with the least access to traditional services also tend to have the least well developed infrastructure and often lack the economies of scale characteristic of larger centres. While in some quarters, attention has been riveted on 'leading edge', high bandwidth options in an effort to "push the envelope", in other quarters, the concern is to pay the telephone bill, to get access to the electronic 'dirt roads". Access issues are not confined to the question of physical access or affordability. There are other barriers such as the lack of easy to use interfaces, appropriate appliances, awareness and skills. Cultural diversity adds another level of complexity particularly if culture is understood broadly to include not just ethno-linguistic differences, but gender, ability, age and so on.

If the information highway is viewed as the critical infrastructure to the emergent "information economy", the same questions of equity and wealth redistribution which surround the industrial economy must be considered. The technology has the potential, on a national and international basis, to extend access to information or, on the other hand, to increase the gap between the information rich and the information poor. This has been characterized by some as the widening gap between the "knows" versus the "know nots". It is fair to assume that industry is best suited to defining and pursuing what it thinks will be profitable. Governments, however, must not confuse this with the public interest. In my view, government may play a role in facilitating economic development, for example in removing barriers or in fulfilling a coordinating role, but should concentrate on the issues of access, broadly defined. The model I have proposed of the "Electronic Highway" joins the technological infrastructure, with content and user applications, and recognizes the full range of stakeholders associated with each one. The hard questions about the "Electronic Highway" which remain, in my view, are not so much focused on which technology will prevail but: Where will it go? Who will be able to use it? At what cost?

Cross Cultural Issues in Electronic Communications

Wendy Cukier, Professor, Administration and Information Management
Ryerson Polytechnic University, Toronto ON CANADA M5B 2K3
416-979-5000 x.6740

Mary OHara Devereux, Research Fellow
Institute for the Future, Menlo Park CA 94025
415-854-6322

Executive Abstract

Introduction

This paper explores the implications of "cross cultural" issues, broadly defined, to the implementation and use of electronic communications tehnology in organizations. Electronic communications technology is allowing companies to create teams across time and distance. Often groups from different countries are brought together to work on a regular basis electronically and increases the complexity of "cross cultural communications".

"Cross cultural communications are affected by several factors. Nationality may not be the only or principal determinant of values and beliefs. There are other dimensions to cultural diversity - profession, age, gender, etc.- which may also contribute to "multi-culturalism" and the emergence of organizational "sub-cultures". Electronic communications also changes the nature of inter-personal communications and management issues. Some studies have examined the potential effects of particular attributes (age, gender, profession) on the implementation of technology. Others have explored the interactions of organizational culture and technology. This exploratory paper is an effort to apply the lens of "cultural diversity", broadly defined, to the implementation and applications of electronic communications technology.

Methodology

This exploratory paper is based on a review of the literature as well as the themes which emerged from interviews with over 40 key informants working in electronically supported teams in Canada (French and English) and the United States and Mexico. The paper explores issues which may warrant further investigation.

Discussion

With growing diversity in the workplace and increased globalization, much has been written about "cross cultural" issues focusing on the implications of "national" cultures, for instance, between Japanese and American, on management. Little has been written on the nature or implications of the subtle but real cultural differences between Canada and the United States or Mexico or on the regional variations within either country. Moreover, "cultural identity" has tended to be defined primarily in terms of nationality even though one individual may belong to a range of different groups which tend to share certain value and belief systems. A broader definition of cultural diversity that includes ethno-racial, national, linguistic, gender, age and professional culture suggests more heterogeneity than traditional approaches to cross cultural communication tend to acknowledge.

Organizations are recognizing the need to accommodate layers of diversity. A corporation's "culture" may be understood as not homogeneous but consisting of diverse sub-cultures. The relative strength of the organizational culture relative to the sub cultures may vary. For example, the cultures of Canadian companies may share certain characteristics which distinguish them from their American counterparts. At the same time, there may be more common values within certain professional groups (eg. engineers) across companies than there are between professional groups within the same company.

On top of this diverse cultural context, we can add the complexity of communications technologies which are being used to link increasingly diverse teams electronically. Studies of "cross cultural communications" have tended to focus on traditional forms - face to face interactions, correspondence etc. - rather than on emerging electronic forms such as electronic mail, teleconferencing, groupware etc. Given the ways in which these technologies interact with organizational structures and processes, viewing them through the lens of "cultural diversity" may provide new insights into their development and application.

Culture is an enacted systems of beliefs, symbols and behaviours which binds individuals in groups. An individual may belong to many groups with distinct or overlapping cultures. Cultures can be viewed from many perspectives. Value and belief systems, power and relationships, language and physical differences are among the many lenses which we can use to view cultural differences. One particularly important dimension of culture, defined as the context of communications, relates to the elements that surround and give meaning to a communication event, the conventions, understood assumptions and protocols which shape it.

Differences in culture, broadly defined, have implications for the implementation of electronic communications technologies. Some propositions which emerged from the interviews may warrant further exploration. There were differences, for example, in the ways in which French and English Canadians viewed work and family boundaries which may have implications.for their acceptance of anytime/anyplace technologies associated with telecommuting and wireless telephones. People working in a second language who have a better command of the written as opposed to oral language may be better served by text-based communication systems as are people with some forms of physical disability. Differences in attitudes towards competitiveness and individualism are often associated with certain cultures. These may be amplified or mitigated by electronic communications. For instance, in cultures where approaches to conflict are more indirect, electronic communications may present certain barriers to understanding. For cultures where individualism is considered less acceptable, more emphasis may need to be placed on encouraging interaction through the introduction of "polling" techniques. In consensus oriented cultures, the "voting" features of some group decision support systems may be inappropriate.

Physical differences must also be considered. Skin colour, for example effects the lighting and exposure requirements in photography but lighting and cameras used in most videoconferencing systems are set for Caucasian skin tones. The continuum of "low context" to "high context" cultures may have implications for media richness. Electronic mail systems, for example, may be less well-suited to "high context' environments than other forms such as voice mail or audioteleconferencing. Within organizations, the contrasts between the contextual needs of professional cultures, for example, of engineering compared to marketing, may also influence preferences for media richness. The importance of "context" and interpersonal interaction also affects the learning environment. The paradigm of the videogame, for example, which is shaping much of the discussion around the emerging "multimedia" educational neglects potential gender differences in communications, learning styles and preferences.

Conclusions

The interactions between technology and organizations have been explored in the past and there is growing recognition of the relevance of organizational culture. At the same time, there is growing recognition of the role of diversity in organizations. This paper has suggested that examining cultural diversity adds a layer of complexity to the study of communications technologies in organizations. It raises a number of issues and questions which need to be further explored.

Managing Information Technology Networking Objectives

Charles K. Davis & Charlene A. Dykman
University of Houston - Downtown
One Main Street, Houston TX 77002, (713) 221-8017
and
Loren E. Davis, Texas A&M - Kingsville
Kingsville, TX 77363, (512) 595-2690

Executive Abstract

INTRODUCTION

Advances in networking and telecommunications are having profound impacts throughout our world. For example, in Desert Storm we could witness the impact of rapid dissemination of news through networking. Certainly this capability had a direct impact on policy-making and on the citizens of the countries involved.

In some instances this technology has enabled the dissemination of knowledge that has led to social progress. Witness the satellite television links into the remotest regions of the earth. The social and economic impacts have been both positive and negative. Sophisticated telecommunications linkages provide access to a tremendous amount of knowledge. However, the more advanced and dominant groups providing the networks may tend to interject their cultures into the culture of the receiving country.

The potential power and influence of telecommunications technology mandates that organizations gain control of the management of their networks. Corporations and governments must be positioned to provide stable, consistent, secure, and reliable networks that will serve as the "super highways" of the future. Telecommunications networks can no longer be allowed to passively evolve one step behind the needs of the organization.

This paper presents a methodology for the systematic management of information technology networks in order to achieve the objectives that have been articulated by the organization. Such a methodology is needed to assure that the impact of this technology is controlled and understood and that society is able to utilize the power of telecommunications for positive social and economic gains.

SETTING OBJECTIVES

A major corporation headquartered in Houston conducted a one day meeting. The meeting included all of the key managers and executives in the company who had responsibility for operating or using the corporation's computer networks. There were dozens of people in the room with widely diverse backgrounds and perspectives. The meeting agenda had only one item on it: "*Network Management Objectives.*" The goal of the meeting was to arrive at a consensus as to what the objectives of the corporation's network man-

agement team should be. By the end of the day, the following list had emerged from extensive and thoughtful discussions:

- Satisfy current needs for services in a cost effective, systematic manner.
- Position the organization to meet future service requirements without costly network re-design or unnecessary user disruption.
- Achieve a balance between shorter-term and longer-term objectives to help control business risk due to network change.
- Establish user profiles for computer applications that help to identify strategic and tactical requirements for the network.
- Construct service level agreements between network management and users that include performance measures that are meaningful in terms of the users' work environments and are based upon an understanding of costs for different service levels.
- Maintain transparency of the network from the users' perspectives as modifications are applied over time.
- Establish techniques for anticipating changes in network requirements and for predicting the impacts of network change.
- Standardize network specifications and configurations to the extent possible within limits of user requirements, cost, and management strategy.
- Establish a network design that facilitates support and service of networking equipment with an architecture that provides for centralized network management and control whenever feasible.
- Establish policies to control and minimize the complexity of the network and to instill ease of maintenance as a selection criterion for equipment selection.
- Achieve interconnection flexibility for network components and subnetworks that may be specialized to particular application areas.
- Develop and implement cost vs. benefit analyses to support acquisition of networking equipment.
- Establish a standardized primary network backbone to interconnect with subnetwork as required.
- Integrate network usage files with other files for computer use reporting, capacity analysis, and performance analysis into one consistent database system.
- Achieve a flexible networking environment that can be easily

upgraded when needed and provides users with consistent, uncomplicated interfaces to applications systems as needed.

While the consensus was achieved, the fundamental issue is this, "How do you assure that these objectives are met with any reasonable level of consistency and regularity?" Today even large corporations and many governments are *bogged down* with outdated, almost primitive, network management tools and techniques that leave well-meaning, but inadequately prepared, network staffs forced to rely on intuition, guesswork, and trial-and-error approaches. This is a serious problem for organizations trying to handle the growing demand for modern network services. In today's highly competitive global marketplace, organizations simply cannot afford reliance on outdated modes of computer network management and the inevitable loss of competitiveness.

Achieving the goals outlined above, consistently and reliably, means migrating network management away from the realm of art toward the realm of science, to move away from a reactive reliance on educated guesswork toward a proactive reliance on sound principles of information management. In other words, the answer is to establish and utilize a method-ology that will provide a framework for gaining control of network growth and expansion.

This paper presents a methodology for managing a telecommunications network utilizing a *delivery systems* perspective that addresses both the computing and networking portions of the information services component of the organization. The following areas are examined within this methodology:

- Documentation of existing network facilities
- Examination of workload statistics
- Selection of data collection intervals
- Identification of usage measurement criteria
- Review of subnetwork characteristics
- Establishment of utilization reporting criteria
- Profile of network traffic patterns
- Development of network simulation models
- Establishment of baseline and trendlines
- Development of planning scenarios
- Forecasting of capacity, workload, and costs

Each of these areas is discussed, resulting in a methodology that leads managers through the various steps involved in providing a telecommunications facility that can be relied upon by all of the stakeholders involved.

More Than Just Email: The Internet
for Information Systems Education

Dr. Mary J. Granger
Assistant Professor
Management Science Department
George Washington University
Washington, DC 20052
202-994-7159
GRANDER@GWUVM

Dr. David L. Schroeder
Assistant Professor of Decision Sciences
College of Business Administration
Valparaiso University
Valparaiso, Indiana 46383
219-464-5050
DLSCHROED@VALPO

ABSTRACT

Many students in undergraduate Information Systems (IS) courses have little or no previous exposure to either the nature or the use of information technologies. The Internet offers vast communication resources through email, but also provides access to numerous information sources to enhance Information Systems education. This paper reviews some of the email possibilities and summarizes additional resources, providing specific examples for their use in computer literacy, management information systems, database, programming and systems design courses. The technology blends with the subject matter and becomes an integral part of the course. Included from several sources are several popular Internet definitions.

INTRODUCTION

Bill Clinton, Al Gore, members of Congress, the Library of Congress, museums, databases, journals and more than twenty million people in over 60 countries are on it. It is a means of almost instantaneous, low-cost global communications. Business organizations design new products, order equipment and conduct daily transactions across it. Nearly every university is connected to it, thereby enabling students access to it for the asking. For many users it has become indispensable; they cannot imagine being without its communications facilities.

The Internet is a Wide Area Network available at most universities and many business organizations enabling worldwide electronic communications. On the Internet, time and space almost have no meaning (LaQuey, 1992). Users of the Internet are in distant locations, in different time zones and often have never met each other face to face. "In short, Internet gives you access to more people and more information faster than you can imagine, including online catalogs from most major U.S. academic and research libraries and from more and more foreign libraries." (LaQuey, 1992, p. 7)

Using the Internet it is possible to receive a file from Austria, visit New Zealand, chat with someone from the United Kingdom, check the weather on both coasts of the United States, and see whether a text is available in the local library or the state-wide network all within a matter of moments and all without leaving the comfort of the office chair next to the personal computer terminal.

Personal computers, increasingly more powerful and less expensive, enable unprecedented access to computer networks. These networks are replacing and enhancing previous means of communication. No longer is text the only mode of communications; graphics and video are routinely transmitted. The workplace is no longer one specific location; employees communicate from home, hotels, airplanes, automobiles and trains from over the world. The Internet's computer-based communications are producing many business, political, legal and social reorganizations; the communications manner and methods are rapidly changing.

Many students in undergraduate Information Systems (IS) courses have little or no previous exposure to either the nature or the use of information technologies. A recent study (Grover and Goslar, 1993) identified key communication technologies. Two of these technologies, networks and email, play important roles in the way international organizations conduct business and engage in the everyday transfer of information. Information Systems' students need to appreciate the power of electronic communications; cooperative work, using electronic media, should be encouraged.

As the Internet revolutionizes the workplace, it is beginning to transform the classroom. There are studies detailing K-12 usage (Cannon 1993; Fromme 1993; Grigas 1993;), but few offer suggestions for incorporation into a university setting. Current university students leaving academia need exposure to technologies that are changing the way organizations conduct business; Internet is one of the ubiquitous technologies. The objective of this paper is to explore opportunities, within the undergraduate IS curriculum, which allow students attending universities to become familiar with the resources on the Internet. Some of the questions that will be addressed are: 1) What are benefits derived from the experience? 2) What are the major problems for faculty and students? 3) What IS courses are appropriate for cooperative work using the Internet?

Employing email and networks simultaneously enables students to master the course material and learn to use the technologies to exchange information and ideas. Additionally, utilizing the Internet provides an opportunity to add an international dimension to their knowledge. A new category of student emerges; one that learns about interacting groups participating in technological situations.

INTERNET RESOURCES

What are some of the resources available on the Internet? Among the most popular resources are electronic mail (email), usergroups or newsgroups and databases. Electronic mail is similar to the Postal Service; the computers involved are not necessarily directly connected to each other and messages travel to the recipients on a 'store and forward' network (Krol 1993).

Originally, email facilitated the exchange of academic research; today email transfers both text and multimedia messages. However, due to the potential volume of messages, email rapidly becomes cumbersome for those interested in multiple discussion groups; news groups relieve this bottle-neck. The Internet news is similar to the physical bulletin board with posted paper messages. Questions and answers are electronically posted; readers with similar interests can start their own news groups. USENET is a collection of over 3,000 established news groups that have world wide readership and is available on most nodes of the Internet. Usenet offers multiple hierarchies, including research biology (bionet), conferences from listserv mailing lists (bit.listserv), business (biz), computers and related subjects (comp), hobbies, games and recreation (rec), science (sci), sociologically oriented groups (soc), politically related topics (talk), and even contro-versial or unusual topics (alt). There are financial, scientific, marketing, literature, environmental, legal and employment databases available on the Internet. It is hard to imagine any hobby or special interest, whether frivolous or serious, that is not represented by an Internet news group.

Gophers and Wide-Area Information Servers (WAISs) provide for menu driven access to many resources on the Internet. Based on software created at the University of Minnesota (home of the golden gophers), many Internet sites have their own gopher server. Most all gophers are intercon-nected to most all other gopher locations; the student needs to know only one interface instead a different one for each autonomous site. There is access, not only to the card catalogs, but also to full text and multimedia from university libraries, public libraries and the Library of Congress. Publications (Li 1993) detailing citing on-line bibliographies are beginning to appear. More information is easily available to more people. Providing a common query interface to hundreds of databases and library catalogs, WAISs offer another search route for resources on the Internet. The program hides the complexity of doing the actual search, allowing the user to focus only on the topic of the search.

UTILITIES

The two basic Internet utilities are Telnet and File Transfer Protocol (FTP). Telnet capability enables access to remote computers; this is not a dial up utilizing a modem. A remote computer is accessed through the local computer and the user interacts with the resources at the remote location. Once files are located, they can be transferred to the local site.

Several menu driven programs offer a catalog of telnet sites. One such program is Hytelnet, which provides hypertext access to over 1400 sites, including libraries, campus-wide information systems, gopher, WAIS, and WWW systems, freenets, and more.

Through use of FTP, a program that facilitates transferring files between different locations, data is transferred at a very high speed. The most common use is transfer of files from a remote site to the local, originating site. Locating files at remote sites can be accomplished using archie, a database utility which views multiple remote sites in an attempt to completely or partially match keywords provided to it.

INTEGRATING INTERNET INTO THE CURRICULUM

Today's students will utilize and manage technology in the business organization and they need exposure to these ad-vances throughout their curriculum. Not only IS majors, but also all business majors, need this experience. Following are specific examples for use of the Internet in computer literacy, management Information Systems, programming, systems design and database courses; these courses tend to appear in almost every Information Systems curriculum. Since illus-trations for combining the Internet and a telecommunications or networking course are intuitive, examples for this course are omitted.

Computer Literacy Course

The introductory computer literacy course, required for every student majoring in the business curriculum, is part of almost every business school core. Most university students have easily accessible connections to email; some are linked to the host computer through PC LANS, while others are di-rectly connected through dedicated terminals in a computer labatory or in the dorms. Many students own a PC with a modem, but many have not used the communications capa-bilities. There are tremendous differences in the computer skills and interest levels of the students enrolled in this course. In spite of all the efforts being made to introduce computers and telecommunications into the K-12 grades, in this course, 10% familiarity with email is high.

Students enrolled in this course need to be introduced to basic email functions: sending and receiving messages. How-ever, most students do not immediately think that email is very exciting and do not voluntary begin using it. Just offering a grade for utilizing email is not sufficient, neither is setting up pen pals with another university. Some students become very enthusiastic, while the majority view the exer-cise as meaningless and a waste of time. This attitude of indifference poses an obstacle for faculty attempting to intro-duce the technology into the curriculum. The technology must integrate with course logistics.

Email used for posting assignments, class messages and, test topics and formats, provides a 'real' reason to learn email. Instead of printing assignments, require the students to re-trieve them from the Internet. Students find any modifica-tions, or clarifications to homework using email, thereby, obliging them to constantly monitor their mail for new messages. They become responsible for any course related messages, changes or directions that are sent to their accounts. Depending upon the facilities at the university or at home, and the type of student, commuter or resident, initial introduction to the Internet communications may be fairly time consuming, but eventually the benefits outweigh the negatives. Use of the Internet email becomes a habit and the more students utilize it, the more they appreciate its power.

Depending upon the course workload, the type of facilities available and the interest of the students, uploading and download files or news groups may be introduced. Unless there is a specific need for this feature, such as a joint project, students will not perceive its importance. Therefore, these topics are often beyond the scope and time of this course, and are better introduced in the MIS course.

Management Information Systems (MIS) course

The Management Information Systems (MIS) course is either the second required IS course in the business core, or an elective for anyone in the business school. The focus of this course is primarily the strategic implications and importance of IS within a business organization. The Internet's USENET provides many interesting news groups that are relevant to topics covered in the MIS course; additionally, local discussion groups can be established. Groupware, software which allows "several users to work on the same document at the same time" (von Biel 1991), should be encouraged for team projects and papers.

Gopher servers and WAISs provide access to written documents, files, programs, graphics and databases. Where students previously had little or no opportunity to touch a working database, the Internet provides myriads of examples. The menu driven Hytelnet program lists multiple databases for easy access. Using these existing examples of databases allows a dramatic understanding of the strategic use of information.

Programming Courses

Students in any level programming course require assistance with their program logic and debugging. Since students often work on their assignments during evening and weekend hours, these are the times they need aid. Using the Internet is a perfect way to provide support during those hours. Students leave messages or send their programming files to the instructor, who attempts to solve the problem. A return message or solution is forwarded to the student and is waiting at the next system logon. The instructor does not have to be physically in the computer laboratory, but provides a high level of support. There must be a dedication and willingness on the part of the instructor to monitor their Internet accounts during weekend and evening hours. This is assuming the instructor has the capability of accessing the Internet account from off campus sites.

If the instructor is unavailable or unable to solve the problem, students are able to post questions and receive answers within a short period of time from USENET sub-

scribers who have encountered the same questions or bugs. There are USENET groups interested in almost every programming language; each group believing that their language is superior to all others. Many commercial developers such as Borland and Microsoft, have FTP sites that are readily available. Programming examples may be located at FTP sites using an archie search, Additionally, students create their own user group: a help group where they can post questions and receive answers. Students will learn by seeing and solving other students' problems; they might even avoid same mistake. Because students perceive there is always someone there to help them, they feel more comfortable with the material and the instructor usually gets very high ratings for availability and helpfulness.

Information Systems Design (with CASE)

Information Systems design in the business organization is being done across international boarders, with experts from all over the world. The development of systems from remote sites, can be incorporated into the IS design course. Since the Internet enables the transfer of graphics, data flow diagram, structure charts, entity relationship diagrams, etc, now flow along the net.

Students are able to send and retrieve designs, and/or telnet into another location to create or modify a design. Therefore, the design is created under the guidance of different professors, and by students with potentially varied backgrounds and abilities. Initially, select a university within the same country using the same system development methodology and, ideally the same Computer-Aided Software Engineering (CASE) tools. After the course is running smoothly with a same-country university, expand into the global arena by contacting a university in a different country. Time differences introduce new dimensions into the system development process. One team may continue project work long after another team has gone for the day.

Incorporating the Internet into IS design requires a great deal of co-ordination both for faculty and students, but the simulation of real world experience for students is worth the time and effort.

Database Management and Design

Students enrolled in the Database Management course design logical and physical aspects of databases. Similar to the System Design course, the student can use the Internet to accomplish these goals.

Upon graduating, the many undergraduate IS students are involved with database maintenance projects. Since the Internet enables sharing of many network connected database, students from different locations are able to use the same database for different applications. There is also the potential of creating new applications for an existing database designed at another location. Instead of developing the initial database, students may examine the design of an existing database and learn about the different type of designs and management features. They may determine there is some data they are able to access but not update nor delete; there is some data they are not able to access. Using the Internet to investigate an existing database enables them to discover some of the maintenance and security issues that they will face in a real world situation. These maintenance and security issues related to database are usually discussed but never implemented in the undergraduate IS curriculum. The Internet usage provides the hands-on, real-world experiences with databases that will benefit students in their careers. For success, this endeavor will also require a great deal of faculty and student co-ordination.

SUMMARY

The major beneficiary of integrating the Internet into the undergraduate IS curriculum is the student. They are better prepared for the every changing demands of the undergraduate business curriculum and their future work environment. Use of the Internet fosters independent learning; students set their own agendas and explore different interests.

The Internet provides opportunities for enhancement of not only the courses which rely heavily on the net for the actual implementation of the course work, but other courses in the curriculum. The students will also bring strengthened communication and telecommunication skills to their professional endeavors. The computer is viewed as a medium of communication, not just another technology.

Expertise with the Internet will serve the students in their capstone policy course. In order to accomplish the goals of this senior level course, the instructors expect the students to be able to access financial and marketing databases. The entire undergraduate business student body can benefit from the additional telecommunication proficiencies.

Integration of the Internet in the undergraduate Information Systems curriculum pose several problems for both faculty and students. Students may have problems learning how to use some of the resources available. Additionally, they may not have daily access to the Internet and may consider it's usage an imposition; this is particularly true of commuter students. As they explore the Internet for new opportunities for their classes, faculty also invest learning time. Numerous publications/tutorials (Dern 1994; Krol 1993; Lambert 1993; LaQuey 1993; Marine 1993) are readily available. Faculty may sacrifice some of their weekend hours helping students through the Internet, however, they may be able to shorten the time physically spent on campus. The Internet permits communication between students and faculty that does not occur in the classroom; students are often reluctant to ask questions or join in discussions in the classroom, but will using the Internet. Communication barriers between students and instructors disappear.

One of the major criticisms of graduates from business school are their lack of communications and telecommunications skills. Introducing the Internet across the undergraduate Information Systems curriculum forces the students to address this issue. As students work on email, participate in newsgroups and develop project on the Internet, they concentrate on their communication skills. They are exposed to the

communications networks that competitive business organizations are currently employing; they realize the Internet and other networks are ubiquitous. Eventually, they form the Internet mentality. Instead of using the telephone to communicate, they use the Internet.

REFERENCES

Cannon, John R. (1993) "Telecommunications for Public Schools: A Need More Than Ever Before," *Interpersonal Computing and Technology: An Electronic Journal for the 21st Century*, Vol.1 No. 4, October 1993, Archived as CANNON IPCTV1N4 on LISTSERV@GUVM.CCF.GEORGETOWN.EDU and available via gopher from GUVM.CCF.GEORGETOWN.EDU (141.161.71.1).

Dern, Daniel P. (1994) *The Internet Guide for New Users*. Meckler, Westport, Ct., 1994.

Electronic Frontier Foundation (1993) *Big Dummy's Guide to the Internet*.

Fromme, Robert A. (1993) "'Project Ecology': An International Exchange of Student Art," *Interpersonal Computing and Technology: An Electronic Journal for the 21st Century*, Vol.1 No. 4, October 1993, Archived as FROMME IPCTV1N4 on LISTSERV@GUVM.CCF.GEORGETOWN.EDU and available via gopher from GUVM.CCF.GEORGETOWN.EDU (141.161.71.1).

Grigas, Gintautas (1993) "An Experiment of Computer Programming Practice by E-mail," *Interpersonal Computing and Technology: An Electronic Journal for the 21st Century*, Vol.1 No.2, April 1993, Archived as GRIGAS IPCTV1N2 on LISTSERV@GUVM.CCF.GEORGETOWN.EDU and available via gopher from GUVM.CCF.GEORGETOWN.EDU (141.161.71.1).

Grover, Varun and Goslar, Martin (1993) "Technical Correspondence - Information Technologies for the 1990s: The Executives' View," *Communications of the Association of Computing Machinery*, March 1993, Vol. 36, No. 3, 17-19, 102-103.

Krol, Ed (1993) *The Whole Internet User's Guide and Catalog*. O'Reilly and Associates, Sebastopol, California, 1993.

Lambert, Steve and Howe, Walt (1993) *Internet Basics: A Guide to the World's Electronic Highway*. Random House, New York, 1993.

LaQuey, Tracy with Ryer, Jeanne C. (1992) *The Internet Companion: A Beginner's Guide to Global Networking*, Addison-Wesley, 1992.

Li, Xia and Crane, Nancy B. (1993) *Electronic Style: A Guide to Citing Electronic Information*. Meckler, Westport, Ct. 1993.

Marine, April; Kirkpatrick, Susan; Neou, Vivian and Ward, Carol (1993) *Internet: Getting Started*. Prentice-Hall, Englewood Cliffs, New Jersey, 1993.

Scott, Peter (1994) *Hytelnet 6.6*, a hypertext database of publicly accessible Internet sites. The program is available for viewing via telnet to access.usask.ca and is available for anonymous ftp from ftp.usask.ca (128.233.3.11), in the /pub/hytelnet directory.

von Biel, V. (1991) "Groupware Grows Up," *MacUser*, June 1991, 207-211.

GLOSSARY - INTERNET DEFINITIONS
Definitions from Hytelnet (1994)

Anonymous FTP (File Transfer Protocol) -- The procedure of connecting to a remote computer, as an anonymous or guest user, in order to transfer public files back to your local computer. (See also: FTP and Protocols)

BITNET -- A cooperative computer network interconnecting over 2,300 academic and research institutions in 32 countries. Originally based on IBM's RSCS networking protocol, BITNET supports mail, mailing lists, and file transfer. Now merging with CSNET and running the RSCS protocol over TCP/IP protocol (BITNET II), the network will be called

Computer Research and Education Network (CREN).

Client-Server Interface -- A program that provides an interface to remote programs (called clients), most commonly across a network, in order to provide these clients with access to some service such as databases, printing, etc. In general, the clients act on behalf of a human end-user (perhaps indirectly).

CREN -- Computer Research and Education Network is the new name for the merged computer networks, BITNET and Computer Science Network (CSNET). It supports electronic mail and file transfer.

Domain Name System (DNS) -- The Internet naming scheme which consists of a hierarchical sequence of names, from the most specific to the most general (left to right), separated by dots, for example nic.ddn.mil.

Electronic Bulletin Board -- A shared file where users can enter information for other users to read or download. Many bulletin boards are set up according to general topics and are accessible throughout a network.

FTP -- File Transfer Protocol allows a user to transfer files electronically from remote computers back to the user's computer. Part of the TCP/IP/TELNET software suite.

Gateway -- Used in different senses (e.g., Mail Gateway, IP Gateway), but most generally, a computer that forwards and routes data between two or more networks of any size.

Host Computer -- In the context of networks, a computer that directly provides service to a user. In contrast to a network server, which provides services to a user through an intermediary host computer.

Internet -- The series of interconnected networks that includes local area, regional, and national backbone networks. Networks in the Internet use the same telecommunications protocol (TCP/IP) and provide electronic mail, remote login, and file transfer services.

IP (Internet protocol) -- The Internet standard protocol that provides a common layer over dissimilar networks, used to move packets among host computers and through gateways if necessary.

IP Address -- The numeric address of a computer connected to the Internet; also called Internet address.

Listserv Lists (or listservers) -- Electronic discussion of technical and nontechnical issues conducted by electronic mail over BITNET using LISTSERV protocols. Similar lists, often using the UNIX readnews or rn facility, are available exclusively on the Internet. Internet users may subscribe to BITNET listservers. Participants subscribe via a central service, and lists often have a moderator who manages the information flow and content.

NREN -- The National Research and Education Network is a proposed national computer network to be built upon the foundation of NSF backbone network, NSFnet. NREN would provide high speed interconnection between other national and regional networks. SB 1067 is the legislative bill proposing NREN.

OPAC -- Online Public Access Catalog, a term used to describe any type of computerized library catalog.

OSI (Open Systems Interconnection) -- This is the evolving international standard under development at ISO (International Standards Organization) for the interconnection of cooperative computer systems. An open system is one that conforms to OSI standards in its communications with other systems.

Protocol -- A mutually determined set of formats and procedures governing the exchange of information between systems.

Remote Access -- The ability to access a computer from outside a building in which it is housed, or outside the library. Remote access requires communications hardware, software, and actual physical links, although this can be as simple as common carrier (telephone) lines or as complex as Telnet login to another computer across the Internet.

Shareware -- Microcomputer software, distributed through public domain channels, for which the author expects to receive compensation.

TCP/IP -- Transmission Control Protocol/Internet Protocol is a combined set of protocols that performs the transfer of data between two computers. TCP monitors and ensures correct transfer of data. IP receives the data from TCP, breaks it up into packets, and ships it off to a network within the Internet. TCP/IP is also used as a name for a protocol suite that incorporates these functions and others.

TELNET -- A portion of the TCP/IP suite of software protocols that handles terminals. Among other functions, it allows a user to log in to a remote computer from the user's local computer.

Terminal Emulation -- Most communications software packages will permit your personal computer or workstation to communicate with another computer or network as if it were a specific type of terminal directly connected to that computer or network.

Additional definitions from Big Dummy's Guide (1993)

WAIS: Wide-area Information Server; a program that can search dozens of databases in one search.

Gopher: A program that gives you easy access to dozens of other online databases and services by making selections on a menu. You'll also be able to use these to copy text files and some programs to your mailbox.

IRC: Internet Relay Chat, a CB simulator that lets you have live keyboard chats with people around the world.

Clarinet: News, sports, feature stories and columns from Universal Press International; Newsbytes computer news.

Local Area Network Implementation

Manfred W. Hopfe, PhD
Nancy Tsai, PhD
Frank Lowery MS(MIS) (Candidate)
School of Business Administration
California State University, Sacramento

Executive Abstract

Local Area Networks (LANs) not only facilitate the accessibility of valuable information through the integration of a common organization data base, but also lower the maintenance costs through sharing of the various expensive computer resources. Consequently, more and more organizations adopt LANs to gain the competitive edge with its resulting cost savings.

It is paramount that an organization carefully consider the technical and managerial issues prior to deciding to implement a LAN. Failure to do so will increase the risk of a poor LAN configuration which could result in inconsistent system performance, inaccurate information, low system reliability, significant maintenance costs, inferior user confidence, and proliferation of incompatible LANs.

This paper investigates some of the important technical and managerial issues involved in a LAN implementation and concludes with a case study on the LAN systems implementation by the State of California's Office of Emergency Services. The technical issues refer to the primary components to be used when installing a LAN. The managerial issues portion addresses the selection criteria to be considered when choosing a LAN to be implemented in an organization.

A Framework for MIS Research in Telecommunications

Jerry D. McCreary and Chetan S. Sankar
Dept. of Management
415 W. Magnolia Avenue
Auburn University
Auburn AL 36849

Executive Abstract

BACKGROUND

The melding of computers and communications, the deregulation of the telecommunications industry and the globalization of business have necessitated that the domain of information system include telecommunications. However, business research on telecommunications is not well reported. This indicates the need for a comprehensive telecommunications framework to aid MIS researchers.

Existing telecommunications frameworks deal with a subset of the topic germane to a specific reference discipline. The most significant framework associated with telecommunications is the Open Systems Interconnect (OSI) model developed by the International Standards Organization. Closely related are proprietary communications models developed by major computer vendors. Examples are IBM's Systems Network Architecture (SNA) and Digital Equipment Corporation' Digital Network Architecture (DNA). Keen's stages of telecommunications management (Keen, 1988) model could be used as a framework to classify telecommunications research. This model concerns the attitude of an organizations management toward the value of their telecommunications system. King and Premkumar (1989) use an input-process-output approach to model telecommunications planning. The focus of their work was to identify and organize the key issues of telecommunications planning. A framework for understanding the "business value and potential applications" of telecommunications is presented by Hammer and Mangurian (1987). This framework combines the impact of telecommunications on time, geography and relationships. Economic models of telecommunications exist which demonstrate some aspect of pricing or welfare related to telecommunications. None were developed to cover the integrative nature of the IT field and to facilitate identification and analysis of management issues and applications.

A FRAMEWORK FOR TELECOMMUNICATIONS

The framework has two dimensions: (1) stakeholders and (2) networks and services. The stakeholder dimension represents people or companies that use telecommunications. The networks and services dimension represents the type of telecommunications services provided or used by the stakeholders.

Stakeholders of Telecommunications. Stakeholders are those who use or provide telecommunications networks on a continuous basis. Five categories of stakeholders are: (1) managers - those people who manage the telecommunications networks of client organizations or are managers of companies that provide the services, (2) providers of telecommunications - organizations that manufacture telecommunications equipment, provide telecommunications services and support the telecommunications industry, (3) governments - those political bodies having legal and regulatory authority over the telecommunications industry, (4) intergovernmental organizations - those organizations whose influence on telecommunications spans governmental boundaries and/or whose membership is drawn from many nations, and (5) customers - organizations or individuals that acquire telecommunications services or technologies from providers.

Telecommunications Networks and Services. The networks and services dimension define the type of services provided and the management issues in providing the services. It also includes the applications, such as electronic mail, EDI, that are used by the stakeholders. This dimension is divided into five categories: (1) domain - this refers to geopolitical coverage and is further subdivided into local, national/regional and international, (2) type - this defines the kind of service used by a stakeholder and is describes by its subdivisions of voice, data video/image and integrated networks and services, (3) technology - this concerns the underlying technical aspects (what and how) associated with telecommunications systems, (4) management - this defines the managerial issues that are important in planning, deploying, using or operating telecommunications technology, and (5) applications - this category encompasses the uses of telecommunications by the stake holders.

VALIDATION OF THE FRAMEWORK

The framework was validated by using it to categorize existing telecommunications literature from six major MIS journals: Decision Sciences, Harvard Business Review, Information & Management, MIS Quarterly, Management Science and Sloan Management Review. The search spanned the time period from December, 1984 through November, 1992. Articles relating to telecommunications were identified using a key word search of an on-line database. The abstract and associated keywords were used by two MIS researchers to classify each article according to the framework. This methodology is similar to that adopted by Ives, et al., (1980), Nolan and

Wetherbe (1980) and Adams, Lacity & Mullins (1990). Each researcher independently recorded the relevant framework categories and sub-categories covered by each article. Their classification were then compared and differences resolved.

RESULTS AND CONCLUSIONS

From December, 1984, through November, 1992, the six journals analyzed published over 3100 articles. Of these articles, 101 were found to concern telecommunications. Most of the articles were found to deal with the customer category of stake holder (94%) and the management category of services and networks (89%). Almost no research is found dealing with inter-governmental organizations (1 article) or government (6 articles) and very little research (13 articles) is found dealing with telecommunications providers. Given the importance of applications of information technology to MIS there are a surprisingly small number of articles that describes MIS applications supported by telecommunications.

While the telecommunications budget in many organizations may approach or even exceed that for DP/MIS, the number of research articles published on telecommunications in business journals seems to be disproportionally low (3%). The analysis further suggests that there are major needs for research on the impace of telecommunications in the following areas: (1) vendors as stakeholders, (2) government and intergovernment agencies as stakeholders, and (3) application nature of telecommunications.

Downsizing: A Paragidm Shift in Information Processing

Mustafa A. Kamal
Curtis Coleman
Computer and Office Information Systems
Central Missouri State University
Warrensburg, MO 64093
Phone : (816) 543-4767

Executive Abstract

INTRODUCTION

The restructuring of organizations, recessionary pressures, and global competition are forcing businesses to change. This change in how business operates began slowly with the processing of data and information through a single, centralized, mainframe computer -- until the invention of large-scale computer networks. This new technology with its powerful client-server facilities is giving rise to the new concept of Information Systems Downsizing. However, with this technology, personnel and system resources required to maintain this enterprise-wide data access and distribution is phenomenal -- and expensive. This latter issue, expense, is the driving force behind the downsizing of mainframe computers to Personal Computers (PCs). Downsizing is based on transfer of large-system applications to cheaper, more flexible networks, usually using personal computers and local area networks (LANs). Any shift, however, that is more productive, gives more access of information to users, and saves money can be called downsizing.

THE TREND IS DOWN

In 1991, a survey sponsored by *PC Week* found that 57% of the nation's largest PC sites had done one of two things: Either they had shifted applications from a mainframe to LAN within the past 18 months, or they plan to within the next 18 months. The survey covered over 200 corporations, institutions, or government agencies, each having at least 250 PCs. Computer Intelligence, a market research firm located in San Diego, CA, completed a survey in 1993 of 671 mainframe sites. The survey concluded that only 39% of the applications being planned in these organizations were designed to run on mainframes. Additionally, 40% of the applications that currently run on mainframes are being redesigned to run on other platforms, such as client/server environments. Although many application are rapidly moving into the PC environment, the use of mainframes will continue to play a critical role in business.

WHY SHOULD CORPORATIONS DOWNSIZE

The three major reasons to downsize are to: 1) Reduce Processing Cost, 2) Increase Flow of Information, 3) Increase Sales. The reduction in cost is amongst the three top reasons for downsizing. Today some of the most powerful PC-based systems can match some of the larger mainframe computers in capacity and performance. However, when the overall price is considered, the PC-based systems can do that at a fraction of the cost. Although reduced costs is listed as a major reason to downsize, unexpected expenses can sharply cut the savings. Another reason to downsize is to provide increased access of information to users. The information should be available in real-time, so that good decisions can be made in a timely manner. Using the PC-based networks, data can be easily accessed and analyzed. Third, by downsizing many organizations will increase their sales. This is due to the fact that information may be available on-line, in a timely fashion. With downsizing, a sales representative has immediate access to information that can be used to help make more sales. Other reason for downsizing is reliability. In 1988, on the eve of a new election, the *Washington Post* experienced the complete failure of the computer system that the editors and reporters used. For over two hours no one could accomplish anything. The system also was a one-of-a-kind operating system, and over 10 years old. The *Post* needed a solution that would guarantee this would never happen again. The answer was to install over 700 PC workstations, with servers running OS/2 and LAN Manager.

PROBLEMS WITH DOWNSIZING

Downsizing is not nearly as simple as replacing an expensive old computer with inexpensive new ones. Typical problem areas are: 1) Hidden costs, 2) Support problems with LANs, 3) Human factors. The hardware/ software to support downsized applications costs only a fraction of the same capacity in a larger system. But conversion of applications to the PC-based environments can eat up much of the savings. Nearly every one, from the system's programmers to the data entry clerks, have to be retrained. The technology and the tools are different, which means people will need new knowledge and new skills. In the arena of support, customers require a high degree of support that they often don't get. Security and reliability still work against downsizing. These considerations are particularly important because the term *mission critical* appears so often in discussions of what applications are to be downsized. The most serious obstacles to successful downsizing are not technical, but human factors. The people who must live with the new system, including those who must give up the old ways of doing things, will cause more troubles than the technical problems. What this means is that downsizing will save significant amounts of money, give employees better, more productive access to corporate data, but the conversion cycle must be well planned to keep from stumbling over the many obstacles along the path to success.

WHO SHOULD DOWNSIZE

Databases are the leading candidates for two reasons: usually databases can readily be moved to downsized systems, and they often have a high degree of interactive use. Amongst the database applications for which downsizing is often fruitful:1) Billing and invoicing, 2) Maintaining customer lists, particularly for direct mail, 3) Inventory and sales records. Another good candidate for consideration are office systems. Office systems usually are designed to improve the productivity of individuals or small groups, yet many are centrally controlled. Large system applications are being operated with dumb terminals in many office environments making these systems ripe of both downsizing and modernization. Some typical office system conversions include: 1) Storing and tracking legal documents, 2) Developing group documents, 3) Filing and retrieving business records.

THE CLIENT / SERVER ARCHITECTURE

For companies that have mainframe databases, the client/server model for downsizing presents an opportunity to share information more widely and more flexibly than ever before. In today's multi-platformed environments, an organization might have a mainframe, two or more DEC VAXes, and possibly several hundred users on a LAN. The drawback to this arrangement is that the only way to share data between environments is by multiple file transfers. In some instances, data is entered twice: once for the LAN, and once for the mainframe. The client/server approach is to move a portion of the mainframe system's processing functions onto intelligent, PC-based nodes (the clients). By continuing to have all the data residing on the servers, each accessible to any client workstation, file transfers are no longer required, and up-to-the-moment data is available. An existing mainframe can become a database server to many more users, or it can be replaced with smaller, less costly equipment. For companies that have many PCs, but have not yet incorporated them into networks, the client/server model will provide a more versatile and attractive architecture than the local area network using file servers. The client/server architecture is also the best solution for those companies that find the performance level of their LANs have reached their limits.

CONCLUSIONS

Downsizing (or Rightsizing) will continue to be the trend in Information Systems area for the rest of this century. Corporate pressure to increase productivity and maintain an upperhand in the global competitive market would force the DP managers to streamline information processing paradigm by restructuring around efficient and interconnected LAN based client/server computing architecture. The profit for the corporation would come from the ultimate reduced cost in building and maintaining the system and from the increased efficiency of the system. The transition from purely mainframe to LAN based client server environment would not be easy.

Usage Patterns and Perceptions of Voice Mail in a University Setting

Karen S. Nantz, Ph.D.   Marilyn L. Wilkins, Ed.D.
Lumpkin College of Business and Applied Sciences
Eastern Illinois University
Charleston, IL 61920, (217) 581-2627

Executive Abstract

A number of electronic technologies have substantially changed the way organizations communicate, including voice mail--"a network of answering machines" (Menkus) with message recording, retrieval, storage, and forwarding features. Voice mail allows the caller to leave electronic messages and the receiver to access messages at any times from any phone. Many companies report productivity gains of 20-30% with voice mail because the problem of telephone tag is eliminated.

Some executives are questioning the appropriateness of voice mail. Issues include internal versus external calling, potential for messages being received by inappropriate parties, costs associated with message storage, and direct marketing through voice mail.

The university setting offers a unique opportunity to assess voice mail because of the diversity of the workforce. Administrators who work a typical 8-hour day closely appropriate the schedules of business executives. Faculty, on the other hand, have schedules more like a sales force that is out of the office more than in. Faculty have erratic schedules, depending on class days, times of classes, and other commitments. Many faculty conduct their research activities at home, thus using a remote office. Students, as university consumers, also have varied schedules and may not be able to meet faculty members during scheduled office hours. Potentially, the opportunity for voice mail to succeed is great. Many schools are using voice mail to help communicate with parents, alumni, and on- and off-campus groups.

RESEARCH PLAN

This study was conducted during 1993 as part of a 5-year longitudinal study of electronic communications at a business college of a midwestern university. The population consisted of all faculty members and administrators with faculty rank. Of the faculty surveyed, 46 of 69 (67%) responded.

A survey was developed, validated, and pilot tested and included sections on voice mail, local area networks, electronic mail, mainframe use, and demographic data. Respondents included all professorial ranks; the median age of respondents was 45 with 8 years teaching experience and a full-time teaching appointment.

FINDINGS

Respondents were asked how often they checked their telephone voice mailboxes. Faculty are unable to use the phone without hearing a signal that indicates voice messages exist. Of the faculty responding, 70 percent checked their voice messages at least once a day or more. About 13 percent indicated that they do not use voice mail, while the remaining 17 percent checked their voice mail less than once a day but more than once a week. Those accessing voice mail less than once a day are ignoring the voice mail signal.

Respondents were also asked how often they used additional voice mail features, such as message archiving and forwarding. The university routinely saves messages 29 days, but messages can be flagged for retention. The majority of users (over 50 percent indicated that they used none of the additional voice mail features. However, about 30 percent of the users indicated that they archived messages and reviewed archived messages. However, fewer than 10 percent forwarded messages or used the group mail feature.

Faculty were asked about their impressions of voice mail using a 5-point scale consisting of 8 opposite modifiers. While faculty believe that voice mail improves productivity and is easy to use, they also consider it to be work, to be impersonal, and to be more welcomed by the receiver than the caller. These findings are similar to other research studies.

Finally, faculty were asked if they had experienced annoying or harassing voice mail calls. This was an initial concern since callers can remain anonymous. Most users (78%) indicated that they had not. The remaining users had received annoying calls, although these calls were few in number.

CONCLUSION

The findings from this study parallel what has been found in industry. Voice mail can effect productivity gains, but can be impersonal and an inconvenience to both the caller and receiver. Users were overall neither very positive or very negative about voice mail. Users tend to access it at least once a day, but some users refuse to use it, therefore restricting its usefulness to the organization. New users tend to stick to the basic features. This could indicate a need for training on the advanced features.

On-campus use of voice mail is relatively new compared to other technologies. If voice mail is accepted by university personnel, there exists the opportunity to use it as a recruiting and retention tool. This preliminary study only looked at one faction of the campus community. Additional research needs to be completed to determine 1) if attitudes and usage patterns change over time and 2) if voice mail can be as effective on campus as it has been in industry.

Satellite Based Distance Learning Environment: The New Horizon for Productive Utilization of IT in Managing Organizational Changes

Dr. sc. Fjodor Ruzic, info.sci.
Institute for Informatics,
Markusevacka 7, Zagreb, Croatia

Executive Abstract

1 INTRODUCTORY REMARKS

In a world of ever-accelerating competition and change in the conditions of the workplace, of ever-greater danger, and of ever-larger opportunities for those prepared to them, educational reform should focus on the goal of creating an open learning environment with the commitment to a set of values and to a system of education that permits all members the opportunity to stretch their minds to full capacity. The new open learning environment has the idea that education is important not only because it contributes to one's career goals but also because of the value it adds to the general quality of one's life. Current techniques and information technology development provide the mechanism to be used in distance learning. Thus, we are faced with new generation of education system based on the importance of interpersonal communication and collaborative work in understanding teaching materials and on learning as social process. New communications technology especially satellite-based systems, provide the possibility for removing the barriers of time and space developing new models of distance learning where the priority is given to collaboration between learners, teachers and information resources.

2. SATELLITE BASED COMMUNICATIONS NETWORKS: THE COMMUNICATIONS MILEAGE AT THE END OF 20th CENTURY

The new knowledge-based organizations should find that the crucial factor in determining communications media, protocol and topology, is the distributed multimedia environment. Multimedia is not a single technology, it is a class of technologies and applications that span two or more information types. Speeds required to deliver multimedia of adequate quality range from a lower boundary of 128 Kbps to multimegabit-per-second rates. Currently introduced technological innovations increase operational life-time and capacity of satellites (in terms of number of transponders), and they improve the exploitation of a given space capacity, by capacity sharing among users (Demand Assigned Multiple Access), compression and radio multiplexing techniques. Innovations are currently aimed to introduce multi-beam satellites that have the ability of switching signals providing communication between terminals located in different spot beams. Technically, most of the problems are solved, but the big efforts should be done in the field of network regulation and worldwide coordination.

The new flexibility of VSAT systems is designed to accommodate both low and high speed data rates with equal simplicity to support a variety of applications. For VSAT communications networks, the quantity of user terminals as well the costs of satellite airtime determine the cost-benefit criteria. The cost is depended on frequency used, too. C-band VSATs cost less than Ku-band VSATs. The cost also depends on the type of applications to be shared via VSATs. Costs are influenced by the number and extent of up- and down- converters, modems and baseband equipments. All of these elements make the total cost of the VSATs to be used in entire network architecture. The new satellite technology and VSAT equipments give capability to interconnecting different local area networks (LANs) at remote sites to form a satellite supported wide area network of entire organization. Thus, in the current pilot project HINASAT, each LAN at distributed point has the VSAT node that serves inbound and outbound queues for data packets coming from and to appropriate destination station via satellite. The communications scenario is, in simplified form, based on calling procedures and parties in the communication process. After the calling process (that initiate communication) is established, the data packets are sent from the source point within entire LAN to the VSAT node, from the VSAT node to the satellite (via up- link channel) and from the satellite to the destination VSAT node (via down-link channel), and to the destination point in the destination LAN environment.

3. FINDINGS - VSAT SYSTEMS BASED DISTANCE LEARNING ENVIRONMENT FOR MODERN ORGANIZATION DEVELOPMENT

The main criteria for distance learning is interactivity of communications media so the satellite based telecommunications should provide interactive transmission that can have both audio and video feedback from remote sites. Audio feedback is done by conventional telephone network, and can carry facsimile, electronic mail and computer conferencing. But, for video feedback the media should have high frequencies (for digital video telecommunications 20 GHz is preferable) and wideband channels that can support images, voice and text suitable for interactive learning. This scenario asks for digital images/video multimedia stores to be connected to the central earth station (Hub) for the satellite uplink in Ka-band. The Hub is the point of central Information Depository to which all learners had access for capturing detailed information about multimedia material suitable for developing courseware. Since the costs for making and distributing materials by satellite are very high, it should be noticed that the highest score of the cost list holds the studio (production/support) cost. That is why the central Information Depository at the Hub location reduced the costs effectively by using computerized multimedia information base that is produced and controlled by computer. The currently available 22/30 GHz frequencies (Ka-band) range offers the opportunity to achieve relatively high bit rates with very compact ground signal status that are rearranged Very Small Aperture Terminal (VSAT). Given the identical antenna sizes of VSAT stations, the high frequencies result in higher antenna gains as compared with the 12/14 GHz frequency range mostly in use across Europe. Thus, it is possible to reduce the antenna size and yet achieve the same antenna gain. This is attractive momentum that benefits applications in which knowledge workers in modern organizations are dominantly oriented toward interactive communications services at low costs. The implementation of an interactive VSAT system distribution network should be aimed to users' environment and should provide flexible and variable organization of distance learning; it must be open to various types of contexts in which it can be used.

DISCUSSION

Communications development and group choices in the computer mediated communication is shift away from initial members' preferences because they focus attention on recent arguments or decision proposals contained in the shared task information. Hence, the expected impact of computer-mediated communication on group choice shift is still unclear. Computer Supported Collaborative work systems have emerged as identifiable research area that focuses on the role of the computer in groupwork. The research being undertaken poses a number of questions. How the groupwork can be defined? How can computer and satellite communications system be exploited to maximize the synergy of groups? What kinds of computer and other tools should be developed? The growth of connectivity greatly expands the opportunities for group members to cooperate and work together in the open cooperative environment. A useful view of this cooperative environment is to think of it as an Operating System for Cooperative Applications where a common model for the entire environment facilitates managing users, resources and information. It provides common services (system calls, libraries) to applications, it facilitates inter-process cooperation, it provides different contexts for groups of applications, and it allows users to view and manages several groupware applications together using a shell or desktop tools. This scenario asks for digital images/video multimedia stores to be connected via satellite to the central earth station (Hub) for the satellite uplink as the point of central Information Depository to which all workers (group members) would have access to the information. It also gives access to a wide field of media research and in the sciences of work and communication.

Information Technology's Role in Enhancing Quality in Service Industry

Chetan S. Sankar and Charles A. Snyder
Department of Management
415 West Magnolia Avenue
Auburn University
AL 36849

Tzu-Hui Suzie Liu
Computer Center (Applied Software Section)
Central Weather Bureau
64 Kung Yuan Road
Taipei, Taiwan 100, ROC

ABSTRACT

Worldwide, the service sector now contributes on average 58 percent of the gross national product. Companies in the service sector as major users of information technology (IT) are in a position to enhance the quality of service by exploiting IT capabilities. Information technology is restructuring and redefining the service industry, thoroughly changing the roles of suppliers, intermediaries, and customers. Every part of the service delivery, from concept and strategy to cost, production and delivery can be positively influenced by IT. But, little research has been reported on linking IT to service quality. This paper discusses the role of IT in enhancing quality in the service sector and proposes a framework for analysis. The components of services discussed in this paper are operations, market, employees, and finance. The paper defines and explains the components of the framework by using examples from service companies.

INTRODUCTION

The service industry is the section of economy which supplies the needs of the consumer but produces no tangible goods (Bateson, 1992; Stebbing, 1990). The importance of the service sector is revealed by reviewing some statistics about the contribution to output and employment. Worldwide, the service sector now contributes on average 58 percent of the gross national products (GNP) (Riddle, 1986). The Fortune Global Service 500 firms are large as indicated by their total sales/revenues of $2,938 billion and profits of $126 billions in 1991 (Fortune, 1992). In the United States, the service sector accounts for 72 percent of GNP and 76 percent of employment (Bowen et al., 1990). In most industrialized nations at least 65% of the total work force is involved in the service industry.

Companies in the service sector are major users of information technology (IT). The widespread proliferation of computers and communications technologies has reduced the size of companies, increased the power of top management and increased the number of business applications (Miles, 1990, Brown et al., 1991). Information technology is restruc-turing and redefining the service industry, thoroughly chang-ing the roles of suppliers, intermediaries, and customers (Normann, 1991). IT influences quality in every part of service delivery, from concept and strategy to cost, produc-tion and delivery. But, little research has been reported on linking IT to service quality. Chief Information Officers, MIS managers, and Telecommunications managers need a framework to understand the impact the IT could make to improving the quality in their companies.

This paper discusses the role of IT in enhancing the quality in service industry using a simple framework. The compo-nents of the framework are defined and explained by using examples from service companies. The framework is used to delineate areas for future research by IS professionals.

QUALITY IN THE SERVICE INDUSTRY

A service is an activity or series of activities to satisfy consumer needs and the results are intangible. The service takes place when interactions between the customer and service employees and/or physical resources and/or systems of the service provider occur (Gronroos, 1990).

High service quality should increase organizational effi-ciency and effectiveness by increasing productivity, lower-ing costs, improving responsiveness to customers, and en-hancing reputation. Poor service often entails the hidden costs of rework, market opportunity costs, and lower employee morale (Sasser, et al., 1991). For example, companies can achieve better service by understanding service quality as a series of relationships, the most critical of which is between customers and employees.

Before discussing service quality further, it is important to elaborate on the difference between the manufacturing and service industry. There is a contrast between the tangible products of manufacturing and the intangible nature of ser-vice. Other means of differentiating have been reported and point out the fact that service components exist in manufac-turing as well (Snyder, Cox, and Jesse, 1982). The idea of the existence of a continuum of service intensity makes quality in service even more important than the statistics about the service industry alone.

The manufacturing industry has follow up service; for example, when we buy a VCR, for example, we receive a warranty for repair service. Services are generally delivered and instantly consumed by human beings. It is one thing to guarantee a VCR, which can be inspected before a customer sets eyes on it and can be returned to the factory for repairs. But we cannot send an unsuccessful legal argument or bad haircut back for repair (Hart, 1988). Therefore, enhancing the quality of service in manufacturing and the service industry have a large degree of differences. In this paper, we focus on IT's role in enhancing quality in the service industry.

Quality, and service quality in particular, is such a complex phenomenon that a much more detailed model than the ones normally used is needed (Garvin, 1987). The determinants of service quality have been described as tangibles, reliability, responsiveness, assurance, and empathy (Parasuraman et al., 1986). But, little has been reported about how IT, a major component of providing services, influences these determinants. Discussions on futuristic uses of IT are often made, but, little connection has been established between IT and quality in service industry (Mills, 1986). It is important to understand how IT contributes to quality in the service industry. Next, we examine the contribution of IT to service quality developing a framework.

PROPOSED FRAMEWORK

The proposed framework (Figure 1) divides the role of IT in enhancing service quality into four components. The identification of the four components was done to break down quality into manageable parts. By this breakdown,

managers can define the quality niches in which to compete (Garvin, 1987). Chase and Bowen (1991) used the three components of technology, systems, and people to describe service quality. Malcom Baldrige Award criteria has a section on the contribution of IT to quality. This section concentrates on the potential applications of IT to the different aspects of a business. Similarly, ISO 9000 standards specify the criteria by which IT could contribute to service quality. These standards are generic in nature and do not address the full potential of IT to contribute to service quality.

We wanted to develop a framework that could be useful to the CIO, MIS managers, and telecommunications managers in better targeting their IT organization to improve quality in the service industry. Hence, we used the components of operations, market, employees, and finance to the earlier frameworks to create a new framework (Figure 1). These components are expected to address the needs of the IT managers much more explicitly.

Operations: Operations involve the processing and delivery of the needed service. IT plays a major role in enhancing quality in the service sector by making operations transparent, processing higher volume, enhancing response time, consolidating diverse operations, and tracking quality measures.

Market: The market represents the external customers a company has to serve. Service quality is dependent on effective interactions between customers and employees. IT plays a major role in improving customer satisfaction, retaining customer loyalty, increasing customer involvement in the operations, providing direct links with the customer, and maintaining leadership in the market.

Employee: Employees are all human resources working in

Figure 1: Framework to illustrate role of IT in managing service quality

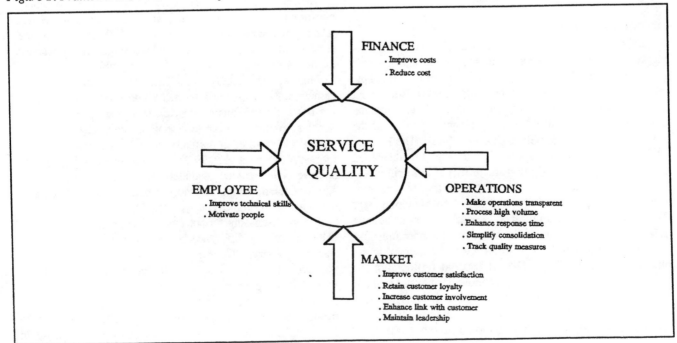

the company workers and management. Employees of a company have the major role in managing the quality in service industry. Service quality is characterized by a high degree of variability and IT frequently capitalizes on the variability, adopting to the expertise of the employee and the customer. IT plays a major role by improving the technical skills of employees, motivating people, and by providing instant communication. Effective use of IT can empower the employees to perform their service functions far better.

Finance: Finance represents the capital needed to operate the company and the funds needed for day-to-day operations. An important aspect of achieving efficiency is by enhancing the financial operations of the company. IT could play a major role in identifying areas where outlays could be improved and identifying areas of lesser profit. Global networks could provide the financial officers the latest information about the markets and opportunities, and provide the company an ability to act promptly by providing instant information on demand.

Effective integration of the use of IT on all four components leads to improved quality in the service industry. We discuss each component of the framework in more detail below. We also cite examples from the literature to illustrate how service quality has been improved by using IT.

Operations

Customers judge the success of service both by the outcome and by the process leading to that outcome. The words "performing" and "producing" express a basic difference between service and production management. Since front-line employees create service experiences with customers, front line employees become a vital link in establishing quality reputation for the company. Information technology can play a major role in enhancing the quality of the experience in the following ways.

1. IT can make operations transparent: An employee or customer may access complex information systems by using simple operations without knowing the complex structure of the networks. Thus, the operations are made transparent and user-friendly to both the employees and customers. For example, banks offer automated teller machines (ATM) to customers who want to withdraw or deposit money from their accounts. The complexities of the information systems and networks that make the ATM function are hidden from the customers. The service representatives at AT&T Universal Card Operations use ISDN (Integrated Services Digital Networks) to retrieve information about the credit card customers instantly. Each customer is identified by the phone numbers from which they call the services most frequently. When a call comes from one of those phones, the ISDN technology provides both the voice call and a screen about that customer's account to the representative. Hence, the representative does not have to make the customer wait for the records to be pulled to their screens. AT&T-Universal Card Operations have been cited for their use of innovative use of IT to improve customer service.

2. IT helps process high volumes of information: With IT, a service company can process huge volumes of information. As an example, Total System Services Inc., (TSYS) has developed a flexible network that allows it to provide complete credit card operations for 34 million credit card customers to banks. The company has built an extensive, nationwide communication network with many nodes and terminals. Customer representatives from the banks can find data within seconds from the main databases. In 1965, when the company first computerized, they had 2,311 disks that held 7.25 million characters of information. By August 1990, they passed the trillion-byte mark in disk space. That represents an increase of about 37,000 times (Ussery et al., 1992).

3. IT can enhance response time: With IT, the speed of the operations can be improved. The package delivery firm, Federal Express, has introduced machines at its customers' sites which weigh a parcel, call for parcel pickup, print shipping labels, calculate the cost, invoice the customer, and (if connected into the customer's information system) charge back that cost to the user department. The same technology can initiate electronic funds transfer from the customer's bank to Federal Express's bank in payment of the invoice. It also allows the customer to conduct an immediate on-line inquiry of where in the Federal Express delivery system their shipment is at any time (Davis, 1987). Thus, Federal Express has been an innovative user of IT in assuring high quality delivery commitment to its customers.

4. IT can simplify consolidation of networks: IT can make it possible for diverse voice, data, video, and fax networks to be consolidated into backbone networks. This reduces costs significantly and improves the efficiency of operations. For example, Citicorp is embarking on a worldwide project to consolidate more than 100 disparate networks into an infrastructure expected to save the firm $100 million a year in telecommunications costs. On the customer service side, the network aims to support globally expanding customers that need their financial needs met simultaneously across geographic boundaries. The firm's cost-cutting crusade includes ongoing data center consolidation, local-area network integration and network management activities that could lead to outsourcing of nonstrategic operations (Wexler, 1991).

5. IT can help track quality measures: There has been emphasis on creating measures to track quality in service industry (Parasuraman, et al., 1986; DiPrimio, 1987) and IT has been helping to track them. Since employees in many service industries use terminals or personal computers for business, it has been possible to measure and control service quality (Zemke, 1992). For example, TSYS measures the quality of its operations using 36 to 45 different measures and produces a daily quality index. These measures include hardware availability, time to mail customers monthly statements, time to mail the credit cards, response time to customers, time to reissue plastic cards, etc. The number of measures varies each day depending on the functions performed on that day. The performance on the quality measures is available on-line to all the employees in the firm. This puts indirect

pressure on all the units to cooperate and achieve or exceed expectations each day. Without the use of a sophisticated IT system, this measurement would not be possible (Ussery, et al., 1992). In addition to enhancing the operations of a company, IT can improve the service quality in dealing with the market.

Market

Quality in service industry requires conformance to the customer's specifications and expectations to the point of delight. Customers decide what they consider good quality, what is important, and what is unimportant (Gronroos 1984; Johnston 1987). IT's role in the market is:

1. IT can improve customer satisfaction: Customer satisfaction is a function of actual service delivered in relation to what is expected from the encounter. The meaning, definition, and evaluation of quality exist in the consumer's mind. Ultimate quality is the difference between service quality expectations and the perceptions of reality (Parasuraman, et al., 1986). IT can help improve the ultimate quality offered to customers. For example, TSYS builds and retains its customer base by providing customized products and prices. A new customized product introduced by TSYS (Ussery, et al, 1992) is an automated voice response system that offers card holders' information about their credit card accounts twenty four hours a day, seven days a week. Using this system, cardholders can determine their balance, credit limit, payment amount and due dates. Other customized products allow primary customers to print statements or find past history of their card holders. One well received product lets the primary customers access TSYS's database in 23 different file formats and produce their own customized reports. Thus, IT enable TSYS to differentiate itself from other processors. All "forms" are customized and personalized to TSYS's customers resulting in thousands of different statements. TSYS ensures that the services are close to what primary customers could offer if they did the work themselves.

2. IT can be used to retain customer loyalty: Existing customers cost less to serve and are generally more profitable than new ones. Loyalty to a service provides results from meeting or exceeding customers' expectations. A few outstanding service organizations not only measure it but go to extraordinary lengths to build and preserve customer loyalty. This requires asking what a targeted customer is worth, measured in terms of the contribution from the stream of purchases the customer may make over time (Sasser et al., 1991). An example is the MBNA credit card issuer providing a free listing of the purchases by categories (such as lodging, gas, restaurants, etc.,) at the end of the year. Another example is Ford or GM Credit card company that rewards purchasers with cash rebates or rebates on car purchases. Airlines provide mileage credit to their customers for purchases made with the credit cards. All these are not possible without the aid of IT to track the purchases of customers individually.

3. IT can increase customer involvement: Another way to improve productivity and quality is to let customers directly impact the production process. There are two principles behind this: customer self-service and participation skills of customers (Gronroos, 1990). Examples of self-service are ATMs and 800-number transactions. When a customer uses an ATM, the account is automatically updated without an employee of the bank spending time on the transaction. ATMs provide customers of financial service institutions with a convenient way of access to routine financial services, such as deposits, withdrawals, and payments. Similarly, mutual fund companies use 800 number lines so that customers can authorize withdrawals or transfers between accounts. Easy-to-read menus and user-friendly options encourage customers to participate in this process.

4. IT can enhance links with customers: Since service, as an intangible commodity, usually requires direct contact with customers, setting a closer relationship with customer is essential. Service is not the end of a "trade" with the customer, but can be the beginning of a long-term relationship with the customer. In order to serve the customer better, getting feedback from the customer is important. A linked relationship with customers can be established by introducing IT into the service process. Some examples of relevant technologies are Electronic Data Interchange (EDI) and Integrated Services Digital Network (ISDN).

EDI can provide computer-to-computer exchange of information between a company, its employees, and customers on standard business documents, such as invoices, bills of lading, and purchase orders. For example, The First National Bank of Maryland (1990) successfully integrated their voice and data networks to serve their branches in Maryland and Virginia (Brown, 1990). In addition, they used this network to let the employees and customers dial in to obtain information about their accounts. A modem combines data from the branches and delivers it to a multidrop analog leased line. The traffic from the analog leased lines is ultimately delivered to the main data center. The bank has a total of 30 multidrop circuits with each circuit supporting an average of six branches. The bank conducts transactions within the branches and with the Federal agencies using EDI standards.

ISDN is a new technology through which voice and data could be transmitted using the same physical line. An example of use of ISDN is by the American Automobile Association (AAA). AAA uses ISDN's automatic number identification capability to assist travelers who are stranded outside their local club areas. Members requiring roadside assistance used to call an 800 number to be referred to the local club. The calls were sent to an office in Heathrow, Fla., where a AAA operator would look up the number and give it to the motorist, who then had to hang up the phone and make another call. ISDN saves AAA money by handling calls in half the time it used to take. It also helps minimize frustration for stranded motorists (Lindstrom, 1992). Thus IT contributes to enhanced customer satisfaction.

5. IT can help maintain a leadership position in the industry: Effective use of IT can assist the company to become a dominant market leader. An example is TSYS's IT business

strategies that provided it leadership in the credit card processing industry. The IT strategies enabled TSYS to win the huge AT&T Universal Card account. Also, these strategies have helped TSYS maintain its position as a leader in highly profitable business where net profit margins are from 15 to 17 percent after tax (Ussery et al, 1992).

Employee

Information technology is important because it shapes or determines, the jobs that people perform in service organizations. This role is quite visible in many service organizations where technology and machines have changed the nature of work. For example, the introduction of automatic teller machines (ATMs) in banks has replaced low-skilled jobs (tellers) and placed more emphasis on high-skilled jobs (programmers, loan officers, etc.). The nature of work has changed dramatically in several service organizations because of IT. Examples abound in overnight parcel delivery business, car rentals, and the travel industry. Further, technology influences the way people are organized or structured, the types of social interactions people engage in, people's attitudes about their organizations, and the behavior they display (Litterer, 1965). This could lead to resistance to the use of IT in many parts of the organization. Employee perceptions of new technology are often negative, particularly in the absence of careful implementation. It could also restrict latitude of their work. Many employees are dragged into using IT by the sheer force of technological change and there are many who use it as an effective tool to advance their career.

1. IT can improve the technical skills of the employees: High-quality service means, among other things that the employees know how to do things correctly the first time. Use of IT to improve the technical skills of the personnel is an important means of simultaneous improvement of quality and productivity (Gronroos, 1990). Video classrooms, videos of customer interactions, computer based learning tools, and recording of customer calls provide a rich source of data for training employees. IT makes it possible to document the interaction between the customers and employees to provide customized training to individual employees. Recent studies indicate that soft skills (oral communications, interpersonal relationships, team working, leadership, etc.) are critical for employees in the service sector (Sankar and Snyder, 1992). IT provides a means to train employees on these skills by videotaping the interactions and bringing in experts by video teleconference to critique the performances.

2. IT can be used to help motivate people: An employee who uses new technology is held in a higher esteem by peer groups (Normann, 1991). An organization where employees use up-to-date IT are proud of their achievements in peer groups and are more motivated. Examples are employees of AT&T Bell Laboratories, IBM Research Laboratories, and NASA discussing their use of IT in business. Similarly, faculty members and industry researchers using electronic mail systems, such as Bitnet and Internet, show creativity in performing joint research. Rapid feedback to service provid-

ers can be one of the most powerful motivators for improved behaviors. IT facilitates this feedback.

3. Provision of instant communication: IT can be used to eliminate lag-time between performance and feedback as noted above. Thus, employees can judge their behaviors and the reactions of customers so that they can adjust to the situation rapidly. This can greatly enhance learning to delight the customers.

4. Enhancement of perceptions by customers: Customers should have enhanced perceptions about employees who are empowered to provide better service through the use of IT. For example, rapid access to databases can reduce waiting and customers will perceive the service employee is more qualified. This use of IT can also improve perception of the overall firm.

Finance

Information technology can be used to improve the quality of financial performance of service companies in the following ways.

1. IT can improve revenues: Customers are normally willing to pay higher prices for they perceive as higher quality and IT could contribute to delivering and maintaining such quality. An example is the computerized reservation systems of large airlines. The entry cost to build a reservation system is millions of dollars, so only the major airlines are in a position to develop such systems. Smaller carriers have to pay to belong to the reservation systems crated by dominant carriers. In addition, reservation terminals are leased to travel agents and small carriers, fostering 'brand' loyalty to the major airline. American Airlines handles $2.5 billion worth of reservations annually. Recently, they have devoted a large investment to build an user-friendly system named QUIK RES (Salamone, 1990). These reservation systems have proved to be a profitable business asset by themselves (Clemons and Row, 1991).

2. IT can reduce costs: Poor quality generates many costs, few of which are measured. Perhaps the most obvious of these is the loss of customer loyalty and the sales and profits that accompany it. Even less likely to be measured are customer costs associated with lost time, expense, and aggravation suffered in correcting problems of poor service. Rarely taken into consideration too are the costs resulting from server dissatisfactions which are evidenced in increased employee turnover, training and yet further service deterioration. These costs suggest the value of developing good quality service (Sasser et al., 1991). They also suggest a need to establish guidelines for amounts that a service provider might spend for the appraisal of service performance and various preventive measures that might be instituted, including service recovery, prior to the loss of a customer (Sasser et al., 1991).

IT can improve quality and decrease costs by providing appropriate information to the customers quickly and cheaply. With the recent flattening of organizations, IT also makes it possible for top management to be award of the performance of lower-level employees without the filtering that formerly took place. Also, Decisions Support Systems and Expert Systems can up-to-date data stored in the company's computers to better control costs of service delivery.

CONCLUSIONS AND DIRECTIONS FOR FUTURE RESEARCH

IT has an important role in enhancing the quality in service industry. The above discussion has focussed on the positive aspects of IT. One must, however, acknowledge that there can also be a downside to the IT application. There must be careful implementations to avoid perverse reactions, but this is beyond the scope of this paper.

Further research needs to be performed to investigate the relative importance of these components in service industry. Focus groups, questionnaire surveys, and interviews with employees in service industry could help refine and delineate its relationships among the components of the framework further. There should be an investigation of the factors that contribute to the successful application as well as those that are barriers.

In a sense, IT transforms the process of creation and provisions of services. It entails all of the activities and techniques involved in the conversion of input into output (Mills, 1986). For a service organization, IT is a major enabler for enhancing the quality of services. This paper discussed how companies can use information technology to enhance quality of services in operations, market, employee, and finance components. Further research employing frameworks such as these should lead to a better understanding of the role of IT in enhancing service quality.

REFERENCES

"Air Freight Progress Report," *Morgan Stanley Investment Research*, New York, January 21, 1985.

Bateson, *Managing Services Marketing*, The Dryden Press, New York, N.Y., 1992.

Bell, C.R., and Zemke, R., "The Performing Art of Service Management," *Management Review*, Vol. 79, Iss. 7, July 1990, pp. 42-45.

Bowen, D.E., Chase, R.B., Cummings, T.G. *Service Management Effectiveness*, Jossey-Bass Publishers, San Francisco, CA, 1990.

Brown, J. "A Good Network is Like Money in the Bank," *Network World*, Vol. 7, No. 48, Nov. 26, 1990, pp. 13, 40, 44, 54.

Brown, S.W., Gummesson, E., Edvardsson, B. and Gustavsson, BengtOve, *Service Quality: Multidisciplinary and Multinational Perspectives*, Lexington Books, 1991.

Chase, R.B. and Bowen, D.E. "Service Quality and the Service Delivery System: A Diagnostic Framework," in *Service Quality: Multidisciplinary and Multinational Perspectives*, edited by Brown, et al., 1991.

Clemons, E.K. and Row, M.C. "Information Technology at Rosenbluth Travel: Competitive Advantage in a Rapidly Growing Global Service Company," *Journal of Management Information Systems*, Vol. 8, No. 2, Fall 1991, pp. 53-79.

Davis, S.M., *Future Perfect*, New York: Addison-Wesley, 1987.

DiPrimio, A. *Quality Assurance in Service Organizations*, Chilton Book Company, Radon, P.A., 1987.

Garvin, G.A., "Competing on the Eight Dimensions of Quality", *Harvard Business Review*, November-December 1987.

Gronroos, C., *Service Management and Marketing*, Canada: Lexington Books, 1990

Hart, C.W.L., "The Power of Unconditional Service Guarantees", *Harvard Business Review*, July/August, 1988.

Lindstrom, A.H., "Users Harvest a Variety of Applications," *Telephony*, Oct. 26, 1992.

Litterer, J. *The Analysis of Organizations*, Wiley, New York, N.Y., 1965.

Miles, I, "Services and Information Technology: Emerging Patterns," in Teare, R., Moutinho, L., and Morgan, N., editors, *Managing and Marketing Services in the 1990s*, Cassell Educational Limited, London, U.K., 1990.

Mills, P.K., *Managing Service Industries*, Cambridge, MA: Ballinger Publishing Co., 1986.

Normann, R., *Service Management: Strategy and Leadership in Service Business*, England: Wiley, 1991.

Parasuraman, A., Zeithaml, V.A., and Berry, L.L., *SERVQUAL: A Multiple-Item Scale for Measuring Consumer Perceptions of Service Quality*, Cambridge, MA: Marketing Science Institute, 1986.

Rajan, A. and Cooke, B., "The Impact of Information Technology on Employment in the Financial Services Industry", *National Westminster Bank Quarterly Review*, August, 1986: 21-35.

Riddle, D.I., *Service-Led Growth*, Westpoint, CT: Praeger, 1986.

Salamone, S. "Airline Reservation Network Flies into New Age of LANs," *Network World*, Vol. 7, No. 48, Nov. 26, 1990, pp. 34-54.

Sankar, C.S., and Snyder, C.A., "Managing Technologists Effectively: Is it an Issue," *1992 International Engineering Management Conference*, Eatontown, N.J., 1992.

Sasser, W.E. Jr., Hart, C.W., and Heskett, J.L., *The Service Management Course: Cases and Readings*, New York, NY: The Free Press, 1991.

Snyder, C.A., Cox, J.F., and Jesse, R.R., Jr., "A Dependent Demand Approach for Service Organization Planning and Control," *The Academy of Management Review*, Vol. 7, No. 3, July 1982, pp. 455-466.

Stebbing, L. *Quality Management in the Service Industry*, Ellis Horwood, N.Y., 1990.

"The Fortune 500 World's Largest Service Corporations," *Fortune*, August 24, 1992, pp. 208-225.

Ussery, R.W., Sankar, C.S., Boulton, W.R., Davidson, N., Snyder, C.A., *Managing Exponential Growth in Credit Card Processing: Strategies to Success*, Working Paper, TSYS, 1992.

Wexler, J.M. "Citicorp Overhauls Corporate Network," *ComputerWorld*, Nov. 18, 1991, Vol XXV, No 46, pp. 117.

Zemke, R. "The Emerging Art of Service Management," *Training*, Vol. 29, Iss. 1, Jan. 1992, pp. 36-42.

The Power of Electronic Data Interchange

Mr. Gary Templeton
Mr. Arthur Chen
Dr. Michael L. Gibson

Executive Abstract

Electronic Data Interchange (EDI) is a rising technology in the area of organizational connectivity and information sharing. The competitive advantages and power that EDI brings to the organization make it an attractive investment for firms of different interest. This paper discusses the origins and characteristics of EDI, the reasons to implement it, its use in relationship to existing strategic models, and its impact on organizational decision making. The intent of the paper is to provide a descriptive view of EDI and its possible impacts on business competitors to encourage that research be conducted on various categories of EDI usage.

EDI technology originated due to the cost of exchanging information between and within companies. It has proliferated in industry due to its use in providing immediate, accurate, and connected information to businesses reducing the cost of trading with the traditional mail system. When used correctly, EDI's characteristics provide a means by which a company can create competitive advantages. Managers should invest in the technology to establish such an advantage, to establish electronic relationships, and to remain competitively proactive. EDI should be considered a backbone technology to the business, one which impacts decisions effecting the business strategy. This is due to the power of EDI in impacting the organization in terms of structure and capability in its functional areas.

Using EDI to Support a Systems Model of Corporate Strategy

Mr. Gary Templeton
Mr. Arthur Chen
Dr. Michael L. Gibson

Executive Abstract

Corporate Strategy involves assessing the organizational strategic position, developing a strategy and strategic plan to carry out the strategy, implementing the strategy, and assessing the impact to maintain organizational strategy. Electronic Data Interchange (EDI) comprises establishing interconnectivity between all stakeholders for an organization. The use of EDI can aid in each phase of strategy development and implementation. This paper provides an organizational strategic model based on existing strategic model principles and the use of EDI to make the strategic model more viable.

The paper views strategy development as a system of managerial activity with components which may be defined, measured, evaluated, and reengineered according to the success of its output. This view of strategy development allows management to reduce the volatility of output, decreasing the likelihood of bad decisions. It allows for a great deal of structure in this highly unstructured decision environment, which allows for a greater amount of information to be used in decisions. It may also be used in finding irrelevant information in the strategic model and spotting information deficiencies. This model should be accompanied by the use of EDI because the characteristics of the technology allows for superior internal and environmental data to be captured for the strategy model builder.

Micro-to Mainframe Link

Ralph R. Gutowski, David (Chi-Chung) Yen, & Sooun Lee
Department of Decision Sciences
Miami University
Oxford, Ohio 45056

Executive Abstract

INTRODUCTION

Advances in communications technologies have permitted the rapid evolution of the microcomputer from a stand-alone processor to an integral part of an organization's information system. Furthermore, the importance of micro-to-mainframe communications in today's corporate computing environment lies in the ability to utilize huge mainframe databases and to solve chronic mainframe backlog problems. At least 45 percent of the PCs used in large corporations already have been connected to a host-based (mainframe or minicomputer) network, and 76 percent of all Fortune 2000 companies want to be able to connect PCs with mainframes. This dramatically increasing demand for micro-to-mainframe connections stems from the benefits that such connections give today's corporate data processing: they satisfy user needs for mainframe data; the use of microcomputers in connection with mainframe provides some relief to mainframe backlog problems; the micro-to-mainframe connection may be viewed as a part of a large scale migration toward end-user computing.

This paper identifies those factors which afford general guidance to build a connection between micro and mainframe and addresses the strategic concerns in building links.

DISCUSSION OF ISSUES

There are four methods for linking microcomputers to a mainframe computer: Terminal emulation, by means of an add-on board in the microcomputer or software; File transfer software, on the micro and/or the host; Protocol converters, automatically translating each device's language into a mutually understandable form; and Local area network, linking not only micros and hosts, but all network resources.

Technological factors affecting micro-to-mainframe connections include: topology (the physical arrangement of the wiring, circuitry, and communications equipment); the communication methodology (asynchronous or synchronous); code conversion (EDCDIC, ASCII); communication protocol standard (ISO, OSI); and network architecture (SNA, OSI).

Allowing a large number of end users, specifically end users with local processing capabilities, to have access to files residing on a corporate mainframe system creates serious managerial problems that are not easily solved. Those problems include data security, political problems, training of end users, and the changing role of information centers.

An analysis framework to facilitate the establishment of a micro-to-mainframe link encompasses three areas.

1. User needs analysis: Network design starts by assessing the requirements by documenting existing resources and current needs. In defining a network, user profile, distance, and applications profiles should be taken into consideration.

2. Technical Analysis: The total amount of data traffic during peak hours includes the length of messages determined by line and protocol control characters such as end of transmission indicator and synchronization characters. The data link control (DLCs) must be known to be able to calculate the ratio of overhead control characters to the applications data. The ratio of applications data to overhead data will be determined by the manner in which the protocol controls the message flow.

   The number of errors that occur effects the total traffic throughput since the messages that are received in error will have to be retransmitted. Therefore, the probable error rates in the total data traffic load should be taken into consideration. Technical analysis should also address protocol conversion across vendor products, methodologies for detecting and isolating technical problems, network performance and the host, and compatibility and non-compatibility of work stations.

3. Performance Analysis: Establishing communication between microcomputers and mainframes is difficult because the independently developed microcomputer architecture is incompatible with that of most mainframes for specifications such as character structure, transfer speed, word size, transfer size. The capacity of the microcomputer is another constraint that may limit communications between microcomputers and mainframes. If the micro does not have disk storage, manipulation of data files too long to be stored on one diskette becomes confusing.

An implementation plan should address the four connection methodologies: simple (dumb and intelligent emulation) asynchronous connection (Xmodem and Kermit); simple synchronous connection; simple 3270 coaxial connection; or integrated async/sync/coaxial connections. Three steps are suggested to facilitate effective implementation: sequential installation, monitoring usage variations, and support to raise user confidence and proficiency.

FINDINGS

Three future trends in micro-to-mainframe connections

are observed:

1. Micro-to-Mini connections: Initially, the larger systems to which micros were connected were almost exclusively mainframes, and development efforts on linkage products reflected this orientation. However, the direct micro-to-mini link scheme does impose demands on mainframe resources that can degrade the system's performance. One answer to this problem has been the use of minicomputers to perform some processing chores and to control communications with a network's micros. The ability to connect minicomputers and micros becomes increasingly important as these systems begin to be used as data computational servers at the departmental level, as decentralized gateways between micros and organizational mainframes, and as primary systems in small organizations.

2. Transparent connectivity between various systems: Among the current trends of the connections between micros and mainframes are the continuing efforts to develop and refine the interaction of end-user programs on a peer-to-peer basis. The goal of these efforts is completely transparent connectivity among the various systems and peripheral components increasingly required in today's integrated computing environments. New advanced communications function/virtual telecommunications access method products allow mainframe machines to achieve peer-to-peer communications with members of incompatible PC product lines. This provides micro users with transparent, concurrent access to multiple databases and with the additional information management capabilities this implies.

3. Products supporting multiple protocols with small package size and low power requirements: Another trend becoming evident is the appearance of micro-to-mainframe communications products that combine support for multiple protocols with small package size and low power requirements. Products combine CPU and transceiver elements on a single chip, allowing design of highly integrated, and highly intelligent, communications devices that take up very little room in a microcomputer. The devices will be programmable, allowing a single product to be adapted to support changes in equipment or protocol occurring after the initial implementation. These products will provide both manufacturers and users of micro-to-mainframe communications with products featuring increased flexibility in design and implementation.

CONCLUSION

Plugging in all shapes and sizes of computers into tomorrow's networks will be as easy as plugging in a telephone today. By the year 2000 IBM likely will have a universal operating system firmly established, and all of its computers will run the same programs. A software will be written for the universal level, with IBM creating translators to allow them to exchange information with older machines. In this scenario the microcomputers running the universal operating system could run all the programs now running on mainframes, allowing mainframes to support hundreds more terminal users. The mainframe will be processed locally by microcomputers, without using mainframe time.

A smoothly functioning network should allow the corporate information staff to monitor and address the performance of every computer on a particular network. By addressing in-house applications needs and existing or projected mainframe capabilities, companies should be able to select linking software that will give non-technical users fast and easy access to the best of both the micro and mainframe worlds.

It appears that the industry is moving toward more consistent interfaces, that both micro and mainframe environments should be the same so the user does not have to confront learning two or more sets of environments. Thus, these products provide flexibility to both manufacturers and users of micro-to-mainframe communications.

Establishing a micro to mainframe link is becoming an important necessity in many organizations. Careful planning and selection of the proper hardware and supporting software can help ensure the success of the effort. In doing so, selecting the correct strategic plan such as terminal emulation, protocol converter, file transfer software, and LAN should be analyzed. In addition, topology, protocols, architecture, transmission method should be taken into consideration for proper implementation of a link.

Section Nine

Accounting Information Systems

The Accountant's Contribution to Executive Information Systems

Mary B. Curtis
School of Accountancy
University of Kentucky
Lexington, KY 40506

ABSTRACT

Accountants can contribute to corporate strategy by participating in the design and operation of strategic information systems. Executive Information Systems (EIS), computerized systems that support top management in their strategic decision making, are one example. During the development of an EIS, accountants can assist in the identification of a sponsor, in cost/benefit determination for the initial proposal, in the analysis phase which will identify management's information and processing needs, and in locating information during the design phase. After the system has been implemented, accountants often serve as on-going Knowledge Providers. In addition, accountants, serving as EDP Auditors, can design and review internal controls to safe-guard the sensitive data utilized by EIS and help ensure data accuracy which is so critical to the development of proper corporate strategy.

THE ACCOUNTANT'S CONTRIBUTION TO EXECUTIVE INFORMATION SYSTEMS

Those who make strategic decisions for an organization have unique information needs that differ from lower-level decision makers because of the unstructured nature of their decisions, the scope of their decisions, and their level of authority (Stambaugh and Carpenter 1992). These decisions are often one-time, ad hoc, unpredictable, and sometimes made on an emergency basis (Turban 1993). The dynamic nature of such decisions has made it difficult, in the past, to support upper-level decision makers with computerized information systems. Instead, in most organizations, the class of middle management was built to function as human information systems.

In the last few years, a new type of information system, Executive Information Systems (EIS), have emerged for purposes of supporting senior management in their strategic decision making tasks. Factors which have led to the evolution of Executive Information Systems include: the need to reduce the large corps of middle-managers (Goldfarb 1990), progress in computer technology to the point where computerized information systems that can support the decision-making requirements of upper-level managers are now possible (Miller 1989), the increased computer literacy of corporate executives today (Roberts 1993), and the increased complexity of decision-making in today's global economy (Miller 1989). Approximately 1,000 EIS were in use worldwide in 1991, with about 600 in the United States and 100 in Canada (Hopkins 1991). EIS are expected to be one of the biggest

software growth markets of the 1990s (Bird 1991).

The purpose of this paper is to discuss the role of accountants in the development and management of Executive Information Systems. The first section will provide a short description of the possible functions of EISs and the technology used to accomplish these. Section two will discuss the development of an EIS and accountants' roles in this process. The third section will present some ideas on accountants as on-going Knowledge Providers. The fourth section will discuss EISs from the EDP Audit point of view. The fifth and final section will summarize by presenting several causes and preventions of EIS failures and accountants' roles in failure prevention.

1. THE FUNCTIONS AND TECHNOLOGIES OF EIS

In order to facilitate company-wide strategic decisions, information systems built to support executives must contain a wide variety of readily available information and provide extremely fast and flexible access to these data. Since EISs are "an emerging technology", no standard, universally accepted definition exists for them as yet (Giordanella 1989). However, EIS can be described by their a) objectives, b) their capabilities, and c) their technological features.

1.1 Objectives

The combination of objectives for each EIS is unique since these systems are designed to meet the needs of individual organizations (Yeo 1991). A few of the more common objectives include: helping an executive make strategic and competitive decisions, keeping track of the overall business operation, facilitating communications between executives, and reducing the time spent on routine tasks (Miller 1989).

1.2 Capabilities

This multiplicity of objectives leads to a wide variety of capabilities for EIS. However, there are some capabilities which are standard in all EISs. Simplistic user interfaces, a wide variety of data, flexible processing capabilities and graphical output facilities are examples of the more common features.

Because of the nature of executive users, EISs must provide interfaces which are easily learned and utilized (O'Brien 1991). Executives seldom have the time or inclination to adequately train in the use of high-technical computer systems. In order to support strategic decision making, extensive information from both inside and outside of the organization

Table 1: Users and Uses of Executive Information Systems

1. CIGNA Corporation, a health care and insurance provider has an EIS that their Employee Benefits Division makes available to customers for information concerning available products and services (Burkan 1992);
2. North American Aircraft division of Rockwell International Corp. uses an EIS to deliver business reports and graphics to executives (Armstrong 1990);
3. Hertz uses an EIS to assess market share in contested areas and facilitate pricing decisions (Stambaugh and Carpenter 1992);
4. Mead Corporation uses their EIS as a corporate information system providing critical success factor analysis to all levels of management (Roberts 1993).
5. Other uses include:
   a. facilitating TQM programs,
   b. overcoming data-sharing problems for geographically dispersed corporate divisions,
   c. linking executives together for communications purposes,
   d. information mining for marketing purposes

must be gathered or accessed to support both quantitative and qualitative analysis. This knowledge must be extremely accurate and is very sensitive from a security stand-point. Processing capabilities must provide the ability to search, ad hoc, through information and compare between factors, companies, divisions, years, or industries. Other pre-programmed processing procedures, such as presentation sets or briefing books, must also be available (Minear 1991). Finally, output in an EIS is typically visual and is often graphical in nature, showing trends and other images, although underlying numbers are usually available in "Drill-Down" form (Minear 1991).

1.3 Technology

Due to the nature of these systems and their data access needs, the information used by EISs is usually stored in databases, either within the EIS application itself or in other accessible systems. Most EIS interaction is performed from microcomputers, although the system itself may reside on any type of computer platform. Networks, both LAN and WAN, are commonly used to facilitate the interaction of these various platforms. Telecommunications, along with E-Mail capabilities, have become an integral part of most EIS. Today, most EISs are implemented using one of many software packages available, which provide extensive capabilities for tailoring the system to a company's particular specifications. There are also many add-on features available from various vendors that will enhance a basic package. EIS software developers are strong supporters of open systems architecture which makes mix-and-match software possible.

2. DESIGNING THE SYSTEM

The steps to designing an EIS include development of a proposal which will specify the expectations of those involved,

analysis to identify the questions that executives want answered, design to find the answers to those questions, and implementation to present the answers in a correct, complete, timely, and understandable manner. Accountants can make unique contributions to the project team in each of these phases.

It is important to recognize at the onset that the development of an EIS is a never-ending project. An effective EIS will continually evolve as new informational possibilities and needs arise, and as new software and hardware are made available (Watson and Glover 1989).

2.1 Proposal Stage

The first and possibly most important step in the development of an EIS is to find an executive sponsor, a high-level executive with decision-making power who understands and supports the EIS project. This champion must have the support of the CEO, able to identify the company's informational needs, and willing to dedicate a significant amount of time to its development. It is widely believed that systems without executive sponsors will most certainly fail, with great financial cost to the organization. Accountants, with their wide access to management, are in a unique position to identify likely candidates within top management who may be amenable to serving in this capacity. Accountants are usually aware of the political and consensus-building strengths of different managers and typically know those who have voiced concern or dissatisfaction with the quality and extent of information currently available. In some organizations, a high-ranking accountant may actually serve as the champion.

A second point in the initial stages of development at which the involvement of accountants will be crucial is in cost/benefit analysis. A feasibility study is usually necessary in order to sell such a system to upper management. Organi-

Table 2: Functions and Features of Executive Information Systems

```
1.   Replacement of paper reports - Briefing Book
2.   Trend analysis
3.   Exception reporting
4.   Drill down
5.   Ad-hoc queries and data analysis
6.   Point or touch access to menus through graphical user interface
7.   Fast response time
8.   Multilevel security
9.   Data validity
10.  Simple data input-output procedures
11.  Extreme user friendliness
12.  Navigational aids
13.  Written interpretations
14.  Hypertext and hypermedia
15.  Communications links to other users and outside data bases
16.  Electronic Mail
17.  Tickler or To-do package to track and schedule events
18.  Office support
19.  Facsimile support
20.  Audio and video teleconferencing
```

zations considering the development of EIS may mistakenly consider the investment in such a system to be unjustified because they are unable to quantify the potential benefits that can be derived from the system. Accountants are often in the position to identify the benefits management could gain from the new information and to measure the potential monetary value of these benefits.

2.2 Analysis

The ultimate goal in designing an EIS is to provide executives with the information they need for decision-making, when they need it, and in the form they find easiest to understand and use. In order to produce such a system, it is necessary to carefully analyze the decision-making informational requirements of company executives and build the simplest means of meeting those needs (Bentley 1989). The first step is to understand what executives do - the nature of their activities.

Since accountants work directly with managers and in many cases are managers themselves, they will have a natural understanding of executives' procedures and tasks. In addition, because they are trained as decision makers and are knowledgeable of corporate strategy, accountants should be able to anticipate many of the strategic decisions that corporate executives must undertake. The accountants' understanding of the types and locations of information available to meet these needs, both inside and outside of the organization, will be invaluable.

2.3 Design

The purpose of the design phase is to determine how to implement the requirements identified in the analysis phase. It is not an easy task to design a system that is simple and relevant to executive users' needs, while providing the advanced capabilities requested by more technical users. The resulting system must be flexible enough to change and expand as its users' needs evolve. The two features considered the most critical to a successful EIS are the user interface and access to a great variety of information.

The design phase encompasses a myriad of tasks. First is the selection of architecture, including software and hard-

Table 3: Potential Benefits of Executive Information Systems

```
1.   Ability to analyze trends
2.   Augmentation of managers' leadership capabilities
3.   Enhanced personal thinking and decision making
4.   Contribution to strategic control flexibility
5.   Enhanced organizational competitiveness in the market place
6.   Ease access to existing information
7.   Instruments of change
8.   Increased executive time horizons
9.   More timely information
10.  Better reporting system
11.  Improved mental model of the business for executives.
12.  Help improved consensus building and communication
13.  Improve office automation efficiency, timeliness, and accuracy
14.  Reduce time for finding and integrating information
15.  Early identification of company problems
16.  Improved analysis of company performance
17.  Detailed examination of critical success factors
18.  Better understanding of enterprise operations
19.  Time management and team coordination can be enhanced, allowing users to
     be more productive
20.  Increased communication capacity and quality
```

ware. Next, the required data must be located and interfaces designed. Prototypes are typically developed during the final design step. While the selection of computer architecture may not be their forte, accountants can be extremely useful in the other two areas.

DATA: The requirements identified during the analysis phase will dictate the information to be utilized by the system. At this point, it is the responsibility of the project team to find that knowledge and determine how access to it will be accomplished. The information may consist of internal information as well as external information, and may be extracted from its source to be stored by the EIS or it may merely be accessed by the EIS when needed (Roberts 1993). The project team may find the required knowledge on a computer system or in manual form. Internally-available information could reside on the same system as the EIS or on a different computer; it may be marketing, financial or production oriented. The external data may be available through a communications network or it could exist only in manual form and so must be transcribed; it may come from databases, newspapers, industry newsletters, or other origins (Turban 1993). Accountants, through their experience, industry contacts, and continual CPE training, may be aware of sources for much of the required information.

Before the EIS can use any knowledge source, however, the content of the data to be employed must be carefully assessed to ensure the data are both timely and accurate. EISs are a part of the answer to harmonizing the use of interlinked databases and communication channels, but they do little to improve security, control information, or improve the quality of available information (Bentley 1989). In most situations, accountants will have a feel for the accuracy of information from within the company and other possible problems that could be encountered with regard to that data, due to their other corporate responsibilities. In addition, as discussed in Section 3, EDP auditors should be included in this evaluation.

PROTOTYPING: Prototyping has been widely acclaimed as an effective approach to requirements definition and systems development, particularly in the development of systems that support executive decision making (Guimaraes & Saraph 1991). These models can be built to elicit reactions from senior management, who can then make suggestions on how to modify the systems to be more responsive to their needs. This method of iterative design and review is an excellent way to develop a user interface that is responsive to user preferences. Accountants can make significant contributions to the initial development and subsequent revisions of prototypes since their knowledge of accounting data and experience with financial forms and reports will give them insights into designs for easily understood computer screens, forms, and reports for the EIS (Stambaugh and Carpenter 1992).

2.4 Implementation

The implementation stage of an EIS is very similar to that in other types of software development projects. Purchase, or development, and installation of the software may actually have been accomplished during prototyping. While much of this phase in system development is highly technical, there are aspects in which the accountant team member can be indispensable. The resulting system must be tested and retested. Users must be trained, but gently since these users tend to be novices in terms of computers. Simple yet complete documentation, to guide executives in their operation of the system, must be written. This documentation should be used during training, so that the executives will be familiar with its contents and format.

3. KNOWLEDGE PROVIDERS

One of the most important types of knowledge utilized by Executive Information Systems is corporate financial information, such as the results of operations, financial position, and cash flows. In addition, once executives become comfortable with the use of EIS, their appetites for data become "insatiable" (Armstrong 1990). Accountants typically serve in the role of Knowledge Providers, where they and their information systems create, collect, maintain, analyze and publish information for use by the corporate EIS (Stambaugh and Carpenter 1992).

EISs can use one of two strategies to access corporate financial information: the systems can pull the data into their own databases on a scheduled basis (periodically refreshed) or they can access the data in its source database. Both of these methods present challenges to the accountants who are responsible for maintaining the knowledge and providing it to the EIS as it is needed.

"As needed" is a critical factor in supplying knowledge to an EIS. Executive decision making does not occur on a schedule that can conform to accounting systems' month-end and year-end closing procedures. There will always be a conflict between the accountant's perceived need for extensive review of data before it is released and the need for immediate access by users (Reese 1993). This is the age-old conflict between accuracy and timeliness. For example, Sprint found that their executives, who assumed that any information provided by the EIS was accurate, would sometimes accessed accounting data before it had been reviewed and adjusted. The result was miscues and confusion. On other occasions, they experienced data conflict when seemingly similar information was pulled from two different source databases (Reese 1993).

One solution to this problem is the replacement of immediate, on-line access to accounting data with periodically prepared, reformatted reports or slide-shows for viewing on the screen (Stambaugh and Carpenter 1992). Although this greatly limits management's interactive analytical capabilities, it does ensure that decisions based on financial information are based on accurate data. Others suggest that training users of the system as to how and when to use various sources of data is the preferred solution.

Table 4: Applications Controls Risks Often Found in EIS

```
Input:
    1: Dependency on the input controls within the many, widely dispersed
       source systems.
    2: Lack of standard input controls over external data.
    3: Internal control concerns over qualitative data.
    4: Pressure on Knowledge Providers to supply data before review completed.
    5: Source-database access may prevent adequate review prior to release.
    6: Unauthorized access through simplistic interface.
    7: Extensive requirements to restrict and manage access to system.
Processing:
    1: It is essential that all of this software operate accurately.
    2: Constant modification to software inhibits maintenance controls.
    3: Lack of structured development process.
Output:
    1: Output can be sent through E-mail to unauthorized recipients.
    2: Graphical output is more difficult to verify.
```

Another alternative to the use of financial knowledge by EIS is to change the nature of data provided to the systems from a time-period basis to an event basis (Benbasat and Dexter 1979, Stambaugh and Carpenter 1992). Using this approach, individual events are recorded and made available for use by the EIS as they occur. Management will essentially be given the details of the financial dealings of the company. It is then the EIS's responsibility to group and summarize financial events into what ever basis for summarization needed: type of transaction, time period, customer, product type, etc. Since adjusting, closing and reversing journal entries will not be reflected in the event-based data, the EIS will never be able to recreate the financial statements presented by the accounting department. This approach will, however, provide management with fairly accurate data on a more timely basis than could otherwise be achieved and with the details needed for drill down purposes.

4. EDP AUDITORS

It is the responsibility of internal auditing to review "the reliability and integrity of financial and operating information" (Standards 1978). Because of this role, the emergence of new systems will have an immediate impact on internal auditors (Paul 1992). Although auditor involvement in the EIS is critical "to ensure that the system includes adequate preventive, detective and corrective controls and that the integrity of data is safeguarded" (Stambaugh and Carpenter 1992), this involvement is often accomplished with very little training or guidance. Standards and educational programs seldom precede the implementation of new technology.

The identification of control risks and concerns will require that EDP auditors invest considerable time determining the exact composition of their company's EIS, both in terms of critical capabilities and the technology employed to achieve these capabilities (Simon 1993). Although these capabilities and technological components may exist individually in other systems, the number, variety, and particular combination may not have been encountered previously. In addition, the objectives of an EIS may result in data characteristics and processing procedures unfamiliar to auditors, certainly be different from transaction processing systems (Floryan 1993, Simon 1993). This, in turn, will lead to a different set of control risks and new control procedures that have not been encountered previously. The control risks of an EIS may be

Table 5: General Controls Risks Often Found in EIS

```
    Data:
        1: Data may be accessed outside of the application, through the DBMS.
        2: Data may be stored on less secure personal computers.
        3: Use of laptops allow data to be carried out of secure environments.
        4: Downloading capabilities make theft of EIS data easier.
        5: Unauthorized EIS users have authorized access to the network.
        6: Standard telecommunications control procedures are not feasible.
    Software:
        1: Open systems architecture exposes the system to control leaks.
        2: Rapid Development could lead to a analysis or design failure.
    Hardware:
        1: The backup of data residing on micros is not always performed.
        2: Ensuring a consistent backup policy for all locations is difficult.
        3: Contingency plans may not include microcomputers applications.
    Procedures and People:
        1: Executives often resist security measures and control procedures.
```

defined in terms relating to EIS capabilities (which is an application controls approach), or in terms of EIS technological capabilities (a general controls approach) (IAPC 1991, Simon 1993).

Internal controls within EISs present a peculiar problem to EDP auditors. Since a fundamental principle of EISs is that they be very easy to manipulate by relatively unskilled and often impatient users, internal controls inhibiting this flexibility will be rejected or ignored. The internal controls must, therefore, be extremely sophisticated in order to provide maximum security, but function behind the scenes. The internal controls must be "seamless" (Harper 1993).

The two problems mentioned above suggest the need for EDP auditor involvement in the systems development process. This is and will remain, however, a major point of disagreement between many systems developers and EDP auditors (Rittenberg and Davis 1979, Grabski et al. 1987).

5. DISCUSSION AND SUMMARY

When the development of an Executive Information System fails to reach implementation, due to any number of reasons, it is said that there was an "EIS failure" (Barrow 1990). Systems failures can occur at many junctures. Systems, which are implemented, may never be used or systems that are used for a time may eventually fall out of use. The possible causes of EIS system failure are wide-ranging, including inability to secure a champion for the system, political infighting within upper management, inadequate analysis by the project team, poor software or overly complex user interfaces, or inadequate system maintenance during times of changing management needs (Eckerson 1990, Watson and Glover 1989).

The failure of an EIS to satisfy its users can have devastating affects on an organization. Paller and Laska (1990) contend that there are more EIS failures than successes. This is a

Table 6: Causes of EIS Failure

1. **Management Failures and/or Political Problems**
   a. Lack of sponsorship
   b. Perception of the system as unimportant
   c. Lack of commitment by management
   d. Resistance by middle management
   e. Misrepresentation of true potential
   f. Unknown objectives or inability to define information requirements
   g. Requirement for cost-justification of the EIS
   h. Insufficient information system department resources
   g. Loss of interest by executives
   i. Unwillingness to train

2. **Developer Failures**
   a. Failure of the system to meet objectives
      1. Inadequate consideration of the reasons for developing an EIS
      2. Inadequate analysis of needs
      3. Poor development tool selection
   b. Doubtful data integrity,
   c. Insufficient depth of information
   d. Slow applications development.

3. **Technology Failures**
   a. Hardware
      1. Problems accessing data
      2. Inability to support required functions including simultaneous processing
      3. Inadequate capacity and speed, resulting in poor response time
   b. Software
      1. Problems accessing data
      2. Insufficient functions
      3. Lack of user friendliness
      4. Inability to integrate software packages
   c. Users
      1. Inability to maintain databases
      2. Inability to learn to use the system
      3. Resistance to the system or its use

4. **Cost**
   a. In dollars, to develop
   b. In users' time, to analyze and train
   c. In political terms

5. **Time**
   a. Too much time to develop
   b. Too much time to train
   c. Too much time to maintain

shocking statement and not necessarily supported by other researchers, but if making organizations aware of the possibility of failure will help to prevent it, then this forewarning should be highly publicized.

The potential repercussions of system failure are great. Most certainly the careers of the developers will suffer from this failure. The executives and other managers who were depending on the system to solve some of their problems may not have anywhere else to turn. The money invested, or wasted, could have been put into alternate forms of information systems which might have solved some of the organization's informational problems. The organization will certainly be hesitant to delve into the development of other EIS, and may possibly shy away from even DSS systems due to lack of confidence.

Certain steps can be taken to help a company avoid experiencing an EIS failure, including many of those mentioned previously. An EIS must have not only a champion, but also a broad base of executive support. Offering senior managers the opportunity to attend computer appreciation seminars to remove the mystery of computer terminology is one approach companies can take (Karten 87). To prevent management support from dwindling, the benefits detailed in the system proposal should be explained and discussed as often as possible. A competent and enthusiastic project team, especially the project manager, is critical for the success of an EIS development project. A thorough evaluation of informational and analytical requirements must be completed. To guard against unidentified objectives and help reduce the possibility of loosing management's interest, fast prototyping is often suggested (Eckerson 1990, Barrow 1990). In order to meet the demands of the users, appropriate technology must be selected to fit their styles and environments (Turban 1993). Finally, to ensure that the system continues to meet users' needs after implementation, an appropriate support staff should be assembled (Holmes 1993, Watson 1990). Usage reports can help pinpoint the elements of the system that are more highly utilized (Floryan 1993). The accountant's role in all of these phases of the development and continuing operation of an EIS is essential to prevent systems failure.

REFERENCES

Armstrong, David. 1990. The People Factor in EIS Success. *Datamation* (April 1): 73-79.

Barrow, Craig. 1990. Implementing an Executive Information System: Seven Steps for Success. *Journal of Information Systems Management* 7 (Spring): 41-49.

Benbasat, I. and Dexter, A.S. 1979. Value and Events Approaches to Accounting: An Experimental Evaluation. *The Accounting Review* (October): 735-749.

Bentley, Trevor. 1989. Computer Threats and Opportunities. *Management Accounting* (UK) 67 (November): 45.

Bird, Jane. 1991. Managing Information Technology: Let Your Fingers Do the Walking. *Management Today* (November): 97-104.

Eckerson, Wayne. 1990. Politics, Technology Woes Hinder the Success of EIS. *Network World* 7 (November 12): 1,77.

Floryan, Chris. 1993. Director of Executive Support for the Information Systems Department, Aetna Life and Casualty. Interview on November 18.

Friend, David. 1989. Benefits of an Executive Information System. *Information Management Review* 4, Issue 3: 7-15.

Giordanella, Richard. 1989. Choosing an Executive Information System. *Journal of Accounting & EDP* 5 (Spring): 10-16.

Goldfarb, Eric. 1990. Think Develop a Winning EIS Mind-Set. *Computerworld* (June 25): 91.

Grabski, Severin V., Reneau, J. Hal, and West, Stephen G. 1987. A Comparison of Judgement, Skills, and Prompting Effects Between Auditors and Systems Analysts. *MIS Quarterly* (June): 151-61.

Guimaraes, Tor and Saraph, Jayant V. 1991. The Role of Prototyping in Executive Decision Systems. *Information & Management* 21 (December): 257-267.

Harper, John. 1993. Director of EDP Audit for Sprint Corporation. Interview on November 22.

Holmes, Thomas. 1993. Former Director of Architecture and Planning for Information systems. Interview on November 8.

Hopkins, Bob. 1991. Executive Information Systems Take Off. *CMA Magazine* 65 (October): 31-35.

Internal Auditing Practices Committee. 1991. *Risk Assessment and Internal Control - EDP Characteristics and Considerations*. Addendum 1 to International Standard on Auditing. International Federation of Accountants, NY, NY.

Karten, Naomi. 1989. Why Executives Don't Compute. *Information Strategy: The Executive's Journal* 4 (Fall): 38-39.

Miller, Robert. 1989. Executive Information Systems Help You Conduct Your Business. *Today's Office* (April): 16-24.

Minear, Michael N. 1991. Implementing an Executive Information System. *Computers in Healthcare* 12 (July): 34-40.

O'Brien, Rita Cruise. 1991. Brief Case: EIS and Strategic Control. *Long Range Planning* 24 (October): 125-127.

Paller, Alan; Laska, Richard. 1990. Executive Information Systems: What Users Want Today. *Personal Computing* 14 (Apr 27): 72-74.

Paul, Ross G. 1992. Open Systems Architecture: A New Challenge for EDP Auditors. *The EDP Auditor Journal* 1: 45-52.

Reese, Bob. 1993. Director of Security for Information systems Department for Sprint corporation. Interview on November 16.

Rittenberg, Larry E. and Davis, Gordon B. 1979. The Roles of Internal and External Auditors in Auditing EDP Systems. *The Internal Auditor* (February): 58-68.

Roberts, Burnell. 1993. Former CEO of Mead Corporation. Interview on November 12.

Simon, Jeffrey. 1993. Director of EDP Audit for Colgate-Palmolive Co. Interview on November 18.

Stambaugh, Clyde T. and Carpenter, Floyd W. 1992. The Roles of Accounting and Accountants in Executive Information Systems. *Accounting Horizons* 6 (September): 52-63.

Standards for the Professional Practice of Internal Auditing. 1978. Altamonte Springs, FL: The Institute of Internal Auditors, Section 300.

Turban, Efram. 1993. *Decision Support Systems and Expert Systems: Management Support Systems*. MacMillan Publishing Company (New York, Third edition).

Watson, Hugh. 1990. Avoiding Hidden EIS Pitfalls. *Computerworld* 24 (June 25): 87-91.

Watson, Hugh and Glover, Harry. 1989. Common and Avoidable Causes of EIS Failure. *Computerworld* 23 (Dec 4): 90-91.

Yeo, Hilary. 1991. MCI Counts on Intuitive Systems to Help Make Decisions. *Computing Canada* (January 17): 43.

An Object-Oriented Paradigm for Modeling Financial Systems

Anil Kumar
Department of MIS and DS
Fogelman College of Business and Economics
Memphis State University
Memphis, TN 38152
Telephone # : 901-678-2462

Amarnath Prakash
Department of MIS and DS
Fogelman College of Business and Economics
Memphis State University
Memphis, TN 38152
Telephone # : 901-678-2462

INTRODUCTION

Business firms are dependent on critical accounting information to perform many tasks such as reporting profit, calculating cash flows, evaluating assets, analyzing performance, and developing financial strategies. The criticality of these tasks underscores the indispensability of developing computerized financial accounting systems in most business firms.

BACKGROUND

One important issue in implementing a computerized financial accounting systems in a shared environment is the selection of an appropriate data model to capture the essence of accounting practices. Designing a generic data model to accommodate environment-specific variables and procedures has to take into account a complex set of building blocks that contribute to the configuration of new accounting systems. In addition, there are some aspects of financial accounting structures, accounting procedures, and the linkage between structures and procedures that present special requirements that only an appropriately designed data model can fulfill.

There are a few relational data models that are used in the design and development of financial systems. Inspite of the prevalence of the use of these relational models in the market today, the inability of these models to integrate various accounting structures and procedures leaves a vacuum to be filled. The advent of object-oriented technology has provided fresh impetus to the search of an optimal and generic model that is both adaptive and user-friendly.

DISCUSSION OF ISSUES

The intrinsic incapability of a relational data model to generalize abstractions and complex structures and the inability of exercising a tighter control over accounting procedures are a few critical drawbacks. On the other hand, in an object-oriented model the encapsulation of behavior within an object provides a means for modeling accounting procedures. Such advanced features promote a design that integrates accounting structures and accounting procedures and helps create an user-friendly, modular, and reliable system. The object-oriented paradigm can be used effectively as a conceptual foundation for modeling financial accounting systems. The idea of frames as a knowledge representation scheme, the concepts of inheritance, behavior encapsulation, and polymorphism are central in the design of an object-oriented model.

Despite the diverse paths along which object-oriented concepts have been developed, a set of core object-oriented concepts common to most object-oriented programming languages and database systems has emerged. The object-oriented concepts of class and class hierarchy match the accounting concepts of account categories and account hierarchy. Hence, it would be appropriate to model account categories as classes. Similarly, the concept of behavior encapsulation provides a means to incorporate accounting procedures in the design thereby allowing the integration of accounting structures and accounting procedures. This integration, essentially, imbues objects with accounting knowledge, which makes them powerful building blocks that can be used to construct a system quickly.

Reusability is a powerful feature of object-oriented systems. It refers to reusing the methods and the structure of previously defined classes with the objective of improving the efficiency in developing software systems. An object is a collection of modules in the form of methods which serve as its public interface. This means that modularity is an innate feature of object-oriented models. Accounting objects, as a repertory of accounting procedural knowledge, can serve as basic building blocks for rapid development of accounting systems. A logical extension of this concept is the idea of establishing a library of financial accounting objects whereby the process of building financial accounting systems can be automated and simplified to a large extent. This not only improves the efficiency of the systems development process but also promotes standardization within and across various industries.

CONCLUSION

Accounting methods are relatively well structured. The object-oriented paradigm utilizes this fact to leverage and incorporate such methods into the behavioral components of objects. In addition, the objects of a financial accounting system are easily identifiable from a firm's chart of accounts. Firms within the same industry most likely work within the same variety of objects and use the same methods. Thus, there is a scope for building on this commonality and producing a generic model that accommodates industry-specific variations in the work environment.

Object-oriented concepts can and should be profitably applied in traditional areas of business. Object-oriented concepts provide system developers with flexibility, versatility, and modularity. Model building and system development could benefit greatly from object-oriented technology. Familiarity with these concepts is bound to stimulate innovative ideas on their application in many business areas. Object-oriented models are rapidly becoming mainstream tools for developing software systems. Businesses should learn to adopt and adapt these new tools and technologies for improving the efficiency and effectiveness of their operations.

DIRECTIONS FOR FURTHER RESEARCH

The design of a generic object-oriented model that can incorporate the dynamic set of variables operating in a heterogenous business environment will provide optimal design solutions. There is also a need for modification in the systems analysis and design methodologies to guide the construction of object-oriented financial information systems. Research in the areas of cross-functional impacts, object standardization, and modeling looks promising and beneficial for the development of object-oriented methodology as a emerging technology.

An Entity-Relationship View of the Third Wave Accounting Paradigm

P. Paul Lin and Lijen Ko
Department of Accounting
College of Management Science
National cheng Kung University
Tainan, Taiwan
Tel: (6) 2757575 ext 53428
Fax: (6) 2744104

Executive Abstract

The world is fast emerging from the clash of new values, new technologies, and new geopolitical relationships. Consequently, the greatest challenge for chief executive officers (CEOs) in the 90s is to reengineer their companies to meet the ever-changing and increasingly competitive global market. Organizations rely on, among others, accounting information systems (AIS) to run their businesses and stay competitive. Nonetheless, information technology is creating significant impacts on the accounting professionals. AIS provide information for decision-making and can be a key role of the business reengineering processes in the 90s.

Elliott (1992) envisioned several differences between the conventional and the third wave accounting information systems (TWAIS). First, TWAIS will focus on changes in resources and processes and, the resources and obligations measured in TWAIS may also change. Second, third wave organizations are focused on their customers, and their AIS must deal with measuring the values created for customers. Finally, TWAIS must provide real-time dials on the business rather than waiting for events to occur before recording them, thus providing only retrospective information about the enterprise.

Chen's (1976) Entity-Relationship (ER) model has been widely used by information professionals in database design. The ER approach uses *entity*, *relationship*, and *attributes* to represent the enterprise view of a database system. Entities are distinct objects that are of interest to the firm. Relationships are the meaningful interactions between (among) entities. Attributes are the data items that describe entities and relationships. Each attribute is defined on a value set (domain) and can take a value from its domain.

A company's competitive advantage is a function of how well a company can manage its five competitive forces—the threat of new entrants, the threat of substitute products or services, the bargaining power of suppliers, the bargaining power of buyers, and the rivalry among the existing competitors (Porter 1990). A company can create competitive advantage by better optimizing or coordinating these five competitive forces. Consequently, TWAIS should provide the information concerning Porter's five competitive forces. Information concerning these five competitive forces can be obtained from information services such as DIALOG, LEXIS/NEXIS, CompuServ, BRS, Orbit, OCLC or Dow Jones. Using the available information technology and information services, TWAIS can hook up information databases services to collect relevant information of each competitive force.

The ER diagram can be used to represent a firm's enterprise view of its database system and is an effective tool to describe the business environment. The ER Approach is used to capture the semantic features of a company's business activities. The enterprise view of a firm faithfully represents the real business environment and Porter's (1990) five competitive forces that determine industry competition. Third wave companies conduct businesses and collect the information concerning the five competitive forces. These competitive forces are represented as the entities in an ER diagram, and the important interactions among entities as the relationships in the ER diagram. The entities and relationships are described using the attributes of ER diagram, which contain the information that should be maintained in TWAIS.

Accounting professionals of the second wave paradigm do not have enough skill and/or knowledge to provide information effectively in third wave companies. Third wave companies constantly utilize information technology to compete with domestic and international rivals. As a consequence, accounting educators should employ the student(customer)-oriented approach and create the third wave values (skills) for the students. In fact, for the accountants to continue to sell their services at a premium price, they must be the producers of "state-of-the-art" information. Since the curriculum should prepare graduates to enter third wave companies, accounting educators must teach students an accounting model which is suitable to the third wave world.

Third wave accountants should not be content with applying debit/credit rules to prepare financial statements. The role of accountants may be at stake if they attempt to isolate themselves from the rapid changes of information technology and the impacts thereof. Computer systems can be designed to perform accounting procedures provided that transactions are recorded in the computer-readable format. Third wave accounting professionals are information specialists and have the capability to effectively and economically prepare or collect relevant information for decision-making, regardless of its location. As a result, accounting professionals should focus on using information technology to improve the information quality. Accounting professionals may adapt to change and thrive, or they may ignore change and wither. The opportunity for accounting professionals is to be part of an information age. The danger is that accounting professionals may be stereotyped as conservative and may try to stay in the world they understood and in which they have been successful.

The Influence of Evolution on Computer Accounting Systems

Donald D. Martin
Central Missouri State University
405 A Dockery
Warrensburg, MO 64093
(816) 543-8560

Executive Abstract

The chronological aging of a computer accounting system increases greatly the difficulty in operating the system. The older an accounting program or application is, the more susceptible it is to various types of error. This phenomena is easily illustrated by the difficulties often encountered in using a program which has been stored and idle for a period of time. Frequently, the program will not run, even if previously operational. Similar observations can be found when changing parameters in an on-going application or when adding programs to an existing system. These obvious difficulties seem to be totally unrelated. However, the following discussion will show that continual evolution of computer accounting systems can be applied to the process of natural selection, thought formerly by most to be limited to living organisms.

NATURAL SELECTION

The theory of natural selection was first explained in 1859 by Charles Darwin's *On The Origin Of Species* (1859). He postulated that each living system constantly adapted to the environment of its existence. The principle of adaptation by which each slight variation is preserved, if useful, was named natural selection. Later, works by Spencer, Fisher, and Weinberg extended Darwin's natural selection phenomena to various non-living systems and finally to abstract ideas. Evolution through natural selection exists in a population if: (1) successive reproductions occur, (2) the reproduction process is not exact, and (3) the environment favors certain variations. The population increase in "fitness" is judged by the environment.

When applied to systems, the theory of natural selection has two basic theorems:(1) the existence theorem--The fitness of a population as measured by its environment will improve with time, and (2) the evolutionary potential theorem--describes the conflicting role played by variation. Because a population must reduce variation to be better suited to a particular environment, the theorem becomes: the more suited and adapted a population becomes to an environment, the less adaptable it is to other environments.

MODELING COMPUTER ACCOUNTING SYSTEM FOR NATURAL SELECTION

With this modified theory, the behavior of computer accounting systems can be modeled to fit the three prerequisites of natural selection. The computer system is said to reproduce at the end of each time period, T, as the life cycle. If during time period T system modifications have occurred then exactness is not maintained. The variation may be caused by program modification, or even by component structure difference. But, if these variations do occur, their assignment to select periods through the arbitrary T is possible. This creation of T periods and modifications satisfies successive reproductions. Since modification is arbitrarily assigned to various T's, prerequisite two is also satisfied. (the reproduction process is not exact).

Prerequisite three (the environment favors certain variations) is satisfied because of the imperfect detecting ability of programmers and analysts. Some undesirable variations are eliminated only by chance. The programmers and analysts by their diagnostic procedures provide a selective environment which is constantly removing certain variations from the population. The environment is selective because each variation does not have a similar probability of detection. Eventually, following the two theorems of evolution, the system has adapted well to its environment but contains the potential for non-acceptance of new programs, applications, etc. Adaptation or evolution has occurred so well that the system has bred itself into an undesirable status.

To illustrate, think of the data as the environment. The planned data changes alter the net of existing data relationships are altered. These alterations of data relationships are less immediately apparent and ominous but just as potent in eventual effect. By the time the trouble is encountered, the initializing influence may even be forgotten, making recovery extremely difficult. Programs not consistently ran and updated on comprehensive test data will soon run counter to the net's unexplored data cases. Most programmers and analysts can recall at least on instance of this. Soon the programs are not operational, a victim of uncontrolled evolution.

A second example is the environment in the computer supporting the program. When an error is detected maintenance, changes are made in the program's population of instructions. If successful, nothing further is done and the program has adapted to the computer. But, how can the less obvious errors be detected and corrected? Such error types are therefore often corrected without investigating the underlying reasons. Returning the program to operating status is deemed sufficient. As the computer accumulates these changes, the programs supported must also change. This evolution soon places these programs in an non-operative mode when a run is attempted in another computer environment.

SYSTEM EVOLUTION'S USEFULNESS AND POSTPONEMENT

Viewing accounting computer systems in this evolutionary manner helps explain why various things happen as they do. The duplicate versions of an accounting program will change significantly over time, when running on different computers. The natural selection helps predict that different versions will become more dissimilar over time. Because of this evolutionary effect, standardization, a long sought goal, becomes even more elusive.

Moreover, evolution is helpful in explaining the bowl shape of the reliability curve for systems. Based on the works by Eisenhut (1973) and Ogdin (1972), system evolutionary influence should help predict this upturn in failure per unit point in which implementation is complete. The actual shape of the curve could be shown a variable of the particular evolutionary environment the system exists within.

The major use of recognizing the effect of evolution on systems is to postpone its effect. The best method would seem to be the use of continuous diagnostic procedures. A continuing stream of diagnostics would have the effect of constantly shifting the relevant environment in which the system operates, ensuring dynamic coverage of the system. The environment would therefore remain standard and the system would not be subjected to abnormal evolutionary stress. This could best be accomplished by assignment to a specific unit, segregated from most day-to-day operational pressures. The internal "diagnostic" team would effectively counter the evolutionary pressure.

CONCLUSION

Darwin's original thesis on natural selection is modified and shown applicable to non-living systems. With this modification, a theory of the evolution of computer systems become possible. Examination of specific environments, illustrate that evolution in computer systems does occur. The interactions and influences are shown to constantly favor change, leading to natural selection and evolution.

Can IT Help Recurrent Accounting Problems?

Athar Murtuza, Ph. D., CMA
David A. Rosenthal, Ph. D.
W. Paul Stillman School of Business
Seton Hall University
South Orange, NJ 07079
201-761-9233   Fax: 201-761-9217

Executive Abstract

It is well recognized that the productive use of information technology (IT) can help an organization improve its effectiveness and even enhance its evolutionary potential. The improvement in the effectiveness of an organization with the help of IT can be exemplified by surveying how IT has helped improve the everyday effectiveness of accounting departments by providing solutions to problems that have long burdened the accounting profession.

In his 1982 *Management Accounting* paper, "Accounting Problems Nobody Talks About," Vincent Giovinazzo, discussed a number of everyday problems that plague accounting departments in all sorts of organizations. Despite their universality, the problems listed by Giovinazzo lacked the chic or the glamour which might have allowed them to be discussed systematically and frequently in the professional literature. Such persistent, universally occurring but rarely discussed problems, according to Giovinazzo were:

Source data vulnerability; Involvement of non-accounting personnel

Non-integrated accounting systems; Processing and reporting lags

Uneven workload; Under-estimating time requirements; Human relations problems

The list includes problems having to do with the use of IT to help perform accounting functions as well as problems that pre-existed the advent of IT. While past performance is no guarantee of future success, the progress made in addressing 11 year old problems would seem to be an appropriate reference point for an analysis of the effectiveness of IT solutions to persistent accounting problems.

The balance of this paper explore the extent to which these problems still plague accounting departments. For each, we describe (1) the problem in 1982 terms, (2) Giovinazzo's proposed solution(s), and (3) the extent to which IT solutions exist today. In order to avoid reliance on untested technology, we will limit the solutions to commercially available products. In addition, we will compare 1993 solutions with the 1982 proposals.

ASSESSING THE PROMISE OF IT

At the time Giovinazzo wrote his article, the technology was less advanced. Using the IT then available, Giovinazzo recognized the need (1) for the use of integrated systems, (2) the importance of on-line capabilities, and (3) a greater involvement of the accountants in the design and operation of the IS systems. However, he expected the main thrust for solving the problems to come from non-technical steps such as:

Better forms to reduce data entry errors.

Cooperation between information producers and information users to insure that the information being reported is relevant.

Better relationships between accountants and operating departments so that data concerning operations could be communicated expeditiously.

Need to analyze and measure work done by accounting workers with a view toward the elimination of logjams.

As one looks at the current environment and technology, it is quite clear that IT currently available has reduced the problem of accuracy and speed. Today, it is feasible to have on-line, integrated accounting systems with built-in controls available to insure accurate data input. Clearly, the price/performance ratios are improving and the systems are easier to use. In addition, accountants are becoming more knowledgeable about IT. Clearly, the predictions made about technology have been greatly exceeded. The solution that IT can provide today can be both "specific" to a given problem or "general" but easily customized to meet a particular need. The growth of the IT industry can support general and customized solutions.

CONCLUSION

Clearly, IT is useful. Indeed, one could say that technology has almost always worked. Applications of IT fail because of misunderstanding(s) of the problem(s), improper application/implementation of the technology, and/or the embryonic nature of the IT itself. Many of the problems that occurred with IT were due to the administration of the technology.

What are the chances of a "misfit" between IT purchased today and the problem(s) to be addressed? One will do well to first identify the needs that IT is expected to satisfy. The likelihood of an IT failure can be greatly reduced by (1) a clear understanding the needs to be met, (2) careful planning of the change-over, and (3) proper training of the employees. Contrary to the impression of the Charlie Chaplin tv commercial, merely purchasing computers will not make one's business operate like clockwork. When we buy clothes, we try them on for size; when doctors prescribe medication, they make it specific to the symptoms. The same holds true for decisions for IT and IT applications.

However, IT cannot help accounting information become more relevant or make the controller's department become more productive if the same old ways of doing business survives. If this happens, then IT will only have replaced the calculators, without fully realizing its potential. There is a need to redesign procedures that comprise accounting function, keeping in mind the IT presently available. If one is buying IT to solve systemic problems, it is better to first address the systemic problem itself and while investigating the problems, one can explore the potential use of IT to solve the problem or to design a way around the problem. To better address systemic problems, changes in accounting functions are needed and such changes can be done through Reengineering and by applying cross functional approaches to many accounting function. Indeed, to facilitate changes in accounting functions, it may be better to think of accounting as a part of the information resource management function, rather than a distinct entity. Audit and internal control constraints may dictate the separation of accounting and IS, however there ought to be greater coordination between the two departments in order to insure effective management of information resources. Accounting department will never be problem-free, but it can become a more optimumly-used resource for decision-makers in the Information Age by rethinking and redesigning its functions with the help of emerging IT.

Accounting, MIS or Information Resource Management: The Department of the Future

Athar Murtuza
Seton Hall University
Accounting Department
School of Business
South Orange, NJ 07079
Phone: Home 201-691-1065
Office 201-761-9233

William Brunsen
Eastern New Mexico University
College of Business
Portales, NM 88130
Phone: Home 505-356-6905
Office 505-562-2744

Gerry Huybregts
Eastern New Mexico University
College of Business
Portales, NM 88130
Phone: Home 505-356-6439
Office 505-562-2737

BACKGROUND

The re-structuring/re-engineering of American industry continues; after almost ten years of down-sizing, re-structuring and/or re-engineering, companies continue to adjust their work force and organizational structure to remain competitive. As these efforts continue, several patterns have become clear: the organizational structure typically leads to a "flatter" organization chart; the role of the employee becomes more general -- less of an expert; and there is a far greater emphasis on teamwork and the ability of the employee to work with others. A result of these changes is that traditional departments within the company and/or their relationships are changing. It is this aspect of re-structuring that is addressed in this paper.

ISSUES

Departments of Accounting and Management Information Systems (MIS) have historically been separate and distinct entites -- entities that are frequently at odds with each other. Turf battles occur, even though both are a part of the same firm. What is needed is the adoption of the concept known as Information Resource Management (IRM); a concept based on the recognition that information cuts across departmental boundaries and functions. Under IRM, Accounting and MIS are not seen as self-contained departments, but as elements of a system working together to provide appropriate information for all users. Indeed, the organization's information system is too important to be left entirely to the care of either the Accounting or the MIS personnel. The organization's information system should reflect the information needs of the entire organization. Such a perspective will serve to assure the relevance of output and the availability of appropriate information to all decisionmakers.

FINDINGS

During the 1960s corporate America invested significant amounts of money in the establishment of computer departments and/or MIS operations under a variety of names. Also during the 1960s, the (sub)discipline of Managerial Accounting became reasonably well defined. The academic definition of Managerial Accounting and its role would function very nicely to describe/define the role of the Information Resource Management function for today's environment. This paper discusses the role of Management Accounting and Information Resources Management and how the two fit into the corporate environment of today. The paper then addresses the expected impact on the traditional Accounting and MIS departments. The paper concludes with a discussion of some of the mechanical and personnel problems that may be expected as this change occurs.

CONCLUSIONS

The "new" globally competitive environment provides little opportunity for the inefficient business firm. Survival will require current, accurate information in a timely manner. The Information Resource Management concept which reflects the Management Accounting approach offers a string tool to meet the information needs of the firm. The issue is not whether the business firm should adopt such an approach; the issue is how quickly can the transition be made.

Yes, there will be costs and there will be internal resistance and changing personnel needs. There may even be a need to reduce or replace specific individuals. However, the changes required are a necessary cost for those firms where survival may be questionable.

The theoretical discussion of this approach began almost thirty years ago. Those firms that have failed to respond and continue to ignore the need are already at a competitive disadvantage. Further delays will only result in greater disadvantages and possibly higher costs when the changes are finally made.

Issues in Economic Justification for Flexible Manufacturing Systems and Some Guidelines for Managers

Somendra Pant
School of Management
Rensselaer Polytechnic Institute
Troy NY 12180-3590

Lawrence Ruff
Senior Project Manager
Design and Manufacturing Institute
Rensselaer Polytechnic Institute
Troy, NY 12180-3590

ABSTRACT

Information Technology has enabled substantial automation of manufacturing functions by way of computer integrated manufacturing and flexible manufacturing systems. These systems offer many benefits but also require substantial long term capital investment. Traditional cost accounting and capital budgeting techniques fail to fully justify installation of these systems. A substantial quantity of literature in this field is reviewed to come up with the existing state of affairs in manufacturing automation and economic justification of flexible manufacturing systems. Economic justification of flexible manufacturing systems on broader basis than provided by traditional methods appears to be not only desirable but also imperative for manufacturing firms going in for them. Based on literature review, some guidelines have been culled for managers to enable them to invest in these systems on a more rational basis and with more confidence. A bibliography of articles and research papers provides further references and readings to practitioners in this area.

1. INTRODUCTION

In the beginning of this century, manufacturing was revolutionized with the introduction of "transfer line" technology for mass production where, basic inputs are processed in a fixed sequence of steps using equipment specifically designed to produce a single standardized product in extremely large quantities for extended periods of time. In the late twentieth century, there is again a revolution in manufacturing. The specialized, single-purpose equipment that characterized transfer lines is being replaced by flexible machine tools and programmable, multi-task production equipment. These systems provide a wide range of benefits including great improvements in quality, customization of products, extremely high output efficiencies of production in very small batches, etc. At the same time these systems are expensive and require a commitment of sizable funds for a long time to implement them. The question of economic justification of these systems assumes importance in this context.

Flexible Manufacturing System (FMS) is an integrated system of machine tools and material-handling equipment designed to manufacture a variety of parts at low or medium volumes. It can also be viewed as an integrated system for automatic random processing of work units through various workstations in the system. FMS actually is an umbrella term, which in turn refers to flexible assembly, fabrication, machine and welding systems. An FMS is characterized by its ability to process many variations within a single-product family as well as ability to make rapid extensions of an existing product line.

There are many motivations for adopting FMS. These are:

- Cost Reasons
- Lower inventory levels
- Reduced labor costs
- Reduced scrap and rework
- Reduced floor space requirements
- Reduced information tracking costs
- Time Reasons
- Sizable reductions in production-cycle times due to:
- The ability to route around bottlenecks and machine breakdowns
- Lower set up times
- Reduction in fixture and tooling errors
- Reduced human intervention in all phases of manufacturing
- Marketing Reasons
- Shorter delivery times
- Ability to maintain production of low-volume products

- Ability to make rapid changes in product mix and volume to accommodate market shifts
- Quicker introduction of new and modified products
- Quality Reasons
- Very high first-time-through quality levels
- Maintain high consistency levels with which parts are processed
- Technology Reasons
- Creates or maintains a competitive advantage
- Desire to experiment with new technology
- Desire to be on the technology frontier

Different firms acquire FMS for different reasons. Usually, a common reason is competition from other firms. With increased customization of products, the firms which can deliver the desired product to customers at the right time, in the right quantity and at the right price turn out to be winners. Time, quality and meeting customer requirements are the main reasons for adopting FMS.

There are a number of positive consequences as also a few negative consequences associated with adopting FMS. Based on a survey of twenty US firms[25], these consequences are:

- Positive consequences of adopting FMS:
- Reductions in direct labor ranging from 50 percent to 88 percent;
- Increase in machinery efficiency ranging from 15 percent to 90 percent;
- Reductions in production-cycle time ranging from 30 percent to 90 percent and;
- Reductions in floor space ranging from 30 percent to 80 percent

A survey of thirty UK engineering companies reported the following[25]:

- Mean reduction in work in process of 68 percent; and
- Mean increase in machine use from 40-50 percent with conventional machine tools to over 90 percent with FMS.

Other benefits of adopting FMS are:
- The ability to produce a wide variety of products in a wide range of volumes.
- The ability to respond quickly to customer demands and product design changes.
- The ease of adding new members to a product line and accommodating a change in volume in existing products.
- Vastly improved product quality; almost zero defect in some cases.
- Less setup time because of better computer scheduling and setups performed at the load/unload station instead of at each machine.
- Better information on production, system utilization, tooling, maintenance and the like.
- Negative consequences of adopting FMS:

Four main classes of negative experiences have been reported:

- *Cost related*. This class includes dramatic underestimation of the cost of installing the FMS, not being able to eliminate the labor time predicted in the proposal, and not achieving the planned machine use.
- *Time related*. Long delays in making the FMS operational have been reported by several firms.
- *Technology related*. This class includes break-downs in hardware (e.g. automated guided vehicles, machines, and tools) or software (e.g. tool record programs and system supervisory programs).
- *Labor related*. Problems with labor unions have been reported at many firms.

Usually protracted negotiations over labor issues delay the implementation of FMS.

Because of so many benefits of having FMS, a number of firms have adopted and are in the process of adopting them. As reported by Ranta and Tchijov [70], FMS can be divided into two categories: compact systems costing less than US $4 million and high-efficiency systems costing more than US $5 million. A typical compact system consists of 2-4 CNC-tool or machining centers, conveyor or/and automatic storage and retrieval systems and two robots for material handling and a programmable controller for systems control. A typical large scale system consists of 15-30 CNC-tools, automated guided vehicles and an automated storage and retrieval system for material handling, a local area network and distributed micro-computer based cell and machine control systems and usually two VAX-type computers for coordination, scheduling and database management. It usually has a backup computer system

Table 1: Implemented and estimated FMSs

Year	Total Number	Compact Systems	High-efficiency Systems
1980	80	20	60
1988	1000	800	200
2000	3000	1600	1400

Table 2: FMS Distribution Over Investments

Investment (Million US dollars)	No. of FMS	Percentage
0-5	188	64%
5-10	68	23%
10-15	17	6%
15-20	17	4%
>30	9	3%

and a software system for the coordination of the systems. According to this study in spring 1989 there were around 1200 flexible systems worldwide and at least a 15% annual growth rate of FMS population is predicted for the rest of this century. The number of implemented FMS and estimated numbers in future is given in table 1.

Based on 293 documented cases, Table 2. shows the FMS distribution over investment [70].

In 1985, there were approximately 50 fully computerized FMS installations in the United States. By 1990, close to 300 complete FMS installations were expected to be operative. In addition, 250 flexible manufacturing cells (compact systems) were in operation in 1985 and their number was expected to rise to 1900 by 1990. The major US. users of FMS are the automotive, aerospace, defense, and construction industries [4]. Investment in automation by American manufacturers has been on the rise. In 1987 this investment went up by $17 billion[25]. In 1964 there were fewer than 100 graphics terminal installations in the United States. By the end of 1985, the level had reached 8.8 millions with an annual growth rate of 30%. In 1987 there were about 6000 CAD/CAM systems and more than 80,000 workstations in operation[4]. As reported in [Ranta, 1990], the growth rate in new installations has been 20%-25% towards the end of 1980s and even after considering a saturation of the diffusion process as well as application barriers, the growth rate is expected to be at least 15% through the end of this century. The main reason behind adoption of automated manufacturing systems has been to boost productivity and to remain competitive in the world market.

2. ECONOMIC JUSTIFICATION: TRADITIONAL METHODS

One major problem associated with the adoption of FMS has been their economic justification. Traditional cost accounting methods are either inadequate or fail completely when used for accounting for FMS. In one instance when the traditional cost accounting methods were used, the company found that it was beneficial for it to farm out certain parts and retain the others. In actuality, it should have been just the opposite[4]. When a traditional cost-benefit analysis is done for

FMSs, these systems are doubly disadvantaged: while calculating the cash outflows and inflows, discounted cash flow technique unduly penalizes these long-term projects and at the same time major benefits of adopting these systems like flexibility of switching from one product to another, improved quality, reduced throughput and lead-times, etc. are not considered.

There are a number of reasons why traditional cost accounting methods fail when applied to FMS. The principles of current cost-management systems were laid down soon after the Securities Exchange Act of 1934 in an era when labor was the chief variable cost. Then mass production was the theme and Frederick W. Taylor's time and motion studies were the paradigm of efficiency. That system served its purpose fully and the US. industry came up at the top in the world. Now the scene has made a U-turn. Automation has brought direct labor down to 8% to 12% of total production costs at an average. It is much less in electronics, which is America's fastest growing and third-largest industry. This trend is demonstrated by a company like the Beckman Instruments Inc. which has eliminated labor as a separate cost category and merged it with other overheads[4]. Apart from its emphasis on allocating overheads based on direct labor, traditional cost accounting methods are inadequate to account for FMS because of their inability to fully or even partially account for some major benefits of FMS like reduced inventory levels, reduced floor space requirements, reduced scrap and rework, flexibility, improved quality and reduced throughput and lead times. There is every indication that as manufacturing becomes more and more automated, these benefits will become more pronounced and will provide vital competitive advantage to firms. These traditional financial evaluation models are more suited to short-term profitability goals rather than long-term strategic goals [61].

Another issue related to economic justification of FMS is product costing. These systems, as has been pointed out, are characterized by their capability to produce diverse products and in small lot sizes. Traditional product costing systems allocate overheads on some direct basis like direct labor, machine hours or material dollars. This cost accounting system works well for machine systems that produce a single product in large quantities. For multiple product-low volume systems, such a costing system returns highly distorted product costs. Traditional or volume based costing, in fact over-costs high-volume products and under-costs low volume products [12]. Obviously, such a distortion works against economic justification of FMS which specialize in diverse and low volume products. This aberration in product costing can be corrected by resorting to an Activity Based Costing System (ABCS). Activity Based Costing Systems focus on activities rather than products. They use secondary bases other than direct labor, machine hours or material dollars for allocation of overheads. These bases include setup hours, number of setups, material handling hours and the like. Consumption of these bases varies directly with the number of items produced and thereby returns much accurate product costs.

The traditional cost accounting practices have their basis in discounting procedure for evaluating investments in long-lived assets. These procedures became widely adopted in corporations during the mid-1950s. There are many reasons to believe that discounted cash flow (DCF) techniques may not be fully adequate to evaluate important corporate investments like in FMS. Some of the principal reasons why DCF techniques may not be fully adequate to justify investment in FMS are:

1. They require payback over arbitrarily short time periods. Many companies demand that investments, particularly new investments in new technologies pay back their initial investment within two or three years. Reasons offered to justify include the distrust of the management of the estimates of future cash flow savings and need to stay liquid and self financing so as to reduce the financial risk of the company. For new investments in FMS or Computer-Integrated Manufacturing (CIM), arbitrarily short time periods make it difficult to justify the extra investment required to achieve flexibility. The benefits from flexibility allow for the accommodation of products and their variants in future years.

2. Excessively high discount rates in excess of 20%-25% unduly penalize a long-term investment. Instead a more realistic rate of 12%-13% would make the investment in long-term projects like FMS look not so unattractive.

Other problems associated with applying traditional capital budgeting techniques to FMS reported in literature are:

1. Inaccurate Cash Flows: Any alternative to new investment assumes that the present cash flows can be maintained with no investment in new technology. A better way of looking at this situation will be that if a new investment is made in technology now, the future cash flows will be improved due to lower labor, material or energy costs, better quality, etc.

2. Piecemeal Development: The capital approval process for many companies specifies different levels of authorization as a function of the size of the request. This creates an incentive for managers to propose a series of small projects instead of going in for a major investment in technology. Because of this the division or the company never gets the full benefit from a completely redesigned and re-equipped plant. As an alternative to this piecemeal approach, the company should forecast the remaining technological life of the plant and then not accept any process improvements that will not be repaid within this period. At the end of the specified period, the old facility would be scrapped and replaced with the new one with latest technology. It is possible that the collection of incremental decisions could have a lower net present value than the alternative of deferring most investment during a terminal period, earning interest on the unexpended funds, and then replacing the plant.

3. Quality Benefits: It is necessary to measure all the benefits from the new process. It is especially necessary to measure the benefits mentioned earlier and which are not tracked well by the traditional cost accounting and project appraisal systems. Benefits accruing out of reduced inventory levels and reduced floor space are comparatively easy to measure. Quality improvements, which are a major source of tangible benefits from new technology investments are not so easy to measure. The opportunities for savings in quality can be estimated by first collecting information on how much the company is currently spending on producing, repairing, replacing, and discarding poor-quality items.

4. Level of Precision: Another point which has to be kept in mind while quantifying benefits mentioned above is that these savings can not be estimated with the customary precision from the financial and cost accounting systems. But this should not be construed to mean that difficult-to-estimate benefits are zero. For purposes of financial justification, less rigorous precision could be considered. This will be better than ignoring such benefits altogether.

5. Flexibility Benefits: Computer based process technologies provide very great flexibility in accommodating changes in product specifications, process improvements, schedule changes and implementing new products and variants on existing equipment. Such a capability permits efficient manufacturing at much smaller scale than before and even batch sizes of one can be run efficiently. The flexibility in FMS equipment gives it useful life beyond the life cycle of the product for which it was purchased. These benefits should be accounted for while justifying investment.

6. Benefits Due To Reduced Throughput Time: Successful adoption of FMS technology results in great reductions in throughput processing times. In some cases the processing times have been reduced to one or two days for products that formerly took months to process. Besides these dramatic reductions in some cases, other installations have reported time savings ranging from 50% to 95%. The obvious benefit of such a reduction in throughput processing time is by way of greatly reduced inventory. Other benefits are: (a) ability to meet customer demands with much shorter lead times and (b) an ability to respond quickly to changes in market demands. Both these factors will provide major marketing advantage to the company and the benefits

flowing from that should be considered in any justification decision.

7. Organizational Learning: Another benefit of investing in new-process technologies which is ignored is opportunity afforded to the entire organization to learn about the capabilities of such processes. Thus, many of the start-up costs of any new project will eventually be shared by other projects which use similar technologies. An investment in the training of employees in new technologies also gives the organization an opportunity to participate in future enhancements.

3. ECONOMIC JUSTIFICATION: ALTERNATIVE METHODS

Many organizations have realized the limitations of traditional accounting and capital budgeting methods, especially DCF method, in justifying investments in FMS. According to a Management Accounting survey[36], the alternatives and extensions to DCF and other guidelines which are considered by managers while accounting for FMS are:

1. Investments in FMS should be made in the belief that if the right strategic decisions are made, the future will be as good as the past.

2. Intangible benefits should also be taken into account and managers should try to quantify these benefits as much as possible. An educated guess about the value of these benefits is better than leaving them out altogether.

3. In conjunction with a DCF primary capital budgeting technique, payback may be a useful secondary technique because it indicates how long it will take to recover the initial outlay. The primary and secondary capital budgeting techniques used by the survey respondents to justify expenditures for factory automation are shown in figure 1.

Some salient points which emerge from the above study are:

(a) Only about two-thirds of the respondents now use a DCF technique as a primary technique in justifying expenditure for factory automation and 14% do not use a DCF technique as either a primary or secondary technique.

(b) About one half of the respondents use payback as a secondary evaluation technique. Also, about one-half use subjective evaluation as a secondary technique in conjunction with a quantitative primary technique; the reason being that they may not be comfortable with their quantification of the more intangible benefits.

Ideally, all expected benefits and costs should be quantified and included in a DCF model when evaluating capital expenditures for factory automation. The benefits that survey respondents quantify and those they consider qualitative only are shown in the figure 2.

Figure 1: Capital Budgeting Techniques (Source: Management Accounting, December, 1988, p. 25)

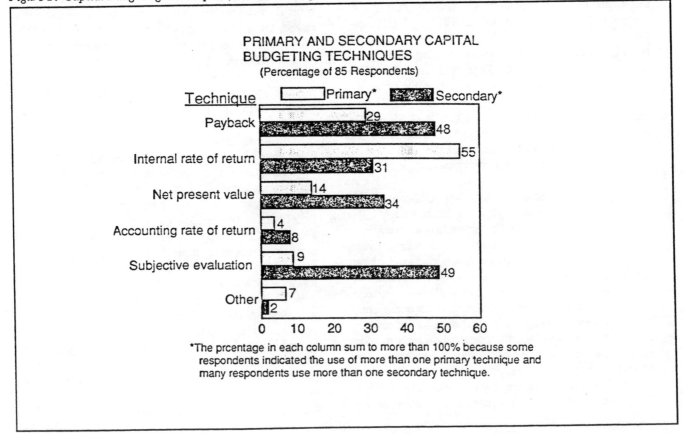

Figure 2: Benefits of FMS (Source: management Accounting,December, 1988, p. 26)

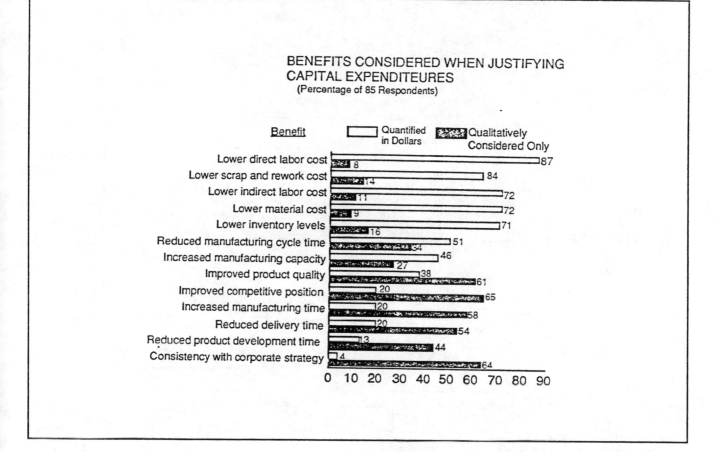

Quantification of Intangible Benefits:

Most companies quantify the first five benefits listed in figure 2 because they are more tangible and easy to quantify. While justifying investment in FMS, first easily quantifiable benefits like reductions in labor, rework, material and inventory costs need to be considered. If investment in FMS can be justified on the basis of these benefits alone, the management should go for it with confidence as many benefits ranging from reduced cycle time to improved quality have not yet been taken into account. However, if the project cannot be justified on the basis of easily quantifiable benefits alone, then other benefits should be evaluated before making a decision on rejecting the project. In conjunction with a discounted cash flow primary capital budgeting technique, payback may be a useful secondary technique as it indicates the time in which initial outlay will be recovered. Methods which need to be tried at this second stage of evaluating FMS make use of heuristics where experienced managers try to assign weights and valued to likely benefits. Use of probability factors for cash flows, sensitivity analysis, or other risk analysis techniques can be employed. Another rigorous evaluation method is the modeling method [61]. This method develops mathematical models for each manufacturing system. These models consist of both stochastic and deterministic variables and capture the important flexibility

components for the particular problem. Simulation is another powerful method to study the cash flows and the effects of variables on the NPV of a firm, etc.

Based on the above discussion, steps needed for justifying investment in automated equipment can be summarized as follows:

1. The firm must consider its products, markets, customer demands, and domestic and foreign competition. This will help the company to determine its long-term strategic goals and the manufacturing strategy to achieve these goals. This strategy may or may not require investment in automated equipment.

2. If the firm comes to a conclusion that it is desirable to acquire automated equipment, the second step consists of listing all expected benefits and costs associated with the automated equipment.

3. The third step is to quantify those items listed in step 2 that can be estimated with a reasonable degree of accuracy, for example the first five benefits shown in figure 2.

4. The fourth step is calculating internal rate of return or net present value and payback for those items quantified in step 3. These calculations may justify acquisition. If not, the next step should be considered.

5. Quantify the remaining benefits and costs using a team

Figure 3: Steps in Justifying Investment in FMS

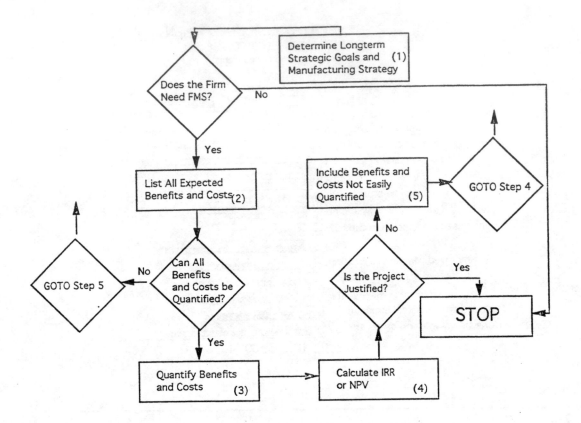

approach and risk analysis. Calculate internal rate of return or net present value and payback to determine if project is now financially acceptable.

These steps are shown in the flow chart in figure 3.

4. CONCLUSIONS:

1. Flexible Manufacturing Systems offer unprecedented promise in manufacturing discrete parts in mid-volume range. These systems have grown at a fast pace all over the industrialized world and will continue to grow in the years to come. With increased customization and competition, these systems are expected to provide vital competitive advantage to manufacturing firms.

2. These systems are expensive and require long-term capital commitment. The benefits deriving out of the implementation of these systems are not easily quantifiable. This makes economic justification of these systems difficult. The popular DCF capital budgeting technique may not favor investment in FMS. This method needs to be extended or modified to fully justify investment in FMS.

3. Apart from the DCF capital budgeting techniques being

unfavorable to adoption of FMS, traditional volume-based product costing techniques return distorted (lower) product costs for systems which produce multiple products and in small lot sizes. this can be corrected by switching over to Activity Based Costing Systems to get accurate product costs. Organizations which are considering adoption of FMS or already have one in place, should look at their product costing system and assess if they need to switch to an Activity Based Costing System. A series of four articles referenced in [12] to [15] provide a good starting point for such an evaluation.

4. It is recommended that some of the techniques outlined in this paper and the literature should be applied to fully justify investment in flexible manufacturing systems.

5. ACKNOWLEDGMENTS

The authors would like to acknowledge partial financial support for this survey from the Automated Assembly Program of the Design and Manufacturing Institute at the Rensselaer Polytechnic Institute, Troy, NY. We would also like to thank Dr. Kathy Silvester Assistant Professor, School of Management, Rensselaer Polytechnic Institute, Troy, NY for her help in this project.

6. REFERENCES AND BIBLIOGRAPHY

1. Baldwin, William, "This is the Answer," Forbes, July 5, 1982, pp. 50-52.

2. Banks, Robert L. and Steven C. Wheelwright, "Operations vs. Strategy: Trading Tomorrow for Today," Harvard Business Review, May-June 1979, pp. 112-120.

3. Behuniak, J.A., "Economic Analysis of Robot Applications," Proceedings of Robots IV Conference, Society of Manufacturing Engineers, 1979.

4. Bennett, Robert E., and Hendricks, James A., "Justifying the Acquisition of Automated Equipment," Management Accounting, July 1987, pp. 39-46.

5. Blackburn, Joseph D., "The New Manufacturing Environment," Cost Management, Summer, 1988, pp. 4-10.

6. Borus, Michael G. and Cohen, Stephen S., "The Economic Angle," IEEE Spectrum, September 1993, pp. 67-68.

7. Bublick, T., "The Justification of an Industrial Robot," Proceedings of Finishing '77 Conference and Exposition, Society of Manufacturing Engineers, 1977.

8. Buehler, Vernon M. and Y. Krishna Shetty, Productivity Improvement: Case Studies of Proven Practice, (New York: AMACOM. 1981).

9. Bylinsky, Gene, "The Race to the Automatic Factory," Fortune, February 21, 1983, pp. 52-64."

10. Canda, J.R., "Non-Traditional Methods for Evaluating CIM Opportunities: Assign Weights to Intangibles," Vol. 18, No. 3, Industrial Engineering, March 1986.

11. Carr, Lawrence P. and Cma, Thomas Tyson, "Planning Quality Cost Expenditures-How Much Should a Company Spend on Improving Quality?," Management Accounting, October 1992.

12. Cooper, Robin, "The Rise of Activity Based Costing-Part One: What Is an Activity-Based Cost System?," Journal of Cost Management, Summer, 1988, pp. 45-54.

13. Cooper, Robin, "The Rise of Activity Based Costing-Part Two: When Do I Need an Activity-Based Cost System?," Journal of Cost Management, Fall, 1988, pp. 41-48.

14. Cooper, Robin, "The Rise of Activity Based Costing-Part Three: How Many Cost Drivers Do You Need, and How Do You Select Them?," Journal of Cost Management, Winter, 1989, pp. 34-46.

15. Cooper, Robin, "The Rise of Activity Based Costing-Part Four: What Do Activity Based Cost Systems Look Like?," Journal of Cost Management, Spring, 1989, pp. 38-49.

16. Craig, Charles E. and R. Clark Harris, "Total Productivity Measurement at the Firm Level," Sloan Management Review, Spring 1973, pp. 13-38.

17. Crosby, Philip B., Quality is Free, McGraw-Hill, New York 1979.

18. Downing, Thomas, "Eight New Ways To Evaluate Automation," Mechanical Engineering, July 1989, pp. 82-86.

19. Drucker, P., "We Need to Measure, Not Count," The Wall Street Journal, April 13, 1993.

20. ECE, Recent Trends in Flexible Manufacturing, United Nations, New York, 314 pp., (October 1986).

21. Edmonds, Thomas P., Tsay, Bor-Yi, and Lin, Wen-Wei, "Analyzing Quality Costs," Management Accounting, November 1989, pp. 25-29.

22. Engelberger, J., Robotics in Practice, Kogan Page Ltd., 1980.

23. Engelberger, J., "Robots Make Economic and Social Sense," Atlanta Economic Review, July/August, 1977.

24. Fine, Charles, Quality Control and Learning in Productive Systems, Working Paper, Graduate School of Business, Stanford University, January 1982.

25. Forster, George, and Horngren, Charles T., "Flexible Manufacturing Systems: Cost Management and Cost Accounting Implications," Cost Management, Fall 1988, pp. 16-24.

26. Fotsch, R. J., "Machine Tool Justification Policies: Their Effect on Productivity and Profitability," Vol. 3, No. 2, Journal of Manufacturing Systems, pp. 169-195.

27. Fox, Robert E., "MRP, Kanban, or OPT: What's Best?" Inventories and Production Magazine, July-August 1982".

28. Godfrey, James T., and Pasewark, William R., "Controlling Quality Costs," Management Accounting, March 1988, pp. 48-51.

29. Hayashin Hideyuki, "A Preview of the 21st Century," IEEE Spectrum, September 1993, pp. 82-84.

30. Hayes, Robert H., A Note on Productivity Accounting, HBS 0-682-084 (Boston: Harvard Business School, 1982), July-August 1981, pp. 57-66.

31. Hayes, Robert H., and Joseph A. Limprecht, "Germany's World Class Manufacturers," Harvard Business Review, November-December 1982, pp. 137-145.

32. Hayes, Robert H., and Abernathy, William J., "Managing Our Way to Economic Decline," Harvard Business Review, July-August 1980, pp. 67-77.

33. Hayes, Robert H., "Why Japanese Factories Work," Harvard Business Review, July-August 1981, pp. 57-66.

34. Hayes, Robert H., and Steven C. Wheelwright, "The Dynamics of Process-Product Life Cycles," Harvard Business Review, March-April 1979b, pp. 127-136.

35. Hayes, Robert H., and Steven C. Wheelwright, "Link Manufacturing Process and Product Life Cycles," Harvard Business Review, January-February 1979a, pp. 133-140.

36. Hendricks, James A., "Applying Cost Accounting To Flexible Automation," Management Accounting, December 1988, pp. 24-30.

37. Holt, Charles, Franco Modigliani, John Muth, and Herbert Simon, Planning, Production, Inventories, and Work Force, Englewood Cliffs, NJ: Prentice Hall, 1960.

38. Howell, Robert A. and Soucy, Stephen R., "The New Manufacturing Environment: Major Trends in Management Accounting," Management Accounting, July 1987,

39. Huang, P.Y., and Ghandfaroush, P., "Procedures Given for Evaluating, Selecting Robots," Industrial Engineering, April 1984.

40. Hutchinson, George K., and Holland, John R., "The Economic Value of Flexible Automation," Vol. 1, Number 2, Journal of Manufacturing Systems, pp. 215-227.

41. "In Search of Agile Manufacturing," Feature Article, Manufacturing Engineering, February 1993, pp. 24-26.

42. Johnston, R., and Lawrence, P. R., "Beyond Vertical Integration - The Rise of the Value-added Partnership," Harvard Business Review, July-August 1988, pp. 94-101.

43. Juran, J.M, "Japanese and Western Quality—A Contrast," Management Review, November 1978, pp. 27-38, 39-45.

44. Juran, J.M, "Japanese and Western Quality- A Contrast," Quality Progress, December 1978, pp. 10-18.

45. Kaplan, Gadi, "Manufacturing A' La Carte: Agile Assembly Lines, Faster Development Cycles," IEEE Spectrum, September 1993, pp. 25-27.

46. Kaplan, Robert S., "Measuring Manufacturing Performance: A New Challenge for Managerial Accounting Research," The Accounting Review, October 1983, pp. 686-705.

47. Kendrick, John W. and Daniel Creamer, Measuring Company Productivity: Handbook with Case Studies , Revised Edition , New York: The Conference Board, 1965.

48. Koten, John, "Auto Makers Have Trouble with 'Kanban'," Wall Street Journal, April 7, 1982.

49. Krasa-Sethi, A. and Sethi, S.P., "Flexibility in Manufacturing: A Survey," TIMS/ORSA Meeting, April 21-23, 1988, Washington, DC.

50. Kulatilka, N., "Financial, Economic and Strategic Issues Concerning the Decision to Invest in Advanced Automation," International Journal of Prod. Res., Vol. 22(6), pp. 949-968.

51. Kulatilka, N., "A Managerial Decision Support System to Evaluate Investments in FMSs," Proceedings of First ORSA/TIMS Special Interest Conference on FMS, Ann Arbor, Michigan, August 1984.

52. Liberatore, M.J. (Ed.), Selection and Evaluation of Advanced Manufacturing Technologies, Springer-Verlag, New York (1990).

53. Ligus, Rich, " The Agile Enterprise," Manufacturing Engineering, September, 1990, p.120.

54. Mammone, James L., "Productivity Management: A Conceptual Overview," Management Accounting, July 1980b, pp. 40-44.

55. Manuel, William G., Productivity Experiences at Nucor, in Buehler and Shetty, Productivity Improvement: Case-Studies of Proven Practice, New York: AMACOM, 1981, Chapter 4.

56. Meredith, J. R., and Mantel, S. J., Jr., Project Management: A Managerial Approach, John Wiley and Sons, 1985.

57. Meredith, J. R., "Implementing an Automated Factory," Vol. 6, No. 2, Journal of Manufacturing Systems, 1987.

58. Meredith, J. R., "Strategic Planning for Factory Automation by the Championing Process," Vol. 33, No. 3, IEEE Transactions on Engineering Management, August 1986.

59. Michael, G.J. and Meredith, J.R., "Economic Justification of Modern Computer-Based Factory Automation Equipment: A Status Report," Proc. First ORSA/TIMS Conf. FMS, 1984, pp. 30-35.

60. Milgram, Paul and Roberts, John, "The Economics of Modern Manufacturing: Technology, Strategy, and Organization," The American Economic Review, June 1990,

61. Miltenburg, G.J., "Economic Evaluation and Analysis of Flexible Manufacturing Systems," Engineering Costs and Production Economics, 12 (1987), pp. 79-92.

62. Monden, Yashurio "Production Smoothing Part II," Industrial Engineering, January 1981d, pp. 22-30.

63. Monden, Yashurio, "Kanban System," Industrial Engineering, May 1981a, pp. 29-66. 65. Monden, Yashurio, "Production Smoothing," Industrial Engineering, January 1981a, pp. 42-51.

64. Monden, Yashurio, "What Makes the Toyota Production System Really Tick," Industrial Engineering January 1981a, pp. 36-48.

65. Murrin, Thomas, Rejecting the Traditional Ways of Doing Business, Chicago: American Production and Inventory Control Society, October 1982.

66. Nagrur, Nagen, "Some Performance Measures in Flexible Manufacturing Systems," International Journal of Production Res., Vol. 30, No. 4, 1992, pp. 799-809.

67. Parasi, Hamid and R., Karwoski, "Measuring Monetary and Non-Monetary in Economic Justification of Computer Integrated Manufacturing Systems," Proceedings of the First Symposium on Advanced Manufacturing, Lexington, Kentucky, September, 1987.

68. Pinches, George E., "Myopia, Capital Budgeting and Decision Making," Financial Management, Autumn 1982, pp. 6-19.

69. Primrose, P.L., and Leonard, R., "Selecting Technology for Investment in Flexible Manufacturing," The International Journal of Flexible Manufacturing Systems, Vol. 4, 1991, pp. 51-77

70. Ranta, J., and Tchijov, I., "Economics and Success Factors of Flexible Manufacturing systems: The Conventional Explanation Revisited," The International Journal of Flexible Manufacturing Systems, Vol. 2, 1990, pp. 169-190.

71. Rappaport, Alfred, "Executive Incentives vs. Corporate Growth," Harvard Business Review, January 1981a, pp. 81-88.

72. Reich, Robert "The Next American Frontier," The Atlantic Monthly, March 1983,

73. Reich, Robert, "The Next American Frontier," The Atlantic Monthly, April 1983,

74. Richardson, Peter R. and John R. M. Gordon, "Measuring Total Manufacturing Performance," Sloan Management Review, Winter 1980, pp. 47-58.

75. Santos, Brian L. Dos., "Justifying Investments in New Information Technologies," Journal of Management Information Systems , Vol. 7, No. 4, Spring 1991, pp. 71-90.

76. Schonberger, Richard, Japanese Manufacturing Techniques, New York: Free Press, 1982.

77. Skinner, Wickham, "Manufacturing-Missing Link in Corporate Strategy," Harvard Business Review,May-June 1969, pp. 136-145.

78. Skinner, Wickham, "The Focused Factory," Harvard Business Review, May-June 1974, pp. 113-121.

79. Son, Y. K., and Park, C. S., "Economic Measure of Productivity, Quality and Flexibility in Advanced Manufacturing Systems," Vol. 6, No. 3, Journal of Manufacturing Systems, 1987.

80. Stalk, G., "Time— The Next Source of Competitive Advantage," Harvard Business Review, Vol. 66, No. 4, July-August 1988, pp. 41-51.

81. Sullivan, W.G., "Models IEs Can Use to Include Strategic, Non-monetary Factors in Automation Decisions," Vol. 18, No. 3, Industrial Engineering, March 1986.

82. Suresh, N.C., and Meredith, J.R., "A Generic Approach to Justifying Flexible Manufacturing Systems," Proc. First ORS/TIMS Conf. FMS, 1984, pp. 36-42.

83. Suresh, Nallan C., and Meredith, Jack R., "Justifying Multimachine Systems: An Integrated Strategic Approach," Vol. 4, No. 2, Journal of Manufacturing Systems, 1985, pp. 117-134.

84. Takeuchi, Hirotaka, "Productivity: Learning from the Japanese," California Management Review, Summer 1981, pp. 87-95.

85. Tchijov, I., and Alabian, A., Flexible Manufacturing Systems (FMS): Main Economic Advantages , WP-88-IIASA, Laxenburg, Austria, September 1988.

86. Tchijov, I., and Sheinin, R., "Flexible Manufacturing Systems (FMS): Current Diffusion and Main Advantage," Technological Forecasting and Social Change, Vol. 35, No. 2-3, April 1989, pp. 277-293.

87. Tchijov, I., FMS World Data Bank, WP-89-33, IIASA, Laxenburg, May 1989a.

88. Tchijov, I., "CIM Introduction: Some Socioeconomic Aspects," Technological Forecasting and Social Change, Vol. 35, No. 2-3, April, 1989a, pp. 261-275.

89. "The Productivity Paradox," Feature Article, Business Week, June 6, 1988, pp. 99-108.

90. "The Technology Payoff," Feature Article, Business Week, June 14, 1993, pp. 57-68.

91. Tsurumi, Yoshi, "Japan's Challenge to the U.S.: Industrial Policies and Corporate Strategies," Columbia Journal of World Business, Summer 1982, pp. 87-95.

92. Tsurumi, Yoshi, "Productivity: The Japanese Approach," Pacific Basin Quarterly, Summer 1981.

93. Van Blois, J.P., "Economic Models: The Future for Robotics Justification," Proceedings of 13th Industrial Symposium on Industrial Robots and Robots 7, Society of Manufacturing Engineers, April 1983, pp. 4-24 to 4-31.

94. Weimer, George A., "Is An American Renaissance At Hand?," Industry Week, May 4, 1992, pp. 48-51.

95. Weimer, George, "U.S.A. 2006: Industry Leader Or Loser?," Industry Week, January 20, 1992, p.68.

96. Wheelwright, Steven C., "Japan-Where Operations Really are Strategic," Harvard Business Review, July-August 1981, pp. 67-74.

97. Worthy, Ford S., "Japan's Smart Secret Weapon," Fortune, August 12, 1991, pp. 72-75.

98. Youssef, Mohamed A., "Agile Manufacturing: A Necessary Condition For Competing In Global Markets," Industrial Engineering, December 92, pp. 18-20.

A Transaction Processing Emphasis for the Introductory Accounting Information Systems Course

Andrew D. Schiff, PhD, CPA
Department of Accounting
University of Baltimore
1420 North Charles Street
Baltimore, MD 21201
410-837-5095
eajqads@ube.ub.umd.edu

Executive Abstract

BACKGROUND AND ISSUES

There is no single approach for teaching the introductory course in accounting information systems (Bagranoff and Simkin, 1994). Some instructors stress training in the use of general purpose business software such as spreadsheets and databases. This approach helps students learn how to use such software, but focuses on tools that accountants utilize, rather than the flow of accounting information through an organization. Some other instructors utilize concepts such as events accounting and data modeling as the basis for the AIS course (Grabski, 1993). This approach introduces students to new and innovative ways of thinking about accounting information, but does not necessarily lead to the development of skills and knowledge which are critical to entry-level job success.

An alternative approach concentrates on the processing of accounting transactions. An emphasis on transaction processing offers a number of advantages:

1. It bridges the gap between a student's knowledge of journal entries obtained in the accounting principles course and elsewhere, and the real world of transaction processing cycles and activities. This real-world knowledge can contribute significantly to the student's productivity and success as an entry-level accountant or auditor.

2. If the AIS course is established as a prerequisite for the auditing course, this approach reduces the need for a detailed coverage of transaction processing in the auditing course.

3. A transaction processing emphasis can incorporate important aspects of the other two approaches above. For example, training in the use of software tools and a study of database designs and features can both be covered, as discussed below.

4. An emphasis on transaction processing is consistent with the following recommendation of the Accounting Education Change Commission (Kinard, 1991):

"The heart of the AIS course is accounting record keeping, in a cycle framework. The general ledger and subsystem modules (accounts payable, payroll, accounts receivable, inventory, fixed assets) need to be understood in both manual and automated forms" (114).

COURSE CONTENT

The following is a structure for an AIS course with a transaction processing emphasis. Each topic and project is listed in the order in which it is presented, followed by a description of the way the topic or project contributes to a knowledge of transaction processing.

TOPIC 1: Flowcharts, Data Flow Diagrams and Other Systems Documentation. A review of these techniques provides a foundation for understanding subsequent illustrations of transaction processing systems.

TOPIC 2: Computer Hardware, Software and Configurations. Concepts which are essential to understanding transaction processing technology are emphasized. Examples include application and systems software, and the differences between centralized and distributed computer configurations.

TOPIC 3: Traditional Data File Organization, Data Base Organization, and Approaches to Data Processing. Students who will use and audit transaction processing software must understand the different ways in which data can be stored and accessed. Since most transaction processing software is moving from traditional files toward data bases, the design and benefits of an online, real-time data base environment are discussed in detail.

PROJECT 1: A Manual Transaction Processing System. Students use a comprehensive and realistic practice set to record transactions for the final week of a fiscal year, and to complete the accounting records for the year. While manual (and batch-oriented) transaction processing systems are steadily being eliminated, and source documents are gradually being replaced by EDI and image processing, a study of these early approaches helps students understand the complexities of newer transaction processing systems more easily. Flowcharts which illustrate how sales, purchases, payroll and other transactions should be processed are studied during class sessions.

TOPIC 4: Revenue, Expenditure, Conversion and Financial Cycles. The classes for Project 1 and this topic are alternated, so that the study of a transaction processing cycle in a manual system is followed by a study of that cycle in a computerized environment. The source documents, reports and processing steps associated with each cycle are stressed.

TOPIC 5: Internal Controls and System Controls. Basic objectives and concepts of internal control, and the implementation of controls in computer-based transaction processing systems, are introduced.

PROJECT 2: A Computer-Based Transaction Processing System. Students learn how to use a commercial accounting software package to set up general and subsidiary ledgers, to process transactions in different modules, and to produce reports. They develop an understanding of the integrated modular structure of these packages, and of the need to comply with rules for transaction processing and error correction which are more restrictive than those in manual systems. An entry-level accounting software package is studied rather than an advanced one to allow coverage of more modules in a brief period of time.

TOPIC 6: Systems Development Processes. The traditional systems development life cycle approach to creating transaction processing systems is reviewed. This is followed by a discussion of some contemporary trends in systems design, including downsizing and systems reengineering.

FINDINGS AND DISCUSSION

The success of a transaction processing emphasis for the introductory AIS course has been demonstrated in several ways. First, while there is some evidence (Bhada, 1992) that AIS instructors receive relatively lower student evaluations than other accounting instructors due to the nontraditional nature of the course material, this has not been the case at the author's institution since the implementation of a transaction processing emphasis in the AIS course. Interestingly, while Project 1 is rather tedious, students have found it to be such a beneficial learning experience that they have recommended retaining it in the course by a ratio of four to one.

Other findings which support a transaction processing emphasis include the placement experiences of students. Several former students have obtained positions as EDP auditors despite their lack of a substantial technical background in EDP beyond this course. Additionally, student enthusiasm for the introductory course has made it possible to offer an advanced course in accounting systems at the undergraduate level for the past three years. In 1994, enrollment in the advanced AIS course exceeded the official limit by nearly 20 percent. Topics in the advanced course include current and emerging trends and technologies, the use of advanced transaction processing software, and the use of database software through the development of a small transaction processing system (Schiff, 1994).

REFERENCES

Available from the author upon request.

Privacy and Software Piracy: An Investigation of Peer Pressure Effect

Abdulla H. Abdul-Gader
Ibrahim M. Al-Jabri

Department of Accounting and MIS
King Fahd University of Petroleum and Minerals
Dhahran, Saudi Arabia

ABSTRACT

With the high advancements in information technology (IT) and the simplicity of disseminating and exchanging information between computer users, the attitudes toward some ethical issues have led to unethical or illegal practices. This study empirically investigates the impact of peer pressure on behaviour regarding ethical issues that can arise when confronted with ethical dilemmas. The objective is to assess the relevance and applicability of group pressure in a culture fundamentally different from those of the developed countries (e.g., U.S.). Emphasising individual privacy and software piracy issues in Saudi Arabia, this study strives to stimulate interest in ethical issues where there is no previous empirical investigation. The scenario method has been used to collect data from 278 university students. The results show significant effect of peer pressure on ethical decision. The findings and their implications are discussed.

INTRODUCTION

With the high advancements in information technology (IT) and the simplicity of disseminating and exchanging information between computer users, the attitudes toward some ethical issues have led to unethical or illegal practices. Since IT personnel posses the technical skills to manipulate information systems, several professional societies in developed countries have enacted ethics codes for information systems professionals. Among these are the Data Processing Management Association (DPMA), the Association for Computing Machinery (ACM), the Canadian Information Processing Society (CIPS), and the British Computer Society (BCS). Certainly professional ethics codes are not the only remedy but it can be of help in determining what is ethical and what is not.

Lacking computer code of ethics as defined by developed countries professional societies, developing countries are subjecting their citizens and software developers to dangers of invasion of privacy and software piracy. Furthermore, culture plays a fundamental role in determining whether a certain behaviour is viewed ethical or unethical. A behaviour can be viewed as ethical in one nation and unethical in another. Unwritten ethical codes in different countries have similarities and differences (Oz, 1992).

This study empirically investigates the impact of peer pressure on behaviour regarding ethical issues that can arise when confronted with ethical dilemmas. The objective is to assess the relevance and applicability of group pressure in a culture fundamentally different from those of the developed countries (e.g., U.S.). Emphasising individual privacy and software piracy issues in Saudi Arabia, this study strives to stimulate interest in ethical issues where there is no previous empirical investigation. Although the computing environment in Saudi Arabia is still in its infancy stage, it is emerging rapidly (Abdul-Ghani and Al-Sakran, 1988; Abdul-Ghani and Al-Meer, 1989; Abdul-Gader, 1990; Rahman and Abdul-Gader, 1993). As computing practices grow, information technology management needs to investigate computer ethical issues and implications.

ETHICS AND BEHAVIOUR

The term ethics designates a collection of moral principles or cultural values that guide people's behaviour. Behaviour is the act that people actually practice (Watson and Pitt, 1993). The ethics of business practices have been tackled extensively in various areas, especially in marketing (Chonko and Hunt, 1985; Murphy and Laczniak, 1981). Although interest in ethical dimensions of computers has been gaining momentum (Anderson, et al., 1993; Harrington and McCollum 1990; Alder, et al., 1985; Couger, 1989; Mason, 1986; Parker, 1990; Garner and Fidel 1990; Paradice, 1990), empirical studies are very scarce. This can be attributed to the fact that very few people are willing to allow their ethical behaviour to be observed (Trevino, 1986).

Many ethical issues have been identified in the literature (Mason, 1986; Straub and Collins, 1990). Among these

Acknowledgment: The authors are grateful to the administration, faculty, and students of King Fahd University of Petroleum and Minerals.

issues are privacy, accuracy, property, and accessibility. Individuals need to protect their intellectual property and privacy. On the other hand, they have obligations towards society, employer, client, colleagues, and professional organizations. For this study, privacy and software piracy were chosen primarily because of their significance in countries like Saudi Arabia. Privacy is one's right to keep data about himself or herself private (Mason 1986) and is subject to strict usage rules (Roos 1981). Unlike many developed countries, Saudi Arabia has what is known as extended family notion. Totalism rather than individualism pertains in many situations. In spite of many benefits of such notion, it is sometimes difficult to draw a line between what is personal and what is public information.

Software market in Saudi Arabia is in its infancy. Unauthorized copies can be obtained from several sources. The presence of off-the-shelf software companies is almost non existence. This has lead to insufficient after sale software support, encouraging many computer users to find excuses for not buying original software. It is believed that investigating software copying views is very important in such unique market circumstances.

Many scholars have tried to identify the variables that may influence computing behaviour (Hunt and Vitell, 1986; Ferrel and Gresham, 1985; Watson and Pitt, 1993). Five broad categories of variables are said to affect ethical

behaviours: perceived implications, culture, peer pressure, management actions and perceived policies, and opportunity to commit an action (Watson and Pitt, 1993).

This paper emphasizes the peers' pressure effects on ethical decision making concerning privacy and software piracy. Southerland and Cressey (1970) theorized that association of peers shapes ethical behaviour. The actual behaviour of peers and the perception about their ethical beliefs contribute to the making of the individuals behaviour.

METHODOLOGY

The scenario method has been used to collect data for this study. This method has been extensively used in ethics research (Gifford and Norris, 1987; Ferrel and Gresham, 1985; Nel, et al., 1989). Three scenarios were carefully designed, based on ethics literature and the authors' knowledge of Saudi environment. Describing situations calling for ethical decision making, two scenarios focused on software piracy and the third on individual right for privacy.

Responses from 278 Saudi college students were gathered. Each subject was asked to read the scenarios and make an ethical decision. Then, each respondent was provided with a list of statements and was asked to indicate his level of agreement on a seven-point scale (1 = strongly agree, 2 = agree, 3 = moderately agree, 4 = neutral, 5 = moderately disagree, 6 = disagree, 7 = strongly disagree).

Table 1. Sample Characteristics

Variable	Number of Respondents	Percentage
ACADEMIC MAJOR:		
Engineering	120	43.2
Business	62	22.3
MIS, ICS, & COE	96	34.5
COMPLETED COMPUTER CREDIT HOURS:		
None	19	6.8
1-8 hours	125	45.0
9-24 hours	68	24.5
25 or more	66	23.7
EDUCATIONAL LEVEL:		
Freshmen	11	4.0
Sophomore	30	10.8
Junior	66	23.7
Senior	156	56.1
Graduate	15	5.4
WEEKLY COMPUTER USE:		
None user	38	4.0
Low user	111	10.8
Heavy users	129	46.4
PERSONAL COMPUTER OWNERSHIP:		
Yes	94	33.8
No	184	66.2
AGE:		
Less than 20	7	2.5
20-25	245	88.1
More than 25	26	9.4

Demographic data were collected on academic major, number of completed computer credit hours, educational level, weekly computer use, personal computer ownership, and age. The profile of the respondents is summarized in Table 1.

FINDINGS

Each scenario is presented along with a brief discussion. The scenarios were phrased to force the respondent to make a decision toward an action.

Scenario I:

After graduation, you were employed by a major business firm located in Saudi Arabia. During the past few years, the firm invested a lot of money in building a computerized system for automating its accounting and financial operations. Management has made it clear that making copies of the system is forbidden. A friend of yours asked you for a copy of this system to be used in his business. Would you give him?

The respondents' decision was:

	frequency	percent
Give (Unethical)	38	13.7
Undecided	11	4.0
Won't give (Ethical)	229	82.0

More than 80 percent of the subjects decided not to give a copy to their friends and abide with the firm's policies and regulations.

Sometimes it is difficult to get the real intended action from respondents, especially if it is illegal or violates certain traditional norm. One way to go around it is to ask about their perceptions of what their peers would do in similar situations (Wilkes 1978). Below is the distribution of the respondents' assessment of their peer's response to the scenario.

	frequency	percent
Give (Unethical)	79	28.41
Undecided	31	11.15
Won't give (Ethical)	168	60.41

Majority of respondents felt that their peers won't act unethically and make unauthorized copies. This is consistent with the result of own action seen previously. However, to further explore the relationship between own and peer behaviours, a breakdown of personal decision by peer decision is shown in Table 2.

To test the significance of the relationship, Chi-square test was computed. Chi-square value was 32.5. It is statistically significant at (p>.000). The result shows that the respondent decision is related to his perception of his peer's

Table 2. Peer Pressure and Ethical Decision in Scenario I

	Respondent's Decision		
	Give (Unethical)	Undecided	Won't give (Ethical)
Peer Decision:			
Give (Unethical)	65.79%	18.18%	22.71%
Undecided	7.89%	0.0%	12.23%
Won't give (Ethical)	26.32%	81.82%	65.07%

behaviour. Peer pressure is an influential factor in determining ethical behaviour. This is in congruency with the differential association theory (Sutherland and Cressey, 1970) that postulate the ethical/unethical behaviour is learned through association with peers.

Scenario II:

As an independent programmer, you were asked to develop a personnel system for a client. You recommended the client to buy an of-the-shelf package. But the client opposed the recommendation on the ground that this package is very expensive and he cannot afford buying it because of financial problems. Instead, he expressed a willingness to buy an unauthorized copy of the same package. The copy is available in the local market. Would you buy the unauthorized copy?

The respondent's decision distribution was:

	frequency	percent
Buy (Unethical)	122	43.9
Undecided	52	18.7
Won't buy (Ethical)	104	37.4

A positive response to the client's request is apparently software piracy. It is prohibited by the software vendor and a violation of the copyright. The result is alarming. It shows that the number of respondents who express a willingness to buy unauthorized copy is more than the ones who do not, 43.9 percent against 37.4 percent. At least two interesting observations emerge from the result. First, it seems that the respondents are trapped by the financial position of the client's business and eventually becoming teleologists (Hunt and Vitell 1986). A teleologist emphasizes the consequences of actions or behaviours. Therefore, he may argue that software copying is acceptable because of the financial situation of the client.

Second, the results show discrepancies between the ethical decisions in the first and the second scenario. While 82.0 % of the respondents have refused to give the software to their friend (ethical) in the first scenario, only 37.4 % have objected buying unauthorized copy in the second scenario.

This can be attributed to the nature of software in question. In the first scenario, the software was an in-house developed system, whereas in the second scenario it was an off-the-self system.

With regard to the subjects' perception of their peers' decision on buying unlicensed software package, the distribution was as follows:

	frequency	percent
Give (Unethical)	199	71.58
Undecided	43	15.47
Won't give (Ethical)	36	12.95

More than 70 % of the respondents perceive that their peers consider buying unlicensed copy is ethical; an alarming finding indeed. Table 3 crosstabulates respondent and peer actions.

A chi-square test supports that the peer pressure affects the respondent's decision, as suggested by the chi-square value of 28.7 (p>.000).

Scenario III:

You are working in the Registrar office of a Saudi university and have the privilege to access students' database. One of your friends has asked you to provide him with a private information about one of the university students (e.g. Grade Point Average). Would you give the information?

Unlike the other scenarios, scenario III addresses individual privacy. The responses were distributed as follows:

	frequency	percent
Give (Unethical)	17	6.1
Undecided	20	7.2
Won't give (Ethical)	241	86.7

As students, the respondents have expressed enthusiasm to protect students' information. More than 86% de-clared that they won't release the information. That is to protect the individual rights to privacy. Similar pattern also emerged in the perceived peer action.

	frequency	percent
Give (Unethical)	29	10.41
Undecided	42	15.11
Won't give (Ethical)	207	75.46

Respondents reported that more than 75.7% of their peers feel that revealing private information is clearly unethical, whereas only 10.41% consider the action ethical.

To test the relationship between the individual and peer actions, a breakdown of the responses is shown in Table 4.

The peer's influence on the subject decision is very obvious, as indicated by the chi-square value of 51.76 (p>.000).

SUMMARY AND CONCLUSION

The findings of this study suggest that there is a strong association between the subject's decision in all the three scenarios and his perception of his peers' act. Saudi organizations must have a clear policy that is communicated clearly to all personnel. Employees awareness must be enhanced by communicating a sound advice about how to interpret codes and resolve conflicts. The "word" should be spread all over the organization about the rules and regulations, since peers affect each other as illustrated in all the scenarios. Conflicts always arise but can be eliminated or minimized by reducing the inducements of conflicts and suggesting a procedure that helps people to keep away from unethical acts (Gellerman, 1989). Others (McKibben, 1983; Straub and Nance, 1990) have shown that policies coupled with assignments of penalties and criminal liabilities to violators can effective.

Computer ethics awareness campaigns need to be designed to address property rights and privacy issues. One of the misconceptions that has emerged in this study is the way respondents view off-the-self software. Majority of them do not equate off-the-shelf software with in-house software in

Table 3. Peer Pressure and Ethical Decision in Scenario II

Respondent's Decision			
	Give (Unethical)	Undecided	Won't give (Ethical)
Peer Decision:			
Give (Unethical)	85.25%	67.31%	57.69%
Undecided		8.20%	9.62%
26.92%			
Won't give (Ethical)	6.56%	23.08%	15.38%

Table 4. Peer Pressure and Ethical Decision in Scenario III

	Respondent's Decision		
	Give (Unethical)	Undecided	Won't give (Ethical)
Peer Decision:			
Give (Unethical)	41.18%	15%	7.88%
Undecided	23.53%	55%	11.2%
Won't give (Ethical)	35.29%	30%	80.91%

term of software piracy.

Saudi organizations need to establish a clear policy statement that distinguishes between behaviour that is acceptable and behaviour that is not. In the first scenario, regulations were stated clearly that the software is for exclusive internal use of the organization. Most of the respondents (82%) abide with the regulations.

Although Saudi Computer Society (the only computer professional entity) is fairly young, it needs to adopt code of ethics as soon as possible. The code should document the objective of the code, the responsibilities and obligations of employees, the ethical and unethical practices, and the sanctions for violations and mechanisms for dealing with conflicts. In the second scenario, the client was almost about to persuade the software programmer to buy unlicensed copy (44% agreed with the client) due to the absence of the code.

REFERENCES

Abdul-Gader, A. (1990) "End-User Computing Success Factors: Further Evidence from a Developing Nation," Information Resources Management Journal, 3, 1, pp. 1-13.

Abdul-Ghani, J. and Al-Meer, A. (1989). "Effect of End-User Computing on Job Satisfaction: An Exploratory Study," Information and Management, 17, pp. 1-5.

Abdul-Ghani, J. and Al-Sakran, S. (1988). The Changing Data Processing Environment in Saudi Arabia. Information and Management, 14, 61-66.

Alder, P., Parsons, C., and Zolke, S. (1985), "Employee Privacy: Legal and Research Developments and Implications for Personnel Administration," Sloan Management Review, 26, 2, pp. 13-22.

Anderson, R., Johnson, D., Gotterbarn, D. and Perrolle, J. (1993), "Using the New ACM Code of Ethics in Decision Making," Communications of the ACM, 36, 2, pp. 98-107.

Chonko, L., and Hunt, S. (1985), "Ethics and Marketing Management: An empirical Examination," Journal of Business Research, 13, 4, pp. 339-359.

Couger, J. (1989), "Preparing IS Students to Deal With Ethical Issues," MIS Quarterly, 13, 2, pp. 211-216

Ferrel, O. and Gresham, L. (1985), "A Contingency Framework for Understanding Ethical Decision Making in Marketing," Journal of Marketing, 49, pp. 87-96.

Gamer, R., and Fidel, K. (1990), "Computer Workers: Professional Identity and Societal Concern," Computers and Society, 20, 3, pp. 153-156

Gellerman, S. (1989), "Managing Ethics from the Top Down," Sloan Management Review, 30, 2, pp. 73-79

Gifford, J. and Norris, D. (1987), "Ethical Attitudes of Retail Store Managers: A Longitudinal Analysis, Journal of Retailing, Vol. 63, No. 3, pp. 298-311.

Harrington, S. and McCollum, R. (1990), "Lessons from Corporate America Applied to Training in Computer Ethics," Computers and Society, 20, 3, pp. 167-173.

Hunt, S., and Vitell, S. (1986), "A General Theory of Marketing Ethics," Journal of Macromarketing, Spring, pp. 5-16.

Mason, R. (1986), "Four Ethical Issues of the Information Age," MIS Quarterly, 10, 1, pp. 5-12.

McKibben, W. (1983), "Who Gets the Blame for Computer Crime?" Infosystems, 5, 7, pp. 34-36

Murphy, P. and Laczniak, G. (1981), "Marketing ethics: A review with Implications for Managers, Educators and Researchers" in Enis and Roering, Review of Marketing, American Marketing Association, Chicago, Illinois, pp. 251-266.

Nel, D., Pitt, L., and Watson, R. (1989), "Business Ethics: Defining the Twilight Zone," Journal of Business Ethics, 8, 10, pp. 781-791.

Oz, E. (1992), "Ethical Standards for Information Systems Professionals: A Case for a Unified Code," MIS Quarterly, 16, 4, pp. 423-433.

Paradice, D. (1990), "Ethical Attitudes of Entry-Level MIS Personnel," Information and Management, 18, 3, pp. 143-151.

Parker, R. (1990), "Computer-Related Crime: Ethical Considerations," Computers and Society, 20, 3, pp. 180-191.

Rahman, M. and A. Abdul-Gader (1993), Knowledge Workers' Use of Support Software in Saudi Arabia, Information and Management, 25, 6, pp. 303-311.

Roos, H. (1981), "Confidentiality of Information," Information and Management, 4, 1, pp. 17-21.

Straub, D. and Collins, R. (1990), "Key Information Issues Facing Managers: Software Piracy, Proprietary Databases, and Individual Rights to Privacy," MIS Quarterly, 14, 2, pp. 143-156.

Straub, D. and W. Nance (1990), "Discovering and Disciplining Computer Abuse in Organizations: A Field Study," MIS Quarterly, 14, 1, pp. 45-60

Sutherland, E., and Cressey, D. (1970), Principles of Criminology, Lippincott, Chicago, Illinois.

Trevino, L. (1986), "Ethical Decision Making in Organizations: A Person-Situation Interactionist Model," Academy of Management Review, 11, 3, pp. 601-617.

Watson, R. and Pitt, L. (1993), "Determinants of Behavior Towards Ethical Issues in Personal Computing," OMEGA, 21, 4, pp. 457-470.

Wilkes, R. (1978), "Fraudulent Behavior by Consumers," Journal of Marketing, 42, 4, pp. 67-75.

Section Ten

Information Technology in Libraries

Faculty and Administrators Access and Usage of Information Resources in a University Library

Carl Lorber
Reference Librarian
Booth Library

Janet F. Iaribee
Acting Assistant Dean
Graduate School

Eastern Illinois University, Charleston, IL 61920. (217) 581-6072

Executive Abstract

Recent technological advances in the storage, retrieval, and dissemination of information have had a major impact on libraries. Common trends in university libraries have been to replace conventional card catalogs with on-line public access catalogs, and to acquire state-of-the-art electronic resources. According to Daniel (1986), such actions follow stage one of technology adoption whereby technology replaces manual or traditional methods. In the second stage "technology fosters new applications and things are done that were never done before" (Daniel, 1986). Boolean techniques, for instance, enable patrons to perform more complex searches than they could with conventional print sources. During the third and final stage of technology adoption, technology itself changes lifestyles and the patterns of people. Daniel (1986) goes on to describe the library of the future as "a smaller facility functioning as a gateway agency, a node in a comprehensive information network".

The premise of this paper is that today's university libraries are in the process of moving from stage two to stage three of this model. It is becoming more and more apparent, for example, that information is being accessed by end-users from their homes and/or offices. In other words, it is no longer necessary to physically be within the library facility itself to access information. More recently, the wide popularity and acceptance of the Internet has made it easier and faster to retrieve all types of information. In both of these situations libraries have been at the core, acting as a gateway and facilitator of information access and distribution. Also, as predicted by Daniel(1986), the lifestyles and patterns of people (mainly the librarians and patrons) involved with storing, retrieving and disseminating information have also been changed by technology. From the librarians' point of view, from a simpler provider of information, they are increasingly becoming responsible for not only selecting and purchasing electronic resources such as computers, printers, and CD-ROM titles, but also for troubleshooting hardware problems, and instructing patrons on how to operate or search these new resources. From the end-users' point of view they welcome any technology that makes it easier and faster to access information.

With todays' technological advances, however, university librarians face new responsibilities and concerns. One of them is to determine the degree of effectiveness these resources offer. Librarians should strive to know the answers to questions such as: To what degree are these resources being utilized? Do patrons know that these resources exists and are available? How often and how well do patrons use these resources and for what purpose? In other words, what is the information access and usage pattern of end-users in regards to the new technologies in university libraries, and how well these new technologies are being utilized. A survey was conducted to attempt to find answers to these questions. A questionnaire was developed and distributed to 785 faculty and administrators. Two hundred-and-fifty questionnaires were returned.

The library in this study is centrally located in one facility in a Midwest, traditional residential university. This university is a regional accredited institution with over 10,600 students and 1800 employees. It offers both undergraduate and graduate (Master's) degree programs. The library's collection, in excess of 640,000 cataloged volumes and more than one-and-one-half million microforms, supports the educational mission of the university. This mission is to provide superior yet accessible undergraduate and graduate education, where students learn the methods and outcome of free inquiry in the arts, sciences, humanities, and professions guided by a faculty known for its commitment to teaching. The library's online catalog has been available since September 1988 and end-user access to additional databases has been offered since 1989. These holdings are accessible in various ways: via the campus-wide Local Area Network, a statewide computerized network , and through dedicated workstations in the library. The Local Area Network in turn provides access to the university's computing resources, the Internet, and the library's own file servers (with access to several databases).

CONCLUDING REMARKS

New electronic resources in university libraries present new responsibilities for librarians, as managers of these information sources. An area of concern is to determine the effectiveness or level of utilization of these resources. The survey conducted and described in this paper produced results worthy of consideration and perhaps further investigation:

1. In general, half of the patrons with access to library electronic resources utilize them.

2. Some reasons suggested by this study as to why some patrons do not opt for realizing the full potential of the electronic resources available through libraries include:
   a. Apathy towards computers in general.
   b. Perceived lack of easy-to-read documentation and training of electronic resources.
   c. Lack of time to properly learn and to actually use the electronic resources.

3. At least in the institution where the study was conducted, the respondents are utilizing the library electronic resources at about the same rate, regardless of age, rank, or purpose (teaching, research, or service).

Electronic Knowledge:
The Future Alternatives of Libraries

Andrew S. Targowski
Professor of Computer Information Systems
Department of Business Information Systems
WESTERN MICHIGAN UNIVERSITY
Kalamazoo, MI 49008
(616) 375-5406
fax (616) 375-8762
targowski@hcob.wmich.edu

Abstract

The correlation among literacy, productivity, innovations, democracy and libraries are analyzed. The role of information technology in libraries is evaluated in the areas of online database services, library communications networks, electronic bulletin boards, optical disks, and facsimile. Alternative futures of libraries are defined: Status Quo, Automated Library, Electronic Library, Virtual Library. The systems architecture for those libraries is presented. Libraries have a mission of informing the nation and the world. Some rules and premises of this mission are analyzed. If the evolution of libraries will reach the electronic level, then it may mean the death of the classic library. If the virtual library becomes a reality, then libraries will evolve into clearinghouses and distributors of information services.

A Pathway for Literacy, Productivity, Innovations, and Democracy

The explosion of innovative technologies in 1980s and 1990s, initiated by the rapid electronic information creation and utilization has been dramatic. The now identifiable developing trend challenges the former national economic cornerstone of reliance on manufacturing productivity with the need to enhance literacy, increase productivity of services and production, accelerate innovations, and strengthen democracy to meet the requirements of an information-dependent world. As a result the pivotal need for libraries has to be defined in order to store and disseminate public information and knowledge, which are instrumental in improving literacy, productivity, innovations, and democracy. These qualities are critically based on the storage and dissemination of information and knowledge.

Literacy and Libraries

The effects of illiteracy permeate the fiber of the nation, undermining the ability of its citizens to live and work in the world of today and to meet the challenges of a rapidly changing world of tomorrow. The globalization of the world marketplace and its information resources dictates what, where, and how we educate our citizens. These citizens must compete in the world arena and develop literacy in all forms to effectively absorb information in many new forms and formats.

Though the United States boasts one of the highest standards of living, literacy remains a vexing problem: The U.S. ranks 49th in literacy among the 158 member countries of the United Nations. In real terms, Project Literacy U.S. estimates that as many as 23 million adult Americans are functionally illiterate, lacking skills beyond the fourth-grade level, with another 35 million being semi-literate, lacking skills beyond the eight-grade level. One state, Texas, estimates in 1988 that illiteracy cost that state $17.2 billion yearly through lost productivity, unrealized tax revenue, and welfare and crime-related costs. With literacy's integral role in an individual's self-image and as a common denominator that bringing people together, the toll in human terms is evident.

Trends show that diversity will increase during the 21st century. Fully 30 percent of U.S. school children are from racial or cultural minority families. Early in the next century that percentage is projected to increase to 35 percent. Some states are expected to have no "majority" group by the Year 2000. Coupled with this trends is the representation of every known religious denomination, more than 100 different languages, and the spectrum of special-need Americans from the gifted and talented to those with learning difficulties and physical limitations. The need and scope of the task become apparent.

In addition, some trend data project an increase in the number of children living below the poverty line, which has been shown to create further challenges to learning and literacy. The current national high school dropout rate of over 30 percent is another measure of literacy.

Literacy provides leverage for responding to the needs of the increasingly diverse population in a fast-paced, competitive world. Literacy is, in fact, the fulcrum for increasing productivity, creating innovations, and strengthening democracy. Libraries and information services are at the heart of the Nation's education program which fights illiteracy.

Productivity and Libraries

Old definitions give way to new. Productivity, the measure of a worker's output in relation to resources, most often has been associated with raw materials and tangible resources. But a labor-intensive economic system is being supplemented by an information-based economy. That old definition now has expanded to include information and knowledge as a resource — and involves reliance on judgments about source credibility, timeliness, format, and utility for application to the end product. These factors are not easily measured by traditional productivity standards, but are critical in an Information Age which can cloud a worker's sense of productive contribution to society.

The abundance of technologies and associated information places new demands on people in the work force who must adapt to these changes. The velocity and rapid turnover of information has created today's "knowledge worker" who must be prepared with lifelong learning habits, access to relevant information, and analytical skills to remain productive in his/her chosen field. Some estimates indicate that today's worker will have to update skills every three years.

Collection, preservation, and retrieval of information and knowledge in a timely and useful form for the end user is a major goal if we are to build and maintain a productive, competitive work force in an interconnected global market. The nation which moves to an information-based economy, harnessing knowledge through technology, and applying it through an educated work force will assure its people economic independence and the standard of living they desire.

The emergence of the "knowledge worker" requires us to recognize libraries and information services as educational institutions for lifelong learning of "knowledge skills." The Information Superhighway built by the National Research and Education Network should encourage the creation of cooperative information and technology partners at all levels of the economy. The sharing of national intellectual resources should lead to higher productivity.

Innovations and Libraries

The competition among nations and companies in developed environments is more and more relying on innovations. Citizens, workers, firms, and nations should actively seek out pressure and challenge, not try to avoid them. The task is to take advantage of sources of information and knowledge and thus create the impetus for innovation.

Innovations are generated by imagination and knowledge. Imagination alone is not good enough to create worthy innovation. Knowledge is a key ingredient of innovating power and a library and information services is a tool to disseminate that knowledge.

Beyond the pressure to innovate, one of the most important advantages a society, individual or firm can have a source of early insight into needs, environmental forces and trends that others have not noticed, but will be important in the future. This can be done through the intensive application of library and information services.

Democracy and Libraries

As dependence of information grows, the potential increases for emergence of an Information Elite — the possibility of a widening gap between those who possess facility with information resources and those denied the tools to access, understand, and use information.

This dichotomy could threaten to send fissures into the democratic base of the Nation. Thomas Jefferson's warning that the success of a democratic society depends upon an "informed and educated" populace could well have been proclaimed today. The intellectual freedom to access information and pursue truths, makes judgments, and achieve goals as full participants in society is the bedrock of a strong democracy.

Today, more than ever, information and knowledge is power. Access to it — and the skill to understand and apply it — increasingly is the way power is exercised. Information has become so essential that a large and growing part of federal, state, and local government, academic institutions, and the private sector work force is engaged in information-related activities. Tens of thousands of organizations, from small businesses, publishers, and associations to global industries, work in the trade of information distillation and delivery.

In the U.S., information delivery systems include more than 30,000 public, academic, and special libraries, and an estimated 74,000 school libraries and media centers. It is a telling testimony to the insight of Benjamin Franklin that, in 1731, he established the Nation's first library, the Philadelphia Library Company. In the world, there are an estimated 750,000 public, academic and special libraries containing about 100 billion volumes.

As literacy is a key to productivity, innovations, and democracy, so literacy, productivity, and innovations are essential to a strong "educated" democracy. All are intertwined, interconnected, interdependent, and inseparable. Thus, the role of libraries as "schoolrooms for lifetime education" is central to the nation's long-term political stability and prosperity. The democratic Nation should afford equal information opportunity to the broadest number of citizens for their full and informed participation in all aspects of the nation's economic, political, cultural, and intellectual life. The support of a strong democracy is the intellectual freedom to inquire, discover, question, validate, and create.

The challenge remains to provide integrated, cohesive, cooperative national policies and programs to crystallize the continued educational contribution of libraries to enhance literacy, productivity, innovations, and democracy [1].

Role of Information Technology in Libraries

All libraries employ a variety of information technologies in support of their mission of "allowing people to utilize information," (Turoff and Spector 1976). A library is an institution that acquires, manages, and disseminates information. Moreover, "a library is a bibliographic system regardless of the situation in which is placed, and the task of the librarian is to bring people and graphic records together in a meaningful relationship that will be beneficial to the user," (Wilson 1977).

Information technologies are not "new" to libraries. A broad scope of IT have been applied by libraries for years and have effected all aspects of library operations and services. In fact, almost every library function has been altered to some extend by electronics, computers, and telecommunications.

Libraries may employ one or more of the following technologies and/or technological applications: microcomputers, on-line data services (bibliographic search), networks such as OCLIN (On-line College Library Center) and RLIN (Research Libraries Information Network (RLIN), automated information systems, electronic bulletin boards, optical disk technologies such as videodisk and CD-ROM, facsimile, and microfiche and related equipment.

On-line Database Services

On-line database services, such as DIALOG, BRS, and other computerized retrieval systems, cover a wide array of continually expanding subject areas. Each database is a compilation of textual, statistical, and/or bibliographic information. Bibliographic and referral databases are sometime called reference databases, whereas numeric and textual-numeric databases are called source databases. In 1979-80 there were 400 databases, 221 database producers, and 59 on-line service available. By 1987, there were 3,169 databases, 1,494 database producers, and 486 on-line services [2].

These services allow rapid access to information sources, integrate information for the user, permit libraries greater flexibility in a choice of format, and provide access to previously unavailable information. Use of these services also allows the library to be less dependent on paper or hard-copy indexing materials.

Library Communications Networks

Two or more libraries may form communication networks utilizing information technologies to enhance the exchange of materials, information, or other services. The formation of local, state, regional, and national networks has significantly altered the operation of libraries. There are several types of networks — bibliographic utility, regional service organizations, and others. WESTNET, SOLINET, AMOGOS, CLASS, and the like are regional service networks that facilitate the expansion of the bibliographic utility. Although bibliographic utilities began as a means for libraries to reduce cost of cataloging, their primary function today is for sharing of resources. One example of bibliographic utility is OCLC, a major computer-based cooperative network with over 8,000 members and employed by all types of libraries nationally and internationally. The OCLC network assists librarians in:

- acquiring materials
- cataloging materials
- ordering custom-printed catalog cards
- initiating interlibrary loans
- locating materials in member libraries
- accessing other databases
- searching for government documents.

Many depository libraries use OCLC with management information systems [3].

Electronic Bulletin Boards

Libraries are applying electronic bulletin boards in support of library operations such as:

- interlibrary loan (ILL)
- resource-sharing functions
- access to current information located elsewhere
- professional dialogue on library development and operations
- managerial communication

The Wisconsin Interlibrary Service (WILS) network is one example of the growing use of bulletin boards in libraries. The WILS network is used by 30 member libraries and handle over 90,000 requests a year [3]. Libraries are subscribing to governmental bulletin boards. For example, the Remote Bulletin Board System (RBBS) of the National Science Foundation contains useful information for research activities.

Optical disks technologies include videodisks, compact audio disks, CD-ROMs, optical digital disks, and others. Despite of a lack of common information access and retrieval standards, an increasing number of vendors are introducing database services on optical disks (they use the differential reflection of light from a mirror disk surface as a means of reading information). Databases are popular on this type of a medium, among many, one can list: the Wilson business database, Books in Print, Ulrich's Periodicals Directory, Forthcoming Books, AGRICOLA on agriculture, and so forth. The Library Corporation sells Library of Congress (LOC) MARC catalogue records on four optical disks.

Since CD-ROM disks cannot be updated (they are replaced), therefore they are not practical for time-sensitive data.

Facsimile

Facsimile machines are a very quick method of transmitting printed information between libraries. For example, the National Library of Medicine will send up to 20 pages of professional literature to a member in support of emergency patient care.

Alternative Futures for Libraries

With the increasing number of information technology-driven projects in libraries, the impetus to automate and to include electronic information in depositories and disseminate it is strong. IT products improve access to library information and negligence to include these products/systems could limit the public access to information and knowledge. The following alternatives of libraries futures are offered:

Alternative I: Status Quo, where information is stored and disseminated in paper and microfiche formats with a few CD-ROMs and a few on-line files.

Alternative II: Automated Library, where information is stored in a paper format, however, cataloging, retrieval and circulation of information is automated by computer information systems and services.

Alternative III: Electronic Library, where information is stored and disseminated in the electronic format via telecommunications and computer networks, however, there is a depository (Information Museum) of books, journals, and documents, and only certain type of information and services are provided locally in a timely manner.

Alternative IV: Virtual Library, where information is stored and disseminated in the electronic format to the end users at workplaces, schools and colleges, as well as at homes. Furthermore, a depository type of a library is eliminated.

The last two alternatives of the future libraries implicate the loss of many patrons to private sector information providers. Libraries, particularly public ones, will lose business, and more important, will lose the financial and political support of middle-class citizens. This group of citizens constitute the major group of home computer systems users with access to electronic or virtual libraries dispersed in the world. They will support scope (niche) electronic information providers rather than near-by libraries of scale.

Table 1 compares goals and solutions of the four library alternatives.

This comparison implicates a radical change in the library organization. Large collections of paper information are becoming more a matter of history than a goal of improving the access and choice. Those libraries with more gateways to electronic information and services will achieve the higher status than those with large old library buildings.

Automated Library

The Automated Library Alternative dominates the present level of academic and research libraries development paradigm. Its architecture is depicted on Figure 1, applying the Targowski model (Targowski 1990)..

The Automated Library aims to improve services to the patrons either through widely available services (OCLC) or via a so-called the library integrated system. The integrated systems are usually installed by software providers, such as Library Corporation, Information Dimension, multiLIS, Data Trek, CARL, NOTIS, CoBIT, CARL, and others.

A library at this stage of development is at a cross-

Table 1: A Comparison of Library Alternatives

Alternative	Goal	Information	Maintain info.	Gateways
STATUS QUO	Growing Collection	Paper, Microfiche CD-ROM	Catalog Cards	Very Limited
AUTOMATED LIBRARY	Improved Service	Paper, Microfiche CD-ROM	Automated	To Several On-line DB and Info Services
ELECTRONIC LIBRARY	Improved Access	Electronic Format, Local Services of Scope	Automated and Networked	To Many On-line DB and Info Services
VIRTUAL LIBRARY	Improved Choice	Electronic Format	Automated and Networked	To All Available On-line DB and Info Services

Figure 1: The Architecture of Autoamted Library

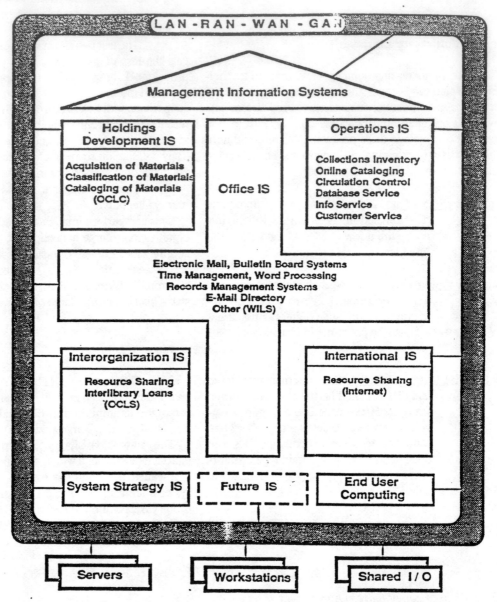

roads. It is a "prisoner" of its own old holdings and wants to improve its general library services via automation. It maintains its presence in two opposite environments. By the tradition, it wants to expand its own holdings, but being under pressure for cutting edge solutions, it wants to apply as many resources as possible for the automated services. Of course, such libraries face a lack of funds and staff support. These libraries may be in a state of confusion with a lack of vision (unfulfilled promises and expectations).

Electronic Library

The Electronic Library Alternative is a solution of a new quality. It is still a "library" which provides the automated services and electronic easy access to holdings stored electronically. While these holdings may be stored locally, it will be more probable that more and more holdings will be stored elsewhere. A library gateway will transmit patron requests through LANs, MAN, WANs, and GANs to other electronic libraries. The old type of a status quo library will disappear. The electronic library will become a place where a certain type of information or service is available, perhaps, locally oriented. The architecture of this library is illustrated on Figure 8-2.

This type of a library will prevail in academic and research institutions. Public libraries can survive only if they will develop locally-oriented holdings and services. The public libraries cannot be so general anymore. They will find that library services have to be provided to some people in specialized areas only. The public libraries may change from store-

Figure 2: The Architecture of Electronic Library

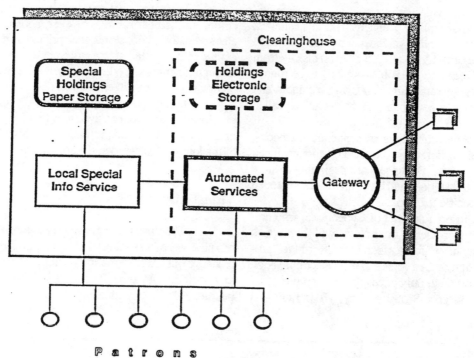

house of books and other materials to clearinghouses or that of repository of programmed experiences.

Shuman (1989) names such a library an "Experience Parlour." According to the quoted author the staff now call themselves *experience facilitators* or *neotravel agents*. People are not looking any more for passive usage of two-dimensional films and pages. They seek "all-at-onceness" and actual participation in the experiences they witness. People don't just want entertainment anymore, they want roles. Users of the experience parlour visit them for the following reasons: (1) to escape routine, (2) to test a new lifestyle before abandoning their own, (3) to be entertained in novel, involving ways, (4) to be challenged by different or exciting circumstances, (5) to learn about something new, and (6) to realize fantasies which, for a multiplicity of reasons, will have to remain fantasies.

Such television shows as "Fantasy Island," "Lifestyles of the Rich and Famous," "The Millionaire," "Dynasty," "Dallas," motivated people to become these "fortunate" people from the shows. Therefore, if they cannot immigrate to the United States or Western Europe or other developed countries to fulfill their dreams, they would like at least to experience dreams under conditions as realistic as possible. Needless to say, the majority of North Americans, West Europeans, and so forth would like to implement their dreams too.

The successful development of the electronic library depends on the development and cooperation of other electronic libraries. This process will be incremental, mostly driven by private information vendors and the climate created by government for the application of the electronic infrastructure. Libraries, however, cannot wait for a "supply of ready solutions." They have to define a vision of their own environment

and experience pilot and demo systems.

The electronic library is not far away, since the first electronic books are already "in print." Electronic books read on computer screens are popping up everywhere — anything from baseball-trivia collections in the shape of tiny pocket calculators to elaborate $2000 software creations that require state-of-the-art desk top-computers. Some electronic books are already more popular than their print counterparts. Random House sold 400,000 electronic encyclopedias, which is four times more than the printed version was sold.

Print evolved in the last 500 years, while electronic printing is only a few years old. It will take some time until electronic books will eliminate printed books. Electronic books, however, will deliver new features that are not available in printed books. A click of the mouse should make the print four times larger. Footnotes can be read when they are needed or a search for some names or events can be done for a reader throughout the whole electronic book.

Tom Clancy's "Hunt for Red October" if published on a disk, could have a plain text, maps, submarine blueprints and other toys for the techno-thriller junkie. If a reader is tired of reading on screen, can put on headphones and listen to an audio version played from the same disk. Sony's multimedia Player and Franklin's Digital Book are examples of this trend which is tested in practice.

In 1992, IBM begun selling schools the tools students need to create their own electronic books. The Illuminated Books and Manuscripts system is pricey — $2000 for the software and about $8000 for the adapted PC. It comes with five documents already "illuminated" — each one appears on the computer screen as a printed page, and the students can easily order up sound and video presentations to accompany the text. Actors, for example, provide various readings of "Hamlet;" politicians, including Joseph P. Kennedy II and Daniel K. Inouye, discuss the Declaration of Independence. The IBM package also includes an additional 100 books on disk — from the collected Shakespeare to the Bible — ready to be illuminated by the students by attaching their own text, audio and images, linking them all together through the technique called hypertext.

In 1990s some publishers of academic textbooks, such as McGraw Hill, offered instructors a custom designed textbook for a given class. Publishers are beginning to store electronically written textbooks and later can assemble needed chapters into one specific textbook.

William Gibson a prophet of Cyberspace, who created much of computer-hacker mythology with cyberpunk novels like "Neuromancer" and "Mona Lisa Overdrive" produced a limited edition of "Agrippa." It is an electronic book that can read on a computer only once. After that it turns into nonsense. The book cost $1500 a copy. It is rather an investment than fun to read (Rogers 1992).

Paper and electronic books will coexist for decades to come. In the near future, however, books will be delivered electronically to bookstores, then printed on demand, one copy at time or down loaded to a customer computer on location or through a network. Today, this type of a readership requires computers that are still expensive.

In the coming future, if a public library will able to provide easy and inexpensive access to many electronic works of artists, scientists, and professionals. This will be a beginning of the knowledge democratization process.

Virtual Library

The Virtual Library Alternative is the implementation of a new way of accessing information. So far people have been reaching out for information, visiting libraries, news stands, and so forth. In this alternative, information will come to people, even "automatically." An user not only will look for

Figure 3: The Architecture of Virtual Library

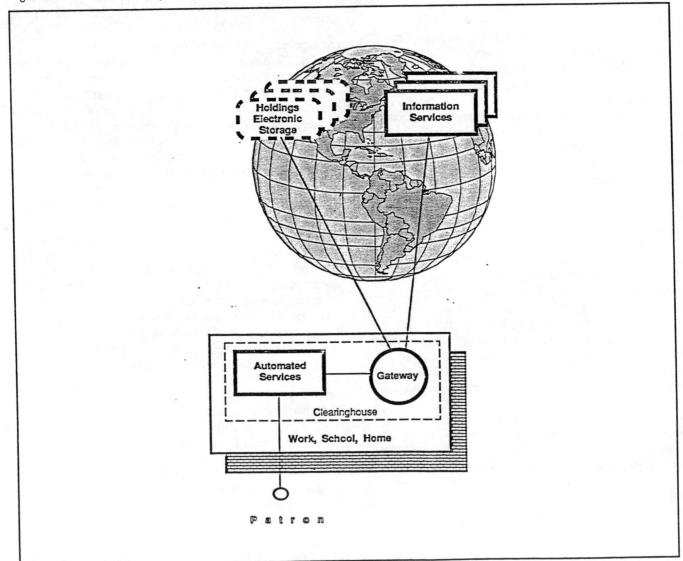

bigger choice of information via global networks and electronic holdings but will be receiving information via smart "info absorbers." The user will program an info absorber that will look for electronic information of interest anywhere on the Globe. Even without patron intervention, such information may soon flow to his/her work-school-home computer.

The architecture of the virtual library is shown on Figure 3.

Readers will find it more convenient to search for information from their own place of work rather than visiting libraries or even using/buying libraries intermediate services. A library's classic functions are downloaded and carried-out from the user's location. A virtual library, however, provides not only convenience, but more important, it provides a much larger choice of information. At this stage of information infrastructure development, private and governmental information providers will take over library services. A patron will be able to access electronic sources of information directly and also get direct information services.

Informing the Nation

The libraries, regardless of their alternatives are depositories of human culture. They preserve and disseminate information, concepts, knowledge, and wisdom. They are tools of human cognition which make us wiser and more aware of our needs to survive and blossom. An informed man is a free man who knows how to sustain healthy environments in economy, education, and politics. " If a Nation expects to be ignorant and free in a state of civilization, it expects what never was and never will be...if we are to guard against ignorance and remain free, it is the responsibility of every American to be informed." (Thomas Jefferson, July 6, 1816).

In the 1990s, the U.S. is "A Nation at Risk" which, with the help of better information, concepts, knowledge and wisdom should become "A Learning Nation" and eventually "A Nation of the Informed." Libraries and information services are essential to a learning and informed nation.

To be an informed nation, some solutions for the information infrastructure have to be provided. The nation has to be led, focused, and facilitated in order to implement these solutions. The executive and legislative branches of the federal (national) government should serve as a catalyst to energize the local, state, federal, and private sector in information areas.

The focus on ways of achieving the informed nation can be explained by the list of following recommendations groups (that include 95 specific recommendations), by the 1991 White House Conference on Library and Information Services (with 984 participants, this conference was a summary of 100,000 Americans participating in local, state conference forums who provided 2,500 policy proposals) [4]:

- Availability and access to information
- National information policies
- Information networks through technology
- Structure and governance
- Service for diverse needs
- Training to reach end users
- Personnel and staff development
- Preservation of information
- Marketing to Communities

To be informed, a person has to have information rights, something like *habeus corpus* or rather *habeus scriptus*. The mentioned conference offered the following People's Information Bill of Rights [4]:

- All people are entitled to free access to the information and services offered by libraries, clearinghouse, and information centers
- All people are entitled to obtain current and accurate information on any topic
- All people are entitled to courteous, efficient, and timely service
- All people are entitled to assistance by qualified library and information services personnel
- All people are entitled to the right of confidentiality in all of their dealings with libraries, clearinghouses, information centers, and their staff
- All people are entitled to full access and services from library and information network on local, state, regional, and national levels
- All people are entitled to the use of a library facility or information center that is accessible, functional, and comfortable
- All people are entitled to be provided with a statement of policies governing the use and services of the library, clearinghouse, or information center
- All people are entitled to library and information services that reflects the interests and needs of the community.

The attention has to be brought to the need for appropriate reading materials and programming for children and youth adults with assorted disabilities: Perceptual, neurological, binocularity, ocular motility, dyslexia, etc., as well as blindness, and to increase the education of librarians adequately to meet the demands of handicapped young and old people.

The growth and augmentation of the Nation's libraries and information services are essential if all citizens, without regard to race, ethnic background, or graphic location are to have reasonable access to adequate information and lifelong learning.

Informing the World

The access to information and ideas is indispensable to the development of human potential, the advancement of civilization, and the continuance of enlightened self-government. The emerging satellite communication networks and other technologies offer unparalleled opportunity for access to education opportunities in all parts of the world. The emergence of the Electronic Global Village (Targowski 1991) offers the opportunity that the learning potential inherent in all children and youth, will be reinforced throughout the Globe, especially in the scope of literacy, reading, research, and retrieving skills.

Libraries and information services available electronically at all corners of the world should limit existing information ignorance among the world's almost 4.5 billion people. These people do not necessarily have access to good information sources. With the help of their electronic public libraries and Global Area Networks, these libraries should provide information to uninformed people. The uncensored information and knowledge is the first prerequisite to abolish "information slavery." in the world

"Information slavery" is one of main sources of the growing spread of fundamentalism, racism, and nationalism in the Second and Third World countries. Conflicts in the 1990s, such as in former Yugoslavia, the former Soviet Union, the Middle East, or some African countries are the result of a lack of education and still existing mentality of the 18th and 19th centuries. In times when Western Europe eliminates its own borders, in Southern Europe, former Yugoslavia, thousands of people are killed just in order to keep strong ethnic lines.

The people from all countries need to be informed and better educated through their whole life to know of all their options and be wise to solve their own problems in a rational manner. At the stake is "to be or not to be" of human kind and..... each of us.

Conclusion

The development of libraries and information services is driven by accelerated information technology progress and a national strategy of using information as a key resource in supporting the economy and democracy. The eclectic influx of automated and electronic systems causes some confusion among library management, sponsors, and patrons. This need to be replaced with a vision of ultimate solutions and needs for given library services. On the one hand, the strong pressure by private information vendors will move libraries on the higher levels of solutions. On the other hand the patrons will search for better information services and choices. In effect, it may lead to the death of the classic library. Certainly, if the virtual library becomes a reality, then libraries will evolve into clearinghouses and distributors of information services.

End Notes

1. This overview of challenges facing libraries draws from remarks to the 1991 White House Conference on Libraries and Information Services by President George Bush and keynote speakers Congressman Major R. Owens

(D, N.Y.); William T. Esrey, Chairman and Chief Executive Officer, United Telecommunications, Inc.; and Mary Hatwood Futrell, Senior Fellow and Associate Director of the Center for the Study of Education and National Development, George Washington University.

2. Cuadra Associations, Directory of On-line Databases, New York, NY: 1986, vol. 7, No. 3, p.v.

3. U.S. Congress, Office of Technology Assessment, Informing the Nation: Federal Information Dissemination in an Electronic Age, OTA-CIT-396, Washington, DC: U.S. Government Printing Office, October 1988.

4. Information 2000, Library and Information Services for the 21st Century., Washington, DC: the U.S. Government Printing Office, ISBN 0-16-035978-3, 1991

References

Rogers, M. (1992), "The Literary Circuitry," Newsweek, June 29, pp.66-67

Shuman, B, A. (1989), The Libraries of the Future, Englewood, CO: Libraries Unlimited, Inc. p.89.

Targowski, A. (1990), The Architecture of Enterprise-wide Information Management Systems, Harrisburg, PA: Idea Group Publishing

Targowski, A. (1991), "Strategies and Architecture of the Electronic Global Village," The Information Society, vol. 7, No. 3. pp. 187-202.

Turoff, M and M. Spector (1976), "Libraries and the Implications of Computer Technology," Proceedings of the AFIPS National Computer Conference, vol. 45.

Wilson, P. (1977), A Community Elite and the Public Library: The Uses of Information in Leadership, Westport, CT. p.xii.

Section Eleven

Database Technologies

Quality Issues in Database Reverse Engineering: An Overview

Roger H. L. Chiang
School of Management
Syracuse University
Syracuse, NY 13244

Terry M. Barron
William E. Simon Graduate School of Business Administration
University of Rochester
Rochester, NY 14627

1 DATABASE REVERSE ENGINEERING

It is often difficult to obtain a good conceptual understanding of an old and ill-designed database, especially when there is a lack of documentation. Database reverse engineering provides solutions for this problem, which recovers domain semantics of an existing database and represents them as a conceptual schema that corresponds to the possible (most likely) design specifications of the database. Three specific motivations of the application of database reverse engineering are:

Semantic Degradations.

During the design and maintenance of a database, some domain semantics might not be captured, or else are captured but removed due to representation limitations and implementation considerations of the database system. Therefore, design specifications of an existing database cannot be easily recognized by referring to information provided by the target database management system (DBMS). However, a conceptual schema can help users understand the database and retrieve the required data correctly, as well as help designers and maintainers.

Maintenance and Redesign.

Database design is oriented toward design from scratch. However, database design is often actually redesign. It is essential to obtain a conceptual schema in order to develop a new executable schema for an existing database.

Change of Data Models.

A conceptual schema is useful as an intermediate design when converting an existing database into a different data model (e.g., an IMS database into a DB2 database, or a relational database into an object-oriented database).

2 QUALITY ISSUES

Three quality issues are discussed here. These issues should be addressed for any reverse engineering method so that it can be implemented at a high level of automation, and the resulting conceptual schema will be semantically rich and correct.

2.1 Database Design versus Reverse Engineering

The problem of a database's meaning is subtle; there are at least three ways in which it might be interpreted:

1. What the original designers and maintainers intended the database to represent.

2. What its users understand the database to mean.

3. What a rational designer, using a particular design method, would use the structures appearing in the database to represent.

The "rational designer" interpretation appears to make the most sense since it will yield a broadly useful tool whose output can then be revised by an appropriate combination of users and designers to produce a final conceptual schema. Therefore, in designing a generic reverse engineering method, one should assume the third of the above viewpoints. As a result, the output of any reverse engineering method can only be a best guess as to what the designers intended any particular database to represent.

The assumption about the design method then form the basis for rules and heuristics used to interpret the database structures. An open question is the extent to which different design approaches will lead to different rules and heuristics, and whether they in turn lead to significantly different conceptual schemas when applied to a given database. Thus one major determinant of the quality of results produced by a reverse engineering method may be the degree of congruence between the forward engineering process it assumes and the approaches actually used in the design and maintenance of the subject database. Existing research has generally been weak on this dimension.

2.2 Thoroughness of Domain Semantics Acquisition

There are at least two ways in which a conceptual schema produced by reverse engineering can improve upon an executable schema: 1) by making the existing database more meaningful by providing an understanding of how its parts relate to each other, and 2) by having the conceptual schema incorporate more information than the executable schema. The first kind of improvement is usually useful since it provides a more abstract and holistic view than is available from the database itself. However, the true promise of reverse engineering lies in achieving the second kind of improvement. Clearly, in order for such improvements to be made, sources of semantic information beyond the executable schema are needed. They are classified into three categories: 1) domain semantics that can be obtained directly from the target DBMS, 2) domain semantics obtainable by analysis of the executable schema and data instances, and 3) domain semantics obtained from knowledgeable persons. Reverse engineering methods that do not fully exploit all of these information sources are unlikely to be able to provide improvements much beyond the first type noted above, providing just a graphical means of representing the physical implementation of the database. We recommend the following directions for future research:

- Greater understanding of the kinds of information that can be extracted from the stored data, and methods for doing so, are needed. Results from research on knowledge discovery in databases may be useful for domain semantics acquisition.
- What can be acquired from other machine-analyzable sources? Examples of potential sources include views, canned queries, programs that do data entry checking, and other programs that use the existing database.

2.3 Performance Evaluation Criteria

Research on database reverse engineering has largely ignored performance evaluation issues. There are at least four fundamental performance evaluation perspectives to consider. Completeness considers the extent to which a reverse engineering method incorporates rules to handle the full array of structures that might be found in existing databases. Robustness considers how a reverse engineering process will perform when presented with database structures that were not explicitly anticipated by the method's creators. Obviously completeness and robustness are largely empirical ques-

tions that can best be answered by testing the reverse engineering process on real databases. Considerable work remains to be done in applying and evaluating existing methods on these two dimensions, and is clearly a fertile area for academic-industry cooperation.

Two essential criteria for performance efficiency are: 1) determining which operations can be fully automated, and 2) whether these operations can be implemented efficiently on a computer. The latter question can be evaluated by analyzing the time complexity of the algorithms that implement a reverse engineering process. The key issue addressed by correctness is how faithfully a database will be represented by a conceptual schema produced from it. "Faithfulness" has several dimensions. For example, one can ask whether a database that was designed via the forward engineering process assumed by the reverse engineering method will, when reverse engineered, yield a conceptual schema identical to the one used in the initial design. This can be tested empirically by controlled experiment, by reverse engineering databases whose design was done for the experiment. The focus here is to test the method (i.e. rules and algorithms) rather than the implementation; we call this validation (of the method). Additionally, once a conceptual schema is generated, it must be evaluated as a representation of the portion of the real world the users of the database understand it to represent. We call this validation (of the output), and can only be done by people who are familiar with the database and also understand the domain in question.

A Comparison of Three Data Models for Text Storage and Retrieval Systems: The Relational Model Revisited

Morten Hertzum
Dept. of Computer Science
University of Copenhagen

A number of software toolkits exist for the development of text storage and retrieval systems (TSARS). This study compares three data models applicable to such toolkits and discusses the suitability of one of them as the basis of a toolkit unifying all three data models. The three data models are: (1) the text model, also known as the inverted file approach, (2) the hypertext model, and (3) the relational model. In the design of the relational model changeability was a key consideration, but more often it is sacrificed to save development resources or improve performance. As it is not uncommon to see successful TSARS exist for 15-20 years and be subject to manifold changes during their lifetime, it is the relational model which is considered for use in the unified toolkit. It seems as if the relational model can be enhanced to incorporate the text model and the hypertext model.

1. Introduction

Text storage and retrieval systems (TSARS) are systems intended to support the organization of and access to bodies of texts. To avoid developing TSARS from scratch, they are mostly based on a more or less application-specific toolkit, i.e. a set of integrated software tools covering large or all parts of an application. The purpose of this study is twofold: (1) To review the strengths and weaknesses of three data models applicable to such toolkits, namely the text model which is also known as the inverted file approach, the hypertext model, and the relational model. (2) To discuss the suitability of the relational model as the basis of a toolkit unifying all three data models. In the literature, the relational model is generally considered inferior to other data models for the development of TSARS (van Rijsbergen, 1979; Lynch & Stonebraker, 1988). From the present author's point of view this reflects an underestimation of the need for adapting TSARS to changes during their lifetime.

In the next section the three data models are introduced and their main properties as well as major aspects of their implementations are discussed, based on the literature. Section 3 briefly describes three commercially available toolkits implementing the data models and, to some extent, combining facilities from them. Section 4 concerns the possibility of developing a toolkit having the major strengths of all three data models. The choice of the relational model as the basis of this toolkit implies that it is expected to be suited for this purpose; it does not imply that the two other data models are judged unsuited.

2. The three data models

TSARS share a number of properties, but there are also fundamental differences which have motivated the development and use of different data models. A couple of the differences are highlighted in the following simple classification which distinguishes two types of systems and three types of text involvement, see figure 2.1 which also includes examples. The two types of systems are: (1) *Text retrieval systems*, which provide access to fixed or externally updated corpora. (2) *Text filing and retrieval systems*, which provide facilities for both filing and, subsequently, retrieving texts. The three types of text involvement are: (1) *Registering*, in which the system handles fields with information about the texts, sometimes known as text surrogates, but not the text itself. (2) *Storing*, in which the system handles the text itself along with certain attribute fields. However, each text is treated as an atomic entity. (3) *Modelling*, in which the system handles information about the internal structure of the texts along with the text itself and certain attribute fields. Here, the retrieval facilities allow exploitation of the text structure, for example by providing access both to entire texts at a time and to individual parts while retaining their relation to the entire text.

2.1 The text model

The majority of text retrieval systems with little or no modelling of the texts are based on what Macleod (1991) terms the text model. The text model is little more than a generalized description of the way in which these systems are currently implemented and have been implemented for years without major modifications. Texts are conceived of as independent documents with two major components, a set of attributes and a content. The attributes vary with the application area, but bibliographic information, such as title, author, and date of

Figure 2.1 A Simple Classification of TSARS, including examples

type of system	type of text involvement		
	registering	storing	modelling
text retrieval systems	keyword-based information retrieval systems	full-text information retrieval systems	hypertext 'books'
text filing and retrieval systems	journalization systems	archival systems	electronic publishing

publication, is almost always present. The contents is the text from which the document is composed and may or may not be included in actual systems. To improve performance an index is established containing all the words appearing in the attributes and, if part of the system, in the contents. This index is commonly implemented as an inverted file, hence the designation the inverted file approach (Salton & McGill, 1983; Macleod, 1991).

The major strength of the text model is that it is developed specifically for text storage and retrieval (van Rijsbergen, 1979). The text model allows a reasonable natural representation of the documents, including the possibility to subdivide documents into a sequence of paragraphs. Retrieval can be conditioned on the contents of particular paragraphs and document display can be restricted to specific paragraphs. The boolean logic query language is syntactically simple, and in combination with the index it provides fast performance even on very large text databases. However, it is well-known that many users fail to understand the semantics of boolean retrieval and, thus, experience manifold difficulties in dealing with the query language, see e.g. (Borgman, 1986). Furthermore, the text model is easy to implement and most systems include text related facilities, such as data entry tools, automatic creation of the index, and query constructs for phrase handling and proximity searching.

The major weaknesses of the text model is the crude, slow update facilities and the lack of flexibility and extensibility. As argued by Hertzum et al. (1993), one reason for this is that the traditional applications of the text model are text retrieval systems, not text filing and retrieval systems. This issues in the assumption that the demands on the systems are rather stable and that updates are sufficiently rare to be collected over a period of time and then executed collectively. Some systems have these characteristics, others do not, and still others evolve from having to not having them. With the current emphasis on interactivity and integrated information handling environments the size of the last two categories is likely to be considerable and increasing. The lack of flexibility is also evidenced by most implementations allowing only one document format per application.

cation.

A further weakness of the text model is the limited possibilities of modelling inter- and intra-document structure and the exclusive provision of querying as the way to access the documents. This separates the text model fundamentally from the hypertext model.

2.2 The hypertext model

The hypertext model was first described by Bush (1945), Engelbart (1963), and Nelson (1967) in their attempts to devise the ultimate way of interaction between humans and TSARS. With its emphasis on non-linear reading and text organization the hypertext model has evolved around an idea of associative structuring. The characteristic feature of hypertext systems is that the text database is a network of interlinked text chunks. However, contemporary hypertext systems vary considerably in their definitions of the network concept. Recently, the Dexter hypertext reference model (Halasz & Schwartz, 1990) has been proposed in an effort to standardize the terminology and provide a basis for comparing hypertext systems.

The major strengths of the hypertext model are the straightforward representation of texts, the flexible, powerful linking facilities, and the interactive annotation and extension facilities. The emphasis on human-computer interaction has equipped most systems with graphical user interfaces manipulated by mouse-clicking on buttons embedded in the texts and elsewhere on the screen (Conklin, 1987). Typically, hypertext systems support text as well as graphics; thus, figures and the like found in many printed texts are not lost when the text is turned into hypertext. Furthermore, some systems support hypermedia. The hypertext model emphasizes interactivity. This is apparent in the facilities allowing new links and text chunks to be created. However, it is even more apparent in the facilities providing access to the texts. The way to access the texts is browsing, i.e. exploring text chunks and following links between them. To help the users stay oriented while browsing, the links are often supplemented by a visual representation of the network, such as a map or tree.

The major weaknesses of the hypertext model are inad-

Figure 2.2: Major strengths (+) and weaknesses (-) of the three data models

	Text model	Hypertext model	Relational model
Representation of documents	+ reasonably natural representation of documents - usually, only one document format per application	+ natural representation of documents, including graphics or even hypermedia	- difficulties modelling text with normalized relations - problems handling long texts (a strongly decreasing problem)
Data entry	+ automatic indexing and other data entry tools	+ tools to turn text with special markup into hypertext	- no data entry tools for text
Links	- lack of linking facilities	+ flexible, powerful linking facilities	+ versatile linking facilities; links may involve texts and other objects
Query language	+ syntactically simple query language + specific text related functions, such as phrase handling and proximity searching - inflexible query language	- inadequate query facilities	+ flexible, powerful query language - lack of text related query facilities - SQL unsuited as an end-user query language
User interface	- rather predefined, command or menu based user interfaces	+ direct manipulation, graphical user interfaces	- the user interface is not part of the relational model
Performance	+ fast performance, even on very large text databases	+ satisfactory performance	- performance is a bottleneck; large space requirements
Update	- crude, slow update facilities	- crude update facilities	+ high-level update functions, possibly including integrity constraints
Extensibility	- weak on extensibility	+ straightforward annotation facilities - weak facilities for larger extensions	+ extensibility without affecting applications, including openness towards other systems
Application range	- limitation to a single application area, thus little like recovery routines and such	- lack of many database management facilities, such as performance measuring facilities	+ designed to address a broad range of applications

equate query facilities, crude update facilities, and the closedness of most hypertext systems. Browsing is an exploratory search strategy well-suited in situations where understanding is given priority to retrieval (Marchionini & Shneiderman, 1988). The hypertext model practically lacks query facilities to support the situations in which retrieval is the major objective, for instance because the subject is understood but a certain fact forgotten. Usually, the update facilities affect a single link or text chunk at a time and are unsuited for making significant restructurings or global changes. Part of the explanation for the humble query and update facilities is that higher level facilities require the imposition of some structure on the network—and structure is contrary to the ideal of freedom permeating hypertext work (Parsaye et al., 1989). Most hypertext systems are closed systems where texts must be copied into the system before links can be attached to them (Puttress & Guimaraes, 1990). A few systems provide a link service instead and thereby make it possible to create links, for instance, to texts which are currently under preparation in a text processing system.

2.3 The relational model

The relational model was introduced by Codd in 1970 (Codd, 1970). During the 1980s systems implementing it have become dominant for all database applications, except those involving large amounts of text. However, as TSARS in which the texts are merely registered are rather similar to traditional applications of the relational model, such systems are sometimes relational. In the relational model data is arranged as rows (tuples) in 2-dimensional tables (relations), each tuple consisting of a number of attributes. The relational model has succeeded in providing systems developers with a more declarative, set-at-a-time programming language which leaves the translation into a record-at-a-time access path to the database management systems (DBMS). The goal was to take care of the file handling details of a broad range of applications, not to support all aspects of a certain class of applications (Codd, 1982).

The major strengths of the relational model are its simplicity, flexibility, extensibility, and the powerful data manipulation facilities. The data manipulation facilities, commonly SQL, include a query language as well as update facilities, both of which operating on sets. Links are modelled easily and may reference texts as well as any other object. In the design of the relational model change was considered an essential and unavoidable property of information systems (Codd, 1982). Thus, new relations and new attributes can be added in a piecemeal fashion without affecting existing applications. It is also possible to experiment with the effects of having or not having particular indexes on the relations without affecting the applications in any other way than in performance. Furthermore, relational DBMS include numerous facilities for managing databases, such as recovery routines, performance measuring facilities, and authorization mechanisms; Blair (1988) lists many more such facilities.

The major weaknesses of the relational model are difficulties modelling text with relations, problems achieving satisfactory performance, and the efforts required to build the user interface on top of the relational DBMS. Some TSARS reference the texts at several levels, for example at document level, chapter level, and paragraph level. This makes retrieval from a relational database somewhat cumbersome as relations must be normalized, i.e. all attributes must be atomic. Thus, the texts must be divided into paragraphs to allow retrieval of individual paragraphs, and then a document or chapter can only be retrieved as a sequence of paragraphs, not as one unbroken entity. Preferably, it should be possible to access the texts at different levels of detail depending on the situation. Normalized relations may be normalized further to reduce redundancy, a process dividing the database into a larger number of relations. Having divided the database into a large number of relations, it is typically necessary to combine—join—data from several relations to answer a query. Thus, a lot of *joins* are required, and each *join* is a time-consuming operation (Lynch & Stonebraker, 1988). Date (1986b) admits that there is some truth in regarding normalization as optimizing for update at the expense of retrieval. Furthermore, a decade ago relational DBMS lacked data structures for storing long texts (Codd, 1982); now this problem has been significantly reduced, e.g. Sybase can handle up to 2 Gb of text as a single attribute.

Many critics of basing TSARS on the relational model have focused on the unsuitability of SQL as a query language for the end-user, see for example Morissey et al. (1986) and Macleod (1991). From the present author's point of view, SQL was never intended for this purpose, but as the internal interface between the database and the application program. Because of its generality SQL is much more complicated than the query language of virtually all TSARS need to be. Furthermore, equating the query language with SQL restricts the system to a command line dialogue. However, compared to the text model and the hypertext model it is no doubt a weakness that the relational model provides part of the system only. The user interface to be build on top of the relational DBMS must also implement any text related facilities as the relational model lacks such facilities.

3. Examples

Data models are abstractions and often more rigid than the systems implementing them. By briefly describing three commercially available toolkits, the following examples supplement the above discussion and illustrate certain combinations of facilities from different data models. The examples are BRS/Search (version 6.0) based on the text model, Folio Views (version 2.1) based on the hypertext model, and Oracle, including version 1.1 of the special purpose text retrieval module, based on the relational model. The examples summarize a case study in which the toolkits were used to develop three prototypes of a full-text legal information retrieval system comprising 4 Mb of text from Karnov's Lawbook, a leading body of laws in Denmark. The case study was performed by this author and nine graduate students, see Andersen et al. (1992). Figure 3.1 lists the differences between the major strengths and weaknesses discussed in the literature and whose of the toolkits investigated.

BRS/Search is a widespread and comprehensive toolkit for development of TSARS. It has the strengths of the text model and avoids a number of the weaknesses. The boolean query facilities are available with several user interfaces, menu based as well as command based and basic as well as comprehensive. Querying is supported by a thesaurus facility and supplemented by the possibility of establishing links in or between documents. Furthermore, applications may include documents in different formats. The weaknesses center around the extensibility and the update facilities. Finally, it is apparent from the development of the prototype that the data entry tools are inadequate for nontrivial applications.

Folio Views builds upon the hypertext model in that the texts are divided into chunks, called folios, and retrieval consists of creating and selecting groups of folios, called views. Views can be created by following links and by posing queries. The query facility is based on an inverted file which includes all words in the texts as well as the attributes assigned to the text chunks. The query facility is central to Folio Views, actually links are implemented as static, embedded queries. The toolkit has the strengths of the hypertext model and, in addition, a reasonable

query facility. However, the prototype shows that utilizing the possibilities of the toolkit requires careful and heavy use of attributes, and this leads to a inflexible system as both data entry and update facilities are rather crude.

Oracle is a relational DBMS around which a number of special purpose tools have been built. The toolkit used in the case study consisted of the relational DBMS, the text retrieval module SQL*Textretrieval, and the user interface module SQL*Forms. The text retrieval module extends the relational DBMS with facilities comparable to a simple text model system. These facilities include an unsophisticated mapping of text onto relations, the addition of a text related query sublanguage to SQL, a thesaurus facility, and a number of library functions to support applications development. Furthermore, the toolkit supports form based user interfaces well, and the prototype has satisfactory response times. The weaknesses include that: (1) text is limited to 64 Kb chunks, and handling texts consisting of multiple chunks is the responsibility of the applications developers; (2) the versatile facilities for modelling links are not supported by facilities for link following in the user interface; and (3) the data entry tools are inadequate.

4. Discussion

The following discussion concerns the possibility of developing toolkits having the strengths of all three data models. It

Figure 3.1: Difference between the major strengths and weaknesses of the data models, as discussed in the literature, and the toolkits, as found in the case study

	BRS	Folio Views	Oracle
Representation of documents	+ an application may include several document formats	+ strong facilities for handling attributes assigned to the texts	- text limited to 64 Kb chunks
Data entry	- inadequate data entry tools	- inadequate data entry tools	- inadequate data entry tools
Links	+ reasonable linking facility		
Query language	+ a thesaurus facility	+ reasonable query facilities	+ SQL is extended with a text related query sublanguage + several text related facilities, including word indexes and thesaurus
User interface	+ user interfaces for different kinds of users + the link facility has a hypertext-like user interface		+ form based user interfaces are well-supported - inadequate support for link following in the user interface
Performance			+ satisfactory performance

begins by motivating such a unification and by emphasizing changeability as a major property of a unified toolkit. Providing changeability is central to the relational model while it has only had a minor impact on the design of the two other data models. Mainly for this reason, it is the relational model which is considered for use as the nucleus of a unified TSARS development environment.

4.1 A unified toolkit approach

The text model, the hypertext model, and the relational model have different origins—library automation, human-computer interaction, and database theory, respectively. However, in recent years their application areas have come to overlap significantly. Thus, while some application areas are supported better by systems based on one of the data models, more and more applications seem to require facilities from two or all three classes of toolkits. Electronic publishing is one example: To provide online retrieval services, such a system requires some of the text related query facilities of the text model and some of the browsing facilities of the hypertext model; and to enable extraction of text for inclusion in various, possibly overlapping, publications, the system also needs the data modelling and structured retrieval facilities of the relational model.

The advantages of using toolkits in software development rest on the assumption that the toolkit fits the application. Thus, a situation where facilities from more than one toolkit seem to be needed is a critical one. Furthermore, what appears to be needed when the choice of toolkit is made will inevitably be subject to subsequent modifications. The importance of this aspect is emphasized by it not being uncommon to see successful TSARS exist for 15-20 years. During their lifetime these systems are subject to manifold changes, and their continued success is largely due to the changes being incorporated into the original structure and idea of the system in a smooth way, see Naur (1985). This places high demands on the changeability of the toolkits used. The applications must, at the same time, be adaptable to manifold changes and manage to preserve their basic structure during this evolution. Thus, the toolkits must provide a flexible, yet stable, platform. Among other things, the stability should enable applications to benefit from achievements incorporated into new versions of the toolkit without more or less rewriting the systems. On the other hand, the flexibility should enable the systems to meet application-specific demands for tailoring and evolution.

Nishimoto & Ura (1989) note that in systems development response time and space requirements are mostly favoured at the expense of changeability. Probably, this reflects both an underestimation of the need for changeability and a pragmatic tendency to solve immediate problems before addressing longer term problems. This emphasizes that to reach a proper balance between performance and changeability both must be inherent in the toolkit—providing good performance without changeability is common and results in inflexible systems, providing changeability without good performance is research only.

4.2 Extending the relational model

The relational model focuses on one part of the application and is intended to be supplemented with tools handling, among other things, the user interface. Thus, relational DBMS have the openness required to form part of a TSARS development environment. Subject to meeting certain challenges, discussed below, the relational model is found capable of incorporating both the text model and the hypertext model:

- Incorporating the text model. As one of the examples in section 3 shows, the relational model can be extended with an inverted file, boolean retrieval, and other specific text related facilities. In the example, boolean retrieval is achieved by extending SQL with a special text retrieval clause; alternatively, Macleod (1979) shows how it can be implemented by adding a macro facility. Thus, provided the relational model is enhanced slightly, it seems suited for text model systems.

- Incorporating the hypertext model. The file and data structures used to implement the hypertext model are mostly special purpose ones, specific to the toolkit. However, larger applications place higher demands on the file and data structures and, partly for this reason, some hypertext toolkits are built on top of DBMS. Relational DBMS seem suited for this purpose, as they have the facilities for modelling all sorts of links. These links may refer to texts stored inside the database or in files external to it; thus, both closed systems and link services are supported.

There seems to be three major challenges involved in extending the relational model into a viable TSARS development environment incorporating the text model and the hypertext model: First, the development of user interface tools for TSARS. Ready-made user interfaces should be provided for common applications. These user interfaces should be templates which may be used without modifications or refined to suit application-specific needs. As TSARS have a broad range of application, see figure 2.1, there is also a need for tools from which to build user interfaces, for example facilities creating relationships between the database and objects in the user interface. The user interface tools should support the development of TSARS combining facilities from the three data models. Currently, little guidance is available on how to combine for instance browsing and querying, but the importance of the subject is widely acknowledged, see for example Halasz (1988) and Marchionini & Shneiderman (1988).

Second, the need to access the texts at different levels of detail at different times. Many text model systems allow retrieval at two levels—document level and paragraph level, the paragraphs being defined by tags inserted into the texts. To allow retrieval of individual paragraphs, the relational model requires that the texts are divided into paragraphs, but then entire documents are necessarily retrieved as sequences of paragraphs. The need to access texts or other objects at several levels is the motivation for suggesting nested relations, see for example Jaeschke & Schek (1982) and Roth et al. (1988). However, a much simpler solution would be to allow concatenation of multiple paragraphs at retrieval time, much in line with for example the *sum* aggregate function.

Third, the performance costs of the high level of changeability. The response times of relational DBMS appear to be acceptable at least for small and medium sized TSARS, i.e. text databases less than 100 Mb of text. However, experimental evidence is scarce, especially concerning large and very large text databases. Many resources are invested in improving response times. Typically, these efforts focus on reducing the number of joins by abandoning the first normal form or on improving the query optimizer, for example through preprocessing and lazy evaluation, see for instance Graefe (1993) and Lynch (1991). A more narrowly focused effort could be to tune the query optimizer especially for text retrieval.

The space requirement is large; it is comparable to the 50-300% storage overhead seen in connection with the text model (Faloutsos, 1985). This is, partly, due to the duplication of keys needed to establish connections between the relations. Hertzum et al. (1993) report a storage overhead of 400% using a relational DBMS, but also find that this is of minor importance due to the rather low price of high volume storage media. Date (1986a) agrees that the space requirement is large in most current relational DBMS, because the relations are mapped into stored files. However, Date notes that due to the physical data independence a relational database could use any storage structure. This means that, in principle, the space requirement can be reduced to the same as any other system requires.

5. Conclusion

This study has reviewed the major strengths and weaknesses of three data models for the development of TSARS—the text model, the hypertext model, and the relational model. All three data models have unique, valuable properties, but more and more applications seem to require facilities from more than one of the data models. This requirement is recognized in the three commercially available toolkits described, and it is the motivation for the unified TSARS development environment discussed.

The unified toolkit is based on the relational model though this choice is contrary to most of the literature. The relational model was chosen because of its emphasis on changeability and without implying that the two other data models are unsuited. In general, the relational model seems capable of providing a flexible, yet stable, platform incorporating the text model and the hypertext model. Specifically, the study points to three areas where relational DBMS should be improved to function as the basis of an efficient TSARS development environment: (1) Relational DBMS should be supplemented with user interface tools specifically for TSARS. On this point, much inspiration and experience can be gained from hypertext systems due to their emphasis on human-computer interaction. (2) Relational DBMS should be extended to provide access to the texts at several, application defined levels of detail. It seems possible to achieve this with simple means at retrieval time. (3) Performance, especially response times, should be improved to reduce the costs of the high level of changeability. However, though response times are important, they must be balanced with the decrease in overall performance caused by lack of changeability, for example prolonged system down time during maintenance and evolution.

Acknowledgments

I am grateful to Erik Frøkjær for stirring and spurring my interest in using the relational model as the basis for TSARS and to Kaj Grønbæk and Jørgen Lindskov Knudsen for volunteering their informed opinions on the status and directions of hypertext.

References

Andersen, K. H., Davidsen, P., Foldbjerg, M., Göttsche, P., Hertzum, M., Jensen, J., Jensen, L. G., Lund, K., Rehn, M. & Rungø, P. (1992). *Undersøgelse af værktøjer til opbygning af tekstsøgesystemer*. student report 92-4-12. DIKU, Copenhagen. In Danish.

Blair, D. C. (1988). An extended relational document retrieval model. *Information Processing & Management*, **24**(3), 349-371.

Borgman, C. L. (1986). Why are online catalogs hard to use? Lessons learned from information-retrieval studies. *Journal of the American Society for Information Science*, **37**(6), 387-400.

Bush, V. (1945). As we may think. *Atlantic Monthly*, **176**(1), 101-108.

Codd, E. F. (1970). A relational model of data for large shared data banks. *Communications of the ACM*, **13**(6), 377-387.

Codd, E. F. (1982). Relational database: a practical foundation for productivity. *Communications of the ACM*, **25**(2), 109-117.

Conklin, J. (1987). Hypertext: an introduction and survey. *IEEE Computer*, **20**(9), 17-41.

Date, C. J. (1986a). Some relational myths exploded. In *Relational Database: Selected Writings*. pp. 77-123. Addison-Wesley, Reading, Massachusetts.

Date, C. J. (1986b). A practical approach to database design. In *Relational Database: Selected Writings*. pp. 417-470. Addison-Wesley, Reading, Massachusetts.

Engelbart, D. C. (1963). A conceptual framework for the augmentation of man's intellect. In *Vistas in Information Handling*. Vol. 1. pp. 1-29. Spartan Books, London.

Faloutsos, C. (1985). Access methods for text. *ACM Computing Surveys*, **17**(1), 49-74.

Graefe, G. (1993). Query evaluation techniques for large databases. *ACM Computing Surveys*, **25**(2), 73-170.

Halasz, F. (1988). Reflections on Notecards: seven issues for the next generation of hypermedia systems. *Communications of the ACM*, **31**(7), 836-852.

Halasz, F. & Schwartz, M. (1990). The Dexter hypertext reference model. In *Proceedings of the Hypertext Standardization Workshop*. pp. 95-133. NIST Special Publication 500-178. National Institute of Standards and Technology, Gaithersburg, Maryland.

Hertzum, M., Søes, H. & Frøkjær, E. (1993). Information retrieval systems for professionals: a case study of computer supported legal research. *European Journal of Information Systems*, 2(4), 296-303.

Jaeschke, G. & Schek, H.-J. (1982). Remarks on the algebra of non first normal form relations. In *Principles of database systems. Proceedings of the ACM SIGACT-SIGMOD Symposium* (Los Angeles, California). pp. 124-138.

Lynch, C. A. (1991). Nonmaterialized relations and the support of information retrieval applications by relational database systems. *Journal of the American Society for Information Science*, 42(6), 389-396.

Lynch, C. A. & Stonebraker, M. (1988). Extended user-defined indexing with application to textual databases. In *Proceedings of the fourteenth international conference on very large databases, VLDB*. pp. 306-317. Morgan Kaufman, Palo Alto, California.

Macleod, I. A. (1979). SEQUEL as a language for document retrieval. *Journal of the American Society for Information Science*, 30, 243-249.

Macleod, I. A. (1991). Text retrieval and the relational model. *Journal of the American Society for Information Science*, 42(3), 155-165.

Marchionini, G. & Shneiderman, B. (1988). Finding facts vs. browsing knowledge in hypertext systems. *IEEE Computer*, 21(1), 70-80.

Morissey, J. M., Harper, D. J. & van Rijsbergen, C. J. (1986). Interactive querying techniques for an office filing facility. *Information Processing & Management*, 22(2), 121-134.

Naur, P. (1985). Programming as theory building. *Microprocessing and Microprogramming*, 15(5), 253-261.

Nelson, T. H. (1967). Getting it out of our system. In *Information Retrieval: A Critical Review*. Thompson Books, Washington, D. C.

Nishimoto, H. & Ura, S. (1989). Complex view support for a library database system. *Information Processing & Management*, 25(5), 515-525.

Parsaye, K., Chignell, M., Khoshafian, S. & Wong, H. (1989). *Intelligent databases. Object-oriented, deductive hypermedia technologies*. Wiley & Sons, New York.

Puttress, J. J. & Guimaraes, N. M. (1990). The toolkit approach to hypermedia. In *Hypertext: concepts, systems and applications. Proceedings of the First European Conference on Hypertext*. pp. 25-37. Cambridge University Press, Cambridge.

Roth, M. A., Korth, H. F. & Silberschatz, A. (1988). Extended algebra and calculus for nested relational databases. *ACM Transactions on Database Systems*, 13(4), 389-417.

Salton, G. & McGill, M. J. (1983). *Introduction to modern information retrieval*. McGraw-Hill, New York.

van Rijsbergen, C. J. (1979). *Information Retrieval*. Second edition. Butterworths, London.

The Impact of Distributed Database Technology on the Business Environment

Nadesan S. Kumar, Balaji Rajagopalan and Amarnath Prakash
University of Memphis, Dept. of MIS/DS
Memphis, TN 38152
(901) 678-3802/2462

Executive Abstract

INTRODUCTION

In recent times, distributed databases have generated enough interest to merit extensive research in academic institutions, research laboratories and industrial laboratories.

This paper attempts to study to impact of the distributed databases on the business environment. The areas examined include the nature of distributed database processing and distinguishing it from other computer systems, benefits derived from it, the technical shortcomings of distributed databases, the client/server architecture and the strategy adopted by computer vendors in this field.

THE NATURE OF DISTRIBUTED DATABASE PROCESSING

A distributed database consists of several CPUs and the data is stored in various mass storage devices. The actual location of any item of data does not have to be known in order to make an inquiry. In addition, the process of finding, retrieving, and storing records from the correct mass storage device is completely transparent to the users.

On the other hand, in a centralized system, the entire database would be stored on one computer, which in reality is also the sole mass storage device. Although the centralized systems provide access to remote databases, the user will have to know the location and perform the necessary operations to obtain data. In the case of a distributed system, data access is transparent (Date, 1987).

In his study, Barsook (1988) classified three major types of distributed databases: traditional remote processing (applications/database- central; users-remote), more distributed (applications - remote; database - central) and real distributed (application/database-remote.

In terms of cost/benefit ration, distributed database technology is more applicable for larger organizations to supplement the heavy data distribution across geographic regions. A centralized system would be more appropriate for smaller organization.

FACTORS THAT LED TO THE DEVELOPMENT OF DISTRIBUTED DATABASE

The development of distributed database technology was facilitated by a host of factors. Some of these factors are:

- the globalization of many firms increased the need for accessing data from several remote databases.
- changing user needs. Users needed timely and accurate information to enhance their performance (Hurst, 1987).
- better computer connectivity (Hurst, 1987).
- reduction in hardware and transmission cost.
- the advent of relational database technology made it possible to overcome the inherent deficiencies of hierarchical and network databases.

SEVEN FUNCTIONS OF DISTRIBUTED DATABASE

Gartner Groups Inc., a Stanford based marked research firm, came up with seven standards (based on transparency) to evaluate distributed databases. They are retrieval transparency, update transparency, schema transparency, performance transparency, transaction transparency, copy transparency, and tool transparency.

BENEFITS OF DISTRIBUTED DATABASE

Basically, distributed database offers five important benefits:

1) A distributed database has the capability to accommodate multiple computers and allow numerous users to operate in that environment.
2) Most of the distributed databases have simple user interfaces and this supports the work of users in a significant manner.
3) Davis (1990) indicated in her study that the adoption of distributed technology should enable an organization to have a better price/performance ratio.
4) In the event of a computer breakdown or site crash, the disaster is confined to the point of occurrence.
5) Distributed databases are not dependent on the physical organization of the data.

TECHNICAL PROBLEMS

Some key problems inherent in the distributed databases are:

- the problem of connectivity between distributed and other databases (vendors are trying to come up with gateways to

solve this problem).
- the problem of resource contention and data contention at the nodes and the links.
- the existence of "antirelational data" within the databases poses a problem.
- lack of "success" of the two-phase commit process.

CLIENT-SERVER ARCHITECTURE

Ideally, a distributed database system is conducive for large organizations that have data dispersed over wide geographic regions. For smaller organizations, a form of distributed database system called the client-server architecture is seen as a viable alternative. By implementing this technology, smaller organizations can receive the benefits of the distributed technology.

STRATEGY OF COMPUTER VENDORS

The complex nature of the distributed technology has hindered vendors in the development of products that performs ll the seven major functions of the distributed database.

The strategy developed by the computer vendors is to introduce distributed products in various stages. That is, each stage having enhanced product capabilities over the previous one. Relational Technology, during the first stage brought distributed products that furthered location transparency and multi-site read transaction. The second stage products were equipped with powerful updating and data replication features. In the third stage, Relational's distributed DBMS products will be furnished with gateways to provide access to DBMS that do not use SQL (Yalonis, 1988).

The future of the distributed database products rests on the development of powerful querying capabilities. According to Davis, the strategy adopted for distributed querying will have a three-fold objective. First, products would be embedded with a comprehensive distributed query functions. Second, vendors would build products that have not only a query feature, but also facilitate multi-site updating on homogenous databases. Third, products will be able to perform querying and updating functions on heterogenous database (Davis,1990).

CONCLUSIONS

The impact of distributed database is highly visible through the business environment. Notwithstanding the many promises it offers, the success of distributed technology would to a large extent depend on the resolution of their effort towards building distributed products which have the capability to perform the major functions and removing the barriers erected by SQL. They have totally neglected the security considerations within the distributed environment. Future research should concentrate on the security issues and on the issue of database connectivity.

Heterogeneous Databases: An Evaluation of PEGASUS and MULTIBASE

Balaji Rajagopalan
Dept. of MIS/DS
Fogelman College of Business and Economics
Memphis State University
Memphis, TN 38152
Ph: (901)-678-2462

Ravi Krovi
Dept. of Accounting & CIS
College of Business
Southern Arkansas University
Magnolia, AR 71753.
Ph: (501)-235-5161

Nadesan S. Kumar
Dept. of MIS/DS
Fogelman College of Business and Economics
Memphis State University
Memphis, TN 38152
Ph: (901)-678-2462

Amarnath Prakash
Dept. of MIS/DS
Fogelman College of Business and Economics
Memphis State University
Memphis, TN 38152
Ph: (901)-678-2462

1.0 INTRODUCTION

Distributed database technology has undoubtedly been one of the architects of business success in the recent years. Moreover, the promise of a database management system allowing the integration of multiple databases (with varied schemas) has been touted as a major development in recent times. Systems that help accomplish this objective of integration are refered to as Heterogeneous Distributed Database Management Systems (HDDBMS). Heterogeneous databases are attractive because of their supposed ability to connect a set of preexisting local DBMS's without changing the existing software, database operations etc. at a local DBMS level. Several such systems are now in place but not without any problems. The focus of this paper will be to identify the significant issues in developing HDDBMS and look at several solutions to address these (existing and proposed models will be examined for solutions). Moreover the issues will be examined in the light of two HDDBMS: Multibase and Pegasus.

2.0 BACKGROUND

A plethora of issues concern the development of HDDBMS. We restrict our discusion to the more significant ones. Each one of the following issues will be disscussed at length:
1. The Mapping Problem.
2. Schema Integration.
3. Invisibility.
4. Query Management.
5. Update Synchronization.
6. Security - Access and Authorization.
7. Database Failure.
8. Concurrency Control.

It should be noted that several of these issues might appear the same as for any distributed database environment but it is important to realize that they have an added non-trivial dimension of heterogeneity. This makes the issues extremely complex.

3.0 EVALUATION OF EXISTING SYSTEMS:

The two well known approaches to establish a heterogeneous distributed database system are a unified schema and a multidatabase. Multibase is a frontend system supporting only retrieval operations against a heterogeneous set of DBMS's. It consists of a global schema expressed in a language called DAPLEX; a set of local schemas expressed in DAPLEX and data definitions of local DBMS's. On the other hand the Pegasus system is a more comprehensive database management system that integrates various native and local databases. It uses both functional and type abstractions to resolve the mapping and integration problems. It is based on a object oriented model that serves as a framework for multiple data sources with different DBMS. Both PEGASUS and MULTIBASE do not support data fragmentation. PEGASUS also uses an object oriented global schema which is comparable to DAPLEX. In both cases, global optimization is used from local optimization. PEGASUS is able to provide partial support for concurrency control and transactions management. MULTIBASE is restricted because it does not provide any of the above functions.

4.0 CONCLUDING REMARKS:

The technical bottlenecks should not in any way undermine the technological progress and growing interest in HDDBMS. HDDBMS creates a simplistic data model from an enduser point of view, where the user is completely shielded from the intricacies of a typical database environment with varying data models.

So far in the heterogeneous environment the transaction protocol has not been the same. Pegasus in the near future will move towards a protocol that will provide the user with added flexibility. Work is also underway to provide more flexibility in defining local database relations and concurrency control.

Systems in the future will be based on a heterogeneous architecture and research in this field needs to focus continuing to develop systems like pegasus that can pave the way for implementing better systems.

Section Twelve

Expert Systems Technology

Expert Systems and Their Applications: An Overview and a Synthesis

Nishat Abbasi
Israr Khan
Department of Accounting & MIS
King Fahd University of Petroleum & Minerals
Dhahran, Saudi Arabia

Executive Abstract

BACKGROUND

Expert Systems (ES), an application of Artificial Intelligence, represent one of the most promising areas of contemporary applications of Information Technology to decision making. This paper presents an overview of ES and their applications and comprises three parts. The first part gives an overview of ES, the second part presents some examples ES applications, and the final part proposes a synthesis of this area.

AN OVERVIEW OF EXPERT SYSTEMS

An Expert System has been defined as a computer system that contains an organised body of specialist "knowledge" in a bounded domain of expertise that emulates expert problem solving skills by applying an inference mechanism to this knowledge. Expert systems imitate the reasoning process of human experts and provide decision makers with optimal solutions to complex problems. Expert systems can be constructed through the use of three types of tools: AI languages (e.g. LISP, PROLOG), ES shells (e.g. VPExpert, EXSYS), and knowledge-engineering tool-kits. The greatest advantage of ES lies in their replication, distribution, and archiving of human expertise at minimal replication cost after their construction. Their greatest limitations lie in knowledge-acquisition problems, limited focus, and developmental cost. Expert systems can be operated in consultative, batch or real-time modes.

The architecture of an ES has the following components: (a) the knowledge base representing the expertise of human experts in a specific problem domain, (b) the inference engine, which is the software portion that operates on the knowledge base and uses a control strategy (for instance, backward or forward chaining) and user's inputs to provide conclusions about the problem, (c) the user interface, which manages the exchanges that take place between the user and the system, (d) the knowledge acquisition sub-system, that acquires, transfers, and transforms the expertise to the computer programs, (e) blackboard which is the workplace or an area in working memory set aside for a current problem, and (f) justifier, which is an explanation ability to trace the ES behaviour employed to reach the conclusions. Most expert systems on market are capable of handling binary logic, i.e.

true-false, yes-no type of logic. Recently, however, some work has been done in the field of fuzzy logic, where the patterns are not binary but based upon reasoning and thinking as human do in terms of the most appropriate solution to a problem.

SOME EXAMPLES OF ES APPLICATIONS

Expert Systems are currently used in decision making worldwide. This part of paper describes ES applications. A classic application of ES is MYCIN, that is employed in the medical diagnosis and treatment of infectious blood diseases. MYCIN asks a series of questions about the condition of a patient. Based on the answers to these questions and using approximately 400 IF/THEN rules, the system concludes whether an infection exists, suggests the probable cause, identifies possible treatment, and explains the reasons for arriving at the conclusions.

Finance/Accounting area provides a fertile ground for ES applications. There are many ES in use in corporate financial planning. Examples of such ES are FAME and CAPITAL INVESTMENT SYSTEM. FAME, and IBM product, is directed towards providing investment information by IBM sales personnel to customers. Texas Instruments uses the CAPITAL INVESTMENT SYSTEM to make internal investment decisions. PLANPOWER serves as an assistant on financial planning advice on investment, tax, et. EXPERTAX helps auditors and tax professionals collect and evaluate data for tax accrual and planning. TAXADVISOR is an ES for estate planning, while FOLIO supports portfolio management. RISKEVALUAION is an ES for evaluating risks for financial operations. CORPORATE LENDING ADVISOR and LOAN RISK ADVISOR are used in lending, whereas SIS is used in business intelligence and CIM in project evaluation and management. Arthur D. Little has developed an ES for variance analysis, and REGEX is developed by William W. Gale for regression analysis. DEC's famed X-CON is used in VAX configuration.

ES are widely used in public accounting. Some examples of such systems are EASY and EY DECISION SUPPORT in work program development, C & L CONTROL RISK ASSESSMENT and INTERNAL CONTROLS EXPERT in evaluation of internal control, INHERENT RISK ANALYSIS in risk analysis, and D&TEXPERT in software development. Some other ES applications are IBM's INTEGRATED MANUFACTURING SYSTEM for operations management, PROMOTER that assists in sales promotion, AMEX's credit authorisation ES, ACE for diagnosing trouble spots in telephone networks, DART for spotting faults in computer hardware, and DENDRAL for inferring the molecular structure of unknown compounds.

A SYNTHESIS

This part has two sections. The first section presents a conceptual model of ES, while the second section classifies ES applications into various generic categories. The model of Expert Systems proposed in this paper has the following conceptual facets or dimensions: architecture, fundamental qualities, and relationships with other types of computer-based systems. The conceptual architecture of an ES has the following essential components: the knowledge base, the inference engine, the user interface, the knowledge acquisition sub-system, the blackboard, and the justifier.

Some fundamental qualities of Expert Systems are: (1) Expertise that can lead to an effective and efficient achievement of goals, (2) symbolic manipulation and reasoning, (3) general problem-solving ability in a domain, (4) complexity and difficulty of problems and domains, (5) reformulation of problems in a form capable of processing by the ES, (6) abilities requiring reasoning about self, and (7) the ability to work on one or of the following types of tasks: interpretation, prediction, diagnosis, design, planning, monitoring, debugging, repair, instruction, and control. Expert systems differ from other computer systems basically in ability to reason and explain, and in terms of the other fundamental qualities listed above.

There are many ways to classify ES applications. This paper is rounded off by a summary of a scheme that classified ES applications into various application areas and uses [courtesy Information Builders, Inc.]

Decision management : Loan portfolio analysis, employee performance, insurance underwriting, demographic forecasts

Diagnostic/trouble shooting : equipment calibration, help desk operations, software debugging, medical diagnosis

Maintenance/scheduling : maintenance, production, and education scheduling, project management

Intelligent Text/documentation : Building Regulations, OSHA Safety standards, employee benefits, EEPO employment codes.

Design/configuration : computer option installation, optimum assembly plans, manufacture studies, communications networks

Selection/classification : material selection, delinquent account identification, information classification, suspect identification

Process monitoring/Control : machine and inventory control, production monitoring, chemical testing

The Impact of Expert Systems on Social and Economic Change

Dr. Robert L. Mullen

School of Business, Department of Management

Southern Connecticut State University

501 Crescent Street

New Haven, Connecticut 06515

203-284-2692

Executive Abstract

OBJECTIVE OF THE RESEARCH

The purpose of this research was to determine whether or not expert systems are being used to replace highly skilled workers in large corporations which have developed such systems to a significant degree that we should consider some intervention to protect those effected by these systems.

BACKGROUND INFORMATION

Expert system technology grew in the 1980's as a subset of a computer application specialty known as "artificial intelligence." These applications are also often included as a subset of "decision support systems" in studies of business at a university due to their decision-making nature. Interest in their use in business came from Computer Science specialists looking for yet another application of computer hardware through software.

Expert Systems are computer applications that contain the knowledge, experience, and judgement of skilled professionals. They suggest decisions and often the reasoning behind their recommendations.[1]

The initial use of expert systems was limited to a very few specific areas such as problem diagnosis in the maintenance and medical fields. Some use was found in the early days in the 1980's in the area of training new employees. In the mid-1990's, however, there seems to be no limit where and how expert systems are used.

Expert system techniques can be used to preserve and disseminate scarce expertise by encoding the relevant experience of an expert and making this expertise available as a resource to the less experienced person.[2]

This quote indicates that use of expert systems can be very beneficial to an organization. These systems allow for the experience of retiring experts to be captured before they leave the organization. This benefits new employees by giving them an opportunity to learn their jobs faster. But, what if the expertise is captured before an employee is ready to retire and then used to force the employee out of his or her job as a means to save the organization some money?

Many well-known companies have reported huge savings from the use of expert systems. What has not been reported is the impact of these systems on jobs. Does their use reduce the challenge to the jobs effected? Has the savings resulted from the loss of jobs from the use of these systems? We need to understand if this use is a real threat to employees, with regard to their skill level and their very jobs.

RESEARCH VARIABLES

The following variables were defined for this research:

U = rating of the extent of expert system use.

S = rating of the level of satisfaction with results of use.

E = rating of how expectations have been met by these systems.

F = rating of expected growth in the use of these systems.

R = percentage that use of systems has reduced skills in jobs.

J = percentage where use of systems has caused loss of jobs.

RESEARCH HYPOTHESES OF ISSUES OF CONCERN

There were six research questions and related hypotheses. Statistical testing was done at the .05 level of significance.

A. *Are expert systems used extensively in large corporations?*

$$H_o : U \le 3; \quad H_a : U > 3$$

B. *Are the top level executives in satisfied with the present use of expert systems in their organization?*

$$H_o : S \le 3; \quad H_a : S > 3$$

C. *Does the present use of expert systems meet the expectations of these systems for the top executives?*

$$H_o : E \le 3; \quad H_a : E > 3$$

D. *If expert systems are not now extensively used, do top executives see an expected future use of such systems?*

$$H_o : F \le 3; \quad H_a : F > 3$$

E. *Has use of expert systems resulted in reducing the skill level of the jobs affected?*

---

[1] Ralph H. Sprague and H. J. Watson, editors, "Decision Support Systems: Putting Theory into Practice", Prentice Hall, 3rd Edition, Englewood Cliffs, NJ, 1993, p363.

[2] Fred L. Luconi, Thomas W. Malone, and Michael S. Scott Morton, "Expert Systems: The Next Challenge for Managers", *Sloan Management Review*, (Summer 1986), p3.

$$H_o : R \leq 50\,\%; \quad H_a : R > 50\,\%$$

F. *Has the use of expert systems in large organizations resulted in the loss of jobs?*

$$H_o : J \leq 50\,\%; \quad H_a : J > 50\,\%$$

SUMMARY OF FINDINGS

1. The results of this research indicate that expert systems are not now used extensively in large organizations.
2. However, top level executives reported that they expect more use of expert systems in the future.
3. Top level executives in organization using expert systems are satisfied with the present use of these expert systems.
4. Expert systems are not meeting the expectations of the executives who invested millions of dollars to develop them.
5. Use of expert systems in large organizations has reduced the skill level needed in the jobs affected by these systems.
6. Top executives in large organizations using expert systems do not see them as eliminating or replacing jobs.

MAJOR CONCLUSIONS AND RECOMMENDATIONS

1. The majority of those responding indicated that the use of expert systems in their organizations has reduced the skill level required of the jobs involved but has not reduced the number of jobs significantly.
2. Job seekers should focus on their communication skills and a positive attitude toward serving others rather than on their technical skills which can be replaced by expert systems.
3. We should be concerned with the reduction in skill level. Eventually, this will reduce wages and impact the economy.

FUTURE RESEARCH

There may be more cases of job elimination than these executives were willing to admit. This should be a subject for future research on this topic.

A Hypermedia Based Intelligent System for Business Training

Mihir Parikh
Alok Srivastava
Department of Decision Sciences
College of Business Administration
Georgia State University
Atlanta, GA 30303
Tel: 651-4000, Fax: 651-3498
Internet: qmdmapx@gsusgi2.gsu.edu

Executive Abstract

INTRODUCTION AND BACKGROUND

Intelligent System for Business Training (ISBT) can be complimented as an artificial intelligent version of traditional computer-based training (CBT). In addition, ISBT focuses on several issues which were not previously addressed by CBT such as customized instructions, quick response to the needs of trainee, diagnosis of knowledge state, prescription of remedial measures, and reinforcement of current knowledge.

Recently, a lot of research has been done on different components of intelligent tutoring systems (ITS). ISBT adds a new dimension to the development of ITS with inclusion of hypermedia. ISBT includes both object-oriented approach for system structuring and hypermedia for advanced user interface. Previously, CBT and ITS were designed with highly supervisory environment, in which control over communication of information was with the system rather than the trainee. This instructor imparted training may not necessarily help in maintaining learner's attention and interest. In ISBT, this control has been transferred to the trainee which permits him or her to explore domain knowledge in a variety of ways and increases effectiveness of training. So, behavioristic precepts of programmed learning is rejected in favor of cognitive considerations.

CONCEPTUAL DESIGN OF ISBT

ISBT is designed on the principle of dynamic interaction between human trainer and trainee. Like human instructor, ISBT must be able to diagnose knowledge state of the trainee and determine the learning needs of the trainee. This intelligent diagnosis provides intelligent prescription and modification of instructional strategies that truly reflects learning needs of the trainee. The role of ISBT is extended from instructor in CBT to advisor, counselor, and coach in ISBT.

It is an integrated product of information technology and artificial intelligent techniques. Technological components such as data-based, model-based and knowledge-based decision support systems are fully integrated to the evolution of ISBT. Data-based system provides vital information to the system. Model-based system classifies and generates specific information. Knowledge-based system provides interpretation of information. All components data, model and knowl-edge of the system are objects which are grouped into classes. An inheritance relation between the classes is used to express specializations and generalizations of the concepts, such as diagnosis or prescriptive.

ISBT has rules and inference engine. The inference engine is made up of two component: the searching engine and the reasoning engine. The searching engine executes intelligent searches based on heuristic. The reasoning engine provides analytical tool for inferencing.

A system with quick feedback is a key aspect of ISBT. Immediate feedback about errors makes it easier for the trainee to integrate the instruction about the errors into the next learning step. The feedback mechanism can be in four different modes: warning, interrupt, help, and input feedback. Warning and interrupt are proactive feedback triggered by the system, while help and input feedback are reactive feedback initiated by the trainee. Proactive feedback gives guidance to the trainee when flaw in trainee's learning process is detected or performance is degraded. It also provides useful tips for solving the problem, when delays in answering is detected. Reactive feedback can help trainee at different level depending on type of help is required. As input feedback, the system can provide useful hints for solving the exercise problems.

Hypermedia, an integration of hypertext and hypergraphs, liberates the learning process by offering self-defined exploratory access to unfamiliar territory. It allows fluent access to fragments of material from any source and in any format to be stored and linked, and thus provides comprehensive frame of reference which can be customized for each trainee. Since the pieces of information are held as linkable segments of any size, this approach provides multiple paths to the trainee for learning. The trainee can freely explore what seems personally relevant, and linger or backtrack as he or she wants. This linking can be recorded and traced back to see any pattern forming, which can reflect cognitive style of the trainee and can be used in future for individualized instruction.

CONCLUSION AND FUTURE RESEARCH

Development of general paradigm for training systems as proposed in this paper will facilitate rapid development of flexible and adaptable systems for computer aided instruction. By utilizing such a framework applications can be developed without the constraints of domain-specificity. Context-based learning and rapid feedback can prove to be very effective in teaching difficult concepts in relatively specialized areas. The use of multiple media (like hypertext, graphics, and voice) can facilitate customization of instruction based on trainee's needs.

Trainees will have access to the knowledge of experts (master teachers). Training systems such as ISBT will provide multiple sources of expertise from diverse areas integrated in a single environment. ISBT will offer flexibility (can be used anytime and anywhere), adaptability (can customize instruction based on a student's unique needs and characteristics), and interactability that may be superior to human interaction.

Student Personality Traits and Expert Systems

Marcus D. Odom
and
Hamid Pourjalali
Assistant Professors of Accounting
Department of Accounting
The University of Southwestern Louisiana
Lafayette, LA 70504

ABSTRACT

The recent increase in development and use of expert systems and computer-assisted instruction has resulted in a need for research in the effectiveness of such instructional methods. Expert systems are computer programs that are designed to emulate the analysis (thinking) process an expert uses in reaching a judgment regarding a particular problem. Expert systems may be used for (1) retention and preservation of expertise, (2) distribution of expertise to others, (3) assistance in quality control, and (4) education or training.

Research on the use of expert systems as pedagogical tools is limited. Odom and Murphy (1992) examine the use of expert systems as a pedagogical device in the teaching of transfer pricing to accounting students. Three different teaching methods--"only instruction," "only expert system," and "a combination of the two"--were used in their research to develop the student's knowledge of the subject domain. Their results provided some evidence that expert-system-use facilitated the development of knowledge in some instances.

The purpose of an educational system is to facilitate the process of learning. Odom and Murphy (1992) evaluated the use of expert systems by measuring the development of declarative and procedural knowledge. Knowledge, which is obtained through the presentation of new information (data), is stored in long-term memory using the human information processing system. Gagné (1985) defines two types of knowledge--declarative knowledge and procedural knowledge. Declarative knowledge is *factual* knowledge, and procedural knowledge is the knowledge of *how* to do something. The educational process is designed to facilitate learning both types of knowledge. An expert system may facilitate this learning process.

This research extends Odom and Murphy (1992) by introducing the students' personality traits as a variable that may have had an impact on their results. Personality traits differ among individuals; however, the degree of difference varies. One individual may have traits that are similar (though not identical) to those of another, but differ completely from a third individual. Psychologists have tried to group people based on different personality traits. Given that people have these measurable differences in personality, it is highly possible that these differences will affect their learning processes.

This study is limited to the effect of the students' personality traits and the teaching method employed on their learning at both levels of knowledge--declarative and procedural.

The experiment was a pretest-treatment-posttest design. The pretest measures, declarative and procedural, were used as a covariate in an ANCOVA analysis with the dependent variables being the posttest measures. Both pretest and posttest variables were measured without the use of the expert system.

The results indicate that both expert system and instruction, as well as one personality trait, significantly affected the development of declarative knowledge. Two interactive variables were also found to be significant. These findings demonstrate that personality traits do affect the development of declarative knowledge. The results for the development of procedural knowledge also show a significant main effect for both teaching methods and for two personality traits. Two of the interactive variables were also significant. These results suggest that personality traits affect the development of procedural knowledge.

We limited the scope of this study to the analysis of the effects of four aspects of students' personalities on their learning. Further analysis is needed to determine which of the individual personality types caused the effects and to determine the direction of the effects. This will be necessary for both declarative and procedural knowledge. Additionally, research is needed to determine if these findings are generalizable to other subject domains.

The limitations of this project are the general limitations related to a laboratory experiment. The use of a single instructor for all subjects controlled for any instructor effects, but may limit the generalizability.

Gagné, E. D., (1985) *The Cognitive Psychology of School Learning*, Boston: Little Brown and Company.

Odom, M. D. and D. S. Murphy, (1992). Expert Systems Versus Traditional Methods for Teaching Accounting Issues. *Developments in Business Simulation & Experiential Exercises*, Vol. 19, pp. 131-35.

Key: Expert Systems, Personality Traits, Education, Accounting

DSS Maintenance Process

Bel Gacem Raggad
Norfolk State University
Norfolk, VA 23504

Executive Abstract

Background

The objective of an on-line maintenance process is to recognize and analyze DSS deficiencies and generate recommendations for immediate corrections. The maintenance process consists of six phases: Information Requirement, Measurement and Control, Homogenization, Design of Diagnostic Models, Inference Process, Correction Generation Management.

In order to design such a process it is first necessary to identify all controllable and measurable variables relevant to DSS evaluation. In the information requirement phase the designer defines the role of each data or information item useful for the DSS evaluation process. For example, data related to task structure, task uncertainty, task variety, and task difficulty are used in assessing DSS usefulness. If data analysis shows that tasks are often structured, routine, or deterministic then a program approach is a more appropriate alternative for decision support than the DSS approach.

The second phase of the DSS maintenance process consists of filtering data and information items so that only those controllable, measurable and interpretable variables are retained. For example, Turing's effect representing the extent to which a computer-based decision support is "human", is an important determinant of DSS success that is not retained because it cannot be easily measured or controlled. Input variables like user involvement in the DSS development process, top management support, or user training are retained because they are controllable, measurable, and interpretable.

In the homogenization phase a strategy will be employed for grouping system variables into homogeneous groups according to a subset of pre-defined concepts. Groups may contain duplicate variables, as long as all variables within one group remain significantly correlated. The minimum significant level of variable intercorrelation is determined by the DSS designer. We will refer to those concepts, in the rest of the paper, as parity concepts. Possible grouping strategies include segmentation, factorial analysis, correlation techniques, etc. At the end of this phase, a set of DSS variable groups is available for the DSS maintenance process.

The fourth phase consists of designing, for every group of variable, a qualitative and quantitative multiple diagnostic model based on its parity concepts. For every parity concept, a threshold should be determined by management, according to management predefined performance standards. The parity concept is said to fire when the threshold, set for it, is violated. Firing of a parity concept is an indication of possible DSS deficiencies.

Following the recognition of deficiencies, an inference process will produce the names of suspect DSS variables. This inference process is designed at the fifth phase of the DSS maintenance process. What would be system deficiencies when a subset of parity concepts of some diagnostic models fire. How is evidence combined facing conflicting conclusions produced by various firing diagnostic models. Those questions are answered in the inference phase.

At the sixth phase, recommendations are generated based on accepted evidence concerning DSS deficiencies. The maintenance process provides suspect DSS variables and their belief values. For each subset of suspect variables, the maintenance subsystem suggests guide lines and strategies concerning how to solve DSS deficiencies. This methodology is further illustrated in Figure 2. Figure 1 proposes a model for the development of an on-line DSS maintenance process, based on the proposed methodology.

Discussion of DSS maintenance issues

Information requirement for the proposed DSS maintenance process is based on the current DSS literature. There are mainly six composite DSS variables emphasizing six different aspects of DSS evaluation: development process, DSS usefulness, end user, DSS functionality, DSS success, and DSS profitability.

1. Process:
-top management support
-user training
-user involvement

2. Usefulness:
-structure
-difficulty
-uncertainty
-variability
-independence

3. End user:
-organizational level
-DSS experience

4. DSS functionality:
-supported phase
-level of managerial activity
-source of information

5. DSS success
-overall satisfaction
-decision making satisfaction
-user perception of DSS benefits

6. DSS profitability:
-time delay due to DSS duration

-Bayesian update time
    -Bayesian update cost
    -operating cost
    -uncertainty reduction

Conclusion and directions for future research

The article developed an on-line maintenance process capable to recognize and analyze DSS deficiencies and generate recommendations for immediate corrections. We intend, in the near future, to extend this research study by proposing a new architecture for a DSS where a computer-based DSS maintenance subsystem is added to the original configuration of a DSS. This new model of a DSS will have the capability to recognize it own deficiencies and invoke its own correction procedures. The new DSS model, for example, will only allow invocations that are expected to participate in enhancing DSS profitability, usefulness and success by satisfying a pre-defined subset of quantitative and qualitative parity concepts.

Intelligent Coaching System

Bijan Fazlollahi, Alok Srivastava, Sameer Verma
Department of Decision Sciences,
Georgia State University,
Atlanta, GA, 30303
Phone: (404) 651-4000
e-mail qmdbbf@gsusgi2.gsu.edu

Executive Abstract

INTRODUCTION

Recent developments demonstrate the viability, cost-effectiveness and benefits of Computer Assisted Instruction (CAI). Computers are providing not only support services such as word processing, data retrieval, and computations, but are also creating interactive learning environments. Intelligent tutoring and guiding tools are increasingly becoming available to facilitate the learning processes. The design of intelligent tutoring systems (ITS) are also evolving. ITSs are geared to provide expertise through effective teaching and communication techniques while allowing the student to control the learning situation. ITSs are providing student-centered reactive environments.

Intelligent Tutoring Systems (ITS) environment has two primary components. One is of the student, who is human, and the other is the tutor, which is a computer. The metamorphosis of the two domains is difficult. This is primarily because the perspectives of the two domains are different. Human part of the system emphasizes on the psychological aspect of ITS. It delves deep into the issues regarding methods of learning, memory retention, pedagogical models, student needs and other parameters. From the tutors viewpoint, the computer requires intelligence and expertise to emulate a teacher. The proper merger of psychology and ES/AI is in ITS. Due to so many factors, the system tends to be highly complex. The main components of the system are the domain expert, the instructional expert, and the student needs profile.

INTELLIGENT COACHING SYSTEM

Intelligent coaching system (ICS) is an intelligent tutoring system that creates a learning environment similar to the relationship between a master and an apprentice. A master considers the instructional context and knows what the student does not know in terms of knowledge, and perceives what the student can and can not do in terms of skill. ICS provides a framework for exploring and learning with a feedback from time-to-time. Its function resembles the Intelligent Process Control Systems (IPCS) used to control industrial processes. IPCS monitors the industrial process for proper functioning and when it encounters an abnormality or a faulty pattern, it takes corrective action through some feedback mechanism. Systems having a built-in feedback can prompt the user at various stages of decision-making.

ICS knowledge base includes different categories of knowledge such as knowledge of the subject matter, knowledge of applicable teaching methodology, applicable teaching plans, and student needs profile. Needs can be categorized into some quantized needs profiles. A needs profile is established by asking the student some basic questions about his/her familiarity with the domain. ICS then revises the needs profile as the learning process progresses.

ICS monitors student performance ansd provides guidance. It presents knowledge so that the student can comprehend the knowledge while exercising and mastering the skill. A student with little, or no knowledge about the domain would requires explanation and guidance at all levels of decision making. On the other hand, a student with a good understanding and familiarity of the domain would need very little prompting from the system. ICS automatically adjusts its relationships with its domain, a specific student, and its instructional repertoire.

ICS major issue is when to interrupt the student and what advice to give. ICS monitors student task performance and generate the response on the basis of student model, dialogue history, and the knowledge base. ICS must decide whether or not to talk *about* the student response, provide *motivational* feedback, say *whether* an approach is appropriate, *what* a correct response would be, and *why* the student's response is correct or incorrect. The ICS must also provide hints, leading questions, or counter-suggestions.

The ICS responses to the student in a manner best understood by the student. ICS critiquing style of instruction requires a critiquing style of communication. Where dialogue is non-sequential, asynchronous, multithread, or event-based. Here a number of tasks are available to the student at any one time. Student may select any sequence of tasks and every action a student may take can not be anticipated. ICS customizes its presentations to the needs of the current student and dialogue because student backgrounds are different and tutoring sessions proceed in unpredictable fashion.

REQUIREMENTS

The system has to be more than an on-line help system. Some "intelligence" has to be coded into the system in order to create an Interactive Learning Environment. The system requires Intelligent guidance, real-time response, controlled access to information, and the use of multiple tools such as spreadsheets. The system interaction has to be at various levels of abstraction.

OBJECT ORIENTED IMPLEMENTATION

Using smart objects will result in a system that can easily evolve to higher levels of sophistication. This is appropriate because ICSs are evolving systems. The system may be developed as a set of smart objects that pass data and control information among each other. The knowledge in a smart object is divided into domain knowledge and supervisory control knowledge. Domain knowledge consists of application data and application rules which work on data. Supervisory control knowledge consists of control data states and control rules which work on control data and determine which application rules to use in a given situation. For example, a situation may be defined by the student needs profile. Encapsulation of control abstractions within an object makes an object more independent, by giving it more control over how the application knowledge is used.

INTELLIGENT COACHING PROTOTYPE SYSTEM

We have selected the *guided-example exercises or the coaching* phase of learning. Here the student is presented with an specific example and is guided or coached through it. We assume that the student has the necessary *enabling* skills such as basic computer skills, algebra, etc. We also assume that the student has received in class room instructions in the knowledge-rich-domain of model-based decision support systems.

STATEMENT OF THE PROBLEM

Build a model-based-DSS in Excel spreadsheet to calculate the relative volatility of a stock in relation to one of the stock market indices. A spreadsheet template is provided which contains the headings for the structure of the spread sheet. The student is responsible to complete the spread sheet such that it performs the following: (1) import stock history, (2) calculate rate of change in the stock, (3) import stock market index of choice, (4) calculate rate of change in the stock market index, (5) use simple regression to find volatility measure for the particular stock, (6) perform what-if analysis.

Three modules are needed: expert (knows how to perform the task and can demonstrate it). Instructional module (is capable of generating alternative instructional approaches based on the current state of the student), student (represents the current state of the student needs profile). This prototype does no include a student needs profile. The student is assumed to be knowledgeable. The student interaction intelligent object is used to represent the student module.

ICS ARCHITECTURE

The architecture consists of the following objects, with their individual tasks listed below:
·Tutor intelligent object with the following functions

Prototype System Architecture

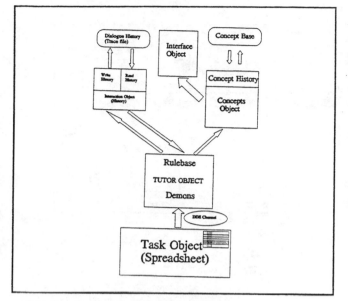

Monitor the student task performance
Determine appropriate instructional strategy
Select appropriate action for intervention
Perform selected action
·Task object
Generate messages as to current state of task performance
Concept intelligent object
Monitor history of concept presentation
Select concepts to be presented
·Student interaction history intelligent object
Monitor history of interactions
Determine the current state of task performance
Determine the current state of the student needs

HARDWARE/SOFTWARE:

The ICS requires Microsoft Windows 3.1 and Microsoft Excel 4.0 to run the programs. The monitor has been developed in KnowledgePro for Windows (KPWIN), however, a runtime version can run on MS Windows independently. The hardware requirements are the same as for MS Windows 3.1.

OPERATION

Microsoft Excel is used in this case, for the Task object. A template developed in Excel, guides the user to import data into columns and write formulas in cells. Sequence of actions, for importing data, writing formulas etc., are reported to the monitoring module.

The monitoring module has been developed in KPWIN. This module encapsulates within itself, the DDE channel monitors, or demons, the rulebase, and dialogue history write objects. The Dynamic Data Exchange (DDE) channels report each action, which is evaluated by the monitoring Tutor object, and rules are fired accordingly. This Dialogue history is recorded in a trace file. A concepts object keeps a track of the

Task and Interface objects

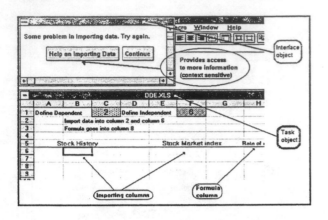

concepts that have already been presented to the user. Based on this concept history, and a rulebase, the concepts are presented in the proper sequence. The text and graphics are retrieved from the concept base, and presented to the user through automatically sized windows and hypertext/buttons. The types and detail of concepts presented to the user vary depending on the type of problem and the stage at which the user commits a mistake. The concepts that are presented are financial concepts, market index, volatility, statistical concepts, spreadsheet concepts and information on importing data, writing formulas, and using analysis tools. Help regarding spreadsheet usage is provided through the Excel Help. The concept base adds on some minor details, that might be required for the specific problem.

CONCLUSIONS

The goal was to create an intelligent coaching system to provide tutoring to students following formal class-room instruction. Our approach reduces the difficulty of integrating intelligent tutors into existing curriculums and educational systems. ICSs can monitor student performance of course specific projects and exercises and provide timely and appropriate guidance. The ICS will serve as a research tool to study the learning patterns of students and develop strategies to intervene in the learning process. The research has the potential to improve the effectiveness of teachers by allowing them to create computerized one-on-one learning environments.

Section Thirteen

Computer-Aided Software Engineering Tools

CASE Technology vs. the Software Maintenance Crisis:

What Will It Take to Win?

Judith D. Ahrens
Drexel University

Abstract

The software maintenance crisis - escalating costs and sluggish responsiveness to changing requirements - is a complex problem intertwining aspects of software menagement, work flow coordination, human cognition, and technological infrastructure support. To untangle these elements, this article asks: What precisely do maintenance activities consist of? How do we manage them? What does it mean to understand software? How well does the current generation of CASE technology support forward software development and the maintenance processes of software reengineering? What capabilities would a CASE technology infrastructure supporting the entire software life cycle possess? After exploring these issues, three integrated, multi-tool CASE environments are proposed as the technological infrastructure for the next generation of CASE technology. These advanced prototype environments include the Software Specification Environment, the Software Engineering Environment, and the Software Reengineering Environment. Scenarios are presented illustrating how these integrated environments can leverage human resources for all software engineering processes and life cycle models.

1. INTRODUCTION

Maintenance consumes up to 70-75 percent of a software system's cost over its lifetime, dwarfing the phases of requirements analysis, specification, design, implementation, testing, and production (Bloom, 1990; CSTB Report, 1990). This statistic is even more stunning when combined with the opportunity cost of diminished funds for replacing existing systems and lengthened payback periods for justifying new systems. The maintenance crisis justifies a radical reconceptualization of maintenance processes. Only by challenging prevailing assumptions can we hope to invent CASE tools for facilitating maintenance in a timely and cost-effective manner.

Maintenance is a complex problem intertwining aspects of software management, work flow coordination, human cognition, and technological infrastructure support. To untangle these elements, we need to ask penetrating questions such as: What precisely do maintenance activities consist of? How do we manage them? What does it mean to understand software,

and how can we improve the process? How well does the current generation of CASE technology support the processes of forward software development and maintenance? What are the requirements for a CASE technology infrastructure that supports the actual processes enountered during the software life cycle? This article explores these issues and proposes the necessary technological infrastructure.

The remainder of the article is organized as follows. The process of fundamental rethinking about maintenance is initiated in Section 2 by examining its long-held assumptions. This examination reveals that software maintenance is assumed to be either as separate and distinct from software development, or that it can be accomplished by CASE tools supporting forward software development, i.e. one simply redesigns the software and generates new source code. As a result of these assumptions, CASE technology has been neglected that integrates capabilities for forward engineering, domain engineering and software reuse, with "maintenance" capabilities for reengineering (Forte and Norman, 1992). Reengineering capabilities include reverse engineering, program understanding and restructuring.

In Section 3, maintenance and the software life cycle are reconceptualized. Reengineering, i.e. maintenance processes, are seen to be present in forward engineering's iterative phases, as well as in domain and application engineering for software reuse. Although the reasons for initiating these activities differ, *they employ identical technical processes*. Therefore, no justification exists for separating software development from maintenance with respect to software engineering technology, jobs, organizational structures, management and measurement systems, and the cultural values and beliefs ascribed to maintenance activities. Capabilities needed in a new generation of CASE technology to support these integrated processes are identified.

Section 4 describes these capabilities as proposed in three advanced prototype environments: the Software Specification Environment, the Software Engineering Environment, and the Software Reengineering Environment. Section 5 presents scenarios illustrating the CASE environment integration, and Section 6 presents conclusions and ideas for further research.

2. WIDELY HELD ASSUMPTIONS ABOUT MAINTENANCE

Assumption 1: Maintenance starts after the software is released

In the software engineering literature, several authors have criticized the prevailing assumption about software maintenance because it portrays software practice in an unrealistic manner (Paul and Simon, 1989). This assumption, which originated with the Waterfall model (Pressman, 1992), views maintenance as a separate software life cycle that begins *after* software enters production. That is, before the first release of the software, all software activities are assumed to be associated with forward engineering.

Assumption 2: Maintenance is defined by administrative concerns

In assumption 2, similarities between development and maintenance activities are recognized, but the separation is justified based on administrative concerns. Both new software development and perfective, adaptive, and preventive maintenance (described in Section 3) involve requirements analysis, specification, design, implementation, and testing. The difference lies in how these activites are *constrained* and *controlled*.

New software development is constrained by customer requirements, as well as by their budgets, existing resources, and acquisition policies. Additionally, software maintenance is constrained by a preexisting software system (Ford and Gibbs, 1989). Control over new software development is mandated by distinct developmental phases defined in military standards, (e.g. DoD-STD-2167A, 1988), but control over software maintenance activities *per se* are set forth in scattered change control administrative procedures that do not define maintenance processes (Forte and Norman, 1992).

This is a serious problem because software developers know that change occurs from the earliest design stages as initial expressions of customer requirements are refined. After implementation, controlling changing requirements involves controlling ongoing iterations that mix old code (typically with inadequate documentation of original specifications as well as modifications made over time), new programmers, and new technology. The control process is *ad hoc* and the problem grows over time: the larger the installed base of legacy software (old software written in obsolete languages), the more formidable the problems.

Assumption 3: Forward CASE technology can perform almost all maintenance

Under this assumption, maintenance is understood to involve more than fixing bugs that emerge after the new system is released. Maintenance involves responding to changes in customer requirements, to new technology, and to changes in the external environment, e.g. regulatory changes. Under this broader definition, maintenance is assumed to be a component of the forward development process, involving configuration management, modifications to requirements specifications, designs, and source code, followed by testing. Therefore, most maintenance can be performed with the same techniques and products used during forward software development, but some more specific tasks such as reverse engineering must be approached with *ad hoc* techniques and tools (Fuggetta, 1993). Since CASE technology now permits code to be generated directly from design specifications, most "maintenance" activities can be accomplished through software redesign followed by source code generation, e.g. the Design Maintenance System (Baxter, 1992).

Discussion of Maintenance Assumptions

These assumptions have had consequences for software management, software practice, and CASE technology. This section discusses the consequences of the assumptions. Assumption 1 seems to have legitimized the high costs, poor technological support, and poor management of maintenance activities (CSTB Report, 1990). For example, the management of the same software system may be split between a development manager and a maintenance manager. Similarly, the development and maintenance tasks are frequently allocated to different developmental and maintenance software engineers. In general, maintenance work is perceived as less desirable than new software development, and few programmers aspire to a career in maintenance.

Rather than dividing software into specialized development and maintenance activities, we should instead conceptualize software as a process that originates with customer need and ends with software that meets that need. Conceptualizing all software practice in terms of processes will change the structure of software engineering jobs, the associated management and measurement systems, and people's values and beliefs about the value of their work.

Assumption 2 errs in its tendency to organize work processes around administrative concerns rather than around the work itself. This leads to a process characterized by highly specialized jobs and fragmented administrative and control procedures. Each separate software task thus requires a "handoff" to the next task and person. Each handoff in turn requires administrative coordination or control, adding to the overhead associated with the work process. CASE tool integration will enable seamless transitions between forward and reverse software engineering processes, eliminating the necessity for both administrative and technical handoffs. This technology-enabling integration should be reflected in integrated software administration.

Assumption 3 depicts unrealistically the cognitive processes involved in software understanding. It suggests that human software engineers should adapt themselves to the capabilities of available CASE tools, rather than having tools support the actual work and cognitive processes of software engineers. For example, bugs appearing during testing or after the software is released into production typically require analysis and manipulation at a lower level of abstraction than that provided by program design specifications in today's CASE tools. Software engineers frequently need to understand software at the level of source code. Therefore, the software engineer should have the capability to (1) reverse engineer from the source code to the program specification, (2) correct and/or restructure the software, and (3) forward engineer the new source code automatically from the new program design specification. Unfortunately, such an integration of tools for forward and reverse engineering is not proposed (Fuggetta, 1993).

These assumptions may have influenced developers of CASE technology to neglect tools that support maintenance in favor of tools that support forward software development (Chen and Norman, 1992). Consequently, the current generation of CASE technology does not support software engineering activities present in the entire life cycle (Forte and Norman, 1992).

To support the entire life cycle, integrated tools are needed having capabilities not only for software specification, design, code generation and testing, but also for reverse engineering, reengineering legacy software, evaluating and generating software system components from a reuse library. Modern software practice thus requires a new generation of integrated CASE technology that supports the complete software life cycle. Furthermore, this technology should support alternative software development models, such as the spiral model (Boehm, 1988), the evolutionary model (Gilb, 1988), and the prototyping model (Boar, 1984). Unlike the traditional Waterfall model (Pressman, 1992) which mandated separate, non-iterative phases of software development, these alternative models recognize the necessity of iteration within and between life cycle phases. Once it is recognized that "maintenance activities" include an intensive mix of forward and reverse engineering processes, integrated tools and environments can be developed that reduce the time needed to transition between these processes. Administrative cost controls linked to CASE technology usage can be introduced that monitor and control all software activity, including maintenance. The next section provides a closer look at maintenance activities, and the CASE tool capabilities required for their support.

3. CASE TOOL CAPABILITIES FOR MAINTENANCE SUPPORT

Since maintenance and software development require many capabilities in common, integrated toolsets and environments are needed. Maintenance activites have been studied by the National Institute of Standards and Technology (NIST) (CSTB

Report, 1990). A description of each maintenance activity and the percentage of time devoted to each follows:

• *Perfective maintenance, or enhancements* (50% or more), introduces major transformations in form, functions, and objectives.

• *Adaptive maintenance*, (25%) responds to changes in the external environment, including conversion of legacy code into modern programming languages.

• *Corrective maintenance*, (20%) includes diagnosis and correction of design, logic or coding errors.

• *Preventive maintenance*, (5%) improves future maintainability and reliability.

Along the horizontal axis of Table 1 are listed the maintenance activities and the percentage of time devoted to each. Along the vertical axis are listed the CASE tool capabilities required by a software engineer to perform these activities effectively and efficiently. Note that some capabilities, such as testing, understanding the existing system's software architecture and interfaces, and configuration management, apply to multiple activities.

Software engineers spend most of their time thinking about software. A perusal of these required capabilities suggests that software engineers could devote less time to maintenance activities if tools were available for facilitating the *understanding* of complex software relationships and the performance of *thought-intensive cognitive tasks*. For example, tools for software understanding could reduce the time needed for all maintenance activites. Tools for creating and updating requirements specifications could reduce the time devoted to perfective and adaptive maintenance. Finally, tools for automating the translation of legacy software into modern programming languages and platforms could significantly impact adaptive maintenance.

4. INTEGRATED ENVIRONMENTS FOR THE CASE TECHNOLOGY INFRASTRUCTURE

Today's corporations depend for their survival upon their information technology infrastructure, i.e., the integrated databases, networks, computer-supported cooperative work environments, and client-server architectures. Similarly, the software maintenance crisis requires a CASE technology infrastructure. This section describes such an infrastructure based on the research and development work at Computer Command and Control Company (CCCC), Philadelphia, PA. CCCC has been engaged in developing software reengineering and specification technology as part of the research and development programs at the Department of Defense. The capabilities inherent in this technology are readily transferrable to the non-

Table 1: Maintenance Process/Required Capabilities Matrix

Required Capabilities	Maintenance Process			
	Perfective (50%)	Adaptive (25%)	Corrective (20%)	Preventive (5%)
Generate current software abstractions (specifications) from implemented software	X	X	X	X
Generate/revise/confirm software specifications from a specification reuse repository.	X			
Reengineer/update a domain from specification.	X	X	X	X
Analyze commonality/variability in the domain to engineer the application.	X	X		
Query, retrieve, analyze, and understand reuse repository of code specifications.	X			
Generate code from specifications.	X	X	X	X
Perform software concurrency analysis.	X	X	X	X
Perform software simulation.	X	X	X	X
Testing.	X	X	X	X
Configuration management.	X	X	X	X
Convert from legacy language to modern language.		X		X
Understand converted legacy software.		X		X
Restructure system boundaries to support partial retirement of legacy systems.		X		X
Reorganize/restructure converted legacy code into new programming paradigms, e.g. object-oriented.		X		X
Extract components from legacy systems for reuse libraries and/or new systems.		X		X
Migrate to new development and production environments, e.g. open systems.		X		
Understand code visually, (i.e. graphically) from different perspectives.	X	X	X	X
Manipulate visual code representations.	X	X	X	X
Generate new code from visual representations.	X	X	X	X

military public and private sectors.

Figure 1 shows how these environments are integrated to support the complete software life cycle processes. The next sections describe the environments.

Software Specification Environment (SSE)

The SSE appears at the top left of Figure 1. SSE was created specifically to facilitate the creation and updating of software specifications conforming to Department of Defense Standard 2167A (DoD-STD-2167A, 1988), but the capabilities apply equally well to current software development methodologies for information systems in the public and private sectors.

The inclusion of SSE reflects the importance of software specifications for an orderly software life cycle. SSE is an integrated set of information repositories and tools. SSE guides, instructs and informs staff in composing, updating and evaluating preliminary requirements and specifications. Typical users of SSE are development managers, software engineers, or contractors. SSE allows a user to manage, query and update its repository of application system documents. Staff may ask complex technical questions about the software specifications and retrieve answers. Fragments of retrieved answers can be extracted for inclusion as updates to relevant new documents. SSE leads the inexperienced specifier in a "step-by-step" manner and provides traceability to the source documents used to update specifications.

SSE subsystems include:

- Document Manager: This is used by the data administrator to create and catalog documents in in the repository
- Assignment Manager: This is used by the manager to enter the work plan for subordinates who compose or update documents
- Step-by-step: This is used to guide specifiers in searching previous documents and in composing or updating requirements

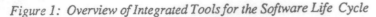

Figure 1: Overview of Integrated Tools for the Software Life Cycle

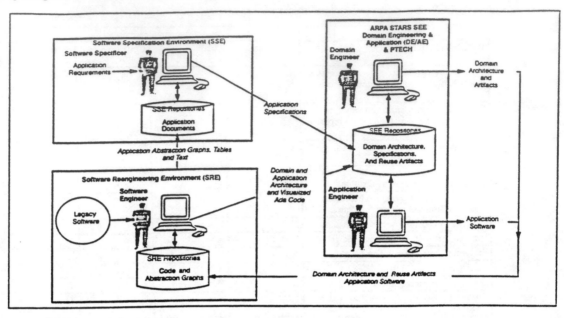

• Evaluate: This is used to provide feedback on completeness of requirements' coverage

Software Engineering Environment (SEE)

The SEE (Foreman, 1992) is shown at the top right of Figure 1. SEE incorporates new software development technology for software reuse and for automatic program generation, following the Advanced Research Project Agency's (ARPA) Domain Specific Software Architecture (DSSA) Program (Mettala and Graham, 1992). This technology includes domain engineering (DE) and application engineering (AE). Domain engineering enables a domain engineer to define the process of producing software for a class of related applications in a domain. Application engineering enables an application engineer to produce software for an application that belongs to the domain (SPC, 1992).

The domain engineering and application engineering (DE/AE) facilities are employed as follows. A specific domain is comprised of all software developed for a closely related family of applications, e.g. order processing. A domain software architecture (Agrawala, 1992) is a set of functions common to these applications. Once a domain software architecture is developed by a domain engineer, new applications can be generated from the domain repository by comparing new application specifications to the domain software architecture and identifying commonalities and variabilities with respect to functions. The common functions constitute the reusable software, which can be employed directly and without modification. The variable functions require software development.

The domain repository contains software artifacts, i.e., the reusable source code and software specifications. The DE/AE capabilities facilitate selection of reuse software and generation of new software to create a specific application system. Thus, the domain engineer creates the domain software architecture, and the application engineer uses the software selection and generation tools to create a specific application (SPC, 1992).

The reuse software is part of the DE/AE repository (see Figure 1). The reuse software is organized as a hierarchy of software artifacts that follows the domain architecture. For example, software created for the Department of Defense follows a standard hierarchical tree structure of software units called System, Segment, Computer Software Configuration Item (CSCI) and Software Unit (DOD-Standard 2167A). Each software unit in the hierarchy has a specification of its position in the architecture hierarchy, its capabilities, interfaces and dependencies on other software units.

The capabilities of the hierarchical software units determine commonality and variability between them. It is possible to navigate through the domain hierarchy tree by referring to capabilities and selecting hierarchical software units based on commonality and variability of their respective capabilities. Hierarchical software units may be parameterized and a code generation tool may be used to select parameters from the generic software. Alternatively, hierarchical units may be completely generated based on models of their functionality. A series of tools is also available in the DE/AE for application modelling, unit testing and conversion to concurrent operations. The SEE also permits a software engineer to design object-oriented software and to generate object-oriented programs in Ada and in C++ automatically. Finally, the SEE incorporates meta-tools for tool integration.

Software Reengineering Environment (SRE)

The SRE (CCCC, 1992) is shown at the bottom left of Figure 1. The same approach used to re-engineer obsolete and poorly documented programs into modern languages for the Department of Defense and can also be used to re-engineer obsolete programming languages found in business and industry. For example, softare reengineering capabilities are needed to translate FORTRAN, PL/1 and COBOL programs into the C programming language. Furthermore, the SRE incorporates state-of-the-art techniques for software understanding such as interactive software visualization and visual programming that will enhance the software engineer's cognitive processes in any software environment. Each of these techniques is discussed below.

Software visualization overcomes the essential invisibility (i.e. non-physical quality) of software by representing the program structure, control flow, and data graphically. An abstract, graphical representation can facilitate a software engineer's visual perception and cognitive understanding of complex software during debugging, monitoring, and program restructuring (Roman and Cox, 1993; Meyers, 1990).

Visual programming is a methodology of programming as well as of program maintenance. In visual programming, a graph is composed and edited on the screen of a terminal, primarily through use of a pointing device. This is contrasted with conventional programming which consists of keying-in textual statements.

To date, software visualization and visual programming tools have been developed for forward software engineering, facilitiating software design to be followed by implementation. Software code can be generated from the design diagrams by these tools, partially automatically and partially manually. In contrast, the integrated tools enable the process to be reversed by deriving design diagrams from software code. In this way, maintenance can be performed on the reverse engineered design which is consistent with the old code, and the entire new code can be forward engineered automatically.

The foregoing capabilities are incorporated into the three SRE components: software capture and transformation, software abstraction and documentation, and software understanding. Following is a description of each component.

Software capture and transformation

The SRE was developed to translate software written in a legacy software language (CMS II) into Ada, the current Department of Defense standard programming language. The same technological approach is presently being developed to translate other legacy languages into modern operating environments and languages, specifically, UNIX and C. We will use Ada to illustrate the approach.

First, the SRE translates the old language, statement by statement, into a pseudo-Ada, called Elementary Statement Language (ESL) Ada. Next, the ESL-C programs are transformed into the Ada programming paradigm in a series of passes that achieve 100% translation to Ada. Each pass translates different aspects of the programming paradigm of the source language into the Ada programming paradigm. During the transformation process, seven different sets of relations are generated, each defining a different view of the associations among programming objects. At the end of the transformation process, these relations are converted into graphic structures in the form of Entity-Attribute-Relation (EAR) diagrams. The EAR representation is the main vehicle for graphic program analysis and visualization. Visualization is used to query, retrieve, understand, restructure and generate program documentation.

Software abstraction and documentation

SRE partitions the software into multi-level hierarchical software units conforming to the 2167A standards for describing the software architecture. Software Abstraction Documents are then generated that describe the architecture of these units from different perspectives. Six types of Software Abstraction Documents are created to document the architecture. Note that these documents permit the software to be viewed from perspectives common to contemporary methods of software development. Where applicable, these methods are noted below:

• *Hierarchical decomposition diagram:* This graph shows the decomposition of the overall software into hierarchical units, corresponding to the HIPO diagrams of the structured techniques

• *Flow diagram:* This graph shows the flow of data and control within and between hierarchical units, corresponding to Data Flow Diagrams for information systems, and to Ward Mellor (data and control flow) diagrams for representing real time systems (Pressman, 1992)

• *Interface table:* These tables show the structure of inputs and outputs of each hierarchical unit, corresponding to the IPO diagrams of the structured techniques

• *Object/Use diagram:* This graph shows, for each hierarchical unit, where types or generics are defined and where they are used, corresponding to a class hierarchy in the object-oriented methodology

• *Context diagram:* This graph shows library units and where they are used

• *Comments text*: This text records the software comments found in each hierarchical unit. They are assumed to contain information on the hierarchical unit's capabilities

Software understanding:

Software understanding consists of query and retrieval of the Software Abstraction Documents that illustrate the software from various perspectives. These diagrams are used to visualize specific aspects of the software. The diagrams are first divided into in-the-large and in-the-small diagrams. In-the-large diagrams help a software engineer to visualize declarations of objects. In-the-small diagrams help a software engineer to visualize execution statements within individual program units.

Program diagrams are stored in a graphic form in the repository of a customized CASE system. A graphic query language is provided for ad-hoc browsing of the software abstraction documents in the graphic repository. These graphs show relations between high or low level hierarchical units. This facilitates understanding both the software architecture and its detailed source code. Changes to the program for debugging or program restructuring can be made via the graphics used for visualization.

Examples of graphic query retrieval capabilities in the SRE for understanding and creating reusable software include:

• Display Base View
• Query Base View to create Subview
• Select root node, e.g. "within Program x..."
• Select node type, e.g. "show me all of the subprograms..."
• Select relations, e.g. "and their Input/Output"
• Select depth, e.g. "any children...?"
• Query subviews as needed for progressive graphical browsing
• Save subviews as needed for documentation
• Generate new software code from any view

Two interfaces integrate the three environments.

Interface between SRE and SSE:

This interface is shown at the middle left of Figure 1 (Prywes et al., 1993a). This interface provides a reverse process to produce information for the software requirements and specifications and other documentation from program code. SSE receives the documentation from the SRE. The Software Abstraction Documents map into specific paragraphs of the Department of Defense requirements specifications. For example, the Hierarchy software abstraction document can be

Table 2: Required Capabilities/CASE Technology Matrix

Required Capabilities	Software Specification Environment				Software Engineering Environment			Software Reengineering Environment		
	Document Manager	Assignment Management	Step-by-Step	Evaluate	Domain Engineering	Applic. Engineering	Define Domain Specific Reuse Oriented Processes	Capture and Transformation	Understanding	Abstraction and Documentation
Generate current software abstractions (specifications) from implemented software.					X	X				Software Abstraction Documents
Generate/revise/confirm software specifications from a specification reuse repository.					X					
Reengineer/update a domain from specification.						X				
Analyze commonality/variability in the domain to engineer the application.			X			X				
Query, retrieve, analyze, and understand reuse repository of code specifications.			X						Graphic query & retrieval	X
Generate code from specifications.						X				
Perform software concurrency analysis.						X				
Perform software simulation.							X			
Testing.								X		X
Configuration management.	X	X		X	X	X	X	X		X
Convert from legacy language to modern language.									X	
Understand converted legacy software.			X						Structured Repository	X
Restructure system boundaries to support partial retirement of legacy systems.					X	X		X	Graphic query & retrieval	Visualization from different perspectives
Reorganize/restructure converted legacy code into new programming paradigms, e.g. object-oriented.					X	X	X	X	X	X
Extract components from legacy systems for reuse libraries and/or new systems.	Specification Repository	Process Mgt.			X	X	X	X	X	X
Migrate to new development and production environments, e.g. open systems.					X	X		X		
Understand code visually, (i.e. graphically) from different perspectives.			X						X	X
Manipulate visual code representations.									X	X
Generate new code from visual representations.						X				

used for the System Architecture diagram required in those specifications.

Interface Between SRE and SEE

This interface is shown in the left-hand portion of Figure 1 (Prywes and Lee, 1993b). The SRE provides DE/AE with software documentation in the form of high-level graphic views of the architecture (the software abstraction documents) as well as detailed graphic views of algorithms. The SRE can process legacy source code as well as reuse source code from the DE/AE repository. The SRE generates key parts of the specifications of each hierarchical software unit. These are used to establish commonality and variability among the domain architecture's hierarchical software units in the SEE. Tools for the SSE and SRE environments and their interfaces were developed by CCCC.

The required maintenance capabilities listed in (Table 1) are now mapped into their respective integrated CASE tool environments in Table 2.

5. ILLUSTRATIONS

Several scenarios illustrating alternative paths through the environments shown in Figure 1 are possible. Taken together, they support the entire life cycle. Typically, the tools will be used iteratively until a desired new or upgraded application system is obtained. The following four scenarios illustrate the need for integrated forward, reverse, and reengineering capabilities in the software life cycle. The first scenario illustrates how the integrated capabilities facilitate software development in those environments having reuse repositories. The second illustrates how the reverse engineering capability allows an organization to confirm that outsourced software meets its specifications. The third illustrates how alternative models of software development will increase the need for integrated CASE environments. Finally, the fourth illustrates how these environments facilitate creating specifications for code where none exists, or bringing specifications in line with current software implementations.

Facilitating Software Development with Domain and Application Engineering Reuse Repositories

For the first scenario, assume that totally new application software is desired. The preliminary requirements have been generated by the program manager (Figure 1). The platform to be used and its dynamics may be derived through modelling and simulation. The software specifier, with the aid of the SSE, composes hierarchically structured specifications based on the requirements. The specifications are then communicated to the application engineer who uses them to select architectural units from the domain and to generate new source code to create

application software. The application engineer then uses the SRE to reverse engineer software abstractions from the application software. The application engineer then compares these software abstractions to the specifications for the new application, verifying that the reusable software actually meets the requirements. The software abstractions are next used by the specifier, who employs SSE to update the high level software specifications. This cycle may be repeated a number of times until satisfactory application software is realized.

Note that the integrated capabilities assist all human participants and update repositories as required. The SRE processes software from various sources (domain, application, legacy) and augments the domain architecture to satisfy new capabilities. Visualization graphs and software abstractions portray the architecture of the system as well as source code artifacts. The software abstractions are communicated to the SSE so that the specifiers can incorporate them in updated specifications. The abstractions and code are communicated to the domain engineer who can use them to update the domain. The abstractions and program visualizations are communicated to the application engineer who can use them to create documentation of the implemented application software.

Confirming that Outsourced Software meets Specifications

Not every software environment today has implemented domain and application engineering for software reuse. Instead, many organizations outsource their software development to software vendors or consultants. It is vital in such situations that the contracting company has the capability to confirm that the outsourced software actually meets the specifications. This confirmation can be accomplished by reverse engineering the delivered software and comparing the generated to the original specifications. The earlier that deviations are found, the greater the future savings in development time and cost. The reverse specification capability would also enable more objective formal reviews during the outsourced software development process because the specifications reverse engineered from the software can be compared to the original specifications.

Facilitating Software Development with Alternative Models.

Alternative software life cycle models, such as those that include prototyping, joint application development, and evolutionary development, do not assume the existence of a complete set of requirements before design and program development begins. This assumption is expected to *increase* the frequency with which the reverse specification capability will be needed. For example, in prototyping and evolutionary development, changes may be made quickly at a user's request at the level of source code, not specifications. Therefore, software abstractions generated automatically from evolutionary or prototype software can keep the specifications current at very little cost.

Creating/Updating Software Specifications

The reverse engineering capability is also needed for the software maintenance activity of updating obsolete specifications or creating specifications for undocumented software. Software managers are continually confronted by problems associated with outdated or unavailable software specifications. Updates to specifications typically lag updates to software. Pressured by time and budget constraints, it is convenient to make modifications to the code and neglect the corresponding changes to software specifications. This is a critical problem since the specification plays a central role in the contracting, scheduling, planning, design, implementation and post-deployment support. The reverse specification capability will make it easier for software managers to update obsolete specifications and create specifications where none existed.

6. CONCLUSIONS AND FUTURE RESEARCH

A realistic assessment of software activities clearly indicates that many more cycles of forward and reverse engineering are involved in the software life cycle than originally imagined. Furthermore, assumptions suggesting that software techniques required for maintenance are somehow different from those actually required for forward software development are seen to be obsolete and incorrect. Nevertheless, these assumptions have shaped our attitudes and our behaviors towards software maintenance and software development. Major changes are needed to begin reversing the software maintenance crisis.

These changes fall into two categories: technological changes and organizational changes. The integrated software engineering environments described above can provide the technological infrastructure needed for those in the software engineering community to begin changing their understanding of the processes involved in the software life cycle. However, technology alone cannot reverse the upwardly spiralling time and cost trends associated with the maintenance crisis. Concomitant changes are needed in the job descriptions of software engineers and programmers that make distinctions based on skill rather than on obsolete notions of "development" vs "maintenance." Organizational structures that previously separated development units from maintenance units should be combined. The same management planning and control systems should be applied equally to "development" and "maintenance." Employee evaluation and reward systems should be based on skill and performance rather than on "development" vs "maintenance" classes of personnel. Finally, the software culture that extols development and demeans maintenance needs to change. Clearly, there are many software maintenance

battles to fight, and they need to be fought on several fronts!

References

Agrawala, A., et al, (1992). "Domain-Specific Software Architectures for Intelligent Guidance, Navigation & Control," *Proceedings of the DARPA Software Technology Conference 1992*, Los Angeles, CA, April.

Baxter, I. (1992). "Design Maintenance Systems," *CACM*, Vol. 35, No. 4, pp. 73-89.

Bloom, P. (1990). *CASE Market Analysis*, Volpe, Welty and Co., San Francisco.

Boar, B. (1984). *Application Prototyping*, Wiley-Interscience.

Boehm, B.(1988)., "A Spiral Model for Software Development and Enhancement," *IEEE Computer*, Vol. 21, No. 5, May, pp. 61-72.

Chen, M., and Norman, R.(1992). "A Framework for Integrated CASE," *IEEE Software*, March, pp.18-22.

Computer Command and Control Company (1992). "Software Intensive Systems Reverse Engineering," *Final Report for Contract No. N60921-90-C-0298*, April.

CSTB Report, (1990). "A Research Agenda for Software Engineering," *CACM* Vol. 33, No. 3, March , 1990,pp.281-293.

DoD-STD-2167A, (1988). "Defense System Software Development," September.

Ford. G., and Gibbs, N. (1989). "A Master of Software Engineering Curriculum," *IEEE Computer*, September, pp.59-70.

Foreman, J. (1992). "STARS: State of the Program," *STARS '92 Conference*, pp. 20-41.

Forte, G. and Norman, R., (1992). A Self-Assessment by the Software Engineering Community," *CACM*, Vol. 35, No. 4, April, pp. 28-32.

Fuggetta, A.(1993). "A Classification of CASE Technology," *IEEE Computer*, December, pp. 25-38.

Gilb, T.(1988). *Principles of Software Engineering Management*, Addison-Wesley.

Mettala, E., and Graham, M. (1992). "Domain Specific Software Architecture Program," *Proceedings of the DARPA Software Technology Conference*, Los Angeles, CA, April.

Meyers, B. (1990). "Taxonomies of Visual Programming and Program Visualization." *J. Visual Languages and Computing*, Vol. 1, No. 1, pp. 97-123.

Paul, J. and Simon, G. (1989). "Bugs in the system: Problems in federal government computer software development and regulation," *U.S. Government Printing Office*, Washington, D.C., September.

Pressman, R. (1992). *Software Engineering: A Practitioner's Approach*, 3rd ed, McGraw Hill, NY: pp 680-683.

Prywes, N., Ingargiola, G., and Ahrens, J., (1993a). "Automatic Reverse Engineering of Software to Confirm/Update Requirements Specification," Computer Command and Control Company, Philadelphia, PA, 19103, June.

Prywes N., and Lee, I. (1993b). "Integration of Software Specification, Reuse and Reengineering," Computer Command and Control Company, Philadelphia, PA, 19103, June.

Roman, G. and Cox, K. (1993). "A Taxonomy of Program Visualization Systems," *IEEE Computer*, December, pp. 11-24.

SPC (1992). "Domain Engineering Guidebook," *Technical Report SPC-92019-CMC, Software Productivity Consortium*, 1992.

Issues on Designing a Client/Server-Based CASE System

David C. Chou
Department of Computer Information Systems
West Texas A&M University
Canyon, Texas 79016

Reed Helmly
Seagull Energy Inc.
905 S. Fillmore, Suite 400
Amarillo, Texas 79101

ABSTRACT

A powerful CASE tool can be used to assist software analysis, design, code generation, maintenance, and re-engineering tasks. However, most CASE tools are supported by either PC-based or PC-mainframe-interacted development environment. Since these CASE tools must be developed under a single workstation/user, the developing cost is considerably higher than that of a shared or distributed environment.

This paper discusses the important issues relating to designing a client/server-based CASE tool. It includes the benefits of moving to a distributed CASE environment, the implication of the distributed computing environment, and the various techniques of designing a distributed CASE tool.

INTRODUCTION

A computer-aided software engineering (CASE) tool is software which aids in the construction of other software products. Currently, a powerful CASE tool can be used to assist software analysis, design, code generation, maintenance, and re-engineering tasks. However, most CASE tools are supported by either PC-based or PC-mainframe-interacted development environment. Since these CASE tools must be developed under a single workstation/user, the developing cost is considerably higher than a shared or distributed environment.

Another trend in the software industry is downsizing. These expectations are putting the pressure on Information System (IS) department to be more productive with less resources. The fruit of these movements is the client/server architecture. CASE tool industry must turn its direction to a multiuser/multitasking, networking supported environment if it is to survive in the future. This paper discusses the important issues relating to designing a client/server-based CASE tool. The benefits of moving to a distributed CASE environment are addressed in the first section. The implication of the distributed computing environment is deliberated next. It includes the concepts of the distributed model, distributed CASE repository, and cooperative CASE-client/server processing. The various techniques of designing a distributed CASE tool are discussed in the next section. These methodologies include

distributed processing, two-phase commit, collaborative programming, and distributed CASE repository. A conclusion is made after this section.

THE BENEFITS OF A DISTRIBUTED CASE ENVIRONMENT

Berson (1992, p. 8) describes an advantage of the client/server processing by comparing a file server and a database server. For example, if a PC application needs a particular record from a shared file, it sends a request to read the entire file to a file server. The file server then makes this entire file available to the PC. The application running on the PC has to search the file to select the requested records. The computing resources of the file server are used to process the entire file, while the PC's resources are used to run an application that reads every record of the file. If every record is sent to the PC for processing, a significant portion of the available resources are used inefficiently, and communication lines are overloaded.

However, in the case of a database server, an application running on a PC sends a record request to the database server. The database server then processes the database file locally and sends only the requested records to the PC application. Both the client and the server use computing resources to perform the requested query. This is a much more efficient method in that both the client and server cooperatively use their computing resources and the traffic along the communication lines is minimized.

Berson (1992, pp. 11-12) also identifies a number of real benefits in adopting a client server model. Many of these benefits directly relate to the importance of this environment in conjunction with CASE tools. These benefits are:

1. It allows corporations to leverage emerging desktop computing technology better. Today's workstations deliver considerable computing power at a fraction of mainframe costs.
2. It allows the processing to reside close to the source of data being processed. The network traffic and response time can be significantly reduced.

3. It facilitates the use of graphical user interfaces (GUI) available on powerful workstations. These new interfaces can be delivered to customers in a variety of visual presentation techniques together with easy navigation and standards-compliant consistency.

4. It allows for and encourages the acceptance of open systems. Servers can run on different hardware and software platforms. This allows the end users to free themselves from particular proprietary architectures and take advantage of the open market of available products.

The client server model has some disadvantages as well. They are:

1. If a significant portion of application logic is moved to a server, the server may become a bottleneck in the same fashion as a mainframe in a master-slave architecture. The server's limited resources will be in high demand by the increasing number of end users.

2. Distributed applications, especially those designed for cooperative processing, are more complex than non-distributed applications. However, some of this complexity can be offset by reducing a large problem into a set of smaller, possibly interdependent problems, as in modular system design.

3. Increased cost of administrative and support personnel to maintain the database server may also be an issue. On a small network (generally under 20 users) the network administrator can usually maintain the database server, the users access to it and support the front end applications. However, as the number of users increases, or the database itself grows, a database administrator may be needed just to run the DBMS and support the front ends.

4. Training may also add to the startup cost. The DBMS may be run on an operating system unfamiliar to support personnel.

A properly implemented client/server model will reduce some software maintenance costs, while increasing costs associated with network administration. It is clear that software portability will be increased. The application backlog will be reduced or eliminated by increasing the developer's productivity and shortening the development life cycle. These are the main driving factors of implementing CASE products in a client server environment. These advantages lead us to the next evolutionary step beyond simple file sharing. This higher step is that of distributed computing.

THE DISTRIBUTED COMPUTING ENVIRONMENT

A distributed computing environment such as the Open Software Foundation's Distributed Computing Environment, makes a collection of loosely connected systems appear to be a single system. Distributed computing makes it easier to develop and run applications that use resources throughout a computer network. Applications can be distributed to run on the computers best suited for the task. Various tasks can be run in parallel, providing higher performance and better resource utilization. A client/server architecture is built on, and it represents a special case of distributed computing.

The Distributed Model

There are two major forces at work in the distributed model. One force breaks up applications and pushes the resulting pieces toward the end users. By pushing this data toward the end users, the system is able to take advantage of significant price and performance gains on the workstations as well as meeting the user's demands for local autonomy and additional functions that can increase the user's productivity.

The second, opposing force, consists of the user's need to access corporate data. This need results in the centralization of applications on large powerful mainframes. To meet both of these requirements, a distributed model is developed which consists of a large powerful platform connected to a network of sufficiently powerful workstations operating in a local area network.

Berson (1992) proposed a three-tiered architecture. The top tier of this environment consists of the most powerful system which holds the corporate data. The second tier contains powerful LAN servers which serve as top tier servers to the PCs as well as sending appropriate requests to the mainframe. The PCs that reside on the third tier are served by the server positioned in the middle tier. All information that they get either comes from or via that server.

An example of this three tiered architecture would be a corporation that extends its central data center capabilities by building LANs in each of its headquarters and connecting those LANs to the host.

Distributed CASE Repository

The basic premise of the client/server model is its capability of conducting the distributed processing. An equally important piece of the client/server puzzle is how the data is distributed over the network. A database server contains the DBMS software and the data itself. One of the main objectives of the client/server model is to allow a client-based application to access its remote data in the most efficient manner. Advanced DBMS implementations allow for the placement of common procedures in the server DBMS which necessitates its' central position in the client server architecture. Advanced DBMS implementations include DBMS resident data dictionaries that facilitate application development, support data location transparency, and provide for more efficient data administration.

In determining the proper architectural decisions for data, it is important to place the DBMS software and all shared data on a database server. At the same time, if client applications require some unique applications and client-specific data, the proper place for the data would be a data store located on the client system. These two situations determine the way a client application connects to a server running the DBMS. With the direct application to DBMS connection, the client application would use communication protocols and some kind of remote transaction processing to request a server-resident DBMS to access data. The situation can become more complicated if multiple servers have to be accessed.

With an indirect application to DBMS, the client requests remote data through an intermediary. This intermediary is the local (client-resident) DBMS. The benefit of such an indirect connection is that the client can access both local and remote data, hopefully using the same data manipulation language. One problem with the indirect connection is that the data is distributed between at least the client and the server. Once again we must guarantee the integrity of the data by distributed transaction management or by distributed request processing with the two-phase commit. Data location transparency must also be supported to provide the single system image.

Data integrity and administration issues have to be resolved. For example, if the application data is spread across multiple servers, distributed database management, or distributed request processing with the two-phase commit will be required to guarantee data integrity across servers.

Erickson (1993) points out that multiple CASE repositories can greatly improve the responsiveness of the CASE tool. These distributed databases must be efficiently accessed by the CASE tool. Multiple developers must have the ability to concurrently access the repository to create, read, update and delete information. It is also important for one developer to have the ability to view the work of other developers across the network. These benefits will lead to a high degree of coordination, communication, and an increase of productivity.

Cooperative CASE-Client/Server Processing

Cooperative client/server processing is the foundation for the client/server architecture. The distinguishing characteristic of a cooperative processing application is the high degree of interaction between various application components. In a client/server architecture, these interactions take place between the clients request and the servers reactions to those requests. Berson (1992) proposed the components of general client/server distributed processing and it can serve as the foundation of a client/server-based CASE system design.

The typical CASE application consists of the following components:

1. Presentation processing logic. This is a part of the application code that interacts with a device such as an end user's terminal or workstation. Presentation logic performs such tasks as screen formatting, reading, and writing of the screen information, window management, keyboard, and mouse handling.
2. CASE processing logic. This is a part of the software development application code that uses the input data from

a screen and/or database to perform CASE tasks. Usually this code is developed in a third generation language.
3. Database Processing Logic. This is a part of the application code that manipulates data within the application. The data is managed by a DBMS. Data manipulation in relational DBMSs is done using some dialect of the Structured Query Language (SQL). SQL's data manipulation language is typically embedded into the 3GL or 4GL application code.
4. Database processing. This is the actual processing of the database data that is performed by the DBMS. Ideally, the DBMS processing is transparent to the CASE logic of the application. However, from the architectural point of view, database processing is an essential part of the cooperative processing interactions, and should be considered as a component of cooperative application processing.

In host-based processing, these application components reside on the same system and are combined into one executable program. No distribution is taking place and the application is restricted by the limited resources of the platform on which it runs. With the advent of distributed computing, new opportunities are being opened to system developers and end users. Portable scalable applications capable of running on networks of open systems that are transparent to the end users can now be developed. By distributing computing resources across the network, significant cost-benefits can be achieved.

The critical questions in the determination of client/server distribution are what resources should be distributed and what are the consequences of such a distribution. When only data is distributed several locations, a single application can conceivably access the data from any location in a fashion totally transparent to the application. Certain benefits, like placing the data close to its source and data distribution for greater availability, can be derived from such a distribution. However, the singularity of an application can create a bottleneck (Berson, 1992). This bottleneck can be relieved by placing some application processing, in addition to data, across the network. Doing this will better utilize various computing resources. This becomes a valuable benefit when the significant price/performance characteristics of modern workstations are considered. The client/server architecture employs distributed cooperative processing to distribute application processing components between clients and servers and to support cohesive interactions between clients and servers in a cooperative fashion.

One of the main concerns of client/server design is how to distribute application components between clients and servers. The following guidelines can be observed for designing a client/server-based CASE system:

1. The presentation logic component with its screen input/output facilities is placed on a client system and these clients are placed on the lowest tier of the environment.
2. Some of the CASE logic should be placed on the client system. This takes advantage of the power of the local client

system. This is especially true for the part of the application logic that deals with the screen-related editing and maybe those pieces of the code that are specific to a particular client.

3. If the database logic is embedded into the CASE logic and if clients maintain some low-interaction, then the database processing logic can be placed on a client system.

4. Given the fact that a typical LAN connects clients within a common-purpose workgroup, and assuming that the workgroup shares a database, all common, shared fragments of the CASE and database processing logic and DBMS itself should be placed on the server.

TECHNIQUES OF DESIGNING A DISTRIBUTED CASE TOOL

In order to design a distributed CASE tool, the following software techniques are needed: distributed processing, two-phase commit, collaborative programming, and distributed CASE repository.

Distributed Processing

While cooperative client/server processing is the key toward optimization of the computing resources in a network, it is really the CASE and repository logic that represent the essence of the application. One of the critical design steps in the client/server process is the placement of the CASE and repository logic (together referred to as the application processing). Berson (1992) offers three possible solutions to this placement:

1. Application processing logic is placed entirely on the client system.
2. Application processing logic is placed entirely on a server.
3. Application processing logic is fragmented, with the fragments distributed between the client and the server.

Each solution has its advantages and disadvantages. However, solution 3 can combine the advantages of the first two scenarios, while reducing the other approaches' disadvantages.

Indeed, the distributed approach provides the most benefits. It is also the most complicated one. Proper fragmentation is very important to the success of the distribution. The correct balance between client resident and server resident application processing logic is application-dependent.

The Two-Phase Commit

Another critical issue of application processing logic distribution is the issue of synchronization in distributed transaction processing. A client resident application logic fragment interacts with the server resident fragment in cooperative fashion by exchanging requests and responses. In general, interactions in the distributed transaction processing between a client and a server are synchronous. A client issues a request to a server and waits for the request to be processed. A positive or

negative result is to be returned to the client before the next request is issued.

The problem arises when, in the course of the transaction, both a client and a server modify their respective resources. If both the client and the server have been successful in their parts of a transaction process, they can commit the changes permanently. If one of the client/server interaction partners fails, another partner should reverse the changes made in the course of the transaction to the original state the resources were in before the transaction started. These rules are called a two-phase commit protocol (Berson, 1992). Even though it is often associated with distributed database processing, the two-phase commit protocol guarantees the integrity of the transaction resources.

Collaborative Programming

Coordinating a programming team requires a powerful set of repository-based tools built around a multi-user data dictionary. As groups of programmers work on large projects, it is very important for them to function as a team in their production of a fully functional enterprise-wide software system (Moad, 1992). The programmers need to share code, keep code updated, keep track of the updates and do this all with a minimum amount of effort. It is important to keep the effort associated with the menial administration functions to a minimum. This enables the programmers to work on the creative art of producing code.

As the versions change that are associated with multiple pieces of code, a code library must be developed and updated. This library must have all the information about current versions and historical information. The detail included in this library must contain the information about the versions of all the particular parts of a system that were used to compile a version of a system.

Another part of collaborative programming that is extremely important is the ability of code to be reusable by all of the developers in a programming group. This reusable code not only saves time and increases productivity, it also enables team leaders to set standards for various key components of the code.

Collaborative programming also allows programmers within a team to specialize within certain areas. For example, some programmers may specialize in building screens, others in the construction of reports, and still others may work on object classes and overall program design.

Collaborative programming can give the development team many advantages in their use of the CASE tool. It improves the productivity of the individual programmer and the team leaders. It also improves the coordination of the entire team.

Distributed CASE Repositories

The CASE repository contains all the rules of code construction along with all of the code that has ever been created. This is an extremely important part of the entire client/server system. An AI-enhanced CASE tool makes it easy to use (Chou, 1994).

One of the main objectives of the client/server CASE architecture is the efficient ability to remotely access data. That access is provided by a database server. That database server contains the DBMS software and the data itself. Some of the characteristics of this environment as listed by Berson (1992) are:

1. DBMS software is common, shared software.
2. In a client/server environment the server is the focal point of all client requests.
3. Advanced DBMS implementations allow for the placement of common procedures and even certain business rules into the server DBMS, which necessitates its central position in a client/server architecture.
4. In a workgroup environment, the majority of the data to be processed needs to be shared among all clients.
5. Advanced DBMS implementations include DBMS resident data dictionaries that facilitate application development, support data location transparency, and provide for more efficient data administration.
6. Placing data and the DBMS together on a database server makes it easier to implement facilities that provide data integrity and availability.

Therefore, the proper architectural decision would be to place the DBMS software and all shared data on a database server. At the same time, if client applications require some unique applications and client specific data, the proper place for them would be a data store located in a client system. These two situations would determine the way a client application could connect to a server running a DBMS. With the direct application-to-DBMS connection, the client application would use communication protocols and some kind of remote transaction processing to request a server resident DBMS to access data. This situation can become more complicated if multiple servers have to be accessed.

In either case, data integrity and administration issues would have to be resolved (Salemi, 1993). For example, if the application data is spread across multiple servers, distributed database management or distributed request processing with the two-phase commit will be required to guarantee data integrity across servers.

CONCLUSIONS

The near future will bring landmark advancements in the field of client/server computing. As this architecture becomes more robust, CASE tools will become more important. Perhaps the most important technology that will be made available in the near future is the ability for software design teams to construct software by using cooperative programming techniques in a client/server environment. The repositories that hold all the rules and construction parts for the code development will be distributed across the network in a manner that provides a high degree of efficiency and optimum speed. The data locations will be transparent to the programmer developing code in this environment. In addition to the databases being distributed, parts of the CASE application itself will reside in different locations in the client/server environment. The operating efficiencies that this type of architecture will bring to the development teams will greatly enhance the productivity of CASE tools. This enhanced productivity in the client/server environment will allow the production of client/server applications to become even more efficient and robust. This is bound to be one of the most important technological contributions that will reshape the way many organizations develop and use software.

REFERENCES

Alexander, Michael. (1991, September 30). Taking Five Top Technologies Into the Future. Computerworld, p20.

Andrews, Dorine C. and Naomi S. Leventhal. (1993). Fusion - Integrating IE, CASE and JAD. Englewood Cliffs, NJ: Prentice Hall.

Berson, Alex. (1992). Client/Server Architecture. New York, NY: McGraw-Hill, Inc.

Booker, Ellis. (1992, June 1). 4GL Development Tool Targets Images. Computerworld, p61.

Catchings, Bill and Mark L. Van Name. (1992, March 2). Client/Server Computing Needs Big-Time Tools. PC Week, p71.

Champy, James A. (1992, January). Mission: Critical, With the recession putting the squeeze on IS budgets everywhere, CIO's must learn to do more with less - and be able to prove it too. CIO, p18.

Chou, David C. (1993). Computer-Aided Software Engineering: Issues and Trends for the 1990s and Beyond. Using CASE in Expert Systems Design, Chapter 13

Chou, David C. (1994). Software Quality Assurance in CASE Tools. Information Systems Management, Spring 1994, pp. 56-61.

Currid, Cheryl. (1993, August). A Case against CASE: It's Expensive and Often Unsuccessful. Infoworld, p68.

Dodge, Frank. (1992, December 7). A Winning Client/Server Formula. Computerworld, p85.

Eckerson, Wayne. (1993, October 25). KnowledgeWare deploys Client/Server Repositories. Network World, p33.

Ferranti, Marc. (1992, August 3). Startup Ships Client/Server Wares for Customer Support. PC Week, p29 (2).

How IS Can Answer Corporate Needs With Client/Server Computing. (1993, June 15). Datamation, p S.2 (19).

Jones, Bob. (1992, March 9). Client/Server Development Tools. Computerworld, p73 (8).

Knight, Robert M. (1993, October 18). Software Engineering, CASE Studies. Information Week, p36 (2).

McClure, Carma. (1989). CASE is Software Automation. Englewood

Cliffs, NJ: Prentice Hall

Moad, Jeff. (1991, September 15). Where to Turn for Client/Server Skills. Datamation, p79 (2).

Moad, Jeff. (1992, August 1). Gupta's Double Impact. Datamation, p28 (5).

Pinella, Paul. (1992, March 1). The Race for Client/Server CASE. Datamation, p51 (3).

Polilli, Steve. (1992, November). TI Banking on CASE to Reach $1B Target; Executive Shakeout Revamped Sales Force Plans for IEF Platform Expansion. Software Magazine, p106 (3).

Ryan, Hugh W. (1993, Spring). Adopting Client-Server Technology. Information Systems Management, p62 (3).

Salemi, Joe. (1993). PC Magazine Guide to Client/Server Databases. Emeryville, CA: Ziff-Davis Press.

Schwartz, Evan I. (1993, March 15). Finally, Software that Slays Giants, Client-Server programs Let PCs do Mainframe Work. Business Week, p96 (3).

Stahlman, Mark. (1993, November 1). The Future of Clennt/Server Computing: Part 2. Network Computing, p67 (2).

Van Name, Mark l. and Bill Catchings. (1991, November 4). Client/Server Apps Demand New Blend of Developer Skills. PC Week, p65.

Ware, Rob. (1992, October). Client/Server Ststems: The Next Wave? Journal of Systems Management, p39.

What You Always Wanted to Know About Client/Server, But Were Afraid to Ask. (1992, March 9). Computerworld, p84.

Yourdon, Edward. (1992). Decline and Fall of the American Programmer Englewood Cliffs, NJ: Prentice Hall.

Object Analyzer for CASE

Sue Ho C.S.
Hong Kong Polytechnic
Hong Kong

Abstract

This paper aims at describing the object analyzer for CASE. The object analyzer is part of the analysis tool which is used for selecting objects from the existing documents. The documents are either the existing documentations of the system or any documents such as interview notes collected during fact finding. Usually before any physical system is built the designer required to produce a logical model for the new system. A logical model is conceptualised based on ones understanding of a problem domain. The activity which followed is to identify the required functions and objects. Selecting and identifying objects in this case is one of the main issues in adopting object analyzer.

Introduction

CASE is a system and software engineering tool which is designed to support the software development process. The main reason of using the tool is to increase productivity and to improve software quality. Basically it is a tool which consists of a project planning capability, analysis, design, implementation and maintenaince. There are others which fall outside these specific lifecycle categories such as tools for designing graphical user interface (GUI) to existing applications, tools for designing applications for specific GUI environments, tools for designing of object-oriented systems and metatools.

CASE tools are further classified into Upper CASE, Lower CASE, and Integrated CASE. Upper CASE automates the analysis and design aspects of the system development. Whereas Lower CASE aims at automating the later parts of the system development mainly code generation. Integrated CASE commonly known as I-CASE is an integration of both Upper and Lower CASE. On the main, all these CASE tools available on the market are vendor dependent. An obvious example is to be able to use a CASE tool one has to know a specific systems development methodology.

The adoption of object oriented approach to systems analysis is still at a very early stage.. Even though there are all kinds of object oriented or object based products continues to expand at a very rapid rate. The emphasis is very much still on languages like Smalltalk and C++. Therefore in order to bridge the gap a hybrid approach may be adopted. This means that one can use structured approach to analysis and design and be able to implement the system using an object oriented language. For those system people who are to use Structure system analysis and design in the '80 would certainly require to retrain their mindset so as to be able to adopt object oriented approach to system development.

In this paper the main issue is on Upper CASE focussing on capturing the objects from documents . For any software systems to be durable it has to have a properly organised software production environment with documents and documentation standard . Having collected the documents and created the documentation they have to be properly filed with appropriate references. So the emphasis is not solely on just identifying objects but also setting up proper links with the documents.

Objective

The main objective is to build Object Analyzer which can be incorporated with CASE tool mainly the analysis tool. This particular tool which will help analyst to create objects based on the existing documents. One of the many techniques which the analyst used when defining objects within the problem domain is searching through the existing documents for objects and analysing the selected objects. Common techniques used for fact finding such as interviewing, sampling questionaires and observation which required a fair amount of recording and documentation. These of course if they are recorded on documents would required a fair amount of time to pick up the objects. As an analyst this could be one of the most difficult and time consuming task.

Object Analyzer will assists the analyst in selecting the right objects. This is vital because objects selected are not only used in the current problem domain but will be reused in future systems. Software designers must be able to define and understand the current system. The process begins with defining objects which are related to the problem at hand.

Problem/scope

In this paper I will assume that document files are created by using the appropariate scanning utilities. The tool consists of two parts. The first part, Object specifier, will browse through the text from the document file and each word is compared with the objects kept in the dictionary. A searching algorithm is used for finding the object in the dictionary. Hypertext documents are created whereby there are links between documents and objects. In this case each processed document has a unique identity and they are filed according to the identity sequence. Similarly objects will bare the same identity as the source documents.

The second part of the Object analyzer will pick up objects from the dictionary when initiated by the user . With the help of the tool the user will be able to identify objects within the problem domain. Here one will expect to eliminate objects or introduce new objects and therefore require to update the dictionary. A browser is provided for viewing the object repository and make amendments when necessary.

Implementation

Scanner is used as a basic tool for capturing documents. Individual document is created with a unique identity. All the object names are created and kept in the Object Dictionary. While analysing the document , each word will be retrieved and compared with the object names kept in the Object Dictionary. A search algorithm will be used for finding the object. If the object is found it will be created in theObject Repository. Initially each object will bear a document identity indicating the object origin.

Initial objects can be amended by using Browser. Browsing will enable user to browse through the repository and identify which objects require modification. Once object is identified Editing Function can be called up to perform any necessary amendments. Here descriptions can be added or deleted from the objects. Browser will also enable user to cross-check with the documents once the object is identified.There is a possibility that an object will appear in more than one documents. Therefore there will be multiple links between documents and objects.

Object Analyzer will retrieve each object and prompt the user by displaying a number questions for identifying the object. For instance "Has it contained any descriptions or attributes?" , " If not is it an attribute of another object ?" "Does user need to keep it", "Does it have life in it?". At this stage some objects will be weeded off and descriptions or attributes will be created for the remaining objects. Again documents can be retrieved whenever it is necessary.

Alternative approach.

Scanner is used as a tool for capturing documents. Each document created will have a unique identity. Document will be displayed on the screen and user selects the objects based on his/her intuition. Browser is used for checking any redundant objects and for introducing new objects into the repository. Each object will bear a document identity.Descriptions may be added to each object. Object analyser will serves similar functions as the above. This approach eliminates the step of weeding off the redundant objects. In this case objects created in the repository have cross references to the source documents.

Limitations.

This automatic process will lead to a lot of redundant objects created. Therefore the weeding process may take a lot longer than expected. The second approach may proved a lot more useful in this sense as the user has to scan through the documents first before selecting the objects. Based on the users intuition and understanding, together with the assistant of the tool the releveant objects will be selected.

Searching through the Object Dictionary may take too long. The search algorithm of course plays a vital role here. The added problem here is that every single word on the document needs to cross-check with the dictionary. Also there is a chance that objects on the documents may be missed if the names do not appear in the dictionary.

Building hypertext database for object analyser

The hypertext database will provide active cross-references so that users can retrieve relevant documents or information as required. It does not place any restriction on node format which makes it specially useful for holding the wide variety of information. Conceptually there will be network of nodes and links. Nodes in this case are documents and objects which can be photographs, graphics, sound and text. Links are cross-references between documents and objects. Cross-references can be arranged in hierarchical structures which facilitate easy access to information.

Conclusion.

Whenever there are lots of documents involved during the initial stage of the analysis the object analyzer will help not only in performing automatic documentation for the system but also help in getting the right objetcs for the system. If the objects are carefully selected this will produce reusable objects. Objects in the respository can be shared with other systems. The tool can be improved by introducing AI techniques which provide a basis for defining new formal languages and an appropriate way to represent the large amount of analysis knowledge to support the specification and design of a software system.

Prototype Object analyser

The following main modules will be used for the prototype.

Documents function.

This will enable user to browse through the documents and select the relevent objects. Both objects and documents have a unique identifier and they will be kept in the repository.

Object analyser/browser.

Browser will enable user to scan through both the objects and the related documents.Each selected object will be prompted with questions which assist the analyst to define appropriate objects within the system domain. Object descriptions may be created at this stage. In addition a checking facility is provided for checking the multiple occurences of an object. The same object appears in more than one document will need to reprocess i.e. to consolidate all the documents identifiers into one object. Synonym of an object can be added at this stage.

Object maintenance.

This will enable the creation of new objects, the deletion of redundant objects and updating the object descriptions.

Hardware requirements:

IBM PC 486 or compatible/4 MB memory/ VGA monitor/ Micrsoft serial mouse.

Software requirements:

Microsoft window 3.0 or above/ Borland C++ version 3.1/ window word 2.0 for preparing documents.

References:

Object-Oriented modelling and design,J.Rumborgh, M.Blaha, Premerlan,F.Eddy,W.Lorensen(Prentice-Hall 1991)

Object-Oriented design, Coad and Yourdon(prentice-Hall 1991)
Object-Oriented analysis,Coad and Yourdon (Prentice-Hall 1990)

Software Engineering and CASE - Building the culture Gap,Fletcher and Hunt (Mcgraw-Hill 1993).
Hypertext 87: Keynote address,Van Dam (Communications of the ACM, July 1988).

Cognitive tools for locating and comprehending software objects for reuse, Fisher,Henninger, Redmiles (!3th international conference on software engineering May)

CASE and reengineering: Elliot J. Chikofsky, Index Technology Corporation and Northeastern University.
CASe: reliability for information systems, E Chikofsky and B.RRubenstein, Index Technology.
Reengineering: Can a program put intelligence in stupid program,M.Maiocchi, University og Milan.

Hypertext and CASE, James Bigelow, IEEE software Development CASE.

ASPIS: A knowledge based CASE environment, Puncullo, Torrigiani, Pietri, Burlon, Cardile andConti.
A laboratory for teaching Object Oriented thinking , Kent Beck, Apple Computer,Wyatt Software services.

CASE strategies, Jan.1993, Feb.1993 March 1993 April 1993, May 1993.
Object oriented strategies, Feb. 1992, March 1992, April 1993, June 1993.

Computer-Aided Systems Engineering Support for Structured Analysis

David Jankowski
Assistant Professor of Management Information Systems
Center for High Technoogy Manufacturing
College of Business Administration
San Marcos, California
619-752-4235
FAX 619-752-4250
internet: david_jankowski@csusm.edu

1. INTRODUCTION

System specification consistency, or adherence to a development methodology, has been identified as one of the criteria affecting software quality factors (McCall, Richards, & Walters, 1977). Consistency is defined to be the software attributes that provide uniform design and implementation techniques and documentation (Arthur, 1985). Consistency has been identified as directly impacting the following software quality factors: correctness, flexibility, maintainability, and reliability.

Computer-aided systems engineering (CASE) tools have been proposed as one of many "silver bullets" to improve system quality and eliminate the development and maintenance backlog of information systems applications (Brooks, 1987). One important role of a CASE tool is to serve as a methodology companion, i.e., to assist an analyst in the creation of documentation passed to succeeding phases of the life cycle, and to guide the analyst through a particular systems development methodology (McClure, 1989). The level of methodology assistance provided by a CASE tool varies from product to product and may include a graphics tool to support various diagramming techniques, a data dictionary for storing entities associated with a systems project, and automated checks, which serve to enforce a particular methodology and help ensure completeness and consistency of the resulting specifications.

Unfortunately, while many vendors claim their product supports a particular information systems development methodology, the actual level of methodology support varies greatly from one CASE tool to another. The level of support ranges from the simple existence of methodology diagramming symbols to methodology rules that are enforced in realtime. Teresko (1990) describes the current status of methodology support thusly: "CASE tools impose a development methodology as a primary benefit to developers. Some may dictate very strict methods. Others may be more flexible" (p. 83).

There are many advocates of CASE who believe the level of methodology support provided by the tools is insufficient. Alavi (1993) suggests that CASE might be more well-received if systems development methodology support was embedded in the CASE tools. Loy (1993) states, "The tools do not yet adequately support the methods as promised" (p. 31). Page-Jones (1992) further adds that the current level of methodology support provided by CASE tools is unacceptable. Yourdon (1992) states that a "CASE tool without methodology support is nothing more than a glorified drawing tool" (p. 144). A recent survey of CASE experts indicates that the integration of CASE tools and methodologies must be improved in the future (Crosslin, Bergin, & Stott, 1993), while Henderson and Cooprider (1990) state, "CASE products support a weak level of analysis functionality ... increasing the level of analysis technology holds strong promise" (p. 251). Sumner's (1993) case study of thirteen firms that use CASE concludes that one of the top two success factors for implementing CASE is the adherence to the chosen methodology.

In this paper the feasibility of automating support for structured analysis will be examined. The levels of methodology support described are based upon previous work in decision support system (DSS) restrictiveness. The various levels of automated methodology support available have been applied to the rules of structured analysis in order to determine the feasibility of automating the structured analysis methodology. The feasibility study presented can then be used as a basis of comparison for current CASE tools in order to determine the extent to which they support structured analysis.

2. A FRAMEWORK FOR CLASSIFYING CASE METHODOLOGY SUPPORT

The first substantial work aimed at classifying CASE tools based upon their level of methodology support is presented in a study by Vessey, Jarvenpaa, & Tractinsky (1992). Using terminology taken from the decision support system (DSS) literature, the authors describe methodology support as being either restrictive, guided, or flexible. Specifically, two attributes of a DSS, system restrictiveness and decisional guidance (as defined in Silver [1990]), have been redefined and applied to CASE tools.

The remainder of this section examines the concepts of restrictiveness and guidance as they apply to CASE tools and the execution of the systems development process. By examining both restrictiveness and guidance, it will be possible to look at the extent to which it is feasible to automate support for structured analysis. By understanding the feasibility of automating a methodology we will be able to not only answer the question, "Does CASE tool X support methodology Z?", but also, "*To what extent* does CASE tool X support methodology Z?".

2.1 CASE Tool Restrictiveness

CASE tool restrictiveness may be formally defined as follows: *The degree to which and the manner in which a CASE tool limits its users' software development processes to a subset of all possible processes* (adapted from Silver, [1990]). A CASE tool may restrict the execution of the systems development process by placing restrictions upon the procedures used to create the product of a particular systems development activity as well as restrictions upon the products themselves. To illustrate this consider the methodology rules for structured analysis. These rules apply to either the *process* of structured analysis, i.e., ensuring that the specification is constructed in a top-down manner, or to the *products* of structured analysis, i.e., syntax rules for data flow diagrams and minispecs. The product rules can be further broken down into those rules that ensure the internal consistency of a product (e.g., ensuring that data stores are connected to processes) and those rules that ensure the hierarchical consistency between products (e.g., ensuring that data flows are balanced between levels) (Vessey, et al., 1992).

In order to restrict the execution of systems development, rules must be embedded within a CASE tool that serve to force the analyst to rigorously follow the rules of a chosen operator (e.g., data flow diagramming). In order to determine if a rule has been implemented in a restrictive fashion, three properties of the rule must be examined: the timing of the rule, the invocation of the rule, and the enforcement of the rule (see Figure 1). The *timing* of a rule refers to when a rule violation

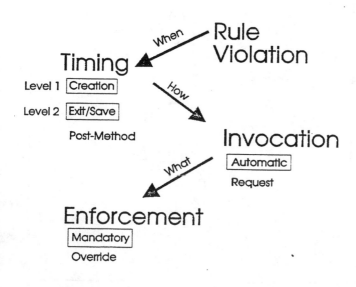

Figure 1: Restricting the Execution of the Systems Development Process

is presented to the analyst. A rule that is implemented in a restrictive fashion by a CASE tool will allow violations to be checked as soon as is feasible to do so. Restriction implies that an analyst is being forced to conform to the rules of the chosen operator. Therefore, it is imperative that the analyst be given the opportunity to fix a violation as soon as the violation is detected by the CASE tool in order to keep the violation from propagating through the system specification. This implies that rule violations must be detectable while in the process of using an operator (Level 1 Restriction). Other rule violations may not be detectable until the analyst is finished using an operator (e.g., while saving and/or exiting the operator) (Level 2 Restriction). The *invocation* of a rule refers to the mechanism by which the rule violation is presented to the analyst. A rule that is implemented in a restrictive fashion (Level 1 or Level 2) by a CASE tool will be automatically presented to the analyst as soon as it is detected by the CASE tool. The *enforcement* of the rule refers to the set of options available to the analyst once a rule violation has been detected by the CASE tool. The analyst may be forced to correct the violation before proceeding further (mandatory) or the analyst may be allowed to continue working and ignore the error (override). In summary, a rule will be considered to be implemented within the CASE tool in a restrictive fashion if the analyst is automatically presented with the rule violation while using an operator, or while terminating use of an operator, and is forced to correct the violation before proceeding.

2.2 CASE Tool Development Guidance

An alternative to restricting the execution of the systems development process is to provide suggestions and information that serve to guide the analyst through the development process. CASE tool development guidance may be formally defined as follows: *The degree to which and the manner in which a CASE tool guides its users in executing the systems development process and constructing its resultant products, by assisting them in choosing and using its methods* (adapted from Silver, [1990]). A CASE tool may guide the execution of the systems development process by providing the analyst with suggestions and information regarding the procedures of a particular systems development activity as well as the resultant product of that activity. By definition, the word "guidance" implies the existence of an underlying choice, i.e., a decision must be made as to whether or not to accept the guidance. The guidance provided by the CASE tool to the analyst must be flexible enough so that the analyst can ignore the embedded advice. Two types of guidance can be made available to the analyst by the CASE tool: active guidance and passive guidance. Active guidance is informative and suggestive advice that is unsolicited, i.e., the CASE tool delivers the guidance to the analyst when the CASE tool detects a need for guidance (see Figure 2). Active guidance can be provided by the CASE tool while the analyst is using an operator (Level 1 Active Guidance) or it may be provided by the CASE tool when the analyst is finished using an operator (e.g., while saving and/or exiting the operator) (Level 2 Active Guid-

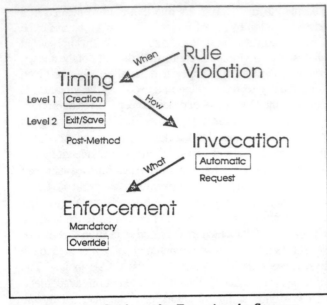

Figure 2: Active Guidance for Executing the Systems Development Process

ance). The violation must be presented to the analyst in the form of an informative message or suggestion for correcting the violation. It is then left to the discretion of the analyst to determine whether or not to correct the violation. For example, if the analyst tries to delete an input data flow from a child diagram the CASE tool could immediately warn the analyst that the deletion may result in a methodological inconsistency. The analyst should then have the option of continuing or aborting the operation.

A second type of guidance provided by a CASE tool is passive guidance. Passive guidance is informative and suggestive advice that is solicited by the analyst from the CASE tool (see Figure 3). For example, if the analyst is unsure if a parent and child data flow diagram are balanced he can request that the CASE tool check the balancing and report any inconsistencies. Passive guidance may be requested by the analyst from within an operator (Level 1 Passive Guidance) or it may be implemented as a separate function outside of the operator (Level 2 Passive Guidance). For example, Visible Analyst Workbench 3.1 allows the analyst to validate work in progress by requesting a consistency check from within the data flow diagramming tool. Excelerator 1.9, on the other hand, requires the analyst to save the diagram, exit the diagramming tool, and then execute a separate analysis function. As with active guidance any violations must be presented to the analyst in the form of informative messages or suggestions for correcting the violations.

An alternative to embedding restrictiveness and guidance within a CASE tool is the complete lack of support for a methodology or a particular methodology rule. For example, a CASE tool may not contain any embedded checks of the internal consistency of a diagram. Rather, the analyst is left with the responsibility of making certain the diagram adheres to the rules of the chosen methodology.

3. FEASIBILITY OF CASE SUPPORT FOR STRUCTURED ANALYSIS

By adopting a particular systems development methodology and mandating its use, an organization is expecting the products of the systems development activities to conform to the chosen methodology. To achieve the objective of methodology prescription an organization, in theory, should be able to purchase a CASE tool that supports the chosen methodology. However, the concept of methodology support can be handled differently from one CASE tool to another. Further complicating the issue is the fact that some methodology rules cannot, for practical reasons, be implemented in a restrictive fashion.

When discussing the enforcement of methodology rules in a restrictive fashion the conflict between an actual methodology violation and work in progress must be addressed. The CASE tool should not interrupt the analyst's work to report a violation if the suspected violation may be a symptom of unfinished work. For example, if an analyst tries to connect two data stores with a data flow then this violation may be immediately presented to the analyst by the CASE tool. However, if an analyst has just entered a new process on a diagram it would be counter-productive for the CASE tool to immediately stop the analyst to indicate that the process has no inflows or outflows. The second example is a suspected rule violation and may be flagged automatically but it would be more appropriate to do so at the request of the analyst. However, the suspected violation could be automatically presented when the analyst attempts to save the diagram and/ or exit the diagramming tool. To account for this, a rule violation which may be the result of unfinished work should be handled in one of two ways: 1) The violation may be automatically presented to the analyst only when the analyst is finished with an operator (e.g., while saving and/or exiting

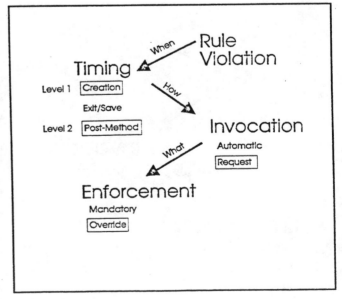

Figure 3: Passive Guidance for Executing the Sytems Development Process

the operator) (Level 2 Active Guidance), or 2) The violation is only presented to the analyst upon the request of the analyst (Level 1 or Level 2 Passive Guidance). In either of the above methods, the analyst is not bothered with an erroneous interruption while using the operator. Notification of violations via active guidance would have the probable effect of identifying possible inconsistencies earlier than would passive guidance; however, active guidance might also prove to be a nuisance to the analyst by forcing the analyst, every time an operator is terminated, to read through a list of violations that can be attributed to unfinished work. The remainder of this section examines the feasibility and practicality of automating the rules of structured analysis. The feasibility of automating structured analysis methodology rules will be reported with respect to the scale shown in Figure 4. The scale displays the previously discussed methods of notifying an analyst of a rule violation, arranged in order of strong to weak enforcement rigidity.

Process Rule

1. A parent process must be specified before a child process. This is the only methodology rule which enforces the process of top-down design. This rule may be restrictively (Level 1) enforced by a CASE tool by not allowing processes to be linked post-hoc, i.e., the only way new processes (with the exception of the context diagram process) may be created is through the decomposition and subsequent refinement of a parent process.**Product Rules (Internal Consistency)**

2. A data flow diagram must have at least one process. This rule cannot be enforced in a restrictive fashion because doing so will not take into account unfinished work. For example, a diagram in progress may contain data flows and data stores but not processes. Passive guidance (Level 1 or Level 2) can be provided if the analyst does not wish to be distracted with automatic internal consistency checks on work in progress.

3. A data flow diagram must have no more than seven processes. This rule can be restrictively (Level 1) enforced by a CASE tool by not allowing the analyst to access a new process symbol if seven processes already exist on the data flow diagram.

4. A context diagram must exist. This rule can be restrictively (Level 1) enforced by a CASE tool by defining the first data flow diagram to be the context diagram and applying all other context diagram rules to this diagram.

5. The context diagram must contain only one process. This rule can be restrictively (Level 1) enforced by a CASE tool by not allowing the analyst to access a new process symbol if a process already exists on the diagram. However, the requirement that the context diagram must have a process cannot be restrictively enforced in order to account for unfinished work. Passive guidance (Level 1 or Level 2) can be provided if the analyst does not wish to be distracted with automatic internal consistency checks on work in progress.

6. The context diagram must contain at least one input from an external entity and one output to an external entity. This rule cannot be enforced in a restrictive fashion because doing so will not take into account unfinished work. For example, an unfinished context diagram might contain input from an external entity but no output to an external entity. Passive guidance (Level 1 or Level 2) can be provided if the analyst does not wish to be distracted with automatic internal consistency checks on work in progress.

7. The context diagram process must be numbered zero (0). This rule can be restrictively (Level 1) enforced by a CASE tool by automatically numbering the context process for the analyst when the process is created and not allowing the analyst to change the numbering.

8. A process must have at least one input data flow and one output data flow. This rule cannot be enforced in a restrictive fashion because doing so will not take into account unfinished work. For example, an unfinished diagram might contain a process with an output data flow but no input data flow. Passive guidance (Level 1 or Level 2) can be provided if the analyst does not wish to be distracted with automatic internal consistency checks on work in progress.

9. A process must be connected to at least one of the following: data store, process, external entity. This rule cannot be enforced in a restrictive fashion because doing so will not take into account unfinished work. For example, immediately after a process is drawn it is free-standing. Passive guidance (Level 1 or Level 2) can be provided if the analyst does not wish to be distracted with automatic internal consistency checks on work in progress.

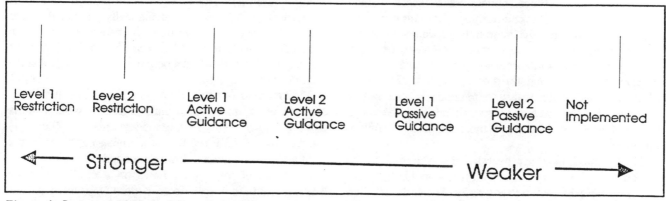

Figure 4: Spectrum of Methodology Enforcement

10. A process must be labeled. This rule can be restrictively (Level 1) enforced by a CASE tool by automatically prompting the analyst to enter a label when the process is created and requiring the analyst to enter a label at the prompt.

11. An external entity must appear for the first time on the context diagram. This rule can be restrictively (Level 1) enforced by a CASE tool by verifying the name of any external entity placed below the context diagram with a list of names of those external entities appearing on the context diagram. If the external entity is appearing for the first time in the diagram set (but not on the context diagram) the CASE tool can disallow the placement of the external entity.

12. An external entity must be connected to a process. This rule has two possible scenarios, each of which requires a different enforcement mechanism. In the first scenario the external entity is free-standing and, therefore, in violation of the methodology rule. However, this may be attributed to work in progress rather than an error by the analyst. Active (Level 2) or passive (Level 1 or Level 2) guidance can be used to detect a free-standing external entity. In the second scenario, the analyst attempts to connect the external entity to a data store or another external entity. A CASE tool may prohibit this type of connection from being made (Level 1 Restriction).

13. An external entity must be labeled. This rule can be restrictively (Level 1) enforced by a CASE tool by automatically prompting the analyst to enter a label when the external entity is created and requiring the analyst to enter a label at the prompt.

14. A data flow must be an interface between a process and either a second process, a data store, or an external entity. This rule may be enforced in a restrictive (Level 1) manner by not allowing a data flow to be drawn as a free-standing object. Instead, a data flow can be created by indicating the two existing objects that the flow is connecting. If one of the objects is not a process the CASE tool can prevent the data flow from being created.

15. A data flow into a data store must have a composition that is a subset of the data store's composition. This rule cannot be enforced in a restrictive fashion because doing so will not take into account unfinished work. For example, the analyst can choose not to explicitly define, via the data dictionary, the composition of the data stores and/or data flows until after the diagram has been drawn. In this case, active guidance (Level 2) or passive guidance (Level 1 or Level 2) can be used to indicate any potential inconsistencies or the existence of an undefined data flow/store. Even if the CASE tool required the analyst to immediately enter the data dictionary after creating a data store or a data flow, the analyst must still be allowed to leave the composition definition unfinished.

16. A data flow must be labeled. This rule can be restrictively (Level 1) enforced by a CASE tool by automatically prompting the analyst to enter a label when the data flow is created and requiring the analyst to enter a label at the

prompt.

17. A data store can only exist as an interface between two processes. This rule has two possible scenarios, each of which requires a different enforcement mechanism. In the first scenario the data store is free-standing or connected to only one process (and is not connected to the parent process) and, therefore, in violation of the methodology rule. However, this may be attributed to work in progress rather than an error by the analyst. Active (Level 2) or passive (Level 1 or Level 2) guidance can be used to detect this situation. In the second scenario, the analyst attempts to connect a data store to anything but a process. The CASE tool may prohibit this type of connection from being made (Level 1 Restriction).

18. A data store must be labeled. This rule can be restrictively (Level 1) enforced by a CASE tool by automatically prompting the analyst to enter a label when the data store is created and requiring the analyst to enter a label at the prompt.

Product Rules (Hierarchical Consistency)

19. A parent data flow diagram must exist unless it is a context diagram. This rule can be restrictively (Level 1) enforced by a CASE tool by only allowing a new diagram to be created (except for the context diagram) from a process decomposition resulting in a new (child) diagram level.

20. A process must decompose to either another data flow diagram or a primitive process specification. This rule cannot be enforced in a restrictive fashion because doing so will not take into account any unfinished leveling. Level 1 Active Guidance can be provided to the analyst by giving the analyst the option of creating a primitive process specification after creating the process. Passive guidance (Level 1 or Level 2) can be provided if the analyst does not wish to be distracted with automatic completeness checks on work in progress.

21. A process must be numbered with respect to its parent. This rule can be restrictively (Level 1) enforced by a CASE tool by automatically numbering all processes when they are created and not allowing the analyst to change the numbering.

22. An input (output) data flow on a parent data flow diagram must appear on a child data flow diagram as input (output). This rule can be restrictively (Level 1) enforced by a CASE tool by automatically carrying down all input and output data flows from the parent process to the child diagram when moving between diagram levels and not allowing the net input and net output data flows to be deleted from the child diagram.

23. An input (output) data flow on a child data flow diagram must appear on a parent data flow diagram as input (output). This rule can be restrictively (Level 1) enforced by a CASE tool by not allowing insertions of net input and net output data flows on a child diagram.

24. A set of input data flows on a child data flow diagram that were split from a data flow on a parent data flow diagram must match the parent data flow's

composition. This rule can be restrictively (Level 1) enforced by a CASE tool by automatically carrying down input data flows from the parent process to the child diagram when moving between diagram levels. Further, the CASE tool should not allow any of the sub-flows to be deleted from the child diagram nor may any sub-flows be added to the child diagram.

25. A data flow must decompose to either a record definition or an element definition. This rule cannot be enforced in a restrictive fashion because doing so will not take into account unfinished work. Level 1 Active Guidance can be provided to the analyst by giving the analyst the option to enter the definition in the data dictionary after creating the data flow. Passive guidance (Level 1 or Level 2) can be provided if the analyst does not wish to be distracted with automatic completeness checks on work in progress.

26. A data store must decompose to either a file definition or a record definition. This rule cannot be enforced in a restrictive fashion because doing so will not take into account unfinished work. Level 1 Active Guidance can be provided to the analyst by giving the analyst the option to enter the definition in the data dictionary after creating the data store. Passive guidance (Level 1 or Level 2) can be provided if the analyst does not wish to be distracted with automatic completeness checks on work in progress.

27. All inputs and outputs of a primitive process specification must match those of the corresponding parent process on the data flow diagram. This rule can be restrictively (Level 1) enforced by a CASE tool by automatically carrying down input and output data flows from the parent process to the primitive process specification upon creation of the primitive process specification. Further, the CASE tool should not allow any of the inputs or outputs to be deleted from the primitive process specification nor may any inputs or outputs be added to the primitive process specification.

28. A primitive process specification must be labeled with the same identifier as the corresponding primitive process on the data flow diagram. This rule can be restrictively (Level 1) enforced by a CASE tool by automatically labeling the primitive process specification with the corresponding process label and not allowing the analyst to change the label.

Table 1 summarizes the methodology enforcement feasibility discussion presented in this section. From the table it can be seen that it is not feasible to automate the entire structured analysis methodology in a restrictive fashion. Eight of the twenty-eight methodology rules cannot be feasibly implemented in a restrictive fashion. It should also be noted that some form of methodology enforcement is possible for all of the 28 rules investigated in this study.

4. CONCLUSION

Computer-aided systems engineering tools have the potential to improve system quality and increase analyst productiv-ity. Unfortunately, this potential has largely gone unrealized. The lack of methodology support offered by commercial CASE products may be seen as one of the barriers to CASE fulfilling its potential. The feasibility of automating the rules of structured analysis presented here may be used to compare CASE tools that claim to support structured analysis (as is done in Jankowski [1993]). The rule classification may also be used to generate hypotheses regarding the "optimal" enforcement mechanism for each rule (as is done in Jankowski [1994]). Further research may show that only a small subset of rules account for a majority of the violations, and it is these rules that should be restrictively enforced. Alternatively, there may be a subset of rules that should not be enforced in order to allow the analyst the greatest degree of flexibility and creativity possible. Further, CASE tool selection criteria, of which support for a particular methodology is a particularly important criteria (Baram & Steinberg, 1989), will be refined by identifying differences in the level of methodology support provided by various CASE products.

REFERENCES

Alavi, M. (1993). Making CASE an organizational reality. Strategies and new capabilities needed. *Information Systems Management. 10*(2), 15-20.

Arthur, L. J. (1985). *Measuring programmer productivity and software quality.* New York: John Wiley & Sons.

Baram, G., & Steinberg, G. (1989). Selection criteria for analysis and design CASE tools. *Software Engineering Notes. 14*(6), 73-80.

Brooks, F. P. (1987). No silver bullet: Essence and accidents of software engineering. *Computer. 20*(4), 10-19.

Crosslin, R. L., Bergin, T. J., & Stott, J. W. (1993). Critical factors influencing the future of computer-aided software engineering. In T. J. Bergin (Ed.), *Computer-aided software engineering: Issues and trends for the 1990s and beyond* (pp. 616-637). Harrisburg, PA: Idea Group.

Henderson, J. C., & Cooprider, J. G. (1990). Dimensions of I/S planning and design aids: A functional model of CASE technology. *Information Systems Research. 1*, 227-254.

Jankowski, D. J. (1993). The feasibility of CASE structured analysis methodology support. To appear in *Software Engineering Notes.*

Jankowski, D. J. (1994). *Computer-aided systems engineering methodology support and its effect on the output of structured analysis.* Unpublished doctoral dissertation, University of Arizona.

Loy, P. (1993). The method won't save you (but it can help). *Software Engineering Notes. 18*(1), 30-34.

McCall, J.A., Richards, P.K., & Walters, G.F. (1977). *Factors in software quality: Vol. 1. Concept and definitions of software quality.* (Contract No. F030602-76-C-0417). Sunnyvale, CA: General Electric Company.

McClure, C. (1989). *CASE is software automation.* Englewood Cliffs, NJ: Prentice Hall.

Page-Jones, M. (1992). The CASE manifesto. *CASE Outlook. 6*(1), pp. 33-42.

Silver, M. S. (1990). Decision support systems: directed and nondirected change. *Information Systems Research. 1*, 47-70.

Sumner, M. (1993). Factors influencing the adoption of CASE. In T. J. Bergin (Ed.), *Computer-aided software engineering: Issues and trends for the 1990s and beyond* (pp. 130-155). Harrisburg, PA: Idea Group.

Teresko, J. (1990, April 2). What MIS should be telling you about CASE. *Industry Week*, pp. 82-85.

Vessey, I., Jarvenpaa, S. L., & Tractinsky, N. (1992). Evaluation of vendor products: CASE tools as methodology companions. *Communications of the ACM. 35*(4), 90-105.

Yourdon, E. (1992). *Decline & fall of the American programmer.* Englewood Cliffs, NJ: Yourdon Press.

Table 1: Summary of CASE Tool Methodology Enforcement Feasibility

Rule #	Upon Creation			Upon Exit/Save		Post-Method	Not
	Automatic		On	Automatic		On	Feasible
	Mandatory	Override	Request	Mandatory	Override	Request	
1	X						
2			X				
3	X						
4	X						
5	X		X				
6			X				
7	X						
8			X				
9			X				
10	X						
11	X						
12	X		X				
13	X						
14	X						
15			X				
16	X						
17	X		X				
18	X						
19	X						
20		X	X				
21	X						
22	X						
23	X						
24	X						
25		X	X				
26		X	X				
27	X						
28	X						
	Level 1 Restriction	Level 1 Active Guidance	Level 1 Passive Guidance	Level 2 Restriction	Level 2 Active Guidance	Level 2 Passive Guidance	Not Feasible

Understanding the Benefits of Integrating Case Tools with Work Flow, Decision Support and Expert Systems

William H. Money, Ph.D.
Associate Professor
The George Washington University
Executive Masters In Information System Program
20201 Academic Way, Rm 309
Ashburn, VA 22011-2604
(703)729-8335   FAX (703)729-8311

BACKGROUND INFORMATION

For many years, CASE has promised significant system development and organizational paybacks, yet the elusive cost reduction and code generation benefits have been difficult to document in adopting organizations. During its initial period of development, CASE technology was viewed as the application of the systems development technologies to automation of the step-by-step methodologies for software and systems development. It was envisioned as a comprehensive methodology covering all the aspects of the development cycle from planning through maintenance. The broad functions performed by the tools documented inputs to the design of systems, provided enhanced diagramming techniques, maintained design specifications which can produce code when fed into code generators, and incorporated testing and debugging tools to speed the testing of software.

The development requirements of organizations have now changed dramatically, and CASE tools must now be selected to fit the business problems of organizations that are downsizing units and eliminating some of the tasks performed by previous employees and departments. With the new problems have come a set of new criteria for assessment of the success of CASE tools. This paper analyzes these new criteria and documents the experience of a property and casualty insurance organization that has met these new requirements with a CASE approach and methodology.

ISSUES: BUSINESS PROBLEMS OF THE MID 90's

Companies now face complex re-engineering and process innovation problems that redefine the role of information systems.

Systems supported by these tools must combine many different features such as a GUI for front end capture of information with a relational database, an expert system, an optical imaging system, and systems management using a work flow system. The CASE tool may be added to the project mix after the optical system had been installed. These systems must store the terms in a form that can used by the organization members, serve as a design and development data dictionary, and support the ability to utilize the data model as a tool that can be used to demonstrate the characteristics of the business relationships among the business units in the organization. The data model is used in systems design and during imple-mentation to illustrate how departments and units are related. The CASE tools must be able to link to the front end PC based development environment of the organization, prototype evolving applications, and integrate the various databases of the organization (Oracle is utilized in the insurance company in this study).

The development of the system by the property and casualty insurance company discussed in this paper was a strategic move away from what the organization perceived to be the previously old and incomplete mainframe environment. The new system is a conscious effort to modify the hierarchial flow of information in the organization that primarily supported the mainframe. In the old system, selected data for policy creation and billing was entered from paper documents into screens. The remaining data were only stored via the digitized scanner. Managers had no query capability, and no ability to model or modify the processing of the application data entered into the system.

This straight forward system posed four critical business problems. First, there was significant information loss in the method used to store data. Secondly, poor storage techniques required that large fields be available to store data (and remain blank if data didn't exist), and the attributes of the data stored in these field was relatively inaccessible because it could not be searched for specific values or conditions. Thirdly, the mandatory codification of data terms and rules for action into currently "available" numbers and letters (codes) implemented in the mainframe information system prevented the business from updating its profiles of preferred customers and further detailed analysis of risks. Finally, the previous system offered very limited ability to manage the flow of information among the various units in the organization, and improve the service levels and performance of the individual departments.

FINDINGS: USING CASE TO INTEGRATE ORGANIZATIONAL SYSTEMS

The problem solved through CASE integrative efforts is one of recomposing the segmented subsystems and environments of an organization into a totally managed organization responding to a complete environmental problem, uncertainty or demand. The recomposition is necessary for the differentiated components of the organization which may have adopted different goals and objectives.

The system utilized by the insurance company required a organizational data model and a relational database that allowed for creative use of the relationships to identify and solve data association business problems. The goal was to utilize the model to eliminate redundancy in entries in the database by avoiding storing complex rules that must be memorized by employees. The data model and database were constructed with the CASE tool. The entities and their attributes were associated with requirements, problems, and business solutions available to the firm.

The new system differs in data capture and front end editing when it is compared to the old process. Previously, underwriters reviewed applications for completeness, data was then entered into CICS screens, and scanned into the system as digitized paper. Repetitive editing was often continued on the data entered into the CICS screens, and frequent rejections for incomplete data or incorrect coding could delay the issuing of the policy from an application.

The optical system is a window product with GUI screens that has been customized to the organization's operations. The optical image no longer limits the access to the policy data to the one department that has been able to locate and maintain control of the image folder. It is now possible for the accounting department to access an image of the policy folder and all associated data on its screens while the claims personnel analyze a claim. The claims department may even obtain a printed copy of the documents in the folder. The system also maintains a "sticky" or comment capability that permits extensive notes and documentation to be attached to the information in the folder. This permits the staff to document actions, note missing information, alert other department to problems, and even make comments on special folders that are protected by levels of security.

The benefits from integrating the optical storage of information include speeding up the customer service activities of the organization, and reducing the telephone "tag" that develops between the company, customer, and sales agent for a policy. There is no repetitive edit of the data entered into the system that forces company representatives to call back to the agent or customer to obtain more information. The company has used this feature to maintain a high level of service to the agents who sell its policies.

The implementation of the basic system only begins to utilize the potential of the CASE tools and the integrated system for decision making support and management information. The insurance company analyzed in this paper documents the different levels of decision making support and management information support available form an integrated system. They levels vary from sophisticated expert and decision support system capabilities to analytical control of the distribution of the data in the system itself.

The expert system is a vendor supplied product written in C that has been customized with the company's underwriting rules. It contains some five hundred business rules for one line of business and one state. It is utilized as a primary logic editor for the application and will increase in rule numbers and capabilities as the business and systems mature. It operates in a OS/2 environment and uses DB2/2 as its relational database. It is updated with specific tables to maintain currency with the applications in use via an integrated Novell network and ORACLE database. Documentation for the system includes the rating information and related data that are stored in MS word documents. These documents include the underwriting manual, business rules for the company, filed ratings guidelines, and procedural manuals.

The outputs of this expert system flows through to the application processing in the organization. The system replaces the previous edit reports with system edits of inputs against the rules that are filed (with the state commission) in the organizations underwriting guidelines. The rules are incorporated into the screens used to collect the policy data. Validations occur on-line, and queries are issued for more information when it is required.

CONCLUSION: IMPACT ON ORGANIZATIONAL VARIABLES

Corporate culture is now captured and recorded by storing agreed to definitions, terms, and making these data available to all individuals in the company. This has been a previous problem for the company because the underwriters seem to disagree when presented with similar data. In effect, the system creates a level playing field for the customer. One is able to get concurrence on a specific policy, risk and rating problem. Definitions are frozen for the questions and the data that has been collected from the customer.

The system has radically changed the training requirements of the data entry processors by eliminating the requirements to use arbitrary codes to represent field values, and rules which state which codes to use under what circumstances. This position had taken from 3-4 months of training in processing, coding, and error handling. This has now been shortened because clerks do no have to memorize information that is presented to on the screen.

FUTURE DIRECTION: IMPLEMENTATION CONCERNS

The question of "how to change" is a primary concern of managers that face similar problems. It is far easier to describe what has happened rather than to proactively state how new development systems and environments can be implemented. For this organization, the change appears to have been both strategic and incremental. The managers indicated that the changes were a clear objective of the organization. However, many factors including the timing of the change, business goals, and technical motivations of managers were important. In addition, the availability of the CASE tools, GUI front end, database, expert system, business rules, and optical scanning and storage capability all appear critical. Managers should continually develop an ongoing approach to strategic information planning that involves comprehensive strategies for adopting CASE and other tools that upgrade organizational support capabilities.

Functional Requirements Elicitation AND Application Domain Modelling: A Knowledge-based Approach

Alessandro Cucchiarelli, Maurizio Panti, Salvatore Valenti
Computer Science Dept - University of Ancona - 60131 Ancona - Italy.
Silab@anvax2.cineca.it
Tel. +39 71 2204825

Executive Abstract

Introduction

Functional requirements are the description of the external behaviour (from the user point of view) of a software system, and their determination and description are recognised as "not trivial" activities performed through an interactive process, involving the end-user and the analyst. One of the major problems in this process comes from the lack of homogeneous knowledge between actors, both as concepts and as lexicon, acting as an obstacle in establishing the proper correspondence between the analyst's general knowledge on automation process and the specific application.

This paper presents a model for functional requirements elicitation through application domain modeling. In order to overcome the highlighted problem such an approach is aimed to: a) give capability to objectify the lexicon of actors; b) use extensively the actors' common knowledge and c) "really" involve the user in the definition of domain components. The ultimate goal of the assistant is to extract semi-formal description of functional requirements in terms of object and activities on them, defined as components of a specific application domain, and to permit an "user_driven" elicitation process.

The elicitation model

The elicitation model is founded on the definition of a functional requirement as "the need to carry out an activity on a set of objects defined in an application specific domain" so that the elicitation process stems from the definition of objects and activities, and the application domain model is defined in an incremental way through close co-operation between the user and the analyst by a refinement process of the former functional needs. Domain components are defined in terms of their structural properties (sub-components for objects, sets of sub-activities and related objects for activities) and the application domain is a collection of objects and activities that create, delete or modify them. This description, based on physical and procedural properties, permits a user-analyst interaction using components on which both raised a conceptual agreement .

The analyst's skill in domain description is represented as a knowledge base and is organised into two levels: that of stereotypes and that of application instances (istantiated stereotypes). Stereotypes are conceptual descriptions of domain components having common functional and/or structural properties, from which objects and activities in the application domain can be derived as instances. This knowledge organisation allows: a) to obtain a logical separation among general skills, related to sets of objects with the same characteristics, and particular ones, associated with instances of stereotypes and defined for a specific application domain, and b) the definition of a mechanism of unification by analogy (structural and/or functional) among entities (object and activities) described by the user and stereotypes known by the analyst.

The definition of the application domain starts from the user's needs, communicated to the system by the analyst who acts as interface between the formal language of the machine and the informal one of the user. New information allows the identification of new entities as instances of related stereotypes by an interactive process among user, analyst and system, directed to finding, among all known stereotypes in the system, the one that best fits the characteristics of the component under investigation. When both actors agree on the characteristics between a component in the user's world and a stereotype, a new component, resulted by filling the stereotype with information supplied by user, can be added to the application domain description.

The elicitation process goes on with a new request of information to the user, until all domain components, (i.e. all the objects or activities directly specified by the user or implied by them) are defined. Once the relevant activities and objects of the domain are known, the system is able to list all the functional requirements of the application in a semi_formal language.

Domain Representation: Objects & Activities

To implement the elicitation process, the object representation must provide: a) an homogeneous description of objects and stereotypes; b) the capability to grant a mechanism of classification by abstraction and c) the capability to link activities and objects. To satisfy these needs we adopted a description model based on semantic networks; in our framework, object stereotypes are in close correspondence with the concept of 'class', and objects with the concept of 'instances' of a class. In this way the link between a stereotype and an object is represented by a class-instance relation, so satisfying the requirements for a proper application of the association by analogy mechanism (an object is related to a given stereotype if the attributes of the former totally or partially match those of the latter). Moreover, the semantic model allows the realisation of two different types of classification by abstraction: generalisation/specification through the class-subclass relation IS-A; and aggregation/decomposition through the PART-OF relation.

Activities related to an object stereotype can be easily represented as assertional attributes inside the model of objects: the attribute defines the type of activity, while its instance maps the particular activity related to an object. The use of assertional attributes gives the possibility to obtain two interesting results: first, an activity is not a necessary property for an object classification, and the mapping process of an object into a stereotype is partially independent from its functional characteristics; second, the possibility to have multiple instances for a single attribute allows the functional specialisation of each domain object generated by a single stereotype.

The activity stereotype is modelled through the following template:

Name: <Activity name>
Objects: <Objects involved by the activity>
Preconditions: <Conditions that must be satisfied in order to carry on the activity >
Structure: <Sequence of the subtasks that compose the activity>

The Objects are classified into Input, Output and Instrumental. The Output Objects are those produced as the result of an activity, the Input and the Instrumental Objects are represented by those objects needed by the activity in order to produce the Output Objects: the difference between Input and Instrumental objects relying in the fact that the former must be specified when an activity is called, while the latter represent those objects that, although not belonging to one of the previously outlined classes, are still required to carry on an activity.

In this model a stereotype identifies a class of activities that can be applied to different objects (note that the preconditions have effect only on the structure of the objects involved in a given activity, and so they must not be regarded as conditions that need to be satisfied at run-time to apply an activity). The Structure slot contains the sequence of sub-activities required to carry it on.

The Model at Work

The described model has been used to implement a prototype of a knowledge-based system supporting a junior analyst in the task of functional requirements elicitation (SS). The prototype supports the construction of the application-domain model switching from objects' world into the activities' world and vice versa. The deduction chain is activated by an information need expressed by the user, as for instance from the well known example of a library system: <u>The system should allow the compilation of borrow cards for books.</u> (R1)

The SS starts the analysis of the sentence R1 to identify the objects involved (note that since we do not want to face the problems related to Natural Language Processing, a simple menu, containing all objects mentioned in the boot requirement and known to the system, can be listed) and asking the user to choose between <u>borrow-cards</u> and <u>books</u>. Selecting <u>borrow-card</u> the SS switch in the object world, looks for the stereotype of the <u>borrow-card</u> and activates a subtask for instantiating it (i.e. defining all its components). From the boot sentence R1 the system can infer that the <u>borrow-card</u> will contain data about books, while from the structure of the object <u>borrow-card</u> and interacting with the analyst the system can infer that the requester is a user. Now the stereotype of the object borrow-card is instantited into the object: borrow_card_for_books_from_users, and is added to the description of the application domain. Once the description of an object is complete, the SS starts to verify which activities are associated to such an object. In our example, once defined the object borrow_card_for_books_from_users, the SS looks in the boot requirement R1 to verify the presence of any of the activities associated with the object stereotype. Since the search is successful for the presence of the term <u>compilation</u> in the boot requirement the SS starts working in the activities' world, with the goal of instantiating the stereotype of the <u>compilation</u> activity. The description of the domain will become the input of a Requirement Generator that produces the associated functional requirements, as for instance:

-the system shall allow the borrow of books (R2.1);

-the borrow of a book will require the compilation of a card containing data about the book to be borrowed and about the user requesting the book (R2.2);

-data for a book will be found by searching by title a data store of books (R3.2).

Furthermore, the following requirements may be generated:

-the system shall accept new items in the data_store of books (R4.1);

-the system shall allow cancellation of an item in the data_store of books (R4.2);

-the system shall allow the search by title in the data_store of books (R4.3);

-the system shall allow the list of all items in the data_store of books (R4.4).

The requirements identified with numbers 4.1-4.4 are generated under the agreement between the user and the analyst on: the structure of the data_store object, its necessity in the considered domain and the assumption that the activities associated with the book data_store are add, erase, list and search.

Open Problems and Future Developments

In order to build a prototype that fully supports the analyst in the elicitation phase of the requirements engineering through the model described in this paper, we must face a number of issues. Firstly, a solution must be found to the problems arising when the user and the analyst do not agree on the structure of any object (and/or activity), or when an object (activity) is known to the user but is unknown to the analyst.

Furthermore, some mechanisms for the acquisition of the initial competence by the support system must be provided, and some protocols for the growing and consistence maintenance of such knowledge must be defined.

Product Comparisons of CASE Tools: Excelerator and IEF

Sung Y. Shin, Ali R. Salehnia, Zahra Alishiri, and Kwangsoo Ko

Computer Science Department
South Dakota State University
Brookings, SD 57007

College of Business and Public Adm.
University of Guam
Mangilao, Guam 96923

Executive Abstract

I. Introduction

There are many powerful CASE tools in widespread use, but the many user still have a hard time to find a suitable CASE tool for their project. This paper made comparisons between Execlerator and IEF CASE tools based on many different criteria. Those are two leading brand CASE Tools in the market. We also have researched on the criteria for comparing CASE tools. The result of the paper would be very important information for selecting a right CASE tool. It can also be used on feasibility study of CASE tools for a specific project.

CASE tools are used to improve the practice of designing and building computer software using structured methods. The ultimate goal of the CASE technology is to automate the entire software life cycle process with a set of integrated software tools. The CASE attitude is that software development and maintenance should be viewed as a formal, disciplined activity to enable more extensive correctness checking and automation of the process [8]. The only realistic way to increase software quality and productivity significantly is through automation. Gary Ray [1] quotes that "Productivity improvements of 50% are gained at the US patent and trademark office from use of an integrated CASE".

CASE tools that help from having a good word processor to actually doing code generation. It is also vitally important to have various diagrams to support systems development, and these diagrams, hierarchical tree structured diagrams, detailed procedural logic diagrams. and also screen and report layout, and proper user interfaces. CASE tools support wide range of structured methodologies, and design flexibility, hence software developer can choose the methods most appropriate for the design task at hand. In this paper, we have made a comparison of Excelerator and IEF based on wide range of structured methodologies and design flexibilities. Excelerator is one of the leading brand CASE tools in the market [8]. Excelerator is a mature product that delivers quality tools to help supports the system analysis and design phases of the software cycle [5]. IEF (Information Engineering Facility) is available on a variety of workstations and can generate systems to run on multiple platforms ranging from workstations to mainframes [7].

II. Criteria to compare the CASE tools

The idea behind CASE technology dramatically changes the way software systems are built now and will be built in the future. CASE technology provides following key advancements that need to be evaluated when looking at individual CASE tool packages.

— Software lifecycle phases supported
— Type of software development supported
— Languages supported
— Development methodologies supported
— Development platforms supported
— Operating systems supported
— Graphical user interface supported
— Network supported
— Database supported
— Reverse engineering features
— Repository/Data Dictionary support

Each of these criterias should be considered when evaluating a CASE tool. If almost all of those can be met it should mean that the CASE tool selected will provide an efficient, productive, hopefully user friendly environment that greatly aid the progress of the application being developed.

III. SUMMARY:

In comparison of Excelerator and IEF, we think Excelerator is one of the few products that offers extensive support for creating, maintaining, and printing documentation or presentation materials. The document graph and presentation graph types in Excelerator allow the developer to lay out and print report, entity descriptions, prototypes, and diagram and will automatically generate the finished document. While it has many strengths, it has some weakness. The product does not currently support shared access to objects or diagrams in a LAN environment, as do some of the other front-end CASE tools. Another weakness of Excelerator is that it uses a proprietary user interface and currently does not support viewing or updating of multiple objects on a single screen. The lack of Version control capabilities in Excelerator is also found. IEF is the most fully integrated CASE product that currently available for the IBM environment. IEF provides run-time system testing tools that uses the developed diagrams to view executing systems. IEF generates code based on the business model defined by the users. It checks for consistency at every stage to eliminate incomplete model specifications, compilation errors or system errors. IEF permits multiple develops to work on a project simultaneously without work overlap. IEF maintains extensive flexibility within the framework of Informative Engineering. Compare to Excelerator IEF is not having major limitation for the software development. But on the other hand, notice that IEF is much more expensive system than Excelerator.

The Importance of Cost Drivers Used in Cost Estimation Models: Perceptions of Project Managers

Girish Subramanian
School of Business Administration
Pennsylvania State University, Harrisburg

Steven Breslawski
School of Business and Economics
State University of New York, College at Brockport

Cost estimation models such as COCOMO ([13],[14]) Bailey-Basili Model [6], Function Points [4] use variables believed to influence the cost of software development in arriving at effort and cost estimates for the software project. These variables are often referred to as cost drivers. Examples of such cost drivers include programmer experience, software complexity, required reliability among others. The choice of cost drivers to be factored in the estimation model is decided by the model developers. For example, Boehm [1981] uses 15 cost drivers in the COCOMO intermediate model which are not entirely identical to the cost drivers used in Bailey-Basili model. These estimation models typically arrive at a nominal estimate based solely on program size in lines of code or function points. This nominal estimate is refined based on the values or ratings for the cost drivers.

Several studies on variables influencing productivity have each arrived at their own set of variables that have significant influences on software development productivity. These studies include Walston-Felix study [33], and the ITT study [32]. Other studies examined the influence of one variable on productivity such as the influence of team size [31] or structured programming [17]. Jones [1986] and Conte et al [1986] point to the problems associated with the productivity measure used in most of these studies which is the size in lines of code / development effort.

We feel that it is necessary to assess the opinions of project managers, drawn from different organizations and project environments, on the importance of these cost drivers in estimating effort and cost for software projects. It will be interesting to contrast the results of such a study with the set of cost drivers that were found to influence productivity in the productivity studies and the cost drivers used in the estimation models.

Through the use of a survey research method, this study obtains the opinions of project managers on the importance of the cost drivers. This study will identify cost drivers that are considered important by managers in different organizations, projects, and application areas. In addition, this study will provide a more recent report of the importance of cost drivers as perceived by project managers.

COST DRIVERS USED IN PRODUCTIVITY STUDIES AND ESTIMATION MODELS

Individual capability [34], programmer experience ([13],[30]), computer response time [30], structured programming [17], and hardware constraints [13] are some of the variables or cost drivers found significant in their influence on software development productivity. Walston and Felix [1977] identified a set of 29 variables significant in their influence on productivity. Eight product variables and five project variables are identified as the list of variables with the greatest impact on productivity in the ITT study [32].

The cost estimation model developed at Systems Development Corporation [27] uses fourteen cost drivers. Bailey and Basili [1981] use four major attributes and 21 variables in their estimation model developed on NASA projects. The COCOMO intermediate model [13] uses four attributes and fifteen cost drivers as shown in table 1. The COPMO model

Table 1: Variables used in COCOMO model

Product variables.
Required Software Reliability Database Size Product Complexity
Computer Variables.
Execution time constraint Main storage constraint Virtual machine volatility Computer turnaround time
Personnel variables.
Analyst capability Applications Experience Programmer capability Virtual machine experience Programming language experience
Project variables.
Modern programming practices Use of software tools Required development schedule

[31] studies the effect of team size on development effort. The function points method has an adjustment scheme to factor in the use of reused code and software complexity. Empirical studies ([24], [26]) on the effectiveness of cost estimation models also examine the effectiveness of cost drivers.

BACKGROUND ON THE SURVEY RESEARCH METHOD

A survey questionnaire was designed to obtain information about the software project, project manager, and the importance of cost drivers. The survey questionnaire obtained the following information among other things :

a. Project manager's experience in project segments, and application areas.

b. Project manager's rating of the importance of a set of variables in estimating development effort on a scale of "very important" {1} to "not important" {5}. This set of variables are chosen based on the survey of the literature presented in the earlier section and by incorporating recent technological developments such as CASE tools. Care is taken to omit duplicate variables and variables similar in meaning used in the studies covered in the survey section. This set of variables are presented in table 2.

In obtaining this information, the project manager is assured complete confidentiality. The survey was administered to a small, random sample of project managers in the Northeast U. S. A. The survey instrument was mailed out to about 140 software professionals who are members of the ACM Special Interest Group on Software Engineering (SIGSOFT). Since the unit of analysis for this study are project managers, the instrument clearly stated that software professionals complete the questionnaire only if they have managed software projects or are managing projects. However, these professionals were requested to pass on the surveys to project managers in their organization if they were not project managers. The survey administration was followed up with a reminder and a follow up administration. Thirty two project manager responses were useable for this study. Some software professionals returned the surveys back indicating their unwillingness or unsuitability for participation in this survey. There are two reasons indicated in the literature that works against the collection of a large sample. The reasons are :

a. lack of systematic and detailed data collection for software projects in the U. S. A., and

b. the reluctance to divulge project related data due to competitive reasons even when confidentiality is promised [19].

These reasons could also explain the small sample size associated with this study. It should be noted that this survey requires managers to provide data for these projects. This data, however, is not used in this paper and is intended for future research work. In the tables below, some background information on the experience of the project managers in project segments and application areas is provided. Number of managers with experience in project segments and application areas.

RESULTS OF THE SURVEY

The cost drivers presented in table 2 were rated by the project managers on a scale of "1 - Very Important" to "5 -

Table 2: Variables used in this survey

Applications Variables	People Variables
1. Development team's understanding of application 2. Development team's rapport with users 3. User Participation in requirements specification 4. Novelty of requirements 5. Legal and statutory requirements	1. Project manager's knowledge of application 2. Analyst knowledge of application 3. Programmers knowledge of application 4. Project team composition 5. Project manager's experience 6. Analyst experience 7. Programmers experience with language 8. Programmers experience with operating system
Project variables	Product variables
1. Use of program generators 2. Binding time schedule for completion 3. Changes in requirements 4. Use of fourth generation languages/productivity tools 5. Use of software engineering tools like CASE tools 6. Design method followed e.g., life-cycle, prototyping 7. Use of structured programming 8. Use of object-oriented programming 9. Use of chief programmer team 10 Use of design and code inspections 11 Standards at the site constraint	1. Required reliability 2. Software complexity 3. Total lines of code 4. Percentage of reused code 5. Data base size
	Computer variables
	1. Response time constraint 2. Distributed processing 3. Execution time constraint 4. Main storage

Table 3 and 4: Number of managers with experience in project segments and application areas.

Project segments	No.
Government-non-military	2
Government-military	7
Business	18
Scientific	11
Other	4
	42

Applications	No.
Expert Systems/AI	3
Scientific	12
Real-Time	10
Systems Software	10
DSS	10
Communications	6
Transaction Processing	9
Report Generation	7
Other	5
	72

Table 5:"Very Important" variables

Very Important variables *Experience and Knowledge of the Development Team*	Mean	S.D.
1. Development team's understanding of application	1.258	0.63
2. Analyst knowledge of application	1.393	0.49
3. Analyst experience	1.821	0.55

Table 6: "Important" Variables

Experience and knowledge of the team	Mean	S.D.
4. Project manager knowledge of application	1.8	0.85
5. Project manager experience	2.0	0.81
6. Programmers knowledge of application	2.0	0.85
Development team's interaction with users		
7. Development team's rapport with users	2.367	0.77
8. User participation in requirements specification	1.667	0.80
Development team's job satisfaction		
9. Project team composition	2.0	1.11
10. Morale of project personnel	1.93	1.11
11. Compensation of project personnel	2.91	1.04
Project constraints/environment		
12. Binding time schedule for completion	2.27	1.23
13. Changes in requirements	1.53	0.86
14. Required reliability	1.90	1.06
15. Software complexity	1.87	0.94
16. Response time constraint	2.20	1.06
17. Execution time constraint	2.17	1.00
18. Distributed processing	2.41	1.08
Software Development tools		
19. Use of fourth generation languages/ productivity tools	2.70	1.07
20. Use of software engineering tools like CASE tools	2.46	1.14
21. Design method followed e.g., life-cycle, prototyping	2.43	1.14
Experience in programming		
22. Programmers experience with language	2.13	0.87
23. Programmers experience with operating system	2.44	0.89
Software development and programming discipline		
24. Use of structured programming	2.10	1.21
25. Use of design and code inspections	2.35	1.01
26. Standards at the site	2.17	0.99

Not Important" with the mid point of the scale standing for "Important". Statistically significant differences from the mid point of the scale helps identify variables that are considered as "very important" by the project managers who participated in the survey. The statistic used for this purpose is :

$$Z = [Mean - 3] / \text{standard deviation.}$$

The magnitude (without sign) of the difference between mean and 3 is used to arrive at the value of Z. If Z is greater than 1.96, then the variable is "very important" at p=0.05. Similarly, statistically significant differences from the end point of the scale "5 - Not Important" helps identify variables that are considered "important" by the project managers. The statistic used for this purpose is : $Z_1 = [Mean - 5] /$ standard deviation.

Again, the magnitude of the difference between the mean and 5 is the value of Z_1. If Z_1 is greater than 1.96, then the variable is "important" at p=0.05. The "very important" and "important" variables are presented in tables 5 and 6. Seven major factors emerge as the major determinants of cost and productivity in software development.

Experience and knowledge of the development team.

All the three "very important" variables emphasize the importance of the analyst's knowledge and experience in addition to the development team's understanding of the application. The project manager's knowledge of the application and experience along with the programmers knowledge of the application also emerge as "important" variables. These results confirm Kendall and Lamb's [1977] assertion that "management can have more influence on productivity of the programming staff than any technology now in use". Further, the higher the programmer's perception of the manager's and analyst's knowledge, the higher the productivity of programmers [22]. Boehm and Papaccio [1990] also point to the employment of the best software people as the most significant influence on software costs. Jeffery [1987] reports in his empirical study that good experience and positive attitude of the software development staff reduces the cost of adding extra staff to projects.

Development team's interaction with users.

The development team's rapport with users and the user participation in the requirements specifications phase are the two variables that stress the importance of the interaction of the development team with the users. User participation in requirements specification is needed as "the requirements document has a unique role in the development of a software system : It is the basis for communication among customers, users, designers, and implementers of the system, and unless it represents an informed consensus of these groups, the project is not likely to be a success" [36].

Development team's job satisfaction.

The morale and compensation of the development team reflects the job satisfaction level of the development team and influences the productivity of software development. The composition of the development team would influence the satisfaction level of the team and thus affect the development productivity. Basili and Reiter [1981] found that chief programmer teams performed better on a number of programming metrics than individuals or ad hoc teams which adds support to the importance of the team composition. The cost estimation models often fail to factor these human resources variables and issues. This observation is in line with Bartol and Martin [1982]'s conclusion that more research still needs to be done in the areas of motivation, work groups, and leadership in software development. While it is difficult for the estimation models to account for these subjective and qualitative variables, the project manager needs to consider these issues in assessing the cost of software development or the productivity levels in projects.

Project constraints/environment.

The variables that constrain the software project and considered important by project managers are requirement changes, binding time schedule, required reliability, software complexity, response time constraint, distributed processing, and execution time constraint. As these variables are largely fixed features of the software product and not management controllable, these variables are referred to as project constraints/environment. Qualitative comments of the project managers does indicate the presence of requirement changes and binding time schedules in software projects. Boehm and Papaccio [1988] do note that requirements volatility (changes) is an important and neglected source of cost savings and control. Response times have a significant effect on programmer productivity as confirmed in [30]. Requirements volatility is included in the COCOMO detailed model. Required reliability, software complexity, response time constraint, and execution time constraint are also part of the COCOMO intermediate model.

Software development tools.

Fourth generation and productivity tools, Computer-Aided Software Engineering (CASE) tools, and design method employed are considered important in their influence on development effort, cost, and productivity. This result confirms the belief of the project managers in the use of appropriate development tools to effectively build software. In their comparison of software development practices in the American and Japanese companies, Cusumano and Kemerer [1990] report the use of software development tools as indicated in table 7. Other examples of software development tools are process construction systems ([8], [20]); software standard checkers and other quality assurance functions ([12], [28]); and requirements and design consistency checkers ([5], [8], [11]).

Experience in programming.

The programmers experience in the language and operating systems is considered important in its influence on develop-

TABLE 7: *Software development tools*

| Analysis/Design |
| Design support |
| Automated Flow-chart |

| Coding |
| Utilities (Domain-specific editing, |
| Specialized compilers) |
| Environmental Management |
| Data Management |
| Code generators |
| Reuse/Program libraries |

| Testing |
| Test/Debug |
| Simulators |
| Performance testing |

| Other tools |
| Documentation support |
| Schedule tracking |
| Problem tracking |
| Metrics collection |

ment effort and productivity. Project managers definitely need the right people with the right programming experience for effective software development. Programming experience is especially valuable in countering the "90 % syndrome" in software project management as reported in [3].

Software development and programming discipline.

Structured programming, design and code inspections, and project development standards are considered important by project managers in their influence on development effort and cost. Cusumano and Kemerer [1990] report an increased use of debugging and testing tools in software projects in the U.S. and Japan which adds support to the importance of design and code inspections. Software engineering project standards [SEPS] is considered important as it is needed to establish the development methods to be used; the specific requirements, design, and coding techniques and languages; the verification, validation and testing approach; the form and type of records to be kept and controlled; and the official documents that should be produced [16].

CONCLUSION

In capturing the perceptions of project managers on the importance of cost drivers used in current estimation models, this study identifies seven major factors into which the twenty six variables considered "very important" or "important" are classified. These variables represent an exhaustive set of "very important" or "important" variables across different project segments and application areas. So, a subset of these variables may be important in any particular project segment or application area.

Project managers need to closely monitor and control these

seven factors in order to control costs and effectively manage projects. Most of these factors are already incorporated in current estimation models or are found important by productivity studies. The factors less emphasized by these models and studies are the development team's job satisfaction, software development tools used, and software development and programming discipline. Future models and studies have to emphasize the importance of these factors in their work.

A subset of variables from this exhaustive list of twenty six can be chosen by the project manager or model developer based on their understanding of the importance of each of these variables in their influence on cost or productivity of the software project under development. In addition, each of these factors can be captured by estimation models by including the subset of variables for which data is available. Thus, data availability will not be a deterrent to the use of cost estimation tools and techniques.

Field studies examining the impact of each of these factors on cost and productivity in different project segments and application areas need to be done. Specifically, simulation based studies ([1], [2]) enjoy merit as they provide insights into the software development process.

REFERENCES

[1]Abdel-Hamid, Tarek A. "The Dynamics of Software Project Staffing : A System Dynamics Based Simulation Approach", *IEEE Transactions on Software Engineering*, V 15, N 2, February 1989, 109-119.

[2]Abdel-Hamid, Tarek. A., "The Economics of Software Quality Assurance : A Simulation-Based Case Study", *MIS Quarterly*, September 1988, 395-411.

[3]Abdel-Hamid, Tarek A. "Understanding the "90% Syndrome" in Software Project Management : A Simulation-Based Case Study", *The Journal of Systems and Software*, Vol 8, 1988, pp 319-330.

[4]Albrecht, Allan J. and John E. Gaffney, Jr. " Software Function, Source Lines of code, and development effort prediction : A software science validation ", *IEEE Transactions on Software engineering*, SE-9, No. 6, November, 1973, pp 639-648.

[5]Alford, M. W. "A Requirements Engineering Methodology for Real-Time Processing Requirements", *IEEE Transactions on Software Engineering*, V 3, Jan 1977, 60-68.

[6]Bailey, J.W. and V.R. Basili. "A meta-model for software development resource expenditures", *Proceedings of the Fifth international conference on Software Engineering*, 1981, 107-116.

[7]Barstow, D. R. "Domain-specific Automatic Programming", *IEEE Transactions on Software Engineering*, V 11, Nov 1985, 1321-1336.

[8]Barstow, D. R, Shrobe, H. and Sandewall, E. *Interactive Programming Environments*, McGraw-Hill, New York, 1984.

[9]Bartol, K.M. and Martin, D. C. "Managing Information Systems Personnel: A Review of the Literature and Managerial Implications", *MIS Quarterly/Special Issue*, 1982, 49-70.

[10]Basili, V. R. and Reiter, R. W. "A Controlled Experiment Quantitatively Comparing Software Development Approaches", *IEEE Transactions on Software Engineering*, V 7, N 3, 1981, 299-320.

[11]Bell, T. E., Bixler, D. C., and Dyer. M. E. "An Extendable Approach to Computer-Aided Software Requirements Engineering", *IEEE Transactions on Software Engineering*", Jan 1977, 49-59.

[12]Boehm, B. H., Brown. J. R., Kaspar. H., Lipow. M., MacLeod. E. J. and Merritt, M. J., *Characteristics of Software Quality*, Amsterdam, The Netherlands : North-Holland, 1978.

[13]Boehm, B.W. *Software Engineering Economics*, Englewood Cliffs, NJ : Prentice-Hall, 1981.

[14]Boehm, B.W. "Software Engineering Economics", *IEEE Transactions on Software Engineering*, SE-10, N 1, Jan 1984, pp 4 - 21.

[15]Boehm, B.W., and Papaccio, P. N. "Understanding and Controlling Software Costs", *IEEE Transactions on Software Engineering*, V 14, N 10, October 1988, pp 1462 - 1477.

[16]Branstad, M. and Powell, P. B. "Software Engineering Project Standards", *IEEE Transactions on Software Engineering*, V 10, N 1, January 1984, 73-78.

[17]Brooks, W. D. "Software Technology Payoff - Some Statistical Evidence", *Journal of Systems and Software*, V 2, 1981, 3-9.

[18]Conte, S.D., Dunsmore, H.E. and Shen, V.Y. *Software Engineering metrics and models*, Benjamin/Cummings Publishing Co, CA, 1986.

[19]Cusumano, M. A. and Kemerer, C. F. "A Quantitative Analysis of U. S. and Japanese Practice and Performance in Software Development", *Management Science*, V 36, N 11, Nov. 1990, 1384-1406.

[20]Feldman, S. I. "MAKE-A Program for Maintaining Computer Programs", *UNIX Programmers' Manual*, V 9, April 1979, 255-265.

[21]Jeffery, D. R. "A Software Development Productivity Model for MIS Environments", *Journal of Systems and Software*, V 7, 1987, 115-125.

[22]Jeffery, D.R. and Lawrence, M. J. "Managing Programming Productivity", *The Journal of Systems and Software*, V 6, N 1, 1985.

[23]Jones, Capers. *Programming Productivity*, New York, Mc Graw-Hill, 1986.

[24]Kemerer, Chris F. "An empirical validation of software cost estimation models", *Communications of the ACM*, V30, N5, May 1987, pp 416-429.

[25]Kendall, R. C., and Lamb, E. C. "Management Perspectives on Programs, Programming and Productivity", presented at Guide 45, Atlanta, GA, November 1977, 201-211.

[26]Kitchenham, Barbara. A. and Taylor, N.R. "Software project development cost estimation", *Journal of Systems and Software*, V5, N4, Nov 1985, 267-278.

[27]Nelson, E.A. "Management development handbook for the estimation of computer programming costs", *AD-A648750, Systems Development Corporation*, October 31, 1966.

[28]Sneed, H. M. and Marey, A. "Automated Software Quality Assurance", *IEEE Transactions on Software Engineering*, V 11, Sept. 1985, 909-916.

[29]Teichroew, D. and Hershey, E. A. III, "PSL/PSA: A Computer-Aided Technique for Structured Documentation and Analysis of Information Processing Systems", *IEEE Transactions on Software Engineering*, V 3, Jan 1977, 41-48.

[30]Thadani, A. J. "Factors Affecting Productivity during Application Development", *IBM Systems Journal*, V 23, 1984, 19-35.

[31]Thebaut, S.M. and V.Y. Shen. "An analytic resource model for large-scale software development", *Information Processing and Management*, V 20, N 1-2, 1984, pp 293-315.

[32]Vosburgh, J, et. al. "Productivity Factors and Programming Environments", *Proceedings of the Seventh International Conference on Software Engineering*, 1984, 143-152.

[33]Walston, C.E. and C.P. Felix. "A method of programming measurement and estimation", *IBM Systems Journal*, V 16, N 1, 1977, pp 54-73.

[34]Wang, A. S. "The Estimation of Software Size and Effort : An Approach Based on the Evolution of Software Metrics". *Doctoral Dissertation*, Department of Computer Science, Purdue University, August 1984.

[35]Williams, R. D. "Managing the Development of Reliable Software", in *Proceedings of the International Conference on reliable Software, IEEE/ACM*, April 1975, 3-8.

[36]Yeh, R. T., Zave, P., Conn, A. P., and Cole, G. E. "Software Requirements : New Directions and Perspectives" in *Handbook of Software Engineering*, (eds.) Vick, C. R. and Ramamoorthy, C. V., Van Nostrand Reinhold, New York, N. Y., 1985, 519-543.

Section Fourteen

Multimedia Technologies

An Integrated Multimedia System (IMS) for Plastic Parts Price Quoting at High-Tech Companies

Dr. Kuriakose Athappilly
Department of Business Information System
Hearth College of Business
Kalamazoo, MI 49008
Ph: (616) 387-5405   Office

Executive Abstract

In many plastic molding companies, price quoting often becomes inaccurate and time consuming. Since the survival and success of these companies primarily depend on accurate quoting improvements in quoting through the application of advanced computer aided system are deemed to be a necessity today. A successful attempt has been undertaken by a high-tech company in Vicksburg, Michigan to come up with an integrated computer system that substantially reduces the cycle time for the introduction of new product. The architecture of this Integrated Multimedia System (IMS) consists of two layers: 1. The front line user modules consisting of four sub systems: i) the Neural Networks, ii) Expert Systems, iii) Multimedia Computing, and iv) Communication Networks and 2. the rear line support modules consisting of typical MIS capabilities which provides access to a i) data base sub system, ii) model base sub system and iii) a sub system for procedural languages. This paper explains the context and development of this system.

Introduction

This is an integrated system to help high-tech injection molding supplier companies i) quote prices accurately and efficiently, ii) reduce the cycle time, iii) upgrade quality, and thereby iv) bring about a healthy relationship between the suppliers and Original Equipment Companies (OEMs) for the development of plastic parts.

For introduction of new products, **time, cost, and quality** are deemed to be the critical success factors. Of which the most significant is the first one, the cycle time - the time taken from the inception of an original idea to the entry of the product into the market place. During this cycle time, the most critical process is prototyping, the process of translating the newly defined concept into the desired reality. For, the sooner the prototype, the earlier is the entry and penetration of the new product into the market.

Cost is an essential factor for the OEMs as well as the suppliers. If quoted high, the suppliers loose their customers, and if quoted low, they loose money from their pocket. The quotes, therefore, should reflect accurate costs in today's competitive environment.

Quality of the product depends on the supplier's adherence to the OEM's specifications. This adherence is possible only through an effective communication, enhanced through audio/visual representation, especially in the context of new product development which will require several engineering changes.

But the pivotal factor of the entire process of product development is a dynamic price quoting - a factor whose critical importance is often not fully understood. Hence the present system is developed taking the price quoting as the most central issue to be addressed.

By making the price quoting process most efficient, accurate, and dynamic, the critical success factors, such as time, cost and quality can be addressed more systematically and successfully. The present system, IMS, is developed to address issues and bottlenecks related to the aforesaid factors and thereby make the entire process of product development most efficient and effective to the satisfaction of both the suppliers and the OEMs.

Bottlenecks in Product Development Process

Engineering changes and Lack of proper and effective documentation: The most unpleasant bottleneck occurs when engineering changes are deemed to be necessary after the initial specifications are defined and designed. However, for major product developments, it is almost impossible to avoid engineering changes. Engineering changes involve more time, labor and cost, and as a result, substantial variations from the initial quote occur necessarily . In the rush of making the desired part according to changing specifications, many a time, CAD operators fail to document these variations properly. Consequently, full accountability of these changes is not known to either the supplier or the customer. This situation leads to disputes over cost figures and the relationship becomes bitter for both the parties. Needless to say, in the long run both lose.

Lack of efficient and timely communication and the delay in the production process: Another bottle neck is the delay of the production process in the absence of fast and effective communication between the suppliers and OEMs about the nature of changes in the design and other related factors of change. Usually several visits take place to confirm and reconfirm the engineering changes and to settle the disputes over cost figures. and the waiting periods before these meetings for settlements causing substantial delay to the development process.

Mistrust: A serious byproduct results from these bottle-necks. Mistrust! The customer, not having the actual documentation and timely report is in no way comfortable with the huge bill that comes after the engineering changes. The suppliers believe that any change is double the task, undoing what is done and reworking on most everything. They suspect the intention of the customer. Thus both are on their guard not to be exploited by the other. A totally unhealthy partnership!

It is, therefore, almost imperative to develop a system that makes provision for an accurate documentation, effective communication and a healthy relationship between the suppliers and the customers in order to reduce cycle time and cost and enhance quality.

Background Information

Ronningen/Emergent Technologies Group, located in Vicksburg, Michigan, is a high-tech company catering to the Fortune 100 and 500 OEM companies. It is one of the first 13 companies in the world which introduced fully integrated CAD/CAM capabilities for product development. Ronningen's forte is its fast track product development through fully integrated CAD/CAM capabilities. Speed and quality are their motto. Mr. Jon Eickhoff envisioned that the time taken for price quoting could considerably be reduced by employing a well developed expert system. The system was successfully developed by team of four computer scientists headed by the author of this paper. The system was known as Marty's Quest (Quoting Expert System), a name after the Mr. Marty Eickhoff, the Vice President of Manufacturing, who used to make the quotes prior to the implementation of the expert system. This was the first module of the integrated system. It turned out to be a highly successful project - "**a three hundred percent success!**" according to the Mr. Jon Eickhoff, the CEO at Ronningen. The project leader later suggested the enhancement of the present system by incorporating other relevant modules into it. Hence is the configuration of the present system.

Rationale for the Enhanced System

The enhanced system takes into account all the issues and concerns mentioned previously. The new system once developed properly the author believes, could become the industry standard for the next decade. The system described here further will reduce the cycle time for prototype development from months and weeks according to today's standards of operation to tao or three days. It will allow the suppliers adhere to the OEM's specification easily and exactly even with engineering changes, through dynamic communication through interactive multimedia capabilities. Also, it will dispel the shady areas of re-engineering costs. More importantly, it will create an environment for a partnership between the OEMs and the suppliers for the entire product development process.

Architecture and Functionalities

The architecture of this integrated system consists of two layers. The front line user modules consist of four sub systems: the Neural Networks, Expert Systems, Multimedia Computing, and Communication Networks and the rear line support modules consist of typical MIS which provides access to a data base sub system, model base sub systems and a sub system for procedural languages.

Briefly, the functions of each component are as follows:

1) **The Neural Networks System** categorizes the quotes according to the pre-specified parameters. The parameters include complexity level, the desired cycle time, the material category, and the decried service category (samples only or samples cum pre-production)

2) **The Expert System** does the actual quoting according to the specified conditions of the customer and the parameters set by the neural networks system. The quoting process is an exercise of both quantitative and qualitative decision making process. The people who quote rely heavily on the wealth of knowledge they accumulated over years of experience in the field. The expert systems aptly portrays the expertise of the senior vice of manufacturing who used to do the quoting for Ronningen. Thus, the neural networks and the expert systems are complementary units which share the task of quoting

3) **The Multimedia Computing System** is an interactive system in two respects: A) At the suppliers cite, it accomplishes two major tasks: i) It interacts with the expert system and neural networks systems on one end and the CAD system on the other. Thus it combines the quote received from the ES/NN with the design created by CAD and adds its own audio/visual information describing the quote and design, ii) It dynamically records all the engineering changes that take place after the initial quote. Many a time, for large projects particularly, several engineering changes take place before it is finalized. Often, these changes are the reasons for "bad business deals." The time, labor and cost incurred due to the engineering changes are often not properly recorded. The engineers, busy with their designing process to make sure that they comply with the customers demand, frequently fail to record the labor they put in. The accounting department usually gets data pertaining to the extra time and labor almost at the end of the project, that too inaccurate. Even with accurate recording of the time and labor spent, it is hard to convince the customer of the accountability of the time and labor. With multimedia, every change can be recorded, with changed design and added time and labor for it. Instantly, the data can be transferred to the accounting department for computing the cost figures attached to it. Thus, the Multimedia provides a verifiable, accurate information about the changes that are made along with each change in drawing, time needed for it, and the kind of labor that went along with that. Even, in dispute, it becomes a verifiable legal document. B) It transmits this integrated information to the Communication Network System.

4) **The Communication Network** carries the package of

information to the OEM which has the other end of the interactive Multimedia station. Thus the multimedia system provides a live audio/visual representation of the proposed part for development. Also, it opens a communication channel between the OEM and the suppliers with the real part in front of their respective screen. It saves time, travel, and cost to the OEM, and adds efficiency and effectiveness to the entire process of price quoting and part design, and consequently to the prototyping and pre-production services and early market penetration.

Once the idea is proposed by the prospective OEM, the NN takes about 10 minutes to classify the quoting request. Then the ES makes the quote in about 20 minutes. The CAD engineers complete the design in day or two. The design is immediately transferred to the MMC for the addition of audio/visual information to go along with the part design. The quote and design along with the audio/visual explanation material explaining the quote and the design are then transferred electronically to the MMC at the desk top of the concerned engineers at the OEM's cite. Typically, this takes weeks and sometimes months according to present day technology. But with the new system this is done in three to four days!

Advantages

A tremendous reduction of cycle time for the introduction of a new product from months and weeks to days!

A verifiable record of all engineering changes and its accountability!

Possibility for a dynamic team approach between the customer and the supplier for product development process!

A Potent catalyst for continued customer relationship - no more the bad business deals!

Multimedia Engineering Information System for Operation and Maintenance of Power Transmission Network

K.C.K.Law, H.H.S.Ip, F.Y.Mong, H.T.F.Wong
Image Computing Group,
Department of Computer Science,
City Polytechnic of Hong Kong
83 Tat Chee Avenue, Kowloon, Hong Kong
Tel:(852)7888618, Fax:(852)7888614, Email:cskckl@cphkvx.cphk.hk

INTRODUCTION

A multimedia based system for handling engineering information for the power transmission industry is presented. The project is collaborated with China Light and Power Limited (CLP), a large power generating, transmission and distributing company in Hong Kong which provide valuable engineering data, technical comments and advices. The aims is to allow efficient and accurate access to necessary engineering information to carry out project reviews, commissioning, operation, maintenance and repair, training and also be able to provide necessary preliminary engineering data for emergency situations. The engineering information to support the operation in the transmission industry consists of :

(1) Technical drawings on paper with sizes range from A0 to A4 include information such as : (a) Detail design drawings for engineering component, (b) Schematic drawings, and (c) Technical drawings such as electrical circuit drawing, cable segments, hydraulic drawings and land profile diagrams for cable segments.

(2) Engineering Data which are directly related to elements in the circuits provide identity of the equipments that include, (a) Identification reference, (b) Rating and capacity of the equipment, (c) Nominal settings, (d) Physical location, (e) Technical reference, and (f) Other information related to supplier, component availability in store, preventive maintenance data etc..

(3) Photographs and Images which are widely used as (a) A way of identifying a needed spare part from store or outside purchase, location identification of underground cables and overhead line sites, (b) To allow the frame by frame recorded sequence for a engineering assembly to aid maintenance operations, and (c) To give information for the engineers on access to maintenance in substations and overhead lines.

(4) Sound recording and video sequence

The use of sound recording describing the operation together with video images to demonstrate the sequence provide a powerful means of training engineer to perform maintenance and repair on existing and new equipments. Sound annotations can also provide help and warning for certain critical operations.

Currently all these information are mostly paper based

information that bear high risk of damage, losing, misfiling and very time consuming for retrieval and cross referencing between different information are not possible. The speedy access to engineering information are especially critical for urgent repairs and during non-office hours where staff support is not available. Training new engineers for maintenance operations also become time consuming.

LOGICAL STRUCTURE OF THE ENGINEERING DOCUMENT

The logical structure of engineering information provides a framework for organizing the structure and contents of the data. The structure also represent the logical sequence of accessing the engineering information. Figure 1 shows the information tree representing the types of media and the node contents.

Circuit representing two main connecting points which usually are two main sub-stations in the transmission network. The circuit information generally consists of: (i) substations, (ii) cable systems, (iii) over-head-lines. Each circuit

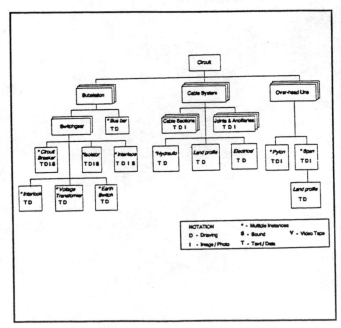

Figure 1: Logical Structure of Engineering Information

can have multiple instances of the components such as a number of substations, a number of cable segments connecting the substations and one or more over-head line segments. Substations with sub-node switchgear with leaf-nodes include circuit breaker, voltage transformer, isolator, interface, earth switch, interlock and bus bar. Cable systems with leaf-nodes include cable sections, joints and ancillaries, hydraulic, land profile, electrical. Over-head line with leaf-nodes include pylon, span and land profile.

MULTIMEDIA DOCUMENT PRESENTATION

Based on the design studies, a prototype multimedia engineering information presentation sub-system has been developed on a PC platform with additional multimedia functional boards.

Circuits can be searched and selected through the embedded Structured Query Language (SQL) from the database storage. The prototype presentation system directly interfaces and retrieves information from the database. The procedures of accessing the engineering information is programmed logically the same as the paper based searching and retrieval operations.

Microsoft Windows provides a flexible user interface of accessing engineering information. Multi-Document-Interface (MDI) feature in windows allows different media in the information set to be presented as child windows or icons within a parent frame window that also allows control such as moving, re-sizing of the child windows. Hyper-text concept is applied in the system which allows user to link and browse various parts of the associated information in a non-linear manner. The use of hyper-text concept greatly aided the clarity on the presentation system especially for first-time user and greatly reduced the time it take to familiarize with the system.

Figure 2 shows a screen containing a typical Circuit information :

(i) Circuit window - a schematic representation for the circuit connecting sub-stations TYA, TYS and KCA, with three underground cable systems and one overhead cable system. The underground Cable System is highlighted.

(ii) Cable System window - a schematic representation for the highlighted underground cable section, a cable section with related joint information are highlighted.

(iii) Joint, Hydraulic, Hydraulic and Land Profile, Landscape #1, Landscape #2 windows

CONCLUSIONS

The results of applying multimedia technology to support the operational information for the CLP engineers has been discussed. The benefits of adopting such a system for a power transmission system greatly benefits in the areas of project reviews, commissioning, operation, maintenance and repair, emergency response, administration, and training.

Engineering information are presented using the prototype system. Favourable responses has been received from engineers on the prototype. It is concluded that,

(i) The system can be used to display complex related engineering information effectively.

(ii) The system can search and retrieve these information far more efficient with more informative and accurate information presented by the prototype than the currently used manual method.

(iii) Other supporting sub-systems (such as the database, document construction sub-systems) are needed to verify the design and to support pilot scale implementation of such a system at CLP.

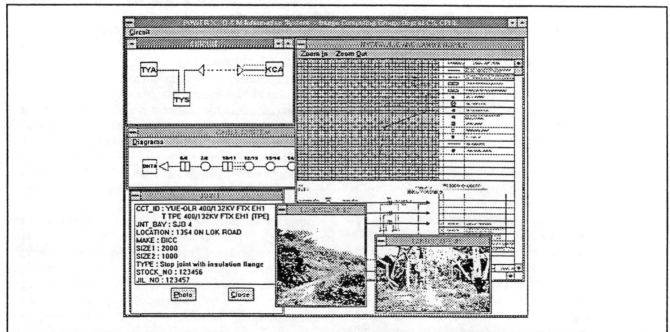

Figure 2   A typical screen of circuit information with details on a cable segment

Multimedia Computing: A Forward Looking Retrospective Analysis

Dr. S. Reisman

Department of Management Science/Information Systems

California State University

Fullerton, CA 92634

OFFICE: (714) 773-3325

FAX: (714) 281-6742

Executive Abstract

Multimedia computing has a history that reaches back almost 30 years, almost to when the industry of computing was just beginning. Multimedia is not new, but rather the natural evolution of the computer, an evolution that by the beginning of the 21st Century will be almost one half century old. If MMC is a phase in the evolution of computing, then a study of its history can provide insight into the future of computing.

A REVIEW OF THE PAST

In 1964, IBM developed the IBM 1500 System, a computer-assisted instruction (CAI) system. Later in the 1960s, the University of Illinois developed the PLATO CAI system. Both the IBM 1500 and PLATO used host-driven time-shared computers to control analog audio and video (A/V) devices locally attached to student workstations. Both systems delivered multimedia applications with integrated audio, graphics, animation, and video. Applications running on both systems were based on authoring languages that were models for the procedural languages that would be used to develop multimedia applications for the next 25 years.

Towards the end of the 1960s and early in the 1970s, Mitre Corporation experimented with the TICCIT system, which used standard TV technology, and was based on a centralized host computer that controlled and distributed host-based A/V to TV-based terminals.

Probably the first, truly available multimedia computer was the Apple II+ which was not only function-rich, it also supported inexpensive and easy-to-use printers and floppy disk drives. With its ROM-BASIC anyone could easily develop applications that used all the functions of the machine.

At about the same time Philips NV, Pioneer Electronics, Thomson CSF, RCA Corp., and Sony Corp. experimented with low cost mass storage technologies for audio and full motion video. From the mid 1970s through the mid 1980s these companies carried on relentless technology and marketing wars in an effort to produce a single A/V storage standard. In 1979 IBM, MCA, and Pioneer formed the joint venture DiscoVision Associates (DVA) which pioneered the development and marketing videodiscs, trademarked as LaserDiscs.

In the early 1980s many small companies developed multimedia computing systems with configurations based on the Apple II+ connected to and controlling LaserDisc players. Clever system integrators developed mixing/switching electronics that mixed the computer's digital output and the videodisc player's analog output for display on a single screen. These systems allowed application developers to deliver the digital outputs of an Apple II+ computer together with the analog outputs of video and stereo audio - all integrated at a single workstation.

While it was not apparent in 1984, the introduction of the Macintosh was a major milestone in the evolution of MMC. The Mac was the first product to make computing easy and popular. Within only a few years GUIs became the only feasible interface for really personal computing. The use of implied that interactions should be as natural as possible and that that even more natural interfaces, including the use of color, images, audio, and video could even further facilitate user/computer interaction. However, in 1984 when the Mac was first introduced, technology had still not advanced sufficiently to allow engineers to build cost-effective all-digital multimedia systems.

In 1986 IBM introduced the videodisc-based InfoWindow System. With the "endorsement" of IBM, MMC in the form of InfoWindow Systems became a "legitimate" expenditure by Corporate America. The InfoWindow System gave notice that LaserDisc-based multimedia, controlled by an IBM Personal Computer, could provide cost-benefits in such commercial applications as training, marketing, and corporate communications. The InfoWindow System established a de facto MMC standard that, despite severe shortcomings, was an important factor in the continuation of MMC hardware, software, and application development work for the next five years.

Ever since the early 1960s, multimedia systems designers had been forced to integrate two incompatible technologies to deliver digital and A/V output at a workstation. Digital computers have, since their first introduction, been high speed electronic devices. On the other hand, audio and video devices have always been low speed, unreliable electromechanical devices. The introduction of LaserDiscs increased the reliability and performance of devices that could deliver MMC A/V. It did not remove the inherent incompatibilities between digital text/graphics output and analog audio/video output. In the late 1980's however, even this barrier began to fall.

Throughout the 1980s, laser optical scientists/engineers improved LaserDisc technologies. Many companies and international committees standardized upon the physical characteristics of audio Compact Discs (CDs). From the mid 1980's, as CDs virtually replaced tape as the audio medium of choice, the price of volume-manufactured CD players plummeted.

The same committees that established standards for audio CDs also developed logical file format standards for optical disc data files. CD-ROMs provide an integrated storage medium for all-digital data of text, audio, and full motion video, retrievable and manipulable by a "host" personal computer.

A LOOK AT THE PRESENT

MMC is of interest to i) industrial/commercial, and ii) consumer markets, and these markets do have much in common. Apple II+ computers found their way into Corporate America long before IBM announced and "legitimized" the PC. The Apple II+, running the first electronic spreadsheet, VisiCalc, was a salvation from the logjam of requests awaiting service by overworked MIS departments.

Accounting department personnel had seen Apple II's in use at their children's schools, and were astounded at their simplicity and affordability. It was relatively easy for a department in a company to budget a few thousand dollars for new "office equipment." By the time IBM announced the PC, it was easy to cost-justify the purchase of personal computers, especially if the manufacturer was IBM.

So too may MMC become pervasive in business. Today, MMC has captured the interest of the consumer market with a myriad of companies offering so-called "multimedia up-grade kits" for the consumer-base of "home office" PCs. As these kits grow in popularity (and as the price of CD-ROMs and sound boards drops), application developers will develop diverse CD-ROM-applications. Industrial acceptance of MMC is more conservative. For companies to adopt MMC as enthusiastically as the consumer market, the MMC development community there must be i) improvements in MMC technology and ii) the emergence of a discipline of MMC application development.

Technology. Today, popular CISC and RISC PC microprocessors can barely keep up with the demands to process digital audio and video. Fortunately, unlike conventional computer data, with contemporary microprocessors it is possible, with trade-offs in the quality of audio and/or video, to run reasonable multimedia applications. Such trade-offs are most apparent in the characteristics of video. "Software-only" methods of manipulating motion video (i.e., methods in which the PC's microprocessor can only barely process the volumes of digital video data), fail to deliver true full motion). are Microsoft's Indeo and Apple's QuickTime.

Currently, the only way to deliver true full motion video is to supplement the power of the PC microprocessor with some kind of A/V coprocessor. Even with an A/V coprocessor, the processing task is only barely manageable. In order to reduce the task 1) the volume of data must be reduced, 2) processor/coprocessors must be more efficient, or 3) a combination of both solutions is required. Computer scientists and engineers are currently working on a variety of solutions to these challenges. Ultimately, standards will emerge, benefiting the hardware manufacturers whose products will provide the sought-after solutions. Because Intel Corporation had an early start in these debates, the company's Digital Video Interactive (DVI) technology has already been endorsed and adopted as a corporate favorite. It is now clear though, that newer methods (and products) may be superior.

Another issue today concerns the "best" operating system

TECHNOLOGIES	PRODUCTS	ISSUES
Artificial intelligence	Cellular communications	Cable/Phone company disputes
Battery power	Graphical user interfaces	Copyrights, patents, and standards
Character recognition	Local and wide area networking	Electronic media publishing
Fiber optics	Operating systems	Globalization & world trade
Future generation programming languages	Pen computing	IBM and Apple
Flat screens	Personal digital assistants	Information superhighway
Neural networks	RISC and CISC processors	Mainframe and minicomputers
Parallel processors		Teleconferencing
Robotics		The art of computer programming
Speech recognition		Videoconferencing
Storage technologies		Workgroups
Three dimensionality		
Virtual systems		

Table 1: Some Factors Affecting the Future of Computing

for multimedia. For the foreseeable future the choices will include GUIs based on Apple's Macintosh System/7, Microsoft's Windows (with or without DOS), IBM's OS/2, or a rendition of UNIX.

Application Development. Although object oriented programming languages and design methodologies are becoming popular, a significant amount of excellent MMC application code is still being written with third generation, procedural programming languages. This situation too, is unlikely to change much in the foreseeable future. While languages and systems like C++, ObjectVision, SmallTalk, HyperCard, ToolBook, and VisualBasic can provide a bridge to the future of application development, these systems are really not a significant departure from the programming systems of the past. To use any of them to create a really terrific MMC application, programmers must be more than skillful, they must be creative "artists."

WHAT OF THE FUTURE?

When the computer industry began in the 1950s, no one could have predicted the pervasiveness of PCs only 30 years later. Even today, with each announcement of a new generation of microprocessor, experts declare that the new chips will not be useful in single user desktop machines, but are really suited for file servers or front end processors. If those early experts had been correct, there would never have been a need for personal computers. And if later experts had been any wiser, no desktop PC would have ever have used a 16 or 32 bit microprocessor. Each of these processors, at the time of their announcement, was declared to be overkill for personal, desktop applications. Not surprisingly, the same story is true about memory (RAM) and data storage (tape/disk/disc) devices. Because of such predictions, one forecast that we can now comfortably make is that no amount of computing power, RAM, or data storage will ever be enough. Each new generation of processor and memory technology will be just a little bit less than new applications will really require.

Today, the computer industry has become truly personalized. Every popular magazine and daily newspaper is replete with stories about computers and related technologies. Unfortunately, much of this information is often distorted, exaggerated, or simply incorrect. Despite this, as Table 1 illustrates, there are a number of emerging technologies, products, and unresolved issues which will converge from time to time to produce both incremental as well as monumental advances in the evolutionary continuum of computing. As the these factors evolve and/or become resolved, personal computing, today mostly highlighted by the phenomenon of "multimedia computing" will continue to evolve beyond any paradigm that we might today be able to perceive.

The Emergence of Multimedia Computing in Support of Knowledge Work and Group Collaboration

Jerry A. Van Os
Westminster College of Salt Lake City
1840 South 1300 East
Salt Lake City, Utah 84106

Executive Abstract

BACKGROUND INFORMATION

Multimedia refers to the delivery of information in intuitive, multisensory ways through the integration of previously, independent and distinctive media--sound, still images, live-action video, animation and text--in a single presentation under the control of a computer platform. Multimedia has the potential to provide designers with more freedom of communication and users with an effective form of information delivery.

The concept of multimedia computing recognizes that different information can be represented in different ways. Complexity in a knowledge-task environment can be effectively reduced when problem representations support the strategies and cognitive capabilities required to perform the task. This notion is termed cognitive fit, and supports the theory that knowledge work will be more effective and efficient if decision-making tasks are matched with the appropriate media representation. Multimedia platforms support intellectual technologies that give organizations the ability to compete in an information economy based on their ability to manage abstract and complex information. In reviewing organizational theory and MIS literature, the following organizational constraints can be overcome with a properly designed multimedia application: time and space, cognitive limitations and limited expert resources.

DISCUSSION OF THE ISSUES

A large part of what is known about the factors affecting organizational processes, structures, and performance were developed when the nature and mix of communication technologies were relatively constant, both across time and across organizations of the same general type. The implementation of computer-assisted communication technologies facilitate access to people inside and outside of organizations with an ease that previously was not possible.

The introduction of multimedia computing platforms can facilitate decision-making at organizational levels lower that if such technologies were not available. Organizations are increasingly moving towards the concepts of high-performance-high commitment collaborative work systems. These high performance teams are designed to foster a work culture having the following characteristics: delegation, teamwork across boundaries, empowerment, integration of people and technology and a shared sense of purpose.

Multimedia computing and other advanced information technologies are likely to be used as supplements and complements to traditional technologies, rather than as substitutes. It is anticipated that people within organizations will substitute multimedia applications for traditional communication forms if it seems efficacious to do so. Overall, the affect of multimedia computing is to increase the range of communication options for the organization.

FINDINGS

Multimedia applications that have considerable potential for supporting knowledge works and collaborative work groups include: Computer-Based Training, Video Conferencing, Intelligent Hypermedia Systems, Groupware Support Systems, and Informal Media Spaces.

Computer-Based Training (CBT) is on-demand, interactive, specific to immediate tasks, performed where and when the user desires, and does not require a human instructor to be active in the training process. CBT was found to effective in organizations that require continuous training of complex, non-repetitive tasks to support knowledge work.

Video Conferencing was found to most effective in conjunction with collaborative work groups that require on-going coordination and control. Earlier limitations of video conferencing have been overcome by enhanced technology and increased access to high-bandwidth communication networks making videoconferencing available to large and small groups.

Intelligent Hypermedia Systems benefit organizations by combining multimedia applications with artificial intelligence capabilities. This combination give designers more freedom in communication and knowledge workers more ways to access information. It provides a non-sequential search methodology that combines the benefits of artificial intelligence and the communication effectiveness of graphics, sound, animation and video.

Groupware Support Systems, utilizing a multimedia computer platform, are able to overcome previous limitations of group support systems by providing capabilities for "different time, different place" applications. In organizations where the culture supports teamwork and sharing over individual contributions, groupware has the potential to make a significant organizational impact.

Finally, when people are not located near each other, information technology can be used to support group work and collaboration by creating an Informal Media Space. The concept of informal media spaces, a technologically created environment, provides a way of working that allows social and task specific activities to come together across time and space by placing multimedia technology in common areas.

SUMMARY AND CONCLUSIONS

This paper summarizes how knowledge workers and collaborative work groups can overcome organizational constraints utilizing various multimedia applications. The creation of multimedia application platforms requires the coordination of heterogeneous tools, considerable technical expertise, the need to think and utilize information in multidimensional ways, and a considerable investment in complex hardware and software. The benefit derived from this investment is the creation of multimedia applications that support knowledge workers and collaborative teams in overcoming organizational limitations of time and space, cognitive fit and expert resources.

Multimedia applications that have considerable potential for supporting knowledge workers and collaborative work groups include: Computer-Based Training, Video Conferencing, Intelligent Hypermedia Systems, Groupware Support Systems, and Informal Media Spaces. Future applications in multimedia computing will continue to leverage the effectiveness of knowledge workers and collaborative work groups by allowing people to deal with large amounts of interrelated information through visualization and providing ways to manipulate and access information quickly and easily across organizational boundaries.

Enhancing MIS Education Through

Multimedia Technology: A Case Study

F. Stuart Wells
Tennessee Technological University
Department of Decision Sciences, Box 5022
Cookesville TN 38505
(615) 372-3334

Russell C. Kick
Tennessee Technological University
Department of Decision Sciences, Box 5022
Cookeville TN 38505

Executive Abstract

The purpose of this paper is to show the effectiveness of multimedia technology in education and how it is employed in the MIS program at Tennessee Technological University (TTU). Multimedia can be defined as a multisensory, participative experience with the emotional impact of audio, image, and video information. Applications of this technology which have been successfully used to enhance the quality of education and marketability of MIS graduates will be described and demonstrated.

A NEW LEARNING PARADIGM

Multimedia technology is gaining acceptance in both academic and business settings. Besides enhancing traditional instructional delivery, multimedia workstations enable students to explore MIS topics and concepts independently and at their own pace. A new learning paradigm is thus created through the use of hypermedia in an interactive computer environment. Students can navigate through a networked multimedia knowledgebase on an individual basis. In depth exploration of MIS concepts is facilitated through personal selection of both breadth and depth of relevant topics.

Pedagogically, multimedia augments and strengthens the instructional process while providing students with valuable MIS tools. These tools enhance the student's ability to analyze, design, develop and market their systems products. Inherent in the process is the vastly improved interactivity between management, user groups and systems personnel.

MULTIMEDIA AS A SYSTEMS DEVELOPMENT TOOL

Communication between MIS development personnel and between systems personnel and users is one of the outstanding benefits of employing multimedia technology in the systems development process. There are two reasons why the communications process is better than ever. First, communications between users and IS personnel becomes an ongoing process, whereas before communications occurred periodically and often at long intervals. Second, the employment of multimedia in the communications process enhances the assimilation of knowledge transfer. For example, multimedia encourages the sue of rapid prototyping and total user involvement. Cognitive science has shown that multiple forms of communication such as sound, video, graphics, etc. enhance the transfer of knowledge between human beings. Thus, the meeting of minds between users and systems personnel, which is essential to successful systems development, is facilitated by the utilization of multimedia technology.

Other significant benefits include improvement in the user interface design, better data modeling through the visualization provided by the technology, and more effective project management. Quasi-voice mail mode of interaction between user and IS (information systems) personnel exists, where both parties have the ability to verbally annotate their thoughts on disk, often attaching them to depicted components of the system. Thus, a new channel of communication is opened. This channel provides continuous feedback throughout the development process. Multimedia improves both process and product.

MULTIMEDIA AT TENNESSEE TECHNOLOGICAL UNIVERSITY

The College of Business Administration at TTU has two classrooms committed to multimedia instruction. Decision Sciences' Advanced Applications Lab, the more technologically advanced of the two, is dedicated to MIS instruction. Features of this classroom include multimedia workstations, state-of-the-art sound and video system, full-motion projection system, and leading edge software for presentation and systems development.

Multimedia technology presents and elaborates upon such topics as data modeling, knowledge engineering, prototyping and knowledge acquisition. An integral part of the pedagogy is utilization of hypermedia to link relevant ideas often overlooked by students. For example, the logical organization required by good form design is better understood through visualization. The subtle problems of eliciting requirements from users is brought to the surface by the interactivity made possible by multimedia technology. Client-server architectures and groupware problems are likewise illuminated by pictorially depicting the systems's environment.

Besides enhancing traditional instructional delivery, multimedia workstations enable students to explore MIS topics and concepts independently and at their own pace. As presented above these topics and concepts include user interface design, knowledge engineering, data modeling, query design and process flow. Students are required to use multimedia in several of their major courses in the process of developing and implementing information systems for local organizations. Students actually use multimedia authoring software to present their concepts to users in a "real-world" setting.

MIS MAJOR MARKETABILITY

There is an obvious interest by industry recruiters in the multimedia skills of TTUs MIS graduates. Recruiters are increasingly interested in infusing this technology into their organizations. Multimedia skills differentiate these graduates and thereby provide them with a distinct advantage in today's competitive job market.

SUMMARY

Use of multimedia technology has become an integral part of the MIS curriculum at TTU. Students are emerging with a new set of IS tools that enhance rather than replace time-proven traditional ones. The success of this effort has been shown through the successful development of "real-world" systems by student project-teams. Further evidence of the importance of this pedagogy is exhibited in the placement of TTUs MIS graduates, their starting salaries and the rapid career advancement achieved by many. TTUs intent is to continue using multimedia in the education of MIS majors and to seek out new and better ways to further incorporate it into the curriculum.

Section Fifteen

End User Computing

End-User Support and IT Adoption

Harry C. Benham
College of Business
Montana State University
Bozeman, MT 59715
406-994-6196
ubmhb@msu.oscs.montana.edu
and
Bruce Raymond
College of Business
Montana State University
Bozeman, MT 59715
406-994-4322
ibmbr@msu.oscs.montana.edu

Executive Abstract

BACKGROUND

Understanding how to assure that end-users adopt information technology (IT) innovations continues to be a challenging issue in information systems. Information systems or technologies which are not used cannot be effective. Thus, it is important to understand the end-user's adoption decision and what management can do to influence that decision. Management can influence the adoption decision through selection of which ITs to introduce and the degree to which they support end-users with training, documentation, and help facilities. This study seeks to assess the impact of end-users' perceptions of 1) the characteristics of a voice mail system and 2) the voice mail support available to them on their voice-mail adoption decisions.

MAIN ISSUES

Adoption of systems based on IT innovations such as voice mail is part of the implementation phase of an information system's life cycle. Recently, researchers have framed their information systems/information technology adoption studies within the context of an accepted theory. One approach offering a flexible, general representation of the innovation adoption decision can be found in the theory of planned behavior (TPB) attributed to Fishbein and Ajzen (1975), Ajzen and Fishbein (1980), and Ajzen (1985). Davis (1986, 1989) and Mathieson (1991) have adapted TPB to IT innovation adoptions.

TPB can be viewed as describing the process taking place within diffusion theory's persuasion stage. Figure 1 depicts how attitudes, subjective norms, and perceived behavioral control influence behavioral intent and ultimately actual behavior. Attitudes, subjective norms, and perceived behavioral control in turn depend upon the individual's beliefs and evaluations.

TPB addresses internal psychological variables through which numerous external variables achieve their influence. From an information systems management perspective, end-user support influences the beliefs and evaluations underlying perceived behavioral control. Managerial actions in the provision of end-user support are likely to influence an individual user's perceptions of the "presence of requisite resources and opportunities" to successfully use the system. Thus the primary research question is

R1:To what extent do an end-user's perceptions of user support influence perceived behavioral control and through it the user's intent to use voice mail?

a.)To what extent do an end-user's perceptions of access to and the effectiveness of training opportunities influence perceived behavioral control and through it the user's intent to use voice mail?

b.)To what extent do an end-user's perceptions of access to and the effectiveness of documentation influence perceived behavioral control and through it the user's intent to use voice mail?

c.)To what extent do an end-user's perceptions of access to and the effectiveness of help facilities influence perceived behavioral control and through it the user's intent to use voice mail?

Although it would appear that managerial actions in the provision of end-user support are most likely to influence the adoption decision through perceived behavioral control, it is also possible that the provision of end-user support influences end-users' perceptions about the advantages of using the system, its ease of use, or other behavioral beliefs. Thus the following research question.

R2:To what extent do an end-user's perceptions of user support influence beliefs about the system's characteristics?

a.)To what extent do an end-user's perceptions of access to and the effectiveness of training opportunities influence beliefs about the system's characteristics?

b.)To what extent do an end-user's perceptions of access to and the effectiveness of documentation influence beliefs about the system's characteristics?

c.)To what extent do an end-user's perceptions of access to and the effectiveness of help facilities influence beliefs about the system's characteristics?

STATUS OF PROJECT

Survey responses are being coded. Preliminary analysis of the results should be available at the conference. Reference are available upon request.

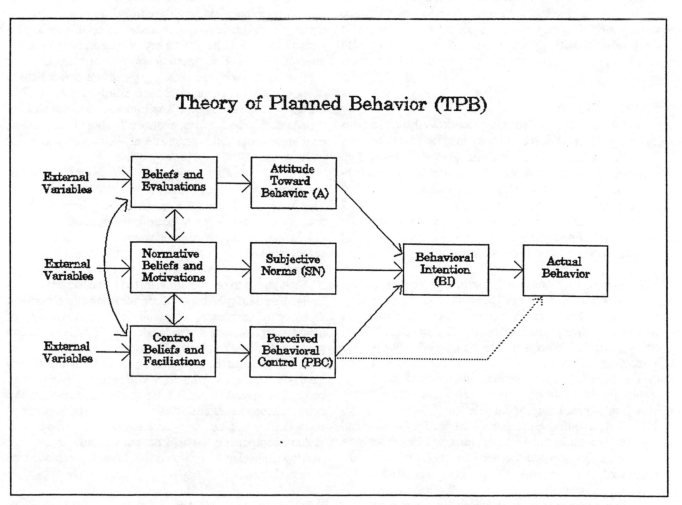

Theory of Planned Behavior (TPB)

Figure 1

Defining Computer Literacy for the End-User

Nancy Wilson Head
Purdue University
4601 Central Avenue
Columbus, IN 47203
(812) 372-8266 ext 7211

Executive Abstracts

INTRODUCTION

During the early 1980's, businesses of all sizes began to increase their dependency upon information systems. This was due mostly to the drastic increase of microcomputers and application software. As a result, the numbers of employees involved in end-user computing exploded.

When this end-user computing revolution began, business began training their employees in the use of computers and computer applications. Often, the employer preferred to train only for specific jobs. This training took place in-house or was provided by vendors. Universities played a small part in training the work force.

By the mid-1980's, it was obvious that computers would be standard business tools. Most employers began to require some degree of literacy as a prerequisite for employment. It also became increasingly obvious that college graduates needed to be computer literate to compete successfully in the business market.

BACKGROUND

In 1984 the state of Tennessee mandated that all students graduating from schools of higher education should be computer literate. Several other states quickly followed suit. However, the exact definition of computer literacy was unclear. At that time, many colleges and universities already had introductory computer literacy courses in place. At first glance, the solution to producing computer literate graduates seemed easy. However, most literacy courses were designed for Information Systems (IS) students and not for the end-user.

Institutions soon began offering literacy courses as electives for nontechnical majors. Students majoring in nursing, engineering, liberal arts, or business were all enrolling in courses specifically designed for the IS curriculum. These courses included information on the history, evolution, and terminology of computers. Students learned how to support the computer's physical functions, and how to produce information for the end-user. Students also had to prove proficiency in programming, usually learning BASIC or FORTRAN on a mainframe computer. Eventually, this programming requirement became a major concern. Many department heads began to question the need for this component, and requested literacy courses designed specifically for nontechnical majors.

As this movement toward change in the literacy course was taking place, two major trends in IS were also occurring. The first was the evolution away from mainframe applications and toward the use of microcomputers. The second was the trend toward non-procedural fourth generation tools. These trends helped convince universities that modifying their literacy courses was necessary.

FINDINGS

Today there is general agreement that all college students should complete an elementary computer course. To design that course, we first need to identify the classifications of end-users and examine today's literacy courses.

In most businesses, there is a small group of employees who use computers occasionally. They are not interested in experimenting with computer use. Another group utilizes a computer frequently on the job. They are comfortable with that requirement and often volunteer to adapt existing computer applications to their jobs. Possibly the fastest growing group of end-users utilizes computers continuously on the job. They often seek out new computer applications and tools to help in their jobs. Some are even enthusiastic about building their own applications, and can create new computing tools for others to use.

A newly emerging group of end-users is more than just computer literate. They are known as "information literate". They know how information can be used and have the ability to apply that knowledge to achieve the business' goals and objectives. Business owners/managers are now beginning to expect more end-users to interpret computerized information and make business decisions based on that information.

There seems to be a common thread in the literacy courses being offered today. Almost all courses feature the history and evolution of computers, and focus on the terminology of hardware, software, and peripherals. Typically, a microcomputer tools component has replaced the programming component. It includes basic operating system commands and hands-on experience with microcomputer packages (word processing, spreadsheets, and databases). Occasionally, this course utilizes integrated software packages, or packages of the revolutionary graphical user interfaces genre. Some courses include components on telecommunications, networking, desktop publishing, or non-procedural fourth generation software packages.

RECOMMENDATIONS

An exact definition of computer literacy is not available today, and that definition and the content of literacy courses should not be standardized. Educators and business must constantly assess literacy programs and end-user needs. As these end-user needs and classifications change, so should literacy education.

In the future, effective literacy courses will prepare students to be comfortable with computers in all business situations. These courses will help them in their other classes, in their chosen field of study, and in future employment. They will provide education in how computers work, what computers can and cannot do, and cover the impact that computers have on society.

College graduates will need to know what computers should and should not be allowed to do, should have the skills necessary to apply computers to common business problems, and should be able to determine which problems can and cannot be solved using computers. In addition, the computer literate end-user should be aware of supplementary sources of computer information and training available. They should have the skills to use on-line tutorial programs and appropriate manuals, and be able to teach themselves new skills as they are needed. End-users of the future must be capable of using the computer as a total business resource.

One has to wonder if the complete migration of literacy course offerings away from mainframe applications and toward microcomputer applications is wise. Isn't this trend ignoring the needs of a vital part of the end-user community? After all, not all businesses have migrated to an end-user environment equipped only with microcomputers. By eliminating mainframe access and exposure we may be short-changing students in their career preparation. In the future, students should exit any computer literacy course with an understanding of (if not experience with) both mainframe and microcomputer environments.

CONCLUSION

The real issue here is to decide the best way to prepare college students to enter the computerized professional work force. This issue will influence the preparation of future end-users as well as the preparation of IS professionals. It sometimes appears that the computer skills needed for end-users are somewhat job or industry specific. If this is true, business needs to take a more active role in defining literacy requirements at the college level. This can be accomplished through existing advisory board relationships. However, this will require increased discussion on specific skills needed for new employees. Business should be responsible for constantly reexamining the literacy needs of the end-user community. The advisory board should be the tool to communicate changes in those needs to educators. Educators must constantly reevaluate literacy course content. In addition, each must pursue an on-going evaluation of trends in the Information Systems industry. Literacy offerings for students who will be end-users must be more than state-of-the-art. They must be "state-of-the-future." Our graduates of today must be prepared to meet the needs that business and industry will have five years from today.

Employee Perceptions on Outsourcing: Preliminary Empirical Results

Mehdi Khosrowpour and Girish H. Subramanian
School of Business Administration
Penn State Harrisburg

John Gunterman
EDS, Harrisburg, Pa.

Executive Abstract

Outsourcing is the contracting out of all or part of a company's information systems functions to outside parties. In general business terms, outsourcing can be used to reference other contracting out arrangements not associated with information systems, however, in the context of this paper, the term will refer to information systems functions. Due [1992] defines outsourcing as "the transfer of a part or all of an organization's existing data processing hardware, software, communications network, and systems personnel to a third party."

This research presents the potential problems and concerns of information systems (IS) employees who may be affected by outsourcing. This research also provides preliminary findings of a survey on outsourcing. These preliminary results summarize the perceptions of IS professionals on the topic of outsourcing.

Problems and concerns

Most of the current literature available on the topic of outsourcing deals with the business considerations of outsourcing. The business issues covered in the literature include outsourcing rationale, potential cost savings, selecting the right outsourcing vendor, contract negotiation, mistakes to avoid and the identification of good candidates for outsourcing. Very few articles deal with the human aspects of outsourcing, either from the client's point of view, the outsourcing vendor's point of view or the Information System professional's point of view.

Favorable reactions

Other employees have favorable reactions to the outsourcing. Many find the new work environment to be stimulating and challenging. Opportunities for learning new technologies, advancing in a company whose main business is information technology, and the challenge of serving a genuine customer were all things which were received positively in Due's [1992] discussions with outsourced employees.

RESEARCH METHODOLOGY AND RESULTS

A survey was developed to gather data reflecting the outsourcing perceptions of a cross section of information systems professionals. The survey was mailed to 1000 information systems professionals. The survey used to collect data was designed specifically for this research. The survey was mailed to 1000 information systems professionals throughout the United States. The professionals surveyed were all members of the Association for Systems Management (ASM) and were randomly selected from the membership roles. The survey consisted on twenty-nine questions. Of the twenty-seven selection questions, the first eleven were designed to determine the respondent's situational variables. There were also eleven questions designed to gauge the respondents perceptions on various aspects of outsourcing. Five questions were designed to register the respondent's opinions on questions dealing directly with an outsourcing event. The two open-ended questions at the end of the survey asked the respondents to provide their opinions in free-form text response. A copy of the survey is available to interested readers upon request.

Of the 1000 surveys sent out, 146 surveys were returned which could be used in full, or in part, in the survey. Several preliminary findings are reported as a result of this survey of IS professionals. Almost all of the respondents indicated that they had heard the term "outsourcing" and knew what it meant. A majority of the respondents had neutral or negative feelings about outsourcing. This points out to the indifferent and negative views of client IS employees on outsourcing. Respondents were equally (in percentage terms) on whether they would be affected by outsourcing. The popularity of outsourcing is evident from the fact that 34 % felt that they would be affected by outsourcing.

A majority of the respondents agreed or strongly agreed that outsourcing could be an appropriate business decision. A majority either disagreed or strongly disagreed that the IS professionals were a key factor in the minds of management when making the outsourcing decision. One of the justifications of outsourcing is that companies which do not specialize in information technology can no longer keep up with the rate of change in the industry, and should therefore let a specialist assume the role of service provider. A majority of the respondents felt that it was difficult for companies to keep up with the latest developments.

Compensation and career opportunities were perceived to be better in IT companies while respondents perceived no difference between IT and non-IT companies with respect to job security. A majority of respondents did not find it appropriate for management to withhold outsourcing decision information. The respondents also had clear preferences for the person in the organization who should communicate the outsourcing decision to them.

To effectively deal with the human aspects of outsourcing, management must understand what perceptions exist within the employee ranks and develop a plan which addresses employee needs and perceptions, even if the perceptions are without basis. This research has indicated that I.S. professionals have different perceptions on outsourcing depending on what their particular personal and professional situations are. It is in the best interest of all parties to treat the affected I.S. professionals in a fair manner. A smooth outsourcing evaluation and transition period is not possible without their cooperation. Productivity losses and low morale associated with employee anxieties not only hurt the current business, but could also prevent the outsourcing arrangement from being successful. Other repercussions of an improperly handled transition include potential lawsuits and the loss of key talent.

Supporting Appropriate User-Developed Applications: Guidelines for Managers

Laura Lally
Hofstra University
BCIS/QM Department
134 Hofstra
Hempstead, NY 11550

Executive Abstract

CHARACTERIZING USER-DEVELOPED APPLICATIONS

Organizations have invested in user development of applications by providing PC-hardware, user-friendly application software, and technical support to end-users. These investments are motivated by the desire to reduce: 1) the overhead costs associated with mainframes, 2) the large application backlogs in traditional IS departments, and 3) the communication gap that arises between professional analysts and their business oriented clients. With organizational support, end-users can develop applications without spending a great deal of time and effort developing analytical or programming skills.

The resulting systems, user-developed applications (UDAs) are likely to differ from traditionally developed systems in a number of ways. First, UDAs are likely to be developed to support the user's own job. Second, UDAs are more likely than traditional systems to be developed using productivity tools. Third, UDAs are more likely than traditional systems to be developed on personal computers.

Studies of end-user computing tend to focus on end-user satisfaction, rather than the ultimate fate of the applications users develop. A lack of emphasis on application quality and usefulness can lead to a number of problems with UDAs. Users lacking analytical skills can design systems which are error-prone, inappropriate for a given productivity tool or for a PC-based platform, or beyond the abilities of the end-user to develop to completion. An end-user's job-oriented perspective may lead to the development of systems with too narrow a focus or systems which duplicate applications already in the firm.

The goal of this study is to provide guidelines for managers in choosing appropriate systems for end-user development, and for supporting the development of logically correct and usable applications. To provide a framework for the key issues involved, traditional systems analysis and design is compared to the development of UDAs and the tradeoffs mapped to a systems design life cycle (**SDLC**) model. By following this model, managers can: 1) minimize the costs associated with inappropriate or incorrect systems, 2) make a cost efficient use of resources used to support UDAs, and 3) maximize the possibility that the benefits of UDAs will be realized. Areas where further research is need will also be indicated.

THE SDLC AND USER-DEVELOPED APPLICATIONS

Planning. During the planning phase, end-users are less likely to define their problem independently of their available tools, engage in alternative structuring of the problem, or see their application in a larger, organizational context. Guidance should be provided at this point by professional analysts to ensure that the end-user's problem fits his or her application software, hardware platform, and abilities. If the application is time-consuming, the salary of the end-user, and conflicts with other job duties must be considered. Existing applications, either off-the-shelf or in-house, may suit the user's problem with only minor modifications. The source of the data for the application must be considered in terms of its security and the ease with which it can be transferred to a PC environment. Finally, if the system is an integral part of the user's job, arrangements must be made as to who will own the system should the user leave.

One strong factor favoring UDAs during the planning phase is the user's superior understanding of just what the problem is. An end-user's previous experience designing systems may mitigate the impact of a lack of formal training in analysis and programming.

Analysis and Design. This phase of a UDAs life cycle can be better supported by the development of tools and methodologies aimed at supporting the analysis and design of productivity tool based systems. End-users need to be encouraged to document their applications carefully, especially if they will not be used continually or are to be used by others.

Implementation. UDAs require rigorous testing if they are to be used to support critical tasks. Here again, guidance from professional analysts is needed.

If UDAs have survived until this point, however, the benefits of user-development can come increasingly into play.

Maintenance. Updating and upgrading the program should not be such a dismal task for an end-user who will be the primary beneficiary of a correct and efficient system. Professional analysts and programmers are more likely to have moved on to a new projects and be reluctant to make changes.

Even more promising is the potential for UDAs to **evolve** beyond their original specifications. In the process of developing a system, an end-user may gain new insight into the nature of the underlying problem. As the system is used, new ideas for enhancements may emerge. UDAs provide a greater potential for iterative application development, use, and enhancement than do traditional systems.

Case studies of successful and unsuccessful UDAs will provide greater insight into the choice of appropriate candidates for user-development. The development of analysis and design methodologies to be used with productivity tools will help ensure UDA quality.

Performance Concepts for Information Technologists: Reexamining the Components of Productivity

Dr. William L. Lomerson
Assistant Professor of Computer Science
School of Business
Hardin-Simmons University
Box C HSU Station
Abilene, TX 79698
(915)670-1503
and
Dr. Nancy J. Hard
Assistant Professor
General Business and Systems Management
East Texas State University
Commerce, TX 75429
(903)886-5687

Executive Abstract

End-users and information technology processes have become the focus of increasing interest and importance as organizations strive to improve their performance. In the few articles that address performance issues for end users or information technology processes, a substantial amount of inconsistent and inappropriate use of the concepts of productivity exists. The term, **productivity**, has been misused to imply the existence of causal and measurable relationships between inputs, processes and outputs of information technology systems. These relationships generally do not exist.

Using the economic and mathematical foundations of productivity concepts, this paper develops definitions that can be applied consistently and appropriately to information technology research. These definitions are based upon well-grounded economic concepts extended from the sectors of business that make and move things. This methodology provides consistency and congruity between the historical use of these terms and the developing use of these terms by information technologists.

THE COMPONENTS OF PRODUCTIVITY

Productivity describes the observable outputs of a physical or intellectual process, often called products. **Effectiveness** refers to the quality of the result or accomplishment. **Efficiency** refers to the use of resources in the operation of a process. **Productiveness** refers to the operation of a process or the process itself, rather than the result. While both **efficiency** and **effectiveness** affect **productivity**, they are independent of one another.

The term, **productivity**, has its origins in the process-product paradigm (P-PM) of manufacturing and is based upon the notion that a set of inputs is physically changed by a process into a set of outputs. This paradigm makes two important assumptions. First, organizations exercise control over the inputs to the process to insure consistency of the inputs. Second, the production process causes the inputs to be converted to outputs.

It is most likely that measurable products do not constitute the primary outputs from IT systems. Unfortunately, the concept of measurable products being produced by information technology processes has become axiomatic within the information technology community. The source of the information-as-product concept can be seen as the extension of this P-PM to information technology systems. Most researchers would agree that knowledge creation, rather than the physical conversion of inputs into outputs, is the objective of most information technology processes.

THE ROLE OF THE END USER

The users and creators of information, collectively called knowledge workers, form the largest category of individuals that are generally referred to as end-users. It is through the activities of the end-user that the benefits of IT are actually realized. Many of the relationships and factors associated with knowledge creation and use, however, are ill defined. As a result, many of the theories and practices based upon the application of P-PM have produced results that are neither very predictable nor very uniform.

The process-service model (P-SM) is distinguished from the P-PM by its explicit recognition that the outputs of the service process are highly dependent upon the process inputs. By analogously recognizing the consumer role of end-users, the P-SM might provide a more useful model for researchers in analyzing and improving the performance of information technology processes. The actual results of this interaction can only be determined by examining the outcomes that result from the knowledge user's activities.

THE BASICS OF PRODUCTIVITY MEASUREMENT

Productivity measurement requires the measurable results that exist after changing a particular defined set of inputs into an expected set of outputs. To obtain a meaningful interpretation of a productivity measure, it must be compared to a similar criterion measure or an earlier measurement of the subject process. The measure of productivity improvement, however, has no meaning if the non-quantitative dimensions of the inputs and/or the outputs are not essentially the same at both measurement instances. A principal difficulty in developing a valid and reliable measure of productivity in information technology occurs because most of the system inputs are different each time the process begins.

The concept of **productiveness** can serve to guide our investigative methodologies. This is achieved by refocusing the analysis from the immeasurable outcomes of the IT process to the process itself. Productivity improvement still remains the objective but recognition is made that the outcomes must be intuitively or managerial evaluated rather than measured. Attention is directed toward identifying and examining the factors that contribute both to **effectiveness** and to **efficiency** in the process. The **productivity** of an end-user or a system is then improved by improving **effectiveness** and/or **efficiency** of the process. The attempt to measure productivity improvement is not pursued.

PERFORMANCE CONCEPTS FOR INFORMATION TECHNOLOGISTS

The following definitions differentiate and delineate the concepts of **productivity**, **productiveness**, **effectiveness** and **efficiency** as they relate to the environment of information technology systems.

Productivity Concepts for Information Technology Systems (ITS)

ITS Productivity- the conversion of physical resources into an environment that supports and facilitates the processes of knowledge creation and use.

ITS Productiveness- the ability of an information technology process to affect a desired change in the outcomes sought by an end user interacting with this process.

ITS Effectiveness - the ability of an information technology process to integrate the available information technology resources and the end user's interaction efforts such that the opportunity for the maximum outcome sought by the end user can occur.

ITS Efficiency- the ability of an information technology process to minimize the number of knowledge creating and using tasks that must be performed to achieve an outcome desired by an end user.

Productivity Concepts for End Users (EU)

EU Productivity- the quantitative output of the clerical and administrative processes performed by an end user.

EU Productiveness- the ability of an end user to apportion his/her efforts so that as much time as possible is allocated to knowledge creating and using functions.

EU Effectiveness- the ability of a end user to manipulate the available information technology resources such that the maximum outcome sought by the end user occurs.

EU Efficiency- the ability of an end user to accomplish his/her knowledge creation and using tasks with as few organization resources in as short a time as possible.

This paper provides a clear definition and differentiation of **productivity**, **productiveness**, **effectiveness** and **efficiency** for both processes and end users. These definitions are developed from well-established concepts that exist within the making and moving sectors of the business world. They provide the firm conceptual foundation required to develop, evaluate and discuss tools, activities and procedures that can improve the performance of information technology systems.

Market Driven Quality from the Perspective of Application Software Development and Maintenance

Ramamurti Sridar

Project Manager - ISSC/NOVA University Doctoral Student

P.O. Box 1232

La Canada, Ca 91012

Tel: (310) 447-4579/(310) 297-4665 (Office)

(818) 790-5515 (Home)

Executive Abstract

BACKGROUND INFORMATION

For more than a decade, every facet of the organizations in U.S. is subjected to tremendous pressure from global competition. The key element of this competition has always been the pursuit of excellence in quality. Besides the manufacturing and service industries, the word 'Quality' has become an inseparable entity in the computing environment.

In this current era of information age, Information System organizations have become a strategic unit in almost all businesses. Having attained this kind of high visibility in the corporate world, Information Systems are focussing more and more on quality in delivering services to end user community.

DISCUSSION OF ISSUES

The management and the employees of IBM together have defined the Quality to be: customer satisfaction, management leadership, people involvement and empowerment, definable, repeatable, and predictable processes measurable for improvement, and continuous improvement. The above definitions of quality are applicable in software development and maintenance environment, where the key issue is to address the needs of end users to the best of their satisfaction. In order to achieve this goal, the project manager has to perform the following tasks: define the process which entails the identification of various sub steps starting from the application development/maintenance task to final delivery of end products to end users; define the functions under each process; Define Quantification parameters from functions for measurement of Quality; and Measurement and Tracking of the performance of functions as identified above.

As a project manager of a document retrieval system called PSAPPLIC, the author used the above procedures to implement the quality program.

DISCUSSION OF FINDINGS

There were four processes defined for PSAPPLIC: Application Development, End User Interface, Monitor PSAPPLIC Usage, and PSAPPLIC planning. For Application Development process, the functions related to system requirement definition and system implementation. For End User Interface process, the functions related to the interaction between the end user and system developer on the useability of the system. For Monitor PSAPPLIC usage process, the functions related to keeping track of PSAPPLIC usage statistics. For PSAPPLIC planning process, the functions related to the

Quantification parameter	Measurement and Achievement Tracking
Reduction in Lines of system code, Percentage reduction in code maintenance time per month (Development process)	950 lines of redundant system code reduction achieved over 3 months time. 30 percent reduction in hours of system code maintenance time per month achieved over a period of 3 months time.
Reduction in number of retest attempts by independent system test team before code promotion (Development process)	0 retest attempt was achieved over a period of 3 months time from 3 retest attempts.
Percentage reduction in end user interface time on data file update (End User interface process)	75 percent reduction in hours of end user interface time per month achieved over a period of 3 months
Reduction in number of business days to respond to end user problems/concerns (End User Interface process)	One business day turnaround time achieved over a 3 months time from 3 business day turnaround time.

interaction between the project manager and end users on system code release schedule.

The quantification, measurement and achievement tracking for the functions are summarized as follows:

The achievement of the goals was possible by the following actions:

1. Standardization of common function code.
2. Provide the end users the necessary tools to update files in the system.
3. Involve Independent System Test team from the very early stage of system development.
4. Streamline the end user problem routing mechanism such that appropriate system people are notified of the end user problems without delay.

CONCLUSION

This case in point clearly demonstrates how one can visualize the quality attainment once all the processes and their related functions are defined. There was a total buy in of the quality target by both IS professionals as well as the end users. All the players were empowered to offer any suggestion which would enable the attainment of quality target. The two key results of attaining the quality target were cycle time reduction in delivery of service to end users, defect free computing environment. The former result caused an enhancement to productivity and cost savings while the latter result caused an efficient and reliable computing environment.

"Prototyping Information Systems Development for Commercial and Administrative Organizations in Hong Kong: Developer and End-User Perspectives"

David W. Wilson & Yip Hon Fai, Willie
Hong Kong Polytechnic
Department of Computing
Hung Hom
Kowloon
Hong Kong
Tel. (852) 367 4914

Executive Abstract

BACKGROUND

The term "prototyping" has been in common usage with reference to information systems development for more than the last ten years. Over the last three years the authors have led a number of studies into the use of prototyping in organizational information systems development situations.

DISCUSSION

If only one eventual target object is to be produced, as with Information Systems, there need to be compelling reasons why an expensive period of experiment and stakeholder / developer dialogue is justified. If we can "make do" with the product of the imagination of the developer, how can we justify taking up the time of the user, perhaps users at various levels and with different roles in the organization?

FINDINGS

Prototyping was less popular than had been expected, a number of organisations having tried it out before rejecting it. Developers stated they believed prototyping appropriate to design with physical design and analysis also being favored strongly. They also said that there was not enough software education or training based on a prototyping approach.

The developers asserted that there is a need for education on both the user and developer side. The approach should be promoted in tertiary level curricula. There is a requirement for methods of prototyping which can fit in with project management methods. Tools should be simple, easy to use, well supported by vendors and generate products for use throughout the life-cycle including code and high quality documentation.

The user participants asserted prototyping is the best vehicle to involve the user. They stated that users only really have a chance to perceive systems errors in the cascade model after implementation. Although they may participate in structured walkthroughs and be presented with proposals in "user friendly" documentation using data flow diagrams and entity models they could not really accept responsibility for non-working models expressed in the notation of another profession.

Further they identified that through providing the user with a tangible means of understanding and evaluating the proposed system a stimulus to user input was created. Users asserted that they were adept at criticizing an existing tangible artefact whereas envisioning a system from traditional documentation to the level of confidently criticizing it was more difficult. Also, User ownership of the system was established and this was accompanied by commitment and even enthusiasm. The activity fosters better relations between developers and users.

CONCLUSIONS

There are some very clear lessons from the evidence collected and analysed. There is not a great deal of tension between the end-user and the practitioner as to whether prototyping should be used. Rather the decision is left to the professional judgement of the practitioner as to whether the approach is desirable and to what extent it should be practised. Both developers and users have strong positive feelings about the ability of a prototyping approach to serve them well in the fitting of automated infor mation systems to organizations. Both parties acknowledge that the approach is likely to improve the probability of the delivered system being close to the required system. This effects an actual productivity gain.

However, use of the approach is not yet widespread in Hong Kong. It would be possible to parallel the study in other territories. Further investigation in Hong Kong should con-

The Impact of Management Information

Systems on Management Structure:

A comparative empirical analysis of 500 organisations

Prof Dr Ad Teulings, University of Amsterdam
Rijnsburgerweg 5, 2334 BA Leyden, The Netherlands
Tel (31)-71-170973. Fax (31)-71-156402

Executive Abstract

This study presents some results of the POISON research project (University of Amsterdam), a comparative structured case study analysis of the adoption and implementation of management information systems (MIS) in 500 Dutch firms and institutions. The rate and scope of adoption and utilization is compared across organizations and functional areas of management. The data show major differences between innovative and imitative cultures. Innovative informatization has considerable impact on organisational structure and design. Imitative processes (the majority of all informatization projects) are marginal as inductors of organisational change and reinforce established management structures.

Methodology

The spectrum of management information systems technologies is categorised in a two-dimensional typology, by level and by scope. By level, MIS may support operational, intermediate (structuring), or strategic management. By scope, it may support a single management activity (such as inventory management), a management function (a cluster of functionally related activities such as production control, sales, or distribution), or the integration of two or more managerial functions. A checklist of management activities is used to analyse patterns of adoption over time (Kraemer et al, 1989; Bikson et al., 1987; Attewell & Rule, 1992). Retrospective interviews with management provide starting dates for each system adopted in support of a management activity, management function or coupling of functions. Other relevant aspects, such as system change and future investment plans are also reviewed.

Diffusion analysis: five stages in the diffusion process

The year of first adoption ranges from 1960 to 1993. The rate of innovation follows a sigmoidal growth curve (s-form). Multivariate analysis of the resulting time series shows that the time span of 33 years is divided in five coherent waves, each wave carried by a distinctive cohort of organisations and information technologies. The first three waves (60-69, 70-74, 75-85) coincide with hardware developments, the last two (86-89 and 90-93) tend to be more related to software developments.

Cohort analysis: divergent patterns of Informatization

Early cohorts leap ahead of their successors up to the present time, both in scope of management activities supported by MIS and in technological sophistication. The earliest adopters are today's most advanced users. Late entrants however adopt primarily the standardised plain vanilla systems available on PC's.

Impact analysis: coupling of management activities and decoupling of management functions

The extending scope of MIS applications has a significant impact on the structuring (= division and co-ordination) of managerial activities. Although polarisation may be too strong a label to depict this development, our data analysis reveals a clear tendency for some management functions towards increased interdependency, whereas others tend become more dissociated from the core of general management. First, and not very surprisingly, MIS tends to glue management activities more closely together in traditional functional areas of management. Integration of activities implies at the same time a more pronounced separation of management functions, leading to an increase in functional specialisation. Next, implementation of MIS may sometimes facilitate functional integration, or even produce a merger of departments. In contrast with widespread assumptions (Nolan, 1979, 1982; Ward et al., 1990; Zeffane, 1992) this is not the only, and today not even the predominant pattern. In many organisations we also observe tendencies towards functional dissociation and isolation (in Dutch consultancy speak: functional "chutes").

Integrative tendencies: IT support for core functions of management

Coupling of management functions is typical for organizations who start MIS early on in core areas of line management. Integration occurs in particular between production, sales and distribution control systems supporting intermediate management levels. Ultimately, financial modelling, planning and control systems may link executive levels of management more closely to these core functions. This development seems to head directly towards integrated line management with IS technology as a dominant co-ordinating mechanism. Strong cases pointing in this direction are at present in a minority, mainly multinational industrial and business corporations belonging to the Ivy League of early adopters.

Decoupling: IT support for operational staff support functions

The opposite tendency, towards functional "chuting", is observed when organisations start with MIS as a support of operational staff functions (i.e. finance, salary or personnel administration. These areas remain isolated from the core of line management at various levels, and from each other. The concept of polarisation therefore seems adequate as a description of the present stage of informatisation.

Adoption and implementation patterns: IT as an imitation processes

Recent adopters of MIS era differ significantly from early entrants. They select the standard applications (accounting, personnel administration, inventory management) available on the market, and do so in large numbers. Its implementation has little impact on the co-ordination and integration of management functions. They stay away from opportunities for MIS in core operations. The implementation of MIS does not engage management in a long term learning process. Informatization tends to reinforce bureaucratic tendencies of functional specialisation and staff centralisation. The steep slope of the S-curve of adoption for recent cohorts reflects an imitation process, very distinct from the gradual inclination of innovative development observable in earlier cohorts.

Early adopters: IT as an innovation and organisational learning process

For earlier cohorts, informatization is directed towards the core functions of management, first in operations, then at higher levels. Implementation requires the development of tailor-made applications and management is confronted continuously with severe implementation problems and steep learning curves. Taking this road is still a capital intensive affair. Their systems have to be continuously redesigned in order to be effective. This requires that full attention is paid to competence development.

Organizations taking the innovative course in MIS adoption are marked by well known contingency factors such as size and scale, technological complexity of the production process and market instability. *Informatization is used as an instrument to cope with these uncertainties by taking advantage of the co-ordinating capacities of MIS.* The steep adoption curve of recent times is created by newcomers absorbing standard, ready made applications. For these organizations, Structural and environmental contingency factors play hardly a role and the laws of imitation are prevailing.

Information Technology to the Aid of Higher Education Administration

Ms. Mary T. Knepp
Systems Analyst
Registrar
Southwest Texas State University
601 University Drive
San Marcos, TX 78666
and
Marcos P. Sivitanidess, Ph.D.
Assistant Professor
Computer Information Systems
School of Business
Southwest Texas State University
San Marcos, TX 78666

I. GENERAL DESCRIPTION OF THE TRANSCRIPT SERVICE PROCESS

In an educational or academic environment, the registrar's office is responsible for updating, maintaining, and reporting academic data for all students. One of the ways this data is reported is in the form of the academic transcript which provides the requestor or recipient with a history of attempted course work. The release of transcripts must always be authorized by the student and may be sent to other educational institutions for admissions processing or to government agencies and businesses for employment purposes.

II. CURRENT SYSTEM

Southwest Texas State University (SWT) opened its doors in 1903 and has a current enrollment of approximately 20,000 students. The Registrar's Office has four full-time employees and hires a number of student workers each semester to provide transcript service at a volume of about two hundred requests daily.

Processing:

Requests arrive by mail, telephone and walk-up with service provided on-demand if the requestor wishes to pick up the transcript, or by sending the transcript directly to the recipient specified on the request form. When the Registrar's Office receives the request, one of three things occurs:

1) The transcript is prepared and distributed.
2) Service is denied due to an account hold. The student is notified and request is held, pending resolution of the hold.
3) Service is denied due to inadequate fees submitted with the request. The student is notified and request is held, pending receipt of the appropriate fees.

Transcript records for academic activity prior to the late 1970's are maintained in a hard copy filing area. Transcripts showing more recent academic work are stored on a VAX mainframe computer with transcript data batched and sent to a printer. Mail-in requests are opened and enclosed fees logged. Details about requests are tracked for later research. Receipts are written and cash activity is balanced for accounting purposes. Transcripts are printed, validated, and prepared for mailing. Request forms are then marked to indicate action taken and filed for later reference. Telephone requests also require obtaining and verifying credit card payment authorization.

Research for requestor:

Once a transcript request has been placed, the requestor may contact the Registrar's Office to check the status of the request. In order to respond the employee must provide details of the service provided including number of copies sent, destination or recipient, date sent and method of transmission.

Research for management:

Management (transcript service supervisor, registrar, or other administrative personnel) requires information for budget, planning and resource management. The information requested may include processing data about the volume of requests processed for specific time periods, the number of requests reported by destination, associated processing costs, the number of requests denied for non-payment of fees, the number of requests denied for hold enforcement, or time elapsed for denied requests in a pending state.

III. PROBLEMS WITH CURRENT SYSTEM

Manual processing:

SWT employs a manual system and there are concerns about the level of efficiency and production. Each request form is handled an average of ten times from receipt to completion. As a result, providing service is time consuming. At the end of each semester the volume of requests received increases dramatically and production suffers so much that turnaround time usually doubles or triples. In order to adhere to auditing guidelines and maintain some level of efficiency, it is necessary to break the process into individual steps for batch processing. The larger the batches, the more time spent on each level of manual processing.

Management reporting and request query capabilities are unwieldy at best and non-existent at worst. In a manual system the only history maintained for transcript service is in the form of hard copy storage of each original transcript request. Individual status checks involve looking in a manually maintained transaction log and retrieving the original request form from file storage for details and then refiling the document. The production of management reports requires compiling information obtained from original request forms and presenting the data in a format appropriate for the specified report. Processing one recent request for information about transcript activity for a specific three month period took over one month to complete.

Costs:

The cost associated with producing and sending transcripts is presently only about fifty cents per transcript, excluding manpower costs. However, measuring the cost in terms of public image and employee morale is more difficult. Public image suffers on at least two levels. Perception is often worse than reality. Since many requestors doubt the efficiency of the system they place many calls to check the status of requests. The prospective employer of SWT alumni may question the wisdom of considering someone from an institution that cannot provide transcripts in a timely manner. "If transcript service (read university administration) is so poor, what are the academic standards?" Registrar employee morale suffers because of the frustration and boredom associated with the manual systems and the awareness that automation could be provided that could help improve efficiency.

Security:

In any environment where money and private or protected information is involved, security is an important consideration. With a manual system, security is often difficult to maintain. At each of the more than ten steps in SWT's manual process, there exists at least one opportunity for security breaches (money mismanagement, theft, release of information to unauthorized persons, etc).

IV. WHAT CAN IT DO FOR SWT's TRANSCRIPT SERVICE?

First, data management and planning resulting in the development and implementation of an *automated transcript request system* for production of the transcript, receipt, mailing label (if necessary), or other documents would simplify and streamline the transcript service process. Features like: the ability to batch or sort transcripts based on recipient so that

transcripts could be sent together to save postage and staff time; allowing the user to designate sort order on receipts and labels to save sort and document matching time; allowing immediate printing of transcripts for walk-up service without interruption of print batches in process; and the ability to automatically produce the appropriate correspondence for holds or fees required would amount to increased efficiency and decreased processing time. Automating the process would also provide easier and more immediate access of the data necessary for transcript request tracking, status inquiries, and management reports. Institutions that have converted from manual to automated systems have realized remarkable improvements in processing time, accuracy and employee morale.[1]

Second, *optical scanning* could be used to log incoming mail. This would eliminate the hand posting of fees enclosed with transcript requests and provide better documentation (proof) when the required fees are not included. Mailed in requests would logged faster, cutting down on overall processing time. Occasionally, employees must provide copies of original request forms. These copies could be printed from a scanned and stored computer record and would, in most cases, be visually clearer than a photographic copy taken of the original paper request.

Third, introducing *electronic data interchange* (EDI) for all transcripts sent to other colleges, universities, government agencies or businesses approved for receipt and identified as having the ability to receive data electronically could result in the student's academic record being received more quickly than it would via regular postal service. Currently, over twenty five institutions in Texas transmit and receive academic transcripts electronically.[2] With states including Florida, California, Wisconsin, Oregon and Canadian provinces involved as well, EDI may become the primarily accepted means of communicating standard data between academic institutions.[3] Additionally, many EDI software applications allow for a level of transmission tracking not easily accomplished in a manual system. Data files containing academic information are created using an approved American National Standards Institute standard format with header and trailer records attached. A transmittal record can include destination, identifier for each transcript sent (often student social security number or student identification number), date and time of transmission, and acknowledgement of receipt by the destination institution, along with individual student information.

Fourth, use *optical scanning and disc storage* to store all hard copy pre-1980 original transcripts. Older records are often difficult to locate in the manual system due to unreported name changes or errors that sometimes occur during refiling. Scanning systems have sophisticated indexing capabilities that allow retrieval of records via a number of identifiers as opposed to the strict alphabetical filing system currently used.[4] Optical storage would allow scanned and stored transcript files to be retrieved from disc and sent to a laser printer for completion of the requested transcript service without the time delays associated with the current manual retrieval and reproduction process.

Fifth, employ *voice technology* to enable students to request transcripts without restrictions based on time of day, day of week, or staff availability. An automated telephone answering system would prompt the caller for information necessary to complete transcript service (name, social security number, number of transcripts requested, destination, contact phone number, credit card number and expiration date, etc.)[5]. This system would be available during all non-business hours and any time callers encounter busy signals. The recorded information would then be stored and available for later retrieval and processing. Staff would organize their work load to process these requests within the expected time frame.

V. BENEFITS

Improved service:

Taking advantage of the above mentioned technologies would improve service to requestors in a number of ways. The time necessary to produce transcripts would be reduced because the automated system would eliminate many manual steps. Matching documents (transcripts to request form, to address label, to receipt, to request log, to user of entry) in preparation for mailing and filing would be virtually eliminated by the use of sort routines built into the system. The research tasks associated with status inquiries by requestors would be simplified with the creation of a request query screen where any authorized user could enter an identifier and see a record of past requests received and details associated with each request in seconds or minutes instead of the current time required (often hours).

EDI would benefit the customer since, with appropriate security features, transcripts are more tamper proof than hard copy form[6], records are processed more quickly; they arrive at their destinations in a more timely manner; and validation of transmission is more reliable than the standard phrase, "That transcript went in the mail yesterday and should arrive shortly."

Allowing customers to request a transcript twenty four hours a day is the kind of enhancement almost always positively perceived by the requestor because it allows them to take care of business at their convenience.

Improved reporting:

Reports could be produced much more quickly to provide information necessary to ensure that adequate staffing and supplies are available, especially for peak production periods. For example, with data available about EDI transmission volume, management may be able to reduce on-hand inventory levels of transcript safety paper and laser printer toner cartridges - both costly items. These reports could also pinpoint times during semesters where it would be most effective to have additional student worker help and when such help might be unnecessary, thus helping to control staffing costs.

Other pluses:

The use of optical scanning for logging mailed requests and for storage of older transcript records provides additional benefits. First, logging incoming requests by scanning them would improve the quality of the original document in most cases, since the operator can adjust the image being scanned for clarity and, if a laser printer were used for hard copy, the document would not have fold marks or other physical defects that detract from readability. Improved audit tracking from mail room to transcript request processing desk is another benefit. From the aspect of permanent record storage, scanning and storing old transcript records would allow the original hard copy records to be relocated to secure, off-site archival. Less space devoted to storage means more space for staff and equipment. The same considerations with document quality mentioned for logging mail apply to transcript production, along with the possibility of using safety-type laser printer paper for those transcript records which cannot be sent electronically to provide additional protection from document forgery.

Electronic transcript transmission would improve office tasks by removing the steps required to process transcripts for mailing (printing, validating, folding, stuffing, addressing). Postage costs would decrease since fewer transcripts would be produced for mailing. With manual transfer of transcript by mail and hand delivery, there is a possibility for records to be misplaced or misdirected. Since transcripts sent electronically are always sent in packets and collected only by designated users at the receiving station, the occurrence of misplaced or misfiled transcripts would be greatly reduced.

Electronic transcript transmission and verification of credit card payments in batch during off-hour periods when lower telephone rates are in effect also means increased savings to the institution.

VI. CONCLUSIONS

Expanding our thinking about information technology and its use in the business world to include possible applications in the education industry where low budgets and traditional methods predominate will result in improved service to our students. Although many of the technologies mentioned in this document are new to the higher education industry, there has been much interest. The SPEEDE (Standardization of Postsecondary Education Electronic Data Exchange) Committee sponsored by AACRAO (American Association of Collegiate Registrars and Admissions Officers) has been instrumental in gaining the adoption of a national standard format to be used for electronically transmitting academic transcript data. New users of EDI technology throughout North American are enthusiastically accepting this standard.[7] The U.S. Department of Commerce prepared and presented a workshop focusing on security issues for EDI.[8] A recent conference in Vancouver, British Columbia was held for educational institutions for the express purpose of examining electronic data interchange and how it can be used in the academic environment. According to a SPEEDE Internet conference note posted by Mary Neary, Associate Registrar at Arizona State University, Canada and thirty two states were represented with an attendance of over 250.

"The times, they are a-changing" to the ultimate benefit of institutions, their employees, their current and former students, alumni, and the outside organizations they communicate with. Taking advantage of current technologies to manage academic records is the best way to realize these benefits.

NOTES

1. Stephens, Gail, "A Dynamic Transcript Request System" (University of South Carolina, 1992); Clawson, David, University of Texas at Austin, Assistant Registrar. 1992. Interview by author, May 27. Austin. University of Texas at Austin Registrar's Office.

2. Clawson, David and Stones, David H., University of Texas at Austin, Assistant Registrar. 1992. Interview by author, May 27. Austin. University of Texas at Austin Registrar's Office.

3. Stones, David H. 1992. Electronic Transcripts: The SPEEDE/ExPRESS Perspective. Paper presented at the 71st Annual Meeting of the Texas Association of Collegiate Registrar and Admissions Officers. 8-11, November, Odessa.; "Vancouver Workshop Fall 1993," *SPEEDE/ExPRESS Newsletter* 1 (July 1993) 2.

4. Barta, James and Smith, Mike. 1993. Imaging as a Workflow. Paper presented at the 72nd Annual Meeting of the Texas Association of Collegiate Registrar and Admissions Officers. 1-3, November , San Antonio.

5. Easter, Deanna and Long-Phinney, Kathryn. 1993. Imaging: Admitting Students Without Paper .. and other paperless technology too! Paper presented at the Brigham Young University Exploring Technologies Conference: Progressing Toward the Paperless Admissions and Records Office. 22-25, June. Provo.

6. Palmer, Barbara H. and Wei, P. Betty. 1993. "SPEEDE Made Easy," *College and University*, Fall 1993.

7. *SPEEDE/ExPRESS Newsletter* 1 (July 1993).

8. U.S. Department of Commerce, Technology Administration, National Institute of Standards and Technology, Computer Systems Laboratory, *Workshop on Security Procedures for the Interchange of Electronic Documents: Selected Papers and Results*. Gaithersburg, MD. 1992.

BIBLIOGRAPHY

Committee on the Standardization of Postsecondary Education Electronic Data Exchange (SPEEDE) of the American Association of Collegiate Registrars and Admissions Officers and Exchange of Permanent Records Electronically for Students and Schools (ExPRESS) of the National Center for Education Statistics and the Council of Chief State School Officers. 1992. *A Guide to the Implementation of the SPEEDE/ExPRESS Electronic Transcript.*

Skeel, R. 1992. The manager's view of SPEEDE: How do I handle this new technology. Paper presented at the 78th Annual Meeting of the American Association of Collegiate Registrars and Admissions Officers, 17-24, April, Dallas.

Gunter, T. Luther. 1993. Data Storage: What is the Best Way to Archive the Volume of Data We Collect? Paper presented at the 72nd Annual Meeting of the Texas Association of Collegiate Registrars and Admissions Officers. 1-3, November, San Antonio.

Barta, James and Smith, Mike. 1993. Imaging as a Workflow. Paper presented at the 72nd Annual Meeting of the Texas Association of Collegiate Registrars and Admissions Officers. 1-3, November, San Antonio.

Stones, David H. 1992. Electronic Transcripts: The SPEEDE/ExPRESS Perspective. Paper presented at the 71st Annual Meeting of the Texas Association of Collegiate Registrar and Admissions Officers. 8-11, November, Odessa.

Easter, Deanna and Long-Phinney, Kathryn. 1993. Imaging: Admitting Students Without Paper...and other 'paperless' technology too! Paper presented at the Brigham Young University Exploring Technologies Conference: Progressing Toward the Paperless Admissions & Records Office. 22-25, June. Provo.

Stones, David H., University of Texas at Austin Database Administrator and SPEEDE Committee Member. 1993. Interview by author, December 1. San Marcos. Southwest Texas State University of Texas.

Clawson, David and Stones, David H., University of Texas at Austin, Assistant Registrar. 1992. Interview by author, May 27. Austin. University of Texas at Austin Registrar's Office.

Palmer, Barbara H. and Wei, P. Betty. 1993. "SPEEDE Made Easy," *College and University*, Fall 1993.

U.S. Department of Commerce, Technology Administration, National Institute of Standards and Technology, Computer Systems Laboratory, *Workshop on Security Procedures for the Interchange of Electronic Documents: Selected Papers and Results*. Gaithersburg, MD. 1992.

Stephens, Gail, "A Dynamic Transcript Request System" (University of South Carolina, 1992), Photocopied.

"Vancouver Workshop Fall 1993," *SPEEDE/ExPRESS Newsletter* 1 (July 1993) 2.

"Florida Moves to SPEEDE/ExPRESS Format," *SPEEDE/ExPRESS Newsletter* 1 (September 1993) 3.

"State of Oregon Update," *SPEEDE/ExPRESS Newsletter* 1 (March 1993) 1.

Factors Influencing the Success of Computer-Assisted Software Engineering

Mary Sumner
Department of Management Information Systems
Southern Illinois University at Edwardsville

BACKGROUND

The need to improve the productivity of systems development professionals is one of the motivations for introducing CASE. Lengthy project backlogs, high cost, increasing pressure to upgrade existing systems, and the shortage of MIS professionals are all concerns with current systems development processes.

Many claims have been made about the benefits of CASE. A number of industry reports show that CASE improves productivity, reduces costs, and results in higher quality software (Perrone, 1988; Orikowski, 1988). One of the major benefits of CASE is the introduction of engineering-like discipline into the systems development process. Another benefit of CASE is the creation of a common repository of design documentation. By providing a single source of project information, CASE enables analysts and designers to coordinate their work more effectively (McClure, 1989).

In summary, CASE tools enable systems developers to build quality, maintainability, and reliability into software. The introduction of design discipline, the standardization of systems development methodology, and the creation of a central repository for design documentation are all major benefits attributed to the adoption of CASE.

With all of the benefits of CASE, most organizations have found it difficult to implement CASE technology. Some of the commonly mentioned obstacles to CASE are cost, resistance by systems developers, and unacceptable learning curve (Yourdon, 1989). Experienced designers feel that highly-structured CASE tools interfere with their job autonomy and creativity (Kull, 1987).

A number of issues, including technology issues, economic issues, cultural issues, and organizational issues complicate the transition to CASE. Successful use of CASE may require changes in the way in which information systems are developed. Managers need to understand the factors which influence the transition to CASE.

OBJECTIVES OF THE STUDY

The primary objective of this study is to identify the factors which facilitate the successful use of CASE. The factors under review will include "internal integration" strategies and "external integration" strategies.

The *internal integration* strategies will be related to the maturity of the systems development environment, the overall compatibility of CASE with existing skills, and the internal support of management for the use of CASE. In the analysis of the maturity of the software development environment, the Process Maturity Model will be used as a guideline (Humphrey, 1989).

External integration strategies are related to the extent of user involvement in information systems development activities, the alignment of information systems plans and business plans, and user responsibility for project management and control. Strategies such as Joint Application Development (JAD), rapid prototyping, and the appointment of a user manager as project leader are designed to enhance effective communications with users.

The study will depict the success of CASE in each of four different development environments. These development environments will include four quadrants in the following diagram:

The major research question is: What is the success of CASE in each of the four development environments? Do firms with high external integration and high internal integration, for example, make the most successful transition to using CASE in a systems development project(s)? Or does another combination of factors (high internal integration, low external integration) contribute to the successful use of CASE?

REVIEW OF THE LITERATURE

In the context of this study, the successful use of CASE in a systems development project will depend upon the use of internal integration strategies and external integration strategies. The importance of some of these factors is defined in the research.

External Integration Strategies:
The external integration strategies to be assessed in this

EXTERNAL INTEGRATION STRATEGIES		
	LOW	HIGH
INTERNAL INTEGRATION STRATEGIES — LOW	low int low ext	low int high ext
INTERNAL INTEGRATION STRATEGIES — HIGH	high int low ext	high int high ext

Table 1: Four Systems Development Environments

study are Integration, Alignment, Effective Communications with Users, and the Role of the User in Project Management.

Integration. An organizational variable which may be related to the adoption of CASE is integration. Lawrence and Lorsch (1967) define integration as the collaboration between technical specialists and line managers in the achievement of functional goals. Shrivastava and Souder (1987) note that successful management of technological innovation requires high levels of integration across departments and levels. In the context of making the transition to CASE, it would seem that a coalition of users, information technology professionals, and general managers are needed to align information systems development priorities with business needs. Strategies which facilitate effective integration are Joint Application Design (JAD) and Rapid Prototyping.

Alignment. An organizational factor which should be related to successful use of CASE is the process of aligning information systems plans with business plans. In organizations in which information technology is being used to achieve a competitive advantage, the need to integrate information systems plans with business plans is critical (Porter and Millar, 1985; Parsons, 1983; McFarlan, 1984).

Effective Communications. Effective communications with the user is a critical strategy in information systems development. In a number of studies of effective skills of systems analysts, the ability to create effective communications and to understand user requirements is critical to success (Green, Vitalari).

User Responsibility in Project Management. Another set of external integration strategies deals with user responsibility. User responsibilities include: selection of a user as project manager, participation of users on project steering committees, and giving users the responsibility for approving changes in design.

Internal Integration Strategies:
Internal integration factors relate to the maturity of the systems development environment and the overall compatibility of CASE with existing work methods and procedures in systems development.

Compatibility. An important factor introducing effective diffusion of innovations is compatibility. Compatibility means the extent to which an innovation is consistent with the existing beliefs, values, and experiences of potential adopters (Rogers, 1983). Effective introduction of a technological innovation depends upon the existence of technical skills available to use the innovation (Utterback, 1974).

Process Maturity. The Process Maturity Model for software provides a framework for assessing the extent of software engineering excellence a firm has achieved (Humphrey, 1989). The model was designed to guide software development organizations in selecting process improvement strategies. The staged structure of the Process Maturity Model is based upon total quality management principles elaborated by Crosby, Deming, and Juran. The framework was adapted to the software process by Watts Humphrey at IBM.

The five maturity levels define an ordinal scale for measuring the maturity of an organization's software development capability. At each stage of maturity, the organization achieves a set of process goals that make additions to the sophistication and capability of the software development process.

The success of CASE should be more realistic at high levels of compatibility and at high levels of process maturity.

Support Factors. The last set of internal integration factors influencing innovation are support factors. Most researchers conclude that highly enthusiastic individuals that become "champions" of the innovation play a vital role in influencing the process of innovation (Madique, 1980). The positive role of the champion is related to both adoption of an innovation and success of its implementation (Kimberly and Evanisko, 1981).

Other support factors influencing the success of an innovation are vendor support, top management support, and user involvement. In high-technology innovations, effective ven-

Level	Focus	Key Process Areas
5 OPTIMIZING	Continuous process improvement	Defect prevention, Technology innovation, Process change management
4 MANAGED	Product and process quality	Process measurement and analysis, Quality management quality
3 DEFINED	Engineering process	Organization process focus, Organization process definition, Peer reviews, Training program, Intergroup coordination, Software product engineering, Integrated software management
2 REPEATABLE	Project management	Software project planning, Software project tracking, Software subcontract mgmt, Software quality assurance, Software configuration mgmt, Requirements mgmt
1 INITIAL	Immature software development organization	

Table 2: Process Maturity Model for Software

dor support may be critical to success (Ettlie, 1986). Top management commitment and support for an innovation is also critical (Quinn, 1985; Burgleman, 1983). Effective marketing of the innovation has also been discussed by researchers as a key factor to success. Robertson and Gatignon (1986), for example, conclude that effective "selling" of an innovation is important in influencing the speed of its diffusion.

The Success of CASE

The successful implementation of CASE will be measured in terms of a number of factors, including the perceived success of CASE, the percentage of projects in which CASE is used, and the extent of use of CASE in the systems development life cycle.

PROCEDURES FOR THE STUDY

Data was collected through a field survey using an interview and questionnaire. Members of the St. Louis *CASE Users' Group* were asked to identify CASE users within their respective organizations. A total of 15 CASE users were identified. Each of these users was asked to participate in an interview and to complete a questionnaire.

Development of the Questionnaire

The questionnaire included ten items dealing with external integration strategies characterizing a systems development project in which CASE tools were being used. Some of the factors included were:

Each of these items was scored using a Likert-type scale, with a response of 5 indicating a higher level of external integration and a response of 1 indicating a low level of external integration. The sum of the scores for the ten items was derived to obtain the external integration score for each project in which a CASE tool was used.

An additional twelve items were used to assess the extent of internal integration characterizing the application development environment in which CASE was being used. These questions dealt with compatibility, process maturity, and support factors:

FINDINGS

The findings of the study are based upon the experiences of 15 respondents in 15 different organizations. Each of these respondents reported on experiences using CASE in a particular systems development project. In four cases, multiple respondents working on the same project were interviewed.

INTEGRATION	User participation on the project team; Extent of user knowledge in the application area; Extent of user commitment to the project.
ALIGNMENT	Criticality of the information system to achieving business plans; Basis for project justification.
EFFECTIVE COMMUNICATIONS	Use of processes to develop a better understanding of user requirements (JAD, etc.); Use of development methods to facilitate effective communications (prototyping, etc.)
USER RESPONSIBILITY IN PROJECT MANAGEMENT	User participation in approving systems design changes; Extent of user involvement in monitoring project activities and outcomes; Level of management responsible for project approval.

Table 3: External Integration Strategies

COMPATIBILITY	Extent of use of structured methods in systems analysis and design; Existing commitment to an organization-wide data dictionary
PROCESS MATURITY	Extent of continuous process improvement of software development processes; Effectiveness of the project management and control system in managing change; Level of job specialization within the application development function; Extent of use of standardized, reusable specifications in software design; Extent of use of "off-the-shelf" components vs. custom design in application engineering; Evolution and comprehensiveness of the software design repository; Extent of use of metrics in assessing software development productivity.
SUPPORT FACTORS	Evidence of internal support for CASE; Extent of commitment of MIS management to CASE; Effectiveness of the marketing of CASE within the organization.

Table 4: Internal Integration Factors

A variety of CASE tools were used in a number of different projects, as shown in Table 5:

Project Name:	CASE Tool:
Quality Manufacturing	OracleCASE
Accounts Payable	IEF
Personal Injury Liability	IEF
Alarm Tracking	IEF
Misc. Projects	IEF
Provider I/S	IEF
Retail	ADW
Inventory Management	ADW
MRP	Prokit Workbench
Misc. Projects—Investments	Visible Analyst
Evidence Tracking	PCPrism
Marketing Database	Bachman
Misc. Projects—Insurance	Excelerator
Misc. Projects—Consulting	Excelerator
Purchase Order	Synon

Table 5: Projects and CASE Tools

In the organizations using IEF and OracleCASE, the tool was used throughout the systems development life cycle, including analysis, systems design, and construction. In the other organizations, CASE was being used primarily to automate certain activities within the life cycle such as data flow diagramming, data modeling, and the drawing of structure charts. In these environments, CASE was being "plugged into" the life cycle, rather than being integrated throughout. One could also argue that without a commitment to application engineering and software design discipline, the CASE tools being used could not have a greater impact.

Analysis of External Integration and Internal Integration Strategies

For each organization involved in a CASE project, the scores for external integration and internal integration were calculated. Firms with scores in the 75th percentile and above for external and internal integration were categorized as "high" in external and internal integration respectively. Firms with scores equal to or less than the 65th percentile for external and internal integration were categorized as "low" in external and internal integration respectively.

Based upon an analysis of the scores, nine of these firms were placed in one of the four quadrants, as you can see from Table 6:

	External Integration Score	Integration Quadrant	Internal Integration Score	Integration Quadrant
Financial institution	48	High	48	High
Transportation company	32	Low	45	High
Regional government agency	40	High	28	Low
Health care provider	42	High	37	Low
Retail chain	48	High	32	Low
Aerospace manufacturing	46	High	37	Low
Investment brokerage	42	High	30	Low
Chemical company	32	Low	26	Low
Food products	30	Low	38	Low

Table 6: External and Internal Integration Scores

Nine of the fifteen organizations were placed into one of the four quadrants based upon their external and internal integration scores. The majority of firms in the study were placed in the High External Integration/Low Internal Integration quadrant. Only one firm was categorized as High External Integration/High Internal Integration, and one additional firm was included in the Low External Integration/High Internal Integration quadrant. (Table 7.)

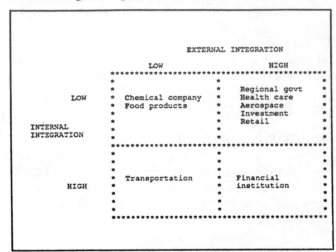

Table 7: Four Software Development Environments

Five of the firms did not have scores which were in the 75th percentile or above or in the 65th percentile or below to place them into either the "high" or "low" categories in external or in internal integration. One firm was not included in the analysis because interview results were not available and the questionnaire data were incomplete. One aspect of the scores which is worth noting is that there were only two organizations in the entire sample of 15 firms which had high internal integration scores. In contrast, seven of the fifteen firms reported high external integration scores. This finding indicates that CASE was being introduced into many environments in which the process maturity scores were relatively low and in which software engineering discipline and structured methods were not fully integrated.

The Impact of CASE

The main research question addressed in this study was the extent of the success of CASE in the four different software development environments. Each of the respondents was asked to report on the overall success of CASE in their organizations. These findings were reported as "high level of success," a "moderate level of success," and "limited success."

As you can see from Table 8, the success of CASE varied in the four application development environments. CASE was considered highly successful in the firm reporting high external integration/high internal integration. CASE was considered moderately successful in the firms with low external integration/high internal integration and with high

Type of Firm	Ext. Integr.	Int. Integr.	Success of CASE
Financial institution	HIGH	HIGH	HIGH
Transportation co.	LOW	HIGH	MODERATE
Regional government	HIGH	LOW	MODERATE
Health care provider	HIGH	LOW	MODERATE
Retail	HIGH	LOW	MODERATE
Aerospace	HIGH	LOW	MODERATE
Investment brokerage	HIGH	LOW	LOW
Chemical company	LOW	LOW	LOW
Food products	LOW	LOW	MODERATE

Table 8: Success of CASE in Four Different Environments

external integration/low internal integration. CASE was "of limited success" in the firm reporting low internal and low external integration.

CASE in the Four Different Environments

Low Internal Integration/Low External Integration. As you can see from the findings, two of the firms were in the LOW/LOW quadrant. In one of these firms, CASE was reported to be of limited success, and in the other of moderate success. In the firm in which CASE was of limited success, the manager reported skepticism about its benefits. Without cost/benefit data to justify this kind of investment, senior MIS management was hesitant to make a commitment to CASE. The CASE tool being used was OracleCASE. Because of limited training in the use of the data dictionary accompanying the tool, the staff couldn't get the code generator to work initially. One interesting comment was that the users were pleased when MIS used CASE because it represented a systematic method.

In the second firm in the LOW/LOW quadrant, top management recommended that the MIS group start using CASE. Since the firm was in an AS/400 environment, they chose SYNON. SYNON generates RPGIII code from action diagrams, although it does not provide a facility for using entity-relationship diagrams or data flow diagrams in analysis and design. Used within the context of its methodology, SYNON works successfully.

Although this food products manufacturer was placed in the LOW/LOW quadrant because of its scores, the CASE tool was working moderately well. The Information Services group consisted of only six individuals, and some of the strategies which characterize systems engineering and project control in larger organizations were not applicable to this shop.

Low External Integration/High Internal Integration. As noted earlier, only two firms in the sample reported "high internal integration" scores. In the case of the transportation firm, a project team used Texas Instruments' IEF tool throughout a project—in analysis, design, and construction. The project was not a "mission critical" system, which may explain the lesser need for user involvement and the lower external integration score.

Because of the use of IEF, adherence to an information engineering methodology was important. IEF built a repository of design documentation, including entity-relationship diagrams, process action diagrams, and other design specifications. The discipline being enforced by the tool may be influencing higher internal integration scores. In the judgment of the user, the CASE experience was moderately successful. "Management needs to recognize that the transition to a CASE environment entails a major learning curve," he argued; "CASE is not just another programming tool."

Low internal integration/high external integration. As noted earlier, five of the nine firms in the matrix fit into this quadrant. In the overall sample of 15 firms, 10 reported "low internal integration" scores. This is indicative of the early stages of process maturity depicting the software development environments within most of these firms.

One of the issues which was indicative of CASE in these organizations was a lack of commitment to the underlying software engineering methodologies being supported by CASE tools. This led to a "piecemeal" approach to their use. In two of the organizations in which Texas Instruments' IEF was being used, managers were interested in moving into an "application engineering" environment, but project members were hesitant to conform with the systems development practices which were enforced by the use of the tool. The learning curve, complicated with limited resources for training, was a factor which caused its evaluators to consider their current experiences with CASE "moderately successful."

In the other three organizations in the LOW INT/HIGH EXT quadrant, CASE tools were being used to support data and process modeling rather than being integrated throughout the entire life cycle. This was partly a result of the capabilities of the CASE tools.

For example, at the investment brokerage firm, Visible Analyst was used primarily to draw data flow diagrams and structure charts, because the tool does not generate code. At the retailing firm, the use of ADW was limited to data and process modeling in the planning phases of a project. At the aerospace firm, Prokit Workbench was used to create an integrated data dictionary for multiple systems. While this did prevent re-inventing the wheel in establishing data names and data definitions for commonly used data elements, it did not create a major culture change. With the absence of code-generation, systems developers in these shops were continuing to use traditional custom-design and implementation practices. In contrast, in an integrated CASE environment, a tool would be used to generate code from high-level design specifications.

Interestingly, the use of CASE in these environments reinforced effective external integration. In several cases, users felt that the CASE tool provided graphical process and data modeling techniques which facilitated user involvement. This helps to explain the higher external integration scores and reinforces the "moderate success" being experienced with the use of CASE.

High internal/high external integration. The responding

organization in the HIGH/HIGH quadrant had been using Texas Instruments' IEF tool for five years. A "critical mass" of its I/S professionals (15 of 50) were trained in the IEF toolkit and used it in a number of projects. IEF was fully integrated with the systems development life cycle and was used to generate code. In addition to the high degree of MIS commitment, there was a high user commitment. The high "internal integration" scores were indicative of the fact that IEF supports a systematic information engineering methodology.

Internal and External Integration Strategies

One of the related findings in this study was that the presence of high internal integration or high external integration was not sufficient to assure success with CASE. Of the 14 organizations which comprised the useable sample, seven respondents reported "high external integration," which meant effective user communications, user participation in project management and control, and effective alignment of project plans with business plans. While "high external integration" is important for project success, CASE does not work without an underlying commitment to software engineering methodology and design discipline. Of the 14 organizations in the sample, only two reported "high internal integration" scores.

The reason for the moderate to low success with CASE overall can be attributed to the relatively low process maturity in software development environments in which CASE is being implemented. If CASE is superimposed upon a work system in which there is lack of standardization, lack of job specialization, and lack of commitment to an underlying information engineering methodology, then it will probably not be effective. The reason for the moderate success of CASE in many of the firms studied was that the software development environments in which CASE was being introduced were relatively immature and unstandardized.

The combination of effective external integration strategies and internal integration strategies is important for the success of CASE. In the area of external integration, CASE provides tools which can facilitate user involvement in prototyping, effective communications, and project control. In the organizations reporting "high external integration," CASE was a significant factor.

In the area of internal integration, CASE can reinforce the use of a disciplined application engineering methodology. But this can only happen if the organization first makes the commitment to the underlying information engineering methodology which the CASE tool supports. In the company in the HIGH/HIGH quadrant, the commitment to the methodology was an important factor in the successful use of CASE.

SUMMARY AND CONCLUSIONS

This study was designed to determine the factors which facilitate the successful use of CASE. Both internal integration strategies and external integration strategies were taken into account. Internal integration strategies are related to the compatibility of CASE with current skills, the maturity of software development processes, and support factors. External integration strategies are related to user involvement in systems development activities, user responsibility for project management and control, and alignment of project objectives and business plans.

Firms in each of the four quadrants were compared with respect to their success with CASE. The two firms in the LOW/LOW (low internal integration/low external integration) quadrant experienced low success with CASE. The firm in the high internal integration/low external integration quadrant experienced moderate success, and a number of organizations in the low internal integration/high external integration quadrant experienced moderate success. The one firm in the HIGH/HIGH (high internal integration/high internal integration) experienced high levels of success with CASE.

While these results are based upon case studies of 14 software development environments, they point to the importance of multiple strategies in facilitating the transition toward CASE. External integration strategies such as effective communications with users and effective project management are traditionally associated with systems development success; but these strategies are not sufficient to move into the CASE environment.

The successful transition to CASE means making the transition to a disciplined, standardized software engineering environment in which knowledge of the underlying information engineering methodology is a fundamental premise. Based upon these findings, the introduction of an integrated CASE tool can help reinforce the use of a systematic methodology.

However, without an underlying management commitment to making the change, the transition to CASE will not work. The interview findings consistently said that CASE is not only a technical challenge but also an organizational challenge which requires top management support and user involvement to be effective.

REFERENCES

Burgelman, R.A., "Corporate Entrepreneurship and Strategic Management; Insights from a Process Study," *Management Science*, V. 28, December, 1983, pp. 1349-1364.

Ettlie, J.E., "Implementing Manufacturing Technologies: Lessons from Experience," in *Managing Technological Innovation*, Jossey-Bass Publishers, San Francisco, 1986.

Green, Gary I., "Perceived Importance of Systems Analysts' Job Skills, Roles, and Non-Salary Incentives," *MIS Quarterly*, June 1989, pp. 115-133.

Humphrey, Watts. *Managing the Software Process*. Reading, MA: Addison-Wesley, 1989.

Kimberly, J. R. and Evanisko, M. J., "Organizational Innovation: The Influence of Individual, Organizational, and Contextual Factors on Hospital Adoption of Technological and Administrative Innovations," *Academy of Management Journal*, V. 24, 1981, pp. 689-713.

Kull, David, "The Rough Road to Productivity," *Computer Decisions*, February 23, 1987, pp. 30-41.

Madique, M.A. and Zirger, B.J., "A Study of Success and Failure in Product Innovation: The Case of the U.S. Electronics Industry," *IEEE Transactions on Engineering Management*, November 1984, pp. 192-203.

McClure, Carma, "SThe CASE Experience," *Byte Magazine*, April 1989.

Orikowski, Wanda J., "CASE Tools are the IS Workplace," *Proceedings of the 1988 ACM SIGCPR Conference on the Management of Information Systems Personnel*, College Park, Md, April 7-8, 1988, pp. 88-97.

Parsons, G. L., "Information Technology: A New Competitive Weapon," *Sloan Management Review*, Fall, 1983, pp. 3-14.

Perrone, Giovanni, "Primary Product in the Development Life Cycle," *Software Magazine*, August 1988, pp. 35-41.

Quinn, J. B., "Managing Innovation: Controlled Chaos," *Harvard Business Review*, May-June, 1985, pp. 73-84.

Robertson, T.S. and Gatignon, H., "Competitive Effects on Technology Diffusion," *Journal of Marketing*, V. 50, July, 1986, pp. 1-12.

Rogers, E. M., *Diffusion of Innovations*, Free Press, New York, 1983.

Shrivastava, P. and Souder, W. E., "The Strategic Management of Technological Innovation; A Review and a Model," *Journal of Management Studies*, V. 24, January, 1987, pp. 25-41.

Utterback, J. M., "Innovation in Industry and the Diffusion of Technology," *Science*, V. 183, February, 1974, pp. 620-626.

Vitalari, Nicholas, "Knowledge as a Basis for Expertise in Systems Analysis: An Empirical Study," *MIS Quarterly*, Vol. 9, No. 3, September 1, 1985, pp. 221-241.

Yourdon, Edward, "Serious CASE in the 90's: What Do We Do When the Novelty Wears Off?" Presentation at the ShowCASE Conference IV, Washington University, St. Louis, October 10, 1989.

Panel and Workshop Summaries

Managing Ethically in an International Environment

MODERATOR
Eli B. Cohen
College of Business
Eastern New Mexico University
Portales, NM 88130-7031

PANELISTS
Frank W. Connolly
Department of Computer and Information Systems
The American University
119 Clark Hall
Washington, DC 20016-8116

Karen Forcht
Information and Decision Sciences
College of Business
James Madison University
Harrisonburg, VA 22807

Thomas Hilton
Business Information Systems and Education
Utah State University
UMC 3515, Logan, UT 84322

Abbe Mowshowitz
Department of Computer Science
The City College (CUNY)
New York, NY 10031

The focus of this panel session is to explore the impact of multi-national environments on firms that would like to manage their affairs ethically. In recent years, many writers have expressed concern regarding the explosion of ethical dilemmas as business takes on transnational/transcultural dimensions. Choosing an ethical course of action is non-trivial because even single-national firms find difficulty arriving at consensus as to what is the ethical course of action. The multinational environment exacerbates the issue of ethics. The manager in a global firm who wishes to make ethical decisions is faced with concerns of cultural, language, and historical diversity as well as the demands of competition. The panelists in this session will explore these issues from their own research perspectives. They include individuals who have made major contributions to the areas of IS ethics and multinational IS. The topics of discussion include the following:

- An overview of Cultural Diversity and its Impact on IT.
- An overview of Classical and Neoclassical Ethical Theory
- Problems in applying ethical norms from one society to other societies
- Some attempts at resolving this dilemma

A major purpose of this panel is to draw together individuals (from the panel and the audience) interested in this area with an eye toward developing future cooperative research.

The Differences Between CD-ROM and Videodisc Technology

Peter Fenrich
Interactive Multimedia Development Centre
British Columbia Institute of Technology
Tel: (604) 432-8817   Fax: (604) 436-0286

PRIMARY FOCUS
This presentation will enable you to:
o compare and contrast CD-ROM and videodisc technology
o describe the strengths and weaknesses of both CD-ROM and videodisc technologies
o make informed purchasing decisions for CD-ROM and videodisc technology.

DISCUSSION
The choice between adopting either CD-ROM or videodisc technology is not necessarily clear or simple. There are many similarities and critical differences between CD-ROMs and videodiscs.

The similarities between CD-ROMs and videodiscs include:
o being a relatively permanent storage medium
o being able to store a large amount of data such as high quality motion visuals, still visuals, graphics, audio, and text
o having access to the data through computers
o being proven and accepted technologies
o having low reproduction costs
o having flexible uses.

The major differences between CD-ROMs and videodiscs include:
o storage capacity
o quality of motion visuals
o data access and retrieval
o data storage (e.g. digital versus analog)
o their uses
o the present and future hardware base.

CONCLUSION
In general, both CD-ROM and videodisc technologies are

excellent and have different strengths and weaknesses. Carefully determine your present and future needs before deciding on adopting one or both of these technologies. Adopting one technology will not necessarily mean that the other is not needed or useful. Many sites use and need both technologies.

Quality of Teaching Information Systems in Multicultural Classes

Panel Chair:
Lech J. Janczewski, *University of Auckland*
Panelists:
Andrew S. Targowski, *Western Michigan University*
Judith D. Ahrens, *Drexel University*
Karen D. Loch, *Georgia State University*
Abdula Abdul-Gadar, *King Fahd University of Petroleum & Minerals*

Very rarely in university classes do we face students of a uniform background. Basically, the differences may be of the following three types:
* The language of instruction may be new for some students,
*Different general background (or, in the other words, different culture),
* Different knowledge of the technical domain.

University administrators and didactic staff place the most attention on the last point. The whole system of prerequisites, corequisites, crosscrediting, etc is aimed on making the entry - student level of knowledge more or less uniform.

The question of a different previous language of instruction is usually addressed through imposing some language tests or other proofs of proficiency in a language used at the particular university.

But the problem of a different cultural background is rarely taken care of. Universities administrators seem to be only forced by communities to take some actions but do not address these issues for themselves. In all known cases, the actions are limited to organising study or social groups rather than dealing with the problem through lectures/labs/tutorial presentations.

The aim of the panel is therefore to discuss
* if cultural difference may inhibit the efficiency of a didactic process. If the answer is positive then,
* how such questions should be address by IS lecturers?

Other purpose of this panel is to draw together individuals (both from the panel and the audience) who are interested in this area towards developing future cooperative research.

IT Outsourcing in a Global Context:

Current Practice and Future Directions

Panel Chair:
Jaak Jurison
Graduate School of Business Administration
Fordham University, New York, NY 10023
(212) 636-6183

Panelists:
P. Candace Deans, Thunderbird - American
Graduate School of International Management
Edward M. Roche, Seton Hall University
R. Ravichandran, Ball State University

Outsourcing, the practice of subcontracting some or all of the information systems functions to another firm, is becoming an important alternative for managing IS resources. Modern high speed telecommunications have made outsourcing across country borders a viable option for many firms. Many U.S. firms are having software developed offshore in countries which have highly skilled computer professionals and significantly lower labor rates than in the U.S. While these arrangements can offer significant cost advantage to many U.S. firms and contribute to the economic development of some countries, there is also a growing concern about the potential migration of U.S. programming jobs to foreign countries.

The purpose of this panel is to examine the major issues surrounding global outsourcing practices from several different perspectives and explore future opportunities and challenges for both practitioners and academic researchers.

Panel chair Jaak Jurison will introduce the subject, present an overview of the current state of global outsourcing practice, identify the major issues, and moderate the remaining presentations and discussion.

Issues to be explored by the panel are: What are the opportunities and challenges of offshore software development? What type of projects are good candidates for offshore development? What are the managerial issues? What is the long-term impact of global IT outsourcing on the U.S software community? What are the opportunities for research in this area?

Representatives from outsourcing firms and offshore vendors will be invited to present their perspectives and describe their experiences.

After presentations by panelist the audience will be encouraged to participate in the discussion.

The Influence of Personality Type on Systems Work

Eugene Kaluzniacky
Business Computing Program
University of Winnipeg
Winnipeg, Manitoba, Canada

A WIDELY-USED PERSONALITY INDICATOR

It is currently an accepted principle that MIS is a socio-technical field in which personality characteristics of the people involved in the area do play an influential role. The **Myers-Briggs Personality Type Indicator** is a widely-used, applied psychological instrument which identifies one's personality preferences along four dimensions: Introversion / Extraversion, Intuition / Sensing, Thinking / Feeling, and Judging / Perception. It has been used in MIS research on team effectiveness, Information Center staffing, programming ability, and computer anxiety.

CONTRIBUTION FROM VARIOUS PERSONALITIES

The system development function consists of a number of different tasks which would seem to correspond to different dimensions in the Myers-Briggs Indicator. For example, soliciting requirements from an end-user may require extraversion, developing detailed program specifications may need sensing and thinking, maintenance programming may involve perception (open-endedness), and long-range IS planning may fit very well with open-ended intuitive thinking. Edward Yourdon, in his recent book, *The Decline and Fall of the American Programmer*, specifically discusses use of Myers-Briggs typing on software development teams and indicates that world-class software organizations are providing training to their professional staff in such areas.

AN OPPORTUNITY FOR AWARENESS

The workshop will have not only an informative, but also a developmental character. Participants will receive a basic understanding of the nature and characteristics of the 16 MBTI types (and the derived four temperaments). Research results and relevant literature quotations will be highlighted. Video clippings from interviews with IS personnel will be shown to emphasize how different types will react to a particular task, and how their assessment of their work and their intended career direction is corroborated by MBTI type theory. Career planning and stress management issues in IS, as related to type, will be discussed. A literature list will be distributed, as will be a list of suggested MBTI-related projects which can be implemented in the participants' organizations.

Enhancing Classroom Learning and Group Work with Groupware

Workshop Leaders
Peggy M. Beranek , Georgia State University
Karen D. Loch, Georgia State University

As organizations rely more and more on groups and teams to accomplish their goals, collaborative computer technologies have evolved and developed to support the problem solving, communication and decision making efforts of these teams. Group support systems (GSS) exemplify group technology which has evolved in response to the need to increase efficiency and effectiveness of group meetings and cooperative work.

As educators it is our charge to keep students abreast of these new technological developments and business trends. In response to this we have developed a workshop which will provide insights on:

• How a GSS can be used to learn and enhance group and meeting skills
• How a GSS can be used in a classroom setting
• Methodology and procedures for the introduction, use, and evaluation of GSS technology in a classroom environment.

The workshop is divided into three sections. The first part begins with a general introduction to GSS and the various technology configurations that exist. The second section presents two meeting models: Team Performance (Drexler et al) and Bostrom, Anson, and Clawson model. The first model focuses on the meeting process and describes the stages a team moves through as it solves a problem. The second model presents the meeting as a series of tasks and activities in those tasks, and maps the activities to the various electronic tolls which can be used. The third part of the workshop presents decision making models and describes the process of integrating a GSS into a decision-making class and how we can use electronic tools at the various stages of the formal decision-making process.

This workshop will be of value to those interested in the use of GSS technologies and/or other Information Technologies in a classroom environment. The workshop may also be of value for industry trainers and consultants.

Critical Success Factors for Development and Implementations International Information Systems

Panel Chairs

Shailendra C. Palvia
Kenny F. Lee
Information Management Research Centre (IMARC)
School of Accountancy and Business (SAB)
Nanyang Technological University (NTU)
Singapore 2263

Panelists

Candace Deans
Thunderbird American International School of Management

Two More to be Appointed

A limited survey of multinational companies in Singapore revealed three major issues confronting the CIOs: choosing the right information architecture; implementing an optimum mix of outsourcing and insourcing for IS functions; and identifying factors critical to the successful development and implementation of an International Information System (IIS). This paper will explore the last issue i.e., identifying and analyzing critical success factors (CSFs) for the successful development of an IIS and then succeeful worldwide or regional implementation and adoption.

The initial list of issues will arise from a research that will be completed in Singapore by the end of April, 1994. Singapore setting for this research is very pertinent and relevant since Singapore is home to the largest number of MNCs in this part of the world. The research results will be based on 3-phase research methodology. First interviews will be conducted with the CIOs or systems development managers of three companies in Singapore to gain basic understanding of issues related to development and implementation of IIS. Second, a detailed research instrument will be designed to probe deeper into the issues unraveled in the first phase. This instrument will be then administered to CIOs or systems development managers of about 40 regional or global companies who have developed and implemented at least one IIS in the recent past. Thirdly, after an initial analysis of the responses to the research instrument, structured interviews will be conducted with selected respondents to gain a better understanding of the factors critical to successfully developing and implementing an IIS.

We hope that the above methodology will provide us rich data on the CSFs for the development and implementation of an IIS. Based on extensive literature survey, we will identify and analyze CSFs commons to the development and implementation of both National Information Systems (NISs) and IISs. We will also identify and analyze CSFs that are primarily applicable to the development and implementation of IISs.

Author Index